DANISH DICTIONARY

DANISH DICTIONARY

English–Danish
Danish–English

Edited by Anna Garde.
Additional material by W. Glyn Jones

London and New York

First published 1991
by G · E · C Gads Forlag,
Copenhagen

Republished 1995
by Routledge
11 New Fetter Lane, London EC4P 4EE

Simultaneously published in the USA and Canada
by Routledge
29 West 35th Street, New York, NY 10001

Reprinted 1999, 2001

Routledge is an imprint of the Taylor & Francis Group

Printed and bound in Great Britain by
TJ International Ltd, Padstow, Cornwall
Printed on acid-free paper.

British Library Cataloguing in Publication Data
A catalogue record for this book is available from the British Library

Library of Congress Cataloging in Publication Data
Danish dictionary : English–Danish, Danish–English / edited by Anna Garde; additional material by W. Glyn Jones.
p. cm.
ISBN 0–415–10803–9
1. Danish language–Dictionaries–English. 2. English language–Dictionaries–Danish. I. Garde, Anna. II. Jones, W. Glyn.
PD3640.D36 1994
439.8′1321–dc20 93-40631
CIP

CONTENTS

A GUIDE TO DANISH PRONUNCIATION

STRESS

The stress will normally fall on the first syllable of a Danish word, with a secondary stress on the first syllable of each element in a compound:

hoved – ***ho*****ved*****bane*****gård**

This rule does not, however, apply to certain prefixes, which are not stressed, e.g. **be-**, **er-**: **be*****ta*****le**; **er*****hverv***. Not does it apply to foreign loan words, where the stress tends to follow the pattern of the original: **restaur*****ant***; **mu*****se*****um**; **bibliot*****ek***.

LENGTH

All vowels can be both long and short, and their quality is usually apparent from the orthography. A vowel followed by a single consonant and a further vowel will be long; one followed by a double consonant will be short:

Short vowel	*Long vowel*
glad	**glade**
han	**hane**
du	**dukke**
dyster	**dyne**
død	**døde**

In addition, the sole vowel in many monosyllables will be long: **hus**; **is**; **tur**; **dyb**.

It should be noted that the immediate proximity of the letter **-r-** will affect the quality of certain vowels.

STØD

The **stød**, or glottal stop, can occur virtually anywhere in Danish words. The written language gives no indication of whether there is a **stød** or not, and the dictionary makes no attempt to show it.

VOWELS

Letter	*Quality*	*Description*	*Examples*
a	short	as in northern English 'm*a*n'	**mand, kat**
	long	more open, as in 'm*a*re'	**bane, hane**
	with **-r-**	as in 'p*a*rk'	**bare, klar**
e	short	half way between English 'm*e*n' and 'p*i*n', 'sl*i*d'	**pen, ven**
	long	rather like the English *ai* in 'p*ai*n', but slightly more closed	**mene, sten**
	as final, unstressed	rather like the final *-er* in 'moth*er*'	**gøre, smukke**
	with **-r-**	slightly more open	**ren, rest**
	de	in the plural article/pronoun **de**, the **-e** is pronounced as the English *-ee* in 'b*ee*'	
i	short	similar to short **-e-**	**ind, ingen**
	long	as in English 't*ea*' or 'b*ee*'	**pine, mine**
	with **-r-**	little change	**ride, rive**
o	short	as in English 'm*o*th'	**som, nok**
	long	as in northern English 'c*oa*l'	**god, love**
	with **-r-**	little change	**rolig, mor**
u	short	as in northern English 'b*u*t'	**mut, kutter**
	long	as in English 'b*oo*t'	**du, hus**
	with **-r-**	little change	**krut, rude**
y	short	with lips formed to say **o**, try to say **ee**. Compare French *eu*	**lykke, stykke**
	long	with lips formed to say **u**, try to say **ee**. Compare German *müde.*	**dyb, lyder**
	with **-r-**	little change	**rydde, dyr**
æ	short	similar to English 'b*e*st'	**tænke, bænk**
	long	similar but longer	**pæne, glæde**

	with **-r-**	little change	**pære,lære**
ø	short	as short **y** above	**død, blød**
	long	similar but longer	**døde, bløde**
	with **-r-**	slightly more open	**rød, tør**
å	short	as in English *o*ften	**måtte, blåt**
	long	as in English s*aw*	**må, blå**
	with **-r-**	little change	**råbe, råde**

DIPHTHONGS

Single Danish vowels do not show the tendency towards diphthongization that is found in English. There are, however, diphthongs in Danish, though the following letter combinations do not always form diphthongs, e.g. the **-ag-** in **dag** does not, whereas in **daglig**, it does.

-aj-	as English 'm*y*'	**bajer, hajer**
af-	diphthongized as prefix only; as English 'h*ow*'	**afgang, afsked**
-ag-	as English 'h*ow*'	**daglig, fagbog**
-av-	as English 'h*ow*'	**tavs, navn, rav**
	but not always diphthongized	**lav, brav**
-au-	as English 'h*ow*'	**pause**
-eg-	as English 'm*y*'	**meget, bleg, jeg**
	sometimes not diphthongized	**eg, steget**
-ej-	as English 'm*y*'	**nej, sejle**
-ek-	pronounced as English 'm*y*' in **seksten**, but otherwise not diphthongized	
-ig-	as in English 'm*y*'	**mig, sig**
	this combination is not always a diphthong	**sige, vige, lig**
-og-	rather like the English 'bel*ow*'	**og, dog**
-ov-	as **-og-**, above	**sove, over**
-øg-	as English 'b*oy*'	**døgn, møg, løg**
	this combination is not always a diphthong	**Køge, søge**
-øj-	as **-øg-**, above	**skøjte, tøj, højre, støj**

CONSONANTS

Danish consonants are 'lighter', less aspirated, than their English equivalents. Danish consonants do not lengthen, except in a few compounds such as **nattog**, where the first element ends on the same consonant as that starting the second element.

Consonants requiring special comment are as follows:

Letter	*Quality*	*Description*	*Examples*
c		only found in loan words	
	k	before **-a**, **-o**, **-u** and consonants	**cardigan, clips**
	s	before **-e**, **-i**, **-y**	**celle, civil**
	sj	in combination **ch-**	**chokolade**
d	**d**	initially	**dag, dejlig**
	silent	after **l**, **n**, **r**	**sild, bord**
	'soft'	at end of syllable, rather like English *-th*, though lighter.	**gade, rød**
g	**g**	initially	**god, gerne**
	silent	in combination with **-ig**	**dejlig, rolig**
	'soft'	formed by bringing vocal chords together as though to say **g**, but not allowing them to touch. In practice, the soft **g** is often almost silent.	**pige, sørge, hage, krage**
	-sj-	in certain French loan words, an approximation is made to the French pronunciation	**bagage, ravage, plamage**
	-ng	as in English	**sang, længe**
h	silent	before **j-** and **v-**	**hvem, hvor, hvilken**
j		as English *y* in '*y*es'	**jeres, jord**
		occasionally keeps foreign pronunciation in loan words	**jeton, job**
k		as in English	
	-kk-	slightly voiced: **-gg-**	**ikke, dukke**
	kn-	The **k** is always pronounced along with the **n**	**kniv, knude**
p	**-pp-**	slightly voiced: **-bb-**	**oppe, glippe**
r		uvular **r**, pronounced deep in the throat	**ren, rar, rør**
s	**s**	as in English	**som, slem**

	sj-	similar to English *sh-*	**sjov, sjælden**
t	**t**	in initial position similar to English	**tage, trin**
	-t	in final position after unstressed **-e-**, **-t** is pronounced as a 'soft' **-d**	**gået, elsket, mærket**
	-tt-	slightly voiced: **-dd-**	**satte, putte**
	silent	entirely silent in **det**	
v		initially as in English	**vil, virke**
	silent	after **-l-**	**sølv, tolv**
	-w-	often after **o** or **i**	**sove, hive**
		see also under Diphthongs	
w		only occurs in foreign place names and personal names. For dictionary purposes treated as **-v-**, and pronounced as such	
x		only in loan words. Normally replaced by **-ks-**	
z	**s**	only in loan words	**zink, zone, zebra**

NOTES ON DANISH NOUNS AND VERBS

This dictionary was originally intended for Danish learners of English. Consequently, certain information of use to English learners of Danish is omitted, in particular relating to verb forms and noun plurals. The *gender* of nouns is indicated in the italicized *-en* or *-et* after each noun, but the *plural* is not. The following, then, contains a brief guide to the typical ways of pluralizing Danish nouns. Nouns are grouped, and within each group their endings are listed alphabetically, followed by the most common ways of pluralizing them. The lists are not intended to be comprehensive, but to act as a guide only.

Similarly, the notes of verb conjugation can only provide a general guideline, but it is worth remembering that seventy-five per cent of Danish regular verbs belong to the first conjugation. There is, of course, no guidance on usage, which really belongs in a grammar. The list of irregular verbs corresponds to those included in the dictionary.

NOUN PLURALS

There are three main ways of forming the plural of Danish nouns: by adding **-(e)r** to the singular, by adding **-e** to the singular, or by leaving the singular unchanged. In addition, a small number of nouns undergo a vowel mutation, and there are a few irregular and foreign plurals. To facilitate the use of this dictionary, the following list of noun endings will give an indication of the patterns of plurals.

Unstressed noun endings

-dom

doubles the **-m-** and adds **-e**: **sygdom/sygdomme**; **ungdom/ungdomme**. Compare also **brudgom/brudgomme**.

-e

pluralizes in **-r**: **gade/gader**: **have/haver**; **kande/kander**; **maskine/maskiner**.

Note **tilfælde**, which remains unchanged in the plural.
Note the irregular plural **øje/øjne**.
Note that vowel mutation occurs in **bonde/bønder**.
Note also that in the very few loan words ending in a stressed **-e** (often written **-é**), the plural is **-er**: **ide/ideer (idé/idéer)**; **kafe/kafeer (kafé/kaféer)**.

-ed

always pluralizes in **-er**: **begivenhed/begivenheder**; **enhed/enheder**; **hoved/hoveder**; **måned/måneder**; **sandhed/sandheder**.

-el

loses the **-e-** and adds **-er**: **cirkel/cirkler**; **cykel/cykler**; **kedel/kedler**; **møbel/møbler**.

If the **-el** is preceded by a double consonant, that consonant will be simplified: **fakkel/fakler**.
Exceptions: **engel/engle**; **djævel/djævle**; **himmel/himle**; **apostel/apostle**; **discipel/disciple**.

-else

always adds **-r**: **anelse/anelser**; **fornemmelse/fornemmelser**; **følelse/følelser**; **størrelse/størrelser**; **værelse/værelser**.

-en

adds **-er**, sometimes losing the preceding **-e-**: **dækken/dækkener**; **figen/figener**; **køkken/køkkener**; **lagen/lag(e)ner**; **verden/verdener**.
Exception: **våben/våben**.
Note that this does not apply to monosyllables or compounds based on them, e.g. **ben/ben** and thus **lårben/lårben**; **gren/grene** and thus **sportsgren/sportsgrene**.

unstressed **-er**

normally pluralizes in **-e**, often accompanied by the removal of the preceding **-e-**: **bager/bagere**; **lærer/lærere**; **partner/partnere**; **vælger/vælgere**; **tegner/tegnere**; **cylinder/cylindre**; **teater/teatre**.

If the **-er** is preceded by a double consonant, that consonant will often be simplified: **kammer/kamre**; **nummer/numre**.

Note, however: **svømmer/svømmere**.
Note vowel mutation in: **and/ænder**; **bog/bøger**; **broder/brødre**; **datter/døtre**; **fader/fædre**; **hånd/hænder**; **klo/kløer**; **ko/køer**; **kraft/kræfter**; **moder/mødre**; **nat/nætter**; **so/søer**; **stand/stænder**; **stang/stænger**; **tand/tænder**; **stad/stæder**; **tå/tæer**.
Note also: **fod/fødder**; **rod/rødder**.

-hed

pluralizes in **-er**: **nyhed/nyheder**; **helhed/helheder**; **vanskelighed/vanskeligheder**; **hastighed/hastigheder**.

-se

pluralizes in **-r**: **ekspertise/ekspertiser**; **rejse/rejser**; **ellipse/ellipser**.

-skab

Abstract compounds ending in **-skab** all pluralize in **-er**: **kundskab/kundskaber**; **videnskab/videnskaber**; **regnskab/regnskaber**.

Note, however, that the monosyllable **skab** (meaning cupboard) and compounds based on it pluralize in **-e**. Thus **skab/skabe**; **klædeskab/klædeskabe**.

-um

These Greek and Latin loan words vary between the original and Danish plurals. The older, more established nouns tend to take Danish plurals. **akvarium/akvarier**; **basis/baser**; **konsortium/konsortier**; **krysantemum/krysantemer**; **laboratorium/laboratorier**; **medium/medier**; **ministerium/ministerier**; **museum/museer**; **mysterium/mysterier**; **stadium/stadier**; **verbum/verber**.

Other, less common nouns tend more to the original plurals:

depositum/deposita (or **depositummer**); **faktum/fakta**; **maksimum/maksima**; **minimum/minima**.

Stressed noun endings

stressed vowels normally add **-er**

å/åer; **ble/bleer**; **bro/broer**; **by/byer**; **kopi/kopier**; **mejeri/mejerier**; **ske/skeer**.
Exceptions: **sko/sko**; **strå/strå**.

Note also: **en frø/frøer** (frog/frogs), but **et frø/frø** (seed/seeds).

stressed diphthongs will tend to add **-e**, but are difficult to classify

hav/have; **leg/lege**; **skov/skove**; **steg/stege**; **vej/veje**; **streg/streger**; **haj/hajer**; **kaj/kajer**.
But: **løg/løg**; **spøg/spøg**; **fingerpeg/fingerpeg**.

Note that it is not possible to see from the written language whether vowel–consonant compounds actually form diphthongs or not.

Nouns ending in consonant combinations

-ft

pluralizes in **-er**: **afgift/afgifter**; **bedrift/bedrifter**; **skaft/skafter**; **stift/stifter**; **skrift/skrifter**; **loft/lofter**.
Exceptions: **duft/dufte**; **gift/gifte**.

Note vowel mutation in: **kraft/kræfter**.

-gt

pluralizes in **-er**: **ansigt/ansigter**; **dragt/dragter**; **magt/magter**; **frugt/frugter**; **pligt/pligter**; **udsigt/udsigter**.
Exceptions: **digt/digte**; **lugt/lugte**; **knægt/knægte**; **vægt/vægte**.

-l plus consonant

usually add **-e**: **hals/halse**; **hvalp/hvalpe**; **kalv/kalve**; **skilt/skilte**; **telt/telte**; **tolk/tolke**.

Exceptions: **bælt/bælter; felt/felter; bylt/bylter; valg/valg.**

-m plus consonant

the few nouns of this type divide between **-e** and **-er**: **damp/dampe; gesims/gesimser; kamp/kampe; klump/klumper; svamp/svampe; sump/sumpe; triumf/triumfer; trumf/trumfer.**

Note: **bums/bums.**

-nt

pluralizes in **-er**: **elefant/elefanter; gigant/giganter; kant/kanter; mønt/mønter; spekulant/spekulanter.**

-nk

pluralizes mainly in **-e**: **bænk/bænke; hank/hanke; dunk/dunke; skænk/skænke; stank/stanke; tank/tanke;**
but frequently in **-er**: **bank/banker; skavank/skavanker.**

Note: **blink/blink; stænk/stænk.**

-ns

pluralizes in **-er**: **licens/licenser; prins/prinser; sans/sanser; substans/substanser.**
But: **dans/danse; krans/kranse.**

-rg

pluralizes in **-e**: **bjerg/bjerge; borg/borge; dværg/dværge.**
Exceptions: **dramaturg/dramaturger; sorg/sorger; kirurg/kirurger.**

-rk

plurals occur mainly in **-e**: **birk/birke; fork/forke; stork/storke; skurk/skurke;**
or **-er**: **mark/marker; monark/monarker; park/parker; patriark/patriarker; værk/værker.**

Note: **ark/ark; spark/spark.**

-rm

pluralizes mainly in **-e**: **arm/arme; barm/barme; farm/farme; orm/orme; storm/storme; skærm/skærme.**
Exceptions: **alarm/alarmer; form/former; reform/reformer; term/termer.**

-rn

pluralizes in -e: **bjørn/bjørne; kværn/kværne; torn/torne; tårn/tårne;**
or remains unchanged: **agern/agern; ahorn/ahorn; egern/egern; horn/horn; værn/værn.**

Note vowel mutation in: **barn/børn.**

-rs

pluralizes in **-er**: **kurs/kurser; børs/børser; revers/reverser; univers/universer.**
Exceptions: **kors/kors; vers/vers.**

-rt

pluralizes in **-er**: **art/arter; bommert/bommerter; koncert/koncerter; kikkert/kikkerter; knallert/knallerter; kuffert/kufferter; kuvert/kuverter; part/parter; sort/sorter; start/starter; urt/urter; ært/ærter.**
Exceptions: **port/porte; hjort/hjorte; kort/kort; stjært/stjærte.**

-rv

pluralizes in -e: **kurv/kurve; skærv/skærve; spurv/spurve; torv/torve.**
Exceptions: **hverv/hverv: tørv/tørv.**

-sk

pluralizes in -e: **ask/aske; busk/buske; disk/diske; dusk/duske; kusk/kuske; pisk/piske; visk/viske.**
Exceptions: **kiosk/kiosker; marsk/marsker; slisk/slisker; fisk/fisk; torsk/torsk.**

-st

pluralizes in **-er**: **ateist/ateister; attest/attester; blomst/blomster; fest/fester; gnist/gnister; last/laster; mast/master; dunst/dunster; kyst/kyster; lyst/lyster; racist/racister; rest/rester; svulst/svulster; takst/takster; tingest/tingester; vækst/vækster.**
Exceptions: **hest/heste; hingst/hingste; kost/koste; kvist/kviste; ost/oste; rist/riste; vrist/vriste(r); kast/kast.**

Monosyllables ending in a consonant

long vowels pluralize in **-e**

> **hus/huse**; **klud/klude**; **krig/krige**; **pæl/pæle**; **skab/skabe**.
> Exceptions: **kran/kraner**; **las/laser**; **plan/planer**; **pris/priser**.

short vowels pluralize in **-e**

> **kam/kamme**; **hund/hunde**; **mund/munde**; **pung/punge**.
> Exceptions: **kind/kinder**; **knap/knapper**; **nød/nødder**.
>
> Note that where a short vowel precedes a final single consonant, that consonant is doubled on adding the plural ending. This is to denote the continued short character of the vowel. Examples of this above are **kam/kamme** and **knap/knapper**. Where a short vowel precedes a double consonant, no consonant change is called for, e.g. **mund/munde, kind/kinder**.
>
> Note also **bror/brødre**; **far/fædre**; **mor/mødre**.
> Note also **mand/mænd**.

monosyllables ending in a vowel normally pluralize in **-er**:

> **å/åer**; **by/byer**; **bro/broer**; **ske/skeer**; **sky/skyer**.
> Exceptions: **sko/sko**; **knæ/knæ**; **ski/ski**.
>
> Note: **en frø/frøer** but **et frø/frø**.

Foreign loan words

It is sometimes difficult to adapt foreign loan words to the Danish system of pluralization. There is often some hesitation as to how to pluralize them; for instance, the English word **film** will sometimes pluralize as **films**, though the unchanged form **film** is now becoming established. Other common English loans retaining their English plurals are: **check/checks**; **souvenir/souvenirs** (or **souvenirer**); **album/albummer** (or **albums**, or **album**). Adding the plural definite article to these can be problematic – also for Danes.

A few Italian loan words can pluralize either according to Italian or Danish custom: **konto/konti** (or **kontoer**); **risiko/risikoer** (or **risici**); **tempo/tempi** (rarely **tempoer**). **Villa** always pluralizes as **villaer**.

VERBS

Regular verbs

The verbal form found in the dictionary is the *infinitive*, from which it is necessary to recognize the *stem* in order to form the different tenses. The stem is usually formed by removing the **-e** of the infinitive. If the **-e** of the infinitive is preceded by a double consonant, that consonant will be simplified to form the stem, though it will in practice be doubled again on adding tense endings beginning with **-e**. In the few cases where an infinitive does not end in an **-e**, the stem is identical to the infinitive: **gø/gø**.

There are two conjugations of regular verbs in Danish.

The first conjugation forms its present tense by adding **-er** to the stem, its past tense by adding **-ede** to the stem, and its past participle by adding **-et** to the stem. The present participle, which in Danish has a principally adjectival application, is formed by adding **-ende** to the stem, and is indicated in the following section in parentheses:

elske – **elsker** – **elskede** – **elsket** – **(elskende)**
dufte – **dufter** – **duftede** – **duftet** – **(dustende)**
regne – **regner** – **regnede** – **regnet** – **(regnende)**
nynne – **nynner** – **nynnede** – **nynnet** – **(nynnende)**

The second conjugation forms its present tense by adding **-er** to the stem, its past tense by adding **-te** to the stem, and its past participle by adding **-t** to the stem. If the **-e** of the infinitive is preceded by a double consonant, that consonant will be simplified in the past tense and past participle. As in the first conjugation, the present participle is formed by adding **-ende** to the stem:

besøge – **besøger** – **besøgte** – **besøgt** – **(besøgende)**
spise – **spiser** – **spiste** – **spist** – **(spisende)**
ramme – **rammer** – **ramte** – **ramt** – **(rammende)**
tænke – **tænker** – **tænkte** – **tænkt** – **(tænkende)**

About seventy-five per cent of all Danish verbs, including all new verbs, belong to the first conjugation.

The imperative is identical to the stem in all cases.

The passive

There are two passive forms in Danish, one being formed by means of an auxiliary plus past participle, the other being a verbal form ending in **-s**. In both conjugations the **-e** of the infinitive adds **-s** to form the passive infinitive, the **-er** of the present tense is replaced by **-es** in the present passive, while an **-s** is added to the past tense. There is no **-s** form for the past participle. Thus:

elskes	–	**elskes**	–	**elskedes**
tænkes	–	**tænkes**	–	**tænktes**

Auxiliary verbs

blive	–	**bliver**	–	**blev**	–	**blevet**
få	–	**får**	–	**fik**	–	**fået**
have	–	**har**	–	**havde**	–	**haft**
være	–	**ver**	–	**var**	–	**været**

Modal verbs

burde	–	**bør**	–	**burde**	–	**burdet**
kunne	–	**kan**	–	**kunne**	–	**kunnet**
måtte	–	**må**	–	**måtte**	–	**måttet**
skulle	–	**skal**	–	**skulle**	–	**skullet**
turde	–	**tør**	–	**turde**	–	**turdet**
ville	–	**vil**	–	**ville**	–	**villet**
gide	–	**gider**	–	**gad**	–	**gidet**

Irregular verbs

In the following table, the present tense is only included, in parentheses, when it is irregular. In all other cases the present tense follows the normal pattern of regular verbs. When the infinitive ends in a stressed vowel, the present is formed by adding **-r**.

bede	*bad*	*bedt*
betyde	*betød*	*betydet*
bide	*bed*	*bidt*
binde	*bandt*	*bundet*
blive	*blev*	*blevet*
bringe	*bragte*	*bragt*

briste		*brast/bristede*	*bristet*
bryde		*brød*	*brudt*
byde		*bød*	*budt*
bære		*bar*	*båret*
drage		*drog*	*draget*
drikke		*drak*	*drukket*
drive		*drev*	*drevet*
dø	(*dør*)	*døde*	*død*
falde		*faldt*	*faldet*
fare		*for*	*faret*
finde		*fandt*	*fundet*
fise		*fes*	*fiset*
flyde		*flød*	*flydt*
flyve		*fløj*	*fløjet*
fnyse		*fnøs*	*fnyst*
fortryde		*fortrød*	*fortrudt*
fryse		*frøs*	*frosset*
fyge		*føg*	*føget*
følge		*fulgte*	*fulgt*
få	(*får*)	*fik*	*fået*
gide		*gad*	*gidet*
give		*gav*	*givet*
glide		*gled*	*gledet*
gnide		*gned*	*gnedet*
gribe		*greb*	*grebet*
græde		*græd*	*grædt*
gyde		*gød*	*gydt*
gyse		*gøs/gyste*	*gyst*
gælde		*gjaldt*	*(gjaldt)*
gøre	(*gør*)	*gjorde*	*gjort*
gå	(*går*)	*gik*	*gået*
hedde		*hed*	*heddet*
hive		*hev*	*hevet*
hjælpe		*hjalp*	*hjulpet*
holde		*holdt*	*holdt*
hænge		trans.: *hængte*	*hængt*
		intr.: *hang*	*hængt*
jage		*jog*	*jaget*
klinge		*klang*	*klinget*
knibe		*kneb*	*knebet*
komme		*kom*	*kommet*
krybe		*krøb*	*krøbet*

kvæle		*kvalte*	*kvalt*
lade		*lod*	*ladt*
le	(*ler*)	*lo*	*let*
lide		*led*	*lidt*
ligge		*lå*	*ligget*
lyde		*lød*	*lydt*
lyve		*løj*	*løjet*
lægge		*lagde*	*lagt*
løbe		*løb*	*løbet*
nyde		*nød*	*nydt*
nyse		*nøs/nyste*	*nyst*
pibe		*peb*	*pebet*
ride		*red*	*redet*
rive		*rev*	*revet*
ryge		*røg*	*røget*
række		*rakte*	*rakt*
se	(*ser*)	*så*	*set*
sidde		*sad*	*siddet*
sige		*sagde*	*sagt*
skide		*sked*	*skidt*
skride		*skred*	*skredet*
skrige		*skreg*	*skreget*
skrive		*skrev*	*skrevet*
skyde		*skød*	*skudt*
skælve		*skjalv/skælvede*	*skælvet*
skære		*skar*	*skåret*
slibe		*sleb*	*slebet*
slide		*sled*	*sledet*
slippe		*slap*	*sluppet*
slå	(*slår*)	*slog*	*slået*
smide		*smed*	*smidt*
smøre		*smurte*	*smurt*
snige		*sneg*	*sneget*
snyde		*snød*	*snydt*
sove		*sov*	*sovet*
spinde		*spandt*	*spundet*
springe		*sprang*	*sprunget*
sprække		*sprak/sprækkede*	*sprukket*
spørge		*spurgte*	*spurgt*
stige		*steg*	*steget*
stikke		*stak*	*stukket*
stinke		*stank*	*stinket*

stjæle		*stjal*	*stjålet*
stride		*stred*	*stridt*
stryge		*strøg*	*strøget*
strække		*strakte*	*strakt*
stå	(*står*)	*stod*	*stået*
svide		*sved*	*svedet*
svinde		*svandt*	*svundet*
svinge		*svang*	*svunget*
		svingede	*svinget*
sværge		*svor*	*svoret*
synes	(*synes*)	*syntes*	*syntes*
synge		*sang*	*sunget*
synke		*sank*	*sunket*
sælge		*solgte*	*solgt*
sætte		*satte*	*sat*
tage		*tog*	*taget*
tie	(*tier*)	*tav*	*tiet*
træde		*trådte*	*trådt*
træffe		*traf*	*truffet*
trække		*trak*	*trukket*
tvinge		*tvang*	*tvunget*
tælle		*talte*	*talt*
vide	(*ved*)	*vidste*	*vidst*
vige		*veg*	*veget*
vinde		*vandt*	*vundet*
vride		*vred*	*vredet*
vække		*vakte/vækkede*	*vakt/vækket*
vælge		*valgte*	*valgt*
æde	(*æder*)	*åd*	*ædt*

ABBREVIATIONS

adj **adjectiv, tillægsord,** (adjective)
adm **administrativt** (administration)
adv **adverbium, biord** (adverb)
agr **landbrug** (agriculture)
am **amerikansk** (American)
anat **anatomisk** (anatomy)
arkit **arkitektur** (architecture)
arkæol **arkæologi** (archaeology)
astr **astronomi, astrologi** (astronomy, astrology)
auto **vedr. biler** (automobile)
bibl **biblioteksvæsen** (library)
biol **biologi** (biology)
bot **botanik** (botany)
brit **britisk** (British)
bygn **bygningsfag** (building)
d.s.s. **det samme som** (the same as)
edb **databehandling** (data processing)
elek **elektricitet** (electricity)
F **dagligt talesprog** (familiar)
F! **meget familiært – pas på!** (very familiar)
fig **overført betydning** (figurative)
fodb **fodbold** (football)
fork.f. **forkortelse for** (abbreviation for)
fys **fysik** (physics)
gastr **madlavning og køkken** (cooking and cuisine)
geogr **geografi** (geography)
geom **geometri** (geometry)
gl **gammeldags** (old-fashioned)
gram **grammatik** (grammar)
gymn **gymnastik** (gymnastics)
H **højtideligt** (formal)
hist **historik** (historical)
interj **interjektion, udråbsord** (interjection)
iron **ironisk** (ironical)
jernb **jernbane** (railway)
jur **jura, retsvæsen** (legal)
kem **kemi** (chemistry)
komp **komparativ** (comparative)
mar **maritimt** (maritime/ nautical)
mat **matematik** (mathematics)
med **medicin, lægevidenskab** (medicine)
merk **handel, merkantilt** (trade/ commerce)
met **meteorologi** (meteorology)
mil **militært** (military)
mods **modsat** (in contrast to)
mus **musik** (music)
neds **nedsættende** (derogatory)
ngn **nogen** (somebody)

ngt **noget** (something)
parl **parlamentarisk** (parliamentary)
pl **pluralis, flertal** (plural)
pol **politik** (politics)
pp **perfektum participium, datids tillægsform** (past participle)
præp **præposition, forholdsord** (preposition)
præt **præterium, datid** (preterite)
psyk **psykologi** (pyschology)
rel **religion** (religion)
S **slang** (slang)
S! **grov slang – pas på!** (coarse slang)
s **substantiv, navneord** (substantive, noun)
sby somebody
spøg **spøgende** (jocular)
sth something
sup **superlativ** (superlative)
sv.t. **svarer til** (corresponds to)
teat **teater, dramatik** (theatre, drama)
tekn **teknik** (technology)
tlf **telefon** (telephone)
typ **typografi** (typography)
ubøj **ubøjeligt** (inflexible)
u.pl. **uden pluralis, uden flertal** (no plural)
V **vulgært sprog** (vulgar)
V! **meget vulgært – pas på!** (very vulgar)
v **verbum, udsagnsord** (verb)
zo **zoologi** (zoology)
økon **økonomi** (economics)

ENGLISH–DANISH

A

A, a [ei]; *get an A in maths* få 13 i regning.
a [ei, ə], *an* [æn, ən, n] (ubest. artikel) en, et; om; pr.; ~ *few* nogle få; ~ *little* lidt; ~ *lot* en masse; *three times* ~ *day* tre gange om dagen; *50p a dozen* 50 p pr. dusin.
AA ['ei'ei] *s* (fork.f. *Automobile Association)* brit. pendant til FDM; (fork.f. *Alcoholics Anonymous)* sv.t. Lænken.
aback [ə'bæk] *adv: be taken* ~ blive forbløffet.
abandon [ə'bændən] *s* løssluppenhed // *v* opgive; forlade; ~ *ship* gå i bådene; ~ *oneself to sth* overgive sig til ngt; **~ment** *s* opgivelse; løssluppenhed.
abase [ə'beis] *v* fornedre.
abashed [a'bæʃt] *adj* beskæmmet; forlegen.
abate [ə'beit] *v* aftage, mindske(s); løje af.
abbess ['æbis] *s* abbedisse.
abbey ['æbi] *s* abbedi; klosterkirke.
abbot ['æbət] *s* abbed.
abbreviate [ə'brivieit] *v* forkorte; **abbreviation** [-'eiʃən] *s* forkortelse.
abdomen ['æbdəmən] *s* mave, underliv; underkrop; **abdominal** [-'dɔminəl] *adj* mave-.
abduct [æb'dʌkt] *v* bortføre; **abduction** *s* bortførelse.
aberrant [ə'bɛrənt] *adj* afvigende; **aberration** [æbə'reiʃən] *s* afvigelse; forvildelse.
abet [ə'bɛt] *v: aid and* ~ være medskyldig.
abeyance [ə'beiəns] *s: in* ~ stillet i bero, uafgjort.
abhor [əb'hɔ:*] *v* afsky; **~rence** *s* afsky; **~rent** *adj* afskyelig.
abide [ə'baid] *v* udstå, udholde; vare, holde; ~ *by* overholde, rette sig efter.
ability [ə'biliti] *s* evne; dygtighed; *to the best of one's* ~ så godt man kan.
abject ['æbdʒɛkt] *adj* ynkelig, sølle; ydmyg.
ablaze [ə'bleiz] *adj* i brand, i lys lue; ~ *with light* strålende oplyst.
able [eibl] *adj* dygtig, kompetent; *be* ~ *to* være i stand til (at), kunne; ~ *seaman* helbefaren matros; **~-bodied** *adj* rask og rørig.
ably ['eibli] *adv* dygtigt.
abnormal [æb'nɔ:ml] *adj* unormal, abnorm; **abnormality** [-'mæliti] *s* abnormitet.
aboard [ə'bɔ:d] *adv* ombord // *præp* om bord på.
abode [ə'bəud] *s (gl* el. *spøg): my modest* ~ min ringe bolig.
abolish [ə'bɔliʃ] *v* afskaffe, nedlægge; **abolition** [-'liʃən] *s* afskaffelse.
abominable [ə'bɔminəbl] *adj* afskyelig; gyselig; **abomination** [-'neiʃən] *s* vederstyggelighed; afsky.
aborigine [æbə'ridʒini] *s* indfødt (i Australien).
abort [ə'bɔt] *v* abortere; fremkalde abort (hos); slå fejl; aflyse; **abortion** [-'bɔʃən] *s* (provokeret) abort.
abortive [ə'bɔ:tiv] *adj* mislykket (fx *coup* kup).
abound [ə'baund] *v* findes i overflod; ~ *in (,with)* vrimle med.
about [ə'baut] *adv/præp* omkring; rundt; om; vedrørende; omtrent, cirka; *at* ~ *two o'clock* ved totiden; *it's* ~ *here* det er her et sted; *it's* ~ *time* det er på tide; *that's* ~ *it* det er vist det hele; *walk* ~ *the town* go rundt i byen; *be earnest* ~ *sth* mene ngt alvorligt; *what are we going to do* ~ *it?* hvad skal vi gøre ved det? *be up and* ~ være oppe (af sengen), være på benene; *be* ~ *to cry* være lige ved at græde; *what* ~ *a cup of tea?* hvad med en kop te? *bring* ~ forårsage; *I'm calling* ~ *the advertisement* jeg ringer vedrørende annoncen; **~-turn** *s (fig)* kovending.
above [ə'bʌv] *adv/præp* over; ovenover; ovenpå; mere end; ~ *all* fremfor alt; *be* ~ *sth* være hævet over ngt; *it is not* ~ *him to steal* han undser sig ikke for at stjæle; *from* ~ ovenfra; *it is* ~ *me* det ligger over min forstand; *the* ~ *items* ovennævnte ting; *over and* ~ foruden;

ud over; *be ~ suspicion* være hævet over mistanke; **~board** *adj* ærlig; åben; **~mentioned** *adj* ovennævnt.
abrasion [ə'breiʒən] *s* hudafskrabning.
abrasive [ə'breisiv] *s* slibemiddel // *adj* skarp; slibe-.
abreast [ə'brɛst] *adv: keep ~ of* holde sig ajour med, følge med i; *march four ~* gå fire ved siden af hinanden.
abridge [ə'bridʒ] *v* forkorte.
abroad [ə'brɔ:d] *adj* ud; udenlands; *go ~* tage til udlandet.
abrupt [ə'brʌpt] *adj* brat; pludselig; (om person) kort for hovedet.
abscess ['æbsəs] *s* byld.
abscond [əb'skɔnd] *v* stikke af.
absence ['æbsəns] *s* fravær; mangel (*of* på); *~ of mind* åndsfraværelse.
absent [æb'sɛnt] *v: absent oneself from sth* holde sig væk fra ngt // *adj* ['æbsənt] fraværende; distræt; væk.
absentee [æbsən'ti:] *s* fraværende person; en der pjækker.
absenteeism [æbsən'ti:izm] *s* fravær; pjækkeri.
absentminded ['æbsəntmaindid] *adj* åndsfraværende, distræt.
absolute ['æbsəlu:t] *adj* absolut; fuldstændig; uindskrænket; **~ly** [-'lu:tli] *adv* absolut; fuldstændig, aldeles; simpelthen.
absolution [æbsə'lu:ʃən] *s* syndsforladelse.
absolve [əb'zɔlv] *v: ~ sby from a promise* løse en fra et løfte; *~ sby* give en syndsforladelse.
absorb [əb'zɔ:b] *v* opsuge; suge til sig; opfatte; *be ~ed in a book* være opslugt af en bog; **~ent** *adj* absorberende, sugende; **~ing** *adj* (om fx bog) spændende.
absorption [əb'zɔ:pʃn] *s* opsugning; fordybelse, opslugthed.
abstain [əb'stein] *v* undlade at stemme; *~ from* afstå fra, afholde sig fra.
abstemious [əb'sti:miəs] *adj* afholdende.
abstention [əb'stɛnʃən] *s* afholdenhed; *there were nine ~s* der var ni der undlod at stemme.
abstinence ['æbstinəns] *s* afholdenhed.
abstract *s* ['æbstrækt] uddrag; referat // *v* [æb'strækt] abstrahere; uddrage, udvinde; resumere; optage; fjerne // *adj* ['æbstrækt] abstrakt.
absurd [əb'sə:d] *adj* meningsløs; latterlig; absurd; *don't be ~!* åhr la' vær'! sikke noget sludder!
abundance [ə'bʌndəns] *s* overflod; rigdom; **abundant** *adj* rigelig.
abuse *s* [ə'bju:s] misbrug; mishandling; skældsord // *v* [ə'bju:z] misbruge; mishandle; skade; skælde ud; **abusive** [-'bju:ziv] *adj* grov.
abysmal [ə'bizməl] *adj* afgrundsdyb; elendig, under al kritik; dybt beklagelig.
abyss [ə'bis] *s* afgrund; dybhavsområde.
AC ['ei'si:] (fork.f. *alternating current*) vekselstrøm.
academic [ækə'dɛmik] *s* akademiker // *adj* akademisk; teoretisk.
academy [ə'kædəmi] *s* akademi; *academy of music* musikkonservatorium.
ACAS ['eikæs] *s* (fork.f. *the Advisory, Conciliation and Arbitration Service*) sv.t. Forligsinstitutionen.
accede [æk'si:d] *v: ~ to* gå ind på, tilslutte sig; *~ to the throne* komme på tronen.
accelerate [æk'sɛləreit] *v* fremskynde; accelerere.
acceleration [æksɛlə'reiʃən] *s* acceleration; fremskyndelse.
accelerator [æk'sɛləreitə*] *s* speeder, gaspedal.
accent ['æksənt] *s* accent; tryk (fx på stavelse); tonefald; udtale; hovedvægt.
accentuate [æk'sɛntʃueit] *v* fremhæve, understrege; lægge vægt på.
accept [ək'sɛpt] *v* acceptere; tage imod; tage på sig (fx *the blame* skylden); optage; sige ja til; godtage; **~able** *adj* acceptabel; tilfredsstillende; **~ance** *s* billigelse; accept; modtagelse; optagelse.

access ['æksɛs] *s* adgang; *gain (,have) ~ to* få (,have) adgang til; få (,have) samkvemsret med // *v* få (,skaffe sig) adgang til; ~ **balcony** *s* altangang; ~ **card** *s* hævekort; betalingskort.

accessible [æk'sɛsəbl] *adj* tilgængelig.

accessory [æk'sɛsəri] *s* rekvisit; *(jur)* medskyldig *(to* i); *accessories pl* tilbehør; *toilet accessories* toiletsager.

access road ['æksɛs rəud]] *s* tilkørselsvej.

accident ['æksidənt] *s* tilfælde; uheld; ulykkestilfælde; *by ~* tilfældigt; ved et uheld; *have an ~* komme galt af sted; *~s will happen* det kan ske for enhver.

accidental [æksi'dɛntl] *adj* tilfældig; *~ death* død ved et ulykkestilfælde.

accident-prone ['æksidənt,prəun] *adj: be ~* altid komme galt af sted.

acclaim [ə'kleim] *v* hylde; hilse med bifald.

acclamation [æklə'meiʃən] *s* bifald, akklamation.

acclimatize [ə'klaimətaiz] *v* tilpasse, akklimatisere.

accomodate [ə'kɔmədeit] *v* anbringe; huse; have plads til; tilpasse (sig); imødekomme; *well-~d* bekvem; **accomodating** *adj* imødekommende.

accomodation [əkɔmə'deiʃən] *s* husly; plads; bekvemmelighed; tilpasning; *he's found ~ for 500 guests* han har fundet husly til 500 gæster; *have you got ~ for two adults?* har De værelser til to personer?

accompaniment [ə'kʌmpənimənt] *s* ledsagelse; akkompagnement.

accompany [ə'kʌmpəni] *v* ledsage; akkompagnere.

accomplice [ə'kʌmplis] *s* medskyldig.

accomplish [ə'kʌmpliʃ] *v* udrette; fuldende; gennemføre; **~ed** *adj* gennemført; dannet; dygtig; **~ment** *s* resultat; færdighed; bedrift; *he has many ~ments* han har mange evner.

accord [ə'kɔ:d] *s* enighed; overenskomst, aftale; *of one's own ~* af sig selv; *with one ~* alle som én; i rørende enighed // *v* stemme overens; give, skænke.

accordance [ə'kɔ:dəns] *s: in ~ with* i overensstemmelse med.

according [ə'kɔ:diŋ] *adv: ~ to* ifølge; efter; **~ly** *adv* følgelig; derfor.

accordion [ə'kɔ:diən] *s* harmonika.

accost [ə'kɔst] *v* antaste.

account [ə'kaunt] *s* konto; beretning; *~s* regnskaber; *by all ~s* efter alt at dømme; *by John's ~ she slammed the door* efter hvad John siger smækkede hun med døren; *of no ~* uden betydning; *on ~* à conto; på konto; *on no ~* under ingen omstændigheder; *on ~ of* på grund af; *on that ~ he gave notice* af den grund (,derfor) sagde han op; *take into ~, take ~ of* tage hensyn til; *be called to ~ for sth* måtte stå til regnskab for ngt // *v: be ~ed sth* regnes for ngt; *~ for* gøre rede for; stå for, udgøre **~able** *adj* ansvarlig.

accountancy [ə'kauntənsi] *s* bogføring; revision; **accountant** *s* bogholder; revisor.

account book [ə'kauntbuk] *s* regnskabsbog.

accredit [ə'krɛdit] *v* autorisere, godkende; akkreditere.

accumulate [ə'kju:mjuleit] *v* hobe sig op; vokse; samle(s); **accumulation** [-'leiʃən] *s* samling; ophobning.

accumulative [ə'kju:mjələtiv] *adj* voksende, stigende.

accuracy ['ækjurəsi] *s* nøjagtighed; omhu.

accurate ['ækjurət] *adj* nøjagtig; omhyggelig.

accusation [ækju'zeiʃən] *s* beskyldning; anklage.

accuse [ə'kju:z] *v* beskylde, anklage *(of* for); *the ~d* den anklagede; *stand ~d of* være anklaget for; blive beskyldt for.

accustom [ə'kʌstəm] *v* vænne; **~ed** *adj* vant *(to* til); sædvanlig; *be ~ed to* være vant til.

ace [eis] *s* (kort) es; (person) stjerne; *within an ~ of doing stj* lige ved at gøre ngt; *have an ~ up one's sleeve*

have ngt i baghånden // *adj: it's really ~!* (F) det er alle tiders!
acetic [ə'si:tik] *adj: ~ acid* eddikesyre.
ache [eik] *s* smerte // *v* gøre ondt; være øm; *I'm aching all over* jeg føler mig helt radbrækket; *I'm aching to tell you* jeg kan næsten ikke vente med at fortælle dig det.
achieve [ə'tʃi:v] *v* præstere; udrette; opnå; **~ment** *s* præstation; bedrift; opnåelse.
acid ['æsid] *s* syre; (S) LSD // *adj* sur; syrlig; syre-; **~ity** [æ'siditi] *s* surhed(sgrad); syrlighed; **~ test** *s (fig)* afgørende prøve.
acknowledge [ək'nɔlidʒ] *v* anerkende; bekræfte; indrømme; **~ment** *s* anerkendelse; indrømmelse; *in ~ment of your letter* som svar på Deres brev; *send ~ments* kvittere for modtagelsen.
acme ['ækmi] *s* (H) højdepunkt; indbegreb.
acne ['ækni] *s* akne, bumser.
acorn ['eikɔ:n] *s* agern.
acoustic [ə'ku:stik] *adj* akustisk (fx *guitar)*; **~s** *pl* akustik.
acquaint [ə'kweint] *v: ~ sby with sth* gøre en bekendt med ngt; *be ~ed* kende hinanden; *be ~ed with* kende; *get ~ed* lære hinanden at kende.
acquaintance [ə'kweintəns] *s* bekendtskab; kendskab *(of* til); (om person) bekendt; *make sby's ~* lære en at kende, blive bekendt med en; *have a passing ~ with sth* kende ngt flygtigt, have et overfladisk kendskab til ngt.
acquiesce [ækwi'ɛs] *v* indvillige.
acquiescence [ækwi'ɛsəns] *s* føjelighed; indvilligelse.
acquiescent [ækwi'ɛsənt] *adj* føjelig, medgørlig.
acquire [ə'kwaie*] *v* erhverve sig, få; opnå; **~d** *adj* erhvervet; tillært; *it is an ~d taste* det er ngt man skal vænne sig til.
acquisition [ækwi'ziʃən] *s* erhvervelse.
acquisitive [ə'kwizitiv] *adj* begærlig; 'om sig.
acquit [ə'kwit] *v* frikende; *~ oneself (well)* klare sig (fint); **~tal** *s* frifindelse.
acre ['eikə*] *s* (flademål: 4047 m^2).
acreage ['eikəridʒ] *s* (grund)areal.
acrid ['ækrid] *adj* bitter, skarp.
acrimonious [ækri'məuniəs] *adj* bitter, skarp.
across [ə'krɔs] *adv/præp* (tværs) over; på den anden side af; på tværs; over kors; (i krydsord) vandret; *walk ~ the road* gå over gaden; *a road ~ the wood* en vej tværs igennem skoven; *~ from* lige over for; *come ~* støde på, møde; *~ the EEC* i hele EF; *50 meters ~* 50 m i tværsnit.
act [ækt] *s* handling; akt; lov; *be caught in the ~* blive grebet på fersk gerning; *it was just an ~* det var bare komediespil; *be in the ~ of doing sth* være i færd med at gøre ngt; *get in on the ~* komme 'med; *put on an ~* spille komedie; *they will have to get their ~ together* de må se at finde fælles fodslag // *v* handle; opføre sig; virke; optræde; spille (teater); *~ as* fungere som; *~ out* afreagere; *~ it out on sby* afreagere på en; *~ up* skabe sig; **~ing** *s* skuespilkunst; komediespil // *adj* fungerende.
action ['ækʃən] *s* handling; virkning; funktion; aktion; *(jur)* retssag; *(mil)* kamp; *out of ~* ude af funktion (,drift); *put sth into ~* gennemføre ngt; iværksætte ngt; *take ~* tage affære; anlægge sag; **~ replay** *s (film)* langsom gengivelse, slow motion.
activate ['æktiveit] *v* aktivisere; aktivere; sætte gang i.
active ['æktiv] *adj* aktiv, virksom.
activity [æk'tiviti] *s* aktivitet.
actor ['æktə*] *s* skuespiller.
actress ['æktris] *s* skuespillerinde.
actual ['æktjuəl] *adj* faktisk, virkelig; egentlig; nuværende; *in ~ fact* i virkeligheden, faktisk; **~ly** *adv* faktisk; egentlig; virkelig; for øjeblikket; for resten; *~ly I'm Danish* jeg er faktisk dansk; *no one ~ly saw him* der var faktisk ingen der så ham.

acumen ['ækjumən] *s* skarpsindighed.
acute [ə'kju:t] *adj* akut; skarp; spids (fx *angle* vinkel); skærende (fx *pain* smerte); skarpsindig; ~ *accent* accent aigu.
AD ['ei'di:] *adv* (fork.f. *Anno Domini)* e.Kr. (efter Kristi fødsel).
ad [æd] *s* (kortform af *advertisement)* annonce.
adamant ['ædəmənt] *adj* benhård; ubøjelig.
adapt [ə'dæpt] *v* tilpasse (sig); indrette (sig); bearbejde; **~able** *adj* som kan tilpasses; praktisk; fleksibel.
adaptation [ædæp'teiʃən] *s* tilpasning; bearbejdelse; bearbejdning; ombygning.
adapter [ə'dæptə*] *s (tekn)* mellemstykke.
add [æd] *v* tilføje; tilsætte; lægge til (,sammen); addere; ~ *in* indføje; inkludere; ~ *on* tilføje; bygge til; ~ *up* tælle sammen; *(fig)* stemme; ~ *up to* beløbe sig til; ende med; betyde; *~ed complications* yderligere komplikationer.
adder ['ædə*] *s* hugorm.
addict ['ædikt] *s* narkoman; *(fig)* fanatiker.
addicted [ə'diktid] *adj: be ~ed to* være forfalden til; være vild med.
addiction [ə'dikʃən] *s* hang; (om medicin el. stoffer) tilvænning.
addictive [ə'diktiv] *adj* vanedannende.
addition [ə'diʃən] *s* tilføjelse; sammenlægning; addition; *in ~ to* foruden; **~al** *adj* ekstra; forøget; yderligere.
additive ['æditiv] *s* tilsætningsstof.
address [ə'drɛs] *s* adresse; (højtidelig) tale // *v* tale til; holde foredrag for; henvende (sig til); adressere; **addressee** ['ædrɛsi:] *s* adressat.
adenoids ['ædinɔidz] *pl (med)* polypper.
adept *s* ['ædɛpt] ekspert // *adj* [ə'dɛpt] dygtig, ferm; *be ~ at* være mester i.
adequate ['ædikwit] *adj* tilstrækkelig; fyldestgørende.
adhere [əd'hi:ə*] *v: ~ to* klæbe til; *(fig)* holde fast ved; holde sig til;
adherent *s* tilhænger // *adj* klæbende; *(fig)* forbundet.
adhesion [əd'hi:ʒən] *s* klæben; fastholden; **adhesive** [əd'hi:ziv] *s* klæbestof // *adj* klæbende, klæbe- (fx *tape* strimmel).
adjacent [ə'dʒeisənt] *adj* nærliggende; tilstødende.
adjoin [ə'dʒoin] *v* støde op til; **~ing** *adj* tilstødende.
adjourn [ə'dʒə:n] *adj* udsætte; hæve mødet; fortrække.
adjust [ə'dʒʌst] *v* indstille, justere; tilpasse (sig); ordne; rette på; ~ *to* tilpasse (sig) til; **~able** *adj* indstillelig; fleksibel; **~able spanner** *s* svensknøgle, skruenøgle; **~ment** *s* indstilling; justering; ordning.
ad-lib [æd'lib] *adj* improviseret // *v* improvisere.
administer [əd'ministə*] *v* administrere; tildele; give (fx *medicine* medicin).
administration [ədmini'streiʃən] *s* ledelse, administration; tildeling; *(am)* regering.
administrator [æd'ministreitə*] *s* leder, administrator.
admirable ['ædmərəbl] *adj* beundringsværdig; fortræffelig.
Admiralty ['ædmərəlti] *s: the ~* marineministeriet.
admiration [ædmə'reiʃən] *s* beundring.
admire [əd'maiə*] *v* beundre.
admirer [əd'mairə*] *s* beundrer.
admission [əd'miʃən] *s* indrømmelse; adgang; (på museum etc) entré; (på sygehus) indlæggelse; (på skole etc) optagelse.
admit [əd'mit] *v* indrømme; lukke ind; tillade; indlægge (på sygehus); optage; ~ *defeat* give fortabt; ~ *of* indrømme; tillade; ~ *to* give adgang til; optage i (fx *school* skole); tilstå; **~tance** *s* adgang; **~tedly** *adv* ganske vist.
admonish [əd'mɔniʃ] *v* formane; advare.
admonition [ədmə'niʃən] *s* advarsel.
ad nauseam [æd'nɔ:ziæm] *adj* til ulidelighed.

ado [ə'du:] *s* postyr; *without (any) more* ~ uden videre.

adolescence [ædəu'lɛsns] *s* ungdom; pubertet; **adolescent** *s* ung mand (,pige); teenager.

adopt [ə'dɔpt] *v* adoptere; antage (fx *another name* et nyt navn); vælge; **~ion** *s* adoption; antagelse; vedtagelse.

adorable [ə'dɔ:rəbl] *adj* yndig, henrivende.

adoration [ædə'reiʃən] *s* tilbedelse.

adore [ə'dɔ:*] *v* tilbede, forgude.

adorn [ə'dɔ:n] *v* smykke, pryde; udsmykke; **~ment** *s* pryd; pynt.

Adriatic [eidri'ætik] *s: the* ~ Adriaterhavet.

adrift [ə'drift] *adj: be* ~ drive (for vejr og vind); *(fig)* være overladt til sig selv; *feel* ~ føle sig usikker; *go* ~ gå galt.

adroit [ə'drɔit] *adj* dygtig; behændig.

adult ['ædʌlt] *s* voksen (person) // *adj* voksen; moden.

adulterate [ə'dʌltəreit] *v* forfalske; blande op.

adultery [ə'dʌltəri] *s* utroskab, ægteskabsbrud.

advance [əd'vans] *s* fremskridt; fremrykning; forskud; *in* ~ forud; på forhånd; *make ~s* gøre tilnærmelser // *v* gå frem; fremsætte; fremme; fremskynde; gøre fremskridt; give forskud // *adj: ~ booking* forudbestilling; *~ group* fortrop; **~d** *adj* fremskreden; videregående; avanceret; (højt) udviklet; *of ~d years* i en fremskreden alder; **~ment** *s* forfremmelse; fremme.

advantage [əd'va:ntidʒ] *s* fordel; fortrin; *have the ~ over sby* have fordel frem for en; *take ~ of* benytte sig af.

advantageous [ædvən'teidʒəs] *adj* fordelagtig, gunstig.

advent ['ædvənt] *s* komme; begyndelse; advent.

adventure [əd'vɛntʃə*] *s* eventyr; oplevelse; vovestykke; *~ playground* byggelegeplads; **~er** *s* eventyrer; **adventurous** *adj* eventyrlysten; eventyrlig.

adverb ['ædvə:b] *s* biord, adverbium.

adversary ['ædvəsəri] *s* modstander *(of* af); modspiller.

adverse ['ædvə:s] *adj* ugunstig; uheldig; *be ~ to* være fjendtligt indstillet over for; være skadelig for.

adversity [əd'və:siti] *s* modgang.

advert ['ædvə:t] *s* annonce.

advertise ['ædvətaiz] *v* reklamere, avertere, annoncere; vise.

advertisement [æd'və:tismənt] *s* annonce; reklame.

advertiser ['ædvətaizə*] *s* annoncør.

advertising ['ædvətaiziŋ] *s* reklame; avertering.

advice [əd'vais] *s* råd; (om post) anmeldelse; bevis; *a piece of* ~ et råd.

advisable [əd'vaizəbl] *adj* tilrådelig; ønskelig.

advise [əd'vaiz] *v* råde; rådgive; tilråde; underrette; *be well ~d to* gøre klogt i.

advisedly [əd'vaizidli] *adj* med fuldt overlæg, med vilje.

adviser [əd'vaizə*] *s* rådgiver.

advisory [əd'vaizəri] *adj* rådgivende.

advocate *s* ['ædvəkit] (skotsk) advokat; forkæmper *(of* for) // *v* ['ædvəkeit] gøre sig til talsmand for.

Aegean [i'dʒi:ən] *adj: the ~ (Sea)* Ægæiske Hav.

aegis ['i:dʒis] *s: under the ~ of the UN* under FN's auspicier.

aerial ['ɛəriəl] *s* antenne // *adj* luft-; antenne-; *~ attack* luftangreb; *~ photograph* luftfoto.

aeroplane ['ɛərəplein] *s* fly, flyvemaskine.

aesthetic [is'θɛtik] *adj* æstetisk; fintfølende.

afar [ə'fa:*] *adv: from* ~ langt borte fra; på afstand.

affable ['æfəbl] *adj* venlig, forekommende.

affair [ə'fɛə*] *s* sag; affære; forhold; ting(est); *that's his* ~ det må blive (,være) hans sag; *she was wearing a striped* ~ hun en stribet sag på; *a specialist in Middle East ~s* en specialist i mellemøstlige forhold; **~s** *pl (også)* forretninger.

affect [ə'fɛkt] *v* påvirke; berøre; angribe; foregive; (F) dyrke; *the silk ties which he usually ~ed* de silkeslips han dyrkede.
affectation [æfɛk'teiʃən] *s* affekterethed; krukkeri.
affected [ə'fɛktid] *adj* affekteret.
affection [ə'fɛkʃən] *s* kærlighed; hengivenhed; følelse; påvirkning.
affectionate [ə'fɛkʃənit] *adj* kærlig, hengiven.
affidavit [æfi'deivit] *s (jur)* beediget skriftlig erklæring.
affiliated [ə'filieitid] *adj* tilsluttet, tilknyttet.
affinity [ə'finiti] *s* slægtskab; lighed.
affirmative [ə'fə:mətiv] *adj* bekræftende; *in the ~* bekræftende.
afflict [ə'flikt] *v* plage, hjemsøge; *~ed with* plaget af, ramt af.
affliction [ə'flikʃən] *s* sorg; plage; lidelse.
affluence ['æfluəns] *s* velstand, overflod; tilstrømning.
affluent ['æfluənt] *adj* velstående, velfærds-; tilstrømmende.
afford [ə'fɔ:d] *v* have råd til; kunne tillade sig; yde; byde på; *I can't ~ the time* jeg kan ikke afse tiden.
affront [ə'frɔnt] *s* krænkelse // *v* krænke, støde.
afield [ə'fi:ld] *adv: far ~* langt bort(e); langt ud(e).
afloat [ə'fləut] *adj (mar)* flot; flydende // *adv: stay ~* holde hovedet oven vande; *keep a business ~* holde en forretning kørende; *set sth ~ (fig)* lancere ngt.
afoot [ə'fut] *adv* i gang; i gære.
aforementioned [ə'fɔ:mɛnʃənd], **aforesaid** [ə'fɔ:sɛd] *adj* ovennævnt; førstnævnt.
afraid [ə'freid] *adj* bange; *~ for sby* bange for at der skal ske en ngt; *be ~ of (,to)* være bange for (at); *I'm ~ that...* jeg er bange for at...; *I'm ~ not* desværre ikke; *is he ill? - I'm ~ so!* er han syg? - Ja, desværre!
afresh [ə'frɛʃ] *adv* påny; om igen.
aft [a:ft] *adv* agterud.
after ['a:ftə*] *adj/adv/præp* efter; bagefter; senere // *konj* efter at; *what are you ~?* hvad er du ude efter? *ask ~ sby* spørge til en; *~ all* når det kommer til stykket; alligevel; *take ~ sby* ligne en; **~-care** *s (med)* efterbehandling; kontrol (efter udskrivelse fra sygehus); **~-effects** *pl* eftervirkninger; efterveer; **~life** *s* livet efter døden; **~math** ['a:ftəmæθ] *s* eftervirkning; *in the ~math of* i tiden efter (fx *the war* krigen); **~noon** *s* eftermiddag.
afters ['a:ftəz] *s* dessert, efterret.
afterthought ['a:ftəθɔ:t] *s: have an ~* få en ny indskydelse; være bagklog.
afterwards ['a:ftəwədz] *adv* bagefter; senere; *soon ~* snart efter.
again [ə'gɛn] *adv* igen; på den anden side; desuden; *begin ~* begynde forfra (,igen); *~ and ~* gang på gang; *what did you say ~?* hvad var det du sagde? hvadbehar? *as much ~* lige så meget til, dobbelt så meget.
against [ə'gɛnst] *præp* mod, imod; ud for; ved; *run ~ time* løbe om kap med tiden; *as ~* sammenlignet med, mod.
agape [ə'geip] *adj* gabende; *be ~* måbe.
age [eidʒ] *s* alder; tidsalder; ælde; *it's been ~s since we met* det er hundrede år siden vi sås; *the ~ of consent* sv.t. den kriminelle lavalder; *he's my ~* han er på min alder; *be your ~!* vær nu ikke så barnlig! *come of ~* blive myndig; *under ~* umyndig // *v* ældes, blive gammel.
aged [eidʒd] *adj: a boy ~ ten* en dreng på ti år; ['eidʒid] gammel; oppe i årene.
ageing ['eidʒiŋ] *adj* aldrende.
ag(e)ism ['eidʒizm] *s* ældrediskriminering.
ageless ['eidʒlis] *adj* tidløs.
age limit ['eidʒ,limit] *s* aldersgrænse.
agency ['eidʒənsi] *s* agentur, bureau; virken; kraft; *through (,by) the ~ of sby* ved ens formidling, gennem en.
agenda [ə'dʒɛndə] *s* notesbog, lommebog; dagsorden.
agent ['eidʒənt] *s* agent; middel.
age-old ['eidʒəuld] *adj* ældgammel.

agglomeration [əglɔmə'reiʃən] *s* ophobning.
aggravate ['ægrəveit] *v* forværre; irritere; **aggravation** [-'veiʃən] *s* forværring; skærpelse.
aggregate ['ægrigeit] *s* ophobning; aggregat; samlet sum; *in (the)* ~ tilsammen, i alt.
aggression [ə'grɛʃən] *s* angreb; aggression.
aggressive [ə'grɛsiv] *adj* pågående; aggressiv.
aggressor [ə'grɛsə*] *s* angriber.
aggrieved [ə'gri:vd] *adj* bedrøvet; såret, krænket.
aggro ['ægrəu] *s* (F) aggression; besvær, mas.
aghast [ə'ga:st] *adj* forfærdet.
agile ['ædʒail] *adj* adræt; kvik.
agility [ə'dʒiliti] *adj* smidighed.
aging *adj* d.s.s. *ageing.*
agitate ['ædʒiteit] *v* ophidse; sætte i bevægelse, ryste, røre i; agitere; **~d** *adj* urolig; ophidset.
AGM ['ei,dʒi:'ɛm] *s* (fork.f. *Annual General Meeting)* (ordinær) generalforsamling.
ago [ə'gəu] *adv: long* ~ for længe siden; *not long* ~ for ikke så længe siden; *five years* ~ for fem år siden.
agog [ə'gɔg] *adj: be all* ~ *to see what has happened* være meget spændt på at se hvad der er sket.
agonizing ['ægənaiziŋ] *adj* pinefuld; sindsoprivende.
agony ['ægəni] *s* kval; (stærk) smerte; *be in* ~ lide de frygteligste kvaler; **~ aunt** *s* redaktør af læserbrevkasse; **~ column** *s* (i dameblad) læserbrevkasse.
agrarian [ə'grɛəriən] *adj* landbrugs-.
agree [ə'gri:] *v* være (,blive) enige; stemme (overens); enes; *I* ~ *that...* jeg er enig i at...; ~ *to* gå ind på; gå med til; *they* ~ *on this* de er enige om dette; *they ~d on a price* de enedes om en pris; ~ *with sby* være enig med en; *garlic doesn't* ~ *with me* jeg kan ikke tåle hvidløg; *the mountain air really ~s with him* bjergluften gør ham godt; **~able** *adj* behagelig; velvillig; *are you ~able to this?* er du indforstået med dette?
agreed [ə'gri:d] *adj* enig; aftalt (fx *time* tid).
agreement [ə'gri:mənt] *s* enighed; overenskomst, aftale; *in* ~ *with* i overensstemmelse med.
agricultural [ægri'kʌltʃərəl] *adj* landbrugs-.
agriculture ['ægrikʌltʃə*] *s* landbrug.
aground [ə'graund] *adv: run* ~ løbe på grund, grundstøde.
aha [ə'ha:] *interj* nå; jaså; aha; ja.
ahead [ə'hɛd] *adv* foran; forud(e); fremad; videre; ~ *of* foran; før; forud for; ~ *of time* i god tid; før tiden; *go straight* ~ gå (,køre) lige frem; *they were right* ~ *of os* de var lige foran os; *plan* ~ lægge planer for fremtiden.
aid [eid] *s* hjælp; støtte; hjælpemiddel; *what's that in* ~ *of?* hvad skal det gøre godt for? *hearing* ~ høreapparat // *v* hjælpe; støtte; ~ *and abet (jur)* være medskyldig.
aide [eid] *s* hjælper; **~-de-camp** ['eid-də'kɔŋ] *s* adjudant.
ail [eil] *v* være syg, skrante; *what's ~ing him? (fig)* hvad går der af ham? **~ing** *adj* skrantende (fx *economy* økonomi); **~ment** *s* (lettere) sygdom.
aim [eim] *s* sigte; mål; *take* ~ sigte; lægge an // *v* sigte; kaste; stile; agte; ~ *at* sigte på; stile efter; *she ~ed a kick at his shin* hun gav ham et (velrettet) spark over skinnebenet; ~ *to* agte at, have i sinde at; **~less** *adj* formålsløs.
ain't [eint] (F) d.s.s. *am not; aren't, isn't.*
air [ɛə*] *s* luft; præg; holdning; udtryk, mine; melodi, sang; *I need a change of* ~ jeg trænger til luftforandring; *go by* ~ flyve; *go on the* ~ blive udsendt (,transmitteret); *put on ~s* gøre sig til; *she is floating on* ~ *(fig)* hun svæver helt oppe i skyerne; *out of thin* ~ ud af den blå luft // *v* lufte; ventilere; tørre; **~ base** *s* flyvestation; **~bed** *s* luftmadras; **~borne** *adj* luftbåren; *be*

~borne være i luften; **~-cooled** *adj* luftkølet; **~craft** *s* fly(vemaskine); **~craft carrier** *s* hangarskib; **~crew** *s* flybesætning; **~ force** *s* flyvevåben; **~gun** *s* luftbøsse; **~hostess** *s* stewardesse, flyværtinde.

airily ['ɛərili] *adv* flygtigt; henkastet.

airing ['ɛəriŋ] *s* luftning; udluftning; luftetur.

air... ['ɛər-] sms: **~lane** *s* luftvej; luftkorridor; **~letter** *s* luftpostbrev; **~lift** *s* luftbro; **~line** *s* flyverute; flyselskab; **~liner** *s* rutefly; **~lock** *s* luftsluse; **~mail** *s* luftpost; **~plane** *s* fly; **~ pocket** *s* lufthul; **~ pollution** *s* luftforurening; **~port** *s* lufthavn; **~ raid** *s* luftangreb; **~-raid shelter** *s* beskyttelsesrum; **~-sea rescue** *s* sv.t. flyvevåbnets søredningstjeneste; **~show** *s* flyveopvisning; **~sick** *adj* luftsyg; **~space** *s* luftrum; **~strip** *s* start- og landingsbane; **~tight** *adj* lufttæt; **~ time** *s* *(radio, tv)* sendetid; **~-traffic control** *s* flyveledelse; flyveledere; **~worthy** *adj* flyvedygtig.

airy ['ɛəri] *adj* luftig; luft-; flygtig; nonchalant; **~-fairy** *adj* flyvsk, virkelighedsfjern.

aisle [ail] *s* (i kirke) midtergang; sideskib.

ajar [ə'dʒa:*] *adv* på klem.

akin [ə'kin] *adj: be ~ to* være beslægtet med.

alacrity [ə'lækriti] *s* iver; beredvillighed.

alarm [ə'la:m] *s* alarm(signal); uro, ængstelse; vækkeur; *set the ~ at 7.30* sætte uret til at vække 7.30; *sound the ~* slå alarm // *v* alarmere; forskrække; **~ clock** *s* vækkeur; **~ing** *adj* foruroligende.

alas [ə'la:s] *interj* ak; desværre.

album ['ælbəm] *s* album; LP.

albumen ['ælbjumin] *s* æggehvidestof.

alchemy ['ælkimi] *s* alkymi.

alcohol ['ælkəhɔl] *s* alkohol; sprit; **alcoholic** [-'hɔlik] *s* alkoholiker // *adj* alkoholisk, sprit-.

alder ['ɔldə*] *s* el(letræ).

alderman ['ɔ:ldəmən] *s* rådmand.

ale [eil] *s* lyst øl.

alert [æ'lə:t] *s* alarm; *on the ~* på sin post; i beredskab // *v* alarmere, tilkalde // *adj* vågen; kvik.

A level ['eilɛvəl] *s* (fork.f. *advanced level)* sv.t. uddannelse på gymnasieniveau, studentereksamen.

algebra ['ældʒibrə] *s* aritmetik.

Algeria [æl'dʒiəriə] *s* Algeriet; **Algerian** [æl'dʒiəriən] *s* algerier // *adj* algerisk.

alias ['eiliəs] *s* dæknavn // *adj* også kaldet, alias.

alibi ['ælibai] *s* alibi; undskyldning.

alien ['eiliən] *s* udlænding; fremmed; væsen fra en anden planet // *adj* fremmed; *~ from* forskellig fra; *~ to* fremmed for.

alienate ['eiliəneit] *v* gøre fjendtligt indstillet; fremmedgøre.

alight [ə'lait] *v* stige ned; stå 'af; lande // *adj: be ~* brænde; stråle.

align [ə'lain] *v* stå (,stille sig) på linje med; rette ind; *~ oneself with sth* tilslutte sig ngt; **~ment** *s* stillen på linje; indstilling; *(pol* etc) gruppering; alliance.

alike [ə'laik] *adj/adv* ens; *look ~* ligne hinanden; *it's all ~ to me* det er mig det samme; *it affects Denmark and Sweden ~* det påvirker både Danmark og Sverige.

alimentary [æli'mɛntəri] *adj* fordøjelses-; føde-.

alimony ['æliməni] *s* underholdsbidrag.

alive [ə'laiv] *adj* levende, i live; livlig; *come ~* vågne op; vækkes til live; *be ~ and kicking* leve i bedste velgående; *be ~ to* være opmærksom på; have sans for; *be ~ with* vrimle med.

all [ɔ:l] *adj/pron* al, alt, alle; det hele; helt // *adv* fuldstændig, helt; *~ alone* helt alene; *~ along* hele tiden; *~ but* næsten; *~ his life* hele livet; *~ of them* (dem) allesammen; *~ over the place* over det hele; *not at ~* slet ikke; *~ the same* alligevel; *~ at once* med ét, pludselig; *once (and) for ~* én gang for alle; *~ the better* så meget desto bedre; *he isn't ~ there* han er ikke rigtig klog; han er ikke særlig kvik i pæren.

allegation [æli'geiʃən] *s* påstand.
allege [ə'lɛdʒ] *v* påstå; hævde; **allegedly** [ə'lɛdʒidli] *adv* angivelig; påstået.
allegiance [ə'li:dʒəns] *s* troskab.
all-embracing ['ɔ:lɛm,breisiŋ] *adj* altomfattende.
allergic [ə'lə:dʒik] *adj:* ~ *to* overfølsom for; **allergy** ['ælədʒi] *s* allergi, overfølsomhed.
alleviate [ə'li:vieit] *v* lindre; dæmpe.
alley ['æli] *s* stræde, gyde.
alliance [ə'laiəns] *s* alliance; forbindelse.
allied ['ælaid] *adj* allieret; beslægtet.
all-important ['ɔ:lim'pɔ:tənt] *adj* altafgørende.
all-night ['ɔ:lnait] *adj* helaftens-; døgn-.
allocate ['æləkeit] *v* tildele; fordele; **allocation** [-'keiʃən] *s* tildeling; fordeling; rationering.
allot [ə'lɔt] *v* tildele; uddele; **~ment** *s* andel; kolonihave; tildeling.
all-out ['ɔ:laut] *adj* total.
allow [ə'lau] *v* tillade; lukke ind; lade få, give; indrømme; ~ *for* tage højde for; indkalkulere; regne med.
allowance [ə'lauəns] *s* ration; lommepenge; diæter; rabat; tilskud; (i skat) fradrag; *make ~s for* tage hensyn til; tage højde for.
alloy ['ælɔi] *s* legering // *v* legere.
all right ['ɔ:l'rait] *adj/adv* i orden; rask; udmærket; OK; *it's quite* ~ det er helt i orden; *he'll be here* ~ han skal nok komme.
all-round ['ɔ:l'raund] *adj* alsidig; universal-.
allspice ['ɔ:lspais] *s* (om krydderi) allehånde.
all-time ['ɔ:l'taim] *adj: an ~ record* alle tiders rekord.
allude [ə'lu:d] *v:* ~ *to* hentyde til.
alluring [ə'ljuəriŋ] *adj* forførerisk.
allusion [ə'lu:ʒən] *s* hentydning.
ally ['ælai] *s* forbundsfælle, allieret // [æ'lai] *v:* ~ *oneself with sby* alliere sig med en.
almighty [ɔ:l'maiti] *adj* almægtig; (F) kæmpe-, enorm.
almond ['a:mənd] *s* mandel; ~ **paste** *s* marcipanmasse.
almost ['ɔ:lməust] *adv* næsten.
alms [a:mz] *pl* almisse.
aloft [ə'lɔft] *adv* højt oppe.
alone [ə'ləun] *adj* alene; kun; *go it* ~ køre sit eget løb; *leave sby* ~ lade en være i fred; *all* ~ helt alene; *let* ~... for ikke at tale om...
along [ə'lɔŋ] *adv/præp* langs (med); hen ad; med; af sted; *is he coming ~?* kommer han med? ~ *with* sammen med; foruden; *all* ~ hele tiden; *get ~ with* komme godt ud af det med; klare sig med; ~ *the way (fig)* hen ad vejen; **~side** *præp* ved siden af; langs med.
aloof [ə'lu:f] *adj/adv* reserveret, tilknappet.
aloud [ə'laud] *adv: read* ~ læse højt.
alpine ['ælpain] *adj* alpin; alpe-; ~ **combined** *s* alpine skiløb.
alps [ælps] *pl* alper.
already [ɔ:l'rɛdi] *adv* allerede.
alright ['ɔ:l'rait] *adv* d.s.s. *all right.*
Alsatian [æl'seiʃən] *s* schæferhund.
also ['ɔ:lsəu] *adv* også; ligeledes; desuden; **~-ran** *s (sport, fig)* taber.
altar ['ɔ:ltə*] *s* alter; **~piece** *s* altertavle.
alter ['ɔ:ltə*] *v* ændre, lave om; forandre (sig).
alteration [ɔ:ltə'reiʃən] *s* ændring; (om tøj) omsyning.
alternate ['ɔltəneit] *v* veksle; skifte(s) // *adj* [ɔ:l'tənit] (af)vekslende; skiftevis; alternativ; *on ~ days* hverandden dag; **alternating current** ['ɔ:l-] *s (AC)* vekselstrøm.
alternative [ɔ:l'tə:nətiv] *s* alternativ; valg; anden mulighed; **~ly** *adv: ~ly one could...* man kunne også...; ~ **therapist** *s* alternativ behandler.
alternator ['ɔ:ltəneitə*] *s (auto)* vekselstrømsdynamo.
although [ɔ:l'ðəu] *konj* skønt, selv om.
altitude ['æltitju:d] *s* højde.
alto ['æltəu] *s* alt(stemme); ~ **flute** *s* altfløjte.
altogether ['ɔ:ltə'gɛðə*] *adv* fuldstændig; (alt) i alt; tilsammen; i det hele taget; allesammen; *they came* ~ de kom allesammen; *not* ~ ikke helt // *s: in the* ~ (F) splitternøgen.

always ['ɔ:lweiz] *adv* altid.
am [æm, əm] *v* 1. person sing. af *be; I* ~ jeg er.
a.m. ['ei'ɛm] *adv* (fork.f. *ante meridiem)* om formiddagen, om morgenen; *at seven* ~ klokken syv morgen.
amalgamate [ə'mælgəmeit] *v* sammensmelte; sammenslutte, fusionere.
amass [ə'mæs] *v* samle sammen, opsamle.
amateur ['æmətə*] *s* amatør; **-ish** [-'tə:riʃ] *adj (neds)* amatøragtig.
amaze [ə'meiz] *v* forbløffe; *~d at (,by)* forbløffet over; **-ment** *s* forbløffelse; **amazing** *adj* forbavsende; utrolig.
ambassador [əm'bæsədə*] *s* ambassadør *(to* i).
amber ['æmbə*] *s* rav; (om trafiklys) gult.
ambience ['æmbiəns] *s* atmosfære, stemning.
ambiguity [æmbi'gjuiti] *s* dobbelttydighed; modsigelse.
ambiguous [æm'bigjuəs] *adj* tvetydig; forblommet.
ambition [æm'biʃən] *s* ambition, ærgerrighed; **ambitious** *adj* ambitiøs, ærgærrig.
ambivalence [æm'bivəlʌns] *s* usikkerhed, vaklen; **ambivalent** *adj* usikker.
amble [æmbl] *v: ~ (along)* lunte (af sted).
ambush ['æmbuʃ] *s* baghold // *v* lægge sig (,lokke) i baghold.
ameliorate [ə'mi:liəreit] *v* forbedre (sig).
amenable [ə'mi:nəbl] *adj: ~ to* modtagelig for, tilgængelig for; ansvarlig overfor.
amend [ə'mɛnd] *v* forbedre; rette; forbedre sig; **-ment** *s* forbedring; ændring; *(am)* tilføjelse til lov; **-s** *pl: make ~s* give oprejsning (,erstatning).
amenity [ə'mi:niti] *s* bekvemmelighed; behagelighed; facilitet.
amiable ['eimiəbl] *adj* venlig; elskværdig.
amicable ['æmikəbl] *adj* fredelig; venskabelig.
amid(st) [ə'mid(st)] *præp* midt i; blandt.
amiss [ə'mis] *adj/adv: there's sth ~* der er ngt galt (,forkert); *a holiday wouldn't come ~* jeg ville ikke have ngt imod en ferie; *take sth ~* tage ngt ilde op; *go ~* mislykkes.
ammo ['æməu] *s* (F) ammunition.
ammonia [ə'məuniə] *s* salmiakspiritus, ammoniak.
amnesia [əm'ni:ziə] *s* hukommelsestab.
amnesty ['æmnisti] *s* benådning, amnesti.
among [ə'mɔŋ] *præp* mellem; blandt; *~ other things* blandt andet; *~ others* blandt andre; *~ themselves* indbyrdes; *they kept it ~ themselves* de holdt det for sig selv; **amongst** *præp* d.s.s. *among.*
amoral [ei'mɔrəl] *adj* amoralsk.
amorous ['æmərəs] *adj* forelsket; kælen; *an ~ affair* et kærlighedsforhold.
amount [ə'maunt] *s* beløb; mængde; sum // *v: ~ to* beløbe sig til; være det samme som; *it (all) ~s to the same thing* det kommer ud på ét; *it does not ~ to much* det er ikke meget værd.
amphibian [æm'fibiən] *s* amfibiefartøj; *(zo)* padde.
ample [æmpl] *adj* fyldig; rigelig; vidtstrakt; *this is ~* det (her) er rigeligt; *have ~ time* have rigelig tid.
amplifier ['æmplifaiə*] *s* forstærker.
amplify ['æmplifai] *v* forstærke; udvide; supplere.
amputate ['æmpjuteit] *v* amputere.
amuse [ə'mju:z] *v* more; underholde; **-d** *adj: be ~d* more sig; *keep oneself ~d* underholde sig selv.
amusement [ə'mju:zmənt] *s* underholdning; fornøjelse; ~ **arcade** *s* spillehal; ~ **park** *s* forlystelsespark.
an [æn, ən, n] se *a.*
anaemia [ə'ni:miə] *s* blodmangel, anæmi; **anaemic** *adj* blodfattig, anæmisk.
anaesthetic [ænis'θɛtik] *s* bedøvel-

sesmiddel; *under the* ~ i narkose, bedøvet; **anaesthetist** [æ'ni:sθitist] *s* narkoselæge.
analgesic [ænəl'dʒi:sik] *s* smertestillende middel.
analogy [æ'nælədʒi] *s* parallel; analogi.
analyse ['ænəlaiz] *v* analysere.
analysis [ə'nælisis] *s (pl: analyses* [-si:z]) analyse.
analyst ['ænəlist] *s (brit)* analytiker; *(am)* psykoanalytiker.
anarchy ['ænəki] *s* anarki, lovløshed.
anathema [ə'næθimə] *s: be* ~ være bandlyst; *it is* ~ *to him* det vil han ikke røre med en ildtang.
anatomy [ə'nætəmi] *s* anatomi; (op)bygning; krop.
ancestor ['ænsistə*] *s* forfader, stamfader.
ancestral [æn'sɛstrəl] *adj* familie-, slægts-.
ancestry ['ænsəstri] *s* slægt; forfædre, aner.
anchor ['æŋkə*] *s* anker; *be at* ~ ligge for anker; *weigh* ~ lette anker // *v* ankre op; forankre.
anchorage ['æŋkəridʒ] *s* opankring; ankerplads.
anchovy ['æntʃəvi] *s* ansjos.
ancient ['einʃənt] *adj* ældgammel; oldtids-; *an* ~ *monument* et fortidsminde.
ancillary [æn'siləri] *adj* hjælpe-; assisterende; underordnet; supplerende.
and [ænd, ən] *konj* og; ~ *so on* og så videre; *try* ~ *come* prøv at komme; *do it* ~ *I'll kill you* hvis du gør det slår jeg dig ihjel; *for hours* ~ *hours* i timevis.
anesthetic etc *(am)* se *anaesthetic* etc.
anew [ə'nju:] *adv* på ny; på en frisk.
angina [æn'dʒainə] *s* hjertesygdom (angina pectoris).
angel ['eindʒəl] *s* engel.
angelic [æn'dʒɛlik] *adj* engleagtig; engleblid.
anger ['æŋgə*] *s* vrede // *v* gøre vred.
angle [æŋgl] *s* vinkel; kant; hjørne; *at an* ~ skrå(t); *from their* ~ fra deres synsvinkel // *v* vinkle; give en drejning; ~ *for* fiske efter; ~ **iron** *s* vinkeljern; ~ **parking** *s* skråparkering; **~poise** ® *s* arkitektlampe.
angler ['æŋglə*] *s* lystfisker.
angling ['æŋgliŋ] *s* lystfiskeri.
anglo- ['æŋgləu-] engelsk-; anglo-; **Anglo-Saxon** *adj* angelsaksisk.
angry ['æŋgri] *adj* vred, gal; *be* ~ *with (,at)* være vred på; *get* ~ blive vred; *make sby* ~ gøre en vred.
anguish ['æŋgwiʃ] *s* kval; tortur; **~ed** *adj* forpint.
angular ['æŋgjulə*] *adj* kantet; vinkel-.
animal ['æniməl] *s* dyr // *adj* dyre-; animalsk; *(fig)* instinktiv.
animate ['ænimeit] *v* opmuntre, animere; live op // *adj* ['ænimit] levende; livlig; **~d** *adj* animeret; *~d cartoon* tegnefilm; **animation** [-'meiʃən] *s* livlighed; animering.
animosity [æni'mɔsiti] *s* uvilje; fjendskab.
aniseed ['ænisi:d] *s* anisfrø.
ankle [æŋkl] *s* ankel; ankelled.
anklet ['æŋklit] *s* (om smykke) ankelkæde.
annex(e) ['ænɛks] *s* tilbygning, anneks // *v* [ə'nɛks] indlemme, annektere; **annexation** [-'seiʃən] *s* annektering.
annihilate [ə'naiəleit] *v* tilintetgøre; udslette.
anniversary [æni'və:səri] *s* årsdag; *his twenty-fifth* ~ hans femogtyveårs jubilæum; *wedding* ~ bryllupsdag.
annotate ['ænəuteit] *v* kommentere.
announce [ə'nauns] *v* melde; meddele; bekendtgøre; annoncere; **~ment** *s* bekendtgørelse; annoncering (fx af radioprogram); **announcer** *s (tv, radio)* speaker.
annoy [ə'nɔi] *v* irritere; ærgre; genere; *don't get ~ed!* lad nu være med at blive sur! *~ed with* irriteret på (,over); **~ance** *s* irritation; ærgrelse; gene; **~ing** *adj* irriterende; kedelig.
annual ['ænjuəl] *s* årbog; etårig plante // *adj* årlig; års-; *Annual General Meeting (AGM)* (ordinær) generalforsamling.
annuity [ə'njuiti] *s* årlig ydelse; *life* ~ livrente.

annul [ə'nʌl] *v* annullere; ophæve; **~ment** *s* annullering.
anoint [ə'nɔint] *v* salve; indvi.
anomalous [ə'nɔmələs] *adj* abnorm; uregelmæssig.
anomaly [ə'nɔməli] *s* afvigelse; abnormitet.
anonymous [ə'nɔniməs] *adj* anonym.
another [ə'nʌðə*] *pron* en anden; en til; ~ *cup of tea* en kop te til; ~ *two years* to år til (,endnu); *one* ~ hinanden; *one after* ~ den ene efter den anden; *one way or* ~ på den ene el. den anden måde.
answer ['a:nsə*] *s* svar; løsning; *in* ~ *to* som svar på // *v* svare; besvare; løse (fx *a problem* en opgave); ~ *the door* lukke op (for en der ringer på); ~ *the phone* tage telefonen; ~ *back* svare igen; ~ *for* stå inde for; stå til regnskab for; **~able** *adj* ansvarlig; **~ing machine** *s* telefonsvarer.
ant [ænt] *s* myre.
antagonism [æn'tægənizm] *s* modvilje; modstand; **antagonist** *s* modstander; **antagonistic** [-'nistik] *adj* fjendtlig; modsat.
ante ['ænti] *s* indsats, indskud (i spil); *raise the* ~ sætte indsatsen op; øge sine krav (om penge).
anteater ['ænti:tə*] *s* myresluger.
antecedent [ænti'si:dənt] *s* forgænger; forhistorie; ~*s* forfædre // *adj* forudgående, tidligere.
antedate [ænti'deit] *v* foruddatere.
antediluvian ['æntidi'lu:viən] *adj* (egl. fra før syndfloden), sv.t. oldnordisk.
antemeridian ['æntimə'ridiən] *adj* *(am)* formiddags-.
antenatal ['ænti'neitl] *s* svangrekontrol // *adj* før fødslen, prænatal; ~ **clinic** *s* svangreambulatorium.
antenna [æn'tɛnə] *s* følehorn; antenne.
anterior [æn'tiəriə*] *adj* tidligere, forudgående; forreste.
anteroom ['æntiru:m] *s* forværelse, forkontor.
anthem ['ænθəm] *s* hymne; *national* ~ nationalsang.
ant-hill ['ænthil] *s* myretue.
anthology [æn'θɔlədʒi] *s* udvalg, antologi.
anti... ['ænti-] *sms:* **~-aircraft** *adj* luftværns-; ~*-aircraft defence* luftværn; **~biotic** [-bai'ɔtik] *s* antibiotikum // *adj* antibiotisk; **~body** *s* antistof.
anticipate [æn'tisipeit] *v* vente; se hen til; foregribe; komme i forkøbet.
anticipation [æntisi'peiʃən] *s* forventning; foregribelse; *thanking you in* ~ idet jeg på forhånd takker Dem.
anticlimax [,ænti'klaimæks] *s* antiklimaks.
anticlockwise [ænti'klɔkwaiz] *adj* mod uret; venstredrejet.
antics ['æntiks] *spl* krumspring; kunster.
anti... ['ænti-] sms: **~cyclone** [-'saikləun] *s* højtryk; **~dote** [-dəut] *s* modgift; **~freeze** [-fri:z] *s (auto)* kølervæske; frostvæske; **~-noise campaign** *s* støjbekæmpelse; **~-nuke** [-nu:k] *adj* antiatom-.
antipathy [æn'tipæθi] *s* modvilje, antipati.
Antipodes [æn'tipədi:z] *pl: the* ~ antipoderne (dvs. Australien, New Zealand og Oceanien).
antiquarian [ænti'kwɛəriən] *adj* antikvarisk; ~ **bookshop** *s* antikvariat.
antiquated ['æntikweitid] *adj* gammeldags, antikveret.
antique [æn'ti:k] *s* antikvitet // *adj* antik; gammel; ~ **dealer** *s* antikvitetshandler; ~ **shop** *s* antikvitetshandel.
antiquity [æn'tikwiti] *s* oldtiden; antikken; ælde.
antiseptic [ænti'sɛptik] *s* antiseptisk middel // *adj* steril.
anti-social [ænti'səuʃl] *adj* uselskabelig; usocial; samfundsskadelig.
antlers ['æntləz] *pl* gevir.
ant's nest ['æntsnɛst] *s* myretue.
anvil ['ænvil] *s* ambolt.
anxiety [æŋ'zaiəti] *s* ængstelse, angst; iver.
anxious ['æŋkʃəs] *adj* ængstelig; bekymret *(about* over); ivrig; *be very*

~ *to* være stærkt opsat på (,ivrig efter at).

any ['ɛni] *adv/pron* nogen; enhver; hvilken som helst; *hardly* ~ næsten ingen (,ingenting, intet); *in* ~ *case, at* ~ *rate* i hvert fald; *(at)* ~ *time* når som helst; *(at)* ~ *moment* hvert øjeblik; *does* ~ *of you sing?* er der en af jer der kan synge? *he's not here* ~ *more (,longer)* han er her ikke længere; *he's not just* ~ *old violinist* den violinist er ikke en hr. hvem som helst; *is there* ~ *more tea?* er der mere te?

anybody ['ænibɔdi] *pron* nogen (som helst); hvem som helst; (alle og) enhver; *they jumped about like* ~ de hoppede rundt som gale.

anyhow ['ænihau] *adv* d.s.s. *anyway*.

anyone ['æniwʌn] *pron* d.s.s. *anybody*.

anything ['æniθiŋ] *pron* noget (som helst); hvad som helst; *it was not* ~ *like silk* det lignede overhovedet ikke silke; *it was* ~ *but funny* det var alt andet end morsomt; *I would not miss that for* ~ det ville jeg ikke for min død undvære (,gå glip af); *he had no books or* ~ han havde ingen bøger eller noget.

anyway ['æniwei] *adv* i hvert fald; alligevel; på en hvilken som helst måde; under alle omstændigheder; ~, *we have got to go* nå, men vi er nødt til at gå; *thanks,* ~*!* men tak skal du (,I) have! ~, *John was miffed, so we left him alone* hvorom alting er, John var sur, så vi lod ham passe sig selv.

anywhere ['æniwɛə*] *adv* hvor som helst; alle vegne; *I don't see him* ~ jeg kan ikke se ham nogen steder; *we're not getting* ~ vi kommer ingen vegne; *not* ~ *near enough* ikke på langt nær.

apart [ə'pa:t] *adv* adskilt; afsides; (hver) for sig; fra hinanden; *live* ~ leve hver for sig; være separerede; ~ *from* bortset fra; *take* ~ skille ad.

apartment [ə'pa:tmənt] *s* lejlighed; ~ **house** *s (am)* boligkarré.

apathetic [æpə'θɛtik] *adj* apatisk, sløv, ligeglad.

apathy ['æpəθi] *s* apati, sløvhed.

ape [eip] *s* menneskeabe // *v* abe efter.

aperture ['æpətʃə*] *s* åbning; hul; *(foto)* blænderåbning.

apex ['eipɛks] *s* top; højdepunkt; **Apex ticket** *s (fly)* sv.t. billet til grøn afgang.

aphrodisiac [æfrəu'diziæk] *s* elskovsmiddel.

apiece [ə'pi:s] *adv* pr. styk, stykket; *a pound* ~ et pund stykket.

aplomb [ə'plɔm] *s* (selv)sikkerhed.

apologetic [əpɔlə'dʒɛtik] *adj* undskyldende; *be very* ~ *about sth* være fuld af undskyldninger over ngt.

apologize [ə'pɔlədʒaiz] *v* sige undskyld.

apology [ə'pɔlədʒi] *s* undskyldning; *be an* ~ *for sth* være en dårlig erstatning for ngt; skulle gøre det ud for ngt; *send one's apologies* sende afbud.

apostrophe [ə'pɔstrəfi] *s* apostrof.

appal [ə'pɔ:l] *v* forfærde; **-ling** *adj* rystende, skrækkelig.

apparatus [æpə'reitəs] *s* apparat; redskab; hjælpemiddel.

apparel [ə'pærəl] *s (poet)* dragt.

apparent [ə'pærənt] *adj* synlig, åbenbar; **-ly** *adv* åbenbart, tilsyneladende.

apparition [æpə'riʃən] *s* fænomen, syn; genfærd.

appeal [ə'pi:l] *s* appel; bøn; henvendelse; tiltrækning // *v* appellere; bede; behage, tiltale; ~ *for* anmode indtrængende om; ~ *to* appellere til; virke tiltrækkende på; ~ *to sby for mercy* bede en om nåde; *it doesn't* ~ *to me* jeg synes ikke om det; **-ing** *adj* tiltalende; bønfaldende.

appear [ə'piə*] *v* komme frem, vise sig; møde op; (om bog etc) udkomme; synes; fremgå; *it would* ~ *that* det ser ud til at; *it* ~*s not* åbenbart ikke; ~ *in Hamlet* spille i Hamlet; ~ *on television* komme i tv, optræde i fjernsynet.

appearance [ə'piərəns] *s* forekomst; tilsynekomst; udseende; fænomen;

put in (,make) an ~ møde op; komme til stede; *judge from* ~ dømme efter udseendet; *keep up* ~*s* bevare facaden; *to all* ~*s* efter alt at dømme.

appease [ə'pi:z] *v* berolige; stille.

append [ə'pɛnd] *v* vedlægge, vedføje; **~age** [ə'pɛndidʒ] *s* vedhæng.

appendicitis [əpɛndi'saitis] *s* blindtarmsbetændelse; **appendix** [ə'pɛndiks] *s (pl: appendices* [-si:z]) tillæg, appendiks; blindtarm.

appetite ['æpitait] *s* appetit; lyst.

appetizer ['æpitaizə*] *s* appetitvækker; **appetizing** *adj* appetitvækkende; appetitlig.

applaud [ə'plɔ:d] *v* applaudere, klappe (ad), bifalde.

applause [ə'plɔ:z] *s* bifald.

apple [æpl] *s* æble; *she's the* ~ *of his eye* hun er hans et og alt; ~ **blossom** *s* æbleblomst; **~cart** *s: upset the* ~*cart* vælte ens planer, stikke en kæp i hjulet; ~ **core** *s* kærnehus; ~ **dumpling** *s* sv.t. æbleskive; ~ **pie** *s* æblepie; *in* ~*-pie order* (F) i tip-top form; ~ **sauce** *s* æblemos; ~ **turnover** *s* (sammenfoldet) æbletærte.

appliance [ə'plaiəns] *s* anordning; apparat; instrument.

applicable [ə'plikəbl] *adj* anvendelig; passende.

applicant ['æplikənt] *s* ansøger.

application [æpli'keiʃən] *s* ansøgning; anvendelse; anbringelse; flid; *on* ~ ved henvendelse.

applied [ə'plaid] *adj* anvendt; ~ **art** *s* brugskunst.

apply [ə'plai] *v* anvende; ansøge; henvende sig; anbringe; smøre (,sætte) på; ~ *for* ansøge om; ~ *the brakes* bruge bremsen; ~ *to* gælde for, angå; henvende sig til; ~ *oneself to* gå op i, hengive sig til.

appoint [ə'pɔint] *v* udnævne; udpege; (om tid, sted etc) fastsætte, aftale; **~ment** *s* udnævnelse; stilling; møde; aftale; *make an* ~*ment with sby* aftale et møde (,at mødes) med en.

apportion [ə'pɔ:ʃən] *v* uddele; tildele.

apposite ['æpəzit] *adj* træffende, velvalgt.

appraisal [ə'preizəl] *s* vurdering, bedømmelse; **appraise** *v* vurdere.

appreciable [ə'pri:ʃiəbl] *adj* mærkbar, kendelig.

appreciate [ə'pri:ʃieit] *v* sætte pris på; have sans for; vurdere; **appreciation** [-'eiʃən] *s* påskønnelse; vurdering; *(økon)* værdiforøgelse.

appreciative [ə'pri:siətiv] *adj* taknemmelig; anerkendende.

apprehend [əpri'hɛnd] *v* pågribe; begribe, forstå.

apprehension *s* pågribelse; fatteevne; ængstelse; **apprehensive** *adj* ængstelig.

apprentice [ə'prɛntis] *s* lærling, elev // *v* sætte i lære; **~ship** *s* læretid, elevtid.

approach [ə'prəutʃ] *s* komme; adgang; indkørsel; fremgangsmåde; indstilling // *v* nærme sig; henvende sig til; gribe an; **~able** *adj* omgængelig; tilgængelig.

approbation [əprə'beiʃən] *s* billigelse; samtykke; bifald; *on* ~ på prøve, til gennemsyn.

appropriate *v* [ə'prəuprieit] tilegne sig; bevilge // *adj* [ə'prəupriit] passende, behørig; rammende (fx *remark* bemærkning).

approval [ə'pru:vəl] *s* godkendelse; *on* ~ på prøve, til gennemsyn.

approve [ə'pru:v] *v* godkende; ~ *of* synes om; **approving** *adj* bifaldende.

approximate *v* [ə'prɔksimeit] nærme (sig); tilnærme // *adj* [ə'prɔksimit] tilnærmet, omtrentlig; **~ly** *adv* omtrent, cirka.

approximation [əprɔksi'meiʃən] *s* tilnærmelse.

apricot ['æprikət] *s* abrikos.

April ['eipril] *s* april; ~ **fool** *s* aprilsnar.

apron ['eiprən] *s* forklæde; ~ **string** *s* forklædebånd; *he is tied to her* ~ *strings* han hænger i hendes skørter.

apt [æpt] *adj* passende; træffende; dygtig; *be* ~ *to* være tilbøjelig til (at), have tendens til (at).

aptitude ['æptitju:d] *s* talent, evne;

anlæg; egnethed; ~ **test** *s* færdighedsprøve.
aqualung ['ækwəlʌŋ] *s* iltbeholder (til svømmedykker).
aquarium [ə'kwɛəriəm] *s* akvarium.
Aquarius [ə'kwɛəriəs] *s (astr)* Vandmanden.
aquatic [ə'kwætik] *adj* vand-.
aquatube ['ækwətju:b] *s* vandrutschebane.
aquiline ['ækwilain] *adj* ørne-.
Arab ['ærəb] *s* araber.
Arabia [ə'reibiə] *s* Arabien.
Arabian [ə'reibiən] *s* arabisk; *the ~ Nights* Tusind og én nats eventyr; ~ **camel** *s* dromedar.
Arabic ['ærəbik] *s* (om sprog) arabisk; *~ numerals* arabertal.
arable ['ærəbl] *adj* som kan dyrkes; opdyrket.
arbiter ['a:bitə*] *s* dommer; voldgiftsmand.
arbitrary ['a:bitrəri] *adj* skønsmæssig; egenrådig.
arbitrate *v* (lade) afgøre ved voldgift; dømme.
arbitration [a:bi'treiʃən] *s* voldgift.
arbitrator ['a:bitreitə*] *s* mægler, forligsmand.
arc [a:k] *s* bue // *v* bue.
arcade [a:'keid] *s* arkade; spillehal.
arch [a:tʃ] *s* bue, hvælving; (på foden) svang // *v* krumme (fx ryg); danne en bue (over) // *adj* hoven, overlegen; skælmsk; ærke-.
archaeologist [a:ki'ɔlədʒist] *s* arkæolog; **archaeology** *s* arkæologi.
archaic [a:'keik] *adj* gammeldags, forældet.
archangel ['a:keindʒəl] *s* ærkeengel.
archbishop ['a:tʃbiʃəp] *s* ærkebiskop.
arch-enemy ['a:tʃɛnəmi] *s* ærkefjende.
archer ['a:tʃə*] *s* bueskytte; **archery** *s* bueskydning.
archetype ['a:kitaip] *s* prototype; grundform.
archipelago [a:ki'pɛləgəu] *s* øhav; skærgård.
architect ['a:kitɛkt] *s* arkitekt.
architecture ['a:kitɛktʃə*] *s* arkitektur.
archives ['a:kaivz] *pl* arkiv.
archivist ['a:kivist] *s* arkivar.
archway ['a:tʃwei] *s* bue(gang).
arctic ['a:ktik] *adj* arktisk; *the Arctic* Arktis; *the Arctic Circle* den nordlige polarcirkel; *the Arctic Ocean* Nordlige Ishav.
ardent ['a:dənt] *adj* glødende; ivrig; lidenskablig.
ardour ['a:də*] *s* glød; begejstring; iver.
arduous ['a:djuəs] *adj* besværlig, vanskelig.
are [a:*] *pl* af *be.*
area ['ɛəriə] *s* område; areal; felt; *a sum in the ~ of £50* et beløb på omkring £50; *dining ~* spiseplads; *~ of outstanding natural beauty* sv.t. fredet område, naturpark; ~ **code** *s (tlf)* områdenummer.
aren't [a:nt] d.s.s. *are not; they are nice, ~ they?* de er rare, ikke også?
Argentina [a:dʒən'ti:nə], **Argentine** ['a:dʒəntain] *s* Argentina; **Argentinian** [-'tiniən] *s* argentiner // *adj* argentinsk.
arguable ['a:gjuəbl] *adj* diskutabel; *it is ~ that...* man kan hævde at...; **arguably** *adv* nok, velsagtens.
argue ['a:gju:] *v* diskutere; hævde; overtale; skændes; *~ that* hævde (,påstå) at; *~ out* gennemdiskutere; *~ sby out of doing sth* tale en fra at gøre ngt.
argument ['a:gjumənt] *s* argument; diskussion; skænderi.
argy-bargy ['a:dʒi'ba:dʒi] *s* (F) kævl, vrøvl.
arid ['ærid] *adj* tør, gold; åndløs.
Aries ['ɛəriz] *s (astr)* Vædderen.
arise [ə'raiz] *v (arose, arisen* [ə'reuz, ə'rizn]) opstå; stige op; hæve sig; rejse sig; stå op; *~ from* komme af, skyldes.
aristocracy [əri'stɔkrəsi] *s* aristokrati.
aristocrat [ə'ristəkræt] *s* aristokrat; **aristrocratic** [-'krætik] *adj* aristokratisk.
arithmetic [ə'riθmətik] *s* (om skolefag) regning, matematik.
arm [a:m] *s* arm; gren; ærme; (se også *arms); ~ in ~* arm i arm; *keep sby at ~'s length* holde en tre skridt fra livet (,på afstand); *the ~ of the*

chair armlænet // *v* bevæbne; (op)ruste; armere.
armaments ['a:məmənts] *pl* våben.
armband ['a:mbænd] *s* armbind; (NB! armbånd: *bracelet).*
armchair ['a:mtʃɛə*] *s* lænestol, armstol.
armed ['a:md] *adj* (be)væbnet; ~ *forces* væbnede styrker.
armful ['a:mful] *s* favnfuld.
armhole ['a:mhəul] *s* ærmegab; (NB! armhule: *armpit).*
armistice ['a:mistis] *s* våbenstilstand.
armlock ['a:mlɔk] *s* føregreb.
armour ['a:mə*] *s* rustning, harnisk; pansring; *(mil)* kampvogne; *~ed car* pansret bil; **~ry** *s* arsenal.
armpit ['a:mpit] *s* armhule.
armrest ['a:mrɛst] *s* armlæn.
arms [a:mz] *pl* våben; våbenskjold; *bear* ~ bære våben; *take (up) ~ against* gribe til våben mod; *be up in ~ about sth* være oprørt over ngt; **~ race** *s* våbenkapløb.
army ['a:mi] *s* hær, armé.
A-road ['eirəud] *s* hovedvej.
arose [ə'rəuz] *præt* af *arise.*
around [ə'raund] *adv/præp* rundt (om); omkring (i); om; *is he ~?* er han her (et sted)? *she's been* ~ hun har set (,oplevet) lidt af hvert.
arouse [ə'rauz] *v* vække; ophidse (seksuelt).
arrange [ə'reindʒ] *v* arrangere, ordne; stille op; **~ment** *s* arrangement, ordning; aftale; *make ~ments* gøre forberedelser.
arrant ['ærənt] *adj* gennemført; eklatant.
array [ə'rei] *s* opbud; opstilling // *v* opstille.
arrears [ə'riəz] *pl: be in ~ with one's rent* være bagud med huslejen; *pay in* ~ betale bagud.
arrest [ə'rɛst] *s* standsning; anholdelse; *be under* ~ være anholdt; *make an* ~ foretage en anholdelse // *v* standse; arrestere, anholde; **~ing** *adj* interessant, fængslende.
arrival [ə'raivəl] *s* ankomst.
arrive [ə'raiv] *v* (an)komme; *~ at* finde frem til; nå; ankomme til; ~ *back* komme tilbage; *he has ~d* (også) han har klaret sig godt (, haft succes).
arrogance ['ærəgəns] *s* hovmod; **arrogant** *adj* hovmodig, arrogant.
arrow ['ærəu] *s* pil; **~root** *s* (slags stivelse anvendt til jævning).
arse [a:s] *s* (V) røv; *move (,shift) your ~!* flyt dig! hum dig! *get off your ~!* se at få lettet måsen (og komme i gang)! *he's a pain in the* ~ (V) han er en røvsyg stodder // *v: ~ around* fjolle rundt.
arson ['a:sən] *s* brandstiftelse.
art [a:t] *s* kunst; kunstfærdighed; (se også *arts).*
artefact ['a:tifækt] *s* kunstprodukt.
arterial [a:'tiəriəl] *adj: ~ road* hovedfærdselsåre.
artery ['a:təri] *s* pulsåre, arterie.
artful ['a:tful] *adj* listig, snedig.
art gallery ['a:tgæləri] *s* kunstmuseum; kunstgalleri.
arthritis [a:'θraitis] *s* leddegigt.
artichoke ['a:titʃəuk] *s* artiskok.
article ['a:tikl] *s* genstand; vare; artikel; kendeord; **~s** *pl* elevkontrakt, lærekontrakt.
articulate *v* [a:'tikjuleit] udtale, formulere; give udtryk for // *adj* [a:'tikjulit] leddelt; velformuleret; tydelig; **~d lorry** *s* sættevogn.
artifice ['a:tifis] *s* (krigs)list; påhit; kunstgreb.
artificial [a:ti'fiʃəl] *adj* kunstig; kunst- (fx *manure* gødning); **~ respiration** *s* kunstigt åndedræt.
artillery [a:'tilləri] *s* artilleri.
artisan ['a:tizæn] *s* håndværker.
artist ['a:tist] *s* kunstner.
artiste [a:'tist] *s* artist; entertainer.
artistic [a:'tistik] *adj* kunstnerisk.
artistry ['a:tistri] *s* kunstnerisk dygtighed; kunstfærdighed.
artless ['a:tlis] *adj* ukunstlet, naturlig.
arts [a:ts] *pl: the* ~ de humanistiske videnskaber; *faculty of* ~ humanistisk fakultet; *the (fine)* ~ de skønne kunster.
arty ['a:ti] *adj: be* ~ være kunstfreak.
as [æz, əz] *adv/konj* som, ligesom; da; mens; så; *twice ~ big ~* dobbelt

så stor som; *big* ~ *it is* hvor stort det (,den) end er; ~ *she said* som hun sagde; ~ *if (, though)* som om; ~ *for (, to)* hvad angår; ~ *long* ~ så længe (som); *(for)* ~ *much* ~ så meget som, så vidt som; ~ *soon* ~ så snart (som); ~ *such* som sådan; ~ *well* også; ~ *well* ~ såvel som; ~ *yet* endnu.

ascend [ə'sɛnd] *v* stige (op); gå op ad; bestige.

ascendancy [ə'sɛndənsi] *s* overherredømme.

ascending [ə'sɛndiŋ] *adj* stigende.

ascension [ə'sɛnʃən] *s* opstigning; *Ascension Day* Kristi Himmelfartsdag.

ascent [ə'sɛnt] *s* stigning; bestigning.

ascertain [æsə'tein] *v* forvisse sig om; konstatere.

ascetic [ə'sɛtik] *s* asket // *adj* asketisk.

ascribe [ə'skraib] *v:* ~ *to* tilskrive, tillægge.

ash [æʃ] *s* ask(etræ); (oftest i *pl: ashes)* aske.

ashamed [ə'ʃeimd] *adj* skamfuld, flov: *be* ~ *of* skamme sig over, være flov over; *it's nothing to be* ~ *of* det behøver man ikke at skamme sig over.

ashen ['æʃən] *adj* ligbleg.

ashore [ə'ʃɔ:*] *adv* i land.

ashtray ['æʃtrei] *s* askebæger.

Asia ['eiʃə] *s* Asien; ~ *Minor* Lilleasien; **Asian** *s* asiat // *adj* asiatisk; **asiatic** [eisi'ætik] *adj* asiatisk.

aside [ə'said] *s* sidebemærkning // *adv* til side; ~ *from* bortset fra.

ask [a:sk] *v* spørge; bede, invitere; kræve; ~ *sby to do sth* bede en gøre ngt; ~ *sby about sth* spørge en om ngt; ~ *after sby* spørge til en; ~ *sby out* invitere en ud; ~ *for* spørge efter; bede om; *he was* ~*ing for it* han har selv været ude om det.

askance [ə'ska:ns] *adv: look* ~ *at sby* se skævt til en.

askew [ə'skju:] *adj/adv* skæv(t).

asking price ['a:skiŋ prais] *s* prisforlangende.

asleep [ə'sli:p] *adj* sovende; *be* ~ sove; *fall* ~ falde i søvn; *fast* ~ i dyb søvn.

asparagus [ə'spærəgəs] *s (u.pl)* asparges; *two stalks of* ~ to asparges.

aspect ['æspɛkt] *s* udseende; synsvinkel; aspekt; beliggenhed.

aspen ['æspən] *s* asp(etræ).

asperity [æs'pɛriti] *s* skarphed; barskhed; spydighed.

asphalt ['æsfəlt] *s* asfalt // *v* asfaltere; ~ **paper** *s* tagpap.

asphyxiate [æs'fiksieit] *v* kvæle; blive kvalt.

aspic ['æspik] *s* gelé; sky.

aspiration [æspə'reiʃən] *s* åndedrag, indånding; forhåbning; stræben.

aspire [ə'spaiə*] *v:* ~ *to* stræbe efter.

ass [æs] *s* æsel; *(fig)* fjols, kvaj; *(am)* røv; *make an* ~ *of oneself* kvaje sig.

assail [ə'seil] *v* overfalde; angribe.

assailant [ə'seilənt] *s* voldsmand; angriber.

assassin [ə'sæsin] *s* (snig)morder; **~ate** *v* myrde.

assassination [əsæsi'neiʃən] *s* (snig)mord.

assault [ə'sɔ:lt] *s* angreb; overfald; voldtægtsforsøg; ~ *(and battery) (jur)* vold; legemsbeskadigelse // *v* angribe; overfalde.

assay [ə'sei] *s* prøve.

assemble [ə'sɛmbl] *v* samle; montere; samles.

assembly [ə'sɛmbli] *s* samling; montage; forsamling; ~ **hall** *s* forsamlingshus; ~ **line** *s* samlebånd.

assent [ə'sɛnt] *s* samtykke // *v* samtykke *(to* i).

assert [ə'sə:t] *v* påstå; hævde; bedyre; ~ *oneself* holde på sin ret; føre sig frem; markere sig.

assertion [ə'sə:ʃən] *s* påstand.

assertive [ə'sə:tiv] *adj* påståelig; selvhævdende.

assess [ə'sɛs] *v* vurdere; opgøre, gøre op; **~ment** *s* vurdering; beskatning.

assessor [ə'sɛsə*] *s* ligningsmand; vurderingsmand.

asset ['æsit] *s* aktiv; fordel; **~s** *pl* aktiver; formue.

assiduous [ə'sidjuəs] *adj* ihærdig, utrættelig.
assign [ə'sain] *v* udpege; anvise; overdrage; tillægge; pålægge; tildele.
assignation [əsig'neiʃən] *s* stævnemøde.
assignment [ə'sainmənt] *s* opgave; hverv; overdragelse.
assimilate [ə'simileit] *v* optage; opsuge; fordøje; **assimilation** [-'leiʃən] *s* optagelse; assimilation.
assist [ə'sist] *v* hjælpe; assistere; medvirke.
assistance [ə'sistəns] *s* hjælp, bistand; assistance; medvirken.
assistant [ə'sistənt] *s* assistent; (med)hjælper.
assizes [ə'saiziz] *pl* (i Skotland) nævningeting.
associate *s* [ə'səuʃiit] medarbejder; kollega; medlem // *v* [ə'səuʃieit] forbinde; forene; ~ *with* omgås // *adj* [ə'səuʃiit] tilknyttet.
association [əsəusi'eiʃən] *s* tilknytning *(with* til); forening; association; ~ **football** *s* (almindelig) fodbold.
assort [ə'sɔ:t] *v* sortere; assortere; **~ed** *adj* blandede (fx *chocolates* chokolader); **~ment** *s* blanding; udvalg, sortiment.
assume [ə'sju:m] *v* antage, formode; iføre sig; overtage; tiltage sig; foregive; *~d name* påtaget navn; ~ *one's teeth* sætte protesen på plads; **assuming** *adj* vigtig; *assuming that* under forudsætning af at.
assumption [ə'sʌmpʃən] *s* antagelse; forudsætning; overtagelse; påtagethed; overlegenhed; **Assumption** *s* himmelfart.
assurance [ə'ʃuərəns] *s* forsikring; overbevisning; selvsikkerhed.
assure [ə'ʃuə*] *v* forsikre; garantere; overbevise; *~d of* sikker på, overbevist om; *rest ~d that...* du kan være sikker på at...; **assuredly** [ə'ʃuərədli] *adv* sikkert.
astern [ə'stə:n] *adv* agterud(e).
astonish [ə'stɔniʃ] *v* forbavse, forbløffe; **~ment** *s* forbavselse.
astound [ə'staund] *v* overraske; lamslå.
astray [ə'strei] *adv: go* ~ fare vild; *(fig)* komme på gale veje; *lead sby* ~ vildlede en; få en på gale veje.
astride [ə'straid] *adv* overskrævs // *præp* overskrævs på.
astringent [ə'strindʒənt] *s* adstringerende middel // *adj* sammensnerpende; skarp; skrap.
astrologer [ə'strɔlədʒə*] *s* astrolog; **astrology** *s* astrologi.
astronomer [ə'strɔnəmə*] *s* astronom; **astronomy** *s* astronomi.
astute [ə'stju:t] *adj* snedig, dreven; kvik.
asunder [ə'sʌndə*] *adj* i stykker.
asylum [ə'sailəm] *s* tilflugtssted, asyl; *lunatic ~ (gl)* sindssygeanstalt; *political* ~ politisk asyl.
at [æt, ət] *præp* på; i; ved; hos; ad; til; ~ *the baker's* hos bageren; ~ *school* i skole(n); ~ *table* ved bordet; *be ~ table* sidde til bords; ~ *times* til tider; ~ *that* oven i købet; *laugh* ~ le ad; *throw stones ~ sby* kaste sten efter en; *sell sth ~ 50p* sælge ngt for 50 p; *what are you ~ now?* hvad laver du nu? *what are you driving ~?* hvad hentyder du til? *while you are ~ it...* mens du nu er i gang...
ate [eit] *præt* af *eat.*
Athens ['æθinz] *s* Athen.
athlete ['æθli:t] *s* idrætsmand; atlet; **~'s foot** *s* fodsvamp.
athletic [æθ'lɛtik] *adj* idræts-; atletisk; **athletics** *pl* fri idræt; atletik.
Atlantic [ət'læntik] *s: the ~ (Ocean)* Atlanterhavet // *adj* atlanterhavs-.
atmosphere ['ætməsfiə*] *s* atmosfære; *(fig)* stemning; **atmospheric** [-'fɛrik] *adj* atmosfærisk; **atmospherics** *pl* atmosfæriske forstyrrelser.
atom ['ætəm] *s* atom; *not an ~ of* ikke skygge af.
atomic [ə'tɔmik] *adj* atom-; ~ **bomb** *s* atombombe; ~ **energy** *s* atomkraft.
atomizer ['ætəmaizə*] *s* sprayflaske, forstøver.
atone [ə'təun] *v: ~ for* bøde for; gøre godt igen; **~ment** *s* bod; forsoning.

atrocious [ə'trəuʃəs] *adj* grusom, rædsom; **atrocity** [ə'trɔsiti] *s* grusomhed; rædsel.

attach [ə'tætʃ] *v* fastgøre; hæfte (sammen); vedføje; tilknytte; *be ~ed to sby* være knyttet til en; *no strings ~ed* helt uforpligtende; **-ment** *s* fastgørelse; tilbehør; fæste; *(fig)* hengivenhed; tilknytning.

attack [ə'tæk] *s* angreb; anfald // *v* angribe; kaste sig over; gå i gang med; **-er** *s* angriber.

attain [ə'tein] *v* nå, opnå; **-able** *adj* opnåelig.

attainments [ə'teinmənts] *spl* dygtighed, færdigheder.

attempt [ə'tɛmpt] *s* forsøg; *make an ~ on sby's life* lave attentat mod en // *v* forsøge; **-ed theft** *s (jur)* tyveriforsøg.

attend [ə'tɛnd] *v* deltage i; gå i (fx *church* kirke); gå til (fx *lectures* forelæsninger); *~ (up)on* betjene; være til rådighed for; *~ to* lytte til; passe; tage sig af; ekspedere.

attendance [ə'tɛndəns] *s* tilstedeværelse; deltagelse; fremmøde; tilsyn; betjening.

attendant [ə'tɛndənt] *s* ledsager; tjener; deltager // *adj* tjenstgørende; ledsagende.

attention [ə'tɛnʃən] *s* opmærksomhed; pasning; *at ~ (mil)* i retstilling; *pay ~ to* lægge mærke til; sørge for; høre efter.

attentive [ə'tɛntiv] *adj* opmærksom; påpasselig.

attenuate [ə'tɛnju:eit] *v* svække.

attest [ə'tɛst] *v: ~ to* bevidne, attestere.

attic ['ætik] *s* loft(srum); pulterkammer.

attire [ə'taiə*] *s* dragt, antræk; **-d** *adj: ~d in* klædt i.

attitude ['ætitju:d] *s* stilling; indstilling; holdning.

attorney [ə'tə:ni] *s (am)* advokat; befuldmægtiget; *Attorney General (brit)* medlem af regeringen og dennes juridiske rådgiver; (også:) sv.t. justitsminister; *power of ~* fuldmagt.

attract [ə'trækt] *v* tiltrække (sig).

attraction [ə'trækʃən] *s* tiltrækning; attraktion.

attractive [ə'træktiv] *adj* tiltrækkende; tiltalende.

attribute *s* ['ætribju:t] attribut, egenskab // *v* [ə'tribju:t] tilskrive, tillægge.

attrition [ə'triʃən] *s: war of ~* udmattelseskrig.

auburn ['ɔ:bən] *adj* (om hår) kastaniebrun.

auction ['ɔ:kʃən] *s* auktion; *put sth up for ~* sætte ngt på auktion // *v* sælge på auktion; **auctioneer** [-'niə*] *s* auktionarius.

audacious [ɔ:'deiʃəs] *adj* dristig, fræk; **audacity** [ɔ:'dæsiti] *s* dristighed, frækhed.

audible ['ɔ:dibl] *adj* hørlig.

audience ['ɔ:diəns] *s* publikum; tilskuere; tilhørere; audiens.

audit ['ɔ:dit] *s* revision // *v* revidere.

audition [ɔ:'diʃən] *s* høreevne; høring; prøvesyngning (el. -spilning).

auditor ['ɔ:ditə*] *s* revisor.

auditorium [ɔ:di'tɔ:riəm] *s* tilskuerpladser; auditorium; koncertsal.

augment [ɔ:g'mɛnt] *v* øge(s); gøre (,blive) større.

augur ['ɔ:gə*] *v* varsle, love.

augury ['ɔ:gjuri] *s* varsel.

August ['ɔ:gəst] *s* august.

august [ɔ:'gʌst] *adj* ærefrygtindgydende; ophøjet.

aunt [a:nt] *s* tante; **auntie, aunty** *s* (kæleform af *aunt)* tante.

auspices ['ɔ:spisiz] *pl: under the ~ of* under protektion af; **auspicious** [-'spiʃəs] *adj* lovende; gunstig.

austere [ɔ:'stiə*] *adj* barsk, streng.

austerity [ɔ:stɛriti] *s* barskhed, strenghed; sparsommelighed.

Australia [ɔ:'streiliə] *s* Australien; **-n** *s* australier // *adj* australsk.

Austria ['ɔ:striə] *s* Østrig; **-n** *s* østriger // *adj* østrigsk.

authentic [ɔ:'θɛntik] *adj* ægte, autentisk.

authenticate [ɔ:'θɛntikeit] *v* fastslå ægtheden af; legalisere.

author ['ɔ:θə*] *s* forfatter; ophav(smand).

authoritarian [ɔ:θɔri'tɛəriən] *adj* autoritær.

authoritative [ɔ:'θɔritativ] *adj* autoritativ, myndig.

authority [ɔ:'θɔriti] *s* myndighed; bemyndigelse; autoritet; *the authorities* myndighederne; *have it on good ~ that...* vide fra pålidelig kilde at...

authorize ['ɔ:θəraiz] *v* autorisere; bemyndige.

authorship ['ɔ:θəʃip] *s* forfattervirksomhed; oprindelse.

auto... [ɔ:təu-] *sms:* **~biography** [-bai'ɔgrəfi] *s* selvbiografi; **~cratic** [-'krætik] *adj* enevældig; **~graph** ['ɔ:təgra:f] *s* autograf // *v* signere; **~mate** *v* automatisere; **~matic** [-'mætik] *s* automatpistol // *adj* automatisk; **~mation** [-'meiʃən] *s* automatisering; **~maton** [ɔ:'tɔmətən] *s* robot; **~nomous** [ɔ:'tɔnəməs] *adj* uafhængig, autonom; **~nomy** [ɔ:'tɔnəmi] *s* selvstyre.

autopsy ['ɔ:tɔpsi] *s* obduktion.

autumn ['ɔ:təm] *s* efterår; **~al** [-'tʌmnəl] *adj* efterårs-.

auxiliary [ɔ:g'ziliəri] *s* hjælper // *adj* hjælpe-; reserve-.

avail [ə'veil] *s: of (,to) no ~* til ingen nytte // *v: ~ oneself of* benytte sig af; **~ability** [-'biliti] *s* tilgængelighed; **~able** *adj* disponibel; tilgængelig; til at træffe; *every ~able means* alle til rådighed stående midler.

avalanche ['ævəla:nʃ] *s* sneskred, lavine.

avarice ['ævəris] *s* havesyge, griskhed; **avaricious** [-'riʃəs] *adj* grisk; grådig.

Ave. fork.f. *avenue.*

avenge [a'vɛndʒ] *v* hævne.

average ['ævəridʒ] *s* gennemsnit; middelværdi; *on ~* i gennemsnit; *above (,below) ~* over (,under) gennemsnittet // *v* beregne gennemsnittet; frembringe en gennemsnitlig mængde; *~ out* udligne(s); *~ out at* i gennemsnit blive // *adj* gennemsnitlig; middel-.

averse [ə'və:s] *adj* utilbøjelig; *be ~ to* ikke kunne lide; *I wouldn't be ~ to a drink* jeg ville ikke have ngt imod en drink.

aversion [ə'və:ʃən] *s* modvilje, uvilje, aversion; *pet ~* yndlingsaversion.

avert [ə'və:t] *v* vende bort; afværge.

aviary ['eiviəri] *s* voliere.

aviation [eivi'eiʃən] *s* flyvning.

avid ['ævid] *adj* grisk, begærlig.

avoid [ə'vɔid] *v* undgå; sky; **~able** *adj* til at undgå; **~ance** *s* undgåelse.

avowed [ə'vaud] *adj* erklæret, svoren.

await [ə'weit] *v* afvente, vente på; *~ events* afvente begivenhedernes gang.

awake [ə'weik] *v (awoke, awoken* [ə'wəuk, ə'wəukən]) vække; vågne // *adj* vågen; *be ~ to* være lydhør overfor; være klar over; **~ning** *s* opvågnen.

award [ə'wɔ:d] *s* belønning, præmie // *v* belønne; *(jur)* tilkende, give.

aware [ə'wɛə*] *adj: ~ of* klar over; *become ~ of* blive klar over; *politically ~* politisk bevidst; **~ness** *s* viden; årvågenhed; bevidsthed.

awash [ə'wɔʃ] *adj* overskyllet (af vand); drivende (i vand); *~ with* fuld af.

away [ə'wei] *adj/adv* væk; af sted; bort(e); *Christmas is two weeks ~* der er to uger til jul; *he's ~ for a week* han er væk i en uge; *far ~* langt væk (,borte); *pedal ~* cykle løs; *wither ~* visne hen; *do ~ with* skaffe af vejen; *play ~ (fodb* etc) spille på udebane; *right ~* med det samme, straks; **~ match** *s (sport)* kamp på udebane.

awe [ɔ:] *s* ærefrygt; *stand in ~ of sby* have stor respekt for en; **~-inspiring** *adj* respektindgydende; **~some** *adj* skrækindjagende; formidabel; **~struck** *adj* rædselslagen.

awful ['ɔ:fəl] *adj* skrækkelig, rædsom; mægtig, enorm.

awhile [ə'wail] *adv* en stund, lidt.

awkward ['ɔ:kwəd] *adj* pinlig; kejtet; vanskelig; genert; *it's ~ for me* det passer mig ikke så godt.

awl [ɔ:l] *s* syl.

awning ['ɔ:niŋ] *s* solsejl; markise.

awoke, awoken [ə'wəuk, ə'wəukn] *præt* og *pp* af *awake.*

awry [ə'rai] *adj/adv* skæv(t); *go* ~ slå fejl.
axe [æks] *s* økse; *get the* ~ blive ramt af nedskæringer; *have an* ~ *to grind* have private interesser at pleje, have ngt at skulle have klinket // *v* hugge med økse; afskedige; skære ned (på).
axis ['æksis] *s (pl: axes* ['æksiz]) akse.
axle [æksl] *s* hjulaksel.
ay(e) [ai] *interj* ja; *aye-aye, sir! (mar)* javel! // *s* ja-stemme.
azure ['eiʒə*] *adj* himmelblå, azurblå.

B

B, b [bi:].
BA ['bi:ei] fork.f. *Bachelor of Arts.*
babble [bæbl] *s* pludren // *v* pludre; plapre.
baboon [bə'bu:n] *s* bavian.
babe [beib] *s (gl)* baby; (S) snut, skat; *a* ~ *in arms* en ren novice.
baby ['beibi] *s* spædbarn, baby; *be left holding the* ~ sidde tilbage med alt besværet; **babyish** *adj* barnagtig; **baby-minder** *s* barnepige; dagplejemor.
bachelor ['bætʃələ*] *s* ungkarl; *B~ of Arts (BA)* humanistisk kandidat; *B~ of Science (BSc)* matematisk-naturvidenskabelig kandidat.
back [bæk] *s* ryg; bagside; bageste del; *(fodb)* back; *at the* ~ *of* bagved; *get off my* ~*!* hold op med at plage mig! *go round the* ~ gå ind ad bagdøren (i hus, butik); *get up sby's* ~ gøre en vred; *turn one's* ~ *on sby* vende ryggen til en // *v* gå baglæns; bakke; (også: ~ *up)* støtte, bakke op; *the house is* ~*ing on the park* bagsiden af huset vender ud mod parken; *back out* trække sig ud; springe fra // *adv* bag-; ryg-; tilbage, igen; *answer* ~ svare igen; *ten years* ~ for ti år siden; *he's* ~ han er kommet tilbage; *can I have it* ~*?* må jeg få den igen? *put* ~ *the meal* udsætte måltidet.
backache ['bækeik] *s* hold (,ondt) i ryggen.
backbencher ['bækbentʃə*] *s* menigt medlem af parlamentet.
backbiting ['bækbaitiŋ] *s* bagtalelse.
backbone ['bækbəun] *s* rygrad.
backcomb ['bækkəum] *v* toupere.
backdate ['bækdeit] *v* baguddatere; ~*d pay rise* lønstigning med tilbagevirkende kraft.
backer ['bækə*] *s* bagmand; støtte.
backfire [bæk'faiə*] *v* kikse; give bagslag; (om motor) sætte ud.
background ['bækgraund] *s* baggrund.
backhand ['bækhænd] *s (sport)* baghånd(sslag); **~ed** *adj* tvivlsom; (om skrift) stejl-; **~er** *s* (om bestikkelse) smøring; tvivlsom bemærkning.
backing ['bækiŋ] *s* støtte, opbakning.
backlash ['bæklæʃ] *s* tilbageslag; bagslag.
backlog ['bæklɔg] *s* efterslæb; ugjort arbejde.
back number ['bæk ˌnʌmbə*] *s* gammelt nummer (af blad etc).
back pay ['bæk pei] *s* efterbetaling.
back-pedal [bæk'pɛdl] *v (fig)* hive i land.
back rent ['bæk rɛnt] *s* huslejerestance.
backside [bæk'said] *s* bagside; bagdel.
backstitch ['bækstitʃ] *s* stikkesting.
backstroke ['bækstrəuk] *s* rygsvømning.
back-up [bæk'ʌp] *s* støtte, medhold; backup.
backward ['bækwəd] *adj* tilbage, baglæns; *(fig)* tilbagestående; tilbageholdende; **backwards** *adv* tilbage, bagover; bagfra.
backwash ['bækwɔʃ] *s: in the* ~ *of...* i kølvandet på...
backwater ['bækwɔ:tə*] *s* dødvande; afkrog.
backyard ['bækja:d] *s* baggård.
bacon ['beikən] *s* bacon, flæsk; *save one's* ~ redde skindet.
bacteria [bæk'tiəriə] *spl* bakterier.
bad [bæd] *adj (worse, worst* [wə:s, wə:st]) slem; dårlig; ond; grim; fordærvet; ~ *language* bandeord; *his* ~ *leg* hans dårlige ben; *he's a* ~ *sort* han er en grim karl; *be* ~ *at sth* være dårlig til ngt; *that's too* ~ det

er en skam; det er for galt; *feel ~ about sth* være ked af ngt.
baddy ['bædi] *s* (F) skurk.
bade [beid] *præt* af *bid.*
badge [bædʒ] *s* mærke, emblem; politiskilt.
badger ['bædʒə*] *s* grævling // *v* plage, chikanere.
badly ['bædli] *adv* slemt; dårligt; *~ wounded* hårdt såret; *need sth ~* trænge stærkt til ngt; *be ~ off* være dårligt stillet.
bad-tempered ['bæd,tɛmpəd] *adj* i dårligt humør, sur.
baffle [bæfl] *v* forvirre; forbløffe.
bag [bæg] *s* taske; pose; sæk; kuffert; jagtbytte; *there's ~s of room* der er masser af plads; *it is in the ~* (F) det er i orden, den er hjemme; *be thrown out ~ and baggage* blive smidt ud med alt sit habengut // *v* (F) få fat i; snuppe; **~ful** *s* posefuld.
baggy ['bægi] *adj* poset; løsthængende.
bagpipes ['bægpaips] *spl* sækkepibe.
bag snatcher ['bægsnætʃə*] *s* tasketyv.
bail [beil] *s* kaution; løsladelse mod kaution // *v* gå i kaution for; (også: *~ out)* løslade mod kaution; (om båd) øse, lænse (se også *bale).*
bailiff ['beilif] *s* (kongens) foged; forvalter.
bait [beit] *s* lokkemad; madding; *rise to the ~* bide på krogen (også *fig)* // *v* lokke; tirre, plage.
baize [beiz] *s* grønt filt.
bake [beik] *v* bage; ovnstege; **~d beans** *spl* bønner i tomatsovs.
baker ['beikə*] *s* bager; *~'s dozen* 13 stk.
bakery ['beikəri] *s* bageri.
baking powder ['beikiŋ ,paudə] *s* bagepulver; **baking sheet** *s* bageplade; **baking tin** *s* bageform.
balance ['bæləns] *s* balance, ligevægt; saldo; vægt; *~ of trade* handelsbalance; *~ of payments* betalingsbalance // *v* balancere; afbalancere; afveje; opveje; udligne.
balanced ['bælənsd] *adj* afbalanceret.
balance sheet ['bæləns ʃi:t] *s* statusopgørelse.
balcony ['bælkəni] *s* altan; balkon.
bald [bɔ:ld] *adj* skaldet; bar, nøgen; (om dæk) nedslidt.
balderdash ['bɔ:ldədæʃ] *s* sludder, vrøvl.
baldly ['bɔ:ldli] *adv* uden omsvøb.
bale [beil] *s* balle // *v: ~ out* springe ud med faldskærm.
baleful ['beilful] *adj* olm; ond; ondskabsfuld.
balk [bɔ:k] *s* bjælke; hindring // *v* hæmme; komme på tværs af; (om hest) refusere; *~ at sth (fig)* stejle over ngt.
ball [bɔ:l] *s* bold; bal; kugle; *have a ~* (F) have det skægt; *play ~* spille bold; *(fig)* lege 'med; *a ~ of wool* et nøgle garn; (se også *balls).*
ballad ['bæləd] *s* folkevise.
ball-bearing ['bɔ:lbɛəriŋ] *s* kugleleje.
ballet ['bælei] *s* ballet.
ball game ['bɔ:lgeim] *s* boldspil.
balloon [bə'lu:n] *s* ballon; (i tegneserie) taleboble.
ballot ['bælət] *s* (hemmelig) afstemning; valgresultat // *v* lave opinionsmåling; **~ box** *s* stemmeurne; **~ paper** *s* stemmeseddel.
ballpoint (pen) ['bɔ:lpɔint (pɛn)] *s* kuglepen.
ballroom ['bɔ:lrum] *s* balsal; **~ dancing** *s* selskabsdans.
balls [bɔ:ls] *spl* (V) nosser; *he's lost his ~* (F) der er ikke meget krudt tilbage i ham.
balls-up ['bɔ:lsʌp] *s* (S) koks, "kage"// *v* lave kage i det.
balm [ba:m] *s* balsam; *(bot)* citronmelisse.
balmy ['ba:mi] *adj* balsamisk; livsalig; (F) d.s.s. *barmy.*
Baltic ['bɔ:ltik] *s: the ~ (Sea)* Østersøen // *adj* baltisk; østersø-.
bamboo [bæm'bu:] *s* bambus.
ban [bæn] *s* bandlysning; forbud // *v* forbyde; bandlyse; forvise; *the football player was ~ned for six weeks* fodboldspilleren fik seks ugers karantæne; *~ liquor from football matches* forbyde spiritus ved fodboldkampe.
banana [bə'na:nə] *s* banan; *go ~s* (F)

blive skør; ~ **skin** *s* bananskræl.

band [bænd] *s* bånd; stribe; bande; flok; band // *v: ~ together* slutte (sig) sammen.

bandage ['bændidʒ] *s* forbinding, bandage // *v* forbinde.

Band-Aid ® ['bændeid] *s* hæfteplaster.

B&B, b&b fork.f. *bed and breakfast.*

bandstand ['bændstænd] *s* musikpavillon.

bandwagon ['bændwægən] *s: jump on the ~ (fig)* hoppe med på vognen.

bandy ['bændi] *v* udveksle; *~ about* slå om sig (med); **~-legged** [-lɛgd] *adj* hjulbenet.

bang [bæŋ] *s* brag, knald; smæk; hårdt slag; *~ goes that lunch!* der røg den frokost! // *v* slå (hårdt); smække (i); smække med; banke; hamre; (V!) bolle; *~ the door* dundre på døren; smække med døren.

banger ['bæŋə*] *s* kanonslag; (F) pølse; (om bil) skramlekasse; *~s and mash* (F) pølser med kartoffelmos.

bangle [bæŋgl] *s* armbånd.

bang-on ['bæŋ,ɔn] *adj* lige i øjet.

banish ['bæniʃ] *v* forvise, forjage; bandlyse.

banisters ['bænistəz] *spl* gelænder.

bank [bæŋk] *s* bank; (om flod etc) bred; (om jord etc) vold; dige; *break the ~* sprænge banken // *v* sætte i banken; (om fly) krænge; *~ on* (F) stole på; regne med; *~ up* hobe (sig op); *~ with Clydesdale* have Clydesdale som sin bankforbindelse; ~ **account** *s* bankkonto.

banker ['bæŋkə*] *s* bankmand.

Bank Holiday ['bæŋk ,hɔlidei] *s (brit)* alm. fridag (hvor bankerne holder lukket).

banking ['bæŋkiŋ] *s* bankvæsen; bankvirksomhed; ~ **hours** *spl* bankernes åbningstider.

banknote ['bæŋknəut] *s* pengeseddel; **bank rate** *s* diskonto.

bankrupt ['bæŋkrʌpt] *s* person som er gået fallit, fallent // *v* ruinere // *adj* fallit, konkurs; **bankruptcy** ['bæŋkrʌpsi] *s* konkurs, bankerot.

banns [bænz] *spl* lysning (til ægteskab); *read the ~* lyse til ægteskab.

banquet ['bæŋkwit] *s* banket, festmåltid; **~(ing) hall** *s* festsal.

banter ['bæntə*] *s* smådrilleri // *v* smådrille.

baptism ['bæptizm] *s* dåb.

baptize ['bæptaiz] *v* døbe.

bar [ba:*] *s* stang, tremme; vinduessprosse; stykke (fx *of chocolate* chokolade); bom; hindring; bar, bardisk; *(mus)* takt; (på mål) overligger; *the Bar (jur)* advokatstanden; *be called to the Bar* få advokatbeskikkelse; *behind ~s* bag tremmer // *v* spærre; stænge; udelukke; forbyde // *præp: ~ none* uden undtagelse.

barbarian [ba:'bɛəriən] *s* barbar // *adj* barbarisk.

barbarous ['ba:bərəs] *adj* barbarisk.

barbed wire ['ba:bd'waiə*] *s* pigtråd.

bar code ['ba:'kəud] *s (edb)* stregkode.

bard [ba:d] *s* skjald // *v (gastr)* spække.

bare [bɛə*] *v* blotte; blotlægge // *adj* bar, nøgen; kneben; *lay ~* blotlægge; *the ~ essentials* det nødtørftigste; *the ~ facts* de nøgne kendsgerninger; *~ of* blottet for; **~back** *adv* uden sadel.

barefaced ['bɛəfeisd] *adj* skamløs.

barefoot ['bɛəfut] *adj/adv* barfodet; barfods-.

bareheaded ['bɛəhɛdid] *adj/adv* barhovedet.

barely ['bɛəli] *adv* sparsomt; næppe, dårligt nok; med nød og næppe.

bargain ['ba:gin] *s* handel; køb; aftale; god forretning; *into the ~* oven i købet // *v* købslå; forhandle; bytte; *~ for* regne med, forvente; ~ **basement** *s* (i forretning) kælderetage med tilbudsvarer.

barge [ba:dʒ] *s* pram // *v* mase; *~ in* brase ind; *~ into* løbe 'på; ~ **pole** *s: I would'n touch it with a ~ pole* jeg ville ikke røre den (,det) med en ildtang.

bark [ba:k] *s* (på træ) bark; (H) båd; (om hund) gøen; *his ~ is worse than*

his bite han er ikke så slem som han lyder // *v* afbarke; gø, bjæffe.
barley ['ba:li] *s (bot)* byg.
barmaid ['ba:meid] *s* bardame.
barman ['ba:mən] *s* bartender.
barmy ['ba:mi] *adj* (F) skør, bims.
barn [ba:n] *s* lade.
baronet ['bærənit] *s* (titel) baronet.
barracks ['bærəks] *s* kaserne.
barrage ['bæra:ʒ] *s* spærreild; ['bæridʒ] dæmning, spærring.
barrel ['bærəl] *s* tønde; tromle; (om skydevåben) løb; *I've got them over a ~* jeg har krammet på dem; **~ organ** *s* lirekasse.
barren ['bærən] *adj* ufrugtbar, gold; nøgen; tom.
barricade [bæri'keid] *s* barrikade // *v* barrikadere.
barrier ['bæriə*] *s* barriere; forhindring.
barring ['bariŋ] *præp* undtagen; med mindre.
barrow ['bærəu] *s* gravhøj; (også: *wheel~*) trillebør.
barter ['ba:tə*] *v* bytte; *~ away* forspilde.
base [beis] *s* basis, grundlag; sokkel, fundament; base // *v* basere; *coffee-based* baseret på kaffe; *a London-based firm* et firma med hovedkvarter i London // *adj* lav, gemen; **~less** *adj* grundløs, ubegrundet.
basement ['beismənt] *s* underetage; kælderetage.
bases ['beisi:z] *spl* af *basis;* ['beisiz] *spl* af *base.*
bash [bæʃ] *s* (F) slag, gok; *have a ~ at sth* (også) forsøge sig med ngt // *v* (F) slå, hamre; *~ed in* (om rude) smadret.
bashful ['bæʃful] *adj* genert, undselig.
bashing ['bæʃiŋ] *s* (F) tæv.
basic ['beisik] *adj* fundamental, grundlæggende, basal; grund-; *the ~s of mathematics* elementær matematik; **basically** *adv* i grunden.
basil [bæzl] *s* basilikum.
basin ['beisin] *s* kumme; fad; bassin.
basis ['beisis] *s (pl: bases* ['beisi:z]) basis, grundlag.
bask [ba:sk] *v: ~ in the sun* dase i solen; sole sig (også *fig).*
basket ['ba:skit] *s* kurv; *put all one's eggs in one ~* sætte alt på ét bræt (,kort); **~ chair** *s* kurvestol.
basketry ['ba:skitri] *s* kurvefletning.
bass [beis] *s* bas.
bassoon [bə'su:n] *s (mus)* fagot; (NB! basun: *trombone).*
bastard ['ba:stəd] *s* bastard, uægte barn; (F, om person) lort // *adj* uægte.
baste [beist] *v* ri; kaste; *(gastr)* dryppe (fx en steg).
bat [bæt] *s* boldtræ; bat; ketsjer; *(zo)* flagermus; *have ~s in the belfry* (F) have knald i låget; *do sth off one's own ~* gøre ngt på eget initiativ // *v* slå; blinke med; *he didn't ~ an eyelid* (F) han fortrak ikke en mine.
batch [bætʃ] *s* portion, parti; bunke.
bated ['beitid] *adj: with ~ breath* med tilbageholdt åndedræt.
bath [ba:θ] *s (pl: ~s* [ba:ðz]) bad; badekar; *~s* svømmehal, badeanstalt; *have a ~* tage bad; *run a ~* tappe vand i badekarret // *v* give et bad, bade.
bathe [beið] *v* gå i vandet, bade; *(am)* tage bad.
bather ['beiðə*] *s* badende.
bathing ['beiðiŋ] *s* badning; **~ cap** *s* badehætte; **~ costume** *s* badedragt; **~ trunks** *spl* badebukser.
bath... ['ba:θ-] sms: **~mat** *s* bademåtte; **~robe** *s* badekåbe; **~room** *s* badeværelse; toilet; **~room scales** *spl* badevægt; **~-towel** *s* badehåndklæde; **~tub** *s* badekar.
batman ['bætmən] *s (mil)* oppasser.
baton ['bætən] *s* stav; politistav; *(mus)* taktstok.
batsman ['bætsmən] *s* slåer (i cricket).
batter ['bætə*] *s (gastr)* tynd dej (til pandekager etc) // *v* slå, hamre løs på; tæve; **~ed** *adj* medtaget, ramponeret; *~ed wife (,child)* voldsramt hustru (,barn); **~ing ram** *s* murbrækker.
battery ['bætəri] *s* batteri; *(assault and) ~ (jur)* legemsbeskadigelse; **~ hen** *s* burhøne.

battle [bætl] *s* kamp; slag; *do ~ with* kæmpe med; *fight a losing ~* kæmpe forgæves; være dømt til at mislykkes // *v* kæmpe; bekæmpe; **~-axe** *s* stridsøkse; (om kvinde) strid harpe; **~field** *s* slagmark.
battlements ['bætlmənts] *spl* brystværn (med murtinder).
battleship ['bætlʃip] *s* slagskib.
batty ['bæti] *adj* skør.
bawdy ['bɔ:di] *adj* sjofel.
bawl [bɔ:l] *v* brøle, vræle.
bay [bei] *s* (hav)bugt, indskæring; *(bot)* laurbær(træ); *hold (,keep) at ~* holde stangen // *v* glamme.
bayleaf ['beili:f] *s* laurbærblad.
bay window ['beiwindəu] *s* karnap.
bazaar [bə'za:*] *s* basar.
BBC ['bi:bi:'si:] *s* fork.f. *British Broadcasting Corporation.*
BC ['bi:'si:] *adv* (fork.f. *before Christ)* før Kristi fødsel, f.Kr.
be [bi:] *v (præs: I am, you are, he (,she, it) is, we (,you, they) are; præt: I was, you were, he (,she, it) was, we (,you, they) were; pp: been)* være (til); findes; befinde sig; blive; *how are you?* hvordan har du det? *I am warm* jeg har det varmt; *it is cold* det er koldt; *how much is it?* hvor meget koster det? *how much are the tomatoes?* hvad koster tomaterne? *they are 50p a pound* de koster 50p pundet; *two and two are four* to og to er fire; *how is it that...?* hvordan kan det være at...? *that is (to say)...* det vil sige...; *let it be* lad det være; *have you been to London?* har du været i London?
beach [bi:tʃ] *s* strand; land // *v* landsætte; **~ball** *s* badebold; **~wear** [-wɛə*] *s* strandtøj.
beacon ['bi:kən] *s* fyr; sømærke, vager.
bead [bi:d] *s* perle (af fx glas, træ - ikke ægte); dråbe; *a string of ~s* en perlekæde.
beady-eyed ['bi:diaid] *adj* med små stikkende øjne.
beak [bi:k] *s* næb; tud.
beaker ['bi:kə*] *s* bæger.
beam [bi:m] *s* bjælke; bom; stråle; *broad in the ~* bred over bagen // *v* stråle; sende (via radio); **~ing** *adj* strålende.
bean [bi:n] *s* bønne; *full of ~s* fuld af krudt; *spill the ~s* plapre ud med en hemmelighed; **~pole** *s* bønnestage, langt rær; **~sprout** *s* bønnespire.
bear [bɛə*] *s* bjørn.
bear [bɛə*] *v (bore, born* [bɔ:*, bɔ:n]) bære; udholde; føde; *~ right (,left)* holde til højre (,venstre); *~ comparison with* tåle sammenligning med; *~ down on* styre løs på; lægge pres på; *~ in mind* huske; *~ on* vedrøre, have ngt at gøre med; *~ out* bekræfte; *~ up* holde modet oppe; klare sig; *your arguments do not ~ up* dine argumenter holder ikke; *~ with sby* bære over med en; *bring to ~* tage i brug; gøre gældende; **~able** *adj* tålelig.
beard [biəd] *s* skæg; *grow a ~* lade skægget stå; **bearded** ['biədid] *adj* skægget.
bearer ['bɛərə] *s* bærer; ihændehaver; overbringer.
bear hug ['bɛəhʌg] *s* stort knus.
bearing ['bɛəriŋ] *s* holdning; fremtræden; betydning; retning; *(tekn)* leje; *(ball) ~s* kugleleje; *take a ~* orientere sig, tage pejling; *find one's ~s* finde ud af hvor man står (,er).
bearskin ['bɛəskin] *s* bjørneskind(shue).
beast [bi:st] *s* dyr, bæst; **~ly** *adj* væmmelig, modbydelig.
beat [bi:t] *s* slag; banken; taktslag, rytme; (om politibetjent) runde; *off the ~en track* afsides; væk fra alfarvej // *v (beat, beaten)* slå; banke; piske; *~ about the bush* komme med udflugter; *~ it* stikke af; *~ time* slå takt; *it ~s me* det går over min forstand; *~ off* slå tilbage; *~ up* gennembanke; *~ up eggs* piske æg.
beater ['bi:tə*] *s* (hjul)pisker; (også: *carpet ~)* tæppebanker.
beating ['bi:tiŋ] *s* tæv, prygl.
beatitude [bi:'ætitju:d] *s* salighed.
beat-up ['bi:tʌp] *adj* ramponeret, medtaget.

beau [bəu] *s (pl: ~x)* sheik, fyr.
beaut [bju:t] *s* (F) skøn („fed) ting; mesterstykke.
beautician [bju'tiʃən] *s* skønhedsekspert, kosmetolog.
beautiful ['bju:tiful] *adj* smuk, dejlig.
beauty ['bju:ti] *s* skønhed; pragtstykke; **~ parlour, ~ salon** *s* skønhedsklinik; **~ spot** *s* skønhedsplet; naturskønt sted.
beaux [bəuz] *spl* af *beau.*
beaver ['bi:və*] *s* bæver; *eager ~* morakker // *v: ~ away* pukle løs.
became [bi'keim] *præt* af *become.*
because [bi'kɔz] *konj* fordi, da, eftersom; *~ of* på grund af.
beck [bɛk] *s* vink; *be at sby's ~ and call* stå på pinde for en.
beckon ['bɛkən] *v* vinke; gøre tegn; lokke.
become [bi'kʌm] *v (-came, -come)* blive; klæde; sømme sig for; *~ fat* blive fed; *what's ~ of him?* hvad er der blevet af ham? *that dress ~s you* den kjole klæder dig; **becoming** *adj* passende; klædelig.
bed [bɛd] *s* seng; (i have) bed; (østers)banke; (flod)leje; *(geol)* lag; *make the ~* rede sengen; *go to ~* gå i seng; *~ and breakfast (b&b)* værelse og morgenmad // *v (spøg)* gå i seng med; *~ down* rede seng; lægge sig til at sove; *~ out plants* plante planter ud; **~bug** *s* væggelus; **~clothes** *spl* sengetøj; **~cover** *s* sengetæppe; **~ding** *s* sengetøj; sengeudstyr; underlag.
bedlam ['bɛdləm] *s* kaos, galehus.
bedlinen ['bɛdlinin] *s* sengelinned.
bedpan ['bɛdpæn] *s* bækken.
bedpost ['bɛdpəust] *s* sengestolpe; *between you and me and the ~* mellem os sagt, sagt i fortrolighed.
bedridden ['bɛdridn] *adj* sengeliggende; bundet til sengen.
bedrock ['bɛdrɔk] *s* grundfjeld.
bedroom ['bɛdrum] *s* soveværelse.
bedside ['bɛdsaid] *s* sengekant; **~ book** *s* godnatlekture.
bedsit(ter) ['bɛdsit(ə*)] *s* etværelses lejlighed.
bedsore [bɛdsɔ:*] *s* liggesår.
bedspread ['bɛdsprɛd] *s* sengetæppe.
bedstead ['bɛdstɛd] *s* sengested.
bedtime ['bɛdtaim] *s* sengetid.
bee [bi:] *s* bi; *have a ~ in one's bonnet* have en fiks idé; (F) være blød i bolden.
beech [bi:tʃ] *s* bøg(etræ); **~wood** *s* bøgeskov; (materialet) bøgetræ.
beef [bi:f] *s* oksekød; okse // *v: ~ about sth* (F) brokke sig over ngt; **~ cattle** *s* kødkvæg; **~steak** [-steik] *s* bøf.
beefy ['bi:fi] *adj* kraftig; velnæret; *he's ~* han er et stort brød.
beehive ['bi:haiv] *s* bikube; højt touperet hår.
bee keeper ['bi:ki:pə*] *s* biavler.
beeline ['bi:lain] *s: make a ~ for sth* styre lige mod ngt.
been [bi:n] *pp* af *be.*
beep [bi:p] *s* bip, dut // *v* bippe.
beer [biə*] *s* øl; *it's all small ~* (F) det er bare pebernødder // *v: ~ it up* (S) tylle humle; **~ belly** *s* ølmave; **~mat** *s* ølbrik; **~mug** *s* ølkrus.
beet [bi:t] *s* roe.
beetle [bi:tl] *s* bille.
beetroot ['bi:tru:t] *s* rødbede; **beet sugar** *s* roesukker.
befall [bi'fɔ:l] *v (-fell, -fallen)* tilstøde; hænde; overgå.
befit [be'fit] *v* passe til; passe sig.
before [bi'fɔ:*] *præp* før; inden; foran; forud (for); fremfor; *the week ~* ugen før; *I've seen it ~* jeg har set det før; *~ long* inden længe; *sit ~ the mirror* sidde foran spejlet; **~hand** *adv* i forvejen; på forhånd.
beg [bɛg] *v* tigge, bede, bønfalde; *~ leave to* bede om lov til at; tillade sig at; *~ for mercy* tigge om nåde; *I ~ to differ* undskyld, men jeg er ikke enig.
began [bi'gæn] *præt* af *begin.*
beggar ['bɛgə*] *s* tigger; *poor ~!* stakkels fyr!
begin [bi'gin] *v (began, begun* [bi'gæn, bi'gʌn]) begynde; *to ~ with* til at begynde med; for det første; **~ner** *s* begynder; **~ning** *s* begyndelse.
begrudge [bi'grʌdʒ] *v: ~ sby sth* misunde en ngt; *I don't ~ him his suc-*

cess jeg under ham hans succes.
begun [bi'gʌn] *pp* af *begin.*
behalf [bi'ha:f] *s: on ~ of sby, on sby's ~* på ens vegne.
behave [bi'heiv] *v* opføre sig; optræde; *~ oneself* opføre sig ordentligt; *well ~d* velopdragen.
behaviour [bi'heiviə*] *s* opførsel, optræden; adfærd.
behead [bi'hɛd] *v* halshugge.
beheld [bi'hɛld] *præt* og *pp* af *behold.*
behind [bi'haind] *s* (F) bagdel // *adv/præp* bagved; bagefter; bagud // *præp* bag; *from ~* bagfra; *look ~* se sig tilbage; **~hand** *adj* bagefter, bagud.
behold [bi'həuld] *v (-held, -held)* se; betragte.
being ['bi:iŋ] *s* væsen; tilværelse; *come into ~* blive 'til // *adj: for the time ~* indtil videre, foreløbig; *other things ~ equal* alt andet lige.
belated [bi'leitid] *adj* forsinket.
beleaguer [bi'li:gə*] *v* (H) belejre.
belch [bɛltʃ] *v* bøvse, ræbe; *~ out* udspy.
belfry ['bɛlfri] *s* klokketårn; *have bats in the ~* (F) have knald i låget.
Belgian ['bɛldʒən] *s* belgier // *adj* belgisk.
Belgium ['bɛldʒəm] *s* Belgien.
belie [bi'lai] *v* modsige; stride mod.
belief [bi'li:f] *s* tro; anskuelse; mening; *it is past all ~* det er utroligt; *to the best of my ~* efter min bedste overbevisning.
believe [bi'li:v] *v* tro *(in* på); *make ~* lade som om; **believer** *s* troende; tilhænger.
belittle [bi'litl] *v* forklejne; nedvurdere.
bell [bɛl] *s* klokke; bjælde; *ring (,sound) the ~* ringe med (,på) klokken; *his name rings a ~* hans navn virker bekendt; **~boy** *s* (på hotel) piccolo.
belle [bɛl] *s* (om kvinde) skønhed.
belligerent [bi'lidʒərənt] *adj* krigerisk; krigsførende.
bellow ['bɛləu] *v* brøle.
bellows ['bɛləuz] *s* blæsebælg.
bellpush ['bɛlpuʃ] *s* ringeknap.
belly ['bɛli] *s* mave, vom, bug; **~ ache** *s* mavepine // *v* (F) brokke sig; **~ dance** *s* mavedans; **~flop** *s* maveplaster (ved udspring); **~ful** *s* (F) godt foder; *I've had a ~ful of him* jeg er ved at brække mig over ham.
belong [bi'lɔŋ] *v: ~ to* tilhøre; høre til; *~ together* høre sammen; **~ings** *spl* ejendele; tilbehør.
beloved [bi'lʌvid] *s* elskede // *adj* elsket.
below [bi'ləu] *adv/præp* nedenunder; nede; nedenfor; under; *from ~* nedefra.
belt [bɛlt] *s* bælte; livrem; *(tekn)* drivrem // *v* slå, tæve; (F) flintre af sted; *~ out a song* skråle en sang; *~ up* (F) klappe i; spænde sikkerhedsselen.
bench [bɛntʃ] *s* bænk; høvlebænk; *the B~ (jur)* domstolen, retten.
bend [bɛnd] *s* bøjning; (vej)sving; kurve; (om rør) knæk; *go round the ~* (F) blive skrupskør // *v (bent, bent)* bøje (sig); krumme (sig); svinge, dreje; *~ the rules* omgå reglerne; *~ over* bøje sig fremover; *~ over backwards to do right* stå på hovedet for at gøre det rigtige; *on one's ~ed knee* på sine grædende knæ.
beneath [bi'ni:θ] *adv* nedenunder; nedenfor // *præp* under; *~ contempt* under al kritik; uværdig; *it was ~ him to...* det var under hans værdighed at...
benediction [bɛni'dikʃən] *s* velsignelse.
benefactor [bɛni'fæktə*] *s* velgører; **benefactress** *s* (kvindelig) velgører.
beneficial [bɛni'fiʃəl] *adj* gavnlig; fordelagtig.
benefit ['bɛnifit] *s* fordel; nytte, gavn; støtte; understøttelse; *give him the ~ of the doubt* lade tvivlen komme ham til gode // *v* gavne; *~ from* få (,have) gavn af; nyde godt af; lære af; **~ performance** *s* velgørenhedsforestilling.
benevolence [bi'nɛvələns] *s* velvilje; godgørenhed; **benevolent** *adj* velvillig; godgørende.

benign [bi'nain] *adj* venlig; mild; *(med)* godartet.

bent [bɛnt] *s* tilbøjelighed, hang // *præt* og *pp* af *bend* // *adj* krum, bøjet; buet; *be ~ on sth* være opsat på ngt.

benzine ['bɛnzi:n] *s* rensebenzin.

bequeath [bi'kwi:ð] *v* testamentere; lade gå i arv.

bequest [bi'kwɛst] *s* arv.

bereaved [bi'ri:vd] *adj: the ~* de (sørgende) efterladte; **bereavement** *s* sorg; tab (ved dødsfald).

berry ['bɛri] *s* bær.

berth [bə:θ] *s* køje; kajplads; ankerplads; *give sby a wide ~* gå langt uden om en // *v (mar)* lægge 'til.

beseech [bi'si:tʃ] *v (besought, besought* [bi'sɔ:t]) bønfalde, trygle.

beside [bi'said] *præp* ved siden af; *be ~ oneself with anger* være ude af sig selv af vrede.

besides [bi'saids] *adv* desuden; for øvrigt // *præp* foruden.

besiege [bi'si:dʒ] *v* belejre; *(fig)* bestorme.

besotted [bi'sɔtid] *adj* beruset; betaget; blindt forelsket.

besought [bi'sɔ:t] *præt* og *pp* af *beseech.*

bespectacled [bi'spɛktəkəld] *adj* med briller.

best [bɛst] *adj/adv (sup* af *good)* bedst; mest; højest; *the ~ part of* størstedelen af; *at ~* i bedste fald; *make the ~ of sth* få det mest (,bedst) mulige ud af ngt; *to the ~ of my knowledge* så vidt jeg ved; *to the ~ of my ability* så godt jeg kan; **~ man** *s* forlover.

bestow [bi'stəu] *v* skænke; overdrage.

bet [bɛt] *s* væddemål; *it's a safe ~ that...* jeg tør vædde med at...; *make a ~* lave et væddemål // *v (bet, bet* el. *betted, betted)* vædde; *you ~ I do!* det kan du tro (,bande på) at jeg gør! *he ~ me a fiver I could not do it* han væddede £5 på at jeg ikke kunne gøre det.

betray [bi'trei] *v* forråde; røbe; svigte.

betrayal [bi'treiəl] *s* forræderi; svig.

betrothal [bi'trəuðəl] *s* (H) trolovelse.

better ['bɛtə*] *v* forbedre; (om rekord) slå // *adj (komp* af *good)* bedre; mere; *change for the ~* ændre sig til det bedre; *you'll feel all the ~ for a nice bath* du vil få det meget bedre når du har taget et rart bad; *get the ~ of sby* vinde over en; *you had ~ go now* du må hellere gå nu; *he thought ~ of it* han kom på bedre tanker; *get ~* blive (,få det) bedre; *~ off* bedre stillet.

betting ['bɛtiŋ] *s* væddemål; **~ shop** *s* indskudsbod (for fx tips, trav etc).

between [bi'twi:n] *adv/præp* (i)mellem; *in ~* ind imellem; *~ you and me* mellem os sagt; *~ the two of them* tilsammen.

beverage ['bɛvəridʒ] *s* drik.

beware [bi'wɛə*] *v: ~ (of)* passe på; vogte sig (for).

bewildered [bi'wildəd] *adj* forvirret; desorienteret.

bewitch [bi'witʃ] *v* forhekse; fortrylle; **~ing** *adj* fortryllende.

beyond [bi'jɔnd] *adv* hinsides, på den anden side; længere // *præp* på den anden side af; ud over; over; *it's ~ control* det er ude af kontrol; *~ doubt* uden for enhver tvivl; *~ repair* umulig at reparere; *it's ~ me* det går over min forstand.

bias ['baiəs] *s* forudindtagethed; partiskhed; *on the ~* på skrå; **~ binding** *s* skråbånd; **bias(s)ed** *adj* forudindtaget; partisk.

bib [bib] *s* hagesmæk; klap (på overall etc).

Bible [baibl] *s* bibel; **biblical** ['biblikəl] *adj* bibelsk.

bicarbonate [bai'ka:bənit] *s: ~ of soda* tvekulsurt natron.

bicker ['bikə*] *v* småskændes, kævles.

bicycle ['baisikl] *s* cykel; *ride a ~* cykle // *v* cykle; **~ clip** *s* cykelklemme.

bid [bid] *s* bud; tilbud // *v (bade* el. *bid, bidden* [bæd el. bid, bidn]) byde; befale; *~ for sth* byde på ngt (ved auktion); *~ sby welcome* byde en velkommen.

bidder ['bidə*] *s: the highest ~* den højstbydende.

bidding ['bidiŋ] *s* bud; befaling.

bide [baid] *v: ~ one's time* se tiden an.

biennial [bai'ɛniəl] *adj* to-årig (fx *plant* plante); som sker hvert andet år.

biff [bif] *s* stød, gok // *v* støde; gokke.

big [big] *adj* stor; kraftig; *have a ~ head* være blæret; *in a ~ way* i stor stil; *be ~ with young* (H) være drægtig; *talk ~* prale; *think ~* lægge store planer; *win ~* vinde stort.

bigamy ['bigəmi] *s* bigami.

big game ['big,geim] *s* storvildt.

bigheaded ['bighɛdid] *adj* indbildsk, blæret.

bighearted ['bigha:tid] *adj* ædelmodig.

bigot ['bigət] *s* selvretfærdig (,snæversynet) person; **~ed** *adj* snæversynet.

bigotry ['bigətri] *s* selvretfærdighed; snæversyn.

bigwig ['bigwig] *s* (F) stor kanon, ping.

bike [baik] *s* cykel; *on your ~!* (F) skrid! // *v* cykle; **~mender** *s* cykelsmed.

bilberry ['bilbɛri] *s* blåbær.

bile [bail] *s* galde (også *fig).*

bilge [bildʒ] *s* bavl.

bilingual [bai'liŋgwəl] *adj* tosproget.

bill [bil] *s* regning; pengeseddel; plakat; lovforslag; næb; *fit (,fill) the ~* opfylde forventningerne; *~ of fare* menu; *get a clean ~ of health* blive erklæret sund og rask // *v* fakturere; sætte på plakaten; **~board** *s* plakattavle.

billet ['bilit] *s* indkvartering // *v* indkvartere; (NB! billet: *ticket).*

billfold ['bilfəuld] *s (am)* tegnebog.

billiards ['biljədz] *spl* billard.

billion ['biljən] *s (brit)* billion; *(am)* milliard.

billow ['biləu] *v* bølge.

billy ['bili] *s* kogekar (til camping); **~-goat** *s* gedebuk.

bin [bin] *s* bøtte; kasse; skraldebøtte; *breadbin* brødkasse.

binary ['bainəri] *adj* binær.

bind [baind] *v (bound, bound* [baund]) binde; indbinde; forpligte; **~er** *s* ringbind; **~ing** *s* indbinding // *adj* bindende.

bin liner ['binlainə*] *s* affaldspose (til at fore skraldespanden med).

binge [bindʒ] *s* gilde, abefest.

binoculars [bi'nɔkjuləz] *spl* kikkert.

bio... ['baiəu-] sms: **~chemistry** [-'kɛmistri] *s* biokemi; **~degradable** [-di'greidəbl] *adj* biologisk nedbrydelig; **~graphy** [bai'ɔgrəfi] *s* biografi; **~logist** [bai'ɔlədʒist] *s* biolog.

birch [bə:tʃ] *s* birk(etræ).

bird [bə:d] *s* fugl; (F, om pige) dulle, larve; *old ~* (F) gammel støder; gamle jas; *~ of prey* rovfugl; **~cage** *s* fuglebur; **~-seed** *s* fuglefrø; **~'s-eye-view** *s* fugleperspektiv; **~table** *s* foderbræt; **~watching** *s: go ~watching* tage på fugletur; (S) tage ud og se på damer.

birth [bə:θ] *s* fødsel; herkomst; *Scottish by ~* skotsk af fødsel; *give ~ to* føde; afføde; **~ certificate** *s* fødselsattest; dåbsattest; **~ control** *s* børnebegrænsning; **~day** *s* fødselsdag; **~day suit** *s* fødselsdagstøj; *in one's ~day suit* i Adamskostume; **~mark** *s* modermærke; **~place** *s* fødested; **~ rate** *s* fødselstal.

biscuit ['biskit] *s* småkage; kiks.

bisect [bai'sɛkt] *v* gennemskære; skære over (i to dele).

bishop ['biʃəp] *s* biskop; (i skak) løber.

bishopric ['biʃəprik] *s* bispedømme.

bit [bit] *s* bid, stykke; smule; (om hest) bidsel; *(edb)* bit; *a ~* en smule; lidt; *not a ~* ikke spor; *I'm every ~ as good as he is* jeg er nøjagtig lige så god som han; *do one's ~* gøre sit; gøre sin del; *that's a ~ much* det er lovligt skrapt; *go to ~s* gå i stykker // *præt* af *bite.*

bitch [bitʃ] *s* (om hund) tæve, hunhund; (om kvinde) mær, harpe; *son of a ~* (V!) (forbandet) satan.

bitchy ['bitʃi] *adj* spydig, giftig; led.

bite [bait] *s* bid; stik; mundfuld; *let's have a ~ (to eat)* lad os få en mundfuld mad // *v (bit, bitten* [bit, bitn] bide; stikke; *what's biting you?*

hvad er der i vejen? ~ *the dust* bide i græsset; ~ *off more than one can chew* påtage sig mere end man kan klare.

bit-part ['bitpa:t] *s (teat)* birolle.

bitten [bitn] *pp* af *bite.*

bitter ['bitə*] *s* slags fadøl // *adj* bitter; skarp; *to the ~ end* til den bitre ende; **~s** *s* (mave)bitter.

blabbermouth ['blæbəmauθ] *s* sludrehoved; sladderhank.

black [blæk] *s* sort; neger // *v* sværte; pudse; (i industrien) boykotte; sætte på den sorte liste; ~ *out* mørklægge // *adj* sort; mørk; *give sby a ~ eye* give en et blåt øje; ~ *and blue* (slået) gul og grøn; *get it in ~ and white* få det sort på hvidt.

blackberry ['blækbəri] *s* brombær.

blackbird ['blækbə:d] *s* solsort.

blackboard ['blækbɔ:d] *s* (skole)tavle.

blackcurrant ['blæk,kʌrənt] *s* solbær.

blacken ['blækən] *v* blive (,gøre) sort; formørke(s).

blackhead ['blækhɛd] *s* hudorm.

blackice ['blækais] *s* isslag.

blackleg ['blæklɛg] *s* skruebrækker.

blacklist ['blæklist] *v* sortliste.

blackmail ['blækmeil] *s* pengeafpresning // *v: ~ sby* presse penge af en.

Black Maria ['blæk mə'raiə] *s* (om politibil) salatfad.

black market ['blæk ,ma:kit] *s* sortbørs.

blackout ['blækaut] *s* mørklægning; strømafbrydelse; besvimelse.

black pudding ['blæk 'pudiŋ] *s* blodbudding.

Black Sea ['blæk 'si:] *s: the ~* Sortehavet.

blacksmith ['blæksmiθ] *s* grovsmed.

black tie ['blæk 'tai] *s* sort butterfly; (på indbydelse) smoking.

bladder ['blædə*] *s* blære.

blade [bleid] *s* (om fx kniv, åre) blad; *a ~ of grass* et græsstrå.

blame [bleim] *s* skyld; dadel // *v* bebrejde; give skylden; ~ *sby for sth* give en skylden for ngt; *who's to ~?* hvis skyld er det? **~less** *adj* uskyldig.

blanch [bla:ntʃ] *v* blegne; blege; blanchere.

blancmange [blə'ma:nʒ] *s* maizenabudding.

bland [blænd] *adj* mild; rolig og uforstyrret; (om mad) uden smag.

blank [blæŋk] *s* tomrum; skud med løst krudt; *draw a ~* trække en nitte // *adj* blank, ubeskrevet; tom, udtryksløs; *my mind went ~* der gik en klap ned for mig; *a ~ cheque* en blankocheck.

blanket ['blæŋkit] *s* (uld)tæppe; *he is a wet ~* han er en dødbider.

blare [blɛə*] *s* gjalden // *v* gjalde.

blarney ['bla:ni] *s* smiger, smisken.

blasphemous ['blæsfəməs] *adj* blasfemisk.

blast [bla:st] *s* vindstød; stød; eksplosion // *v* sprænge (væk); ødelægge.

blasted ['bla:stid] *adj* forbandet, pokkers.

blast furnace ['bla:st fə:nis] *s* højovn.

blast-off ['bla:stɔ:f] *s* affyring (af missil etc).

blatant ['bleitənt] *adj* åbenlys, ugenert; skrigende; pågående, grov; *a ~ lie* en fed løgn.

blaze [bleiz] *s* brand; flammer; skær; *do sth like ~s* gøre ngt som en gal // *v* flamme, blusse; stråle; ~ *a trail (fig)* bane (,vise) vej.

bleach [bli:tʃ] *s* blegemiddel // *v* blege; affarve.

bleak [bli:k] *adj* nøgen, forblæst; kold, trist; trøstesløs.

bleary-eyed ['bliəri,aid] *adj* klatøjet.

bleat [bli:t] *s* brægen // *v* bræge.

bleed [bli:d] *v (bled, bled* [blɛd]) bløde; årelade, tappe; *(fig)* flå; **~ing** *s* blødning // *adj* blødende; (F) forbandet.

bleep [bli:p] *s* bip, dut // *v* bippe; **~er** *s* bipper.

blemish ['blɛmiʃ] *s* skavank; plet.

blend [blɛnd] *s* blanding // *v* blande; (om farver) gå over i hinanden; passe sammen.

bless [blɛs] *v (blessed, blessed* el. *blest, blest* [blɛst]) velsigne; *be ~ed with sth* være velsignet med ngt; ~ *me!* du godeste!

blessing ['blɛsiŋ] *s* velsignelse; held; *a ~ in disguise* held i uheld.

blether ['blɛðə*] *v* vrøvle, sludre.
blew [blu:] *præt* af *blow*.
blighter ['blaitə*] *s* karl, fyr.
blind [blaind] *s* skodde; rullegardin; jalousi // *v* gøre blind; blænde // *adj* blind; *turn a ~ eye on (,to) sth* se gennem fingre med ngt; **~ alley** *s* blindgyde; **~fold** *s* bind for øjnene // *v* give bind for øjnene // *adj* i blinde; **~ man's buff** *s* blindebuk; **~ness** *s* blindhed.
blink [bliŋk] *v* blinke, glimte; **~ers** *spl* skyklapper; **~ing** *adj* (F) pokkers, forbandet.
bliss [blis] *s* lyksalighed; **~ful** *adj* salig.
blister ['blistə*] *s* vable, blist; (i maling) blære // *v* danne blærer; få vabler.
blithering ['bliðəriŋ] *adj: a ~ idiot* (F) en kraftidiot.
blitz [blits] *s* luftangreb; lynkrig.
blizzard ['blizəd] *s* snestorm.
bloated ['bləutid] *adj* opsvulmet; oppustet.
blob [blɔb] *s* klat.
bloc [blɔk] *s* blok; *the Eastern ~* Østblokken.
block [blɔk] *s* blok; klods; kliché; blokering, spærring; *a ~ of flats* en boligkarré // *v* blokere, stoppe.
blockade [blɔ'keid] *s* blokade // *v* blokere.
blockage ['blɔkidʒ] *s* blokering.
blockbuster ['blɔkbʌstə*] *s* kæmpesucces.
blockhead ['blɔkhɛd] *s* dumrian.
block letters ['blɔklɛtəz] *spl* blokbogstaver.
bloke [bləuk] *s* (F) fyr.
blonde [blɔnd] *s* blondine // *adj* blond, lyshåret.
blood [blʌd] *s* blod; slægt; *bad ~* ondt blod; *make sby's ~ run cold* få blodet til at isne i årerne på en; **~clot** *s* blodprop; **~curdling** [-kə:dliŋ] *adj* hårrejsende; bloddryppende; **~ group** *s* blodtype; **~less** *adj* ublodig (fx *victory* sejr); bleg, anæmisk; **~ poisoning** *s* blodforgiftning; **~ pressure** *s* blodtryk; **~shed** *s* blodsudgydelse; **~shot** *adj* blodskudt; **~stained** *adj* blodplettet; **~ test** *s* blodprøve; **~thirsty** *adj* blodtørstig; **~ vessel** *s* blodkar.
bloody ['blʌdi] *adj* blodig; (F!) satans, forbandet; *~ good!* skidegodt! **~-minded** [-maindid] *adj* (F) krakilsk.
bloom [blu:m] *s* blomst, blomstring // *v* blomstre.
bloomers ['blu:məz] *spl* svigermorunderbukser.
blooming ['blu:miŋ] *adj* blomstrende; (F) pokkers.
blossom ['blɔsəm] *s* blomst, blomstring // *v* blomstre.
blot [blɔt] *s* klat, plet // *v* klatte, plette; *~ out* udslette; udrydde; *~ one's copybook* ødelægge sit rygte.
blotchy ['blɔtʃi] *adj* skjoldet.
blotting paper ['blɔtiŋ,peipə*] *s* klatpapir.
blotto ['blɔtəu] *adj* (S) skidefuld.
blouse [blauz] *s* bluse.
blow [bləu] *s* slag; stød // *v (blew, blown* [blu:, bləun]) blæse; puste; sprænge (fx *the fuses* sikringerne); *~ one's nose* pudse næse; *~ a tyre* punktere; *~ a whistle* blæse i en fløjte; *~ the expense!* skidt med hvad det koster! *~ the horn* spille på horn; tude i hornet; *~ away* blæse væk; *~ down* blæse ned (,omkuld); *~ off* blæse af; brokke sig; *~ off course* blæse ud af kurs; *~ out* puste ud; springe; *~ up* puste op; sprænge (,springe) i luften; *(foto)* forstørre; **~-dry** *v* føntørre.
blower ['bləuə*] *s* (F) telefon.
blowlamp ['bləulæmp] *s* blæselampe.
blow-out ['bləuaut] *s* forstørrelse; ædegilde; punktering; sprængning.
blubber ['blʌbə*] *s* (hval)spæk; blæverfedt // *v* flæbe; vræle.
bludgeon ['blʌdʒən] *s* kølle // *v* slå med kølle.
blue [blu:] *adj* blå; nedtrykt; *out of the ~* som et lyn fra klar himmel; **~bell** *s* blåklokke; **~bottle** *s* spyflue; **~print** *s* blåkopi; *(fig)* perspektivplan; projekt.
blues [bluz] *spl: have the ~* være deprimeret.
bluff [blʌf] *s* skrænt, klint; bluff(ma-

ger); *call sby's ~* afsløre ens bluff // *v* bluffe // *adj* (om person) bramfri.

blunder ['blʌndə*] *s* dumhed, brøler // *v* kludre, dumme sig.

blunt [blʌnt] *v* sløve(s) // *adj* (om fx kniv) sløv; (om person) brysk, studs.

blur [blə:*] *s* uklarhed; udvisket plet // *v* sløre(s); tvære(s) ud.

blurb [blə:b] *s* reklame (for bog); bagsidetekst.

blush [blʌʃ] *s* rødmen // *v* rødme; *~ one's cheeks* komme kinderødt på; **blusher** *s* kinderødt.

bluster ['blʌstə*] *v* rase, storme.

bn fork.f. *billion.*

boar [bɔ:*] *s* vildsvin.

board [bɔ:d] *s* bræt; tavle; pap; bestyrelse; direktion; komité; *~ and lodging* kost og logi; *full ~* helpension; *above ~* åben og ærlig; helt i orden; *across the ~* generelt, over en bank; *go by the ~* gå i vasken, mislykkes; *be on the ~* være medlem af bestyrelsen // *v* beklæde med brædder; gå ombord i; (om tog) stige op i; *~ up* slå brædder for.

boarder ['bɔ:də*] *s* pensionær; (på skole) kostelev.

board game ['bɔ:d geim] *s* brætspil.

boarding house ['bɔ:diŋ haus] *s* pensionat.

boarding school ['bɔ:diŋ sku:l] *s* kostskole.

boardroom ['bɔ:dru:m] *s* direktionsværelse.

boast [bəust] *s* pral(en); stolthed // *v* prale; kunne prale af; **~ful** *adj* pralende.

boat [bəut] *s* båd; skib; *rock the ~* gøre tingene besværlige, skabe rav i det // *v* sejle; ro.

boater ['bəutə*] *s* flad stråhat.

boat-hook ['bəuthu:k] *s* bådshage.

boatswain [bəusn] *s* bådsmand.

bob [bɔb] *v* hoppe op og ned; neje, knikse; *~ up* dukke op.

bobbin ['bɔbin] *s* (i symaskine etc) spole.

bobby ['bɔbi] *s* (F) politibetjent.

bobsleigh ['bɔbslei] *s* bobslæde.

bodice ['bɔdis] *s* (på kjole) overdel, liv.

bodily ['bɔdili] *adj* korporlig; *~ harm* legemsbeskadigelse; vold // *adv* personlig.

body ['bɔdi] *s* legeme, krop; lig; *(auto)* karrosseri; (om skib) skrog; gruppe, forsamling; masse; *in a ~* i samlet flok; *earn enough to keep ~ and soul together* tjene nok til at opretholde livet; **~-conscious** *adj* kropsbevidst; **~guard** *s* livvagt; **~ odour** *s* kropslugt; svedlugt; **~ repairs** *spl (auto)* karrosseriarbejde; **~work** *s (auto)* karrosseri.

bog [bɔg] *s* mose, sump // *v: get ~ged down* køre fast.

bogey ['bəugi] *s* bussemand; skræmmebillede.

boggle [bɔgl] *v: the mind ~s* det er for utroligt.

bogus ['bəugəs] *adj* falsk, uægte; skin-.

boil [bɔil] *s* byld; kog; *come to the ~* komme i kog // *v* koge; *~ down to (fig)* kunne reduceres til; i al enkelhed gå ud på.

boiler ['bɔilə*] *s* (damp)kedel; varmtvandsbeholder; suppehøne; **~ room** *s* fyrkælder; **~ suit** *s* kedeldragt.

boiling point ['bɔiliŋ pɔint] *s* kogepunkt.

boil-in-the-bag ['bɔilinðə'bæg] *adj* i kogepose.

boisterous ['bɔistərəs] *adj* larmende, støjende.

bold [bəuld] *adj* dristig; fræk; tydelig; *be so ~ as to...* driste sig til at...; *write a ~ hand* have en flot og tydelig håndskrift; **~ type** *s (typ)* halvfed (,fed) skrift.

bollard ['bɔla:d] *s* hellefyr; fortøjningspæl.

bollocking ['bɔləkiŋ] *s* (S) møgfald.

bollocks ['bɔləks] *spl* (V) nosser; vrøvl, forbandet sludder.

bolster ['bəulstə*] *s* pølle // *v: ~ up* stive af, hjælpe på.

bolt [bəult] *s* bolt, slå; *a ~ from the blue* et lyn fra klar himmel // *v* bolte; (om mad) sluge; stikke af; fare af sted.

bomb [bɔm] *s* bombe; *the book goes like a ~* bogen bliver revet væk; *cost a ~* koste en formue // *v* bombe, bombardere; **~ disposal squad** *s* sprængningskommando (,-eksperter).
bomber ['bɔmə*] *s* bombefly.
bombing ['bɔmiŋ] *s* bombning; bombardement.
bomb scare ['bɔmskɛə*] *s* bombetrussel.
bombshell ['bɔmʃɛl] *s (fig)* bombe.
bond [bɔnd] *s* bånd; forskrivning; gældsbevis; obligation; *~s pl* bånd, lænker.
bondage ['bɔndidʒ] *s* trældom.
bone [bəun] *s* ben, knogle; *a ~ of contention* et stridens æble; *make no ~s about it* sige dét som det er; *have a ~ to pick with sby* have en høne at plukke med en // *v* udbene; **~-dry** *adj* knastør.
bonfire ['bɔnfaiə*] *s* bål.
bonkers ['bɔŋkəz] *adj* skør.
bonnet ['bɔnit] *s* hue, kyse; *(auto)* motorhjelm.
bonny ['bɔni] *adj* frisk, sund; (skotsk) smuk, dejlig.
bonus ['bəunəs] *s* tillæg; gratiale.
bony ['bəuni] *adj* benet, radmager; fuld af ben.
boo [bu:] *interj* øv! fy! // *v* hysse ad, råbe øv.
booby trap ['bu:bitræp] *s* fælde // *v* sætte en fælde for.
book [buk] *s* bog; hæfte; *go by the ~* holde sig til reglerne; *in my ~* efter min mening; *be in sby's good books* være i kridthuset hos en // *v* notere; bestille (fx bord, billet); købe billet; *be ~ed for speeding* blive noteret for at køre for stærkt; (se også *books*).
bookable ['bukəbl] *adj: seats are ~* der kan reserveres plads.
bookcase ['bukkeis] *s* bogreol.
bookends ['bukɛndz] *spl* bogstøtter.
bookie ['buki] *s* (F) bookmaker.
booking office ['bukiŋ 'ɔfis] *s* billetkontor.
book-keeping ['bukki:piŋ] *s* bogholderi.
booklet ['buklit] *s* brochure, pjece.
bookmaker ['bukmeikə*] *s* person (el. butik) som tager imod væddemål.
books *spl* regnskab; *cook the ~* pynte på regnskaberne.
bookseller ['buksɛlə*] *s* boghandler.
bookshop ['bukʃɔp] *s* boghandel.
bookstall ['bukstɔ:l] *s* (blad)kiosk.
book token ['buktəukən] *s* gavekort til boghandel.
boom [bu:m] *s* drøn, brag; *(merk)* højkonjunktur, opsving; *(mar)* bom // *v* drøne, buldre; have et opsving.
boor [buə*] *s* tølper.
boost [bu:st] *s* hjælpende skub // *v* hjælpe, sætte skub i; opreklamere.
boot [bu:t] *s* støvle; *(auto)* bagagerum; *give sby the ~* sparke en ud; fyre en; *lick sby's ~* fedte for en; *to ~* oven i købet.
booth [bu:θ] *s* bod; markedstelt; (telefon)boks; stemmeboks.
bootlace ['bu:tleis] *s* snørebånd.
booty ['bu:ti] *s* bytte.
booze [bu:z] *s* (F) sprut // *v* bumle, svire; **~r** *s* (S) pub.
border ['bɔ:də*] *s* kant, rand; grænseegn; kantebånd; blomsterbed; *the Border* grænsen mellem England og Skotland; *the Borders* egnen omkring den engelsk-skotske grænse // *v* kante; *~ on* grænse (op) til; **~line case** *s* grænsetilfælde.
bore [bɔ:*] *s* (om gevær etc) boring, kaliber; (om person) dødbider; *he's a ~* han er dødkedelig // *v* bore; kede; *be ~d (stiff)* kede sig (ihjel) // *præt* af *bear;* **~dom** *s* kedsomhed; **boring** *adj* kedelig.
born [bɔ:n] *adj: be ~* blive født; *~ blind* blindfødt; *in all my ~ days* i alle mine livskabte dage.
borne [bɔ:n] *pp* af *bear.*
borough ['bʌrə*] *s* købstad.
borrow ['bɔrəu] *v* låne; *~ sth from (,off) sby* låne ngt af en.
bosom ['buzəm] *s* (H) barm, bryst; *(fig)* skød; **~ buddy, ~ friend** *s* hjerteven.
boss [bɔs] *s* chef, boss // *v* regere; hundse; bestemme; lede; **~y** *adj* dominerende.

botanical [bə'tænikl] *adj* botanisk (fx *gardens* have).
botanist ['bɔtənist] *s* botaniker.
botany ['bɔtəni] *s* botanik.
botch [bɔtʃ] *s* kludder // *v: ~ (up)* forkludre.
both [bəuθ] *adj/pron* begge; både; *~ of them* dem begge (to); *we ~ came, ~ of us came* vi kom begge to; *~ a and b* både a og b.
bother ['bɔðə*] *s* plage; besvær; *oh, ~!* pokkers også! *it's no ~* det er ingen ulejlighed // *v* plage, genere; gøre sig ulejlighed; *he can't be ~ed to...* han gider ikke...; *~ about* spekulere over; tage sig af; *don't ~!* gør dig ingen ulejlighed! lad det bare være! *~ the money!* skidt med pengene!
bottle [bɔtl] *s* flaske; *hit the ~* (F) slå sig på flasken; *be on the ~* (F) være drikfældig // *v* hælde på flaske(r); henkoge; *~ out (fig)* få kolde fødder; *~ up* tilbageholde; undertrykke (fx *anger* vrede); ~ **bank** *s* beholder til genbrugsflasker.
bottled ['bɔtld] *adj* flaske-; på flaske.
bottle-feed ['bɔtlfi:d] *v* give sutteflaske; opflaske; *bottle-fed baby* flaskebarn.
bottleneck *s* flaskehals (også *fig*).
bottle-opener ['bɔtləupənə*] *s* oplukker.
bottom ['bɔtəm] *s* bund, nederste del; underdel; (F) bagdel; (stole)sæde; *at the ~ of* nederst på (,i); på bunden af; *~ up* med bunden i vejret; *~s up!* skål (og drik ud)! // *adj* lavest, nederst; bund-; under- (fx *floor* etage); underst; ~**less** *adj* bundløs.
bough [bau] *s* (H) gren.
bought [bɔ:t] *præt* og *pp* af *buy*.
boulder ['bəuldə*] *s* kampesten; rullesten.
bounce [bauns] *s* spring, hop; elasticitet; *have ~* fjedre // *v* hoppe; (om bold) hoppe tilbage; (om person) komme farende; (om dækningsløs check) blive afvist; **bouncer** *s* udsmider.
bound [baund] *s* grænse; spring; *out of ~s* på forbudt område // *v* begrænse; grænse (til); springe, hoppe; *præt* og *pp* af *bind* // *adj* bundet; forpligtet; *~ to* nødt til; forpligtet til; *he's ~ to fail* han er dømt til at mislykkes; *he's ~ to come* han 'må komme; han kommer helt bestemt; *~ for* (om skib etc) med kurs mod.
boundary ['baundəri] *s* grænse.
boundless ['baundlis] *adj* grænseløs, uendelig.
bounty ['baunti] *s* gavmildhed; storslået gave; righoldigt udvalg.
bouquet ['bukei] *s* buket.
bourbon ['bə:bən] *s* amerikansk whisky.
bourgeois ['buəʒwa:] *adj* småborgerlig.
bout [baut] *s* omgang; anfald.
bow [bəu] *s* sløjfe; bue; [bau] buk // *v* [bau] bukke; nikke; bøje sig; *~ to (,before)* bøje sig for; være underlegen overfor.
bowels ['bauəlz] *spl* indvolde, tarme; *have bowel movements* have afføring.
bowl [bəul] *s* skål; kumme; (pibe)hoved; kugle // *v* kaste; bowle; *~ over (fig)* vælte omkuld.
bow-legged ['bəulɛgid] *adj* hjulbenet.
bowling alley ['bəuliŋ,æli] *s* bowlingbane.
bowls [beulz] *spl* bowling; bocciakugler.
bow tie ['bəu,tai] *s* butterfly.
bow window ['bəuwindəu] *s* (rundt) karnapvindue.
box [bɔks] *s* æske, kasse; skrin; boks; *(teat)* loge; (på vogn) kuskesæde; *the ~* (F) fjernsynet, flimmerkassen // *v* bokse (med); lægge i æske; deponere; *~ sby's ears* stikke en et par på kassen.
boxer ['bɔksə*] *s* bokser; **boxing** *s* boksning.
Boxing Day ['bɔksiŋ dei] *s* 2. juledag (26. dec).
boxing gloves ['bɔksiŋ glʌvz] *spl* boksehandsker.
box office ['bɔks 'ɔfis] *s* billetkontor.
boxroom ['bɔksru:m] *s* pulterkammer.

boy [bɔi] *s* dreng; ung mand; (om tjener) boy; **-friend** *s* kæreste, fyr, ven; **-hood** *s* drengetid.
boyish ['bɔiiʃ] *adj* drenget.
boyscout ['bɔiskaut] *s* drengespejder.
BR fork.f. *British Rail.*
bra [bra:] *s* (fork.f. *brassiere)* bh.
brace [breis] *s* støtte; stiver; (tand)bøjle; klampe; klamme // *v* støtte, afstive; ~ *oneself* samle alt sit mod; mande sig op; stramme sig an.
bracelet ['breislit] *s* armbånd.
braces ['breisiz] *spl* seler.
bracken ['brækən] *s* bregne.
bracket ['brækit] *s* støtte; hyldeknægt; parentes; gruppe; kategori // *v* sætte i parentes; *(fig)* sidestille; 'sætte i bås'.
brackish ['brækiʃ] *adj:* ~ *water* brakvand.
brag [bræg] *v* prale, skryde; **braggart** ['brægəd] *s* pralhals.
braid [breid] *s* fletning; snor; lidse // *v* flette.
Braille [breil] *s* blindeskrift.
brain [brein] *s* hjerne; *blow sby's ~ out* skyde en en kugle for panden; *he's got ~s* han er intelligent, (F) han er kvik i pæren; *pick sby's ~s* lære af ens ekspertise; spørge en til råds; **-child** *s* fantasifoster; **~ damage** *s* hjerneskade; **~ death** *s* hjernedød; **-less** *adj* ubegavet, tomhjernet; **-wash** *s* hjernevask; **-wave** *s* lys idé.
brainy ['breini] *adj* intelligent, intellektuel.
braise [breiz] *v* grydestege.
brake [breik] *s* bremse; *apply the ~s* træde på bremsen // *v* bremse (op); **~ fluid** *s* bremsevæske; **~ lining** *s* bremsebelægning.
bramble [bræmbl] *s* brombær(busk).
bran [bræn] *s* klid.
branch [bra:ntʃ] *s* gren; afdeling; filial // *v* dele sig; ~ *off* dreje af; forgrene sig; ~ *out* udvide, ekspandere.
brand [brænd] *s* (vare)mærke; slags // *v* brændemærke; ~ *sby a communist (fig)* stemple en som kommunist; **-ed goods** *s* mærkevarer.
brandish ['brændiʃ] *v* svinge (med).
brand-new ['brænd'nju:] *adj* splinterny.
brandy ['brandi] *s* cognac.
brash [bræʃ] *adj* pågående; fræk; (om farve etc) skrigende.
brass [bra:s] *s* messing; (S) gysser, grunker; frækhed; *the ~ (mus)* messingblæserne; **~ band** *s* hornorkester.
brassière ['bræsiə*] *s* brystholder, bh.
brass tacks ['bra:stæks] *spl: let's get down to ~* lad os komme til sagen(s kerne).
brat [bræt] *s (neds)* unge.
brave [breiv] *v* trodse // *adj* modig, tapper; **-ry** ['breivəri] *s* mod, tapperhed.
brawl [brɔ:l] *s* slagsmål // *v* lave optøjer; slås; skændes.
brawn [brɔ:n] *s* muskelkraft, råstyrke; *(gastr)* grisesylte; **brawny** *adj* muskuløs.
bray [bri] *s* skryden // *v* skryde.
brazen ['breizən] *adj* fræk, skamløs.
Brazil [brə'zil] *s* Brasilien; **-ian** *s* brasilianer // *adj* brasiliansk; **~ nut** *s* paranød.
breach [bri:tʃ] *s* brud; revne; breche; ~ *of confidence* tillidsbrud; ~ *of contract* kontraktbrud; ~ *of the peace* forbrydelse mod den offentlige orden; ~ *of promise* brud på ægteskabsløfte // *v* bryde breche i.
bread [brɛd] *s* brød; *a loaf of ~* et brød; *one's ~ and butter* ens levebrød; **-bin** *s* brødkasse; **-board** *s* skærebræt; **-crumbs** *spl* brødkrummer; rasp.
breaded ['brɛdid] *adj* vendt i rasp, paneret.
breadline ['brɛdlain] *s: be on the ~* leve på eksistensminimum.
breadth [brɛdθ] *s* bredde.
breadwinner ['brɛdwinə*] *s* familieforsørger.
break [breik] *s* brud; pause, frikvarter; afbrydelse; chance // *v (broke, broken* [brəuk, brəukn]) ødelægge; slå i stykker; bryde (fx *a promise* et løfte); gå itu; knalde; brække; af-

bryde; begynde; (om vejret) slå om; (om hest) tæmme; ~ *a record* slå en rekord; ~ *service* (i tennis) få servegennembrud; ~ *the news to sby* (skånsomt) fortælle en ngt; ~ *down* bryde ned; bryde sammen; opdele; ~ *even* få det til at gå lige op; ~ *free (,loose)* rive (sig) løs; ~ *in* bryde ind; (om hest) tilride; (om person) oplære; ~ *in on* bryde ind i; afbryde; ~ *into* bryde ind i (fx *a house* et hus); slå over i; ~ *off* afbryde; knække af; ~ *open* bryde (,brække) op; ~ *out* bryde ud; opstå; ~ *out in spots* få udslæt (,knopper); ~ *up* splitte(s); bryde op; sprænge(s); opløse(s); standse.

breakable ['breikəbl] *adj* skrøbelig.

breakage ['breikidʒ] *s* brud; beskadigelse.

breakaway ['breikəwei] *s* løsrivelse; *(pol)* løsgænger.

breakdown ['breikdaun] *s* sammenbrud; skade; motorstop, havari; ~ **lorry** *s* kranvogn; ~ **service** *s* sv.t. fx Falcks vejservice.

breaker ['breikə*] *s* (om bølge) styrtsø; **~s** *spl* brænding.

breakfast ['breikfəst] *s* morgenmad // *v* spise morgenmad; ~ *on toast and jam* spise ristet brød og syltetøj til morgenmad.

break-in ['breikin] *s* indbrud.

breakneck ['breiknɛk] *adj* halsbrækkende.

breakout ['breikaut] *s* flugt (fra fængsel etc); udslæt.

breakthrough ['breikθru:] *s* gennembrud.

breakwater ['breikwɔ:tə*] *s* bølgebryder.

breast [brɛst] *s* bryst; *make a clean ~ of it* tilstå, gå til bekendelse; **~feed** *v* amme, give bryst; **~stroke** *s* brystsvømning.

breath [brɛθ] *s* ånde; åndedrag; pust; *draw* ~ trække vejret; *a ~ of fresh air* en mundfuld frisk luft; *out of* ~ forpustet; *say sth under one's* ~ hviske (,mumle) ngt; *I could have saved my* ~ jeg kunne have sparet mig ulejligheden.

breathalyzer ['brɛθəlaizə*] *s* spritballon (til spiritusprøve).

breathe [bri:ð] *v* ånde, trække vejret; henhånde; ~ *again* ånde lettet op; **~r** *s* (F) pusterum, lille pause.

breathless ['brɛθlis] *adj* åndeløs, forpustet.

breathtaking ['brɛθteikiŋ] *adj* betagende, spændende.

breeches ['bri:tʃəz] *spl* bukser; knæbukser; ridebukser.

breed [bri:d] *s* race; art // *v (bred, bred* [brɛd]) yngle; avle, opdrætte; opdrage.

breeder ['bri:də*] *s* avler.

breeding ['bri:diŋ] *s* formering; opdragelse, dannelse; ~ **ground** *s* yngleplads; *(fig)* udklækningssted.

breeze [bri:z] *s* brise // *v* svanse, sejle.

breezy ['bri:zi] *adj* (om person) munter.

brevity ['brɛviti] *s* korthed.

brew [bru:] *s* bryg // *v* brygge; pønse på; trække op, være i anmarch; *let the tea* ~ lade teen trække.

brewer ['bru:ə*] *s* brygger; **~'s yeast** *s* ølgær.

brewery ['bru:əri] *s* bryggeri.

bribe [braib] *s* bestikkelse // *v* bestikke.

bribery ['braibəri] *s* bestikkelse.

bric-a-brac ['brikəbræk] *s* nipsting; tingeltangel.

brick [brik] *s* mursten, teglsten; byggeklods; *drop a* ~ jokke i spinaten // *v:* ~ *up* mure til (,inde); **~layer** *s* murer; **~work** *s* murværk; **~works** *s* teglværk.

bridal ['braidl] *adj* brude-; bryllups-.

bride [braid] *s* brud; **~groom** *s* brudgom.

bridesmaid ['braidsmeid] *s* brudepige.

bridge [bridʒ] *s* bro; (næse)ryg // *v* slå bro over (også *fig).*

bridging loan ['bridʒiŋ ˌləun] *s* overgangslån.

bridle [braidl] *s* tømme // *v* tøjle, tæmme; **~path** *s* ridesti.

brief [bri:f] *s* resumé; *in* ~ kort sagt // *v* give et resumé af; briefe, informere // *adj* kort, kortfattet.

briefcase ['bri:fkeis] *s* dokumentmappe.
briefing ['bri:fiŋ] *s* instruktioner; information.
briefly ['bri:fli] *adv* kort (og godt).
briefs [bri:fs] *spl* trusser.
brigadier [brigə'diə*] *s* brigadegeneral.
bright [brait] *adj* lys; klar; strålende; glad; kvik; ~ *and early* tidligt (om morgenen).
brighten ['braitən] *v* gøre lysere; lysne; live op; klare op.
brill [bril] *interj* (S) fedt! skønt!
brilliance ['briljəns] *s* glans; skin; intelligens.
brilliant *adj* strålende, fremragende.
Brillo pad ® ['briləupæd] *s* stålulds-svamp.
brim [brim] *s* kant, rand; (hatte)skygge // *v:* ~ *over* svømme over; *be ~ming with sth* vrimle med ngt; **~ful** *adj* fyldt til randen.
brine [brain] *s* lage; saltvand.
bring [briŋ] *v (brought, brought* [brɔ:t] bringe; tage med; skaffe; hente; ~ *about* forårsage, medføre; ~ *back* bringe tilbage; ~ *down* få til at falde; nedlægge; vælte; ~ *forward* fremsætte, fremlægge; ~ *off* gennemføre, klare; ~ *out* få frem; fremhæve; ~ *round (,to)* bringe til sig selv igen; ~ *up* opdrage; bringe på bane; **~-and-buy (sale)** *s* loppemarked.
brink [briŋk] *s* kant, rand.
brisk [brisk] *adj* livlig, kvik; frisk.
brisket ['briskit] *s (gastr)* bryststykke.
bristle [brisl] *s* børste(hår) // *v* rejse børster; få til at stritte; *bristling with* spækket med.
Brit [brit] *s* brite; **Britain** ['britən] *s* Storbritannien.
british ['britiʃ] *adj* britisk; *the British Isles* De Britiske Øer; *British Rail (BR)* de britiske statsbaner.
Briton ['britən] *s* bretoner (person fra Bretagne); **Brittany** ['britəni] *s* Bretagne.
brittle [britl] *adj* skør, skrøbelig; sprød; **~-bone disease** *s (med)* knogleskørhed.
broach [brəutʃ] *v:* ~ *a subject* bringe et emne på bane.
B-road ['bi:rəud] *s* bivej.
broad [brɔ:d] *s (neds)* tøs // *adj* bred; vid; jævn; frisindet; *in ~ daylight* ved højlys dag; *a ~ hint* et vink med en vognstang, et tydeligt vink.
broadcast ['brɔ:dka:st] *s* radioudsendelse // *v* udbrede; udsende, transmittere.
broaden ['brɔ:dn] *v* gøre (,blive) bredere, udvide.
broadly ['brɔ:dli] *adv* i det store og hele; ~ *speaking* stort set.
broadminded ['brɔ:dmaindid] *adj* frisindet.
broiler ['brɔilə*] *s* stegekylling; grill.
broke [brəuk] *præt* af *break* // *adj* (F) "på spanden", helt "flad".
broken ['brəukən] *pp* af *break* // *adj* knust; brækket; brudt; usikker; *in ~ English* på gebrokkent engelsk; *a ~ home* et skilsmissehjem; **~-down** *adj* brudt sammen; faldefærdig; **~-hearted** *adj* sønderknust.
broker ['brəukə*] *s* mægler.
bronze [brɔnz] *s* bronze; **~d** *adj* bronzeret; solbrændt.
brooch [brəutʃ] *s* broche.
brood [bru:d] *s* yngel; kuld // *v* ruge; udruge; spekulere.
broody ['bru:di] *adj* melankolsk; (om høne) liggesyg; (om kvinde) vild efter at få et barn.
brook [bruk] *s* bæk; **~let** *s* lille bæk.
broom [brum] *s* (feje)kost; *(bot)* gyvel; **~stick** *s* kosteskaft.
Bros ['brʌðəz] fork.f. *Brothers* (i firmanavn).
broth [brɔθ] *s* kødsuppe.
brothel ['brɔθəl] *s* bordel.
brother ['brʌðə*] *s* bror; medbror; **~hood** *s* broderskab; **~-in-law** *s* svoger.
brought [brɔ:t] *præt* og *pp* af *bring.*
brow [brau] *s* pande; øjenbryn; *knit one's ~* rynke panden; **~beat** *v* herse med, tromle ned.
brown [braun] *v* brune; blive brun // *adj* brun.
brownie ['brauni] *s* lille pigespejder; slags chokoladekage.

browse [brauz] *v* gå og snuse (i bøger etc); bladre lidt (i).
bruise [bru:z] *s* blåt mærke, blodudtrædning // *v* støde; få blå mærker; **~d** *adj* forslået.
brunch [brʌntʃ] *s* kombineret *breakfast* og *lunch.*
brunt [brʌnt] *s: bear the* ~ måtte tage stødene; måtte trække det tunge læs.
brush [brʌʃ] *s* børste; pensel; krat; *(fig)* sammenstød // *v* børste; stryge; strejfe; ~ *aside* affærdige; feje til side; ~ *up* pudse op; genopfriske; **~off** *s: give sby the ~off* afvise en.
brushwood ['brʌʃwud] *s* kvas; krat.
brusque [brʌsk] *adj* kort for hovedet, studs.
Brussels [brʌslz] *s* Bruxelles.
brussels sprout ['brʌslz ˌspraut] *s* rosenkål.
brutal [bru:tl] *adj* brutal, rå.
brutality [bru:'tæliti] *s* brutalitet.
brute [bru:t] *s* udyr, bæst // *adj: ~ strength* råstyrke.
brutish ['bru:tiʃ] *adj* rå, dyrisk.
BSc ['bi:ɛs'si:] fork.f. *Bachelor of Science.*
BST fork.f. *British Summer Time.*
bubble [bʌbl] *s* boble // *v* boble, sprudle; **~ bath** *s* skumbad; **~ gum** *s* ballontyggegummi.
bubbly ['bʌbli] *adj* boblende; livlig // *s* (S) champagne.
buck [bʌk] *s* (om hare, hjort etc) han, buk; *pass the* ~ (F) lade sorteper gå videre // *v* springe; stange; stejle; ~ *up* skynde sig; ~ *up!* op med humøret!
bucket ['bʌkit] *s* spand; *kick the* ~ (F) kradse af // *v* regne i spandevis, øse ned.
buckle [bʌkl] *s* spænde // *v* spænde(s); *(fig)* slå sig; (om hjul) exe; ~ *in* spænde (sig) fast.
bud [bʌd] *s (bot)* knop; *nip sth in the* ~ standse ngt i opløbet // *v* skyde knopper; spire; **~ding** *adj* spirende; *(fig)* vordende.
buddy ['bʌdi] *s* (F) makker, 'kammerat.
budge [bʌdʒ] *v* flytte (sig); røre (sig); rokke.
budgerigar ['bʌdʒəriga:*] *s* undulat.
budget ['bʌdʒit] *s* budget; finanslov // *v: ~ for sth* optage ngt på budgettet; **~ account** *s* budgetkonto.
budgie ['bʌdʒi] *s* d.s.s. *budgerigar.*
buff [bʌf] *s: in the* ~ (F) splitterfornøjet (dvs. nøgen).
buffalo ['bʌfələu] *s (pl:* ~ el. *~es)* bøffel; *(am)* bisonokse.
buffer ['bʌfə*] *s* stødpude.
buffet *s* ['bufei] buffet; (på tog, station etc) restaurant // *v* ['bʌfit] støde; puffe; bumpe.
buffoon [bə'fu:n] *s* klovn.
bug [bʌg] *s* væggelus; virus (også *edb);* bacille; skjult mikrofon // *v* aflytte; anbringe skjulte mikrofoner i; irritere.
bugger ['bʌgə*] *s* (F) fyr; skiderik // *v: ~ about* (S) fjumre rundt; ~ *off* (S) skride; ~ *up* forkludre.
bugle [bju:gl] *s* (signal)horn.
build [bild] *s* (om person) bygning, skikkelse // *v (built, built)* bygge; ~ *up* opbygge; oparbejde.
builder ['bildə*] *s* bygningshåndværker; entreprenør; bygherre.
building *s* bygning; **~ society** *s* realkreditinstitution.
build-up ['bildʌp] *s* oparbejdning; ophobning; hvervning.
built [bilt] *præt* og *pp* af *build* // *adj* bygget; *well-~* velskabt; **~-in** *adj* indbygget; **~-up area** *s* bebygget område.
bulb [bʌlb] *s* blomsterløg; *(elek)* pære; **bulbous** ['bʌlbəs] *adj* løgformet.
bulge [bʌldʒ] *s* bule // *v* bulne ud; svulme (op); *be bulging with* være ved at revne af.
bulk [bʌlk] *s* omfang; masse; *in ~ (merk)* løst, upakket; *the ~ of* størstedelen af; **~buy** *v* gøre storindkøb; **~head** *s (mar)* skot.
bulky ['bʌlki] *adj* uhåndterlig; voluminøs.
bull [bul] *s* tyr; (om elefant etc) han; (S) vrøvl.
bulldoze ['buldəuz] *s* tromle ned; planere.

bullet ['bulit] *s* kugle, projektil; **~-proof** *adj* skudsikker.
bullfight ['bulfait] *s* tyrefægtning; **~er** *s* tyrefægter.
bullfinch ['bulfintʃ] *s (zo)* dompap.
bullion ['buljən] *s* (guld)barre.
bullock ['bulək] *s* ung tyr, stud.
bull's-eye ['bulsai] *s* (på skydeskive) plet.
bullshit ['bulʃit] *s* (V) vrøvl; lort.
bully ['buli] *s* tyran, bølle // *v* tyrannisere; herse med; skræmme.
bulrush ['bulrʌʃ] *s (bot)* dunhammer.
bum [bʌm] *s* vagabond, bums, sut; (F) bagdel.
bumblebee ['bʌmbl,bi:] *s* humlebi.
bump [bʌmp] *s* bump; stød; bule; (i vej) hul // *v* bumpe; skumple; *~ into* støde mod; *~ sby off* rydde en af vejen; *~ up the price* presse prisen op.
bumper ['bʌmpə*] *s* kofanger, stødfanger.
bumper crop ['bʌmpə krɔp] *s* rekordhøst.
bumptious ['bʌmʃəs] *adj* storsnudet.
bumpy ['bʌmpi] *adj* ujævn; (om vej) hullet.
bun [bʌn] *s* bolle; (om frisure) knude i nakken.
bunch [bʌntʃ] *s* bundt; klump; buket; klase; (om personer) flok.
bundle [bʌndl] *s* bundt; bylt // *v* bundte (sammen); *~ the kids into the car* proppe børnene ind i bilen; *~ off* sende af sted i en fart; *~ out* falde (,vælte) ud.
bungle [bʌŋgl] *v* forkludre; klokke i det; **~r** *s* kludremikkel.
bunion ['bʌnjən] *s* knyst.
bunk [bʌŋk] *s* køje; *do a ~* (S) stikke af; **~ beds** *spl* etageseng.
bunker ['bʌŋkə*] *s* kulkasse; bunker.
bunny ['bʌni] *s* kanin.
bunt [bʌnt] *s* (S) spraydåse (til graffitimaling).
bunting ['bʌntiŋ] *s* flagdug.
buoy [bɔi] *s (mar)* bøje // *v* afmærke; *~ up* bære oppe; *(fig)* holde oppe, støtte.
buoyancy ['bɔiənsi] *s (fig)* livlighed.
buoyant ['bɔiənt] *adj* livlig, let; spændstig; stigende.
burden ['bə:dn] *s* byrde, last; omkvæd; *~ of proof* bevisbyrde // *v* bebyrde.
bureau ['bjuərəu] *s (pl: ~x* [-rəuz]) kontor, bureau; skrivebord; chatol; **~cracy** [-'rɔkrəsi] *s* bureaukrati.
burglar ['bə:glə*] *s* indbrudstyv; **~ alarm** *s* tyverialarm; **burglary** *s* indbrudstyveri.
burgle ['bə:gl] *v* lave indbrud (i).
Burgundy ['bə:gəndi] *s* Bourgogne.
burgundy ['bə:gəndi] *s* bourgognevin; vinrød farve.
burial ['bɛriəl] *s* begravelse; **~ ground** *s* begravelsesplads; kirkegård.
burly ['bə:li] *adj* kraftigt bygget; djærv.
burn [bə:n] *s* brandsår; bæk // *v (~ed, ~ed* el. *~t, ~t)* brænde; svide; *~ down* nedbrænde.
burner ['bə:nə*] *s* brænder.
burning glass ['bə:niŋ gla:s] *s* brændglas.
burnish ['bə:niʃ] *v* polere.
burnt [bə:nt] *præt* og *pp* af *burn* // *adj: ~ sugar* karamel.
burp [bə:p] *s* (F) bøvs // *v* bøvse; *~ the baby* få babyen til at bøvse.
burrow ['bʌrəu] *s* hule, grav // *v* grave.
bursar ['bə:sə*] *s* regnskabsfører; (skotsk) stipendiat.
bursary ['bə:səri] *s* stipendium.
burst [bə:st] *s* eksplosion; brag; sprængt vandrør; *a ~ blood vessel* et sprængt blodkar; *a ~ of energy* et anfald af energi; *a ~ of inflation* en inflationsbølge // *v (burst, burst)* briste, springe; sprænge(s); *~ into flames* bryde i brand; *~ into laughter (,tears)* briste i latter (,gråd); *be ~ing with* være ved at revne af; *~ open* springe op; *~ out of* vælte ud af.
bury ['bɛri] *s* begrave; *~ oneself in sth* fordybe sig i ngt; *~ one's head in the sand* stikke hovedet i busken; *~ the hatchet* begrave stridsøksen.
bus [bʌs] *s (pl: ~es* ['bʌsiz]) bus // *v* køre (,transportere) med bus.
bush [buʃ] *s* busk; krat; *beat about the ~* krybe udenom; **~y** *adj* busket; kratbevokset.

busily ['bizili] *adv* travlt.
business ['biznis] *s* forretning; firma; forretningslivet; erhverv, arbejde; sag, affære; *be away on* ~ være på forretningsrejse; *it's none of your* ~ det kommer ikke dig ved; *mind your own* ~*!* pas dig selv! *he means* ~ han mener det alvorligt; **~like** *adj* forretningsmæssig; saglig; effektiv; **~man** *s* forretningsmand.
busker ['bʌskə*] *s* gademusikant; gadegøgler.
bus lane ['bʌslein] *s* busbane; **bus layby** *s* busholdeplads; **bus shelter** *s* læskur (ved stoppested).
bust [bʌst] *s* buste; brystmål // *v* slå; ødelægge; knuse(s); sprænge(s); ~ *out* bryde ud; ~ *up with sby* slå op med en // *adj* brækket; revnet; i stykker; ruineret; *gå* ~ gå fallit.
bustle [bʌsl] *s* travlhed, tummel // *v* have travlt, skynde sig; **bustling** *adj* travl.
bust-up ['bʌst,ʌp] *s* opgør (mellem kærester etc).
busy ['bizi] *v:* ~ *oneself* være travlt beskæftiget // *adj* travl; trafikeret; **~body** *s* geskæftig (,nævenyttig) person.
but [bʌt, bət] *præp/konj* men; kun; undtagen; *nothing* ~ ikke andet end, bare; ~ *for her* havde det ikke været for hende; *all* ~ *finished* næsten færdig; *anything* ~ alt andet end; langtfra; *the last* ~ *one* den næstsidste.
butcher ['butʃə*] *s* slagter // *v* nedslagte; mishandle; **butchery** *s* slagteri; massakre.
butler ['bʌtlə*] *s* butler, hushovmester.
butt [bʌt] *s* stor tønde; geværkolbe; skæfte; stump; (cigaret)skod; offer, skydeskive *(of, for* for); *get off your* ~*!* (F) se at få lettet måsen! // *v* støde (til); give (,få) en skalle; ~ *in* mase sig på, blande sig.
butter ['bʌtə*] *s* smør // *v* smøre (også *fig);* ~ *sby up* fedte for en; **~cup** *s* smørblomst; **~ dish** *s* smørasiet.
butterfly ['bʌtəflai] *s* sommerfugl; **~ tie** *s* butterfly.
buttermilk ['bʌtəmilk] *s* kærnemælk.
butterscotch ['bʌtəskɔtʃ] *s* slags flødekaramel.
buttery ['bʌtəri] *s* tehus // *adj* smøragtig.
buttocks ['bʌtəks] *spl* bagdel, endebalder.
button ['bʌtn] *s* knap; knop // *v* knappe(s); ~ *up* knappe; *(fig)* klappe i; **~hole** *s* knaphul; knaphulsblomst // *v* hage sig fast i; gribe fat i for at snakke.
buttress ['bʌtris] *s* (stræbe)pille.
buxom ['bʌksəm] *adj* fyldig, yppig, trivelig.
buy [bai] *v (bought, bought* [bɔ:t]) købe; ~ *sby a drink* købe en drink til en; *I'll* ~ *that* den er jeg med på; *he bought it* (F) han hoppede på den; (S) han kreperede; ~ *into a firm* købe sig ind (som partner) i et firma; ~ *off* bestikke; købe fri; ~ *up* opkøbe.
buyer ['baiə*] *s* opkøber; køber.
buzz [bʌz] *s* summen; (F) telefonopringning; *what's the* ~*?* (F) lad mig høre den seneste sladder! // *v* summe; (F) slå på tråden til; ~ *off* (F) gå, skride, smutte; ~ *one's secretary* ringe på sin sekretær.
buzzard ['bʌzəd] *s (zo)* musvåge.
buzzer ['bʌzə*] *s* brummer; ringeklokke.
buzz-word ['bʌzwə:d] *s* (F) modeord.
by [bai] *præp* af; ved; forbi; via; med; *written* ~ *Donne* skrevet af Donne; *a house* ~ *the river* et hus ved floden; *get* ~ klare sig; *pass* ~ gå (,køre etc) forbi; *the train went* ~ *Reading* toget kørte via Reading; *go* ~ *bus* køre med bus; *paid* ~ *the hour* timelønnet; *all* ~ *oneself* helt alene; ~ *the way* for resten; ~ *and* ~ om lidt, snart; ~ *and large* stort set; *multiply* ~ *two* gange med to.
bye(-bye) ['bai('bai)] *interj* farvel! hejhej! *go bye-byes* (F) gå i seng, lægge sig til at sove.
bye-laws ['bailɔ:z] *spl* d.s.s. *bylaws.*
by-election ['baii,lɛkʃən] *s* suppleringsvalg.
bygone ['baigɔn] *s: let* ~*s be* ~*s* lad

det (,fortiden) være glemt // *adj* forgangen, svundet.
by-laws ['bailɔ:z] *spl* vedtægter, statutter.
bypass *s* ['baipa:s] omkørselsvej; ringvej // *v* [bai'pa:s] gå (,køre) uden om; forbigå; springe over.
by-product ['baiprɔdʌkt] *s* biprodukt.
byre [baiə*] *s* kostald.
bystander ['baistændə*] *s* tilskuer.
byway ['baiwei] *s* sidevej.
byword ['baiwə:d] *s: be a ~ for* være et andet ord for.

C

C, c [si:].
C fork.f. *centigrade* celsius.
CA fork.f. *chartered accountant.*
cab [kæb] *s* taxi, drosche; (i bil, tog) førerhus.
cabbage ['kæbidʒ] *s* kål (især hvidkål), kålhoved; *red ~* rødkål.
cabin ['kæbin] *s* hytte, lille hus; *(mar)* kabine, lille kahyt; *(fly)* kabine.
cabinet ['kæbinit] *s* skab; kabinet; regering; *cocktail ~* barskab; *medicine ~* medicinskab.
cabinet-maker ['kæbinitmeikə*] *s* møbelsnedker.
cable [[keibl] *s* kabel; trosse; ledning; telegram // *v* telegrafere; **~-car** *s* (i tovbane) kabine; **~gram** *s* telegram; **~ railway** *s* tovbane; **~stitch** *s* (i strikning) snoninger; **~ television** *s* kabel-tv.
cache [kæʃ] *s* hemmeligt lager (især af våben).
cackle [kækl] *v* kagle; skræppe (op).
cactus ['kæktəs] *s (pl: cacti* ['kæktai]) kaktus.
cadet [kə'dɛt] *s* yngre søn (i fin familie); kadet.
cadge [kædʒ] *v* snylte, nasse; *~ on* nasse på; *~ a meal off sby* redde sig et måltid mad hos en.
cadger ['kædʒə*] *s* snylter, (F) nasserøv.
caesarean [si'sɛəriən] *s (med)* kejsersnit.
caffein ['kæfi:n] *s* koffein.
cage [keidʒ] *s* bur; *(sport)* kurv, net, mål // *v* spærre inde, sætte i bur; **caged** *adj* i bur, bur-.
cagey ['keidʒi] *adj* hemmelighedsfuld; undvigende.
cahoots [kə'hu:ts] *s: be in ~ with* være i ledtog med.
cairn [kɛən] *s* (skotsk) varde; stendysse.
cajole [kə'dʒəul] *v* snakke godt for, smigre, lokke.
cake [keik] *s* kage; stykke; frikadelle; *a ~ of soap* et stykke sæbe; *fish~* fiskefrikadelle; *you can't have your ~ and eat it* man kan ikke få i både pose og sæk; *sell like hot ~s* gå som varmt brød; *it was a piece of ~* det gik som en leg; **~d** *adj: ~d with mud* med kager af mudder; **~ mix** *s* kagemix (færdig blanding til hjemmebagning); **~ tin** *s* bageform; kagedåse.
calamity [kə'læmiti] *s* katastrofe.
calculate ['kælkjuleit] *v* beregne; regne *(on* med); **calculating** *adj* beregnende; regne-.
calculation [kælkju'leiʃən] *s* beregning; udregning.
calculator ['kælkjuleitə*] *s* regnemaskine.
calculus ['kælkjuləs] *s (pl: calculi* [-lai]) *(mat)* -regning; *(med)* sten; *renal ~* nyresten.
calf [ka:f] *s (pl: calves* [ka:vz]) kalv, unge; *(anat)* læg; *elephant ~* elefantunge; **~skin** *s* kalveskind.
calibre ['kælibə*] *s* kaliber; karat; kvalitet.
call [kɔ:l] *s* råb; kalden; opringning, telefonsamtale; opfordring; krav, fordring; besøg; *be on ~* være i beredskab; have tilkaldevagt // *v* råbe; kalde (på); komme på besøg; *(tlf)* ringe til; *he's ~ed John* han hedder John; *~ for* komme for at hente; kalde på; kræve; *~ in* indkalde; komme på besøg; ringe; *~ off* aflyse; *~ on sby to...* opfordre en til at...; *~ up (mil)* indkalde; **~box** *s* telefonboks.
caller ['kɔ:lə*] *s* besøgende, gæst; *(tlf)* en der ringer op.
calling ['kɔ:liŋ] *s* kald; stilling.

callipers ['kælipəz] *spl* passer.
callous ['kæləs] *adj* hård, barket; ufølsom, ubarmhjertig.
callus ['kæləs] *s* hård hud.
calm [ka:m] *s* ro; vindstille; *dead ~* blikstille // *v* berolige; blive rolig; (om blæst etc) lægge sig; *~ down* falde til ro; berolige // *adj* rolig.
calor gas ['kæləgæs] *s* flaskegas.
calve [ka:v] *v* kælve; **~s** [ka:vz] *pl* af *calf*.
camber ['kæmbə*] *s* (om vej) runding; krumning; hældning.
cambric ['kæmbrik] *s* batist.
came [keim] *præt* af *come*.
camera ['kæmərə] *s* foto(grafi)apparat, kamera; filmsapparat; *35 mm ~* småbilledkamera (24x36); *in ~ (jur)* for lukkede døre; **~man** *s* kameramand; fotograf.
camomile ['kæməmail] *s* kamille.
camouflage ['kæməfla:ʒ] *s* camouflage // *v* camouflere.
camp [kæmp] *s* lejr; *make (,pitch) ~* slå lejr; *break (,strike) ~* bryde op // *v* ligge i (,slå) lejr; campere // *adj* overpyntet; lapset; (F) bøsset.
campaign [kæm'pein] *s* kampagne, felttog // *v* deltage i (,organisere) en kampagne.
camp-bed ['kæmpbɛd] *s* feltseng, campingseng; **camp chair** *s* feltstol, campingstol.
camper ['kæmpə*] *s* campist; autocamper.
campfire ['kæmpfaiə*] *s* lejrbål.
campsite ['kæmpsait] *s* campingplads.
campus ['kæmpəs] *s* universitet(sområde), campus.
can [kæn] *s* kande, dunk; *(am)* (konserves)dåse; *carry the ~* måtte tage skylden; *it's in the ~* (F) det er faldet på plads.
can [kæn, kən] *v (præt: could* [kud]) kan; må; *I ~ swim* jeg kan svømme; *I cannot (,can't) see him* jeg kan ikke se ham; *~ I have an apple?* må jeg få et æble? *no, you can't!* nej du må ikke!
Canadian [kə'neidiən] *s* canadier // *adj* canadisk.
canal [kə'næl] *s* kanal.
canary [kə'nɛəri] *s* kanariefugl; kanariegult.
cancel ['kænsəl] *v* aflyse; stryge, strege ud; afbestille; annullere; *~ sth out* opveje ngt; **~lation** [-'leiʃən] *s* aflysning; udstregning; afbestilling; annullering.
cancer ['kænsə*] *s* kræft, cancer; *the Cancer (astr)* Krebsen; *the Tropic of Cancer* krebsens (,den nordlige) vendekreds.
candid ['kændid] *adj* oprigtig, åben; *~ camera* skjult kamera.
candidacy ['kændidəsi] *s* kandidatur.
candidate ['kændideit] *s* kandidat.
candied ['kændid] *adj* (sukker)glaseret; **~ peel** *s* sukat.
candle [kændl] *s* (levende) lys; kærte; *he can't hold a ~ to John* han kan overhovedet ikke måle sig med John; *it's not worth the ~* det er ikke umagen værd; **~light** *s: by ~light* i stearinlysskær; **~stick** *s* lysestage; kandelaber; **~wick** *s* væge; (om stof) chenille.
candour ['kændə*] *s* åbenhed, oprigtighed.
candy ['kændi] *s* kandis; *(am* også) slik; **~-striped** *adj* bolsjestribet.
cane [kein] *s* rør; stok; spanskrør // *v* slå med spanskrør; **~ sugar** *s* rørsukker.
canine ['kænain] *adj* af hundefamilien, hunde-; **~ tooth** *s* hjørnetand.
canister ['kænistə*] *s* dåse; dunk.
canned [kænd] *adj* dåse-; (F) beruset, fuld; *~ fruit* frugt på dåse; *~ music* muzak; **cannery** *s* konservesfabrik.
cannon ['kænən] *s* kanon // *v: ~ into* brase ind i; **~ball** *s* kanonkugle; **~-fodder** *s* kanonføde.
cannot ['kænət] d.s.s. *can not*.
canny ['kæni] *adj* kvik, smart.
canoe [kə'nu:] *s* kano // *v* ro i kano; **~ing** *s* kanosport; **~ist** *s* kanoroer.
canon ['kænən] *s* lov, regel; kannik; *(mus)* 'kanon; **~ize** [-aiz] *v* gøre til helgen, kanonisere.
canoodle [kə'nu:dl] *v* kysse og kramme.

canopy ['kænəpi] *s* baldakin; sengehimmel.

can't [kænt, ka:nt] d.s.s. *can not.*

cantankerous [kæn'tæŋkərəs] *adj* krakilsk, kværulantisk; vrissen.

canteen [kæn'ti:n] *s* kantine, frokoststue.

canter ['kæntə*] *s* kort galop // *v* ride i kort galop.

Canute [kə'nju:t] *s* Knud; *king ~* Knud den Store.

canvas ['kænvəs] *s* lærred, sejldug; (om kunst) maleri; *under ~* i telt; under sejl; **~ chair** *s* liggestol.

canvass ['kænvəs] *v* hverve (stemmer, kunder etc); **~ing** *s* (hus)agitation, stemmehvervning; *(merk)* kolportage; tegning (af abonnementer etc).

canyon ['kænjən] *s* dyb og snæver dal.

cap [kæp] *s* hue; kasket; kalot; kapsel, låg; knaldhætte; pessar; *if the ~ fits* hvis du føler dig truffet; *~ in hand* ydmygt // *v* sætte hue (,låg) på; dække; *be ~ped (sport)* blive udtaget til landsholdet; *to ~ it all...* for at sætte kronen på værket...; *~ped with* dækket af.

capability [keipə'biliti] *s* dygtighed; evne.

capable ['keipəbl] *adj* dygtig, kompetent; *~ of* i stand til.

capacious [kə'peiʃəs] *adj* rummelig.

capacity [kə'pæsiti] *s* evne, anlæg; åndsevner; volumen; kapacitet; *in his ~ of...* i hans egenskab af...; *work at full ~* (om fabrik etc) arbejde (,køre) for fuld kraft; *a ~ audience* fuldt hus.

cape [keip] *s* slag, cape; forbjerg, kap; *the Cape* Kap det Gode Håb.

caper ['keipə*] *s* hoppen og springen; kapers // *v* hoppe rundt.

capital ['kæpitl] *s* hovedstad; kapital, formue; stort bogstav // *adj* kapital-; (F) glimrende, strålende; vigtig; **~ crime** *s* forbrydelse som der er dødsstraf for; **~ gains** *spl* kapitalvinding; **~ punishment** *s* dødsstraf.

capitulate [kə'pitjuleit] *v* kapitulere;

capitulation [-'leiʃən] *s* kapitulation, overgivelse.

capricious [kə'priʃəs] *adj* lunefuld; ustadig.

Capricorn ['kæprikɔ:n] *s (astr)* Stenbukken; *the Tropic of ~* Stenbukkens (,den sydlige) vendekreds.

capsize [kæp'saiz] *v* kæntre.

capsule ['kæpsju:l] *s* kapsel; hylster; beholder.

captain ['kæptin] *s* anfører, leder; kaptajn; *(mar* også) kommandørkaptajn; *(sport)* holdkaptajn // *v* lede, være anfører for.

caption ['kæpʃən] *s* billedtekst.

captivate ['kæptiveit] *v* fængsle, fange; fortrylle.

captive ['kæptiv] *s* fange // *adj* fanget; tryllebundet.

captivity [kæp'tiviti] *s* fangenskab.

capture ['kæptʃə*] *s* erobring; pågribelse; fangst, bytte // *v* erobre; tage; fange.

car [ka:*] *s* bil, vogn.

caravan ['kærəvæn] *s* campingvogn; karavane.

caraway ['kærəwei]: *~ seed* kommen.

carbohydrate [ka:bəu'haidreit] *s* kulhydrat.

carbon ['ka:bən] *s* kulstof; **~ated** *adj* med kulsyre (,brus); **~ copy** *s* gennemslag; **~ dioxide** [-dai'ɔksaid] *s* kultveilte; **~ monoxide** [-mə'nɔksaid] *s* kulilte; **~ paper** *s* karbonpapir.

carburettor [ka:bə'rɛtə*] *s* karburator.

carcass ['ka:kəs] *s* ådsel, kadaver.

card [ka:d] *s* kort; *a pack of ~s* et spil kort; *put one's ~s on the table* lægge kortene på bordet; *have a ~ up one's sleeve* have ngt i baghånden.

cardamom ['ka:dəməm] *s* kardemomme.

cardboard ['ka:dbɔ:d] *s* pap, karton.

card game ['ka:dgeim] *s* kortspil.

cardiac ['ka:diæk] *adj* hjerte-; **~ arrest** *s* hjertestop; **~ infarct** *s* hjerteinfarkt.

cardinal ['ka:dinl] *s* kardinal // *adj* vigtigst; hoved-; *~ number* mængdetal; *of ~ importance* af allerstørste vigtighed.

card index ['ka:d,indɛks] *s* kartotek.

card trick ['ka:dtrik] *s* kortkunst.

care [kɛə*] *s* omhu; pleje, pasning; varetægt; bekymring; *be in sby's* ~ være i ens varetægt; *be taken into care* blive anbragt på institution; *take* ~ passe på; *take* ~ *of* passe, tage sig af; ordne; *handle with* ~*!* forsigtig! // *v* bekymre sig; ~ *about* være interesseret i; tage sig af; ~ *for* tage sig af; kunne lide; holde af; *would you* ~ *to...?* kunne du tænke dig at...? *I don't* ~*!* jeg er ligeglad! *I couldn't* ~ *less!* det rager mig en fjer! *who cares?* og hva' så? det kan være lige meget!

career [kə'riə*] *s* karriere; levnedsløb // *v:* ~ *(along)* fare af sted; **~ist** *s* karrieremenneske.

care... ['kɛə-] sms: **~free** *adj* ubekymret; **~ful** *adj* forsigtig; påpasselig, omhyggelig; *(be)* ~*ful* (vær) forsigtig! pas på! **~less** *adj* uforsigtig; skødesløs, sjusket.

caress [kə'rɛs] *s* kærtegn // *v* kæle for, kærtegne.

caretaker ['kɛəteikə*] *s* vicevært, portner; opsynsmand; pedel; **~ government** *s* forretningsministerium.

car-ferry ['ka:ˌfɛri] *s* bilfærge.

cargo ['ka:gəu] *s (pl:* ~*es)* last; ladning.

car hire ['ka:ˌhaiə*] *s:* ~ *(service)* biludlejning.

Caribbean [kæri'bi:ən] *adj: the* ~ *(Sea)* Caraibiske Hav.

caring ['kɛəriŋ] *adj* kærlig, varmhjertet; engageret.

carnage ['ka:nidʒ] *s* blodbad.

carnal ['ka:nəl] *adj* kødelig, sanselig; verdslig.

carnation [ka:'neiʃən] *s (bot)* nellike.

carnival ['ka:nivəl] *s* karneval.

carnivorous [ka:'nivərəs] *adj* kødædende (fx *plant* plante).

carol ['kærəl] *s: (Christmas)* ~ julesang // *v* synge; gå rundt ved dørene og synge julesange.

car park ['ka: pa:k] *s* parkeringsplads; parkeringshus.

carpenter ['ka:pintə*] *s* tømrer; **carpentry** *s* tømrerarbejde; (i skolen) sløjd.

carpet ['ka:pit] *s* (gulv)tæppe; *be on the* ~ være på tapetet; (F) stå skoleret // *v* lægge tæppe på; give en omgang; **~ing** *s* tæppe(r); **~ sweeper** *s* tæppefejemaskine.

carriage ['kæridʒ] *s* (heste)vogn; togvogn; transport, befordring; holdning; adfærd; **~way** *s* kørebane; *dual* ~*way* vej med midterrabat.

carrier ['kæriə*] *s* bærer; bud; vognmand; bagagebærer; lad; fragtskib; hangarskib; **~ bag** *s* bærepose; **~ pigeon** *s* brevdue.

carrion ['kæriən] *s* ådsel.

carrot ['kærət] *s* gulerød.

carry ['kæri] *v* bære; medføre; transportere, befordre; føre; (om lyd) bære, række; *be carried away* blive revet væk; blive begejstret; ~ *off* gennemføre; løbe af med; ~ *on* føre, drive; fortsætte; opføre sig; skabe sig; ~ *on with sby* have en affære med en; ~ *out* udføre; foretage; **~cot** *s* babylift; **~-on** *s* ballade, halløj.

carsick ['ka:sik] *adj* køresyg.

cart [ka:t] *s* kærre; trækvogn // *v* køre; *(fig)* slæbe; ~ *sby off* slæbe af med en.

cartilage ['ka:tilidʒ] *s* brusk.

carton ['ka:tən] *s* papæske, karton; pakke.

cartoon [ka:'tu:n] *s* vittighedstegning; tegneserie; tegnefilm; **~ist** *s* vittighedstegner; tegneserieforfatter.

cartridge ['ka:tridʒ] *s* patron; filmrulle, kassette; båndkassette.

cartwheel ['ka:twi:l] *s (gymn)* vejrmølle.

carve [ka:v] *v* skære (ud); hugge (ud); *(gastr)* skære 'for, tranchere; ~ *up* skære ud; **carver** *s* forskærerkniv.

carving ['ka:viŋ] *s* billedskærerarbejde; billedhuggerarbejde; træsnit; **~ knife** *s* forskærerkniv.

carwash ['ka:wɔʃ] *s* autovask.

cascade [kæs'keid] *s* vandfald, kaskade // *v* strømme, bruse.

case [keis] *s* sag (også *jur);* tilfælde; kasse, æske, skrin; etui; kuffert; (pude)betræk; *in any* ~ i hvert fald; *in* ~ *he comes* hvis han kommer; *in*

~ *of* i tilfælde af (at); *just in* ~ for alle tilfældes skyld; *upper* ~ store bogstaver; *lower* ~ små bogstaver; ~ **history** *s* (patients) sygehistorie, anamnese.

casement ['keismənt] *s* sidehængt vindue (med hængsler som i DK).

caseworker ['keiswə:kə*] *s* sagsbehandler.

cash [kæʃ] *s* kontanter; *pay (in)* ~ betale kontant; ~ *on delivery (COD)* kontant ved levering // *v* indløse, hæve; ~**-and-carry** *s* lavprisbutik; ~ **book** *s* kassebog; ~ **desk** kasse; ~ **dispenser** *s* pengeautomat.

cashier [kæ'ʃiə*] *s* kasserer.

cashmere ['kæʃmiə*] *s* kashmir(uld).

cash... ['kæʃ-] sms: ~ **payment** *s* kontant betaling; ~**point** *s* pengeautomat; ~ **receipt** *s* kassebon; ~ **register** *s* kasseapparat.

casing ['keisiŋ] *s* beklædning; væg; karm; indfatning.

cask [ka:sk] *s* tønde, fad.

casket ['ka:skit] *s* skrin; *(am)* (lig)kiste.

casserole ['kæsərəul] *s* ildfast fad; gryderet.

cassette [kæ'sɛt] *s* kassette; ~ **player** *s* kassettebåndoptager.

cassock ['kæsək] *s* præstekjole.

cast [ka:st] *s* kast; afstøbning; *(teat)* rollebesætning; gipsbandage // *v (cast, cast)* kaste; (om fjer etc) fælde; støbe; ~ *sby as Hamlet* tildele en rollen som Hamlet; ~ *lots* trække lod; ~ *one's vote* afgive sin stemme; ~ *off (mar)* kaste los; (i strikning) lukke af; ~ *on* (i strikning) slå op.

castaway ['ka:stəwei] *s* skibbruden; udstødt.

caster *s* se *castor*.

casting ['ka:stiŋ] *adj:* ~ *vote* afgørende stemme.

cast iron ['ka:st'aiən] *s* støbejern // *adj* benhård; skudsikker.

castle [ka:sl] *s* slot, borg; herregård; (i skak) tårn; ~*s in the air* luftkasteller; vilde drømme.

castoffs ['ka:stɔ:fs] *spl* aflagt tøj; udstødte (af samfundet).

castor ['ka:stə*] *s* (på rullebord etc) hjul; strødåse; krydderisæt; ~ **oil** *s* amerikansk olie; ~ **sugar** *s* strøsukker.

casual ['kæʒjuəl] *adj* tilfældig; flygtig, henkastet (fx *remark* bemærkning); overlegen; afslappet, uformel; ~ **labour** *s* løsarbejde; ~**ly** *adv* tilfældigt; henkastet.

casualty ['kæʒjuəlti] *s* ulykke; tilskadekommen; skadestue; *casualties pl* tilskadekomne; *(mil)* sårede, faldne.

casual wear ['kæzjuəl 'wɛə*] *s* fritidstøj.

cat [kæt] *s* kat; *let the* ~ *out of the bag* røbe en hemmelighed; plapre ud med det hele; *rain* ~*s and dogs* regne skomagerdrenge.

catalogue ['kætəlɔg] *s* katalog; liste // *v* katalogisere.

catalyst ['kætəlist] *s* katalysator (også *fig)*.

catapult ['kætəpʌlt] *s* slangebøsse; katapult // *v* slynge ud.

cataract ['kætərækt] *s* vandfald; rivende strøm; *(med)* grå stær.

catastrophe [kə'tæstrɔfi] *s* katastrofe; **catastrophic** [-'strɔfik] *adj* katastrofal.

cat burglar ['kætbə:glə*] *s* klatretyv.

catcalls ['kætkɔ:ls] *spl* fy-råb.

catch [kætʃ] *s* fangst; fælde; lås (fx på taske, smykke); *play* ~ lege fangeleg // *v (caught, caught* [kɔ:t]) fange; gribe (fx en bold); nå (fx toget); overraske; opfatte, få fat i; hænge fast (i); ~ *sby's attention (,eye)* fange ens opmærksomhed (,blik); *you'll* ~ *it!* du skal få (fx tæv, en omgang)! ~ *cold* blive forkølet; ~ *fire* antændes; ~ *one's finger in the door* få fingeren i klemme i døren; ~ *sight of* få øje på; ~ *on* komme på mode; fatte; ~ *up (with)* indhente.

catching ['kætʃiŋ] *adj* (om sygdom) smitsom; (om følelse) smittende.

catchment area ['kætʃmənt,ɛəriə] *s* (om fx skole, hospital) opland; befolkningsunderlag; *(geol)* afvandingsområde.

catchphrase ['kætʃfreiz] *s* slagord; **catchword** *s* slogan.

catchy ['kætʃi] *adj* iøjnefaldende; ørefaldende.
categoric(al) [kæti'gɔrik(əl)] *adj* kategorisk, bestemt.
categorize ['kætigəraiz] *v* klassificere, rubricere.
category ['kætigəri] *s* kategori, gruppe.
cater ['keitə*] *v* levere mad *(for* til); ~ *for* appellere til, prøve at gøre tilpas; henvende sig til; sigte imod; betjene.
caterer ['keitərə*] *s* diner transportable; arrangør af (fest)måltider.
catering ['keiteriŋ] *s* forplejning; catering; *the ~ trade* restaurationsbranchen.
caterpillar ['kætəpilə*] *s* kålorm; larve; ~ **tank** *s* kampvogn, tank; ~ **tractor** *s* larvefodstraktor; ~ **vehicle** *s* bæltekøretøj.
cathedral [kə'θi:drəl] *s* domkirke, katedral.
catherine wheel ['kæθərin wi:l] *s* (om fyrværkeri) sol.
Catholic ['kæθəlik] *s* katolik // *adj* katolsk.
catholic ['kæθəlik] *adj* alsidig, omfattende.
catkin ['kætkin] *s (bot)* rakle.
cat litter ['kætlitə*] *s* kattegrus.
catnap ['kætnæp] *s* lille lur.
cat's eye ['kætsai] *s* katteøje.
cattle [kætl] *spl* kvæg, kreaturer; *many ~* meget kvæg; *twenty head of ~* tyve stykker kvæg; **~-grid** *s* kvægrist (i vej).
catty ['kæti] *adj* katteagtig; ondskabsfuld, spydig.
caught [kɔ:t] *præt* og *pp* af *catch*.
cauliflower ['kɔliflauə*] *s* blomkål.
cause [kɔ:z] *s* årsag, grund; sag; *give ~ for* give anledning til; *there is no ~ for concern* der er ingen grund til bekymring // *v* forårsage; bevirke; *~ sby to change his mind* få en til at bestemme sig om.
causeway ['kɔ:zwei] *s* vej på dæmning (over fx sumpet område).
caustic ['kɔ:stik] *adj* ætsende; bidende.
caution ['kɔ:ʃən] *s* forsigtighed; advarsel // *v* advare; tilråde.
cautious ['kɔ:ʃəs] *adj* forsigtig; forbeholden.
cavalry ['kævəlri] *s (mil)* kavaleri.
cave [keiv] *s* hule, grotte // *v: ~ in* (om tag etc) styrte sammen; trykke ind; *(fig)* give efter; **~man** *s* hulemenneske.
cavern ['kævən] *s* stor hule; hulrum.
cavernous ['kævənəs] *adj* hul; bundløs.
cavil ['kævil] *v* kværulere.
cavity ['kæviti] *s* hulhed; hulrum; (i tand) hul; ~ **wall** *s* hulmur.
cavort [kə'vɔ:t] *v* hoppe omkring, lave krumspring.
cc fork.f. *cubic centimetres; carbon copy.*
cease [si:s] *v* standse; høre op; holde op; **~fire** *s* våbenhvile; **~less** *adj* endeløs.
cedar ['si:də*] *s* cedertræ.
cede [si:d] *v* overdrage (fx *the rights* rettighederne); afstå.
ceiling ['si:liŋ] *s* loft (også *fig); (fly)* tophøjde; *(met)* skyhøjde; *hit the ~* ryge helt op i loftet (af raseri).
celebrate ['sɛlibreit] *v* fejre; feste; **~d** *adj* berømt, feteret.
celebration [sɛli'breiʃən] *s* fest; fejren; lovprisning.
celebrity [si'lɛbriti] *s* berømmelse; (om person) berømthed.
celeriac [sə'lɛəriæk] *s* (rod)selleri.
celery ['sɛləri] *s* bladselleri.
celestial [si'lɛstiəl] *adj* himmelsk; himmel-.
celibacy ['sɛlibəsi] *s* cølibat.
celibate ['sɛlibət] *s* person som lever i cølibat (også *fig*).
cell [sɛl] *s* celle; *(elek)* element.
cellar ['sɛlə*] *s* kælder; vinkælder.
cellular ['sɛljulə*] *adj* celle-; cellet; cellulær.
Celtic ['kɛltik, 'sɛltik] *adj* keltisk.
cement [si'mɛnt] *s* cement // *v* cementere.
cemetery ['sɛmitri] *s* kirkegård.
cenotaph ['sɛnəta:f] *s* mindesten (over faldne i krig).
censor ['sɛnsə*] *s* (om film, bøger etc) censor // *v* censurere.

censorious [sən'sɔ:riəs] *adj* fordømmende.
censorship ['sɛnsəʃip] *s* censur.
censure ['sɛnʃə*] *s* kritik // *v* kritisere.
census ['sɛnsəs] *s* folketælling; *traffic* ~ trafiktælling.
centenary [sən'ti:nəri]*s* hundredårsdag.
centigrade ['sɛntigreid] *s* celsius.
centipede ['sɛntipi:d] *s* tusindben.
central ['sɛntrəl] *adj* central(-); ~ **heating** *s* centralvarme.
centralize ['sɛntrəlaiz] *v* centralisere.
central reservation ['sɛntrəl rɛzə'veiʃən] *s* midterrabat.
centre ['sɛntə*] *s* centrum, midtpunkt; center // *v* centrere; ~ *around sth* være koncentreret om, fokusere på; **~board** *s (mar)* sænkekøl; **~piece** *s* midtpunkt.
century ['sɛntʃəri] *s* århundrede.
ceramic [si'ræmik] *adj* keramisk; **~s** *spl* keramik.
cereal ['si:riəl] *s* kornsort; morgendrys (cornflakes, pop-ris, müsli etc).
ceremony ['sɛriməni] *s* ceremoni; *stand on* ~ holde på formerne; *without* ~ uden videre.
cert [sə:t] *s: it's a dead* ~ (F) det er stensikkert.
certain ['sə:tən] *adj* sikker, vis; afgjort; sikker på; *make* ~ sikre sig; *for* ~ bestemt; **~ly** *adv* sikkert, bestemt; (som *interj)* ja absolut; ja endelig; gerne.
certainty ['sə:tənti] *s* vished, sikkerhed.
certificate [sə'tifikət] *s* certifikat, attest, bevis.
certify ['sə:tifai] *v* attestere, bekræfte.
certitude ['sə:titju:d] *s* vished.
cervix ['sə:viks] *s* livmoderhals.
cessation [sɛ'seiʃən] *s* ophør.
cesspool ['sɛspu:l] *s* sivebrønd; *(fig)* sump, kloak.
cf. fork.f. *compare* jf., se.
chafe [tʃeif] *v* gnide; (om sko) gnave; irritere.
chaffinch ['tʃæfintʃ] *s* bogfinke.
chain [tʃein] *s* lænke, kæde; række // *v* lænke; spærre med kæde; ~ **reaction** *s* kædereaktion; **~smoker** *s* kæderyger; ~ **store** *s* kædebutik.
chair [tʃɛə*] *s* stol; *(univ)* lærestol, professorat; formandspost // *v* være formand for, lede (fx *a meeting* et møde); **~lift** *s* svævebane, skilift; **~man** *s* formand; ordstyrer; **~person** *s* ordstyrer, formand m/k; **~woman** *s* forkvinde.
chalice ['tʃælis] *s* bæger; (alter)kalk.
chalk [tʃɔ:k] *s* kridt; *not by a long* ~ (F) ikke på langt nær // *v* kridte; skrive med kridt.
challenge ['tʃælindʒ] *s* udfordring // *v* udfordre; kræve; protestere mod, bestride.
challenger ['tʃælindʒə*] *s (sport)* udfordrer.
challenging ['tʃælindʒiŋ] *adj* udfordrende.
chamber ['tʃeimbə*] *s* kammer, værelse; ~ *of commerce* handelskammer; **~maid** *s* stuepige; ~ **music** *s* kammermusik; **~pot** *s* natpotte; **~s** *spl* ungkarlehybel; advokatkontor; dommerkontor.
chamois ['ʃæmwa:] *s* gemse; ['ʃæmi] vaskeskind.
champ [tʃæmp] *v* gumle
champion ['tʃæmpiən] *s* forkæmper *(of* for); *(sport)* champion, mester // *v* forsvare, støtte; **~ship** *s* mesterskab; mesterskabskonkurrence.
chance [tʃa:ns] *s* chance, mulighed; lejlighed *(of* til); tilfælde(t); *there is little ~ of his coming* der er ikke store chancer for at han kommer; *he doesn't stand a* ~ han har ikke en chance; *take a* ~ tage en chance; løbe en risiko; *by* ~ tilfældigvis; *do you by any ~ know where he is?* du ved vel ikke (tilfældigvis) hvor han er? // *v:* ~ *it* tage chancen, risikere det; ~ *upon sby* tilfældigt møde en, støde på en // *adj* tilfældig.
chancellor ['tʃa:nsələ*] *s* kansler; *Chancellor of the Exchequer* sv.t. finansminister.
chancy ['tʃa:nsi] *adj* risikabel.
chandelier [ʃændə'liə*] *s* lysekrone.
change [tʃeindʒ] *s* ændring; foran-

dring; skifte; omklædning; småpenge, vekselpenge; *a ~ of clothes* skiftetøj; *for a ~* til en forandring; *have you any (small) ~?* har du nogen småpenge? har du vekselpenge? *~ of address* adresseforandring; *the ~ of life* overgangsalderen // *v* ændre(s), forandre (sig); skifte; klæde sig om; bytte, veksle; *~ down* geare ned; *~ into* forvandle sig til; *~ one's mind* ombestemme sig; *~ over* skifte; bytte plads; *~ up* geare op.

changeable ['tʃeindʒəbl] *adj* (om vejret) ustadig, foranderlig.

changeover ['tʃeindʒəuvə*] *s* overgang, omstilling; skifte.

changing ['tʃeindʒiŋ] *s: the ~ of the guards* vagtskifte (i garden) // *adj* skiftende; **~ room** *s* (i butik) prøverum; *(sport)* omklædningsrum).

channel [tʃænl] *s* kanal; *(mar)* sejlrende; (om flod) leje; *the (English) Channel* Kanalen; *the Channel Islands* Kanaløerne // *v* danne kanaler i; kanalisere.

chant [tʃa:nt] *s* (H) sang, messen // *v* messe.

chanterelle ['tʃæntərɛl] *s* kantarel.

chaos ['keiɔs] *s* kaos.

chaotic [kei'ɔtik] *adj* kaotisk.

chap [tʃæp] *s* (F, om mand) fyr // *v* få revner i huden; blive sprukken.

chapel ['tʃæpəl] *s* kapel; mindre kirke; bedehus.

chaplain ['tʃæplin] *s* huskapellan; præst (fx ved hoffet, på skib etc).

chapter ['tʃæptə*] *s* kapitel; *~ and verse* i alle detaljer.

char [tʃa:*] *s* d.s.s. *~woman* // *v* forkulle(s); gå ud og gøre rent.

character ['kærəktə*] *s* karakter; art, natur; (i bog, film etc) person; personlighed; (skrift)tegn; *be in ~* passe i stilen; *be out of ~* ikke passe i stilen; *she is quite a ~* hun er lidt af en personlighed.

characteristic [kærəktə'ristik] *s* karakteregenskab; særligt kendetegn // *adj* karakteristisk (*of* for).

characterize ['kærəktəraiz] *v* karakterisere.

charade [ʃə'ra:d] *s* ordsprogsleg; *(fig)* paradenummer.

charcoal ['tʃa:kəul] *s* trækul.

charge [tʃa:dʒ] *s (jur)* anklage, tiltale, sigtelse; pris, takst; *free of ~* gratis; varetægt; *(mil)* ladning; angreb; *is there a ~?* koster det ngt? *there is no ~* det er gratis; *be in ~ of* have ansvaret for; stå for; *take ~ of* tage sig af; tage i forvaring // *v* beskylde, anklage; (om pris) forlange; debitere; (om gevær etc) lade; *(elek)* oplade; *(mil)* angribe, storme; *~ sby with sth* sigte en for ngt; pålægge en ngt; *they ~d us £10 for the meal* de tog £10 for måltidet; *how much do you ~ for this repair?* hvor meget skal De have for denne reparation? *~ it (,the expenses) to me* sæt det på min regning; *~ in* komme farende ind.

chargeable ['tʃa:dʒəbl] *adj* skattepligtig; afgiftspligtig; at betale.

charges ['tʃa:dʒiz] *spl* omkostninger.

chariot ['tʃæriət] *s* (*hist*) stridsvogn.

charitable ['tʃæritəbl] *adj* næstekærlig; godgørende, velgørende.

charity ['tʃæriti] *s* (næste)kærlighed; velgørenhed; barmhjertighed.

charlady ['tʃa:leidi] *s* d.s.s. *charwoman.*

charm [tʃa:m] *s* charme; ynde; trolddom, tryllemiddel; amulet // *v* charmere; fortrylle; **~er** *s* charmetrold; *snake ~er* slangetæmmer; **~ing** *adj* charmerende; yndig.

chart [tʃa:t] *s* diagram, kurve; tavle; *(mar)* søkort; hitliste // *v* lave kort (,diagram) ove; *(fig)* planlægge.

charter ['tʃa:tə*] *s* dokument; privilegium; fundats; *(mar, fly)* chartring // *v* chartre; **~ed accountant** *s (CA)* statsautoriseret revisor; **~ flight** *s* charterflyvning.

charwoman ['tʃa:wumən] *s* rengøringskone.

chary ['tʃɛəri] *adj: be ~ of doing sth* være forsigtig med at gøre ngt.

chase [tʃeis] *s* jagt, forfølgelse // *v* jage (efter), forfølge; løbe efter.

chaser ['tʃeizə*] *s* forfølger; drink til at skylle efter med.

chasm ['kæzəm] *s* kløft, svælg.
chaste [tʃeist] *adj* kysk, ærbar.
chasten ['tʃeisn] *v* lægge en dæmper på; tøjle, holde i ave.
chastity ['tʃæstiti] *s* ærbarhed; kyskhed.
chat [tʃæt] *s* sludder, snak // *v* sludre, snakke; ~ *up* indynde sig hos, snakke godt for; lægge an på.
chatter ['tʃætə*] *s* snakken, snadren // *v* snakke, pladre, skvadre op; (om tænder) klapre; **~box** *s* sludrebøtte.
chatty ['tʃætti] *adj* snakkesalig.
chauffeur ['ʃəufə*] *s* (privat)chauffør.
cheap [tʃi:p] *adj* billig; tarvelig, simpel; letkøbt; *it did not come* ~ det var ikke billigt; *on the* ~ billigt; **~en** *v* gøre billigere, nedsætte; gøre simpel.
cheat [tʃi:t] *s* snyderi; snyder, bedrager // *v* snyde, bedrage; ~ *at cards* snyde i kortspil; ~ *on sby* bedrage en (i parforhold etc).
check [tʃɛk] *s* standsning; kontrol; kontrolmærke; (restaurations)regning; (kasse)bon; tern; *keep a* ~ *on sby* føre kontrol med en; *hold sby in* ~ holde en skak // *v* standse; holde tilbage; kontrollere, checke; ~ *in* (på hotel etc) indskrive sig, tage ind (på); ~ *off* kontrollere, checke af; ~ *out* (på hotel etc) betale regningen, afrejse; ~ *up on sth* efterprøve (,undersøge) ngt; ~ *up on sby* undersøge ens forhold.
checked [tʃɛkd] *adj* ternet.
checkmate ['tʃɛkmeit] *s* skakmat.
checkout [tʃɛk'aut] *s* kasse.
checkpoint ['tʃekpɔint] *s* kontrolpunkt.
checkup ['tʃɛkʌp] *s (med)* helbredsundersøgelse.
cheek [tʃi:k] *s* kind; (F) frækhed; *what a* ~*!* hvor er det frækt! **~bone** *s* kindben.
cheeky ['tʃi:ki] *adj* fræk, flabet.
cheer [tʃiə*] *s* hurraråb; bifald; (H) humør; ~*s!* skål! // *v* råbe hurra; juble over; opmuntre; ~ *sby on* heppe på en: ~ *up!* op med humøret!
cheerful ['tʃiəful] *adj* munter; frejdig; opmuntrende.
cheerio ['tʃiəri'əu] *intrj* (F) hej! farvel!
cheerleader ['tʃiəli:də*] *s* leder af heppekor.
cheerless ['tʃiəlis] *adj* trist, uhyggelig.
cheery ['tʃiəri] *adj* glad, munter.
cheese [tʃi:z] *s* ost; *say* ~*!* smil til fotografen! **~board** *s* osteanretning; ostebræt; **~cake** *s* slags ostetærte; **~cloth** *s* ostelærred; **~-paring** *adj* hysterisk sparsommelig; **~ spread** *s* smøreost; **~ straw** *s* ostepind.
cheetah ['tʃi:tə] *s (zo)* gepard.
chef [ʃɛf] *s* køkkenchef, kok.
chemical ['kɛmikəl] *s* kemikalie // *adj* kemisk (fx *warfare* krigsførelse); kemi-.
chemist ['kɛmist] *s* kemiker; apoteker.
chemistry ['kɛmistri] *s* kemi.
chemist's (shop) ['kɛmists (ʃɔp)] *s* apotek.
cheque [tʃæk] *s* check; *a* ~ *for £10* en check på £10; **~book** *s* checkhæfte; **~ card** *s* ID-kort (fra bank).
chequered ['tʃɛkəd] *adj* ternet; afvekslende, broget.
cherish ['tʃɛriʃ] *v* værne om, hæge om; elske.
cheroot [ʃə'ru:t] *s* cerut.
cherry ['tʃɛri] *s* kirsebær; kirsebærrødt; **~ brandy** *s* kirsebærlikør.
chervil ['tʃə:vil] *s* kørvel.
chess [tʃɛs] *s* skak; **~board** *s* skakbræt; **~man** *s* skakbræt; **~player** *s* skakspiller.
chest [tʃɛst] *s* kasse, kiste; bryst(kasse); brystmål; *get sth off one's* ~ lette sit hjerte (for ngt); ~ *of drawers* kommode.
chestnut ['tʃɛsnʌt] *s* kastanje(træ); kastanjebrunt.
chew [tʃu:] *v* tygge; ~ *one's nails* bide negle; *bite off more than one can* ~ påtage sig for meget **~ing gum** *s* tyggegummi.
chewy ['tʃu:i] *adj* sej.
chick [tʃik] *s* kylling; fugleunge; (S) pige, dulle.
chicken ['tʃikən] *s* kylling, høne; (S)

bangebuks; *roast* ~ stegt kylling // *v:* ~ *out* få kolde fødder; ~ **broth** [-brɔθ] *s* hønsekødsuppe; ~ **farm** *s* hønseri; ~**feed** *s (fig)* småskillinger, pebernødder; ~**pox** *s* skoldkopper; ~ **wire** *s* hønsetråd.

chickpea ['tʃikpi:] *s (bot)* kikært.

chicory ['tʃikəri] *s (bot)* cikorie; julesalat.

chief [tʃi:f] *s* chef; høvding // *adj* vigtigst; hoved-; over-; ~ **constable** *s* sv.t. politimester; ~ **editor** *s* chefredaktør; ~**ly** *adv* hovedsagelig, først og fremmest.

chieftain ['tʃi:ftən] *s* høvding.

chilblain ['tʃilblein] *s* frostknude; forfrysning.

child [tʃaild] *s (pl: children* ['tʃildrən]) barn; *be with* ~ være gravid; ~**bearing** *s* fødsel // *adj: of* ~*bearing age* i den fødedygtige alder ~ **benefit** *s* børnetilskud; ~**birth** *s* barnefødsel; ~**hood** *s* barndom.

childish ['tʃaildiʃ] *adj* barnlig; barnagtig.

child-minder ['tʃaildmaində*] *s* dagplejemor.

child prodigy ['tʃaild 'prɔdidʒi] *s* vidunderbarn.

childproof ['tʃaildpru:f] *adj* børnesikret.

children ['tʃildrən] *pl* af *child;* ~**'s disease** *s* børnesygdom.

child's play ['tʃaildz plei] *s* barneleg (også *fig).*

child welfare ['tʃaild ˌwɛlfɛə*] *s* børneforsorg.

chill [tʃil] *s* kulde; kuldegysning; snue, forkølelse; *catch a* ~ få snue // *v* få til at fryse; blive (,gøre) kold, afkøle; *serve* ~*ed* serveres afkølet // *adj* kølig, kold.

chilly ['tʃili] *adj* kold, kølig; kuldskær; *feel* ~ småfryse.

chime [tʃaim] *v* kime, ringe (med); (om ur) slå; ~ *in* stemme i; ~ *in with* harmonere med; ~**s** *spl* klokkespil.

chimney ['tʃimni] *s* skorsten; kamin; ildsted; ~**piece** *s* kaminhylde; ~**sweep** *s* skorstensfejer.

chimp [tʃimp] *s* (F) d.s.s. **chimpanzee** [tʃimpæn'zi:] *s* chimpanse.

chin [tʃin] *s (anat)* hage; *keep your* ~ *up!* op med humøret!

China ['tʃainə] *s* Kina.

china ['tʃainə] *s* porcelæn.

Chinese [tʃai'ni:z] *s* kineser // *adj* kinesisk.

chink [tʃiŋk] *s* revne, sprække; klirren.

chip [tʃip] *s* flis; skår, hak; (i spil) jeton; *be a* ~ *off the old block* være som snydt ud af næsen på sin far; *have a* ~ *on one's shoulder* have et kompleks; føle sig forfulgt // *v* snitte; hugge (skår) i; blive skåret; ~ *in with sth* bidrage med ngt; ~**board** *s* spånplade; ~**munk** *s* jordegern; ~**pings** *spl* skærver; spåner.

chippy ['tʃipi] *s* (F) fish and chips-butik; snedker.

chips *spl* pommes frites; *(am)* franske kartofler.

chiropodist [ki'rɔpədist] *s* fodplejer.

chirp [tʃə:p] *v* kvidre, pippe; **chirpy** *adj* kvidrende; i sprudlende humør.

chisel ['tʃizl] *s* mejsel; brækjern; stemmejern // *v* mejsle.

chit [tʃit] *s* kort besked, seddel; gældsbevis.

chitchat ['tʃit,tʃæt] *s* lille sludder, småsnak.

chivalrous ['ʃivəlrəs] *ad* ridderlig.

chivalry ['ʃivəlri] *s* ridderskab.

chives [tʃaivz] *spl* purløg.

chloride ['klɔ:raid] *s (kem)* klorid.

chlorine ['klɔ:rin] *s (kem)* klor.

choc-ice ['tʃɔkais] *s* (F) is med chokoladeovertræk.

chock [tʃɔk] *s* bremseklods; kile; ~**ful** *adj* propfuld.

chocolate ['tʃɔklit] *s* chokolade; *hot* ~ varm chokoladedrik.

choice [tʃɔis] *s* valg; udvalg; *we don't have any* ~ vi har ikke ngt valg; *a large* ~ *in shoes* et stort udvalg af sko // *adj* udsøgt.

choir [kwaiə*] *s* kor; ~**boy** *s* kordreng; messedreng.

choke [tʃəuk] *s (auto)* choker // *v* kvæle; være ved at kvæles; tilstoppe, blokere; ~**d** *adj* halvkvalt.

choker ['tʃəukə*] *s* stiv flip; stram halskæde.

choose [tʃu:z] *v (chose, chosen* [tʃəuz, tʃəuzn]) vælge *(to* at); udvælge; *when he ~s* når det passer ham; *pick and ~* vælge og vrage.
choosy ['tʃu:zi] *adj* kræsen.
chop [tʃɔp] *s* hug; *(gastr)* kotelet; *get the ~* (F) blive fyret; blive ramt af sparekniven // *v* hugge (i småstykker); hakke; *~ down a tree* fælde et træ.
chopper ['tʃɔpə*] *s* hakkekniv; hakkemaskine; (F) helikopter; motorcykel, 'kværn'.
chopsticks ['tʃɔpstiks] *spl* spisepinde.
choral ['kɔrəl] *adj* kor-; sang-; ~ **society** *s* sangforening.
chord [kɔ:d] *s (mus)* streng; akkord; *vocal ~s* stemmebånd.
chore [tʃɔ:*] *s* rutinearbejde; *household ~s* huslige pligter.
choreographer [kɔri'ɔgrəfə*] *s* koreograf.
chorister ['kɔristə*] *s* korsanger (i kirkekor).
chortle [tʃɔ:tl] *v* klukle.
chorus ['kɔrəs] *s* kor; omkvæd // *v* sige i kor.
chose [tʃeuz] *præt* af *choose;* **chosen** ['tʃeuzən] *pp* af *choose.*
Christ [kraist] *s* Kristus.
christen [krisn] *v* døbe; **~ing** ['krisniŋ] *s* dåb.
Christian ['kristiən] *adj* kristen.
Christianity [kristi'æniti] *s* kristenhed; kristendom.
Christian name ['kristiən neim] *s* fornavn.
Christmas ['krisməs] *s* jul; *we're staying over ~* vi bliver julen over; ~ **cracker** *s* knallert; ~ **Eve** *s* juleaften; ~ **present** *s* julegave; ~ **tree** *s* juletræ.
chrome [krəum] *s* krom.
chronic ['krɔnik] *adj* kronisk.
chronicle ['krɔnikl] *s* krønike.
chrysalis ['krisəlis] *s* puppe
chubby ['tʃʌbi] *adj* buttet, rund.
chuck [tʃʌk] *v* kaste, smide; *~ it in* (F) give op; *~ out* smide ud; *~ (up)* (F) opgive; sige op.
chuckle [tʃʌkl] *v* klukle; grine i skægget.
chug [tʃʌg] *v* tøffe.
chum [tʃʌm] *s* kammerat, makker // *v: ~ up* blive gode venner; **chummy** *adj* kammeratlig.
chunk [tʃʌŋk] *s* (om kød) luns; (om brød) humpel.
chunky ['tʃʌŋki] *adj* (F) lækker, 'fed' (fx sweater).
church [tʃə:tʃ] *s* kirke; *go to ~* gå i kirke; **~goer** *s* kirkegænger; **~warden** *s* sv.t. kirkeværge; **~yard** *s* kirkegård.
churlish ['tʃə:liʃ] *adj* strid; ubehøvlet.
churn [tʃə:n] *s* (mælke)junge; smørkærne // *v* kærne (smør); hvirvle rundt; *my stomach ~ed* det vred sig i maven på mig; *~ out* spy ud.
chute [ʃu:t] *s* slisk; rutschebane; (også: *rubbish ~)* affaldsskakt.
CID ['ci:ai'di:] (fork.f. *Criminal Investigation Department)* afd. af *Scotland Yard,* sv.t. kriminalpolitiet.
cigarette [sigə'rɛt] *s* cigaret; ~ **case** *s* cigaretetui; ~ **end** *s* cigaretskod; ~ **holder** *s* cigaretrør.
C-in-C ['si:in'si:] *s* (fork.f. *Commander in Chief).*
cinch [sintʃ] *s: it's a ~* (F) det er en smal sag.
cinder ['sində*] *s* slagge; *~s* (også) aske.
Cinderella [sində'rɛlla] *s* Askepot.
cine-camera ['sini,kæmərə] *s* filmkamera; **cinefilm** *s* (biograf)film.
cinema ['sinəmə] *s* biograf.
cine-projector ['sinioprə,dʒɛktə*] *s* smalfilmsfremviser.
cinnamon ['sinəmən] *s* kanel.
cipher ['saifə*] *s* nul; chifferskrift; chiffer.
circle [sə:kl] *s* cirkel; (rund)kreds; omdrejning; *(teat)* balkon // *v* kredse, cirkle; gå rundt om; omgive.
circuit ['sə:kit] *s* omkreds; kredsløb; runde, kreds; *short ~* kortslutning; **~-breaker** *s* strømafbryder.
circuitous [sə:'kjuitəs] *adj* omstændelig.
circular ['sə:kjulə*] *s* cirkulære, rundskrivelse // *adj* cirkulær; rund.
circulate ['sə:kjuleit] *v* cirkulere; være i omløb; udsprede.

circulation [sə:kju'leiʃən] *s* cirkulation; omløb; kredsløb, blodomløb.
circumcision [sə:kəm'siʒən] *s* omskæring.
circumference [sə'kʌmfərəns] *s* omkreds; periferi.
circumspect ['sə:kəmspɛkt] *adj* forsigtig.
circumstance ['sə:kəmstəns] *s* omstændighed; forhold; *under no ~s* ikke under nogen omstændigheder; *under those ~s* under de omstændigheder (,forhold).
circumstantial [sə:kəm'stænʃəl] *adj: ~ evidence* indicier.
circumvent [sə:kəm'vɛnt] *v* omgå.
circus ['sə:kəs] *s* rund plads; cirkus.
cissy ['sisi] *s* tøsedreng.
cite [sait] *v* citere; påberåbe sig i; *(jur)* stævne (for retten).
citizen ['sitizn] *s* borger; statsborger; **~ship** *s* borgerskab; indfødsret; samfundssind.
city ['siti] *s* by; bymidte; *the City* City (forretningskvarter i London) // *adj* by-, stads-.
civic ['sivik] *adj* borgerlig; by-; kommunal; **~s** *spl* samfundsfag.
civil ['sivil] *adj* civil, borgerlig; høflig; **~ defence** *s* civilforsvar; **~ engineer** *s* civilingeniør.
civilian [si'viliən] *s* civilperson // *adj* civil.
civilization [sivilai'zeiʃən] *s* civilisation.
civilized ['sivilaizd] *adj* civiliseret; kultiveret.
civil... ['sivil-] sms: **~ law** *s (jur)* borgerlig ret, civilret; **~ marriage** *s* borgerligt ægteskab; **~ servant** *s* embedsmand; tjenestemand; **Civil Service** *s* sv.t. statsforvaltningen, civilforvaltningen; **~ war** *s* borgerkrig.
civvies ['siviz] *spl* (F) civil påklædning.
clack [klæk] *v* klapre (med), slå smæld (med).
claim [kleim] *s* krav, fordring; påstand; *lay ~ to* gøre krav på; *(insurance) ~* erstatningskrav // *v* gøre krav på; kræve; påstå.
clam [klæm] *s* musling // *v: ~ up* klappe i.
clamber ['klæmbə*] *v* klatre, kravle.
clammy ['klæmi] *adj* fugtig, klam.
clamour ['klæmə*] *s* høj råben.
clamp [klæmp] *s* skruetvinge; klemme; *(fig)* hindring // *v* spænde fast; *~ down on* slå hårdt ned på; *~ one's teeth* bide tænderne sammen.
clan [klæn] *s* klan, familie.
clandestine [klæn'dɛstin] *adj* hemmelig.
clang [klæŋ] *s* metalklang; klirren.
clap [klæp] *s* brag; smæk; skrald (fx *of thunder* torden-) // *v* brage, smælde; klappe; smække; *~ (one's) hands* klappe i hænderne.
clapped-out ['klæpdaut] *adj* udrangeret, udtjent.
clapperboard ['klæpəbɔ:d] *s (film)* klaptræ.
clapping ['klæpiŋ] *s* applaus, klapsalver.
claret ['klærət] *s* rødvin (især bordeauxvin).
clarification [klærifi'keiʃən] *s* afklaring; klarlæggelse.
clarify ['klærifai] *v* klarlægge; gøre klar.
clarity ['klæriti] *s* klarhed.
clash [klæʃ] *s* klirren; brag; sammenstød; konflikt // *v* klirre; støde sammen.
clasp [kla:sp] *s* spænde; lås; hægte; omfavnelse; greb // *v* spænde; hægte; omfavne; holde op; *~ one's hands* folde hænderne.
class [kla:s] *s* klasse; *have ~* have stil (over sig) // *v* klassificere.
classic ['klæsik] *s* klassiker; *Classics* græsk og latin // *adj* klassisk.
classification [klæsifi'keiʃən] *s* klassificering.
classified ['klæsifaid] *adj* hemmeligstemplet; klassificeret; **~ ads** *spl* rubrikannoncer.
classify ['klæsifai] *v* klassificere; hemmeligstemple.
classmate ['kla:smeit] *s* klassekammerat.
classroom ['kla:sru:m] *s* klasseværelse.

classy ['kla:si] *adj* fornem, fin, smart, med stil.
clatter ['klætə*] *s* klirren; klapren; spektakel // *v* klirre; klapre.
clause [klɔ:z] *s* klausul; bestemmelse; *(gram)* sætning.
claw [klɔ:] *s* klo; klosaks // *v* gribe (med kløerne); kradse, rive.
clay [klei] *s* ler; **~-pipe** *s* kridtpibe.
clean [kli:n] *v* rense; gøre rent; *~ out* udrense; rydde op i; udplyndre; *I am ~ed out* (F) jeg er blanket helt af; *~ up* rydde op; gøre rent; gøre sig i stand // *adj* ren; uplettet; glat, jævn; *a ~ edge* en jævn (,glat) kant; *come ~* indrømme, tilstå // *adv* helt, fuldstændig; *I ~ forgot* jeg glemte det fuldstændig; **~-cut** *adj* veldefineret; med rene træk.
cleaner ['kli:nə*] *s* rengøringsassistent; renseriejer; (om produkt) rensevæske; *take sth to the ~er's* bringe ngt til rensning; *take sby to the ~er's* (F) ribbe en for penge; give et ordentligt møgfald.
cleaning ['kli:niŋ] *s* rensning; rengøring.
cleanliness ['klɛnlinis] *s* renlighed.
cleanse [klɛnz] *v* rense; gøre ren; **~r, cleansing cream** *s* rensecreme; **cleansing tissue** *s* renseserviet.
clean-shaven ['kli:nʃeivn] *adj* glatbarberet.
clean-up ['kli:nʌp] *s* rengøring; oprydning; fed gevinst; godt kup.
clear [kliə*] *s: be in the ~* være uden for fare; være frikendt // *v* klare (op); rydde; rense; tømme; komme over; *(merk)* klarere; *(jur)* frikende; *~ one's throat* rømme sig; *~ up* opklare (fx *a case* en sag); (om vejret) klare op; rydde op i; få af vejen // *adj* klar; ren; *do I make myself ~?* er det forstået? // *adv: ~ of* fri af (,for).
clearance ['kliərəns] *s* rydning; tilladelse; klarering; *slum ~* slumsanering; **~ sale** *s (merk)* udsalg.
clearcut ['kliəkʌt] *adj* klar, tydelig; skarpskåret.
clearing ['kliəriŋ] *s* rydning; lysning; *(merk)* clearing.
clearly ['kliəli] *adv* klart; åbenbart, tydeligvis.
clear-out ['kliəraut] *s* (op)rydning.
clear-sighted ['kliəsaitid] *adj* klarsynet.
clearway ['kliəwei] *s* vej med stopforbud.
cleavage ['kli:vidʒ] *s* (om kjole etc) dyb udskæring; *(spøg)* kavalergang.
cleave [kli:v] *v (cleft, cleft* [klɛft]) kløve, spalte; *(clave, cloven* [kleiv, kləuvn]) klæbe, holde fast ved.
clef [klɛf] *s (mus)* nøgle (fx *G ~* G-nøgle).
cleft [klɛft] *præt* og *pp* af *cleave* // *s* kløft, spalte // *adj* kløvet, spaltet; *~ palate* ganespalte.
clemency ['klɛmənsi] *s* mildhed.
clement ['klɛmənt] *adj* mild.
clench [klɛntʃ] *v* knuge; knytte (fx *one's fist* næven); bide sammen (fx *one's teeth* tænderne).
clergy ['klə:dʒi] *s* gejstlighed; præster; **~man** *s* præst.
clerical ['klɛrikl] *adj* præste-; kontor-.
clerk [kla:k] *s* kontorfunktionær; sekretær.
clever ['klɛvə*] *adj* dygtig *(at* til); kvik, begavet; ferm; smart.
click [klik] *s* klik; smæld // *v* klikke; smælde; klapre med; være på bølgelængde; *~ one's heels* smække hælene sammen; *~ one's tongue* slå smæld med tungen.
client ['klaiənt] *s* klient; kunde.
cliff [klif] *s* klint; klippeskrænt; **~hanger** *s* (F) afsindigt spændende bog (,film etc).
climate ['klaimit] *s* klima.
climb [klaim] *s* bjergbestigning; klatretur; stigning // *v* klatre; kravle (op på); stige (på på); skråne opad.
climber ['klaimə*] *s* klatreplante; stræber; bjergbestiger.
climbing ['klaimiŋ] *s* bjergbestigning; **~ frame** *s* klatrestativ.
clinch [klintʃ] *v* klinke; bekræfte; afgøre endeligt (fx *a deal* en handel).
cling [kliŋ] *v (clung, clung* [klʌŋ]): *~ to* hænge fast ved (,i); klamre sig til; **~film** *s* plastfolie.
clinging ['kliŋiŋ] *adj* (om kjole etc)

tætsiddende; (om lugt) som bliver hængende.
clinic ['klinik] *s* klinik; **~al** *adj* klinisk.
clink [kliŋk] *v* klirre, rasle.
clinker ['kliŋkə*] *s* klinke; slagge.
clip [klip] *s* klemme, holder; cykelklemme; papirclips; klip // *v* klippe; klipse; slå; ~ *together* hæfte sammen.
clippers ['klipəz] *spl* have- el. hækkesaks; neglesaks.
clipping ['klipiŋ] *s* udklip; *nail ~s* afklippede negle.
clique [kli:k] *s* klike.
cloak [kləuk] *s* kappe; slag; **~room** *s* garderobe; toilet.
clobber ['klɔbə*] *v* banke, tæve.
clock [klɔk] *s* ur; klokke; *round the ~* døgnet rundt, dag og nat // *v (sport)* tage tid (på); *~ in to work* stemple ind på arbejdet; *~ off (,out)* stemple ud; **~wise** [-waiz] *adv* med uret; højre om; **~work** *s* urværk; tælleværk; **~work toy** *s* mekanisk legetøj (som trækkes op).
clod [klɔd] *s* klump (jord etc); (F) klods; sløv padde.
clog [klɔg] *s* træsko // *v* hæmme; *~ up* tilstoppe; blive tilstoppet.
cloister ['klɔistə*] *s* klostergård; søjlegang; **~ed** *adj* isoleret fra omverdenen.
clone [kləun] *s (biol)* klon // *v* klone.
close [kləus] *s* indhegning; plads; stræde; [kləuz] afslutning, ophør // *v* [kleuz] lukke; afslutte; slutte; *~ down* lukke; ophøre; nedlægge // *adj/adv* [kləus] nær; tæt; i nærheden, tæt på; lukket; nøje, omhyggelig; (om vejret) lummer; indelukket; *a ~ friend* en nær ven; *~ season* fredningstid (for vildt etc); *a ~ shave* en tæt barbering; *have a ~ shave (fig)* klare sig på et hængende hår; **~-cropped** *adj* tætklippet; **~d shop** ['kləuzd-] *s* virksomhed der kun beskæftiger organiseret arbejdskraft; **~-fisted** *adj* nærig, påholdende; **~fitting** *adj* (om tøj) tætsiddende; **~-knit** [-nit] *adj* fast sammentømret.
closely ['kləusli] *adv* nøje; indgående.
closet ['klɔzit] *s* skab; wc // *v: be ~ed with* være i enrum med.
close-up ['kləusʌp] *s* nærbillede.
closure ['kləuʒə*] *s* lukning; afslutning.
clot [klɔt] *s* klump; blodprop // *v* danne klumper; koagulere.
cloth [klɔθ] *s* klæde; tøj; klud; dug.
clothe [kləuð] *v* klæde på; iklæde; dække.
clothes [kləuðs] *spl* klæder, tøj; **~ basket** *v* snavsetøjskurv; **~ brush** *s* klædebørste; **~ line** *s* tørresnor; **~ peg** *s* tøjklemme; **~ press** *s* klædeskab; kommode.
clothing ['kləuðiŋ] *s* påklædning; tøj.
clotted ['klɔtid] *adj* klumpet; størknet; *~ cream* meget tyk piskefløde.
cloud [klaud] *s* sky; sværm; *be on ~ nine* være i den syvende himmel; *be under a ~* være upopulær // *v* sløre, gøre uklar; fordunkle; *~ over* blive overskyet; *~ up* blive (,gøre) dugget; **~bank** *s* skybanke; **~burst** *s* skybrud; **~ed, ~y** *adj* (over)skyet; uklar, tåget.
clout [klaut] *s* slag, gok; slagkraft // *v* slå.
clove [kləuv] *s* kryddernellike; *a ~ of garlic* et fed hvidløg.
cloven ['kləuvən] *pp* af *cleave;* **~ hoof** *s* klov.
clover ['kləuvə*] *s (bot)* kløver; *be in ~* have kronede dage, være på den grønne gren; **~leaf** *s* kløverblad (også i vejanlæg).
clown [klaun] *s* klovn // *v* klovne.
club [klʌb] *s* klub; kølle; politistav // *v* slå (ned); *~ together* splejse, slå sig sammen; **~ foot** *s* klumpfod.
clubs ['klʌbz] *spl* (i kortspil) klør; *ace of ~s* klør es.
club steak ['klʌb steik] *s (gastr)* oksehøjreb.
cluck [klʌk] *v* (om høne) klukke; (om person) smække med tungen; sige hyp til en hest.
clue [klu:] *s* spor (i en sag); fingerpeg; (i krydsord etc) nøgleord; *I haven't a ~* jeg aner det ikke; **~d-up** *adj* (F) oppe på dupperne, velinformeret.

clump [klʌmp] *s* klump; klynge // *v* trampe; ~ *together* klumpe sig sammen.

clumsy ['klʌmzi] *adj* kluntet; klodset.

clung [klʌŋ] *præt* og *pp* af *cling.*

cluster ['klʌstə*] *s* klynge; (lille) gruppe; klase // *v* samle sig, flokkes.

clutch [klʌtʃ] *s* (stramt) greb; *(auto)* kobling; *be in sby's* ~ være i kløerne på en // *v* gribe fat i; ~ *at* gribe efter; klynge sig til; ~ **bag** *s* kuverttaske.

clutter ['klʌtə*] *s* rod // *v* fylde op; rode; ligge og flyde.

CND (fork.f. *Campaign for Nuclear Disarmament*) antiatomkampagne.

Co fork.f. *company; county.*

coach [kəutʃ] *s* bus; karet; *(jernb)* personvogn; *(sport)* træner // *v* instruere; give lektiehjælp; træne; **~load** *s* busfuld; ~ **station** *s* busterminal.

coagulate [kəu'ægjuleit] *v* størkne, koagulere,

coal [kəul] *s* kul; *haul sby over the ~s* give en en ordentlig opsang; **~field** *s* kulfelt.

coalition [kəuə'liʃən] *s* sammenslutning, forbund, koalition.

coalmine ['kəulmain] *s* kulmine; **~r** *s* kulminearbejder; **coalmining** *s* kulminedrift.

coalpit ['kəulpit] *s* kulmine.

coal scuttle ['kəul skʌtl] *s* kulspand.

coarse [kɔ:s] *adj* grov; rå; *use ~ language* være grov i munden.

coast [kəust] *s* kyst; *the ~ is clear* der er fri bane // *v* sejle langs kysten; (på cykel) køre frihjul; *(auto)* køre med udkoblet motor, rulle; **~al** *adj* kyst-.

coaster ['kəustə*] *s* coaster; flaskebakke, ølbrik.

coastguard ['kəustga:d] *s* kystbevogtning.

coastline ['kəustlain] *s* kystlinje.

coat [kəut] *s* frakke; jakke; (om dyr) pels; fjerdragt; (om maling) lag // *v* overtrække; dække; stryge; smøre; ~ **hanger** *s* (klæde)bøjle.

coating ['kəutiŋ] *s* overtræk; belægning; lag.

coat of arms [kəutəv'a:mz] *s* våbenskjold.

coax [kəuks] *v* lokke; snakke godt for.

cob [kɔb] *s* (majs)kolbe.

cobble [kɔbl] *s* (også *~stone)* brosten // *v: ~ together* flikke sammen.

cobweb ['kɔbwɛb] *s* spindelvæv.

cock [kɔk] *s (zo)* hane; (V) pik // *v* sætte på skrå; dreje, vende; (om gevær) spænde hanen på; ~ *one's ears* spidse ører; ~ *sth up* få ngt til at kokse („gå i fisk); **~crow** [-krəu] *s* hanegal.

cockerel ['kɔkərəl] *s* hanekylling.

cockeyed ['kɔkaid] *adj* skeløjet.

cockle [kɔkl] *s (zo)* hjertemusling; muslingeskal.

cockney ['kɔkni] *s* cockney (person fra London's East End); cockneydialekt.

cockroach ['kɔkrəutʃ] *s (zo)* kakerlak.

cock robin [kɔk'rɔbin] *s* han-rødkælk.

cockscomb ['kɔkskəum] *s* hanekam.

cocksure ['kɔkʃu:ə*] *adj* skråsikker.

cock-up ['kɔkʌp] *s* kludder, klamphuggeri.

cocky ['kɔki] *adj* kæphøj.

cocoa ['kəukəu] *s* kakao.

coconut ['kəukənʌt] *s* kokosnød; ~ **meal** *s* kokosmel.

cocoon [kə'ku:n] *s* kokon, hylster; **~ed** *adj: be ~ed* leve en beskyttet tilværelse, være pakket ind i vat.

COD ['si:əu'di:] (fork.f. *cash on delivery).*

cod [kɔd] *s (zo)* torsk.

coddle [kɔdl] *v* forkæle; (om æg) pochere (i ovnen).

code [kəud] *s* kode; *(jur)* lovsamling kodeks; **~-name** *s* dæknavn.

cod-liver-oil ['kɔdlivər'ɔil] *s* torskelevertran; **cod's roe** *s* torskerogn.

coeducational ['kəuɛdju,keiʃənl] *adj* blandet, fælles- (fx *school* skole).

coerce [kəu'ə:s] *v* tvinge; bruge tvang overfor; **coercion** *s* tvang.

coexistence [kəuig'zistəns] *s* (fredelig) sameksistens.

C of E ['si: ʌv 'i:] (fork.f. *Church of England*).

coffee ['kɔfi] *s* kaffe; ~ **break** *s* kaffepause; ~ **grinder** *s* kaffemølle,

-kværn; ~ **grounds** *spl* kaffegrums; ~**pot** *s* kaffekande; ~ **shop** *s* kafé; ~ **table** *s* kaffebord; sofabord; ~-**table book** *s* pragtudgave (af bog).
coffer ['kɔfə*] *s* skrin, kiste.
coffin ['kɔfin] *s* (lig)kiste.
cog [kɔg] *s* tandhjul; *he's just a ~ in the wheel* han er kun et lille hjul i det store maskineri.
cogent ['kəudʒənt] *adj* overbevisende.
cogitate ['kɔdʒiteit] *v* tænke over.
cogwheel ['kɔgwi:l] *s* tandhjul.
cohabit [kəu'hæbit] *v* leve (papirløst) sammen; ~**ation** [-'teiʃən] *s* (papirløst) samliv.
coherent [kəu'hiərənt] *adj* sammenhængende; logisk.
cohesive [kəu'hi:siv] *adj* sammenhængende; (fast) sammentømret.
coil [kɔil] *s* spiral; spole; rulle // *v* sno (sig); danne spiral.
coin [kɔin] *s* mønt; pengestykke // *v: ~ a phrase* sige det banalt; *to ~ a word...* for nu at sige det sådan..., om jeg så må sige...
coinage ['kɔinidʒ] *s* møntsystem; (om ord) nydannelse.
coin-box ['kɔinbɔks] *s* møntboks; telefonboks.
coincide [kəuin'said] *v* falde sammen; *~ with* indtræffe samtidig med.
coincidence [kəu'insidəns] *s* sammentræf; tilfælde; *by ~* tilfældigvis.
coincidental [kəuinsi'dɛntl] *adj* tilfældig; ~**ly** *adv* tilfældigvis.
coke [kəuk] *s* koks; (S) cola; kokain.
colander ['kɔləndə*] *s* dørslag; *salad ~* salatslynge.
cold [kəuld] *s* kulde; forkølelse; *catch (a) ~* blive forkølet // *adj* kold; *be ~* fryse, være kold; *be out ~* være bevidstløs; *it makes my blood run ~* det får blodet til at stivne i mine årer; ~-**blooded** *adj* kold, hårdhjertet; ~ **cuts** *spl* (*am*) afskåret koldt kød; ~-**shoulder** *v* give den kolde skulder; ~ **snap** *s* (pludselig) kuldeperiode; ~**sore** *s* forkølelsessår; ~ **storage** *s: put sth in(to) ~ storage* lægge ngt på køl; *(fig)* lægge ngt på is, sylte ngt.
coleslaw ['kəulslɔ:] *s (gastr)* råkostsalat (af kål, løg, reven gulerod m.m. i mayonnaise).
colic ['kɔlik] *s* mavekneb, kolik.
collaborate [kə'læbəreit] *v* samarbejde; deltage, medvirke.
collaboration [kəlæbə'reiʃən] *s* samarbejde.
collaborator [kə'læbəreitə*] *s* medarbejder; *(neds)* kollaboratør.
collapse [kə'læps] *s* sammenbrud, kollaps // *v* falde (,bryde) sammen; (kunne) slå(s) sammen.
collapsible [kə'læpsibl] *adj* sammenklappelig, klap-.
collar ['kɔlə*] *s* krave; flip; (om hund) halsbånd // *v* tage i kraven, fange; snuppe, hugge; ~**bone** *s* kraveben.
colleague ['kɔli:g] *s* kollega; medarbejder.
collect [kə'lɛkt] *v* samle (sammen, ind, på); opkræve (fx *taxes* skat); afhente (fx *a parcel* en pakke); samle sig // *adj: call ~ (tlf, am)* ringe på modtagerens regning; ~**ed** *adj: ~ed works* samlede værker.
collection [kə'lɛkʃən] *s* samling; indsamling; opkrævning; afhentning.
collective [kə'lɛktiv] *adj* fælles-; kollektiv-.
collector [kə'lɛktə*] *s* samler; inkassator; indsamler; ~'**s item** *s* samlerobjekt.
college ['kɔlidʒ] *s* kollegium; læreanstalt; privatskole; *(am)* universitet; *~ of education* lærerhøjskole.
collide [kə'laid] *v* kollidere, støde sammen.
colliery ['kɔliəri] *s* kulmine.
collision [kə'liʒən] *s* sammenstød, kollision; ~ **course** *s* kollisionskurs.
colloquial [kə'ləukwiəl] *adj* daglig; ~ **language** *s* (dagligt) talesprog.
collusion [kə'lu:ʒən] *s: in ~ with* i (hemmelig) forståelse med, i ledtog med.
colon ['kəulən] *s (gram)* kolon; *(anat)* tyktarm.
colonel [kə:nl] *s* oberst.
colonial [kə'ləuniəl] *adj* koloni-.
colonize ['kɔlənaiz] *v* kolonisere.
colony ['kɔləni] *s* koloni.

colossal [kə'lɔsl] *adj* kolossal, enorm.
colossus [kə'lɔsəs] *s* kolos, kæmpe.
colour ['kʌlə*] *s* farve, kulør; skær; *have a high* ~ være rød i ansigtet; *local* ~ lokalkolorit // *v* farve; farvelægge; få farve; rødme; præge; (se også *colours);* ~ **bar** *s* raceskel; ~**-blind** *adj* farveblind.
coloured ['kʌləd] *adj* farvet; farve- (fx *photo* foto); ~**s** *spl* (om personer) farvede; (om vasketøj) kulørtvask.
colourfast ['kʌləfa:st] *adj* farveægte.
colourful ['kʌləful] *adj* farverig, farvestrålende.
colouring ['kʌləriŋ] *s* farve(r); farvestof; ~ **book** *s* malebog.
colours ['kʌləz] *spl* fane, flag; (fx fodboldholds) farver.
colour scheme ['kʌləski:m] *s* farvevalg; farvesammensætning.
colour slide ['kʌləslaid] *s* farvedias.
colt [kəult] *s* (om hingst) føl, plag; (om person) nybegynder.
column ['kɔləm] *s* søjle; *(mil)* kolonne; (i avis etc) spalte.
columnist ['kʌləmnist] *s* journalist som skriver fast rubrik.
comb [kəum] *s* (rede)kam // *v* rede (hår), kæmme; finkæmme.
combat ['kɔmbət] *s* kamp // *adj* kamp-, felt- // *v* (be)kæmpe.
combination [kɔmbi'neiʃən] *s* kombination; forbindelse; ~ **lock** *s* kodelås.
combine *s* ['kɔmbain] sammenslutning, kartel // *v* [kəm'bain] kombinere; forene (sig); samarbejde; ~ **harvester** ['kɔmbain-] *s* mejetærsker.
combustible [kəm'bʌstibl] *adj* brændbar.
combustion [kəm'bʌstʃən] *s* forbrænding.
come [kʌm] *v (came* [keim], *come)* komme; ankomme; ~ *into sight (,view)* komme til syne; ~ *to a decision* nå til en beslutning; ~ *undone* gå løs (,op); *how* ~*?* hvorfor? hvordan kan det være? ~ *summer, we will...* når sommeren kommer skal vi...;
~ *about* ske; ~ *across* falde over; støde på; ~ *along!* kom nu! ~ *apart* gå i stykker (,fra hinanden); ~ *away* gå væk; gå af; ~ *back* komme tilbage; ~ *by* få fat i; komme forbi; ~ *down* komme ned; (om priser) gå ned, falde; (om hus) falde sammen; ~ *forward* komme frem; melde sig; ~ *from* komme fra (,af); stamme fra; ~ *in* komme ind; blive aktuel (,in); ~ *in for* komme ud for; få; ~ *into* få; arve; ~ *off* gå løs (,af); foregå; klare sig; ~ *off it!* årh, hold op! ~ *on* udvikle sig; trives; gøre fremskridt; ~ *on!* kom nu! årh, lad vær! ~ *out* komme ud; nedlægge arbejdet, strejke; lykkes; (om blomster) springe ud; ~ *to* komme til sig selv; ~ *up* komme op; dukke op; ~ *up against sth* komme ud for ngt, støde på ngt; ~ *up to expectations* leve op til forventningerne; ~ *up with* komme frem med; ~ *upon* støde på; falde over.
comedian [kə'mi:diən] *s* komiker.
comedown ['kʌmdaun] *s* nedtur, tilbageskridt.
comedy ['kɔmidi] *s* komedie; farce.
come-uppance [kʌm'ʌpəns] *s: get one's* ~ få en over næsen.
comfort ['kʌmfət] *s* trøst; velvære; bekvemmelighed; *too close for* ~ ubehagelig tæt på // *v* trøste.
comfortable ['kʌmfətəbl] *adj* behagelig, magelig; veltilpas.
comforter ['kʌmfətə*] *s* trøster; *(am)* narresut; sjælevarmer.
comforts ['kʌmfətz] *spl* komfort.
comfy ['kɔmfi] *adj* (F) d.s.s. *comfortable.*
comic ['kɔmik] *s* komiker; tegneserie // *adj* komisk; ~ **strip** *s* tegneserie.
coming ['kɔmiŋ] *s* komme; ~*(s) and going(s)* kommen og gåen; anliggender; ~ *of age* det at blive myndig // *adj* kommende; *he has it* ~ *to him* han kan vente sig.
command [kə'ma:nd] *s* ordre; kommando; magt; rådighed; *have sth at one's* ~ have ngt til sin rådighed; *have a good* ~ *of German* beherske tysk // *v* befale; kommandere; have kommandoen over; beherske;

råde over; ~ *sby to* beordre en til at.

commandeer [kɔmən'diə*] *v (mil)* udskrive; beslaglægge.

commander [kə'ma:ndə*] *s* leder, anfører; *(mil)* kommandør; *(mar)* orlogskaptajn; **~-in-chief** *s (C-in-C)* øverstkommanderende.

commanding [kə'ma:ndiŋ] *adj* bydende; med vid udsigt; ~ **officer** *s* befalingsmand.

commandment [kə'ma:ndmənt] *s: the ten ~* de ti bud.

commando [kə'ma:ndəu] *s* kommando // *adj* kommando- (fx *troops* tropper).

commemorate [kə'mɛməreit] *v* fejre; mindes.

commemoration [kəmɛmə'reiʃən] *s* ihukommelse; mindefest.

commemorative [kə'mɛmərətiv] *adj* minde-; jubilæums-.

commence [kə'mɛns] *v* begynde.

commend [kə'mɛnd] *v* rose; anbefale; **~able** *adj* prisværdig.

commendation [kɔmən'deiʃən] *s* anbefaling; lovtale.

comment ['kɔmənt] *s* kommentar, bemærkning // *v* kommentere; ~ *on* udtale sig om.

commentary ['kɔməntəri] *s* kommentar; *(sport* etc) reportage.

commentator ['kɔmənteitə*] *s* kommentator.

commerce ['kɔməs] *s* handel; omgang, samkvem.

commercial [kə'mə:ʃəl] *s (tv etc)* reklameindslag; reklamefilm // *adj* kommerciel; reklame-; handels-, forretnings-; ~ **art** *s* reklametegning; ~ **college** *s* handelsskole; **~ize** [-aiz] *v* udnytte forretningsmæssigt; ~ **television** *s* reklamefjernsyn; reklameindslag; ~ **traveller** *s* handelsrejsende.

commiserate [kə'mizəreit] *v: ~ with* ynke, have ondt af; kondolere.

commission [kə'miʃən] *s* hverv, bemyndigelse; kommission; forøvelse; *out of ~* (om skib) ude af fart // *v* bemyndige; give et hverv.

commissionaire [kəmiʃə'nɛə*] *s* dørvogter, portier.

commissioner [kə'miʃənə*] *s* kommissær; kommitteret; *police ~* sv.t. politidirektør.

commit [kə'mit] *v* begå (fx *a crime* en forbrydelse); overgive *(to* til); sætte (tid, penge) af; ~ *oneself* forpligte sig; røbe sig; udsætte sig *(to* for); ~ *suicide* begå selvmord; ~ *sby to prison* fængsle en; ~ *to writing* nedfælde på papir.

commitment [kə'mitmənt] *s* forpligtelse; engagement.

committee [kə'miti] *s* komité, udvalg.

commodity [kə'mɔditi] *s* vare, produkt.

common ['kɔmən] *s* fælled; *the Commons* (d.s.s. *the House of Commons)* Underhuset // *adj* fælles; almindelig; jævn; simpel; *in ~* fælles; *it's ~ knowledge that...* alle og enhver ved at...; *to the ~ good* til fælles bedste; **~er** *s* borgerlig; ~ **denominator** *s* fællesnævner; ~ **ground** *s: it's ~ ground* det kan vi (kun) være enige om; ~ **law** *s* sv.t. retssædvane // *adj* papirløs (fx *wife* samleverske); **~ly** *adv* sædvanligvis; almindeligt; ~ **market** *s* fællesmarked; **~place** *adj* banal, ordinær; ~ **room** *s* fællesrum; *(univ)* lærerværelse; ~ **sense** *s* sund fornuft; **~wealth** *s* statsforbund; *the British Commonwealth* det Britiske Statssamfund.

commotion [kə'məuʃən] *s* opstandelse, postyr; uro.

communal ['kɔmju:nl] *adj* fælles; kollektiv; ~ **family** *s* storfamilie.

commune *s* ['kɔmju:n] kommune; kollektiv; storfamilie; *people's ~* folkekommune (i Kina) // *v* [kə'mju:n]: ~ *with* omgås fortroligt; tale fortroligt med.

communicate [kə'mju:nikeit] *v* meddele; stå i forbindelse; kommunikere; smitte (med sygdom).

communication [kəmjuni'keiʃən] *s* meddelelse; overføring; forbindelse; kommunikation; ~ **cord** *s* nødbremse(snor).

communicative [kə'mju:nikətiv] *adj* meddelsom.

communion [kə'mju:niən] *s* (også

Holy ~) altergang, nadver.
community [kə'mju:niti] *s* fællesskab; samfund; (befolknings)gruppe; **~ centre** *s* kulturhus; medborgerhus; **~ police** *s* nærpoliti.
commute [kə'mju:t] *v* ombytte; rejse frem og tilbage, pendle; *(jur)* forvandle; **~r** *s* pendler.
compact *s* ['kɔmpækt] pagt; pudderdåse (til at have i tasken) // *adj* [kəm'pækt] fast; tæt; kompakt; (om person) tætbygget.
companion [kəm'pæniən] *s* ledsager; kammerat; **~able** *adj* omgængelig; **~ship** *s* kammeratskab; selskab; **~way** *s (mar)* kahytstrappe.
company ['kʌmpəni] *s* selskab; aktieselskab; kompagni; gæster; *(mar)* besætning; *be seen in sby's ~* blive set i selskab med en; *he's good ~* han er rar at være sammen med; *we have ~* vi har besøg (,gæster); *keep sby ~* holde en med selskab; *keep ~ with* komme sammen med; *part ~ with* skilles fra; **~ law** *s (jur)* selskabsret; **~ secretary** *s* sv.t. direktionssekretær.
comparable ['kɔmpəræbl] *adj* sammenlignelig.
comparative [kəm'pærətiv] *adj* sammenlignende; komparativ; forholdsvis, nogenlunde.
compare [kɔm'pɛə*] *v* sammenligne *(to, with* med); *(gram)* gradbøje; *beyond ~* uden sammenligning.
comparison [kɔm'pærisn] *s* sammenligning; *in ~ to (,with)* i sammenligning med.
compartment [kəm'pa:tmənt] *s* (afgrænset) felt; rum; *(jernb)* kupé.
compass ['kʌmpəs] *s* kompas; omkreds; område.
compasses ['kʌmpəsiz] *spl* passer; *a pair of ~* en passer.
compassion [kəm'pæʃən] *s* medlidenhed; barmhjertighed.
compassionate [kəm'pæʃənit] *adj* medlidende, deltagende.
compatible [kəm'pætibl] *adj* forenelig *(with* med).
compel [kəm'pɛl] *v* tvinge; fremtvinge; aftvinge; **~ling** *adj* tvingende; (om bog etc) fængslende; overbevisende.
compensate ['kɔmpənseit] *v* kompensere; erstatte; *~ for* opveje.
compensation [kɔmpən'seiʃən] *s* erstatning; kompensation; belønning.
compere ['kɔmpɛə*] *s* konferencier // *v* være konferencier (for).
compete [kəm'pi:t] *v* konkurrere *(for* om).
competence ['kɔmpitəns] *s* dygtighed; kompetence; **competent** *adj* dygtig; kvalificeret; kompetent.
competition [kɔmpi'tiʃən] *s* konkurrence.
competitive [kɔm'pɛtitiv] *adj* konkurrencedygtig; konkurrencepræget; konkurrenceminded; *~ sports* konkurrenceidræt.
competitor [kəm'pɛtitə*] *s* konkurrent; konkurrencedeltager.
compile [kəm'pail] *v* samle; udarbejde (fx *a dictionary* en ordbog).
complacency [kəm'pleisənsi] *s* selvtilfredshed; **complacent** *adj* selvglad.
complain [kəm'plein] *v* klage; beklage sig *(about, of* over); **~ant** *s* klager.
complaint [kəm'pleint] *s* klage; reklamation; sygdom, lidelse.
complement ['kɔmplimənt] *s* komplement; *(gram)* omsagnsled, prædikat; tilføjelse; fuldendelse; mandskab.
complementary [kɔmpli'mæntəri] *adj* komplementær.
complete [kɔm'pli:t] *v* fuldende; gøre færdig; opfylde; udfylde (fx *a form* et skema) // *adj* fuldstændig; fuldkommen; komplet; grundig; **~ly** *adv* fuldstændig, helt.
completion [kəm'pli:ʃən] *s* færdiggørelse; opfyldelse; udfyldelse.
complex ['kɔmplɛks] *s* kompleks // *adj* sammensat; indviklet.
complexion [kəm'plɛkʃən] *s* ansigtsfarve, teint.
complexity [kəm'plɛksiti] *s* indviklethed; forvikling.
compliance [kəm'plaiəns] *s* overensstemmelse; føjelighed; *in ~ with* i overensstemmelse med; **compliant**

adj eftergivende; medgørlig.

complicate *v* ['kɔmplikeit] komplicere // *adj* ['kɔmplikit] indviklet, kompliceret; **~d** *adj* indviklet, kompliceret.

complication [kɔmpli'keiʃən] *s* komplikation.

complicity [kəm'plisiti] *s* meddelagtighed.

compliment ['kɔmplimənt] *s* kompliment; *send one's ~s* hilse; *with the ~s of the season* med ønsket om en glædelig jul og et godt nytår // *v* komplimentere; gratulere.

complimentary [kɔmpli'mɛntəri] *adj* smigrende, komplimenterende; **~ copy** *s* frieksemplar; **~ ticket** *s* fribillet.

comply [kəm'plai] *v* føje sig; samtykke; *~ with* rette sig efter; opfylde.

component [kəm'pəunənt] *s* bestanddel, komponent // *adj* del-; **~s** *spl* (også) byggeelementer.

compose [kəm'pəuz] *v* sammensætte; udarbejde; komponere; bringe i orden; *~ oneself* samle sig; tage sig sammen; **~d** *adj* rolig, fattet.

composer [kəm'pəuzə*] *s* komponist; *(typ)* sættemaskine; *photo ~* fotosætter.

composite [kɔm'pɔzit] *adj* sammensat; *(bot)* kurvblomstret.

composition [kɔmpə'ziʃən] *s* sammensætning; udarbejdelse; komposition; *(typ)* sætning, sats.

composure [kəm'pəuʒə*] *s* fatning, ro; ligevægt.

compound ['kɔmpaund] *s* sammensætning; forbindelse (også *kem);* indhegnet område // *adj* sammensat; **~ fraction** *s* brøks brøk; **~ fracture** *s (med)* kompliceret knoglebrud; **~ interest** *s* rentes rente.

comprehend [kɔmpri'hɛnd] *v* forstå, begribe; omfatte.

comprehensible [kɔpri'hɛnsibl] *adj* begribelig; letfattelig.

comprehension [kɔmpri'hɛnʃən] *s* forståelse; fatteevne.

comprehensive [kɔmpri'hɛnsiv] *adj* omfattende; vidtspændende; alsidig; **~ school** *s* sv.t. udelt skole, enhedsskole.

compress *s* ['kɔmprɛs] kompres // *v* [kɔm'prɛs] sammenpresse, komprimere.

compression [kəm'prɛʃən] *s* sammenpresning; kompression.

comprise [kəm'praiz] *v* omfatte; bestå af.

compromise ['kɔmprəmaiz] *s* kompromis // *v* indgå forlig (,kompromis); kompromittere.

compulsion [kəm'pʌlʃən] *s* tvang; tvangstanke.

compulsive [kəm'pʌlsiv] *adj* tvingende; tvangs-; fængslende (fx *book* bog); *a ~ eater* en trøstespiser.

compulsory [kəm'pʌlsəri] *adj* tvungen; obligatorisk.

compute [kɛm'pju:t] *v* beregne.

computer [kəm'pju:tə*] *s* regnemaskine; computer, datamat; *~ game* computerspil; **~ize** [-aiz] *v* databehandle; indføre databehandling; **~ language** *s (edb)* maskinsprog; **~-operated** *adj* datastyret; **~ science** *s* datamatik; informatik.

comrade ['kɔmrid] *s* kammerat; **~ship** *s* kammeratskab.

con [kɔn] *s* svindel; svindelnummer // *v* svindle, narre, tage ved næsen.

conceal [kən'si:l] *v* skjule; fortie.

concede [kən'si:d] *v* indrømme; gå med til; afstå.

conceit [kən'si:t] *s* indbildning; indbildskhed; **~ed** *adj* indbildsk; vigtig.

conceivable [kən'si:vəbl] *adj* tænkelig.

conceive [kən'si:v] *v* finde på; forstå, opfatte; undfange.

concentrate ['kɔnsəntreit] *v* samle (sig); koncentrere (sig); **concentration** [-'treiʃən] *s* koncentration.

concept ['kɔnsɛpt] *s* begreb.

conception [kən'sɛpʃən] *s* opfattelse; begreb; idé; undfangelse.

concern [kən'sə:n] *s* bekymring; virksomhed, koncern; interesse; anliggende // *v* angå, vedrøre; ængste, bekymre; *be ~ed about* være bekymret for (,over); *as far as John is*

~ed... hvad angår John...; *for all ~ed* for alle implicerede; **~ing** *adj* angående, vedrørende.

concert ['kɔnsət] *s* koncert; *in ~ with* i samråd med; **~ed** [kən'sə:tid] *adj* samlet, fælles-; **~-goer** *s* koncertgænger; **~ hall** *s* koncertsal.

concertina [kɔnsə'ti:nə] *s* (om harmonika) koncertina // *v* blive mast sammen som en harmonika.

concerto [kən'ʃə:təu] *s* koncert (for soloinstrument og orkester).

concession [kən'sɛʃən] *s* indrømmelse; koncession.

conch [kɔntʃ] *s* konkylie.

conciliation [kənsili'eiʃən] *s* forsoning; mægling; **conciliatory** [-'siliətəri] *adj* forsonende; forsonlig.

concise [kən'sais] *adj* kortfattet, koncis.

conclude [kən'klu:d] *v* slutte, konkludere; afslutte; beslutte.

conclusion [kən'klu:ʒən] *s* slutning; konklusion; afslutning.

conclusive [kən'klu:siv] *adj* afgørende (fx *evidence* bevis).

concoct [kən'kɔkt] *v* bikse sammen; udpønse.

concoction [kən'kɔkʃən] *s* (sammen)-bryg; løgnehistorie.

concord ['kɔnkɔ:d] *s* sammenhold; overenskomst.

concrete ['kɔnkri:t] *s* beton // *adj* konkret; størknet; beton-.

concur [kɔn'kə:*] *v* stemme overens; være enig(e); falde sammen; **~rent** [-'kərənt] *adj* sammenfaldende, samtidig.

concussion [kən'kʌʃən] *s* rystelse; hjernerystelse.

condemn [kən'dɛm] *v* fordømme; dømme (fx *to death* til døden); (om bygning) kondemnere, dømme til nedrivning; **~ation** [-'neiʃən] *s* fordømmelse; kondemnering.

condensation [kɔndɛn'seiʃən] *s* fortætning; kondens.

condense [kən'dɛns] *v* sammentrænge; fortætte(s).

condescend [kɔndi'sɛnd] *v* nedlade sig; **~ing** *adj* nedladende.

condition [kən'diʃən] *s* tilstand; kondition; betingelse; *he's in no ~ to drive* han er ikke i stand til at køre; *on ~ that* på den betingelse at // *v* bearbejde, forme; præge, behandle; **~al** *adj* betinget; *~al release* prøveløsladelse; *be ~al on* være betinget af.

conditioner [kən'diʃənə*] *s* hårkur; hårbalsam; skyllemiddel.

condolences [kən'dəulənsiz] *spl* kondolence; *send (,give) one's ~* kondolere.

condominium [kɔndə'miniəm] *s (am)* ejerlejlighed; ejendom med ejerlejligheder.

condone [kən'dəun] *v* tilgive; se gennem fingre med.

conduct *s* ['kɔndʌkt] opførsel; førelse // *v* [kən'dʌkt] føre; udføre; *(elek)* lede; *(mus* etc) dirigere; *~ oneself* opføre sig; **~ed tour** [-'dʌktid] *adj* selskabsrejse; rundvisning.

conductor [kən'dʌktə*] *s (mus)* dirigent; (i bus) konduktør; *(elek)* leder.

conduit ['kɔndit] *s* ledning.

cone [kəun] *s* kegle; isvaffel; *(bot)* kogle // *v: ~ off* afspærre (fx vejbane) med plastkegler og snore.

confectioner [kən'fɛkʃənə*] *s* konditor; konfekturehandler.

confectionery [kən'fɛkʃənəri] *s* konditorkager; konfekture.

confederate [kən'fɛdərit] *s* forbundsfælle; medskyldig // *adj* forbunds-.

confederation [kənfɛdə'reiʃən] *s* forbund, føderation.

confer [kən'fə:*] *v* konferere, rådslå; tildele; *(cf.)* jævnfør (jf.); *~ sth on sby* tildele en ngt.

conference ['kɔnfərəns] *s* konference; møde; *he's in ~* han sidder i møde.

confess [kən'fɛs] *v: ~ (to)* tilstå; indrømme, bekende.

confession [kən'fɛʃən] *s* tilståelse; indrømmelse; tro, trosbekendelse.

confessional [kən'fɛʃənəl] *s* skriftestol.

confessor [kən'fɛsə*] *s* skriftefar.

confide [kən'faid] *v: ~ in* betro sig til; stole på; *~ sth to sby* betro en ngt.

confidence ['kɔnfidns] *s* tillid; fortro-

lighed; selvsikkerhed; *in strict* ~ strengt fortroligt; *a vote of no* ~ et mistillidsvotum; ~ **trick** *s* bondefangerkneb.
confident ['kɔnfidnt] *adj* tillidsfuld; tryg; sikker.
confidential [kɔnfi'dɛnʃəl] *adj* fortrolig.
confine [kən'fain] *v* begrænse; indskrænke; **~d** *adj* begrænset; snæver; **~ment** *s* fangenskab; begrænsning; *(med)* nedkomst; **~s** ['kɔnfainz] *spl* grænser; rammer.
confirm [kən'fə:m] *v* bekræfte, bestyrke.
confirmation [kənfə:'meiʃən] *s* bekræftelse; godkendelse; konfirmation.
confirmed [kən'fə:md] *adj* inkarneret; uforbederlig.
confiscate ['kɔnfiskeit] *v* konfiskere.
conflict *s* ['kɔnflikt] konflikt; kamp // *v* [kən'flikt] være i modstrid *(with* med); støde sammen; **~ing** *adj* modstridende.
conform [kən'fɔ:m] *v:* ~ *(to)* tilpasse sig; være i overensstemmelse med.
confound [kən'faund] *v* blande sammen; forvirre; ~ *it!* pokkers også! **~ed** *adj* forvirret; forbistret.
confront [kən'frʌnt] *v* konfrontere; stå ansigt til ansigt med.
confrontation [kənfrən'teiʃən] *s* konfrontation.
confuse [kən'fju:z] *v* blande sammen; forvirre; **~d** *adj* forvirret, forfjamsket.
confusion [kən'fju:ʒən] *s* forvirring; forveksling; uro.
congeal [kən'dʒi:l] *v* størkne, stivne.
congenial [kən'dʒi:niəl] *adj* åndsbeslægtet; af samme slags; rar, sympatisk.
congenital [kən'dʒɛnitl] *adj* medfødt.
congested [kən'dʒɛstid] *adj* (til)stoppet, blokeret.
congestion [kən'dʒɛstʃən] *s* overfyldning; overbefolkning; overbelastning.
conglomeration [kənglɔmə'reiʃən] *s* ophobning.
congratulate [kən'grætjuleit] *v* lykønske; ønske til lykke *(on* med).
congratulation [kəngrætju'leiʃən] *s* lykønskning; ~*s!* tillykke! gratulerer!
congregate ['kɔŋgrigeit] *v* samle sig; forsamles.
congregation [kɔngri'geiʃən] *s* forsamling; menighed.
congress ['kɔŋgrɛs] *s* kongres; **~man** *s (am)* medlem af Kongressen, politiker.
conical ['kɔnikl] *adj* kegleformet, konisk.
conifer ['kɔnifə*] *s* nåletræ.
coniferous [kə'nifərəs] *adj* keglebærende; nåle-.
conjecture [kən'dʒɛktʃə*] *s* gætteri // *v* gætte, gisne.
conjugal ['kɔndʒugl] *adj* ægteskabelig; ægte- (fx *bed* seng).
conjugate ['kɔndʒugeit] *v (gram)* bøje; **conjugation** [-'geiʃən] *s* bøjning.
conjunction [kən'dʒʌŋkʃən] *s* forbindelse; sammentræf; *(gram)* bindeord, konjunktion.
conjunctivitis [kəndʒʌŋkti'vaitis] *s (med)* øjenkatar.
conjure ['kɔndʒə*] *v* trylle; *up* trylle frem; fremkalde.
conjurer ['kɔndʒərə*] *s* tryllekunstner.
conjuring trick ['kɔndʒəriŋ,trik] *s* tryllekunst.
conk [kɔŋk] *s* (F, om næse) snabel; (om hoved) nød // *v* (F) slå (i nødden), "pande"; ~ *out* bryde sammen.
conman ['kɔnmæn] *s* (F) bondefanger.
connect [kə'nɛkt] *v* forbinde; være i forbindelse; *(tlf)* stille ind, *(jernb* etc) korrespondere.
connection [kə'nɛkʃən] *s* forbindelse, tilknyning; *in* ~ *with* i forbindelse med; i anledning af; **connexion** *s* d.s.s. *connection.*
connive [kə'naiv] *v:* ~ *at* se gennem fingre med; ~ *with* konspirere med.
connoisseur [kɔni'sə:*] *s* kender; feinschmecker.
conquer ['kɔnkə*] *v* erobre; (be)sejre, overvinde.

conqueror ['kɔnkərə*] *s* sejrherre; *William the Conqueror* Vilhelm Erobreren.
conquest ['kɔnkwɛst] *s* erobring; *the Norman Conquest* normannernes erobring af England 1066.
cons [kɔnz] *spl* se *pro; convenience.*
conscience ['kɔnʃəns] *s* samvittighed; *in good* ~ med god samvittighed; *have sth on one's* ~ have ngt på samvittigheden.
conscientious [kɔnʃi'ɛnʃəs] *adj* samvittighedsfuld; pligtopfyldende; ~ **objector** *s* militærnægter.
conscious ['kɔnʃəs] *adj* bevidst; ved bevidsthed; *be* ~ *of* være klar over; **~ness** *s* bevidsthed; *regain ~ness* komme til bevidsthed.
conscript ['kɔnskript] *s* værnepligtig.
conscription [kɔn'skripʃən] *s* værnepligt.
consecrate ['kɔnsikreit] *v* indvie, vie; **~ed** *adj* hellig, indviet.
consecutive [kən'sɛkjutiv] *adj* efter hinanden; i træk; fortløbende (fx *numbers* numre); logisk; følge-.
consensus [kən'sɛnsəs] *s* almindelig enighed; almen opfattelse; overensstemmelse.
consent [kən'sɛnt] *s* samtykke; overenskomst; *by mutual* ~ efter fælles overenskomst // *v* samtykke *(to* i).
consequence ['kɔnsikwəns] *s* følge, konsekvens; betydning; *in* ~ derfor, følgelig; *it's of no* ~ det har ingen betydning; det er lige meget; **consequential** [-'kwɛnʃəl] *adj* (deraf) følgende; betydningsfuld.
conservation [kənsə'veiʃən] *s* bevarelse; fredning; konservering.
conservative [kən'sə:vətiv] *adj* bevarende; konservativ; forsigtig; *a* ~ *estimate* et forsigtigt skøn.
conservatory [kən'sə:vətri] *s* vinterhave; (musik)konservatorium.
conserve [kən'sə:v] *v* bevare; spare på; opbevare; sylte.
consider [kən'sidə*] *v* tage hensyn til; betragte; overveje; tænke over; mene; anse for; *all things ~ed* alt i alt.
considerable [kən'sidərəbl] *adj* betydelig; anselig; væsentlig.
considerate [kən'sidərit] *adj* betænksom.
consideration [kənsidə'reiʃən] *s* overvejelse; omtanke; hensyn; betydning; betaling; *out of* ~ *for* af hensyn til; *under* ~ under overvejelse; *for a certain* ~ mod en vis betaling.
considering [kən'sidəriŋ] *præp* i betragtning af (at); (F) efter omstændighederne.
consign [kən'sain] *v* overgive; overdrage; **~ment** *s* forsendelse; sending.
consist [kən'sist] *v:* ~ *in (,of)* bestå af.
consistency [kən'sistənsi] *s* konsistens; konsekvens; overensstemmelse.
consistent [kən'sistənt] *adj* overensstemmende; forenelig; konsekvent; ensartet; *be* ~ *with* stemme (overens) med.
consolation [kɔnsə'leiʃən] *s* trøst; ~ **prize** *s* trøstpræmie.
console *s* ['kɔnsəul] kontrolpanel; rack // *v* [kən'səul] trøste.
consolidate [kən'sɔlideit] *v* befæste, konsolidere; sammenslutte(s).
consort *s* ['kɔnsɔ:t] ledsager; gemal(inde); *Prince Consort* prinsgemal // *v* [kən'sɔ:t]: ~ *with* omgås (med).
conspicuous [kən'spikjuəs] *adj* iøjnefaldende; tydelig; påfaldende.
conspiracy [kən'spirəsi] *s* sammensværgelse, komplot.
conspirator [kən'spirətə*] *s* medsammensvoren.
conspire [kən'spaiə*] *v* sammensværge sig, komspirere.
constable ['kɔnstəbl] *s* politibetjent.
constabulary [kən'stæbjuləri] *s* politi(korps) (i bestemt kommune).
constancy ['kɔnstənsi] *s* bestandighed; uforanderlighed.
constant ['kɔnstənt] *adj* bestandig; konstant; trofast; **~ly** *adv* hele tiden.
constellation [kɔnstə'leiʃən] *s* konstellation (også *fig);* stjernebillede.
consternation [kɔnstə'neiʃən] *s* bestyrtelse; forfærdelse.

constipate ['kɔnstipeit] *v* forstoppe; **constipation** [-'peiʃən] *s* forstoppelse.
constituency [kən'stitʃuənsi] *s* valgkreds.
constituent [kən'stitʃuənt] *s* vælger; nødvendig bestanddel.
constitute ['kɔnstitju:t] *v* udgøre; danne; konstituere; grundlægge, stifte; udnævne til.
constitution [kɔnsti'tju:ʃən] *s* oprettelse; sammensætning; beskaffenhed; forfatning, grundlov; konstitution.
constitutional [kɔnsti'tju:ʃənəl] *s (gl, spøg)* spadseretur // *adj* forfatningsmæssig, konstitutionel; ~ *monarchy* indskrænket monarki.
constrain [kən'strein] *v* tvinge; gøre tvungen; hæmme; **~ed** *adj* tvungen; genert.
constraint [kən'streint] *s* tvang, ufrihed.
constrict [kɔn'strikt] *v* snøre sammen; hæmme.
constrictor [kɔn'striktə*] *s* kvælerslange.
construct [kən'strʌkt] *v* bygge; konstruere; sammensætte.
construction [kən'strʌkʃən] *s* bygning; anlæg; konstruktion.
constructive [kən'strʌktiv] *adj* konstruktiv.
consult [kən'sʌlt] *v* rådspørge, konsultere; benytte; konferere; ~ *a dictionary* slå op i en ordbog.
consultant [kən'sʌltənt] *s* konsulent; overlæge; *legal* ~ juridisk rådgiver; ~ **engineer** *s* rådgivende ingeniør.
consultation [kɔnsʌl'teiʃən] *s* konsultation, samråd.
consulting room [kən'sʌltiŋ ru:m] *s* konsultationsværelse.
consume [kən'sju:m] *v* fortære; opbruge; forbruge.
consumer [kən'sju:mə*] *s* forbruger, konsument; ~ **goods** *spl* forbrugsvarer; ~ **society** *s* forbrugersamfund.
comsuming [kən'sju:miŋ] *adj* altopslugende.
consummate ['kɔnsʌmeit] *v* fuldbyrde.
consumption [kən'sʌmpʃən] *s* fortæring; forbrug; *(gl, med)* tæring.
cont. fork.f. *continued.*
contact ['kɔntækt] *s* kontakt; berøring; kontaktperson // *v* kontakte; få forbindelse med; være i berøring med; møde(s); ~ **lenses** *spl* kontaktlinser.
contagious [kən'teidʒəs] *adj* smitsom; smittende.
contain [kən'tein] *v* indeholde, rumme; beherske; fastholde; ~ *oneself* styre sig, dy sig; **~er** *s* beholder; container.
contaminate [kən'tæmineit] *v* forurene; kontaminere; **contamination** [-'neiʃən] *s* forurening.
contd fork.f. *continued.*
contemplate ['kɔntəmpleit] *v* betragte; overveje; påtænke; **contemplation** [-'pleiʃən] *s* betragten; overvejelse; fordybelse; meditation.
contemporary [kən'tɛmpərəri] *s* jævnaldrende; samtidig // *adj* samtidig; nutids-; moderne (fx *art* kunst).
contempt [kən'tɛmpt] *s* foragt.
contemptible [kən'tɛmptibl] *adj* foragtelig.
contemptuous [kən'temptjuəs] *adj* foragtelig; hånlig.
contend [kən'tɛnd] *v:* ~ *that* hævde at; ~ *with* slås med; rivalisere med.
contender [kən'tɛndə*] *s (sport)* udfordrer; konkurrencedeltager.
content [kən'tɛnt] *s* tilfredshed; ['kɔntɛnt] indhold // *v* tilfredsstille; nøjes *(with* med) // *adj* [kən'tɛnt] tilfreds; *be* ~ *with* være tilfreds med; nøjes med; **~ed** [-'tɛndid] *adj* veltilfreds.
contents ['kɔntənts] *spl* indhold; indbo; *(table of)* ~ indholdsfortegnelse.
contention [kən'tɛnʃən] *s* strid; disput; påstand; *the bone of* ~ stridens æble.
contest *s* ['kɔntɛst] strid; konkurrence // *v* [kən'tɛst] bestride; kæmpe; konkurrere (om); *a ~ed city* en omstridt by; **~ant** [kən'tɛstənt] *s* konkurrencedeltager.
context ['kɔntɛkst] *s* sammenhæng.

continent ['kɔntinənt] *s* kontinent, verdensdel; fastland; *the Continent* det europæiske fastland // *adj* kontinent, i stand til at holde sig.

continental [kɔnti'nɛntl] *s* udlænding (fra Europa) // *adj* kontinental-, fastlands-; ~ **breakfast** *s* let morgenmad, morgenkaffe; ~ **shelf** *s (geogr)* fastlandssokkel.

contingency [kən'tindʒənsi] *s* eventualitet; katastrofe.

contingent [kən'tindʒənt] *s* gruppe; (troppe)kontingent // *adj: ~ on* betinget af.

continual [kən'tinjuəl] *adj* stadig; fortsat.

continuation [kəntinju'eiʃən] *s* fortsættelse; genoptagelse.

continue [kən'tinju:] *v* fortsætte; *to be ~d* (fx i avis) fortsættes; **~d** *adj* fortsat.

continuity [kənti'njuiti] *s* sammenhæng, kontinuitet.

continuous [kən'tinjuəs] *adj* fortsat, uafbrudt, bestandig.

contort [kən'tɔ:t] *v* forvride; forvrænge.

contortion [kən'tɔ:ʃən] *s* forvridning; forvrængning.

contortionist [kən'tɔ:ʃənist] *s* slangemenneske.

contraception [kɔntrə'sɛpʃən] *s* svangerskabsforebyggelse.

contraceptive [kɔntrə'sɛptiv] *s* svangerskabsforebyggende middel // *adj* svangerskabsforebyggende.

contract *s* ['kɔntrækt] kontrakt; aftale; *put sth out to ~* bortlicitere ngt // *v* [kən'trækt] indgå kontrakt; trække sig sammen; fortrække; pådrage sig (fx *a disease* en sygdom).

contraction [kən'trækʃən] *s* forsnævring; sammentrækning.

contractor [kən'træktə*] *s* entreprenør.

contradict [kɔntrə'dikt] *v* modsige; være i modstrid med.

contradiction [kɔntrə'dikʃən] *s* modsigelse; dementi; uoverensstemmelse.

contradictory [kɔntrə'diktəri] *adj* modstridende.

contralto [kən'træltəu] *s* (om dyb altstemme) kontraalt.

contraption [kən'træpʃən] *s* tingest; indretning.

contrary ['kɔntrəri] *s: the ~* det modsatte; *on the ~* tværtimod; *~ to* i modsætning til; *unless you hear to the ~* medmindre du får anden besked // *adj* modsat; [kən'trɛəri] kontrær.

contrast *s* ['kɔntra:st] kontrast, modsætning // *v* [kən'tra:st] stille i kontrast *(with* til); **~ing** ['kɔn-] *adj* kontrasterende; modsat.

contravene [kɔntra'vi:n] *v* handle imod (lov etc), overtræde.

contribute [kən'tribju:t] *v* bidrage (med); medvirke; *~ an article to the magazine* skrive en artikel til bladet; *~ to* bidrage til; medvirke ved.

contribution [kɔntri'bju:ʃən] *s* bidrag.

contributor [kən'tribjutə*] *s* bidragyder.

contributory [kən'tribjətəri] *adj* medvirkende.

contrite [kən'trait] *adj* angrende, sønderknust.

contrivance [kən'traivəns] *s* opfindsomhed; påfund; kunstgreb; indretning; mekanisme.

contrive [kən'traiv] *v* opfinde; udtænke; lægge planer; *~ to* sørge for at; have held med at.

control [kən'trəul] *s* kontrol; herredømme; myndighed; *(tekn)* betjeningshåndtag; *be in ~ of* have magten over; stå for; *circumstances beyond our ~* omstændigheder vi ikke har indflydelse på; *remote ~* fjernstyring // *v* kontrollere; beherske; holde styr på; regulere; **~ler** *s* tilsynsførende; leder; ~ **point** *s* kontrolsted; ~ **tower** *s (fly)* kontroltårn.

controversial [kɔntrə'və:ʃl] *adj* omdiskuteret; kontroversiel.

controversy ['kɔntrəvə:si] *s* disput, kontrovers.

conurbation [kɔnə:'beiʃən] *s* byområde; bymæssig bebyggelse.

convalesce [kɔnvə'lɛs] *v* være rekonvalescent, være i bedring.

convalescence [kɔnvə'lɛsns] *s* bedring; rekonvalescens; **convalescent** [-'lɛsnt] *s* rekonvalescent.

convene [kən'vi:n] *v* træde sammen; samles; sammenkalde.

convenience [kən'vi:niəns] *s* bekvemmelighed; nemhed; *at your earliest* ~ så snart du kan; *all modern ~s* (i annonce: *all mod cons)* alle moderne bekvemmeligheder; *public ~s* offentligt toilet; ~ **food** *s* nem mad, færdigret(ter).

convenient [kən'vi:niənt] *adj* bekvem; belejlig.

convent ['kɔnvənt] *s* (nonne)kloster; ~ **school** *s* klosterskole (for piger).

convention [kən'vɛnʃən] *s* kongres; stævne; konvention.

conventinonal [kən'vɛnʃənl] *adj* konventionel, traditionel.

converge [kən'və:dʒ] *v* samles (i ét punkt), konvergere.

conversation [kɔnvə'seiʃən] *s* samtale; konversation.

converse *s* ['kɔnvə:s] samtale; samkvem // *v* [kən'və:s] samtale, konversere // *adj* ['kɔnvə:s] omvendt, modsat.

conversion [kən'və:ʃən] *s* omdannelse; forvandling; ombygning; omregning; *(rel)* omvendelse; ~ **table** *s* omregningstabel.

convert *s* ['kɔnvə:t] konvertit, omvendt // *v* [kən'və:t] omvende sig; omdanne; forvandle; lave om; omregne; **~er** *s* omformer.

convertible [kən'və:tibl] *s (auto)* cabriolet; bilmodel med kaleche // *adj* konvertibel, som kan forvandles.

convey [kən'vei] *v* transportere; overbringe (fx *our thanks* vores tak); bibringe (fx *an idea* en idé); **~ance** *s* transport, befordring.

conveyer [kɔn'veiə*] *s* transportør.

conveyor belt [kɔn'veiə,bɛlt] *s* transportbånd.

convict *s* ['kɔnvikt] strafafsoner; straffefange // *v* [kən'vikt] erklære skyldig; straffe.

conviction [kɔn'vikʃən] *s* domfældelse; overbevisning.

convince [kən'vins] *v* overbevise (*that* om at).

convoy ['kɔnvɔi] *s* konvoj, eskorte // *v* eskortere.

convulse [kən'vʌls] *v* få krampe; give krampe; vride sig; *be ~ed with laughter* vride sig af grin.

convulsion [kən'vʌlʃən] *s* anfald; *~s* krampe.

coo [ku:] *v* kurre // *interj* (F) gud!

cook [kuk] *s* kok; kokkepige // *v* lave mad; tillave(s); *be ~ing* være i gære; ~ *up a story* brygge en historie sammen; ~ *the books* (F) manipulere med regnskaberne.

cooker ['kukə*] *s* komfur; ovn; madæble.

cookery ['kukəri] *s* madlavning; ~ **book** *s* kogebog.

cookie ['kuki] *s* småkage.

cooking ['kukiŋ] *s* madlavning // *adj* mad-, spise-; ~ **apple** *s* madæble; ~ **film** *s* stegefilm; ~ **oil** *s* spiseolie.

cool [ku:l] *v* køle(s); kølne; ~ *down!* tag den med ro // *adj* kølig; koldblodig; rolig; fræk, smart, rap; *keep* ~ holde hovedet koldt; *a ~ movie* (S) en dødlækker (,fed) film.

coolant ['ku:lənt] *s* kølevæske.

cooler ['ku:lə*] *s* køler.

cool-headed ['ku:lhɛdid] *adj* koldblodig.

cooling tower ['ku:liŋ ,tauə*] *s* køletårn.

coop [ku:p] *s* hønsehus; bur // *v: be ~ed up (fig)* sidde indemuret, sidde inde og lumre.

co-op ['kəuʌp] *s* (fork.f. *co-operative society)* brugs(forening).

cooperate [kəu'ɔpəreit] *v* samarbejde; **cooperation** [-'reiʃən] *s* samarbejde, kooperation.

cooperative [kəu'ɔpərətiv] *s* kooperativ, andelsforetagende // *adj* samarbejdsvillig; andels-; ~ **society** *s* brugsforening.

coordinate [kəu'ɔ:dineit] *v* samordne, koordinere.

coordination [kəuɔ:di'neiʃən] *s* koordination.

cop [kɔp] *s* (F) strisser, strømer; *play ~s and robbers* lege røvere og soldater // *v:* ~ *it* blive taget (,snuppet); få en omgang; ~ *out* bakke ud.

cope [kəup] *v* klare den; ~ *with* klare, overkomme; magte; *can you ~?* klarer du dig?
copier ['kɔpiə*] *s* kopimaskine
copious ['kəupiəs] *adj* omfangsrig; rigelig; vidtløftig.
copper ['kɔpə*] *s* kobber; skilling; (F) strisser, strømer; ~ **beech** *s* blodbøg.
copse [kɔps] *s* krat.
copy ['kɔpi] *s* kopi; eksemplar // *v* kopiere; efterligne; **~book** *s* stilebog; *blot one's ~book* ødelægge sit rygte; **~right** *s* ophavsret; *~right reserved* sv.t. eftertryk forbudt; **~writer** *s* (reklame)tekstforfatter.
coquettish [kə'kɛtiʃ] *adj* koket.
coral ['kɔrəl] *s* koral; koralrødt; ~ **reef** *s* koralrev.
cord [kɔ:d] *s* snor; ledning; fløjl.
cordial ['kɔ:diəl] *s* (alkoholfri) hjertestyrkning // *adj* hjertelig; inderlig.
cordon ['kɔ:dən] *s* (politi)afspærring // *v:* ~ *off* afspærre.
cords [kɔ:ds] *s* (F) d.s.s. *corduroys.*
corduroy ['kɔ:dərɔi] *s* riflet fløjl; **~s** *spl* fløjlsbukser.
core [kɔ:*] *s* kerne; kernehus; marv; *to the ~* helt ind til marven // *v* udkerne; ~ **time** *s* fikstid (mods: flekstid).
cork [kɔ:k] *s* *(bot)* kork; prop // *v* sætte prop i.
corker ['kɔ:kə*] *s* (F) alle tiders fyr (,ting), vidunder; fed løgn.
corkscrew ['kɔ:kskru:] *s* proptrækker.
corky ['kɔ:ki] *adj* korkagtig; livlig.
cormorant ['kɔ:mərnt] *s* *(zo)* ålekrage, skarv.
corn [kɔ:n] *s* korn; *(am)* majs; *(med)* ligtorn; ~ *on the cob* majskolber.
cornea ['kɔ:niə] *s* (øjets) hornhinde.
corned [kɔ:nd] *adj* saltet, konserveret; ~ **beef** *s* sprængt oksekød (på dåse).
corner ['kɔ:nə*] *s* hjørne; krog; *(sport)* hjørnespark // *v* trænge op i en krog; danne hjørne; køre om hjørner; *(auto* etc) tage et sving; *cut ~s* skyde genvej; ~ **shop** *s* nærbutik; døgnkiosk.
cornet ['kɔ:nit] *s* isvaffel; *(mus)* kornet.
cornflour ['kɔ:nflauə*] *s* majsmel.
cornflower ['kɔ:nflauə*] *s* kornblomst.
cornice ['kɔ:nis] *s* gesims.
Cornish ['kɔ:niʃ] *adj* fra Cornwall.
cornucopia [kɔ:nju'kəupiə] *s* overflødighedshorn.
corny ['kɔ:ni] *adj* (F) banal; plat.
coronary ['kɔrənəri] *s* *(med)* blodprop i hjertets kranspulsåre.
coronation [kɔrə'neiʃən] *s* kroning.
coroner ['kɔrənə*] *s* ligsynsmand; **~'s inquest** *s* ligsyn.
corporal ['kɔ:pərl] *s* korporal // *adj:* ~ *punishment* korporlig straf.
corporate ['kɔ:pərit] *adj* fælles; samlet.
corporation [kɔ:pə'reiʃən] *s* korporation; *(am)* aktieselskab; *(brit)* statsligt selskab; (i by) sv.t. magistrat; ~ **tax** *s* selskabsskat.
corporeal [kɔ:'pɔ:riəl] *adj* håndgribelig, legemlig.
corps [kɔ:*] *s* *(pl:* ~ [kɔ:z]) korps.
corpse [kɔ:ps] *s* lig.
correct [kə'rɛkt] *v* rette, korrigere; bøde på; irettesætte; *I stand ~ed* jeg må indrømme at jeg tog fejl // *adj* korrekt, rigtig; **~ing fluid** *s* rettelak, "stræberblæk".
correction [kə'rɛkʃən] *s* rettelse; *he's a spy - correction, agent* han er spion - nej, undskyld, agent.
correlate ['kɔrileit] *v* hænge sammen *(with* med); koordinere.
correspond [kɔri'spɔnd] *v* korrespondere; ~ *with (,to)* svare til; modsvare.
correspondence [kɔri'spɔndəns] *s* korrespondance; overensstemmelse.
correspondent [kɔri'spɔndənt] *s* modstykke; korrespondent // *adj* tilsvarende.
corridor ['kɔridɔ:*] *s* gang, korridor.
corroborate [kə'rɔbəreit] *v* bekræfte; styrke.
corrode [kə'rəud] *v* ætse; ruste; tæres.
corrosion [kə'rəuʒən] *s* tæring, korrosion.
corrugated ['kɔrəgeitid] *adj* bølget; rynket; ~ *cardboard* bølgepap; ~ *iron* bølgeblik.

corrupt [kə'rʌpt] *v* fordærve; korrumpere // *adj* korrupt; rådden; bestikkelig.
corruption [kə'rʌpʃən] *s* korruption.
cosignatory [ˌkəu'signətəri] *s* medunderskriver.
cosiness ['kəuzinis] *s* hygge.
cosmetic [kəs'mɛtik] *s* kosmetisk middel // *adj* kosmetisk; **~s** *spl* kosmetik, sminke.
cosmic ['kɔzmik] *adj* kosmisk.
cosset ['kɔsit] *v* forkæle.
cost [kɔst] *s* pris; omkostning; udgift; *at all ~s* for enhver pris; *at the ~ of* på bekostning af; *free of ~* uden beregning, gratis // *v (cost, cost)* koste; *it will ~ you dear* det bliver en dyr historie for dig; *it ~s the earth* det koster det hvide ud af øjnene.
co-star ['kəusta:*] *s (film, teat)* medspiller // *v* være medspiller.
costly ['kɔstli] *adj* dyr, bekostelig.
cost of living ['kɔst-] *s* leveomkostninger; **cost price** *s* fremstillingspris.
costume ['kɔstju:m] *s* dragt, kostume; spadseredragt; badedragt; **~ jewellery** *s* bijouteri.
cosy ['kəuzi] *s* tevarmer // *adj* hyggelig, rar; lun.
cot [kɔt] *s* barneseng; **~ death** *s* vuggedød.
cottage ['kɔtidʒ] *s* (lille) hus; *(brit)* mindre, ofte gammelt hus på landet, sv.t. husmandssted; hytte; sommerhus; **~ cheese** *s* hytteost; **~ hospital** *s* mindre sygehus på landet; **~ industry** *s* husflid; **~ pie** *s* pie med hakkekød og kartoffelmoslåg.
cotton [kɔtn] *s* bomuld, bomuldstråd // *v: he ~ed on to the fact that...* det gik op for ham at...; **~ wool** *s* vat.
couch [kautʃ] *s* divan; sofa.
cough [kʌf] *s* hoste // *v* hoste; *~ up with* (F) hoste op med, punge ud med; **~ drop** *s* hostepastil.
could [kud] *præt* af *can;* **couldn't** [kudnt] d.s.s. *could not.*
council [kaunsl] *s* råd; *city ~, town ~* byråd; *the British Council* den britiske ambassades kulturafdeling; **~ estate** *s* sv.t. socialt boligbyggeri.
councillor ['kaunsələ*] *s* (by)rådsmedlem.
counsel [kaunsl] *s* råd; rådslagning; juridisk rådgiver; *(pl: counsel)* advokat; *take ~* rådslå.
counsellor ['kaunsələ*] *s* rådgiver.
count [kaunt] *s* tælling; tal; slutsum; (ikke *brit)* greve; fyrste; *keep ~ of* holde tal på; *lose ~ of* ikke kunne holde tal på; *be out for the ~* (i boksning) være ude på tælling // *v* tælle; medregne; regne for; betyde ngt, gælde; *that does not ~* det gælder ikke; *~ on* regne med; stole på; *~ me out* I skal ikke regne med mig; *~ up* tælle op; regne sammen; **~down** *s* nedtælling.
countenance ['kauntinəns] *s* ansigt(sudtryk); fatning; billigelse // *v* støtte; tolerere.
counter ['kauntə*] *s* tæller; disk, skranke // *v* imødegå; modsætte sig; indvende // *adv: ~ to* stik imod (fx *orders* ordre); **~act** *v* modvirke; **~-attack** *s* modangreb // *v* foretage modangreb; **~balance** *v* danne modvægt imod; opveje; *~balance overtime* afspadsere; **~-clockwise** *adv* mod uret, venstre om; **~-espionage** *s* kontraspionage.
counterfeit ['kauntəfit] *s* efterligning; forfalskning // *v* forfalske // *adj* falsk; forloren.
counter... ['kauntə-] sms: **~foil** *s* (i checkhæfte) talon; (på girokort etc) kupon; **~mand** *v* tilbagekalde; **~-measure** *s* modforholdsregel; **~pane** *s* sengetæppe; **~part** *s* sidestykke; modstykke; **~sign** *v* medunderskrive, kontrasignere; **~stroke** *s* modtræk.
countess ['kauntis] *s (brit)* en *earl's* hustru; (ikke *brit)* grevinde; fyrstinde.
countless ['kauntlis] *adj* utallig.
country ['kʌntri] *s* land; område; egn; *in the ~* i landet; på landet; *go into the ~* tage på landet; *go to the ~ (parl)* udskrive valg; **~ dancing** *s* folkedans; **~ house** *s* herregård;

~man *s* landsmand; landbo; **~ seat** *s* landsted; **~side** *s* egn; landskab; *in the ~side* ude på landet.

county ['kaunti] *s (hist)* grevskab; *(adm)* sv.t. amt; **~ council** *s* sv.t. amtsråd; **~ town** *s* sv.t. provinshovedstad.

coup [ku:] *s (pl: ~s* [ku:z]) kup; **~ d'état** ['ku:dei'ta:] *s* statskup.

couple [kʌpl] *s* par; *a ~ of* et par, nogle // *v* koble sammen; kobles; parre(s); gifte sig; parre sig; **~dom** *s* tosomhed, parforhold.

courage ['kʌridʒ] *s* mod; *take ~* fatte mod.

courageous [kə'reidʒəs] *adj* modig.

courier ['kuriə*] *s* kurér; rejsefører.

course [kɔ:s] *s* løb; rute; kurs; forløb; kursus; *(gastr)* ret; (golf)bane; *first ~* forret; *main ~* hovedret; *in due ~* til sin tid; *of ~* naturligvis, selvfølgelig; **~ of action** *s* handlemåde; fremgangsmåde; **~ of life** *s* levnedsløb; livsførelse.

court [kɔ:t] *s (jur)* ret, domhus; retsmøde; *(sport)* bane; *(hist)* slot, hof; gård; *in ~* i retten; *settle a matter out of ~* afgøre en sag i mindelighed; *take to ~* bringe for retten // *v* gøre kur til; tragte efter.

courteous ['kə:tiəs] *adj* høflig; artig.

courtesy ['kə:təsi] *s* høflighed; *~ of the duke* med hertugens tilladelse, takket være hertugen.

courtier ['kɔ:tiə*] *s* hofmand; hofdame.

court-martial [kɔ:t'ma:ʃəl] *s (pl: courts-martial)* krigsret // *v* stille for en krigsret.

courtroom ['kɔ:trum] *s* retslokale.

courtship ['kɔ:tʃip] *s* forlovelsestid; bejlen.

courtyard ['kɔ:tja:d] *s* gård; gårdsplads.

cousin [kʌzn] *s* fætter; kusine.

cove [kəuv] *s* bugt; vig.

cover ['kʌvə*] *s* ly; skjul; dækning; betræk; tæppe; (bog)omslag; *take ~* søge ly; gå i dækning; *under ~ of* i ly af; *under separate ~* særskilt // *v* dække (til); betrække; (om afstand) tilbagelægge; *~ up* dække til; *~ up for* dække over.

coverage ['kʌvəridʒ] *s* dækning; reportage.

cover charge ['kʌvə,tʃa:dʒ] *s* (i restaurant etc) kuvertafgift.

covering ['kʌvəriŋ] *s* dække; dækning; omslag; **~ letter** *s* følgeskrivelse.

covert ['kɔvət] *adj* skjult, fordækt.

covet ['kʌvit] *v* tragte efter; begære.

cow [kau] *s* ko; (om fx giraf, elefant) hun // *v* underkue, true.

coward ['kauəd] *s* kujon.

cowardice ['kauədis] *s* fejhed.

cowardly ['kauədli] *adj* fej.

cower ['kauə*] *v* krybe sammen.

cowl [kaul] *s* munkehætte; røghætte.

cowlick ['kaulik] *s* hvirvel (i håret).

cowpat ['kaupæt] *s* kokasse;

cowshed ['kauʃɛd] *s* kostald.

cowslip ['kauslip] *s (bot)* kodriver.

coxswain ['kɔksn] *s (mar,* på mindre skib) rorgænger, kaptajn, skipper; (i kaproningsbåd) styrmand.

coy [kɔi] *adj* bly; koket.

crab [kræb] *s* krabbe; **~ apple** *s (bot)* vildæble **~bed** *adj* (om skrift) gnidret; **~by** *adj* gnaven.

crack [kræk] *s* revne, sprække; knald, brag; (F) forsøg; vittighed; *at the ~ of dawn* ved daggry, i den årle morgenstund; *have a ~ at it* forsøge sig // *v* revne; knække; gå i stykker; knalde, brage; *~ jokes* rive vittigheder af sig; *~ up* bryde sammen; smadre; *he is ~ing up* det rabler for ham // *adj* (F) førsteklasses; *he's a ~ shot* han er en mesterskytte; **~down** *s* hårdt slag.

cracker ['krækə*] *s* kineser; knallert; usødet kiks; *be ~s* være skør.

cracking ['krækiŋ] *adj: get ~* (F) få fart på.

crackle [krækl] *s* knitren; krakelering // *v* knitre; sprutte; krakelere.

crackling ['krækliŋ] *s* knitren, knasen; sprød flæskesvær.

crackpot ['krækpɔt] *s* skør kule.

cradle [kreidl] *s* vugge // *v* vugge.

craft [kra:ft] *s* (kunst)håndværk; dygtighed; *(pl: craft)* fartøj, båd.

craftsman ['kra:ftsmən] *s* (kunst)-håndværker.

crafty ['kra:fti] *adj* udspekuleret, snu, listig.

crag [kræg] *s* klippefremspring; klippeskrænt; **~gy** *adj* forreven; klippefuld.

cram [kræm] *v* proppe; terpe; ~ *sth with...* stoppe ngt fuldt af...; proppe ngt med...; ~ *sth into the bag* stuve ngt ned i tasken; **~ course** *s* intensivkursus; **~ming** *s* eksamensterperi.

cramp [kræmp] *s* krampe; *(tekn)* skruetvinge // *v* snære; hindre; genere; **~ed** *adj* trang; krampagtig.

cranberry ['krænbəri] *s* tranebær.

crane [krein] *s* trane // *v* strække (fx *one's neck* hals).

crank [kræŋk] *s (tekn)* krumtap; håndsving; (på cykel) krank; (om person) sær snegl; **~shaft** *s (tekn)* krumtapaksel.

cranky ['kræŋki] *adj* mærkelig, sær.

cranny ['kræni] *s* klippespalte, *nooks and crannies* krinkelkroge.

crap [kræp] *s* (F) lort, møg; **~py** *adj* møg-, lorte-.

crash [kræʃ] *s* brag; skrald; *(auto* etc) sammenstød; (med motorcykel etc) styrt; krak // *v* brage; smadre; støde sammen; *(fly)* styrte ned; krakke; ~ *a party* komme uindbudt til en fest; ~ *into* brase ind i; **~ barrier** *s* autoværn; **~ course** *s* lynkursus; **~ helmet** *s* styrthjelm; **~ landing** *s* katastrofelanding.

crass [kræs] *adj* kras, hård, rå.

crate [kreit] *s* pakkasse, (om bil) smadrekasse.

crater ['kreitə*] *s* krater.

crave [kreiv] *v:* ~ *(for)* tørste efter; trænge stærkt til; **craving** *s* begær, stærk trang.

crawl [krɔ:l] *v* kravle, krybe; snegle sig; køre langsomt; crawle; *be ~ing with* vrimle med; *it makes my skin* ~ det giver mig myrekryb.

crayfish ['kreifiʃ] *s* krebs.

crayon ['kreiən] *s* farveblyant; oliekridt; kridttegning.

craze [kreiz] *s* dille, mani; sidste skrig.

crazy ['kreizi] *adj* skør, vild; *be crazy about* være helt fjollet med; *it drives me crazy* det driver mig til vanvid.

creak [kri:k] *v* knage, knirke.

cream [kri:m] *s* fløde; creme; flødefarve; *whipped* ~ flødeskum; *the ~ of sth* det bedste (,blomsten) af ngt // *v* mose; **~ cake, ~ bun** *s* (om kage) flødebolle; **~ cheese** *s* flødeost; fuldfed ost; **creamy** *adj* flødeagtig; cremefarvet.

crease [kri:s] *s* pressefold; rynke // *v* presse (tøj); fure; rynke, krølle.

create [kri:'eit] *v* skabe.

creation [kri:'eiʃən] *s* skabelse; kreation.

creative [kri:'eitiv] *adj* kreativ; skaber-; opfindsom.

creator [kri:'eitə*] *s* skaber.

creature ['kri:tʃə*] *s* skabning; (levende) væsen.

crèche [krɛʃ] *s* vuggestue.

credentials [kri'dɛnʃəlz] *spl* curriculum vitae; (ambassadørs) akkreditiver.

credibility [krɛdi'biliti] *s* troværdighed.

credible ['krɛdibl] *adj* trolig; troværdig.

credit ['krɛdit] *s* tiltro; anerkendelse; ære; kredit(konto); *give ~ to* stole på; *to one's* ~ på ens konto; *take the ~ for* tage æren for; *it does you* ~ det tjener dig til ære // *v* tro (på); give æren *(with* for); kreditere; **~able** *adj* hæderlig, god; **~ card** *s* købekort; **~ ceiling** *s* kreditloft; **~s** *spl (film)* rulletekster.

credulity [kri'dju:liti] *s* godtroenhed.

creed [kri:d] *s* tro, trosretning; *the Creed* trosbekendelsen.

creek [kri:k] *s* bugt, vig; *up the* ~ (F) skør i bolden; *be up the* ~ (også) være på spanden.

creep [kri:p] *s* kryben; *(fig)* ækelt kryb; *it gives me the ~s* det giver mig myrekryb // *v (crept, crept* [krɛpt]) krybe; snige sig; ~ *up on sby* snige sig ind på en.

creeper ['kri:pə*] *s* slyngplante; **~ lane** *s* krybespor; **~s** *spl* kravledragt; listesko.

creepy ['kri:pi] *adj* uhyggelig.

cremate [kri'meit] *v* brænde, kremere.

cremation [kri'meiʃən] *s* ligbrænding, kremering.
crêpe [kreip] *s* crepe; ~ **rubber** *s* rågummi.
crept [krɛpt] *præt* og *pp* af *creep.*
crescent [krɛsnt] *s* halvmåne; halvrund plads (,gade); *(gastr)* horn.
cress [krɛs] *s* karse.
crest [krɛst] *s* (om hane etc) kam; (bjerg)top; (om hjelm) fjerbusk; våbenmærke; (om bølge) skumtop.
crestfallen ['krɛstfɔ:lən] *adj* modfalden.
Crete [kri:t] *s* Kreta.
crevasse [kri'væs] *s* gletscherspalte.
crevice ['krɛvis] *s* sprække; klippespalte.
crew [kru:] *s* besætning, mandskab; ~ **cut** *s* karsehår // *adj* karseklippet; ~**-neck** *s* rund halsudskæring.
crib [krib] *s* krybbe; (i stald) bås; kravleseng // *v* plagiere; skrive af efter hinanden; ~ **death** *s (med)* vuggedød.
crick [krik] *s: a ~ in the neck* et hold i nakken // *v: ~ one's neck* få hold i nakken.
cricket ['krikit] *s (zo)* fårekylling; *(sport)* cricket; *that is not ~!* (F) det er ikke fair! ~**er** *s* cricketspiller.
crime [kraim] *s* forbrydelse; kriminalitet.
criminal ['kriminl] *s* forbryder, kriminel // *adj* kriminel; strafbar; kriminal-; *the Criminal Investigation Department (CID)* sv.t. kriminalpolitiet.
crimp [krimp] *v* kruse, kreppe.
crimson ['krimsən] *adj* højrød; blodrød.
cringe [krindʒ] *v* krybe sammen; krympe sig; *~ to* krybe for.
crinkle [krinkl] *s* rynke // *v* krølle.
cripple [kripl] *s* krøbling // *v* gøre til krøbling; lamme; lemlæste; ~**d** *adj* invalid.
crisis ['kraisis] *s (pl: crises* ['kraisi:z]) krise; kritisk punkt.
crisp [krisp] *adj* sprød; (om frostluft) frisk; *(fig)* klar; skarp; livlig; ~**s** *spl* franske kartofler; ~**y** *adj* sprød.
criss-cross ['kriskrɔs] *adj* på kryds og tværs; i siksak.
criterion [krai'tiəriən] *s (pl: criteria* [-'tiəriə]) kriterium, rettesnor.
critic ['kritik] *s* kritiker, anmelder; ~**al** *adj* kritisk; afgørende.
criticism ['kritisizm] *s* kritik.
criticize ['kritisaiz] *v* kritisere.
croak [krəuk] *v* (om frø) kvække; (om fugl) skrige hæst.
crochet ['krəuʃei] *s* hækling; hæklemaske; *double ~* fastmaske // *v* hækle; ~ **hook** *s* hæklenål.
crockery ['krɔkəri] *s* service; porcelæn.
croft [krɔft] *s* husmandssted; ~**er** *s* husmand.
crony ['krəuni] *s* (F) kammerat; god gammel ven.
crook [kruk] *s* skurk // *v* bøje, krumme; ~**ed** ['krukid] *adj* kroget; krum; skæv; uærlig.
croon [kru:n] *v* nynne; ~**er** *s* refrænsanger.
crop [krɔp] *s* afgrøde, høst; hold; (om fugle) kro // *v* dyrke; høste; *~ up* dukke op; ~ **failure** *s* fejlslagen høst, misvækst.
cropped [krɔpd] *adj* tætklippet.
cropper ['krɔpə*] *s: come a ~* komme galt af sted.
croquet ['krəukei] *s* kroketspil.
cross [krɔs] *s* kors; kryds; krydsning // *v* korse; krydse; rejse (,gå, køre etc) over; *~ off* krydse af; *~ out* overstrege; stryge; *it ~sed my mind that* den tanke strejfede mig at; *~ my heart (and hope to die)!* på æresord! // *adj* sur, tvær; kryds-; tvær-; ~**bar** *s* tværstang; (på fodboldmål) overligger; ~**breed** *s* krydsning, hybrid; ~ **country (race)** *s* terrænløb; ~ **country skiing** *s* langrend; ~**-examination** *s* krydsforhør; ~**-examine** *v* krydsforhøre; ~**-eyed** *adj* skeløjet; ~**fire** *s* krydsild; ~**ing** *s* overfart; overgang; vejkryds; (jernbane)overskæring; fodgængerovergang; ~**-reference** *s* krydshenvisning; ~**roads** *spl* korsvej, vejkryds; ~ **section** *s* tværsnit; ~**wind** *s* sidevind; ~**wise** *adv* over kors; på tværs; ~**word (puzzle)** *s* krydsord, krydsogtværs.

crotch [krɔtʃ] *s* skridt.
crotchet ['krɔtʃit] *s (mus)* fjerdedelsnode.
crouch [krautʃ] *v* krybe sammen; stå på spring.
crow [krəu] *s* krage; hanegal // *v* (om hane) gale; *(fig)* triumfere, juble.
crowbar ['krəuba:*] *s* løftestang; brækjern.
crowd [kraud] *s* (menneske)mængde; opløb; (F) klike, slæng; sværm, mylder // *v* trænges; stimle sammen; myldre; *don't ~ me!* (F) lad være med at presse mig! **~ed** *adj* overfyldt, overlæsset; *~ed with* stuvende fuld af.
crown [kraun] *s* krone; (bjerg)top; (hatte)puld; *(anat)* isse; *the Crown* kronen, staten // *v* krone; fuldende; sætte krone på; *to ~ it all* som kronen på værket.
Crown court ['kraun kɔ:t] *s (jur)* sv.t. overret.
crown jewels ['kraun 'dʒu:əlz] *spl* kronjuveler.
crown prince ['kraun prins] *s* kronprins.
crow's feet ['krəusfi:t] *spl* smilerynker.
crucial ['kru:ʃəl] *adj* afgørende; vanskelig.
crucifixion [kru:si'fikʃən] *s* korsfæstelse.
crucify ['kru:sifai] *v* korsfæste, slå ihjel; *he'll ~ us!* (F) han flår os levende!
crude [kru:d] *adj* rå; grov; umoden; ~ **(oil)** *s* råolie.
cruel ['kru:əl] *adj* grufuld; grusom; **~ty** *s* grusomhed.
cruet ['kru:it] *s* platmenage.
cruise [kru:z] *s* krydstogt; sørejse; langfart // *v* være på krydstogt; køre (,flyve) i passende fart; ~ **missile** *s* krydsermissil; **cruising speed** *s* marchhastighed.
crumb [krʌm] *s* (brød)krumme; rasp; smuld.
crumble [krʌmbl] *v* smuldre; forvitre; **crumbly** *adj* (let)smuldrende.
crumpet ['krʌmpit] *s* slags tekage; (F) laber dulle, godt skår.
crumple [krʌmpl] *v* krølle(s) sammen.
crunch [krʌntʃ] *s* knasen; kritisk øjeblik; afgørelsens time // *v* knase; knuse; mase; **~y** *adj* knasende, sprød.
crusade [kru:'seid] *s* korstog; kampagne; **~r** *s* korsfarer; *(fig)* forkæmper.
crush [krʌʃ] *s* trængsel; *have a ~ on sby* være brændt varm på en; *lemon ~* presset citron, citronsaft // *v* knuse; mase (sig); krølle; ~ **barrier** *s* (ved fodboldkamp etc) gitter om tilskuerpladserne **~ing** *adj* knusende; knugende.
crust [krʌst] *s* skorpe; **~y** *adj* sprød; knotten.
crutch [krʌtʃ] *s* krykke; støtte; *(mar)* åregaffel.
crux [krʌks] *s* vanskeligt punkt.
cry [krai] *s* råb, skrig, brøl; tudetur; *it's a far ~ from what we expected* det er ngt helt andet end det vi forventede // *v* råbe, skrige; udbryde; græde, tude; *~ down* nedgøre, rakke ned på; *~ off* melde afbud til; *~ out for* råbe på; ~ **baby** *s* tudesøren; **~ing** *adj (fig)* himmelråbende; *a ~ing shame* synd og skam.
crystal [kristl] *s* krystal; prisme; **~-clear** *adj* krystalklar; soleklar.
crystallize ['kristəlaiz] *v* krystallisere (sig); kandisere.
cub [kʌb] *s* unge; hvalp; *(fig)* grønskolling; (om spejder) ulveunge.
cube [kju:b] *s* terning; kubus // *v (mat)* opløfte til tredje potens; ~ **root** *s* kubikrod; **cubic** *adj* kubisk; kubik-.
cubicle ['kju:bikl] *s* (sove)kabine; lille aflukke.
cuckold ['kʌkəuld] *s* hanrej // *v* gøre til hanrej, bedrage.
cuckoo ['kuku:] *s* gøg; *go ~* få pip; ~ **clock** *s* kukkeur.
cucumber ['kju:kʌmbə*] *s* agurk; *cool as a ~* kold og rolig, med is i maven.
cud [kʌd] *s: chew the ~* tygge drøv (også *fig*).
cuddle [kʌdl] *v* omfavne, "knuse"; **cuddly** *adj* kælen; nuttet.

cudgel ['kʌdʒəl] *s* knippel.
cue [kju:] *s* billardkø; signal; *(teat)* stikord; ~ **card** *s* tv-oplæsers manuskript.
cuff [kʌf] *s* manchet; ærmeopslag, ærmelinning; håndjern; *off the* ~ på stående fod; ud af ærmet // *v* slå, daske; lægge i håndjern; ~**link** *s* manchetknap.
cuisine [kwi'zi:n] *s* madlavning, kogekunst.
cul-de-sac ['kʌldəsæk] *s* blindgade, lukket vej.
culinary ['kʌlinəri] *adj* kulinarisk, mad-.
cul [kʌl] *v* udvælge
culminate ['kʌlmineit] *v* kulminere; **culmination** [-'neiʃən] *s* kulmination.
culprit ['kʌlprit] *s* "synder", "forbryder".
cult [kʌlt] *s* kult, sekt.
cultivate ['kʌltiveit] *v* dyrke, kultivere; **cultivation** [-'veiʃən] *s* dyrkning; kultivering; afgrøde.
cultural ['kʌltʃərəl] *adj* kulturel, kultur-.
culture ['kʌltʃə*] *s* kultur; dannelse; dyrkning; ~**d** *adj* kultiveret, dannet.
cumbersome ['kʌmbəsəm] *adj* besværlig; uhåndterlig.
cumin ['kʌmin] *s* kommen.
cunning ['kʌniŋ] *s* list, snilde // *adj* listig, snu.
cunt [kʌnt] *s* (V!) kusse.
cup [kʌp] *s* kop; pokal; skål.
cupboard ['kʌbəd] *s* skab.
Cup Final ['kʌpfainəl] *s* (sport) pokalfinale
Cupid ['kju:pid] *s* (gud) Amor; amorin.
cuppa ['kʌpə] *s* (F) kop te.
cup-tie ['kʌptai] *s (sport)* pokalkamp.
curable ['kjuərəbl] *adj* helbredelig.
curate ['kju:rit] *s* (hjælpe)præst.
curator [kju'reitə*] *s* konservator.
curb [kə:b] *s* tømme, tøjle; *(am)* kantsten // *v* tøjle, styre, tæmme.
curdle [kə:dl] *v* stivne, koagulere; (om mælk) skille; *it ~d my blood* blodet stivnede i mine årer.
curds [kə:ds] *spl* kvark, skyr.
cure [kjuə*] *s* helbredelse; (læge)middel; kur // *v* helbrede; kurere; *(gastr)* konservere (,salte, tørre etc); ~-**all** *s* universalmiddel.
curfew ['kə:fju:] *s* udgangsforbud.
curio ['kjuəriəu] *s* kuriositet, souvenir.
curiosity [kjuəri'ɔsiti] *s* nysgerrighed; mærkværdighed.
curious ['kjuəriəs] *adj* nysgerrig; mærkelig.
curl [kə:l] *s* krølle // *v* krølle, kruse; ~ *up* rulle sig sammen; ~**er** *s* curler; *(sport)* curlingspiller; ~**ing tongs** krøllejern; ~**y** *adj* krøllet, kruset.
currant ['kʌrənt] *s* rosin; *red* ~ ribs; *black* ~ solbær.
current ['kʌrənt] *s* (om vand, *elek* etc) strøm; strømning // *adj* gangbar, almindeligt udbredt; aktuel; herskende; løbende; ~ **account** *s* løbende konto; ~ **affairs** *spl (radio, tv)* sv.t. Aktuelt; ~**ly** *adv* for tiden.
currency ['kʌrənsi] *s* valuta; omløb, cirkulation; *foreign* ~ fremmed valuta.
curry ['kʌri] *s* karry; *chicken* ~ høns i karry // *v: ~ favour with* lefle for, indynde sig hos; ~ **powder** *s* karry.
curse [kə:s] *s* forbandelse, ed; (S, *gl)* menses // *v* forbande; bande, skælde ud.
cursory ['kə:səri] *adj* overfladisk, flygtig.
curt [kə:t] *adj* studs, kort for hovedet.
curtail [kə'teil] *v* nedskære; indskrænke.
curtain ['kə:tn] *s* gardin; forhæng; slør; *(teat)* tæppe; ~ **call** *s (teat)* fremkaldelse.
curtsy ['kə:tsi] *s* nejen // *v* neje.
curve [kə:v] *s* kurve; bue; (vej)sving // *v* krumme (sig); svinge (i en bue).
cushion ['kuʃən] *s* pude, hynde // *v* postre; afbøde; danne stødpude.
cushy ['kuʃi] *adj: ~ job* (F) en fed tjans, en loppetjans.
custard ['kʌstəd] *s* vanillecreme; cremebudding.
custodian [kʌs'təudiən] *s* vogter; kustode.

custody ['kʌstədi] *s* varetægt, forvaring; forældremyndighed.
custom ['kʌstəm] *s* skik, sædvane; (om kunder) søgning.
customary ['kʌstəməri] *adj* sædvanlig, almindelig.
custom-built ['kʌstəmbilt] *adj* lavet på bestilling.
customer ['kʌstəmə*] *s* kunde; *a cool ~* (F) en hård banan.
custom-made ['kʌstəmmeid] *adj* lavet på bestilling; (om tøj) syet efter mål.
customs ['kʌstəmz] *spl* told(væsen); **~ duty** *s* toldafgift; **~ officer** *s* toldfunktionær, tolder.
cut [kʌt] *s* snit; hug; skår; udsnit; skive (fx kød, brød); (om plade) skæring; *power ~* strømafbrydelse // *v (cut, cut)* skære; klippe; hugge; nedskære; *~ teeth* (om baby) få tænder; *~ away* skære væk; *~ back* skære ned (på); *~ down (on)* skære ned (på); *~ sby down to size* sætte en på plads; *~ in* afbryde, bryde ind; *~ off* afskære; afbryde; *~ sby off with sth* spise en af med ngt; *~ out* skære (,klippe) ud; udelade; gå i stå; *~ it out!* hold nu op! *~ short* afbryde, gøre en ende på; *~ up* skære ud (,i stykker); dissekere; **~-and-dried** *adj* (om meninger etc) færdigsyet, "fodformet"; **~back** *s* nedskæring.
cute [kju:t] *adj* nuttet, sød; fiffig, snild.
cut glass ['kʌt,gla:s] *s* krystal.
cuticle ['kju:tikl] *s* neglebånd.
cutlery ['kʌtləri] *s* (spise)bestik; knivfabrik.
cutlet ['kʌtlit] *s* kotelet.
cutout *s* påklædningsdukke; *(elek)* HFI-relæ.
cut-price ['kʌtprais] *s* nedsat pris.
cutter ['kʌtə*] *s* skærer; tang; kutter.
cut-throat ['kʌtθrəut] *s* (leje)morder; barberkniv // *adj* hensynsløs, skrap.
cutting ['kʌtiŋ] *s* udklip; *(jernb* etc) gennemskæring // *adj* skærende; skarp; sårende; **~ pliers** *spl* bidetang.
CV fork.f. *curriculum vitae.*
cwt fork.f. *hundredweight.*
cyanide ['saiənaid] *s (kem)* cyanid; *potassium ~* cyankalium.
cyclamen ['sikləmən] *s (bot)* alpeviol.
cycle [saikl] *s* cyklus, kredsløb; cykel // *v* cykle.
cygnet ['signit] *s* svaneunge.
cylinder ['silində*] *s* cylinder, valse, tromle; **~ head** *s (auto)* (cylinder)topstykke; **~ head gasket** *s (auto)* toppakning.
cymbal [simbl] *s (mus)* bækken.
cynic ['sinik] *s* kyniker; **~al** *adj* kynisk.
cynicism ['sinisizəm] *s* kynisme.
cypress ['saipris] *s* cypres(træ).
Cypriot ['sipriət] *s* cypriot // *adj* cypriotisk.
Cyprus ['saiprəs] *s* Cypern.
cyst [sist] *s (med)* cyste.
cystitis [sis'taitis] *s* blærebetændelse.
Czech [tʃɛk] *s* tjekke // *adj* tjekkisk; **Czechoslovakia** ['tʃɛkəusləu'vækiə] *s* Tjekkoslovakiet.

D

D, d [di:].
dab [dæb] *s* lille klat; dråbe; *~s pl* fingeraftryk; *a ~ of paint* et strøg maling // *v* tjatte (til); duppe (fx *eyes* øjne) // *adj: be a ~ hand at sth* være ferm til ngt.
dabble [dæbl] *v: ~ in* fuske med.
dabbler ['dæblə*] *s* fusker.
dad, daddy [dæd, dædi] *s* (F) far(mand); **daddy-long-legs** *s (zo)* stankelben.
daffodil ['dæfədil] *s* påskelilje.
daft [da:ft] *adj* skør; *be ~ about* være skør med.
dagger ['dægə*] *s* daggert, dolk; *be at ~s drawn with sby* have krig på kniven med en; *look ~s at sby* sende en et dræbende blik.
daily ['deili] *s* dagblad; hushjælp (som bor hjemme) // *adj* daglig.
dainty ['deinti] *s* lækkeri // *adj* lækker, fin; raffineret.
dairy ['dɛəri] *s* mejeri // *adj* mejeri-; **~ cattle** *s* malkekvæg; **~ farm** *s* gård

med malkekvæg; ~ **products** *spl* mejeriprodukter.

dais [deiis] *s* podium.

daisy ['deizi] *s* bellis; margerit; **~-wheel** *s (edb)* skrivehjul.

dale [deil] *s* (H) dal.

dally ['dæli] *v* pjanke, fjase; smøle.

dam [dæm] *s* dæmning; dige // *v* opdæmme; *~ up* dæmme op for (også *fig*).

damage ['dæmidʒ] *s* skade; *when the damage is done* når skaden er sket; // *v* beskadige; blive beskadiget; **~s** *spl* skadeserstatning; **damaging** *adj* skadelig; *(jur)* belastende (fx *evidence* bevis).

Dame [deim] *s* titel for kvinder sv.t. *Sir* (fx *~ Judi Dench); **dame*** *s* pige, kvindemenneske.

damn [dæm] *s: I don't give a ~* (F) det rager mig en fjer; *it's not worth a ~* (F) det er ikke en skid værd // *v* forbande; fordømme // *adj* d.s.s. *damned; I should ~ well hope so!* det håber jeg fandeme! *~ (it)!* fandens!

damnation [dæm'neiʃən] *s* forbandelse // *interj* for pokker, fandens.

damned [dæmd] *adj* forbandet, fordømt; *well, I'll be ~ed if I do!* gu' vil jeg ej! *do one's damnedest to* gøre alt hvad man kan for at.

damning ['dæmiŋ] *adj* fældende (fx *evidence* bevis).

damp [dæmp] *s* fugt(ighed) // *v* (også: *~en)* fugte; stænke; dæmpe // *adj* fugtig, klam; **~-course** *s* fugtisolering.

dampen [dæmpən] *v* dæmpe, lægge en dæmper på; fugte.

damper ['dæmpə*] *s* dæmper; *put a ~ on* lægge en dæmper på.

damp-proof ['dæmpru:f] *adj* fugtbeskyttet.

dance [da:ns] *s* dans; bal // *v* danse; **~r** *s* danser; *he's a good ~r* han danser godt; **dancing** *s* dans // *adj* danse-; livlig.

D and C ['di:ən'si:] *s* (fork.f. *dilation and curettage) (med)* udskrabning.

dandelion ['dændilaiən] *s* mælkebøtte.

dandruff ['dændrʌf] *s* skæl (i håret).

dandy ['dændi] *s* laps.

Dane [dein] *s* dansker; *Great Dane* granddanois.

danger ['deindʒə*] *s* fare; *~ of fire* brandfare; *out of ~ danger* uden for fare; ~ **area** *s* farezone; ~ **money** *s* risikotillæg.

dangerous ['deindʒərəs] *adj* farlig; *~ driving* uforsvarlig kørsel.

dangle [dæŋgl] *v* dingle (med); vifte med.

Danish ['deiniʃ] *s/adj* dansk; ~ **pastry** *s* wienerbrød.

dank [dæŋk] *adj* klam.

Danube ['dænju:b] *s: the ~* Donau.

dapper ['dæpə*] *adj* væver; sirlig; smart.

dare [dɛə*] *v* turde; trodse; udfordre; *don't you ~!* du kan lige vove! *I ~ say* jeg tror nok; det kan godt være; *I ~ you to say it* sig det hvis du tør; **~devil** *s* vovehals // *adj* dumdristig.

daring ['dɛəriŋ] *s* dristighed, vovemod // *adj* dristig; vovet.

dark [da:k] *s* mørke; *be in the ~ about sth* være uvidende om ngt; *after ~* efter mørkets frembrud; *before ~* før det bliver mørkt // *adj* mørk; skummel, dyster; *keep sth ~* mørklægge ngt; **~en** *v* blive mørkere; formørke; ~ **glasses** *spl* solbriller; ~ **horse** *s (fig)* person man ikke ved ret meget om; **~ness** *s* mørke; **~room** *s (foto)* mørkekammer.

darling ['da:liŋ] *s* skat; (min) ven; *be a ~ and fetch me my slippers* vær sød at hente mine tøfler // *adj* yndig, sød; yndlings-.

darn [da:n] *v* stoppe (fx *socks* strømper); *~ it!* (F) pokkers! *I'll be ~d!* det var som pokker! **~ing needle** *s* stoppenål.

dart [da:t] *s* kastepil; sæt; figurlæg; indsnit // *v* fare af sted som en pil; sende (fx *an angry look* et vredt blik); **~board** *s* dartskive; **~s** *spl* dartspil.

dash [dæʃ] *s* fremstød; fart; kraft; tår, stænk; knivspids; tankestreg; *make a ~ for it* stikke af; *make a ~ for sth* kaste sig over ngt; styrte hen mod ngt // *v* kaste; slynge; fare, styrte; knuse; stikke af; ~ *away* styrte af sted; ~ *it all!* pokkers! **~board** *s* *(auto* etc) instrumentbræt.

dashing ['dæʃiŋ] *s* flot.

data ['deitə] *spl* data; **~ processing** *s* databehandling.

date [deit] *s* dato; tid(spunkt); stævnemøde; aftale; person man har aftalt stævnemøde med; *(bot)* daddel(palme); *out of* ~ forældet, umoderne; *to* ~ hidtil; *up to* ~ moderne, tidssvarende; ajour // *v* datere, tidsfæste; (F) gå ud med, komme sammen med; *the chapel ~s back to the 1100s* kapellet går tilbage til 1100-tallet; **~d** ['deitid] *adj* forældet; **~line** *s (geogr)* datolinje.

daub [dɔ:b] *v* oversmøre, klatte.

daughter ['dɔ:tə*] *s* datter; **~-in-law** *s* svigerdatter.

daunt [dɔ:nt] *v* tage modet fra; *nothing ~ed* ufortrødent; **~ing** *adj* afskrækkende.

dawdle [dɔ:dl] *v* smøle; slentre.

dawn [dɔ:n] *s* daggry; *(fig)* frembrud, begyndelse; *at* ~ ved daggry // *v* dages, gry; *it ~ed on me* det dæmrede (,gik op) for mig.

day [dei] *s* dag; døgn; tid; vejr; *the ~ before* dagen før; *the ~ before yesterday* i forgårs; *one of these ~s* en af dagene, en skønne dag; *the other ~* forleden dag; *every other ~* hveranden dag; *this ~ week* i dag otte dage; *by ~* om dagen; *in her ~* på hendes tid; *call it a ~* lade det være godt (for i dag); *it's a fine ~* det er dejligt vejr; *make a ~ of it* få en dag ud af det; *some ~* engang; *that'll be the ~*! (F) det vil jeg se før jeg tror det! **~break** *s* daggry; **~ care** *s* dagpleje; **~dream** *v* dagdrømme; **~light** *s* dagslys; *in broad ~light* ved højlys dag; **~ return** *s* endags(retur)billet; **~time** *s: in ~time* ved dagslys, om dagen; **~-to-~** *adj* daglig(dags).

daze [deiz] *s: in a ~* fortumlet, rundtosset // *v* gøre fortumlet; bedøve.

dazzle [dæzl] *v* blænde; **dazzling** *adj* blændende, strålende.

DC fork.f. *direct current*.

deacon ['di:kɔn] *s* hjælpepræst.

deactivate [di:'æktiveit] *v* (om bombe) afmontere.

dead [dɛd] *adj* død; vissen; følelsesløs; mat; *be shot ~* blive skudt (ihjel); *stop ~* standse brat; gå i stå; *in the ~ of winter* midt om vinteren; *I wouldn't be seen ~ in that hat* jeg ville hellere dø end at gå med den hat // *adv* død-; fuldstændig; ~ *on time* lige på klokkeslæt, præcis; ~ *slow* (på skilt) langsom kørsel; **~-beat** *adj* totalt udmattet; **~ duck** *s* klam fidus.

deaden ['dɛdn] *v* dæmpe.

dead end ['dɛd ˌɛnd] *s* blindgade (også *fig*). **dead heat** ['dɛd ˌhi:t] *s* *(sport)* dødt løb.

deadline ['dɛdlain] *s* skæringsdato, frist.

deadlock ['dɛdlɔk] *s* baglås; hårdknude.

deadly ['dɛdli] *adj* dødelig, dræbende; dødkedelig.

deadpan ['dɛdpæn] *adj* udtryksløs; tør.

deaf [dɛf] *adj* døv; *turn a ~ ear on sth* vende det døve øre til ngt; **~-aid** *s* høreapparat.

deafen ['dɛfn] *v* døve; overdøve; dæmpe; **~ning** *adj* øredøvende.

deaf-mute ['dɛfmju:t] *adj* døvstum.

deal [di:l] *s* del; forretning, handel; aftale; fyrretræ; *a big ~* en god (,fed) forretning; *big ~!* og hva' så? ikke andet? *a great ~* en hel del; *have a rotten ~* få en dårlig behandling; *that's a ~!* det er en aftale! *it's your ~* det er din tur til at give kort // *v (dealt, dealt* [dɛlt]) tildele; uddele; give (fx *cards* kort); ~ *in* handle med; ~ *with* have at gøre med; dreje sig om; ordne.

dealer ['di:lə*] *s* -handler, -forhandler; person som giver kort.

dealings ['di:liŋz] *spl* transaktioner; forbindelser.

dean [di:n] *s* (dom)provst; (universitets)dekan.

dear [diə*] *s: my ~* min skat, min ven; *take that, there's a ~* tag den, så er du sød; *she's an old ~* hun er en sød gammel dame // *adj* kær, rar, sød, elskelig; (om pris) dyr; ~ *me! oh* ~*!* du godeste! men dog! **-ly** *adv* inderligt; dyrt.

dearth [də:θ] *s* mangel (*of* på); trange kår, nød.

death [dɛθ] *s* død; dødsfald; *bored to* ~ ved at dø af kedsomhed; *be at* ~*'s door* være på gravens rand; *put to* ~ (om dyr) aflive; **-bed** *s* dødsleje; **-blow** *s* dødsstød; **~ certificate** *s* dødsattest; **~ duty** *s* arveafgift; **-ly** *adj* dødelig; døds-; **~ penalty** *s* dødsstraf; **~ rate** *s* dødelighed; **~ sentence** *s* dødstom; **~ throes** *spl* dødskvaler; **~ toll** *s* antal dødsofre; **~-trap** *s* dødsfælde; **-warrant** *s* dødsdom.

debacle [dei'ba:kəl] *s* katastrofe, fiasko.

debar [di'ba:*] *v* udelukke, formene adgang.

debark [di'ba:k] *v* gå i land; landsætte.

debase [di'beis] *v* forringe; nedværdige; fornedre.

debatable [di'beitəbl] *adj* tvivlsom, diskutabel.

debate [di'beit] *s* debat, drøftelse; *in* ~ under debat, omdiskuteret; tvivlsom; // *v* debattere, drøfte.

debilitate [di'biliteit] *v* svække.

debit ['dɛbit] *s* debet // *v* debitere.

debrief [di'bri:f] *v* udspørge, forhøre (efter endt mission).

debris ['dɛbri] *s* brokker, ruiner; efterladenskaber; affald.

debt [dɛt] *s* gæld; *be in* ~ være forgældet; *run up a debt* sætte sig i gæld; **debtor** ['dɛtə*] *s* debitor, skyldner.

decade ['dɛkeid] *s* tiår.

decadence ['dɛkədəns] *s* forfald; **decadent** *adj* dekadent.

decaffeinated [di'kæfineitid] *adj* koffeinfri.

decamp [di'kæmp] *v* bryde op; fordufte.

decanter [di'kæntə*] *s* (vin)karaffel.

decapitate [di'kæpiteit] *v* halshugge.

decathlon [di'kæθlən] *s* (*sport*) tikamp.

decay [di'kei] *s* forfald; forrådnelse; (*fys*) henfald; karies // *v* forfalde; rådne; gå i opløsning.

decease [di'si:s] *s* død; (se også *disease*); **-d** *adj* (af)død; *the* ~*d* (den) afdøde, de døde.

deceit [di'si:t] *s* bedrageri, svig; **-ful** *adj* løgnagtig; falsk.

deceive [di'si:v] *v* bedrage, narre; *if my eyes don't* ~ *me* hvis ikke jeg tager meget fejl.

decelerate [di:'sɛləreit] *v* sætte farten ned; tage farten af.

December [di'sɛmbə*] *s* december.

decency ['di:sənsi] *s* anstændighed, sømmelighed.

decent ['di:sənt] *adj* pæn, anstændig; flink; *they were very* ~ *about it* de tog det pænt.

deception [di'sɛpʃən] *s* bedrag.

deceptive [di'sɛptiv] *adj* vildledende.

decide [di'said] *v* beslutte, afgøre; ~ *on* træffe beslutning om; *that* ~*d her* det fik hende til at beslutte sig; *that's for you to* ~ det må du bestemme.

decided [di'saidid] *adj* udpræget; afgjort; **-ly** *adv* absolut, bestemt.

deciduous [di'sidjuəs] *adj* løv-.

decimal ['dɛsiməl] *adj* decimal-, titals-; *go* ~ gå over til decimalsystemet; **~ point** *s* sv.t. komma (foran decimalbrøk; NB! *brit* anvendes punktum).

decimate ['dɛsimeit] *v* decimere; (*fig*) tynde ud i.

decipher [di'saifə*] *v* tyde, dechifrere.

decision [di'siʒən] *s* beslutning, afgørelse; beslutsomhed; *make a* ~ træffe en afgørelse; *come to a* ~ tage en beslutning; **~-maker** *s* beslutningstager.

decisive [di'saisiv] *adj* beslutsom; afgørende.

deck [dɛk] *s* (skibs)dæk; spil kort // *v:* ~ *out* udsmykke; **-chair** *s* liggestol.

declaim [di'kleim] *v* deklamere; ~ *against sth* protestere mod ngt.

declamation [dɛklə'meiʃən] *s* deklamation; protesttale.

declaration [dɛklə'reiʃən] *s* erklæring; *tax* ~ selvangivelse.

declare [di'klɛə*] *v* erklære; (i tolden) deklarere; (om skat) opgive; *well, I ~!* det må jeg nok sige! *~ against (,for) en* erklære sig imod (for) en.
declension [di'klɛnʃən] *s* nedgang; *(gram)* (kasus)bøjning.
decline [di'klain] *s* nedgang, tilbagegang // *v* skråne, hælde; dale, aftage; afslå; *(gram)* (kasus)bøje.
declutch [ˌdi:'klʌtʃ] *v* koble ud (,fra).
decode [di'kəud] *v* dechifrere.
decompose [di:kəm'pəuz] *v* opløse(s); nedbryde(s).
decomposition [ˌdi:kɔmpə'ziʃən] *s* opløsning; forrådnelse.
decor ['deikɔ:*] *s* (teater)dekoration, sceneri; udsmykning; indretning.
decorate ['dɛkəreit] *v* pynte, dekorere; (om fx værelse) istandsætte.
decoration [dɛkə'reiʃən] *s* pynt, dekoration; (indvendig) istandsættelse; orden(sdekoration).
decorator ['dɛkəreitə*] *s* dekoratør; *interior ~* indretningsarkitekt.
decorous ['dɛkərəs] *adj* pæn, artig.
decorum [di'kɔ:rəm] *s* sømmelighed.
decoy ['di:kɔi] *s* lokkefugl // *v* lokke.
decrease *s* ['di:kri:s] nedgang, aftagen // *v* [di:'kri:s] aftage, formindske(s).
decree [di'kri:] *s* dekret; påbud // *v* dekretere; påbyde; **~ absolute** *s* skilsmissebevilling; **~ nisi** [-naisai] *s* sv.t. foreløbig skilsmissebevilling.
decrepit [di'krɛpit] *adj* affældig; faldefærdig.
dedicate ['dɛdikeit] *v* indvie; hellige; dedicere; **~d** *adj* hengiven; pligtopfyldende.
dedication [dɛdi'keiʃən] *s* indvielse; dedikation; engagement.
deduce [di'dju:s] *v* udlede, konkludere.
deduct [di'dʌkt] *v* trække fra.
deductible [di'dʌktibl] *adj* fradragsberettiget.
deduction [di'dʌkʃən] *s* udledning; (skatte)fradrag.
deed [di:d] *s* gerning; bedrift, dåd; dokument, skøde.
deem [di:m] *v* skønne; anse for; *he ~ed it necessary* han anså det for (,fandt det) nødvendigt.
deep [di:p] *adj/adv* dyb(t); stor; dybsindig; snu; *~ down* inderst inde; *~ in snow* begravet i sne; *~ in thought* i dybe tanker; *in ~ water (fig)* ude hvor man ikke kan bunde; *stand ten man ~* stå i ti rækker; *he's a ~ one* han er udspekuleret; *go off the ~ end (fig)* blive stiktosset; **~en** *v* uddybe; blive dybere; **~-freeze** *s* dybfryser // *v* dybfryse; **~-fry** *v* friturestege; **~ly** *adv* dybt; *~ly in love* dybt forelsket; **~ red** *adj* mørkerød; **~-rooted** *adj* dybt rodfæstet; **~-sea** *adj* dybhavs-; **~-seated** *adj* indgroet, rodfæstet; **~-set** *adj* dybtliggende (fx *eyes* øjne).
deer [diə*] *s (pl: deer)* hjort; *the ~* hjortefamilien; *red ~* kronhjort; *fallow ~* dådyr; *roe ~* rådyr.
de-escalate [di:'ɛskəleit] *v* nedtrappe.
deface [di'feis] *v* skamfere, overmale.
defamation [dɛfə'meiʃən] *s* bagvaskelse.
default [di:'fɔlt] *s* forsømmelighed; misligholdelse; udebliven; *(edb)* default (på forhånd indlagt værdi el. funktion); *in ~ of* af mangel på // *v* forsømme en pligt; udeblive (fra).
defeat [di'fi:t] *s* nederlag // *v* besejre, slå; forpurre (fx *plans* planer); forkaste (fx *a bill* et lovforslag); **~ist** *s* opgivende person.
defect *s* ['di:fɛkt] mangel, defekt // *v* [di'fɛkt] falde fra, hoppe af; *~ to the enemy* gå over til fjenden.
defective [di'fɛktiv] *adj* mangelfuld.
defector [di'fɛktə*] *s* frafalden; afhopper.
defence [di'fɛns] *s* forsvar; *in ~ of* til forsvar for; *Minister of Defence* forsvarsminister; *counsel for the ~ (jur)* forsvarer; **~less** *adj* forsvarsløs.
defend [di'fɛnd] *v* forsvare.
defendant [di'fɛndənt] *s: the ~ (jur)* den anklagede (,sagsøgte).
defender [di'fɛndə*] *s* forsvarer.
defensive [di'fɛnsiv] *adj* forsvars-, defensiv; *on the ~* i defensiven.
defer [di'fə*] *v* udskyde, udsætte; *~ to sby* bøje sig for en.

deference ['dɛfərəns] *s* agtelse, respekt; **deferential** [-'rɛnʃəl] *adj* ærbødig.
defiance [di'faiəns] *s* trods; udfordring; *in ~ of* til trods for; **defiant** *adj* trodsig; provokerende.
deficiency [di'fiʃənsi] *s* utilstrækkelighed, mangel; underskud; **~ disease** *s* mangelsygdom; **deficient** *adj* utilstrækkelig, mangelfuld.
deficit ['dɛfisit] *s* underskud, minus.
defile [di'fail] *v* forurene, tilsmudse.
define [di'fain] *v* definere; bestemme; angive; afgrænse.
definite ['dɛfinit] *adj* bestemt; klar; afgrænset; *be ~* være sikker (,kategorisk); **~ly** *adv* bestemt, afgjort.
definition [dɛfi'niʃən] *s* definition.
definitive [di'finitiv] *adj* endelig, afgørende, definitiv.
deflate [di'fleit] *v* lukke luften ud af; *(fig)* tage gassen af.
deflation [di'flɛiʃən] *s* deflation.
deflect [di'flɛkt] *v* aflede; afbøje.
deforest [di'fɔrist] *v* rydde for skov.
deform [di'fɔ:m] *v* misdanne, deformere; **~ation** [-'meiʃən] *s* misdannelse; **~ed** *adj* vanskabt.
deformity [di'fɔ:miti] *s* vanskabthed; misdannelse.
defraud [di'frɔ:d] *v* bedrage.
defrost [ˌdi:'frɔst] *v* afrime, afise (fx *the fridge* køleskabet); tø op (fx *the meat* kødet).
deft [dɛft] *adj* fingernem, behændig.
defunct [di'fʌŋkt] *adj* afdød; forsvundet, ikke-eksisterende.
defuse [di'fju:z] *v* desarmere (en bombe); *(fig)* afdramatisere.
defy [di'fai] *v* trodse; udfordre; *it defies description* det trodser enhver beskrivelse; *I ~ you to do it* gør det hvis du tør.
degenerate *v* [di'dʒɛnəreit] udarte, degenerere // *adj* [di'dʒɛnərit] degenereret.
degradation [dɛgrə'deiʃən] *s* nedværdigelse; degradering.
degrade [di'greid] *v* nedværdige; degradere; nedbryde(s); **degrading** *adj* nedværdigende.
degree [di'gri:] *s* grad; rang; (universitets)eksamen; *it is five ~s below (zero)* det er fem graders frost; *by ~s* gradvis; *to a certain ~* til en vis grad; *~ of latitude (,longitude)* bredde- (,længde-)grad.
dehydrated [di:'haidreitid] *adj* (ud)tørret, dehydreret; **~ milk** *s* tørmælk.
de-ice [ˌdi:'ais] *v* afise (fx *the windscreen* forruden).
deign [dein] *v: ~ to* nedlade sig til at.
deity ['di:iti] *s* guddom.
dejected [di'dʒɛktid] *adj* nedslået, modløs; **dejection** *s* modløshed.
dekko ['dɛkəu] *s: have a ~ at sth* (F) kigge på noget.
delay [di'lei] *s* forsinkelse; udsættelse; *without ~* straks, ufortøvet // *v* forsinke; udsætte; nøle; **~ed-action** *adj* tidsindstillet.
delegate *s* ['dɛligit] delegeret // *v* ['dɛligeit] delegere; beskikke.
delegation [dɛli'geiʃən] *s* delegation; beskikkelse.
delete [di'li:t] *v* slette, stryge.
deliberate *v* [di'libəreit] overveje; drøfte // *adj* [di'libərit] bevidst, forsætlig; **~ly** [-'libərətli] *adv* med fuldt overlæg, bevidst.
deliberation [dilibə'reiʃən] *s* overvejelse; overlæg.
delicacy ['dɛlikəsi] *s* sarthed; takt(fuldhed); lækkerbisken; *a matter of ~* en kilden sag.
delicate ['dɛlikit] *adj* sart, skrøbelig; fintfølende; kilden, penibel; delikat.
delicatessen [dɛlikə'tɛsn] *s* viktualieforretning.
delicious [di'liʃəs] *adj* dejlig, lækker.
delight [di'lait] *s* glæde, fryd // *v* glæde; *~ in* nyde, fryde sig ved; **~ed** *adj* henrykt; *I shall be ~ed to* det skal være mig en glæde (at); **~ful** *adj* dejlig; yndig; tiltalende.
delineate [di'linieit] *v* skitsere; skildre.
delinquency [di'liŋkwənsi] *s* forseelse, kriminalitet.
delinquent [di'liŋkwənt] *s* lovovertræder; *juvenile ~* ungdomskriminel // *adj* forsømmelig; kriminel.
delirious [di'liəriəs] *adj* i vildelse; ellevild.

deliver [di'livə*] *v* levere; aflevere; omdele; udbringe (fx *mail* post); befri; nedkomme, føde; ~ *a speech* holde en tale; ~ *the goods* levere varerne; ~ *on expectations* leve op til forventningerne.
delivery [di'livəri] *s* levering; uddeling; (post)ombæring; nedkomst; *take ~ of (merk)* aftage; ~ **van** *s* varevogn.
delude [di'lu:d] *v* narre, bedrage.
deluge ['dɛlju:dʒ] *s* oversvømmelse; *the Deluge* Syndfloden // *v* oversvømme.
delusion [di'lu:ʒən] *s* selvbedrag; vildfarelse; **delusive** *adj* skuffende; illusorisk.
delve [dɛlv] *v:* ~ *into* forske i, bore i; fordybe sig i.
demand [di'ma:nd] *s* krav; efterspørgsel; behov; *in* ~ efterspurgt; *on* ~ efter påkrav; når det ønskes // *v* kræve; forlange; **~ing** *adj* krævende, fordringsfuld.
demean [di'mi:n] *v:* ~ *oneself* nedværdige sig.
demeanour [di'mi:nə*] *s* optræden, opførsel.
demented [di'mɛntid] *adj* afsindig, vanvittig.
demerara [dɛmə'rɛərə] *s:* ~ *sugar* brunt rørsukker.
demi- ['dɛmi-] halv- (fx *god* gud).
demise [di'maiz] *s* (H) død, bortgang.
demist [di'mist] *v* afdugge.
demo ['dɛməu] *s* demo; demonstration.
demob [di:'mɔb] *v* hjemsende (soldater).
democracy [di'mɔkrəsi] *s* demokrati.
democrat ['dɛməkræt] *s* demokrat; **democratic** [-'krætik] *adj* demokratisk.
demoded ['di:məudid] *adj* umoderne.
demolish [di'mɔliʃ] *v* nedrive (fx *a house* et hus); sløjfe; gøre en ende på; **demolition** [-'liʃən] *s* nedrivning; ødelæggelse.
demon ['di:mən] *s* dæmon; djævel.
demonstrable ['dɛmənstrəbl] *adj* beviselig; håndgribelig.
demonstrate ['dɛmənstreit] *v* demonstrere, vise; bevise; lægge for dagen.
demonstration [dɛmən'streiʃən] *s* demonstration; forevisning; bevis.
demonstrator ['dɛmənstreitə*] *s* demonstrant.
demoralize [di'mɔrəlaiz] *v* demoralisere.
demote [di'məut] *v* degradere.
demur [di'mə:*] *v* gøre indsigelse; *without* ~ uden at gøre vrøvl.
demure [di'mjuə*] *adj* dydig, ærbar; nøgtern.
den [dɛn] *s* (dyrs) hule; rovdyrbur; hybel.
denial [di'naiəl] *s* nægtelse; afslag; dementi.
denigrate ['dɛnigreit] *v* rakke ned på.
denim ['dɛnim] *s* cowboystof, denim; **~s** *spl* cowboybukser, jeans.
denomination [dinɔmi'neiʃən] *s* benævnelse, navn; kategori; trosretning; *(økon)* pålydende; møntsort.
denominator [di'nɔmineitə*] *s* nævner; *common* ~ fællesnævner.
denote [di'nəut] *v* betegne, betyde.
denounce [di'nauns] *v* anklage; fordømme; angive, melde.
dense [dɛns] *adj* tæt, kompakt, tyk; (om person) tykhovedet.
density ['dɛnsiti] *s* tæthed; vægtfylde.
dent [dɛnt] *s* fordybning; hak; bule // *v* lave buler i; *(fig)* give et knæk.
dental ['dɛntl] *adj* tand-; ~ **floss** *s* tandtråd; ~ **nurse** *s* klinikassistent; ~ **surgeon** *s* tandlæge.
dentist ['dɛntist] *s* tandlæge.
dentistry ['dɛntistri] *s* tandlægearbejde.
dentures ['dɛntʃəz] *spl* tandprotese.
denunciation [dinənsi'eiʃən] *s* fordømmelse; angivelse; opsigelse.
deny [di'nai] *v* nægte; benægte; *there's no ~ing that* det kan ikke nægtes at.
depart [di'pa:t] *v* rejse væk; afrejse; afgå; *~from* rejse væk fra, forlade; *(fig)* fravige; *~ing trains* afgående tog; *the ~ed* de (,den) afdøde.
department [di'pa:tmənt] *s* afdeling; institut; område, felt; departement; ministerium; ~ **store** *s* stormagasin.
departure [di'pa:tʃə*] *s* afrejse, afgang; fravigelse; afvigelse.

depend [di'pɛnd] *v* være uafgjort; komme an (på); ~ *on* afhænge af; stole på, regne med; *it ~s* det kommer an på omstændighederne; **~able** *adj* pålidelig.

dependant [di'pɛndənt] *s* person som er afhængig.

dependence [di'pɛndəns] *s* afhængighed; tillid.

dependent [di'pɛndənt] *adj* afhængig; *be ~ on* afhænge af.

depict [di'pikt] *v* afbilde; (ud)male; skildre.

deplete [di'pli:t] *v* udtømme; opbruge; forringe.

deplorable [di'plɔ:rəbl] *adj* beklagelig; meget uheldig.

deplore [di'plɔ:*] *v* beklage dybt; sørge over.

deploy [di'plɔi] *v* (om soldater etc) stille (op) med, mønstre; (om missiler, tropper) opstille.

depopulation ['di:pɔpju'leiʃən] *s* affolkning.

deport [di'pɔ:t] *v* udvise, deportere; ~ *oneself* opføre sig; **~ation** [-'teiʃən] *s* deportation; **~ment** *s* optræden, væsen.

depose [di'pəuz] *v* afsætte.

deposit [di'pɔzit] *s* pant, depositum; aflejring // *v* deponere; indsætte (i bank); anbringe; aflejre; **~ account** *s* indlånskonto.

deposition [dɛpə'ziʃən] *s* afsættelse; aflejring.

depositor [di'pɔzitə*] *s* deponent; indskyder.

depot ['dɛpəu] *s* depot, magasin; bus(,fly-)terminal.

deprave [di'preiv] *v* fordærve, demoralisere.

depravity [di'præviti] *s* last; demoralisering.

deprecate ['dɛprikeit] *v* misbillige.

depreciate [di'pri:ʃieit] *v* forringe(s); nedvurdere; nedskrive.

depress [di'prɛs] *v* (ned)trykke; gøre deprimeret; **~ed** *adj* deprimeret; (om område) kriseramt, arbejdsløsheds-; **~ing** *adj* nedslående, deprimerende.

depression [di'prɛʃən] *s* depression; krise(tid); *(geol)* sænkning.

deprivation [dɛpri'veiʃən] *s* berøvelse, tab; afsavn.

deprive [di'praiv] *v: ~ sby of sth* berøve en ngt; unddrage en ngt; **deprived** *adj* fattig, underprivilegeret.

Dept fork.f. *department.*

depth [dɛpθ] *s* dybde, dyb; *in the ~s of* i hjertet af, dybt inde i; *be out of one's ~s (fig)* være ude at svømme; **~ charge** *s (mil)* dybvandsbombe.

deputize ['dɛpjutaiz] *v* være stedfortræder.

deputy ['dɛpjuti] *s* stedfortræder // *adj* vice-; **~ chairman** *s* næstformand; **~ head** *s* vicedirektør; næstkommanderende.

derail [di'reil] *v* (om tog) afspore(s); **~ment** *s* afsporing (også *fig).*

deranged [di'reindʒd] *adj* forstyrret; sindsforvirret; (om fx maskine) i uorden.

derelict ['dɛrilikt] *adj* herreløs; forladt; forsømt.

deride [di'raid] *v* håne, spotte.

derision [di'riʒən] *s* hån, spot.

derisory [di'raisəri] *adj* latterlig.

derivation [dɛri'veiʃən] *s* afledning; udledning; oprindelse; **derivative** [di'rivətiv] *s* afledning // *adj* afledet; udledt.

derive [di'raiv] *v: ~ sth from* få ngt fra; *~ from* stamme fra, komme af.

derogatory [di'rɔgətəri] *adj* nedsættende.

derrick ['dɛrik] *s* boretårn; *(mar)* lossebom.

derv [də:v] *s* diesel (til biler).

descale [di:'skeil] *v* afkalke.

descend [di'sɛnd] *v* komme (,gå, stige etc) ned; dale; *~ from* stå af, komme ned fra; nedstamme fra; *~ on* hjemsøge; *~ to* nedværdige sig til.

descendant [di'sɛndənt] *s* efterkommer.

descent [di'sɛnt] *s* nedstigning; skrånen; afstamning; *(fly)* landing.

describe [di'skraib] *v* beskrive, skildre.

description [di'skripʃən] *s* beskrivelse, skildring; signalement; slags, art; *beyond ~* ubeskrivelig; *of every ~* af alle slags.

descriptive [di'skriptiv] *adj* beskrivende; *a very ~ account* en malende beskrivelse.
desecrate ['dɛsikreit] *v* vanhellige.
desert *s* ['dɛzət] ørken; ødemark // *v* [di'zə:t] forlade; desertere.
desertification [dɛzətifi'keiʃən] *s* ørkendannelse, ørkenvækst.
desertion [di'zə:ʃən] *s* frafald; desertion.
deserts [di'zə:ts] *spl: get one's ~* få hvad man har fortjent.
deserve [di'zə:v] *v* fortjene; **~d** *adj* velfortjent, berettiget; **deserving** *adj* fortjenstfuld; værdig.
desiccate ['dɛsikeit] *v* (ud)tørre.
design [di'zain] *s* udkast, skitse; tegning; mønster; formgivning, design; konstruktion; *have ~s on sth* være ude efter ngt, have ngt i kikkerten // *v* tegne; formgive, designe; konstruere; planlægge.
designate *v* ['dɛzigneit] angive, betegne; udpege // *adj* ['dɛzignit] udpeget, designeret.
designation [dɛzig'neiʃən] *s* betegnelse, titel; udpegning.
designer [di'zainə*] *s* tegner; formgiver, designer; konstruktør; planlægger.
designing [di'zainiŋ] *adj* beregnende.
desirable [di'zaiərəbl] *adj* ønskelig; attråværdig.
desire [di'zaiə*] *s* ønske; begær; anmodning // *v* ønske, begære; anmode om; *it leaves much to be ~d* det lader meget tilbage at ønske.
desist [di'zist] *v* lade være, afstå.
desk [dɛsk] *s* skrivebord; skolebord; (i butik) skranke, kasse; **~ clerk** *s* (hotel)portier; **~ drawer** *s* skrivebordsskuffe.
desolate ['dɛsəlit] *adj* øde; ubeboelig; ulykkelig; **desolation** [-'leiʃən] *s* ødelæggelse; forladthed; fortvivlelse.
despair [dis'pɛə*] *s* fortvivlelse; desperation // *v* fortvivle; *~ of* opgive håbet om (at).
despatch [dis'pætʃ] d.s.s. *dispatch.*
desperate ['dɛspərət] *adj* fortvivlet; håbløs; desperat; **desperation** [-'reiʃən] *s* fortvivlelse; desperation.
despicable [di'spikəbl] *adj* foragtelig, ussel.
despise [di'spaiz] *v* foragte; lade hånt om; forsmå.
despite [di'spait] *præp* trods, til trods for.
despoil [di'spɔil] *v* udplyndre.
despondent [di'spɔndənt] *adj* modløs, mismodig.
dessert [di'zə:t] *s* dessert; **~ wine** *s* hedvin.
destination [dɛsti'neiʃən] *s* bestemmelsessted.
destine ['dɛstin] *v* bestemme, destinere.
destiny ['dɛstini] *s* skæbne.
destitute ['dɛstitju:t] *adj* ludfattig; subsistensløs; *~ of* blottet for.
destroy [di'strɔi] *v* ødelægge; udslette; dræbe; **~er** *s* torbedobåd, destroyer.
destruction [di'strʌkʃən] *s* ødelæggelse; undergang; destruktion.
destructive [di'strʌktiv] *adj* ødelæggende, nedbrydende.
detach [di'tætʃ] *v* tage af; løsne; løsrive; skille ud (,fra); **~able** *adj* aftagelig, udskiftelig.
detached [di'tætʃd] *adj* (om person) reserveret; upartisk; **~ house** *s* villa, parcelhus.
detachment [di'tætʃmənt] *s* adskillelse; objektivitet; *(mil)* afdeling.
detail ['di:teil] *s* detalje; *in ~* indgående, i detaljer; *in every ~* i mindste detalje // *v* fortælle udførligt om; *(mil)* detachere, beordre; **~ed** *adj* detaljeret; omstændelig.
detain [di'tein] *v* opholde, forsinke; tilbageholde, anholde.
detect [di'tɛkt] *v* opdage.
detection [di'tɛkʃən] *s* opdagelse; påvisning; *escape ~* undgå opdagelse.
detective [di'tɛktiv] *s* detektiv; kriminalbetjent.
detector [di'tɛktə*] *s* detektor.
detention [di'tɛnʃən] *s* tilbageholdelse; forvaring; anholdelse; *be in ~* (i skolen) sidde efter.
deter [di'tə:] *v* afskrække; forhindre.
detergent [di'tə:dʒənt] *s* (syntetisk) vaskemiddel; sulfo(sæbe).

deteriorate [di'tiəriəreit] *v* forringe(s); forværre(s); **deterioration** [-'reiʃən] *s* forringelse; forværrelse; svækkelse.
determination [ditə:mi'neiʃən] *s* beslutsomhed, fasthed; bestemmelse, afgørelse.
determine [di'tə:min] *v* bestemme, afgøre; beslutte; afslutte; **~d** [-'tə:mind] *adj* bestemt, beslutsom.
deterrent [di'tɛrənt] *s* afskrækkende middel; *nuclear ~* atomtrussel.
detest [di'tɛst] *v* afsky, hade; **~able** *adj* afskyelig.
detonate ['dɛtəneit] *v* bringe til eksplosion, detonere; sprænges.
detour ['di:tuə*] *s* omvej; omkørsel; afstikker.
detract [di'trækt] *v: ~ from* forringe, skade; bortlede.
detrimental [dɛtri'mɛntl] *adj* skadelig.
detritus [di'traitəs] *s* efterladenskaber, (sørgelige) rester.
deuce [dju:s] *s* (i spil) toer; (i tennis) lige; (F) pokker; *the ~ he did* han gjorde pokker.
devalue [di:'vælju:] *v* devaluere.
devastate ['dɛvəsteit] *v* hærge; ødelægge; *(fig)* sønderlemme; *be ~d* være sønderknust.
develop [di'vɛləp] *v* udvikle (sig) (*into* til); udvide; udnytte; få (fx *cancer* kræft); bebygge; *(foto)* fremkalde.
developer [di'vɛləpə*] *s (foto)* fremkalder; *(bygn)* entreprenør; byggespekulant; selvbrunende creme.
developing country [di'vɛləpiŋ 'kʌntri] *s* udviklingsland, uland.
development [di'vɛləpmənt] *s* udvikling; udbygning; udstykning; bebyggelse.
deviant ['di:viənt] *s* afviger // *adj* afvigende.
deviate ['di:vieit] *v* afvige; **deviation** [-'eiʃən] *s* afvigelse; *(mar)* afdrift.
device [di'vais] *s* indretning, anordning; plan; påhit; list; motto; *leave sby to his own ~s* lade en sejle i sin egen sø.
devil [dɛvl] *s* djævel; **~ish** *adj* djævelsk; **~-may-care** *adj* fandenivoldsk.
devious ['di:viəs] *v* lusket; *by a ~ route* ad omveje; **~ly** *adv* ad omveje.
devise [di'vaiz] *v* udtænke.
devoid [di'vɔid] *adj: ~ of* fri for, blottet for.
devolution [dɛvə'lu:ʃən] *s* overdragelse, afvikling; decentralisering; **devolve** [di'vɔlv] *v* overdrage(s).
devote [di'vəut] *v* hellige, vie; **~d** *adj* hengiven; passioneret; *be ~d to sby* holde meget af en.
devotion [di'vəuʃən] *s* hengivenhed; fromhed; iver.
devour [di'vauə*] *v* fortære, sluge.
devout [di'vaut] *adj* from, andægtig; ivrig.
dew [dju:] *s* dug; **~y** *adj* dugget, dugfrisk.
dexterity [dɛks'tɛriti] *s* fingerfærdighed, behændighed.
dexterous ['dɛkstərəs] *adj* fiks på fingrene.
diabetes [daiə'bi:tiz] *s* sukkersyge.
diabetic [daiə'bɛtik] *s* sukkersygepatient, diabetiker.
diabolic(al) [daiə'bɔlik(l)] *adj* djævelsk.
diagnose ['daiəgnəuz] *v* stille en diagnose, diagnosticere.
diagnosis ['daiəgnəusis] *s (pl: diagnoses* [-si:z]) diagnose.
dial ['daiəl] *s* skive; urskive; solur; *(tlf)* nummerskive // *v (tlf)* dreje; *~ 999 for help* drej 999 for hjælp; **~ling code** *s (tlf)* områdenummer; **~ling tone** *s (tlf)* klartone.
dialogue ['daiəlɔg] *s* samtale, dialog.
diamond ['daiəmənd] *s* diamant; rhombe; **~s** *spl* ruder; *jack of ~s* ruder knægt.
diaper ['daiəpə*] *s (am)* ble.
diaphragm ['daiəfræm] *s (anat)* mellemgulv; *(tekn)* membran; *(med)* pessar.
diarrhoea [daiə'riə] *s* diarré.
diary ['daiəri] *s* dagbog; kalender.
dice [dais] *spl* terninger // *v* rafle; *(gastr)* skære i terninger.
dicey ['daisi] *adj* (F) risikabel.
dictate *s* ['dikteit] diktat, påbud // *v* [dik'teit] diktere, fowreskrive; **dictation** [-'teiʃən] *s* diktat.
dictator [dik'teitə*] *s* diktator.

diction ['dikʃən] *s* udtryksmåde, diktion.
dictionary ['dikʃənəri] *s* ordbog; leksikon; *look sth up in a* ~ slå ngt op i en ordbog.
did [did] *præt* af *do.*
didn't [didnt] d.s.s. *did not.*
die [dai] *s (pl: dice* [dais]) terning.
die [dai] *v* dø; gå i stå; ophøre; *never say ~!* giv aldrig op! ~ *away (,down)* dø hen, stilne af; ~ *out* uddø; (om vind) løje af; **~hard** *s* reaktionær.
diet ['daiət] *s* kost, diæt // *v* holde diæt.
dietician [daiə'tiʃən] *s* ernæringsspecialist.
differ ['difə*] *v* afvige; være anderledes *(from* end); have en anden mening; *I beg to* ~ jeg har nu en anden mening (om det).
difference ['difrəns] *s* forskel; uoverensstemmelse.
different ['difrənt] *adj* forskellig; anderledes; *that's ~!* det er noget andet!
differential [difə'rɛnʃəl] *s* forskel // *adj* differential-.
differentiate [difə'rɛnʃieit] *v* adskille, skelne; gøre forskel; differentiere.
difficult ['difikʌlt] *adj* svær, vanskelig; **~y** *s* vanskelighed; besvær.
diffidence ['difidəns] *s* usikkerhed; generthed; **diffident** *adj* usikker; tilbageholdende.
diffuse *adj* [di'fju:s] spredt, diffus // *v* [di'fju:z] (ud)sprede.
dig [dig] *s* udgravning; puf; hib; (se også *digs) // v (dug, dug* [dʌg]) grave; puffe; (F) slide i det; (F) dyrke, kunne lide; ~ *at sby* stikke til en; ~ *for sth* grave efter ngt; ~ *in one's heels* stå fast; stritte imod; ~ *into sth* kaste sig over ngt; ~ *up* grave op; finde.
digest *s* ['daidʒəst] udtog, sammendrag // *v* [dai'dʒɛst] fordøje.
digestible [di'dʒɛstibl] *adj* letfordøjelig.
digestion [di'dʒɛstʃən] *s* fordøjelse.
digestive [di'dʒɛstiv] *s* fuldkornskiks // *adj* fordøjelses(fremmende).
digit ['didʒit] *s* finger (,tå); (encifret) tal, ciffer.
digital ['didʒitəl] *adj* finger-; digital.
dignified ['dignifaid] *adj* værdig; fornem.
dignify ['dignifai] *v* hædre.
dignitary ['dignitəri] *s* fornem person.
dignity ['digniti] *s* værdighed.
digress [dai'grɛs] *v* afvige; komme væk fra emnet.
digression [dai'grɛʃən] *s* afvigelse; sidespring.
digs [digz] *spl* (F) bolig, hybel.
dike [daik] *s* dige, dæmning // *v* inddige; ~ *up* klæde sig ud (i stadstøjet).
dilapidated [di'læpideitid] *adj* forfalden.
dilate [dai'leit] *v* udvide(s); spile(s) ud.
dilatory ['dilətəri] *adj* sendrægtig; forhalings-.
diligent ['dilidʒənt] *adj* flittig; omhyggelig.
dill [dil] *s* dild.
dilute [dai'lu:t] *v* fortynde // *adj* fortyndet.
dim [dim] *v* dæmpe(s); sløre(s); blænde ned // *adj* svag; tåget, uklar, utydelig; (om person) sløv, dum; omtåget; *take a ~ view of sth* ikke have høje tanker om ngt, misbillige ngt.
dimension [dai'mɛnʃən] *s* dimension, omfang; mål.
diminish [di'miniʃ] *v* formindske(s).
diminutive [di'minjutiv] *adj* lille bitte, minimal.
dimple [dimpl] *s* smilehul; kløft i hagen.
din [din] *s* larm, spektakel.
dine [dain] *v* spise til middag; ~ *in* spise hjemme; ~ *on mince* spise hakkekød til middag; ~ *out* spise ude; være ude til middag.
diner ['dainə*] *s* middagsgæst; *(jernb)* spisevogn.
dinghy ['diŋgi] *s* jolle; *rubber* ~ gummibåd.
dingy ['diŋdʒi] *adj* snusket, nusset.
dining ['dainiŋ] sms: ~ **car** *s (jernb)* spisevogn; ~ **room** *s* spisestue; ~ **table** *s* spisebord.

dinner ['dinə*] *s* middag(smad); middagsselskab; ~ **jacket** *s* smokingjakke; ~ **party** *s* middagsselskab; ~ **service,** ~ **set** *s* spisestel; ~ **suit** *s* smoking; ~**time** *s* spisetid.
diocese ['daiəsis] *s* bispedømme; stift.
dip [dip] *s* dypning; dukkert; dressing, dip; hældning, skråning; lavning; (F) svømmetur // *v* dyppe; dukke; skråne; *~ the (head)lights* blænde (for)lygterne ned; *~ one's flag* kippe flaget; *~ into sth* dykke ned i ngt; *your skirt ~s* din nederdel drypper.
diploma [di'pləumə] *s* diplom.
diplomacy [di'pləuməsi] *s* diplomati.
diplomat ['dipləmæt] *s* diplomat; **diplomatic** [-'mætik] *adj* diplomatisk.
dipper ['dipə*] *s* øse, opøserske.
dipsomania [dipsəu'meiniə] *s* alkoholisme (i perioder).
dipstick ['dipstik] *s (auto)* oliemålepind.
dire [daiə*] *adj* frygtelig; *be in ~ straits* være i nød, være på spanden.
direct [di'rɛkt, dai'rɛkt] *v* dirigere; rette; henlede; vejlede, vise vej; adressere; beordre; iscenesætte; *can you ~ me to Regent Street?* kan De sige mig vejen til Regent Street? // *adj* direkte; ligefrem; ~ **current** *s* jævnstrøm; ~ **debit** *s* sv.t. bankernes betalingsordning; ~ **hit** *s* fuldtræffer.
direction [di'rɛkʃən] *s* retning; ledelse; vejledning; anvisning; direktion; *sense of ~* retningssans; *~s for use* brugsanvisning.
directly [di'rɛktli] *adv* lige, direkte; straks; så snart.
director [di'rɛktə*] *s* leder, direktør; (film)instruktør.
directory [di'rɛktəri] *s* vejviser; adressebog; *telephone ~* telefonbog; ~ **enquiries** *spl (tlf)* nummeroplysningen.
dirt [də:t] *s* snavs, smuds; jord; møg; ~-**cheap** *adj* dødbillig; ~ **road** *s (am)* grusvej; jordvej.
dirty ['də:ti] *adj* snavset; sjofel; fræk; *do the ~ on sby* (S) røvrende en // *v* grise (,svine) til; ~ **trick** *s* tarveligt trick.
disability [disə'biliti] *s* manglende evne; handicap.
disabled [dis'eibld] *adj* uarbejdsdygtig; handicappet.
disadvantage [disəd'va:ntidʒ] *s* mangel, minus, ulempe; *be at a ~* være uheldigt stillet.
disadvantageous [disədvən'teidʒəs] *adj* ufordelagtig; uheldig.
disagree [disə'gri:] *v* være uenig; ikke stemme overens; *~ with* være uenig med; *garlic ~s with me* jeg kan ikke tåle hvidløg; ~**able** *adj* ubehagelig; ~**ment** *s* uoverensstemmelse; uenighed.
disallow ['disə'lau] *v* erklære ugyldig.
disappear [disə'piə*] *v* forsvinde; ~**ance** *s* forsvinden.
disappoint [disə'pɔint] *v* skuffe; ~**ment** *s* skuffelse.
disapproval [disə'pru:vəl] *s* misbilligelse; modvilje.
disapprove [disə'pru:v] *v: ~ of* misbillige.
disarm [dis'a:m] *v* afvæbne; nedruste; ~**ament** *s* nedrustning ~**ing** *adj* afvæbende.
disarrange ['disə'reindʒ] *v* bringe i uorden, rode op i.
disarray [disə'rei] *s* uorden; uordentlig påklædning.
disaster [di'za:stə*] *s* katastrofe.
disastrous [di'za:strəs] *adj* katastrofal.
disband [dis'bænd] *v* opløse (sig).
disbelief [disbi'li:f] *s* vantro; tvivl.
disbelieve ['disbi'li:v] *v* tvivle *(in* på).
disc [disk] *s* skive; (grammofon)plade; p-skive; disk; *slipped ~* diskusprolaps.
discard [dis'ka:d] *v* (af)kaste; kassere; tage af; afskedige.
disc brake ['diskbreik] *s (auto)* skivebremse.
discern [di'sə:n] *v* skelne; skimte, ~**ing** *adj* skarpsindig; kritisk.
discharge *s* ['distʃa:dʒ] udløb, udtømning; *(med)* udflåd; *(elek)* udladning; udskrivelse // *v* [dis'tʃa:dʒ] aflæsse; bortskaffe, fjerne; udsondre; udlade; afskedige; hjemsende, udskrive; løslade, frigive.

disciple [di'saipl] *s* lærling, discipel.
discipline ['disiplin] *s* disciplin; orden // *v* disciplinere, tugte.
disclaim [dis'kleim] *v* frasige sig; benægte; afvise; **~er** *s* dementi, nægtelse.
disclose [dis'kləuz] *v* afsløre; åbenbare.
disclosure [dis'kləuʒə*] *s* afsløring.
discolour [dis'kʌlə*] *v* misfarve; affarve(s).
discomfort [dis'kʌmfət] *s* ubehag; uhygge.
disconcert [diskən'sə:t] *v* bringe ud af fatning.
disconnect ['diskə'nɛkt] *v* afbryde; koble fra; **~ed** *adj* afbrudt; usammenhængende.
disconsolate [dis'kɔnsələt] *adj* utrøstelig.
discontent [ˌdiskən'tɛnt] *s* utilfredshed.
discontinue [diskən'tinju:] *v* afbryde; nedlægge, sløjfe.
discord ['diskɔ:d] *s* uoverensstemmelse; strid; *(mus)* disharmoni.
discordant [dis'kɔ:dənt] *adj* uharmonisk, skærende.
discount *s* ['diskaunt] rabat; diskonto // *v* [dis'kaunt] se bort fra; diskontere.
discourage [dis'kʌridʒ] *v* tage modet fra; afskrække; modvirke, bekæmpe; **discouraging** *adj* nedslående.
discourse [dis'kɔ:s] *s* foredrag // *v* tale; samtale.
discover [dis'kʌvə*] *v* opdage; afsløre; **~y** *s* opdagelse.
discredit [dis'krɛdit] *s* miskredit, dårligt ry // *v* give et dårligt ry; drage i tvivl.
discreet [dis'kri:t] *adj* diskret, taktfuld.
discrepancy [dis'krɛpənsi] *s* uoverensstemmelse; misforhold.
discretion [dis'krɛʃən] *s* diskretion; betænksomhed; *at ~* efter behag; *at your ~* som du selv vil.
discriminate [dis'krimineit] *v* skelne; gøre forskel, diskriminere; *~ between* skelne mellem; gøre forskel på; *~ against sby* diskriminere en; forfordele en; **discriminating** *adj* kræsen; kritisk.
discrimination [diskrimi'neiʃən] *s* skelnen; kritisk sans; kræsenhed; forskelsbehandling, diskrimination.
discursive [dis'kə:siv] *adj* vidtløftig; causerende.
discus ['diskəs] *s (pl: disci* ['diskai]) diskos.
discuss [dis'kʌs] *v* diskutere, tale om; gøre rede for.
discussion [dis'kʌʃən] *s* diskussion, drøftelse; samtale; redegørelse.
disdain [dis'dein] *s* foragt // foragte.
disease [di'zi:z] *s* sygdom, syge; **~d** *adj* syg.
disembark ['disim'ba:k] *v* udskibe; gå i land; stige ud.
disenchanted ['disin'tʃa:ntid] *adj* skuffet.
disengage ['disin'geidʒ] *v* frigøre; udløse; *~ the clutch* slå koblingen fra; **~ment** *s* frigørelse; frigjorthed.
disfavour [dis'feivə*] *s* unåde; mishag.
disfigure [dis'figə*] *v* vansire, skamfere.
disgorge [dis'gɔ:dʒ] *v* spytte ud; spy ud; gylpe op.
disgrace [dis'greis] *s* vanære, skam; *that hat is a ~* den hat er en skandale // *v* bringe skam over; **~ful** *adj* skændig, skammelig.
disguise [dis'gaiz] *s* forklædning; *in ~* forklædt; *a blessing in ~* held i uheld // *v* forklæde; tilsløre; skjule.
disgust [dis'gʌst] *s* afsky, væmmelse // *v* frastøde; chokere, forarge; **~ed** *adj: be ~ed* væmmes; være forarget; **~ing** *adj* afskyelig, led.
dish [diʃ] *s* fad; ret mad; *do (,wash up) the ~es* vaske op // *v: ~ out* uddele; øse op; *~ up* diske op; øse op; **~cloth** *s* viskestykke; karklud.
disheartened [dis'ha:tənd] *adj* modløs, nedslået.
dishevelled [di'ʃɛvəld] *adj* pjusket, sjusket.
dishonest [dis'ɔnist] *adj* uærlig; uhæderlig.
dishonour [dis'ɔnə*] *s* vanære; **~able** *adj* æreløs, vanærende.

dishrack ['diʃræk] *s* opvaskestativ.
dishrag ['diʃræg] *s* karklud.
dishwasher ['diʃwɔʃə*] *s* opvaskemaskine; (om person) opvasker.
dishwater ['diʃwɔ:tə*] *s* opvaskevand.
dishy ['diʃi] *adj* (F) (om fyr) lækker; *a really ~ bloke* en rigtig "steg".
disillusion [disi'luʒən] *s* desillusion // *v* desillusionere.
disinclination [disinkli'neiʃən] *s* ulyst.
disinfect [disin'fɛkt] *v* desinficere.
disinfectant [disin'fɛktənt] *s* desinficerende middel.
disinherit [disin'hɛrit] *v* gøre arveløs.
disintegrate [dis'intigreit] *v* opløse(s); smuldre, forvitre; *(fys)* henfalde.
disinter [disin'tə:*] *v* grave op (,frem) igen (også *fig*).
disinterested [dis'intrəstid] *adj* uselvisk; upartisk.
disjointed [dis'dʒɔintid] *adj* usammenhængende.
disk [disk] *s* d.s.s. *disc.*
dislike [dis'laik] *s* ulyst, uvilje; *take a ~ to* få uvilje mod // *v* ikke kunne lide.
dislocate ['disləkeit] *v* forskubbe, forrykke; *(med)* forvride; *his arm was ~d* hans arm gik af led.
dislodge [dis'lɔdʒ] *v* flytte, få væk.
disloyal [dis'lɔiəl] *adj* illoyal.
dismal ['dizməl] *s* trist, skummel; bedrøvelig.
dismantle [dis'mæntl] *v* afmontere; nedlægge.
dismay [dis'mei] *s* forfærdelse // *v* forfærde; afskrække; chokere.
dismiss [dis'mis] *v* sende bort (,ud); give fri; sende hjem; afskedige; afvise; **~al** *s* afsked; afvisning; frikendelse.
dismount [dis'maunt] *v: ~ (from)* stå af (cykel el. hest).
disobedience [disə'bi:diəns] *s* ulydighed; **disobedient** *adj* ulydig.
disobey [disə'bei] *v* være ulydig, ikke adlyde.
disorder [dis'ɔ:də*] *s* uorden, forstyrrelse; uro; *(med)* sygdom; **~ly** *adj* uordentlig, rodet; *~ly conduct* gadeuorden.
disorganize [dis'ɔ:gənaiz] *v* bringe uorden i.
disorientate [dis'ɔ:riənteit] *v* vildlede, desorientere.
disown [dis'əun] *v* forstøde; nægte at vedkende sig.
disparaging [dis'pæridʒiŋ] *adj* nedsættende.
disparity [dis'pæriti] *s* uensartethed; skævhed, ulighed.
dispatch [dis'pætʃ] *s* afsendelse; ekspedition; hast; *(mil)* depeche // *v* (af)sende; ekspedere; fremme; **~ note** *s* følgeseddel.
dispel [dis'pɛl] *v* sprede, splitte (fx *the crowd* folkemængden); forjage.
dispensary [dis'pɛnsəri] *s* udleveringssted for medicin.
dispense [dis'pɛns] *v* uddele, udlevere; give; dispensere; fritage; *~ with* give dispensation for; se bort fra.
dispenser [dis'pɛnsə*] *s* holder (til fx tape).
dispensing chemist [dis'pɛnsiŋ 'kɛmist] *s* apotek(er).
dispersal [dis'pə:səl] *s* spredning, splittelse.
disperse [dis'pə:s] *v* sprede(s), splitte(s).
dispirited [dis'piritid] *adj* nedslået.
displace [dis'pleis] *v* flytte; forskubbe; forskyde; afskedige; fortrænge; *~d persons* flygtninge; **~ment** *s* forskydning, fortrængning; *(piston) ~ment (auto)* slagvolumen.
display [dis'plei] *s* fremvisning; opvisning; udstilling; *(edb)* skærm, display // *v* fremvise; udstille; (ud)vise; udfolde; **~ unit** *s (edb)* dataskærm; **~ window** *s* udstillingsvindue.
displease [dis'pli:z] *v* mishage; *~d with* utilfreds med.
displeasure [dis'plɛʒə*] *s* mishag; ubehag.
disposable [dis'pəuzəbl] *adj* disponibel; til rådighed; engangs- (fx *plate* tallerken).
disposal [dis'pəuzl] *s* disposition; overdragelse; bortkastning; *at your ~* til din disposition; **~ unit** *s* affaldskværn.
dispose [dis'peuz] *v: ~ of* disponere over; skille sig af med; *~d to* tilbøjelig til; disponeret for.

disposition [dispə'ziʃən] *s* arrangement; anbringelse; gemyt; tilbøjelighed.
disproportionate [disprə'pɔ:ʃənət] *adj* uforholdsmæssig.
disprove [dis'pru:v] *v* gendrive, modbevise.
dispute *s* ['dispju:t] uenighed; disput; *industrial* ~ arbejdskonflikt; *be in* ~ være omdiskuteret (,omstridt) // *v* [dis'pju:t] strides; debattere; bestride.
disqualification [diskwɔlifi'keiʃən] *s* diskvalifikation; ~ *(from driving)* fratagelse af kørekortet.
disqualify [dis'kwɔlifai] *v* diskvalificere; ~ *sby for speeding* fratage en kørekortet for overskridelse af hastighedsgrænserne.
disregard ['disri'ga:d] *v* ignorere; lade hånt om; forbigå.
disrepair ['disri'pɛə*] *s* forfald, dårlig vedligeholdelse; *fall into* ~ forfalde.
disreputable [dis'rɛpjutəbl] *adj* berygtet.
disrespectful [disri'spɛktful] *adj* respektløs.
disrupt [dis'rʌpt] *v* afbryde; splitte, sprænge.
disruption [dis'rəpʃən] *s* afbrydelse; sammenbrud, sprængning.
dissatisfaction ['dissætis'fækʃən] *s* utilfredshed; **dissatisfied** [-'sætisfaid] *adj* utilfreds.
dissect [di'sɛkt] *v* dissekere; analysere; pille fra hinanden.
dissemble [di'sɛmbl] *v* forstille sig.
disseminate [di'sɛmineit] *v* udsprede, udbrede.
dissent [di'sɛnt] *s* meningsforskel, uenighed // *v* være uenig.
dissertation [disə'teiʃən] *s* (doktor)afhandling, disputats.
disservice [di'sə:vis] *s* bjørnetjeneste.
dissident ['disidnt] *s* anderledes tænkende, afviger.
dissimilar [di'similə*] *adj* forskellig *(to* fra); ulig.
dissipated ['disipeitəd] *adj* udsvævende; hærget.
dissociate [di'səuʃieit] *v:* ~ *oneself from sth* tage afstand fra ngt.
dissolute ['disəlu:t] *adj* udsvævende.
dissolve [di'zɔlv] *v* opløse(s); smelte; *(fig)* forsvinde.
dissolvent [di'zɔlvənt] *s* opløsningsmiddel.
dissonant ['disənənt] *adj* disharmonisk.
dissuade [di'sweid] *v:* ~ *sby from doing sth* fraråde en at gøre ngt; få en fra at gøre ngt.
distance ['distns] *s* afstand; *in the* ~ i det fjerne; *from a long* ~ på lang afstand; *go the* ~ stå distancen.
distant ['distənt] *adj* fjern; utilnærmelig.
distaste [dis'teist] *s* afsmag; modvilje; **~ful** *adj* usmagelig; ubehagelig.
distemper [dis'tɛmpə*] *s* limfarve; (om hund) hundesyge.
distend [dis'tɛnd] *v* udspile(s); svulme op.
distil [di'stil] *v* dryppe; destillere(s); **~lery** *s* destilleri, whiskyfabrik; spritfabrik.
distinct [di'stiŋkt] *adj* tydelig, klar; særskilt, særlig; udtalt.
distinction [di'stiŋkʃən] *s* skelnen; forskel; fornemhed, betydning; (ved eksamen) udmærkelse.
distinctive [di'stiŋktiv] *adj* særpræget; karakteristisk; påfaldende; umiskendelig.
distinguish [di'stiŋgwiʃ] *v* skelne; adskille; **~ed** *adj* fornem; fremtrædende; **~ing** *adj:* *~ing feature (,mark)* særligt kendetegn.
distort [dis'tɔ:t] *v* forvrænge, fordreje; **~ion** [-'tɔ:ʃən] *s* forvrængning.
distract [di'strækt] *v* distrahere; plage, genere.
distraction [di'strækʃən] *s* forstyrrelse; adspredelse; *drive sby to* ~ drive en til vanvid.
distraught [di'strɔ:t] *adj* fortvivlet, ude af sig selv.
distress [di'strɛs] *s* sorg, fortvivlelse; nød; kval // *v* volde sorg (etc); pine; forurolige; **~ed area** *s* kriseramt område; ~ **signal** *s* nødsignal.
distribute [di'stribju:t] *v* fordele; uddele; sprede.
distribution [distri'bju:ʃən] *s* fordeling; udbredelse.

distributor [di'stribju:tə*] *s* distributør, grossist; *(auto)* strømfordeler.
district ['distrikt] *s* område, egn; distrikt; ~ **attorney** [ə'tə:ni] *s (am)* offentlig anklager; ~ **nurse** *s* hjemmesygeplejerske.
distrust [dis'trʌst] *s* mistillid *(of* til) // *v* mistro, have mistillid til.
disturb [di'stə:b] *s* forstyrre, bringe uorden i; forurolige.
disturbance [di'stə:bəns] *s* forstyrrelse, uro; *~s* optøjer.
disturbing [di'stə:biŋ] *adj* foruroligende.
disuse [dis'ju:s] *s: fall into ~* gå af brug.
ditch [ditʃ] *s* grøft // *v* grave grøfter; køre i grøften; (F) skille sig af med, smide væk; droppe (fx fyr).
dither ['diðə*] *v* tøve, vakle; fjumre.
dive [daiv] *s* dyk, dykning; udspring // *v* dykke; **~r** *s* dykker; udspringer.
diverge [dai'və:dʒ] *v* afvige, divergere; vige af.
diversify [dai'və:sifai] *v* sprede; variere.
diversion [dai'və:ʃən] *s* afledning; omlægning; omkørsel; adspredelse, underholdning.
diversity [dai'və:siti] *s* afveksling, forskellighed.
divert [dai'və:t] *v* aflede; omlægge, omdirigere; adsprede.
divest [dai'vɛst] *v: ~ of* berøve, fratage.
divide [di'vaid] *s* skel; svælg // *v* dele (sig); adskille; fordele; være uenig; *(mat)* dividere, dele.
divine [di'vain] *v* gætte; spå // *adj* guddommelig.
diving ['daiviŋ] *s* dykning; *(sport)* udspring, svømmedykning; *high ~ (sport)* tårnspring; ~ **board** *s* (til udspring) vippe; ~ **suit** *s* dykkerdragt.
divinity [di'viniti] *s* guddommelighed; *read ~* studere teologi.
division [di'viʒən] *s* division; deling; skel; splid; *(parl)* afstemning; *~ of labour* arbejdsdeling.
divisional [di'viʒənəl] *adj* divisions-; ~ **surgeon** *s* sv.t. politilæge.
divorce [di'vɔ:s] *s* skilsmisse // *v* lade sig skille fra; adskille; **~d** *adj* fraskilt.
divorcé, divorcee [divɔ:'sei, -'si:] *s* fraskilt person.
divulge [dai'vʌldʒ] *v* røbe, afsløre (fx *a secret* en hemmelighed).
DIY, diy (fork.f. *do-it-yourself)* gør det selv-; (om forretning) byggemarked; **~-kit** *s* byggesæt.
dizzy ['dizi] *adj* svimmel; svimlende; *feel ~* være svimmel; ~ **spell** *s* anfald af svimmelhed.
do [du:] *s* gilde, tam-tam // *v (did, done* [did, dʌn]) gøre; bestille; lave, ordne; *how do you ~?* goddag! *how are you ~ing?* hvordan går det? *~ tell me!* sig det nu! vær sød at sige mig; *will this ~?* er det (her) godt nok? er det (her) nok? *that will ~!* det er godt! så er det nok! *~ you agree? I ~!* er du enig? ja, jeg er! *get done (by the police)* (F) blive taget (af politiet);
~ away with skaffe sig af med, rydde af vejen; *~ down* nedgøre; *he's done for* det er ude med ham; *~ sby in* gøre det af med en; *~ up* gøre i stand; pakke ind; knappe (,hægte, lyne); *~ with: I could ~ with a drink* jeg kunne godt trænge til en drink; *can you make ~ with this?* kan du klare dig med det her? *he could ~ with a washing* han trænger til at blive vasket; *~ without* klare sig uden, undvære; *~ sby proud* kræse op for en; *~ one's hair* rede sig, ordne håret; *~ the dishes* vaske op; *what's to ~?* (F) hvad er der i vejen?
docile ['dəusail] *adj* føjelig; lærenem.
dock [dɔk] *s* dok; dokhavn; *(jur)* anklagebænk; *the car is in ~* bilen er på værksted // *v* sætte i dok; gå i dok; beskære, kupere; (om rumskibe) koble(s) sammen; *~ sby's wages* trække fra i ens løn; **~er** *s* havnearbejder; **~land** *s* havnekvarter; **~yard** *s* (skibs)værft.
doctor ['dɔktə*] *s* doktor; læge // *v* doktorere; reparere på; pynte på; forfalske; **~al** *adj* doktor-.

doctrine ['dɔktrin] *s* doktrin.
document ['dɔkjumənt] *s* dokument // *v* dokumentere.
documentary [dɔkju'mɛntəri] *s* dokumentarfilm, -program // *adj* dokumentarisk.
documentation [dɔkjumən'teiʃən] *s* dokumentation.
doddering ['dɔdəriŋ] *adj* lallende, mimrende.
dodge [dɔdʒ] *s* spring til siden; trick, fidus // *v* smutte væk; undgå; lave krumspring.
dodgems ['dɔdʒəms] *spl* radiobiler.
doe [dəu] *s* dådyr.
doer ['du:ə*] handlingsmenneske.
does [dʌz] 3. pers. ental af *do*.
doesn't [dʌzənt] d.s.s. *does not*.
dog [dɔg] *s* hund; *not have a ~'s chance* ikke have en levende chance; *the ~s* (F) hundevæddeløb; *go to the ~s* gå i hundene; *dressed up like a ~'s dinner* (F) ordentlig majet ud; *be ~ tired* være dødtræt // *v* hænge i halen på; nage, plage; ~ **biscuits** *spl* hundekiks; **~-collar** *s* hundehalsbånd; *(fig)* præsteflip; **~-ear** *s* æseløre // *v* lave æselører i; **~fight** *s* hundeslagsmål (også *fig)*.
dogged ['dɔgid] *adj* stædig, udholdende.
doggy ['dɔgi] *s* (F) vovse // *adj* hunde- (fx *smell* lugt).
doghouse ['dɔghaus] *s* hundehus; *be in the ~* være i unåde.
dog licence ['dɔg,laisəns] *s* hundetegn.
dog paddle ['dɔg pædl] *s* hundesvømning.
dogsbody ['dɔgzbɔdi] *s* stikirenddreng.
doily ['dɔili] *s* mellemlægsserviet.
doings ['du:iŋz] *spl: his ~s* det (,hvad) han foretager sig.
do-it-yourself ['du:itjɔ:'sɛlf] *adj* gør det selv-; ~ **kit** *s* byggesæt.
doldrums ['dɔldrʌmz] *spl* død periode; depression; *be in the ~* være langt nede.
dole [dəul] *s* arbejdsløshedsunderstøttelse; *be on the ~* være på understøttelse // *v: ~ out* uddele (i små portioner).
doleful ['dəulful] *adj* sørgmodig; sørgelig.
doll [dɔl] *s* dukke; (F) pige, dulle // *v: ~ oneself up* klæde sig fint på; *all ~ed up* (F) rigtig majet ud.
dollop ['dɔləp] *s* klat.
dolphin ['dɔlfin] *s* delfin.
dolt [dəult] *s* fæ, tumpe.
domain [dəu'mein] *s* (jord)ejendom; domæne.
dome [dəum] *s* kuppel; **~d** *adj* hvælvet.
domestic [də'mɛstik] *adj* hjemlig, huslig; hjemme-; bolig-; indenlands- (fx *flight* flyvning); (om dyr) hus-, tam-.
domesticated [də'mɛstikeitid] *adj* (om dyr) tam; (om person) huslig; hjemme-.
domestic science [də'mɛstik 'saiəns] *s* (som skolefag) hjemkundskab; **domestic staff** *s* tjenestefolk.
dominant ['dɔminənt] *adj* fremherskende, dominerende.
dominate ['dɔmineit] *v* beherske; dominere; have udsigt over.
domination [dɔmi'neiʃən] *s* herredømme.
domineering [dɔmi'niəriŋ] *adj* herskesyg, tyrannisk.
dominion [də'miniən] *s* herredømme, magtområde; dominion.
dominoes ['dɔmineuz] *spl: play ~* spille domino.
don [dɔn] *s* universitetslærer // *v* (H) tage på, iklæde sig.
donate [də'neit] *v* give, skænke (til velgørenhed); **donation** [-'neiʃən] *s* gave, bidrag.
done [dʌn] *pp* af *do* // *adj* gjort; udmattet; færdig; *the potatoes are ~* kartoflerne er færdige (,møre); *that's over and ~ with* det er overstået.
donkey ['dɔŋki] *s* æsel; *it's been ~'s years* det er umindelige tider siden; ~ **work** *s* hestearbejde; rutinearbejde.
don't [dəunt] *v* d.s.s. *do not*.
doodle [du:dl] *v* tegne kruseduller.
doom [du:m] *s* skæbne; undergang // *v: be ~ed* være fortabt; være fordømt; *~ed to failure* dømt til at mislykkes.

doomsday ['du:mzdei] *s* dommedag.
door [dɔ:*] *s* dør; *answer the ~* lukke op (når det ringer el. banker på); *she lives next ~* hun bor inde ved siden af; *out of ~s* udendørs, i det fri; *within ~s* indendørs; *see sby to the ~* følge en til døren; *show sby the ~* smide en på porten; **~bell** *s* dørklokke; **~-handle** *s* dørhåndtag; **~knob** *s* (rundt) dørhåndtag; **~keeper, ~man** *s* dørvogter; portner; **~mat** *s* dørmåtte; **~plate** *s* dørskilt, navneskilt; **~post** *s* dørstolpe; **~step** *s* dørtærskel; trappesten; **~way** *s* dør; indgang.
dope [dəup] *s* (F) narko, stof(fer); (F) idiot // *v* bedøve; dope; **dopey** *adj* (F) sløv (af stoffer); dum.
dormant ['dɔ:mənt] *adj* sovende, slumrende; uvirksom; uudnyttet; *lie ~* henligge, ligge brak.
dormer ['dɔ:mə*] *s* kvistvindue.
dormitory ['dɔ:mitri] *s* sovesal.
dosage ['dəusidʒ] *s* dosering; dosis.
dose [dəuz] *s* dosis; portion // *v* dosere; give medicin.
doss [dɔs] *v: ~ down* overnatte (på provisorisk soveplads); **~er** *s* subsistensløs (der sover på gaden etc); **~-house** *s* (tarveligt) natherberg.
dossier ['dɔsiei] *s* sagsakter.
dot [dɔt] *s* prik; punkt; *at one o'clock on the ~* (præcis) på slaget et; *off one's ~* skør; *in the year ~* i syttenhundrede hvidkål // *v* prikke; punktere (fx en linje).
dotage ['dəutidʒ] *s* senilitet, alderdom.
dote [dəut] *v: ~ on* tilbede, dyrke.
dotted ['dɔtid] *adj* prikket; punkteret.
dotty ['dɔti] *adj* skør, bims.
double [dʌbl] *s* modstykke; dobbeltgænger; *(film)* stand-in, dublant; *at (,on) the ~* i hurtig march; i fuld fart; *cost ~ sth* koste det dobbelte af ngt; *eight six ~ four (tlf)* 8644 // *v* fordoble; folde sammen; dublere; *~ back* vende om og gå (,køre etc) tilbage; *~ up* bøje sammen; dele værelse (,kontor etc); **~ bass** *s* kontrabas; **~ bend** *s* (på vej) S-sving; **~-breasted** *adj* dobbeltradet; **~ cream** *s* piskefløde; **~cross** *v* snyde; **~decker** *s* (om bus etc) todækker; (F) tredobbel sandwich; **~ Dutch** *s* volapyk; **~-edged** *adj* tveægget; tvetydig; **~-glazing** *s* forsatsvindue(r); termorude(r); **~-park** *v* parkere i anden position; **~-quick** *adj* i lyntempo; **~talk** *s* tvetungethed; sort tale.
doubly ['dʌbli] *adv* dobbelt (så).
doubt [daut] *s* tvivl, usikkerhed; *beyond ~* hævet over enhver tvivl; *cast ~ on* så tvivl om; *no ~* uden tvivl, sikkert; *give him the benefit of the ~* lade tvivlen komme ham til gode // *v* tvivle (om, på); *~ that* tvivle på at; **~ful** *adj* tvivlsom; tvivlende; **~less** *adv* utvivlsomt.
dough [dəu] *s* dej; (S) gysser, skillinger; **~nut** *s* friturekogt bagværk, sv.t. munkering.
dour [duə*] *adj* streng, stramtandet; mut.
douse [daus] *v* hælde vand på; slukke.
dove [dʌv] *s* due; **~cote** [-kəut] *s* dueslag.
dowdy ['daudi] *adj* (om påklædning) sjusket, gammeldags.
down [daun] *s* dun, fnug; *have a ~ on sby* være på nakken af en // *v* pille ned, nedgøre; (om drink) skylle ned.
down *adv* ned; (i krydsord) lodret; *be ~ for sth* være skrevet op (på liste) til ngt; *Denmark were two ~ at halftime* Danmark var to mål bagud ved halvlegen; *be ~ with the flu* ligge med influenza; *get ~ to* tage fat på; *~ the road* ned ad vejen; nede på vejen; **~cast** *adj* nedslået; **~fall** *s* fald; regnbyge; snefald; undergang; **~hill** *adv: go ~hill* gå (,køre etc) ned ad bakke; **~hill (skiing)** *s (sport)* styrtløb; **~ payment** *s* udbetaling; **~pour** *s* regnskyl, skylle; **~right** *adv* ligefrem, simpelthen; ren og skær; **~stairs** *adv* nedenunder; ned ad trappe(n); **~stream** *adv* ned ad floden; **~-to-earth** *adj* nøgtern, jordnær; realistisk; **~town** *adj* i bymidten, i centrum; **~ward**

['daunwəd] *adj* skrånende nedad // *adv* (også: *~wards)* nedad.
downy ['dauni] *adj* dunet, dunblød; umoden.
dowry [dauri] *s* medgift.
doz fork.f. *dozen.*
doze [dəuz] *v* døse, blunde; *~ off* døse hen.
dozen [dʌzn] *s* dusin; *a ~ books* en halv snes bøger.
drab [dræb] *adj* gråbrun, trist.
draft [dra:ft] *s* udkast, koncept; plan; *(mil)* indkaldelse // *v* give udkast til; planlægge; indkalde; (se også *draught).*
drag [dræg] *s* bremseklods, hæmsko; trans(vestit); hiv (af cigaret); *be a ~ on sby* være en klods om benet på en // *v* slæbe, trække; *~ out* trække ud; *~ on* slæbe sig af sted, trække i langdrag.
dragon [drægn] *s* drage; **~fly** *s (zo)* guldsmed.
drain [drein] *s* afløb(srør); kloakledning; *go down the ~* ryge i vasken; ende i rendestenen // *v* skabe afløb; tømme, tappe; dræne; afvande(s); **~age** ['dreinidʒ] *s* afløb; dræning; kloakering; **~ hose** *s* afløbsslange; **~ing board** *s* opvaskebakke; **~pipe** *s* afløbsrør; nedløbsrør.
drama ['dra:mə] *s* drama, skuespil; **~tic** [drə'mætik] *adj* dramatisk, skuespil-; **~ school** *s* teaterskole; **~tist** ['dræmətist] *s* dramatiker, skuespilforfatter.
drank [dræŋk] *præt* af *drink.*
drape [dreip] *v* drapere (sig).
draper ['dreipə*] *s* manufakturhandler.
drapery ['dreipəri] *s* draperi; manufakturvare.
drastic ['dræstik] *adj* drastisk, skrap.
draught [dra:ft] *s* (gennem)træk; aftapning; slurk; *(mar)* dybgående; **~ beer** *s* fadøl; **~board** *s* dambræt; **~s** *spl* dam(spil).
draughtsman ['dra:ftsmən] *s* tegner (især teknisk); **~ship** *s* tegnekunst; tegneteknik.
draw [drɔ:] *s* trækning; uafgjort kamp; trækplaster // *v (drew, drawn* [dru:, drɔ:n]) trække; tiltrække; hæve (penge); aftappe; tegne; *(sport)* spille uafgjort; *~ attention to* henlede opmærksomheden på; *~ a bath* fylde vand i badekarret; *~ the curtains* trække gardinerne for (,fra); *~ to a close* lakke mod enden; *~ near* nærme sig; *~ off* tappe (af); *~ on* trække på; *~ out* trække ud; *~ up* trække op; flytte nærmere; udfærdige; standse; **~back** *s* ulempe, minus; **~bridge** *s* vindebro.
drawer [drɔ:*] *s* skuffe; *the top ~* øverste skuffe; **~s** *spl (gl)* underbukser.
drawing ['drɔ:iŋ] *s* tegning; trækning; **~ board** *s* tegnebræt; **~ pin** *s* tegnestift; **~-room** *s* dagligstue.
drawl [drɔ:l] *s* dræven // *v* dræve.
drawn [drɔ:n] *pp* af *draw.*
dread [drɛd] *s* rædsel, skræk // *v* frygte, grue for; **~ful** *adj* frygtelig.
dream [dri:m] *s* drøm; *sweet ~s!* sov godt! *in one's ~(s)* i drømme // *v (~ed, ~ed* el. *dreamt, dreamt* [drɛmt]) drømme; *I would not ~ of it* det ville jeg ikke drømme om; *I never ~ed that...* jeg havde ikke drømt om at...; *~ up sth* udtænke ngt; **~like** *adj* drømmeagtig; **~y** *adj* drømmende; drømmeagtig.
dreary ['driəri] *adj* trist, kedelig.
dredge [drɛdʒ] *v* skrabe (fx *for oysters* (efter) østers).
dredger ['drɛdʒə*] *s (mar)* muddermaskine; (også: *sugar ~r)* strødåse (til sukker).
dregs [drɛgz] *s* bundfald; *to the ~* til sidste dråbe.
drench [drɛntʃ] *v* gennembløde.
dress [drɛs] *s* kjole; dragt; påklædning // *v* klæde (sig) på; (om fjerkræ el. fisk) rense; (om salat) tilberede, komme dressing på; *(med)* forbinde; *~ down* ikke tage for fint tøj på; *~ sby down* sætte en på plads, give en en næse; *~ up* tage fint tøj på; pynte op; *~ a wound* forbinde et sår.
dressage ['drɛsidʒ] *s* dressur.
dress circle ['drɛs ˌsə:kl] *s (teat)* balkon.

dress designer ['drɛs di'zainə*] *s* modetegner.
dresser ['drɛsə*] *s* anretterbord; kommode; *(teat)* påklæder.
dressing ['drɛsiŋ] *s* påklædning; tilberedning; dressing; appretur; *(med)* forbinding; ~ **gown** *s* morgenkåbe; ~ **room** *s* (teat) (skuespiller) garderobe; ~ **table** *s* toiletbord.
dressmaker ['drɛsmeikə*] *s* dameskrædder; **dressmaking** *s* kjolesyning.
dress rehearsal ['drɛs ri'hə:səl] *s* *(teat)* kostumeprøve; generalprøve.
dress shirt ['drɛs ʃə:t] *s* kjoleskjorte.
dressy ['drɛsi] *adj* (for) fint klædt; elegant.
drew [dru:] *præt* af *draw.*
dribble [dribl] *v* sive, sile; (om baby) savle; *(sport)* drible.
dried [draid] *præt* og *pp* af *dry* // *adj* tørret (fx *bean* bønne); tør- (fx *milk* mælk); (se også *cut-and-dried);* **~-up** *adj* udtørret, vissen.
drier ['draiə*] *s* d.s.s. *dryer.*
drift [drift] *s* drift, strøm; driven, flyden; retning; (sne)drive; (sand)klit; mening; *catch the ~ of what he's saying* fatte hvor han vil hen (med det han siger) // *v* (om båd) drive; (om sne, sand) fyge (sammen); glide; **~wood** *s* drivtømmer.
drill [dril] *s* bor, boremaskine; *(mil)* eksercits // *v* bore (hul i); eksercere.
drink [driŋk] *s* drik; slurk; drink; *have a ~* få ngt at drikke; tage sig en drink; *take to ~* slå sig på flasken // *v (drank, drunk* [dræŋk, drʌŋk]) drikke; *~ it in* suge det til sig; sluge det; *~ to sby* skåle for en; *~ up* drikke ud; **~able** *adj* drikkelig; drikke-; **~er** *s* dranker; **~ing water** *s* drikkevand.
drip [drip] *s* dryp; dryppen; *(med)* drop // *v* dryppe; dryppe 'af; **~-dry** *adj* som skal dryptørres; strygefri; **~-feed** *v (med)* sondemade; **~ping** *s* dryppen; *(gastr)* stegesky, stegefedt.
drive [draiv] *s* kørsel; køretur; energi, fremdrift; *(psyk)* drift; indkørsel; *sales ~* salgsfremstød; *left-hand ~* venstrestyring // *v (drove, driven* [drəuv, drivn]) køre; drive, jage; slå (fx *a ball* en bold); trække; køre bil; *~ it home to sby* sørge for at det trænger ind hos en.
drivelling ['drivəliŋ] *adj* savlende, lallende.
driver ['draivə*] *s* chauffør; **~'s licence** *s* kørekort.
driveway ['draivwei] *s* indkørsel.
driving ['draiviŋ] *s* kørsel // *adj* drivende, driv-; *~ rain* øsende regn; ~ **belt** *s* drivrem; ~ **instructor** *s* kørelærer; ~ **lesson** *s* køretime; ~ **licence** *s* kørekort; ~ **seat** *s* førersæde; ~ **test** *s* køreprøve.
drizzle [drizl] *s* støvregn // *v* støvregne.
droll [drəul] *adj* sjov.
drone [drəun] *s* summen; brummen; *(zo)* drone // *v* kværne.
drool [dru:l] *v* savle.
droop [dru:p] *v* hænge slapt; synke sammen.
drop [drɔp] *s* dråbe; fald // *v* dryppe; falde, skråne; falde om; tabe, give slip på; opgive, droppe; udelade; *~ me a line* send mig et par ord; *~ a stitch* tabe en maske; *~ by* lige falde indenfor, lige komme forbi (dvs. besøge); *~ off* falde fra; falde i søvn; *~ out* falde fra; gå ud; **~out** *s* afviger; en der er stået af ræset.
droppings ['drɔpiŋs] *spl: cow ~* kokasser; *dog ~* hundelort; *horse ~* hestepærer.
drought [draut] *s* tørke.
drove [drəuv] *s* flok, hjord; skare // *præt* af *drive.*
drown [draun] *v* drukne; oversvømme; **~ing** *s* drukning.
drowsy ['drauzi] *adj* døsig.
drudge [drʌdʒ] *s* slid og slæb; arbejdsslave; **~ry** ['drʌdʒəri] *s* slid; slavearbejde.
drug [drʌg] *s* lægemiddel, medikament; rusgift; *be on ~s* være på stoffer // *v* bedøve; ~ **abuse** *s* stofmisbrug; ~ **addict** *s* stofmisbruger, narkoman.
druggist ['drʌgist] *s (am)* apoteker.

drugs [drʌgz] *spl* stoffer, narkotika.
drugstore ['drʌgstɔ:*] *s (am)* apotek og materialist (med fx kiosk, bar etc).
drum [drʌm] *s* tromme; tromle // *v* tromme; **~mer** *s* trommeslager; **~stick** *s* trommestik; lår (af kylling).
drunk [drʌŋk] *s* fuld person // *pp* af *drink* // *adj* fuld, beruset; *get* ~ blive (,drikke sig) fuld.
drunkard ['drʌŋkəd] *s* dranker.
drunken ['drʌŋkən] *adj* fuld; fordrukken; **~ driver** *s* spritbilist; **~ driving** *s* spirituskørsel.
dry [drai] *v* tørre; ~ *out* tørre; udtørre; sætte på vandvognen; ~ *up* tørre (ind); løbe tør // *adj* tør; **~ cleaner** *s* renseri; **~-cleaning** *s* kemisk rensning.
dryer ['draiə*] *s* tørreapparat.
dry rot ['drai ,rɔt] *s* (om træværk) svamp.
DTs ['di:'ti:z] *spl: have the* ~ have delirium tremens.
dual [djuəl] *adj* dobbelt; **~ carriageway** *s* vej med midterrabat; **~-purpose** *adj* med dobbelt formål.
dubbed [dʌbd] *adj (film)* eftersynkroniseret.
dubious ['dju:biəs] *adj* tvivlsom; tvivlrådig.
duchess ['dʌtʃis] *s* hertuginde.
duchy ['dʌtʃi] *s* hertugdømme.
duck [dʌk] *s* and; dukkert; *roast* ~ andesteg; *like water off a ~'s back* som at slå vand på en gås; *play ~s and drakes* slå smut // *v* dukke (sig); dykke; **~ling** *s* ælling; **~ shooting** *s* andejagt.
duct [dʌkt] *s* kanal, gang; ledning.
dud [dʌd] *s* (om bombe etc) forsager; **~ cheque** *s* dækningsløs check.
due [dju:] *s: give sby his* ~ give en hvad der tilkommer ham // *adj* skyldig; forfalden; passende // *adv:* ~ *north* stik mod nord; *in* ~ *course (,time)* til sin tid; *the train is* ~ *at 4.15* toget skal efter planen ankomme 16.15; ~ *to* på grund af; *with all* ~ *respect, I think that...* du må meget undskylde, men jeg mener at...; **~s** *spl* kontingent, afgifter.
dug [dʌg] *præt* og *pp* af *dig*.
duke [dju:k] *s* hertug.
dull [dʌl] *adj* kedelig, trist; (om lyd) dump; (om vejr etc) mørk, grå; (om kniv) sløv, stump; (om person) tungnem, træg // *v* dulme; sløve; gøre mat.
duly ['dju:li] *adv* behørigt; i rette tid; som det sig hør og bør.
dumb [dʌm] *adj* stum; tavs; dum; *be struck* ~ blive målløs; **~founded** [-'faundid] *adj* paf, lamslået; **~ waiter** *s* madelevator.
dummy ['dʌmi] *s* attrap, dummy; (voks)mannequin; (til baby) narresut; *(sport)* finte // *adj* forloren; skin-; **~ run** *s* prøvekørsel.
dump [dʌmp] *s* losseplads; affaldsbunke; (om by etc) hul i jorden; *(mil)* depot // *v* læsse af; dumpe (i havet); skaffe sig af med; **~(er) truck** *s* lastvogn med vippelad; **~ing** *s (merk)* dumping (fx *price* pris); dumpning (af giftaffald); *no ~ing* henkastning af affald forbudt.
dumpling ['dʌmpliŋ] *s* bolle; *apple* ~ sv.t. æbleskive.
dunce [dʌns] *s* tumpe, fæ.
dune [dju:n] *s* klit.
dung [dʌŋ] *s* gødning, møg.
dungarees [dʌŋgə'ri:z] *spl* cowboybukser; overalls.
dungeon ['dʌndʒən] *s* fangehul.
dunghill [dʌŋhil] *s* mødding.
duodenal [dju:ə'di:nl] *adj:* ~ *ulcer* sår på tolvfingertarmen.
dupe [dju:p] *v* narre.
duplex ['dju:plɛks] *adj* dobbelt.
duplicate *s* ['dju:plikət] dublet, genpart; *in* ~ i to eksemplarer // *v* [-keit] fordoble; duplikere.
duplicity [dju:'plisiti] *s* dobbelthed; tvetydighed.
durable ['djuərəbl] *adj* holdbar, solid; *consumer ~s* varige forbrugsgoder.
duration [dju'reiʃən] *s* varighed; *for the* ~ så længe det varer; indtil videre; på ubestemt tid.
duress [djuə'rɛs] *s: under* ~ under tvang.
Durex ['djuərɛks] ® *s* kondom.

during ['djuəriŋ] *præp* under (fx *the war* krigen); i løbet af.
dusk [dʌsk] *s* skumring, tusmørke; **~y** *adj* mørk, dyster.
dust [dʌst] *s* støv, pulver; drys // *v* støve; blive støvet; tørre støv af; overstrø, drysse; **~bin** *s* skraldebøtte; **~cart** *s* skraldevogn; **~er** *s* støveklud; strødåse (fx til sukker); **~ jacket** *s* (om bog) smudsomslag; **~man** *s* skraldemand; **~pan** *s* fejeblad; **~-up** *s* (F) slagsmål; **~y** *adj* støvet.
Dutch [dʌtʃ] *s/adj* hollandsk; *go* ~ splejse; *the* ~ hollænderne; *double* ~ volapyk; **~man** *s* hollænder.
dutiful ['dju:tiful] *adj* pligtopfyldende; artig.
duty ['dju:ti] *s* pligt; told, afgift; *be off* ~ have fri; *be on* ~ være i tjeneste; have vagt; **~-free** *adj* toldfri.
duvet ['du:vei] *s* dyne; dynetæppe; **~ cover** *s* dynebetræk.
dwarf [dwɔ:f] *s (pl: dwarves)* dværg // *v* rage op over; undertrykke.
dwell [dwɛl] *v (dwelt, dwelt)* bo; dvæle; ~ *on* dvæle ved; **~ing** *s* bolig.
dwindle [dwindl] *v* svinde, aftage.
dye [dai] *s* farvestof // *v* farve; tage imod farve; **~ing** *s* farvning; **~stuffs** *spl* farvestoffer.
dying ['daiiŋ] *adj* døende; døds-; *be* ~ *for a drink* trænge forfærdeligt til en drink.
dyke [daik] *s* dige, dæmning.
dynamic [dai'næmik] *adj* dynamisk; **~s** *spl* dynamik.
dynamite ['dainəmait] *s* dynamit // *v* sprænge med dynamit.
dynasty ['dinəsti] *s* fyrsteslægt, dynasti.
dyslexic [dis'lɛksik] *adj* ordblind.
dyspepsia [dis'pɛpsiə] *s* fordøjelsesbesvær.

E

E, e [i:].
each [i:tʃ] *pron/adv* hver; hver især; begge (to); ~ *of them has a bike* de har begge to en cykel, de har en cykel hver; *oranges at 20p* ~ appelsiner til 20 p stykket; *they hate* ~ *other* de hader hinanden; *on* ~ *side of* på begge sider af, på hver side af.
eager ['i:gə*] *adj* ivrig; ~ *for* begærlig efter; ~ *to* ivrig efter at; **~ beaver** *s* morakker, arbejdsmyre.
eagle [i:gl] *s* ørn.
ear [iə*] *s* øre; gehør; *(bot)* aks; ~ *of corn* majskolbe; *lend an* ~ *to* høre på; *play by* ~ spille efter gehør; *play it by* ~ *(fig)* improvisere; *I'm all* ~*s* jeg er lutter øre; *be out on one's* ~ være blevet smidt ud; *turn a deaf* ~ *to sth* vende det døve øre til ngt; *be up to one's* ~*s in debt* sidde i gæld til op over ørerne; **~ache** ['iəreik] *s* ørepine; **~drop** *s* hængeørering; **~drops** *spl* øredråber; **~drum** *s* trommehinde; **~ful** *s* omgang (skældud).
earl [ə:l] *s* jarl.
earlier ['ə:liə*] *adj* tidligere; før; **earliest** *adj* tidligste; første; *6 o'clock at the earliest* tidligst kl. 6.
earlobe ['iələub] *s* øreflip.
early ['ə:li] *adj* tidlig; først; snarlig; *make an* ~ *start* tage tidligt af sted; stå tidligt op; *the train was* ~ toget ankom for tidligt; *the* ~ *Iron Age* den ældre jernalder; **~ bird** *s* morgenmenneske; **~ retirement** *s* førtidspensionering.
earmark ['iəma:k] *v* øremærke; *(fig)* reservere, lægge til side.
ear-muffs ['iəmʌfs] *spl* ørevarmere.
earn [ə:n] *v* tjene; indbringe; fortjene; *he* ~*ed his reward* han fortjente sin belønning; ~ *one's living* tjene til livets opretholdelse; **earned income relief** *s* lønmodtagerfradrag.
earnest ['ə:nist] *s* alvor; *in* ~ for alvor; *in dead* ~ i ramme alvor // *adj* alvorlig; oprigtig.
earnings ['ə:niŋs] *spl* indtjening, indtægt, indkomst; **~-related** *adj* indkomstreguleret.
ear... ['iə-] sms: **~phone** *s* hovedtelefon; **~piece** *s (tv)* øresnegl; **~plug** *s* øreprop; **~ring** *s* ørering; **~shot** *s* hørevidde; *within* ~*shot* inden for hørevidde; **~-splitting** *adj* øredøvende.

earth [ə:θ] *s* jord; *(elek)* jordforbindelse; *the* ~ Jorden, jordkloden; *cost the* ~ koste det hvide ud af øjnene; *where (,what) on* ~? hvor (,hvad) i alverden? *go to* ~ gå under jorden; *run sby to* ~ støve en op // *v (elek)* jordforbinde; **~-bound** *adj* jordbunden.

earthenware ['ə:θənwεə*] *s* lertøj; fajance.

earthly ['ə:θli] *adj* jordisk; ~ *remains* jordiske rester; *he has not got an* ~ (F) han har ikke en jordisk chance.

earthquake ['ə:θkweik] *s* jordskælv.

earthworm ['ə:θwə:m] *s* regnorm.

earthy ['ə:θi] *adj (fig)* jordbunden.

earwig ['iəwig] *s* ørentvist.

ease [i:z] *s* velvære; ro; lettelse; lethed; tvangfrihed; *at* ~ i ro og mag; veltilpas; rolig; *ill at* ~ ubehageligt tilpas; urolig; *set sby's mind at* ~ berolige en; *stand at* ~ *(mil)* stå rør; *a life of* ~ en ubekymret tilværelse // *v* lette; lindre; løsne; ~ *sth in (,out)* lempe ngt ind (,ud); ~ *off (,up)* lette; sætte farten ned; slappe af.

easel ['i:zl] *s* staffeli.

easily ['i:zili] *adv* let, med lethed; sagtens; afgjort; *he's* ~ *the best* han er så langt den bedste.

east [i:st] *s* øst; *the East* Østen, orienten; *the Far East* det Fjerne Østen // *adj* østlig; østen-; øst- // *adv* østpå, mod øst.

Easter ['i:stə*] *s* påske.

easterly ['i:stəli] *adj* østlig, østen-.

eastern ['i:stən] *adj* østlig, øst-.

eastward(s) ['i:stwədz] *adv* østpå, mod øst.

easy ['i:zi] *adj* let, nem; bekvem; fri; omgængelig // *adv: take it* ~ tage det med ro; *go* ~ *on sth* spare på ngt; skåne ngt; **~ chair** *s* lænestol; **~-going** *adj* rolig, sorgløs.

eat [i:t] *v (ate, eaten* [eit, i:tn]) spise; fortære; ~ *away at* gøre indhug i; *what's* ~*ing you?* hvad er der i vejen med dig? ~ *in* spise hjemme; ~ *out* spise ude; **~able** *adj* spiselig; **~ables** *spl* mad(varer).

eaves [i:vz] *spl* tagskæg; **~drop** *v* lytte, lure.

ebb [εb] *s* ebbe (mods: flod) // *v* ebbe; synke; ~ *(away)* ebbe ud, svinde.

ebony ['εbəni] *s* ibenholt.

ebullient [i'bʌliənt] *adj* sprudlende, overgiven.

eccentric [ik'sεntrik] *s* excentriker, sær snegl // *adj* excentrisk, sær.

ecclesiastic [ikli:zi'æstik] *s* gejstlig; **~al** *adj* gejstlig, kirkelig.

echelon ['εʃəlɔn] *s (fig)* trin på rangstigen; *the higher (,up-)* ~*s* de højere rangklasser.

echo ['εkəu] *s (pl:* ~*es)* ekko, genlyd; genklang // *v* genlyde; gentage, snakke efter munden.

eclipse [i'klips] *s* formørkelse; *solar* ~ solformørkelse // *v* formørke; stille i skygge.

ecocide ['i:kəusaid] *s* miljøødelæggelse.

eco-friendly ['i:kəu,frεndli] *adj* miljøvenlig.

ecology [i'kɔlədʒi] *s* økologi.

economic [ikə'nɔmik] *adj* økonomisk; rentabel, som kan betale sig; **~al** *adj* økonomisk, sparsommelig; besparende; **~s** *spl* (national)økonomi.

economist [i'kɔnəmist] *s* økonom; **economize** [i'kɔnəmaiz] *v* være sparsommelig, spare *(on* på).

economy [i'kɔnəmi] *s* økonomi; sparsommelighed.

ecstasy ['εkstəsi] *s* ekstase; *go into ecstasies over* falde i svime over.

ecstatic [εks'tætik] *adj* henrykt, ekstatisk.

eczema ['εksimə] *s* eksem.

eddy ['εdi] *s* hvirvel // *v* hvirvle.

edge [εdʒ] *s* kant; (på kniv) æg, skær; skarphed, bid; *take the* ~ *off sth* tage brodden af ngt; *be on* ~ være irritabel; stå på højkant // *v* kante; ligge langs kanten af; ~ *away from* rykke væk fra; ~ *towards* kante sig hen mod; **~ways** *adv* på kant; sidelæns; *he couldn't get a word in* ~*ways* han kunne ikke få et ord indført.

edging ['εdʒiŋ] *s* kantning; kantebånd; bort.

edgy ['ɛdʒi] *adj* irritabel; nervøs; skarp.
edible ['ɛdibl] *adj* spiselig.
edifice ['ɛdifis] *s* stor bygning, bygningsværk.
edit ['ɛdit] *v* redigere; udgive; *(film* etc) klippe.
edition [i'diʃən] *s* udgave; oplag.
editor ['ɛditə*] *s* redaktør; udgiver; *(film)* klippebord.
editorial [ɛdi'tɔ:riəl] *s* leder, ledende artikel // *adj* redaktionel, redaktions-.
EDP ['i:di:'pi:] *s* (fork.f. *electronic data processing)* edb.
educate ['ɛdjukeit] *v* uddanne; opdrage; *an ~d guess* et kvalificeret gæt.
education [ɛdju'keiʃən] *s* uddannelse; undervisning; opdragelse; **educational** [-'keiʃənəl] *adj* uddannelses-; opdragelses-; skole- (fx *books* bøger).
educator ['ɛdjukeitə*] *s* pædagog.
EEC ['i:i:si:] *s* (fork.f. *European Economic Community)* EF (EØF).
eel [i:l] *s* ål; *jellied ~* ål i gele.
eerie ['iəri] *adj* uhyggelig.
efface [i'feis] *v* viske ud, slette; *~ oneself* være selvudslettende.
effect [i'fɛkt] *s* virkning; resultat; effekt; *in ~* faktisk, praktisk talt; *take ~* (om fx maskine) virke; *(jur)* træde i kraft; *sth to that ~* ngt i den retning; *to the ~ that* med det formål at; *to no ~* forgæves.
effective [i'fɛktiv] *adj* virkningsfuld, effektiv.
effects [i'fɛkts] *spl* ejendele, effekter.
effeminate [i'fɛminit] *adj* feminin, kvindagtig.
effervescent [ɛfə'vɛsnt] *adj* sprudlende; brusende.
effete [i'fi:t] *adj* vattet.
efficacy ['ɛfikəsi] *s* virkningsfuldhed.
efficiency [i'fiʃənsi] *s* effektivitet, dygtighed; ydedygtighed; **efficient** *adj* effektiv; dygtig.
effigy ['ɛfidʒi] *s* billede, statue.
effort ['ɛfət] *s* anstrengelse; indsats; præstation; *make an ~* gøre en kraftanstrengelse; **~less** *adj* ubesværet, let.
effrontery [i'frɔntəri] *s* frækhed.
effusive [i'fju:siv] *adj* overstrømmende.
e.g. ['i:'dʒi:] (fork.f. *exempli gratia)* for eksempel, fx.
egg [ɛg] *s* æg; *lay an ~* lægge et æg; (S) kvaje sig; *fried ~s* spejlæg // *v: ~ on* tilskynde, ægge; **~-beater** *s* hjulpisker; **~cup** *s* æggebæger; **~plant** *s* aubergine; **~shell** *s* æggeskal // *adj* æggeskalsfarvet; **~-slice** *s* paletkniv; **~-timer** *s* æggeur; **~ white** *s* æggehvide; **~ yolk** [-jəuk] *s* æggeblomme.
ego ['i:gəu] *s* jeg, ego; (F) forfængelighed; **~centric** [-'sɛntrik] *adj* selvoptaget.
egoist ['ɛgəuist] *s* egoist; **egotist** ['ɛgəutist] *s* selvoptaget person.
Egypt ['i:dʒipt] *s* Egypten; **Egyptian** [i'dʒipʃən] *s* egypter // *adj* egyptisk.
eh [ei] *interj* hva'? hvadbeha'r?
eiderdown ['aidədaun] *s* edderdun; dyne.
eight [eit] *num* otte.
eighteen [ei'ti:n] *num* atten.
eighth [eitθ] *s* ottendedel // *num* ottende.
eighty ['eiti] *num* firs; *in the eighties* i firserne.
Eire ['ɛərə] *s* Den Irske Republik.
either ['aiðə*] *pron* en af to; den ene el. den anden // *adv* heller; *~ a or b* enten a el. b; hverken a el. b; *on ~ side* på begge sider; *I don't like ~ of them* jeg kan ikke lide nogen af dem; *I don't ~* det kan jeg heller ikke; *I didn't see ~ one or the other* jeg så hverken den ene eller den anden; jeg så ingen af dem.
ejaculation [idʒækju'leiʃən] *s* sædudtømmelse, ejakulation; udbrud, udråb.
eject [i'dʒɛkt] *v* udspy; udsende; fordrive, smide ud.
ejector seat [i'dʒɛktə si:t] *s* katapultsæde.
eke [i:k] *v: ~ out* strække, få til at slå til.
elaborate *v* [i'læbəreit] uddybe, udbygge; udarbejde (i detaljer); gå i

detaljer // *adj* [i'læbərit] udførlig, detaljeret; kunstfærdig.

elapse [i'læps] *v* (om tid) gå, forløbe.

elastic [i'læstik] *s* elastik // *adj* elastisk, smidig; ~ **band** *s* elastik, gummibånd.

elasticity [iləs'tisiti] *s* elasticitet, smidighed.

elated [i'leitid] *adj* opløftet; i høj stemning; oprømt.

elation [i'leiʃən] *s* glæde, opløftelse; oprømthed.

elbow ['ɛlbəu] *s* albue; *rub ~s with* gnubbe sig op ad // *v* bruge albuerne; skubbe; *~ one's way forward* albue sig frem; **~-grease** *s* knofedt.

elder ['ɛldə*] *s (bot)* hyld // *adj (komp* af *old)* ældre; *one's ~s* de der er ældre end en selv; *the ~s* fortidens mennesker; menighedens ældste; **~berry** *s* hyldebær; **~ly** *adj* ældre; gammeldags; *the ~ly* de ældre; *care of the ~ly* ældreomsorg; **eldest** ['ɛldist] *adj (sup* af *old)* ældst.

elect [i'lɛkt] *v* vælge; foretrække // *adj* udvalgt; *the president ~* den tiltrædende præsident.

election [i'lɛkʃən] *s* valg; udvælgelse.

electioneering [ilɛkʃə'niəriŋ] *s* valgkampagne, valgagitation.

elector [i'lɛktə*] *s* vælger; valgmand.

electorate [i'lɛktərət] *s* vælgerkorps.

electric [i'lɛktrik] *adj* elektrisk; el-; elektro-; **~al** *adj* elektrisk; ~ **blanket** *s* elektrisk varmetæppe; ~ **cooker** *s* elkomfur; ~ **fire** *s* elvarmeovn.

electrician [ilɛk'triʃən] *s* elektriker.

electricity [ilɛk'trisiti] *s* elektricitet.

electric shock [i'lɛktrik 'ʃɔk] *s* elektrisk stød.

electrify [i'lɛktrifai] *v* elektrificere; opildne.

electrocute [i'lɛktrəkju:t] *v* dræbe ved elektrisk stød; henrette i den elektriske stol.

electron [i'lɛktrən] *s* elektron.

electronic [ilɛk'trɔnik] *adj* elektronisk; ~ **data processing** *s (EDP)* elektronisk databehandling (edb); **~s** *s* elektronik.

elegant ['ɛligənt] *adj* elegant.

element ['ɛlimənt] *s* element; (bestand)del; grundstof; *an ~ of truth* et vist gran af sandhed; *an ~ of danger* et faremoment.

elementary [ɛli'mɛntəri] *adj* elementær; *~ school (brit, gl)* sv.t. folkeskole; *(am)* sv.t. grundskole (1.-6 el. 8. kl).

elephant ['ɛlifənt] *s* elefant.

elevate ['ɛliveit] *v* løfte; forhøje, ophøje.

elevation [ɛli'veiʃən] *s* løften; forhøjning; højde; forfremmelse.

eleven [i'lɛvn] *num* elleve // *s: (football) ~* foldboldhold.

elevenses [i'lɛvənsiz] *spl* formiddagskaffe el. -te.

eleventh [i'lɛvənθ] *s* ellevtedel // *adj* ellevte.

elf [ɛlf] *s (pl: elves* [ɛlvz]) alf; **elfin** *adj* alfe-; alfeagtig; æterisk.

elicit [i'lisit] *v* lokke frem; udløse (fx *a reflex* en refleks).

eligible ['ɛlidʒibl] *adj* valgbar; kvalificeret; passende; *an ~ young man* et passende parti, "drømmen om en svigersøn"; *~ for a pension* pensionsberettiget.

eliminate [i'limineit] *v* bortskaffe, fjerne; udelukke, eliminere.

Elizabethan [ilizə'bi:ðən] *adj* elisabethansk (fra Elisabeth 1.s tid 1558-1603); renæssance-.

elk [ɛlk] *s* elg.

ellipse [i'lips] *s* ellipse.

elliptical [i'liptikəl] *adj* ellipseformet.

elm [ɛlm] *s* elm(etræ); ~ **disease** *s* elmesyge.

elocution [ɛlə'kju:ʃən] *s* talekunst, taleteknik.

elongated ['i:lɔŋgeitid] *adj* forlænget; langstrakt.

elope [i'ləup] *v* løbe bort sammen (for at gifte sig); **~ment** *s* flugt; bortførelse.

eloquence ['ɛləkwəns] *s* veltalenhed; **eloquent** *adj* veltalende; *(fig)* talende, sigende.

else [ɛls] *adv* ellers; anden; andet; *everywhere ~* alle andre steder; *little ~* ikke stort andet; *nothing ~* intet andet; *if nothing ~...* i det mindste...; *or* ~ ellers, eller også; *something* ~ noget andet; *somewhere* ~ andetsteds, et andet sted; **~where** *adv* andetsteds; andre steder.

elucidate [i'lu:sideit] *v* tydeliggøre; belyse, forklare.

elude [i'lu:d] *v* undvige; undgå; slippe fra.

elusive [i'lu:siv] *adj* vanskelig at få fat på; svær at definere; flygtig.

elves [ɛlvz] *spl* af *elf.*

emaciated [i'meisieitid] *adj* udtæret, udmagret.

emanate ['ɛməneit] *v:* ~ *from* udgå fra; udstråle fra; have sit udspring i.

emancipate [i'mænsipeit] *v* frigøre; frigive (fx *the slaves* slaverne); **emancipation** [-'peiʃən] *s* frigørelse; frigivelse.

embalm [im'ba:m] *v* balsamere; fylde med vellugt.

embankment [im'bæŋkmənt] *s* vold, dæmning.

embargo [im'ba:gəu] *s (pl: ~es)* forbud (mod import og eksport), embargo // *v* beslaglægge; lægge embargo på.

embark [im'ba:k] *v:* ~ *on* begynde på; gå ombord i; begive sig ud på; **~ation** [-'keiʃən] *s* indskibning.

embarrass [im'bærəs] *v* gøre forlegen; hæmme; **~ing** *adj* pinlig, flov; **~ment** *s* forlegenhed; generthed.

embassy ['ɛmbəsi] *s* ambassade.

embed [im'bɛd] *v* lægge ned i; indstøbe, indkapsle; *~ded in* begravet i; omgivet af.

embellish [im'bɛliʃ] *v* udsmykke; pynte på; forskønne; **~ment** *s* pynt, forsiring.

ember ['ɛmbə*] *s* glød.

embezzle [im'bɛzl] *v* begå underslæb; **~ment** *s* underslæb.

embitter [im'bitə*] *v* forbitre, gøre bitter.

emblem ['ɛmbləm] *s* symbol; mærke.

embodiment [im'bɔdimənt] *s* legemliggørelse; indarbejdelse.

embody [im'bɔdi] *v* legemliggøre; udtrykke; udforme; inkorporere, indarbejde.

embolism ['ɛmbəlizm] *s (med)* blodprop.

embrace [im'breis] *s* omfavnelse // *v* omfavne (hinanden); tage til sig; omfatte, indbefatte.

embroider [im'brɔidə*] *v* brodere; *(fig)* pynte *(on* på); **embroidery** *s* broderi.

embryo ['ɛmbriəu] *s* foster; *(bot)* kim, spire.

emend [i'mɛnd] *v* forbedre på, rette i.

emerald ['ɛmərəld] *s* smaragd // *adj* smaragdgrøn.

emerge [i'mə:dʒ] *v* dukke op (,frem); fremgå; *it ~d that* det viste sig at; **emergence** [i'mə:dʒəns] *s* tilsynekomst, opdukken.

emergency [i'mə:dʒənsi] *s* nødsituation; *in case of* ~ i nødstilfælde; *state of* ~ undtagelsestilstand; ~ **area** *s* katastrofeområde; ~ **brake** *s* nødbremse; ~ **exit** *s* nødudgang; ~ **ward** *s* skadestue.

emergent [i'mə:dʒənt] *adj:* ~ *countries* udviklingslande.

emery ['ɛməri] *s* smergel; ~ **board** *s* sandfil (til negle).

emigrant ['ɛmigrənt] *s* udvandrer, emigrant.

emigrate ['ɛmigreit] *v* udvandre, emigrere.

eminence ['ɛminəns] *s* høj anseelse; fremtrædende stilling; berømthed.

eminent ['ɛminənt] *adj* høj; fremtrædende, fremragende; enestående.

emissary ['ɛmisəri] *s* udsending.

emission [i'miʃən] *s* udstedelse; (ud)stråling; udstedelse.

emit [i'mit] *v* udsende; udstede; udstråle; udstøde.

emotion [i'məuʃən] *s* følelse; sindsbevægelse; **~al** *adj* følelsesbetonet; følelsesladet; følsom.

emotive [i'məutiv] *adj* følelsesbetonet.

empathy ['ɛmpəθi] *s* indfølingsevne, indlevelse.

emperor ['ɛmpərə*] *s* kejser.

emphasis ['ɛmfəsis] *s (pl: emphases* [-si:z]) eftertryk, vægt.

emphasize ['ɛmfəsaiz] *v* betone, lægge vægt på; understrege.

emphatic [ɛm'fætik] *adj* eftertrykkelig, udtrykkelig; iøjnefaldende.

empire ['ɛmpaiə*] *s* kejserdømme, imperium; *the Roman Empire* romerriget; *French Empire* empirestil.
empirical [ɛm'pirikəl] *adj* erfaringsmæssig.
employ [im'plɔi] *s* beskæftigelse, tjeneste // *v* ansætte, beskæftige; anvende, bruge.
employee [implɔi'i:] *s* ansat; funktionær.
employer [im'plɔiə*] *s* arbejdsgiver.
employment [im'plɔimənt] *s* beskæftigelse; ansættelse; arbejde; ~ **agency** *s* privat arbejdsanvisningsbureau.
empower [im'pauə*] *v:* ~ *sby to* bemyndige en til (at); sætte en i stand til (at).
empress ['ɛmpris] *s* kejserinde.
empty ['ɛmpti] *v* tømme(s), blive tom // *adj* tom; øde, ubeboet; **~-handed** *adj* tomhændet; **~-headed** *adj* tomhjernet.
emulate ['ɛmjuleit] *v* efterligne; prøve at leve op til.
emulsifier [i'mʌlsifaiə*] *s* emulgator.
enable [i'neibl] *v:* ~ *sby to* gøre det muligt for en at, gøre en i stand til at.
enact [i'nækt] *v* (om lov) vedtage; *(fig)* spille.
enamel [i'næməl] *s* emalje // *v* emaljere, lakere.
encased [in'keist] *adj:* ~ *in* indkapslet i; indesluttet af.
enchant [in'tʃa:nt] *v* fortrylle; henrykke; **~ing** *adj* fortryllende, besnærende.
encircle [in'sə:kl] *v* indkredse, omringe; omkredse.
enclose [in'kləuz] *v* omgive; indhegne; indeslutte; *please find ~d* (i brev) vedlagt følger.
enclosure [in'kləuʒə*] *s* indhegning, indelukke; (i brev) bilag.
encode [in'kəud] *v* kode.
encompass [in'kʌmpəs] *v* omgive; omringe; omfatte.
encore ['ɔŋkɔ:*] *s* ekstranummer, dacapo.
encounter [in'kauntə*] *s* møde, sammentræf // *v* møde, træffe (på).
encourage [in'kəridʒ] *v* opmuntre; tilskynde, fremme; **~ment** *s* opmuntring; tilskyndelse.
encroach [in'krəutʃ] *v:* ~ *on* trænge sig ind på; gøre indgreb i.
encumber [in'kʌmbə*] *v* hindre, besværliggøre; tynge.
encumbrance [in'kʌmbrəns] *s* belastning.
encyclopaedia [ɛnsaikləu'pi:diə] *s* leksikon, opslagsværk.
end [ɛnd] *s* ende, slutning; spids; stump; skod; endeligt; mål; *at an ~* færdig; *come to an ~* slutte, høre op; *put an ~ to* gøre en ende på; sætte en stopper for; gøre kål på; *in the ~* til sidst, til slut; *it's no ~ difficult* (F) det er mægtig svært; *this is the ~!* nu er det altså nok! *he's got no ~ of money* (F) han er fuld af penge; *be on ~* stå på den anden ende; være på højkant; *for days on ~* i dagevis; *for five hours on ~* i fem timer i træk; *to that ~* med det formål; *to no ~* uden formål; *make ~s meet* få pengene til at slå til, få det til at løbe rundt // *v* ende, slutte; afslutte; holde op; ~ *up with* ende med.
endanger [in'deindʒə*] *v* bringe i fare, sætte på spil.
endearing [in'diəriŋ] *adj* indtagende; **endearment** *s* kærtegn.
endeavour [in'dɛvə*] *s* bestræbelse, stræben // *v:* ~ *to* bestræbe sig på at.
ending ['ɛndiŋ] *s* ende, (af)slutning; endelse.
endive ['ɛndaiv] *s* julesalat.
endless ['ɛndlis] *adj* endeløs, uendelig.
endorse [in'dɔ:s] *v* (om check) skrive bag på, endossere; påtegne; skrive under på; **~ment** *s* påtegning; endossering; tilslutning.
endow [in'dau] *v* skænke (et beløb), betænke; ~ *with* udstyre med; skænke.
end product ['ɛndprɔdəkt] *s* slutprodukt, slutresultat.
endurable [in'djuərəbl] *adj* udholdelig, tålelig.

endurance [in'djuərəns] *s* udholdenhed; modstandskraft; trængsler, lidelser.
endure [in'djuə*] *v* tåle, udholde; lide, udstå; vare (ved).
endways *adv: a house built ~ to the road* et hus der vender gavlen ud mod vejen.
enemy ['ɛnəmi] *s* fjende // *adj* fjendtlig.
energetic [ɛnə'dʒɛtik] *adj* energisk, aktiv; handlekraftig.
energy ['ɛnədʒi] *s* energi, kraft.
enervating ['ɛnə:veitiŋ] *adj* enerverende; udmattende.
enforce [in'fɔ:s] *v* bestyrke; fremtvinge, gennemtvinge; *(jur)* håndhæve (fx *the laws* lovene); **~d** *adj* påtvungen; ufrivillig.
engage [in'geidʒ] *v* engagere; ansætte; reservere; optage; påtage sig *(to* at); *(mil)* angribe; *(tekn)* tilkoble; *~ in* tage del i; indlade sig på; indlede; **~d** *adj* optaget, travl; forlovet; *be ~d in* være beskæftiget med; *number ~d (tlf)* optaget; **~ment** *s* beskæftigelse; ansættelse; aftale; forpligtelse; forlovelse; *(mil)* træfning; **~ment ring** *s* forlovelsesring.
engaging [in'geidʒiŋ] *adj* indtagende, vindende.
engine ['ɛndʒin] *s* maskine, motor; lokomotiv; **~ driver** *s* lokomotivfører.
engineer [ɛndʒi'niə*] *s* ingeniør; maskinist; tekniker; *(fig)* ophavsmand // *v* konstruere; *(fig)* iscenesætte, arrangere; **engineering** [-'niəriŋ] *s* teknik; ingeniørarbejde // *adj* maskin-.
engine failure ['ɛndʒin 'feiljə*] *s* motorstop, motorskade; **engine room** *s (mar)* maskinrum; (i fabrik) maskinhal; **engine trouble** *s (auto* etc) vrøvl med motoren.
English ['iŋgliʃ] *s/adj* engelsk; *the ~* englænderne; **~ breakfast** *s* stor morgenmad med varme retter; **~man** *s* englænder.
engrave [in'greiv] *v* gravere, præge; **engraving** *s* gravering.
engrossed [in'grəust] *adj: ~ in* opslugt af, fordybet i.
engulf [in'gʌlf] *v* opsluge.
enhance [in'ha:ns] *v* forøge; forhøje; forbedre.
enigma [i'nigmə] *s* gåde; **~tic** [-'mætik] *adj* gådefuld.
enjoy [in'dʒɔi] *v* nyde; more sig over; synes om; *~ oneself* more sig; have det rart; *~ good health* have et godt helbred; **~able** *adj* morsom; hyggelig; **~ment** *s* nydelse; glæde.
enlarge [in'la:dʒ] *v* forstørre; udvide; blive større; *~ on* udbrede sig om; **~ment** *s* forstørrelse; udvidelse.
enlighten [in'laitn] *v* oplyse; **~ed** *adj* oplyst; **~ment** *s* oplysning; *the Enlightenment (hist)* oplysningstiden.
enlist [in'list] *v* hverve, rekruttere; melde sig (fx *in the army* til hæren).
enliven [in'laivn] *v* oplive, kvikke op.
enmity ['ɛnmiti] *s* fjendskab, uvenskab.
enormity [i'nɔ:miti] *s* uhyrlighed.
enormous [i'nɔ:məs] *adj* enorm, uhyre, drabelig; **~ly** *adv* enormt.
enough [i'nʌf] *adj/adv* nok; *~ is ~* nu kan det være nok; *~ to drive you crazy* til at blive vanvittig over (,af); *strangely ~* mærkeligt nok; *and sure ~, he forgot!* og han glemte det ganske rigtig!
enquire [in'kwaiə*] *v* d.s.s. *inquire.*
enrage [in'reidʒ] *v* gøre rasende.
enrich [in'ritʃ] *v* berige; *~ with* berige med; tilsætte.
enrol [in'rəul] *v* indføre på liste, indskrive; tilmelde sig; **~ment** *s* indskrivning; tilmeldelse; medlemskab.
ensconced [in'skɔnst] *adj: ~ in* forskanset i; plantet i (fx *the sofa* sofaen).
ensign ['ɛnsain] *s* fane, flag; ['ɛnsn] *(am)* søløjtnant.
enslave [in'sleiv] *v* gøre til slave, underkue.
ensue [in'ʃu:] *v* følge (lige) efter; være resultatet af; **ensuing** *adj* efterfølgende.
ensure [in'ʃuə*] *v* garantere, sikre.
entail [in'teil] *v* medføre; kræve.
entangle [in'tæŋgl] *v* filtre sammen, vikle ind; *get ~d in* blive blandet

ind i, rode sig ind i; *be ~d with sby* have rodet sig ud i ngt med en.
enter ['ɛntə*] *v* gå (,komme) ind (i); anføre, indføre; optage; indskrive; melde sig til; *(edb)* gemme; *~ for* indskrive sig til; *~ into* gå ind i; indlade sig på; komme ind på; *~ upon* slå ind på; tiltræde.
enterprise ['ɛntəpraiz] *s* foretagende; foretagsomhed; virksomhed; **enterprising** *adj* foretagsom.
entertain [ɛntə'tein] *v* underholde; traktere, have gæster; gøre sig (fx *illusions* illusioner); overveje; **~er** *s* varietékunstner, entertainer; **~ing** *s* selskabelighed, repræsentation // *adj* underholdende, morsom; **~ment** *s* underholdning; **~ment allowance** *s* repræsentationstillæg.
enthralled [ɛn'θrɔ:ld] *adj* fængslet, betaget.
enthuse [in'θju:z] *v* være begejstret; falde i svime.
enthusiasm [in'θju:ziæzəm] *s* entusiasme, begejstring; **enthusiast** *s* varm tilhænger, entusiast; **enthusiastic** [-'æstik] *adj* entusiastisk, begejstret.
entice [in'tais] *v* lokke; forlede.
entire [in'taiə*] *adj* hel, komplet, i ét stykke; **~ly** *adv* helt, fuldstændig; udelukkende; **~ty** [-'tairəti] *s* helhed; *in its ~ty* i sin helhed.
entitle [in'taitl] *v: be ~d to* være berettiget til, have krav på; *~ sby to sth* give en ret til ngt.
entity ['ɛntiti] *s* væsen, individ.
entrails ['ɛntreilz] *spl* indvolde; indmad.
entrance *s* ['ɛntrəns] indgang; adgang, entré; *gain ~ to* få adgang til; blive optaget på (fx *university* universitetet) // *v* [in'tra:ns] henrykke, tryllebinde.; **~ examination** *s* adgangseksamen; **~ fee** *s* entré(afgift); indmeldelsesgebyr.
entreat [in'tri:t] *v* bønfalde (,bede indtrængende) om; **entreaty** *s* bøn(faldelse).
entrenched [in'trɛntʃd] *adj* forskanset; rodfæstet, indgroet.
entrust [in'trʌst] *v: ~ sth to sby* betro en ngt; *~ him with the money* betro ham pengene.
entry ['ɛntri] *s* det at komme ind; indtræden; indkørsel; indtog; adgang; indmeldelse, indskrivning; *no ~* indkørsel (,adgang) forbudt; *make an ~ in a book* indføre (,skrive) ngt i en bog; **~ form** *s* indmeldelsesblanket; **~ permit** *s* indrejsetilladelse; passérseddel.
entwine [in'twain] *v* flette sammen, omvinde.
enumerate [i'nju:məreit] *v* optælle, opregne.
enunciate [i'nʌnsieit] *v* udtale, formulere.
envelop [in'vɛləp] *v* indhylle; skjule; omgive, omringe.
envelope ['ɛnvələup] *s* konvolut, kuvert.
enviable ['ɛnviəbl] *adj* misundelsesværdig; **envious** ['ɛnviəs] *adj* misundelig *(of* på).
environment [in'vairənmənt] *s* omgivelser, miljø; **~al** [-'mɛn-] *adj* miljø-; **~alist** [-'mɛn-] *s* miljøforkæmper; **~al pollution** *s* miljøforurening; **~al protection** *s* miljøbeskyttelse.
environs [in'vairənz] *spl* omgivelser; omegn.
envisage [in'vizidʒ] *v* se på; forudse; forestille sig; se i øjnene.
envoy ['ɛnvɔi] *s* udsending, sendebud.
envy ['ɛnvi] *s* misundelse // *v* misunde.
EOC ['i:əu'si:] *s* fork.f. *Equal Opportunities Commission.*
ephemeral [i'fɛmərəl] *adj* kortvarig, flygtig.
epic ['ɛpik] *s* epos // *adj* episk; storslået.
epidemic ['ɛpidɛmik] *s* epidemi // *adj* epidemisk.
epilogue ['ɛpilɔg] *s* efterskrift, slutningstale, epilog.
Epiphany [i'pifəni] *s* helligtrekongersdag (6.jan).
episode ['ɛpisəud] *s* episode; (i fx tv-serie) afsnit.
epitaph ['ɛpita:f] *s* gravskrift, epitaf.
epithet ['ɛpiθɛt] *s* tilnavn, øgenavn.
epitome [i'pitəmi] *s: be the ~ of (fig)* være indbegrebet af.

epitomize [i'pitəmaiz] *v* resumere, sammenfatte; være indbegrebet af.

epoch ['i:pɔk] *s* tid(s)alder, epoke; **~-making** *adj* epokegørende.

equable ['ɛkwəbl] *adj* rolig, ligevægtig.

equal ['i:kwəl] *s* lige(mand) // *v* være lig med; kunne måle sig med // *adj* lige; ligelig; ligestillet; *The Equal Opportunities Commission* sv.t. Ligestillingsrådet; *~ to* lig med; jævnbyrdig med; *be ~ to* (også) kunne magte; *on ~ terms* på lige fod; *other things being ~* alt andet lige.

equality [i'kwɔliti] *s* lighed; ligestilling.

equalizer ['i:kwəlaizə*] *s (sport)* udligning(smål).

equally ['i:kwəli] *adv* lige(ligt), lige så.

equal(s) sign ['i:kwəl(z) sain] *s* lighedstegn.

equanimity [ɛkwə'nimiti] *s* ligevægt, sindsro.

equation [i'kweiʃən] *s (mat)* ligning.

equator [i'kweitə*] *s* ækvator; **~ial** [ɛkwə'tɔ:riəl] *adj* ækvatorial-.

equestrian [i'kwɛstriən] *s* (skole)rytter // *adj* rytter-.

equilateral ['i:kwi'lætərəl] *adj* ligesidet.

equilibrium [i:kwi'libriəm] *s* ligevægt.

equine ['ɛkwain] *adj* hesteagtig; heste-.

equinox ['i:kwinɔks] *s* jævndøgn.

equip [i'kwip] *v* udstyre, udruste; ekvipere; **~ment** *s* udrustning; udstyr; tilbehør; installation.

equity ['ɛkwiti] *s* retfærdighed; *equities* stamaktier.

equivalent [i'kwivələnt] *s* modstykke, ækvivalent // *adj* tilsvarende; *be ~ to* svare til; være det samme som.

equivocal [i'kwivəkəl] *adj* tvetydig; usikker; tvivlsom.

er [ə:*, ɛ:*]: *~, ladies and gentlemen* øh, mine damer og herrer.

era ['iərə] *s* epoke, tidsalder, æra.

eradicate [i'rædikeit] *v* udrydde.

erase [i'reiz] *v* viske ud; radere (ud), slette.

eraser [i'reizə*] *v* viskelæder.

ere [ɛə*] *præp* (H) før, inden.

erect [i'rɛkt] *v* rejse (fx *a monument* et monument); opføre; oprette // *v* oprejst; opret, rank.

erection [i'rɛkʃən] *s* rejsning; opførelse; oprettelse; erektion.

ermine ['ə:min] *s* hermelin, lækat.

erode [i'rəud] *v* erodere(s), nedbryde(s); *(fig)* undergrave.

erosion [i'rəuʒən] *s* erosion, nedbrydning.

erotic [i'rɔtik] *adj* (let *neds)* erotisk.

erotica [i'rɔtikə] *s* erotiske billeder; erotisk litteratur.

eroticism [i'rɔtisizm] *s* erotisk præg, erotik.

err [ə:*] *v* tage fejl, fejle; *(gl)* flakke om, fare vild.

errand ['ɛr(ə)nd] *s* ærinde; **~ boy** *s* bydreng; *(fig)* stikirenddreng.

errant ['ɛrənt] *adj* omstrejfende; (om ægtemand) utro, vidtløftig.

erratic [i'rætik] *adj* uberegnelig; uregelmæssig; ujævn; omkringflakkende.

erroneous [i'rəuniəs] *adj* fejlagtig, urigtig.

error ['ɛrə*] *s* fejl, fejltagelse; *commit an ~* begå en fejl; *be in ~* tage fejl; *~ of judgment* fejlskøn.

erudite ['ɛrudait] *adj* lærd; belæst.

erupt [i'rʌpt] *v* bryde ud; (om vulkan) komme i udbrud; (om sygdom) slå ud.

eruption [i'rʌpʃən] *s* udbrud; frembrud.

escalate ['ɛskəleit] *v* stige; optrappe; **escalation** [-'leiʃən] *s* optrapning.

escalator ['ɛskəleitə*] *s* rulletrappe.

escape [i'skeip] *s* flugt; rømning; redning; udslip; *fire ~* brandtrappe, flugtvej; *make a lucky ~ from sth* slippe godt fra ngt; *make a narrow ~* undslippe med nød og næppe // *v* flygte; undslippe; undgå; redde sig; strømme ud.

escapee [i'skeipi:] *s* undsluppen, undvegen.

eschew [is'tʃu:] *v* undgå, sky.

escort *s* ['ɛskɔ:t] eskorte; ledsager // *v* [i'skɔ:t] eskortere, ledsage; følge.

esoteric [ɛsə'tɛrik] *adj* kun for særligt indviede.

especially [i'spɛʃli] *adv* specielt, især.
espionage ['ɛspiəna:ʒ] *s* spionage.
esquire [ɛs'kwaiə*] *s (Esq): John Brown* ~ hr. John Brown.
essay ['ɛsei] *s* essay; forsøg; (i skolen) stil.
essence ['ɛsns] *s* det væsentlige; kerne, essens; *in* ~ egentlig.
essential [i'sɛnʃl] *adj* væsentlig; tvingende; uomgængelig; **~ly** *adv* i alt væsentligt; inderst inde.
establish [i'stæbliʃ] *v* oprette, grundlægge; etablere, tilvejebringe; godtgøre, bevise (fx *one's innocence* sin uskyld); ~ *oneself* nedsætte sig; indrette sig; **~ment** *s* oprettelse, etablering; institution; foretagende; *the Establishment* det etablerede samfund, systemet.
estate [i'steit] *s* gods; besiddelse; (døds)bo; *real* ~ fast ejendom; ~ **agent** *s* ejendomsmægler; ~ **car** *s* stationcar.
esteem [i'sti:m] *s* agtelse; *hold sby in great* ~ have stor respekt for en, sætte stor pris på en // *v* sætte stor pris på; anse.
estimate *s* ['ɛstimit] skøn, vurdering; overslag; *at a rough* ~ skønsmæssigt; *at the lowest* ~ mindst // *v* ['ɛstimeit] skønne, vurdere, anslå.
estimation [ɛsti'meiʃən] *s* skøn, vurdering; agtelse, respekt; *go up in sby's* ~ stige i ens agtelse.
estranged [i'streindʒd] *adj: his* ~ *wife* hans fraskilte (,fraseparerede) hustru.
estrangement [i'streindʒmənt] *s* kølighed, fremmedgørelse.
estuary ['ɛstjuəri] *s* flodmunding (med tidevand).
etching ['ɛtʃiŋ] *s* radering; ætsning.
eternal [i'tə:nl] *adj* evig, evindelig.
eternity [i'tə:niti] *s* evighed.
ether ['i:θə*] *s* æter.
etherial [i'θiəriəl] *adj* æterisk, overjordisk.
ethics ['ɛθiks] *s* moral(lære), etik.
ethnic ['ɛθnik] *adj* folke-, etnisk; hedensk; ~ **group** *s* befolkningsgruppe.
Eucharist ['ju:kərist] *s: the* ~ nadveren.
eulogy ['ju:lədʒi] *s* lovtale.
euphemism ['ju:fəmizm] *s* formildende omskrivning, eufemisme.
euphoria [ju:'fɔ:riə] *s* kunstig opstemthed, overdreven optimisme.
Euro-MP ['juərəu,ɛmpi:] *s* medlem af Europaparlamentet.
Europe ['juərəp] *s* Europa.
European [juərə'pi:ən] *s* europæer // *adj* europæisk; *(pol)* EF-tilhænger; ~ **champion** *s* europamester.
euthanasia [ju:θə'neiziə] *s* dødshjælp; medlidenhedsdrab.
evacuate [i'vækjueit] *v* evakuere; tømme; udtømme; rømme.
evacuation [ivækju'eiʃən] *s* evakuering; tømning; rømning.
evade [i'veid] *v* vige udenom, undgå; slippe udenom.
evaluate [i'væljueit] *v* vurdere, evaluere.
evaporate [i'væpəreit] *v* fordampe; få til at fordampe; svinde ind; fordufte; **~d milk** *s* kondenseret mælk.
evaporation [ivæpə'reiʃən] *s* fordampning; forsvinden.
evasion [i'veiʒən] *s* undvigelse; omgåelse; unddragelse.
evasive [i'veisiv] *adj* undvigende; ubestemt.
eve [i:v] *s* dagen (,aftenen) før en helligdag (fx *Christmas Eve* juleaften(sdag)).
even [i:vn] *adj* jævn; flad; ensartet; lige (fx *numbers* tal); *an* ~ *match* en jævnbyrdig kamp; *get* ~ *with* hævne sig på // *adv* lige, netop; selv, tilmed, endog; ~ *if (,though)* selv om; ~ *more* endnu mere; ~ *so* alligevel // *v* jævne ud; ~ *out* udjævne; udligne; fordele ligeligt; ~ *up* (om beløb) runde op; **~-handed** *adj* upartisk, fair.
evening ['i:vniŋ] *s* aften; *in the* ~ om aftenen; *this* ~ i aften; ~ **class** *s* aftenskole; ~ **dress** *s* selskabstøj; (for kvinder) lang kjole; (for mænd) smoking; ~ **duty** *s* aftenvagt; ~ **gown** *s* lang kjole.
evensong ['i:vnsɔŋ] *s* aftenandagt, vesper.
event [i'vɛnt] *s* begivenhed; *(sport)*

disciplin; løb; kamp; *at all ~s* i alle tilfælde; *in that ~* i så fald; *in the ~ of* i tilfælde af; **~ful** *adj* begivenhedsrig.

eventual [i'vɛntʃuəl] *adj* mulig, eventuel; endelig, sluttelig.

eventuality [ivɛntʃu'æliti] *s* mulighed; *in the ~ of* i tilfælde af; **~ly** [-'vɛntʃuəli] *adv* til sidst; efterhånden; senere.

ever ['ɛvə*] *adv* nogensinde; overhovedet; altid; *the best ~* den bedste nogensinde; *if he ~ comes* hvis han overhovedet kommer; *hardly ~* næsten aldrig; *~ since* lige siden; *~ so pretty* noget så pæn; *for ~* for evig; evig og altid; **~green** *s* stedsegrøn plante (,træ); (om melodi) evergreen; **~lasting** *adj* evig; stadig; **~more** *adv* stedse; *for ~more* for al evighed.

every ['ɛvri] *pron* hver; al mulig; *~ day* hver dag; *~ other day* hveranden dag; *~ now and then* hvert øjeblik; nu og da; *in ~ way* på alle måder; *there's ~ hope that...* der er alt muligt håb om at...; *~ bit as good* fuldt ud lige så god; *his ~ word* hvert ord han sagde; **~body** *pron* enhver; alle (og enhver); **~day** *adj* daglig, hverdags-; **~one** *pron* d.s.s. *~body;* **~thing** *pron* alt; det hele; *we had drinks and ~thing* vi fik drinks og alt muligt; **~where** *adv* alle vegne; overalt.

evict [i'vikt] *v* sætte på gaden, sætte ud.

eviction [i'vikʃən] *s* udsættelse (af ejendom, lejlighed etc).

evidence ['ɛvidns] *s* tegn *(of* på); bevis(er); vidneudsagn; *a piece of ~* et bevis; *give ~* vidne, afgive vidnesbyrd; *in ~* tydelig; bemærket; *show ~ of* vise tegn på.

evident ['ɛvidnt] *adj* indlysende, tydelig, åbenbar.

evil [i:vl] *s* ulykke; onde // *adj* ond, syndig; hæslig; dårlig; **~-doer** *s* misdæder; **~-minded** [-maindid] *adj* ondsindet.

evocative [i'vɔkətiv] *adj* tankevækkende; suggestiv; udtryksfuld.

evoke [i'vəuk] *v* fremmane; fremkalde; vække.

evolution [ivə'lu:ʃən] *s* udvikling; udfoldelse.

evolve [i'vɔlv] *v* udvikle; udtænke; udvikle sig.

ewe [ju:] *s* hunfår, moderfår.

ewer [ju:ə*] *s* vandkande.

exact [ig'zækt] *adj* nøjagtig; præcis; rigtig; *or to be more ~...* eller rettere sagt... // *v* kræve, afkræve; inddrive.

exacting [ig'zæktiŋ] *adj* krævende; nøjeregnende; streng.

exactitude [ig'zæktitju:d] *s* nøjagtighed, præcision.

exactly [ig'zæktli] *adv* netop; nøjagtig(t); lige (akkurat); *not ~* ikke ligefrem; *what ~ do you mean?* hvad mener du helt præcis?

exaggerate [ig'zædʒəreit] *v* overdrive; **~d** *adj* overdreven.

exalt [ig'zɔ:lt] *v* opløfte; ophøje; prise.

exaltation [ɛgzɔ:l'teiʃən] *s* ophøjelse; (sygelig) opstemthed.

exam [ig'zæm] *s* (F) eksamen.

examination [igzæmi'neiʃən] *s* undersøgelse; eksamen, prøve; *(jur)* forhør; *medical ~* lægeundersøgelse; *pass an ~* bestå en eksamen.

examine [ig'zæmin] *v* undersøge; eksaminere; afhøre.

examiner [ig'zæminə*] *s* eksaminator; censor; *(jur)* forhørsdommer.

example [ig'za:mpl] *s* eksempel; forbillede; eksemplar; *for ~* for eksempel; *set an ~* foregå andre med et godt eksempel.

exasperate [ig'za:spəreit] *v* irritere, gøre rasende.

excavate ['ɛkskəveit] *v* (ud)grave.

excavation [ɛkskə'veiʃən] *s* udgravning.

excavator ['ɛkskəveitə*] *s* gravemaskine.

exceed [ik'si:d] *v* overskride; overstige; overgå; **~ingly** *adv* yderst; overordentlig.

excel [ik'sɛl] *v* udmærke sig, brillere.

excellence ['ɛksələns] *s* fortræffelighed, fortrin.

Excellency ['ɛksələnsi] *s: His ~* Hans Excellence.

excellent ['ɛksələnt] *adj* glimrende, strålende, udmærket.

except [ik'sɛpt] *v* undtage // *præp* undtagen; ~ *for* bortset fra; ~ *when* undtagen når; **~ing** *præp* undtagen, bortset fra.

exception [ik'sɛpʃən] *s* undtagelse; *make an* ~ gøre en undtagelse; *take* ~ *to* gøre indsigelse mod; tage anstød af; *an* ~ *to the rule* en undtagelse fra reglen; **~al** *adj* usædvanlig, enestående.

excerpt ['ɛksə:pt] *s* uddrag; udtog.

excess [ik'sɛs] *s* overflod; overskud; *drink to* ~ drikke (for) meget; *carry sth to* ~ overdrive ngt; **~ baggage** *s* overvægtig bagage; **~ charge** *s* strafporto; strafgebyr; **~es** *spl* udskejelser; **~ fare** *s* tillægsbillet.

excessive [ik'sɛsiv] *adj* overdreven; umådeholden; urimelig.

excess postage [ik'sɛs 'pəustidʒ] *s* strafporto.

exchange [iks'tʃeindʒ] *s* udveksling; bytte; vekselpenge; valuta; børs; *(tlf)* central; *in* ~ *for* i bytte for; til gengæld for; *foreign* ~ fremmed valuta // *v* udveksle, bytte; veksle, skifte; **~ rate** *s* vekselkurs.

Exchequer [iks'tʃɛkə*] *s: the* ~ *(brit)* statskassen; finansministeriet.

excise ['ɛksaiz] *s* forbrugsafgift (,-skat); **~ duties** *spl* indirekte skatter; toldafgifter.

excite [ik'sait] *v* ophidse; fremkalde, vække; *get* ~*d* blive ophidset; *don't get* ~*d* hids dig nu ikke op; ~ *envy* vække misundelse; **~ment** *s* ophidselse; begejstring; uro; **exciting** *adj* spændende; ophidsende.

exclaim [iks'kleim] *v* udbryde.

exclamation [ɛksklə'meiʃən] *s* udbrud, udråb; ~ *mark* udråbstegn.

exclude [iks'klu:d] *v* udelukke; se bort fra; holde udenfor.

exclusion [iks'klu:ʒən] *s* udelukkelse.

exclusive [iks'klu:siv] *adj* fornem, eksklusiv; speciel; ene- // *adv (merk)* eksklusive; *have the* ~ *right of* have eneretten til; ~ *of VAT* eksklusive moms.

excrete [iks'kri:t] *v* udskille, udsondre; **excretion** *s* udskillelse, udsondring.

excruciating [iks'kru:ʃieitiŋ] *adj* ulidelig; pinefuld.

excursion [iks'kə:ʃən] *s* udflugt, tur; *(fig)* afstikker.

excusable [iks'kju:səbl] *adj* undskyldelig.

excuse *v* [iks'kju:s] undskyldning; anledning; påskud // *v* [iks'kju:z] undskylde; fritage; ~ *me!* undskyld! tillader De! ~ *oneself from* bede sig fritaget fra.

ex-directory [ˌɛksdai'rɛktəri] *adj: be* ~ *(tlf)* have hemmeligt telefonnummer.

execute ['ɛksikju:t] *v* udføre; iværksætte; spille; opføre; henrette; *(jur)* eksekvere.

execution [ɛksi'kju:ʃən] *s* udførelse; henrettelse; eksekution; **~er** *s* bøddel.

executive [ig'zɛkjutiv] *s* leder, chef, direktør // *adj* udøvende; administrativ; administrerende; ledende; (om vare) luksus-; **~ case** *s* attachétaske; **~ committee** *s* bestyrelse; forretningsudvalg.

executor [ig'zɛkjutə*] *s* udøver; *(jur)* eksekutor (af testamente).

exemplary [ig'zɛmpləri] *adj* mønstergyldig, eksemplarisk.

exempt [ig'zɛmpt] *adj:* ~ *from* fritaget for; fri for; *tax-*~ skattefri // *v:* ~ *sby from* fritage en for.

exemption [ig'zɛmʃən] *s* fritagelse; dispensation.

exercise ['ɛksəsaiz] *s* øvelse; motion; udøvelse; anvendelse; (i skolen) opgave, stil; *take* ~ få motion, motionere // *v* øve (sig) træne; udøve; anvende; **~ book** *s* øvehæfte; stilehæfte.

exert [ig'zə:t] *v* anvende, bruge; udøve; ~ *oneself* anstrenge sig; oppe sig.

exertion [ig'zə:ʃən] *s* anvendelse; anstrengelse.

exhale [ɛks'heil] *v* ånde ud; udsende.

exhaust [ig'zɔ:st] *s* udblæsning; udstrømning // *v* opbruge; udtømme; udmatte; **~ed** *adj* udmattet; ud-

tømt; ~ **fumes** *spl* udstødningsgas.
exhaustion [ig'zɔ:stʃən] *s* udtømning; udmattelse.
exhaustive [ig'zɔ:stiv] *adj* udtømmende; grundig.
exhaust pipe [ig'zɔ:st paip] *s* udstødningsrør.
exhibit [ig'zibit] *s* udstillingsgenstand; *(jur)* bilag, bevismateriale // *v* udstille; fremvise; udvise.
exhibition [ɛksi'biʃən] *s* udstilling; fremvisning; tilkendegivelse; *make an ~ of oneself* lave skandale; gøre sig til grin.
exhibitor [ig'zibitə*] *s* udstiller.
exhilarating [ig'zilәreitiŋ] *adj* opmuntrende, opkvikkende.
exhort [ig'zɔ:t] *v* formane.
exhumation [ɛkshju:'meiʃən] *s* opgravning.
exile ['ɛksail] *s* eksil, udlændighed; person der lever i eksil // *v* landsforvise.
exist [ig'zist] *v* eksistere, leve; findes, forekomme.
existence [ig'zistəns] *s* eksistens; tilstedeværelse; liv, tilværelse; *be in ~* være til, findes.
exit ['ɛksit] *s* udgang; (fra motorvej) frakørsel; *(teat)* udgangsreplik, sortie; ~ **permit** *s* udrejsetilladelse.
exodus ['ɛksədəs] *s* udvandring; *Exodus* 2. Mosebog.
exonerate [ig'zɔnəreit] *v* frifinde; fritage.
exorbitant [ig'zɔ:bitənt] *adj* urimelig; ublu (fx *prices* priser).
exorcise ['ɛksɔ:saiz] *v* uddrive (fx *an evil spirit* en ond ånd); foretage djævleuddrivelse.
exotic [ig'zɔtik] *adj* eksotisk, fremmedartet.
expand [iks'pænd] *v* udvide; udvide sig; vokse; udbrede sig *(on* om); uddybe nærmere.
expanse [iks'pæns] *s* vid udstrækning; vidtstrakt flade.
expansion [iks'pænʃən] *s* udvidelse; ekspansion; udbredelse.
expansive [iks'pænsiv] *adj* meddelsom.
expatriate [ɛks'pætrieit] *v* landsforvise; *Danish ~s in Spain* udlandsdanskere i Spanien // *adj* [ɛks'pætriit] bosiddende i udlandet.
expect [iks'pɛkt] *v* vente; forvente; kræve, forlange; regne med; antage; *be ~ing* (også) vente sig; *~ sby to* forvente af en at; forlange af en at.
expectant [iks'pɛktənt] *adj* ventende; forhåbningsfuld; vordende; forventet.
expectation [ikspɛk'teiʃən] *s* forventning; *~s* forhåbninger; fremtidsudsigter.
expedience, expediency [ɛk'spi:diən-s(i)] *s* middel; udvej; hensigtsmæssighed.
expedient [ɛks'pi:diənt] *s* udvej; middel // *adj* formålstjenlig; hensigtsmæssig.
expedite ['ɛkspidait] *v* fremskynde; gøre hurtigt.
expedition [ɛkspi'diʃən] *s* ekspedition; opdagelsesrejse; hurtighed.
expeditious [ɛkspi'diʃəs] *adj* hurtig.
expel [iks'pɛl] *v* kaste ud; uddrive, fordrive; bortvise.
expend [iks'pɛnd] *v* anvende; forbruge, bruge op; **~able** *adj* som kan opbruges; til at undvære.
expenditure [iks'pɛnditʃə*] *s* forbrug; udgift.
expense [iks'pɛns] *s* udgift; omkostning; bekostning; *at great ~* med store omkostninger; i dyre domme; *at the ~ of* på bekostning af; *at his ~* på hans regning; ~ **account** *s* udgiftskonto.
expensive [iks'pɛnsiv] *adj* dyr, kostbar.
experience [iks'piəriəns] *s* erfaring; oplevelse // *v* opleve, komme ud for; erfare; **~d** *adj* erfaren, rutineret.
experiment [iks'pɛrimənt] *s* erfaring; oplevelse // *v* eksperimentere, lave forsøg; **~al** [-'mɛntl] *adj* forsøgs-, eksperimentel.
expert ['ɛkspə:t] *s* ekspert, specialist // *adj* sagkyndig; dygtig, erfaring; ekspert-.
expiate ['ɛkspieit] *v* sone.
expiration [ɛkspi'reiʃən] *s* udånding;

udløb; ~ *date* sidste salgsdato, "bruges inden".
expire [iks'paiə*] *v* ånde ud; udånde, dø; (om fx kontrakt) udløbe; ophøre.
expiry [iks'paiəri] *s* udløb; forfald.
explain [iks'plein] *v* forklare; gøre rede for; ~ *away* bortforklare.
explanation [iksplə'neiʃən] *s* forklaring.
explanatory [iks'plænətri] *adj* forklarende.
expletive [iks'pli:tiv] *s* udråb; ed, banden.
explicit [iks'plisit] *adj* tydelig; bestemt; udtrykkelig.
explode [iks'pləud] *v* eksplodere, springe i luften; sprænge(s).
exploit *s* ['ɛksplɔit] bedrift, dåd // *v* [iks'plɔit] udnytte; udbytte; **~ation** [-'teiʃən] *s* udnyttelse; udbytning.
exploration [ɛksplə'reiʃən] *s* udforskning; undersøgelse.
exploratory [iks'plɔrətri] *adj* forberedende, orienterende (fx *talks* forhandlinger).
explore [iks'plɔ:*] *v* udforske, undersøge; gå på opdagelse i.
explosion [iks'pləuʒən] *s* eksplosion, sprængning.
explosive [iks'pləusiv] *s* sprængstof // *adj* eksplosiv, spræng-.
exponent [iks'pəunənt] *s* eksponent; repræsentant.
export *s* ['ɛkspɔ:t] eksport, udførsel // *v* [ɛks'pɔ:t] eksportere, udføre; **~ation** [-'teiʃən] *s* eksport; **~ duty** *s* eksportafgift; **~er** *s* eksportør; **~ licence** *s* udførselstilladelse.
expose [iks'pəuz] *v* udsætte (*to* for); fremvise; udstille; afsløre (fx *a crime* en forbrydelse); *(foto)* belyse, eksponere; ~ *oneself (jur)* krænke blufærdigheden, blotte sig.
exposition [ɛkspə'ziʃən] *s* fremlægning; redegørelse; forklaring; udstilling.
exposure [iks'pəuʒə*] *s* det at være udsat; fremvisning; *(foto)* belysning; optagelse; *suffer from* ~ være medtaget af kulde, vejr, vind etc.
expound [iks'paund] *v* forklare, udlægge.
express [iks'prɛs] *s* eksprestog; ekspresbesørgelse // *v* udtrykke, udtale; sende ekspres // *adj* udtrykkelig; ekspres-.
expression [iks'prɛʃən] *s* udtryk; tilkendegivelse.
expressive [iks'prɛsiv] *adj* udtryksfuld; udtryks-.
expressly [iks'prɛsli] *adv* udtrykkelig; specielt.
expropriate [ɛks'prəuprieit] *v* ekspropriere.
expulsion [iks'pʌlʃən] *s* udstødning; bortvisning; eksklusion.
exquisite ['ɛkskwizit] *adj* udsøgt; meget fin; dejlig.
ext. (fork.f. *extension)*: ~ *344* lokal 344.
extend [iks'tɛnd] *v* udstrække, udvide; forlænge; række (ud), strække (ud); **~ed family** *s* storfamilie.
extension [iks'tɛnʃən] *s* udstrækning; udvidelse; forlængelse; tilbygning; *(elek)* forlængerled; *(tlf)* lokalnummer; ekstraapparat.
extensive [iks'tɛnsiv] *adj* udstrakt, vidtstrakt; omfattende (fx *damage* skader); vidtgående; *he has travelled ~ly* han har rejst vidt omkring.
extent [iks'tɛnt] *s* størrelse, udstrækning; omgang; grad; *to some* ~ i nogen grad, til en vis grad; *to what ~?* i hvor høj grad?
extenuating [iks'tɛnjueitiŋ] *adj* formildende.
exterior [ɛks'tiəriə*] *s* ydre, yderside // *adj* ydre, udvendig.
exterminate [iks'tə:mineit] *v* udrydde, tilintetgøre.
extermination [ikstə:mi'neiʃən] *s* udryddelse, tilintetgørelse.
external [ɛks'tə:nl] *adj* ydre; udvendig; ekstern; **~ examiner** *s* (til eksamen) censor; **~ly** *adv* udvendigt, udadtil.
extinct [iks'tiŋkt] *adj* udslukt (fx *volcano* vulkan); uddød.
extinction [iks'tiŋkʃən] *s* slukning; udslettelse; ophævelse.
extinguish [iks'tiŋgwiʃ] *v* slukke; udslette; **~er** *s* ildslukker.
extort [iks'tɔ:t] *v* afpresse; ~ *sth from sby* aftvinge en ngt.

extortion [iks'tɔ:ʃən] *s* afpresning.
extortionate [iks'tɔ:ʃənət] *adj* ublu, åger- (fx *prices* priser).
extra ['ɛkstrə] *s* ekstraudgave; *(teat, film)* statist; ekstranummer; *~s* ekstraudgifter, det ekstra // *adj* ekstra(-).
extract *s* ['ɛkstrækt] ekstrakt; uddrag // *v* [iks'trækt] trække ud (fx *a tooth* en tand); hale ud *(from* af); lave uddrag *(from* af).
extraction [iks'trækʃən] *s* udtrækning; udpresning; udvinding; afstamning.
extractor [iks'træktə*] *s* saftpresser; udsugningsanlæg.
extradite ['ɛkstrədait] *v* udlevere (en forbryder til et andet land).
extramarital ['ɛkstrə'mæritl] *adj* udenomsægteskabelig.
extramural ['ɛkstrə'mjuərəl] *adj* uden for murene (,institutionen).
extraneous [iks'treiniəs] *adj* ydre, udefra kommende; uvedkommende.
extraordinary [iks'trɔ:dnri] *adj* ekstraordinær; usædvanlig; mærkværdig.
extraterrestrial ['ɛkstrəti'rɛstriəl] *adj* rum-.
extra time ['ɛkstrə'taim] *s (fodb)* forlænget spilletid.
extravagant [iks'trævəgənt] *adj* ødsel, flot; ekstravagant; urimelig; overdreven; overspændt.
extravaganza [ɛkstrævə'gænzə] *s* flot show; udstyrsstykke.
extreme [iks'tri:m] *s* yderlighed; yderpunkt; *in the ~* i allerhøjeste grad; *go to ~s* gå til yderligheder // *adj* yderst; yderlig; yderliggående; overordentlig; *the ~ left* det yderste venstre.
extremist [iks'tri:mist] *s* ekstremist // *adj* yderliggående.
extremity [iks'trɛmiti] *s* yderpunkt; højdepunkt; det yderste; *extremities* arme og ben, lemmer.
extricate ['ɛkstrikeit] *v: ~ sth (from)* befri (,frigøre) ngt (fra).
extrovert ['ɛkstrəvə:t] *adj* udadvendt.
exuberant [ig'zju:bərənt] *adj* overstrømmende; frodig; overdådig.
exude [ig'zju:d] *v* udsondre; udsive; *(fig)* udstråle (fx *charm* charme).
exult [ig'zʌlt] *v* juble; triumfere.
eye [ai] *s* øje; blik; *before (,under) her very ~s* lige for øjnene af hende; *catch his ~* fange hans blik; *it caught my ~* jeg fik øje på det; *cast an ~ on* kaste et blik på; *do sby in the ~* (S) tage røven på en; *keep an ~ on* holde øje med; *keep one's ~s peeled* holde skarpt udkig, passe på; *run an ~ over sth* lade blikket løbe hen (,ned) over ngt; *in the public ~* i offentlighedens søgelys; *see ~ to ~ with sby* have samme syn på tingene som en; *with an ~ to* med henblik på (at) // *v* se på; mønstre; **~ball** *s* øjeæble; **~bath** *s* øjenbadeglas; **~brow** ['aibrau] *s* øjenbryn; *up to the ~brows* til op over ørerne; **~-catching** *adj* iøjnefaldende; **~drops** *spl* øjendråber; **~ful** *s* (S) flot pige, sejt skår; **~glass** *s* monokel; **~lash** *s* øjenvippe; **~let** *s* snørehul; lille åbning; **~lid** *s* øjenlåg; *without batting an ~lid* uden at blinke; **~-opener** *s* overraskelse; **~-patch** *s* klap for øjet; **~shadow** *s* øjenskygge; **~sight** *s* syn(sevne); *her ~sight is failing* hendes syn er ved at blive svækket; **~sore** *s* skamplet, noget hæsligt; **~ test** *s* synsprøve; **~tooth** *s* hjørnetand; **~wash** *s* øjenbadevand; *(fig)* bluff; **~ witness** *s* øjenvidne.
eyrie ['iəri] *s* rovfuglerede; (om hus) ørnerede.

F

F, f [ɛf].
F fork.f. *Fahrenheit.*
fab(bo) ['fæb(əu)] *adj* (S) skøn, fantastisk.
fable [feibl] *s* fabel, sagn; løgn; **~d** *adj* berømt, legendarisk.
fabric ['fæbrik] *s* (vævet) stof, tekstil; vævning; struktur; *a ~ of lies* et væv af løgne.
fabricate ['fæbrikeit] *v* opdigte, finde på; forfalske; **fabrication** [-'keiʃən] *s* opspind; forfalskning; fremstilling.

fabulous ['fæbjuləs] *adj* fantastisk; fabelagtig; fabel-.

face [feis] *s* ansigt; ansigtsudtryk; forside; facade; overflade; *in the ~ of* over for; *on the ~ of it* tilsyneladende; *lose ~* tabe ansigt; *pull a ~ (at)* vrænge ansigt (ad); *put on a brave ~* lade som ingenting; *save ~* redde ansigt // *v* vende ansigtet mod; stå overfor; vende ud mod; beklæde; *~ the music* tage skraldet; *~ up to* se i øjnene; **~ cloth, ~ flannel** *s* vaskeklud; **~ lift** *s* ansigtsløftning (også *fig,* fx om hus); **~ pack** *s* ansigtmaske.

facetious [fə'si:ʃəs] *adj* spottende, "morsom".

face value ['feis'vælju:] *s: take sth at ~ (fig)* tage ngt for pålydende.

facial ['feiʃəl] *adj* ansigts-.

facile ['fæsail] *adj* let; letkøbt.

facilitate [fə'siliteit] *v* gøre lettere; lette; hjælpe.

facility [fæ'siliti] *s* lethed; mulighed; behændighed; **facilities** *spl* hjælpemidler, faciliteter; bekvemmeligheder.

facing ['feisiŋ] *s* (på væg etc) beklædning; (på tøj) besætning, opslag, revers // *adj* med front mod, overfor.

fact [fækt] *s* kendsgerning; omstændighed; realitet; *in ~* faktisk; endog; *in actual ~* i virkeligheden; *the ~ is* sagen er; *as a matter of ~* faktisk; *the ~ remains that...* ikke desto mindre...; *know sth for a ~* vide ngt med bestemthed; *tell sby the ~s of life* give en seksualundervisning; **~finding** *adj* undersøgelses- (fx *commission* kommission); informationssøgning.

faction ['fækʃən] *s* klike, partigruppe, fraktion; splittelse.

factitious [fæk'tiʃəs] *adj* kunstig, uægte.

factory ['fæktəri] *s* fabrik; **~ farming** *s* industrielt landbrug, det at opføde tremmekalve, burhøns etc; **~ hand** *s* fabriksarbejder.

factual ['fæktʃuəl] *adj* faktisk, virkelig; nøgtern.

faculty ['fækəlti] *s* evne, anlæg; fakultet.

fad [fæd] *s* kæphest, mani.

faddy ['fædi] *adj* fuld af nykker; meget kræsen.

fade [feid] *v* falme, visne; *~ away* svinde bort, dø hen; *~ out (film)* tone ud.

fag [fæg] *s* slid, mas; (F) cigaret, smøg; (*am*,S) bøsse; **~-end** *s* (F) cigaretskod; sidste del af ngt; **~ged** [fæ:gd] *adj: ~ged out* udkørt.

faggot ['fægət] *s (brit)* kødbolle; *(am,* S) bøsse.

Fahrenheit ['færənait] *s* Fahrenheit (temperaturskala).

fail [feil] *v* svigte; slå fejl, mislykkes; fejle; dumpe; lade dumpe; blive svagere; mangle; *his courage ~ed* modet svigtede ham; *~ in sth* være mangelfuld på et punkt; *~ to* ikke kunne; undlade at; *without ~* helt bestemt; **~ing** *s* svaghed, fejl, skavank // *præp* i mangel af; **~-safe** *adj* fejlsikret.

failure ['feiljə*] *s* fiasko; nederlag; svigten; sammenbrud.

faint [feint] *s* besvimelse // *v* besvime // *adj* svag, mat; *feel ~* være utilpas (,svimmel); *I have not the ~est (idea)* jeg har ingen andelse (om det).

fair [fɛə*] *s* marked, basar; messe // *adj* retfærdig; ærlig, reel; rimelig; smuk; (om kvalitet etc) god, nogenlunde; (om farve) lys, blond; *~ and square* ligeud, åbent og ærligt; præcis, i plet; *the ~ sex* det smukke køn; **~ copy** *s* renskrift; **~ground** *s* markedsplads; tivoli; **~ly** *adv* temmelig; retfærdigt; **~-minded** *adj* retfærdig; **~ness** *s* retfærdighed; *in all ~ness* retfærdigvis; **~ play** *s* ærligt spil.

fairy ['fɛəri] *s* fe, alf; (S) bøsse; **~ lights** *spl* kulørte elektriske pærer (til juletræ); **~ tale** *s* eventyr.

faith [feiθ] *s* tro, tillid; troskab; **~ful** *adj* tro, trofast; nøjagtig; troende; **~fully** *adv: yours ~fully* ærbødigst, med venlig hilsen.

fake [feik] *s* forfalskning; svindel; (om person) svindler, simulant; *his illness is a ~* han spiller syg // *v* forfalske; simulere // *adj* uægte, falsk.

falcon ['fɔ:lkən] *s* falk.
fall [fɔ:l] *s* fald; nedgang; *(am)* efterår // *v (fell, fallen* [fɛl, fɔ:lən]) falde; aftage; blive; *her face fell* hun blev lang i ansigtet; ~ *back on* falde tilbage på; ~ *behind* komme bagefter (,bagud); ~ *down* falde ned; (om hus etc) styrte sammen; ~ *down on* svigte; ~ *flat* falde på næsen (,pladask); ~ *for* falde for; hoppe på; ~ *in* styrte sammen; *(mil)* træde an; ~ *in love* blive forelsket *(with* i); ~ *in with* gå ind på; stemme overens med; ~ *off* falde af; gå tilbage; blive mindre; ~ *out* falde ud; blive uvenner; ~ *over backwards to do sth* være helt vild efter at gøre ngt; ~ *through* falde igennem; mislykkes.
fallacy ['fæləsi] *s* fejlslutning; vildfarelse.
fallen ['fɔ:lən] *pp* af *fall* // *adj* faldet; falden; ~ *arches* platfod.
fallible ['fæləbl] *adj* fejlbarlig; som kan tage fejl.
falling ['fɔliŋ] *adj* faldende; **~-off** *s* nedgang, svækkelse; **~ star** *s* stjerneskud.
fallout ['fɔ:laut] *s* (radioaktivt) nedfald.
fallow ['fæləu] *adj* gulbrun; brak; **~ deer** *s* rådyr.
falls [fɔ:ls] *spl* vandfald.
false [fɔ:ls] *adj* falsk; urigtig; forkert; forloren; utro; **~hood** *s* usandhed, løgn; **~ start** *s (sport)* tyvstart; **~ teeth** *spl* forlorne tænder, protese.
falsify ['fɔ:lsifai] *v* forfalske.
falter ['fɔ:ltə*] *v* vakle, snuble; (om tale) stamme.
fame [feim] *s* rygte, ry; berømmelse; *of ill* ~ berygtet; **~d** *adj* berømt.
familiar [fə'miliə*] *adj* kendt, velkendt; fortrolig; *be ~ with* kende.
familiarity [fəmili'æriti] *s* fortrolighed.
familiarize [fə'miliəraiz] *v: ~ oneself with* gøre sig fortrolig med.
family ['fæmili] *s* familie; slægt; *start a* ~ få (kone og) børn; *he has a wife and* ~ han har kone og børn; *be in the ~ way* vente familieforøgelse; **~ allowance** *s* børnetilskud; **~ doctor** *s* huslæge; **~ man** *s* familiefar; familiemenneske; **~ name** *s* efternavn; **~ planning** *s* familieplanlægning.
famine ['fæmin] *s* hungersnød.
famished ['fæmiʃt] *adj* skrupsulten, "ved at dø af sult".
famous ['feiməs] *adj* berømt; **~ly** *adv* glimrende, fortræffeligt.
fan [fæn] *s* vifte; ventilator; (om person) tilhænger, fan // *v* vifte; ~ *out* spredes (i vifteform); ~ *the flame* puste til ilden.
fanatic [fə'nætik] *s* fanatiker // *adj* (også *~al)* fanatisk.
fan belt ['fæn,bɛlt] *s* ventilatorrem.
fancier ['fænsiə*] *s* -ynder, -elsker; **fanciful** *adj* lunefuld; lige lovlig fantasifuld.
fancy ['fænsi] *s* fantasi; indbildning; indfald; lyst; *take a ~ to* få lyst til; kaste sin kærlighed på; *it took (,caught) my* ~ det faldt i min smag // *v* mene, tænke sig; have lyst til; være lun på; ~ *that...* forestille sig at...; ~ *that, now!* nej, tænk bare! *he fancies her* han sværmer for hende; *he fancies himself* han føler sig rigtigt; ~ *meeting you here!* tænk at jeg skulle møde dig her! // *adj* kunstfærdig; dyr, fin; **~ dress** *s* karnevalsdragt; **~-dress ball** *s* karneval, kostumebal; **~-free** *adj* fri, ugift.
fang [fæŋ] *s* hugtand, gifttand.
fan heater ['fæn,hi:tə*] *s* varmeblæser; **fan oven** *s* varmluftsovn.
fantasize ['fæntəsaiz] *v* fantasere, drømme.
fantastic [fæn'tæstik] *adj* fantastisk.
fantasy ['fæntəsi] *s* fantasi; grille.
far [fa:*] *adj (farther, farthest* ['fa:ðə*, 'fa:ðist] el. *further, furthest* ['fə:ðə*, 'fə:ðist]) fjern; lang; vid // *adv* fjernt; meget; *as ~ as I know* så vidt jeg ved; *as ~ as possible* så vidt muligt; ~ *away* langt væk, langt borte; ~ *better* meget bedre; *by ~ the best* langt det (,den) bedste; ~ *from* langt fra; *so ~ I have not seen him* hidtil har jeg ikke set ham; *so ~ so good* så langt så godt; det var det.
farcical ['fa:sikəl] *adj* farceagtig, latterlig.

fare [fɛə*] *s* kost, mad; billetpris, takst, kørepenge; (i taxi) passager, kunde; *~s please!* billettering! // *v* klare sig.

Far East ['fa:r'i:st] *s: the ~* Det Fjerne Østen // *adj* fjernøstlig.

farewell ['fɛə'wɛl] *s* farvel, afsked.

far-fetched ['fa:fɛtʃd] *adj* usandsynlig, søgt.

far-flung ['fa:flʌŋ] *adj* vidt udbredt; fjern.

fargone ['fa:gɔn] *adj* langt nede (,ude).

farm [fa:m] *s* (bonde)gård, farm // *v* drive landbrug; dyrke jorden; *~ out work* lade arbejde blive lavet ude i byen.

farmer ['fa:mə*] *s* landmand, bonde.

farmhand ['fa:mhænd] *s* landarbejder.

farmhouse ['fa:mhaus] *s* bondegård, stuehus.

farming ['fa:miŋ] *s* landbrug.

farmland ['fa:mlənd] *s* landbrugsjord.

farmstead ['fa:mstɛd] *s* bondegård.

farmyard ['fa:mja:d] *s* gårdsplads.

Faroe ['fɛərəu] *s: the ~ Islands* Færøerne.

Faroese [fɛərəu'i:z] *s* færing // *adj* færøsk.

far... ['fa:*-] sms: **~-off** *adj* fjern; **~-out** *adj* fjern; yderliggående, langt ude; fantastisk; **~-reaching** *adj* vidtrækkende; **~-sighted** *adj* fremsynet; vidtskuende; langsynet.

fart [fa:t] *s* prut, fis // *v* prutte, fise; *~ about* (F) fise rundt.

farther ['fa:ðə*] *(komp* af *far)* fjernere; længere; **farthest** ['fa:ðist] *(sup* af *far)* fjernest; længst; *at the farthest* højst.

fascinate ['fæsineit] *v* fængsle; betage; **fascinating** *adj* betagende; spændende.

fascination [fæsi'neiʃən] *s* fortryllelse.

fascist ['fæʃist] *s* fascist // *adj* fascistisk.

fashion ['fæʃən] *s* mode; manér; facon; *after a ~* på en måde; *in ~* på mode; *out of ~* gået af mode // *v* danne, forme; **~able** *adj* moderne; mondæn, fashionabel; **~ show** *s* modeopvisning.

fast [fa:st] *s/v* faste // *adj/adv* hurtig, rask; (om ur) for stærkt, foran; gjort fast; (om farve) vaskeægte; *fall ~ asleep* falde i dyb søvn; *the ~ lane* (på motorvej) overhalingsbanen; *pull a ~ one on sby* (S) tage røven på en.

fasten [fa:sn] *v* gøre fast; lukke; hæfte; knappe; hænge fast; *~ down* fæstne; *~ on an idea* bide sig fast i en idé; **~er** *s* lukker; **~ing** *s* lukkemekanisme; lukning.

fastidious [fæs'tidiəs] *adj* kræsen; forvænt.

fat [fæt] *s* fedt(stof); *the ~ is in the fire* (F) nu brænder lokummet // *adj* fed; tyk; *a ~ lot of good that is going to do!* (F) det skal fedt hjælpe! *~ chance!* det er der ikke store chancer for!

fatal ['feitl] *adj* skæbesvanger, fatal; dødelig (fx *wound* sår); **~ism** ['feitəlizm] *s* fatalisme.

fatality [fə'tæliti] *s* farlighed; dødsoffer; dødsulykke.

fate [feit] *s* skæbne; død, undergang; *as sure as ~* så sikkert som amen i kirken; **~d** *adj: ~d to* dømt til at; **~ful** *adj* skæbnesvanger; vigtig.

fathead ['fæthɛd] *s* (F) grødhoved.

father ['fa:ðə*] *s* fader, far // *v* avle; være (,blive) far til; *~ sth on sby* give en skylden for ngt; *Father Christmas* julemanden; **~hood** *s* faderskab; **~-in-law** *s* svigerfar.

fathom ['fæðəm] *s* favn *(6 feet,* 1,8 m) // *v (mar)* lodde, måle dybden; *(fig)* sondere; komme til bunds i; **~less** *adj* bundløs; afgrundsdyb.

fatigue [fə'ti:g] *s* træthed; udmattelse; *(mil)* arbejdsuniform // *v* trætte, udmatte.

fatless ['fætlis] *adj* fedtfri.

fatten [fætn] *v* fede; blive fed; **fatty** ['fæti] *adj* fed; fedtet.

fatuous ['fætʃuəs] *adj* dum; indbildsk.

faucet ['fɔ:sit] *s (am)* (vand)hane.

fault [fɔ:lt] *s* fejl; *(geol)* forkastning; *it's my ~* det er min fejl (,skyld);

find ~ with bebrejde; kritisere; *be at ~* have skylden; have uret; *(fig)* være på vildspor; *to a ~* til overmål; i urimelig grad; **~-finder** *s* krakiler; **~less** *adj* fejlfri; **faulty** ['fɔ:lti] *adj* fuld af fejl, mangelfuld, defekt.

favour ['feivə*] *s* gunst, velvilje; tjeneste; *do sby a ~* gøre en en tjeneste; *in ~ of* til fordel for; *out of ~* i unåde // *v* støtte, billige; begunstige, favorisere; **~able** *adj* gunstig; imødekommende; favorabel.

favourite ['feivərit] *s* yndling, favorit // *adj* yndlings-.

fawn [fɔ:n] *s* hjortekalv, råkid // *v* (om hjort) kælve; (om hund) logre; *~ (up)on sby* sleske (,krybe) for en // *adj* lysebrun.

faze [feiz] *v* tage pippet fra.

fear [fiə*] *s* frygt, angst; *for ~ of* af frygt for; *be in ~ of* være bange for; *no ~!* det er der ingen fare for! ikke tale om! // *v* frygte, være bange (for); **~ful** *adj* frygtsom; frygtelig; **~less** *adj* uforfærdet; **~some** *adj* skrækkelig.

feasibility [fi:zə'biliti] *s* gennemførlighed.

feasible ['fi:zibl] *adj* gennemførlig; mulig; rimelig.

feast [fi:st] *s* fest; banket; *(rel)* højtid // *v* holde gilde; traktere; *~ on* nyde, fryde sig over.

feat [fi:t] *s* dåd, bedrift.

feather ['fɛðə*] *s* fjer; *they are birds of a ~* de er to alen af et stykke; *in fine ~* i fin form // *v: ~ one's nest* mele sin egen kage; **~ed** *adj* med fjer; **~-weight** *s (sport)* fjervægt.

feature ['fi:tʃə*] *s* ansigtstræk; karakteristisk træk; (i avis) kronik, avisrubrik; indslag // *v* kendetegne; byde på; fremvise; *a film featuring Daniel Massey* en film med Daniel Massey i hovedrollen; **~ film** *s* spillefilm; **~less** *adj* uinteressant, uden særpræg; **features** *spl* (ansigts)-træk.

February ['fɛbruəri] *s* februar.

feckless ['fɛklis] *adj* uduelig.

fed [fɛd] *præt* og *pp* af *feed; ~ up with* led og ked af, træt af.

federal ['fɛdərəl] *adj* forbunds-.

federation [fɛdə'reiʃən] *s* forbund, føderation.

fee [fi:] *s* honorar; afgift, gebyr; skolepenge.

feeble [fi:bl] *adj* svag, mat; hjælpeløs; **~-minded** *adj* åndssvag.

feed [fi:d] *s* foder, føde; (F) måltid // *v (fed, fed* [fɛd]) fodre, give mad; ernære; (om baby) amme, give flaske; (om maskine) tilføre, påfylde; (om plante) gøde; *~ on* leve af; *~ up* opfodre; **~back** *s* tilbagemelding, feedback; **~er** *s* sutteflaske; foderautomat; biflod; bivej.

feel [fi:l] *s* følelse; stemning; præg; *get the ~ of a place* lodde stemningen på et sted // *v (felt, felt* [fɛlt]) føle, mærke; have på fornemmelsen; synes, tænke; *~ about (,around)* famle; *~ bad about* ikke rigtig kunne lide; have dårlig samvittighed over; *~ better* have det bedre; *~ hungry* være sulten; *~ like screaming* have lyst til at skrige; *it ~s like silk* det føles som silke; *it ~s soft* det er blødt at føle på; *~ sorry for* have ondt af.

feeler ['fi:lə*] *s (zo)* følehorn; *put out ~s (fig)* stikke en føler ud.

feeling ['fi:liŋ] *s* følelse, fornemmelse; stemning; *without (,no) hard ~s* uden bitterhed.

feet [fi:t] *spl* af *foot;* (som mål) fod.

feign [fein] *v* foregive, simulere.

feint [feint] *s* finte; skinmanøvre.

felicitations [filisi'teiʃəns] *spl* lykønskninger.

felicitous [fi'lisitəs] *adj* lykkelig; heldig.

feline ['fi:lain] *adj* katteagtig; katte-.

fell [fɛl] *v* fælde, hugge om; slå ned; sy kapsøm; *præt* af *fall.*

fellow ['fɛləu] *s* fyr, kammerat; kollega; medlem (af selskab etc); stipendiat; *(univ)* lærer ved kollegium; *their ~ students* deres studiekammerater (,studenterkammerater); **~ being** *s* medmenneske; **~ citizen** *s* medborger; **~ countryman** *s* landsmand; **~ men** *spl* medmennesker; **~ship** *s* fællesskab, kammeratskab;

selskab; sammenslutning; *(univ)* stipendium; ~ **sufferer** *s* lidelsesfælle; ~ **traveller** *s* medrejsende.
felony ['fɛləni] *s* (grov) forbrydelse.
felt [fɛlt] *s* filt; (filt)hat // *præt* og *pp* af *feel;* **~-tip (pen)** *s* filtpen, spritpen, (F) tusse.
female ['fi:meil] *s* kvinde; *(neds)* kvindemenneske; *(zo)* hun(dyr) // *adj* kvindelig; *(zo)* hun-; ~ **impersonator** *s* drag; transvestit.
feminine ['fɛminin] *adj* kvindelig, feminin; *(gram)* hunkøns-.
feminist ['fɛminist] *s* kvindesagsforkæmper, feminist.
fen [fɛn] *s* engmose.
fence [fɛns] *s* hegn, stakit, plankeværk // *v* indhegne // *v* fægte; *(fig)* vige udenom.
fencing ['fɛnsiŋ] *s (sport)* fægtning; hegnsmateriale.
fend [fɛnd] *v* afværge; ~ *for oneself* klare sig (selv); ~ *off* undgå, afværge.
fender ['fɛndə*] *s* kamingitter; stødfanger, kofanger.
fennel [fɛnl] *s* fennikel.
ferment *s* ['fə:mənt] gæring // *v* [fə'mɛnt] gære.
fermentation [fə:mən'teiʃən] *s* gæring.
fern [fə:n] *s* bregne.
ferocious [fə'rəuʃəs] *adj* vild; grusom; glubsk.
ferocity [fə'rɔsiti] *s* vildskab; grusomhed.
ferret ['færit] *v:* ~ *out* opsnuse; ~ *out the secret* lokke hemmeligheden ud af en.
Ferris wheel ['fɛris ,wi:l] *s* pariserhjul.
ferrous ['fɛrəs] *adj* jern-.
ferry ['fɛri] *s* færge // *v* færge, overføre; transportere.
fertile ['fə:tail] *adj* frugtbar; frodig (fx *imagination* fantasi).
fertility [fə:'tiliti] *s* frugtbarhed.
fertilize ['fə:tilaiz] *v* gøde; befrugte.
fertilizer ['fə:tilaizə*] *s* (kunst)gødning.
fervent ['fə:vənt] *adj* varm, glødende, ivrig.
fervour ['fə:və*] *s* varme, glød.
fester ['fɛstə*] *v* blive betændt; nage.
festival ['fɛstivəl] *s (rel)* højtid; fest, festival.
festive ['fɛstiv] *adj* festlig, glad; *the ~ season* julen.
festivities [fɛ'stivitiz] *spl* festligheder.
festoon [fɛ'stu:n] *s* guirlande.
fetch [fɛtʃ] *v* hente; (ved salg) indbringe; ~ *sby a blow* lange en et slag; **~ing** *adj* charmerende, fængslende.
fete [feit] *s* (udendørs) fest // *v* fejre, fetere.
fetid ['fɛtid] *adj* ildelugtende.
fetters ['fɛtəz] *spl* lænker, tvang.
feud [fju:d] *s* fejde.
feudalism ['fju:dəlizm] *s* feudalisme.
fever ['fi:və*] *s* feber; **~ish** *adj* febril, med feber; febrilsk.
few [fju:] *adj* få; ikke mange; *a ~* nogle få; *quite a ~* ret mange, en hel del; *in a ~ days* om et par dage.
fey [fei] *adj* (lidt) skør.
fiancé, fiancée [fi'a:ŋsei] *s* forlovede.
fib [fib] *s* (F) hvid løgn.
fibre [faibə*] *s* fiber, trævl; *(fig)* karakter, kaliber; **~-board** *s* træfiberplade; **~glass** *s* glasfiber.
fickle [fikl] *adj* svingende, vægelsindet, skiftende.
fiction ['fikʃən] *s* skønlitteratur, prosa; opspind.
fictitious [fik'tiʃəs] *adj* opdigtet; fiktiv; fingeret.
fiddle [fidl] *s* violin; (F) fupnummer, fusk; *as fit as a ~* (F) frisk som en fisk // *v* (F) lave fup med; forfalske; ~ *with* pille ved; **~-proof** *adj* pillesikker (fx *switch* kontakt).
fiddler ['fidlə*] *s* spillemand; (F) fupmager.
fiddlesticks ['fidlstiks] *spl* vrøvl, sludder.
fiddling ['fidliŋ] *adj* ubetydelig, ligegyldig.
fidelity [fi'dɛliti] *s* troskab; omhu.
fidget ['fidʒit] *v* være rastløs, vimse rundt; pille, fingerere; **fidgety** ['fidʒiti] *adj* rastløs, febrilsk.
field [fi:ld] *s* mark; område, felt; *(sport)* bane // *v* give (kvikt) svar; ~ **day** *s* stor dag, skøn dag; ~ **glasses** *spl* (felt)kikkert; **~work** *s* arbejde i marken.

fiend [fi:nd] *s* djævel, satan; (F) fanatiker; **-ish** *adj* djævelsk.
fierce [fiəs] *adj* vild; rasende; voldsom, barsk (fx *wind* blæst).
fiery ['faiəri] *adj* brændende, hed; heftig, fyrig.
fifteen ['fif'ti:n] *num* femten.
fifth [fifθ] *s* femtedel // *adj* femte.
fiftieth ['fiftiiθ] *adj* halvtredsindstyvende.
fifty ['fifti] *num* halvtreds.
fig [fig] *s* figen(træ).
fight [fait] *s* kamp; slagsmål; skænderi; *have a* ~ slås; skændes; *put up a* ~ kæmpe bravt // *v (fought, fought* [fɔ:t]) kæmpe, slås; bekæmpe; ~ *back* kæmpe imod; slå tilbage; ~ *down* nedkæmpe; ~ *off* holde på afstand; jage væk; ~ *over sth* slås om ngt; **-er** *s* kriger; slagsbror; bokser; *(fly)* jager.
fighting ['faitiŋ] *s* kamp // *adj* kæmpende; *a* ~ *chance* en fair chance; ~ *fit* i topform; ~ *mad* lynende gal; **- spirit** *s* kampgejst.
figurative ['figjurətiv] *adj* billedlig; overført; blomstrende.
figure ['figə*] *s* figur, skikkelse; tal // *v* afbilde; optræde; figurere; beregne; ~ *out* regne ud; finde ud af; *that* ~*s!* det stemmer! **-head** *s (mar)* galionsfigur; *(fig)* stråmand; **- of speech** *s* talemåde; **- skating** *s* kunstskøjteløb.
filament ['filəmənt] *s* tråd, fiber; (i pære) glødetråd; *(bot)* støvtråd.
filch [filtʃ] *v* hugge, stjæle.
file [fail] *s* fil; brevordner, arkiv, kartotek; akter, sag; *(edb)* fil; *in single* ~ i gåsegang // *v* file; ordne, arkivere; indgive ansøgning; ~ *in* komme ind en og en; ~ *past* defilere forbi.
filing ['failiŋ] *s* arkivering; **- cabinet** *s* arkivskab.
Filipino [fili'pi:nəu] *s* filippiner // *adj* filippinsk.
fill [fil] *v* fylde; udfylde; optage; stoppe; ~ *a tooth* plombere en tand; ~ *in* udfylde; fylde op; ~ *sby in* orientere (,informere) en; ~ *up* (ud)fylde; fylde op; ~ *it up, please! (auto)* fyld tanken op! *eat one's* ~ spise sig mæt; *he had his* ~ han fik nok; **-er** *s* spartelmasse.
fillet ['filit] *s* filet, mørbrad // *v* filere, filetere.
filling ['filiŋ] *s* (om mad) fyld; fyldning; (om tand) plombe(ring); **- station** *s* benzinstation.
fillip ['filip] *s* incitament.
filly ['fili] *s* avlshoppe.
film [film] *s* film; hinde // *v* filme; ~ *over* sløres; **- star** *s* filmstjerne.
filmy ['filmi] *adj* tynd, let.
filter ['filtə*] *s* filter // *v* filtrere; sive igennem; **- lane** *s* frakørselsbane; **- tipped** *adj* (om cigaret) med filter.
filth [filθ] *s* snavs, skidt; *(fig)* sjofelheder.
filthy ['filθi] *adj* snavset, beskidt; sjofel; ~ *rich* (F) stenrig.
fin [fin] *s* (om fisk) finne.
final [fainl] *s* slutkamp, finale // *adj* endelig, afsluttende; afgørende.
finalize ['fainəlaiz] *v* afslutte; godkende.
finally ['fainəli] *adv* endelig, til sidst.
finals ['fainəlz] *spl* afsluttende eksamen; finale.
finance [fi'næns] *s* finans // *v* finansiere.
financial [fi'nænʃəl] *adj* finans-, penge-.
financier [fi'nænsiə*] *s* finansmand, financier.
finch [fintʃ] *s* finke.
find [faind] *s* fund // *v (found, found* [faund]) finde; opdage; skaffe; ~ *sby guilty (jur)* kende en skyldig; ~ *one's way* finde vej; ~ *out* opdage, finde ud af; **-ings** *spl (jur)* kendelse; konstatering.
fine [fain] *s* bøde // *v (jur)* idømme en bøde, give bødeforlæg // *adj* fin; glimrende; smuk; *the* ~ *arts* de skønne kunster; *I'm* ~ jeg har det fint; jeg klarer mig; *you are a* ~ *fellow!* du er en køn en! *cut it a bit* ~ ikke have meget tid at løbe på.
finery ['fainəri] *s* pynt, stads.
finger ['fiŋgə*] *s* finger; (ur)viser *keep one's* ~*s crossed for sby* krydse fingre for en; *put one's* ~ *on sth* sætte fingeren (,pege) på ngt; *have a* ~ *in*

every pie stikke sin næse i alting // *v* fingerere (ved); berøre; **~ing** *s* berøring; pillen; *(mus)* fingersætning; **~nail** *s* negl; **~print** *s* fingeraftryk // *v* tage fingeraftryk af; **~tip** *s* fingerspids.

finicky ['finiki] *adj* pertentlig; kræsen; pillen.

finish ['finiʃ] *s* afslutning; efterbehandling; overfladebehandling; *(sport)* opløb // *v* ende, gøre færdig, (af)slutte; færdigbehandle; *~ sby off* gøre det af med en; *~ sth off* gøre ngt færdigt; *~ up with* slutte (af) med; **~ing line** *s* mållinje; **~ing school** *s* privat skole for unge piger; **~ing touch** *s* en sidste afpudsning.

finite ['fainait] *adj* begrænset.

Finn [fin] *s* finne; **~ish** *s/adj* finsk.

fir [fə*] *s* gran(træ); **~ cone** *s* grankogle.

fire [faiə*] *s* ild; (ilde)brand; bål; lidenskab; *set ~ to* sætte ild til, (an)tænde; *catch ~* komme i brand; *on ~* i brand; *open ~* åben ild (,pejs) // *v* affyre; fyre; *~ away!* fyr bare løs! **~arm** *s* skydevåben; **~bomb** *s* brandbombe; **~brand** *s* urostifter; **~break** *s* brandbælte; brandmur; **~ brigade** [bri'geid] *s* brandvæsen; **~ drill** *s* brandøvelse; **~ engine** *s* brandbil; **~ escape** *s* brandtrappe; **~ extinguisher** *s* brandslukker; **~ hydrant** *s* brandhane; **~-irons** *spl* pejsesæt; **~ master** *s* brandchef; **~place** *s* kamin, ildsted, pejs; **~proof** *adj* brandsikker; ildfast; **~side** *s: sit by the ~side* sidde ved kaminen; **~station** *s* brandstation; **~ trap** brandfælde **~wood** *s* brænde; **~works** *spl* fyrværkeri.

firing ['faiəriŋ] *s* skydning; **~ squad** *s* henrettelsespeloton.

firm [fə:m] *s* firma // *adj* fast; bestemt; **~ness** *s* fasthed; bestemthed.

first [fə:st] *s* førsteplads; (ved eksamen) første karakter; *(auto)* første gear // *adj* først // *adv* før; hellere; for det første; *at ~* i begyndelsen, først; *in the ~ place* for det første; *~ of all* allerførst, først og fremmest; *~ thing in the morning* straks i morgen tidlig; **~ aid** *s* førstehjælp; **~-aid kit** *s* førstehjælpskasse; **~-class** *adj* førsteklasses; *travel ~-class* rejse på første klasse; **~-hand** *adj* førstehånds; **~ly** *adv* for det første; **~ name** *s* fornavn; **~ night** *s* premiere(aften); **~-rate** *adj* førsteklasses, førsterangs.

firth [fə:θ] *s* fjord.

fiscal ['fiskəl] *adj* skatte-; **~ year** *s* skatteår.

fish [fiʃ] *s (pl: ~* el. *~es)* fisk; *~ and chips* friturestegt fisk og pommes frites; *have other ~ to fry (fig)* have andet at lave (,tage sig af); *feel like a ~ out of water* føle sig som en spurv i tranedans; *he is a queer ~* han er en sær snegl // *v* fiske (i); *~ a river* fiske i en flod; *~ for* fiske efter; *go ~ing* tage på fisketur; **~cake** *s* fiskekrokette.

fisherman ['fiʃəmən] *s* fisker.

fishery ['fiʃəri] *s* fiskeri.

fish fingers ['fiʃ ˌfiŋgəz] *spl (gastr)* fiskestave.

fishing ['fiʃiŋ] *s* fiskeri // *adj* fiske-; **~ boat** *s* fiskebåd; **~ line** *s* fiskesnøre; **~ rod** *s* fiskestang; **~ tackle** *s* fiskeredskaber.

fishmonger ['fiʃmɔŋgə*] *s* fiskehandler.

fish slice ['fiʃslais] *s* paletkniv.

fishy ['fiʃi] *adj* fiske- (fx *smell* lugt); *(fig)* mistænkelig, suspekt; *there's sth ~ about it* der er ngt muggent ved det.

fissure ['fiʃə*] *s* spalte, revne.

fist [fist] *s* næve; (om skrift) klo.

fit [fit] *s* anfald, tilfælde; pasform; *this dress is a good ~* denne kjole passer (,sidder) godt; *by ~s and starts* i ryk, rykvis; *he had a ~ when he saw it* han blev helt vild (af raseri) da han så det // *v* udstyre; indrette; tilpasse; (om tøj) passe; passe til; *~ in* passe ind; få plads til; *~ out (,up)* udstyre, ekvipere // *adj* passende; egnet; i god form; veltrænet; *keep ~* holde sig i form; *as you think (,see) ~* som du synes; *~ for* egnet til; ~ *to* egnet til at; værdig til at; lige ved at; **-ful** *adj* stødvis; urolig.

fitment ['fitmənt] *s* tilbehør; indbygget skab; element.

fitness ['fitnis] *s* egnethed; duelighed; form, kondition.

fitted ['fitid] *adj* egnet; specielt fremstillet; ~ *carpet* heldækkende tæppe; ~ *cupboards* skabselementer; ~ *kitchen* elementkøkken; ~ *sheet* faconsyet lagen.

fitter ['fitə*] *s* montør; tilskærer.

fitting ['fitiŋ] *s* montering; (om tøj) prøvning // *adj* passende; **-s** *spl* (faste) installationer.

five [faiv] *num* fem.

fiver ['faivə*] *s* (F) fempundseddel.

fix [fiks] *s: be in a* ~ være i knibe; *get a* ~ (S) få en sprøjte, "fikse"; *get a* ~ *on* tage pejling på // *v* fæste, gøre fast; reparere; klare, fikse, ordne; fastsætte; *it's* ~*ed in my mind* det står prentet i min hukommelse; ~ *up* ordne, fikse.

fixation [fik'seiʃən] *s* fiksering.

fixative ['fiksətiv] *s* fikserbad.

fixed [fikst] *adj* fast (fx *price* pris); fiks (fx *idea* idé), stiv.

fixture ['fikstʃə*] *s* fast tilbehør (,inventar); *(sport)* sportskamp (som led i turneringsplan).

fizz [fiz] *s* sodavand; (S) boblevand // *v* bruse, moussere; syde.

fizzle [fizl] *v* bruse; ~ *out* fuse ud, mislykkes.

fizzy ['fizi] *adj* med brus.

flabbergasted ['flæbəga:stid] *adj* lamslået, paf.

flabby ['flæbi] *adj* slatten, lasket; holdningsløs.

flaccid ['flæksid] *adj* slatten, slap.

flag [flæg] *s* flag; flise; ~ *of convenience* bekvemmelighedsflag; *fly the* ~ flage, lade flaget vaje; *with* ~*s flying* med bravour // *v* hænge slapt; dø hen; ~ *down* (begynde at, få til at) standse; ~ *out (mar)* flage ud.

flagged ['flægd] *adj* flisebelagt.

flagpole ['flægpəul] *s* flagstang.

flagrant ['fleigrənt] *adj* åbenbar; skrigende; skamløs.

flagstone ['flægstəun] *s* flise.

flail [fleil] *v* fægte med.

flair [flɛə*] *s* sans, næse.

flake [fleik] *s* flage; (sne)fnug; (sæbe)spån // *v:* ~ *(off)* skalle af, ~ *out* kokse ud.

flamboyant [flæm'bɔiənt] *adj* festlig; farvestrålende; overlæsset, prangende.

flame [fleim] *s* flamme, lue; *in* ~*s* i lys lue; *burst into* ~*s* bryde i brand // *v* flamme, blusse; **~-thrower** *s* flammekaster.

flaming ['fleimiŋ] *adj* flammende; (F) forbandet, fandens.

flammable ['flæməbl] *adj* brændbar.

flan [flæn] *s (gastr)* tærte.

flank [flæŋk] *s* flanke, side // *v* flankere.

flannel [flænl] *s* (om stof) flannel, flonel; vaskeklud; (F) smiger; **-s** *spl* flannelsbukser.

flap [flæp] *s* klap, lem; snip; hatteskygge // *v* daske, baske; hænge slapt ned; (F, også: *be in a* ~) blive (,være) forfjamsket; **~-eared** *adj* med flyveører.

flare [flɛə*] *s* flakkende lys; nødblus, signallys; (om skørt) svaj, strutten // *v:* ~ *up* blusse op; *(fig)* fare op; **~d, flaring** *adj* (om bukser el. skørt) med svaj.

flash [flæʃ] *s* blink; lynglimt; kort nyhedsindslag; *(foto)* blitz, flash; *in a* ~ på et øjeblik // *v* blinke, lyne; lade skinne frem; prale med; være exhibitionist; ~ *one's headlights* blinke med forlygterne; ~ *by (,past)* stryge (,drøne) forbi; **~back** *s (film)* tilbageblik; **~bulb** *s (foto)* blitzpære; **~ cube** *s* blitzterning.

flasher ['flæʃə*] *s (auto)* blinklys; exhibitionist.

flashlight ['flæʃlait] *s* signallampe; blitz.

flashy ['flæʃi] *adj (neds)* smagløs, overlæsset, prangende.

flask [fla:sk] *s* flaske, lommelærke; termoflaske.

flat [flæt] *s* lejlighed; flade; punktering; *B-flat minor (mus)* b-mol; *E-flat major (mus)* es-dur // *adj* flad;

jævn; direkte; (om smag) fad, doven; (om lyd) tonløs; *(mus)* for lav, falsk; *you can't, and that's ~!* det kan du ikke og dermed basta! *in two seconds ~* på to sekunder rent; *~ out* helt udmattet; *work ~ out* ligge vandret i luften; **~-footed** *adj* platfodet; **~let** *s* lille lejlighed; **~ly** *adv* direkte, rent ud sagt; kategorisk; **~-nose pliers** *spl* fladtang.

flatten [flætn] *v* gøre flad; jævne med jorden.

flatter ['flætə*] *v* smigre; **~er** *s* smigrer; **~ing** *adj* smigrende; flatterende.

flattery ['flætəri] *s* smiger.

flatulence ['flætjuləns] *s* tarmluft, fjert; *(fig)* svulstighed.

flaunt [flɔ:nt] *v* flagre; knejse; skilte med.

flavour ['fleivə*] *s* aroma, smag; *(fig)* duft; *add ~ to* krydre, tilsætte smagsstoffer til // *v* give aroma (,smag); smagsætte; *vanilla ~ed* med vaniljesmag; **~ing** *s* krydderi; tilsmagning; kunstigt smagsstof.

flaw [flɔ:] *s* (skønheds)fejl; mangel; svaghed; **~less** *adj* fejlfri.

flax [flæks] *s (bot)* hør; **flaxen** *s* hør-; hørgul, blond.

flay [flei] *v* flå (også *fig*).

flea [fli:] *s* loppe; **~ market** *s* loppemarked.

fleck [flɛk] *s* plet, stænk.

fled [flɛd] *præt* og *pp* af **flee** [fli:] *v* flygte fra.

fledgling ['flɛdʒliŋ] *s* flyvefærdig (fugle)unge; nybegynder.

flee [fli:] *v (fled, fled)* flygte (fra).

fleece [fli:s] *s* skind, uld // *v* (F) plukke, flå.

fleet [fli:t] *s* flåde; flådestyrke; (om lastbiler etc) konvoj; vognpark.

fleeting ['fli:tiŋ] *adj* flygtig, forbigående.

flesh [flɛʃ] *s* kød; *in the ~* i egen høje person; **fleshy** *adj* kødfuld.

Flemish ['flɛmiʃ] *adj* flamsk.

flew [flu:] *præt* af *fly*.

flex [flɛks] *s (elek)* ledning // *v* bøje; *~ the muscles* spille med musklerne.

flexibility [flɛksi'biliti] *s* bøjelighed; smidighed.

flexible ['flɛksibl] *adj* bøjelig; smidig, fleksibel.

flexitime ['flɛksitaim] *s* flekstid.

flick [flik] *s* knips, svirp; *the ~s* (F) biffen // *v* knipse; svirpe; slå med; *~ on* tænde for, slå til; *~ through* bladre igennem.

flicker ['flikə*] *s* flakken; flagren // *v* flimre, flakke.

flick knife ['fliknaif] *s* springkniv.

flier ['flaiə*] *s* (også: *flyer)* (om person) flyver.

flight [flait] *s* flugt; flyvning, flyvetur; *put to ~* jage på flugt; *take ~* flygte; *a ~ of stairs* en trappe; **~ deck** *s* startdæk (på hangarskib); cockpit.

flighty ['flaiti] *adj* flyvsk; forfløjen.

flimsy ['flimzi] *adj* tynd; spinkel; overfladisk.

flinch [flintʃ] *s* vige tilbage; krympe sig *(from* for).

fling [fliŋ] *s* kast; *have a ~* slå sig løs // *v* kaste, smide, kyle.

flip [flip] *s* knips; lille tur // *v* daske, tjatte; (F) flippe ud // *adj* rapkæftet.

flippant ['flipənt] *adj* næsvis, flabet.

flipper ['flipə*] *s* luffe, svømmefod.

flipside ['flipsaid] *s* (på LP etc) b-side.

flirt [flə:t] *s* kokette, flirt // *v* filme, flirte.

flirtation [flə:'teiʃən] *s* flirt, koketteri.

flit [flit] *v* flagre; flyve; svæve; flytte i hemmelighed.

float [fləut] *s* tømmerflåde; (til fiskeri) flåd; *(tekn)* svømmer // *v* flyde, drive; oversvømme; (om tømmer) flåde; *(merk,* om kurs) lade flyde; **~ing** *adj* flydende.

flock [flɔk] *s* flok; hob; (om dyr) hjord // *v* flokkes; strømme.

floe [fləu] *s* isflage; isskosse.

flog [flɔg] *v* piske, banke, slå.

flood [flʌd] *s* højvande; oversvømmelse; strøm; *the Flood* Syndfloden // *v* oversvømme; *~ed with light* badet i lys; **~gates** *spl* sluseporte, sluser (også *fig*); **~light** *s* projektør // *v* projektørbelyse.

floor [flɔ:*] *s* gulv; etage; bund; *ground ~* stueetage; *wipe the ~*

with sby jorde en // *v* lægge gulv i; jorde, sætte til vægs; **~board** *s* gulvbræt; **~ing** *s* gulvbelægning; **~ polish** *s* bonevoks; **~ show** *s* varietéshow.

flop [flɔp] *s* fiasko; klask // *v* baske; klaske; plumpe ned; have fiasko.

floppy ['flɔpi] *adj* slatten, løsthængende; **~ disk** *s (edb)* diskette.

floral [flɔ:rl] *adj* blomster-.

florid ['flɔ:rid] *adj* blomstrende; rødmosset; svulstig.

florist ['flɔ:rist] *s* blomsterhandler.

flotation [fləu'teiʃən] *s* flyden; *(merk)* dannelse; 'gåen på børsen'.

flotilla [flə'tilə] *s* flåde.

flotsam ['flɔtsəm] *s* vraggods.

flounce [flauns] *s* flæse // *v* svanse, spankulere.

flounder ['flaundə*] *s* flynder, skrubbe // *v* sprælle; hakke i det.

flour [flauə*] *s* mel // *v* mele.

flourish ['flʌriʃ] *s* sving; forsiring, krusedulle; *(mus)* fanfare, touche // *v* blomstre, trives; svinge med; prale med.

flow [fləu] *s* strøm; (mods: ebbe) flod // *v* strømme, flyde; (om vand også) stige; (om hår) hænge løst; **~ chart** *s* (rute)diagram.

flower ['flauə*] *s* blomst; blomstring; *in* ~ i blomst, blomstrende // *v* blomstre; **~bed** *s* blomsterbed; **~ed** *adj* blomstret; **~pot** *s* urtepotte; **~y** *adj* blomstrende; med blomster.

flown [fləun] *pp* af *fly*.

fl.oz. fork.f. *fluid ounce*.

flu [flu:] *s* (F) influenza; *be down with the* ~ ligge med influenza.

fluctuate ['flʌktʃueit] *v* svinge, variere.

fluctuation [flʌktʃu'eiʃən] *s* vaklen, svingning; *(merk)* kurssvingning.

flue [flu:] *s* skorstenskanal.

fluency ['flu:ənsi] *s* lethed, talefærdighed; *with* ~ flydende.

fluent ['flu:ənt] *adj* flydende.

fluff [flʌf] *s* dun, fnug.

fluffy ['flʌfi] *adj* dunet, blød; **~ toy** *s* blødt legedyr.

fluid [flu:id] *s* væske // *adj* flydende; **~ ounce** *s* sv.t. 0,028 liter.

fluke [flu:k] *s* held, lykketræf.

flung [flʌŋ] *præt* og *pp* af *fling*.

flunk [flʌŋk] *v* dumpe (fx *an exam* til eksamen); lade dumpe.

flunkey ['flʌŋki] *s (neds)* lakaj.

fluorescent [fluə'rɛsnt] *adj* fluorescerende; **~ light** *s* lysstofrør; neonlys.

fluoride ['fluəraid] *s*, **fluorine** ['fluərin] *s* fluor.

flurry ['flʌri] *s* hastværk; uro; vindstød; snebyge; *a ~ of activity* hektisk aktivitet.

flush [flʌʃ] *s* rødmen; opbrusen; hedetur // *v* rødme; skylle ud; *~ the toilet* skylle ud, trække i snoren // *adj* fuld, svulmende; i plan; velbeslået; **~ed** *adj* rød i hovedet.

fluster ['flʌstə*] *s* forfjamskelse; **~ed** *adj* forfjamsket; forskræmt.

flute [flu:t] *s* fløjte; **~d** *adj* riflet.

flutter ['flʌtə*] *s* flagren, basken; nervøsitet; *in a* ~ forfjamsket // *v* baske med; blafre; (om person) være nervøs (,ophidset).

flux [flʌks] *s* strøm; flyden; *(med)* udflåd.

fly [flai] *s* flue; (i bukser) gylp // *v (flew, flown* [flu:, fləun]) flyve; fare; flygte; lade vaje (fx *the flag* flaget); *~ at* fare løs på; *let ~ at* gå løs på; give den store tur; *~ open* (om dør etc) springe op; **~catcher** *s* fluefanger; (om fugl) fluesnapper.

flyer ['flaiə*] *s* (også: *flier) s* (om person) flyver).

flying ['flaiing] *s* flyvning // *adj* flyvende; hurtig; *a ~ start* en flyvende start; *a ~ visit* en lynvisit; *with ~ colours* med glans; **~ fish** *s* flyvefisk; **~ squad** *s* sv.t. rigspolitiets rejsehold.

flyover ['flaiəuvə*] *s* overføring (over vej).

flypast ['flaipa:st] *s* forbiflyvning (i formation).

flysheet ['flaiʃi:t] *s* (på telt) oversejl.

fly-swatter ['flaiswɔtə*] *s* fluesmækker.

flywheel ['flaiwi:l] *s* svinghjul.

foal [fəul] *s* føl // *v* fole.

foam [fəum] *s* skum, fråde; skumgummi // *v* skumme.

fob [fɔb] (fork.f. *free on board) (merk)* frit ombord // *v: ~ sby off with sth* spise en af med ngt; *~ sth off on sby* prakke en ngt på.
focal [fəukl] *adj* fokal; *the ~ point* brændpunktet.
focus ['fəukəs] *s* brændpunkt, fokus; *in ~* skarp; *out of ~* uskarp // *v* indstille, fokusere; (om lys) samle, koncentrere.
fodder ['fɔdə*] *s* foder // *v* fodre.
foe [fəu] *s* (H) fjende.
foetus ['fi:təs] *s* foster.
fog [fɔg] *s* tåge // *v*: **~-up** *adj* dugge (til); **~gy** *adj* tåget; dugget; sløret; *I haven't the ~giest* jeg har ikke den fjerneste anelse.
foible [fɔibl] *s* svaghed.
foil [fɔil] *s* (metal)folie; aluminiumsfolie; sølvpapir // *v* forpurre; narre.
foist [fɔist] *v: ~ sth off on sby* prakke en ngt på.
fold [fəuld] *s* fold, ombøjning; fårefold // *v* folde, lægge sammen; *~ up* folde, lægge sammen; bryde sammen; måtte lukke.
folder ['fəuldə*] *s* folder, brochure; chartek.
folding ['fəuldiŋ] *adj* sammenklappelig; *~ bed* klapseng; *~ chair* klapstol.
fold-up ['fəuldʌp] *adj* folde-; klap-.
foliage ['fəuliidʒ] *s* blade, løv.
folk [fəuk] *spl* folk, mennesker // *adj* folke-.
folklore ['fəuklɔ:*] *s* folkeminder, folklore.
folks [fəuks] *spl* familie.
follow ['fɔləu] *v* følge (efter); efterfølge; følge med; være en følge (af); *as ~s...* som følger..., følgende...; *it ~s that...* heraf følger at...; *~ suit* følge trop, gøre ligeså; *~ up* følge op; forfølge; *with drinks to ~* med drinks ovenpå (,bagefter); **~er** *s* ledsager; tilhænger; **~ing** *s* følge, tilhængere // *adj* følgende // *præp* efter; **~-up** *s* opfølgning; efterkontrol.
folly ['fɔli] *s* dumhed, dårskab.
fond [fɔnd] *adj* kærlig, øm; *be ~ of* holde af, kunne lide, elske.
fondle [fɔndl] *v* kæle for.
fondness ['fɔndnis] *s* kærlighed, ømhed; *a special ~ for* en særlig svaghed for.
food [fu:d] *s* mad, føde; *be off one's ~* have tabt appetitten; *it's ~ for thought* det giver stof til eftertanke; **~ chain** *s* fødekæde; **~ mixer** *s* køkkenmaskine; **~ poisoning** *s* madforgiftning; **~ processor** *s* universal(køkken)maskine; **~stuffs** *spl* fødevarer.
fool [fu:l] *s* fjols, nar; *(gastr)* flødeskum med frugtpuré (fx *strawberry ~* jordbærskum); *make a ~ of oneself* gøre sig til grin // *v* narre; fjolle, pjatte; *~ around* fjolle rundt.
foolery ['fu:ləri] *s* fjolleri, pjat.
foolhardy ['fu:lha:di] *adj* dumdristig.
foolish ['fu:liʃ] *adj* dum; latterlig.
foolproof ['fu:lpru:f] *adj* idiotsikker.
foot [fu:t] *s (pl: feet* [fi:t]) fod; sokkel; engelsk fod *(12 inches,* 30,48 cm); *on ~* til fods; *put one's ~ down* slå i bordet; træde på speederen; *put one's ~ in it* jokke i spinaten; *set ~ in* sætte sine ben i, betræde; *fall on one's feet* slippe godt fra det; *get under sby's feet* komme i vejen for en; **~ and mouth (disease)** *s* mund- og klovsyge; **~ball** *s* fodbold; **~baller** *s* fodboldspiller; **~brake** *s* fodbremse; **~bridge** *s* gangbro; **~fall** *s* fodtrin; **~hills** *spl* udløbere (af bjerg); **~hold** *s* fodfæste; **~ing** *s* fodfæste; fundament; *lose one's ~ing* miste fodfæstet; *on an equal ~ing* på lige fod; **~lights** *spl* rampelys; **~man** *s* tjener; lakaj; **~-mark** *s* fodspor; **~note** *s* fodnote; **~path** *s* gangsti; fortov; **~print** *s* fodspor; **~prints** *spl (tekn)* rørtang; **~rest** *s* fodstøtte; **~sore** *adj*: *be ~sore* have ømme fødder; **~step** *s* fodtrin; fodspor; **~wear** *s* skotøj; **~work** *s* benarbejde.
foppish ['fɔpiʃ] *adj* lapset.
for [fɔ:*] *præp* for; til; (om tidsrum) i // *konj* for, thi; *~ all I know* så vidt jeg ved; *I haven't seen him ~ weeks* jeg har ikke set ham i flere uger; *leave ~ France* tage af sted til

Frankrig; *as ~ him* hvad ham angår; *~ fear of doing sth* af frygt for at gøre ngt; *he went down ~ the paper* han gik ned efter avisen; *~ sale* til salg; *you're ~ it!* nu hænger du på den!

foray ['fɔrei] *s* strejftog; udflugt.

forage ['fɔridʒ] *s* foder // *v* fouragere.

forbad(e) [fə'bæd] *præt* af *forbid.*

forbearing [fɔ:'bɛəriŋ] *adj* tålmodig; overbærende.

forbid [fɔ:'bid] *v (forbad(e), forbidden* [fə'bæd, fə'bidn]) forbyde; hindre; **~den** *adj* forbudt; **~ding** *adj* afskrækkende; uhyggelig.

force [fɔ:s] *s* kraft, styrke; magt; *the Forces* militæret; *by ~ of* i kraft af; *in ~* i stort tal, mandstærkt; *come into ~* træde i kraft; *join ~s with* slå sig sammen med, slutte sig til // *v* tvinge; presse; forcere; *~ an entry* tiltvinge sig adgang; **~d** *adj* tvunget; unaturlig; **~-feed** *v* tvangsfodre; **~ful** *adj* kraftig, stærk; **~meat** *s* kødfars.

forceps ['fɔ:sɛps] *spl* tang.

forcibly ['fɔ:sibli] *adv* med magt.

ford [fɔ:d] *s* vadested // *v* vade (over).

fore... [fɔ:*-] sms: **~arm** *s* underarm; **~boding** [-'bəudiŋ] *s* forudanelse; *~bodings pl* bange anelser; **~cast** *s* forudsigelse, prognose; vejrudsigt // *v* [-'ka:st] forudsige; forudse; **~fathers** *spl* forfædre; **~finger** *s* pegefinger; **~go** [-'gəu] *v* se *forgo;* **~ground** *s* forgrund; **~head** ['fɔrid] *s* pande.

foreign ['fɔrin] *adj* fremmed, udenlandsk; udenrigs- (fx *trade* handel); **~ body** *s* fremmedlegeme; **~er** *s* udlænding; **~ exchange rate** *s* valutakurser; **~ minister** *s* udenrigsminister; *the* **Foreign Office** *s (brit)* udenrigsministeriet.

foreleg ['fɔ:lɛg] *s* forben.

foreman ['fɔ:man] *s* (arbejds)formand.

foremost ['fɔ:məust] *adj* forrest, først; mest fremragende.

forensic [fə'rɛnsik] *adj: ~ medicine* retsmedicin.

forerunner ['fɔ:rʌnə] *s* forløber; forgænger.

foresee [fɔ:'si:] *v (-saw, -seen* [-'sɔ:, -'si:n]) forudse; **~able** *adj* til at forudse.

foresight ['fɔ:sait] *s* forudseenhed, fremsynethed.

forest ['fɔrist] *s* skov.

forestall [fɔ:'stɔ:l] *v* komme i forkøbet.

forestry ['fɔristri] *s* skovbrug, forstvæsen.

foretaste ['fɔ:teist] *s* forsmag.

foretell [fɔ:'tɛl] *v (-told, -told)* forudsige.

forethought ['fɔ:θɔ:t] *s* omtanke.

forever [fə'rɛvə*] *adv* (for) altid, (for) bestandig; konstant.

forwarn [fɔ:'wɔ:n] *v* advare i forvejen.

forfeit ['fɔ:fit] *s* bøde; pant; ngt man har mistet retten til // *v* fortabe, sætte over styr.

forgave [fə'geiv] *præt* af *forgive.*

forge [fɔ:dʒ] *s* smedje // *v* smede; forfalske; *~ documents* lave dokumentfalsk; *~ money* lave falskmøntneri.

forger ['fɔ:dʒə*] *s* forfalsker.

forgery ['fɔ:dʒəri] *s* falskneri; forfalskning.

forget [fə'gɛt] *v (-got, -gotten)* glemme; have glemt; *...not ~ing John* ...John ikke at forglemme; **~ful** *adj* glemsom; *~ful of* uden at tænke på; **~-me-not** *s (bot)* forglemmigej.

forgive [fə'giv] *v (-gave, -given)* tilgive; eftergive; **~ness** *s* tilgivelse, forladelse; barmhjertighed.

forgo [fɔ:'geu] *v (-went, -gone)* undvære; forsage; give afkald på.

forgot [fə:'gɔt] *præt* af *forget;* **~ten** [fə'gɔtn] *pp* af *forget.*

fork [fɔ:k] *s* gaffel; høtyv; greb; skillevej // *v* dele sig; gafle, skovle; *~ out* punge ud; **~ed** *adj* gaffelformet; kløftet; *~ed lightning* siksaklyn; **~-lift truck** *s* gaffeltruck.

forlorn [fə'lɔ:n] *adj* forladt; ynkelig; fortvivlet.

form [fɔ:m] *s* form; skikkelse; formular; (skole)klasse; *a matter of ~* en formssag; *that is bad ~* sådan gør

(,siger) man ikke; *be on (,off)* ~ være i (,ude af) form; *true to* ~ som sædvanlig // *v* forme, danne; udgøre.

formal ['fɔ:məl] *adj* formel; (om person) stiv, højtidelig; afmålt.

formality [fɔ:'mæliti] *s* formalitet.

format ['fɔ:mæt] *s* format // *v (edb)* formatere.

formation [fɔ:'meiʃən] *s* dannelse, tilblivelse; formation.

former ['fɔ:mə*] *adj* tidligere, forhenværende; *the* ~ førstnævnte; *in* ~ *times* i gamle dage; **~ly** *adv* tidligere.

formidable ['fɔ:midəbl] *adj* frygtindgydende, drabelig, formidabel.

formula ['fɔ:mjulə] *s* formel; formular; opskrift.

formulate ['fɔ:mjuleit] *v* udforme; formulere

fornication [fɔ:ni'keiʃən] *s* hor, utugt.

forsake [fə'seik] *v (-sook, -saken* [-'suk, -'seikn]) svigte; forlade (fx *one's children* sine børn); opgive (fx *an idea* en idé).

forte ['fɔ:tei] *s: cooking is not his* ~ madlavning er ikke hans stærke side.

forth [fɔ:θ] *adv* frem(ad), videre; *back and* ~ frem og tilbage; *and so* ~ og så videre; *from this day* ~ fra i dag af; fra denne dag af; *put* ~ fremlægge; *set* ~ (H) drage af; **~coming** *adj* forestående, kommende; imødekommende; **~right** *adj* ligefrem, oprigtig; **~with** *adv* straks, sporenstregs.

fortieth ['fɔ:tiiθ] *num* fyrretyvende.

fortification [fɔ:tifi'keiʃən] *s* befæstning; forstærkning.

fortify ['fɔ:tifai] *v* befæste; styrke.

fortitude ['fɔ:titju:d] *s* mod, fatning.

fortnight ['fɔ:tnait] *s* fjorten dage; *once a* ~ en gang hver fjortende dag (,hveranden uge); *this day* ~ i dag fjorten dage; **~ly** *adv* hver fjortende dag, hveranden uge.

fortress ['fɔ:tris] *s* fæstning.

fortuitous [fɔ:'tju:itəs] *adj* tilfældig; **~ly** *adv* på slump.

fortunate ['fɔ:tjunit] *adj* heldig; **~ly** *adv* heldigvis.

fortune ['fɔ:tjun] *s* formue; lykke; skæbne; held; *bad* ~ uheld; *make a* ~ tjene en formue; *tell* ~*s* spå; **~-teller** *s* spåmand, -kone.

forty ['fɔ:ti] *num* fyrre; *have* ~ *winks* tage sig en lur.

forward ['fɔ:wəd] *v* fremme; fremsende; (for)sende; ekspedere; *please* ~ bedes eftersendt // *adj* forrest; småfræk, ubeskeden; fremmelig // *adv* fremad, videre; forover; fremme; *be looking forward to* glæde sig til, se frem til; **~ing address** *s* adresse til videresendelse.

forwards ['fɔ:wədz] *s (sport)* angrebskæde // *adv* fremad.

forwent [fɔ:'wɛnt] *præt* og *pp* af *forgo.*

fossilized ['fɔsilaizd] *adj* forstenet; forbenet.

foster ['fɔstə*] *v* fremme, støtte; opfostre; pleje; fostre; **~ child** *s* plejebarn; **~ mother** *s* plejemor; *(agr)* rugemaskine.

fought [fɔ:t] *præt* og *pp* af *fight.*

foul [faul] *s (fodb)* ureglementeret spil // *v* svine til; forpeste; *(fodb)* lave frispark (imod); ~ *up* svine til; forkludre, ødelægge // *adj* modbydelig, uhumsk; fordærvet; *a* ~ *temper* et rædsomt humør (,temperament); *by fair means or* ~ med alle midler; *fall* ~ *of sby* rage uklar med en; **~ play** *s* uærligt spil; luskeri.

found [faund] *v* grundlægge, oprette; bygge; *(tekn)* støbe // *præt* og *pp* af *find.*

foundation [faun'deiʃən] *s* grundlæggelse; stiftelse; fond; pudderunderlag; ~*s* grundvold; **~ stone** *s* grundsten.

founder ['faundə*] *s* grundlægger, stifter; *(tekn)* støber // *v* (om skib) gå under; (om hus) styrte sammen; *(fig)* mislykkes.

foundling ['faundliŋ] *s* hittebarn.

foundry ['faundri] *s* støberi; støbegods.

fount [faunt] *s* kilde.

fountain ['fauntin] *s* springvand; **~ pen** *s* fyldepen.

four [fɔ:*] *num* fire; *on all* ~*s* på alle fire; **~-letter word** *s* uartigt ord (fx *arse, fuck);* **~-ply** [-plai] *adj* firetrådet; **~-poster** [-pəustə*] *s* himmelseng; **~some** *s* spil mellem to par; selskab (,dans) for fire; **~-stroke** *adj* firetakts-.

fourteen [fɔ:'ti:n] *num* fjorten; **fourteenth** *num* fjortende // *s* fjortendedel.

fourth ['fɔ:θ] *num* fjerde // *s* fjerdedel; *(mus)* kvart.

fowl [faul] *s* (stykke) fjerkræ.

fox [fɔks] *s* ræv; *(fig)* snu person // *v* narre, snyde; gøre paf; **~glove** [-glʌv] *s (bot)* digitalis, fingerbøl; **~hunt(ing)** *s* rævejagt.

foxy ['fɔksi] *adj* snu; lusket.

fraction ['frækʃən] *s* brøk(del); smule.

fracture ['fræktʃə*] *s* brud, fraktur // *v* brække (fx *one's leg* benet).

fragile ['frædʒail] *adj* skrøbelig; spinkel.

fragment ['frægmənt] *s* brudstykke, fragment; skår; stump // *v* gå i stykker; knuses; slå i stykker; **~ary** *adj* brudstykkeagtig.

fragrance ['freigrəns] *s* duft, vellugt // *v* perfumere.

fragrant ['freigrənt] *adj* vellugtende.

frail [freil] *adj* skrøbelig; svag, svagelig; **~ty** *s* svaghed.

frame [freim] *s* ramme, stel; bygning; stativ; stillads; (om person) skikkelse, form; *~ of mind* sindsstemning // *v* indramme; udforme, danne; lave falske beviser mod; **~work** *s* skelet; struktur; system.

France [fra:ns] *s* Frankrig.

franchise ['fræntʃaiz] *s* rettighed, privilegium; valgret.

frank [fræŋk] *adj* åben, oprigtig // *v* frankere.

frankincense ['fræŋkinsəns] *s* røgelse.

frankly ['fræŋkli] *adv* ærlig talt; rent ud sagt.

frantic ['fræntik] *adj* hektisk; vild; ude af sig selv.

fraternal [frə'tə:nl] *adj* broderlig.

fraternity [frə'tə:niti] *s* broderlighed; broderskab.

fraternize ['frætənaiz] *v* fraternisere, omgås.

fraud [frɔ:d] *s* bedrageri; (om person) bedrager; *he is a ~* han er en svindler; *the Fraud Squad* sv.t. bagmandspolitiet.

fraudulent ['frɔ:djulənt] *adj* bedragerisk, svigagtig.

fraught [frɔ:t] *adj: ~ with* fyldt af, ladet med.

fray [frei] *v* slide i laser; trævle, flosse.

frazzle ['fræzəl] *s: worn to a ~* slidt i laser; *burned to a ~* forkullet; **~d** *adj* udmattet, udslidt.

freak [fri:k] *s* kuriositet; grille; original; (F) flipper; *(biol* etc) mutant; *a ~ of nature* et af naturens luner; *a health ~* en sundhedsapostel // *v: ~ out* (F) flippe ud.

freckle [frɛkl] *s* fregne; **~d** *adj* fregnet.

free [fri:] *v* befri, frigøre // *adj* fri; tvangfri; ligefrem; gratis; rigelig; ledig; *set ~* slippe fri, løslade; *feel ~!* lad som om du var hjemme! *for ~* gratis; *you are ~ to do so* det står dig frit for at gøre det; *make ~ with sth* (hæmningsløst) udnytte ngt; **~-and-easy** *adj* tvangfri, afslappet.

freedom ['fri:dəm] *s* frihed; **~ fighter** *s* frihedskæmper.

Freefone ['fri:fəun] *s (tlf)* direkte kald (betales af det modtagende firma).

free-for-all ['fri:fər,ɔ:l] *s* almindeligt slagsmål; åben konkurrence.

free-handed ['fri:hændid] *adj* rundhåndet, large.

freehold ['fri:həuld] *s* selveje.

free kick ['fri: kik] *s (fodb)* frispark.

freely ['fri:li] *adv* frit, utvunget; rigeligt.

Freepost ['fri:pəust] *s* sendes ufrankeret (modtageren betaler portoen).

free... ['fri:-] sms: **~mason** *s* frimurer; **~-range** *adj* (om æg etc) skrabe-; **~skating** *s* friløb (på skøjter); **~-spoken** *adj* åbenhjertig; **~style** *s* fri svømning; **~ trade** *s* frihandel; **~wheel** *v* køre på frihjul.

freeze [fri:z] *s* frost; fastfrysning // *v (froze, frozen* [frəuz, frəuzn]) fryse; være (,blive) iskold; stivne; nedfryse; fastfryse (fx *the prices* priserne); *~ over (,up)* fryse til; **~-dry** *v* frysetørre.

freezer ['fri:zə*] *s* dybfryser.

freezing ['fri:ziŋ] *adj: ~ cold* iskold; **~ point** *s* frysepunkt.

freight [freit] *s* fragt; gods, last; fragtpenge; **~er** *s (mar)* fragtskib.

French [frɛntʃ] *s* (om sproget) fransk // *adj* fransk; *the ~* franskmændene; **~ beans** *spl* haricots verts; **~ bread** *s* flute; **~ fries** *spl* pommes frites; **~ horn** *s (mus)* valdhorn; **~ loaf** *s* flute; **~ window** *s* fransk dør, glasdør ud til det fri.

frenetic [frə'nɛtik] *adj* vild, rasende.

frenzy ['frɛnzi] *s* vanvid, raseri(anfald); raptus.

frequency ['fri:kwənsi] *s* hyppighed; frekvens.

frequent *v* [fri'kwɛnt] besøge hyppigt, omgås, frekventere // *adj* ['fri:kwənt] hyppig; **~ly** ['fri:-] *adv* ofte, tit.

fresh [frɛʃ] *adj* frisk; ny; fræk; *~ paint* nymalet; *we're ~ out of sherry* (F) vi er løbet helt tør for sherry; *be ~ with sby* være nærgående over for en, gøre (uønskede) tilnærmelser til en; **~en** *v* friske op; *~en up* friske sig op; **~er, ~man** *s* (om studerende) rus; **~ly** *adv* ny-, frisk-; **~water** *adj* ferskvands-.

fret [frɛt] *s* (om guitar etc) bånd (på gribebrættet) // *v* være bekymret; ærgre sig; beklage sig; **~ful** *adj* irritabel; (om barn) klynkende; **~saw** *s* løvsav.

friar ['fraiə*] *s* munk.

friction ['frikʃən] *s* gnidning, friktion.

Friday ['fraidi] *s* fredag; *on ~* på fredag; *on ~s* om fredagen, hver fredag; *man ~* Fredag (i Robinson Crusoe); *(fig)* tjener, tro følgesvend; *girl ~* privatsekretær; *Good ~* langfredag.

fridge [fridʒ] *s* (F) køleskab.

fried [fraid] *præt* og *pp* af *fry* // *adj* stegt; *~ egg* spejlæg.

friend [frɛnd] *s* ven, veninde; bekendt; *make ~s with* blive (gode) venner med; *a ~ of mine* en ven af mig; **~liness** *s* venlighed; **~ly** *adj* venlig; **~ship** *s* venskab.

frieze [fri:z] *s* frise.

frigate ['frigit] *s (mar)* fregat.

fright [frait] *s* skræk; forskrækkelse; *(fig)* rædsel; *give sby a ~* gøre en forskrækket; *she looks a ~* hun ligner et fugleskræmsel.

frighten ['fraitn] *s* forskrække, skræmme; **~ed** *adj: be ~ed of* være bange for; **~ing** *adj* skræmmende; afskrækkende.

frightful ['fraitful] *adj* skrækkelig.

frill [fril] *s* flæse; kalvekrøs; **~s** *spl* falbelader.

fringe [frindʒ] *s* frynse; krans; rand; udkant; **~ benefits** *spl* frynsegoder; **~ theatre** *s* sv.t. alternativteater.

frippery ['fripəri] *s* overflødig pynt, stads.

frisk [frisk] *v* kropsvisitere; boltre sig; **~y** *adj* sprælsk, kåd.

fritter ['fritə*] *s* (om bagværk) "æblefisk" // *v: ~ away* klatte væk.

frivolous ['frivələs] *adj* overfladisk; fjantet.

frizz [friz] *v* (om hår) kruse.

frizzle [frizl] *v* brase; sprutte.

fro [frəu] *adv: to and ~* frem og tilbage.

frock [frɔk] *s* kjole; kittel, busseronne; præstekjole.

frog [frɔg] *s (zo)* frø; *(neds, spøg)* franskmand; *have a ~ in one's throat* have en tudse i halsen; **~-march** *v* slæbe af sted med i føregreb.

frolic ['frɔlik] *s* løssluppenhed, kådhed; spøg // *v* springe rundt; fjolle.

from [frɔm] *præp* fra; på grund af; *~ childhood* fra barndommen af; *~ what he says* efter hvad han siger; *safe ~* sikker mod.

front [frɔnt] *s* forside; forende; front; *(fig)* ydre; mine; *in ~ (of)* foran; *in ~ of the class* i klassens påhør; *up ~* henne foran // *v* vende ud mod; lede, styre // *adj* forrest; for-.

frontage ['frɔntidʒ] *s* facade.

front door ['frɔnt,dɔ:r] *s* gadedør; hoveddør; *(auto)* fordør.

frontier ['frɔntiə*] *s* grænse (mellem stater).

front... sms: **~ page** *s* (om avis etc) forside; **~ room** *s* værelse til gaden;

~-runner *s* spidskandidat; **~-wheel drive** *s (auto)* forhjulstræk.
frost [frɔst] *s* frost, rimfrost; kulde; **~bite** *s* forfrysning.
frosted ['frɔstid] *adj* (om glas) matteret; *(am)* glaseret.
frosting ['frɔstiŋ] *s* (om glas) mattering; *(am*, om kage etc) glasur.
frosty ['frɔsti] *adj* frossen; kølig.
froth [frɔθ] *s* skum, fråde; *(fig)* gas // *v* skumme; fråde.
frown [fraun] *s* rynket pande; skulende blik // *v* rynke panden; skule, se truende ud; *~ on sth* misbillige ngt.
froze [frəuz] *præt* af *freeze;* **~n** *pp* af *freeze* // *adj* nedfrosset; indefrosset; iskold, stivfrossen.
frugal [fru:gl] *adj* sparsommelig; beskeden; tarvelig.
fruit [fru:t] *s (pl: ~)* frugt; *(fig)* resultat, udbytte; *be in ~* om træ etc) bære frugt(er); **~ful** *adj* frugtbar; udbytterig.
fruition [fru:'iʃən] *s: come to ~* blive realiseret.
fruit... ['fru:t-] sms: **~ machine** *s* spilleautomat; **~ salad** *s* frugtsalat; **~ sundae** *s* is med frugt og flødeskum; **~y** *adj* frugtagtig; saftig.
frustrate [frʌ'streit] *v* tilintetgøre, forpurre; modarbejde; skuffe; **~d** *adj* utilfreds, frustreret.
frustration [frʌ'streiʃən] *s* skuffelse, frustration.
fry [frai] *s: small ~* småfisk; unger; småtterier // *v (fried, fried* [fraid]) stege; blive stegt; **~ing pan** *s* stegepande.
ft fork.f. *foot, feet.*
fuck [fʌk] *v* (V!) bolle, knalde; *~ all* ikke en skid; *~ it!* satans også! *~ off!* skrub af! *~ that car!* den lortebil! *~ you!* gå ad H til! *~ up* lave koks i, ødelægge; **~ing** *adj* (V!) satans, forpulet.
fuddled [fʌdld] *adj* forvirret; omtåget.
fudge [fʌdʒ] *s* slags blød karamel; fusk; vrøvl // *v* fuske; krybe udenom.
fuel [fju:əl] *s* brændsel; brændstof; *add ~ to the flames* puste til ilden // *v* fyre; give næring til; **~ oil** *s* fyringsolie.
fug [fʌg] *s* (F) møf, hørm.
fugitive ['fju:dʒitiv] *s* flygtning // *adj* flygtet; *(fig)* flygtig.
fulfil [ful'fil] *v* opfylde; udføre; fuldføre; tilfredsstille; **~ment** *s* opfyldelse; indfrielse; fuldførelse; tilfredsstillelse.
full [ful] *adj* fuld, opfyldt; mæt; fuldstændig; fyldig; vid; *I'm ~* jeg er mæt; *in ~* fuldt ud; i sin helhed; *a ~ skirt* en vid nederdel; *at ~ speed* for fuld fart; *a ~ two hours* fulde (,hele) to timer; *be ~ of oneself* være stærkt selvoptaget // *adv* helt, fuldt; **~-blown** *adj* fuldt færdig, gennemført; komplet; vaskeægte; **~ board** *s* helpension; **~ dress** *s* festdragt, galla; **~-face** *adj* en face, lige forfra; **~gown** *adj* fuldvoksen; **~-length** *adj* i hel figur; uforkortet; hellang; **~ moon** *s* fuldmåne; **~ness** *s* fylde; vidde; **~-page** *adj* helsides; **~-sized** *adj* i legemsstørrelse; **~ stop** *s* punktum; **~ time** *s (sport)* tid (dvs. slut for kampen).
fully ['fuli] *adv* helt, fuldstændigt; **~-fledged** [-flɛdʒd] *adj* flyveværdig (også *fig).*
fulminate ['fulmineit] *v* rase (*against* imod).
fumble [fʌmbl] *v* famle, fumle (med); forkludre; *~ with* pille ved.
fume [fju:m] *v* dampe, ryge; *(fig)* rase, fnyse; **~s** *spl* dampe; giftige gasser.
fumigate ['fju:migeit] *v* desinficere med røg.
fun [fʌn] *s* sjov, løjer; *have ~* more sig; *it's not much ~* der er ikke meget grin ved det; *make ~ of* gøre grin med; *for the ~ of it* for sjovs skyld; *he's great ~* han er mægtig sjov; *~ and games* fis og ballade.
function ['fʌnkʃən] *s* funktion; hverv; fest, højtidelighed // *v* fungere, virke; **~al** *adj* funktions-.
fund [fʌnd] *s* fond, kapital; forråd // *v* anbringe penge i; *~ sby's schooling* betale for ens skolegang; **funds** *spl* obligationer, fonds; midler.
fundamental [fʌndə'mɛntl] *adj* grundlæggende, fundamental; **~ research**

s grundforskning; **~ly** *adv* principielt; i bund og grund; **fundamentals** *spl* grundbegreber.
fund-raising ['fʌndreiziŋ] *s* (penge)indsamling.
Funen ['fju:nən] *s* Fyn.
funeral ['fju:nərəl] *s* begravelse; **~ director** *s* bedemand; **~ service** *s* begravelse(sgudstjeneste).
funereal [fju:'niəriəl] *adj* begravelsesagtig; grav-.
funfair ['fʌnfεə*] *s* forlystelsespark, tivoli.
fungus ['fʌŋgəs] *s (pl: fungi)* svamp.
funk [fʌŋk] *s* skvat, tøsedreng // *v* være bange; krybe udenom.
funnel [fʌnl] *s* tragt; (på skib el. lokomotiv) skorsten.
funny ['fʌni] *adj* morsom, sjov; mærkelig, underlig; *feel ~* være utilpas; have en underlig fornemmelse.
fur [fə:*] *s* pels(værk); skind; kedelsten; belægning (på tungen) // *v: ~ up* kalke til.
furbish ['fə:biʃ] *v* pudse op.
furious ['fjuəriəs] *adj* rasende, voldsom.
furl [fə:l] *v* rulle sammen.
furnace ['fə:nis] *s* (smelte)ovn; fyr, ildsted.
furnish ['fə:niʃ] *v* yde, levere, skaffe; møblere, udstyre; **~ings** *spl* møbler; boligudstyr; *soft ~ings* boligtekstiler.
furniture ['fə:nitʃə*] *s* møbler; udstyr; inventar; *a piece of ~* et møbel; *he's part of the ~* (F, *fig)* han er fast tilbehør; **~ van** *s* flyttebil.
furrier ['fʌriə*] *s* buntmager.
furrow ['fʌrəu] *s* plovfure; fure.
furry ['fʌri] *adj* pelsagtig; pelsklædt; lodden.
further ['fə:ðə*] *v* fremme, befordre // *adj/adv (komp* af *far)* fjernere; yderligere; mere; videre; *until ~ notice* indtil videre; **~more** *adv* desuden, endvidere.
furthest ['fə:ðist] *adj (sup* af *far)* fjernest, længst (væk).
furtive ['fə:tiv] *adj* stjålen, hemmelighedsfuld; listig.
fury ['fjuəri] *s* raseri; *(myt)* furie; *in a ~* rasende.
fuse [fju:z] *s* lunte; detonator; (el)sikring; *blow the ~s* få sikringerne til at springe // *v* smelte; sammensmelte; sammenslutte; *the bulb has ~d* pæren er sprunget; **~ box** *s (elek)* sikringskasse.
fuselage ['fju:zəlidʒ] *s (fly)* krop, skrog.
fusion ['fju:ʒən] *s* sammensmeltning, fusion.
fuss [fʌs] *s* ståhej, vrøvl; forvirring; *make a ~* lave ballade; gøre vrøvl; *make a ~ of sby* gøre et stort nummer af en; pylre om en // *v* gøre vrøvl; skabe sig; pylre; *~ around* vimse rundt; **~pot** *s* pylrehoved.
fussy ['fʌsi] *adj* nervøs; kræsen; geskæftig; pertentlig; vanskelig.
futile ['fju:tail] *adj* unyttig; resultatløs, forgæves, omsonst; indholdsløs.
futility [fju:'tiliti] *s* ørkesløshed; tomhed.
future ['fju:tʃə*] *s* fremtid; *(gram)* futurum; *in ~* for fremtiden // *adj* fremtidig, kommende.
fuzz [fʌz] *s* dun; fnug; uskarphed; *the ~* (S) strisserne.
fuzzery ['fʌzəri] *s* (S) politistation.
fuzzy ['fʌzi] *adj* dunet; omtåget; (om hår) kruset; *(foto* etc) uskarp, sløret.

G

G, g [dʒi:].
g. fork.f. *gramme(s); gram(s).*
gab [gæb] *s* snak // *v* snakke.
gabble [gæbl] *v* plapre; lire af.
gable [geibl] *s* gavl.
gadget ['gædʒit] *s* (F) tingest, dippedut; indretning; påfund.
Gaelic ['gælik] *s/adj* gælisk.
gaff [gæf] *s: blow the ~* plapre ud med det hele.
gaffe [gæf] *s* bommert, brøler.
gaffer ['gæfə*] *s* (F) boss, formand, chef.
gag [gæg] *s* knebel; mundkurv; *(fig)* fup(nummer); spøg // *v* kneble; være ved at brække sig; stoppe munden på.
gaiety ['geiəti] *s* lystighed, munterhed.

gaily ['geili] *adv* livligt, muntert (se *gay).*
gain [gein] *s* gevinst, profit; fremgang, forøgelse // *v* vinde; tjene; tage på i vægt; (om ur) gå for hurtigt; ~ *ground* gribe om sig; ~ *ground on sby* vinde ind på en; ~ *a living* tjene til livets ophold; ~ *strength* komme til kræfter; **~ful** *adj* indbringende; **~say** [gein'sei] *v (-said, -said)* sige imod; bestride.
gait [geit] *s* gang(art).
gaiter ['geitə*] *s* gamache.
gal fork.f. *gallon* // *s* [gæl] (F) d.s.s. *girl.*
gala ['ga:lə] *s* gallaforestilling.
galaxy ['gælæksi] *s* mælkevej, galakse.
gale [geil] *s* storm, stærk blæst; *~-force winds* vindstød af stormstyrke; **~ warning** *s* stormvarsel.
gall [gɔ:l] *s* bitterhed; frækhed; galde // *v* ærgre, krepere.
gallant ['gælənt] *adj* tapper, ædel, ridderlig; galant.
gallantry ['gæləntri] *s* tapperhed, ridderlighed.
gall-bladder ['gɔ:lblædə*] *s* galdeblære.
gallery ['gæləri] *s* galleri; kunstmuseum; kunstgalleri; (på hus) svalegang.
galley ['gæli] *s (mar)* kabys; galej; **~ proof** *s (typ)* spaltekorrektur.
galling ['gɔ:liŋ] *adj* kreperlig; utålelig.
gallivant [gæli'vænt] *v* føjte rundt; slå til søren.
gallon [gælən] *s* rummål *(brit:* 4,546 liter; *am:* ca. 3,8 liter).
gallop ['gæləp] *s* galop // *v* galopere.
gallows ['gæləuz] *s* galge.
gallstone ['gɔ:lstəun] *s* galdesten.
galore [gə'lɔ:*] *adv* i massevis.
gambit ['gæmbit] *s* indledende manøvre.
gamble [gæmbl] *s* hasardspil; lotteri // *v* spille (hasard); ~ *on (fig)* løbe an på, satse på.
gambler ['gæmblə*] *s* (hasard)spiller.
gambling ['gæmbliŋ] *s* hasardspil; *(merk)* spekulation.
gambol ['gæmbəl] *v* boltre sig, tumle.
game [geim] *s* leg, spil; kamp; (ved jagt) vildt; *be easy* ~ være et let bytte (,offer); *big* ~ storvildt; *give the* ~ *away* røbe det hele; *see through sby's* ~ gennemskue en; *the* ~ *is up* spillet er ude // *adj* modig; kampklar, parat; *be* ~ *for sth* være med på ngt; **~keeper** *s* skytte, jagtbetjent; **~ licence** *s* jagttegn; **~ reserve** *s* vildtreservat.
gammon ['gæmən] *s (gastr)* (røget) skinke.
gamut ['gæmət] *s* register, skala.
gander ['gændə*] *s* gase.
gang [gæŋ] *s* bande; hob; hold // *v:* ~ *up with sby* rotte sig sammen med en; ~ *up on sby* mobbe en.
gangling ['gæŋgliŋ] *adj* ranglet.
gangrene ['gæŋgri:n] *s (med)* koldbrand.
gangway ['gæŋwei] *s* landgang(sbro); midtergang; gangbro.
gaol [dʒeil] *s* d.s.s. *jail.*
gap [gæp] *s* åbning; kløft; afbrydelse; *(fig)* tomrum, hul.
gape [geip] *v* måbe, glo; **gaping** *adj* måbende, gabende.
garage ['gæra:ʒ, 'gæridʒ] *s* garage; benzinstation; bilværksted.
garb [ga:b] *s* antræk.
garbage ['ga:bidʒ] *s* (køkken) affald; skrald; bras.
garden [ga:dn] *s* have // *v* lave havearbejde; **~ centre** *s* planteskole, handelsgartneri.
gardener ['ga:dnə*] *s* gartner, havemand.
gardening ['ga:dniŋ] *s* havearbejde; havedyrkning.
garfish ['ga:fiʃ] *s* hornfisk.
gargle [ga:gl] *s* mundskyllemiddel // *v* gurgle.
garish ['gɛəriʃ] *adj* skrigende, grel.
garland ['ga:lənd] *s* (blomster)krans; hæderskrans.
garlic ['ga:lik] *s* hvidløg.
garment ['ga:mənt] *s* klædningsstykke.
garnet ['ga:nit] *s* (om ædelsten) granat.
garnish ['ga:niʃ] *s* garnering, pynt // *v* garnere, pynte.

garret ['gærit] *s* kvist(værelse).
garrison ['gærisn] *s* garnison.
garrulous ['gærələs] *adj* snakkesalig.
garter ['ga:tə*] *s* strømpebånd; *the Order of the Garter* hosebåndsordenen; ~ **belt** *s* strømpeholder.
gas [gæs] *s* gas; luftart; (øre)gas; *step on the* ~ træde på speederen // *v* gasse; (F) sludre, vrøvle; ~**bag** *s* sludrehoved; ~ **cooker** *s* gaskomfur; ~ **cylinder** *s* gasflaske; ~ **fire** *s* gasradiator; gaskamin.
gash [gæʃ] *s* flænge, gabende sår // *v* flænge; skramme.
gasket ['gæskit] *s* (i vandhane etc) pakning.
gasman ['gæsmən] *s* måleraflæser; **gas meter** *s* gasmåler.
gasoline ['gæsəli:n] *s (am)* benzin.
gasp [ga:sp] *s* gisp // *v* gispe, stønne; ~ *for breath* hive efter vejret.
gas ring ['gæsriŋ] *s* gasapparat; **gas station** *s (am)* benzinstation; **gas stove** *s* gaskamin; gaskomfur.
gassy ['gæsi] *adj* med brus.
gastric ['gæstrik] *adj* mave-; ~ **ulcer** *s* mavesår.
gasworks ['gæswə:ks] *s* gasværk.
gate [geit] *s* port; låge; indgang; (jernbane)bom; ~**crash** *v* komme uindbudt (til selskab); ~**way** *s* port(åbning); *(fig)* indfaldsport; vej.
gather ['gæðə*] *v* samle(s); (om blomster) plukke; samle sammen; (om håndarbejde) rynke; *(fig)* forstå; ~ *speed* få farten op; ~**ing** *s* samling; forsamling; sammenkomst.
gauche [gəuʃ] *adj* kejtet, kluntet.
gaudy ['gɔ:di] *adj* skrigende, stærkt spraglet.
gauge [geidʒ] *s* mål; måleinstrument; *(tekn)* lære; kaliber; *(jernb)* sporvidde // *v* måle; justere.
gaunt [gɔ:nt] *adj* mager, udhungret; øde, barsk.
gauntlet ['gɔ:ntlit] *s: run the* ~ løbe spidsrod.
gauze [gɔ:z] *s* gaze.
gave [geiv] *præt* af *give.*
gawky ['gɔ:ki] *adj* klodset.
gawp [gɔ:p] *v* glo, måbe.
gay [gei] *s* bøsse // *adj* homoseksuel; *(gl)* lystig, munter; ~ **lib** *s* bøssebevægelsen; ~ **place** *s* bøssebar.
gaze [geiz] *s* blik, stirren // *v:* ~ *at* stirre på, se stift på.
gazette [gə'zɛt] *s* avis.
GB ['dʒi:'bi:] (fork.f. *Great Britain).*
GCSE ['dʒi:si:ɛs'i:] *s* (fork.f. *General Certificate of Secondary Education:* ~ *A level* sv.t. studentereksamen; ~ *O level* sv.t. folkeskolens afgangsprøve.
Gdns fork.f. *gardens.*
GDR (fork.f. *German Democratic Republic) (hist)* DDR.
gear [giə*] *s* udstyr, grej; apparat; gear; *in* ~ i gear; *(fig)* i gang; *out of* ~ ude af gear; *(fig)* i uorden; *top* ~ fjerde gear; *low* ~ andet gear; *bottom* ~ første gear // *v* indstille; ~*ed to* beregnet til; ~**box** *s* gearkasse; ~ **lever** *s* gearstang.
gee [dʒi:] *interj (am)* gud! ih!
geese [gi:s] *spl* af *goose.*
gelignite ['dʒɛlignait] *s* plastisk sprængstof.
gem [dʒɛm] *s* ædelsten; *(fig)* klenodie, perle.
Gemini ['dʒɛminai] *s (astr)* Tvillingerne.
gender ['dʒɛndə*] *s* køn.
gene [dʒi:n] *s* gen.
general ['dʒɛnərl] *s* general // *adj* almindelig, generel; almen; hoved-; *in* ~ i almindelighed; *the* ~ *idea is to...* det drejer sig om at...; ~ **election** *s* valg til underhuset.
generality [dʒɛnə'ræliti] *s* almindelighed; almindelig udbredelse.
generally ['dʒɛnərəli] *adv* sædvanligvis; ~ *speaking* stort set.
General Post Office ['dʒɛnərl 'pəust 'ɔfis] *(GPO) s* hovedpostkontor.
general practitioner ['dʒɛnərl præk'tiʃənə*] *(GP) s* almenpraktiserende læge.
general-purpose ['dʒɛnərl,pə:pəs] *adj* universal-.
general science ['dʒɛnərl 'saiəns] *s* (i skolen) naturfag.
general store ['dʒɛnərl 'stɔ:*] *s* landhandel.
generate ['dʒɛnəreit] *v* udvikle, frem-

bringe; (om afkom) avle; *(fig)* afføde.

generation [gʒɛnə'reiʃən] *s* generation; udvikling; avl; *the ~ gap* generationskløften.

generosity [dʒɛnə'rɔsiti] *s* gavmildhed; ædelmodighed.

generous ['dʒɛnərəs] *adj* gavmild, rundhåndet; ædelmodig; rigelig, stor; *a ~ helping* en stor portion.

Genesis ['dʒɛnisis] *s* 1. Mosebog; **genesis** *s* kilde, oprindelse.

genetic [dʒi'nɛtik] *adj* genetisk; gen-; **~ engineering** *s* genmanipulation, gensplejsning.

geneticist [dʒi'nɛtisist] *s* genetiker.

genetics [dʒi'nɛtiks] *s* arvelighedslære, genetik.

genial ['dʒi:niəl] *adj* gemytlig, hyggelig; (om klima) mild.

genitals ['dʒɛnitlz] *spl* kønsorganer.

genius ['dʒi:niəs] *s* geni; genialitet; skytsånd.

genned [dʒɛnd] *adj: ~ up* (F) velorienteret, ajour.

genocide ['dʒɛnəsaid] *s* folkedrab.

gent [dʒɛnt] *s* fork.f. *gentleman;* se også *gents.*

genteel [dʒɛn'ti:l] *adj* fisefornem, snobbet; standsmæssig, herskabelig.

gentile ['dʒɛntail] *s* ikke-jøde; hedning.

gentle [dʒɛntl] *adj* blid, venlig; mild; (fx om skråning) jævn; **~man farmer** *s* bybonde; **~ness** *s* mildhed, venlighed; **gently** *adv* blidt, stille; jævnt.

gentry ['dʒɛntri] *s* lavadel; *(iron)* fine folk; *landed ~* landadel.

gents [dʒɛnts] *s* (F) herretoilet.

genuine ['dʒɛnjuin] *adj* ægte, virkelig; autentisk; oprigtig.

geographer [dʒi'ɔgrəfə*] *s* geograf;

geographic(al) [dʒiə'græfik(l)] *adj* geografisk.

geography [dʒi'ɔgrəfi] *s* geografi.

geologic(al) [dʒiə'lɔdʒik(l)] *adj* geologisk; **geologist** [dʒi'ɔlədʒist] *s* geolog.

geology [dʒi'ɔlədʒi] *s* geologi.

geometric(al) [dʒiə'mɛtrik(l)] *adj* geometrisk.

geometry [dʒi'ɔmətri] *s* geometri.

geranium [dʒi'reinjəm] *s* pelargonie, geranium.

geriatric [dʒɛri'ætrik] *s* ældre (person), gammel // *adj* geriatrisk, ældre-.

germ [dʒə:m] *s* bakterie; *(bot, fig)* spire, kim.

German ['dʒə:mən] *s* tysker; tysk (sprog) // *adj* tysk; **Germanic** [-'mænik] *adj* germansk; **German measles** [-mi:zlz] *spl (med)* røde hunde; **Germany** *s* Tyskland.

germination [dʒə:mi'neiʃən] *s* spiring.

germ warfare ['dʒə:m,wɔ:fɛə*] *s* bakteriologisk krigsførelse.

gestation [dʒɛs'teiʃən] *s* svangerskab, drægtighed.

gesticulate [dʒɛs'tikjuleit] *v* fægte med armene, gestikulere.

gesture ['dʒɛstʃə*] *s* håndbevægelse, gestus.

get [gɛt] *v (got, got* [gɔt]) få; skaffe, hente; forstå, begribe; blive; nå,; komme; *go and ~ sth* (gå hen og) hente ngt; *~ it?* forstår du? er du med?

~ about komme omkring; brede sig; *~ across* komme over; slå an; *~ an idea across* vinde gehør for en idé; *~ along* klare sig; gøre fremskridt; komme videre; *~ along with* komme (godt) ud af det med; *~ at* komme til; drille, stikke til; nå; *what are you ~ting at?* hvad hentyder du til? *~ away* slippe væk; *~ away with* komme godt fra; klare;

~ back få igen (,tilbage); komme tilbage; *~ one's own back* få hævn; *~ by* komme forbi; få fat i; klare sig;

~ down gå ned; stige ned; *he ~s me down* han går mig på nerverne; *~ down to* tage fat på;

~ in komme ind; komme hjem; ankomme; *~ into* komme ind i; trænge ind i; *what got into you?* hvad gik der af dig? *~ into bed* gå i seng; *~ in with* komme i lag med, holde sig til hos;

~ off stå af; slippe væk; (om tøj) tage af; tage af sted; få af (,løs); *~ on* klare sig; komme videre; (om tøj)

tage på; ~ *on (with)* komme videre med; komme (godt) ud af det med; ~ *on with it!* skynd dig nu! se nu at komme i gang! ~ *out* komme (,stå, gå etc) ud; ~ *out of* stå ud af; slippe godt fra; ~ *over* overvinde; komme over;
~ *rich* blive rig; ~ *ready* gøre sig parat; ~ *round* komme ud; omgå; komme om ved;
~ *through* komme (,slippe) igennem; ~ *sby to do sth* få en til at gøre ngt; ~ *together* komme sammen; samles;
~ *up* stå op (af sengen); få op; klæde ud; ~ *up to* indhente.
getaway ['gεtəwei] *s* flugt; tilflugtssted; fritidshus; ~ *car* flugtbil.
get-together ['gεtəgεðə*] *s* komsammen; sammenslutning, fusion.
getup ['gεtʌp] *s* udstyr; antræk.
geyser ['gi:zə*] *s* gasvandvarmer; gejser.
ghastly ['ga:stli] *adj* uhyggelig, grufuld; gyselig.
gherkin ['gə:kin] *s* sylteagurk.
ghost [gəust] *s* spøgelse, genfærd; ånd; *the Holy Ghost* helligånden; *give up the* ~ opgive ånden, dø; (om motor) bryde sammen; **~ly** *adj* spøgelsesagtig; *(fig)* åndelig; **~ writer** *s* "neger" (der skriver bøger etc for andre).
ghoulish ['gu:liʃ] *adj* rædselsvækkende, bloddryppende.
giant [dʒaiənt] *s* kæmpe // *adj* kæmpemæssig, kæmpe-; **~ slalom** *s* storslalom.
gibberish ['dʒibəriʃ] *s* volapyk.
gibe [dʒaib] *s* spydighed, hib // *v* håne, gøre nar af.
giblets ['dʒiblits] *spl* (fjerkræ)indmad.
giddiness ['gidinis] *s* svimmelhed.
giddy ['gidi] *adj* svimmel, ør; svimlende; kåd.
gift [gift] *s* gave; begavelse; talent; **~ed** *adj* begavet, talentfuld; **~ token** *s* gavekort; **~-wrapped** *adj* i gaveindpakning.
gigantic [dʒai'gæntik] *adj* enorm, gigantisk.
giggle [gigl] *s* fnisen; *have the ~s* fnise // *v* fnise.
gild [gild] *v (~ed, ~ed)* forgylde.
gill [dʒil] *s* rummål *(0,25 pints,* 0,14 liter).
gills [gilz] *spl* gæller.
gilt [gilt] *s* forgyldning // *adj* forgyldt; **~-edged securities** *spl* guldrandede papirer.
gimcrack ['dʒimkræk] *s* billigt stads.
gimlet ['gimlit] *s* håndbor, vridbor.
gimmick ['gimik] *s* trick, fidus; modedille; dims.
ginger ['dʒindʒə*] *s* ingefær // *adj* rød(gul) // *v: ~ up* sætte fut i, friske op; **~ ale, ~ beer** *s* sodavand med ingefærsmag; **~bread** *s* ingefærkage (sv.t. honningkage); **~ group** *s* aktivistgruppe, pressionsgruppe; **~-haired** *adj* rødblond; **~ly** *adv* forsigtigt.
gipsy ['dʒipsi] *s* sigøjner.
girdle [gə:dl] *s* bælte; hofteholder // *v* omgive, omgjorde.
girl [gə:l] *s* pige; datter; *go with ~s* gå på pigesjov; *old ~* gamle tøs; **~ Friday** *s* privatsekretær; **~friend** *s* veninde; **~ guide** *s* pigespejder; **~hood** *s: in her ~hood* da hun var pige.
girlie ['gə:li] *adj: ~ magazines* pornoblade, blade med nøgne piger.
girlish ['gə:liʃ] *adj* pige-; ungpigeagtig; tøset.
giro ['dʒairəu] *s* giro.
gist [dʒist] *s: the ~* det væsentlige.
give [giv] *s* (om stof) elasticitet, stræk // *v (gave, given* [geiv, givn]) give; forære; give efter, vige; *don't ~ me that!* årh, hold op! *I'll ~ you that* det må jeg indrømme; *~ as good as you get* give igen af samme mønt; give svar på tiltale; *~ away* give væk; røbe; *~ back* give tilbage (,igen); *~ in* give efter; indgive; *~ off* afgive; udsende (fx *steam* damp); *~ out* uddele; meddele; udbrede; *~ out a sigh* udstøde et suk; *~ up* opgive; give afkald på; *~ oneself up* melde sig; *~ up smoking* holde op med at ryge; *~ way* holde tilbage, vige.
give-away ['givəwei] *s* gave, foræring; afsløring // *adj* gratis.
given [givn] *adj: ~ to* tilbøjelig til; *~ that...* forudsat at...

glacial ['gleisjəl] *adj* is-; iskold.
glacier ['gleisiə*] *s* gletscher, bræ.
glad [glæd] *adj* glad, glædelig.
gladden [glædn] *v* glæde.
glade [gleid] *s* lysning (i skov).
gladly ['glædli] *adv* med glæde, gerne.
glamorous ['glæmərəs] *adj* strålende, betagende.
glamour ['glæmə*] *s* glans; fortryllelse; romantik; ~ **girl** *s* (film)skønhed.
glance [gla:ns] *s* blik; glimt; *at a ~* ved første blik // *v: ~ at* se (,kikke) på; *~ off* (om kugle) prelle af.
glancing ['gla:nsiŋ] *adj* forbigående; *a ~ blow* et slag der lige strejfer.
gland [glænd] *s* kirtel.
glandular ['glændjulə*] *adj* kirtel-; ~ **fever** *s (med)* mononukleose, kyssesyge.
glare [glɛə*] *s* blændende lys; olmt blik; *(fig)* søgelys; *in the ~ of publicity* i offentlighedens søgelys // *v* blænde, skinne; (om farver) skrige; (om person) glo.
glaring ['glɛəriŋ] *adj* blændende; skærende, skrigende.
glass [gla:s] *s* glas; spejl; kikkert; **~es** *spl* briller; **~ware** *s* glasvarer; **~works** *s* glasværk.
glassy ['gla:si] *adj* glasagtig; spejlklar; *(fig,* om blik) stiv, udtryksløs.
glaze [gleiz] *s* glasur; politur; glans // *v* sætte glas i; (om keramik etc) glasere; polere; **~d** *adj* (om blik) udtryksløs, tom; (om keramik) glaseret.
glazier ['gleiziə*] *s* glarmester.
gleam [gli:m] *s* glimt; stråle (af lys, lyn) // *v* glimte, stråle; lyse, lyne.
glean [gli:n] *v* indsamle, opsnuse.
glee [gli:] *s* fryd; skadefryd.
glen [glɛn] *s* (især skotsk) dal, bjergkløft.
glib [glib] *adj* glat, mundrap.
glide [glaid] *s* gliden; svæven // *v* glide; svæve.
glider ['glaidə*] *s* svævefly.
gliding ['glaidiŋ] *s* svæveflyvning.
glimmer ['glimə*] *s* glimten; flimren; *(fig)* antydning, svagt glimt // *v* flimre, skinne mat.
glimpse [glimps] *s* glimt; strejf; flygtigt blik // *v* skimte, få et glimt af.
glint [glint] *s* blink, glimt // *v* glimte, funkle.
glisten [glisn] *v* funkle, skinne.
glitter ['glitə*] *s* glitren, glans // *v* glitre, funkle.
gloat [gləut] *v: ~ (over)* fryde sig, godte sig (over).
glob [glɔb] *s* (F) klat, sjat.
globe [gləub] *s* globus, klode; kugle; *~ of the eye* øjeæble.
globule ['glɔbju:l] *s* lille klump; dråbe.
gloom [glu:m] *s* mørke; tristhed, melankoli; **~y** *adj* mørk, dyster; nedtrykt, melankolsk.
glorification [glɔ:rifi'keiʃən] *s* lovprisning; forherligelse; (F) fest.
glorify ['glɔrifai] *v* lovprise, forherlige.
glorious ['glɔ:riəs] *adj* strålende, prægtig; pragtfuld.
glory ['glɔ:ri] *s* pragt; ære; storhed, herlighed // *v: ~ in* fryde sig over, nyde; sole sig i.
gloss [glɔs] *s* glans, skin // *v: ~ (over)* besmykke, pynte på.
glossary ['glɔsəri] *s* glosebog, glosar.
gloss paint ['glɔspeint] *s* emaljelak, højglansmaling.
glossy ['glɔsi] *adj* skinnende, blank; blankslidt; *~ magazine* kulørt ugeblad.
glove [glʌv] *s* handske; *be hand in ~ with sby* være pot og pande med en; ~ **compartment** *s (auto)* handskerum.
glow [gləu] *s* glød, rødme; varme // *v* gløde, blusse.
glower ['glauə*] *s* skulen // *v* skule.
glow-worm ['gləuwə:m] *s* sankthansorm.
glue [glu:] *s* lim // *v* lime, klistre.
gluey ['glu:i] *adj* klistret.
glum [glʌm] *adj* trist; mut; nedtrykt.
glut [glʌt] *s* overflod, overskud, "pukkel" // *v* oversvømme, overfylde.
glutton ['glʌtn] *s* grovæder, ædedolk; *he is a ~ for work* han er arbejdsliderlig.
gluttonous ['glʌtənəs] *adj* grådig, forslugen.
gluttony ['glʌtəni] *s* grådighed; frådseri.
gm, gms fork.f. *gramme(s).*

GMT (fork.f. *Greenwich Mean Time)* Greenwichtid.
gnarled [na:ld], **gnarly** ['na:li] *adj* knudret, kroget.
gnash [næʃ] *v:* ~ *one's teeth* skære tænder.
gnat [næt] *s* myg.
gnaw [nɔ:] *v* gnave; nage, pine.
GNP ['dʒi:ɛn'pi:] (fork.f. *gross national product)* bruttonationalprodukt (BNP).
go [gəu] *s (pl: -es)* forsøg; chance; historie; omgang; *have a* ~ gøre et forsøg; *have a* ~ *at* forsøge sig med; *be on the* ~ være i gang; *it's no* ~ den går ikke; *it's all the* ~ det er sidste skrig.
go [gəu] *v (went, gone* [wɛnt, gɔn] gå; afgå; rejse; tage (til); bevæge sig; køre; blive; forsvinde; ~ *shopping* gå på indkøb; *he's not* ~*ing to do it* han gør det ikke; *let* ~ *of sth* slippe ngt;
~ *about* gå (,løbe) omkring; være i omløb; *how do I* ~ *about this?* hvordan skal jeg gribe det her an? ~ *ahead* gå i forvejen; komme videre, fortsætte; ~ *along* gå videre; ~ *along with* høre sammen med; være enig med; *as you* ~ *along* efterhånden, hen ad vejen; ~ *away* gå væk; tage af sted; ~ *away!* forsvind! skrub af!
~ *back on one's word* svigte sit løfte; ~ *by* gå forbi; (om tid) gå; ~ *by train* tage med toget; *give us sth to* ~ *by* giv os nogle retningslinjer;
~ *down* gå ned; (om skib etc) gå under; vinde bifald; *the concert went down well* koncerten blev godt modtaget; ~ *down in history* gå over i historien;
~ *for* gå efter; regnes for; falde 'over; gå ind for; ~ *for a walk* gå en tur; *they all went for him* de kastede sig allesammen over ham; *the painting went for £100* maleriet gik (,blev solgt) for £100;
~ *in* gå ind; begynde; ~ *in for* beskæftige sig med; dyrke; gå ind for; ~ *in for football* dyrke fodbold; ~ *in for a competition* melde sig til en konkurrence; ~ *into* gå ind i; ~ *into publishing* blive forlægger; *let's not* ~ *into that!* lad os ikke komme nærmere ind på det!
~ *off* gå, tage af sted; (om mad) blive fordærvet; forløbe; *our holiday went off well* vores ferie forløb (,gik) godt; *the gun went off* geværet gik af; ~ *off to sleep* falde i søvn; *I've gone off meat* jeg har tabt lysten til kød;
~ *on* fortsætte, gå videre, foregå; *what's* ~*ing on!* hvad foregår der! ~ *on talking* blive ved med at snakke; ~ *on with* fortsætte (,blive ved) med;
~ *out* gå ud; slukkes; ~ *out of one's way to* gøre sig særlig umage for at; ~ *over* gennemgå (nøje); (om skib) kæntre;
~ *round the back* gå ind ad bagindgangen; ~ *round the bend* blive skør;
~ *through* gå igennem; gennemgå; ~ *through with* gennemføre; ~ *together* følges ad; passe sammen;
~ *up* gå op; springe i luften; (om priser) stige;
~ *with* ledsage; være enig med; passe sammen med; ~ *without* undvære; *it* ~*es without saying* the siger sig selv.
goad [gəud] *v* drive, anspore.
go-ahead ['gəuəhɛd] *s* startsignal, grønt lys // *adj* fremadstræbende, dynamisk.
goal [gəul] *s* mål; *keep* ~ stå på mål; **~ie** *s* (F) d.s.s. **~keeper** *s* målmand; **~post** *s* målstolpe.
goat [gəut] *s* ged; *he gets my* ~ han irriterer mig vanvittigt.
goatee [gəu'ti:] *s* fipskæg.
gobble [gɔbl] *v* sluge; pludre; ~ *up* opsluge.
gobbledygook ['gɔbldi,gu:k] *s* blabla, forvrøvlet sludder; kancellisprog; politikerjargon.
go-between ['gəubi,twi:n] *s* mellemmand, mægler.
goblet ['gɔblit] *s* bæger; pokal.
goblin ['gɔblin] *s* nisse, trold.
go-cart ['gəuka:t] *s* klapvogn; gokart.

god [gɔd] *s* gud; *God knows* guderne skal (,må) vide; *God willing* om Gud vil; *I hope to God that...* jeg håber og beder til at...; *thank God* Gud være lovet; **~child** *s* gudbarn.

goddess ['gɔdis] *s* gudinde.

god... ['gɔ:d-] sms: **~father** *s* gudfar; (F) mafialeder; **~-fearing** [-fiəriŋ] *adj* gudfrygtig; **~-forsaken** *adj* gudsforladt; **~ly** [gɔdli] *adj* from, hellig; **~mother** *s* gudmor; **~send** *s* uventet held; *it is a ~send* det kommer som sendt fra himlen.

go-getter ['gəugɛtə*] *s* stræber.

goggle [gɔgl] *v* glo, måbe; **~ box** *s* (F, om tv) tossekasse.

goggles [gɔglz] *spl* motorbriller; beskyttelsesbriller.

going ['gəuiŋ] *s: stop while the ~ is good* holde op mens legen er god // *adj: get ~* se at komme i gang (,af sted); *keep ~* blive ved; holde i gang; *the ~ rate* den gældende tarif; *a ~ concern* en igangværende (,fremgangsrig) virksomhed; **~-over** *s: give sth a good ~-over* (F) gå ngt efter i sømmene.

goitre ['gɔitə*] *s* struma.

gold [gəuld] *s* guld; *be as good as ~* være så god som dagen er lang // *adj* guld-; **~en** *adj* guld-; gylden; **~fish** *s* guldfisk; **~ leaf** *s* bladguld; **~ rush** *s* guldfeber.

golf [gɔlf] *s* golf(spil); **~ ball** *s* golfkugle; kuglehoved; **~ club** *s* golfkølle; golfklub; **~ course** *s* golfbane; **~er** *s* golfspiller; **~ links** *s* golfbane.

golly ['gɔli] *interj* ih du store! Gud!

gone [gɔn] *pp* af *go* // *adj* borte, væk; *be far ~* være langt ude; *it is ~ seven* klokken er over syv.

goner ['gɔnə*] *s: he's a ~* (F) han er færdig, det er ude med ham.

goo [gu:] *s* (F) nas, klistret stads.

good [gud] *s* gode; det gode; *it's for your own ~* det er til dit eget bedste // *adj (better, best)* god; dygtig; venlig; egnet; *as ~ as blind* så godt som blind; *be ~ at* være god til; *would you be ~ enough to move over?* vil De være så venlig at give plads? *a ~ deal, a ~ many* en hel del; *be ~ with children* have tag på børn; *for ~* for bestandig; *it's ~ for you* det er sundt; *that's no ~* det går ikke; **~bye** *s* farvel; **~-for-nothing** *adj* uduelig; **Good Friday** *s* langfredag; **~-humoured** *adj* godmodig, rar; **~-looking** *adj* pæn; køn.

goodness ['gudnis] *s* godhed; *for ~ sake!* for Guds skyld! *~ gracious!* du godeste!

goods [gudz] *spl* ting; gods; varer.

goody ['gudi] *s* pænt menneske; godte, lækkerbisken; **goody-goody** *s* dydsmønster // *adj* dygtig.

goofy ['gu:fi] *adj* (F) dum; (om tænder) udstående; *Goofy* (i tegneserie) Fedtmule.

goose [gu:s] *s (pl: geese* [gi:s]) gås.

gooseberry ['guzbəri] *s* stikkelsbær; *play ~ (fig)* være femte hjul til en vogn.

gooseflesh ['gu:sflɛʃ] *s* gåsehud.

gorge [gɔ:dʒ] *s* svælg; slugt, kløft; snævert pas // *v: ~ oneself* proppe i sig.

gorgeous ['gɔ:dʒəs] *adj* strålende, pragtfuld, (F) dødflot.

gorilla [gə'rilə] *s* gorilla (også *fig);* (S) £1000; *it cost 30 ~s* det kostede £30.000.

gory ['gɔ:ri] *adj* bloddryppende.

go-slow ['gəusləu] *s* arbejde langsomt-aktion.

gospel ['gɔspəl] *s* evangelium; **~ truth** *s* den rene sandhed.

gossip ['gɔsip] *s* hyggesnak; sladder; (om person) sladdertaske // *v* sludre; sladre.

got [gɔt] *præt* og *pp* af *get*.

gouge [gaudʒ] *v* udhule; *~ out sby's eyes* stikke øjene ud på en.

gourd [guəd] *s* græskar.

gout [gaut] *s* gigt, podagra.

govern ['gʌvən] *v* styre, regere; (be)herske.

governess ['gʌvənis] *s* guvernante.

government ['gʌvnmənt] *s* ledelse; regering; ministerium // *adj* regerings-; stats-.

governor ['gʌvnə*] *s* leder, hersker; guvernør; (F) du gamle; *board of ~s* bestyrelse; *the ~* den gamle, bossen.

Govt fork.f. *government.*
gown [gaun] *s* kappe; (dame)kjole, robe.
GP ['dʒi:'pi:] *s* fork.f. *general practitioner.*
GPO ['dʒi:pi:'əu] fork.f. *General Post Office.*
grab [græb] *s* greb; grab; *it's up for ~s* der er frit frem for enhver; *make a ~ at* gribe efter // *v* gribe, snuppe; rage til sig.
grace [greis] *s* ynde; elskværdighed; nåde; bordbøn; *five days' ~* fem dages henstand; *be in sby's bad ~* være i unåde hos en; *do sth in good ~* gøre ngt uden at mukke; *do sth in bad ~* gøre ngt modvilligt; *fall from ~* falde i unåde; *say ~* bede bordbøn // *v* smykke; hædre; benåde; **~ful** *adj* yndefuld, graciøs; smuk.
gracious ['greiʃəs] *adj* nådig; venlig; *good ~!* du godeste! *~ living* høj levestandard; *be ~ in defeat* være en god taber.
gradation [grə'deiʃən] *s* gradvis overgang; trindeling.
grade [greid] *s* kvalitet, sort; kategori; grad, rang; karakter; *(am)* klasse // *v* sortere; inddele; udjævne.
gradient ['greidiənt] *s* hældning, skråning.
gradual ['grædʒuəl] *adj* gradvis, trinvis.
graduate *s* ['grædʒuit] kandidat; en der har taget afsluttende eksamen // *v* ['grædʒueit] tage afsluttende eksamen; graduere.
graduation [grædʒu'eiʃən] *s* gradinddeling, gradering; afgang fra læreanstalt.
graft [gra:ft] *s* podning; *(med)* transplantat (fx organ, hud); transplantering // *v* pode; transplantere.
grain [grein] *s* korn, kerne; struktur; (i træ) årer; *with a ~ of salt* med et gran salt; *not a ~ of truth* ikke skygge af sandhed.
grammar ['græmə*] *s* grammatik; **~ school** *s (gl)* gymnasium, latinskole.
grammatical [grə'mætikl] *adj* grammatisk.
gramme [græm] *s* gram.
gramophone ['græməfəun] *s* grammofon; **~ record** *s* grammofonplade.
gran [græn] *s* (F) bedstemor.
granary ['grænəri] *s* kornmagasin; *(fig)* kornkammer.
grand [grænd] *adj* stor; storslået; fornem; stor på den; (F) glimrende.
grandad ['grændæd] *s* (F) bedstefar.
grandchild ['græntʃaild] *s* barnebarn.
grandeur ['grændʒə*] *s* storslåethed, pragt.
grandfather ['grænfa:ðə*] *s* bedstefar; **~ clock** *s* bornholmerur.
grandiose ['grændiəus] *adj* storslået; svulstig.
grandma, grandmother ['grænma:, -mɔðə*] *s* bedstemor.
grandpa ['grænpa:] *s* bedstefar.
grand piano ['grænd pi'ænəu] *s* flygel.
grandstand ['grændstænd] *s (sport)* tilskuertribune.
granny ['græni] *s* bedstemor.
grant [gra:nt] *s* bevilling, stipendium; (stats)støtte // *v* skænke, bevilge; indrømme; *take sth for ~ed* anse ngt for givet.
granulated ['grænjuleitid] *adj: ~ sugar* krystalmelis, perlesukker.
granule ['grænjəl] *s* korn.
grape [greip] *s* (vin)drue; **~fruit** *s* grapefrugt; **~vine** *s* vinranke; *hear it on the ~vine* høre det i jungletelegrafen.
graph [gra:f] *s* kurve, diagram.
graphic ['græfik] *adj* grafisk; **~s** *spl* grafik.
grapple [græpl] *v* kæmpe; klamre sig til.
grasp [gra:sp] *s* greb, tag; *(fig)* opfattelsesevne; forståelse; *it's beyond my ~* det går over min fatteevne; det er uden for min rækkevidde // *v* gribe, tage fat i; begribe; **~ing** *adj* grisk; gerrig.
grass [gra:s] *s* græs; græsgang; (S) hash; *a blade of ~* et græsstrå; *put out to ~* sætte på græs; (F, *fig)* pensionere; **~hopper** *s* græshoppe; **~land** *s* græsjord; **~-roots** *spl* græs-

rødder; ~ **snake** *s* snog; ~ **widow(er)** *s* græsenke(mand).

grassy ['gra:si] *adj* græsagtig; græsklædt.

grate [greit] *s* rist, gitter // *v* gnide; rive (på rivejern); (om lyd) skurre.

grateful ['greitful] *adj* taknemmelig.

grater ['greitə*] *s* rivejern.

gratify ['grætifai] *v* glæde; tilfredsstille; **~ing** *adj* opmuntrende.

grating ['greitiŋ] *s* gitter(værk); rist // *adj* skræppende, grel.

gratitude ['grætitju:d] *s* taknemmelighed.

gratuitous [grə'tju:itəs] *adj* unødvendig; uønsket.

gratuity [grə'tju:iti] *s* gratiale; drikkepenge.

grave [greiv] *s* grav // *adj* alvorlig; højtidelig; **~digger** *s* graver.

gravel [grævl] *s* grus, ral; ~ **pit** *s* grusgrav.

gravestone ['greivstəun] *s* gravsten; **graveyard** ['greivja:d] *s* kirkegård.

gravity ['græviti] *s* alvor, højtidelighed; vægt; tyngdekraft; vægtfylde.

gravy ['greivi] *s* kødsaft, sky; sovs; ~ **boat** *s* sovsekande.

graze [greiz] *s* hudafskrabning // *v* græsse; strejfe; skrabe; (S) zappe, tage på kanalrundfart (i tv).

grease [gri:s] *s* fedt, smørelse; (F) bestikkelse // *v* fedte, smøre; (F) bestikke; ~ **gun** *s* smørepistol; **~paint** *s* teatersminke; **~proof paper** *s* smørrebrødspapir.

greasy ['gri:zi] *adj* fedtet, smattet.

great [greit] *adj* stor; fremragende; mægtig; (F) storartet; olde-; **Great Britain** *s* Storbritannien; **Great Dane** *s* granddanois; **~-grandfather** *s* oldefar; **~ly** *adv* i høj grad, meget.

Grecian ['gri:ʃən] *adj* græsk; **Greece** [gri:s] *s* Grækenland.

greed [gri:d] *s* grådighed; begærlighed; **~y** *adj* grådig; begærlig; gerrig.

Greek [gri:k] *s* græker; græsk (sprog); *it's ~ to me* det er det rene volapyk // *adj* græsk.

green [gri:n] *s* grønt; (på golfbane) green; (også: *village ~*) grønning // *adj* grøn; ung, umoden, naiv.

greenery ['gri:nəri] *s* grønne planter, grøn bevoksning.

greenfly ['gri:nflai] *s* bladlus.

greengage ['gri:ngeidʒ] *s* reineclaude.

greengrocer ['gri:ngrəusə*] *s* grønthandler.

greenhouse ['gri:nhaus] *s* drivhus; *the ~ effect* drivhuseffekten.

greenish ['gri:niʃ] *adj* grønlig.

green-labelled ['gri:n,leibəld] *adj* (om vare) mærket som miljøvenlig el. biodynamisk.

Greenland ['gri:nlənd] *s* Grønland; **~er** *s* grønlænder.

greenlight ['gri:nlait] *v* give grønt lys for.

greens [gri:ns] *spl* grøntsager.

greenster ['gri:nstə*] *s* miljøforkæmper, økobevidst person.

greet [gri:t] *v* hilse.

greeting ['gri:tiŋ] *s* hilsen; **~(s) card** *s* lykønskningskort.

gregarious [gri'gɛəriəs] *adj* selskabelig.

grenade [gri'neid] *s* *(mil)* granat.

grew [gru:] *præt* af *grow*.

grey [grei] *adj* grå; trist; mørk; *the future looks ~* der er dystre udsigter for fremtiden; *go (, turn) ~* blive gråhåret; **~hound** *s* mynde.

grid [grid] *s* rist; net; *(elek)* strømnet; **~iron** *s* (stege)rist.

grief [gri:f] *s* sorg; *come to ~* komme galt af sted; *good ~!* du godeste! **~-stricken** [-strikn] *adj* knust.

grievance ['gri:vəns] *s* klage(punkt).

grieve [gri:v] *v* sørge; græmme sig; volde sorg; *~ at* sørge over.

grievous ['gri:vəs] *adj* alvorlig, svær; bitter.

grill [gril] *s* gitter, rist; grill // *v* stege, grille(re); krydsforhøre, holde på pinebænken.

grille [gril] *s* gitter(værk); *(auto)* kølergitter.

grim [grim] *adj* streng, barsk; grusom.

grimace [gri'meis] *s* grimasse.

grime [graim] *s* snavs; **grimy** *adj* beskidt, bemøget.

grin [grin] *s* grin // *v* grine, smile.

grind [graind] *s* knusning; slibning; *(fig)* slider; *the daily ~* det daglige

slid // *v* *(ground, ground* [graund]) knuse; male, kværne; (om kniv etc) slibe, hvæsse; terpe; *~ one's teeth* skære tænder; *~ to a halt* standse med en hvinen; gå i stå.
grinder ['graində*] *s* kindtand; mølle, kværn.
grindstone ['graindstəun] *s* slibesten.
grip [grip] *s* greb, tag; håndtag; hårklemme; rejsetaske; *come to ~s with* give sig i kast med; komme ind på livet af; *take a ~ on oneself* tage sig sammen. // *v* gribe; få tag i.
gripe [graip] *v* (F) brokke sig.
grisly ['grizli] *adj* uhyggelig.
gristle [grisl] *s* brusk.
grit [grit] *s* grus, sand; *(fig)* ben i næsen // *v* (om fx vej) gruse; *~ one's teeth* skære tænder; bide tænderne sammen.
grizzle [grizl] *s* grå farve // *v* klynke, beklage sig; **~d** *adj* gråsprængt.
grizzly bear ['grizli bɛə*] *s* gråbjørn.
groan [grəun] *s* støn(nen); knagen // *v* stønne.
groats [grəuts] *spl* gryn.
grocer ['grəusə*] *s* købmand; *~'s (shop)* købmandsbutik; **groceries** *spl* købmandsvarer.
groin [grɔin] *s* lyske.
groom [gru:m] *s* tjener, karl; brudgom // *v* pleje; (om hest) strigle.
groove [gru:v] *s* fure; skure; rille.
groovy ['gru:vi] *adj* (F) smart, in, spændende.
grope [grəup] *v* famle *(for* efter).
gross [grəus] *adj* stor, tyk; grov; *(merk)* brutto-; **~ national product** *s (GNP)* bruttonationalprodukt (BNP).
grotto ['grɔtəu] *s* grotte.
grotty ['grɔti] *adj* væmmelig; elendig; mærkværdig.
grouch [grautʃ] *s* surhed; *have a ~ against sby* have et horn i siden på en // *v* skumle, mukke.
ground [graund] *s* jord; grund; terræn; plads; *(sport)* bane; *(fig)* årsag; *below ~* under jorden; *gain (,lose) ~* vinde (,tabe) terræn; *go to ~* holde sig skjult; *hold one's ~* holde stand; *prepare the ~ for sth* bane vejen for ngt; *hold one's* stå fast; *it suits me down to the ~* det passer mig fint; *on the ~(s) that* af den grund at // *v* (om fly) give flyveforbud; (om skib) gå på grund; sætte på grund // *præt* og *pp* af *grind;* **~floor** *s* stueetage.
grounding ['graundiŋ] *s* grundlag.
groundless ['graundlis] *adj* ubegrundet.
groundnut ['graundnʌt] *s* jordnød.
grounds [graundz] *spl* (i væske) bundfald, grums; (til hus) have, park.
groundsheet ['graundʃi:t] *s* teltunderlag.
groundsman ['graunzmən] *s (sport)* banemand.
ground staff ['graund,sta:f] *s (sport)* banepersonale.
groundwork ['graundwə:k] *s* grundlag; forarbejde.
group [gru:p] *s* gruppe, hold // *v* gruppere (sig); **~ing** *s* gruppering; gruppe.
grouse [graus] *s* rype // *v* knurre, brokke sig.
grove [grəuv] *s* lund, lille skov.
grovel [grʌvl] *v: ~ (before) (fig)* krybe (for), ligge på maven (for).
grow [greu] *v (grew, grown* [gru:, grəun]) vokse, gro; blive; dyrke, anlægge; *~ a beard* anlægge skæg; *~ old* blive gammel; *~ apart* vokse fra hinanden; *it ~s on you* man bliver mere og mere glad for det; *~ out of* vokse fra; *~ up* vokse op; blive voksen.
grower ['grəuə*] *s* dyrker; producent.
growing ['grəuiŋ] *adj* voksende, tiltagende; **~ pains** *spl* vokseværk; **~ season** *s* vækstid, dyrkningsperiode.
growl [graul] *v* knurre; rumle.
grown [grəun] *pp* af *grow* // *adj* voksen; **~-over** *adj* tilgroet; **~-up** *s* voksen.
growth [grəuθ] *s* vækst, tiltagen; dyrkning, avl; *(med)* svulst; gevækst.
grub [grʌb] *s* maddike; (F) ædelse.
grubby ['grʌbi] *adj* snusket, ulækker.

grudge [grʌdʒ] *s* nag; uvilje; *bear sby a ~* bære nag til en; have et horn i siden på en // *v* ikke unde; *I don't ~ him the success* jeg under ham succesen.
grudgingly ['grʌdʒiŋli] *adv* modstræbende.
gruel [gru:əl] *s* havresuppe, vælling.
gruelling ['gru:əliŋ] *adj* anstrengende, enerverende.
gruesome ['gru:səm] *adj* makaber, rædselsfuld.
gruff [grʌf] *adj* barsk, bøs.
grumble [grʌmbl] *v* brumme, knurre; brokke sig.
grumpy ['grʌmpi] *adj* sur, gnaven.
grunt [grʌnt] *s* grynten, grynt // *v* grynte.
guarantee [ˌgærən'ti:] *s* garanti, kaution // *v* garantere (for).
guarantor [ˌgærən'tɔ:*] *s* garant, kautionist.
guard [ga:rd] *s* vagt; bevogtning; garde; vogter; *(jernb)* togfører; *catch him off his ~* overrumple ham; *be off one's ~* ikke tage sig i agt; *be on one's ~* være på vagt; *the changing of the ~s* vagtskiftet // *v* (be)vogte, beskytte; **~ed** *adj* bevogtet; forsigtig, reserveret.
guardian ['ga:diən] *s* beskytter; *(jur)* værge; **~ angel** *s* skytsengel.
guardsman ['ga:dzmən] *s* gardist, garder.
guess [gɛs] *s* gæt, gætning; *at a ~...* skønsvis..., jeg vil gætte på at...; *have a ~* prøve at gætte; *it's anybody's ~* det må guderne vide // *v* gætte; *~ what!* ved du hvad?
guesstimate ['gɛstimit] *s* (F) slag på tasken.
guesswork ['gɛswə:k] *s* gætteri.
guest [gɛst] *s* gæst; *be my ~!* ja endelig! det er du velkommen til! *~ of honour* æresgæst; **~-house** *s* (hotel)pension; **~room** *s* gæsteværelse.
guffaw [gʌ'fɔ:*] *s* skraldlatter // *v* skraldgrine.
guidance ['gaidəns] *s* ledelse; vejledning; *under the ~ of* under ledelse af.
guide [gaid] *s* fører; vejleder; (turist)guide; (om bog) rejsefører; *(girl) ~* pigespejder // *v* føre, lede; vejlede; **~book** *s* rejsefører; **~d missile** *s* fjernstyret missil; **~ dog** *s* førerhund; **~d tour** *s* rundvisning; **~line** *s* retningslinje.
guild [gild] *s* lav.
guilder ['gildə*] *s* (hollandsk) gylden.
guile [gail] *s* svig, list.
guilt [gilt] *s* skyld; **~less** *adj* uskyldig.
guilty ['gilti] *adj* skyldig *(of* i); skyldbevidst; *a ~ conscience* en dårlig samvittighed.
guinea ['gini] *s* 105 p (tidl. 21 shillings); **~ fowl** *s* perlehøne; **~ pig** *s* marsvin; *(fig)* forsøgskanin.
guise [gaiz] *s* skikkelse, dragt; forklædning; *in the ~ of* i skikkelse af; under dække af.
gulf [gʌlf] *s* (hav)bugt, golf; afgrund; *the Gulf* Den Persiske Bugt, Golfen.
gull [gʌl] *s* måge.
gullet ['gʌlit] *s* spiserør.
gullible ['gʌlibl] *adj* godtroende, blåøjet.
gully ['gʌli] *s* slugt, kløft.
gulp [gʌlp] *s* slurk, drag; *at one ~* i ét drag, i én mundfuld // *v* sluge, synke, nedsvælge.
gum [gʌm] *s* gumme, tandkød; lim; vingummi; tyggegummi // *v* klæbe, gummiere; **~boil** *s* tandbyld; **~boots** *spl* gummistøvler; **~drop** *s* vingummi.
gummy ['gʌmi] *adj* klæbende.
gumption ['gʌmpʃən] *s* (F) omløb (i hovedet), gåpåmod.
gun [gʌn] *s* gevær; kanon; revolver; *jump the ~ (sport)* tyvstarte; *stick to one's ~s* stå fast // *v: ~ down* skyde ned; *be ~ning for sby* være ude efter en; **~boat** *s* kanonbåd; **~fire** *s* skydning; **~man** *s* revolvermand; gangster; **~ner** *s* artillerist, skytte; **~point** *s: at ~point* med skydevåben parat; under trussel om skydning; **~powder** *s* krudt; **~-runner** *s* våbensmugler; **~shot** *s* skud; *within ~shot* inden for skudvidde.
gunwale [gʌnl] *s (mar)* ræling, lønning.
gurgle [gə:gl] *s* gurglen; skvulpen // *v* gurgle; skvulpe.

gush [gʌʃ] *s* strøm, væld // *v* strømme, vælde frem; *(fig)* falde i svime, svømme hen.
gusset ['gʌsit] *s* (i tøj) kile, spjæld.
gust [gʌst] *s* vindstød, pust; *(fig)* udbrud.
gusto ['gʌstəu] *s* veloplagthed; begejstring, entusiasme.
gut [gʌt] *s* tarm; *hate sby's ~s* ikke kunne udstå en; **~ reaction** *s* instinktiv reaktion; **~s** *spl* indvolde; *(fig)* rygrad, mod.
gutter ['gʌtə*] *s* tagrende; rendesten; *the ~ press* skandalebladene.
guttural ['gʌtərəl] *adj* strube-, guttural.
guvnor ['gʌvnə*] *s* (F) chef, boss.
guy [gai] *s* (F) fyr; (telt)bardun.
guzzle [gʌzl] *v* proppe sig, æde; bælle (sig), tylle (i sig).
gym [dʒim] *s* gymnastik; gymnastiksal.
gymkhana [dʒim'ka:nə] *s* ridestævne.
gymnasium [dʒim'neizjəm] *s* gymnastiksal.
gymnast ['dʒimnəst] *s* gymnast.
gymnastics [dʒim'næstiks] *spl* gymnastik.
gym shoes ['dʒim,ʃu:z] *spl* gymnastiksko.
gymslip ['dʒimslip] *s* gymnastikdragt.
gynaecology [gainə'kɔlədʒi] *s* gynækologi.
gypsum ['dʒipsəm] *s* gips.
gypsy ['dʒipsi] *s* sigøjner.
gyrate [dʒai'reit] *v* rotere.

H

H, h [eitʃ]; *drop one's h's* ikke udtale h'erne (dvs. tale udannet).
haberdasher ['hæbədæʃə*] *s (brit)* butik der handler med sytilbehør; *(am)* herreekviperingshandel.
habit ['hæbit] *s* vane; dragt; *be in the ~ of* pleje at; *make a ~ of it* gøre det til en vane.
habitable ['hæbitəbl] *adj* beboelig.
Habitat ® ['hæbitət] *s* butikskæde der sælger boligudstyr etc (à la Ikea).
habitation [hæbi'teiʃən] *s* beboelse.
habitual [hə'bitʃuəl] *adj* sædvanlig;vane-.
hack [hæk] *s* hak; snit; spark; tør hoste; krikke; (blad)neger // *v* hakke; hoste.
hackney ['hækni] *s: ~ (cab) (gl)* hyrevogn; **~ed** *adj* fortærsket, slidt.
hacksaw ['hæksɔ:] *s* nedstryger.
had [hæd] *præt* og *pp* af *have.*
haddock ['hædək] *s (pl: ~)* (om fisk) kuller.
hadn't [hædnt] d.s.s. *had not.*
haemorrhage ['hɛmərid3] *s* stærk blødning.
hag [hæg] *s* heks; kælling.
haggard ['hægəd] *adj* mager, udtæret; uhyggelig, vild.
haggis ['hægis] *s* (skotsk ret:) hakket fåreindmad og krydderier kogt i en fåremave.
haggle [hægl] *v* tinge, prutte (om pris); parlamentere.
Hague [heig] *s: the ~* Haag (i Holland).
hail [heil] *s* hagl; *(fig)* byge // *v* hilse; praje; hagle; **~stone** *s* hagl; **~storm** *s* kraftig haglbyge.
hair [hɛə*] *s* hår; *do one's ~* sætte sit hår; *keep your ~ on!* tag det nu roligt! *get in sby's ~* irritere en; *let one's ~ down* slå håret ud; *(fig)* slå sig løs; *she didn't turn a ~* hun fortrak ikke en mine; *split ~s* strides om ord; **~brush** *s* hårbørste; **~cut** *s* klipning; frisure; **~do** ['hɛədu:] *s* frisure; **~dresser** *s* frisør; **~-drier** *s* hårtørrer; **~-grip** *s* hårklemme; **~piece** *s* (om kunstigt hår) top; **~pin** *s* hårnål; **~pin bend** *s* hårnålesving; **~-raising** *adj* hårrejsende; **~ remover** *s* hårfjerner; **~ slide** *s* skydespænde; **~-splitting** *s* ordkløveri; **~style** *s* frisure.
hairy ['hɛəri] *adj* lodden, be(håret); *(fig)* farlig; stærk.
halcyon ['hælsiən] *adj: ~ days* lykkelige (,gyldne) dage.
half [ha:f] *s (pl: halves* [ha:vz]) halvdel; *(sport)* halvleg; *go halves* dele (beløb) lige // *adj/adv* halv, halvt; *~-an-hour* en halv time; *a week and a ~* halvanden uge; *~ (of it)* halvdelen; *~ (of)* det halve (af); *cut sth in ~* dele ngt i to; *not ~!* (F) virkelig! overhovedet ikke! **~baked**

adj halvfærdig (især *fig*); **~board** *s* halvpension; **~-breed, ~-caste** *s* halvblods, mestits; **~-hearted** *adj* halvhjertet, lunken; ligegyldig; **~-hour** *s* halv time; **~-life** *s (fys)* halveringstid; **~-mast** *s*: *at ~-mast* på halv stang; **~penny** ['heipni] *s (gl)* halv penny; **~-term** *s* kort ferie midt i et semester; **~-timbering** *s* bindingsværk; **~-time** *s (sport)* halvleg // *adj* halvdags, halvtids; *be on ~-time* arbejde halvdags; **~way** *adv* på halvvejen; halvvejs; **~way line** *s (fodb)* midtlinje.

halibut ['hælibət] *s* helleflynder.

hall [hɔ:l] *s* hal, sal; entré, vestibule; herregård, stor bygning; *~ of residence* (universitets)kollegium.

hallmark ['hɔ:lma:k] *s* stempelmærke (i sølvtøj); *(fig)* kendetegn.

hallowed ['hæləud] *adj* indviet (fx *ground* jord); hellig.

Halloween ['hæləu'i:n] *s* allehelgensdag (31. okt.).

hallstand ['hɔ:lstænd] *s* stumtjener.

halo ['heiləu] *s* glorie, strålekrans; halo, ring om solen.

halt [hɔ:lt] *s* holdt; holdeplads; *call a ~ to* gøre en ende på // *v* standse, stoppe; halte.

halve [ha:v] *v* halvere, dele; **~s** *spl* af *half*.

ham [hæm] *s* skinke; knæhase; bagdel; radioamatør; (om skuespiller etc) flødebolle; **~-fisted** *adj* med store næver; klodset.

hamlet ['hæmlit] *s* (lille) landsby.

hammer ['hæmə*] *s* hammer; *throwing the ~ (sport)* hammerkast; *work ~ and tongs* (F) give den hele armen // *v* hamre, banke; *(fig)* kritisere, angribe; *~ it down to sby that...* banke det ind i knolden på en at...

hammock ['hæmək] *s* hængekøje.

hamper ['hæmpə*] *v* genere; hindre.

hand [hænd] *s* hånd; (ur)viser; håndskrift; korthånd; arbejder, mand; (F) bifald; *change ~s* skifte ejer; *give sby a ~* klappe ad en; *lend sby a ~* give en en hånd med; hjælpe en; *shake ~s* give (hinanden) hånden; *work ~ in glove with sby* have et nært samarbejde med en; *be ~ in glove with* være pot og pande med; *at ~* ved hånden; nær ved; *by ~* i hånden, med håndkraft; *made by ~* håndlavet; *in ~* under kontrol; (om arbejde) i gang; *get sth off one's ~s* slippe af med ngt; *~s off!* ikke pille! *on the right ~ side* på højre side; *on the other ~* på den anden side; *out of ~* ude af kontrol; // *v* række, give; *~ around* byde (,sende) rundt; *~ down* lade gå i arv; *~ in* indlevere; *~ out* udlevere, uddele; *~ over* aflevere; **~bag** *s* håndtaske; **~basin** *s* vandfad; håndvask; **~bill** *s* løbeseddel; reklame; **~book** *s* håndbog; **~brake** *s* håndbremse; **~cart** *s* trækvogn; **~cuffs** *spl* håndjern; **~ful** *s* håndfuld; *she's quite a ~ful* hun er svær at styre; **~grenade** [-gri'neid] *s* håndgranat.

handicraft ['hændikra:ft] *s* (kunst)håndværk; håndarbejde.

handiwork ['hændiwə:k] *s* arbejde, værk.

handkerchief ['hæŋkətʃif] *s* lommetørklæde.

handle [hændl] *s* håndtag; hank, skaft; *fly off the ~* ryge helt op i loftet (af raseri) // *v* røre ved, håndtere; tumle, klare; ekspedere; *~ with care* forsigtig; **~bars** *spl* cykelstyr.

hand... ['hænd-] sms: **~-luggage** *s* håndbagage; **~made** *adj* håndlavet; **~-me-down** *s* aflagt stykke tøj; **~out** *s* tildeling; brochure (el. andet papir) som uddeles; **~-picked** *adj* håndplukket; **~rail** *s* gelænder; ræling; **~shake** *s* håndtryk.

handsome ['hænsəm] *adj* smuk; anselig, klækkelig.

handwriting ['hændraitiŋ] *s* håndskrift; **handwritten** [-ritn] *adj* håndskrevet.

handy ['hændi] *adj* praktisk, bekvem; ved hånden, nær ved; (om person) behændig, fiks på fingrene; **~man** *s* altmuligmand; gør det selv-mand.

hang [hæŋ] *v (hung, hung* [hʌŋ]) hænge (op); være hængt på; *(hanged, hanged)* hænge (i galge); *~ wallpa-*

per sætte tapet op; ~ *one's head* hænge med næbbet; ~ *it!* pokkers også! *he can go* ~! (F) han kan rende mig! ~ *about* stå og hænge; drive rundt; ~ *on* hænge ved; vente; ~ *up (tlf)* lægge røret på.

hangdog ['hæŋdɔg] *adj* ydmyg, sønderknust, flov.

hanger ['hæŋə*] *s* (klæde)bøjle; (i fx frakke) strop.

hang-gliding ['hæŋglaidiŋ] *s (sport)* drageflyvning.

hanging ['hæŋiŋ] *s* hængning; opsætning (af tapet); forhæng.

hangman ['hæŋmən] *s* bøddel.

hangout ['hæŋaut] *s* tilholdssted.

hangover ['hæŋəuvə*] *s* tømmermænd.

hangup ['hæŋʌp] *s* kompleks, dille.

hanker ['hæŋkə*] *v:* ~ *after* hige efter.

hankie, hanky ['hæŋki] *s* (F) lommetørklæde.

hanky-panky ['hæŋki'pæŋki] *s* (F) luskeri; kissemisseri.

hansom ['hænsəm] *s:* ~ *(cab) (gl)* hestedroske.

haphazard [hæp'hæzəd] *adj* tilfældig, på lykke og fromme.

happen ['hæpən] *v* ske, hænde; *these things* ~ det er hvad der kan ske; *as it* ~*s* tilfældigvis; forresten; *do you* ~ *to know...?* ved (,kender) du tilfældigvis...? // *adv* måske; **~ing** *s* hændelse; happening.

happily ['hæpili] *adv* lykkeligt; lykkeligvis; *they lived* ~ *forever after* de levede lykkeligt til deres dages ende.

happiness ['hæpinnəs] *s* lykke.

happy ['hæpi] *adj* lykkelig, glad; heldig; *I'd be* ~ *to come* jeg vil meget gerne komme; ~ *birthday!* tillykke med fødselsdagen! ~ *with* tilfreds med; glad for; **~-go-lucky** *adj* ubekymret; ligeglad.

harangue [hə'ræŋ] *s* moralpræken.

harass ['hærəs] *v* plage, chikanere; **~ment** *s* plagerier, chikane.

harbour ['ha:bə*] *s* havn // *v* huse, rumme; (om følelse etc) nære; **~-master** *s* havnefoged.

hard [ha:d] *adj/adv* hård; stærk; streng; (om blik) stift; *drink* ~ drikke tæt; *as* ~ *as nails* benhård; *think* ~ tænke sig grundigt om; ~ *luck!* det var uheldigt! *no* ~ *feelings!* skal vi lade det være glemt? ~ *of hearing* tunghør; ~ *done by* uretfærdigt behandlet; ~ *on sby* hård ved en; *be* ~ *up* have lavvande i kassen; *be* ~ *up for sth* mangle ngt; **~back** *s* indbunden bog; **~-bitten** *adj* hård; hærdet; **~board** *s* træfiberplade; **~-boiled** *adj* hårdkogt; **~-earned** [-ə:nd] *adj* surt tjent.

harden ['ha:dn] *v* gøre hård; hærde(s); **~ing** *s* hærdning; forhærdelse.

hardiness ['ha:dinis] *s* hårdførhed; udholdenhed.

hard labour ['ha:d 'leibə*] *s* tvangsarbejde, strafarbejde.

hardliner ['ha:dlainə*] *s (pol)* strammer.

hardly ['ha:dli] *adv* næppe, knap; *it's* ~ *enough* det er sikkert ikke nok, det er nok ikke tilstrækkeligt; ~ *anything* næsten intet.

hardness ['ha:dnis] *s* hårdhed.

hardsell ['ha:dsɛl] *s (merk)* pågående reklame.

hardship ['ha:dʃip] *s* prøvelse, lidelse; ~*s pl* afsavn.

hard shoulder ['ha:d 'ʃəuldə*] *s* (vej)rabat.

hard-up [ha:d'ʌp] *adj: be* ~ sidde hårdt i det.

hardware ['ha:dwɛə*] *s* isenkram; *(edb)* udstyr, maskinel; **~ shop** *s* isenkramforretning.

hard-wearing ['ha:dwɛəriŋ] *adj* slidstærk, solid.

hard-working ['ha:dwə:kiŋ] *adj* flittig, arbejdsom.

hardy ['ha:di] *adj* hårdfør, modstandsdygtig.

hare [hɛə*] *s* hare; **~-brained** *adj* skør; **~lip** *s* hareskår.

harlot ['ha:lət] *s (gl)* tøjte.

harm [ha:m] *s* skade, fortræd; *he meant no* ~ han mente det ikke så slemt; *no* ~ *done* der er ingen skade sket; *there's no* ~ *in trying* det skader ikke at prøve, man kan da altid forsøge; *out of ~'s way* i sikkerhed // *v* skade, gøre fortræd; **~ful** *adj* skadelig; ond; **~less** *adj* uskadelig, harmløs.

harmonic [ha:'mɔnik] *adj* harmonisk.

harmonica [ha:'mɔnikə] *s* mundharmonika.

harmonics [ha:'mɔniks] *spl (mus)* harmonilære.

harmonious [ha:'məuniəs] *adj* harmonisk; **harmonize** ['ha:mənaiz] *v* harmonisere; afstemme; harmonere.

harmony ['ha:məni] *s* harmoni; fredelighed, fordragelighed.

harness ['ha:nis] *s* (til hest) seletøj; (til barn) sele // *v* give sele(tøj) på; *(fig)* udnytte.

harp [ha:p] *s (mus)* harpe // *v: ~ on* tale konstant om; **~ist** *s* harpenist.

harpsichord ['ha:psikɔ:d] *s* cembalo.

harrow ['hærəu] *s (agr)* harve; **~ing** *adj* sindsoprivende.

harsh [ha:ʃ] *adj* streng, hård, brutal; barsk; (om lyd) skurrende; (om farve) grel; (om smag) besk, harsk.

harvest ['ha:vist] *s* høst // *vv* høste; **~er** *s* høstmaskine; høstarbejder.

has [hæz] se *have.*

hash [hæʃ] *s (gastr)* hakkemad, biksemad; *(fig)* kludder; (fork.f. *hashish)* hash; *make a ~ of sth* forkludre ngt // *v: ~ up* hakke; forkludre.

hashish ['hæʃiʃ] *s* hash.

hasn't [hæznt] d.s.s. *has not.*

hassle [hæsl] *s* skænderi; problem // *v* plage.

haste [heist] *s* hast, fart; hastværk; *in a ~* i en fart; *make ~* skynde sig.

hasten [heisn] *v (gl)* fremskynde; haste, ile.

hasty ['heisti] *adj* hastig; forhastet.

hat [hæt] *s* hat; *talk through one's ~* vrøvle; *keep sth under one's ~* holde ngt for sig selv; *that's old ~!* det er ikke nogen nyhed!

hatch [hætʃ] *s (mar* også: *~way)* luge, lem; (om fugl) udklækning; kuld // *v* ruge; udruge; udklække; **~back** *s (auto)* (bil med) hækdør.

hatchet ['hætʃit] *s* lille økse; *bury the ~* begrave stridsøksen.

hate [heit] *s* had // *v* hade, afsky; være ked af; *I would ~ to* jeg vil meget nødig; *I ~ to disturb* jeg er ked at af forstyrre; **~ful** *adj* væmmelig, modbydelig.

hatred ['heitrid] *s* had.

haughty ['hɔ:ti] *adj* overlegen, arrogant.

haul [hɔ:l] *s* træk; strækning; bytte, fangst // *v* hale, slæbe.

haulage ['hɔ:lidʒ] *s* transport(omkostninger).

haulier ['hɔ:liə*] *s* vognmand.

haunch [hɔ:ntʃ] *s* hofte; (om dyr) kølle; *~ of venison* dyrekølle.

haunt [hɔ:nt] *s* tilholdssted // *v* hjemsøge, plage; spøge (i); *the house is ~ed* det spøger i huset; *a ~ed look* et jaget udtryk (,blik).

have [hæv, həv] *v (had, had* [hæd, həd]) have; være; eje; (F) narre; *~ done (with)* være færdig (med); *~ a dress made* få syet en kjole, *~ to* være nødt til, skulle, måtte; *I had better* jeg må hellere; *~ sby on* gøre grin med en, narre en; *~ it in for sby* have et horn i siden på en; *~ it out with* få talt ud med; *I won't ~ it* jeg vil ikke finde mig i det; *he has had it* han er færdig; han har fået nok; *he has been had* han er blevet snydt; *~ tea* drikke te; *~ a drink* få sig en drink.

haven ['heivən] *s* (H) tilflugtssted; *tax ~* skattely.

haves [hævz] *spl: the ~ and the have-nots* de rige og de fattige.

havoc ['hævək] *s* ødelæggelse; ravage; *cry ~* råbe gevalt; *play ~ with* hærge, ødelægge.

hawk [hɔ:k] *s* høg (også *pol); **~er*** *s* falkejæger; gadesælger.

hawthorn ['hɔ:θɔ:n] *s* tjørn.

hay [hei] *s* hø; *hit the ~* (S) hoppe i dynerne, gå til køjs; **~fever** *s* høfeber; **~wire** *adj: go ~wire* blive skør; gå i skuddermudder.

hazard ['hæzəd] *s* tilfælde; fare, risiko // *v* vove, risikere.

hazardous ['hæzədəs] *adj* risikabel, hasarderet.

haze [heiz] *s* dis, tåge; *(fig)* uklarhed.

hazel ['heizəl] *s* hassel // *adj* nøddebrun; **~nut** *s* hasselnød.

hazy ['heizi] *adj* diset, tåget; *(fig)* ubestemt, vag; *(foto)* uskarp.

he [hi:] *pron* han; den, det; ham; ~ *who* den som; *it is ~ who...* det er ham som...

head [hɛd] *s* hoved; leder, forstander; (i avis) overskrift; (om kvæg) stykke; *(fig)* intelligens, forstand; *at the ~ of* i spidsen for; øverst på; *laugh one's ~ off* le sig fordærvet; *~ over heels* til op over begge ører; hovedkulds; *put one's ~s together* stikke hovederne sammen; *keep one's ~* holde hovedet koldt; *she lost her ~* hun mistede besindelsen // *v* lede, stå i spidsen for; gå forrest; *(fodb)* heade, lave hovedstød; *~ for* sætte kursen (,styre) imod; *~ off* aflede; afværge; **~ache** ['hɛdeik] *s* hovedpine; **~er** *s* hovedspring; hovedstød; **~first** *adv* på hovedet; **~gear** *s* hovedtøj; hat; **~-hunter** *s* hovedjæger; **~ing** *s* titel, overskrift; afsnit; **~lamp** *s (auto)* forlygte; **~land** *s* odde, forbjerg; **~light** *s (auto)* forlygte; **~line** *s* overskrift; *hit the ~lines* komme på forsiden; **~long** *adv* på hovedet, hovedkulds; **~master** *s* skolebestyrer; rektor; **~mistress** *s* skolebestyrerinde; rektor; **~ office** *s* hovedkontor; **~-on** *adj* frontal (fx *collision* sammenstød); **~phones** *spl* hovedtelefoner; **~quarters** *spl* hovedkvarter; **~-rest** *s* nakkestøtte; **~room** *s* fri højde; **~s** *spl: ~s or tails* plat el. krone; **~scarf** *s* hovedtørklæde; **~set** *s* hovedtelefoner; **~ start** *s* (solidt) forspring; **~stone** *s* gravsten; **~strong** *adj* stædig, egentådig; **~way** *s* fart; fremskridt; **~wind** *s* modvind.

heady ['hɛdi] *adj* impulsiv; berusende, som stiger til hovedet.

heal [hi:l] *v* hele(s), læge(s); helbrede.

health [hɛlθ] *s* sundhed; helbred; *in good ~* ved godt helbred; *drink (to) sby's ~* skåle for en; **~ centre** *s* lægehus; **~ food** *s* helsekost; **~ freak** [-fri:k] *s* sundhedsapostel; **~ resort** *s* kursted; *the* **Health Service** *s* sygesikringen; **~ visitor** *s* sundhedsplejerske.

healthy ['hɛlθi] *adj* sund, rask.

heap [hi:p] *s* bunke, dynge; masse; *a ~ of, ~s of* en mængde, masser af // *v* samle i bunke; *(fig)* ophobe, dynge sammen; *a ~ed spoonful* en topskefuld.

hear [hiə*] *v (heard, heard* [hə:d]) høre; erfare; lytte; lystre; *make oneself heard* skaffe sig ørenlyd; *~ about* høre om; *~ from* høre fra; *they wouldn't ~ of it* de ville ikke høre tale om det; *do you ~ me?* hører du? *~ sby out* lade en få lov at tale færdig.

hearing ['hiəriŋ] *s* hørelse; høring; *hard of ~* tunghør; **~ aid** *s* høreapparat.

hearsay ['hiəsei] *s* rygter.

hearse [hə:s] *s* ligvogn, rustvogn.

heart [ha:t] *s* hjerte; mod; kerne; *at ~* inderst inde; *by ~* udenad; *he didn't have the ~ to do it* han nænnede ikke at gøre det; *have a ~!* vær nu lidt rar! *have a change of ~* bestemme sig om; *lose ~* tabe modet; *set one's ~ on* være opsat på; *take ~* tage mod til sig; *to your ~'s content* af hjertens lyst; (se også *hearts); ~* **attack** *s* hjerteanfald; **~beat** *s* hjertebanken; hjertets slag; **~breaking** *adj* hjerteskærende; **~broken** [-brəukn] *adj* sønderknust; **~burn** *s* halsbrand, sure opstød; **~ condition** *s* dårligt hjerte.

heartening ['ha:təniŋ] *adj* opmuntrende.

heart failure ['ha:t ,feiljə*] *s* hjertestop.

heartfelt ['ha:tfɛlt] *adj* hjertelig, inderlig.

hearth [ha:θ] *s* kamin; esse.

heartily ['ha:tili] *adv* hjerteligt, inderligt; *agree ~* være helt enig(e).

heartless ['ha:tlis] *adj* hjerteløs.

hearts [ha:ts] *spl* (om kort) hjerter; *queen of ~* hjerter dame.

heartthrob ['ha:rtθrɔb] *s* (om mand) hjerteknuser, drømmefyr.

heart-to-heart ['ha:təha:t] *s* fortrolig snak.

hearty ['ha:ti] *adj* hjertelig; ivrig; sund; (om appetit etc) solid.

heat [hi:t] *s* varme, hede; *(fig)* glød, ophidselse; (om dyr) brunst; *(sport)* løb, heat; *put the ~ on sby* lægge pres på en // *v* varme (op); blive varm; **~ed** *adj* opvarmet; ophedet, hidsig; **~er** *s* varmeapparat; varmelegeme.

heath [hi:θ] *s* hede.

heathen ['hi:ðən] *s* hedning // *adj* hedensk.

heather ['hɛðə*] *s* lyng // *adj* lyngfarvet, lilla.

heating ['hi:tiŋ] *s* opvarmning // *adj* varmende; varme-; **~ oil** *s* fyringsolie.

heatrash ['hi:træʃ] *s* varmeknopper.

heatstroke ['hi:tstrəuk] *s* hedeslag.

heatwave ['hi:tweiv] *s* hedebølge.

heave [hi:v] *s* træk; kast; bølgen, dønning // *v* løfte; kaste; hive; drage; svulme; *~ a sigh* drage et suk; *it makes my stomach ~* det får det til at vende sig i mig; *~ to (mar)* dreje bi.

heaven [hɛvn] *s* himmel(en); *~ forbid* Gud forbyde; *~ knows* det må guderne vide; **~ly** *adj* himmelsk; dejlig; **~ly body** *s* himmellegeme; **~-sent** *adj* som sendt fra himmelen.

heavily ['hɛvili] *adv* tungt; svært; meget; dybt.

heavy ['hɛvi] *s* stærk mand, gorilla // *adj* tung, stor, stærk, svær; *it's ~ going* det er besværligt; *~ industry* sværindustri; *a ~ smoker* en storryger; *the car is ~ on petrol* bilen sluger meget benzin; **~-handed** *sdj* hårdhændet; **~-weight** *s (sport)* sværvægt.

Hebrew ['hi:bru:] *s* hebræer // *adj* hebraisk.

heck [hɛk] *interj: oh ~!* pokkers!

hectic ['hɛktik] *adj* hektisk.

he'd [hi:d] d.s.s. *he had; he would.*

hedge [hɛdʒ] *s* hegn, hæk // *v* tøve, vakle; *~ in* indhegne; *~ one's bets* (i tipning etc) foretage helgarderinger; **~hog** *s* pindsvin; **~row** [-rəu] *s* levende hegn.

heed [hi:d] *s: pay ~ to* tage sig af, ænse // *v* ænse, bryde sig om, lægge mærke til; **~less** *adj* ligegyldig; ubetænksom.

heel [hi:l] *s* hæl; endeskive; (S, om person) lort; *click one's ~s* smække hælene sammen; *dig one's ~s in* (kridte skoene og) stå fast; *be hard on sby's ~s* være lige i hælene på en; *take to one's ~s* stikke af // *v* (om sko) sætte hæle på.

hefty ['hɛfti] *adj* stor, velvoksen, solid.

heifer ['hɛfə*] *s* kvie.

height [hait] *s* højde; højdedrag; højdepunkt; **~en** *v* forhøje, øge; *(fig)* tage til.

heir [ɛə*] *s* arving.

heiress ['ɛərəs] *s* kvindelig arving.

heirloom ['ɛəlu:m] *s* arvestykke.

held [hɛld] *præt* og *pp* af *hold.*

helipad ['hɛlipæd] *s* helikopterlandingsplads (fx på skib el. hustag).

hell [hɛl] *s* helvede; *a ~ of a...* en allerhelvedes...; *give them ~* gøre helvede hedt for dem; *oh ~!* så for pokker! pokkers! *get the ~ out of here!* se at skrubbe ud! *raise ~* lave en farlig ballade; *like ~ I will!* gu' vil jeg ej! *for the ~ of it* (F) for sjov; *come ~ or high water* hvad pokker der så end sker.

he'll [hi:l] d.s.s. *he shall; he will.*

hell-bent ['hɛlbɛnt] *adj*: *~ on* (F) fast besluttet på.

hellish ['hɛliʃ] *adj* helvedes, infernalsk.

hello [hə'ləu] *interj* goddag! hej! hovsa! hallo!

helm [hɛlm] *s (mar)* ror, rat.

helmet ['hɛlmit] *s* hjelm.

helmsman ['hɛlmzmən] *s* rorgænger.

help [hɛlp] *s* hjælp; hjælper; hushjælp // *v* hjælpe; støtte; *~ yourself (to bread)* værsgo at tage (brød); *I can't ~ saying it* jeg kan ikke lade være med at sige det; *he can't ~ it* han kan ikke gøre for det; *be of ~* være til hjælp; *~ sby out* hjælpe en igennem en vanskelighed, komme en til hjælp; **~er** *s* hjælper; **~ful** *adj* hjælpsom; nyttig.

helping ['hɛlpiŋ] *s* portion.

helpless ['hɛlplis] *adj* hjælpeløs.

helter-skelter ['hɛltə'skɛltə*] *adv* i vild forvirring, hulter til bulter.

hem [hɛm] *s* søm, kant // *v* sømme, kante; *~ in* omringe, indeslutte.

hemisphere ['hɛmisfiə*] *s* halvkugle, hemisfære.
hemline ['hɛmlain] *s* søm (på kjole etc).
hemp [hɛmp] *s (bot)* hamp.
hemstitch ['hɛmstitʃ] *s* hulsøm.
hen [hɛn] *s* høne; hunfugl.
hence [hɛns] *adv* deraf; derfor; fra nu af; *two years* ~ om to år fra nu af; **~forth** *adv* fra nu af, for fremtiden.
henchman ['hɛntʃmən] *s* håndlanger.
hen party ['hɛnpa:ti] *s* dameselskab; polterabend (for kvinder).
henpecked ['hɛnpɛkd] *adj* (om ægtemand) under tøflen.
hepatitis [hɛpə'taitis] *s* leverbetændelse.
her [hə:*] *pron* hende, sig; hendes.
herald ['hɛrəld] *s* herold, budbringer // *v* forkynde, bebude; **~ry** ['hɛrəldri] *s* heraldik.
herb [hə:b] *s* urt; krydderurt.
herbaceous [hə:'beiʃəs] *adj* urteagtig; ~ *border* staudebed.
herbal ['hə:bl] *adj* urte-.
herd [hə:d] *s* hjord, flok // *v:* ~ *together* genne sammen.
here [hiə*] *adv* her, herhen; *from* ~ herfra; *~'s my sister* dette (,her) er min søster; ~ *she comes* der kommer hun; ~ *you are* værsgo; ~ *goes!* så, nu går det løs! *now, look ~!* hør nu engang! **~abouts** *adv* her omkring, her i nærheden; **~after** *adv* herefter // *s: the ~after* det hinsides; **~by** *adv* herved.
hereditary [hi'rɛditri] *adj* arvelig, arve-; **heredity** *s* arvelighed.
heresy ['hɛrəsi] *s* kætteri.
heretic ['hɛrətik] *s* kætter; **heretical** [hi'rɛtikl] *adj* kættersk.
herewith [hiə'wið] *adv* hermed.
heritage ['hɛritidʒ] *s* arv.
hermit ['hə:mit] *s* eremit, eneboer.
hernia ['hə:niə] *s (med)* brok.
hero ['hiərəu] *s* helt.
heroic [hi'rəuik] *adj* heltemodig, heroisk.
heroin ['hɛrəuin] *s* heroin.
heroine ['hɛrəuin] *s* heltinde.
heroism ['hɛrəuizm] *s* heltemod.
heron ['hɛrən] *s* hejre.
herring ['hɛriŋ] *s* sild; *a red* ~ et falsk spor; *smoked* ~ røget sild; **~bone** *s* sildeben; sildebensmønster; **~bone stitch** *s* heksesting.
hers [hə:z] *pron* hendes; sin, sit, sine.
herself [hə:sɛlf] *pron* hun selv; hende selv; sig selv; *she did it* ~ hun gjorde det selv.
he's [hi:z] d.s.s. *he has; he is.*
hesitant ['hɛzitənt] *adj* tøvende, usikker.
hesitate ['hɛziteit] *v* tøve, vakle; ~ *about* være i tvivl om; ~ *to* tøve med at; **hesitation** [-'teiʃən] *s* tøven; usikkerhed.
het-up [hɛt'ʌp] *adj* (F) ophidset.
hew [hju:] *v (~ed, ~ed* el. *~n)* hugge.
heyday ['heidei] *s* velmagtsdage.
HGV [eitʃdʒi:'vi:] *s* (fork.f. *heavy goods vehicle)* lastvogn.
hi [hai] *interj* hej! davs!
hibernate ['haibəneit] *v* overvintre; ligge i dvale (,hi).
hiccough, hiccup ['hikʌp] *s/v* hikke.
hid [hid] *præt* af *hide;* **~den** [hidn] *pp* af *hide.*
hide [haid] *s* skind, hud // *v* banke, prygle; *(hid, hidden)* skjule, gemme; skjule sig; ~ *from* gemme sig for; ~ *sth (from sby)* skjule (,gemme) ngt for en; **~-and-seek** *s* (om leg) skjul; **~away** *s* skjulested.
hidebound ['haidbaund] *adj* forstokket, reaktionær.
hideous ['hidiəs] *adj* hæslig, skrækkelig.
hideout ['haidaut] *s* gemmested.
hiding ['haidiŋ] *s* tæsk, prygl; skjul; *give sby a good* ~ give en en ordentlig omgang tæv; *be in* ~ holde sig skjult; **~ place** *s* gemmested.
higgeledy-piggledy ['higəldi,pigəldi] *adv* hulter til bulter.
high [hai] *adj* høj; stor; stærk; voldsom (fx *wind* blæst); (S) høj, skæv (af stoffer); *leave sby* ~ *and dry* lade en i stikken; ~ *and mighty* stor på den; *in* ~ *spirits* i højt humør; *it's* ~ *time* det er på høje tid; *from on* ~ fra højeste sted; **~brow** [-brau] *s* intellektuel; åndssnob; **~-class** *adj* topklasse-.
High Court ['haikɔ:t] *s* overret.

high... ['hai-] sms: **~diving** *s (sport)* tårnspring; **~ flier** *s* stræber; succesdreng; **~-handed** *adj* storsnudet; **~-heeled** *adj* højhælet; **~ jump** *s (sport)* højdespring.

Highlander ['hailəndə*] *s* skotsk højlænder; *the* **Highlands** *spl* det skotske højland.

high... ['hai-] sms: **~-level** *adj* på højeste niveau, top-; **~light** *s (fig)* højdepunkt // *v* kaste lys over; fremhæve; **~ly** *adv* i høj grad, meget, højt; *~ly strung* overspændt, nervøs.

Highness ['hainis] *s: Your ~* Deres højhed.

high... ['hai-] sms: **~-pitched** *adj* (om stemme, tone) skinger, høj; **~-powered** *adj* kraftig; dynamisk; **~-pressure** *adj* højtryks-; **~-priced** *adj* dyr; **~rise block** *s* højhus; **~ school** *s* højere skole (11-18 år); **~-speed** *adj* hurtig-; **~-spirited** *adj* livlig; **~ spot** *s* højdepunkt; **~ tea** *s* eftermiddagsmåltid; **~ street** *s* hovedgade; **~-tension** *adj* højspændings-; **~-ups** *spl* pinger; **~way** *s* hovedvej; **~wayman** *s* landevejsrøver.

hijack ['haidʒæk] *v* (om fly) kapre, bortføre; **~er** *s* flykaprer.

hike [haik] *s* travetur, vandretur; (F) stigning (i priser etc) // *v* være på travetur; *~ up* hive op i; **~r** *s* vandrer; **hiking** *s* vandring.

hilarious [hi'lɛəriəs] *adj* kåd, løssluppen.

hilarity [hi'læriti] *s* munterhed, løssluppenhed.

hill [hil] *s* bakke; (især skotsk) bjerg; *as old as the ~s* urgammel.

hillock ['hilɔk] *s* lille bakke.

hillside ['hilsaid] *s* (bjerg)skråning.

hill start ['hilsta:t] *s (auto)* start op (,ned) ad bakke.

hilly ['hili] *adj* bakket; bjergrig.

hilt [hilt] *s: up to the ~ (fig)* helt igennem.

him [him] *pron* han; ham; den, det; sig.

himself [him'sɛlf] *pron* han selv; sig selv; *(all) by ~* (helt) alene; *he did it ~* han gjorde det selv.

hind [haind] *s* hind // *adj* bagest, bag-.

hinder ['hində*] *v* hindre; sinke.

hindrance ['hindrəns] *s* hindring.

hindsight ['haindsait] *s* bagklogskab.

hinge [hindʒ] *s* hængsel // *v: ~ on (fig)* komme an på.

hint [hint] *s* antydning, vink; *drop sby a ~* give en et vink // *v* antyde, insinuere; *~ at* hentyde til.

hip [hip] *s* hofte; *(bot)* hyben // *adj* (F) med på noderne; **~ flask** *s* lommelærke.

hippopotamus [hipə'pɔtəməs] *s (pl: ~es* el. *hippopotami* [-'pɔtəmai]) flodhest.

hire [haiə*] *s* leje; løn; hyre; *for ~* til leje; (på taxi) fri // *v* leje; hyre, ansætte; *~ out* leje ud; **~ purchase** *s (HP)* køb (,salg) på afbetaling.

his [hiz] *pron* hans; sin, sit, sine.

hiss [his] *s* hvæsen; hvislen // *v* hvæse, hvisle; hysse.

historian [hi'stɔ:riən] *s* historiker.

historic(al) [hi'stɔrik(əl)] *adj* historisk.

history ['histəri] *s* historie; *make ~* skabe historie; *have a ~ of violence* være kendt som voldsmand; *go down in ~* gå over i historien; *that's past ~* det er fortid.

hit [hit] *s* stød, slag; succes, hit; (fuld)træffer // *v (hit, hit)* ramme; støde, slå; nå; støde sammen med; finde, støde på; *~ the bottle* slå sig på flasken; *~ the ceiling* flyve helt op i loftet; *~ the headlines* komme i avisen; *~ the road* (F) tage af sted; *~ the sack* (F) gå til køjs; *~ it off with sby* komme godt ud af det med en; **~-and-run driver** *s* flugtbilist.

hitch [hitʃ] *s* hindring, standsning; *(mar)* stik // *v* sætte fast; spænde for; *~ a lift* blaffe, køre på tommelfingeren; **~-hike** *v* blaffe.

hitman ['hitmən] *s* (F) lejemorder.

hive [haiv] *s* bikube.

HMS fork.f. *Her (,His) Majesty's Ship.*

hoard [hɔ:d] *s* forråd, reserver; skat // *v* samle sammen, hamstre.

hoarding ['hɔ:diŋ] *s* plankeværk.

hoarfrost ['hɔ:frɔst] *s* rimfrost.

hoarse [hɔ:s] *adj* hæs.

hoax [həuks] *s* spøg, nummer; skrøne // *v* narre.

hob [hɔb] *s* bordkomfur; kogesektion; varmeplade (oven på komfur); pind (i ringspil).
hobble [hɔbl] *v* halte, humpe.
hobby ['hɔbi] *s* hobby; *ride one's* ~ *(fig)* ride sin kæphest; **-horse** *s* (om legetøj) kæphest.
hobnailed ['hɔbneild] *adj* (om støvle) sømbeslået.
hobnob ['hɔbnɔb] *v*: ~ *with* mænge sig med, gnubbe skuldre med.
hock [hɔk] *s* rhinskvin; (om hest) hase // *v* pantsætte.
hoe [həu] *s* hakke, lugejern.
hog [hɔg] *s* (vild)svin; *go the whole* ~ tage skridtet fuldt ud // *v (fig)* rage til sig.
Hogmanay [hɔgmə'nei] *s* (skotsk) nytårsaften.
hogwash ['hɔgwɔʃ] *s* (F) pladder, bavl.
hoist [hɔist] *s* hejs, spil // *v* hejse, løfte.
hoity-toity ['hɔiti'tɔiti] *adj* storsnudet.
hold [həuld] *s* hold, tag; støtte, fodfæste; *(mar)* lastrum; *catch (,get)* ~ *of* få fat i; *get* ~ *of oneself* tage sig sammen // *v (held, held)* holde; indeholde, rumme; eje; mene, anse for; gælde; ~ *it!* vent lige lidt! ~ *the line! (tlf)* et øjeblik! ~ *one's own (fig)* holde stand; ~ *one's drink* kunne tåle at drikke meget; *don't* ~ *it against me!* lad mig ikke høre for det! ~ *back* holde tilbage; skjule (fx *a secret* en hemmelighed); ~ *down* holde nede; blive i (fx *a job* et job); ~ *off* holde borte; holde på afstand; ~ *on* holde sig fast; holde ud; fortsætte; ~ *on!* stop lidt! ~ *on to* holde fast i (,på); beholde; ~ *out* holde ud; love; tilbyde; ~ *out for sth* stædigt forlange ngt, holde fast ved ngt; ~ *out on sby* skjule ngt for en; ~ *up* række op; støtte, holde oppe; holde i skak; lave holdup; **-all** *s* rejsetaske, weekendtaske.
holder ['həuldə*] *s* indehaver; holder.
holding ['həuldiŋ] *s* beholdning; aktiepost; *(agr)* gård, brug; ~ **company** *s* holdingselskab.
hold-up ['həuldʌp] *s* holdup, væbnet røveri; trafikstandsning.
hole [həul] *s* hul; *be in a* ~ være i knibe; *be in* ~*s* være hullet // *v* hulle, lave huller i; *be* ~*d up* gemme sig, forskanse sig.
holiday ['hɔlidei] *s* ferie; fridag; helligdag; *go on* ~ tage på ferie; **-maker** *s* ferierejsende, turist; ~ **resort** [-ri'zɔ:t] *s* feriested.
holiness ['həulinis] *s* hellighed.
holler ['hɔlə*] *s* skrål, brøl // *v* brøle, skråle.
hollow ['hɔləu] *s* hulning; hul; *in the* ~ *of one's hand* i sin hule hånd // *adj* hul; *(fig)* falsk.
holly ['hɔli] *s* kristtorn.
hollyhock ['hɔlihɔk] *s* stokrose.
holocaust ['hɔləkɔ:st] *s* storbrand; massakre, massedrab.
holster ['həulstə*] *s* pistolhylster.
holy ['həuli] *adj* hellig; *Holy Communion* nadver; *the Holy Ghost (,Spirit)* helligånden; ~ *smoke!* milde Moses! *holier than thou (neds,* om person) frelst, hellig; ~ **orders** *spl: take* ~ *orders* blive præsteviet; *the* **Holy See** *s* pavestolen; *the* **Holy Writ** *s* den hellige skrift, Bibelen.
homage ['hɔmidʒ] *s* hyldest; *pay* ~ *to* hylde.
home [həum] *s* hjem; *at* ~ hjemme; *make oneself at* ~ lade som om man er hjemme; *he lives away from* ~ han bor ikke hjemme // *adj* hjemlig; hjemme-; indenrigs, national // *adv* hjem; hjemme; i mål; *it came* ~ *to me* det gik op for mig; *go* ~ gå hjem; *(fig)* ramme; *his remark went* ~ hans bemærkning ramte (,traf) // *v*: ~ *in* (om missil) få kontakt med målet; (om fugl) vende hjem; **--brew** *s* hjemmebryg; **-coming** *s* hjemkomst; ~ **economics** *s* (i skolen) hjemkundskab; **--grown** *adj* hjemmedyrket; ~ **help** *s* hjemmehjælper; **-land** *s* fædreland; (i Sydafrika) reservat (for sorte); **-less** *adj* hjemløs; husvild; **-ly** *adj* hjemlig, hyggelig; jævn, folkelig; **--made** *adj* hjemmelavet; *the* **Home Office** *s* indenrigsministeriet; ~ **rule** *s* selvstyre, hjemmestyre; **Home Secretary** *s* sv.t. indenrigsminister;

~sick *adj: be ~sick* have hjemve; **~ stretch** *s* (i løb og *fig*) opløb; **~ward(s)** *adv* hjemad, hjem-; **~work** *s* hjemmearbejde, lektier.

homey ['həumi] *adj* hyggelig, hjemlig.

homicide ['hɔmisaid] *s* drab; drabsmand.

homily ['hɔmili] *s* præken.

homing ['həumiŋ] *adj* målsøgende; *~ pigeon* brevdue.

homogeneous [hɔməu'dʒi:niəs] *adj* ensartet, homogen.

hone [həun] *v* slibe, hvæsse; *(fig)* oplære, 'slibe af'.

honest ['ɔnist] *adj* ærlig; hæderlig; *be ~ with* være ærlig overfor; **~ly** *adv* ærligt; ærligt talt.

honesty ['ɔnisti] *s* ærlighed.

honey ['hʌni] *s* honning; (F) skat // *v* snakke godt for, smøre; **~dew melon** [-dju:] *s* honningmelon.

honeymoon ['hʌnimu:n] *s* bryllupsrejse, hvedebrødsdage.

honeysuckle ['hʌnisʌkl] *s (bot)* kaprifolium.

honk [hɔŋk] *v* dytte, tude (med hornet).

honorary ['ɔnərəri] *adj* æres- (fx *member* medlem).

honour ['ɔnə*] *s* ære, hæder; *in ~ of* til ære for; *guest of ~* æresgæst; *maid (,lady) of ~* hofdame; *be on one's ~* have givet sit æresord; *do the ~s* spille vært (,værtinde) // *v* ære, hædre; opfylde, indfri; *~ a bill (merk)* acceptere en veksel; **~able** *adj* hæderlig, retskaffen; æret; *the ~able member (parl)* det ærede medlem; **~s degree** *s* kandidateksamen *(BA)* med specialisering i ét fag.

hood [hu:d] *s* hætte; *(auto)* kaleche; emhætte.

hoodlum ['hu:dləm] *s* bølle.

hoodwink ['hudwiŋk] *v* bluffe, narre.

hoof [hu:f] *s (pl: hooves* [hu:vz]) hov (på dyr).

hook [hu:k] *s* krog; knage; hægte; fiskekrog; *swallow sth ~, line and sinker* sluge ngt råt // *v* få på krogen; hægte; bøje, krumme; *~ on* hægte (sig) på; hænge på; *~ up* hægte sammen; koble til; **~ed** *adj* krum; *~ on* grebet (,fanget) af, vild med; afhængig af.

hooker ['hu:kə*] *s* (S) luder.

hooligan ['hu:ligən] *s* bølle, voldsmand; *(brit* især) fodboldbølle.

hoop [hu:p] *s* tændbånd, ring; *put sby through the ~s* sætte en på en hård prøve.

hoot [hu:t] *s* hujen, tuden; *not give a ~* være revnende ligeglad; *he's a ~* han er hylende grinagtig // *v* tude, huje; *~ with laughter* hyle af grin.

hooter ['hu:tə*] *s* bilhorn; *(mar)* signalhorn, sirene; (S) tud, gynter.

hoover® ['hu:və*] *s* støvsuger // *v* støvsuge.

hooves [hu:vz] *spl* af *hoof.*

hop [hɔp] *s* hop, spring; *(bot)* humle // *v* hoppe; hinke; *~ping mad* flintrende gal.

hope [həup] *s* håb; *in the ~ of...* i håb om at...; *be past all ~* ikke stå til at redde; *some ~!* det er der ikke store chancer for! // *v* håbe (på); *I ~ not* det håber jeg ikke; *I ~ so* det håber jeg; **~ful** *adj* forhåbningsfuld; lovende; **~fully** *adv* forhåbentlig; **~less** *adj* håbløs.

hopscotch ['hɔpskɔtʃ] *s: do ~* hinke.

horizon [hə'raizən] *s* horisont; **~tal** [hɔri'zɔntl] *adj* vandret.

hormone ['hɔ:məun] *s* hormon; **~ deficiency** [-də'fiʃənsi] *s* hormonmangel.

horn [hɔ:n] *s* horn; *blow the ~ (auto)* tude i hornet; *(mus)* blæse i hornet; *~ of plenty* overflødighedshorn; **~ed** *adj* med horn; horn-.

hornet ['hɔ:nit] *s* gedehams; **~'s nest** *s* hvepserede (også *fig).*

horn-rimmed ['hə:nrimd] *adj: ~ spectacles* hornbriller.

horny ['hɔ:ni] *adj* med hård hud; (F) (om mand) liderlig.

horrendous [hə'rɛndəs] *adj* grufuld; enorm.

horrible ['hɔribl] *adj* frygtelig, grufuld; afskyelig.

horrid ['hɔrid] *adj* væmmelig, gyselig.

horrific [hɔ'rifik] *adj* skrækkelig; rædselsfuld.

horrify ['hɔrifai] *v* forfærde, skræmme.

horror ['hɔrə*] *s* rædsel, skræk; afsky; *she looks a ~* hun ser skrækkelig ud; *have a ~ of spiders* have en skræk for edderkopper; *have the ~s* have delirium tremens; **~ film** *s* skrækfilm, gyser; **~-stricken** [-strikn] *adj* rædselslagen.

horse [hɔ:s] *s* hest; (sav)buk; **~back** *s* hesteryg; *on ~back* til hest; **~flesh** *s* hestekød; heste; **~fly** *s* hestebremse; **~man** *s* rytter; **~power** *s (hp)* hestekraft; hestekræfter (hk); **~-racing** *s* hestevæddeløb; **~radish** *s* peberrod; **~-trading** *s (fig)* studehandel; **~whip** *s* ridepisk.

hors(e)y ['hɔ:si] *adj* hesteagtig; heste-; vild med heste.

horticulture ['hɔ:tikʌltʃə*] *s* havedyrkning.

hose [həuz] *s* (også: *~ pipe)* (vand)slange; (også: *garden ~)* haveslange // *spl* strømper // *v* vande; sprøjte.

hosiery ['həuziəri] *s* trikotage; (i forretning) strømper, strømpeafdeling.

hospitable ['hɔspitəbl] *adj* gæstfri.

hospital ['hɔspitl] *s* sygehus, hospital; *in ~* på sygehuset, indlagt.

hospitality [hɔspi'tæliti] *s* gæstfrihed.

hospitalize ['hɔspitəlaiz] *v* indlægge (på sygehus).

host [həust] *s* vært; (hær)skare, mængde.

hostage ['hɔstidʒ] *s* gidsel; *be taken ~* blive taget som gidsel.

hostel [hɔstl] *s* hjem, herberg; (også: *youth ~)* ungdomsherberg, vandrerhjem.

hostess ['həustis] *s* værtinde; (også: *air ~)* stewardesse, flyværtinde.

hostile ['hɔstail] *adj* fjendtlig.

hostility [hɔ'stiliti] *s* fjendtlighed.

hot [hɔt] *adj* varm, hed; krydret, stærk; *(fig)* hidsig, lidenskabelig; *you are getting ~* tampen brænder; *be ~ at sth* være skrap til ngt; *he's ~ on football* han er vild med fodbold // *v*: *~ up a car* tune en bil; **~bed** *s* drivbænk; *(fig)* arnested.

hotchpotch ['hɔtʃpɔtʃ] *s* ruskomsnusk, rodsammen.

hotel [həu'tɛl] *s* hotel.

hotelier [həu'tɛliə*] *s* hotelejer, hotelvært.

hot... ['hɔt-] sms: **~foot** *v: ~foot it* skynde sig, spurte // *adv* sporenstregs; **~headed** *adj* hidsig, opfarende; **~house** *s* drivhus; **~plate** *s* kogeplade; varmeplade; **~pot** *s (gastr)* ragout af kød og kartofler; **~ spot** *s* urocentrum; sted med mange aktiviteter; **~-water bottle** *s* varmedunk.

hound [haund] *s* jagthund; *ride to ~s* drive rævejagt // *v* jage, forfølge.

hour [auə*] *s* time; stund; tid; *an ~ and a half* halvanden time; *strike the ~* (om ur) slå hel; *after ~s* efter lukketid; *at an early ~* tidligt; *paid by the ~* timelønnet; *for ~s and ~s* i timevis; *on the ~* på slaget (hel); *work long ~s* have en lang arbejdsdag; *out of ~s* uden for arbejdstid; **~ hand** *s* lille viser; **~ly** *adj* time- // *adv* i timen; hver time.

house *s* [haus] *(pl: ~es* ['hauziz]) hus (også om firma etc); *(teat)* forestilling; tilskuerpladser; *be getting on like a ~ on fire* klare sig strålende; komme fint ud af det (med hinanden); *it's on the ~* huset betaler; *bring the ~ down (fig)* vælte huset; *the House of Commons* underhuset; *the House of Lords* overhuset // *v* [hauz] huse; give husly; **~ agent** *s* ejendomsmægler; **~bound** *adj* ude af stand til at gå ud; **~breaking** *s* indbrud; **~hold** *s* husstand; husholdning; **~-hunt** *v* søge bolig; **~keeper** *s* husholderske; husbestyrerinde; **~keeping** *s* husholdning; **~plant** *s* stueplante; **~top** *s* hustag; **~train** *v* gøre stueren; **~wife** *s* husmor; **~work** *s* husligt arbejde.

housing ['hauziŋ] *s* boliger, huse // *adj* bolig; **~ association** *s* boligselskab; **~ benefit** *s* boligtilskud; **~ development** *s* boligbyggeri; **~ estate, ~ scheme** *s* boligkvarter; **~ shortage** *s* boligmangel.

hovel ['hʌvəl] *s* ussel hytte, skur.

hover ['hɔvə*] *v* svæve; vakle, tøve; *~ about (,round) sby* kredse om en; **~craft** *s* luftpudebåd; luftpude-.

how [hau] *adv* hvordan; hvor; *~ are you?* hvordan har du det? (ofte som hilsen) goddag! *~ come? ~ so?* hvordan kan det være? hvordan det? *~ could you!* hvordan kunne du gøre det! *~ lovely!* hvor skønt! *~ many?* hvor mange? *~ much is it?* hvad koster det? *~ about a drink?* hvad med en drink? **~ever** [hau'ɛvə*] *adv* hvordan end; *~ever that may be...* hvorom alting er... // *konj* imidlertid, alligevel.

howl [haul] *s* hyl, brøl, tuden // *v* hyle, tude, vræle.

howler ['haulə*] *s* brøler, bommert.

howling ['həuliŋ] *adj* hylende, vrælende; *(fig)* drønende.

HP, hp fork.f. *hire-purchase; horsepower.*

HQ ['eitʃ'kju:] fork.f. *headquarters.*

HRH fork.f. *His Royal Highness.*

hr(s) fork.f. *hour(s).*

ht fork.f. *height.*

hub [hʌb] *s* (hjul)nav; *(fig)* centrum; (F) (også: *hubby)* (ægte)mand.

hubbub ['hʌbʌb] *s* ståhej, larm.

hubcap ['hʌbkæp] *s* hjulkapsel.

huddle [hʌdl] *v: ~ together* stimle sammen; trykke sig op ad hinanden.

hue [hju:] *s* farve; anstrøg; *~ and cry (fig)* ramaskrig, alarm; klapjagt, hetz.

huff [hʌf] *s: in a ~* mopset // *v: ~ and puff* puste og stønne; rase og regere; **~y** *adj* fornærmet, mopset.

hug [hʌg] *s* omfavnelse, knus // *v* omfavne, knuge (ind til sig); holde sig tæt ved.

huge [hju:dʒ] *adj* enorm, kæmpestor.

hulk [hʌlk] *s* stort klodset skibsskrog; (om person) klods; **~ing** *adj* enorm, kæmpe-.

hull [hʌl] *s* skibsskrog; *(bot)* bælg, skal.

hullabaloo [hʌləbə'lu:] *s* (F) ståhej.

hum [hʌm] *s* nynnen; (om insekt) brummen, summen // *v* nynne; summe, brumme; *~ and haw* sige "øh" og "æh"; ikke ville ud med sproget.

human ['hju:mən] *s* (også: *~ being)* menneske // *adj* menneskelig; menneske-; *I'm only ~* jeg er kun et menneske; **~ error** menneskelig fejl; **~ rights** *spl* menneskerettigheder.

humane [hju'mein] *adj* menneskekærlig, human.

humanitarian [hju:mæni'tɛəriən] *adj* humanitær.

humanities [hju'mænitiz] *spl* humaniora.

humanity [hju'mæniti] *s* menneskelighed; menneskehed.

humble [hʌmbl] *adj* ydmyg; beskeden, tarvelig; *eat ~ pie* krybe til korset; ydmyge sig; **humbly** *adv* ydmygt; beskedent.

humbug ['hʌmbʌg] *s* vrøvl; humbug; svindler; pebermyntebolsje.

humdrum ['hʌmdrʌm] *adj* kedsommelig, ensformig.

humid ['hju:mid] *adj* fugtig.

humidifier [hju:'midifaiə*] *s* befugtningsanlæg, luftfugter.

humidity [hju:'miditi] *s* fugtighed.

humiliate [hju:'milieit] *v* ydmyge; **humiliation** [-'eiʃən] *s* ydmygelse.

humility [hju:'militi] *s* ydmyghed.

hummingbird ['hʌmiŋbə:d] *s* kolibri.

humorous ['hju:mərəs] *adj* humoristisk.

humour ['hju:mə*] *s* humor; humør // *v* føje.

hump [həmp] *s* pukkel; tue; bakke; (indbygget) bump (i vejbane) // *v* slæbe på; tage op på skulderen; **~back** *s* pukkelrygget person.

hunch [hʌntʃ] *s* klump, luns; *(fig)* forudanelse; *have a ~ that...* have på fornemmelsen at... // *v: ~ one's back* krumme ryg; **~back** *s* pukkel; pukkelrygget person; **~ed** *adj* ludende, bøjet.

hundred ['hʌndrəd] *num* hundrede; **~s and thousands** *s (gastr)* farvet krymmel.

hundredth ['hʌndrədθ] *s* hundrededel.

hundredweight ['hʌndrədweit] *s* centner *(brit: 112 lb,* 50,8 kg; *am: 100 lb,* 45,3 kg).

hung [hʌŋ] *præt* og *pp* af *hang.*

Hungarian [hʌn'gɛəriən] *s* ungarer //

adj ungarsk; **Hungary** ['hʌŋgəri] *s* Ungarn.
hunger ['hʌŋgə*] *s* sult; *(fig)* trang *(for* til) // *v: ~ for* tørste efter, ønske brændende.
hung over ['hʌŋ əuvə*] *adj* plaget af tømmermænd.
hungry ['hʌŋgri] *adj* sulten; begærlig *(for* efter); *it's ~ work* det giver appetit.
hung up [ˌhʌŋ'ʌp] *adj* slået ud; *be ~ about sth* (også) tabe hovedet over ngt; være fikseret på ngt.
hunk [hʌŋk] *s* luns, humpel; (S, om mand) flot steg.
hunt [hʌnt] *s* jagt // *v* jage (efter); søge; gå på jagt; *~ for* lede efter; *~ the thimble* lege gemme fingerbøl; *~ out* opstøve, opsnuse.
hunter ['hʌntə*] *s* jæger.
hunting ['hʌntiŋ] *s* jagt (især rævejagt til hest); **~ box** *s* jagthytte.
huntsman ['hʌntsmən] *s* jæger.
hurdle [hə:dl] *s* gærde; *(sport)* hæk, forhindring; **~ race** *s* (også: *hurdles)* hækkeløb; forhindringsløb.
hurl [hə:l] *v* slynge, kyle.
hurly-burly ['hə:li,bə:li] *s* virvar, tummel.
hurricane ['hʌrikən] *s* orkan.
hurried ['hʌrid] *adj* hastig, fortravlet; hastværks-.
hurry ['hʌri] *s* hast(værk); fart; travlhed; *be in a ~* have travlt; *do sth in a ~* skynde sig med ngt; *there's no ~* det jager ikke // *v* skynde sig, haste; skynde på; fremskynde; *~ up!* skynd dig (,jer)!
hurt [hə:t] *s* skade, fortræd; sår // *v (hurt, hurt)* skade; slå, støde; *(fig)* såre; gøre ondt; *it won't ~ you to...* du tager ikke skade af at... // *adj* såret; **~ful** *adj* sårende.
hurtle [hə:tl] *v* slynge, kaste; styrte, suse; *~ down* rasle ned; *~ past* suse forbi.
husband ['hʌzbənd] *s* (ægte)mand // *v: ~ sth* holde hus med ngt, spare på ngt.
husbandry ['hʌzbəndri] *s* (H) landbrug.
hush [hʌʃ] *s* stilhed // *v* berolige, dysse ned; *hush!* hys! stille! **hush-hush** *adj* meget hemmelig, tys-tys.
husk [hʌsk] *s (bot)* avne, skal; kapsel; bælg.
husky ['hʌski] *s* slædehund // *adj* (om stemme) hæs, grødet.
hustle [hʌsl] *s* trængsel; *~ and bustle* liv og røre // *v* jage med; skubbe til.
hut [hʌt] *s* hytte; skur; *(mil)* barak.
hutch [hʌtʃ] *s* bur.
hybrid ['haibrid] *s* bastard; hybrid, krydsning.
hydrate ['haidreit] *s (kem)* hydrat // *v* hydrere.
hydroelectric ['haidrəui'lɛktrik] *adj* vandkraft-.
hydrogen ['haidrədʒən] *s* brint, hydrogen; **~ peroxide** *s* brintoverilte.
hydrophobia [haidrə'fəubiə] *s* vandskræk; *(med)* hundegalskab, rabies.
hygiene ['haidʒi:n] *s* hygiejne.
hymn [him] *s* salme, hymne.
hypertension [haipə'tɛnʃən] *s* forhøjet blodtryk, hypertension.
hyphen [haifn] *s* bindestreg.
hyphenation [haifə'neiʃən] *s* orddeling.
hypnosis [hip'nəusis] *s* hypnose; **hypnotic** [-'nɔtik] *adj* hypnotisk.
hypnotist ['hipnətist] *s* hypnotisør.
hypochondriac [haipə'kɔndriæk] *s* hypokonder.
hypocrisy [hi'pɔkrisi] *s* hykleri.
hypocrite ['hipəkrit] *s* hykler.
hypodermic [haipə'də:mik] *s* sprøjte; indsprøjtning // *adj: ~ needle* kanyle.
hypothesis [hai'pɔθəsis] *s (pl: hypotheses* [-si:z]) antagelse, hypotese.
hypothetic(al) [haipə'θɛtik(l)] *adj* antaget, hypotetisk.
hysterectomy [histə'rɛktəmi] *s* fjernelse af livmoderen, hysterektomi.
hysteria [hi'stiəriə] *s* hysteri; **hysterical** [-'stɛrikl] *adj* hysterisk.
hysterics [hi'stɛriks] *spl* hysterianfald; *go into ~* blive hysterisk.

I

I, i [ai].
I [ai] *pron* jeg; mig.
ice [ais] *s* is; *he cuts no ~ with me* han

gør ikke indtryk på mig // *v* afkøle; lægge på is; glasere; ~ *over (,up)* overise; **~ age** *s* istid; **~bag** *s* ispose; **~berg** *s* isbjerg; **~box** *s* frostboks; iskasse; **~breaker** *s* isbryder; **~cap** *s* indlandsis; evig sne; **~-cream** *s* (fløde)is; **~ cube** *s* isterning.

iced [aisd] *adj* iskold; isafkølet; is-; glaseret.

ice fern ['aisfə:n] *s* isblomst.

Iceland ['aislənd] *s* Island; **~er** *s* islænding; **Icelandic** [-'lændik] *s/adj* islandsk.

ice lolly ['aislɔli] *s* ispind; **ice rink** *s* skøjtebane.

icicle ['aisikl] *s* istap.

icing ['aisiŋ] *s* isslag; overisning; *(gastr)* glasur (på kage etc); **~ sugar** *s* glasursukker, flormelis.

icy ['aisi] *adj* iskold, isnende; isglat.

I'd [aid] d.s.s. *I had; I would.*

ID ['ai'di:] *s* fork.f. *identification; identity.*

idea [ai'diə] *s* idé; begreb; tanke; mening; *get the* ~ fatte meningen; *I have no* ~ jeg aner (det) ikke; *have you any* ~ *where?* har du ngt begreb om hvor? *that's the* ~*!* sådan skal det være! *what's the big* ~*?* hvad er meningen? *put* ~*s into sby's head* sætte fluer i hovedet på en.

ideal [ai'diəl] *s* forbillede, ideal // *adj* ideel; fuldendt.

idealist [ai'diəlist] *s* idealist; **idealistic** [-'listik] *adj* idealistisk.

identical [ai'dɛntikl] *adj* ens, identisk; **~ twins** *spl* enæggede tvillinger.

identification [aidɛntifi'keiʃən] *s* legitimation; identifikation; **~ parade** *s* konfrontation (i mordsag etc).

identify [ai'dɛntifai] *v* identificere.

identikit [ai'dɛntikit] *s* fantombillede.

identity [ai'dɛntiti] *s* identitet.

ideological [aidiə'lɔdʒikəl] *adj* ideologisk.

ideology [aidi'ɔlədʒi] *s* ideologi.

idiocy ['idiəsi] *s* idioti.

idiom ['idiəm] *s* sprog; talemåde.

idiosyncrasy [idiə'sinkrəsi] *s* overfølsomhed; særhed.

idiot ['idiət] *s* idiot, fjols; **idiotic** [-'ɔtik] *adj* idiotisk.

idle [aidl] *v* drive *(about* rundt); *(auto)* gå i tomgang // *adj* ledig, ubeskæftiget; doven; ude af drift; intetsigende; håbløs, forgæves; *lie* ~ ligge stille.

idler ['aidlə*] *s* lediggænger; dovendidrik.

idol [aidl] *s* afgud, idol.

idolize ['aidəlaiz] *v* forgude, tilbede.

i.e. ['ai'i:] (fork.f. *id est)* dvs.

if [if] *konj* hvis, dersom; om; selv om; *as* ~ som om; ~ *not* hvis ikke; ellers; ~ *only* hvis bare, gid; ~ *so* i så fald.

iffy ['ifi] *adj* (F) i tvivl, usikker.

ignition [ig'niʃən] *s* antændelse; *(auto)* tænding; *turn on the* ~ slå tændingen til; **~ key** *s (auto)* startnøgle.

ignominy ['ignəmini] *s* skændsel, vanære.

ignorance ['ignərəns] *s* uvidenhed; ukendskab.

ignorant ['ignərənt] *adj* uvidende *(of* om).

ignore [ig'nɔ:*] *v* ignorere; overse; overhøre.

I'll [ail] d.s.s. *I shall; I will.*

ill [il] *adj* syg, dårlig; ond; *take (,be taken)* ~ blive syg; *be* ~ *in bed* ligge syg; *for good or* ~ på godt og ondt; ~ *will* ond vilje; *speak* ~ *of* tale ondt om; **~-advised** *adj* ubetænksom; uovervejet; **~-at-ease** *adj* ilde til mode; **~-bred** *adj* uopdragen; **~-disposed** *adj* uvenligt stemt, uvillig.

illegal [i'li:gl] *adj* ulovlig, illegal.

illegible [i'lɛdʒibl] *adj* ulæselig.

illegitimate [ili'dʒitimət] *adj* uberettiget; ulovlig; (om barn) uægte, illegitim.

ill-fated ['ilfeitid] *adj* ulyksalig; skæbnesvanger.

ill feeling ['il,fi:liŋ] *s* fjendskab; nag.

ill-gotten ['ilgɔtn] *adj* uretmæssig.

illicit [i'lisit] *adj* ulovlig.

illiterate [i'litərət] *s* analfabet // *adj* som ikke kan læse el. skrive; uvidende.

ill-mannered ['il'mænəd] *adj* uopdragen.

ill-natured ['ilneitʃəd] *adj* ondsindet; gnaven.

illness ['ilnis] *s* sygdom.
illogical [i'lɔdʒikl] *adj* ulogisk.
ill-timed ['iltaimd] *adj* malplaceret.
ill-treat [il'tri:t] *v* mishandle.
illuminate [i'lu:mineit] *v* oplyse, belyse; illuminere; **~d sign** *s* lysskilt.
illumination [ilu:mi'neiʃən] *s* belysning, illumination.
ill-use [,il'ju:z] *v* mishandle; behandle dårligt.
illusion [i'lu:ʒən] *s* illusion; indbildning; (falsk) forhåbning; *be under the ~ that...* bilde sig ind at...
illusive [i'lu:siv], **illusory** [i'lu:səri] *adj* uvirkelig; illusorisk.
illustrate ['iləstreit] *v* illustrere; belyse.
illustration [ilə'streiʃən] *s* illustration; billede; *by way of ~* som (et) eksempel.
illustrious [i'lʌstriəs] *adj* berømt; strålende.
ill-will ['ilwil] *s* ond vilje, uvenskab.
I'm [aim] d.s.s. *I am.*
image ['imidʒ] *s* billede; spejlbillede; image; *she's the spitting ~ of her mother* hun er sin mors udtrykte billede.
imagery ['imidʒri] *s* billedverden; billedsprog.
imaginary [i'mædʒinəri] *adj* indbildt, imaginær.
imagination [imædʒi'neiʃən] *s* fantasi; indbildning.
imaginative [i'mædʒinətiv] *adj* opfindsom, fantasifuld.
imagine [i'mædʒin] *v* forestille sig; tro; bilde sig ind; *I can't ~ what...* jeg kan ikke forestille mig (,begribe) hvad...; *imagine!* tænk bare!
imbecile ['imbəsi:l] *s* tåbe // *adj* dum, imbecil.
imitate ['imiteit] *v* efterligne.
imitation [imi'teiʃən] *s* efterligning, parodi, imitation; ~ **leather** *s* kunstlæder.
imitator ['imiteitə*] *s* efterligner.
immaculate [i'mækjulət] *adj* ren, uplettet; ulastelig; *(rel)* ubesmittet.
immaterial [imə'tiəriəl] *adj* uvæsentlig; ligegyldig.
immature [imə'tjuə*] *adj* umoden.
immediate [i'mi:djət] *adj* øjeblikkelig; nærmest; direkte; **~ly** *adv* straks, umiddelbart; *~ly next to* lige ved siden af.
immemorial [imi'mɔ:riəl] *adj: from time ~* i umindelige tider, fra tidernes morgen.
immense [i'mɛns] *adj* enorm, vældig.
immerse [i'mə:s] *v* dyppe (helt ned); nedsænke; *be ~d in* (også) være opslugt af; **immersion heater** *s* dypkoger.
immigrant ['imigrənt] *s* indvandrer; **immigration** [-'greiʃən] *s* indvandring.
imminent ['iminənt] *adj* nært forestående; truende, overhængende.
immobile [i'məubail] *adj* ubevægelig.
immobilize [i'məubilaiz] *v* gøre ubevægelig; stoppe, standse.
immoderate [i'mɔdərət] *adj* umådeholden; overdreven.
immodest [i'mɔdist] *adj* ubeskeden; fræk; uanstændig.
immoral [i'mɔrl] *adj* umoralsk.
immortal [i'mɔ:tl] *s/adj* udødelig; **~ize** *v* udødeliggøre.
immune [i'mju:n] *adj* immun *(to* mod); uimodtagelig *(from* for).
immunization [imjunai'zeiʃən] *s* immunisering, vaccination.
imp [imp] *s* (om barn) trold, gavstrik.
impact ['impækt] *s* stød, slag; træfning; *make an ~ on sby* gøre indtryk på en.
impair [im'pɛə*] *v* svække(s); forværre(s).
impale [im'peil] *v* spidde.
impartial [im'pa:ʃl] *adj* upartisk.
impasse [im'pa:s] *s (fig)* blindgyde.
impatience [im'peiʃəns] *s* utålmodighed; iver.
impatient [im'peiʃənt] *adj* utålmodig; *be ~ of* ikke kunne tage; *be ~ to* være utålmodig efter at.
impeach [im'pi:tʃ] *v* anklage, drage i tvivl.
impeccable [im'pɛkəbl] *adj* ulastelig; fejlfri.
impede [im'pi:d] *v* hindre; vanskeliggøre.
impediment [im'pɛdimənt] *s* hindring; gene; (også: *speech ~)* talefejl.

impel [im'pɛl] *v* tvinge; drive, tilskynde.
impending [im'pɛndiŋ] *adj* nært forestående; truende.
impenetrable [im'pɛnitrəbl] *adj* uigennemtrængelig.
imperative [im'pɛrətiv] *s (gram)* bydemåde, imperativ // *adj* bydende; påkrævet.
imperceptible [impə'sɛptibl] *adj* umærkelig; ganske lille.
imperfect [im'pə:fikt] *s (gram)* datid, imperfektum // *adj* ufuldkommen; defekt; mangelfuld.
imperfection [impə'fɛkʃən] *s* ufuldkommenhed; skavank.
imperial [im'piəriəl] *adj* kejserlig; imperie-; (om mål og vægt) britisk standard.
imperialism [im'piəriəlizm] *s* imperialisme.
imperil [im'pɛril] *v* bringe i fare.
imperious [im'piəriəs] *adj* myndig, bydende.
impermeable [im'pə:miəbl] *adj* uigennemtrængelig.
impersonal [im'pə:sənl] *adj* upersonlig.
impersonate [im'pə:səneit] *v* udgive sig for; *(teat* etc) spille, parodiere.
impersonation [impə:sə'neiʃən] *s* personifikation; parodi.
impertinence [im'pə:tinəns] *s* næsvished, uforskammethed.
impertinent [im'pə:tinənt] *adj* næsvis, uforskammet.
imperturbable [impə'tə:bəbl] *adj* uforstyrrelig; uanfægtet.
impervious [im'pə:viəs] *adj* uimodtagelig *(to* for); *~ to water* vandtæt.
impetuous [im'pɛtʃuəs] *adj* voldsom; fremfusende.
impetus ['impətəs] *s* drivkraft; *(fig)* incitament.
impinge [im'pindʒ] *v: ~ on* trænge sig ind på; ramme, støde imod.
impish ['impiʃ] *adj* drilsk.
implacable [im'plækəbl] *adj* uforsonlig.
implant [im'pla:nt] *v* indpode; implantere.
implement *s* ['implimənt] redskab // *v* [-'mɛnt] opfylde; realisere.
implicate ['implikeit] *v* indebære, implicere; **implication** [-'keiʃən] *s* indblanding; underforståelse; antydning.
implicit [im'plisit] *adj* underforstået; ubetinget.
implore [im'plɔ:*] *v* bønfalde, bede indstændigt.
imply [im'plai] *v* medføre, indebære; antyde; lade formode.
impolite [ˌimpə'lait] *adj* uhøflig.
import *s* ['impɔ:t] indførsel, import; betydning, mening // *v* [im'pɔ:t] indføre, importere; indebære, betyde.
importance [im'pɔ:təns] *s* betydning, vigtighed; *it's of no ~* det betyder ikke ngt.
important [im'pɔ:tnt] *adj* vigtig.
importation [impə'teiʃən] *s* import.
import permit ['impɔ:t 'pə:mit] *s* indførselstilladelse.
impose [im'pəuz] *v* påtvinge; *~ on sby* benytte sig af (,bedrage) en.
imposing [im'pəuziŋ] *adj* imponerende; statelig.
impossibility [impɔsə'biliti] *s* umulighed.
impossible [im'pɔsibl] *adj* umulig.
impostor [im'pɔstə*] *s* svindler, bedrager.
impotence ['impətns] *s* afmagt, svaghed; impotens.
impotent ['impətənt] *adj* kraftesløs, afmægtig; impotent.
impound [im'paund] *v* beslaglægge, konfiskere.
impoverished [im'pɔveriʃt] *adj* forarmet, ludfattig.
impracticable [im'præktikəbl] *adj* uigennemførlig; umulig; (om vej etc) ufremkommelig.
impractical [im'præktikl] *adj* upraktisk.
impregnable [im'prɛgnəbl] *adj* uindtagelig; *(fig)* uangribelig; urokkelig.
impregnate ['imprɛgneit] *v* imprægnere; præparere; gennemtrænge; befrugte.
impress [im'prɛs] *v* gøre indtryk på; trykke; (ind)præge; *~ sth on sby* indprente en ngt.
impression [im'prɛʃən] *s* indtryk; aftryk; *be under the ~ that...* tro at...; **~able** *adj* letpåvirkelig.

impressive [im'prεsiv] *adj* imponerende; slående.
imprint *s* ['imprint] aftryk; mærke, spor; stempel // *v* [im'print] trykke på; mærke; indprente; **~ed** [-'printid] *adj:* *~ed on* prentet i (fx *the memory* hukommelsen).
imprison [im'prizn] *v* fængsle; **~ment** *s* fængsling; fængsel.
improbable [im'prɔbəbl] *adj* usandsynlig.
improper [im'prɔpə*] *adj* upassende; uanstændig; urigtig.
impropriety [imprə'praiəti] *s* uanstændighed; urigtighed.
improve [im'pru:v] *v* forbedre(s); blive bedre; gøre fremskridt; *~ on* forbedre, pynte på; **~ment** *s* forbedring; fremskridt.
improvise ['imprəvaiz] *v* improvisere.
imprudence [im'pru:dns] *s* ubetænksomhed.
imprudent [im'pru:dənt] *adj* uforsigtig; uklog.
impudent ['impjudənt] *adj* uforskammet, fræk.
impulse ['impʌls] *s* impuls; tilskyndelse; skub; (instinktiv) lyst; *on an ~* impulsivt.
impulsive [im'pʌlsiv] *adj* impulsiv.
impunity [im'pju:niti] *s* straffrihed.
impure [im'pjuə*] *adj* uren.
impurity [im'pjuəriti] *s* urenhed.
in [in] *adj* inde; ved magten; på mode // *adv/præp* i; (om retning) ind; (om tid) om; på; *their party is ~* deres parti er ved magten; *~ two weeks* om to uger; *~ a second* om (,på) et sekund; *a man ~ ten* en mand ud af ti; *~ hundreds* i hundredvis; *is he ~?* er han hjemme? *he's ~ the country* han er på landet; *~ town* i byen; *~ English* på engelsk; *~ my opinion* efter min mening; *ask sby ~* invitere en indenfor; *know the ~s and outs of sth* kende ngt ud og ind; *~ that* idet, derved at; *you are ~ for it now* nu hænger du på den; *sby has got it ~ for me* der er ngn der er ude efter mig.
in., *ins.* fork.f. *inch(es).*
inability [inə'biliti] *s* manglende evne; uduelighed.
inaccessible [inək'sεsibl] *adj* utilgængelig; uopnåelig; uimodtagelig.
inaccuracy [in'ækjurəsi] *s* unøjagtighed.
inaccurate [in'ækjurit] *adj* unøjagtig.
inaction [in'ækʃən] *s* uvirksomhed.
inactive [in'æktiv] *adj* uvirksom, passiv.
inadequacy [in'ædikwəsi] *s* utilstrækkelighed.
inadequate [in'ædikwət] *adj* utilstrækkelig.
inadvertently [inəd'və:tntli] *adv* uforvarende.
inadvisable [inəd'vaizəbl] *adj* ikke tilrådelig, uklog.
inane [i'nein] *adj* åndsforladt, dum.
inanimate [in'ænimət] *adj* død, livløs.
inappropriate [inə'prəupriət] *adj* upassende.
inapt [i'næpt] *adj* klodset; upassende.
inarticulate [ina:'tikjulət] *adj* umælende; som har svært ved at udtrykke sig; uartikuleret.
inasmuch [inəz'mʌtʃ] *adv:* *~ as* for så vidt som; eftersom.
inattention [inə'tεnʃən] *s* uopmærksomhed.
inattentive [inə'tεntiv] *adj* uopmærksom.
inaudible [in'ɔ:dibl] *adj* uhørlig.
inaugural [in'ɔ:gjurəl] *s* åbningstale // *adj* åbnings-.
inaugurate [in'ɔ:gjureit] *v* åbne; indvi; indlede.
in-between ['inbi'twi:n] *adj* (ind)imellem; mellem-.
inborn ['inbɔ:n] *adj* medfødt.
inbred ['inbrεd] *adj* indavlet; medfødt.
inbreeding ['in'bri:diŋ] *s* indavl.
inbuilt ['inbilt] *adj* indbygget; medfødt.
Inc (fork.f. *incorporated)* A/S.
incalculable [in'kælkjuləbl] *adj* utallige; uoverskuelig.
incapability [inkeipə'biliti] *s* manglende evne; uduelighed.
incapable [in'keipbl] *adj* ude af stand (*of* til); uduelig.
incapacitate [inkə'pæsiteit] *v* gøre uarbejdsdygtig (,ukampdygtig).

incarnate *v* ['inka:neit] legemliggøre // *adj* [in'ka:neit] indkarneret.
incendiary [in'sɛndiəri] *s* brandbombe // *adj* brand-.
incense *s* ['insɛns] røgelse // *v* [in'sɛns] opflamme, ophidse; gøre vred.
incentive [in'sɛntiv] *s* tilskyndelse, spore.
incessant [in'sɛsnt] *adj* ustandselig, uophørlig.
incest ['insɛst] *s* blodskam.
inch [intʃ] *s* sv.t. tomme (2,5 cm); *within an ~ of* lige ved (at); *he is every ~ an actor* han er helt igennem skuespiller // *v* rykke gradvis; kante sig; **~ tape** *s* målebånd.
incidence ['insidəns] *s* forekomst; hyppighed.
incident ['insidənt] *s* hændelse; begivenhed; episode.
incidental [insi'dɛntl] *adj* tilfældig; *~ to* som følger med; *~ expenses* diverse udgifter; **~ly** *adv* for resten; tilfældigvis.
incinerator [in'sinəreitə*] *s* forbrændingsovn.
incipient [in'sipiənt] *adj* begyndende; spirende.
incision [in'siʒən] *s* indsnit.
incisive [in'saisiv] *adj* skærende; skarpsindig; træffende.
incisor [in'saizə*] *s* fortand.
incite [in'sait] *v* tilskynde; anspore.
incl fork.f. *including*.
inclination [inkli'neiʃən] *s* bøjning; hældning; tilbøjelighed.
incline *s* ['inklain] hældning, skråning // *v* [in'klain] bøje; skråne; *~ to* hælde til, have tilbøjelighed til; *be ~d to* være tilbøjelig til (at); *well ~d* venligt indstillet.
include [in'klu:d] *v* omfatte; medregne, inkludere; **including** *præp* iberegnet, inklusive.
inclusion [in'klu:ʒən] *s* medregning.
inclusive [in'klu:siv] *adj* samlet; *~ of* inklusive.
incoherent [inkəu'hiərənt] *adj* usammenhængende; uklar.
income ['inkʌm] *s* indkomst, indtægt; **~ tax** *s* indkomstskat; **~ tax return** *s* selvangivelse.
incoming ['inkʌmiŋ] *adj* ankommende (fx *trains* tog); indløbende (fx *letters* breve); *~ tide* stigende tidevand.
incomparable [in'kɔmpərəbl] *adj* uforlignelig.
incompatible [inkəm'pætibl] *adj* uforenelig.
incompetent [in'kɔmpitnt] *adj* uduelig, umulig.
incomplete [inkəm'pli:t] *adj* ufuldstændig.
incomprehensible [inkəmpri'hɛnsibl] *adj* uforståelig.
inconceivable [inkən'si:vəbl] *adj* ufattelig, ubegribelig.
inconclusive [inkən'klu:siv] *adj* ufyldestgørende; uafgjort.
incongruous [in'kɔngruəs] *adj* upassende; uoverensstemmende; urimelig.
inconsequential [inkənsi'kwɛnʃəl] *adj* ligegyldig.
inconsiderate [inkən'sidərət] *adj* ubetænksom; tankeløs.
inconsistent [inkən'sistnt] *adj* usammenhængende; ulogisk; uoverensstemmende.
inconsolable [inkən'səuləbl] *adj* utrøstelig.
inconspicius [inkən'spikju:əs] *adj* ikke særlig i øjnefaldende, ubetydelig; *make oneself ~* gøre sig lille, holde en lav profil.
inconstant [in'kɔnstnt] *adj* ustadig, foranderlig.
inconvenience [inkən'vi:niəns] *s* ulejlighed; besvær; ulempe // *v* ulejlige; forstyrre; **inconvenient** *adj* ubelejlig; upraktisk.
incorporate [in'kɔ:pəreit] *v* indlemme; indkorporere; omfatte; optage (som medlem); (om firmaer) fusionere; **~d** *adj: ~ company (Inc) (am)* aktieselskab.
incorrect [inkə'rɛkt] *adj* ukorrekt; forkert.
incorrigible [in'kɔridʒibl] *adj* uforbederlig.
incorruptible [inkə'rʌptibl] *adj* ubestikkelig.
increase *s* ['inkri:s] stigning, vækst; forøgelse; *on the ~* i tiltagen, tilta-

gende // *v* [in'kri:s] forøge(s); vokse, tiltage; **increasing** [-'kri:siŋ] *adj* voksende, tiltagende.

incredible [in'krɛdibl] *adj* utrolig.

incredulous [in'krɛdjuləs] *adj* vantro; skeptisk.

increment ['inkrimənt] *s* stigning, tilvækst; løntillæg; værdistigning.

incriminate [in'krimineit] *v* anklage; rette mistanke imod; kompromittere.

incubation [inkju'beiʃən] *s* udrugning; inkubation.

incubator ['inkjubeitə*] *s* rugemaskine; varmeskab; kuvøse.

incur [in'kə:*] *v* pådrage sig; lide.

incurable [in'kjuərəbl] *adj* uhelbredelig.

incursion [in'kə:ʃən] *s* indtrængen.

indebted [in'dɛtid] *adj* forgældet; i taknemmelighedsgæld; *be ~ to sby* være en tak skyldig.

indecent [in'di:snt] *adj* uanstændig; usømmelig; *~ exposure* blufærdighedskrænkelse.

indecision [indi'siʒən] *s* ubeslutsomhed, rådvildhed.

indecisive [indi'saisiv] *adj* svævende (fx *answer* svar); ubeslutsom.

indeed [in'di:d] *adv* virkelig; i virkeligheden; ganske vist; rigtignok; *thank you very much ~!* tusind tak! *he is rather handsome! - Yes, ~!* han er ret flot! - Ja, 'det er han! // *interj: ~!* minsandten! virkelig! *~?* nej, virkelig? såh?

indefinable [indi'fainəbl] *adj* ubestemmelig, udefinerlig.

indefinite [in'dɛfinit] *adj* ubestemt; utydelig; **~ly** *adv* i det uendelige, på ubestemt tid.

indelible [in'dɛlibl] *adj* uudslettelig; *~ ink* mærkeblæk.

indelicate [in'dɛlikət] *adj* taktløs, ufin; smagløs.

indemnity [in'dɛmniti] *s* skadeserstatning; forsikring.

indentation [indən'teiʃən] *s* indsnit, hak; *(typ)* indrykning.

independence [indi'pɛndns] *s* uafhængighed; selvstændighed.

independent [indi'pɛndənt] *adj* uafhængig; **~ly** *adv* hver for sig.

in-depth [in'dɛpθ] *adj* indgående, dybdeborende.

indescribable [indis'kraibəbl] *adj* ubeskrivelig.

indeterminable [indi'tə:minəbl] *adj* ubestemmelig.

indeterminate [indi'tə:minət] *adj* ubestemt; uvis; uklar.

index ['indɛks] *s (pl: ~es)* (i bog) register; (på bibliotek etc) kartotek, katalog; indeks; viser; **~ card** *s* kartotekskort; **~ finger** *s* pegefinger; **~-linked** *adj* pristalsreguleret; **~ regulation** *s* dyrtidsregulering.

India ['indiə] *s* Indien.

Indian ['indjən] *s* inder; indianer // *adj* indisk; indiansk; indianer-; **~ file** *s: in ~ file* i gåsegang; **~ ink** *s* tusch; *the* **~ Ocean** *s* Indiske Ocean.

indicate ['indikeit] *v* angive; betegne; vise; antyde; tyde på.

indication [indi'keiʃən] *s* angivelse; tegn.

indicative [in'dikətiv] *adj: be ~ of* tyde på, vise; være et tegn på.

indicator ['indikeitə*] *s* viser; (signal)tavle; *(auto)* blinklys.

indict [in'dait] *v* tiltale; strafforfølge; **~able** *adj* strafbar; **~ment** *s* tiltale, anklage.

indifference [in'difrəns] *s* ligegyldighed; **indifferent** *adj* ligeglad, ligegyldig; middelmådig.

indigenous [in'didʒinəs] *adj* indfødt; medfødt.

indigestible [indi'dʒɛstibl] *adj* ufordøjelig.

indigestion [indi'dʒɛstʃən] *s* fordøjelsesbesvær; dårlig mave.

indignant [in'dignənt] *adj* indigneret, forarget; **indignation** [-'neiʃən] *s* harme, forargelse.

indignity [in'digniti] *s* ydmygelse, tort.

indirect [indai'rɛkt] *adj* indirekte.

indiscreet [ˌindi'skri:t] *adj* ubetænksom; indiskret.

indiscretion [indi'skrɛʃən] *s* taktløshed, indiskretion.

indiscriminate [indi'skriminət] *adj* kritikløs; tilfældig, i flæng, planløs (fx *bombing* bombning).

indispensable [indis'pɛnsəbl] *adj* uundværlig.

indisposed [ˌindis'pəuzd] *adj* utilpas, indisponeret.
indisposition [indispə'ziʃən] *s* utilpashed.
indisputable [indis'pju:təbl] *adj* ubestridelig; uimodsigelig.
indistinct [indi'stiŋkt] *adj* utydelig; vag.
individual [indi'vidʒuəl] *s* individ, person // *adj* individuel, enkelt, særlig.
individuality [individʒu'æliti] *s* særpræg, egenart; særegenhed.
individually [indi'vidʒuəli] *adv* hver for sig, enkeltvis.
indivisible [indi'vizibəl] *adj* udelelig.
indolent ['indələnt] *adj* lad, ugidelig.
indomitable [in'dɔmitəbl] *adj* ukuelig.
indoor ['indɔ:*] *adj* indendørs-; inde- (fx *football* fodbold); stue- (fx *plant* plante).
indoors [in'dɔ:z] *adv* inde, inden døre.
indubitable [in'dju:bitəbl] *adj* utvivlsom; ubestridelig.
induce [in'dju:s] *v* formå, bevæge; forårsage; fremkalde; **~ment** *s* tilskyndelse; *(neds)* returkommission.
induction [in'dʌkʃən] *s* induktion; igangsættelse (af fødsel); indsættelse (i embede etc).
indulge [in'dʌldʒ] *v* føje; forkæle; give efter for; nyde; (F) nyde alkohol; *~ in sth* hengive sig til (,dyrke, nyde) ngt; **indulgence** *s* overbærenhed; (overdreven) nydelse; luksus; **indulgent** *adj* overbærende, svag.
industrial [in'dʌstriəl] *adj* industriel; industri-; faglig; *take ~ action* gå i strejke; **Industrial Court** *s* arbejdsret; **~ dispute** [-dis'pju:t] *s* arbejdskonflikt; **~ estate** *s* industriområde; **~ medicine** *s* arbejdsmedicin.
industrialist [in'dʌstriəlist] *s* industrimand, fabrikant.
industrious [in'dʌstriəs] *adj* flittig, arbejdsom.
industry ['indʌstri] *s* industri; erhverv; flid.
inebriated [i'ni:brieitid] *adj* beruset.
inedible [i'nεdibl] *adj* uspiselig.
ineffective [ini'fεktiv] *adj* virkningsløs; unyttig.
ineffectual [ini'fεktʃuəl] *adj* virkningsløs; uduelig.
inefficient [ini'fiʃənt] *adj* udygtig, uduelig; ineffektiv.
ineligible [in'εlidʒəbl] *adj: be ~ for sth* ikke være berettiget til ngt.
inept [i'nεpt] *adj* kluntet; ufiks.
ineptitude [in'εptitju:d] *s* kluntethed, udygtighed.
inequality [ini'kwɔliti] *s* ulighed; uregelmæssighed.
inert [i'nə:t] *adj* død, træg, inaktiv.
inertia [i'nə:ʃə] *s* træghed, sløvhed; inerti; **~-reel seat belt** *s* rullesele.
inescapable [ini'skeipəbl] *adj* uundgåelig.
inessential [ini'sεnʃl] *adj* uvæsentlig.
inestimable [in'εstiməbl] *adj* uvurderlig; umådelig.
inevitable [in'εvitəbl] *adj* uundgåelig; **inevitably** *adv* uvægerlig.
inexact [inig'zækt] *adj* upræcis.
inexusable [iniks'kju:zəbl] *adj* utilgivelig.
inexhaustible [inig'zɔ:stibl] *adj* utrættelig; uudtømmelig.
inexorable [in'εksərəbl] *adj* ubønhørlig.
inexpensive [iniks'pεnsiv] *adj* billig.
inexperienced [iniks'piəriənsd] *adj* uerfaren, uøvet.
inexpert [in'εkspə:t] *adj* ukyndig.
inexplicable [iniks'plikəbl] *adj* uforklarlig.
inextricable [iniks'trikəbl] *adj* uløselig; indviklet.
infallibility [infæli'biliti] *s* ufejlbarlighed.
infallible [in'fælibl] *adj* ufejlbarlig.
infamous ['infəməs] *adj* nederdrægtig, infam; berygtet.
infamy ['infəmi] *s* skændsel, vanære.
infancy ['infənsi] *s* barndom; mindreårighed; *be in its ~* være i begyndelsesfasen.
infant ['infənt] *s* lille barn, spædbarn; **~ food** *s* babymad.
infantile ['infəntail] *adj* barne-, børne-; barnlig.
infantry ['infəntri] *s (mil)* infanteri.
infant school ['infənt,sku:l] *s* forskole for børn under syv år; sv.omtr.t. børnehaveklasse.
infatuated [in'fætʃueitid] *adj: ~ with* forblindet af; vildt forelsket i.

infatuation [infætʃu'eiʃən] *s* forgabelse; forelskelse.
infect [in'fɛkt] *v* inficere, smitte; *(neds)* besmitte.
infection [in'fɛkʃən] *s* smitte, infektion; smitsom sygdom.
infectious [in'fɛkʃəs] *adj* smitsom; smittende.
infer [in'fə:*] *v* slutte, udlede.
inference ['infərəns] *s* (følge)slutning.
inferior [in'fiəriə*] *s* underordnet // *adj* lavere; dårlig, ringe; underordnet.
inferiority [infiəri'ɔriti] *s* lavere rang; dårligere kvalitet; ~ **complex-** [-'kɔmplɛks] *s* mindreværdskompleks.
infernal [in'fə:nl] *adj* helvedes, infernalsk.
infertile [in'fə:tail] *adj* ufrugtbar.
infested [in'fɛstid] *adj: ~ (with)* plaget (af); angrebet (af).
infidelity [infi'dɛliti] *s* utroskab; vantro.
infiltrate ['infiltreit] *v* trænge ind i, infiltrere.
infinite ['infinit] *adj* uendelig.
infinitesimal [infini'tɛsiməl] *adj* uendelig lille.
infinity [in'finiti] *s* uendelighed; det uendelige.
infirm [in'fə:m] *adj* svag(elig).
infirmary [in'fə:məri] *s* sygehus.
infirmity [in'fə:miti] *s* svagelighed; skavank.
inflame [in'fleim] *v* opflamme; blive opflammet; blive (,gøre) betændt.
inflammable [in'flæməbl] *adj* letantændelig, brandfarlig.
inflammation [inflə'meiʃən] *s* antændelse; betændelse.
inflate [in'fleit] *v* puste (,pumpe) op; udspile(s); **~d** *adj* (om fx stil) oppblæst, svulstig; overdreven.
inflation [in'fleiʃən] *s* oppustning; udspilning; inflation.
inflect [in'flɛkt] *v (gram)* bøje.
inflection [in'flɛkʃən] *s* bøjning.
inflexible [in'flɛksibl] *adj* ubøjelig; urokkelig.
inflict [in'flikt] *v: ~ on* påføre, tildele; volde.
infliction [in'flikʃən] *s* tildeling; plage; straf.
inflow ['infləu] *s* tilstrømning; tilgang.
influence ['influəns] *s* indflydelse; *under the ~ of* påvirket af // *v* have indflydelse på; påvirke.
influential [influ'ɛnʃl] *adj* inflydelsesrig.
influx ['inflʌks] *s* d.s.s. *inflow.*
info ['infəu] *s* (F) d.s.s. *information.*
inform [in'fɔ:m] *v* meddele, oplyse- *(of* om); *~ against (,on)* angive, stikke.
informal [in'fɔ:ml] *adj* uformel, tvangfri; *dress ~* daglig påklædning; *~ language* (dagligt) talesprog.
informality [infə'mæliti] *s* tvangfrihed.
information [infə'meiʃən] *s* oplysning(er); underretning; viden; *a piece of ~* en oplysning.
informative [in'fɔ:mətiv] *adj* oplysende, belærende; meddelsom.
informer [in'fɔ:mə*] *s* anmelder; angiver, stikker.
infra dig ['infrədig] *adj* under ens værdighed.
infrequent [in'fri:kwənt] *adj* sjælden; ualmindelig.
infringe [in'frindʒ] *v* overtræde, bryde (fx *the law* loven); *~ on* krænke; **~ment** *s: ~ment (of)* overtrædelse (af); krænkelse (af).
infuriate [in'fjuərieit] *v* gøre rasende; **infuriating** *adj* til at blive rasende over.
infuse [in'fju:z] *s* lave et udtræk af; indgyde; gennemtrænge.
infusion [in'fju:ʒən] *s* urtete, udtræk; tilførsel.
ingenious [in'dʒi:niəs] *adj* genial; snild.
ingenuity [indʒi'nju:iti] *s* genialitet.
ingenuous [in'dʒɛnjuəs] *adj* naiv, troskyldig.
ingot ['iŋgɔt] *s* (om metal) barre; blok.
ingrained [in'greind] *adj* indgroet; helt igennem.
ingratiate [in'greiʃieit] *v: ~ oneself with sby* (prøve at) indynde sig hos en.
ingratitude [in'grætitʃu:d] *s* utaknemmelighed.
ingredient [in'gri:diənt] *s* bestanddel, ingrediens.

ingrown ['ingrəun] *adj* indgroet; (om tånegl) nedgroet.
inhabit [in'hæbit] *v* bebo; **~able** [-əbl] *adj* beboelig.
inhabitant [in'hæbitənt] *s* beboer; indbygger.
inhale [in'heil] *v* ånde ind; indånde; inhalere.
inherent [in'hiərənt] *adj: ~ in (,to)* (uløseligt) forbundet med; rodfæstet i; iboende.
inherit [in'hɛrit] *v* arve; **~ance** *s* arv; *law of ~ance* arveret.
inhibit [in'hibit] *v* hæmme; undertrykke; forbyde; *~ sby from doing sth* forhindre en i at gøre ngt.
inhibition [inhi'biʃən] *s* hæmning.
inhospitable [in'hɔspitəbl] *adj* ugæstfri.
inhuman [in'hju:mən] *adj* umenneskelig.
inimical [i'nimikl] *adj* uvenlig; fjendtlig.
inimitable [i'nimitəbl] *adj* uforlignelig.
iniquity [i'nikwiti] *s* uhyrlighed; misdåd; synd.
initial [i'niʃl] *s* forbogstav; initial // *adj* indledende, første; begyndelses-; **~ly** *adv* i begyndelsen.
initiate [i'niʃieit] *v* indvi; indlede; påbegynde; *~ sby into a secret* indvi en i en hemmelighed.
initiative [i'niʃətiv] *s* initiativ; foretagsomhed.
inject [in'dʒɛkt] *v* indsprøjte; indgyde.
injection [in'dʒɛkʃən] *s* indsprøjtning.
injunction [in'dʒʌŋkʃən] *s (jur)* forbud; pålæg; tilhold.
injure ['indʒə*] *v* såre, skade, kvæste; beskadige.
injury ['indʒəri] *s* skade, kvæstelse; fornærmelse; **~ time** *s (fodb)* forlænget spilletid (p.g.a. skader).
injustice [in'dʒʌstis] *s* uretfærdighed; *do sby an ~* gøre en uret.
ink [iŋk] *s* blæk; *write sth in ~* skrive ngt med blæk.
inkling ['iŋkliŋ] *s* mistanke; anelse.
ink pad ['iŋkpæd] *s* stempelpude.
inkwell ['iŋkwɛl] *s* blækhus.
inlaid ['inleid] *adj* indlagt (fx træ).
inland *adj* ['inlənd] indlands-; indenrigs- // *adv* [in'lænd] ind (,inde) i landet; **Inland Revenue** [-'rɛvənju:] *s (brit)* skattevæsenet; **inland waterways** *spl* vandveje (floder, kanaler etc).
in-laws ['inlɔ:z] *spl* svigerforældre.
inlay ['inlei] *s* indlagt arbejde; indlæg.
inlet ['inlɛt] *s* stræde, vig; åbning; tilløb.
inmate ['inmeit] *s* beboer; (i fængsel) indsat.
inmost ['inməust] *adj* d.s.s. *innermost.*
inn [in] *s* kro.
innards ['inədz] *spl* indmad.
innate [i'neit] *adj* medfødt; naturlig.
inner ['inə*] *adj* indre; inder-; **~most** *adj* inderst(e); **~ tube** *s* (i dæk) slange.
innkeeper ['inki:pə*] *s* kroVært.
innocence ['inəsns] *s* uskyld(ighed).
innocent ['inəsnt] *adj* uskyldig *(of* i); troskyldig.
innocuous [i'nɔkjuəs] *adj* uskadelig.
innovation [inəu'veiʃən] *s* fornyelse.
innuendo [inju'ɛndəu] *s* hentydning, insinuation.
innumerable [i'nju:mərəbl] *adj* utallig(e).
inoculation [inɔkju'leiʃən] *s* vaccination; podning.
inoffensive [inə'fensiv] *adj* uskadelig.
inopportune [in'ɔpətju:n] *adj* ubelejlig.
inordinately [in'ɔ:dinətli] *adv* uforholdsmæssigt.
inorganic [inɔ:'gænik] *adj* uorganisk.
in-patient ['in,peiʃənt] *s* indlagt patient (mods: ambulant).
input ['input] *s* tilførsel; *(edb)* inddata.
inquest ['inkwɛst] *s* retslig undersøgelse, ligsyn.
inquire [in'kwaiə*] *v* (fore)spørge; *~ about* forhøre sig om; *~ after* spørge til (fx *the patient* den syge); *~ into* undersøge.
inquiry [in'kwaiəri] *s* forespørgsel; undersøgelse; efterforskning.
inquisitive [in'kwizitiv] *adj* videbegærlig; nysgerrig.
inroad ['inrəud] *s* indfald; overfald; indgreb; *make ~s into* gøre indhug i.
insane [in'sein] *adj* sindssyg.
insanitary [in'sænitəri] *adj* uhygiejnisk; usund.
insanity [in'sæniti] *s* sindssyge.

insatiable [in'seiʃəbl] *adj* umættelig.
inscribe [in'skraib] *v* indskrive; inskribere; (i bog) dedicere, tilegne.
inscription [in'skripʃən] *s* indskrivning; indskrift; dedikation.
inscrutable [in'skru:təbl] *adj* uudgrundelig.
insect ['insɛkt] *s* insekt.
insecticide [in'sɛktisaid] *s* insektdræbende middel.
insecure [insi'kjuə*] *adj* usikker, utryg.
insecurity [insi'kjuəriti] *s* usikkerhed.
insensible [in'sɛnsibl] *adj* følelsesløs; ufølsom; bevidstløs.
insensitive [in'sɛnsitiv] *adj* ufølsom; upåvirkelig.
inseparable [in'sɛprəbl] *adj* uadskillelig(e).
insert *s* ['insə:t] (i avis etc) tillæg; bilag // *v* [in'sə:t] indføje; indskyde; indlægge.
insertion [in'sə:ʃən] *s* indføjelse; indskud; (i avis) indrykning.
inset ['insɛt] *s* bilag; indlæg.
inshore ['in'ʃɔ:*] *adj* mod land // *adv* inde ved land; ~ **fisheries** *spl* kystfiskeri.
inside ['in'said] *s* inderside // *adj* indvendig; indenfor; inder-; ~ *ten minutes* indenfor ti minutter; *he's been* ~ (også) han har siddet inde // *præp* inde; ~ *of three weeks* inden for tre uger; *turn sth* ~ *out* vende vrangen ud af ngt; *know sth* ~ *out* kende ngt ud og ind.
insidious [in'sidiəs] *adj* lumsk.
insight ['insait] *s* indsigt; forståelse.
insignificant [insig'nifikənt] *adj* ubetydelig.
insinuate [in'sinjueit] *v* insinuere, antyde.
insinuation [insinju'eiʃən] *s* antydning.
insipid [in'sipid] *adj* (om mad) uden smag, fad; udvandet.
insist [in'sist] *v* insistere; påstå; understrege; ~ *on doing sth* absolut ville gøre ngt; ~ *that* hævde at; påstå at; holde på at.
insistence [in'sistəns] *s* insisteren; stædighed.
insistent [in'sistənt] *adj* vedholdende; ihærdig; stædig.
insofar [insəu'fa:*] *adv:* ~ *as* for så vidt som.
insolence ['insələns] *s* frækhed, uforskammethed.
insolent ['insələnt] *adj* uforskammet.
insoluble [in'sɔljubl] *adj* uopløselig; (om gåde etc) uløselig.
insomnia [in'sɔmniə] *s* søvnløshed.
inspect [in'spɛkt] *v* inspicere; efterse; kontrollere.
inspection [in'spɛkʃən] *s* eftersyn; inspektion.
inspector [in'spɛktə*] *s* inspektør; kontrollør; *police* ~ politiassistent.
inspiration [inspi'reiʃən] *s* inspiration.
inspire [in'spaiə*] *v* inspirere; indgyde; ånde ind; **inspiring** *adj* inspirerende.
install [in'stɔ:l] *v* indsætte; installere, indlægge (fx *gas* gas).
installation [instə'leiʃən] *s* indsættelse; installering.
instalment [in'stɔ:lmənt] *s* afdrag; rate; (om tv-serie) afsnit.
instance ['instəns] *s* eksempel; instans; *for* ~ for eksempel; *in many* ~*s* i mange tilfælde.
instant ['instənt] *s* øjeblik // *adj* øjeblikkelig; *(gastr)* pulver- (fx *coffee* kaffe); ~ *food* færdigret(ter); ~ *potatoes* kartoffelmospulver; *the tenth* ~ den tiende dennes.
instantaneous [instən'teiniəs] *adj* øjeblikkelig.
instantly ['instəntli] *adv* øjeblikkelig, straks.
instead [in'stɛd] *adv* i stedet; ~ *of* i stedet for.
instep ['instɛp] *s* vrist.
instigate ['instigeit] *v* anstifte; tilskynde; sætte i gang.
instil [in'stil] *v:* ~ *(into)* indpode, indgyde; vække.
instinct ['instiŋkt] *s* instinkt; *do sth by* ~ gøre ngt pr. instinkt.
instinctive [in'stiŋktiv] *adj* instinktiv.
institute ['institju:t] *s* institut // *v* indføre, indstifte; iværksætte (fx *an enquiry* en undersøgelse).
institution [insti'tju:ʃən] *s* institution; indførelse; iværksættelse.

instruct [in'strʌkt] *v* instruere, undervise; informere.
instruction [in'strʌkʃən] *s* undervisning; vejledning; *~s for use* brugsanvisning.
instructor [in'strʌktə*] *s* lærer, instruktør.
instrument ['instrumənt] *s* instrument; redskab; **~ panel** *s* instrumentbræt.
insubordinate [insʌb'ɔ:dinit] *adj* ulydig; **insubordination** [-'neiʃən] *s* ulydighed.
insufferable [in'sʌfrəbl] *adj* ulidelig; uudholdelig.
insufficient [insʌ'fiʃənt] *adj* utilstrækkelig.
insular ['insjulə*] *adj* ø-, øbo-; (om person) som er sig selv nok.
insulate ['insjuleit] *v* isolere; **insulating tape** *s* isolerbånd.
insulation [insju'leiʃən] *s* isolation.
insult *s* ['insʌlt] fornærmelse // *v* [in'sʌlt] fornærme, krænke; **~ing** [-'sʌltiŋ] *adj* fornærmelig.
insuperable [in'su:prəbl] *adj* uovervindelig.
insupportable [insə'pɔ:təbl] *adj* uudholdelig.
insurance [in'sjuərəns] *s* forsikring; **~ broker** *s* forsikringsagent; **~ policy** *s* forsikringspolice.
insure [in'sjuə*] *v* forsikre; (NB! se også *ensure).*
insurrection [insə'rɛkʃən] *s* opstand, oprør.
intact [in'tækt] *adj* uskadt, hel, intakt.
intake ['inteik] *s* tilførsel; indånding; indtagelse (fx *of food* af mad).
intangible [in'tændʒibl] *adj* uhåndgribelig; ubestemt; immateriel.
integral ['intigrəl] *adj* integral-; nødvendig; komplet.
integrate ['intigreit] *v* integrere; indordne (sig).
integrity [in'tɛgriti] *s* hæderlighed; integritet.
intellect ['intəlɛkt] *s* forstand; intelligens; **intellectual** [-'lɛktjuəl] *adj* intellektuel.
intelligence [in'tɛlidʒəns] *s* intelligens; underretning; efterretning; **~ service** *s* efterretningsvæsen.
intelligent [in'tɛlidʒənt] *adj* intelligent.
intelligible [in'tɛlidʒibl] *adj* tydelig, forståelig.
intend [in'tɛnd] *v* have i sinde, agte (*to* at); *be ~ed for* være beregnet til (,på); **~ed** *adj* tilsigtet; planlagt.
intense [in'tɛns] *adj* intens; stærk; (om person) lidenskabelig; sammenbidt.
intensify [in'tɛnsifai] *v* intensivere; forstærke.
intensity [in'tɛnsiti] *s* styrke; intensitet.
intensive [in'tɛnsiv] *adj* intensiv, stærk; **~ care (unit)** *s* (på sygehus) intensivafdeling.
intent [in'tɛnt] *s* hensigt; *to all ~s and purposes* praktisk talt; i alt væsentligt; *with ~ to* i den hensigt at // *adj* anspændt; *~ on* stærkt opsat på; fordybet i.
intention [in'tɛnʃən] *s* hensigt; mening; **~al** *adj* forsætlig; tilsigtet.
inter [in'tə:*] *v* (H) begrave.
interact [intər'ækt] *v* påvirke hinanden.
interaction [intər'ækʃən] *s* vekselvirkning.
intercede [intə'si:d] *v* gå i forbøn.
intercept [intə'sɛpt] *v* opsnappe; opfange; afskære, spærre (vejen) for.
interchange *s* ['intətʃeindʒ] udveksling; (motorvejs)udfletning // *v* [intə'tʃeindʒ] udveksle; ombytte; **~able** *adj* udskiftelig.
intercom ['intəkɔm] *s* samtaleanlæg.
interconnect [intəkə'nɛkt] *v* (om fx værelser) stå i forbindelse med hinanden.
intercourse ['intəkɔ:s] *s* samkvem; forbindelse; *sexual ~* samleje.
interest ['intrist] *s* interesse; *(økon)* rente(r); *take an ~ in* interessere sig for; *repay with ~* betale tilbage med renter // *v* interessere; *be ~ed in* være interesseret i; *I'd be ~ed to see...* det ville være interessant at se...; **~-free** *adj* rentefri; **~ing** *adj* interessant.
interface ['intəfeis] *s* berøringsflade; interface.
interfere [intə'fiə*] *v: ~ in* blande sig

i; ~ *with* forstyrre; gribe ind i; pille ved.
interference [intə'fiərəns] *s* indblanding; forstyrrelse.
interim ['intərim] *s: in the* ~ i mellemtiden // *adj* foreløbig, konstitueret.
interior [in'tiəriə*] *s* indre; interiør // *adj* indre; indenrigs-; ~ **decorator** *s* indretningsarkitekt.
interjection [intə'dʒɛkʃən] *s* udråb(sord), interjektion.
interlaced ['intəleist] *adj* (sammen)flettet.
interlock [intə'lɔk] *v* gribe ind i hinanden; sammenkoble(s).
interlude ['intəlu:d] *s* mellemspil; *(teat)* mellemakt.
intermediary [intə'mi:diəri] *s* mellemmand; formidler.
intermediate [intə'mi:djət] *adj* mellemliggende, mellem-.
interminable [in'tə:minəbl] *adj* uendelig, endeløs.
intermingle [intə'miŋgl] *v* blande (sig) med hinanden.
intermission [intə'miʃən] *s* afbrydelse; pause, mellemakt.
intermittent [intə'mitənt] *adj* periodisk, som kommer og går; **~ly** *adv* med mellemrum, ind imellem.
intern *s* ['intə:n] *(am)* yngre reservelæge; turnuskandidat // *v* [in'tə:n] internere; *(am)* gøre turnustjeneste.
internal [in'tə:nl] *adj* indre, intern; *not to be taken ~ly* kun til udvortes brug.
international [intə'næʃənl] *s (sport)* landskamp // *adj* international.
internment [in'tə:nmənt] *s* internering.
interplay ['intəplei] *s* samspil.
interpose [intə'pəuz] *v* indskyde; sætte imellem.
interpret [in'tə:prit] *v* (for)tolke; tyde.
interpretation [intə:pri'teiʃən] *s* (for)tolkning.
interpreter [in'tə:pritə*] *s* tolk.
interpreting [in'tə:pritiŋ] *s* tolkning.
interrelated [intəri'leitid] *adj* indbyrdes beslægtet.
interrogate [in'tɛrəugeit] *v* udspørge; forhøre; spørge.
interrogation [intɛrəu'geiʃən] *s* forhør; ~ **mark** *s* spørgsmålstegn.
interrogative [intɛ'rɔgətiv] *adj* spørgende, spørge-.
interrogator [in'tɛrəgeitə*] *s* forhørsleder.
interrupt [intə'rʌpt] *v* afbryde.
interruption [intə'rʌpʃən] *s* afbrydelse.
intersect [intə'sɛkt] *v* (gennem)skære; (om fx veje) skære hinanden.
intersection [intə'sɛkʃən] *s* gennemskæring; vejkryds.
interspersed [intə'spə:sd] *adj: ~ with sth* med ngt ind imellem; spækket med ngt.
intertwine [intə'twain] *v* slynge (,flette) (sig) sammen.
interval ['intəvəl] *s* pause; mellemrum; frikvarter; *(sport)* halvleg; *at ~s* med mellemrum; til tider; *bright ~s* (i vejrudsigt) til tider opklaring.
intervene [intə'vi:n] *v* skride ind; komme imellem; **intervening** *adj* mellemliggende.
intervention [intə'vɛnʃən] *s* indgriben; intervention.
interview ['intəvju:] *s* interview // *v* interviewe.
intestate [in'tɛsteit] *adj: die ~* dø uden at have lavet testamente.
intestine [in'tɛstin] *s* tarm; *large ~* tyktarm; *small ~* tyndtarm; **~s** *spl* indvolde.
intimacy ['intiməsi] *s* intimitet; fortrolighed.
intimate *v* ['intimeit] tilkendegive; antyde; meddele // *adj* ['intimət] intim, nær.
intimation [inti'meiʃən] *s* tilkendegivelse; antydning.
intimidate [in'timideit] *v* skræmme.
into ['intu, 'intə] *præp* ind i; ned (,op) i; ud i; til; *translate sth ~ English* oversætte ngt til engelsk; *far ~ the night* (til) langt ud på natten; *turn ~* blive til; lave om til; *he's ~ computers* (F) han er interesseret i computere; han arbejder i computerbranchen.
intolerable [in'tɔlərəbl] *adj* utålelig, uudholdelig.
intolerant [in'tɔlərənt] *adj* intolerant.

intoxicate [in'tɔksikeit] *v* beruse; **~d** *adj* beruset.

intractable [in'træktəbl] *adj* uregerlig, umedgørlig, genstridig.

intransigent [in'trænsidʒənt] *adj* ubøjelig, stejl.

intra-uterine [intrə'ju:tərain] *adj* i livmoderen; **~ device** *(IUD) s* spiral.

intrepid [in'trɛpid] *adj* dristig.

intricacy ['intrikəsi] *s* indviklethed; *intricacies* forviklinger.

intricate ['intrikət] *adj* indviklet, kompliceret.

intrigue [in'tri:g] *s* intrige(r); (i bog) handling // *v* intrigere; optage, fængsle; *be ~d with* være fascineret af; **intriguing** *adj* spændende.

intrinsic [in'trinsik] *adj* egentlig; iboende; indre.

introduce [intrə'dju:s] *v* indføre; indlede; præsentere; *~ oneself* præsentere sig; *~ sby to sth* gøre en bekendt med ngt.

introduction [intrə'dʌkʃən] *s* introduktion; indledning.

introductory [intrə'dʌktəri] *adj* indledende.

introspective [intrə'spɛktiv] *adj* indadvendt.

introvert ['intrəvə:t] *adj* indadvendt.

intrude [in'tru:d] *v: ~ (on)* trænge sig på; forstyrre.

intruder [in'tru:də*] *s* ubuden gæst.

intrusion [in'tru:ʒən] *s* indtrængen; forstyrrelse.

intuit [in'tju:it] *v* opfatte intuitivt.

intuition [intju:'iʃən] *s* intuition.

intuitive [in'tju:itiv] *adj* intuitiv.

inundate ['inʌndeit] *v* oversvømme, drukne.

invade [in'veid] *v* trænge ind i, invadere.

invader [in'veidə*] *s* indtrængende person (,fjende).

invalid *s* ['invəlid] kronisk syg person; invalid // *adj* ['invəlid] invalid; [in'vælid] ugyldig; **~ chair** ['in-] *s* kørestol.

invalidate [in'vælideit] *v* invalidere; annullere, gøre ugyldig; modbevise.

invaluable [in'væljuəbl] *adj* uvurderlig.

invariable [in'vɛəriəbl] *adj* uforanderlig.

invariably [in'vɛəriəbli] *adv* konstant; uvægerlig.

invective [in'vɛktiv] *s* skældsord.

invent [in'vɛnt] *v* opfinde; finde på.

invention [in'vɛnʃən] *s* opfindelse; opfindsomhed; løgnehistorie.

inventive [in'vɛntiv] *adj* opfindsom.

inventor [in'vɛntə*] *s* opfinder.

inventory ['invəntri] *s* lagerliste.

inverse [in'və:s] *adj* omvendt.

invert [in'və:t] *v* vende om på; spejlvende; *~ed commas* anførselstegn, gåseøjne; *~ed snobbery* snobben nedad.

invest [in'vɛst] *v* investere; anbringe; udstyre; indhylle; belejre.

investigate [in'vɛstigeit] *v* undersøge; efterforske.

investigation [invɛsti'geiʃən] *s* undersøgelse; efterforskning.

investment [in'vɛstmənt] *s* investering; indeslutning.

investor [in'vɛstə*] *s* investor; aktionær.

inveterate [in'vɛtərət] *adj* uforbederig; indgroet.

invigorating [in'vigəreitiŋ] *adj* styrkende, forfriskende.

invincible [in'vinsibl] *adj* uovervindelig.

inviolable [in'vaiələbl] *adj* ukrænkelig.

invisible [in'vizibl] *adj* usynlig.

invite [in'vait] *v* invitere; bede om; opfordre til; *~ offers* indhente tilbud; **inviting** *adj* indbydende; fristende.

invoice ['invɔis] *s* faktura // *v* fakturere.

invoke [in'vəuk] *v* påkalde; påberåbe sig; tilkalde.

involuntary [in'vɔləntri] *adj* ufrivillig; uvilkårlig.

involve [in'vɔlv] *v* inddrage; indebære; medføre; *~ sby in sth* blande en ind i ngt; **~d** *adj* indblandet, impliceret; *be ~d with* have et forhold til; **~ment** *s* indblanding; engagement.

invulnerable [in'vʌlnərəbl] *adj* usårlig.

inward ['inwəd] *adj* indre; indvendig; indadgående; **~ly** *adv* i sit stille sind.

inward(s) ['inwədz] *adv* indad.
iodine ['aiəudi:n] *s* jod.
IOU ['aiəu'ju:] *s* (fork.f. *I owe you)* gældsbrev.
IQ ['ai'kju:] *s* (fork.f. *intelligence quotient)* intelligenskvotient (IK).
IRA ['ai'a:'ei] *s* (fork.f. *Irish Republican Army)* den irske revolutionshær (IRA).
Iran [i'ra:n] *s* Iran; **Iranian** [i'reiniən] *s* iraner // *adj* iransk.
Iraq [i'ra:k] *s* Irak; **Iraqi** [i'ra:ki] *s* iraker // *adj* irakisk.
irascible [i'ræsibl] *adj* hidsig, arrig.
irate [ai'reit] *adj* harmdirrende, rasende.
Ireland ['aiələnd] *s* Irland.
iridescent [iri'dɛsnt] *adj* changerende, som spiller i alle regnbuens farver.
Irish ['airiʃ] *s: the ~* irerne // *adj* irsk.
irk [ə:k] *v* ærgre, krepere.
iron ['aiən] *s* jern; strygejern; *rule with a rod of ~* styre med jernhånd; *strike while the ~ is hot* smede mens jernet er varmt // *v* stryge; *~ out* udglatte; bringe ud af verden // *adj* jern-; **~ age** *s* jernalder; *the* **~ curtain** *s* jerntæppet.
ironic(al) [ai'rɔnik(l)] *adj* ironisk.
ironing ['aiəniŋ] *s* strygning; strygetøj; **~ board** *s* strygebræt.
iron... ['aiən-] sms: **~monger** *s* isenkræmmer; **~ ore** *s* jernmalm; **~work** *s* jernbeslag; jern; **~works** *s: an ~works* et jernværk.
irony ['airəni] *s* ironi.
irradiate [i'reidieit] *v* udstråle; bestråle.
irradiation [ireidi'eiʃən] *s* stråling; bestråling; udstråling; *~ therapy* strålebehandling.
irrational [i'ræʃənl] *adj* ufornuftig; ulogisk.
irredeemably [iri'di:məbli] *adv: ~ lost* uigenkaldeligt fortabt.
irregular [i'rɛgjulə*] *adj* uregelmæssig; ureglementeret.
irregularity [irɛgju'læriti] *s* uregelmæssighed; ukorrekthed.
irrelevance [i'rɛləvəns] *s* ngt sagen uvedkommende; **irrelevant** *adj* uvedkommende, irrelevant.
irreparable [i'rɛprəbl] *adj* uoprettelig.
irreplaceable [iri'pleisəbl] *adj* uerstattelig.
irrepressible [iri'prɛsibl] *adj* ukuelig, optimistisk.
irreproachable [iri'prəutʃəbl] *adj* uangribelig; upåklagelig.
irresistible [iri'zistibl] *adj* uimodståelig.
irresolute [i'rɛzəlu:t] *adj* ubeslutsom; vaklende.
irrespective [iri'spɛktiv] *adj: ~ of* uden hensyn til, uanset.
irresponsible [iri'spɔnsibl] *adj* uansvarlig; ansvarsløs.
irretrievable [iri'tri:vəbl] *adj* uoprettelig; uigenkaldelig.
irreverent [i'rɛvərənt] *adj* uærbødig, respektløs.
irreversible [iri'və:sibəl] *adj* uigenkaldelig.
irrigate ['irigeit] *v* vande, overrisle; **irrigation** [-'geiʃən] *s* overrisling, kunstig vanding.
irritable ['iritəbl] *adj* irritabel.
irritate ['iriteit] *v* irritere.
is [iz] 3. person ental af *be*.
island ['ailənd] *s* ø; (også: *traffic ~)* helle; **~er** *s* øbo.
isle [ail] *s* ø (fx *the British Isles*); **islet** ['ailit] *s* lille ø.
isn't [iznt] d.s.s. *is not*.
isolate ['aisəleit] *v* isolere, afskære fra omverdenen; **~d** *adj* afsides; isoleret; enkeltstående.
isolation [aisə'leiʃən] *s* isolation.
Israel ['izreil] *s* Israel.
Israeli [iz'reili] *s* israeler // *adj* israelsk.
issue ['isju:] *s* udstedelse; (om blad etc) udgave, nummer; (strids)spørgsmål; resultat, udfald; afkom; *be at ~* være under debat; *evade the ~* vige uden om sprøgsmålet (,problemet); *make an ~ of sth* gøre et stort nummer ud af ngt; *take ~ with sth* tage afstand fra ngt // *v* udsende; fordele; udstede; udgive.
isthmus ['isməs] *s* landtange.
it [it] *s/pron* den, det; *it's raining* det regner; *that's ~* det er rigtigt; der har vi det; *run for ~* stikke af; *have a good time of ~* more sig godt.
Italian [i'tæljən] *s* italiener // *adj* italiensk.
italics [i'tæliks] *spl* kursiv.
Italy ['itəli] *s* Italien.

itch [itʃ] *s* kløe; voldsom trang *(for* til) // *v* klø; *be ~ing to* brænde efter at; *have an ~ing palm* være gerrig; **~y** *adj* kløende, kradsende.
it'd [itd] d.s.s. *it had; it would.*
item ['aitəm] *s* punkt; nummer; (også: *news ~)* nyhed(sartikel).
itemize ['aitəmaiz] *v* specificere.
itinerant [i'tinərənt] *adj* omrejsende.
itinerary [ai'tinərəri] *s* rejseplan, rejserute.
it'll [itl] d.s.s. *it shall; it will.*
its [its] (genitiv af *it)* dens, dets; sin, sit, sine.
it's [its] d.s.s. *it has; it is.*
itself [it'sɛlf] *pron* selv, selve; sig; *by ~* alene, af sig selv; *in ~* i sig selv; *not in the house ~* ikke i selve huset; *he's kindness ~* han er lutter venlighed.
itsy-bitsy [itsi'bitsi] *adj* kælen, puttenuttet (fx *voice* stemme).
IUD *s* (fork.f. *intra-uterine device)* spiral.
I've [aiv] d.s.s. *I have.*
ivory ['aivəri] *s* elfenben; *ivories* (F) tangenter (på klaver).
ivy ['aivi] *s* vedbend, efeu.

J

J, j [dʒei].
jab [dʒæb] *s* stik; stød; indsprøjtning, sprøjte // *v* stikke; støde.
jabber ['dʒæbə*] *s* plapren // *v* plapre.
jack [dʒæk] *s* donkraft; (i kortspil) knægt // *v: ~ it in* holde op, droppe det; *~ up* løfte (med donkraft).
jackal ['dʒækəl] *s* sjakal; håndlanger.
jackass ['dʒækæs] *s* hanæsel; *(fig)* fæ, fjols.
jackdaw ['dʒækdɔ:] *s* allike.
jacket ['dʒækit] *s* jakke; trøje; *(tekn)* kappe; (om bog) omslag; *potatoes in their ~s* kartofler med skræl på.
jackknife ['dʒæknaif] *s* foldekniv; lommekniv // *v: the lorry ~d* (om lastvogn) anhængeren kom på tværs.
jack-of-all-trades ['dʒækəv,ɔ:ltreidz] *s* tusindkunstner.
Jacobean [dʒækə'bi:ən] *adj* fra James 1s tid (1603-42).
Jacuzzi ® [dʒə'ku:zi] *s* boblebad.
jade [dʒeid] *s* jade; krikke, tøs; **~d** *adj* udkørt, træt.
jag [dʒæg] *s* tak, spids; **~ged** ['dʒægid] *adj* hakket, takket, forreven.
jail [dʒeil] *s* fængsel; **~bird** *s* fange; vaneforbryder; **~break** [-breik] *s* fangeflugt.
jailer ['dʒeilə*] *s* fangevogter.
jam [dʒæm] *s* syltetøj; vrimmel; (også: *traffic ~)* trafikprop; *be in a ~* være i knibe // *v* blokere; sidde fast, binde; mase, proppe; blive blokeret; *the door ~med* døren bandt; *~ things into a bag* proppe ting ned i en taske; *~ on the brakes* hugge bremserne i; *~ up* blive blokeret.
jangle [dʒæŋgl] *v* rasle (med), klirre (med).
janitor ['dʒænitə*] *s* portner, vicevært; (i skole) pedel.
January ['dʒænjuəri] *s* januar.
Japan [dʒə'pæn] *s* Japan;
Japanese [dʒæpə'ni:z] *s* japaner // *adj* japansk.
jar [dʒa:*] *s* krukke; glas; ryk, stød; chok; (om lyd) skurren; *on the ~* på klem // *v* skurre; ryste, chokere; (om farver) skrige.
jaundice ['dʒɔ:ndis] *s* gulsot; **~d** *adj* misundelig; misbilligende.
jaunt [dʒɔ:nt] *s* udflugt, lille tur; **~y** *adj* kæk, kry, flot.
javelin ['dʒævlin] *s* kastespyd; **~-throwing** *s (sport)* spydkast.
jaw [dʒɔ:] *s* kæbe; hage; snak, sludder; moralpræken; *his ~ fell* han blev lang i ansigtet // *v* sludre; kæfte op.
jay [dʒei] *s (zo)* skovskade; **~walker** *s* fumlegænger.
jazz [dʒæz] *s* jazz; (F) fut; sludder // *v: ~ up* (F) sætte fut i; **~y** *adj* (F) kvik; (over)smart; (om tøj) spraglet.
jct fork.f. *junction.*
jealous ['dʒɛləs] *adj* misundelig, jaloux; **jealousy** *s* misundelse, jalousi.
jeans [dʒi:ns] *spl* cowboybukser.
jeer [dʒiə*] *v: ~ (at)* håne, spotte; **~s** *spl* hånlige tilråb.
jellied ['dʒɛlid] *adj* i gelé.
jelly ['dʒɛli] *s* gelé, sky; **~baby** *s* sv.t.

vingummibamse; **~fish** *s* vandmand.

jeopardize ['dʒɛpədaiz] *v* sætte på spil.

jeopardy ['dʒɛpədi] *s* fare.

jerk [dʒə:k] *s* ryk, sæt; (om person) skid // *v* rykke; spjætte; ~ *to a stop* standse med et ryk; **~y** *adj* rykvis, stødvis.

jerry-building ['dʒɛribildiŋ] *s* byggesjusk; spekulationsbyggeri.

jerry-can ['dʒɛrikæn] *s* benzindunk.

jersey ['dʒə:zi] *s* jersey(stof); trøje; jumper.

jest [dʒɛst] *s* spøg, morsomhed // *v* spøge; **~er** *s* spøgefugl; *(hist)* hofnar.

jet [dʒɛt] *s* stråle, sprøjt; jetfly // *v* flyve (med jetfly); **~-black** *adj* kulsort; **~ engine** *s* jetmotor; **~ fighter** *s* jetjager; **~lag** *s* ubehag p.g.a. rejse med jetfly gennem flere tidszoner.

jetsam ['dʒɛtsəm] *s* strandingsgods, vraggods.

jettison ['dʒɛtisn] *v* kaste over bord (også *fig*); tilintetgøre.

jetty ['dʒɛti] *s* mole, anløbsbro.

Jew [dju:] *s* jøde.

jewel ['dʒu:əl] *s* juvel, ædelsten.

jeweller ['dʒu:ələ*] *s* juvelér; **~'s (shop)** *s* guldsmedebutik.

jewellery ['dʒu:əlri] *s* smykker.

Jewess ['dʒu:is] *s* jødisk kvinde.

Jewish ['dʒu:iʃ] *adj* jødisk.

jibe [dʒaib] *s* spydighed, hib // *v* håne, gøre nar af.

jiffy ['dʒifi] *s: in a* ~ (F) på (,om) et øjeblik; **Jiffy Bag**® *s* foret kuvert.

jig [dʒig] *v* danse; hoppe; vippe.

jiggle [dʒigl] *v* dingle med; vippe (med).

jigsaw ['dʒigsɔ:] *s:* ~ *(puzzle)* puslespil.

jilt [dʒilt] *v* give løbepas.

jingle [dʒiŋgl] *s* klirren, ringlen; reklameslogan (på vers) // *v* klirre (med), rasle (med).

jinx [dʒiŋks] *s* (F) ulykke(sfugl).

jitters ['dʒitəz] *spl: get the* ~ (F) blive helt ude af det, blive nervøs.

job [dʒɔb] *s* arbejde; stilling; affære; (S) bræk, kup; tingest; *give sth up as a bad* ~ opgive ngt som håbløst; *it's a good* ~ *we came* det var heldigt vi kom; *it's just the* ~ det er lige sagen; *it's fine as long as it does the* ~ det er fint, bare det virker; **~ber** *s* akkordarbejder; børsspekulant; **~centre** *s* arbejdsformidling; **~less** *adj* arbejdsløs; **~ lot** *s* parti billige varer; **~ sharing** *s* arbejdsdeling.

jockey ['dʒɔki] *s* jockey; svindler // *v* manipulere.

jockstrap ['dʒɔkstræp] *s (sport* etc) skridtbind.

jocular ['dʒɔkjulə*] *adj* jovial; munter; humoristisk.

jodphurs ['dʒɔdpəz] *spl* ridebukser.

jog [dʒɔg] *s* skub, puf; trav // *v* skubbe (til); jogge; ~ *along* lunte, skumple; ~ *sby's memory* friske op på ens hukommelse.

join [dʒɔin] *s* sammenføjning // *v* forbinde (sig med); sammenføje; slutte sig til; melde sig ind i; *will you* ~ *me for dinner?* skal vi spise middag sammen? ~ *in* tage del i; stemme i (med); ~ *up* gå med; melde sig som soldat.

joiner ['dʒɔinə*] *s* snedker; **~y** *s* snedkeri.

joint [dʒɔint] *s* sammenføjning; *(anat)* led; *(gastr)* steg; (F) bule, biks; (S) hash-cigaret; *out of* ~ af led; af lave // *adj* fælles; forenet; *by* ~ *efforts* ved fælles anstrengelser; **~ed** *adj* (om fjerkræ) parteret; **~ly** *adv* i fællesskab; **~ owner** *s* medindehaver; **~ venture** *s* konsortium.

joist [dʒɔist] *s* tværbjælke.

joke [dʒəuk] *s* spøg, vittighed; *the* ~ *is on you* det er dig der er til grin // *v* spøge; drille; *you must be joking!* det er ikke sandt! det må være din spøg!

joker ['dʒəukə*] *s* spøgefugl; joker; fyr.

joking ['dʒəukiŋ] *s* spøg; ~ *apart* spøg til side.

jollity ['dʒɔliti] *s* lystighed; festlighed.

jolly ['dʒɔli] *adj* lystig, munter; gemytlig // *adv* mægtigt, enormt (fx ~ *hungry* sulten); *you'll* ~ *well have*

to det bliver du knageme nødt til.
jolt [dʒəult] *s* stød, bump; chok // *v* støde; ryste; give et chok; ~ *sby's memory* friske ens hukommelse op.
josh [dʒɔʃ] *s* (små)drille.
joss stick ['dʒɔsstik] *s* røgelsespind.
jostle ['dʒɔsl] *v* skubbe (til); mase.
jot [dʒɔt] *s* tøddel // *v:* ~ *down* kradse ned, notere; **~ter** *s* notesbog (,-blok).
journal ['dʒə:nl] *s* (dag)blad; tidsskrift; dagbog; **~ism** *s* journalistik.
journey ['dʒə:ni] *s* rejse (især til lands) // *v* rejse; **~man** *s* (håndværks)svend.
Jove [dʒəuv] *s* Jupiter; *by ~!* du store! for pokker!
jovial ['dʒəuviəl] *adj* munter, gemytlig, jovial.
jowl [dʒaul] *s* (under)kæbe; kind; *cheek by ~* side om side.
joy [dʒɔi] *s* glæde; lykke; *I wish you ~ of it! (iron)* god fornøjelse! **~ful, ~ous** *adj* glad, lykkelig; **~ride** *s* fornøjelsestur (oftest i stjålen bil og med stor fart).
jubilant ['dʒu:bilənt] *adj* jublende; triumferende.
jubilation [dʒu:bi'leiʃən] *s* jubel, fest.
jubilee ['dʒu:bili:] *s* jubilæum.
judge [dʒʌdʒ] *s* dommer; kender; *I'll be the ~ of that* det skal jeg nok selv afgøre // *v* dømme; skønne; anse for; ~ *by (,from)* dømme efter; *judging from...* at dømme efter...
judg(e)ment ['dʒʌdʒmənt] *s* dom; dømmekraft; mening, skøn; *an error of ~* en fejlbedømning, et fejlskøn; **~ day** *s* dommedag.
judicial [dʒu:'diʃl] *adj* dommer-; retslig; upartisk; justits-.
judicious [dʒu:'diʃəs] *adj* klog; velovervejet.
jug [dʒʌg] *s* kande.
juggernaut ['dʒʌgənɔ:t] *s* (om lastbil) mastodont.
juggle [dʒʌgl] *v* jonglere; manipulere med; **~r** *s* jonglør; svindler.
juice [dʒu:s] *s* saft; (F) benzin; *(elek)* strøm.
juicy ['dʒu:si] *adj* saftig (også *fig*).
July [dʒu:'lai] *s* juli.
jumble ['dʒʌmbl] *s* virvar, rod // *v:* ~ *(up)* rode sammen; **~ sale** *s* loppemarked.
jump [dʒʌmp] *s* spring, hop; sæt // *v* springe, hoppe; give et sæt; ryge i vejret; *he ~ed at the offer* han tog straks mod tilbudet; ~ *the lights* køre over for rødt; ~ *the queue* springe over i køen; ~ *sby* overfalde en; **~ed-up** *adj* højrøvet.
jumpy ['dʒʌmpi] *adj* nervøs, urolig.
junction ['dʒʌnkʃən] *s* forbindelse, knudepunkt.
juncture ['dʒʌnktʃə*] *s: at this ~* på dette tidspunkt; i dette kritiske øjeblik.
June [dʒu:n] *s* juni.
jungle [dʒʌngl] *s* jungle; vildnis.
junior ['dʒu:niə*] *s* junior // *adj* yngre; junior-; *he's ~ to me by two years, he's my ~ by two years* han er to år yngre end jeg; *he's ~ to me* (også) han har lavere anciennitet end jeg; **~ aspirin** *s* sv.t. børnemagnyl; **~ school** *s* sv.t. folkeskolens mellemtrin.
juniper ['dʒu:nipə*] *s* enebærtræ (,-busk); **~ berry** *s* enebær.
junk [dʒʌŋk] *s* skrammel; *(mar)* junke; (S) heroin.
junket ['dʒʌŋkit] *s* tykmælk; offentlige personers "studierejse" for statens midler.
junkfood ['dʒʌŋkfu:d] *s* usund færdigmad og snacks, tomme kalorier; **junk mail** *s* uønsket post (reklametryksager etc), adresseløse forsendelser; **junkshop** *s* marskandiserbutik.
jurisdiction [dʒuəris'dikʃən] *s* embedsområde; retskreds.
jurisprudence [dʒuəris'pru:dəns] *s* retsvidenskab.
juror ['dʒuərə*] *s* nævning.
jury *s* nævninge, jury.
just [dʒʌst] *adj* retfærdig; rigtig // *adv* lige, kun, bare, netop; *he has ~ left* han er lige gået; ~ *as he was leaving* lige da han var ved at gå; ~ *as I expected* lige som jeg havde ventet; *it's ~ as well!* det er godt det samme; ~ *right* præcis rigtig; ~

about right næsten rigtig; *it's ~ me* det er bare mig; *I ~ caught the bus* jeg nåede lige netop bussen; *~ then* netop da, i samme øjeblik; *I saw him ~ now* jeg har lige set ham; *~ listen to this!* hør nu bare her!
justice ['dʒʌstis] *s* retfærdighed; dommer; *be brought to ~* få sin straf; *do sby ~* yde en retfærdighed; vide at sætte pris på en; *Lord Chief Justice* sv.t. højesteretspræsident; **Justice of the Peace** *s* fredsdommer.
justifiable [ˌdʒʌsti'faiəbl] *adj* forsvarlig.
justification [dʒʌstifi'keiʃən] *s* retfærdiggørelse; undskyldning.
justify ['dʒʌstifai] *v* retfærdiggøre; undskylde; berettige.
justly ['dʒʌstli] *adv* med rette.
jut [dʒʌt] *v: ~ (out)* rage frem (,ud).
Jutland ['dʒʌtlənd] *s* Jylland; **-er** *s* jyde.
juvenile ['dʒu:vənail] *adj* ungdoms-, børne-; **~ delinquent** [-də'liŋkwənt] *s* ungdomskriminel.
juxtapose ['dʒʌkstəpəuz] *v* sidestille.

K

K, k [kei].
kail, kale [keil] *s* grønkål.
kangaroo [ˌkæŋgə'ru:] *s* kænguru.
kayak ['kaiæk] *s* kajak.
kedgeree [kɛdʒə'ri:] *s (gastr)* indisk ret af ris og fisk.
keel [ki:l] *s* køl; *on an even ~* på ret køl; støt og roligt // *v: ~ over* kæntre; **-haul** [-hɔ:l] *v* kølhale.
keen [ki:n] *adj* stærk, intens (fx *interest* interesse); skarp (fx *edge* kant); ivrig; *~ to* ivrig efter at; *~ on sby* begejstret for (,lun på) en; *~ on sth* opsat på ngt; begejstret for ngt; **-ness** *s* iver, entusiasme; **--sighted** *adj* skarpsynet.
keep [ki:p] *s* borgtårn; kost, underhold; *earn enough for one's ~* tjene til livets opretholdelse // *v (kept, kept* [kɛpt]) beholde; holde; drive (fx *a shop* en forretning); underholde, ernære; opretholde; ophold; holde sig; *don't let me ~ you* jeg skal ikke opholde dig; *will this fish ~?* kan denne fisk holde sig? *~ going* blive ved; *~ doing sth* blive ved med at gøre ngt; *~ in with sby* holde sig gode venner med en; *~ off sth* holde sig fra ngt; *~ on (with)* blive ved (med); *~ up* holde oppe; holde i gang; *~ up with sby* holde trit med en.
keeper ['ki:pə*] *s* vogter; dyrepasser.
keeping ['ki:piŋ] *s* forvaring; underhold; *in ~ with* i overensstemmelse med.
keeps [ki:ps] *spl: for ~* (F) til at beholde.
keepsake ['ki:pseik] *s* minde, souvenir.
keg [kɛg] *s* lille tønde (,fad)
Kelt [kɛlt] *s* kelter; **-ic** *adj* keltisk.
kennel [kɛnl] *s* hundehus; rendesten; **kennels** *s* kennel, hundepension; *a kennels* en kennel.
kept [kɛpt] *præt* og *pp* af *keep.*
kerb [kə:b] *s* (på fortov) kantsten; rendesten.
kerfuffle [kə'fʌfəl] *s* halløj, ståhej.
kernel ['kə:nl] *s* kerne; sten.
kerosene ['kɛrəsi:n] *s* petroleum.
kettle [kɛtl] *s* kedel; *that's a different ~ of fish* det er en helt anden historie; **-drum** *s (mus)* pauke.
key [ki:] *s* nøgle; tangent, tast; *(mus)* toneart; kode; facitliste // *v: ~ in (edb)* indtaste; indkode; *~ up (mus)* stemme; *(fig)* stramme op; *all ~ed up* nervøs.
keyboard ['ki:bɔ:d] *s* nøglebræt; klaviatur; tastatur // *v* (ind)taste; **~ operator** *s* tasteoperatør.
keynote ['ki:nəut] *s* grundtone; grundtema.
keystone ['ki:stəun] *s (bygn)* slutsten; *(fig)* hovedpunkt.
khaki ['ka:ki] *s* kaki; *~s pl* kakiuniform // *adj* kakifarvet.
kick [kik] *s* spark; slag; (F) spænding; sjov; *get the ~* blive fyret; blive smidt ud; *get a ~ out of doing sth* finde fornøjelse i at gøre ngt; *for ~s* for sjov // *v* sparke; sprælle; *~ the bucket* (F) kradse 'af; *~ about* mishandle; drive rundt; *~ out* smide

ud; fyre; *~ up a fuss* lave ballade; **~back** *s* returkommission; **~-off** *s (fodb)* begyndelsesspark; **~-up** *s* (F) ballade.

kid [kid] *s* barn, unge, kid // *v* narre, drille; *I was only ~ding* det var bare for sjov; *no, ~ding!* nej, nu driller du! nej, det er da løgn! **~ gloves** *spl: treat sby with ~ gloves* tage på en med fløjlshandsker.

kidney ['kidni] *s* nyre; **~ bean** *s* snittebønne; **~ machine** *s* dialyseapparat, kunstig nyre.

kill [kil] *s* bytte; *be in at the ~* være med når det sker // *v* dræbe, slå ihjel; slagte; ødelægge; *~ off* gøre det af med; *dressed to ~* dødsmart klædt på; *~ oneself laughing* være ved at dø af grin.

killer ['kilə*] *s* morder; dræber.

killing ['kiliŋ] *s* drab; *make a ~* få en fed fortjeneste // *adj* dræbende.

killjoy ['kildʒɔi] *s* (om person) lyseslukker.

kiln [kiln] *s* (stor) ovn; tørreovn // *v* brænde; tørre.

kilt [kilt] *s* kilt // *v* kilte op; lægge i læg.

kin [kin] *s* slægt, slægtninge; *next of ~* nærmeste slægtning(e); *kith and ~* venner og slægtninge.

kind [kaind] *s* slags, art; *pay in ~* betale i naturalier; *repay in ~* give igen af samme mønt; *all ~s of...* alle mulige...; *they are two of a ~* de er to alen af samme stykke; *he's ~ of funny* han virker underlig; *he's a football player of a ~ (neds)* han skal forestille at være fodboldspiller // *adj* venlig, rar; *would you be so ~ as to...?* vil du være så rar at...?

kindergarten ['kində,ga:tn] *s* børnehave.

kindle [kindl] *v* fænge, tænde; *(fig)* ophidse, vække.

kindly ['kaindli] *adj* venlig; velvillig // *adv* venligt; *will you ~ lend me your pen?* vil du være så sød at låne mig din pen? *take ~ to* se med velvilje på.

kindness ['kaindnis] *s* venlighed; velvilje; god gerning.

kindred ['kindrid] *adj* beslægtet; *a ~ spirit* en bror (,søster) i ånden.

king [kiŋ] *s* konge; *King's English* dannet sprog // *v: ~ it* spille konge; **~dom** *s* (konge)rige; *the animal ~dom* dyreriget; **~fisher** *s* isfugl; **~ship** *s* kongeværdighed.

kink [kiŋk] *s* bugt, snoning; karakterbrist; fiks idé; **~y** *adj* bugtet; (om hår) kruset; *(fig)* sær, speciel.

kinsfolk ['kinsfəuk] *spl* slægtninge; **kinship** *s* slægtskab; **kinsman** *s* slægtning.

kip [kip] *s* (F) lur, søvn // *v* sove.

kipper ['kipə*] *s (gastr)* saltet og røget sild.

kirk [kə:k] *s* (skotsk) kirke.

kiss [kis] *s* kys; *the ~ of life* mund til mund-metoden; *blow sby a ~* sende en et fingerkys // *v* kysse; kysse hinanden; *~ the dust* måtte bide i græsset; **~er** *s* (S) kyssetøj; **~-proof** *adj* kysægte.

kit [kit] *s* udstyr; værktøj; samlesæt; **~bag** *s* køjesæk.

kitchen ['kitʃən] *s* køkken; **~ette** [-'nεt] *s* tekøkken; **~ range** *s* komfur; **~ sink** *s* køkkenvask; **~ware** *s* køkkenudstyr.

kite [kait] *s* drage (af papir etc); *(merk)* dækningsløs check; *fly a ~* sætte en drage op; *(merk)* udstede en dækningsløs check; *(fig)* opsende en prøveballon.

kith [kiθ] *s: ~ and kin* venner og slægtninge.

kitten [kitn] *s* kattekilling; *have ~s* (F) få et føl på tværs.

Kitty ['kiti] *s* pulje.

knack [næk] *s* håndelag, tag; *have the ~ for it* kende taget; *have the ~ of disappearing* have en vis evne til at forsvinde.

knapsack ['næpsæk] *s* rygsæk, tornyster.

knead [ni:d] *v* ælte.

knee [ni:] *s* knæ; *go on one's ~s* falde på knæ; **~cap** *s* knæskal; **~-deep** *adj* op til knæene.

kneel [ni:l] *v (knelt, knelt* [nεlt]) knæle.

knees-up ['ni:zʌp] *s* (S) abegilde.

knell [nɛl] *s* (klokke)ringning.
knew [nju:] *præt* af *know.*
knickers ['nikəz] *spl* (dame)underbukser; knæbukser.
knick-knack ['niknæk] *s* nipsting.
knife [naif] *s (pl: knives* [naivz]) kniv // *v* dolke, stikke med kniv; **~ edge** *s* knivsæg.
knight [nait] *s (gl)* ridder; (i skak) springer; titel der giver ret til at kalde sig *Sir // v* slå til ridder; **~hood** *s* ridderskab; rang af *knight.*
knit [nit] *v (knit, knit* el. *~ted, ~ted)* strikke; knytte; forene; vokse sammen; *~ one's brows* rynke panden; **~ting** *s* strikning; strikketøj; **~ting needle** *s* strikkepind; **~wear** [-wɛə*] *s* strikvarer, strik.
knives [naivz] *spl* af *knife.*
knob [nɔb] *s* knop, kugle; dørhåndtag; (på radio) knap; *a ~ of butter* en klat smør.
knobbly ['nɔbli] *adj* knudret.
knock [nɔk] *s* slag; banken // *v* slå; banke; (F) dupere; *~ (on) the door* banke på døren; *~ about* flakke om; mishandle; *~ back a drink* skylle en drink ned; *~ down* slå ned; rive ned (fx *a house* et hus); *~ off* (om pris) slå af på; (F) holde fyraften; *~ it off!* hold op! *~ sby off his feet* slå benene væk under en; *~ out* slå ud; *~ over* vælte; *~ up* bikse sammen; (V) gøre gravid.
knocker ['nɔkə*] *s* dørhammer; **~s** *spl* (V) store patter.
knock-kneed ['nɔkni:d] *adj* kalveknæet.
knoll [nəul] *s* lille høj, bakketop.
knot [nɔt] *s* knude; sløjfe; klynge; vanskelighed; *(mar)* knob // *v* binde, knytte; **~ty** *adj* knudret, vanskelig.
know [nəu] *v (knew, known* [nju:, nəun]) vide; kende; kunne (fx *one's lessons* sine lektier); *~ about* kende til; *for all I ~* så vidt jeg ved; *there is no ~ing* man kan aldrig vide; det er ikke godt at vide; *not that I ~ of* ikke så vidt jeg ved; *you wouldn't ~* det kan du jo ikke vide; det ved du jo alligevel ikke; *you ~* du ved (nok); ved du (nok); **~-all** *s (neds)* alvidende person; **~-how** *s* ekspertise, sagkundskab.
knowing ['nəuiŋ] *adj* kyndig; sigende; indforstået; **~ly** *adv* med vilje.
knowledge ['nɔlidʒ] *s* viden, kendskab; lærdom; vidende; *that is common ~* det ved alle og enhver; *to the best of my ~* så vidt jeg ved; **~able** ['nɔlidʒəbl] *adj* velinformeret.
known [nəun] *pp* af *know.*
knuckle [nʌkl] *s* kno; skank // *v* banke; *~ down (,under)* bøje sig; give efter; **~duster** *s* knojern.
kph (fork.f. *kilometres per hour)* km/t.
Kremlin ['krɛmlin] *s: the ~* Kreml (i Moskva).
kudos ['kju:dɔs] *s* ære, berømmelse.

L

L, l [ɛl].
L (fork.f. *learner (car))* skolevogn.
l. fork.f. *litre.*
lab [læb] *s* fork.f. *laboratory.*
label [leibl] *s* mærkeseddel, etiket; mærke // *v* mærke; rubricere; stemple.
laboratory [lə'bɔrətəri] *s* laboratorium.
laborious [lə'bɔ:riəs] *adj* arbejdsom; træls, slidsom.
labour ['leibə*] *s* arbejde; arbejdskraft; besvær, mas; *(med)* fødselsveer; *be in ~* have veer // *v* arbejde; slide (i det); **~-intensive** [-tɛn-] *adj* arbejdskrævende; *the* **Labour party** *s* arbejderpartiet; **~-saving** *adj* arbejdsbesparende; **~ camp** *s* arbejdslejr.
laboured ['leibəd] *adj* besværlig; besværet; kunstlet.
labourer ['leibərə*] *s* arbejder.
labour force ['leibə fɔ:s] *s* arbejdskraft.
lace [leis] *s* snørebånd; knipling, blonde // *v* snøre; tilsætte, blande *(with* med); **~-up** *s* snøresko.
lack [læk] *s* mangel; *through (,for) ~ of* af mangel på // *v* mangle; savne; *be ~ing in* mangle.

lackey ['læki] *s* lakaj (også *fig).*
lacklustre ['læklʌstə*] *adj* trist, farveløs; mat.
lacquer ['lækə*] *s* lak // *v* lakere.
lad [læd] *s* knægt, stor dreng; fyr, gut.
ladder ['lædə*] *s* stige; (i strømpe) løben maske // *v: I've ~ed my tights* det er løbet en maske i mine strømpebukser.
la-di-da ['la:di:'da:] *adj* affekteret, 'fin'.
ladle [leidl] *s* stor ske, opøseske; slev // *v* øse op.
lady ['leidi] *s* dame, frue; *Our Lady* Jomfru Maria; **~bird** *s* mariehøne; **~-in-waiting** *s* hofdame; **~killer** *s* kvindebedårer; **~like** *adj* dannet; damet.
Ladyship ['leidiʃip] *s: your (,her) ~* Deres (,hendes) nåde.
lag [læg] *s* forsinkelse; (også: *time ~)* tidsafstand; straffefange // *v* varmeisolere; *~ behind* komme (,være) bagefter (,bagud).
lager ['la:gə*] *s* pilsner(øl).
lagging ['lægiŋ] *s* isoleringsmateriale.
laid [leid] *præt* og *pp* af *lay; get ~* (S) blive bollet; **~-back** *adj* afslappet.
lain [lein] *pp* af *lie.*
lair [lɛ:ə*] *s* (dyrs) hule; *(fig)* tilflugtssted.
laity ['leiti] *s* lægfolk.
lake [leik] *s* sø; *Lake Garda* Gardasøen; *the Lake District* egn med søer og bjerge i Nordvestengland.
lamb [læm] *s* lam; lammekød; *leg of ~* lammekølle; **~ chop** *s* lammekotelet; **~s·wool** *s* lammeuld.
lame [leim] *adj* halt; vanfør; *(fig)* tam; **~ duck** *s* (om person) fiasko.
lament [lə'mɛnt] *s* klage(sang) // *v* klage (sig); sørge over; **~able** ['læməntəbl] *adj* sørgelig, beklagelig.
laminated ['læmineitid] *adj* lamineret.
lamp [læmp] *s* lampe, lygte.
lampoon [læm'pu:n] *s* satirisk skrift // *v* smæde, satirisere.
lamppost ['læmppəust] *s* lygtepæl; **lampshade** [-ʃeid] *s* lampeskærm.
lance [la:ns] *s* lanse, spyd.
land [lænd] *s* land; jord; *extensive ~s* vidtstrakte jorder; *live off the ~* leve af hvad man selv dyrker; *on ~* til lands; *on dry ~* på landjorden // *v* lande; gå i land; landsætte; ende, havne; *be ~ed in jail* havne i fængsel; *~ sby (fig)* få en på krogen; *~ up with* ende med; **~ed gentry** *s* landadel; godsejere; **~fall** *s* landkending; **~holder** *s* jordejer; forpagter.
landing ['læmdiŋ] *s* landing; landsætning; (trappe)afsats, repos; **~ craft** *s* landgangsfartøj; **~ strip** *s* (mindre) startbane.
land... ['lænd-] sms: **~lady** *s* værtinde; kroværtinde; **~locked** *adj* omgivet af land på alle sider; **~lord** *s* vært; krovært; godsejer; **~lubber** *s* landkrabbe; **~mark** *s* landemærke; vartegn; **~owner** *s* jordbesidder; **~scape** *s* landskab; **~slide** *s* jordskred; *(pol)* stemmeskred; **~ surveyor** *s* sv.t. landinspektør.
lane [lein] *s* smal vej, stræde; vejbane, kørebane; *bus ~* busbane; *a six-~ motorway* en seksssporet motorvej.
language ['læŋgwidʒ] *s* sprog; *bad ~* grimt sprog, skældsord.
languid ['læŋgwid] *adj* ligeglad, sløv, mat.
languish ['læŋgwiʃ] *v* blive mat; sygne hen; dø hen; sukke.
languor ['læŋgə*] *s* smægten; kraftesløshed; sløvhed.
lanky ['lænki] *adj* ranglet.
lap [læp] *s* skød; overlapning; (om bane) omgang, runde; etape; *sit on sby's ~* sidde på skødet hos en; *~ of honour* æresrunde // *v: ~ (up)* labbe i sig; (om bølge) skvulpe; **~dog** *s* skødehund.
lapel [lə'pɛl] *s* opslag, revers.
Lapp [læp] *s* same // *adj* samisk.
lapse [læps] *s* fejl, lapsus; udløb; tidsrum; pause; *~ of time* tidsforløb // *v* forse sig; henfalde *(into* til); *(jur)* bortfalde.
lapwing ['læpwiŋ] *s* vibe.
larceny ['la:səni] *s* tyveri.
larch [la:tʃ] *s* lærk(etræ).
lard [la:d] *s* spæk, svinefedt // *v* spække; **~er** *s* spisekammer.

large [la:dʒ] *adj* stor; omfattende; *at ~* på fri fod; i al almindelighed; *by and ~* i det store og hele; **~ly** *adv* i høj grad; overvejende; **~-scale** *adj* i stor målestok; storstilet.
largess(e) [la:'dʒɛs] *s* rundhåndethed.
largish ['la:dʒiʃ] *adj* temmelig stor.
lark [la:k] *s* lærke; (F) fest, halløj // *v: ~ about* rende rundt og lave fis og ballade.
larva ['la:və] *s (pl: larvae* ['la:vi]) larve.
laryngitis [lærin'dʒaitis] *s* halsbetændelse.
larynx ['læriŋks] *s* strubehoved.
lascivious [lə'siviəs] *adj* lysten, liderlig.
lash [læʃ] *s* piskeslag; piskesnert; (oftest: *eye~)* øjenvippe // *v* piske; gennemhegle; surre (fast); *~ out at* lange ud efter; angribe.
lass [læs] *s* ung pige.
lassitude ['læsitju:d] *s* træthed.
last [la:st] *s* (sko)læst // *v* vare (ved); holde (sig) // *adj* sidst(e) // *adv* sidst; til sidst; *~ week* i sidste uge; *~ night* i aftes, i nat; *at ~* til sidst, endelig; *at long ~* langt om længe; *~ but one* næstsidst; *the year before ~* i forfjor; forrige år; *I can't wait to see the ~ of him* jeg glæder mig virkelig til at blive af med ham.
lasting ['la:stiŋ] *adj* vedvarende; varig; holdbar.
lastly ['la:stli] *adv* til slut.
last-minute ['la:stminit] *adj* sidste (øjebliks).
latch [lætʃ] *s* klinke, smæklås // *v: ~ onto* klynge sig til klæbe til.
latchkey [lætʃki:] *s* gadedørsnøgle; **~ child** *s* nøglebarn.
late [leit] *adj/adv* sen; forsinket; sent; længe; afdød; *in ~ May* i slutningen af maj; *the ~ Mr. Johnson* afdøde hr. Johnson; **~comer** *s* person der kommer for sent; **~ly** *adv* i den senere tid.
latent [leitnt] *adj* skjult, latent.
later ['leitə*] *adj/adv* senere; nyere; *~ on* senere; *see you ~!* farvel så længe! *sooner or ~* før eller senere.
lateral ['lætərəl] *adj* side-; til siden; *~ thinking* uortodoks tænkning.
latest ['leitist] *adj/adv* senest, sidst; nyest; *at the ~* (aller)senest.
lath [læθ] *s* liste, tremme.
lathe [leið] *s* drejebænk.
lather ['læðə*] *s* (sæbe)skum; *be all in a ~* (F) være helt ude af flippen // *v* sæbe ind; skumme.
Latin ['lætin] *s* latin // *adj* latinsk, latiner-.
latitude ['lætitju:d] *s (geogr)* bredde(grad); *(fig)* spillerum.
latter ['lætə*] *adj* sidste; *the ~* sidstnævnte (af to).
lattice ['lætis] *s* gitter, tremmeværk.
Latvia ['lætviə] *s* Letland.
laudable ['lɔ:dəbl] *adj* prisværdig.
laudatory ['lɔ:dətəri] *adj* rosende.
laugh [la:f] *s* latter; *have a good ~ at sby* få sig et billigt grin over en; *get a ~* få folk til at grine; *what a ~!* hvor morsomt! // *v* le, grine; smile; *it's no ~ing matter* det er ikke ngt at grine ad; *~ at* le ad; *~ it off* slå det hen i spøg; **~able** *adj* latterlig; **~ing** *adj* leende; *be the ~ing stock of* være til grin for.
laughter ['la:ftə*] *s* latter.
launch [lɔ:ntʃ] *s* søsætning; (om raket) affyring; (om båd) chalup; (større) motorbåd // *v* søsætte; affyre; starte; iværksætte; lancere; **~ing** *s* søsætning; affyring; **~(ing) pad** *s* affyringsrampe.
launder ['lɔ:ndə*] *v* vaske og stryge (,rulle); kunne vaskes; (om penge) renvaske.
launderette [lɔ:n'drɛt] ® *s* møntvaskeri.
laundry ['lɔ:ndri] *s* vaskeri; vasketøj; *do the ~* vaske (og stryge) tøj.
laureate ['lɔ:riit] *adj: poet ~* hofdigter.
laurel ['lɔ:rl] *s* laurbær(træ).
lavatory ['lævətəri] *s* toilet, wc.
lavender ['lævəndə*] *s* lavendel.
lavish ['læviʃ] *v* ødsle med; overøse // *adj* ødsel, rundhåndet, flot.
law [lɔ:] *s* lov; jura; *by ~* efter loven; *go to ~* gå til domstolene; *read ~* studere jura; **~-abiding** *adj* lovlydig; **~breaker** *s* lovbryder; **~ court** *s* domstol, ret; **~ful** *adj* lovlig; retmæssig; **~fully** *adv* lovformeligt (fx *married* gift); **~less** *adj* retsløs.

lawn [lɔ:n] *s* græsplæne; **~-mower** *s* græsslåmaskine.
law... ['lɔ:-] sms: **~ school** *s* juridisk fakultet; **~ student** *s* jurastuderende; **~suit** [-su:t] *s* retssag.
lawyer ['lɔ:jə*] *s* jurist; advokat.
lax [læks] *adj* slap, løs; *~ bowels* tynd mave.
laxative ['læksətiv] *s* afføringsmiddel.
laxity ['læksiti] *s* slaphed.
lay [lei] *v (laid, laid* [leid]) lægge // *præt* af *lie; ~ aside (,by)* lægge til side; *~ down* lægge ned; nedlægge; *~ down a rule* fastsætte en regel; *~ off* holde op (med); *~ on* lægge på; indlægge (fx *gas* gas); smøre på, overdrive; *~ hands on sth* få fat i ngt; *~ the blame on sby* give en skylden for ngt; *~ out* lægge ud; anlægge; slå ud; tegne, layoute; *~ up* lægge hen, gemme; spare op; *(auto)* klodse op; (om skib) lægge op; *be laid up* måtte holde sengen; *~ the table* dække bordet // *adj* læg.
layby ['leibai] *s* vigeplads; (på motorvej) rasteplads; holdeplads.
layer ['leiə*] *s* lag; **~ed** *adj* lagdelt, i lag.
layette [lei'ɛt] *s* babyudstyr.
layman ['leimən] *s* lægmand.
layoff ['leiɔf] *s* fyring; pause.
layout ['leiaut] *s* plan; opsætning, layout.
laze [leiz] *v* dovne, dase; *~ around* drive rundt.
laziness ['leizinis] *s* dovenskab.
lazy ['leizi] *adj* doven, lad; **~bones** *s* dovendidrik.
lb fork.f. *pound(s).*
lead [li:d] (se også næste opslagsord) *s* ledelse, føring; vink, fingerpeg; (til hund) snor; *(teat)* hovedrolle; *have the ~* have føringen, ligge i spidsen // *v (led, led* [lɛd]) lede, føre; stå i spidsen (for); *~ astray* føre på afveje; *~ back to* føre tilbage til; *~ on* opmuntre; gå i forvejen; *~ sby on* (også) forlede en; tage en ved næsen; *~ on to* føre ind på; *~ to* føre til; medføre; *~ up to* lægge op til; stile imod; *~ sby up the garden path* tage en ved næsen.
lead [lɛd] (se også foregående opslagsord) *s* bly; (bly)lod; (i blyant) stift; **~ed** *adj* blyindfattet; **~en** *adj* bly-; blygrå; tung som bly.
leader ['li:də*] *s* fører, leder; (i avis) leder(artikel); *(mus)* koncertmester; **~ship** *s* ledelse; førerskab.
leading ['li:diŋ] *adj* ledende, førende; **~ lady** *s (teat)* primadonna; **~ man** *s (teat)* mandlig hovedkraft.
leaf [li:f] *s (pl: leaves* [li:vz]) blad; løv; flage; broklap; (på bord) (udtræks)plade; *come into ~* (om træ) springe ud // *v: ~ through* blade (,bladre) igennem.
leaflet ['li:flit] *s* brochure, folder.
leafy ['li:fi] *ad* bladrig; løv-.
league [li:g] *s* forbund; liga; *be in ~ with* stå i ledtog med.
leak [li:k] *s* utæthed, læk; udslip; *go for a ~* (F) gå ud og tisse // *v* være utæt, lække; sive; *~ sth to the Press* lade ngt sive ud til pressen.
leakage ['li:kidʒ] *s* utæthed, læk; udsivning.
leaky ['li:ki] *adj* utæt, hullet.
lean [li:n] *s* hældning // *v (~ed, ~ed* el. *leant, leant* [lɛnt]) hælde, stå skråt; læne (sig); støtte (sig); *~ against* stille (ngt) op ad; læne sig op ad; *~ on* støtte sig til; *~ over* hælde; *~ over backwards to do sth* stå på hovedet for at gøre ngt; *~ towards* hælde til // *adj* mager.
leaning ['li:niŋ] *s* tilbøjelighed, tendens *(towards* i retning af) // *adj* hældende, skrå.
lean-to ['li:ntu] *s* halvtag; skur.
leap [li:p] *s* spring // *v (leapt, leapt* [lɛpt] el. *~ed, ~ed)* springe (over) (fx *a fence* et stakit); *~ at* gribe ivrigt efter; **~frog** *v* springe buk; **~ year** *s* skudår.
learn [lə:n] *v (~ed, ~ed* el. *learnt, learnt* [lə:nt]) lære; erfare, få at vide, høre; *I have yet to ~ that...* jeg har endnu aldrig hørt at...
learned ['lə:nid] *adj* lærd.
learner ['lə:nə*] *s* elev, begynder; **~ (car)** *s (L)* skolevogn.
learning ['lə:niŋ] *s* lærdom.
lease [li:s] *s* leje; forpagtning; lejekontrakt // *v* leje; lease; udleje;

~hold [-həuld] *s* lejet (,forpagtet) ejendom (,jord); lejemål.
leash [li:ʃ] *s* (hunde)snor; (hunde)kobbel; *on a ~* i snor.
least [li:st] *adj/adv* mindst; *at ~* i det mindste; i hvert fald; *not in the ~, not the ~ bit* ikke det mindste; på ingen måde; *~ of all* mindst af alt (,alle); *to say the ~ of it* mildest talt; **~ways** *adv* (F) i det mindste.
leather ['lɛðə*] *s* læder, skind // *adj* læder-, skind-.
leave [li:v] *s* tilladelse, lov; orlov; *be on ~* have orlov; *take one's ~* tage afsked, sige farvel; *take ~ of one's senses* gå fra forstanden; *~ of absence* orlov, tjenestefri // *v (left, left* [lɛft]) tage af sted; forlade; efterlade; levne; *be left* blive forladt; være til overs; *take it or ~ it* så kan du selv vælge, du kan selv vælge; *~ school* gå ud af skolen; *~ home* gå (,flytte) hjemmefra; *~ sby alone* lade en være (i fred); *let's ~ it at that* lad det nu ligge; *~ behind* efterlade; *~ off!* hold så op! *~ out* udelade; *~ it to me!* det skal jeg nok klare! *there's some milk left* der er ngt mælk til overs.
leaven [lɛvn] *s* surdej.
leaves [li:vz] *spl* af *leaf.*
Lebanese [lɛbə'ni:z] *s* libaneser // *adj* libanesisk; **Lebanon** ['lɛbənən] *s* Libanon.
lecherous ['lɛtʃərəs] *adj* liderlig.
lecture ['lɛktʃə*] *s* forelæsning; foredrag // *v* forelæse; docere; *~ on* holde forelæsning over; **~ course** *s* forelæsningsrække.
lecturer ['lɛktʃərə*] *s* foredragsholder; lektor, docent.
lectureship ['lɛktʃəʃip] *s* lektorat, docentur.
led [lɛd] *præt* og *pp* af *lead.*
ledge [lɛdʒ] *s* fremspring; (smal) hylde; (klippe)afsats.
ledger ['lɛdʒə*] *s (merk)* hovedbog.
lee [li:] *s* læ.
leech [li:tʃ] *s (zo)* igle; (om person) snylter.
leek [li:k] *s* porre.
leer [liə*] *v: ~ at* kaste et olmt blik på; skæve til.
leery ['liəri] *adj: ~ of* (F) forsigtig med, mistænksom over for.
leeward ['li:wəd] *s/adj* læ.
leeway ['li:wei] *s: make up ~* indhente det forsømte; *have some ~* have spillerum.
left [lɛft] *præt* og *pp* af *leave* // *adj* venstre; *on the ~* på venstre hånd; til venstre; *keep ~* holde til venstre; *the Left* venstrefløjen; **~-hand driving** *s* venstrestyring; **~-handed** *adj* kejthåndet; **~-hand side** *s* venstre side; **~ist** *s/adj* venstreorienteret; **~-luggage (office)** *s* (banegårds)garderobe; bagageopbevaring; **~overs** *spl* levninger; **~-wing** *adj* venstreorienteret; venstrefløjs-.
leg [lɛg] *s* ben; støtte; *(gastr)* kølle, lår; *pull sby's ~* tage gas på en; *take to one's ~s* tage benene på nakken; *he does not have a ~ to stand on* der er overhovedet ikke ngt hold i det han siger; *be on one's last ~s* synge på sit sidste vers; *have one's ~ over* (V) lægge en pige ned // *v: ~ it* bene af.
legacy ['lɛgəsi] *s* arv.
legal ['li:gl] *adj* lovlig; legal; lovbestemt; retlig; rets-; **~ aid** *s* retshjælp for ubemidlede; **~ adviser** *s* juridisk rådgiver.
legalize ['li:gəlaiz] *v* gøre lovlig, legalisere.
legend ['lɛdʒənd] *s* legende, sagn; indskrift; (i bog etc) billedtekst; **~ary** *adj* legendarisk, sagn-.
leggings ['lɛgiŋs] *spl* (lange) gamacher; benvarmere.
leggy ['lɛgi] *adj* langbenet; med flotte ben.
legible ['lɛdʒibl] *adj* let læselig, tydelig.
legion ['li:dʒən] *s* legion; mængde, hærskare.
legionary ['li:dʒənəri] *s* legionær.
legislate ['lɛdʒisleit] *v* lovgive; **legislation** [-'leiʃən] *s* lovgivning.
legislative ['lɛdʒislətiv] *adj* lovgivende.
legislature ['lɛdʒislətʃə*] *s* lovgivningsmagt.

legitimacy [li'dʒitiməsi] *s* lovlighed; rimelighed.
legitimate [li'dʒitimit] *adj* lovlig; legitim; ~ *children* børn født i ægteskab.
leisure ['lɛʒə*] *s* fritid; otium; *be at* ~ have god tid; *at* ~ i ro og mag; *do it at your* ~ gør det når du har tid; ~ **centre** *s* fritidsklub; **~ly** *adv* magelig; i ro og mag.
lemon ['lɛmən] *s* citron(træ); citronsaft; ~ **balm** *s* citronmelisse; ~ **squeezer** *s* citronpresser.
lend [lɛnd] *v (lent, lent)* låne (ud); give; ~ *sth to sby* låne en ngt; ~ *a hand* give en hånd med; ~ *aid* give hjælp; ~ *oneself to* være med til; nedværdige sig til; ~ *one's name to* lægge navn til; **~er** *s* (penge)udlåner.
length [lɛŋθ] *s* længde; varighed; strækning; stykke; (stof)bane; ~ *of time* varighed; *at* ~ endelig; langt om længe; udførligt; *at some* ~ ret langtrukkent; *go to the* ~ *of...* gå så vidt som til at...; **~en** *v* forlænge(s); **~ways, ~wise** *adv* i længden; på langs.
lengthy ['lɛŋθi] *adj* langtrukken.
leniency ['li:niənsi] *s* mildhed.
lenient ['li:niənt] *adj* mild; lemfældig.
lens [lɛns] *s* linse; *(foto)* objektiv.
Lent [lɛnt] *s* faste(tid).
lent [lɛnt] *præt* og *pp* af *lend.*
lentil [lɛntl] *s (bot)* linse.
Leo ['li:əu] *s (astr)* Løven.
leotard ['li:əta:d] *s* trikot.
leper ['lɛpə*] *s* spedalsk.
leprosy ['lɛprəsi] *s* spedalskhed.
lesbian ['lɛzbiən] *s* lesbe // *adj* lesbisk.
lesion ['li:ʒən] *s* kvæstelse, skade, læsion.
less [lɛs] *adj/adv* mindre; færre; ringere; ~ *and* ~ mindre og mindre; *more or* ~ mere el. mindre; ~ *than* mindre end; ringere end; ~ *than half* under halvdelen; *the* ~ *you say, the better* jo mindre du siger, des bedre; *no* ~ ingen (,intet) mindre end // *præp* minus; *three* ~ *two is one* tre minus to er en; *a year* ~ *five days* et år minus fem dage.
lessen [lɛsn] *v* (for)mindske(s); aftage; undervurdere.
lesson [lɛsn] *s* lektie; (skole)time; lærestreg; *take dancing* ~*s* gå til dans; *prepare one's* ~*s* læse sine lektier; *let that be a* ~ *to you* lad det være dig en lærestreg; *teach sby a* ~ give en en lærestreg.
lest [lɛst] *konj* for at ikke; for at; *I hid it* ~ *it was stolen* jeg gemte den for at den ikke skulle blive stjålet; *we were afraid* ~ *he should forget* vi var bange for at han skulle glemme det.
let [lɛt] *v (let, let)* lade; leje ud; ~ *me go!* lad mig gå! giv slip! ~*'s go!* lad os gå! kom, nu går vi! *to* ~ til leje; ~ *alone* lade være i fred; *he never laughed,* ~ *alone smiled* han lo aldrig, for slet ikke at tale om at smile; ~ *be* lade være; ~ *down* sænke; (om tøj) lægge ned; *(fig)* svigte, skuffe; ~ *go* give slip *(of* på); give los; ~ *in* lukke ind; ~ *in the clutch* slippe koblingen; ~ *sby in on sth* indvi en i ngt; ~ *off* fyre af; lade slippe; slippe ud (fx *steam* damp); ~ *on abouth sth* sladre om ngt; ~ *out* lukke ud, slippe ud; (om tøj) lægge ud; løslade; udstøde (fx *a scream* et skrig); ~ *up* holde op; slappe af; aftage; **~-down** *s* (F) skuffelse.
lethal ['li:θl] *adj* dødelig; dødbringende.
lethargic [li'θa:dʒik] *adj* sløv, apatisk; **lethargy** ['lɛθədʒi] *s* sløvhed; døsighed.
let's d.s.s. *let us.*
letter ['lɛtə*] *s* brev; bogstav; *to the* ~ nøjagtigt, til punkt og prikke; **~box** *s* brevkasse; postkasse; **~head** *s* brevhoved; **~ing** *s* bogstaver; skrift; tekstning; **letters** *spl* litteratur.
lettuce ['lɛtis] *s* salat(hoved).
let-up ['lɛtʌp] *s* pause, ophold.
leukaemia [lu:'ki:miə] *s* leukæmi.
level [lɛvl] *s* niveau, plan; (også: *spirit* ~) vaterpas; *on the* ~ vandret; *(fig)* regulær, ærlig // *v* planere, udjævne; bringe i vater; gøre lige; jævne med jorden; ~ *down* runde ned; ~ *off (,out)* udjævne(s); flade ud //

adj plan, jævn; flad; jævnbyrdig; *be ~ with* være på højde med; ~ **crossing** *s* jernbaneoverskæring; ~-**headed** *adj* klarhovedet, fornuftig; ~**ling** *s* planering; udjævning; nivellering.

lever ['li:və*] *s* løftestang; (også *fig*); stang (fx *gear~* gearstang) // *v* løfte.

leverage ['li:vəridʒ] *s* (*fig*) magt, indflydelse.

levity ['lɛviti] *s* letsindighed, overfladiskhed.

levy ['lɛvi] *s* skat, afgift; udskrivning, opkrævning // *v* udskrive, opkræve; pålægge.

lewd [lu:d] *adj* sjofel, anstødelig; smudsig.

liability [laiə'biliti] *s* ansvar; tilbøjelighed; ulempe; handicap; *liabilities* passiver.

liable ['laiəbl] *adj: ~ for* ansvarlig for; *~ to* forpligtet til; tilbøjelig til; modtagelig for.

liaise [li'eiz] *v* stå i kontakt med, samarbejde med.

liaison [li:'eizən] *s* forbindelse.

liar [laiə*] *s* løgner, løgnhals.

libel [laibl] *s* injurier; bagvaskelse // *v* bagvaske; smæde; ~**lous** *adj* ærekrænkende.

liberal ['libərl] *adj* gavmild, large; rigelig; liberal, frisindet.

liberate ['libəreit] *v* befri, frigive.

liberation [libə'reiʃən] *s* befrielse; frigivelse.

liberty ['libəti] *s* frihed; *at ~* fri, ledig; på fri fod; *be at ~ to* have lov til at; *take the ~ of* tillade sig.

libidinous [li'bidinəs] *adj* liderlig, lysten.

Libra ['li:brə] *s* (*astr*) Vægten.

librarian [lai'brɛəriən] *s* bibliotekar.

library ['laibrəri] *s* bibliotek; ~ **ticket** *s* lånerkort; ~ **van** *s* bogbus.

Libya ['libiə] *s* Libyen; ~**n** *s* libyer // *adj* libysk.

lice [lais] *spl* af *louse*.

licence ['laisəns] *s* tilladelse; bevilling; licens; (om restaurant etc) udskænkningsret; (også: *driving ~*) kørekort // *v* give tilladelse (,bevilling); autorisere; ~**d** *adj* med bevilling.

licensee [laisən'si:] *s* bevillingshaver.

licence plate ['laisəns pleit] *s* nummerplade.

licensing hours ['laisənsiŋ auəz] *spl* pubbernes åbningstider.

lichen ['laikən] *s* (*bot*) lav.

lick [lik] *s* slik; anelse; *a ~ of paint* et strøg maling // *v* slikke; tæve, banke; *~ sby's boots* sleske for en; *~ one's lips* slikke sig om munden; ~**ing** *s* omgang tæv.

licorice ['likəris] *s* d.s.s. *liquorice*.

lid [lid] *s* låg; (også: *eye~*) øjenlåg.

lie [lai] *s* løgn // *v* lyve; (se også næste opslagsord).

lie [lai] *s* beliggenhed; *the ~ of the land* som landet ligger; *have a long ~* sove længe; *have a ~ down* lægge sig; *have a ~-in* sove længe // *v* (*lay, lain* [lei, lein] ligge; *~ about* ligge og flyde; *take sth lying down* tage ngt yden at kny; *~ low* holde en lav profil; (se også foregående opslagsord).

lieu [lju:] *s: in ~ of* i stedet for.

lieutenant [lɛf'tɛnənt] *s* løjtnant.

life [laif] *s* (*pl: lives* [laivz]) liv; levevis; levetid; livet; menneskeliv; *enjoy ~* nyde livet; *bring to ~* bringe til live igen; skabe liv i; *for ~* for livet; *not for the ~ of me* ikke for min død; *come to ~* live op; *he got ~ for it* han fik livstidsfængsel for det; *take one's ~ in one's hands* vove pelsen; *not on your ~!* ikke på vilkår! *true to ~* virkelighedstro; *fifty lives were lost* halvtreds menneskeliv gik tabt; ~ **assurance** *s* livsforsikring; ~**belt** *s* redningsbælte; ~**boat** *s* redningsbåd; ~**buoy** [-bɔj] *s* redningskrans; ~ **expectancy** *s* forventet levetid; ~**guard** *s* livredder; *the* **Life Guards** *s* livgarden; ~ **jacket** *s* redningsvest; ~**less** *adj* livløs; ~**like** *adj* livagtig, naturtro; ~**long** *adj* livslang; for livstid; ~**r** *s* livstidsfange; ~-**raft** *s* redningsflåde; ~-**saver** *s* livredder; ~ **sentence** *s* livsvarigt fængsel; ~-**sized** *adj* i legemsstørrelse; ~ **support system** *s* (*med*) respirator;

~time *s* levetid; menneskealder; *the chance of a ~time* alle tiders chance.
lift [lift] *s* løft; elevator; lift; *give sby a ~* give en et lift // *v* løfte, hæve; (om tåge) lette; **~-off** *s* (om raket) start.
light [lait] *s* lys; lampe; vindue; *have you got a ~?* har du ngt ild? *come to ~* komme for en dag; *in the ~ of* på baggrund af; *put a ~ to, set ~ to* sætte ild til; *see the ~ of day* se dagens lys // *v (~ed, ~ed* el. *lit, lit)* tænde(s); oplyse; *~ a fire* tænde op; *~ up* oplyse; tænde lys; lyse op // *adj/adv* lys; lyse-; let, mild, svag; *with a ~ touch* med let hånd.
lighten ['laitn] *v* oplyse, gøre lysere; lysne; lette; blive lettere.
lighter ['laitə*] *s* tænder, lighter; (om båd) lastepram.
light... ['lait-] sms: **~ fixture** *s* fatning; lampet; **~-headed** *adj* uklar; svimmel; kåd; **~-hearted** *adj* munter; letsindig; **~house** *s* fyrtårn; **~ing** *s* belysning; **~ing-up time** *s* lygtetændingstid; **~ meter** *s (foto)* belysningsmåler.
lightning ['laitniŋ] *s* lyn; *like ~* lynhurtigt; *like a greased ~* hurtigere end lynet; **~ conductor** *(brit)*, **~ rod** *(am) s* lynafleder.
light... ['lait-] sms: **~ship** *s* fyrskib; **~weight** *adj* letvægts- (fx *suit* habit); **~ year** *s* lysår.
like [laik] *s: the ~* magen; *and the ~* og lignende; *the ~s of you* sådan nogle som du // *v* kunne lide; holde af; *I would ~ to* jeg vil(le) gerne // *adj/adv/præp* lignende; ens; som, ligesom; som om; *be (,look) ~ sby* ligne en; *what's it ~?* hvordan er det? *she screamed ~ mad* hun skreg som en gal; *that's just ~ him!* hvor det ligner ham! *something ~* omkring, cirka; sådan ngt som; ngt lignende; *that's more ~ it!* det er (,var) bedre! det begynder at ligne! *~ as not* sandsynligvis, sikkert; *feel ~* have lyst til; føle sig som; **~able** *adj* tiltalende.
likelihood ['laiklihud] *s* sandsynlighed.
likely ['laikli] *adj* sandsynlig; rimelig // *adv: as ~ as not* sandsynligvis; *most ~* højst sandsynligt; *not ~!* bestemt nej!
like-minded ['laikmaindid] *adj* ligesindet.
liken ['laikn] *v: ~ to* sammenligne med.
likeness ['laiknis] *s* lighed.
likewise ['laikwaiz] *adj* på samme måde, ligeså.
liking ['laikiŋ] *s: have a ~ for* godt kunne lide; have smag for; *take a ~ to* få sympati for; få smag for; *to his ~* efter hans smag.
lilac ['lailək] *s (bot)* syren // *adj* lille.
Lilo ® ['lailəu] *s* gummimadras.
lilt [lilt] *s* syngende tonefald; munter sang.
lily ['lili] *s* lilje; **~ of the valley** *s* liljekonval; **~ pond** *s* åkandedam.
limb [lim] *s* (om arm, ben etc) lem; *risk life and ~* risikere liv og lemmer // *v* sønderlemme.
limber ['limbə*] *v: ~ up (sport)* varme op.
limbo ['limbəu] *s* glemsel; *be in ~* svæve i det uvisse.
lime [laim] *s* kalk; *(bot)* lind(etræ); lime(frugt).
limelight ['laimlait] *s* rampelys; *in the ~* i søgelyset.
limestone ['laimstəun] *s* kalksten, limsten.
limit ['limit] *s* grænse; *that's the ~!* nej, nu kan det være nok! *he's the ~!* han er altså noget så! *within ~s* inden for visse grænser; *off ~s* (om sted) forbudt område // *v* begrænse.
limitation [limi'teiʃən] *s* begrænsning.
limited ['limitid] *adj* begrænset; indskrænket; **~ (liability) company** *s (Ltd)* aktieselskab (med begrænset ansvar).
limp [limp] *s: walk with a ~* halte // *v* halte, humpe // *adj* slap, slatten.
limpid ['limpid] *adj* (krystal)klar.
Linden ['lidən] *s: ~ (tree)* lindetræ.
line [lain] *s* linje; line, snor; kæde, række; (om bus etc) rute; branche; *along these ~s* omtrent sådan her; *all along the ~* over hele linjen;

draw the ~ at sth trække grænsen ved ngt; *get a ~ on sby* (F) få ngt at vide om en; *take a firm ~ with sby* stå fast over for en; være streng mod en; *what's your ~?* hvad laver du? *in his ~ of business* i hans branche; *in ~ with* på bølgelængde med; i overensstemmelse med // *v* kante; (om tøj) fore; beklæde; *~ up* stille op (på rad); arrangere.

lineage ['liniidʒ] *s* afstamning, herkomst; ['lainidʒ] linjeantal.

linear ['liniə*] *adj* linje-; lineær.

lined ['laind] *adj* furet; linieret.

line drawing ['lain,drɔ:iŋ] *s* stregtegning.

linen ['linin] *s* lærred; linned.

liner ['lainə*] *s* rutebåd.

linesman ['lainzmən] *s (fodb)* linjevogter; (i tennis) linjedommer; telefonarbejder; ledningsarbejder.

line-up ['lainʌp] *s* række, geled; *(sport)* holdsammensætning.

linger ['liŋgə*] *v* tøve, nøle; drysse; (fx om lugt) blive hængende; **~ing** *adj* tøvende; langsom; langvarig.

lingo ['liŋgəu] *s (pl: ~es)* sprog.

linguist ['liŋgwist] *s* sprogforsker, lingvist.

linguistics [liŋ'gwistiks] *spl* sprogvidenskab, lingvistik.

liniment ['linimənt] *s* salve, liniment.

lining ['lainiŋ] *s* (om tøj) for; forstof; *brake ~* bremsebelægning.

link [liŋk] *s* (i kæde) led; forbindelse; tilknytning // *v* sammenkæde; koble (sammen); *~ up* knytte sammen; hænge sammen.

linkage ['liŋkidʒ] *s* sammenknytning, kobling.

links [liŋks] *spl* golfbane.

link-up ['liŋkʌp] *s* forbindelse; telefonmøde; (i rumfart) sammenkobling.

lino ['lainəu] *s* (F) linoleum.

linseed ['linsi:d] *s* hørfrø; **~ oil** *s* linolie.

lion ['laiən] *s* løve; *the ~'s share* broderparten; **~ cub** *s* løveunge.

lioness ['laiənis] *s* hunløve.

lip [lip] *s* læbe; (på kop etc) rand, overkant; (F) frækhed; *lower ~* underlæbe; *upper ~* overlæbe; *keep a stiff upper ~* ikke fortrække en mine; bide tænderne sammen; *my ~s are sealed* jeg siger ikke et ord; **~block** *s* læbepomade med solfilter; **~read** *v* mundaflæse; **~ service** *s: pay ~ service to* lefle for; **~stick** *s* læbestift.

liqueur [li'kjuə*] *s* likør.

liquid ['likwid] *s* væske // *adj* flydende; klar; strålende; **~ assets** *spl* likvider, disponible midler.

liquidate ['likwideit] *v* likvidere; **liquidation** [-'deiʃən] *s* likvidation.

liquidizer ['likwidaizə*] *s* blender.

liquor ['likə*] *s* væske, spiritus, alkohol.

liquorice ['likəris] *s* lakrids; **~ allsorts** *s* lakridskonfekt.

lisp [lisp] *s* læspen // *v* læspe.

list [list] *s* liste; (om skib) slagside // *v* skrive op; føre (på) liste; (om skib) krænge over; *~ed building* fredet bygning; *Grade One ~ed* fredet i klasse A.

listen [lisn] *v* lytte, høre efter; *~ to* lytte til; høre (på); høre efter; **~er** *s* tilhører; (radio)lytter.

listless ['listlis] *adj* sløv, ligeglad.

lit [lit] *præt* og *pp* af *light.*

literacy ['litərəsi] *s* det at kunne læse og skrive.

literal ['litərəl] *adj* bogstavelig; ordret; **~ly** *adv: ~ly speaking* bogstavelig talt; så at sige.

literary ['litərəri] *adj* litterær.

literate ['litərət] *adj* som kan læse og skrive; kultiveret.

literature ['litrətʃə*] *s* literatur.

lithe [laið] *adj* smidig; bøjelig.

Lithuania [liθu'einiə] *s* Litauen.

litmus ['litməs] *s* lakmus; **~ test** *s (fig)* afgørende prøve.

litre ['li:tə*] *s* liter.

litter ['litə*] *s* affald; efterladenskaber; rod; (om dyr) kuld; strøelse; kattegrus // *v* lave rod, rode til; (om dyr) få unger; *be ~ed with* flyde med; **~ bin** *s* affaldsspand; **~ bug, ~ lout** *s* natursvin.

little [litl] *adj/adv* lille; lidt; lidet; *a ~* en smule, lidt; *~ by ~* lidt efter lidt; *~ better* ikke stort bedre; *make*

~ *of* ikke gøre ngt stort nummer ud af; ~ *ones* børn; unger; ~ *or nothing* så godt som ingenting.
live *v* [liv] leve; bo; ~ *in* bo i; bo på stedet; ~ *off the land* leve af hvad man dyrker; ~ *on* leve af (fx *milk* mælk); leve på; ~ *on* leve videre; ~ *out of tins* leve af dåsemad; ~ *up to* leve op til; ~ *it up* (F) leve livet, slå sig løs // *adj* [laiv] levende; virkelig; livlig; (om udsendelse) direkte; ~ *wire* højspændingsledning; **~-in** [liv'in] *adj* som bor på stedet.
livelihood ['laivlihud] *s* levebrød.
liveliness ['laivlinəs] *s* livlighed; **lively** ['laivli] *adj* livlig; levende.
liven ['laivən] *v:* ~ *up* sætte fut i; muntre op.
liver ['livə*] *s* lever.
liveried ['livərid] *adj* i liberi.
lives [laivz] *spl* af *life*.
livestock ['laivstɔk] *s* (husdyr)besætning.
livid ['livid] *adj* gusten; ligbleg; hvidglødende (af raseri).
living ['liviŋ] *s* levevis; underhold; præstekald; *standard of* ~ levefod; *earn (,make) one's* ~ tjene til livets opretholdelse // *adj* levende; leve-; **~ room** *s* opholdsstue; **~ standards** *spl* levestandard; **~ wage** *s* løn der er til at leve af.
lizard ['lizəd] *s* firben; øgle.
load [ləud] *s* byrde; læs; belastning; *that was a ~ off my mind* der faldt en sten fra mit hjerte; *a ~ of, ~s of* masser af // *v* læsse; laste; belæsse; belaste; (om kamera, gevær etc) lade; **~ed** *adj* belæsset; ladt; følelsesladet; (F) stenrig; fuld, beruset.
loaf [ləuf] *s (pl: loaves* [ləuvz]) brød; *two loaves of bread* to brød // *v* (også: ~ *about)* drysse rundt; **~er** *s* drivert; collegesko.
loam [ləum] *s* lermuld.
loan [ləun] *s* lån; *have the ~ of sth* have ngt til låns, låne ngt; *on* ~ til låns // *v* udlåne.
loath [ləuθ] *adj: be ~ to* nødigt ville.
loathe [ləuð] *v* hade, afsky; væmmes ved; **loathing** *s* lede, væmmelse; **loathsome** ['ləuðsʌm] *adj* ækel, væmmelig, led.
loaves [ləuvz] *spl* af *loaf*.
lobby ['lɔbi] *s* forværelse; vestibule; *(pol)* interessegruppe // *v* lave korridorpolitik.
lobe [ləub] *s (anat)* lap (fx i hjernen); (også: *ear* ~) øreflip.
lobster ['lɔbstə*] *s* hummer.
local [ləukl] *s: the ~* det lokale værtshus; *the ~s* folkene på stedet // *adj* stedlig, lokal; stedvis; **~ call** *s (tlf)* lokalsamtale; **~ colour** *s* lokalkolorit; **~ government** *s* kommunalt selvstyre.
locality [ləu'kæliti] *s* sted, lokalitet.
locate [ləu'keit] *v* lokalisere; finde; placere; *be ~d at* være beliggende ved.
location [ləu'keiʃən] *s* lokalisering; placering; sted; *on* ~ udendørs (film)optagelse.
loch [lɔχ] *s* (skotsk) sø.
lock [lɔk] *s* lås; (i kanal) sluse; (om hår) lok, tot; ~, *stock and barrel* rub og stub; *under ~ and key* under lås og slå // *v* låse; blokere; kunne låses; ~ *up* låse af; spærre inde.
locker ['lɔkə*] *s* skab; kasse; **~ room** *s* omklædningsrum.
locket ['lɔkit] *s* (om smykke) medaljon.
lock gate ['lɔkgeit] *s* sluseport.
lockjaw ['lɔkdʒɔ:] *s* stivkrampe.
locksmith ['lɔksmiθ] *s* klejnsmed.
locum ['ləukəm] *s* (om læge el. præst) vikar.
locust ['ləukəst] *s* græshoppe.
locution [lə'kju:ʃən] *s* talemåde.
lodge [lɔdʒ] *s* lille hus; gartnerbolig; portnerbolig; loge // *v* logere, bo; indkvartere; deponere; indsende; ~ *in* sætte sig fast i, blive hængende i; ~ *with* bo hos; **lodger** *s* lejer, logerende; **lodgings** *spl* logi; lejet værelse.
loft [lɔft] *s* (hø)loft; loftrum.
lofty ['lɔfti] *adj* højtbeliggende; overlegen; højtravende.
log [lɔg] *s* tømmerstok, stamme; brændeknude; (også: *~book)* skibsjournal, logbog; kørselsbog; *sleep like a* ~ sove som en sten // *v* skrive ned (,ind); **~ cabin** *s* tømmerhytte.

loggerheads ['lɔgəhɛdz] *spl: be at ~ with sby* ligge i strid med en.
logic ['lɔdʒik] *s* logik; **~al** *adj* logisk.
loin [lɔin] *s: ~ of veal* kalvenyresteg; **~s** *spl* lænd(er).
loiter ['lɔitə*] *v* drive; slentre *(about* rundt); *no ~ing* ophold forbudt.
loll [ləul] *v* sidde (,stå) og hænge.
lollipop ['lɔlipɔp] *s* slikkepind; **~ lady, ~ man** *s* person med funktion som skolepatrulje.
lolly ['lɔli] *s* slikkepind; ispind.
lone [ləun] *adj* ensom; enlig; **~ly** *adj* ensom; enlig.
loner ['ləunə*] *s* enspænder.
lonesome ['ləunsəm] *adj* ensom.
long [lɔŋ] *v* længes *(for* efter; *to* efter at) // *adj* lang; stor // *adv* længe; *all night ~* hele natten (lang); *~ before* længe før (,inden); *before ~* inden længe, snart; *at ~ last* endelig langt om længe; *no ~er, not any ~er* ikke længere; **~-awaited** *adj* længe ventet; **~-distance** *adj (sport)* distance-; *(tlf)* sv.t. mellembys, udenbys; (om lastbil) langturs-; **~drink** *s* stort glas med (oftest) alkoholfri drik.
longevity [lɔn'dʒɛviti] *s* lang levetid.
long-haired ['lɔŋhɛəd] *adj* langhåret.
longhand ['lɔŋhænd] *s* almindelig skrift (mods: *shorthand* stenografi).
longing ['lɔŋiŋ] *s* længsel *(for* efter) // *adj* længselsfuld.
longitude ['lɔŋgitju:d] *s (geogr* etc) længde; **longitudinal** [-'tju:dinəl] *adj* på langs; længde-.
long... ['lɔŋ-] sms: **~ johns** *spl* lange underbukser; **~ jump** *s* længdespring; **~-lasting** *adj* varig, langvarig; **~-lived** [-livd] *adj* som lever længe; langvarig; **~-lost** *adj* længe savnet; langsigtet; **~-range** *adj* langdistance; **~-sighted** *adj* langsynet; **~-standing** *adj* gammel; mangeårig; **~-suffering** *adj* langmodig; **~-term** *adj* langsigtet, langtids-; **~-wave** *s* langbølge; **~-winded** [-windid] *adj* langtrukken; omstændelig.
loo [lu:] *s* (F) toilet, wc.
look [luk] *s* blik; udseende; udtryk; *can I have a ~?* må jeg se? *have a ~ round* se sig om; *I don't like the ~ of it* det ser ikke godt ud; det tegner ikke godt // *v* se, kigge; se 'ud; vende (ud); *~ after* se efter; tage sig af, passe; *~ after oneself* passe på sig selv; *~ at* se på; undersøge; *~ down on* se ned på; *~ for* lede efter; *~ forward to* glæde sig til; se frem til; *~ like* ligne; *~ on* se 'til; *~ out* passe på; *~ out (for)* være forberedt på; være ude efter; *~ to* passe på; se hen til; regne med; *~ up* slå op (fx *in a dictionary* i en ordbog); opsøge; besøge; se op; *~ up!* op med humøret! *~ up to* beundre, se op til.
look-alike ['lukalaik] *s* (om person) dobbeltgænger.
looker ['lukə*] *s: be a (good) ~* se godt ud; **~-on** *s* tilskuer.
looking glass ['lu:kiŋgla:s] *s* spejl.
look-out ['lukaut] *s* udkigspost; *be on the ~ for* være på udkig efter.
looks [luks] *spl* udseende.
loom [lu:m] *s* væv // *v* tårne sig op; virke truende.
loony ['lu:ni] *adj* (S) skør; **~ bin** *s* (S) galeanstalt.
loop [lu:p] *s* løkke; bugtning; (som prævention) spiral; *~ the ~ (fly)* loope; **~hole** *s* smuthul.
loose [lu:s] *adj* løs; (om tøj) vid, løstsiddende; løs på tråden; slap; *be at a ~ end* ikke vide hvad man skal finde på; *run ~* løbe frit omkring; være sluppet løs; *let (,set) ~* slippe løs (,fri); **~-leaf** *adj* løsblads-.
loosen ['lu:sn] *v* løsne (på), slække (på); *~ up!* slap af!
loot [lu:t] *s* bytte // *v* plyndre.
lop [lɔp] *v* (om træ) beskære; *~ off* skære (,hugge) af.
lope [ləup] *v* løbe, storke.
lopsided ['lɔpsaidid] *adj* skæv, usymmetrisk.
loquacious [lə'kweiʃəs] *adj* snakkesalig.
lord [lɔ:d] *s* herre; *Lord* lord (adelstitel); *the Lord* Vorherre; *good Lord!* du gode Gud! *the (House of) Lords* overhuset // *v: lord it*; spille stor på den; **lordly** *adj* fornem; storslået;

hoven; *the* **Lord Mayor** *s* overborgmesteren (især i London); **Lordship** *s: your Lordship* Deres Nåde; *the* **Lord's Prayer** *s* fadervor.
lorry ['lɔri] *s* lastvogn; *articulated* ~ sættevogn; ~ **driver** *s* lastbilchauffør.
lose [lu:z] *v (lost, lost* [lɔst]) tabe; miste; komme væk fra; ~ *heart* tabe modet; ~ *(time)* (om ur) gå for langsomt; *be lost* gå tabt; være faret vild; være fortabt; *get lost* fare vild; *get lost!* skrub af! forsvind! *kindness is lost on him* venlighed er spildt på ham; ~ *sight of sth* tabe ngt af syne; **loser** ['lu:zə*] *s* (om person) taber.
loss [lɔs] *s* tab; spild; (om skib) forlis; *be at a* ~ være i vildrede; ikke begribe et muk; *sell at a* ~ sælge med tab; *he's a dead* ~ han er håbløs; ~ *of life* tab af menneskeliv.
lost [lɔst] *præt* og *pp* af *lose // adj* fortabt; ~ **property** *s* (kontor for) glemte sager.
lot [lɔt] *s* lodtrækning; skæbne; jordlod; (vare)parti; *the* ~ det altsammen; *a* ~ meget; *a* ~ *of* mange; *be a bad* ~ være en kedelig type; ~*s of* masser af; *draw* ~*s* trække lod.
lottery ['lɔtəri] *s* lotteri.
loud [laud] *adj* (om lyd etc) høj, kraftig; larmende; højrøstet; (om farve etc) skrigende; *say it out* ~ sige det højt; ~**hailer** *s* råber; ~**mouth** *s* skrålhals, gabhals; ~**speaker** *s* højttaler.
lounge [laundʒ] *s* salon; vestibule // *v* stå og hænge; sidde henslængt; ~ **bar** *s* (i pub el. hotel) finere bar; ~ **suit** *s* habit.
louse [laus] *s (pl: lice* [lais]) lus // *v:* ~ *up* lave rav i.
lousy ['lauzi] *adj (fig)* modbydelig; (F) luset, elendig; fornæret.
lout [laut] *s (neds)* drønnert.
lovable ['lʌvəbl] *adj* elskelig.
love [lʌv] *s* kærlighed; elskede, skat; *be (,fall) in* ~ *with* være (,blive) forelsket i; *make* ~ elske, have samleje *(to* med); *send sby one's* ~ sende en en kærlig hilsen; ~ *fifteen* (i tennis) nul-femten // *v* elske; holde af; ~ *to* elske at; gerne ville; ~ **affair** *s* kærlighedsforhold; ~**birds** *spl* to forelskede, "turtelduer"; ~ **letter** *s* kærestebrev; ~ **life** *s* kærlighedsliv.
lovely ['lʌvli] *adj* yndig; dejlig.
love-making ['lʌvmeikiŋ] *s* erotik; samleje.
lover ['lʌvə*] *s* elsker, kæreste; ynder.
loving ['lʌviŋ] *adj* kærlig, øm.
low [ləu] *adj* lav, dyb; ringe, dårlig; gemen, tarvelig; ved at være opbrugt; *feel* ~ være deprimeret; *be lying* ~ holde sig skjult; *he's very* ~ han er langt nede; *he's running* ~ *on jokes* han er ved at løbe tør for vittigheder // *v* (om ko) brøle; ~-**cal,** ~-**calorie** *adj* kalorielet; ~-**cut** *adj* udringet.
lower ['ləuə*] *v* sænke; dæmpe; hale ned (fx *the blind* gardinet); ~ *oneself* nedværdige sig.
low... sms: ~-**grade** *adj* (om benzin) med lavt oktantal; ~-**key** [-ki:] *adj* afdæmpet; ~**lands** *spl* lavland; ~**ly** *adj* beskeden, simpel; ~-**minded** [-maindid] *adj* lavsindet, vulgær; ~-**paid** *adj* lavtlønnet; ~-**pitched** *adj* dyb; dæmpet; ~ **tide** *s* ebbe.
loyal ['lɔiəl] *adj* tro, loyal; trofast; ~**ty** *s* troskab; trofasthed.
lozenge ['lɔzindʒ] *s* tablet, pastil; rombe.
L-plate ['ɛlpleit] *s* L-skilt (på bil hvis fører er *learner* begynder).
Ltd ['limitid] (fork.f. *limited)* A/S.
lubricant ['lu:brikənt] *s* smøremiddel.
lubricate ['lu:brikeit] *v* smøre.
lucent [lu:sənt] *adj* strålende.
lucid ['lu:sid] *adj* klar; lysende.
luck [lʌk] *s* skæbne; lykke, held; *bad* ~ uheld; *good* ~*!* held og lykke! *have* ~ være heldig; *be in* ~ sidde i held; *just my* ~*! (iron)* typisk! *he's down on his* ~ han har modgang; han sidder hårdt i det; *out of* ~ uheldig; *a piece of* ~ et rent held; *push one's* ~ friste skæbnen; *with any* ~,... med lidt held...; *worse* ~*!* gud bedre det!
luckily ['lʌkili] *adv* heldigvis.
luckless ['lʌklis] *adj* uheldig.
lucky ['lʌki] *adj* heldig; ~*y you!* hvor

er du heldig! ~ **dip** *s* (om leg) fiskedam.
lucrative ['lu:krətiv] *adj* indbringende.
ludicrous ['lu:dikrəs] *adj* latterlig, komisk.
lug [lʌg] *v* slæbe, hale.
luggage ['lʌgidʒ] *s* bagage; ~ **rack** *s* bagagehylde (,-net).
lugubrious [lu'gu:briəs] *adj* trist, bedrøvelig.
lukewarm ['lu:kwɔ:m] *adj* lunken.
lull [lʌl] *s* pause; stille periode; *the ~ before the storm* stilhed før stormen // *v* lulle (et barn); berolige.
lullaby ['lʌləbai] *s* vuggevise.
lumbar ['lʌmbə*] *adj* lænde-.
lumber ['lʌmbə*] *s* tømmer; skrammel // *v* lunte, traske; ~**jack** *s* skovhugger.
luminous ['lu:minəs] *adj* lysende; klar.
lump [ləmp] *s* klump; bule; (om person) sløv padde; klods; *in a ~* på én gang // *v: ~ it* finde sig i det; (også: *~ together)* klumpe (sig) sammen; *(fig)* skære over en kam; ~ **sugar** *s* hugget sukker; ~ **sum** *s* sum betalt én gang for alle; **lumpy** *adj* klumpet.
lunacy ['lu:nəsi] *s* sindssyge, vanvid.
lunar ['lu:nə*] *adj* måne-.
lunatic ['lu:nətik] *s/adj* sindssyg.
lunch [lʌntʃ] *s* frokost // *v* spise frokost; ~ **break** *s* frokostpause.
luncheon ['lʌntʃən] *s* (forretnings)frokost; ~ **meat** *s* sv.t. forloren skinke; ~ **voucher** *s* frokostbillet.
lunch hour ['lʌntʃ auə*] *s* frokostpause.
lung [lʌŋ] *s* lunge.
lunge [lʌndʒ] *s* udfald // *v* kaste sig frem.
lurch [lə:tʃ] *s* slingren; krængning; *leave sby in the ~* lade en i stikken // *v* slingre.
lure [luə*] *v* lokke.
lurid ['ljuərid] *adj* uhyggelig, skummel; gloende; blodig.
lurk [lə:k] *v* lure; ligge (,stå) på lur.
luscious ['lʌʃəs] *adj* lækker; saftig; yppig; overdådig.
lush [lʌʃ] *adj* saftig, frodig.
lust [lʌst] *s* liderlighed; lyst, begær // *v: ~ after* begære, tørste efter.
lustre ['lʌstə*] *s* glans.
lustrous ['lʌstrəs] *adj* skinnende, strålende.
lusty ['lʌsti] *adj* stærk; (kerne)sund; kraftig.
lute [lu:t] *s* lut; ~**nist** ['lu:tənist] *s* lutspiller.
luxuriant [lʌg'zjuəriənt] *adj* overdådig; frodig.
luxuriate [lʌg'zjuərieit] *v: ~ in* svælge i, nyde.
luxurious [lʌg'zjuəriəs] *adj* luksuriøs; overdådig.
luxury ['lʌkʃəri] *s* luksus.
lying ['laiiŋ] *s* løgn // *adj* løgnagtig; ~-**in** *s* barsel.
lynch [lintʃ] *v* lynche.
lynx [liŋks] *s* los.
lyric ['lirik] *adj* lyrisk; ~**s** *spl* lyrik; sangtekst.

M

M, m [ɛm].
m fork.f. *metre, mile, million.*
MA fork.f. *Master of Arts.*
ma [ma:] *s* (F) mor.
ma'am [ma:m] *s* (fork.f. *madam)* frue.
mac [mæk] *s* (F) regnfrakke.
macaroon [mækə'ru:n] *s* makron.
mace [meis] *s* scepter; *(gastr)* muskatblomme.
machinations [mæki'neiʃəns] *spl* intriger.
machine [mə'ʃi:n] *s* maskine; maskineri; automat // *v* sy på maskine; ~ **gun** *s* maskingevær; ~**ry** [mə'ʃi:nəri] *s* maskineri; ~ **tool** *s* værktøjsmaskine; **machinist** *s* maskinist.
mackerel ['mækərəl] *s* makrel.
mackintosh ['mækintɔʃ] *s* regnfrakke.
macrobiotic [mækrəubai'ɔtik] *adj* mikro-makro.
mad [mæd] *adj* sindssyg, gal; skør; *~ about* vred over; skør med; *like ~* som en gal; *drive sby ~* drive en til vanvid; *~ as a hatter* bindegal.
madam ['mædəm] *s* (i tiltale) frue.
madcap ['mædkæp] *adj* forfløjen, skør.
madden [mædn] *v* drive til vanvid; ~**ing** *adj* irriterende, kreperlig.

made [meid] *præt* og *pp* af *make;* **~-to-measure** *adj* syet (,lavet) efter mål; **~-up** *adj* opdigtet; sminket; færdig(lavet).
madhouse ['mædhaus] *s* galeanstalt.
madly ['mædli] *adv* vanvittigt; ~ *in love* dødeligt forelsket.
madman ['mædmən] *s: like a* ~ som en gal.
madness ['mædnis] *s* sindssyge; galskab, raseri.
magazine [mægə'zi:n] *s* tidsskrift; magasin, depot.
maggot ['mægət] *s* maddike, larve.
magic ['mædʒik] *s* magi, trylleri, trolddom; *work like* ~ gå som smurt // *v:* ~ *away* trylle væk; ~ *up* trylle frem; **~al** *adj* magisk; **~ carpet** *s* flyvende tæppe.
magician [mə'dʒiʃən] *s* troldmand; tryllekunstner.
magistrate ['mædʒistreit] *s* fredsdommer; underretsdommer.
magnanimous [mæg'næniməs] *adj* storsindet, ædelmodig.
magnate ['mægneit] *s* magnat, matador.
magnet ['mægnit] *s* magnet.
magnetic [mæg'nɛtik] *adj* magnetisk.
magnetism ['mægnitizəm] *s* magnetisme.
magnificent [mæg'nifisnt] *adj* storslået, herlig.
magnify ['mægnifai] *v* forstørre; **~ing glass** *s* forstørrelsesglas.
magnitude ['mægnitju:d] *s* størrelse(sorden) *of the first* ~ af allerstørste betydning; *a fool of the first* ~ alle tiders idiot.
magpie ['mægpai] *s (zo)* skade.
mahogany [mə'hɔgəni] *s* mahogni.
maid [meid] *s* pige; jomfru; *old* ~ gammeljomfru; **~en** *s* ung pige // *adj* ugift; uberørt; uprøvet; **~en name** *s* pigenavn; **~en voyage** *s* jomfrurejse; **~-of-honour** *s (am)* brudepige.
mail [meil] *s* post; breve; ringbrynje // *v* poste, sende (med posten); **~-order** *s* postordre; **~van** *s* postbil.
maim [meim] *v* kvæste; lemlæste.
main [mein] *s* hovedledning; *in the* ~ i hovedsagen // *adj* hoved-; **~ branch** *s* (om firma) hovedafdeling; **~ course** *s (gastr)* hovedret; **~frame** *s (edb)* central computer; **~land** *s* fastland.
mainly ['meinli] *adv* hovedsagelig, især.
main road ['meinrəud] *s* hovedvej.
mains [meinz] *spl* lysnet; forsyningsnet; hovedkontakt; hovedhane; ~ *operated* tilsluttet nettet.
mainspring ['meinspriŋ] *s* drivkraft.
mainstay ['meinstei] *s (fig)* grundpille.
mainstream ['meinstri:m] *s* hovedstrømning // *adj* fremherskende.
maintain [mein'tein] *v* opretholde, bevare; vedligeholde; hævde; forsørge.
maintenance ['meintənəns] *s* opretholdelse; vedligeholdelse; underhold(sbidrag); understøttelse.
maisonette [meizə'nɛt] *s* toetages lejlighed i større hus.
maize [meiz] *s* majs; majsgult.
majestic [mə'dʒɛstik] *adj* majestætisk.
majesty ['mædʒəsti] *s* majestæt.
major ['meidʒə*] *s* major; myndig (person); *(mus)* dur // *v:* ~ *in French* have fransk som hovedfag // *adj* større; betydningsfuld; størst, hoved-.
majority [mə'dʒɔriti] *s* flertal; myndighedsalder.
make [meik] *s* fabrikat, mærke; (om tøj etc) snit; *be on the* ~ være på vej frem (,opad) // *v (made, made* [meid]) lave; fremstille; gøre (til); ~ *sby sad* gøre en bedrøvet; ~ *sby do sth* få en til at gøre ngt; ~ *it* klare den; *two and two* ~ *four* to og to er fire; ~ *friends with* blive ven(ner) med; ~ *peace* slutte fred; *let's* ~ *it 8 o'clock* lad os sige kl. 8; ~ *sth happen* få ngt til at ske; ~ *as if to do sth* lade som om man skal til at gøre ngt; ~ *away with* skille sig af med; stikke af med; ~ *do with* klare sig med; ~ *for* sætte kurs efter; fare løs på; ~ *off* tage afsted; ~ *out* skimte, ane; forstå; udfærdige, skrive (fx *a bill* en regning); ~ *over* overdrage;

~ *up* udgøre; opdigte, finde på; pakke ind; rede (op) (fx *the bed* sengen); sminke sig; ~ *up for* erstatte, opveje; ~ *up one's mind* bestemme sig; ~ *it up to sby for sth* gøre ngt godt igen for en; ~ *it up with sby* blive gode venner igen med en.
make-believe ['meikbili:v] *adj* påtaget; skin-.
maker ['meikə*] *s* fabrikant, producent; skaber.
makeshift ['meikʃift] *s* nødhjælp // *adj* improviseret, nød-.
make-up ['meikʌp] *s* sminke, make-up; sammensætning.
making ['meikiŋ] *s: in the* ~ under udarbejdelse; *she has the* ~ *of a good pianist* hun har det der skal til for at blive en god pianist.
maladjusted [mælə'dʒʌstid] *adj* dårligt tilpasset; miljøskadet.
maladroit [mælə'drɔit] *adj* kluntet, ubehændig.
malady ['mælədi] *s* sygdom, onde.
male [meil] *s* mand; (om dyr) han; *(neds)* mandsperson // *adj* mandlig; mandig; han-; ~ **child** *s* dreng(ebarn).
malevolent [mə'lɛvələnt] *adj* ondsindet.
malformation ['mælfɔ:'meiʃən] *s* misdannelse.
malfunction [mæl'fʌŋkʃən] *s* funktionsfejl // *v* være i uorden; være defekt.
malice ['mælis] *s* ondsindethed; skadefryd.
malicious [mə'liʃəs] *adj* ondskabsfuld; skadefro; *(jur)* i ond hensigt.
malign [mə'lain] *v* bagtale.
malignant [mə'lignənt] *adj* ondartet, malign.
malingerer [mə'liŋgərə*] *s* simulant.
mall [mɔ:l, mæl] *s* promenade, indkøbsstrøg (bilfrit).
mallard ['mæla:d] *s* gråand.
malleable ['mæliəbl] *adj* som kan formes, blød.
mallet ['mælit] *s* (træ)kølle; kødhammer.
malnutrition ['mælnju:'triʃən] *s* underernæring.
malpractice [mæl'præktis] *s* forsømmelse; uagtsomhed; embedsmisbrug.
malt [mɔ:lt] *s* malt; maltwhisky.
maltreat [mæl'tri:t] *v* mishandle.
mammal ['mæməl] *s* pattedyr.
man [mæn] *s (pl: men)* mand; menneske; (i skak etc) brik; ~ *of war* krigsskib; ~ *of the world* verdensmand; *to a* ~ alle som én; *that* ~ *Hardy* ham Hardy; // *v* bemande.
manacles ['mænəkəls] *spl* håndjern.
manage ['mænidʒ] *v* klare; styre, lede; manipulere; ~ *to* klare at; **~able** *adj* medgørlig; til at styre; overskuelig; **~ment** *s* ledelse; administration; direktion.
manager ['mænidʒə*] *s* leder; direktør; impresario.
managing *adj:* ~ *director* administrerende direktør.
mandarin ['mændərin] *s* mandarin; (F) ping.
mandatory ['mændətəri] *adj* obligatorisk.
mane [mein] *s* manke.
maneater ['mæni:tə*] *s* menneskeæder; (om kvinde) mandfolkejæger.
manful ['mænful] *adj* mandig, tapper.
manganese [mæŋgə'ni:z] *s* mangan.
manger ['meindʒə*] *s* krybbe.
mangle [mæŋgl] *s* (tøj)rulle // *v* rulle (tøj); *(fig)* lemlæste.
manhandle ['mænhændl] *v* mishandle; bakse med.
manhood ['mænhud] *s* manddom; mandighed.
manhunt ['mænhʌnt] *s* menneskejagt.
mania ['meiniə] *s* mani; vanvid.
maniac ['meiniæk] *s* sindssyg.
manic ['mænik] *adj* manisk; **~-depressive** *adj* maniodepressiv.
manifest ['mænifɛst] *v* manifestere; (ud)vise; give udtryk for // *adj* åbenbar.
manifestation [mænife'steiʃən] *s* tilkendegivelse; manifestation.
manifold ['mænifəuld] *adj* mangfoldig; alsidig // *v* mangfoldiggøre.
manila [mə'nilə] *s:* ~ *envelope* brun kuvert.
manipulate [mə'nipjuleit] *v* manipulere; betjene, manøvrere.

mankind [mæn'kaind] *s* menneskeheden.
manly ['mænli] *adj* mandig, viril.
man-made ['mænmeid] *adj* menneskeskabt; syntetisk.
manned ['mænd] *adj* bemandet.
manner ['mænə*] *s* måde, facon; maner; væremåde; *all ~ of* alle slags; *in a ~ of speaking* om man så må sige; *in the grand ~* i den store stil; **~ed** *adj* affekteret.
mannerism ['mænərizm] *s* affekterethed.
manners ['mænəz] *spl* opførsel; væsen; *bad ~* uopdragenhed.
mannish ['mæniʃ] *adj* (om kvinde) mandhaftig.
manoeuvre [mə'nu:və*] *s* manøvre // *v* manøvrere (med); lempe.
manor ['mænə*] *s* herregård, gods.
manpower ['mænpauə*] *s* arbejdskraft.
manse [mæns] *s* præstegård.
manservant ['mænsə:vnt] *s (pl: menservants)* tjener.
mansion ['mænʃən] *s* palæ; **~s** *spl* (finere) beboelseshus.
manslaughter ['mænslɔ:tə*] *s* manddrab.
mantelpiece ['mæntəlpi:s] *s* kaminhylde.
mantle [mæntl] *s* kappe; dække.
manual ['mænjuəl] *s* håndbog; lærebog // *adj* manuel, hånd-.
manufacture [mænju'fæktʃə*] *s* fabrikation; produkt, vare // *v* fremstille, forarbejde; **~r** *s* fabrikant, producent.
manure [mə'njuə*] *s* gødning; møg; *liquid ~* ajle; gylle.
Manx [mæŋks] *adj* fra øen Man.
many ['mɛni] *adj* mange; *a great ~* en mængde; *as ~ (as)* så mange (som); *as ~ again* dobbelt så mange; *~ a time* mange gange; *~'s the time they have...* de har tit og ofte...; *too ~* for mange; *one too ~* en for meget; *he has had one too ~* han har fået en tår over tørsten.
map [mæp] *s* (land)kort // *v* kortlægge.
maple [meipl] *s (bot)* ahorn, løn.
mar [ma:*] *v* skæmme; ødelægge.
marble [ma:bl] *s* marmor; gravsten; statue; (glas)kugle; *he's lost his ~s* han er gået fra forstanden; **~s** *spl* kuglespil.
March [ma:tʃ] *s* marts.
march [ma:tʃ] *s* march // *v* marchere; *~ sby off* slæbe af med en; *~ on Moscow* marchere mod Moskva; **~-past** *s* forbidefilering.
mare [mɛə*] *s* (om hest) hoppe.
margarine ['ma:dʒə,ri:n] *s* margarine; **marge** [ma:dʒ] *s* (F) margarine.
margin ['ma:dʒin] *s* margen; rand, kant; spillerum.
marginal ['ma:dʒinəl] *adj* underordnet, marginal; rand-; **~ly** *adv* en anelse.
marigold ['mærigəuld] *s (bot)* morgenfrue.
marinate ['mærineit] *v* marinere.
marine [mə'ri:n] *s* marine, flåde; marineinfanterist; *tell that to the ~s!* den må du længere ud på landet med! ja god morgen! // *adj* hav-, marine-.
mariner ['mærinə*] *s (gl)* sømand; matros.
marital ['mæritəl] *adj* ægteskabelig.
maritime ['mæritaim] *adj* sø-; sømands-, maritim.
marjoram ['ma:dʒərəm] *s (bot)* merian.
mark [ma:k] *s* mærke, spor; tegn; (i skolen) karakter; (ved skydning) mål; *be up to the ~* leve op til standarden; være oppe på mærkerne; *be slow off the ~* være sen til at komme ud af starthullerne; *hit the ~* ramme plet; *wide of the ~* helt ved siden af // *v* mærke, sætte mærke på; plette; kendetegne; markere; lægge mærke til; (i skolen) rette, give karakterer; *~ my words!* husk det! du skal se jeg får ret! *he's a good pianist, ~ you* han er vel at mærke en god pianist; *~ time* slå takt; *~ down* skrive ned; nedsætte (pris); give lav karakter; *~ off* afmærke; *~ out* afmærke; udpege; *~ up* sætte (pris) op; **~ed** *adj* markeret; tydelig; **~er** *s* markør; bogmærke; filtpen.

market ['ma:kit] *s* marked; *be in the ~ for sth* være liebhaver til ngt; *the single ~* (om EF) det indre marked // *v* markedsføre; forhandle; **~able** *adj* salgbar; **~ day** *s* torvedag.
marketeer [ma:ki'tiə*] *s* EF-tilhænger.
market garden ['ma:kit ˌga:dn] *s* handelsgartneri.
marketing ['ma:kitiŋ] *s* markedsføring.
marketplace ['ma:kitpleis] *s* markedsplads, torv.
marking ['ma:kiŋ] *s* markering; retning (af opgaver); **~ ink** *s* mærkeblæk.
marksman ['ma:ksmən] *s* (dygtig) skytte; **~ship** *s* skydefærdighed; træfsikkerhed.
marmalade ['ma:məleid] *s* appelsinmarmelade; citrusmarmelade.
maroon [mə'ru:n] *v* lade i stikken // *adj* kastaniefarvet; *be ~ed* (også) blive efterladt på en øde ø.
marquee [ma:'ki:] *s* stort telt (til havefest etc).
marquess, marquis ['ma:kwis] *s* (som titel) markis.
marriage ['mæridʒ] *s* ægteskab; bryllup; **~able** *adj* giftefærdig; **~ guidance** [-gaidəns] *s* ægteskabsrådgivning; **~ licence** *s* vielsesattest.
married ['mærid] *adj* gift *(to* med); ægteskabelig; *he's ~ with two children* han er gift og har to børn; *a ~ couple* et ægtepar.
marrow ['mærəu] *s* marv; livskraft; *(bot)* græskar.
marry ['mæri] *v* gifte sig (med); vie; forene; *get married* blive gift, gifte sig; *~ off* gifte væk.
marsh [ma:ʃ] *s* sump, mose; eng.
marshal ['ma:ʃəl] *s* marskal // *v* bringe orden i; **~ling yard** *s* rangerbanegård.
marshmallow ['ma:ʃmæləu] *s* slags slik, sv.omtr.t. skumfiduser.
marshy ['ma:ʃi] *adj* sumpet.
marsupial [ma:'su:piəl] *s* pungdyr.
marten ['ma:tin] *s* mår.
martial ['ma:ʃl] *adj* krigs-, militær-; **~ law** *s* undtagelsestilstand.
Martian ['ma:ʃən] *s* marsbeboer // *adj* mars-.
martyr ['ma:tə*] *s* martyr // *v* gøre til martyr; **~dom** *s* martyrium.
marvel ['ma:vəl] *s* under; vidunder; mirakel // *v: ~ (at)* undre sig (over).
marvellous ['ma:vələs] *adj* fantastisk, vidunderlig, herlig.
masculine ['mæskjulin] *adj* maskulin, mandig; hankøns-.
mash [mæʃ] *s (gastr)* mos; *bangers and ~* (F) pølser med kartoffelmos // *v* mose; *~ed potatoes* kartoffelmos.
mask [ma:sk] *s* maske // *v* maskere; skjule; dække; **~ing tape** *s* malertape.
mason [meisn] *s* murer; stenhugger; frimurer; **~ry** *s* murværk.
masquerade [mæskə'reid] *s* maskerade // *v* spille komedie; *~ as* udgive sig for.
mass [mæs] *s* masse; mængde; (i kirke og *mus)* messe; *the ~es* de store masser // *v* samle sig (i mængder).
massacre ['mæsəkə*] *s* massakre // *v* nedslagte, massakrere.
massage ['mæsa:dʒ] *s* massage // *v* massere; *(fig)* manipulere (med).
massed [mæst] *adj* samlet.
massif ['mæsif] *s* bjergmassiv.
massive ['mæsiv] massiv.
mast [ma:st] *s* mast.
master ['ma:stə*] *s* herre, mester; (på skib) kaptajn; (i skole) lærer; *Master John* (om dreng) den unge hr. John; *Master's degree* kandidateksamen // *v* beherske; styre; lære sig; mestre; **~ copy** *s* original; **~ful** *adj* mesterlig; myndig; **~ key** *s* universalnøgle; **~ly** *adj* mesterlig; **~mind** *s* hjerne (bag ngt) // *v* være hjernen i (,bag); **Master of Arts** *(MA) s* sv.t. magister; **Master of Science** *(MSc) s* sv.t. mag.scient; **~piece** *s* mesterstykke; **~ plan** *s* overordnet plan; **~stroke** *s* mesterværk; genialt indfald; **~ switch** *s* hovedkontakt.
mastery ['ma:stəri] *s* herredømme; beherskelse; kunnen.
mat [mæt] *s* måtte; løber; lunchserviet.

match [mætʃ] *s* tændstik; kamp, match; sidestykke; ligemand; parti; *be a ~ for sby* kunne måle sig med en; *be a good ~* være et godt parti; passe godt; *meet one's ~* møde sin ligemand // *v* svare til, passe til; sammenholde, afpasse; være på højde med; leve op til; *be well ~ed* passe godt sammen; *~ up* assortere (varer); *~ up to* leve op til; **~box** *s* tændstikæske; **~ing** *adj* som passer til; **~less** *adj* mageløs; **~maker** *s* Kirsten giftekniv.

mate [meit] *s* makker, kammerat; ægtefælle; mage; *(mar)* styrmand // *v* gifte sig (med); (om fugle etc) parre sig // *adj* (i skak) mat.

material [mə'tiəriəl] *s* materiale; stof, tøj; *raw ~s* råstoffer // *adj* materiel; legemlig; væsentlig.

materialize [mə'tiəriəlaiz] *v* blive til virkelighed; dukke op.

maternal [mə'tə:nl] *adj* moderlig; mødrene.

maternity [mə'tə:niti] *s* moderskab; barsel; **~ leave** *s* barselsorlov; **~ ward** *s* fødeafdeling; **~ wear** [-wɛə*] *s* ventetøj.

matey ['meiti] *adj* kammeratlig.

mathematical [mæθə'mætikl] *adj* matematisk.

mathematician [mæθəmə'tiʃən] *s* matematiker.

mathematics [mæθə'mætiks] *spl* matematik.

maths [mæθs] *spl* (F) matematik.

mating ['meitiŋ] *s* parring.

matrimony ['mætriməni] *s* ægteskab.

matrix ['meitriks] *s (pl: matrices)* matrice.

matron ['meitrən] *s* økonoma; (på hospital) forstanderinde.

matt [mæt] *adj* matteret; mat.

matted ['mætid] *adj* (sammen)filtret.

matter ['mætə*] *s* sag; spørgsmål; *(fys* etc) stof, substans; indhold; *(med)* materie, pus; *no ~ what* lige meget hvad; *what's the ~?* hvad er der i vejen? *that's another ~* det er en anden sag; *as a ~ of course* selvfølgeligt, helt naturligt; *as a ~ of fact* faktisk; i virkeligheden; *it's a ~ of habit* det er en vanesag; *it's a ~ of opinion* det er en smagssag; *it's a ~ of time* det er et spørgsmål om tid; *printed ~* tryksag // *v* betyde ngt; *it does not ~* det er lige meget (,ligegyldigt) **~-of-fact** *adj* nøgtern; med begge ben på jorden.

matting ['mætiŋ] *s* måttevæv (fx kokostæppe etc).

mattress ['mætris] *s* madras.

mature [mə'tjuə*] *v* modne(s); udvikle (sig) // *adj* moden; voksen; (om ost) lagret.

maturity [mə'tjuəriti] *s* modenhed.

maudlin ['mɔ:dlin] *adj* sentimental, rørstrømsk.

maul [mɔ:l] *v* mishandle; *~ed* ilde tilredt.

mauve [məuv] *adj* lyslilla.

maverick ['mævərik] *s* enspænder, løsgænger.

mawkish ['mɔ:kiʃ] *adj* sentimental, overstrømmende.

max fork.f. *maximum.*

maxim ['mæksim] *s* leveregel, maksime.

maximum ['mæksiməm] *s (pl: maxima)* højdepunkt, maksimum // *adj* højest, maksimal-.

May [mei] *s* maj; *~ Day* 1. maj.

may [mei] *v (præt: might* [mait]) kan (,vil) måske; må godt; *he ~ come* han kommer måske; han må godt komme; *~ I smoke?* må jeg godt ryge? *be that as it ~* lad det nu ligge; *~ God bless you!* Gud velsigne dig! *I might as well go* jeg kan lige så godt gå; *you might like to try* du vil måske gerne prøve; *~ we all meet next year!* jeg håber vi alle ses igen næste år!

maybe ['meibi:] *adv* måske.

mayday ['meidei] *s* nødsignal, SOS.

mayhem ['meihɛm] *s: create ~* hærge, rase, fare ødelæggende frem.

mayor ['mɛə*] *s* borgmester; **mayoress** *s* borgmesterfrue.

maypole ['meipəul] *s* majstang.

maze [meiz] *s* labyrint.

MCP ['ɛmsi:'pi:] *s* (F) (fork.f. *male chauvinist pig)* mandschauvinist.

MD (fork.f. *Doctor of Medicine)* læge.

me [mi:] *pron* mig; *dear ~!* men dog! *~ too!* også mig! jeg med!
mead [mi:d] *s* mjød.
meadow ['mɛdəu] *s* eng.
meagre ['mi:gə*] *adj* mager, tynd; sparsom, knap.
meal [mi:l] *s* måltid; (groft) mel; **~s-on-wheels** *spl* madudbringning (til pensionister etc); **~time** *s* spisetid.
mealy-mouthed ['mi:limauðd] *adj* forsigtig, spagfærdig; skinhellig.
mean [mi:n] *s* middeltal; gennemsnit; middelvej; (se også *means) // v (meant, meant* [mɛnt]) betyde; mene; have i sinde; *be meant for* være bestemt for (,til); *I meant to tell you* jeg ville have fortalt dig det; *~ well* mene det godt *// adj* nærig, smålig; middel-; mellem-; *he's no ~ lover* han er slet ikke nogen dårlig elsker; *the ~ value* middelværdien.
meander [mi'ændə*] *v* (om flod) bugte sig; (om person) slentre omkring.
meaning ['mi:niŋ] *s* betydning; mening **~ful** *adj* betydningsfuld; (om blik etc) sigende; **~less** *adj* meningsløs.
meanness ['mi:nnis] *s* smålighed, nærighed.
means [mi:ns] *s* middel; midler; penge; *by ~ of* ved hjælp af; *by all ~* hellere end gerne; naturligvis; *by no ~* under ingen omstændigheder; på ingen måde; *by some ~ or other* på en el. anden måde; *a man of ~* en formuende mand.
meant [mɛnt] *præt* og *pp* af *mean.*
meantime ['mi:ntaim], **meanwhile** ['mi:nwail] *adv* i mellemtiden.
measles [mi:zlz] *s* mæslinger; *German ~* røde hunde.
measly ['mi:zli] *adj* elendig, sølle.
measure ['mɛʒə*] *s* mål; målebånd; grad; forholdsregel; *take ~s to do sth* tage skridt til at gøre ngt; *in some ~* til en vis grad *// v* måle; registrere; tage mål af; *give sth for good ~* give ngt i tilgift; *~ for ~* lige for lige *~ up to* kunne måle sig med; **~d** *adj* afmålt; taktfast; velovervejet; **~ments** *spl* mål; *chest ~ments* brystmål.
meat [mi:t] *s* kød; **~ ball** *s* kødbolle; frikadelle; **~ loaf** *s* forloren hare; **~ pie** *s* kødpostej.
meaty ['mi:ti] *adj* kødfuld; (om person) kraftig, svær.
mechanic [mi'kænik] *s* mekaniker; **~al** *adj* mekanisk; **~s** *spl* mekanik.
mechanism ['mɛkənizm] *s* mekanisme.
mechanization [mɛkənai'zeiʃən] *s* mekanisering.
medal [mɛdl] *s* medalje.
medallist ['mɛdəlist] *s (sport)* medaljevinder.
meddle [mɛdl] *v: ~ in* blande sig i; *~ with* rode med; pille ved; **~some** *adj* geskæftig.
media ['mi:diə] *s: the ~* medierne.
mediaeval [mɛdi'i:vl] *adj* d.s.s. *medieval.*
median ['mi:diən] *adj* middel-, gennemsnitlig.
mediate ['mi:dieit] *v* mægle; formidle.
mediation [mi:di'eiʃən] *s* mægling; formidling.
medic ['mɛdik] *s* (F) læge.
medical ['mɛdikl] *adj* læge-; lægelig; medicinsk; medicinal-; **~ student** *s* lægestuderende.
medication [mɛdi'keiʃən] *s* (medicinsk) behandling; ordinering; medicin.
medicinal [mɛ'disinəl] *adj: ~ plant* lægeurt.
medicine ['mɛdisin] *s* lægevidenskab; medicin; **~ chest** *s* medicinskab.
medieval [mɛdi'i:vl] *adj* middelalderlig.
mediocre [mi:di'əukə*] *adj* middelmådig.
mediocrity [mi:di'ɔkriti] *s* middelmådighed.
meditate ['mɛditeit] *v* meditere; gruble, pønse på.
meditation [mɛdi'teiʃən] *s* meditation; eftertanke.
meditative ['mɛditətiv] *adj* tænksom, spekulativ.
Mediterranean [mɛditə'reiniən] *adj* middelhavs-; *the ~* Middelhavet.

medium ['mi:diəm] *s (pl: media)* middel; *(pl: ~s)* medie; *the happy ~* den gyldne middelvej // *adj* medium, mellem; **~-range** *adj* mellemdistance-.
medley ['mɛdli] *s* blanding, sammensurium.
meek [mi:k] *adj* ydmyg; forsagt.
meet [mi:t] *s* (sports)stævne // *v (met, met* [mɛt]) møde(s); træffe(s); ses; tage imod; tilfredsstille; *I'll ~ you at the station* jeg henter dig på stationen; vi mødes på stationen; *~ with* møde; komme ud for; *make both ends ~* få det til at løbe rundt.
meeting ['mi:tiŋ] *s* møde; *(sport* etc) stævne; *she's at a ~* hun er til møde.
megalomania [mɛgələ'meiniə] *s* storhedsvanvid.
melancholy ['mɛlənkəli] *s* melankoli, tungsind(ighed) // *adj* melankolsk.
mêlée ['mɛlei] *s* tummel; håndgemæng.
mellifluous [mi'lifluəs] *adj* honningsød, blid.
mellow ['mɛləu] *v* modne(s) // *adj* moden; blød; (om farve etc) mættet; (om lyd) fyldig.
melodious [mi'ləudiəs] *adj* melodisk, melodiøs.
melody ['mɛlədi] *s* melodi; velklang.
melt [mɛlt] *v* smelte; blive rørt; *~ away* smelte væk; *~ down* smelte om; **~-down** *s* nedsmeltning (af atomreaktor); **~ing point** *s* smeltepunkt; **~ing pot** *s* smeltedigel.
member ['mɛmbə*] *s* medlem; element; lem; *~s only* kun for medlemmer; **Member of Parliament** *(MP) s* parlamentsmedlem.
membership ['mɛmbəʃip] *s* medlemskab; medlemstal; medlemmer.
memo ['mɛməu] *s* (F) d.s.s. *memorandum.*
memorable ['mɛmərəbl] *adj* mindeværdig.
memorandum [mɛmə'rændəm] *s (pl: memoranda* [-'rænda]) notat, optegnelse; memorandum.
memorial [mi'mɔ:riəl] *s* mindesmærke; minde // *adj* minde-.
memorize ['mɛməraiz] *v* lære udenad; notere.
memory ['mɛməri] *s* hukommelse; minde, erindring; *(edb)* lager; *in ~ of* til minde om; *not within my ~* ikke så længe jeg kan huske; *within living ~* i mands minde.
men [mɛn] *spl* af *man.*
menace ['mɛnəs] *s* trussel; *that boy's a ~* (F) den dreng er livsfarlig // *v* true.
mend [mɛnd] *s* reparation; bedring; *be on the ~* være i bedring // *v* reparere; stoppe, lappe; bedres, få det bedre; *~ one's ways* forbedre sig.
mendacious [mən'deiʃəs] *adj* løgnagtig.
mendacity [mən'dæsiti] *s* løgnagtighed.
mending ['mɛndiŋ] *s* reparation; lapning; stopning; lappetøj.
menial ['mi:niəl] *adj* underordnet.
menservants *spl* af *manservant.*
men's room ['mɛnzru:m] *s* herretoilet.
menstruate ['mɛnstrueit] *v* have menstruation.
menswear ['mɛnzwεə*] *s* herretøj.
mental [mɛntl] *adj* mental; åndelig; sindssyge-; hjerne-; *he's a ~ case* han er sindssyg; *make a ~ note of sth* skrive sig ngt bag øret; *~ arithmetic* hovedregning.
mentality [mɛn'tæliti] *s* mentalitet; indstilling.
mention ['mɛnʃən] *s* omtale; *get a ~* blive nævnt; få rosende omtale // *v* omtale, nævne; *don't ~ it!* ikke ngt at takke for! *not to ~ John* for ikke at tale om John.
MEP ['ɛmi:'pi:] *s* (fork.f. *Member of the European Parliament)* medlem af Europaparlamentet.
mercenary ['mə:sinəri] *s* lejesoldat // *adj* beregnende; pengegrisk.
merchandise ['mə:tʃəndaiz] *s* vare(r).
merchant ['mə:tʃənt] *s* købmand; grosserer; **~ bank** *s* forretningsbank; **~ navy** *s* handelsflåde.
merciful ['mə:siful] *adj* barmhjertig, nådig; **merciless** *adj* ubarmhjertig.
mercury ['mə:kjuri] *s* kviksølv.

mercy ['mə:si] *s* barmhjertighed, nåde; *have ~ on* have medlidenhed med; *be at sby's ~* være i ens vold; **~ killing** *s* medlidenhedsdrab.
mere [miə*] *adj* ren (og skær); kun; *the ~st suggestion of* den mindste antydning af; *a ~ boy* kun en dreng; **~ly** *adv* kun, udelukkende; slet og ret; *not ~ly...* ikke bare...
merge [mə:dʒ] *v* smelte sammen; forene(s); slå sammen; fusionere; **~r** *s* *(merk)* fusion.
meringue [mə'ræŋ] *s* marengs.
merit ['mɛrit] *s* fortjeneste; fortrin; udmærkelse // *v* fortjene.
meritocracy [mɛri'tɔkrəsi] *s* præstationsræs.
mermaid ['mə:meid] *s* havfrue.
merrily ['mɛrili] *adv* lystigt, muntert.
merriment ['mɛrimənt] *s* lystighed.
merry ['mɛri] *adj* lystig, glad; *~ Christmas!* glædelig jul! **~-go-round** *s* karrusel; **~-making** *s* fest(lighed), festivitas.
mesh [mɛʃ] *s* (i net) maske; net(værk).
mesmerize ['mɛzməraiz] *v* hypnotisere; tryllebinde.
mess [mɛs] *s* rod, uorden; kludder; *(mil)* messe, kantine; *look a ~* se herrens (,rædselsfuld) ud; *in a ~* rodet, uordentlig; i ét rod; *make a ~* svine; rode; kludre // *v* rode; lave kludder i; grise til; *~ around* (F) rode rundt; fumle; gå og svine; *~ about with* bikse (,fumle) med; have en affære med; *~ up* lave rod i; grise til.
message ['mɛsidʒ] *s* meddelelse; besked; budskab; *do the ~s* (især skotsk) købe ind; *did you get the ~?* (F) er det sivet ind?
messenger ['mɛsindʒə*] *s* bud; budbringer.
Messrs ['mɛsəz] *spl* de herrer.
messy ['mɛsi] *adj* rodet; snavset, griset; *a ~ divorce* en skilsmisse med en masse ballade.
met [mɛt] *præt* og *pp* af *meet* // fork.f. *meteorological; Metropolitan (Opera).*
metabolism [mɛ'tæbəlizm] *s* stofskifte.
metal [mɛtl] *s* metal; asfalt.
metallic [mi'tælik] *adj* metallisk; metal-.
mete [mi:t] *v: ~ out* udmåle; tildele.
meteorological [mi:tiərə'lɔdʒikl] *adj* meteorologisk.
meteorology [mi:tiə'rɔlədʒi] *s* -meteorologi.
meter ['mi:tə*] *s* måler; tæller; (også: *parking ~)* parkometer; *(am)* meter // *v* måle; **~ man** *s* måleraflæser.
method ['mɛθəd] *s* metode.
methodical [mi'θɔdikl] *adj* metodisk, systematisk.
meths [mɛθs] *s* d.s.s. *methylated spirits.*
methylated ['mɛθileitid] *adj: ~ spirits* denatureret sprit.
meticulous [mɛ'tikjuləs] *adj* omhyggelig, pertentlig.
metre ['mi:tə*] *s* meter.
metric ['mɛtrik] *adj* meter- (fx *system* system); **~al** *adj* metrisk; på vers.
metropolis [mə'trɔpəlis] *s* hovedstad; storby.
metropolitan [mɛtrə'pɔlitən] *adj* hovedstads-; *the Metropolitan Opera* berømt opera i New York; **~ police** *s* Londons politi.
mettle [mɛtl] *s* mod; fyrighed; *show one's ~* vise hvad man har i sig.
mew [mju:] *v* (om kat) mjave.
mews [mju:z] *s: ~ house* (hus indrettet i tidl. staldbygninger) sv.t. atelierlejlighed.
miaow [mi:'au] *v* (om kat) mjave.
mice [mais] *pl* af *mouse.*
mickey ['miki] *s: take the ~ out of sby* drille en.
microphone ['maikrəfəun] *s* mikrofon.
microscope ['maikrəskəup] *s* mikroskop; **microscopic** [-'skɔpik] *adj* mikroskopisk.
microwave ['maikrəweiv] *s: ~ (oven)* mikro(bølge)ovn // *v* tilberede i mikroovn.
mid- [mid-] midt (i); i midten af; *in mid-air* i luften; *in mid-morning* midt på formiddagen; *in mid-ocean* midt ude på havet.
midday ['middei] *s* middag.
middle [midl] *s* midje, bæltested;

midte; *in the ~ of* midt i // *adj* midterst, mellemst; mellem-; midter-; **~-aged** *adj* midaldrende; *the* **Middle Ages** *spl* middelalderen; **~-class** *adj* sv.t. borgerlig; *the ~ class(es)* middelstanden; *the* **Middle East** *s* Mellemøsten; **~ finger** *s* langfinger; **~man** *s* mellemmand; **~ name** *s* mellemnavn.
middling ['midliŋ] *adj* mellemgod; middelmådig // *adv* nogenlunde.
midge [midʒ] *s* myg.
midget ['midʒit] *s* dværg // *adj* dværg-; mini- (fx *submarine* ubåd).
midnight ['midnait] *s* midnat.
midriff ['midrif] *s (anat)* mellemgulv.
midshipman ['midʃipmən] *s* kadet.
midst [midst] *s: in the ~ of* midt i; *in our ~* i vores midte, iblandt os.
mid... ['mid-] sms: **~summer** *s* midsommer; **~way** *adj/adv* midtvejs; **~week** *s* midt i ugen; **~wife** *s* jordemor; **~wifery** *s* fødselshjælp; **~winter** *s* midvinter.
miff [mif] *s: in a ~* fornærmet, mopset; **~ed** *adj* fornærmet, mopset.
might [mait] *s* magt; styrke; *with all one's ~* af al (sin) magt // *præt* og *pp* af *may*.
mighty ['maiti] *adj* mægtig // *adv* gevaldig; storsnudet.
migrant ['maigrənt] *s* trækfugl; (om dyr, person) omstrejfer // *adj* som flyver på træk, træk-; omvandrende; *~ worker* gæstearbejder.
migrate ['maigreit] *v* emigrere; drage bort; trække.
migration [mai'greiʃən] *s* vandring; (om fugle) træk.
mike [maik] *s* (fork.f. *microphone)* mikrofon.
mild [maild] *adj* mild, blid; let (fx *ale* øl).
mildew ['mildju:] *s* meldug; skimmel, mug.
mildly ['maildli] *adv* mildt, let; *to put it ~* mildt sagt.
mile [mail] *s* engelsk mil (1609 m); *for ~s* milevidt; *he's ~s better* han er 100 gange bedre; *we could see him a ~ off* vi kunne se ham på lang afstand; *it sticks out a ~* det kan man se med et halvt øje, det er soleklart.
mileage ['mailidʒ] *s* afstand i *miles;* sv.t. kilometergodtgørelse; (også) antal km pr. gallon benzin.
milestone ['mailstəun] *s* sv.t. kilometersten; *(fig)* milepæl.
militant ['militənt] *adj* krigerisk, militant.
military ['militəri] *s: the ~* militæret // *adj* militær(-).
militia [mi'liʃə] *s* milits.
milk [milk] *s* mælk; *full-cream (, whole) ~* sødmælk; *skimmed ~* skummetmælk; *semi-skimmed ~* letmælk // *v* malke (også *fig);* **~ chocolate** *s* flødechokolade; **~float** *s* mælkebil; **~ing** *s* malkning; **~man** *s* mælkemand; mælkebud.
milky ['milki] *adj* mælkeagtig; *the* **Milky Way** *s (astr)* mælkevejen.
mill [mil] *s* mølle, kværn; maskine; tekstilfabrik // *v* male; valse; knuse; hvirvle rundt.
millennium [mi'lɛniəm] *s (pl: ~s* el. *millennia)* årtusind.
miller ['milə*] *s* møller.
millet ['milit] *s* hirse.
milliner ['milinə*] *s* modehandler; modist; **~y** *s* modevarer; modehandel.
millipede ['milipi:d] *s* tusindben.
millstone ['milstəun] *s* møllesten.
millwheel ['milwi:l] *s* møllehjul.
milometer [mai'lɔmitə*] *s* sv.t. kilometertæller.
mime [maim] *s* mimekunstner // *v* mime; parodiere.
mimic ['mimik] *s* mimiker // *v* efterligne; parodiere.
mimicry ['mimikri] *s* efterligning.
min. fork.f. *minute(s); minimum.*
mince [mins] *s* hakket oksekød // *v* hakke; trippe; *not ~ one's words;* ikke lægge fingrene imellem; **~meat** *s* blanding af tørret, hakket frugt (brugt i bagværk); **~ pie** *s* tærte med *~meat.*
mincer ['minsə*] *s* (kød)hakkemaskine.
mincing ['minsiŋ] *adj* affekteret; trippende.
mind [maind] *s* sind, sjæl; hjerne; forstand; indstilling; *bear in ~* tænke på; huske; *change one's ~* bestem-

me sig om; *at the back of one's ~ (fig)* i baghovedet; *to my ~* efter min mening; *make up one's ~* bestemme sig; *have in ~* have i tankerne; *I have a ~ to tell him* jeg har lyst til at sige det til ham; *I'll give him a piece of my ~* jeg skal sige ham min ærlige mening; *be out of one's ~* være ude af sig selv; *it calls sth to my ~* det minder mig om ngt; *it takes your ~ off the problems* det får dig til at glemme problemerne; *it slipped my ~* jeg glemte det; *put his ~ at rest* berolige ham; *be in two ~s about sth* være i tvivl om ngt // *v* passe (fx *children* børn); passe 'på; bryde sig om; have ngt imod; *I don't ~ the noise* jeg har ikke ngt mod støjen; *do you ~ if I borrow your pencil?* har du ngt imod at jeg låner din blyant? *never mind* det gør ikke ngt! skidt med det! *don't ~ me* tag dig ikke af mig; *I would not ~ a drink* jeg ville ikke have ngt imod en drink; *~ your language!* pas på dit sprog! tal ordentligt! *~ the step!* pas på trinet! **~-blowing, ~-boggling** *adj* (F) utrolig; **~ful** *adj: ~ful of* opmærksom på; **~less** *adj* tankeløs, sjælløs; **~ reader** *s* tankelæser.

mine [main] *s* mine, bjergværk // *v* grave efter, bryde (fx *coal* kul); minere.

mine [main] *pron* (se *my*) min, mit, mine; *a friend of ~* en af mine venner.

mine detector ['maindi,tɛktə*] *s* minesøger.

minefield ['mainfi:ld] *s* minefelt.

miner ['mainə*] *s* minearbejder.

mineral ['minərəl] *s* mineral // *adj* mineralsk, mineral-.

minesweeper ['mainswi:pə*] *s* minestryger.

mingle [miŋgl] *v* blande (sig) *(with* med).

mingy ['mindʒi] *adj* fedtet, nærig; snoldet, sølle.

minicab ['minikæb] *s* minitaxi.

minim ['minim] *s (mus)* helnode.

minimal ['minimәl] *adj* mindste-; minimal-.

minimize ['minimaiz] *v* formindske; undervurdere.

minimum ['minimәm] *s* minimum; laveste punkt // *adj* minimums-; mindste-.

mining ['mainiŋ] *s* minedrift; brydning // *adj* mine- (fx *town* by).

minister ['ministə*] *s* præst; (i Skotland) sognepræst; *(pol)* minister.

ministerial [minis'tiəriəl] *adj* ministeriel; minister-.

ministry ['ministri] *s* ministerium; regering.

minor ['mainə*] *s* mindreårig; *(mus)* mol // *adj* underordnet; ubetydelig; side-.

minority [mai'nɔriti] *s* mindretal, minoritet; mindreårighed.

minster ['minstə*] *s* domkirke; klosterkirke.

minstrel ['minstrәl] *s (hist)* trubadur

mint [mint] *s (bot)* mynte; pebermyntebolsje // *v* præge (mønter); *the Royal Mint* den kongelige mønt; *in ~ condition* som ny; ubrugt; **~ sauce** *s* myntesovs (med eddike, sukker og mynte).

minuet [minju'ɛt] *s* menuet.

minus ['mainəs] *s* minus(tegn) // *præp: five ~ three is two* fem minus tre er to.

minute ['minit] *s* minut; øjeblik; notat; *do it this ~!* gør det straks! *at any ~* hvert øjeblik; *the ~ he comes, call me* ring til mig så snart han kommer // *v* skrive (møde)referat.

minute [mai'nju:t] *adj* minutiøs, lille bitte; udførlig.

minutes ['minits] *spl* referat (af møde etc).

miracle ['mirәkl] *s* mirakel; vidunder.

miraculous [mi'rækjuləs] *adj* mirakuløs; mirakel-.

mire [maiə*] *s* sump, morads; smuds.

mirror ['mirə*] *s* spejl // *v* (af)spejle.

mirth [mә:θ] *s* munterhed.

misadventure [misәd'vɛntʃə*] *s* uheld; *death by ~* død ved et uheld.

misanthropist [mi'zænθrәpist] *s* menneskehader, misantrop.

misapprehend [misæpri:hɛnd] *v* misforstå.

misappropriate [misə'prəuprieit] *v* tilegne sig; forgribe sig på.
misbehave [misbi'heiv] *v* opføre sig dårligt; være uartig; **misbehaviour** *s* dårlig opførsel.
miscalculate [mis'kælkjuleit] *v* regne forkert; fejlbedømme; **miscalculation** [-'leiʃən] *s* regnefejl; fejlbedømmelse.
miscarriage [mis'kæridʒ] *s (med)* (spontan) abort; ~ *of justice* justitsmord.
miscellaneous [misə'leiniəs] *adj* blandet; uensartet; diverse.
miscellany [mi'sɛləni] *s* blanding; mangfoldighed.
mischief ['mistʃi:f] *s* gale streger; fortræd, skade; *stay out of* ~ lade være med at lave ulykker.
mischievous ['mistʃivəs] *adj* drillesyg; skælmsk; skadelig.
misconduct [mis'kɔndʌkt] *s* utroskab; *professional* ~ tjenesteforseelse; embedsmisbrug.
misconstrue [miskən'stru:] *v* misfortolke.
misdemeanour [misdi'mi:nə*] *s* forseelse.
miser ['maizə*] *s* gnier.
miserable ['mizərəbl] *adj* elendig, ulykkelig.
miserly ['maizəli] *adj* gerrig.
misery ['mizəri] *s* elendighed; ulykke; jammer.
misfire [mis'faiə*] *v* klikke; slå fejl.
misfit ['misfit] *s* (om person) mislykket individ; afviger.
misfortune [mis'fɔ:tʃən] *s* uheld, ulykke.
misgiving(s) [mis'giviŋ(z)] *s(pl)* bange anelser; betænkeligheder.
misguided [mis'gaidid] *adj* vildledt.
mishap ['mishæp] *s* lille uheld.
mishear [mis'hiə*] *v* høre forkert.
mishmash ['miʃmæʃ] *s* miskmask, rod.
misinform [misin'fɔ:m] *v* give forkerte oplysninger.
misinterpret [misin'tə:prit] *v* misfortolke.
misinterpretation [misintə:pri'teiʃən] *s* misforståelse.
misjudge [mis'dʒʌdʒ] *v* fejlbedømme.
mislay [mis'lei] *v* forlægge; ikke kunne finde.
mislead [mis'li:d] *v* vildlede; føre vild.
mismanage [mis'mænidʒ] *v* bestyre (,forvalte) dårligt.
misplace [mis'pleis] *v* anbringe forkert, fejlplacere; **~d** *adj* malplaceret.
misprint ['misprint] *s* trykfejl.
mispronounce ['misprə'nauns] *v* udtale forkert.
misquote [mis'kwəut] *v* fejlcitere.
misread [mis'ri:d] *v* læse forkert.
Miss, miss [mis] *s* frøken.
miss [mis] *s* kikser, forbier; fejlskud; *that was a near* ~ det var lige ved; *give sth a* ~ blive væk fra ngt; give pokker i ngt // *v* skyde (,ramme) forbi (,ved siden af); savne; overse; gå glip af; komme for sent til; *you can't* ~ det kan ikke slå fejl; *you can't* ~ *it* du kan ikke undgå at se det; *you didn't* ~ *much* du er ikke gået glip af ngt; ~ *the train* komme for sent til toget; ~ *out* udelade; overse; komme til kort.
misshapen [mis'ʃeipn] *adj* misdannet, vanskabt.
missile ['misail] *s* kasteskyts; missil, raketvåben.
missing ['misiŋ] *adj* manglende; (om person) ikke til stede; savnet; forsvundet; *go* ~ forsvinde, blive væk.
mission ['miʃən] *s* mission; delegation; ærinde.
missionary ['miʃənəri] *s* missionær.
misspell ['mis'spɛl] *v* stave forkert.
missus ['misiz] *s (spøg)* kone.
mist [mist] *s* dis, let tåge // *v* sløres; (om vinduer, også: ~ *over*, ~ *up)* dugge.
mistake [mis'teik] *s* fejl, fejltagelse; misforståelse; *make a* ~ tage fejl; *by* ~ ved en fejltagelse; *make no* ~ *about it!* det kan du være stensikker på! // *v* misforstå; ~ *a for b* forveksle a med b; *it is a case of* ~*n identity* der er sket en forveksling; *be* ~*n* tage fejl.
mister ['mistə*] *s* se *Mr.*
mistletoe ['misltəu] *s* mistelten.

mistook [mis'tuk] *præt* af *mistake.*
mistreat [mis'tri:t] *v* behandle dårligt; mishandle.
mistress ['mistris] *s* frue; (skole)lærerinde; herskerinde; mester; elskerinde.
mistrust [mis'trʌst] *s/v* mistro.
misty ['misti] *adj* diset; sløret; dugget; ~ *rain* finregn.
misunderstand [ˌmisʌndə'stænd] *v* misforstå; **-ing** *s* misforståelse; uoverensstemmelse.
misuse *s* [mis'ju:s] misbrug; forkert brug // *v* [mis'ju:z] misbruge; bruge forkert.
mite [mait] *s* mide; (lille) smule; (om barn) lille myr.
mitigate ['mitigeit] *v* lindre, mildne; **mitigating** *adj* formildende.
mitt(en) [mit(n)] *s* vante, luffe.
mix [miks] *s* blanding; kludder // *v* blande; mixe; ~ *up* blande sammen; *be ~ed up in sth* være indblandet i ngt; ~ *with* blande (sig) med; omgås; **-ed** *adj* blandet; fælles-; *a ~ed bag* en broget (for)samling; (,blanding); **-ed-up** *adj* forvirret, desorienteret.
mixer ['miksə*] *en* røremaskine; *he's a good ~er* han har let ved at omgås folk.
mixing bowl ['miksiŋ ˌbəul] *s* røreskål.
mixture ['mikstʃə*] *s* blanding; mikstur.
mix-up ['miksʌp] *s* forvirring.
moan [məun] *s* stønnen, jamren; klage // *v* stønne, sukke; klage (sig); ~ *about* klage over; **-ing** *s* klagen, jamren.
moat [məut] *s* voldgrav.
mob [mɔb] *s* hob, flok; pøbel; bande // *v* overfalde i flok; mobbe; **-bing** *s* mobning.
mobile ['məubail] *s* uro (til pynt) // *adj* mobil, bevægelig; transportabel; ~ *home* husvogn; campingvogn; ~ *library* bogbus.
mobility [məu'biliti] *s* bevægelighed.
mobilize ['məubilaiz] *v* mobilisere.
mock [mɔk] *v* håne; gøre nar ad; efterligne // *adj* forloren, falsk; kunstig.
mockery ['mɔkəri] *s* spot, hån; parodi.
mock exam ['mɔk ik'zæm] *s* prøveeksamen, sv.t. terminsprøve.
mocking-bird ['mɔkiŋbə:d] *s* spottefugl.
mock turtle ['mɔk 'tə:tl] *s* forloren skildpadde.
mock-up ['mɔkʌp] *s* model, simulator; attrap.
MoD [ɛməu'di:] *s* fork.f. *Ministry of Defence.*
mod cons [mɔd'kɔnz] *spl* (i annonce: *modern conveniences)* moderne udstyr (,faciliteter).
mode [məud] *s* måde; mode; toneart.
model [mɔdl] *s* model; gine; mønster; forbillede // *v* modellere; forme; stå model; ~ *clothes* gå mannequin // *adj* eksemplarisk; model-.
moderate *v* ['mɔdəreit] beherske; dæmpe, moderere; (om vind) tage af // *adj* ['mɔdərit] moderat.
moderation [mɔdə'reiʃən] *s* mådehold; *in* ~ med måde.
modern ['mɔdən] *adj* moderne; nyere.
modernize ['mɔdənaiz] *v* modernisere.
modest ['mɔdist] *adj* beskeden; undselig; anstændig.
modesty ['mɔdisti] *adj* beskedenhed; ærbarhed.
modicum ['mɔdikəm] *s* smule, minimum.
modification [mɔdifi'keiʃən] *s* tillempning; modifikation.
modify ['mɔdifai] *v* modificere; lempe; ændre.
module ['mɔdju:l] *s* modul.
moist [mɔist] *adj* fugtig; ~ *tissue* vådserviet; **-en** [mɔisn] *v* fugte, væde.
moisture ['mɔistʃə*] *s* fugt(ighed).
moisturizer ['mɔistʃəraizə*] *s* fugtighedscreme.
molar ['məulə*] *s* kindtand.
molasses [məu'læsiz] *s* (mørk) sirup.
mole [məul] *s* skønhedsplet; muldvarp (også *fig);* bølgebryder.
molecule ['mɔlikju:l] *s* molekyle.
molehill ['məulhil] *s* muldvarpeskud; *make a mountain out of a* ~ gøre en myg til en elefant.

molest [məu'lɛst] *v* genere, forulempe; **~er** *s* seksualforbryder.
mollify ['mɔlifai] *v* blødgøre; formilde.
mollusc ['mɔləsk] *s* bløddyr.
mollycoddle ['mɔlikɔdl] *v* pylre om.
molten ['məultn] *adj* smeltet.
mom [mɔm] *s* (F) mor.
moment ['məumənt] *s* øjeblik; betydning; *at the* ~ i øjeblikket, *for a* ~ et øjeblik; *in a* ~ om et øjeblik; *just a* ~ et øjeblik; *of no* ~ uden betydning; *the* ~ *he said it*... i samme øjeblik han sagde det...; *he has his* ~*s* han har sine lyse øjeblikke; han har sine gode sider.
momentary ['məuməntəri] *adj* øjeblikkelig; forbigående.
momentous [məu'mɛntəs] *adj* vigtig, betydningsfuld.
momentum [məu'mɛntəm] *s* fart; styrke; *gather* ~ få fart på.
monarch ['mɔnək] *s* konge, monark.
monarchy ['mɔnəki] *s* kongedømme, monarki.
monastery ['mɔnəstəri] *s* (munke)-kloster.
Monday ['mʌndi] *s* mandag; *last* ~ i mandags; *on* ~*s* om mandagen, hver mandag.
monetary ['mʌnitəri] *adj* penge-; valuta-.
money ['mʌni] *s* penge; *make* ~ tjene penge; *much* ~ mange penge; *danger* ~ risikotillæg; *get one's* ~*'s worth* få valuta for pengene; *he has* ~ *to burn* han har penge som græs; *be in the* ~ være ved muffen, være velbeslået; **~-grubbing** *adj* pengegrisk; **~lender** *s* pengeudlåner; **~-maker** *s* person der forstår at tjene penge; firma med stor indtjening; **~ order** *s* postanvisning (på under £100).
mongrel ['mɔŋgrəl] *s* (om hund) køter, bastard.
monitor ['mɔnitə*] *s* monitor; kontrolapparat; overvågningsudstyr; fjernsynsskærm; (i skole) ordensduks; // *v* aflytte; kontrollere; overvåge.
monk [mʌŋk] *s* munk.
monkey ['mʌŋki] *s* abe // *v:* ~ *about* fjolle rundt; **~ business** *s* hundekunster, fikumdik; **~ tricks** *spl* hundekunster; **~ wrench** *s* svensknøgle; skruenøgle.
monologue ['mɔnəlɔg] *s* enetale, monolog.
monopolize [mə'nɔpəlaiz] *v* få (,have) monopol på; lægge beslag på.
monopoly [mə'nɔpəli] *s* eneret, monopol; *Monopoly* ® (om spil) Matador.
monosyllabic ['mɔnəusi'læbik] *adj* enstavelses-; (om person) fåmælt.
monotone ['mɔnətəun] *s* ensformig tone.
monotonous [mɔ'nɔtənəs] *adj* ensformig, monoton; kedelig.
monotony [mɔ'nɔtəni] *s* ensformighed, monotoni.
monoxide [mɔ'nɔksaid] *s: carbon* ~ kulilte.
monster ['mɔnstə*] *s* monstrum, uhyre.
monstrosity [mɔn'strɔsiti] *s* uhyre; skrummel; rædsel.
monstrous ['mɔnstrəs] *adj* kolossal, monstrøs; uhyrlig.
month [mʌnθ] *s* måned; *for* ~*s (and* ~*s)* i månedsvis; *last* ~ (i) sidste måned; *next* ~ (i) næste måned; **~ly** *s* månedsblad // *adj* månedlig // *adv* månedsvis; om måneden.
monument ['mɔnjumənt] *s* monument, mindesmærke; **~al** [-'mɛntl] *adj* storslået, monumental.
mooch [mu:tʃ] *v:* ~ *about* daske rundt.
mood [mu:d] *s* humør, sindsstemning; *be in the* ~ *for* være i humør til, have lyst til; *he's in one of his* ~*s* han er i dårligt humør igen; *I'm in no* ~ *to argue* jeg er ikke i humør til at diskutere.
moody ['mu:di] *adj* humørsyg; lunefuld; nedtrykt; mut.
moon [mu:n] *s* måne; *be over the* ~ *with joy* være helt oppe i skyerne af glæde // *v:* ~ *around* drysse rundt; ~ *over sby* drømme forelsket om en; **~beam** *s* månestråle; **~light** *s* måneskin; **~lighting** *s* måneskinsarbejde; **~lit** *adj* måneklar; **~shine** *s* måneskin; (F) hjemmebrændt whisky.

moor [muə*] *s* hede // *v* (om skib) lægge til, fortøje.
mooring ['muəriŋ] *s* fortøjningsplads; **~s** *spl* fortøjninger.
moorland ['muələnd] *s* hede.
moose [mu:s] *s* elg, elsdyr.
moot [mu:t] *adj: it's a ~ question whether...* det er et spørgsmål om..., det kan diskuteres om...
mop [mɔp] *s* svaber; *a ~ of hair* en manke // *v* svabre; tørre (op).
mope [məup] *v* hænge med næbbet.
moped ['məupɛd] *s* knallert.
moral [mɔrl] *s* morale // *adj* moralsk; moral-.
morale [mɔ'ra:l] *s* kampmoral.
morality [mə'ræliti] *s* moral; moralfølelse.
morally ['mɔrəli] *adv* moralsk.
morals ['mɔrəlz] *spl* moral; sæder.
morbid ['mɔ:bid] *adj* sygelig; makaber.
more [mɔ:*] *adj/adv* mer(e); flere; *~ people* flere mennesker; *the ~ he gets, the ~ he wants* jo mere han får, des mere vil han have; *I want two ~ bottles* jeg vil gerne have to flasker til; *no ~* ikke mere; ikke længere; *~ or less* mere el. mindre; *~ than ever* mere end nogensinde; *and what's ~...* og desuden..., dertil kommer at...; **~over** *adv* desuden.
morgue [mɔ:g] *s* lighus.
morning ['mɔ:niŋ] *s* morgen; formiddag; *in the ~* om morgenen; om formiddagen; *yesterday ~* i går morges; *this ~* i morges, i formiddags; *tomorrow ~* i morgen tidlig (,formiddag); **~-afterish** *adj: feel ~-afterish* have tømmermænd; **~-after pill** *s* fortrydelsespille (mod svangerskab); **~ coat** *s* jaket; **~ room** *s* opholdsstue; **~ sickness** *s* graviditetskvalme; **~ suit** *s* citydress (jaket, stribede bukser og bowlerhat).
Moroccan [mə'rɔkən] *s* marokkaner // *adj* marokkansk; **Morocco** [-'rɔkəu] *s* Marokko.
moron ['mɔ:rən] *s* tåbe, idiot.
morose [mə'rəus] *adj* sur, gnaven.
morphia ['mɔ:fiə], **morphine** ['mɔ:fi:n] *s* morfin.
morsel [mɔ:sl] *s* bid; nip; stump.
mortal [mɔ:tl] *s/adj* dødelig.
mortality [mɔ:'tæliti] *s* dødelighed.
mortal sin ['mɔ:tl 'sin] *s* dødssynd.
mortar ['mɔ:tə*] *s* mørtel; morter; **~board** *s* flad, firkantet sort hat (bæres af studerende og lærere ved universiteter).
mortgage ['mɔ:gidʒ] *s* pant; prioritet (i ejendom) // *v* belåne; prioritere.
mortician [mɔ:'tiʃən] *s (am)* bedemand.
mortified ['mɔ:tifaid] *adj* sønderknust, ved at dø af skam.
mortify ['mɔ:tifai] *v* såre, krænke.
mortuary ['mɔ:tʃuəri] *s* lighus, ligkapel.
mosaic [məu'zeiik] *s* mosaik.
Moscow ['mɔskəu] *s* Moskva.
Moslem ['mɔzləm] *s/adj* d.s.s. *Muslim.*
mosque [mɔsk] *s* moské.
mosquito [mə'ski:təu] *s (pl: ~es)* moskito; myg; **~ repellent** *s* myggebalsam.
moss [mɔs] *s (bot)* mos; tørvemose; **~ stitch** *s* perlestrikning.
mossy ['mɔsi] *adj* mosbegroet.
most [məust] *adj/adv* mest; det meste; flest; de fleste; højst; *~ interesting* interessantest; yderst interessant; *~ people think that it is wrong* de fleste mennesker mener at det er forkert; *~ of them* de fleste af dem; *~ of all* allermest; *at the (very) ~* (aller)højst; *make the ~ of* få det mest mulige ud af; **~ly** *adv* hovedsagelig; især.
MoT *s* (fork.f. *Ministry of Transport)* trafikministeriet; *the ~ (test)* årligt bilsyn (på over tre år gamle biler).
moth [mɔθ] *s* natsværmer; møl; **~ball** *s* mølkugle // *v* lægge i mølpose (også *fig);* **~-eaten** *adj* mølædt.
mother ['mʌðə*] *s* mor, moder; *shall I be ~?* skal jeg skænke (,øse) op? // *v* tage sig moderligt at; **~hood** *s* moderskab; **Mothering Sunday** *s* mors dag; **~-in-law** *s* svigermor; **~ly** *adj* moderlig; **~-of-pearl** *s* perle-

mor; **~-to-be** *s* vordende mor; **~-tongue** *s* modersmål.

mothproof ['mɔθpru:f] *adj* mølsikret; møltæt.

motif ['məutif] *s* motiv; mønster.

motion ['məuʃən] *s* bevægelse; tegn, vink; forslag; *(med)* afføring; *the ~ was carried* forslaget blev vedtaget; *set sth into ~* sætte ngt i gang (,bevægelse); *go through the ~s of doing sth* lade som om man gør ngt // *v* vinke til; gøre tegn til; **~less** *adj* ubevægelig; **~ picture** *s* film; **~ sickness** *s* transportsyge.

motivated ['məutiveitid] *adj* motiveret; begrundet; **motivation** [-'veiʃən] *s* motivering.

motive ['məutiv] *s* motiv; hensigt // *adj* bevægende; bevæg- (fx *force* kraft).

motley ['mɔtli] *adj* broget, spraglet.

motor ['məutə*] *s* motor; bil; *(fig)* drivkraft // *v* køre i bil // *adj* motor-; bil-.

Motorail ['məutəreil] *s* biltog.

motor... ['məutə-] sms: **~bike** *s* motorcykel; **~boat** *s* motorbåd; **~cade** *s* bilkortege; **~cycle** *s* motorcykel; **~cyclist** *s* motorcyklist.

motoring ['məutəriŋ] *s* bilkørsel; motorsport; **~ accident** *s* bilulykke; **~ holiday** *s* bilferie.

motorist ['məutərist] *s* bilist.

motor... ['məutə-] sms: **~ oil** *s* bilolie; **~ racing** *s* motorvæddeløb; **~ scooter** *s* scooter; **~ vehicle** *s* motorkøretøj; **~way** *s* motorvej.

mottled [mɔtld] *adj* broget; marmoreret.

mould [məuld] *s* form; støbeform; budding (lavet i form); mug, skimmel; *cast in the same ~* af samme støbning // *v* forme; støbe; mugne.

moulder ['məuldə*] *v* mugne; rådne; forfalde; smuldre hen.

moulding ['məuldiŋ] *s* formning; støbning; *(auto)* pynteliste.

mouldy ['məuldi] *adj* muggen.

moult [məult] *v* (om dyr) fælde.

mound [maund] *s* høj; bunke.

mount [maunt] *s* bjerg; ridehest; (om billede etc) indfatning // *v* stige (op); bestige; gå op ad; montere; indfatte; få stablet på benene.

mountain ['mauntin] *s* bjerg; **~ ash** *s* røn.

mountaineer [maunti'niə*] *s* bjergbestiger; **~ing** *s* alpinisme.

mountain lion ['mauntin ˌlaiən] *s* puma.

mountainous ['mauntənəs] *adj* bjergrig; bjerg-; enorm.

mountain range ['mauntin reindʒ] *s* bjergkæde.

mountainside ['mauntinsaid] *s* bjergside; bjergskråning.

mounted ['mauntid] *adj* til hest, bereden.

mourn [mɔ:n] *v* sørge; græde; *~ (for)* sørge over; **~er** *s* sørgende; efterladt; **~ful** *adj* bedrøvet, trist; **~ing** *s* sorg; sørgedragt.

mouse [maus] *s* *(pl: mice* [mais]) mus; **~trap** *s* musefælde.

moustache [mə'sta:ʃ] *s* overskæg.

mousy ['mauzi] *adj* (om person) grå, trist; (om hår) gråbrunt, leverpostejsfarvet.

mouth [mauθ] *s* *(pl: ~s* [mauðz]) mund; åbning; *be down in the ~* hænge med næbbet; *get it straight from the horse's ~* høre det fra sikker kilde; *by word of ~* mundtligt; *it makes your ~ water* det får tænderne til at løbe i vand // *v* [mauð] smage på ordene, forme (fx ord) med læberne; **~ful** *s* mundfuld; **~ organ** *s* mundharmonika; **~piece** *s* mundstykke; telefontragt; *(fig)* talsmand, talerør; **~wash** *s* mundskyllemiddel; **~-watering** *adj* som får tænderne til at løbe i vand.

movable ['mu:vəbl] *adj* bevægelig; transportabel; *~s* løsøre.

move [mu:v] *s* træk; skridt; flytning; *get a ~ on* få fart på; flytte sig; *make a ~* røre på sig; tage affære; *on the ~* i gang, på farten; *make the first ~* tage initiativet // *v* bevæge (sig); flytte (sig); færdes; gribe, betage; fremsætte forslag om; *be ~d* være rørt (,grebet); *~d to tears* rørt til tårer; *~ about* bevæge sig rundt; rejse rundt; *~ along* gå (,køre) videre; ~ *away* fjerne sig; flytte væk; ~ *house* flytte; ~ *in* flytte ind (i et hus); ~ *over* flytte (sig); ~ *on* komme videre; ~ *out* flytte ud (af et hus); ~ *up* rykke sammen; avancere; **-ment** *s* bevægelse; *(mus,* del af symfoni etc) sats.

movie ['mu:vi] *s* (især *am)* film; *the ~s* biografen.

moving ['mu:viŋ] *adj* som bevæger sig; gribende, rørende; rulle-, rullende.

mow [məu] *v (~ed, ~ed* el. *mown)* meje, slå (fx *grass* græs); **-er** *s* slåmaskine.

MP ['ɛm'pi:] *s* fork.f. *Member of Parliament.*

mpg fork.f. *miles per gallon* (30 mpg sv.t. 29,5 liter pr. 100 km).

mph fork.f. *miles per hour* (60 mph sv.t. 96 km i timen).

Mr ['mistə*] *s: ~ Ford* hr. Ford.

Mrs ['misiz] *s: ~ Miller* fru Miller; *Doctor and ~ Smith* doktor Smith og frue.

Ms [miz] *s* fr. (dækker både *Miss* og *Mrs).*

MSc fork.f. *Master of Science.*

Mt fork.f. *Mount.*

much [mʌtʃ] *adj/adv* meget; omtrent; absolut; langt; *how ~ is it?* hvad koster det? *it's not ~* det er ikke meget; det er ikke ngt særligt; *it was not ~ of a party* der var ikke meget ved det selskab; *it is ~ the same* det er nogenlunde det samme; *this is ~ better* det her er meget bedre; *this is ~ the best* den her er langt den bedste; *so ~ for him!* færdig med ham! det var så ham! *make ~ of sth* gøre et stort nummer ud af ngt.

muck [mʌk] *v: ~ about* nusse rundt; *~ in* give en hånd med; *~ out* muge ud; *~ up* (F) ødelægge; **--raking** *s* dybdeborende journalistik; *(neds)* skandalejournalistik; **--up** *s* rod, "koks"; fiasko.

mucky ['mʌki] *adj* (F) bemøget; sjofel, smudsig.

mucus ['mju:kəs] *s* slim.

mud [mʌd] *s* mudder; slam; skidt.

muddle [mʌdl] *s* forvirring; roderi, kludder; *be in a ~* (om person) være forvirret // *v* (også: *~ up)* forkludre; forvirre; *~ through an exam* klare en eksamen som man nu bedst kan.

muddy ['mʌdi] *adj* pløret, sølet; uklar.

mud flats ['mʌd,flæts] *spl* mudderbanke.

mudguard ['mʌdga:d] *s (auto)* stænkeskærm.

mudpack ['mʌdpæk] *s* muddermaske.

muff [mʌf] *s* muffe; *make a ~ of it* forkludre det.

muffin ['mʌfin] *s* slags flad bolle.

muffle [mʌfl] *v* pakke ind; dæmpe; **-d** *adj* formummet; dæmpet.

muffler ['mʌflə*] *s* halstørklæde; *(am, auto)* lydpotte.

mufti ['mʌfti] *s: in ~* civilklædt.

mug [mʌg] *s* krus; (F) fjæs; flab; tosse // *v* overfalde; **-ger** *s* voldsmand, røver; **-ging** *s* røverisk overfald.

muggy ['mʌgi] *adj* lummer.

mulatto [mju:'lætəu] *s (pl: ~es)* mulat.

mulberry ['mʌlbəri] *s* morbær; mørkviolet.

mule [mju:l] *s* muldyr; tøffel.

mull [mʌl] *v: ~ over* spekulere over.

mulled [mʌld] *adj: ~ wine* sv.t. gløgg.

multiple ['məltipl] *adj* sammensat; mangfoldig; **~ crash** *s* harmonikasammenstød; massesammenstød; **~ store** *s* kædeforretning.

multiplication [mʌltipli'keiʃən] *s* mangfoldiggørelse; multiplikation.

multiply ['mʌltiplai] *v* mangfoldiggøre, formere (sig); gange, multiplicere.

multi-storey ['mʌltistɔ:ri] *adj* fleretages.

multitude ['mʌltitju:d] *s* mængde; sværm; vrimmel.

mum [mʌm] *s* (F) mor; *~'s the word!* vi må ikke lade et ord slippe ud! // *adj: keep ~* ikke sige et ord.

mumble [mʌmbl] *s* mumlen // *v* mumle.

mumbo jumbo ['mʌmbəu'dʒʌmbəu] *s* bunke sludder, volapyk.

mummy ['mʌmi] *s* mumie; (F) mor.

mumps [mʌmps] *s* fåresyge.

munch [mʌntʃ] *v* gumle, gnaske (på).

mundane [mʌn'dein] *adj* jordbunden, prosaisk.
Munich ['mju:nik] *s* München.
municipal [mju:'nisipl] *adj* kommunal, kommune-; ~ **council** *s* kommunalbestyrelse; ~ **heating** *s* fjernvarme.
municipality [mju:nisi'pæliti] *s* kommune; kommunal myndighed.
munitions [mju:'niʃəns] *spl* krigsmateriel.
mural ['mjuərəl] *s* vægmaleri, fresko.
murder ['mə:də*] *s* mord, drab; *he can get away with* ~ han kan tillade sig hvad som helst // *v* myrde, dræbe.
murderer ['mə:dərə*] *s* morder, drabsmand.
murderous ['mə:dərəs] *adj* morderisk; dræbende.
murky ['mə:ki] *adj* tåget; mørk, skummel.
murmur ['mə:mə*] *s* mumlen; murren // *v* mumle; knurre; (om flod etc) bruse; (om skov) suse.
muscle [mʌsl] *s* muskel; muskelkraft // *v:* ~ *in on* mase sig ind på.
muscular ['mʌskjulə*] *adj* muskuløs; muskel-.
muse [mju:z] *s* muse // *v* gruble, spekulere.
museum [mju:'ziəm] *s* museum; ~ **piece** *s* museumsstykke.
mush [mʌʃ] *s* (F) klistret masse, grød.
mushroom ['mʌʃrum] *s (bot)* svamp, (især:) champignon // *v (fig)* skyde op som paddehatte.
mushy ['mʌʃi] *adj* blød, grødet; moset; (F) rørstrømsk.
music ['mju:zik] *s* musik; noder; *set sth to* ~ sætte musik til ngt; *face the* ~ tage skraldet.
musical ['mju:zikl] *s* musical // *adj* musikalsk; musik-; ~ **instrument** *s* musikinstrument.
music hall ['mju:zik ,hɔ:l] *s* varieté.
musician [mju:'ziʃən] *s* musiker.
music paper ['mju:zik ,peipə*] *s* nodepapir.
music stand ['mju:zik ,stænd] *s* nodestativ.
musk [mʌsk] *s* moskus.
Muslim ['mʌzlim] *s* muslim // *adj* muslimsk.
muslin ['mʌzlin] *s* musselin.
mussel [mʌsl] *s* musling.
must [mʌst] *s* nødvendighed; noget man 'skal // *v* må, måtte; skal, skulle; være nødt til; *I* ~ *do it* jeg må (,er nødt til at) gøre det; ~ *you go now?* skal du (absolut) gå nu? *well, if you* ~ siden du absolut vil.
mustard ['mʌstəd] *s* sennep; sennepsfarve.
muster ['mʌstə*] *v* mønstre; samle.
mustn't [mʌsnt] d.s.s. *must not.*
musty ['mʌsti] *adj* muggen.
mute [mju:t] *adj* stum // *v* dæmpe; **~d** ['mju:tid] *adj* dæmpet; med sordin.
mutilate ['mju:tileit] *v* skamfere.
mutilation [mju:ti'leiʃən] *s* lemlæstelse; skamfering.
mutinous ['mju:tinəs] *adj* oprørsk; som gør mytteri.
mutiny ['mju:tini] *s* mytteri.
mutter ['mʌtə*] *v* mumle, brumme, rumle.
mutton [mʌtn] *s* fårekød; *leg of* ~ lammekølle; ~ **chop** *s* lammekotelet.
mutual ['mju:tʃuəl] *adj* gensidig; indbyrdes; fælles.
muzzle [mʌzl] *s* snude; mule; (gevær)munding // *v:* ~ *sby* give en mundkurv på.
muzzy ['mʌzi] *adj* omtåget; tåget.
my [mai] *pron* min, mit; mine // *interj* du store! ih!
myopic [mai'ɔpik] *adj* nærsynet.
myself [mai'sɛlf] *pron* jeg selv; selv; mig; *I did it* ~ jeg gjorde det selv; *by (,for)* ~ alene, på egen hånd.
mysterious [mi'stiəriəs] *adj* mystisk.
mystery ['mistəri] *s* mysterium.
mystic ['mistik] *s* mystiker // *adj* mystisk.
mystify ['mistifai] *v* mystificere; forvirre.
myth [miθ] *s* myte; sagn; **mythical** *adj* mytisk; sagn-; opdigtet.
mythological [miθə'lɔdʒikl] *adj* mytologisk.
mythology [mi'θɔlədʒi] *s* mytologi.

N

N, n [ɛn].
nab [næb] *v* snuppe.
nag [næg] *s* krikke; sur kælling; småskænden // *v* (konstant) småskænde; **~ging** *adj* (om smerte) murrende; (om fx kone) som skælder og smælder.
nail [neil] *s* negl; søm; *hard as ~s* benhård; *on the ~* (F) lige på stedet // *v* få fat i; (F) negle, hugge; slå søm i; *~ sby down to sth* holde en fast ved ngt; **~brush** *s* neglebørste; **~file** *s* neglefil; **~ polish** *s* neglesaks; **~ scissors** *spl* neglesaks; *a pair of ~ scissors* en neglesaks; **~ varnish** *s* neglelak.
naïve [na'i:v] *adj* naiv; ukunstlet.
naked ['neikid] *adj* nøgen, bar; utilsløret; *it's the ~ truth* det er den rene sandhed; *with the ~ eye* med det blotte øje.
namby-pampy [næmbi'pæmpi] *v* pylre om, forkæle // *adj* blødsøden; krukket.
name [neim] *s* navn; ry; *a man by the ~ of* en mand ved navn; *in the ~ of B* i B's navn; *lend one's ~ to* lægge navn til; *make a ~ for oneself* skabe sig et navn; *get a bad ~* få et dårligt ry; *put down one's ~ for sth* lade sig skrive op til ngt; *call sby ~s* skælde en ud // *v* nævne; give navn, kalde; *he does skiing, swimming, running, you ~ it!* han løber på ski, svømmer, løber og alt hvad man i øvrigt kan komme på; **~dropping** *s* pralen af sine fine bekendte; **~less** *adj* navnløs; unævnelig.
namely ['neimli] *adv* nemlig; det vil sige.
namesake ['neimseik] *s* navnebror (,-søster).
nanny ['næni] *s* *(pl: nannies)* barnepige; **~ goat** *s* (hun)ged.
nap [næp] *s* lur; (om stof) luv // *v* tage sig en lur; *be caught ~ping* blive taget på sengen.
nape [neip] *s: the ~ of the neck* nakken; nakkeskindet.
napkin ['næpkin] *s* serviet; ble.
nappy ['næpi] *s* (F) ble.
narcissus [na:'sisəs] *s (pl: narcissi* [-'sisai]) narcis; pinselilje.
narcotic [na:'kɔtik] *s* bedøvelsesmiddel; narkotisk middel; **~s** *spl* narkotika, stoffer.
nark [na:k] *s* (F) stikker // *v* ærgre; irritere; stikke.
narrate [næ'reit] *v* fortælle.
narrative ['nærətiv] *s* beretning, fortælling.
narrator [nə'reitə*] *s* fortæller; kommentator.
narrow ['nærəu] *v* indsnævre(s); (i strikning) tage ind; *~ sth down* indskrænke (,reducere) ngt // *adj* smal, trang; snæver; kneben; *have a ~ escape* undslippe med nød og næppe; *have a ~ mind* være smalsporet; **~ly** *adv: he ~ly missed the tree* han undgik lige at ramme træet, han var lige ved at ramme træet; *he ~ly missed the target* han ramte lige ved siden af målet; **~-minded** *adj* indskrænket, snæversynet.
nasal ['neizl] *adj* nasal, næse-.
nasty ['na:sti] *s* væmmelige ting; voldsfilm // *adj* væmmelig, ækel, modbydelig; *a ~ piece of work* en led karl.
natal [neitl] *adj* føde-.
nation ['neiʃən] *s* nation; folk.
national ['næʃənəl] *adj* national; folke-; landsomfattende; **~ anthem** *s* nationalsang; **~ call** *s (tlf)* udenbys samtale; **~ costume** *s* nationaldragt; *the* **National Health Service** *s (NHS)* sv.t. sygesikringen.
nationalism ['næʃənəlizm] *s* nationalisme.
nationality [næʃə'næliti] *s* nationalitet.
nationalization [næʃənəlai'zeiʃən] *s* nationalisering.
mational park ['næʃənəl pa:k] *s* nationalpark.
national service ['næʃənəl 'sə:vis] *s* militærtjeneste.
National Trust ['næʃənəl 'trʌst] *s* fredningsforeningen (i Storbritannien).
nationwide ['neiʃənwaid] *adj* landsomfattende.

native ['neitiv] *s* indfødt // *adj* indfødt; medfødt; føde-; hjem-; *a ~ speaker of English* en person med engelsk som modersmål; ~ **language** *s* modersmål.
natter ['nætə*] *s* vrøvl; snak // *v* snakke.
natural ['nætʃrəl] *adj* naturlig; natur-; medfødt; født; *she's a ~ leader* hun er den fødte leder; *~ parents* biologiske forældre; ~ **gas** *s* naturgas.
naturalist ['nætʃrəlist] *s* naturalist; naturforsker.
naturalize ['nætʃrəlaiz] *v* give statsborgerskab, naturalisere.
naturally ['nætʃrəli] *adv* naturligt; naturligvis.
natural wastage ['nætʃrəl 'weistidʒ] *s* naturlig afgang.
nature ['neitʃə*] *s* natur; art, beskaffenhed; temperament; sind; *by ~* af naturen; *follow the call of ~* træde af på naturens vegne; *it's second ~ to him* det er gået ham i blodet, han har det i rygmarven; *in the ~ of things* ifølge sagens natur; ~ **reserve** *s* naturreservat.
naughty ['nɔ:ti] *adj* uartig; vovet.
nausea ['nɔ:siə] *s* kvalme; væmmelse; **nauseate** ['nɔ:sieit] *v* give kvalme.
nautical ['nɔ:tikl] *adj* nautisk; sø-, sømands-; ~ **chart** *s* søkort; ~ **mile** *s* sømil (1852 m).
naval ['neivl] *adj* maritim, flåde-; ~ **officer** *s* søofficer.
nave [neiv] *s* (hjul)nav; (i kirke) midterskib.
navel [neivl] *s* navle.
navigable ['nævigəbl] *adj* sejlbar; manøvredygtig.
navigate ['nævigeit] *v* sejle; besejle; navigere.
navigation [nævi'geiʃən] *s* navigation; sejlads.
navigator ['nævigeitə*] *s* navigatør; *(hist)* søfarer.
navvy ['nævi] *s* vejarbejder; jord- og betonarbejder.
navy ['neivi] *s* flåde, marine; ~ **blue** *adj* marineblå.
nay [nei] *s* nej-stemme; *the ~s have it* der er flest nej-stemmer, forslaget er forkastet.
near [niə*] *adj/adv/præp* nær; i nærheden; næsten; *~ by* lige ved, i nærheden; *~ to* nær ved; *draw ~* komme nærmere; *it's nowhere ~ enough* det er ikke på langt nær nok; *it was a ~ thing* det var på et hængende hår, det var lige før det gik galt; **~by** *adv* nærliggende; i nærheden; *the* **Near East** *s* Det Nære Østen.
nearly ['niəli] *adv* næsten; *I ~ fell* jeg var lige ved at falde.
near miss ['niə 'mis] *s* ngt der rammer lige ved siden af; *it was a ~* det var lige ved.
nearside ['niəsaid] *s (brit)* venstre side (af bilen); *the ~ lane* inderbanen.
nearsighted ['niəsaitid] *adj* nærsynet.
neat [ni:t] *adj* ordentlig, ryddelig; velplejet, pæn; sirlig; pertentlig; (om alkohol) ublandet, ren; *a ~ whisky* en tør whisky; **~ly** *adv* propert, pænt; behændigt.
necessarily ['nɛsisrili] *adv* nødvendigvis.
necessary ['nɛsisri] *adj* nødvendig.
necessitate [ni'sɛsiteit] *v* nødvendiggøre.
necessity [ni'sɛsiti] *s* nødvendighed; fornødenhed; trang, nød; *the bare necessities* det allernødvendigste.
neck [nɛk] *s* hals; halsudskæring; *breathe down sby's ~* ånde en i nakken; *wring sby's ~* dreje halsen om på en; *stick one's ~ out* stikke snuden for langt frem; *get it in the ~* få på pelsen; *be up to one's ~ in work* være begravet i arbejde; *save one's ~* redde pelsen // *v* (F) kæle.
necklace ['nɛklis] *s* halssmykke.
neckline ['nɛklain] *s* halsudskæring.
née [nei] *adj: ~ Scott* (om kvinde) født Scott.
need [ni:d] *s* trang; nødvendighed; fornødenhed; nød, behov; *if ~ be* om nødvendigt; *there's no ~ to...* der er ingen grund til at... // *v* behøve; trænge til; *he ~s watching* man er nødt til at holde øje med ham; *a much ~ed break* en stærkt tiltrængt pause; **~ful** *adj: the ~ful* det nødvendige.

needle [ni:dl] *s* nål; strikkepind; viser; *be on the* ~ (S) være på sprøjten // *v* sy; stikke; prikke til, irritere; **~cord** *s* babyfløjl.
needless ['ni:dlis] *adj* unødvendig; ~ *to say*... selvfølgelig..., det siger sig selv at....
needlework ['ni:dlwə:k] *s* håndarbejde, syning, broderi.
needy ['ni:di] *adj* trængende; nødlidende.
negation [ni'geiʃən] *s* (be)nægtelse.
negative ['nɛgətiv] *s (foto)* negativ; *(gram)* nægtelse; *answer in the* ~ svare benægtende // *adj* negativ.
neglect [ni'glɛkt] *s* forsømmelse; vanrøgt; ligegyldighed; forsømthed; *in a state of* ~ forsømt, forfalden // *v* forsømme; negligere; vanrøgte.
negligence ['nɛglidʒəns] *s* forsømmelighed; uagtsomhed; **negligent** *adj* forsømmelig, skødesløs.
negligible ['nɛglidʒibl] *adj* ubetydelig; minimal.
negotiable [ni'gəuʃiəbl] *adj (merk)* omsættelig; som der kan forhandles om; (om vej) fremkommelig, farbar.
negotiate [ni'gəuʃieit] *v* forhandle (om); omsætte; klare, komme over; passere.
negotiation [nigəuʃi'eiʃən] *s* forhandling; omsætning; passage; overvindelse.
negress ['ni:gris] *s* negerkvinde.
negro ['ni:grəu] *s* neger // *adj* sort, neger-.
neigh [nei] *v* vrinske.
neighbour ['neibə*] *s* nabo; sidemand; næste // *v:* ~ *on* støde op til, grænse op til; **~hood** *s* nabolag; omegn; egn; nærhed; **~ing** *adj* tilstødende; nabo-.
neither ['naiðə*] *pron* ingen; intet (af to) // *adv:* ~ *a nor b* hverken a el. b; *that's* ~ *here nor there* det gør hverken fra el. til; det kan ikke bruges til ngt // *konj* heller ikke; *I didn't move and* ~ *did he* jeg rørte mig ikke og han heller ikke; ingen af os rørte os.
neon ['ni:ən] *s* neon; **~ light** *s* neonlys; **~ sign** *s* neonskilt, lysreklame; **~ tube** *s* neonrør, lysstofrør.
nephew ['nɛfju:] *s* nevø.
nerve [nə:v] *s* nerve; *(fig)* mod, kraft; *he's got a* ~ han er ikke bange af sig, han er ikke så lidt fræk; *his* ~*s are on edge* hans nerver står på højkant; *he gets on my* ~*s* han går mig på nerverne; *touch a raw* ~ ramme et ømt punkt; *lose one's* ~ gå i panik; *have the* ~ *to*... være fræk nok til at...; *what a* ~*!* hvor er det frækt! // *v:* ~ *oneself* mande sig op; **~-racking** *adj* enerverende.
nervous ['nə:vəs] *adj* nervøs; nerve-; **~ breakdown** *s* nervesammenbrud; **~ system** *s* nervesystem; **~ wreck** *s* nervevrag.
nervy ['nə:vi] *adj* (F) nervøs.
nest [nɛst] *s* rede, bo; sæt; *a nest of tables* indskudsborde // *v* bygge rede.
nestle [nɛsl] *v* sætte (,lægge) sig godt til rette; putte sig, *(up to* hos, ind til); hygge sig.
net [nɛt] *s* net // *v* få i nettet; tjene (netto) // *adj* netto.
Netherlands ['nɛðələndz] *spl: the* ~ Holland, Nederland.
netting ['nɛtiŋ] *s* netværk, net; trådnet.
nettle [nɛtl] *s (bot)* nælde // *v* ærgre, irritere; provokere; **~ rash** *s* nældefeber, udslæt.
network ['nɛtwə:k] *s* netværk; system; *(radio, tv)* sendernet.
neurotic [njuə'rɔtik] *s* neurotiker // *adj* neurotisk.
neuter ['nju:tə*] *s (gram)* intetkøn, neutrum // *v* (om dyr) kastrere.
neutral ['nju:trəl] *s (auto)* frigear // *adj* neutral.
neutrality [nju:'træliti] *s* neutralitet.
never ['nɛvə*] *adv* aldrig; ikke; ~ *again* aldrig mere; ~ *ever* aldrig nogensinde; ~ *mind!* skidt med det! ~ *fear!* bare rolig! *well, I* ~*!* nej, nu har jeg aldrig (hørt mage)! **~-ending** *adj* endeløs; **~-never** *s: buy sth on the* ~*-never* købe ngt på afbetaling.
nevertheless [ˌnɛvəðə'lɛs] *adv* ikke desto mindre, alligevel.

new [nju:] *adj* ny; frisk; moderne; **~born** *adj* nyfødt; **~comer** *s* nyankommen; tilkomling; **~-fangled** *adj* nymodens.
newly ['nju:li] *adv* nylig, ny-; ~ *married* nygift; **~weds** *spl* nygift par.
news [nju:z] *s* nyhed(er); *the ~ in brief (tv, radio)* nyhedsoversigten; *a piece of ~* en nyhed; *what's the ~?* hvad nyt? **~ agency** *s* pressebureau, nyhedsbureau; **~agent** *s* bladhandler; **~caster** *s* nyhedsoplæser; **~ flash** *s* højaktuel nyhed; *(radio, tv)* nyhedsindslag; ekstraudsendelse; **~men** *spl* pressefolk; **~paper** *s* avis, (dag)blad; **~print** *s* avispapir; **~ stand** *s* aviskiosk.
newt [nju:t] *s* salamander.
New Year ['nju:jiə*] *s* nytår; **~'s Day** *s* nytårsdag; **~'s Eve** *s* nytårsaften.
next [nɛkst] *adj* næste; førstkommende; nærmest; nabo-; ~ *to* ved siden af; ~ *to nothing* så godt som ingenting // *adv* derefter, så; næste gang; *when do we meet ~?* hvornår ses vi igen? *who's ~?* hvis tur er det? *he's ~* det er hans tur; **~-door** *adv: he lives ~-door* han bor i huset) ved siden af; *he's my ~-door neighbour* han er min nærmeste nabo; **~-of-kin** *s* nærmeste slægtning.
NHS fork.f. *National Health Service.*
nibble [nibl] *v* nippe til; gnaske.
nice [nais] *adj* pæn; flink, rar; god; dejlig; ~ *and warm* dejlig varm; *he's a ~ one!* han er en køn (,værre) en! *she was very ~ about it* hun tog det pænt; *have a ~ time!* god fornøjelse!
nicety ['naisiti] *s* finesse; nøjagtighed; *to a ~* pinlig nøjagtgigt.
nick [nik] *s* hak; (F) fængsel, brumme; *in the ~ of time* i sidste øjeblik // *v* snuppe; *be ~ed* (F) blive taget (af politiet).
nickname ['nikneim] *s* øgenavn, tilnavn // *v* kalde.
niece [ni:s] *s* niece.
nifty ['nifti] *adj* smart, fiks.
niggardly ['nigədli] *adj* nærig, fedtet.
niggle [nigl] *v* kritisere, hakke på; plage.
night [nait] *s* nat; aften; mørke; *at ~* om aftenen (,natten); *by ~* om natten; *last ~* i går aftes; i nat; *have an early (,late) ~* gå tidligt (,sent) i seng; *make a ~ of it* få sig en glad aften; *stay the ~* overnatte; **~cap** *s* godnatdrink; **~dress** *s* natkjole; **~ duty** *s* nattevagt; **~fall** *s* mørkets frembrud, mørkning.
nightie ['naiti] *s* (F) natkjole.
nightingale ['naitiŋgeil] *s* nattergal.
nightly ['naitli] *adj/adv* natlig, nat-; hver nat (,aften).
nightmare ['naitmɛə*] *s* mareridt.
night school ['nait ˌsku:l] *s* aftenskole.
night-time ['naittaim] *s* nattetid.
night watchman ['nait ˌwɔtʃmən] *s* nattevægter.
nightwear ['naitwɛə*] *s* nattøj.
nil [nil] *s* nul; intet.
nimble [nimbl] *adj* adræt, let, rap, kvik.
nine [nain] *num* ni; *she was dressed to the ~s* hun var ordentlig majet ud; **~pins** *s* keglespil.
nineteen ['nainti:n] *num* nitten.
ninety ['nainti] *num* halvfems.
ninth [nainθ] *num* niende // *s* niendedel.
nip [nip] *s* bid, nap; frisk kulde; lille drink // *v* knibe, nappe, nippe; smutte; ~ *along* smutte af sted; ~ *sth in the bud* standse ngt i opløbet.
nipper ['nipə*] *s* tang; klosaks; lille fyr.
nipple [nipl] *s* brystvorte; (på flaske) sut.
nippy ['nipi] *adj* (om kulde etc) bidende; (om person el. bil) rap, kvik.
nit [nit] *s* fæ, tumpe; **~picking** *s* pindehuggeri.
nitric ['naitrik] *adj: ~ acid* salpetersyre.
nitrogen ['naitrədʒən] *s (kem)* kvælstof.
nitwit ['nitwit] *s* fæhoved, tumpe.
no [nəu] *s* nej; afslag; *I won't take ~ for an answer* jeg accepterer ikke et nej // *adj/pron* ingen, intet // *adv* ikke // *interj* nej! *there's ~ denying that* man kan ikke nægte at; *there's ~ mistaking that* der er ingen tvivl

om at; ~ *entry* adgang forbudt; ~ *dogs* hunde må ikke medtages.

nobble [nɔbl] *v:* ~ *sby* lokke en over på sit parti.

nobility [nəu'biliti] *s* adel, adelskab; ædelhed.

noble [nəubl] *adj* adelig, ædel, fornem, fin; **~man** *s* adelsmand.

nobody ['nəubədi] *pron* ingen // *s: he's a mere* ~ han er et rent nul.

nod [nɔd] *s* nik; lille lur // *v* nikke; sove; ~ *off* falde i søvn.

node [nəud] *s* knude; knudepunkt.

no-go ['nəugəu] *adj:* ~ *area* forbudt område.

noise [nɔiz] *s* støj, spektakel; ståhej, postyr; *make a* ~ larme, støje; *make a* ~ *about sth* lave et stort nummer ud af ngt; *he's a big* ~ han er en stor kanon; **~less** *adj* lydløs.

noisey ['nɔizi] *adj* støjende; højlydt.

no-man's-land ['nəumænzlænd] *s* ingenmandsland.

nominal ['nɔminəl] *adj* symbolsk, nominel.

nominate ['nɔmineit] *v* opstille; udpege, nominere; udnævne; **nomination** [-'neiʃən] *s* opstilling; udnævnelse.

non... ['nɔn-] i sms: ikke-; non-; **~-aggression pact** *s* ikke-angrebspagt; **~-alcoholic** [-'hɔlik] *adj* alkoholfri; **~-aligned** [-ə'laind] *adj (pol)* alliancefri; **~-breakable** *adj* brudsikker; **~-committal** [-kə'mitl] *adj* uforpligtende; diplomatisk; neutral; **~descript** *adj* ubestemmelig.

none [nɔn] *pron* ingen, intet; ~ *of them* ingen af dem; *you have money but I have* ~ du har penge men jeg har ingen; *it's* ~ *of your business* det kommer ikke dig ved; *he's* ~ *the worse for it* han tog ingen skade af det.

nonentity [nɔ'nɛntiti] *s* (om person) nul; (om ting) ubetydelighed.

nonetheless [ˌnɔnðə'lɛs] *adv* ikke desto mindre.

non... ['nɔn-] ikke-; non-; sms: **~-fiction** *s* fagbog; faglitteratur; **~-flammable** [-'flæməbl] *adj* ildfast; brandsikker; **~-iron** *adj* strygefri; **~-payment** *s* manglende betaling; **~plussed** [-'plʌsd] *adj* paf, perpleks; **~-profit** *adj* almennyttig; ikke for fortjenestens skyld.

nonsense ['nɔnsəns] *s* vrøvl, sludder; pjat, idioti.

non... ['nɔn-] i sms: ikke-; non-; **~-shrink** *adj* krympefri; **~-smoker** *s* ikke-ryger; **~-stick** *adj* (om pande, gryde etc) slip-let; **~-union** *adj* uorganiseret (fx *labour* arbejdskraft); **~-violence** *s* ikke- vold.

noodles [nu:dlz] *spl (gastr)* nudler.

nook [nuk] *s* krog, hjørne; *~s and crannies* krinkelkroge.

noon [nu:n] *s* middag (kl. 12); *at* ~ ved middagstid, ved tolvtiden.

noose [nu:s] *s* løkke.

nor [nɔ:*] *konj* heller ikke (se også *neither).*

Nordic ['nɔ:dik] *adj* nordisk.

normal ['nɔ:məl] *adj* normal(-); **~ly** *adv* normalt; i reglen; ellers.

Norman ['nɔ:mən] *adj* normannisk; *(brit,* om stil) romansk, rundbue-.

Normandy ['nɔ:məndi] *s* Normandiet.

Norse [nɔ:s] *adj (hist)* nordisk; norsk; *Old* ~ oldnordisk; **~man** *s (hist)* nordbo.

north [nɔ:θ] *s* nord // *adj* nord-; nordlig; mod nord // *adv* nordpå; **~-east** *s* nordøst.

northerly ['nɔ:ðəli] *adj* nordlig.

northern ['nɔ:ðən] *adj* nordlig, nordre; nordisk; **Northern Ireland** *s* Nordirland.

North Pole ['nɔ:θ 'pəul] *s: the* ~ Nordpolen; *the* **North Sea** *s* Nordsøen, Vesterhavet.

northward(s) ['nɔ:θwədz] *adv* mod nord, nordpå.

north-west [nɔ:θ'wɛst] *s* nordvest.

Norway ['nɔ:wei] *s* Norge.

Norwegian [nɔ:'wi:dʒən] *s* nordmand // *adj* norsk.

nose [neuz] *s* næse; lugtesans; *blow one's* ~ pudse næse; *it's right under your* ~ det ligger lige for næsen af dig; *look down one's* ~ *at sth* se ned på ngt; *pay through the* ~ betale det hvide ud af øjnene; *it gets up my* ~

det kreperer mig; *turn up one's* ~ *at sth* rynke på næsen ad ngt // *v:* ~ *around* snuse rundt; ~ *out* opsnuse; **~bag** *s* mulepose; **~bleed** *s* næseblod; **~dive** [-daiv] *s (fly)* styrtdyk; **~gay** *s* (lille) blomsterbuket.

nosey ['nəuzi] *adj* nysgerrig; **~-parker** *s* nysgerrigper.

nosh [nɔʃ] *s* (F) mad, ædelse.

nostril ['nɔstril] *s* næsebor.

nosy ['nəuzi] *adj* d.s.s. *nosey.*

not [nɔt] *adv* ikke; ~ *at all* slet ikke; åh, jeg be'r; *you must* ~ *(,mustn't) do it* du må ikke gøre det; *he is* ~ *(,isn't) here* han er ikke her; *so as* ~ *to* for ikke at; ~ *that he is not nice* det er ikke fordi han ikke er rar; *he is good,* ~ *to say a wizard, at skiing* han er god, for ikke at sige en ørn, til skiløb.

notable ['nəutəbl] *adj* bemærkelsesværdig; anset; kendelig.

notably ['nəutəbli] *adv* navnlig, især.

notch [nɔtʃ] *s* hak, indskæring; skår.

note [nəut] *s* tone, node; klang; undertone; notat, optegnelse; seddel; *make a* ~ *of sth* notere sig ngt; *take* ~ *of sth* tage ngt til efterretning; *an actor of* ~ en anset skuespiller; *worthy of* ~ bemærkelsesværdig // *v* lægge mærke til, konstatere; notere, skrive op; **~book** *s* notesbog; lommebog; **~-case** *s* seddelmappe.

noted ['nəutid] *adj* kendt; fremtrædende.

notepad ['nəutpæd] *s* notesblok.

notepaper ['nəutpeipə*] *s* brevpapir.

noteworthy ['nəutwə:ði] *adj* bemærkelsesværdig.

nothing ['nɔθiŋ] *s* nul, ubetydelighed // *pron* ingenting, intet, ikke ngt; *come to* ~ ikke blive til ngt; ~ *doing* den går ikke; *for* ~ gratis; uden grund; forgæves; *there's* ~ *for it but to leave* der er ikke andet for end at gå; *there's* ~ *to it* det er ganske let; *to say* ~ *of John* for ikke at nævne John; *next to* ~ næsten ingenting; ~ *less than* intet mindre end; *it's all been for* ~ det har altsammen været forgæves; **~ness** *s* intethed, tomhed.

no-thoroughfare ['nəu'θʌrəfɛə*] *s* blindgade.

notice ['nəutis] *s* meddelelse; varsel; notits; *at short* ~ med kort varsel; *bring to* ~ henlede opmærksomheden på; *it has come to my notice that...* jeg har erfaret at...; *it has escaped my* ~ det er undgået min opmærksomhed; *give* ~ sige op; *take* ~ *of* lægge mærke til; *take no* ~ *of it!* ignorer det! *until further* ~ indtil videre // *v* lægge mærke til, bemærke; mærke; **~able** *adj* synlig, mærkbar; påfaldende; **~ board** *s* opslagstavle.

notify ['nəutifai] *v* bekendtgøre; underrette.

notion ['nəuʃən] *s* begreb, idé; opfattelse; *I have no* ~ *of what...* jeg har ingen anelse om hvad...

notorious [nəu'tɔ:riəs] *adj* berygtet; bekendt; notorisk.

notwithstanding [nɔtwiθ'stændiŋ] *adv* ikke desto mindre // *præp* trods, uanset // *konj* uagtet.

nought [nɔ:t] *s (mat* etc) nul; ~*s and crosses* (om spil) kryds og bolle.

noun [naun] *s (gram)* navneord, substantiv.

nourish ['nʌriʃ] *v* ernære; nære (også *fig);* **~ing** *adj* nærende; **~ment** *s* (er)næring.

novel [nʌvl] *s* roman // *adj* ny (og usædvanlig); original.

novelist ['nʌvəlist] *s* romanforfatter.

novelty ['nʌvəlti] *s* nyhed.

November [nəu'vɛmbə*] *s* november.

now [nau] *adv/konj* nu; nu (da); ~ *and then* nu og da; ~ *and again* fra tid til anden; *from* ~ *on* fra nu af; *by* ~ nu, ved denne tid; ~ *then!* se så! ~, *I told you he would say that!* jamen, jeg sagde jo at han ville sige sådan!

nowadays ['nauədeiz] *adv* nutildags, nu for tiden.

nowhere ['nəuwɛə*] *adv* ingen steder, intetsteds; ingen vegne; *out of* ~ ud af det blå; *live in the middle of* ~ bo i en fjern afkrog; ~ *near as pretty* ikke nær så pæn.

noxious ['nɔkʃəs] *adj* skadelig.

nozzle [nʌzl] *s* mundstykke, tud.
nr (fork.f. *near)* pr.
nth [ɛnθ] *adj: for the ~ time* for 117. gang.
nub [nʌb] *s* pointe, (sagens) kerne.
nuclear ['nu:kliə*] *adj* kerne-, atom-; **~ disarmament** *s* atomnedrustning; **~ energy** *s* atomenergi, kernekraft; **~ family** *s* kernefamilie; **~-free** *adj* atomfri; **~ fuel** *s* atombrændstof; **~ physics** *s* atomfysik; **~-powered** *adj* atomdrevet; **~ power station** *s* atomkraftværk; **~ waste** *s* atomaffald.
nude [nju:d] *s* nøgenmodel; *in the ~* i bar figur, nøgen // *adj* nøgen, bar.
nudge [nʌdʒ] *v* puffe til (med albuen); lempe, lirke.
nudity ['nju:diti] *s* nøgenhed.
nugget ['nʌgit] *s* guldklump.
nuisance ['nju:sns] *s* plage, gene; onde; (om person) plageånd; *don't be a ~!* lad nu være med at plage (mig)! *it's a ~* det er irriterende (,ærgerligt).
nuke [nju:k] *v: ~ sby (am* S) smide en atombombe over ngn.
null [nʌl] *adj: ~ and void* ugyldig.
nulliify ['nʌlifai] *v* annullere; ophæve.
numb [nʌm] *v* dulme; gøre følelsesløs // *adj* følelsesløs, stiv (af kulde).
number ['nʌmbə*] *s* nummer; antal; tal; *a ~ of people* et antal mennesker, en del mennesker; *any ~ of things* et utal af ting; *without ~* talløse; *his opposite ~* hans kollega (dvs. person i tilsvarende stilling som hans) // *v* tælle; udgøre, omfatte; nummerere; *the staff ~s ten* personalet omfatter (,består af) ti; *his days are ~ed* hans dage er talte; **~ plate** *s* nummerplade.
Numbers ['nʌmbəz] *spl* (i bibelen) 4. Mosebog.
numbskull ['nʌmskʌl] *s* (F) grødhoved.
numeral ['nju:mərəl] *s* tal; *(gram)* talord, numerale.
numerical [nju:'mɛrikl] *adj* numerisk; nummer-.
numerous ['nju:mərəs] *adj* talrig(e); talstærk.
nun [nʌn] *s* nonne; **~nery** *s* nonnekloster.
nuptial ['nʌpʃəl] *adj* bryllups-.
nurse [nə:s] *s* sygeplejerske; barnepige // *v* amme; passe (børn); pleje; ruge over, nære (fx *hopes* håb).
nursery ['nə:səri] *s* børneværelse; planteskole; **~ school** *s* sv.t. børnehaveklasse (3-5 år); **~ slope** *s* begynderløjpe.
nursing ['nə:siŋ] *s* sygepleje; **~ home** *s* (privat)klinik; plejehjem; (privat) fødeklinik.
nurture ['nə:tʃə*] *v* nære, ernære; opfostre.
nut [nʌt] *s (bot)* nød; *(tekn)* møtrik; (F) hoved, nød; (om person) skør kule; *go off one's ~* (F) blive skør; **~case** *s* (F) skør kule; **~cracker** *s* nøddeknækker; **~meg** *s* muskatnød.
nutrient ['nju:triənt] *s* næringsstof.
nutrition [nju:'triʃən] *s* (er)næring; ernæringstilstand.
nutritious [nju:'triʃəs] *adj* nærende.
nuts [nʌts] *adj: he's ~* (F) han er skrupskør.
nutshell ['nʌtʃɛl] *s* nøddeskal.
nutty ['nʌti] *adj* nøddeagtig.
nuzzle [nʌzl] *v* rode op i; *~ up to sby* putte sig ind til en.
nymph [nimf] *s* nymfe; puppe.

O

O, o [əu]; *O* (i talesprog) nul.
oaf [əuf] *s (pl: oaves* [əuvz]) fjols, klodrian.
oak [əuk] *s* eg(etræ); **~en** *adj* ege-, egetræs-.
OAP (fork.f. *old-age-pensioner)* pensionist.
oar [ɔ:*] *s* åre; roer; *put an ~ in (fig)* blande sig, give sit besyv med.
oarsman ['ɔ:zmən] *s* roer.
oasis [əu'eisis] *s (pl: oases* [-si:z]) oase.
oatcake ['əutkeik] *s* havrekiks.
oath [əuθ] *s* ed; banden; *take an ~* aflægge ed; *on (,under) ~* under ed.
oatmeal ['əutmi:l] *s* havregryn; **~ porridge** *s* havregrød.
oats [əuts] *spl* havre; *be off one's ~* have tabt madlysten; *feel one's ~* (F) være i stødet.

oaves [əuvz] *spl* af *oaf.*
obdurate ['ɔbdjurit] *adj* hårdnakket, forstokket.
OBE fork.f. *Order of the British Empire* britisk orden.
obedience [ə'bi:djəns] *s* lydighed; *in ~ to* i lydighed mod; **obedient** *adj* lydig *(to* mod).
obese [əu'bi:s] *adj* fed, lasket; **obesity** *s* fedme; overvægt.
obey [ə'bei] *v* adlyde; rette sig efter (fx *rules* reglerne).
obituary [ə'bitjuəri] *s* nekrolog.
object *s* ['ɔbdʒikt] genstand, ting; hensigt, mål; hindring; *(gram)* objekt // *v* [əb'dʒɛkt] indvende; protestere; *~ to* protestere mod; ikke kunne lide; *I ~!* jeg protesterer! *he ~ed that* han indvendte at.
objection [əb'dʒɛkʃən] *s* indvending; protest; *if you have no ~* hvis ikke du har ngt imod (det); **~able** *adj* ubehagelig; stødende.
objective [əb'dʒɛktiv] *s* mål; objektiv // *adj* saglig, objektiv.
object lesson ['ɔbdʒikt 'lɛssən] *s* anskuelsesundervisning.
objector [əb'dʒɛktə*] *s* modstander; *conscientious ~* militærnægter.
obligation [ɔbli'geiʃən] *s* forpligtelse; skyldighed; *be under an ~ to do sth* være forpligtet til at gøre ngt.
obligatory [ə'bligətəri] *adj* tvungen, obligatorisk; bindende.
oblige [ə'blaidʒ] *v* tvinge; nøde; imødegå; *~ sby* gøre en tjeneste; *~ sby to* tvinge en til; *I am much ~ed to you* mange tak skal du have.
obliging [ə'blaidʒiŋ] *adj* imødekommende; elskværdig.
oblique [ə'bli:k] *adj* skrå; skrånende; indirekte (fx *threats* trusler).
obliterate [ə'blitəreit] *v* udviske; tilintetgøre; udslette.
oblivion [ə'bliviən] *s* glemsel; *fall into ~* gå i glemmebogen.
oblivious [ə'bliviəs] *adj: be ~ of* glemme, være ligeglad med.
oblong ['ɔblɔŋ] *adj* aflang.
obnoxious [ɔb'nɔkʃəs] *adj* modbydelig; utålelig.
oboe ['əubəu] *s* obo.
obscene [əb'si:n] *adj* sjofel, obskøn.
obscenity [əb'sɛniti] *s* uanstændighed, obskønitet; *(jur)* utugt.
obscure [əb'skjuə*] *v* formørke; skjule; tilsløre // *adj* mørk; utydelig; uklar.
obscurity [əb'skjuəriti] *s* dunkelhed; uklarhed; ubemærkethed.
obsequies ['ɔbsikwiz] *spl* (H) begravelse.
obsequious [əb'si:kwiəs] *adj* servil, krybende, slesk.
observable [əb'zə:vəbl] *adj* bemærkelsesværdig; mærkbar.
observance [əb'zə:vns] *s* overholdelse (fx *of rules* af regler); højtideligholdelse; skik.
observant [əb'zə:vənt] *adj* opmærksom, agtpågivende.
observation [əbzə'veiʃən] *s* iagttagelse; observation; bemærkning.
observe [əb'zə:v] *v* iagttage; observere; overholde (fx *the law* loven); bemærke, udtale.
observer [əb'zə:və*] *s* iagttager; observatør.
obsess [əb'sɛs] *v* besætte; forfølge; *~ed with* besat af; opslugt af.
obsession [əb'sɛʃən] *s* besættelse; fiks idé.
obsessive [əb'sɛsiv] *adj* næsten sygelig; *~ thought* tvangstanke.
obsolescence [ɔbsə'lɛsns] *s* forældethed; *built in (,planned) ~ (merk)* indbygget forældelse.
obsolete ['ɔbsəli:t] *adj* forældet, gammeldags.
obstacle ['ɔbstəkl] *s* hindring; ~ **race** *s* forhindringsløb.
obstetrician [ɔbstə'triʃən] *s* fødselslæge.
obstinacy ['ɔbstinəsi] *s* stædighed; genstridighed.
obstinate ['ɔbstinit] *adj* stædig; vedvarende (fx *pain* smerte); hårdnakket.
obstreperous [əb'strɛpərəs] *adj* uregerlig; larmende.
obstruct [əb'strʌkt] *v* spærre, blokere; hindre; tilstoppe.
obstruction [əb'strʌkʃən] *s* spærring; tilstopning; hindring.

obstructive [əb'strʌktiv] *adj* hæmmende; spærrende.
obtain [əb'tein] *v* opnå, få, skaffe sig; gælde; **~able** *adj* opnåelig; til at skaffe.
obtrusive [əb'tru:siv] *adj* påtrængende; gennemtrængende (fx *smell* lugt).
obtuse [əb'tju:s] *adj* stump (fx *angle* vinkel); *(fig)* afstumpet.
obvious ['ɔbviəs] *adj* tydelig, åbenbar; indlysende; påfaldende; **~ly** *adv* åbenbart.
occasion [ə'keiʃən] *s* lejlighed; begivenhed; grund, anledning; *no ~ for...* ingen grund til...; *on ~(s)* lejlighedsvis; *on the ~ of* i anledning af; *rise to the ~* være situationen voksen.
occasional [ə'keiʒənl] *adj* tilfældig; lejlighedsvis; **~ly** *adv* af og til, en gang imellem.
occupant ['ɔkjupənt] *s* beboer; besætter; indehaver.
occupation [ɔkju'peiʃən] *s* erhverv; beskæftigelse; *(mil)* besættelse; *unfit for ~* ubeboelig; **~al disease** *s* erhvervssygdom; **~al therapy** *s* ergoterapi.
occupy ['ɔkjupai] *v* bebo; besidde; beklæde (fx *a position* en stilling) optage (fx *a seat* en plads); beskæftige; besætte.
occur [ə'kə:*] *v* hænde; forekomme; *it ~s to me* jeg kommer i tanke om; *it never ~red to me* det har jeg slet ikke tænkt på; det er aldrig faldet mig ind; **~rence** *s* hændelse; forekomst.
ocean ['əuʃən] *s* hav, ocean; **~ climate** *s* kystklima; **~ liner** *s* stort passagerskib.
ochre ['əukə*] *adj* okker(gul).
o'clock [ə'klɔk] *adv: it is five ~* klokken er fem.
octane ['ɔktein] *s: ~ number, ~ rating* oktantal.
October [ək'təubə*] *s* oktober.
octogenarian [ɔktədʒi'nɛəriən] *s/adj* firsårig.
octopus ['ɔktəpəs] *s* blæksprutte.
oculist ['ɔkjulist] *s* (især *am)* øjenlæge.
OD ['əu'di:] (fork.f. *overdose)* overdosis // *v* tage en overdosis.
odd [ɔd] *adj* mærkelig, underlig; ulige; umage; overskydende; *sixty ~* nogle of tres; *at ~ times* fra tid til anden, af og til; *the ~ one out* den der er tilovers; *two ~ socks* to umage sokker; *he would give the ~ lecture* han holdt en forelæsning nu og da; **~ball** *s* særling.
oddity ['ɔditi] *s* særhed; sjældenhed; særling.
odd-job man [ɔd'dʒɔb,mæn] *s* altmuligmand; **odd jobs** *spl* tilfældigt arbejde.
oddments ['ɔdmənts] *spl* rester; småting; pakkenelliker.
odds [ɔdʒ] *spl* chancer; fordel; ulighed; odds; *the ~ are against his coming* der er ikke store chancer for at han kommer; *it makes no ~* det gør ingen forskel; *at ~ with* uenig med; *~ and ends* diverse småting.
odds-on [ɔdz'ɔn] *adj: it's ~ that he's hooked* det er højst sandsynligt at han har bidt på krogen; *an ~ favourite to win the match* en klar favorit til at vinde kampen.
odious ['əudiəs] *adj* modbydelig, frastødende.
odour ['əudə*] *s* lugt, duft; **~less** *adj* lugtfri.
of [ɔv, əv] *præp* (udtrykker ofte genitiv:) *a friend ~ ours* en af vore venner, vores ven; *the son ~ the boss* chefens søn; (andre betydninger:) *the fifth ~ June* den femte juni; *south ~ London* syd for London; *~ late* i den senere tid; for nylig; *a boy ~ ten* en dreng på ti år; *think ~ sth* tænke på ngt; *complain ~* klage over; *all ~ you* jer allesammen; *all four ~ us* os alle fire.
off [ɔf] *adj/adv* bort, af sted; af; (om kontakt) slukket; (om vandhane) lukket; (om mad) dårlig; (om mælk) sur; (om vare) udgået; (om møde etc) aflyst; *~ and on* nu og da; *I must be ~* jeg er nødt til at gå (,tage af sted); *she is well ~* hun er velhavende; *be ~ sick* være fraværende på grund af sygdom; *a*

day ~ en fridag; *have an* ~ *day* have en dårlig dag (,en minusdag); *our engagement is* ~ vores forlovelse er hævet; *he had his coat* ~ han gik uden frakke; *the hook is* ~ krogen er taget af (dvs. døren er åben); *hands* ~*!* fingrene væk! *we dined* ~ *the remains of the stew* vi spiste resten af den sammenkogte ret til middag; *10%* ~ 10% rabat (,nedslag); *5 km* ~ *the road* 5 km (borte) fra vejen; ~ *the coast* ud for kysten; *a house* ~ *the main road* et hus et stykke fra hovedvejen; *I'm* ~ *meat* jeg er holdt op med at spise kød; *on the* ~ *chance that* i det svage håb at; for det tilfældes skyld at.

offal ['ɔfəl] *s* affald; indmad.

off-balance ['ɔfˌbæləns] *adj* ude af balance; uforvarende.

offbeat ['ɔfbi:t] *adj* (F) utraditionel; excentrisk.

off-colour ['ɔfkʌlə*] *adj* sløj, uoplagt; tvivlsom (fx *joke* vits).

offence [ə'fɛns] *s* fornærmelse; anstød; forseelse; forbrydelse; *give (,cause)* ~ *to* såre, krænke; støde; *take* ~ *at* tage anstød af.

offend [ə'fɛnd] *v* fornærme; støde; forse sig.

offender [ə'fɛndə*] *s* forbryder, lovovertræder.

offensive [ə'fɛnsiv] *s (mil)* angreb, offensiv; *take the* ~ gå i offensiven // *adj* fornærmelig; anstødelig; ækel (fx *smell* lugt).

offer ['ɔfə*] *s* tilbud; *make an* ~ *of sth* tilbyde ngt; ~ *of marriage* ægteskabstilbud; *be on* ~ være på tilbud // *v* tilbyde; byde (på); fremføre (fx *one's opinion* sin mening); tilbyde sig; **~ing** *s* gave, offer.

off-guard ['ɔfga:d] *adj: be taken* ~ blive overrumplet.

off-hand ['ɔfhænd] *adj* improviseret; henkastet; nedladende // *adv* uden forberedelse, på stående fod.

office ['ɔfis] *s* kontor; ministerium; embede; *be in* ~ være ved magten; have regeringsmagten; være minister; *Bush' second year in* ~ Bush' andet år i præsidentembedet; ~ **block** *s* kontorbygning; ~ **hours** *spl* kontortid; ~ **party** *s* sv.t. julefrokost (på arbejdspladsen); firmafest.

officer ['ɔfisə*] *s* officer; embedsmand; politibetjent.

official [ə'fiʃl] *s* tjenestemand; embedsmand; funktionær // *adj* offentlig, officiel.

officious [ə'fiʃəs] *adj* nævenyttig, geskæftig.

offing ['ɔfiŋ] *s: in the* ~ i sigte; i farvandet.

off... ['ɔf-] sms: **~-key** [-ki:] *adj* falsk; **~-licence** [-'laisəns] *s* (forretning med) ret til at sælge vin, øl og spiritus ud af huset; **~-load** *v* læsse af; **~-peak** [-pi:k] *adj* (om el-tarif etc) lavpris-; *at* ~*-peak hours* udenfor myldretiden; **~print** *s* særtryk; **~putting** *adj* frastødende, lidet tillokkende; nedslående; **~-season** *adj/adv* uden for sæsonen; **~set** *s* udløber; modvægt; *(typ)* offset // *v* modregne; kompensere; opveje; **~shoot** *s* udløber; sidegren; **~shore** *adj* fralands; fra land; ud for kysten (fx *oil rig* boreplatform); kyst- (fx *fishing* fiskeri); **~side** *s* (om bil) højre side (mod vejmidten); *(sport)* offside; **~spring** *s* afkom; *(fig)* produkt; **~stage** *adv* uden for scenen; i kulissen; **~-the-cuff** *adj* henkastet; på stående fod; **~-the-peg** *adj* konfektionssyet; **~-the-record** *adj* uofficiel; fortrolig.

often [ɔfn] *adv* ofte, tit; *as* ~ *as not* i de fleste tilfælde.

ogle [əugl] *v* lave øjne (til); se på.

ogre ['əugə*] *s* uhyre, udyr.

oil [ɔil] *s* olie // *v* smøre, oliere; ~ *sby's palm* bestikke (,smøre) en; **~can** *s* smørekande; oliedunk; **~ers** *spl* olietøj; **~field** *s* oliefelt; **~-fired** *adj* oliefyret; ~ **heater** *s* oliefyr; ~ **painting** *s* oliemaleri; ~ **refinery** *s* olieraffinaderi; ~ **rig** *s* boretårn; (til søs) boreplatform; **~skins** *spl* olietøj; **~slick** *s* oliepøl (på vand); ~ **strike** *s* oliefund; ~ **well** *s* oliekilde.

oily ['ɔili] *adj* olieagtig; olieret; (om mad) fed, fedtet; *(fig)* slesk.

ointment ['ɔintmənt] *s* salve.

OK, okay ['əu'kei] *v* godkende // *adj* i orden, ok // *interj* i orden, ok.

old [əuld] *adj (~er, ~est* el. *elder, eldest)* gammel; aldrende; erfaren; *how ~ are you?* hvor gammel er du? *he's ten years ~* han er ti år gammel; **~ age** *s* alderdom; **~-age pensioner** *(OAP) s* pensionist; **~-fashioned** *adj* gammeldags; **~ hat** *adj* gammeldags; **~ish** *adj* ældre; **~ maid** *s* gammeljomfru; **~ man** *s* (F, tiltale) gamle ven; du gamle; *the ~ man* chefen; far; **~ people's home** *s* plejehjem; **~ wives' tale** *s* ammestuehistorie; **~-world** *adj* gammeldags.

olive ['ɔliv] *s* oliven(træ) // *adj* olivengrøn.

Olympic [ə'limpik] *adj* olympiade-, olympisk; **~s** *spl* OL, de olympiske lege.

omen ['əumən] *s* varsel; *bird of ill ~* ulykkesfugl.

ominous ['ɔminəs] *adj* ildevarslende; uheldsvanger.

omission [əu'miʃən] *s* undladelse, forsømmelse.

omit [əu'mit] *v* undlade, forsømme; udelade.

omnipotent [ɔm'nipətənt] *adj* almægtig.

omnipresent ['ɔmni'prɛzənt] *adj* allestedsnærværende.

omniscient [ɔm'nisiənt] *adj* alvidende.

omnivorous [ɔm'nivərəs] *adj* altædende.

on [ɔn] *adv/præp* på; om; ved; i gang; (om lys, radio) tændt; (om vandhane) åben; *is the meeting still ~?* er der stadig møde? skal der stadig være møde? *when is this film ~?* hvornår bliver denne film vist? *have you got anything ~ tonight?* skal du ngt i aften? *a house ~ the river* et hus ved floden; *~ learning this, I left* da jeg hørte det, gik jeg; *~ arrival* ved ankomsten; *~ the left* på venstre side; *~ Friday* på fredag; *a week ~ Friday* fredag otte dage; *it's getting ~ for one o'clock* klokken nærmer sig et; *go ~* gå videre, fortsætte; *it's not ~!* ikke tale om! *~ and off* nu og da; *be ~ about sth* ustandselig tale om ngt; *this is ~ me* det her betaler jeg; *I'm ~ to her* jeg ved hvad hun er ude på.

once [wʌns] *adv* en gang; engang // *konj* når først; så snart; *at ~* straks; med det samme; samtidig; *all at ~* pludselig; på én gang; *~ a week* en gang om ugen; *~ more* en gang til; *~ and for all* en gang for alle; *~ upon a time* (der var) engang; **~-over** *s: give sby the ~-over* kaste et hurtigt blik på en.

oncoming ['ɔnkʌmiŋ] *adj* (om trafik) modgående.

one [wʌn] *num* én, et // *pron* en; nogen; man; *this ~* denne (her); *that ~* den (der); *the ~ book which...* den eneste bog som...; *~ by ~* en ad gangen, en efter en; *~ never knows* man kan aldrig vide; *~ another* hinanden; *be at ~ with sby* være helt enig med en; *the little ~s* de små, børnene; **~-man** *adj* enmands; **~-night stand** *s* engangsforestilling (også *fig); ~-***parent family** *s* familie med enlig forsørger; **~-piece** *adj* ud i ét.

oneself [wʌn'sɛlf] *pron* sig; sig selv; *be by ~* være alene; *do sth by ~* gøre ngt selv (,på egen hånd).

one-time ['wʌntaim] *adj* tidligere, forhenværende.

one-way ['wʌnwei] *adj* (om gade, trafik) ensrettet.

ongoing ['ɔngəuiŋ] *adj* igangværende.

onion ['ʌnjən] *s* løg; *know one's ~s* kunne sit kram.

onlooker ['ɔnlukə*] *s* tilskuer.

only ['əunli] *adj* eneste // *adv* kun, blot // *konj* men; *an ~ child* et enebarn; *not ~* ikke alene; *if ~* hvis bare, gid; *~ just* kun lige akkurat; først nu; *he told me, ~ I didn't believe him* han sagde det, men jeg troede ikke på ham.

onset ['ɔnsɛt] *s* begyndelse; angreb.

onshore ['ɔnʃɔ:*] *adj* pålands-; kyst-; i land.

onslaught ['ɔnslɔ:t] *s* stormløb.

onto ['ɔntu] *præp* op på; over på; ned på.

onward(s) ['ɔnwəd(z)] *adv* fremad; *from this time* ~ fra nu af, fremover.

ooze [u:z] *v* sive, pible frem; *he ~d satisfaction* han emmede af veltilfredshed.

opacity [əu'pæsiti] *s* uigennemsigtighed.

opaque [əu'peik] *adj* uigennemsigtig.

open [əupn] *v* åbne, lukke op; ~ *on to* vende ud mod; føre ud til; ~ *out* brede ud; udvikle; ~ *up* åbne, lukke op // *adj* åben; (om fx møde) offentlig; (om beundring) uforbeholden; (om stilling) ledig; *in the ~ (air)* i det fri; *an ~ and shut case* en oplagt sag; *wide* ~ på vid gab; *an ~ secret* en offentlig hemmelighed; **~-air** *adj* frilufts-; **~-ended** *adj* uformel, uforpligtende; **~er** *s* åbner; **~-handed** *adj* gavmild, rundhåndet; **~ing** *s* åbning; indledning; ledigt job; chance; **~-minded** *adj* frisindet; **~ sandwich** *s* stykke smørrebrød; **~ shop** *s* arbejdsplads som også beskæftiger uorganiseret arbejdskraft.

opera ['ɔpərə] *s* opera; **~ glasses** *spl* teaterkikkert.

operate ['ɔpəreit] *v* virke; arbejde; betjene (fx *a machine* en maskine); operere; ~ *on* virke på; operere.

operatic [ɔpə'rætik] *adj* opera-.

operating ['ɔpəreitiŋ] *adj:* ~ *costs* driftsomkostninger; ~ *table* operationsbord; ~ *theatre* operationsstue.

operation [ɔpə'reiʃən] *s* virksomhed; funktion; drift; betjening; operation.

operative ['ɔpərətiv] *s* arbejder // *adj* virksom; gyldig; operativ.

operator ['ɔpəreitə*] *s* operatør; tasteoperatør; telefonist.

opinion [ə'piniən] *s* mening; synspunkt; opfattelse; udtalelse; *get a second* ~ spørge en anden også; *in my* ~ efter min mening; *it's a matter of* ~ det er en skønssag, det afhænger af hvordan man ser på det; *have a high ~ of sby* have høje tanker om en; **opinionated** *adj* stædig; selvhævdende; **opinion poll** *s* meningsmåling.

opponent [ə'pəunənt] *s* modstander, opponent.

opportune ['ɔpətju:n] *adj* belejlig, opportun.

opportunity [ɔpə'tjuniti] *s* lejlighed; chance; rette øjeblik; *take the ~ to* benytte lejligheden til at; *at the earliest* ~ ved førstkommende lejlighed.

oppose [ə'pəuz] *v* modsætte sig; *as ~d to* i modsætning til; **opposing** *adj* modsat.

opposite ['ɔpəzit] *s* modsætning // *adj* modsat *(to, from* af); overfor // *præp* over for; *his ~ number* hans kollega; hans modstykke; **opposition** [-'ziʃən] *s* modstand; modsætning; *(pol)* opposition.

oppress [ə'prɛs] *v* undertrykke, kue; tynge.

oppression [ə'prɛʃən] *s* undertrykkelse; nedtrykthed.

oppressive [ə'prɛsiv] *adj* trykkende.

opt [ɔpt] *v:* ~ *for* vælge; ~ *out* (F) bakke ud, stå 'af.

optical ['ɔptikl] *adj* optisk; ~ *illusion* synsbedrag.

optician [ɔp'tiʃən] *s* optiker.

optics ['ɔptiks] *spl* optik.

optimum ['ɔptiməm] *adj* optimal.

option ['ɔpʃən] *s* valg; valgmulighed; *(merk)* forkøbsret, option; *keep one's ~s open* lade alle muligheder stå åbne; **~al** *adj* valgfri; frivillig.

opulent ['ɔpjulənt] *adj* rig; overdådig, opulent.

or [ɔ:*] *konj* eller; ellers; ~ *else* eller også.

oral ['ɔ:rəl] *s* (F) mundtlig eksamen // *adj* mundtlig, mund-; *(med)* som indtages gennem munden, oral.

orange ['ɔrindʒ] *s* appelsin // *adj* orangefarvet; **~ peel** *s* appelsinskal; **~ stick** *s* neglepind.

oration [ɔ'reiʃən] *s* højtidelig tale; præk.

orator ['ɔrətə*] *s* taler.

orbit ['ɔ:bit] *s* kredsløb (i verdensrummet); bane; **~al** *s* ydre ringvej.

orchard ['ɔ:tʃəd] *s* frugtplantage.

orchestra ['ɔ:kistrə] *s* orkester.
orchestrate ['ɔ:kistreit] *v* organisere, iscenesætte.
orchid ['ɔ:kid] *s* orkidé.
ordain [ɔ:'dein] *v* ordinere; fastsætte.
ordeal [ɔ:'di:l] *s* prøvelse.
order ['ɔ:də*] *s* orden; ro; rækkefølge; ordning; ordre; bestilling; befaling; *in* ~ i orden; *in* ~ *of size* i størrelsesorden; *in* ~ *to (,that)* for at; *in working* ~ funktionsdygtig; *made to* ~ lavet på bestilling; *out of* ~ i uorden // *v* ordne; beordre; bestille; ~ *sby around* koste rundt med en; ~ **form** *s* ordreseddel.
orderly ['ɔ:dəli] *s (mil)* ordonnans; *(med)* sygepasser; (hospitals)portør // *adj* ordentlig, metodisk.
ordinal ['ɔ:dinl] *s* ordenstal.
ordinary ['ɔ:dənri] *adj* ordinær, almindelig; *(neds)* tarvelig, middelmådig; *sth out of the* ~ ngt ud over det almindelige, ngt for sig selv.
ordnance ['ɔ:dnəns] *s (mil)* materiel; **Ordnance Survey map** *s* sv.t. generalstabskort.
ore [ɔ:*] *s* malm; metal.
organ ['ɔ:gən] *s* organ; *(mus)* orgel; **~-grinder** *s* lirekassemand.
organic [ɔ:'gænik] *adj* organisk.
organize ['ɔ:gənaiz] *v* organisere; **~r** *s* organisator.
orgy ['ɔ:dʒi] *s* orgie.
orient ['ɔ:riənt] *v:* ~ *oneself to sth* vænne (,tilpasse) sig til ngt; ~*ed to* orienteret mod, vendt mod.
orientation [ɔ:riən'teiʃən] *s* orientering.
orienteering [ɔ:riən'tiəriŋ] *s* orienteringsløb.
orifice ['ɔrifis] *s* åbning.
origin ['ɔridʒin] *s* oprindelse, herkomst; kilde; *the* ~ *of species* arternes oprindelse.
original [ɔ'ridʒinəl] *s* original // *adj* oprindelig, original; ægte; ~*al sin* arvesynd; **~ly** *adv* oprindelig, fra første færd.
originate [ɔ'ridʒineit] *v:* ~ *from* stamme (,hidrøre) fra; ~ *in* hidrøre fra.
originator [ɔ'ridʒineitə*] *s* ophavsmand.
ornament ['ɔ:nəmənt] *s* ornament; pynt; smykke; udsmykning.
ornamental [ɔ:nə'mɛntl] *adj* ornamental; til pynt.
ornamentation [ɔ:nəmən'teiʃən] *s* udsmykning; dekoration.
ornate [ɔ:'neit] *adj* overpyntet.
orphan ['ɔ:fən] *s* forældreløst barn // *v: be* ~*ed* blive (gjort) forældreløs.
orphanage ['ɔ:fənidʒ] *s* børnehjem.
OS [əu'ɛs] fork.f. *outsize; Ordnance Survey.*
oscillate ['ɔsileit] *v* svinge; vibrere.
osier ['əuʒə*] *s* pil, vidje; ~ *basket* vidjekurv.
osprey ['ɔsprei] *s* fiskeørn.
ossify ['ɔsifai] *v* forbene(s).
ostensible [ɔs'tɛnsibl] *adj* påstået; tilsyneladende; **ostensibly** *adv* angivelig.
ostentatious [ɔstɛn'teiʃəs] *adj* pralende; demonstrativ.
osteopath ['ɔstiəpæθ] *s* kiropraktor.
ostracize ['ɔstrəsaiz] *v* fryse ud; udelukke; boykotte.
ostrich ['ɔstritʃ] *s* struds.
other ['ʌðə*] *adj* anden, andet; andre; *the* ~ *day* forleden dag; *every* ~ *week* hveranden uge; *sth or* ~ et el. andet; *among* ~ *things* blandt andet; ~ *than* andet end; anderledes end; ud over.
otherwise ['ʌðəwaiz] *adv/konj* anderledes; ellers.
otter ['ɔtə*] *s* odder.
ouch [autʃ] *interj* av!
ought [ɔ:t] *v* bør, burde; skulle; *I* ~ *to do it* jeg burde gøre det; *this* ~ *to have been done* dette skulle have været gjort; *he* ~ *to win* han vinder sandsynligvis; han skal nok vinde.
ounce [auns] *s* (vægtenhed: 28,35 gram); *not an* ~ *(fig)* ikke en disse.
our [auə*] *pron* vores, vor, vort, vore; *Our Lord* Vorherre; **~s** *pron* vores, vor, vort, vore; *a friend of* ~*s* en ven af os, en af vores venner.
ourselves [auə'sɛlvz] *pron pl* os; (forstærkende) selv; *let us do it* ~ lad os gøre det selv.
oust [aust] *v* fordrive; fortrænge.
out [aut] *adv* ud; ude; udenfor; op-

brugt; (om fx lys) slukket; *he's ~* han er ikke hjemme; han er besvimet; *these hats are ~* disse hatte er gået af mode; *he's ~ for money* han er ude efter penge; *be ~ in one's calculations* regne forkert; forregne sig; *~ here* herude; *~ loud* højt; med kraftig stemme; *~ of* udenfor; på grund af (fx *anger* vrede); ud af; *~ of breath* forpustet; *~ of petrol* løbet tør for benzin; *made ~ of wood* lavet af træ; *~ of order* ude af funktion; i uorden; *~ there* derude; **~-and-out** *adj* gennemført; helt igennem, komplet.

outbalance [aut'bæləns] *v* opveje.

outbid [aut'bid] *v* overbyde.

outboard ['autbɔ:d] *adj* udenbords; *~ (motor)* påhængsmotor.

outbreak ['autbreik] *s* udbrud (fx *of war* krigs-); pludselig opståen; bølge (fx *of riots* af optøjer); opstand.

outburst ['autbə:st] *s* udbrud.

outcast ['autka:st] *s* paria; *an ~ of society* en social taber.

outclass [aut'kla:s] *v* langt overgå.

outcome ['autkʌm] *s* resultat; udslag.

outcry ['autkrai] *s* råb; nødråb; *start an ~* opløfte et ramaskrig.

outdated [aut'deitid] *adj* forældet; umoderne.

outdistance [aut'distəns] *v* distancere.

outdo [aut'du:] *v* overgå.

outdoor ['autdɔ:*] *adj* udendørs; frilufts-; **~s** *adv* udendørs, i fri luft.

outer ['autə*] *adj* ydre, yder-; **~ space** *s* det ydre (verdens)rum.

outfit ['autfit] *s* udstyr; udrustning; mundering; grej; (F) foretagende; **~ter's** *s* herreekviperingshandler.

outgoing ['autgəuiŋ] *adj* udadvendt; udgående (fx *mail* post).

outgrow [aut'grəu] *v* vokse fra.

outing ['autiŋ] *s* udflugt.

outlandish [aut'lændiʃ] *adj* fremmed; aparte; forskruet; hårrejsende.

outlast [aut'la:st] *v* holde (,leve) længere end.

outlaw ['autlɔ:] *s* fredløs // *v* gøre fredløs; forvise; forbyde ved lov.

outlay ['autlei] *s* udlæg, udgifter.

outlet ['autlɛt] *s* udløb, afløb (også *fig); (elek)* stikkontakt; *(merk)* afsætningssted.

outline ['autlain] *s* omrids, kontur; *(fig)* resumé; skitse; oversigt.

outlive [aut'liv] *v* overleve; komme over.

outlook ['autluk] *s* udsigt; (livs)syn; (fremtids)udsigter.

outlying ['autlaiiŋ] *adj* fjern, afsidesliggende.

outmoded ['autməudid] *adj* gammeldags, umoderne.

outnumber [aut'nʌmbə*] *v* være overlegen i antal; *be ~ed* være i mindretal.

out-of-date [autəv'deit] *adj* gammeldags, forældet.

out-of-the-way [autəvðə'wei] *adj* afsides; usædvanlig.

outpatient ['autpeiʃənt] *s* ambulant patient.

outpost ['autpəust] *s* forpost.

output ['autput] *s* produktion; ydelse; udbytte; *(elek)* udgangseffekt; *(edb)* uddata.

outrage ['autreidʒ] *s* vold; krænkelse; skandale; *bomb ~* bombeterror // *v* øve vold imod; krænke.

outrageous [aut'reidʒəs] *adj* skandaløs, oprørende.

outright *adj* ['autrait] fuldstændig; gennemført (fx *lie* løgn); kategorisk (fx *denial* nægtelse) // *adv* [aut'rait] straks; fuldstændigt; direkte, lige ud.

outset ['autsɛt] *s* begyndelse; *from the ~* fra første færd.

outshine [aut'ʃain] *v* overskygge.

outside *s* ['autsaid] ydre; yderside; *at the ~ (fig)* højst; *the ~ world* omverdenen *at an ~ estimate* højt regnet; *an ~ chance* en meget lille chance // *adj/adv* [aut'said] udvendig; yderst; udendørs; udenpå; udenfor; yder-.

outsider [aut'saidə*] *s* fremmed; udenforstående; outsider.

outsize ['autsaiz] *s* stor størrelse, fruestørrelse // *adj* ekstra stor.

outskirts ['autskə:ts] *spl* udkant; *on the ~ of London* i udkanten af London.

outspoken [aut'spəukən] *adj* (lovlig) åbenhjertig; frimodig.
outspread [aut'sprεd] *adj* udbredt, udstrakt.
outstanding [aut'stændiŋ] *adj* fremragende; fremtrædende; udestående; ['aut-] udstående.
outstay [aut'stei] *v:* ~ *one's welcome* blive for længe.
outstretched [aut'strεtʃt] *adj* udstrakt (fx *hand* hånd).
outward ['autwəd] *adj* ydre, udvendig; udgående; ~ *bound* (om skib) for udgående; **~ly** *adv* udadtil; udvendigt.
outweigh [aut'wei] *v* opveje; veje mere end.
outwit [aut'wit] *v* narre; være snedigere end.
ovary ['əuvəri] *s* æggestok, ovarie; *(bot)* frugtknude.
oven [ʌvn] *s* ovn; **~glove** [-glʌv] *s* grillhandske; **~proof** *adj* ovnfast; **~-ready** *adj* ovnklar; **~ware** *s* ovnfaste fade etc.
over ['əuvə*] *adj/adv* forbi, ovre, omme; over, mere end; via // *præp* (ud) over; på den anden side af; mere end; ~ *here* her ovre („over); ~ *here* der ovre („over); *all* ~ over det hele, overalt; forbi, overstået; ~ *and* ~ *(again)* igen og igen; ~ *and above* ud over; ~ *the last three years* i de sidste tre år; *is there any food* ~*?* er der ngt mad tilovers? *ask sby* ~ invitere en (over til sig); *stay* ~ *the weekend* blive weekenden over.
overall ['əuvərɔ:l] *s* kittel // *adj* total (fx *length* længde); samlet; generel; *an* ~ *majority* absolut flertal // *adv* [əuvər'ɔ:l] alt i alt; overalt; **~s** *spl* overall, arbejdstøj.
overawed [əuvər'ɔ:d] *adj* benovet.
overbalance [əuvə'bæləns] *v* få overbalance; vælte.
overbearing [əuvə'bεəriŋ] *adj* myndig; overlegen.
overboard ['əuvəbɔ:d] *adv* overbord; udenbords.
overcast ['əuvəka:st] *adj* overskyet; overtrukket.
overcome [əuvə'kʌm] *v* overvinde, besejre; sejre; ~ *by* overmandet af; ~ *with* overvældet af (fx *grief* sorg).
overdo [əuvə'du:] *v* overdrive; *don't* ~ *it* overanstreng dig ikke; lad være med at overdrive.
overdone [əuvə'dʌn] *adj* kogt („stegt) for længe.
overdose ['əuvədəus] *s* overdosis // *v* overdosere; tage en overdosis.
overdraft ['əuvədra:ft] *s* overtræk (på konto).
overdrawn [əuvə'drɔ:n] *adj* overtrukket.
overdrive ['əuvədraiv] *s (auto)* 5. gear, økonomigear.
overdue [əuvə'dju:] *adj* forsinket; for længst forfalden.
overeat [əuvə'i:t] *v* spise for meget.
overestimate [əuvə'εstimeit] *v* overvurdere.
overflow *s* ['əuvəfləu] oversvømmelse; overflod // *v* [əuvə'fləu] flyde („strømme) over; oversvømme.
overgrown [əuvə'grəun] *adj* overgroet; tilgroet.
overhang ['əuvəhæŋ] *s* (klippe)fremspring.
overhaul *s* ['əuvəhɔ:l] eftersyn og reparation; overhaling; nøje gennemgang // *v* [əuvə'hɔ:l] foretage grundigt eftersyn; gennemgå nøje.
overhead *adj* ['əuvəhεd] luft- (fx *line* ledning); oven- (fx *light* lys) // *adv* [əuvə'hεd] ovenover, oppe i luften; **~s** *spl* faste udgifter.
overhear [əuvə'hiə*] *v* høre; komme til at høre.
overheated ['əuvə'hi:tid] *adj* overophedet; ophidset.
overjoyed [əuvə'dʒɔid] *adj* himmelhenrykt.
overkill ['əuvəkil] *s* stærk overdrivelse; *(mil)* mere end rigelig våbenstyrke (til at slå fjenden).
overlap *s* ['əuvəlæp] overlapning; delvis dækning // *v* [əuvə'læp] overlappe; falde (delvis) sammen.
overleaf ['əuvə'li:f] *adv* på næste side.
overload ['əuvə'ləud] *v* overbelaste; overlæsse.
overlook [əuvə'luk] *v* vende ud imod

(fx *the river* floden); overse; ignorere; lade passere; *~ing the valley* med udsigt over dalen.

overmanned ['əuvəmænd] *adj* overbemandet.

overnight ['əuvə'nait] *adv* i nattens løb; natten over; *(fig)* fra den ene dag til den anden, pludselig; *he stayed ~* han blev natten over; han overnattede; *he'll be away ~* han er væk til i morgen; **~ bag** *s* weekendkuffert.

overpower [əuvə'pauə*] *v* overmande; overvinde; **~ing** *adj* overvældende; uimodståelig.

overrate ['əuvə'reit] *v* overvurdere.

overreach [əuvə'ri:tʃ] *v: ~ oneself (fig)* gabe over for meget på en gang.

override [əuvə'raid] *v* tilsidesætte (fx *rules* regler); negligere; underkende (fx *a decision* en beslutning); **overriding** *adj* altovervejende.

overrule [əuvə'ru:l] *v* underkende; afvise.

overseas ['əuvə'si:z] *adj (merk)* udenrigs- (fx *trade* handel) // *adv* oversøisk; udenlands.

oversight ['əuvəsait] *s* forglemmelse; uagtsomhed.

oversleep [əuvə'sli:p] *v* sove over sig.

overstate ['əuvə'steit] *v* overdrive; angive for højt; **~ment** *s* overdrivelse.

overt [əu'və:t] *adj* åben; åbenlys.

overtake [əuvə'teik] *v* indhente; overhale (fx *a car* en bil).

overthrow [əuvə'θrəu] *v* kaste omkuld; vælte, styrte.

overtime ['əuvətaim] *s* overarbejde; *(sport)* forlænget spilletid; omkamp.

overturn [əuvə'tə:n] *v* vælte.

overview ['əuvəvju:] *s* overblik.

overweight ['əuvəweit] *s* (fx om bagage) overvægt // *adj* overvægtig.

overwhelm [əuvə'wɛlm] *v* overvælde; overmande; **~ing** *adj* overvældende.

overwork *s* ['əuvəwə:k] overanstrengelse; overarbejde // *v* [əuvə'wə:k] overanstrenge sig.

overwrought [əuvə'rɔ:t] *adj* overanstrengt; overspændt.

ovulation [ɔvju'leiʃən] *s* ægløsning.

owe [əu] *v* skylde; have at takke for.

owing ['əuiŋ] *adj* skyldig; *~ to* på grund af.

owl [aul] *s* ugle.

own [əun] *v* eje; indrømme; *~ up* tilstå // *adj* egen, eget, egne; *a room of one's ~* eget værelse; *get one's ~ back* få revanche; *on one's ~* alene; på egen hånd.

owner ['əunə*] *s* ejer; **~-occupied** *adj* ejer- (fx *flat* lejlighed); **~ship** *s* ejendomsret.

ox [ɔks] *s (pl: oxen)* okse; **~eye** *s (bot)* margerit; **~tail** *s: ~tail soup* oksehalesuppe.

oxygen ['ɔksidʒin] *s* ilt; **~ mask** *s* iltmaske.

oyster ['ɔistə*] *s* østers; **~ bed** *s* østersbanke.

oz [auns, aunsiz] fork.f. *ounce(s)* (28,35 gram).

ozone ['əuzəun] *s; ~ layer* ozonlag.

P

P, p [pi:].

p [pi:] fork.f. *penny; pence; page.*

PA ['pi:'ei] fork.f. *personal assistant; public address system.*

pa [pa:] *s* (F) papa, far.

p.a. ['pi:'ei] fork.f. *per annum.*

pace [peis] *s* skridt; gangart; fart, tempo; *keep ~* holde trit; følge med; *at one's own ~* i sit eget tempo; *set the ~* bestemme farten // *v* skridte (af); *~ up and down* gå (utålmodigt) frem og tilbage.

pacific [pə'sifik] *adj* fredelig; freds-; *the* **Pacific Ocean** *s* Stillehavet.

pacify ['pæsifai] *v* berolige; tilfredsstille; pacificere.

pack [pæk] *s* pakke; bylt; indpakning; (om hunde) kobbel; (om røvere etc) bande, flok; (om kort) spil; *a ~ of lies* (tyk) løgn // *v* pakke (ind, ned); fylde op, proppe; *~ed lunch* madpakke; *~ (one's bags)* pakke (sin bagage); *the bus was ~ed* bussen var stopfuld; *send sby ~ing* smi-

de en ud; ~ *it in!* (F) hold op! ~ *up* pakke sine ting; *(fig)* pakke sammen; *the fridge has ~ed up* (F) køleskabet er "stået af".
package ['pækidʒ] *s* pakning; pakke, balle; **~ deal** *s* samlet overenskomst; pakkeløsning; **~ tour** *s* færdigpakket rejse.
packet ['pækit] *s* (lille) pakke; *it cost a ~* (F) det kostede det hvide ud af øjnene.
packing ['pækiŋ] *s* emballage; emballering // *adj: send sby ~* give en løbepas; smide en ud; **~ slip** *s* pakseddel.
pact [pækt] *s* pagt.
pad [pæd] *s* pude; hynde; (fedt)delle; trædepude; (ben)beskytter; stempelpude; skulderpude; helikopterlandingsplads; affyringsrampe; (papir)blok; (hygiejne)bind; (F) hybel, lejlighed // *v* polstre; vattere; lunte, tøffe; **~ded** *adj* polstret; *~ded cell* gummicelle; **~ded envelope** *s* foret kuvert; **~ding** *s* polstring, udstopning.
paddle [pædl] *s* padleåre, pagaj // *v* padle; soppe; **~ steamer** *s* hjuldamper; **paddling pool** *s* soppebassin.
paddock ['pædək] *s* indhegning (til heste.
paddy field ['pædifi:ld] *s* rismark.
padlock ['pædlɔk] *s* hængelås // *v* sætte hængelås for.
paediatrics [pi:di'ætriks] *spl* læren om børnesygdomme, pædiatri.
pagan ['peigən] *s* hedning // *adj* hedensk.
page [peidʒ] *s* (i bog) side, pagina; piccolo, *(gl)* page; brudesvend // *v: ~ sby* kalde en over højttalersystem.
pageant ['pædʒənt] *s* festligt optog; festspil.
pageboy ['peidʒbɔi] *s* piccolo; pagehår.
paid [peid] *præt* og *pp* af *pay* // *adj* betalt; lønnet; *well ~* godt lønnet; *put ~ to* afslutte, gøre en ende på.
pail [peil] *s* spand.
pain [pein] *s* smerte; *be a ~ in the neck* være en plage; *be in ~* have ondt; *on ~ of death* under dødsstraf // *v* pine; **~ed** *adj (fig)* såret, forpint; ilde berørt; **~ful** *adj* smertelig; pinlig; **~killer** *s* smertestillende middel; **~less** *adj* smertefri; *it's quite ~less* det gør slet ikke ondt; **~s** *spl* smerter; veer; umage, ulejlighed; *take ~s to* gøre sig umage for.
painstaking ['peinzteikiŋ] *adj* omhyggelig, samvittighedsfuld.
paint [peint] *s* maling; sminke; *wet ~* (på skilt) nymalet // *v* male; pensle; male sig; *(fig)* skildre, udmale; **~box** *s* farvelade; malerkasse; **~brush** *s* pensel; **~er** *s* maler; kunstmaler; **~ing** *s* malerkunst; maleri; **~-roller** *s* malerrulle; **~-sprayer** *s* sprøjtepistol; **~-stripper** *s* malingsfjerner; lakfjerner; **~work** *s* maling.
pair [pɛə*] *s* par; *in ~s* parvis, to og to; *a ~ of horses* et tospand; *a ~ of scissors* en saks; *the ~ of them* dem begge to; *the ~s* parløb (på skøjter); toer (i roning) // *v* ordne parvis, parre.
Pakistani [pa:ki'sta:ni] *s* pakistaner // *adj* pakistansk.
pal [pæl] *s* (F) kammerat, ven // *v: ~ up with* (F) blive gode venner med.
palace ['pæləs] *s* slot, palads.
palatable ['pælitəbl] *adj* velsmagende; tiltalende; acceptabel.
palate ['pælit] *s* gane; *cleft ~* ganespalte.
pale [peil] *adj* bleg, farveløs, lys; *go (, turn) ~* blegne; *~ blue* lyseblå; **~face** *s* blegansigt.
Palestine ['pælistain] *s* Palæstina; **Palestinian** [-'stiniən] *s* palæstinenser // *adj* palæstinensisk.
palings ['peiliŋz] *spl* pæleværk; stakit.
pall [pɔ:l] *s* tæppe (fx af røg); mørk skygge; ligklæde.
pallet ['pælit] *s* briks; palle.
pallid ['pælid] *adj* bleg, gusten.
pallor ['pælə*] *s* bleghed.
pally ['pæli] *adj* kammeratlig; *get ~* blive gode kammerater; fedte sig ind.

palm [pa:m] *s* håndflade; *(bot)* palme(træ); *have an itching* ~ være grisk; være bestikkelig; *grease sby's* ~ smøre (,bestikke) en // *v* beføle; (om tryllekunstner) palmere; ~ *sth off on sby* (F) prakke en ngt på.

palpable ['pælpəbl] *adj* håndgribelig, til at tage og føle på.

palpitation [pælpi'teiʃən] *s* hjertebanken.

paltry ['pɔ:ltri] *adj* ussel, elendig.

pamper ['pæmpə*] *v* forkæle, spolere.

pamphlet ['pæmflit] *s* pjece, brochure.

pan [pæn] *s* pande; kasserolle; (wc-)kumme // *v* (F) panorere.

panacea [pænə'siə] *s* universalmiddel, patentløsning.

panache [pə'næʃ] *s* flot stil, flot gestus.

pancake ['pænkeik] *s* pandekage; ~ **landing** *s* mavelanding.

pancreas ['pæŋkriəs] *s* bugspytkirtel.

panda car ['pændəka:*] *s* (politi)patruljevogn.

pandemonium [pændi'məuniəm] *s* vildt kaos; øredøvende spektakel.

pander ['pændə*] *v:* ~ *to* lefle for.

pane [pein] *s* rude; felt.

panel [pænl] *s* panel; fyldning; betjeningstavle; *(auto)* instrumentbræt; gruppe, udvalg; (i radio, tv etc) panel; **~ling** *s* paneler, træværk.

pang [pæŋ] *s* smerte, stik; jag; *~s of remorse* samvittighedskvaler.

panic ['pænik] *s* panik, skræk // *v* fremkalde panik; blive panikslagen.

panicky ['pæniki] *adj* panikagtig; som der let går panik i.

panic-stricken ['pænik,strikn] *adj* panikslagen.

pannier ['pæniə*] *s* kurv; cykeltaske.

pan scrubber ['pænskrʌbə*] *s* grydesvamp.

pansy ['pænsi] *s* stedmoderblomst; (F) bøsse.

pant [pænt] *v* stønne, gispe, puste; ~ *for* sukke efter, tørste efter // *s:* se *pants.*

pantechnicon [pæn'tɛknikən] *s* (stor) flyttevogn.

panties ['pæntiz] *spl* (dame)trusser.

pantomime ['pæntəmaim] *s* pantomime; *(brit)* populær eventyrkomedie (oftest opført ved juletid).

pantry ['pæntri] *s* spisekammer; anretterværelse.

pants [pænts] *spl* bukser; underbukser; *catch sby with his ~ down* komme bag på en; *a kick in the* ~ et spark bagi; *wet one's* ~ tisse i bukserne.

panty ['pænti] *s:* ~ *hose* strømpebukser.

papal ['peipəl] *adj* pavelig, pave-.

paper ['peipə*] *s* papir; avis, blad; tapet; artikel, essay; (skriftlig) eksamensopgave; *be in the ~s* stå i avisen; *read a* ~ holde et foredrag // *v* dække med papir; tapetsere // *adj* papir-, papirs-; ~ *over* dække over; **~back** *s* billigbog; **~bag** *s* papirspose; **~-bound** *adj* (om bog) hæftet; **~boy** *s* avisbud; **~clip** *s* clips; ~ **hankie** *s* (F) papirslommetørklæde; ~ **mill** *s* papirfabrik; ~ **money** *s* seddelpenge; ~ **pushing** *s* papirnusseri; ~ **round** *s* (buds) avisrunde; ~ **shop** *s* bladkiosk; **~weight** *s* brevpresser; **~work** *s* skrivebordsarbejde.

par [pa:*] *s* ligestilling; pari; *be below* ~ føle sig sløj (,utilpas); være under normal standard; *on a ~ with* på linje med.

parable ['pærəbl] *s (rel)* lignelse.

parabolic [pærə'bɔlik] *adj:* ~ *antenna* parabolantenne.

parachute ['pærəʃu:t] *s* faldskærm // *v* springe (,kaste) ud med faldskærm; ~ **jump** *s* faldskærmsudspring.

parade [pə'reid] *s* parade; optog, opvisning; promenade // *v (fig)* skilte med; vise frem; gå i optog.

paradise ['pærədais] *s* paradis.

paraffin ['pærəfin] *s* petroleum; ~ **stove** *s* petroleumsovn; ~ **wax** *s* paraffin.

paragon ['pærəgən] *s: a ~ of virtue* et dydsmønster.

paragraph ['pærəgra:f] *s* paragraf; afsnit; artikel (i blad).

parallel ['pærəlɛl] *s* parallel; sammenligning; sidestykke; ~ *(of latitude)* breddegrad // *adj* parallel; tilsvarende.

paralyse ['pærəlaiz] *v* lamme; lamslå.

paralysis [pə'rælisis] *s* lammelse;

paramount ['pærəmaunt] *adj: of ~ importance* af allerstørste vigtighed.

parapet ['pærəpit] *s* rækværk.

paraphernalia [pærəfə'neiliə] *spl* tilbehør, udstyr; habengut.

paraphrase ['pærəfreiz] *s* omskrivning // *v* omskrive.

parasite ['pærəsait] *s* parasit, snylter; (F) nasserøv.

paratrooper ['pærətru:pə*] *s* faldskærmssoldat.

parboil ['pa:bɔil] *v* give et opkog, blanchere; skolde, svitse.

parcel [pa:sl] *s* pakke; jordlod, parcel // *v: ~ out* udstykke; *~ up* pakke ind; ~ **post** *s* pakkepost.

parch [pa:tʃ] *v* svide, tørre ind (,ud); *be ~ed* (om person) være ved at dø af tørst.

parchment ['pa:tʃmənt] *s* pergament.

pardon [pa:dn] *s* tilgivelse; benådning; *I beg your ~!* undskyld! om forladelse! *I beg your ~?* hvad behager? **~able** *adj* tilgivelig.

pare [pɛə*] *v* skrælle (fx *an apple* et æble); klippe (fx *one's nails* negle); nedskære.

parent ['pɛərənt] *s* forælder, far el. mor; *single ~* enlig forsørger // *adj* moder-; **~al** [pə'rɛntl] *adj* faderlig; moderlig; forældre-.

parenthesis [pə'rɛnθəsis] *s (pl: parentheses* [-si:z]) parentes.

parer ['pɛərə*] *s* skrællekniv.

paring ['pɛəriŋ] *s* skræl, afskåret stykke, spån; *nail ~s* afklippede negle.

parish ['pæriʃ] *s* sogn // *adj* sogne-; ~ **council** *s* sogneråd.

parishioner [pæ'riʃənə*] *s* sognebarn; indbygger i sogn.

parish register ['pæriʃ ˌrɛdʒistə*] *s* kirkebog.

parity ['pæriti] *s* ligestilling; ligeberettigelse; *~ of pay* ligeløn.

park [pa:k] *s* park, (offentligt) anlæg; (sports)stadion // *v* parkere; anbringe.

parking ['pa:kiŋ] *s* parkering; *no ~* parkering forbudt; ~ **disc** *s* p-skive; ~ **fine** *s* parkeringsbøde; ~ **lot** *s (am)* parkeringsplads; ~ **meter** *s* parkometer; ~ **place** *s* parkeringsplads; ~ **ticket** *s* parkeringsbøde.

parliament ['pa:ləmənt] *s* parlament; **~ary** [-'mɛntəri] *adj* parlamentarisk; parlaments-.

parlour ['pa:lə*] *s (gl)* stue, salon; modtagelsesværelse; ~ **game** *s* selskabsleg; **~maid** *s* stuepige.

parochial [pə'rəukiəl] *adj* sogne-, kommune-; *(fig)* provinsiel, snæversynet.

parody ['pærədi] *s* parodi // *v* parodiere.

parole [pə'rəul] *s: on ~* prøveløsladt.

parquet ['pa:kei] *s* parket(gulv).

parrot ['pærət] *s* papegøje // *v* snakke efter.

parry ['pæri] *v* afparere, afbøde; *~ a question* vige uden om et spørgsmål.

parsimonious [pa:si'məuniəs] *adj* påholdende, oversparsommelig.

parsley ['pa:sli] *s* persille.

parsnip ['pa:snip] *s* pastinak.

parson [pa:sn] *s* præst, sognepræst; **~age** ['pa:sənidʒ] *s* præstegård.

part [pa:t] *s* del, part; egn, landsdel; *(auto* etc) reservedel; *(mus)* stemme, parti; *(teat)* rolle; *take ~ in* deltage (,tage del) i; *take sth in bad ~* tage ngt ilde op; *take sby's ~* holde med en; *I want no ~ in that* det vil jeg ikke blandes ind i; *on his ~* fra hans side; for hans del; *for my ~* for mit vedkommende; for min del; *for the most ~* for det meste; *for the better ~ of the weekend* størstedelen af weekenden; *be ~ and parcel of sth* være en fast bestanddel af ngt; *~ of speech* ordklasse; *in these ~s* her på egnen; *private ~s (spøg)* ædlere dele // *v* dele, adskille; dele sig; skilles; *~ friends* skilles som venner; *~ with* skilles fra; tage afsked med // *adj* delvis, dels; *~ sugar ~ cream* dels sukker, dels fløde.

partake [pa:'teik] *v (-took, -taken)* tage del (i); *~ of* nyde.

partial [pa:ʃl] *adj* delvis, partiel; partisk; *be ~ to* have en svaghed for.
participant [pa:'tisipənt] *s* deltager.
participate [pa:'tisipeit] *v* deltage *(in* i).
participation [pa:tisi'peiʃən] *s* deltagelse; medbestemmelse.
particle ['pa:tikl] *s* lille del; partikel (også *gram).*
particular [pa:'tikjulə*] *adj* særlig, speciel; (om person) nøjeregnende, kræsen; *in ~* især, specielt; *nothing in ~* ikke ngt særligt; **-ly** *adv* især, navnlig; **-s** *spl* detaljer, enkeltheder; *further ~s* yderligere oplysninger.
parting ['pa:tiŋ] *s* deling; adskillelse; afsked; (i håret) skilning // *adj* afskeds-; **~ shot** *s* afskedssalut.
partition [pa:'tiʃən] *s* deling; skel; skillevæg // *v* opdele.
partly ['pa:tli] *adv* delvis, (til) dels.
partner ['pa:tnə*] *s* deltager; kompagnon, partner; *(sport)* medspiller; makker; **-ship** *s* fællesskab; kompagniskab.
part of speech ['pa:təv'spi:tʃ] *s (gram)* ordklasse.
part payment ['pa:t'peimənt] *s* afdrag, delvis betaling.
partridge ['pa:tridʒ] *s* agerhøne.
part-singing ['pa:tsiŋiŋ] *s* flerstemmig sang.
part-time ['pa:t'taim] *adj/adv* deltids(-), halvdags(-).
party ['pa:ti] *s* selskab, fest; parti; gruppe, part; *throw a ~* holde fest; *be a ~ to* deltage i; være medskyldig i; **~ line** *s (pol)* partilinje; *(tlf)* partstelefon; **~-political broadcast** *s (radio, tv)* partidebat.
pass [pa:s] *s* overgang, passage; (i bjerge) pas; passerseddel; *(sport)* aflevering; *make ~es at sby* gøre tilnærmelser til en; *get a ~ in English* bestå prøven i engelsk // *v* passere, gå (,køre etc) forbi, overhale; række; (om tid) gå, forløbe; bestå (en eksamen); drive over; *~ sth through a ring* stikke ngt gennem en ring; *please ~ me the potatoes* vær rar og række mig kartoflerne; *~ around* sende rundt; *~ away* dø; *~ by* passere, komme forbi; ignorere, negligere; *~ down* overlevere; lade gå i arv; *~ for* gå for at være; *~ off* forløbe; *~sth off as sth* lade ngt gå for at være ngt; *~ on* sende videre; lade gå videre; *~ out* besvime; *~ over* forbigå; *be ~ed over* blive gået; *~ up a chance* lade en chance gå sig forbi; **-able** *adj* fremkommelig, passabel; acceptabel, jævn.
passage ['pæsidʒ] *s* passage, gennemgang; overfart (med skib el. fly); korridor; afsnit (fx i bog); *have you booked your ~?* har du bestilt billet (til båden el. flyet)? **-way** *s* passage.
pass book ['pa:s'bu:k] *s* sparekassebog.
passenger ['pæsindʒə*] *s* passager; **~ liner** *s* passagerskib.
passer-by ['pa:sə,bai] *s* forbipasserende.
passing ['pa:siŋ] *adj* forbigående; *in ~* i forbifarten.
passion ['pæʃən] *s* lidenskab, vrede; forkærlighed; begær; *the Passion* Kristi lidelseshistorie; *fly into a ~* blive helt vild (,skruptosset); *have a ~ for sth* være vild med ngt.
passionate ['pæʃənət] *adj* lidenskabelig.
passive ['pæsiv] *adj* passiv.
pass key ['pa:s,ki:] *s* hovednøgle.
passport ['pa:spɔ:t] *s* pas.
password ['pa:swə:d] *s* feltråb, løsen.
past [pa:st] *s* fortid; *it's a thing of the ~* det tilhører fortiden; *she has a ~ (fig)* hun har en fortid (dvs. tidl. forhold) // *adj* fortidig, tidligere; forløben; forbi; *for the ~ few days* de sidste par dage // *præp* forbi; længere end; ud over; *he's ~ forty* han er over fyrre; *it's ~ midnight* det er over midnat; *at half ~ one* klokken halvto; *it's ten ~* den er ti minutter over; *~ danger* uden for fare; *~ hope* håbløs; *I wouldn't put it ~ him to...* det skulle ikke undre mig hvis han...
paste [peist] *s* masse; pasta; puré; dej; klister; (om smykke) simili // *v*

klistre, lime; ~ *sby* (S) tvære en ud; **~board** *s* karton, pap.
pastime ['pa:staim] *s* tidsfordriv; fornøjelse.
pasting ['peistiŋ] *s: give sby a* ~ (F) give en en hård medfart; give en tæv.
pastoral ['pa:strəl] *adj* hyrde-; *(fig)* idyllisk; *(agr)* græsnings-.
pastry ['peistri] *s* dej; bagværk; kager; *Danish* ~ wienerbrød; **~ brush** *s* kagepensel.
pasture ['pa:stʃə*] *s* græsgang; *put out to* ~ sætte på græs; *(fig)* sende på pension.
pasty *s* ['pæsti] postej // ['peisti] *adj* klæbrig; bleg(fed).
pat [pæt] *v* klappe, glatte; banke let; trippe // *adj/adv* tilpas; i rette øjeblik; *know sth off* ~ kunne ngt flydende.
patch [pætʃ] *s* lap; klud; klap; stykke jord, plet; bed; stykke; periode; *a bad* ~ en uheldig periode; *a* ~ *of land* et stykke jord // *v* lappe; flikke, stykke sammen; ~ *up* lappe sammen; bilægge (fx *a quarrel* en strid); **~y** *adj* uensartet; spredt; mangelfuld.
pâté ['pætei] *s* postej.
patent ['pætənt] *s* patent; ~ *leather shoes* laksko; ~ *pending* patentanmeldt // *v* ['pætənt] patentere // *adj* ['peitənt] åbenbar, tydelig; **~ly** *adv* tydeligt, åbenlyst.
paternal [pə'tə:nl] *adj* faderlig; fædrene; **paternity** *s* faderskab.
path [pa:θ] *s* sti; havegang; passage; (om planet el. fly) bane.
pathetic [pə'θɛtik] *adj* ynkelig, gribende, patetisk; *it's* ~ det er til at græde over.
pathological [pæθə'lɔdʒikl] *adj* patologisk.
pathologist [pæ'θɔlədʒist] *s* patolog.
pathology [pæ'θɔlədʒi] *s* patologi.
pathway ['pa:θwei] *s* (gang)sti; *(fig)* vej, bane.
patience ['peiʃəns] *s* tålmodighed; kabale; *she has no* ~ *with him* han irriterer hende; *try sby's* ~ sætte ens tålmodighed på prøve; *play* ~ lægge kabale.
patient ['peiʃənt] *s* patient // *adj* tålmodig; udholdende.
patio ['pætiəu] *s* gårdhave.
patrol [pə'trəul] *s* patrulje; patruljering; runde // *v* (af)patruljere.
patron ['peitrən] *s* (i butik etc) kunde; velynder, mæcen; ~ *of the arts* kunstmæcen.
patronage ['pætrənidʒ] *s* beskyttelse; protektion.
patronize ['pætrənaiz] *v* beskytte, protegere; handle hos; **patronizing** *adj* nedladende.
patron saint ['peitrən 'seint] *s* skytshelgen.
patter [pætə*] *s* trommen, trippen; remse, snak // *v* trippe, tromme.
pattern ['pætən] *s* mønster; snitmønster; model; strikkeopskrift; stofprøve.
patty ['pæti] *s* lille postej; **~ shell** *s* sv.t. tartelet.
paunch [pɔ:ntʃ] *s* (stor) mave, ølmave.
pauper ['pɔ:pə*] *s* fattiglem; fattig stakkel.
pause [pɔ:z] *s* pause, afbrydelse // *v* holde pause, standse.
pave [peiv] *v* brolægge; ~ *the way for* bane vej for; **~ment** *s* fortov; brolægning.
pavilion [pə'viljən] *s* pavillon.
paving *s* vejbelægning; **~ stone** *s* brosten.
paw [pɔ:] *s* pote, lab; *~s off!* (F) væk med grabberne! // *v* stampe; gramse på.
pawn [pɔ:n] *s* pant; (i skak) bonde; *(fig)* brik // *v* pantsætte; **~broker** *s* pantelåner; **~shop** *s* lånekontor.
pay [pei] *s* betaling, lønning, gage; hyre; *be in sby's* ~ arbejde for en // *v (paid, paid* [peid]) betale; (af)lønne; betale sig; gengælde; ~ *attention (to)* lægge mærke (til); høre efter, lytte (til); ~ *one's way* betale sin del; *(om firma etc)* løbe rundt; ~ *up* punge ud; (se også *paid);* **~able** *adj* at betale; forfalden; **~ day** *s* lønningsdag.
PAYE fork.f. *pay as you earn* kildeskat.

pay... sms: **~ing guest** *s* logerende; **~ing patient** *s* privatpatient; **~master** *s* kasserer; **~ment** *s* betaling; afdrag; *down ~ment* udbetaling; *on ~ment of* mod betaling af; **~off** *s* belønning, bestikkelse; **~ packet** *s* lønningspose; **~phone** *(am) s* mønttelefon; **~roll** *s* lønningsliste; **~-slip** *s* lønseddel; **~ talks** *spl* lønforhandlinger.

PC ['pi:'si:] fork.f. *police constable; personal computer.*

pc fork.f. *per cent; postcard.*

PE fork.f. *physical education.*

pea [pi:] *s* ært.

peace [pi:s] *s* fred, ro; *be at ~ with* leve i fred med; være gode venner med; *hold one's ~* tie stille; *make ~* slutte fred; *~ and quiet* fred og ro; *~ of mind* sindsro; **~able** *adj* fredelig; **~ful** *adj* fredelig, rolig; **~-keeping** *adj* fredsbevarende; **~-loving** *adj* fredselskende, fredelig; **~ talks** *spl* fredsforhandlinger; **~time** *s* fredstid.

peach [pi:tʃ] *s* fersken; *she's a ~* hun er en skat // *adj* ferskenfarvet.

peacock ['pi:kɔk] *s* påfugl.

peak [pi:k] *s* spids; (bjerg)top; højdepunkt // *v* kulminere, toppe; **~ hours** *spl* myldretid; **~ period** *s* periode med spidsbelastning; **~ season** *s* højsæson.

peaky ['pi:ki] *adj* sløj, dårlig.

peal [pi:l] *s* (om klokker) ringen, kimen; *~s of laughter* rungende latter; *a ~ of thunder* et tordenskrald.

peanut ['pi:nʌt] *s* jordnød; *~s* (F) småpenge, pebernødder; *Peanuts* (om tegneserie) Radiserne.

peapod ['pi:pɔd] *s* ærtebælg.

pear [pɛə*] *s* pære.

pearl [pə:l] *s* perle; *a string of ~s* en perlekæde; **~ barley** *s* byggryn, perlebyg; **~ button** *s* perlemorsknap; **~ oyster** *s* perlemusling.

peasant [pɛznt] *s* bonde; husmand; **~ry** ['pɛzntri] *s* bondestand, almue.

peashooter ['pi:ʃu:tə*] *s* pusterør.

pea soup ['pi:su:p] *s* ærtesuppe; **peasouper** *s* tæt, gul londontåge.

peat [pi:t] *s* tørv; **~ bog** *s* tørvemose.

peaty ['pi:ti] *adj* (om whisky) med tørvesmag.

pebble [pɛbl] *s* (lille og rund) sten; *~s* småsten, rullesten.

peck [pɛk] *s* hak(ken), pikken; (let) kys // *v* hakke, pikke; *~ at* hakke efter; stikke til; *(fig)* hakke på; **~er** *s* *(am,* S) pik; *keep up one's ~er (brit)* holde modet oppe; **~ing order** *s* hakkeorden.

peckish ['pɛkiʃ] *adj* (F) sulten.

peculiar [pi'kju:liə*] *adj* mærkelig, sær; særlig, særegen; *~ to* særegen for.

peculiarity [pikju:li'æriti] *s* særhed, særegenhed.

pedagogue ['pɛdəgɔg] *s* pædagog.

pedal [pɛdl] *s* pedal // *v* cykle; træde (pedaler); **~ bin** *s* pedalspand (til affald).

pedalo ['pɛdələu] *s* vandcykel.

peddle [pɛdl] *v* gå rundt og sælge ved dørene, kolportere.

peddler ['pɛdlə*] *s* omvandrende handelsmand, kolportør; *drug ~* narkohandler.

pedestal ['pɛdistəl] *s* piedestal; sokkel.

pedestrian [pi'dɛstriən] *s* fodgænger // *adj* gående, til fods; (F) kedelig, middelmådig; **~ crossing** *s* fodgængerovergang; **~ize** [-aiz] *v* gøre til gågade; **~ precinct** [-'pri:siŋkt] *s* fodgængerområde; **~ street** *s* gågade.

pedigree ['pɛdigri:] *s* stamtavle; **~ horse** *s* racehest.

pee [pi:] *s* tis; *have a ~* tisse // *v* tisse.

peek [pi:k] *v* kigge.

peel [pi:l] *s* skræl, skal, skind // *v* skrælle, pille; skalle af; **~er** *s* skrællekniv; **~ings** *spl* skræller, skaller.

peep [pi:p] *s* kig, glimt; pip, pippen // *v* kigge, titte; pippe; *~ out* titte frem, vise sig; **~hole** *s* kighul; **Peeping Tom** *s* vindueskigger.

peer [piə*] *s* adelsmand; ligemand; medlem af overhuset; *without (a) ~* uforlignelig // *v: ~ at* stirre på.

peerage ['piəridʒ] *s* adelsrang.

peerless ['piəlis] *adj* uden lige.

peeved [pi:vd] *adj* irriteret *(about* over); **peevish** ['pi:viʃ] *adj* sur, vrissen.
peewit ['pi:wit] *s* vibe.
peg [pɛg] *s* pind, pløk; kile; knage; tøjklemme; *be brought down a ~ or two* blive "pillet ned", blive sat på plads; *off the ~* færdigsyet // *v* pløkke; hænge op; fastsætte; *~ out* (F) stille træskoene (dvs. dø).
pejorative [pi'dʒɔrətiv] *s* nedsættende ord // *adj* nedsættende.
peke [pi:k] *s* (F) d.s.s. **pekinese** [pi:ki'ni:z] *s* pekingeser(hund).
pelican ['pɛlikən] *s* pelikan; **~ crossing** *s* fodgængerovergang (hvor gående kan få lyset til at skifte ved tryk på en knap).
pellet ['pɛlit] *s* kugle; hagl; pille.
pell-mell ['pɛl'mɛl] *adv* hulter til bulter.
pelmet ['pɛlmit] *s* gardinkappe.
pelt [pɛlt] *v* bombardere; tæve; drøne af sted; styrte ned.
pelvic ['pɛlvik] *adj (anat)* bækken-.
pelvis ['pɛlvis] *s* bækken(parti).
pen [pɛn] *s* pen; fold, indelukke, bås; kravlegård; *(fig)* skrivestil; forfatter.
penal ['pi:nl] *adj* straffe-; strafbar; **~ code** *s* straffelov; **~ize** [-aiz] *v* straffe; gøre strafbar; **~ offence** *adj* strafbar handling; **~ servitude** *s* strafarbejde.
penalty ['pɛnlti] *s* straf, bøde; *(sport)* straffespark (,-kast); *daily ~* dagbøde; *on ~ of death* under dødsstraf; **~ area** *s (sport)* straffesparkfelt; **~ box** *s* udvisningsbænk.
penance ['pɛnəns] *s* bod.
pence [pɛns] *spl* af *penny.*
pencil [pɛnsl] *s* blyant: *(fig)* strålebundt // *v* skrive (,tegne) med blyant; **~ case** *s* penalhus; **~ sharpener** *s* blyantspidser.
pendant ['pɛndənt] *s* hængesmykke; ørering; hængelampe, pendel.
pendent ['pɛndənt] *adj* hængende; *(fig)* svævende, uafgjort.
pending ['pɛndiŋ] *præp* under, i løbet af; indtil (fx *her arrival* hendes ankomst) // *adj* uafgjort; forestående; som står for døren; *patent ~* patentanmeldt.
pendulum ['pɛndjuləm] *s* pendul.
penetrate ['pɛnitreit] *v* gennemtrænge, trænge ind i; gennembore; **penetrating** *adj* gennemtrængende; skarp(sindig).
penetration [pɛni'treiʃən] *s* indtrængen; gennemtrængen.
penguin ['pɛngwin] *s* pingvin.
peninsula [pə'ninsjulə] *s* halvø.
penitent ['pɛnitnt] *adj* angrende, bodfærdig.
penitentiary [pɛni'tɛnʃəri] *s* forbedringshus; *(am)* fængsel.
penknife ['pɛnnaif] *s* lille lommekniv.
pen name ['pɛnneim] *s* pseudonym.
pennant ['pɛnənt] *s* vimpel.
penniless ['pɛnilis] *adj* fattig, uden en øre.
penny ['pɛni] *s (pl: pence* [pɛns]) penny (1/100 £); *(pl: pennies)* pengestykke; *in for a ~ in for a pound* har man sagt a må man også sige b; *a pretty ~* en pæn sum penge; *spend a ~* (F) gå på toilettet; *a ~ for your thoughts* hvad tænker du på? *he doesn't have a ~ to his name* han er ludfattig; *the ~ dropped* tiøren faldt; **~-pinching** *adj* nærig, fedtet.
pen pal ['pɛnpæl] *s* penneven; **penpusher** *s* kontorslave.
pension ['pɛnʃən] *s* pension; pensionat // *v: ~ off* pensionere; **~able** *adj* pensionsberettiget.
pensioner ['pɛnʃənə*] *s* pensionist.
pension fund ['pɛnʃən ˌfʌnd] *s* pensionskasse.
pension scheme ['pɛnʃən ˌski:m] *s* pensionsordning.
pensive ['pɛnsiv] *adj* tankefuld; tungsindig.
pentagon ['pɛntəgən] *s* femkant; *Pentagon* USA.s forsvarsministerium.
pentathlon [pɛn'tæθlən] *s (sport)* femkamp.
penthouse ['pɛnthaus] *s* (eksklusiv) taglejlighed; overbygning.
pent-up ['pɛntʌp] *adj* indestængt, undertrykt.
penultimate [pə'nʌltimit] *adj* næstsidst.

peony ['piəni] *s* pæon.

people [pi:pl] *spl* folk; man; familie, slægt; *a* ~ et folkeslag; *several* ~ *came* der kom adskillige mennesker; *the room was full of* ~ værelset var fuldt af folk; ~ *say that...* folk siger at...; *why him of all* ~*?* hvorfor netop (,lige) ham? // *v* befolke.

pep [pɛp] *s* fut, pep // *v:* ~ *up* piffe op; sætte fut i.

pepper ['pɛpə*] *s* peber; peberfrugt // *v* pebre; **~ mill** *s* peberkværn; **~mint** *s* pebermynte; **~pot** *s* peberbøsse.

pep pill ['pɛp,pil] *s* (F) ferietablet; **pep talk** *s* opildnende tale.

peptic ['pɛptik] *adj:* ~ *ulcer* mavesår.

per [pə:*] *præp* igennem, ved; pr.; via; ~ *annum* pr. år; ~ *capita* pr. person; ~ *cent* procent; ~ *hour* i timen; *as* ~... ifølge...; *as* ~ *normal* som sædvanlig.

perambulator *s* (H) barnevogn; (d.s.s. *pram).*

perceive [pə'si:v] *v* indse; opfatte, se; fornemme.

percentage [pə'sɛntidʒ] *s* procentdel, procent; *get a* ~ få procenter.

perceptible [pə'sɛptibl] *adj* mærkbar; synlig.

perception [pə'sɛpʃən] *s* opfattelse(sevne).

perceptive [pə'sɛptiv] *adj* hurtigt opfattende; følsom.

perch [pə:tʃ] *s* aborre // *v* sidde (og balancere); være anbragt højt oppe.

perchance [pə'tʃa:ns] *(gl; spøg)* måske, kanhænde.

percolator ['pə:kəleitə*] *s* kaffemaskine; kaffekolbe.

percussion [pə'kʌʃən] *s* slag, sammenstød; *(mus)* slagtøj; **~ cap** *s* knaldhætte.

peremptory [pə'rɛmtəri] *adj* bydende; kategorisk; *(jur)* afgørende.

perennial [pə'rɛniəl] *s* staude // *adj* evig; (om plante) flerårig.

perfect *s* ['pə:fikt] (også: ~ *tense) (gram)* førnutid, perfektum // *v* [pə'fɛkt] fuldende, fuldstændiggøre // *adj* ['pə:fikt] perfekt, fuldkommen, komplet; *have* ~ *pitch* have absolut gehør.

perfection [pə:'fɛkʃən] *s* fuldkommenhed, fuldendelse.

perfectly ['pə:fiktli] *adv* helt, fuldstændig.

perforate ['pə:fəreit] *v* gennembore, perforere; **perforation** [-'reiʃən] *s* perforering.

perform [pə'fɔ:m] *v* udføre; opfylde; opføre, spille; optræde; yde.

performance [pə'fɔ:məns] *s* udførelse; optræden; fremførelse, forestilling; *(auto* etc) ydeevne.

performer [pə'fɔ:mə*] *s* optrædende, kunstner.

performing [pə'fɔ:miŋ] *adj* dresseret (fx *seal* sæl); (om fx musiker) udøvende.

perfume ['pə:fju:m] *s* parfume; vellugt, duft.

perfunctory [pə'fʌŋktəri] *adj* flygtig, henkastet.

perhaps [pə'hæps, præps] *adv* måske; ~ *so* det kan godt være.

peril ['pɛril] *s* fare, risiko; *in* ~ *of one's life* i livsfare; *at one's own* ~ på eget ansvar; *do it at your own* ~*!* du kan vove på at gøre det!

perilous ['pɛriləs] *adj* farlig.

perimeter [pə'rimitə*] *s* omkreds.

period ['piəriəd] *s* periode, tidsrum; epoke; (i skole) time, lektion; *(am)* punktum; *(med)* menstruation // *adj* stil- (fx *furniture* møbler).

periodic [piəri'ɔdik] *adj* periodisk; **~al** [-'ɔdikl] *s* tidsskrift // *adj* periodisk.

period pains ['piəriəd ,peinz] *spl* menstruationssmerter.

peripheral [pə'rifərəl] *adj* periferisk, perifer; periferi-; **~s** *spl (edb)* periferiudstyr.

periphery [pə'rifəri] *s* periferi.

perish ['pɛriʃ] *v* omkomme, gå til grunde; blive ødelagt; ~ *the thought!* Gud fri mig vel! aldrig i livet! **~able** *adj* forgængelig; letfordærvelig; **~ing** *adj* (F) forbandet; *I'm* ~*ing* jeg er ved at dø af kulde // *adv: it's* ~*ing cold* det er hundekoldt.

perjury ['pə:dʒəri] *s* mened.

perk [pə:k] *v:* ~ *up* kvikke op; ~ *up one's ears* spidse ører.

perks [pə:ks] *spl* frynsegoder; biindtægter.
perky ['pə:ki] *adj* munter; rapmundet.
perm [pə:m] *s* (F) permanent(krølning); *she had a ~* hun blev permanentet.
permanence ['pə:mənəns] *s* varighed, bestandighed.
permanent ['pə:mənənt] *adj* permanent, varig; *a ~ fixture* en fast installation.
permeable ['pə:miəbl] *adj* gennemtrængelig.
permeate ['pə:mieit] *v* trænge igennem.
permissible [pə'misibl] *adj* tilladelig.
permission [pə'miʃən] *s* tilladelse; lov.
permissive [pə'missiv] *adj* (oftest *neds)* tolerant, liberal; frisindet; eftergivende; *lead a ~ life* få lov til alting.
permit *s* ['pə:mit] (skriftlig) tilladelse // *v* [pə'mit] tillade; *be ~ted to* få lov til; *weather ~ting* hvis vejret tillader det.
pernicious [pə:'niʃəs] *adj* skadelig, ondartet.
pernickety [pə'nikiti] *adj* (F) pertentlig; kilden (fx *case* sag).
peroration [pərə'reiʃən] *s* sammenfatning; præken, ordskvalder.
peroxide [pə'rɔksaid] *s: ~ (of hydrogen)* brintoverilte.
perpendicular [pə:pən'dikjulə*] *adj* lodret.
perpetrate ['pə:pitreit] *v* begå.
perpetrator ['pə:pitreitə*] *s* gerningsmand.
perpetual [pə:'pɛtjuəl] *adj* evig; evindelig.
perpetuate [pə:'pɛtjueit] *v* forevige; bevare.
perplex [pə'plɛks] *v* forvirre, gøre perpleks.
persecute ['pə:sikju:t] *v* forfølge; plage, genere.
persecution [pə:si'kju:ʃən] *s* forfølgelse; **~ mania** *s* forfølgelsesvanvid.
persevere [pə:si'viə*] *v* holde ud; blive ved, fremture *(in, with* med);
persevering [-'viəriŋ] *adj* udholdende, ihærdig.
Persian ['pə:ʃən] *adj* persisk; **~ lamb** *s* persianer.
persist [pə'sist] *v: ~ in* blive ved med at, fremture med at; **~ence** *s* ihærdighed, hårdnakkethed; **~ent** *adj* vedholdende, hårdnakket.
person [pə:sn] *s* person; skikkelse, fremtræden; *in ~* personlig, i egen person; *in the ~ of* i skikkelse af; *~ to ~ call (tlf)* personlig samtale; **~able** *adj* præsentabel.
personal ['pə:sənl] *adj* personlig; **~ assistant** *s (PA)* sv.t. privatsekretær; **~ call** *s (tlf)* personlig samtale; privatsamtale.
personality [pə:sə'næliti] *s* personlighed.~
personally ['pə:sənəli] *adv* personlig(t).
personal stereo ['pə:sənl 'stiəriəu] *s* walkman ®, vandremand.
personify [pə'sɔnifai] *v* personificere.
personnel [pə:sə'nɛl] *s* personale; personel; **~ ceiling** *s* personaleloft; **~ manager** *s* personalechef.
perspective [pə'spɛktiv] *s* perspektiv, udsigt.
perspex ® ['pə:spɛks] *s* gennemsigtig plastic, slags plexiglas.
perspicacious [pə:spi'keiʃəs] *adj* skarpsindig.
perspicuous [pə:'spikjuəs] *adj* klar; indlysende.
perspiration [pə:spi'reiʃən] *s* sved, transpiration.
perspire [pə'spaiə*] *v* svede, transpirere.
persuade [pə'sweid] *v* overtale; overbevise; *he ~d me to do it* han overtalte mig til at gøre det; *he ~d me that* han overbeviste mig om at.
persuasion [pə'sweiʃən] *s* overtalelse; overbevisning; anskuelse.
persuasive [pə'sweisiv] *adj* overbevisende.
pert [pə:t] *adj* næsvis, rapmundet.
pertaining [pə'teiniŋ] *adj: ~ to* angående, vedrørende.
pertinacious [pə:ti'neiʃəs] *adj* ihærdig; hårdnakket.

pertinent ['pə:tinənt] *adj* relevant; træffende.
perturb [pə'tə:b] *v* forurolige; forstyrre.
perusal [pə'ru:zl] *s* (grundig) gennemlæsning, granskning.
peruse [pə'ru:z] *v* granske.
Peruvian [pə'ru:viən] *s* peruaner // *adj* peruansk.
pervasive [pə'veisiv] *adj* gennemtrængende; med stor gennemslagskraft.
perverse [pə'və:s] *adj* forstokket; urimelig.
perversion [pə'və:ʃən] *s* fordrejelse; fordærv; perversion.
perversity [pə'və:siti] *s* urimelighed; trodsighed.
pervert *s* ['pə:və:t] pervers person // *v* [pə'və:t] fordreje; fordærve; **~ed** [-'və:tid] *adj* pervers.
pessary ['pɛsəri] *s* pessar.
pessimism ['pɛsimizm] *s* pessimisme.
pessimist ['pɛsimist] *s* pessimist, sortseer; **pessimistic** [-'mistik] *adj* pessimistisk.
pest [pɛst] *s* plage, plageånd; skadedyr; pest; **~er** *v* genere, plage.
pesticide ['pɛstisaid] *s* skadedyrsmiddel.
pestilence ['pɛstiləns] *s* pest; *(fig)* pestilens.
pestle [pɛsl] *s* støder (til morter).
pet [pɛt] *s* kæledyr; yndling; (F) skat; *he's such a ~* han er simpelthen så sød // *v* kæle for; forkæle // *adj* yndlings-; kæle-.
petal [pɛtl] *s (bot)* kronblad.
pet aversion ['pɛtə'və:ʃən] *s* yndlingsaversion.
Pete [pi:t] d.s.s. *Peter; for ~'s sake* for Guds skyld.
peter ['pi:tə*] *v: ~ out* løbe ud i sandet, ebbe ud; (om vind) løje af.
petite [pə'ti:t] *adj* lille og net, som en nipsgenstand.
petition [pə'tiʃən] *s* ansøgning; bønskrift // *v* ansøge, indgive anmodning om.
pet name ['pɛtneim] *s* kælenavn.
petrified ['pɛtrifaid] *adj* forstenet; *(fig)* stiv af skræk.
petrify ['pɛtrifai] *v* forstene; blive forstenet.
petrol ['pɛtrəl] *s* benzin; *run out of ~* løbe tør for benzin.
petroleum [pə'trəuliəm] *s* råolie; *~ jelly* vaseline.
petrol... ['pɛtrəl-] sms: **~ gauge** [-geidʒ] *s* benzinmåler; **~ station** *s* tankstation, benzintank; **~ tank** *s* benzintank (i bil).
pet shop ['pɛt,ʃɔp] *s* dyrehandel.
petticoat ['pɛtikəut] *s* underkjole.
pettifogging ['pɛtifɔgiŋ] *adj* smålig, pedantisk.
pettiness ['pɛtinis] *s* smålighed.
petty ['pɛti] *adj* smålig; ubetydelig; små-; **~ cash** *s* småpenge; **~ officer** *s (mar)* underofficer.
petulant ['pɛtjulənt] *adj* gnaven, irritabel.
pew [pju:] *s* kirkestol; *have a ~! (spøg)* sid ned!
pewter ['pju:tə*] *s* tin; **~ ware** *s* tinvarer.
phallic ['fælik] *adj* fallos-.
phantom ['fæntəm] *s* fantasibillede, fantom; spøgelse.
pharmaceutical [fa:mə'su:tikl] *adj* medicinal-; farmaceutisk; **~s** *spl* lægemidler, medicin.
pharmacist ['fa:məsist] *s* farmaceut; sv.t. apoteker.
pharmacy ['fa:məsi] *s* apotek.
phase [feiz] *s* fase, periode; stadie // *v: ~ in (,out)* gradvis indføre (,afskaffe).
phasing ['feiziŋ] *s* synkronisering.
PhD ['pi:eitʃ'di:] (fork.f. *Doctor of Philosophy)* sv.t. dr.phil.
pheasant ['fɛznt] *s* fasan.
phenomenon [fə'nɔminən] *s (pl: phenomena)* fænomen, foreteelse.
phew [fju:] *interj* pyh! føj! pyha!
phial [faiəl] *s* lille flaske, medicinglas.
philanthropic [filən'θrɔpik] *adj* menneskekærlig, filantropisk; **philanthropist** [-'lænθrəpist] *s* menneskeven, filantrop.
philatelist [fi'lætəlist] *s* frimærkesamler, filatelist.
Philippines ['filipi:nz] *spl* Filippinerne.

Phillips ® ['filips] *s: ~ screwdriver* stjerneskruetrækker.
philology [fi'lɔlədʒi] *s* sprogvidenskab, filologi.
philosopher [fi'lɔsəfə*] *s* filosof.
philosophize [fi'lɔsəfaiz] *v* filosofere.
philosophy [fi'lɔsəfi] *s* filosofi.
phlegm [flɛm] *s* koldinsighed, flegma; *(med)* (ophostet) slim.
phobia ['fəubjə] *s* fobi.
phone [fəun] *s* (F) telefon; *be on the ~* have telefon; være ved at telefonere // *v* telefonere (,ringe) (til); **~ booth** *s* telefonboks; **~-in** *s (radio, tv)* telefonprogram.
phonetics [fə'nɛtiks] *s* lydskrift; fonetik.
phon(e)y ['fəuni] *s* (F) fupmager; humbug // *adj* falsk, forloren.
phosphorescent [fɔsfə'rɛsnt] *adj* fosforescerende; selvlysende.
phosphorus ['fɔsfərəs] *s* fosfor.
photo ['fəutəu] *s* foto(grafi); **~ composer** *s (typ)* fotosætter; **~copier** *s* (foto)kopimaskine; **~copy** *s* fotokopi; **~ finish** *s: it was a ~ finish* der måtte målfoto til; **~genic** *adj* fotogen; **~graph** *s* foto(grafi) // *v* fotografere; *~graph well* være god på billeder; **~grapher** [fə'tɔgrəfə*] *s* fotograf; **~graphy** [fə'tɔgrəfi] *s* fotografering; foto(grafi).
phrase [freiz] *s* udtryk, talemåde; frase // *v* udtrykke; frasere; **~book** *s* parlør.
phraseology [freizi'ɔlədʒi] *s* udtryksmåde; ordvalg.
physical ['fizikl] *adj* fysisk, legemlig; sanselig; *~ education (PE)* gymnastik, idræt; *~ punishment* korporlig straf.
physician [fi'ziʃən] *s* læge.
physicist ['fizisist] *s* fysiker.
physics ['fiziks] *s* fysik.
physiology [fizi'ɔlədʒi] *s* fysiologi.
physiotherapist [fiziəu'θɛrəpist] *s* fysioterapeut.
physique [fi'zi:k] *s* legemsbygning, fysik; *a person of strong ~* en fysisk stærk person, en person med et godt helbred.
pianist ['pi:ənist] *s* pianist.
piano [pi'ænəu] *s* klaver; flygel; **~ tuner** *s* klaverstemmer.
piccalilli ['pikəlili] *s (gastr)* slags stærk pickles.
pick [pik] *s* hakke; valg; udvalg; *take your ~* værsgo at vælge; *the ~* det bedste; eliten // *v* hakke; plukke (fx *flowers* blomster); tage, stjæle; vælge (ud); *~ a bone* gnave et ben; *~ a lock* dirke en lås op; *~ a fight* starte et slag; *~ sides* vælge side; *~ one's way* finde vej; *~ one's nose* pille næse; *~ pockets* være lommetyv; *~ at sth* pirke til ngt; *~ at sby* hakke på en; *~ one's teeth* stange tænder; *~ sby's brains* hugge ens ideer; pumpe en for oplysninger; *~ on sby* være på nakken af en; *~ out* udvælge; skelne; *~ up* samle op; få, skaffe sig; lære; kvikke op; *the trade is ~ing up* det begynder at gå fremad med salget; *~ up speed* sætte farten op.
pickaxe ['pikæks] *s* hakke.
picket ['pikit] *s* pæl; strejkevagt, blokadevagt // *v* lave blokade imod; stille strejkevagter op ved.
pickings ['pikiŋs] *spl* udbytte; bytte; rester.
pickle [pikl] *s* lage, eddike; pickles; (F) knibe; *be in a nice ~* være i en køn suppedas // *v* marinere, lægge i lage; *~d herrings* marinerede sild.
picklock ['piklɔk] *s* dirk; indbrudstyv.
pick-me-up ['pikmi:ʌp] *s* opstrammer.
pickpocket ['pikpɔkit] *s* lommetyv.
pickup ['pikʌp] *s* pick-up; opsamling; ngt (,en) man har samlet op, tilfældigt bekendtskab; *(om bil etc)* acceleration(sevne).
picnic ['piknik] *s* skovtur, udflugt; medbragt mad; *go for a ~* tage på skovtur.
pictorial [pik'tɔ:riəl] *adj* illustreret; malerisk; billed-.
picture ['piktʃə*] *s* billede; *let's go to the ~s* lad os gå i biografen; *her face was a ~* hendes ansigt var et syn for guder; *look a ~* være billedskøn; *be out of the ~* være ude af billedet; *I get the ~* jeg forstår hvor

du (,I) vil hen; *put sby in the ~* orientere en // *v* afbilde; forestille sig; **~-goer** *s* biografgænger.
picturesque [piktʃə'rɛsk] *adj* malerisk, pittoresk.
picture tube ['piktʃə tju:b] *s* billedrør; **picture window** *s* panoramavindue.
piddle [pidl] *v* (F) tisse.
piddling ['pidliŋ] *adj* (F) sølle, ussel.
pidgin ['pidʒin] *adj: ~ English* kineserengelsk.
pie [pai] *s* pie, postej; *have a finger in every ~* blande sig i alting; *as easy as ~* pærelet; **~bald** *adj* broget.
piece [pi:s] *s* stykke; *a ~ of furniture* et møbel; *a nasty ~ of work* en led karl; *a ~ of news* en nyhed; *in one ~* uskadt; *give sby a ~ of one's mind* sige en et par borgerlige ord; *in ~s* i stykker, itu; *go to ~s* gå i stykker; bryde sammen; *take sth to ~s* skille ngt ad; *a nice little ~* (F, om kvinde) en lækker lille sag // *v* lappe, sy sammen; *~ together* stykke sammen; **~meal** *adj* stykke for stykke; **~work** *s* akkordarbejde.
pier [piə*] *s* mole, anløbsbro.
pierce [piəs] *v* gennembore, trænge ind i; *have one's ears ~d* få lavet huller i ørerne; **piercing** *adj* gennemtrængende (fx *cry* skrig).
piety ['paiəti] *adj* fromhed, pietet.
piffling ['pifliŋ] *adj* latterlig.
pig [pig] *s* gris, svin (også *fig) // v: ~ oneself* æde løs.
pigeon ['pidʒən] *s* due; **~hole** *s* hul; dueslag; (i reol etc) rum.
piggery ['pigəri] *s* svinefarm; **piggish** ['pigiʃ] *adj* svinsk; grådig; nærig.
piggy bank ['pigibæŋk] *s* sparegris.
pigheaded ['pighɛdid] *adj* stædig.
piglet ['piglit] *s* griseunge; *~s* smågrise.
pigmy d.s.s. *pygmy.*
pigskin ['pigskin] *s* svinelæder; **pigsty** ['pigstai] *s* svinesti; **pigswill** *s* svinefoder; hundeæde; **pigtail** *s* grisehale; **pigtails** *spl* rottehaler.
pike [paik] *s* gedde.
pilchard ['piltʃəd] *s* sardin.
pile [pail] *s* stabel; dynge; *(fys)* atomreaktor; (om tæppe) luv // *v* (også: *~ up)* stable (op); dynge (op); hobe sig op; **~s** *spl* hæmorroider; **~-up** *s* harmonikasammenstød.
pilfer ['pilfə*] *v* rapse; **~ing** *s* rapseri.
pilgrimage ['pilgrimidʒ] *s* pilgrimsfærd; valfart.
pill [pil] *s* pille; *be on the ~* tage p-piller.
pillage ['pilidʒ] *s* plyndring // *v* (ud)plyndre.
pillar ['pilə*] *s* søjle, pille; støtte; **~ box** *s* (fritstående) postkasse; **~-box red** *adj* postkasserød.
pillion ['piljən] *s* bagsæde (på motorcykel); *ride ~* sidde på bagsædet.
pillory ['piləri] *s* gabestok // *v* hænge ud, sætte i gabestokken.
pillow ['piləu] *s* hovedpude; **~ case, ~ slip** *s* (hoved)pudebetræk.
pilot ['pailət] *s* lods; pilot // *v* lodse; føre (et fly); styre // *adj* forsøgs-, pilot-; **~ light** *s* vågeblus; kontrollampe; **~ plant** *s* forsøgsanlæg; **~ scheme** *s* pilotprojekt.
pimento [pi'mɛntəu] *s* spansk peber; allehånde.
pimp [pimp] *s* alfons.
pimple [pimpl] *s* filipens, bums; **pimply** *adj* bumset.
pin [pin] *s* knappenål; stift; kegle; *I have ~s and needles* mit ben (etc) sover // *v* fæste (med nåle); hæfte; *~ down sth* præcisere ngt; sætte fingeren på ngt; *~ sby down to sth* holde en fast ved ngt; *~ sth on sby* hænge en op på ngt; *~ up* (om plakat etc) slå op; (om hår) sætte op.
pinafore ['pinəfɔ:*] *s* (barne)forklæde.
pinball ['pinbɔ:l] *s: ~ (machine)* flippermaskine.
pincers ['pinse:ʒ] *spl: a pair of ~* en knibtang.
pinch [pintʃ] *s* kniben, klemmen; nød, klemme; så meget man kan have mellem to fingre (fx *a ~ of salt); at a ~* i en snæver vending // *v* knibe, klemme; (F) stjæle; *~ and scrape* måtte vende hver øre.
pinched [pintʃt] *adj* udtæret; forfrossen; udmattet; *~ for sth* i bekneb for ngt.
pincushion ['pinkuʃən] *s* nålepude.

pine [pain] *s* fyr(retræ) // *v:* ~ *for* længes efter; ~ *away* hentæres.
pineapple ['painæpl] *s* ananas.
pin holder ['pinhəuldə*] *s* blomsterfakir.
pinion ['pinjən] *v* holde fast; bagbinde.
pink [piŋk] *s* *(bot)* nellike; lyserød farve; *in the* ~ i fin form; *he was tickled* ~ han var virkelig smigret // *adj* lyserød.
pinkie ['piŋki] *s* lillefinger.
pinnacle ['pinəkl] *s* tinde, spir; bjergtop.
pinpoint ['pinpɔint] *s* nålespids; prik // *v* ramme præcis; præcisere // *adj* nøjagtig.
pinstriped ['pinstraipt] *adj* nålestribet, smalstribet.
pinprick ['pinprik] *s* nålestik; *(fig)* hib.
pint [paint] *s* måleenhed sv.t. 0,56 liter; (F) et stort glas øl.
pinta ['paintə] *s* (F) d.s.s. *pint of* (oftest om mælk), sv.t. 1/2 sød; papvin.
pioneer [paiə'niə*] *s* pioner; foregangsmand; nybygger // *v* være banebryder for.
pious ['paiəs] *adj* from.
pip [pip] *s* kerne; bip, dut.
pipe [paip] *s* rør, rørledning; (tobaks)pibe; fløjte; sækkepibe // *v* pibe; lægge rør i; lede gennem rør; fløjte; ~ *down* (F) stikke piben ind, holde mund; ~ *up* (F) åbne munden, give sit besyv med; **~d music** *s* muzak, dåsemusik; **~ dream** *s* ønskedrøm.
pipeline ['paiplain] *s* rørledning (især til olie el. gas).
piper ['paipə*] *s* fløjtespiller; sækkepibespiller; *pay the* ~ betale regningen (for festen).
pipe wrench ['paip rɛntʃ] *s* rørtang.
piping ['paipiŋ] *s* rørsystem; piben // *adj* fløjtende // *adv:* ~ *hot* kogende varm; **~ bag** *s* sprøjtepose.
pipsqueak ['pipskwi:k] *s* pjevs.
piquant ['pi:kənt] *adj* pikant.
piqued [pi:kd] *adj* stødt, pikeret.
piracy ['paiərəsi] *s* sørøveri; *(fig)* plagiat.
pirate ['paiərət] *s* sørøver, pirat.
Pisces ['paisi:z] *s* *(astr)* Fiskene.
piss [pis] *s* (V) pis; *take the* ~ *out of sby* røvrende en // *v* (V) pisse; ~ *around* (V) fjolle rundt; ~ *off!* (V) skrid! skrub af! *be* ~*ed* (V) være skidefuld.
piston ['pistən] *s* *(tekn)* stempel; *(mus)* ventil; **~ engine** *s* stempelmotor.
pit [pit] *s* grav, hule; grube, skakt, mine; kule; smøregrav; (i motorløb) depot; *(teat)* parterre; *coal* ~ kulmine; *orchestra* ~ orkestergrav // *v* kule (ned); lave huller i; ~ *sby against sby* sætte ngn op mod hinanden.
pitch [pitʃ] *s* kast; *(mus)* tone, tonehøjde; højdepunkt; hældning; salgstaktik; *(sport)* bane; *perfect* ~ *(mus)* absolut gehør // *v* falde; skråne, hælde; kaste; ~ *camp* slå lejr; *be* ~*ed forward* blive kastet forover; ~ *one's aspirations too high* spænde forventningerne for højt; **~-black** *adj* kulsort; **~ed roof** *adj* skråtag.
pitcher ['pitʃə*] *s* *(am)* krukke; *(sport)* kaster (i fx baseball).
pitchfork ['pitʃfɔ:k] *s* høtyv, greb.
piteous ['pitiəs] *adj* ynkelig, sørgelig.
pitfall ['pitfɔ:l] *s* faldgrube, fælde.
pith [piθ] *s* marv; *(fig)* kerne, kraft; *orange* ~ det hvide under appelsinskallen; **~y** ['piθi] *adj* marvfuld, kraftig.
pitiable ['pitiəbl] *adj* ynkelig, jammerlig; **pitiful** *adj* medlidende; ynkelig; **pitiless** *adj* ubarmhjertig.
pittance ['pitəns] *s* sulteløn; smule.
pituitary [pi'tju:itəri] *s:* ~ *(gland)* *(anat)* hypofyse.
pity ['piti] *s* medlidenhed; *what a* ~*!* det var en skam! *for* ~*'s sake* for Guds skyld; *take* ~ *on* forbarme sig over; *more's the* ~*!* desværre! det er bare ærgerligt!
pivot ['pivət] *s* tap; akse; tyngdepunkt // *v* dreje (om en tap).
pixie ['piksi] *s* nisse; **~ hat** *s* nissehue.
placard ['plaka:d] *s* opslag, plakat; transparent.

placate [plə'keit] *v* formilde.

place [pleis] *s* sted; plads; (om arbejde) stilling; (om hus) hjem; landsted; *all over the ~* over det hele; *at his ~* hjemme hos ham; *in his ~* i hans sted; *to his ~* hjem til ham; *where's your ~?* hvor bor du? *it's not my ~ to do that* det tilkommer ikke mig at gøre det; *put sby in his ~* sætte en på plads; *go ~s* rejse, se sig om i verden; *he's going ~s* han skal nok nå langt (her i livet); *take ~* finde sted, foregå; *out of ~* malplaceret; *in ~s* nogle steder, her og der; *in the first ~* for det første; *out of ~* malplaceret; *in ~ of* i stedet for // *v* anbringe, placere; identificere, bestemme; *~ an order* afgive en bestilling; **~ card** *s* bordkort; **~ mat** *s* dækkeserviet; **~ment** *s* placering; **~name** *s* stednavn; **~ setting** *s* kuvert, opdækning.

placid ['plæsid] *adj* fredsommelig, rolig.

plagiarism ['pleidʒərizm] *s* plagiat.

plague [pleig] *s* pest; plage // *v* plage.

plaice [pleis] *s* rødspætte.

plaid [plæd] *s* skotskternet stof; klantern; plaid.

plain [plein] *s* slette; retmaske // *adj* klar, tydelig; enkel; ensfarvet; (om person) jævn, ligefrem; (om udseende) grim; (om cigaret) uden filter; (i strikning) ret; *~ chocolate* mørk (letbitter) chokolade; *in ~ clothes* (om politi) i civil; *say it in ~ English* sige det ligeud; *it was ~ sailing* det gled smertefrit; *the ~ truth* den rene sandhed // *adv* (F) direkte, simpelthen; *it's ~ stupid* det er simpelthen åndssvagt; **~ly** *adv* ligeud, uden omsvøb; tydeligvis, åbenbart; **~ness** *s* simpelhed; grimhed; enkelhed; **~spoken** *adj* ligefrem, oprigtig.

plaintiff ['pleintif] *s* klager, sagsøger.

plaintive ['pleintiv] *adj* klagende; lidende.

plait [plæt] *s* fletning; læg // *v* flette.

plan [plæn] *s* plan, projekt; *draw up a ~* lægge en plan; *according to ~* efter planen; *make ~s* lægge planer // *v* planlægge; organisere; have i sinde, agte; *~ned obsolescence* indbygget forældelse; *~ ahead* lægge planer i forvejen; *~ for sth* indstille sig på ngt; *~ on sth* regne med ngt; *~ out* planlægge.

plane [plein] *s* platan(træ); *(tekn)* høvl; *(fly)* flyvemaskine; flade, plan; niveau // *v* høvle // *adj* flad, plan.

planet ['plænit] *s* planet.

planetary ['plænitəri] *adj* planet-, planetarisk.

plank [plæŋk] *s* planke; *main ~* hovedprogrampunkt.

planner ['plænə*] *s* planlægger; planlægningskalender.

planning ['plæniŋ] *s* planlægning.

plant [pla:nt] *s* plante; (om maskineri) materiel; virksomhed, anlæg, fabrik // *v* plante; beplante; anlægge, grundlægge; placere, lægge, anbringe.

plantation [plæn'teiʃən] *s* plantage; plantning.

planter ['pla:ntə*] *s* plantageejer.

plaque [plæk] *s* platte; mindeplade; tandbelægning, plak.

plaster ['pla:stə*] *s* gips, puds; hæfteplaster; *in ~* (om ben etc) i gips(bandage) // *v* kalke, gipse; pudse; oversmøre; *~ with* overdænge (,oversmøre) med; **~ cast** *s* gipsbandage; gipsafstøbning.

plastered ['pla:stəd] *adj* klistret; (F) fuld, pløret.

plastic ['plæstik] *s* plastic, plast // *adj* plastisk; plastic-, plast-; **~ bag** *s* plastpose; **~ explosive** *s* plastisk sprængstof.

plasticine ® ['plæstisi:n] *s* modellervoks.

plastic surgery ['plæstik 'sə:dʒəri] *s* plastikkirurgi.

plate [pleit] *s* plade; planche; tallerken; portion; (sølv)plet; (også: *dental ~*) protese; *have a lot on one's ~* have meget at se til.

plateau ['plætəu] *s* højslette; plateau.

plateful ['pleitful] *s* tallerken(fuld), portion.

plate glass ['pleit,gla:s] *s* spejlglas (fx til butiksruder).

platen [plætn] *s* (på skrivemaskine) valse.
platform ['plætfɔ:m] *s* perron; forhøjning, tribune; valgprogram; **~ shoes** *spl* sko med plateausåler; **~ ticket** *s* perronbillet.
plating ['pleitiŋ] *s* forsølvning; forgyldning; pansring.
platinum ['plætinəm] *s* platin.
platitude ['plætitju:d] *s* banalitet; flad bemærkning.
platoon [plə'tu:n] *s (mil)* deling.
platter ['plætə*] *s* tallerken, fad; serveringsbræt.
plausible ['plɔ:zibl] *adj* plausibel, ret sandsynlig.
play [plei] *s* leg, spil; (teater)stykke, skuespil; spillerum; *do sth in ~* gøre ngt for sjov // *v* lege, spille; *~ at sth* lege ngt; *what are you ~ing at?* hvad skal det forestille? *~ down* bagatellisere; *~ for time* prøve at vinde tid; *~ up* skabe sig; opreklamere; *~ up to* spille op til; støtte, bakke op; **~act** *v* spille teater; **~bill** *s* teaterplakat.
player ['pleiə*] *s* spiller; musiker; skuespiller.
playful ['pleiful] *adj* legesyg; munter.
playgoer ['pleigəuə*] *s* teatergænger.
playground ['pleigraund] *s* legeplads.
playgroup ['pleigru:p] *s* legestue.
playing card ['pleiiŋ,ka:d] *s* spillekort.
playing field ['pleiiŋ,fi:ld] *s* sportsplads.
playmate ['pleimeit] *s* legekammerat.
play-off ['pleiɔ:f] *s (sport)* forlænget spilletid.
playpen ['pleipɛn] *s* kravlegård.
playtime ['pleitaim] *s* frikvarter; fritid.
playwright ['pleirait] *s* skuespilforfatter, dramatiker.
PLC, plc ['pi:ɛl'si:] (fork.f. *public limited company)* A/S.
plea [pli:] *s* bøn, appel; *(jur)* påstand.
plead [pli:d] *v* bede indtrængende, trygle; *(jur)* plædere, føre en sag; *~ with sby* anråbe en; *~ guilty* erkende sig skyldig; *~ not guilty* nægte sig skyldig.
pleasant [plɛznt] *adj* behagelig; rar, elskværdig; hyggelig.
pleasantry ['plɛzntri] *s* vittighed; spøgefuldhed; *pleasantries* venligheder.
please [pli:z] *v* behage, tiltale; *~!* vær så venlig! *my bill, ~!* må jeg få regningen? *yes, ~!* ja tak! *~ yourself* gør som du vil; *there's no pleasing him* han bliver aldrig tilfreds; **~d** *adj* tilfreds; *be ~d with* være tilfreds med; være glad for; *~d to meet you!* det er hyggeligt at hilse på Dem! goddag! **pleasing** *adj* behagelig, tiltalende.
pleasure ['plɛʒə*] *s* glæde, fornøjelse; nydelse; ønske; *take ~ in* nyde, finde fornøjelse ved; *with ~!* med fornøjelse! **~ ground** *s* tivoli, (folke)park; **~-seeking** *adj* forlystelsessyg; **~ trip** *s* fornøjelsesrejse.
pleat [pli:t] *s* læg, fold // *v* folde, plissere; *a ~ed skirt* en lægget nederdel.
plebeian [plə'bi:ən] *s* plebejer.
plebiscite ['plɛbisit] *s* folkeafstemning.
pledge [plɛdʒ] *s* pant; løfte // *v* sætte i pant; afgive løfte; forpligte (sig); *he ~d never to return* han lovede at blive væk for bestandig.
plenary ['pli:nəri] *adj: ~ session* plenarforsamling.
plenipotentiary [plɛnipə'tɛnʃəri] *adj* med uindskrænket (fuld)magt.
plentiful ['plɛntiful] *adj* rigelig.
plenty ['plɛnti] *s* overflod, rigdom, velstand; *~ of* nok af, rigeligt med; *there's ~ of time* der er god tid // *adv* (F) rigelig; temmelig; *he was ~ nervous* (F) han var rimelig nervøs.
pleurisy ['pluərisi] *s* lungehindebetændelse.
pliable ['plaiəbl] *adj* bøjelig, smidig; føjelig; **pliant** *adj* d.s.s. *pliable.*
pliers ['plaiəz] *s (tekn): a pair of ~* en tang.
plight [plait] *s* nød; forfald; *economic ~* økonomisk krise.
plimsoll ['plimsəl] *s* gummisko.
plinth [plinθ] *s* sokkel.
plod [plɔd] *v* traske; slide, hænge i; **~der** *s* slider; **~ding** *adj* møjsommelig.
plonk [plɔŋk] *s* bump; (F) billig vin,

sprøjt // *v* plumpe; ~ *away on the piano* tæske i klaveret; ~ *sth down* smække (,smide) ngt ned.

plop [plɔp] *s* plump; plask // *v* plumpe.

plot [plɔt] *s* komplot, sammensværgelse; (i fx bog) handling, intrige; stykke jord // *v* planlægge; pønse på; konspirere; plotte.

plough [plau] *s* plov // *v* pløje; ~ *back (merk)* reinvestere; **~ing** *s* pløjning; **~man's lunch** *s* pubfrokost med brød, ost og pickles.

ploy [plɔi] *s* strategi, taktik.

pluck [plʌk] *s* greb, tag; mod; (om fjerkræ) indmad // *v* plukke; rykke, trække; *(mus,* om strenge) anslå, knipse; ~ *up courage* tage mod til sig; **~y** *adj* modig, tapper.

plunger *s* vaskesuger.

plug [plʌg] *s* prop, pløk; *(elek)* stikprop; stik(kontakt); tændrør; plombe; tampon; gratis reklame // *v* tilproppe, stoppe; (F) pløkke ned; ~ *in (elek)* tilslutte, sætte til; ~ *up* blive tilstoppet.

plum [plʌm] *s* blomme // *adj* blommefarvet; *a* ~ *job* et drømmejob, en ønskestilling.

plumage ['plu:midʒ] *s* fjer(dragt).

plumb [plʌm] *s* blylod, lod // *v* lodde; plombere; ~ *in a toilet* installere et toilet // *adj* lodret, i lod // *adv* fuldstændig; præcis, lige.

plumber ['plʌmə*] *s* blikkenslager.

plumbing ['plʌmiŋ] *s* blikkenslagerarbejde; sanitære installationer; vandrør.

plume [plu:m] *s* fjer(busk); *a* ~ *of smoke* en røgfane; *a* ~ *of spray* et skumsprøjt.

plummet ['plʌmit] *s* lod; *(økon)* styrdyk // *v* styrte (lodret) ned; styrtdykke.

plump [plʌmp] *v* plumpe; lade falde (med et brag); ~ *for sth* beslutte sig for ngt; støtte ngt // *adj* buttet, fyldig.

plunder ['plʌndə*] *s* plyndring, bytte // *v* (ud)plyndre.

plunge [plʌndʒ] *s* dykning, dukkert; *take the* ~ vove springet; kaste sig ud i det // *v* dykke; stikke, jage; springe; kaste sig.

plunger ['plʌndʒə] *s* vaskesuger, svupper.

plunging ['plʌndʒiŋ] *adj:* ~ *neckline* dyb halsudskæring.

plunk [plʌŋk] *v* knipse, klimpre.

pluperfect ['plu:'pə:fikt] *s (gram)* førdatid, pluskvamperfektum.

plural ['pluərəl] *s (gram)* flertal, pluralis // *adj* flertals-.

plus [plʌs] *s* plus, additionstegn; *it's a* ~ det er en fordel; *ten* ~ ti og derover.

plush [plʌʃ] *s* plys // *adj* dyr, luksus-.

ply [plai] *s* (i garn) tråd; (i krydsfinér) lag; *(fig)* tendens; *three* ~ *(wool)* tretrådet (uldgarn) // *v* bruge; arbejde flittigt med; udøve, drive; besejle; ~ *sby with sth* forsyne en rigeligt med ngt; **~wood** *s* krydsfinér.

PM ['pi:'ɛm] fork.f. *post-morten; Prime Minister.*

pm ['pi:'ɛm] (fork.f. *post meridiem)* om eftermiddagen, efter kl. 12 middag.

pneumatic [nju:'mætik] *adj* pneumatisk, luft-, trykluft- (fx *drill* bor).

pneumonia [nju:'məuniə] *s* lungebetændelse.

PO fork.f. *postal order; post office.*

poach [pəutʃ] *v (gastr)* pochere; drive krybskytteri; hugge, stjæle; **~er** *s* krybskytte; **~ing** *s* krybskytteri; *(gastr)* pochering.

pocket ['pɔkit] *s* lomme; hul; *be in* ~ være ved muffen; *be out of* ~ have lommesmerter; *have sby in one's* ~ have en i sin hule hånd; *pick* ~*s* være lommetyv // *v* stikke i lommen; indkassere; skjule; **~book** *s* tegnebog; lommebog; billigbog; *(am)* håndtaske; **~ calculator** *s* lommeregner; **~-knife** *s* lommekniv; **~ money** *s* lommepenge.

pock-marked ['pɔkma:kd] *adj* koparret.

pod [pɔd] *s* bælg // *v* bælge.

podgy ['pɔdʒi] *adj* buttet.

poem ['pəuim] *s* digt.

poet ['pəuit] *s* digter; **poetic** [pəu'ɛtik] *adj* poetisk; digterisk.

poetry ['pəuitri] *s* poesi, digtning.
poignant ['pɔinjənt] *adj* skarp, bitter, intens.
poinsettia [pɔin'sɛtiə] *s (bot)* julestjerne.
point [pɔint] *s* spids; punkt; punktum; sted; sag; hensigt, mening; point; *(elek)* stikkontakt; *two ~ three* to komma tre (NB! skrives på eng: 2.3); *make one's ~* få ret; gøre sin mening klar; *get the ~* forstå (,begribe) ngt; *come to the ~* komme til sagen; *when it comes to the ~* når det kommer til stykket; *be on the ~ of doing sth* skulle lige til at gøre ngt; være lige ved at gøre ngt; *it's beside (,off) the ~* det er sagen uvedkommende; *there's no ~ in doing it* der er ingen mening i at gøre det; *sby's good ~s* ens gode sider; *it has it's ~s* det har sine fordele // *v* spidse; sigte; vende (mod); pege; *~ a gun at sby* sigte på en med et gevær; *~ out* udpege; pointere, understrege; **~-blank** *adv* direkte, ligefrem; *fire ~-blank* skyde på nært hold; **~ed** *adj* spids, skarp; **~edly** *adv* spidst, demonstrativt; **~er** *s* viser; pegepind; vink; pointer; **~less** *adj* meningsløs; **~ of view** *s* mening, synspunkt; **~s** *spl* sporskifte; *(auto)* platiner.
poise [pɔiz] *s* ligevægt, balance; ro // *v* balancere med; *be ~d* balancere; holde sig klar; stå på spring; *be ~d for (fig)* være parat til.
poison ['pɔizən] *s* gift // *v* forgifte, forgive; **~ing** *s* forgiftning.
poisonous ['pɔizənəs] *adj* giftig; skadelig.
poison-pen letter ['pɔizən 'pɛn ˌlɛtə*] *s* anonymt brev.
poke [pəuk] *s* stød; skub; gok // *v* stikke; rode op i; *~ one's nose in(to)* stikke sin næse i; *~ about* snuse rundt; *~ out* stikke ud.
poker ['pəukə*] *s* ildrager; (kortspil) poker.
pok(e)y ['pəuki] *adj* kneben, trang; snoldet.
Poland ['pəulənd] *s* Polen.
polar ['pəulə*] *adj* polar(-); **~ bear** -[-bɛə*] *s* isbjørn; **~ light** *s* polarlys, nordlys.
Pole [pəul] *s* polak.
pole [pəul] *s* pæl, stolpe; *(elek)* mast; *(geogr)* pol; *be up the ~* (F) have en skrue løs; *they are ~s apart (fig)* de står meget langt fra hinanden; **~axed** *adj* lamslået, som ramt af et kølleslag; stangdrukken; **~ star** *s* polarstjerne, nordstjerne; **~ vault** *s (sport)* stangspring.
police [pə'lis] *s* politi; politifolk // *v* holde orden, føre opsyn med; **~ car** *s* politibil; **~ constable** *(PC) s* politibetjent; **~ force** *s* politistyrke; politikorps; **~man** *s* politimand; **~ record** *s* straffeattest, generalieblad; **~ sergeant** *s* sv.t. overbetjent; **~ station** *s* politistation; **~ superintendent** *s* sv.t. politikommissær; **~woman** *s (PW)* kvindelig politibetjent.
policy ['pɔlisi] *s* politik; taktik; (forsikrings)police.
Polish ['pəuliʃ] *s/adj* polsk.
polish ['pɔliʃ] *s* pudsecreme; politur; bonevoks; neglelak; blank overflade; *(fig)* finhed; *high ~* højglans // *v* pudse, polere; (om gulv) bone; afpudse; *~ off* gøre kål på, ekspedere; **~ed** *adj (fig)* glat, sleben.
polite [pə'lait] *adj* høflig; dannet; *be ~ with* være høflig over for; **~ness** *s* høflighed; velopdragenhed.
politic ['pɔlitik] *adj* snedig, diplomatisk.
political [pə'litikl] *adj* politisk; **~ asylum** [-ə'sailəm] *s* politisk asyl; **~ science** *s* statskundskab.
politician [pɔli'tiʃən] *s* politiker, statsmand.
politics ['pɔlitiks] *spl* politik.
poll [pəul] *s* valg, afstemning; stemmeprocent; meningsmåling // *v* stemme.
pollen ['pɔlən] *s* blomsterstøv, pollen; **~ count** *s* pollentælling.
pollination [pɔli'neiʃən] *s (bot)* bestøvning.
polling station ['pəuliŋ] *s* valgsted.
pollutant [pə'lu:tənt] *s* forureningskilde.

pollute [pə'lu:t] *v* forurene.
pollution [pə'lu:ʃən] *s* forurening; *environmental ~* miljøforurening.
polo-neck ['pəuləunɛk] *s* rullekrave(bluse).
polytechnic [pɔli'tɛknik] *s* sv.t. teknisk skole.
polythene ['pɔliθi:n] *s* polythen, polyethylen; **~ bag** *s* plastpose.
polyunsaturated ['pəuliʌn,sætjəreitid] *adj* flerumættet.
pomegranate ['pɔməgrænit] *s* granatæble.
pomp [pɔmp] *s* pomp, pragt.
pompous ['pɔmpəs] *adj* svulstig; *a ~ ass* (F) en blærerøv.
ponce [pɔns] *s* alfons.
pond [pɔnd] *s* dam; (lille) sø; *the Pond* (F) Atlanterhavet.
ponder ['pɔndə*] *v* overveje, spekulere; tænke over.
ponderous ['pɔndərəs] *adj* tung, massiv.
pong [pɔŋ] *s* (F) hørm.
pontoon [pən'tu:n] *s* ponton.
pony ['pəuni] *s* pony; **~tail** *s* hestehale(frisure); **~ trekking** *s* udflugt (,tur) på pony.
poodle [pu:dl] *s* pudel(hund).
poof(ter) ['pu:f(tə*)] *s* (F) tøsedreng; bøsse.
Pooh [pu:]: *Winnie the ~* Peter Plys.
pool [pu:l] *s* vandpyt; pøl; dam; bassin; svømmebassin (,-pøl); *(merk)* pulje; *(am)* billard; *the ~s* sv.t. tipstjenesten; *do the ~s* tippe; *win the ~s* vinde i tipning // *v* slå sammen (i en pulje); samle; **~s coupon** *s* tipskupon.
poor [puə*] *adj* fattig, stakkels, ringe; dårlig; *you ~ thing!* din stakkel! **~ly** *adj* (F) sløj.
pop [pɔp] *s* knald; skud; *(mus,* F) pop; bedstefar; sodavand // *v* knalde, smælde; affyre; (om prop) springe; putte, stikke; *~ in* lige "kigge indenfor"; *~ off* dø; stikke af; gøre det af med; *~ on* tage på; tænde for; *~ out* smutte ud; *~ up* dukke op; *~ the question* (F) tage sig sammen til at fri.
pope [pəup] *s* pave.
Popeye ['pɔpai] *s: ~ (the Sailor)* Skipper Skræk; **popeyed** *adj* med udstående øjne.
popgun ['pɔpgʌn] *s* legetøjspistol (med prop).
poplar ['pɔplə*] *s* poppel(træ).
popper ['pɔpə*] *s* (F) trykknap.
poppy ['pɔpi] *s* valmue; **~ seed** *s* birkes.
popular ['pɔpjulə*] *adj* populær, folkelig.
popularity [pɔpju'læriti] *s* popularitet.
popularize ['pɔpjuləraiz] *v* popularisere.
populate ['pɔpjuleit] *v* befolke; **population** [-'leiʃən] *s* befolkning; folketal.
populous ['pɔpjuləs] *adj* tæt befolket, folkerig.
pop-up ['pɔpʌp] *adj: ~ toaster* automatisk brødrister.
porch [pɔ:tʃ] *s* vindfang.
porcupine ['pɔ:kjupain] *s* hulepindsvin.
pore [pɔ:*] *s* pore // *v: ~ over* fordybe sig i; hænge over.
pork [pɔ:k] *s* svinekød, flæsk; *roast ~* flæskesteg; **~ chops** *pl* svinekoteletter; **~ loin** *s* stegeflæsk.
pornographic [pɔ:nə'græfik] *adj* pornografisk; **pornography** [-'nɔgrəfi] *s* pornografi.
porous ['pɔ:rəs] *adj* porøs.
porpoise ['pɔ:pəs] *s* (om hvalart) marsvin.
porridge ['pɔridʒ] *s* (havre)grød.
port [pɔ:t] *s* havn; havneby; portvin; *(mar,* også) bagbord.
portable ['pɔ:təbl] *s* bærbar (computer) // *adj* bærbar, transportabel.
portage ['pɔ:tidʒ] *s* transport(omkostninger).
port dues ['pɔ:tdju:s] *spl* havneafgift.
porter ['pɔ:tə*] *s* portner, dørvogter; portier; drager, portør; bærer; (om ølsort) porter.
portfolio [pɔ:t'fəuliəu] *s* (dokument)mappe; portefølje.
porthole ['pɔ:thəul] *s (mar)* koøje.
portico ['pɔ:tikəu] *s* indgang med søjler; søjlegang.
portion ['pɔ:ʃən] *s* del, part; portion;

skæbne, lod // *v:* ~ *out* uddele.
portly ['pɔ:tli] *adj* korpulent; statelig.
portrait ['pɔ:trit] *s* portræt, billede.
portray [pɔ:'trei] *v* portrættere; skildre; **~al** [-'treiəl] *s* portrætmaleri; skildring.
Portuguese [pɔ:tju'gi:z] *s* portugiser // *adj* portugisisk.
pose [pəuz] *s* stilling, positur; stillen sig an // *v* stå model, posere; stille sig an; anbringe; fremsætte; ~ *as* give sig ud for at være; **~r** skabekrukke; hård nød at knække.
posh [pɔʃ] *adj* (F) fin; fisefornem.
posit ['pɔzit] *v* sætte, anslå.
position [pə'ziʃən] *s* stilling, position; indstilling; *be in a* ~ *to* være i stand til; *in* ~ på plads; *you are in no* ~ *to...* du har ingen forudsætninger for at..., det er ikke op til dig at... // *v* bringe på plads; stille op; placere, anbringe.
positive ['pɔzitiv] *adj* positiv; bestemt; direkte; komplet; *a* ~ *fool* en komplet idiot; *be* ~ *(about)* være sikker (på); **~ly** *adv* ligefrem, bogstavelig talt.
possess [pə'zɛs] *v* eje, besidde; beherske; besætte; *be ~ed with (fig)* være besat af; *what ~ed you to do that?* hvad gik der af dig, siden du kunne gøre det?
possession [pə'zɛʃən] *s* ejendom, besiddelse; eje; *take* ~ *of sth* tage ngt i besiddelse.
possessive [pə'zɛsiv] *s (gram)* genitiv // *adj* rethaverisk; begærlig.
possessor [pə'zɛsə*] *s* indehaver, ejer.
possibility [pɔsi'biliti] *s* mulighed *(of* for).
possible ['pɔsibl] *adj* mulig; eventuel; gennemførlig; *as much as* ~ så meget som muligt; *if* ~ om (,hvis det er) muligt.
possibly ['pɔsibli] *adv* måske, eventuelt; *if you* ~ *can* hvis du på nogen måde kan; hvis det er dig muligt; *I can't* ~ *come* det er umuligt for mig at komme.
post [pəust] *s* post, stilling; post(befordring); stolpe; *first* ~ *(mil)* reveille; *last* ~ *(mil)* tappenstreg; *it's in the* ~ det er sendt; *by return of* ~ omgående // *v* poste, sende med posten; postere; (om opslag) slå op; (især *mil)* ansætte; udstationere; *keep sby ~ed* holde en orienteret.
postage ['pəustidʒ] *s* porto; **~ stamp** *s* frimærke.
postal ['pəustəl] *adj* post-; **~ order** *s* postanvisning; **~ vote** *s* brevstemme.
postbox ['pəustbɔks] *s* postkasse; **postcard** *s* postkort; **postcode** *s* postnummer.
postdate ['pəustdeit] *v* (om fx check) fremdatere.
poster ['pəustə*] *s* plakat.
posterior [pɔs'tiəriə*] *s* (F) bagdel // *adj* senere; bag-.
posterity [pɔs'tɛriti] *s* eftertid; efterkommere.
poster paint ['pəustəpeint] *s* plakatfarve.
postgraduate [pəust'grædjuət] *adj:* ~ *studies* videregående studier (efter kandidateksamen).
posting ['pəustiŋ] *s* postering; udstationering.
post... ['pəust-] sms: **~man** *s* postbud; **~mark** *s* poststempel; **~master** *s* postmester; **~ meridiem** *adv (p.m.)* om eftermiddagen; **~-mortem** [pəust'mɔ:təm] *s (PM)* obduktion; **~ office** *s* posthus, postkontor; **~ office box** *s (PO box)* postboks; **~-paid** *adj* portofri.
postpone [pəs'pəun] *s* udsætte, udskyde; **~ment** *s* udsættelse, henstand.
postscript ['pəustskript] *s* efterskrift.
postulate ['pɔstjuleit] *v* hævde, postulere; gøre krav på.
posture ['pɔstjə*] *s* stilling, positur; holdning.
postwar ['pəustwɔ:*] *adj* efterkrigs-.
posy ['pəuzi] *s* (lille) buket.
pot [pɔt] *s* potte, gryde, krukke; (F) marihuana; *go to* ~ gå i fisk; *take a* ~ *at sby* skyde efter en // *v* plante (i potte); nedsylte.
potash ['pɔtæʃ] *s* potaske.
potassium [pə'tæsiəm] *s* kalium; ~

cyanide [-'saiənaid] *s* cyankalium.
potato [pə'teitəu] *s* kartoffel; ~ **chips** *spl* pommes frites; ~ **crisps** *spl* franske kartofler; ~ **flour** *s* kartoffelmel.
pot belly ['pɔtbɛli] *s* topmave.
potency ['pəutənsi] *s* styrke, kraft; indflydelse; potens.
potent ['pəutənt] *adj* stærk (fx *drink);* virkningsfuld; potent.
potential [pə'tɛnʃl] *s* potentiel; muligheder; ydeevne // *adj* mulig, eventuel, potentiel.
pothole ['pɔthəul] *s* hul (i vej); **~r** *s* huleforsker.
potion ['pəuʃən] *s* (gift)drik; medicin.
pot roast ['pɔt,rəust] *s (gastr)* grydesteg; **potshot** *s* slumpskud.
potted ['pɔtid] *adj (gastr)* syltet, nedlagt; forkortet; ~ **plant** *s* potteplante.
potter ['pɔtə*] *s* pottemager // *v: ~ around (,about)* nusse rundt; **pottery** *adj* lervarer; pottemagerværksted.
potty ['pɔti] *s* (F) potte // *adj* (F) skør, småtosset.
pouch [pautʃ] *s* pose, etui; *(zo)* kæbepose; pung.
poulterer ['pəultərə*] *s* vildthandler.
poultice ['pəultis] *s* (varmt) omslag.
poultry ['pəultri] *s* fjerkræ; høns.
pounce [pauns] *s* nedslag; overfald // *v: ~ (on)* slå ned (på); kaste sig over.
pound [paund] *s* pund (453 g; 100 pence) // *v* dundre; male, støde (i morter); stampe, trampe; **~ing** *s* (omgang) tæv, tæsk.
pour [pɔ:*] *v* hælde, skænke (fx *tea* te); øse (ned); vælte frem; *~ in* (om folk) vælte ind; *~ out* hælde op, skænke; hælde ud; øse ud; **~ing** *adj* øsende.
pout [paut] *s* trutmund // *v* lave trutmund, surmule.
poverty ['pɔvəti] *s* fattigdom; **~-stricken** *adj* forarmet; ludfattig.
powder ['paudə*] *s* pudder; pulver; krudt // *v* pudre; pulverisere; *~ one's nose* pudre næsen; *(spøg)* gå på toilettet; ~ **compact** *s* pudderdåse (til at have i tasken); ~ **puff** *s* pudderkvast; ~ **room** *s* dametoilet; **powdery** *adj* støvet; smuldrende; pudret.
power ['pauə*] *s* magt, styrke; evne; *(mat)* potens; *(elek)* strøm; *be in ~* være ved magten; *it will do you a ~ of good* du vil have mægtig godt af det; *come into ~* komme til magten; *the ~s that be* myndighederne // *v* drive (frem); **~-assisted** *adj* servo-; **~boat** *s* motorbåd; ~ **brake** *s* servobremse; ~ **cut** *s* strømafbrydelse; ~ **drill** *s* boremaskine; **~ed** *adj: ~ed by* drevet af; ~ **failure** *s* strømsvigt; **~ful** *adj* mægtig, stærk; **~less** *adj* magtesløs; kraftløs; ~ **of attorney** *s* fuldmagt; ~ **plant** *s* elværk; ~ **point** *s* stikkontakt; ~ **station** *s* kraftværk, elværk; ~ **steering** *s* servostyring.
pox [pɔks] *s: the ~* (F) syfilis (se også: *chicken ~).*
practicable ['præktikəbl] *adj* gennemførlig, mulig; (om vej) fremkommelig, passabel.
practical ['præktikəl] *adj* praktisk; ~ **joke** *s* grov spøg, nummer; **~ly** *adv* praktisk taget, så godt som.
practice ['præktis] *s* praksis (også om læge etc); skik, sædvane; træning; øvelse; udøvelse; *it's common ~* det er almindelig praksis; *in ~* i praksis; *put sth into ~* føre ngt ud i livet; *out of ~* ude af træning; *piano ~* klaverøvelser.
practise ['præktis] *v* øve, træne; udøve; øve sig; praktisere; *~ for a match* træne til en kamp; *~ medicine* være praktiserende læge; *~ the piano* øve sig på klaver.
practitioner [præk'tiʃənə*] *s* praktiker; *general ~* almenpraktiserende læge.
prairie ['prɛəri] *s* prærie, græssteppe.
praise [preiz] *s* ros, pris; *sing sby's ~* rose en til skyerne // *v* rose, prise, berømme; **~worthy** [-wə:ði] *adj* prisværdig.
pram [præm] *s* barnevogn.
prance [pra:ns] *v* spankulere, kro sig.
prank [præŋk] *s* sjov; nummer.
prattle [prætl] *v* sludre, pludre.

prawn [prɔ:n] *s* stor reje.

pray [prei] *v* bede, bønfalde; *and what is that, ~?* og hvad er det, om jeg må spørge? *~ for it to happen* bede til at det sker.

prayer ['prɛə*] *s* bøn; ~ **mat** *s* bedetæppe; ~ **meeting** *s* bønnemøde.

preach [pri:tʃ] *v* prædike, forkynde; *~ at sby* præke for en; **~er** *s* prædikant.

prearranged ['pri:ə'reindʒd] *adj* (forud)aftalt; forberedt.

precarious [pri'kɛəriəs] *adj* prekær; usikker, uholdbar.

precaution [pri'kɔ:ʃən] *s* forsigtighed; forholdsregel; *take ~s against sth* tage sine forholdsregler mod ngt; **~ary** *adj* forsigtigheds-.

precede [pri'si:d] *v* gå forud (for), gå foran; *~d by our teacher we...* med vores lærer i spidsen...

precedence ['prɛsidəns] *s* forrang; *have ~ over* have forrang for; **precedent** ['prɛsidənt] *s* præcedens, fortilfælde.

preceding [pri'si:diŋ] *adj* foregående; forrig.

precept ['pri:sɛpt] *s* forskrift, rettesnor.

precinct ['pri:siŋkt] *s* område, distrikt; grænse; *within the city ~s* inden for bygrænsen; *cathedral ~s* kirkeplads; *pedestrian ~* fodgængerområde; *shopping ~* forretningskvarter.

precious ['prɛʃəs] *adj* kostbar, dyrebar; *(fig)* køn, nydelig; *~ little* ikke ret meget; ~ **stone** *s* ædelsten.

precipice ['prɛsipis] *s* afgrund; stejl skrænt.

precipitate *v* [pri'sipiteit] fremskynde; styrte; *(kem)* udfælde, bundfælde // *adj* [pri'sipitit] forhastet, overilet; hovedkulds; **precipitation** [-'teiʃən] *s* styrt, fald; bundfald; nedbør.

precipitous [pri'sipitəs] *adj* stejl, brat.

précis ['preisi] *s (pl: ~* ['preisiz] resumé.

precise [pri'sais] *adj* præcis, nøjagtig; **~ly** *adv* nøjagtigt, netop.

precision [pri'siʒən] *s* præcision, nøjagtighed.

preclude [pri'klu:d] *v* forebygge; udelukke; forhindre; *~ sby from sth* forhindre en i ngt.

precocious [pri'kəuʃəs] *adj* tidligt moden; fremmelig; gammelklog.

preconceived [pri:kən'si:vd] *adj* forudfattet (fx *opinion* mening).

precondition [pri:kən'diʃən] *s* forudsætning.

precursor [pri'kə:sə*] *s* forløber.

predate ['pri:'deit] *v* foruddatere.

predator ['prɛdətə*] *s* rovdyr; **~y** *adj* rov-; røverisk.

predecessor ['pri:disɛsə*] *s* forgænger; forfader.

predestination [pri:dɛsti'neiʃən] *s* forudbestemmelse.

predestined [pri:'dɛstind] *adj* forudbestemt.

predetermine [pri:di'tə:min] *v* forudbestemme; afgøre i forvejen.

predicament [pri'dikəmənt] *s* forlegenhed, knibe.

predicate ['prɛdikit] *s (gram)* omsagnsled, prædikat.

predict [pri'dikt] *v* forudsige, spå; **~able** *adj* forudsigelig.

prediction [pri'dikʃən] *s* forudsigelse, spådom.

predisposition [pri:dispə'ziʃən] *s* tilbøjelighed, tendens.

predominance [pri'dɔminəns] *s* overvægt; overmagt; **predominant** *adj* dominerende, fremherskende.

predominate [pri'dɔmineit] *v* være fremherskende, dominere.

pre-eminence [pri:'ɛminəns] *s* forrang; overlegenhed.

pre-empt [pri:'ɛmpt] *v* komme i forkøbet; sikre sig på forhånd.

preen [pri:n] *v: ~ oneself* (om fugl) pudse sig; (om person) pynte sig; *~ oneself of sth* blære sig med ngt.

prefab(ricated) ['pri:fæb(rikeitid)] *adj* præfabrikeret; *~ house* elementhus.

preface ['prɛfəs] *s* forord, indledning.

prefer [pri'fə:*] *v* foretrække; *I ~ tea to coffee* jeg foretrækker te fremfor kaffe; **~able** ['prɛfrəbl] *adj* (som er) at foretrække; **~ably** ['prɛfrəbli] *adv* helst, fortrinsvis.

preference ['prɛfrəns] *s* forkærlighed;

fortrinsret; begunstigelse; *in ~ to* fremfor.

prefix ['pri:fiks] *s (gram)* forstavelse, præfiks.

pregnancy ['prɛgnənsi] *s* graviditet, svangerskab.

pregnant ['prɛgnənt] *adj* gravid; betydningsfuld; følelsesladet.

pre-heat ['pri:hi:t] *v* forvarme.

prehistoric ['pri:his'tɔrik] *adj* forhistorisk; **prehistory** *s* forhistorie; forhistorisk tid.

prejudice ['prɛdʒudis] *s* fordom; modvilje; skade, men; *have a ~ against foreigners* være forudindtaget mod udlændinge // *v* forudindtage; være til skade for; **~d** *adj* forudindtaget, partisk.

preliminary [pri'liminəri] *adj* foreløbig; indledende; *preliminaries* indledende forhandlinger.

prelude ['prɛlju:d] *s* forspil; indledning; *(mus)* præludium.

premarital [,pri:'mæritəl] *adj* førægteskabelig.

premature ['prɛmətʃuə*] *adj* for tidlig; overilet; *~ baby* for tidligt født barn.

premeditated [pri'mɛditeitid] *adj* overlagt, forsætlig (fx *murder* mord); **premeditation** [-'teiʃən] *s* overlæg; forsæt.

premier ['prɛmiə*] *s* premierminister // *adj* fornemst; først.

premise ['prɛmis] *s* forudsætning; præmis; **~s** *spl* lokaliteter; ejendom; *on the ~s* på stedet; *keep off the ~s!* adgang forbudt!

premium ['pri:miəm] *s* præmie; bonus; *at a ~* i høj kurs; **~ bond** *s* præmieobligation.

premonition [prɛmə'niʃən] *s* forudanelse; varsel.

prematal [pri:'neitəl] *adj* før fødslen; *~ classes* fødselsforberedelse.

preoccupation [pri:ɔkju'peiʃən] *s* optagethed; åndsfraværelse.

preoccupied [pri:'ɔkjupaid] *adj* optaget; distræt; fordybet.

pre-packed ['pri:'pækd] *adj* færdigpakket.

prepaid ['pri:'peid] *adj* forudbetalt.

preparation [prɛpə'reiʃən] *s* forberedelse; tilberedelse; udfærdigelse.

preparatory [pri'pærətəri] *adj* forberedende; **~ school** *s* (privat) forberedelsesskole (før adgang til *public school*).

prepare [pri'pɛə*] *v* forberede; gøre parat; tilberede; *~ for* forberede sig på; *be ~ed to* være parat til.

preponderance [pri'pɔndərəns] *s* overvægt; overlegenhed.

preposition [prɛpə'ziʃən] *s (gram)* forholdsord, præposition.

preposterous [pri'pɔstərəs] *adj* meningsløs, absurd; latterlig.

prerequisite [pri:'rɛkwizit] *s* betingelse, forudsætning // *adj* nødvendig.

prerogative [pri'rɔgətiv] *s* forret.

presage ['prɛsidʒ] *s* forvarsel; forudanelse // *v* varsle om.

preschool ['pri:sku:l] *adj* førskole-.

prescribe [pri'skraib] *v* foreskrive; skrive recept (på), ordinere.

prescription [pri'skripʃən] *s* forskrift; recept.

presence [prɛzns] *s* tilstedeværelse, nærværelse; *in his ~* i hans nærvær; *~ of mind* åndsnærværelse.

present *s* [prɛznt] gave; *(gram)* nutid, præsens; *at ~* i øjeblikket; *for the ~* indtil videre; *the ~* nutiden // *v* [pri'ʒɛnt] give, forære; fremvise; udgøre; præsentere; *~ sby with sth* overrække (,give) en ngt // *adj* [prɛznt] nærværende; til stede; **~able** [pri'zɛntəbl] *adj* præsentabel; velopdragen; **~ation** [-'teiʃən] *s* overrækkelse; præsentation; forevisning; **~-day** *adj* nutids-, nutidig.

presenter [pri'zɛntə*] *s (tv)* præsentator, studievært.

presentiment [pri'zɛntimənt] *s* forudanelse.

presently ['prɛzntli] *adv* snart, straks; for tiden.

preservation [prɛzə'veiʃən] *s* bevarelse; sikring; fredning; (om mad) konservering; syltning; henkogning.

preservative [pri'zə:vətiv] *s* konserveringsmiddel // *adj* beskyttende, beskyttelses-.

preserve [pri'zə:v] *s* (vildt)reservat; *~s* syltetøj, henkogt frugt etc // *v* beskytte; frede; konservere.
pre-set ['pri:'sɛt] *v* indstille på forhånd // *adj* indstillet på forhånd.
preside [pri'zaid] *v* præsidere, føre forsædet.
presidency ['prɛzidənsi] *s* præsidentperiode.
president ['prɛzidənt] *s* præsident; formand; direktør.
press [prɛs] *s* presse; tryk, pres; trykkeri; (om møbel) kommode, klædeskab; presning; *go to ~* gå i trykken // *v* presse; knuge; tvinge, møde; trænges, mase; presse på, haste; *we are ~ed for time* vi er i tidnød, vi har dårlig tid; *~ for sth* rykke for ngt; *~ on* mase på; køre videre; ~ **agency** *s* nyhedsbureau; ~ **cutting** *s* avisudklip; **~er foot** *s* trykfod; **~ing** *adj* presserende; indtrængende; ~ **release** *s* pressemeddelelse; ~ **stud** *s* trykknap (i tøj); **~-ups** *spl* armbøjninger.
pressure ['prɛʃə*] *s* tryk; pres; pression; ~ **cooker** *s* trykkoger; ~ **group** *s* pressionsgruppe.
pressurized ['prɛʃəraizd] *adj* under tryk, tryk-; *(fig)* under pres.
prestigious [prɛ'stidʒiəs] *adj* anset, velanskrevet.
presumably [pri'zju:məbli] *adv* antagelig, formentlig.
presume [pri'zju:m] *v* antage, formode; tillade sig; gå for vidt.
presumption [pri'zʌmpʃən] *s* antagelse; formodning; indbildskhed; dristighed.
presumptive [pri'zʌmptiv] *adj* sandsynlig.
presumptuous [pri'zʌmptʃuəs] *adj* overmodig; anmassende.
presuppose [pri:sə'pəuz] *v* forudsætte.
pre-tax ['pri:'tæks] *adj* før skat.
pretence [pri'tɛns] *s* påskud; krav *(to* på); indbildskhed; *false ~s* falske forudsætninger; *make a ~ of* lade som om; *on the ~ of* under påskud af.
pretend [pri'tɛnd] *v* foregive, lade som om; lege; *~ to* foregive at; *~ to the throne* gøre krav på tronen; *they are only ~ing* det er bare ngt de leger.
pretentious [pri'tɛnʃəs] *adj* prætentiøs; fordringsfuld.
preterite ['prɛtərit] *s (gram)* datid, præteritum.
preternatural [pri:tə'nætʃrəl] *adj* overnaturlig.
pretext ['pri:tɛkst] *s* påskud; *on the ~ of* under påskud af at.
pretty ['priti] *adj* pæn, køn (også *iron)* // *adv* temmelig; *~ awful* ret slem; *~ well* temmelig godt; næsten; *a ~ penny* en pæn sum penge.
pretzel ['prɛtsəl] *s* (salt)kringle.
prevail [pri'veil] *v* sejre; være fremherskende; *~ (up)on sby to do sth* formå en til at gøre ngt; **~ing** *adj* fremherskende.
prevalence ['prɛvələns] *s* udbredelse; hyppighed; **prevalent** *adj* udbredt; fremherskende; hyppig.
prevaricate [pri'værikeit] *v* komme med udflugter.
prevent [pri'vɛnt] *v* forhindre, forebygge; *~ sby from sth* forhindre en i ngt.
prevention [pri'vɛnʃən] *s* forhindring; forebyggelse; bekæmpelse.
preventive [pri'vɛntiv] *s* forebyggende middel // *adj* hindrende; forebyggende, præventiv.
preview ['pri:vju:] *s* fernisering; forpremiere.
previous ['pri:viəs] *adj* foregående, tidligere; *he had a ~ arrangement* han havde allerede en aftale; *~ to* før.
prewar ['pri:wɔ:*] *adj* førkrigs-.
prey [prei] *s* bytte, rov; *bird of ~* rovfugl; *fall ~ to* blive offer for // *v: ~ on* angribe; udsuge; nage.
price [prais] *s* pris; værdi; *at any ~* for enhver pris // *v* prissætte; prismærke; ~ **freeze** *s* prisstop; **~less** *adj* uvurderlig; kostelig; ~ **range** *s* prisklasse; **~-tag** *s* prisskilt.
pricey ['praisi] *adj* (F) dyr, pebret.
prick [prik] *s* prik; stik; (V) pik; (om person) (S) røvhul // *v* prikke;

stikke; punktere; ~ *up one's ears* spidse ører.

prickle [prikl] *s* (på plante) torn, pig; stikken, prikken.

prickly ['prikli] *adj* tornet; stikkende; *(fig)* vanskelig; (om person) irritabel, prikken; ~ **heat** *s* varmeknopper.

pride [praid] *s* stolthed, hovmod; *take (a) ~ in* sætte en ære i at; *swallow one's ~* bide hovedet af al skam // *v: ~ oneself on sth* være stolt af ngt.

priest [pri:st] *s* (især katolsk) præst; **~ess** *s* præstinde; **~hood** *s* præsteskab; præsteembede.

prig [prig] *s* pedant; stivstikker; snob; dydsmønster; **~gery** *s* selvgodhed; stivstikkeri; **~gish** *adj* dydig; snobbet.

prim [prim] *adj* pæn, sirlig; snerpet.

primal ['praimәl] *adj* oprindelig; vigtigst.

primarily ['praimәrili] *adv* først og fremmest; oprindelig.

primary ['praimәri] *s (am)* primærvalg // *adj* først; primær; grund-; hoved-; oprindelig; ~ **school** *s* grundskole (5-11 år).

prime [praim] *s: in his ~* i sin bedste alder // *v* instruere; præparere; (med maling) grunde // *adj* oprindelig, ur-; fornemst; hoved-; prima; ~ *time (tv)* den bedste sendetid; *in ~ condition* i fineste stand; ~ **minister** *s (PM)* premierminister.

primer ['praimә*] *s* begynderbog; (ved maling) grunder, grundmaling; grunding.

primeval [prai'mi:vәl] *adj* oprindelig, ur-.

primitive ['primitiv] *adj* primitiv.

primrose ['primrәuz] *s* primula, kodriver.

prince [prins] *s* fyrste, prins; ~ **consort** *s* prinsgemal.

princess [prin'sɛs] *s* fyrstinde, prinsesse.

principal ['prinsipәl] *s* chef, arbejdsgiver; (i skole) forstander; (om penge) kapital, hovedstol // *adj* vigtigst, hoved-.

principality [prinsi'pæliti] *s* fyrstendømme; fyrstemagt.

principally ['prinsipli] *adv* hovedsageligt; først og fremmest.

principle ['prinsipl] *s* princip; *in (,on) ~* principielt, af princip; *a man of ~* en principfast mand.

print [print] *s* mærke; aftryk; *(typ)* tryk; *(foto)* kopi; fingeraftryk; *out of ~* udsolgt fra forlaget; *read the small ~* læse det der står med lille skrift // *v* trykke; printe (ud); udgive; skrive med blokbogstaver; ~ **dress** *s* mønstret bomuldskjole; **~ed matter** *s* tryksag.

printer ['printә*] *s* (bog)trykker; *(edb)* printer; **~'s error** *s* trykfejl.

printing ['printiŋ] *s* trykning; bogtryk; *(foto)* kopiering; oplag; ~ **press** *s* trykpresse.

print-out ['printaut] *s (edb)* udskrift.

prior [praiә*] *s* prior // *adj* tidligere; foregående; ~ *to* førend; forud for.

priority [prai'ɔriti] *s* fortrinsret; prioritet; *have top ~* have første prioritet; stå øverst på listen.

priory ['priәri] *s* munkekloster, priorat.

prise [praiz] *v: ~ open* bryde (,lirke) op; *~ sth out of sby* liste ngt ud af en.

prison [prizn] *s* fængsel; ~ **camp** *s* fangelejr.

prisoner ['prizәnә*] *v* fange; *take sby ~* tage en til fange; *~ of war* krigsfange.

prissy ['prisi] *adj* sippet; (om påklædning) kedelig.

pristine ['pristi:n] *adj* uberørt, jomfruelig.

privacy ['privәsi] *s* privatliv; uforstyrrethed.

private ['praivit] *s* menig (fx *soldier* soldat); *in ~* i enrum, under fire øjne // *adj* privat; personlig; ene- (fx *lesson* time); *go ~* blive selvstændig; ~ **eye** *s* privatdetektiv; ~ **parts** *spl* ædlere dele, kønsdele; ~ **tuition** *s* privatundervisning.

privation [prai'veiʃәn] *s* nød, fattigdom; afsavn.

privatize ['praivәtaiz] *v* privatisere.

privet ['privit] *s:* ~ *hedge* ligusterhæk.
privilege ['privilidʒ] *s* privilegium; **~d** *adj* privilegeret.
privy ['privi] *s* (F) wc, lokum // *adj: be ~ to* være medvidende om; *the Privy Council (brit)* gehejmerådet (dronningens politiske rådgivere).
prize [praiz] *s* pris, præmie; skat // *v* sætte pris på; værdsætte; **~ fight** *s* professionel boksekamp; **~-giving** *s* prisuddeling; **~ idiot** *s* kæmpeidiot.
pro [prəu] *s (sport)* professionel; *the ~s and cons* for og imod.
probability [prɔbə'biliti] *s* sandsynlighed; *in all ~* efter al sandsynlighed.
probable ['prɔbəbl] *adj* sandsynlig; **probably** ['prɔbəbli] *adv* sandsynligvis.
probation [prə'beiʃən] *s* prøvetid; *(jur)* betinget dom; *release on ~* prøveløsladelse; **~er** *s* novice; aspirant; prøveløsladt; **~ officer** *s* tilsynsførende (i kriminalforsorgen).
probe [prəub] *s* sonde; undersøgelse // *v* sondere; udforske.
problem ['prɔbləm] *s* problem; *(mat)* opgave.
problematic [prɔblə'mætik] *adj* problematisk.
procedure [prə'si:dʒə*] *s* fremgangsmåde; *(jur)* procedure.
proceed [prə'si:d] *v* gå (,køre etc) fremad, fortsætte; *~ against sby* anlægge sag mod en; **~ing** *s* fremgangsmåde; **~ings** *spl* forhandlinger; *(jur)* sagsanlæg, proces; mødeprotokol; **~s** *spl* udbytte, indtjening.
process ['prəusɛs] *s* proces; metode; *in the ~ of* i færd med (at); *in the ~ of time* i tidens løb // *v* forarbejde; behandle; forædle; **~ed cheese** *s* smelteost; **~ing** *s* behandling; forarbejdning.
procession [prə'sɛʃən] *s* procession, optog.
proclaim [prə'kleim] *v* proklamere; bekendtgøre; erklære (fx *war* krig).
proclamation [prɔklə'meiʃən] *s* bekendtgørelse.
procrastinate [prəu'kræstineit] *v* trække tiden ud, nøle.
procure [prə'kjuə*] *v* skaffe; opdrive.
prod [prɔd] *v* prikke; puffe (til); pirke; *~ sby along* sætte skub i en.
prodigal ['prɔdigl] *adj* ødsel; sløset; *the Prodigal Son* den fortabte søn.
prodigious [prə'didʒəs] *adj* fænomenal, formidabel.
prodigy ['prɔdidʒi] *s* vidunder; *child ~* vidunderbarn.
produce *s* ['prɔdju:s] produktion; produkter; udbytte // *v* [prə'dju:s] producere; frembringe; tage frem; fremvise; skabe, avle; *(teat)* iscenesætte; **~r** *s* producent; *(teat)* instruktør.
product ['prɔdʌkt] *s* produkt; fabrikat.
production [prə'dʌkʃən] *s* produktion; forevisning; fremstilling; værk; iscenesættelse; **~ engineer** *s* driftsingeniør; **~ line** *s* samlebånd; **~ manager** *s* driftsleder, produktionschef.
productive [prə'dʌktiv] *adj* produktiv.
productivity [prədʌk'tiviti] *s* produktivitet.
profane [prə'fein] *adj* verdslig, profan; blasfemisk.
profess [prə'fɛs] *v* erklære; udøve; bekende sig til; *~ to be* give sig ud for at være.
profession [prə'fɛʃən] *s* profession, fag, erhverv; bekendelse; **~al** *s* professionel // *adj* faglig, professionel; *he's a ~al man* han har et liberalt erhverv.
professor [prə'fɛsə*] *s* professor; lærer; **~ship** *s* professorat.
proffer ['prɔfə*] *v* tilbyde.
proficiency [prə'fiʃənsi] *s* dygtighed, færdighed; **proficient** *adj* dygtig; kyndig; kapabel.
profile ['prəufail] *s* profil; omrids.
profit ['prɔfit] *s* udbytte, gevinst; gavn; *sell at a ~* sælge med gevinst; *turn sth to ~* drage nytte af ngt // *v: ~ (by, from)* tjene (på).
profitability [prɔfitə'biliti] *s* lønsomhed, rentabilitet.
profitable ['prɔfitəbl] *adj* gavnlig, nyttig; indbringende.
profiteer [prɔfi'ti:r] *s* profitjæger // *v* spekulere (økonomisk etc).

profitsharing ['prɔfitʃɛəriŋ] *s* udbyttedeling.
profound [prə'faund] *adj* dyb; dybtgående; dybsindig.
profuse [prə'fju:s] *adj* overvældende; rigelig; ødsel; **profusion** [-'fju:ʒən] *s* overflod; ødselhed.
progeny ['prɔdʒini] *s* afkom.
prognosis [prɔg'nəusis] *s* prognose.
program ['prəugræm] *s (edb)* program // *v* programmere.
programme ['prəugræm] *s* progam; **~r** *s* programmør.
progress *s* ['prəugrɛs] fremskridt; fremryken; forløb, udvikling; *in* ~ i gang; *make* ~ gøre fremskridt // *v* [prə'grɛs] skride frem, gå fremad.
progression [prə'grɛʃən] *s* fremgang; rækkefølge.
progressive [prə'grɛsiv] *adj* progressiv; voksende; (om person) fremskridtsvenlig; **~ly** *adv* mere og mere, progressivt.
prohibit [prə'hibit] *v* forbyde; forhindre; ~ *sby from sth* forbyde en at gøre ngt.
prohibition [prəui'biʃən] *s* forbud.
prohibitive [prə'hibitiv] *adj* (om pris) afskrækkende; ~ **sign** *s* forbudsskilt.
project *s* ['prɔdʒɛkt] projekt, plan // *v* [prə'dʒɛkt] planlægge, projektere; rage frem, stikke ud.
projection [prə'dʒɛkʃən] *s* projektering; projicering; fremspring; forudsigelse.
projector [prə'dʒɛktə*] *s* (film- el. dias)fremviser.
proletarian [prəulə'tɛəriən] *s* proletar // *adj* proletarisk.
proliferate ['prə'lifəreit] *v* formere sig (hurtigt); *(fig)* vokse (hurtigt); **proliferation** [-'reiʃən] *s* hurtig formering; hurtig vækst.
prolific [prə'lifik] *adj* frugtbar; *(fig)* frodig; produktiv.
prologue ['prəulɔg] *s* prolog; forord.
prolong [prə'lɔŋ] *v* forlænge; **~ed** *adj* langtrukken.
prom [prɔm] *s* fork.f. *promenade concert.*
promenade [prɔmə'na:d] *s* spadseretur; promenade; ~ **concert** *s* promenadekoncert.
prominence ['prɔminəns] *s* fremspring; *(fig)* betydelighed; **prominent** *adj* fremstående; *(fig)* prominent.
promiscuous [prɔ'miskjuəs] *adj* som har tilfældige forhold.
promise ['prɔmis] *s* løfte; *make a* ~ (af)give et løfte; *show* ~ være lovende; *he shows much* ~ han er meget lovende // *v* love; tegne til; **promising** *adj* lovende.
promontory ['prɔməntri] *s* forbjerg.
promote [prə'məut] *v* fremme, arbejde for (fx *peace* fred); reklamere for; (om person) forfremme; **~r** *s (sport)* promotor.
promotion [prə'məuʃən] *s* fremme, støtte; salgsarbejde; forfremmelse.
prompt [prɔmt] *v* tilskynde; fremkalde; *(teat)* sufflere; ~ *sby to* få en til (at) // *adj* hurtig; beredvillig // *adv* omgående, prompte; **~er** *s* sufflør.
promptitude ['prɔmtitju:d] *s* beredvillighed; hurtighed.
promptly ['prɔmtli] *adv* prompte; præcis.
prone [prəun] *adj* liggende (på maven); tilbøjelig; *he's* ~ *to anger* han bliver let vred; *he's* ~ *to accidents* han kommer altid galt af sted.
prong [prɔŋ] *s* tand (på gaffel); spids.
pronoun ['prəunaun] *s* stedord, pronomen.
pronounce [prə'nauns] *v* udtale; erklære; ~ *(up)on* udtale sig om; ~ *sentence* afsige dom; **~d** *adj* udtalt; udpræget; **~ment** *s* udtalelse.
pronto ['prɔntəu] *adv* straks, omgående.
pronunciation [prənʌnsi'eiʃən] *s* udtale.
proof [pru:f] *s* bevis; (om alkohol) styrke; *(typ)* korrektur; *(foto)* prøveaftryk; *in* ~ *of* som bevis på; *put it to the* ~ sætte det på prøve // *adj* uimodtagelig; tæt; *be* ~ *against* kunne modstå; **~-reader** *s* korrekturlæser.
prop [prɔp] *s* stiver, støtte(bjælke) (se

også *props)* // *v:* ~ *(up)* afstive, støtte; ~ *sth against the wall* stille ngt op ad muren.
propagation [prɔpə'geiʃən] *s* formering; udbredelse.
propel [prə'pɛl] *v* drive (frem).
propellant [prə'pɛlənt] *s* drivmiddel; drivgas.
propeller [prə'pɛlə*] *s* (skibs)skrue; propel.
propelling pencil [prə'pɛliŋ ,pɛnsil] *s* skrueblyant.
propensity [prə'pɛnsiti] *s* hang, tilbøjelighed.
proper ['prɔpə*] *adj* rigtig; egentlig passende, egnet; anstændig; *give sby a* ~ *licking* (F) give en en ordentlig omgang tæv; *in Glasgow* ~ i selve Glasgow; *in the* ~ *sense of the word* i ordets egentlige forstand; **~ly** *adv* egentlig; rigtig; anstændigt; *~ly speaking* strengt taget; **~ noun** *s (gram)* egennavn, proprium.
property ['prɔpəti] *s* ejendom; ejendele; egenskab; *lost* ~ hittegods; **~ man** *s (teat)* rekvisitør; **~ owner** *s* husejer; grundejer.
prophecy ['prɔfisi] *s* forudsigelse, profeti; **prophesy** ['prɔfisai] *v* forudsige, spå.
prophet ['prɔfit] *s* profet.
prophylactic [prɔfi'læktik] *adj* forebyggende.
proponent [prə'pəunənt] *s* fortaler; forslagsstiller.
proportion [prə'pɔ:ʃən] *s* del; forhold; proportion; *in* ~ *to* i forhold til; *out of* ~ *to* ude af proportion med; *sense of* ~ proportionssans // *v* afpasse.
proposal [prə'pəuzl] *s* forslag; frieri.
propose [prə'pəuz] *v* foreslå; forelægge; have i sinde; fri; **~r** *s* forslagsstiller.
proposition [prəpə'ziʃən] *s* forslag; projekt // *v:* ~ *sby* antaste en, lægge an på en.
propound [prə'paund] *v* fremlægge.
proprietary [prə'praiətəri] *adj* navnebeskyttet; ejendoms-; mærke-.
proprietor [prə'praiətə*] *s* ejer.
propriety [prə'praiəti] *s* berettigelse; rigtighed; sømmelighed.
props [prɔps] *spl* (teater)rekvisitter.
propulsion [prə'pʌlʃən] *s* drivkraft, fremdrift.
proscribe [prə'skraib] *v* forbyde.
proscription [prə'skripʃən] *s* forbud; fordømmelse.
prose [prəuz] *s* prosa.
prosecute ['prɔsikju:t] *v* forfølge; udøve; *(jur)* anklage, sagsøge.
prosecution [prɔsi'kju:ʃən] *s* forfølgelse; *(jur)* anklage(myndighed).
prosecutor ['prɔsikju:tə*] *s* anklager; sagsøger; offentlig anklager.
prospect *s* ['prɔspɛkt] udsigt; mulighed, perspektiv; (om person) emne; *~s* udsigter, chancer // *v* [prə'spɛkt] foretage undersøgelser; søge efter olie (,guld etc).
prospective [prə'spɛktiv] *adj* eventuel; fremtidig.
prospector [prə'spɛktə*] *s* guldgraver; en der borer efter olie etc.
prospectus [prə'spɛktəs] *s* prospekt; program.
prosper ['prɔspə*] *v* have fremgang; trives.
prosperity [prɔs'pɛriti] *s* fremgang, held; velstand.
prosperous ['prɔspərəs] *adj* heldig; velstående; blomstrende.
prostate *s:* ~ *(gland)* prostata.
prostitute ['prɔstitju:t] *s* prostitueret, luder.
prostrate ['prɔstreit] *adj* liggende; næsegrus; *(fig)* knust // *v* gøre udmattet, slå ud.
protagonist [prə'tægənist] *s* hovedperson; forgrundsfigur; forkæmper.
protect [prə'tɛkt] *v* beskytte; frede.
protection [prə'tɛkʃən] *s* beskyttelse, værn.
protective [prə'tɛktiv] *adj* beskyttende; beskyttelses-; varetægts-.
protector [prə'tɛktə*] *s* beskytter.
protest *s* ['prəutɛst] protest, indvending // *v* [prə'tɛst] protestere, gøre indsigelse (mod); *she ~ed that...* hun påstod (,hævdede) at...
protracted [prə'træktid] *adj* langtrukken.

protractor [prə'træktə*] *s* vinkelmåler.

protrude [prə'tru:d] *v* stikke ud; rage frem; **protruding** *adj* udstående (fx *eyes* øjne).

protuberant [prə'tju:bərənt] *adj* udstående.

proud [praud] *adj* stolt; hovmodig; *he did me* ~ (F) han diskede op for mig; han gjorde det godt for mig; han gjorde mig ære.

prove [pru:v] *v* bevise; påvise; efterprøve; ~ *correct* vise sig at være rigtig; ~ *oneself* vise hvad man kan; **~n** ['pru:vən] *adj* bevist; notorisk.

proverb ['prɔvə:b] *s* ordsprog.

proverbial [prə'və:biəl] *adj* legendarisk.

provide [prə'vaid] *v* skaffe; forsyne; foreskrive; ~ *sby with sth* skaffe en ngt; ~ *against sth* forbyde ngt; sikre mod ngt; ~ *for* sørge for; tage højde for; ~*d (that)* forudsat (at); på betingelse af (at).

Providence ['prɔvidəns] *s* forsynet.

providential [prɔvi'dɛnʃl] *adj* lykkelig; heldig, gunstig.

provider [prə'vaidə*] *s* forsyner.

providing [prə'vaidiŋ] *konj* forudsat (at).

province ['prɔvins] *s* provins; område, felt.

provincial [prə'vinʃəl] *adj* provinsiel; provins-.

provision [prə'viʒən] *s* anskaffelse; tilvejebringelse; omsorg; bestemmelse; *make* ~ *for sth* tage hensyn til ngt; sørge for ngt; **~al** *adj* foreløbig, provisorisk; **~s** *spl* proviant; forråd; forsyninger.

proviso [prə'vaizəu] *s* forbehold.

provocation [prɔvə'keiʃən] *s* udfordring; provokation.

provocative [prə'vɔkətiv] *adj* provokerende.

provoke [prə'vəuk] *v* fremkalde, vække; tilskynde; provokere.

provost ['prɔvəst] *s* sv.omtr.t. universitetsrektor; (skotsk) borgmester.

prow [prau] *s* forstavn.

prowess ['prauis] *s* tapperhed; stor dygtighed.

prowl [praul] *s* strejftog // *v* strejfe rundt (i).

proximity [prɔk'simiti] *s* nærhed.

proxy ['prɔksi] *s* befuldmægtiget stedfortræder; fuldmagt; *vote by* ~ stemme ved fuldmagt.

prude [pru:d] *s* sippet person.

prudence ['pru:dns] *s* klogskab; forsigtighed.

prudent ['pru:dənt] *adj* klog; forsigtig.

prudery ['pru:dəri] *s* sippethed.

prudish ['pru:diʃ] *adj* sippet.

prune [pru:n] *s* sveske // *v* (om træer, planter etc) beskære.

prussic ['prʌsik] *adj:* ~ *acid* blåsyre.

pry [prai] *v:* ~ *about* snuse rundt; ~ *into* snage i, stikke sin næse i; ~ *out* lirke ud.

psalm [sa:m] *s* salme; *the Psalms* Davids salmer.

pseud(o) ['sju:d(əu)] *adj* pseudo; kunstig.

psych [saik] *v:* ~ *sby out* (F) intimidere (,kyse) en; gennemskue en; ~ *up* lade up (før kamp etc).

psyche ['saiki] *s* psyke, sjæl.

psychiatric [saiki'ætrik] *adj* psykiatrisk; **psychiatrist** [sai'kaiətrist] *s* psykiater; **psychiatry** [-'kaiətri] *s* psykiatri.

psychic(al) ['saikik(l)] *adj* psykisk; (om person) telepatisk.

psycho... [saikəu-] sms: **~analysis** [-æ'nælisis] *s* psykoanalyse; **~analyst** [-'ænəlist] *s* psykoanalytiker; **~logical** [-'lɔdʒikəl] *adj* psykologisk; **~logist** [sai'kɔlədʒist] *s* psykolog; **~path** ['saikəpæθ] *s* psykopat; **~sis** [sai'kəusis] *s* psykose.

pt(s) fork.f. *pint(s)*.

PTO, pto (fork.f. *please turn over)* vend! se næste side!

pub [pʌb] *s* (fork.f. *public house)* kro, værtshus; **~-crawl** ['pʌbkrɔ:l] *s* værtshusturné.

puberty ['pju:bəti] *s* pubertet; **pubic** *adj* pubes-.

public ['pʌblik] *s* publikum; offentlighed; *the general* ~ offentligheden; *in the* ~ *eye* i offentlighedens søgelys; *go* ~ gå på børsen; *in* ~ offentligt; ~ *convenience* offentligt toilet

// *adj* offentlig; almen; ~ **address system** *s (PA)* højttaleranlæg.
publican ['pʌblikən] *s* værtshusholder, pubejer.
publication [pʌbli'keiʃən] *s* publikation; offentliggørelse; udgivelse; bekendtgørelse.
publicity [pʌ'blisiti] *s* reklame, publicity.
publicize ['pʌblisaiz] *v* offentliggøre; lave reklame for.
public... ['pʌblik-] sms: ~ **opinion** *s* den offentlige mening; ~ **prosecutor** *s* offentlig anklager; ~ **relations** *spl (PR)* public relations, reklame; ~ **school** *s* (i England) privat kostskole; (skotsk, *am, Austr)* offentlig skole, kommuneskole; ~ **servant** *s* statstjenestemand; ~-**spirited** *adj* med samfundssind.
publish ['pʌbliʃ] *v* offentliggøre, publicere; udgive; ~ *sth abroad* udbasunere ngt; ~**er** *s* forlægger; ~**ing** *s* forlagsvirksomhed; (om bog) udgivelse.
puce [pju:s] *adj* blommefarvet.
pucker ['pʌkə*] *v* rynke; ~ *one's lips* knibe munden sammen.
pudding ['pudiŋ] *s* budding; dessert; *black* ~ blodpølse; ~**head** *s* (F) grødhoved.
puddle [pʌdl] *s* pyt, pøl.
puerile ['pjuərail] *adj* barnagtig.
puff [pʌf] *s* pust; røgsky; sug (af cigaret etc); pudderkvast; *be out of* ~ have tabt pusten // *v* puste; dampe; ~ *one's pipe* pulse på sin pibe; ~ *and pant* puste og stønne; ~ *out smoke* sende røgskyer ud; ~**ball** *s (bot)* støvbold; ~**ed** *adj* (F) forpustet; oppustet; ~ **pastry** *s* butterdej; ~**fy** *adj* forpustet; oppustet.
pugnacious [pʌg'neiʃəs] *adj* stridbar; aggressiv.
pug nose ['pʌgnəuz] *s* braktud.
puke [pju:k] *s* (F) bræk // *v* brække sig.
pull [pul] *s* træk, ryk; *(fig)* tiltrækning; slurk; sug; *give sth a* ~ rykke i ngt // *v* trække (i), rykke (i); hale (i); (om muskel) forstrække; ~ *a face* skære ansigt; ~ *sth to pieces* rive ngt i stykker; ~ *oneself together* tage sig sammen; ~ *sby's leg* gøre grin med en; bilde en ngt ind; ~ *a fast one on sby* tage gas på en; ~ *apart* rive i stykker; kritisere sønder og sammen; ~ *down* rive (,trække) ned; fælde; slå ned; ydmyge; ~ *in* (om bil) køre ind til siden; (om tog) køre ind på stationen; anholde; ~ *off* trække (,tage) af; klare, gennemføre; ~ *out* trække (sig) ud; gå (,køre) ud; trække sig (tilbage); ~ *round* komme sig; komme til sig selv; ~ *up* standse; trække op; holde an, stoppe.
pulley ['puli] *s* rulle, trisse; *(med)* strækapparat.
pull-in ['pulin] *s* holdeplads; cafeteria (ved bilvej).
pull-out ['pulaut] *s* tag ud-side(r) // *adj* (om bord etc) udtræks-.
pulp [pʌlp] *s* frugtkød; papirmasse; *beat sby to a* ~ slå en til plukfisk; ~ **literature** *s* triviallitteratur.
pulpit ['pulpit] *s* prædikestol.
pulsate [pʌl'seit] *v* pulsere; banke.
pulse [pʌls] *s* puls(slag); (om musik el. maskine) (rytmisk) banken // *v* pulsere; banke.
pulverize ['pʌlvəraiz] *v* pulverisere; forstøve.
pumice ['pʌmis] *s* pimpsten.
pummel ['pʌməl] *v* dunke, banke.
pump [pʌmp] *s* pumpe; vandpost; (om sko) pump // *v* pumpe.
pumpkin ['pʌmpkin] *s* græskar.
pun [pʌn] *s* ordspil.
punch [pʌntʃ] *s* slag, stød; kraft, energi; (om drik) punch; hultang; *Punch and Judy show* mester Jakelteater // *v* slå, støde til; klippe, hulle; ~**bag**, ~**ball** *s* boksebold; ~-**drunk** *adj* groggy; ~**line** *s* pointe; ~-**up** *s* slagsmål.
punchy ['pʌntʃi] *adj* skarp, fyndig; groggy.
punctilious [pʌŋk'tiliəs] *adj* overpertentlig, meget korrekt.
punctual ['pʌŋkʃuəl] *adj* præcis, punktlig.
punctuality [pʌŋkʃu'æliti] *s* punktlighed.

punctuate ['pʌŋktʃueit] *v* pointere; *(gram)* sætte tegn i.
punctuation [pʌŋktʃu'eiʃən] *s (gram)* tegnsætning.
puncture ['pʌŋktʃə*] *s* punktering; stik // *v* punktere, stikke hul i.
pundit ['pʌndit] *s* klogt hoved, orakel.
pungent ['pʌndʒənt] *adj* skarp, kras; sarkastisk.
punish ['pʌniʃ] *v* straffe, afstraffe; **~able** *adj* strafbar; **~ment** *s* straf.
punk [pʌŋk] *s* punker; punk.
punnet ['pʌnit] *s* bakke (fx til jordbær).
punt [pʌnt] *s* fladbundet båd, pram; *(fodb)* flugtning.
puny ['pju:ni] *adj* svagelig; ynkelig, sølle.
pup [pʌp] *s* (hunde)hvalp; (om ræv, ulv etc) unge.
pupa ['pju:pə] *s (pl: pupae)* puppe.
pupil ['pju:pil] *s* elev; *(anat)* pupil.
puppet ['pʌpit] *s* (marionet)dukke.
puppy ['pʌpi] *s* (hunde)hvalp; **~ fat** *s* hvalpefedt.
purchase ['pə:tʃəs] *s* køb, anskaffelse // *v* købe, erhverve; **~r** *s* køber.
purchasing power ['pə:tʃəsiŋ ,pauə*] *s* købekraft.
pure [pjuə*] *adj* ren; ægte; uberørt; *it's ~ nonsense* det er det rene vrøvl; *by ~ chance* ved et rent held, helt tilfældigt; *~ and simple* ren og skær; **~-bred** *adj* raceren.
puree ['pjuərei] *s* puré, mos // *v* purere, mose.
purely *adv* rent; udelukkende; *it's ~ my fault* det er udelukkende min fejl (,skyld).
purgatory ['pə:gətəri] *s* skærsild; lidelse.
purge [pə:dʒ] *s* afføringsmiddel; udrensning; renselse // *v* rense, udrense.
purification [pjuərifi'keiʃən] *s* renselse; oprensning.
purify ['pjuərifai] *v* rense, lutre.
puritan ['pjuəritən] *s* puritaner // *adj* puritansk.
purity ['pjuəriti] *s* renhed.
purl [pə:l] *s* vrangmaske // *v* strikke vrang; *knit one ~ one* en ret en vrang.
purloin [pə:'lɔin] *v* tilvende sig, få fat i.
purple [pə:pl] *adj* violet, lilla.
purport *s* ['pə:pət] betydning, indhold // *v* [pə:'pɔ:t] foregive; påstås; hentyde til.
purpose ['pə:pəs] *s* hensigt, formål; *on ~* med vilje, forsætlig; *to no ~* til ingen nytte; *to all intents and ~s* i alt væsentligt, i det store og hele; *serve a ~* tjene et formål; **~-built** *adj* (om byggeri) integreret; specialbygget; **~ful** *adj* målbevidst; bestemt; **~ly** *adv* med vilje.
purr [pə:*] *s* (om kat) spinden // *v* spinde, snurre.
purse [pə:s] *s* (penge)pung; håndtaske // *v* snerpe sammen.
pursue [pə'sju:] *v* forfølge; tilstræbe; følge; blive ved med; **~r** *s* forfølger.
pursuit [pə'sju:t] *s* forfølgelse, jagt; stræben; beskæftigelse, erhverv; *scientific ~s* videnskabelige sysler.
purveyor [pə'veiə*] *s* leverandør; sælger.
push [puʃ] *s* skub, puf; kraftanstrengelse; fremstød; energi, gåpåmod; *get the ~* blive fyret // *v* skubbe, puffe; trykke på; forcere, tilskynde; opreklamere, promovere; presse på; *don't ~!* lad være med at skubbe! *~ sby about* hundse rundt med en; *~ ahead* komme (,gå, køre, mase) frem; *~ along* (se at) komme videre; *~ aside* skubbe til side; *~ off* (F) komme (,tage) af sted; *~ on* mase på, komme videre; *~ out* spy ud; *~ over* vælte omkuld; *~ through* gennemføre; komme frem; *~ up* presse i vejret (fx *prices* priser); **~-button** *s* trykknap; **~-cart** *s* trækvogn; **~chair** *s* promenadevogn, klapvogn.
pushed [puʃd] *adj: ~ for money* i beknеb for penge; *be hard ~ to do sth* have svært ved at gøre ngt.
pusher ['puʃə*] *s* stræber; pusher.
pushing ['puʃiŋ] *adj* energisk, foretagsom; påtrængende.
pushover ['puʃəuvə*] *s: it's a ~* (F) det er en let sag; *he's a ~* han er ikke svær at få med i seng.

push-ups ['puʃʌps] *spl (am)* armbøjninger.
pushy ['puʃi] *adj (neds)* fremadstræbende, med spidse albuer.
pussy ['pusi] *s* (F) mis(sekat); **~foot** *v* liste på kattepoter; være meget forsigtig.
put [put] *v (put, put)* lægge, sætte, stille, anbringe, putte; fremstille; foreslå; anslå; ~ *about (mar)* gå over stag; udbrede (fx *a rumour* et rygte); *(fig)* ulejlige; *let me ~ it this way* lad mig sige det sådan; ~ *it into Polish* sige det på polsk; oversætte det til polsk;
~ *across* gennemføre, sætte igennem; ~ *the idea across to sby* få en til at gå ind på tanken; ~ *away* lægge til side, gemme væk; (om dyr) aflive; (F) sætte til livs;
~ *back* stille (,lægge etc) tilbage; forsinke; ~ *by* lægge til side, spare op;
~ *down* lægge fra sig; notere, skrive ned; (om paraply etc) slå ned; undertrykke, kvæle; aflive; ~ *down to* tilskrive;
~ *forward* stille frem; fremsætte, foreslå; ~ *in* installere; indgive, indsende; tilbringe, bruge;
~ *off* opsætte, udsætte; sætte af; lægge til side; tage modet fra, skræmme; (om lys etc) slukke, lukke (for);
~ *on* lægge (,sætte) på; tage på (fx *one's clothes* sit tøj); (om lys etc) tænde, åbne for; lave numre med; (om kedel etc) sætte over; ~ *on the brakes* bremse;
~ *out* lægge ud; smide ud; stikke ud; række frem (fx *one's hand* hånden); sætte i omløb (fx *news* nyheder); (om lys etc) slukke, lukke (for); forvirre, irritere; *be quite ~ out* (F) være helt fra den; ~ *out the washing* hænge vasketøjet ud; ~ *together* sætte sammen; lægge sammen;
~ *up* opføre, rejse; hejse; hænge op; give husly; ~ *up with* finde sig i.
put-on ['putɔn] *s* bluff(nummer).
putrid ['pju:trid] *adj* rådden; (F) ækel.
putsch [putʃ] *s* kup.
putter ['pʌtə*] *s* golfkølle // *v* tøffe;
putting green *s* (på golfbane) green.
putty ['pʌti] *s* kit // *v* kitte.
put-up ['putʌp] *adj: a ~ job* aftalt spil.
puzzle [pʌzl] *s* gåde; problem; mysterium; puslespil; krydsord // *v* forvirre; spekulere, bryde sin hjerne; **puzzling** *adj* forvirrende.
pygmy ['pigmi] *s* pygmæ, dværg.
pyjamas [pi'dʒa:məs] *spl* pyjamas.
pylon ['pailən] *s* el-mast, højspændingsmast.
pyramid ['pirəmid] *s* pyramide.
Pyrenees ['pirəni:z] *spl: the ~* Pyrenæerne.
python ['paiθən] *s* pythonslange.

Q

Q, q [kju:].
QC fork.f. *Queen's Counsel.*
quack [kwæk] *s* (om and) rappen, skræppen; kvaksalver.
quad [kwad] *s* (F) firling.
quadrangle ['kwɔdræŋgl] *s* firkant, kvadrat.
quadruped ['kwɔdrupɛd] *s* firbenet dyr.
quadruple [kwɔ'dru:pl] *adj* firedobbelt; firsidet // *v* firdoble.
quadruplet [kwɔ'dru:plit] *s* firling.
quagmire ['kwægmaiə*] *s* hængedynd, sump; *(fig)* dilemma.
quail [kweil] *s* vagtel // *v* tabe modet; ryste af skræk.
quaint [kweint] *adj* mærkelig; kunstfærdig; gammeldags.
quake [kweik] *s* skælven, bæven; (også: *earth~)* jordskælv // *v* skælve, ryste.
Quaker ['kweikə*] *s* kvæker.
qualification [kwɔlifi'keiʃən] *s* kvalifikation; egnethed; forudsætning; eksamen.
qualified ['kwɔlifaid] *adj* kvalificeret, egnet; betinget; uddannet (fx *nurse* sygeplejerske).
qualify ['kwɔlifai] *v* kvalificere; dygtiggøre; give kompetence; uddanne sig; rubricere som; ~ *as* uddanne sig til, tage eksamen som; ~ *(for)* være kvalificeret til.

quality ['kwɔliti] *s* kvalitet; egenskab.
qualm [kwɔ:m] *s* betænkelighed, skrupel.
quandary ['kwɔndəri] *s* forlegenhed, dilemma.
quantitative ['kwɔntitətiv] *adj* kvantitativ.
quantity ['kwɔntiti] *s* mængde, kvantum; kvantitet; størrelse; *an unknown ~ (fig)* en ukendt størrelse; ~ **discount** *s* mængderabat.
quantum ['kwɔntəm] *s (pl: quanta)* kvantum, mængde // *adj (fys)* kvante-.
quarantine ['kwɔrənti:n] *s* karantæne // *v* sætte i karantæne.
quarrel [kwɔrl] *s* skænderi, strid; *pick a ~ with sby* yppe kiv med en // *v* skændes, blive uvenner; **~some** *adj* krakilsk.
quarry ['kwɔri] *s* stenbrud; fangst, bytte // *v (min)* bryde.
quart [kwɔ:t] *s* (rummål: *2 pints* sv.t. 1,136 liter).
quarter ['kwɔ:tə*] *s* fjerdedel, kvart; (om tid) kvarter; kvartal; *(am)* 25 cents; *(brit)* d.s.s. *2 stones* = 12,70 kg; *a ~ of an hour* et kvarter; *a ~ to (,past) two* kvart i (,over) to; *a ~'s rent* kvartalsleje; *in high ~s* på højere sted // *v* dele i fire; partere; indkvartere; **~-deck** *s (mar)* agterdæk; ~ **final(s)** *s* kvartfinale; **~ly** *adj* kvartals- // *adv* kvartalsvis; **~s** *spl* bolig, logi; *(mil)* kvarter; *(mar)* mandskabsrum; *be confined to ~s* have stuearrest; *at close ~s* på nært hold.
quartet [kwɔ:'tɛt] *s (mus)* kvartet.
quartz [kwɔ:ts] *s* kvarts.
quash [kwɔʃ] *v* omstøde, annullere; nedslå.
quasi- ['kweizai-] kvasi-; tilsyneladende, såkaldt.
quaver ['kweivə*] *s* skælven; *(mus)* ottendedelsnode // *v* skælve, dirre.
quay [ki:] *s* kaj; **~side** *s* kaj; havnekvarter.
queasy ['kwi:zi] *adj: feel ~* have kvalme; være utilpas.
queen [kwi:n] *s* dronning; (i kortspil) dame; (S) bøsse; *~ of hearts* hjerter dame // *v: ~ it* kommandere; spille stor på den; ~ **mother** *s* enkedronning (mor til regenten); **Queen's Counsel** *(QC) s* advokat der kan optræde som anklager i kriminalsager (og tage særlige honorarer).
queer [kwiə*] *s* (F) homoseksuel, bøsse // *adj* mærkelig, mistænkelig; sløj; (F) homoseksuel; *be in ~ street* være på spanden.
quell [kwɛl] *v* knuse, undertrykke; dæmpe.
quench [kwɛntʃ] *v* slukke.
querulous ['kwɛruləs] *adj* klynkende; utilfreds; krakilsk.
query ['kwiəri] *s* spørgsmål, forespørgsel; spørgsmålstegn // *v* tvivle på; sætte spørgsmålstegn ved; forespørge.
quest [kwɛst] *s* søgen; *in ~ of* på udkig (,jagt) efter.
question ['kwɛstʃən] *s* spørgsmål; sag; *it's a ~ of* det drejer sig om; *there is no ~ of that* der er ingen tvivl om det; *the house in ~* det pågældende hus; *beyond ~* uden tvivl; *out of the ~* udelukket; *pop the ~* (F) tage sig sammen til at fri; *bring sth into ~* bringe ngt på tale; *it's open to ~ whether...* det er et åbent spørgsmål om ... // *v* (ud)spørge; afhøre; undersøge; drage i tvivl; **~able** [-əbl] *adj* tvivlsom, diskutabel; mistænkelig; **~ing** *s* forhør; undersøgelse; ~ **mark** *s* spørgsmålstegn; **~-master** *s* quizleder.
questionnaire [kwɛstʃə'nɛə*] *s* spørgeskema.
queue [kju:] *s* kø; *jump the ~* springe over i køen // *v: ~ (up)* stille sig (,stå) i kø.
quibble [kwibl] *v* hænge sig i detaljer; være smålig.
quick [kwik] *s: cut to the ~ (fig)* ramme det ømme punkt // *adj* hurtig; kort; kvik; opvakt; (om hørelse, syn) skarp; (om temperament) hidsig; *a ~ one* (F) en hurtig drink; et kort spørgsmål; *be ~!* skynd dig! **~en** *v* fremskynde; sætte fart i; sætte farten op; **~sand** *s* kviksand; **~-setting** *adj* som stivner (,tørrer)

hurtigt; **~silver** *s* kviksølv; **~-tempered** *adj* hidsig; **~-witted** *adj* snarrådig, slagfærdig.
quid [kwid] *s (pl: quid)* (F) pund (sterling); *20 ~* £20.
quiescent [kwi'ɛsnt] *adj* i ro, stille.
quiet ['kwaiət] *s* ro, stilhed; *on the ~* i hemmelighed, i smug // *v: ~ down* falde til ro // *adj* stille, rolig; diskret; *keep ~!* ti stille! vær stille! *keep sth ~* holde ngt hemmeligt; **~ly** *adv* stille; i stilhed; **~ness** *en* stilhed.
quill [kwil] *s* fjer; gåsefjer.
quilt [kwilt] *s* vatteret (,quiltet) tæppe; vattæppe; *(continental) ~* dyne; **~ing** *s* vattering, quiltning.
quince [kwinz] *s* kvæde.
quinine [kwi'ni:n] *s* kinin.
quins [kwins] *spl* (fork.f. *quintuplets)* (F) femlinger.
quintessence [kwin'tɛsns] *s* indbegreb.
quintet(te) [kwin'tɛt] *s* kvintet.
quintuplet [kwin'tju:plit] *s* femling.
quirk [kwə:k] *s* særhed, ejendommelighed; **~y** *adj* ejendommelig.
quit [kwit] *v (~ted, ~ted* el. *quit, quit)* forlade; opgive; fratræde; holde op med, droppe; flytte, gå sin vej; *~ smoking* holde op med at ryge; *notice to ~* opsigelse.
quite [kwait] *adv* helt, fuldkommen; ubetinget; absolut; temmelig, ret; *I ~ understand* jeg forstår udmærket; *~ a few* ikke så få, en hel del; *not ~* ikke helt; *he's not ~ there* (F) han er ikke rigtig med; *~ (so)!* netop! ganske rigtigt!
quits [kwits] *adj* kvit; *I'll be ~ with you!* det skal du få betalt! *cry ~* give op; *call it ~* lade det gå lige op.
quiver ['kwivə*] *s* pilekogger; skælven, bæven // *v* dirre, skælve.
quiz [kwiz] *s* spørgeleg, quiz // *v* udspørge; **~zical** *adj* spørgende; tvivlende.
quoits [kwɔits] *s* ringspil.
quota ['kwəutə] *s* kvota, andel.
quotation [kwəu'teiʃən] *s* citat; *(merk)* notering, kurs; tilbud; **~ marks** *spl* anførselstegn.
quote [kwəut] *s* citat; anførselstegn // *v* citere; *(merk)* notere; give tilbud; *quote ... unquote* citat begynder ... citat slut; *please ~* (i forretningsbrev) sv.t. "vor reference".
quoth [kwəuθ] *v (gl, spøg)* sagde.
quotient ['kwəuʃənt] *s* kvotient.

R

R, r [a:*].
rabbi ['ræbai] *s* rabbiner.
rabbit ['ræbit] *s* kanin.
rabble [ræbl] *s* pak, pøbel; **~-rouser** ['ræblrauzə*] *s* ballademager.
rabid ['ræbid] *adj* gal, rasende; fanatisk, rabiat.
rabies ['reibi:z] *s* hundegalskab, rabies.
raccoon [rə'ku:n] *s* vaskebjørn.
race [reis] *s* race; væddeløb, kapløb; *go to the ~s* gå på galopbanen (,travbanen); *a ~ against time* et kapløb med tiden // *v* løbe (,køre, sejle etc) om kap med; fare af sted, race; *(mek)* løbe løbsk; **~course** *s* væddeløbsbane; **~horse** *s* væddeløbshest; **~ riots** *spl* raceoptøjer; **~track** *s* væddeløbsbane.
racial ['reiʃl] *adj* race-.
racism ['reisizm] *s* racisme.
racist ['reisist] *s* racist // *adj* racistisk.
racing ['reisiŋ] *s* væddeløb; hestesport; motorløb; **~ car** *s* racerbil; **~ driver** *s* væddeløbskører; **~ yacht** *s* kapsejladsbåd.
rack [ræk] *s* stativ; bagagenet; tagbagagebærer; reol; *(hist)* pinebænk; *dish ~* opvaskestativ; *magazine ~* tidsskrifthylde; *toast ~* holder til ristet brød; *go to ~ and ruin* forfalde; gå i hundene // *v* pine; plage; *~ one's brains* bryde sin hjerne; *~ed with pain* forpint.
racket ['rækit] *s* ketsjer; larm, ståhej; liv og glade dage; svindel, fupnummer; *arms ~* illegal våbenhandel; *drugs ~* narkohandel.
racketeer [rækə'tiə*] *s* svindler.
racking ['rækiŋ] rædsom; rystende; dundrende.
racy ['reisi] *adj* smart, dødlækker (fx

car bil); saftig, dristig (fx *story* historie).
radial ['reidiəl] *s* radialdæk // *adj* radial-.
radiance ['reidiəns] *s* stråleglans; udstråling.
radiant ['reidiənt] *adj* strålende.
radiate ['reidieit] *v* udstråle; bestråle.
radiation [reidi'eiʃən] *s* udstråling; stråling; ~ **sickness** *s* strålesyge.
radiator ['reidieitə*] *s* varmeapparat, radiator; *(auto)* køler; ~ **cap** *s* *(auto)* kølerdæksel; ~ **grill** *s* *(auto)* kølergitter.
radical ['rædikəl] *adj* radikal.
radii ['reidiai] *spl* af *radius.*
radio ['reidiəu] *s* radio; *on the* ~ i radioen // *v* radiotelegrafere; **~active** [-'æktiv] *adj* radioaktiv; ~ **announcer** *s* (radio)speaker; ~ **beacon** *s* radiofyr; ~ **broadcast** *s* radioudsendelse; **~-controlled** *adj* radiostyret.
radiographer [reidi'ɔgrəfə*] *s* røntgenassistent, radiograf.
radiology [reidi'ɔlədʒi] *s* radiologi.
radio set ['reidiəu,sɛt] *s* radioapparat.
radiotherapy [reidiəu'θɛrəpi] *s* røntgenbehandling.
radish ['rædiʃ] *s* radise; ræddike.
radius ['reidiəs] *s* *(pl: radii)* radius.
RAF ['a:rei'ɛf] *s* (fork.f. *Royal Air Force)* det britiske flyvevåben.
raffia ['ræfiə] *s* bast.
raffish ['ræfiʃ] *adj* bohemeagtig; småvulgær.
raffle [ræfl] *s* tombola, lotteri.
raft [ra:ft] *s* flåde.
rafter ['ra:ftə*] *s* tagspær.
rag [ræg] *s* klud, las; *(neds,* om avis) sprøjte; sjov, løjer // *v* skælde ud; tage gas på; **~bag** *s* rodsammen; *(fig)* blandet landhandel; ~ **doll** *s* kludedukke.
rage [reidʒ] *s* raseri; mani; *it's all the* ~ det er sidste skrig // *v* rase.
ragged ['rægid] *adj* laset, lurvet; (om fx klippe) forrevet; takket.
raggedy ['rægidi] *adj* flosset.
rag trade ['rægtreid] *s: the* ~ (F) tøjbranchen.
raid [reid] *s* angreb; strejftog; razzia // *v* angribe; lave razzia; plyndre.
rail [reil] *s* gelænder; rækværk; stang; *(jernb)* skinne; *(mar)* ræling; *by* ~ med tog; *go off the* ~*s* løbe af sporet (også *fig); British Rail (BR)* de britiske jernbaner // *v:* ~ *in* indhegne; ~ *off* afspærre; **~bus** *s* skinnebus; **~card** *s* *(jernb)* rabatkort; **~ing(s)** *s(pl)* stakit, rækværk; **~link** *s* (bus)forbindelse mellem fx lufthavn og jernbanestation.
railroad ['reilrəud] *s* *(am)* d.s.s. *railway.*
railway ['reilwei] *s* *(brit)* jernbane; **~man** *s* jernbanefunktionær; ~ **station** *s* jernbanestation.
rain rein] *s* regn; regnvejr; *in the* ~ i regnvejret; *as right as* ~ helt i orden; *come* ~ *or shine* hvad enten vejret er godt eller dårligt // *v* regne; ~ *cats and dogs* styrtregne; *the match was* ~*ed off* kampen blev aflyst på grund af regn; **~bow** [-bəu] *s* regnbue; **~coat** *s* regnfrakke; **~drop** *s* regndråbe; **~fall** *s* regn; regnmængde; **~forest** *s* regnskov; ~ **gauge** [-geidʒ] *s* regnmåler; **~proof** *adj* regntæt; **~storm** *s* voldsomt regnvejr.
rainy ['reini] *adj* regnfuld; regnvejrs-.
raise [reiz] *s* (især *am)* lønstigning // *v* løfte, hæve; opføre, rejse (fx *a building* en bygning); fremkalde; opløfte (fx *a cry* et skrig); dyrke, opdrætte, opdrage; ~ *the alarm* slå alarm; ~ *one's voice* hæve stemmen; ~ *a family* opdrage børn; ~ *the roof* få taget til at lette (med larm, bifald etc); ~ *hell* lave en helvedes ballade.
raisin [reizn] *s* rosin.
rake [reik] *s* rive; ildrager; hældning // *v* rive; skrabe sammen; gennemrode; *(mil)* beskyde; ~ *one's brain* ransage hukommelsen; ~ *in* skrabe til sig; ~ *up* rippe op i; **~-off** *s* (ulovlig) profit.
rakish ['reikiʃ] *adj* flot; fræk.
rally ['ræli] *s* samling, stævne; *(auto)* løb // *v* samle (sig); (om syg person) være i bedring; *(merk,* om kurser) rette sig; ~ *round* samles om; stå sammen om.

ram [ræm] *s* vædder // *v* stampe; vædre; mase; støde; proppe; ~ *sth down sby's throat (fig)* presse ngt ned over hovedet på en; blive ved med at tale til en om ngt.
ramble [ræmbl] *s* (vandre)tur // *v* vandre om; vrøvle, væve; slynge sig; **~r** *s* vandrer; *(bot)* slyngrose; **rambling** *adj* (om tale) usammenhængende; vidtløftig; *(bot)* klatre-.
ramification [ræmifi'kaiʃən] *s* forgrening; *(fig)* udløber.
ramify ['ræmifai] *v* forgrene sig.
ramp [ræmp] *s* rampe.
rampage [ræm'peidʒ] *s* rasen; *go on a ~* slå sig løs // *v* hærge, rase.
rampant ['ræmpənt] *adj* som breder sig stærkt; *be ~* grassere.
ramrod ['ræmrɔd] *s: stiff as a ~* stiv som en pind.
ramshackle ['ræmʃækl] *adj* faldefærdig; vaklevorn.
ran [ræn] *præt* af *run.*
ranch [ra:ntʃ] *s* kvægfarm.
rancid ['rænsid] *adj* harsk.
rancour ['ræŋkə*] *s* bitterhed, nag.
random ['rændəm] *s: at ~* på lykke og fromme; på må og få // *adj* tilfældig; på slump; *~ sample* stikprøve.
randy ['rændi] *adj* (F) liderlig.
rang [ræŋ] *præt* af *ring.*
range [reindʒ] *s* række; (om bjerge) kæde; rækkevidde; udvalg; område; skydebane; skudvidde; (brænde)-komfur // *v* stille op (på række); placere; strejfe om; *~ from ... to ...* variere mellem ... og ...; **~finder** *s* afstandsmåler.
ranger ['reindʒə] *s* skovfoged; parkopsynsmand.
rank [ræŋk] *s* række, geled; *(mil)* grad, rang; (også: *taxi ~*) taxaholdeplads; *close ~s* slutte rækkerne; *the ~ and file (mil)* de menige // *v: ~ among* regnes blandt; være en af; *~ above* stå over, være bedre end // *adj* (alt for) frodig; overgroet; ækel, ram; **~ing-list** *s* rangliste.
rankle ['ræŋkl] *v* nage.
ransack ['rænsæk] *v* ransage; plyndre.
ransom ['rænsəm] *s* løsepenge; *hold sby to ~* kræve løsepenge for en (som man holder fanget).
rant [rænt] *v* skråle, bralre op.
rap [ræp] *s* slag, rap; banken; *take the ~* måtte stå for skud, blive hængt op på det // *v* banke, slå; *~ out* udstøde.
rape [reip] *s* voldtægt; bortførelse; *(bot)* raps // *v* voldtage; røve.
rapid ['ræpid] *adj* hurtig; rivende.
rapidity [ræ'piditi] *s* rivende hast.
rapids ['ræpids] *spl* (i flod) strømhvirvler.
rapist ['reipist] *s* voldtægtsforbryder.
rapport [ræ'pɔ:*] *s* forståelse, bølgelængde.
rapt [ræpt] *adj* betaget; åndeløs; henrykt; *~ in a book* opslugt af en bog.
rapture ['ræptʃə*] *s* henrykkelse, ekstase; *go into ~s over sth* falde i svime over ngt.
rare [rɛə*] *adj* sjælden; usædvanlig; (om bøf etc) halvstegt, rød; (om luft) tynd; **~bit** *s* se *Welsh.*
rarefy ['rɛərifai] *v* fortynde(s); svække.
rarely ['rɛəli] *adv* sjældent.
rarity ['rɛəriti] *s* sjældenhed.
rascal [ra:skl] *s* slyngel, skurk.
rash [ræʃ] *s* udslæt; mylder; stribe; *come out in a ~* få udslæt („røde knopper) // *adj* overilet, forhastet.
rasher ['ræʃə*] *s* tynd skive.
rasp [ra:sp] *s* rasp; raspen // *v* raspe; skurre; snerre.
raspberry ['ra:zbəri] *s* hindbær; *blow a ~* (F) råbe øv.
rasping ['ra:spiŋ] *adj* skurrende (fx *voice* stemme).
rat [ræt] *s* rotte; *smell a ~* lugte lunten, få mistanke // *v: ~ on sby* (F) lade en i stikken; "stikke" en.
rate [reit] *s* takst; procent; sats; *at any ~* i hvert fald; *at this ~* på denne måde // *v* vurdere; regne; regnes; *~ sby among* regne en blandt; **~able value** *s* skatteværdi; **~ of exchange** *s* valutakurs; **~payer** *s* (kommunal) skatteyder.
rates ['reits] *spl* kommunalskat; *~ and taxes* kommune- og statsskatter.

rather ['ra:ðə*] *adv* hellere; helst; snarere; temmelig, ret; *it's ~ expensive* det er temmelig dyrt; *I would ~ you did it* jeg vil helst have at du gør det; *I ~ think he has forgotten* jeg tror næsten han har glemt det; *it's ~ a shame* det er næsten synd; *is he rich? ~!* er han rig? ja, mon ikke!

ratification [rætifi'keiʃən] *s* stadfæstelse.

ratify ['rætifai] *v* stadfæste; anerkende.

rating ['reitiŋ] *s* vurdering; tjenestegrad; klasse; oktantal; **~s** statistiske oplysninger; seertal.

ratio ['reiʃiəu] *s* forhold.

ration ['ræʃən] *s* ration; *on ~* rationeret // *v* rationere; **~al** *adj* rationel, fornuftig.

rationalize ['ræʃənəlaiz] *v* rationalisere.

rationing ['ræʃəniŋ] *s* rationering.

rat-race ['rætreis] *s* rotteræs.

rattle [rætl] *s* raslen, klirren; rallen; rangle, skralde // *v* rasle, klirre; ralle; rasle med; gøre nervøs (,forfjamsket); *~ off* rable af sig; *~ on* knevre videre; **~ snake** *s* klapperslange.

ratty ['ræti] *adj* sær, knotten.

raucous ['rɔ:kəs] *adj* ru, hæs.

ravage ['rævidʒ] *v* plyndre, hærge; **~s** ['rævidʒiz] *spl* plyndring, ødelæggelse.

rave [reiv] *v* fable, tale i vildelse; rase; *~ about sth* fable om ngt, være vild med ngt.

ravel ['rævəl] *v* filtre; trævle; *~ out* trævle op; udrede.

raven ['reivən] *s* ravn // *adj* ravnsort.

ravenous ['rævinəs] *adj* skrupsulten; glubende.

rave-up ['reivʌp] *s* (F) abegilde.

ravine [rə'vi:n] *s* slugt, bjergkløft.

raving ['reiviŋ] *adj: he's a ~ lunatic* han er rablende gal; *~ mad* bindegal.

ravish ['ræviʃ] *v* henrykke; *(gl)* voldtage; **~ing** *adj* henrivende.

raw [rɔ:] *adj* rå; uforarbejdet; hudløs; uøvet; *get a ~ deal* blive skidt behandlet; *touch a ~ nerve* ramme et ømt punkt; *in the ~* (F) splitterfornøjet (,-nøgen) **~ material** *s* råvare, råstof.

ray [rei] *s* stråle; *(zo)* rokke; *a ~ of hope* et svagt håb.

raze [reiz] *v* rive ned til grunden, jævne med jorden.

razor ['reizə*] *s* barbermaskine; barberkniv; **~ blade** *s* barberblad; **~-edge** *s: rest on a ~-edge (fig)* stå på vippen; **~-sharp** *adj* knivskarp.

RC fork.f. *Roman Catholic.*

Rd fork.f. *road.*

R.E. (fork.f. *religious education)* (skolefag) bibelshistorie.

re [ri:] *præp* angående.

reach [ri:tʃ] *s* rækkevidde; strækning; *out of ~* uden for rækkevidde; *within ~* indenfor rækkevidde; *within easy ~ (of)* i umiddelbar nærhed (af) // *v* række, strække; nå (til); kontakte; *~ out for* række ud efter.

react [ri'ækt] *v* reagere *(to* på).

reaction [ri'ækʃən] *s* reaktion.

reactionary [ri'ækʃənri] *adj* reaktionær.

reactor [ri'æktə*] *s* reaktor; reagens.

read [ri:d] *v (read, read* [rɛd]) læse; forstå, opfatte; studere (fx *law* jura; aflæse; *~ out (loud)* læse op; *do you ~ me?* forstår du hvad jeg mener? *have a ~ing knowledge of French* kunne læse fransk; *~ a paper* holde et foredrag // *adj* [rɛd] læst; *be well ~* være belæst; **~able** ['ri:dəbl] *adj* letlæselig; læseværdig.

reader ['ri:də*] *s* læser; oplæser; aflæser; læsebog; litterær konsulent; *(univ)* sv.t. universitetslektor, docent; **~ship** *s* læserskare; lektorat, docentur.

readily ['rɛdili] *adv* gerne; let, hurtigt.

readiness ['rɛdinis] *s* beredskab; beredvillighed; *in ~* parat.

reading ['ri:diŋ] *s* læsning; læsestof; opfattelse; (om måler etc) visning; **~ glasses** *spl* læsebriller; **~ knowledge** *s: have a ~ knowledge of Greek* kunne læse græsk.

readjust ['ri:ədʒʌst] *v* tilpasse; ændre,

omstille; **~ment** *s* tilpasning; ændring.
ready ['rɛdi] *adj* parat, beredt; villig; *be ~ to cry* være lige ved at græde; *get ~* gøre sig klar; *~ wit* slagfærdighed; **~ cash** *s* rede penge; **~-cooked** *adj* (om mad) færdiglavet; **~-made** *adj* færdiglavet; færdigsyet; **~-mix** *s* (til kager, creme etc) færdig pulverblanding; **~-to-serve** *adj* serveringsklar; **~-to-wear** *adj* færdigsyet.
real [riəl] *adj* virkelig, reel; ægte; *is it for ~?* er det for alvor? *it's the ~ thing* det er den ægte vare; **~ beer** *s* fadøl; **~ estate** *s* fast ejendom; **~ estate agent** *s* ejendomsmægler.
realism ['riəlizəm] *s* realisme.
realistic [riə'listik] *adj* realistisk.
reality [ri'æliti] *s* virkelighed.
realization [riəlai'zeiʃən] *s* gennemførelse; opfyldelse; opfattelse.
realize ['riəlaiz] *v* gennemføre; realisere; blive klar over, indse.
really ['riəli] *adv* virkelig; *well, ~ John!* John altså! *no, ~?* nej, er det sandt?
realm [rɛlm] *s* (konge)rige.
ream [ri:m] *s: ~s of* masser af, i lange baner.
reap [ri:p] *v* høste; meje; **~er** *s* høstarbejder; høstmaskine.
reappear ['ri:ə'piə*] *v* vise sig igen; dukke op igen; **~ance** *s* genopdukken.
rear [riə*] *s* bagside; bagtrop; *at the ~ of the plane* i bagenden af flyet; *seen from the ~* set bagfra; *bring up to the ~* danne bagtrop // *v* rejse; stille sig på bagbenene, stejle; opdrætte // *adj* bag-; **~-engined** *adj (auto)* med hækmotor; **~guard** *s* bagtrop; **~ lights** *spl* baglygter.
rearm [ri:'a:m] *v* genopruste; **~ament** *s* genoprustning.
rearmost ['riəməust] *adj* bagest(e).
rearrange ['ri:ə'reindʒ] *v* flytte om på; omorganisere.
rear-view ['riəvju:] *adj: ~ mirror* bakspejl.
rear-wheel drive ['riəwi:ldraiv] *s* baghjulstræk.
reason [ri:zn] *s* grund; fornuft, forstand; *there is every ~ to think that...* der er god grund til at tro at...; *listen to ~* tage imod fornuft; *by ~ of* på grund af; *for no ~ at all* helt uden grund; *it stands to ~* det siger sig selv; *everything within ~* alt inden for rimelighedens grænser // *v: ~ that...* slutte sig til at...; *~ with sby* prøve at tale en til fornuft; *~ sth out* gennemtænke ngt; **~able** *adj* fornuftig, rimelig; **~ably** *adv* rimeligt; nogenlunde; **~ing** *s* ræsonnement; tankegang.
reassemble ['ri:ə'sɛmbl] *v* samle(s) igen.
reassume [ri:ə'sju:m] *v* genoptage; genindtage.
reassure [ri:ə'ʃuə*] *v* berolige; **reassuring** *adj* beroligende.
rebate ['ri:beit] *s* rabat; refusion.
rebel *s* [rɛbl] oprører // *v* [ri'bɛl] gøre oprør // *adj* oprørsk; oprørs-.
rebellion [ri'bɛljən] *s* oprør.
rebellious [ri'bɛljəs] *adj* oprørsk.
rebirth ['ri:'bə:θ] *s* genfødsel.
rebound [ri'baund] *v* springe tilbage; give bagslag.
rebuff [ri'bʌf] *s* afvisning; afslag // *v* afvise.
rebuild ['ri:'bild] *v* genopbygge; ombygge.
rebuke [ri'bju:k] *s* irettesættelse; reprimande // *v* irettesætte.
rebut [ri'bʌt] *v* afvise, afslå; modbevise.
recall [ri'kɔ:l] *s* tilbagekaldelse; *(mil)* genindkaldelse; hukommelse; *beyond ~* uigenkaldelig // *v* tilbagekalde; mindes, huske.
recap [ri:'kæp], **recapitulate** [ri:kə'pitʃuleit] *v* resumere, sammenfatte.
recapture [ri:'kæptʃə*] *v* generobre; genvinde.
recede [ri'si:d] *v* vige; trække sig tilbage; dale, gå ned; **receding** *adj* vigende; skrå; *his hair is receding* han er ved at få høje tindinger.
receipt [ri'si:t] *s* kvittering; modtagelse.
receipts [ri'si:ts] *spl* indtægter.
receive [ri'si:v] *v* modtage; få, tage

imod; opsamle; *be on the receiving end* være den det går ud over; ~ *stolen goods* være hæler.

receiver [ri'si:və*] *s* modtager; telefonrør; hæler; *(jur)* bobestyrer (for konkursbo).

recent [ri:snt] *adj* ny, nyere; *in ~ years* i de senere år; **-ly** *adv* for nylig; *as ~ly as* så sent som.

receptacle [ri'sɛptəkl] *s* beholder.

reception [ri'sɛpʃən] *s* modtagelse; reception; **~ desk** *s* (hotel)reception; **-ist** *s* ansat i hotelreception; (hos læge etc) klinikdame; **~ room** *s* (på hotel etc) selskabslokale; (i privat hjem) stue.

receptive [ri'sɛptiv] *adj* modtagelig.

recess ['ri:sɛs] *s* (i rum) niche; alkove; *(parl* etc) ferie.

recession [ri'sɛʃən] *s (økon)* nedgang, tilbagegang.

recharge ['ri:tʃa:dʒ] *v* genoplade.

recherché [rɛ'ʃɛəʃəi] *adj* raffineret, fin; *(neds)* søgt.

recipe ['rɛsipi] *s* madopskrift.

recipient [ri'sipiənt] *s* modtager.

reciprocal [ri'siprəkl] *adj* gensidig, indbyrdes.

reciprocate [ri'siprəkeit] *v* gengælde; udveksle.

recital [ri'saitl] *s* fortælling, recitation; opregning; koncert.

recite [ri'sait] *v* deklamere; berette om; opregne.

reckless ['rɛkləs] *adj* letsindig; hensynsløs.

reckon ['rɛkən] *v* beregne; regne (for); antage, tro; ~ *in* medregne; ~ *on* regne med; ~ *up* tælle sammen; ~ *without* glemme at regne med, ikke regne med; **-ing** *s* regnskab; *the day of ~ing* regnskabets time, dommens dag.

reclaim [ri'kleim] *v* genvinde, indvinde; udvinde; kræve tilbage.

reclamation [rɛklə'meiʃən] *s* genvinding.

recline [ri'klain] *v* læne (sig) tilbage; **reclining** *adj* tilbagelænet.

recluse [ri'klus] *s* eneboer.

recognition [rɛkəg'niʃən] *s* anerkendelse; erkendelse; genkendelse; *transformed beyond ~* forandret til ukendelighed.

recognize ['rɛkəgnaiz] *v* anerkende; erkende; genkende; *I ~d him by his beard* jeg genkendte ham på skægget.

recoil [ri'kɔil] *v* springe (,vige) tilbage; give bagslag; (om gevær) rekylere.

recollect [rɛkə'lɛkt] *v* mindes; huske; tænke efter.

recollection [rɛkə'lɛkʃən] *s* erindring, minde; tænken efter; *to the best of my ~* så vidt jeg kan huske.

recommend [rɛkə'mɛnd] *v* anbefale; foreslå; **-ation** [-'deiʃən] *s* anbefaling; forslag.

recompense ['rɛkəmpɛns] *s* erstatning, godtgørelse; belønning // *v* erstatte; belønne.

reconcile ['rɛkənsail] *v* forlige; ~ *oneself to sth* forsone sig med ngt.

reconciliation [rɛkənsili'eiʃən] *s* forsoning; forening.

recondition [ri:kən'diʃən] *v* ombygge; hovedreparere.

reconnaissance [ri'kɔnisns] *s (mil)* rekognoscering.

reconnoitre [rɛkə'nɔitə*] *v (mil)* rekognoscere.

reconsider ['ri:kən'sidə*] *v* tage under fornyet overvejelse.

reconstruct ['ri:kən'strʌkt] *v* rekonstruere; genopbygge.

reconstruction [ri:kən'strʌkʃən] *s* genopbygning; ombygning.

record *s* ['rɛkɔ:d] fortegnelse; journal; dokument; fortid; generalieblad; papirer; rekord; grammofonplade; *keep a ~ of* føre protokol over; *off the ~* uden for protokollen, uofficielt; *he's on ~ as being...* han er kendt for at være...; *he holds the ~ for running 500 metres* han er indehaver af rekorden i 500-meter løb // *v* [ri'kɔ:d] skrive ned (,op); skildre; optage, indspille, indsynge etc // *adj* rekord-; *in ~ time* på rekordtid; **~-breaking** *adj* rekord-; **~ed delivery** [ri'kɔ:did-] *s* anbefalet forsendelse.

recorder [ri'kɔ:də*] *s* båndoptager; *(mus)* blokfløjte.

record holder ['rɛkɔ:dhəuldə*] *s (sport)* rekordindehaver.
recording [ri'kɔ:diŋ] *s* indspilning; optagelse.
record library ['rɛkɔ:d ˌlaibrəri] *s* musikbibliotek.
record player ['rɛkɔ:d ˌpleiə*] *s* pladespiller.
recount [ri'kaunt] *v* berette om; **recount** *s* ['ri:kaunt] fintælling // *v* [ri:'kaunt] tælle efter.
recourse [ri'kɔ:s] *s: have ~ to sby* ty til en, tage sin tilflugt til en.
recover [ri'kʌvə*] *v* få tilbage; finde igen; komme sig *(from* efter, over); rette sig.
re-cover ['ri:'kʌvə*] *v* ombetrække.
recovery [ri'kʌvəri] *s* genvinding; bedring; helbredelse; *he is past ~* han står ikke til at redde; **~ vehicle** *s* kranbil.
recreate ['ri:kri'eit] *v* forfriske; rekreere sig.
recreation [ri:kri'eiʃən] *s* adspredelse; hobby; **~ ground** *s* rekreativt område.
recriminations [rikrimi'neiʃəns] *spl* gensidige beskyldninger.
recruit [ri'kru:t] *s* rekrut // *v* rekruttere; **~ment** *s* rekruttering.
rectify ['rɛktifai] *v* rette, korrigere; afhjælpe.
rectitude ['rɛktitju:d] *s* retlinethed.
rector ['rɛktə*] *s* sognepræst; rektor.
rectory ['rɛktəri] *s* præstebolig.
recumbent [ri'kʌmbənt] *adj* liggende, hvilende.
recuperate [ri'kju:pəreit] *v* komme sig.
recur [ri'kə:*] *v* vende tilbage; dukke op; gentage sig; **~rence** *s* gentagelse; **~rent** *adj* tilbagevendende.
recycle [ri:'saikl] *v* genbruge, genanvende; **~d** *adj* genbrugs-.
recycling ['ri:saikliŋ] *s* genbrug.
red [rɛd] *s* rødt; (om venstreorienteret person) rød; *in the ~* i gæld; i farezonen // *adj* rød; **~ alert** *s* katastrofealarm; **~breast** *s (zo)* rødkælk; **~ brick** *s* rødsten; **~-brick university** *s* nyere universitet, universitetscenter; **~ cabbage** *s* rødkål; **~ carpet treatment** *s* fyrstelig modtagelse; **Red Cross** *s* Røde Kors; **~ currant** *s* ribs; **~ deer** *s* kronhjort.
redden [rɛdn] *v* rødme.
reddish ['rɛdiʃ] *adj* rødlig.
redecorate ['ri:'dɛkəreit] *v* nyistandsætte.
redeem [ri'di:m] *v* løskøbe; indløse; indfri; forløse; **~ing** *adj* formildende.
redemption [ri'dɛmpʃən] *s* indløsning; indfrielse; opfyldelse; frelse.
red... [rɛd-] sms: **~-haired** *adj* rødhåret; **~-handed** *adj: be caught ~-handed* blive grebet på fersk gerning; **~head** *s* rødhåret person; **~ herring** *s* falsk spor; **~-hot** *adj* rødglødende; *(fig)* brandaktuel; **Red Indian** *s* indianer.
redirect ['ri:dərɛkt] *v* omdirigere; omadressere.
redistribute ['ri:dis'tribju:t] *v* omfordele.
red led ['rɛd 'lɛd] *s* mønje.
Red-letter day ['rɛdlɛtə ˌdei] *s* mærkedag.
red light district ['rɛd 'lait ˌdistrikt] *s* bordelkvarter.
redo ['ri:'du:] *v* nyistandsætte; gøre igen.
redolent ['rɛdələnt] *adj: be ~ of* smage af; være fuld af; lugte af.
redouble [ri:'dʌbl] *v* fordoble.
redoubtable [ri'dautəbl] *adj* formidabel; frygtindgydende.
redress [ri'drɛs] *v* råde bod på; genoprette.
red-tape ['rɛd'teip] *s* papirnusseri, bureaukrati.
reduce [ri'dju:s] *v* nedsætte; reducere; *~ speed now* sæt farten ned nu; *be ~d to sth* være blevet ngt; være henvist til ngt; *the cottage was ~d to ashes* huset blev lagt i aske (dvs. brændte); *~ sby to tears* få en til at græde.
reduction [ri'dʌkʃən] *s* nedsættelse; indskrænkning; *~ for cash* kontantrabat.
redundancy [ri'dʌndənsi] *s* overskud; arbejdsløshed (p.g.a. nedskærin-

ger); ~ **money** *s* fratrædelsesgodtgørelse.
redundant [ri'dʌndənt] *adj* overflødig; arbejdsløs; ~ *manpower* overskydende (fristillet) arbejdskraft.
reed [ri:d] *s* (tag)rør; (om klarinet etc) rør(blad).
re-edit [ri:'ɛdit] *v* omredigere; genudgive.
reef [ri:f] *s* rev, skær.
reefer ['ri:fə*] *s* vams, pjækkert; (S) cigaret af tobak + marihuana.
reef knot ['ri:f ˌnɔt] *s* råbåndsknob.
reek [ri:k] *s* stank // *v:* ~ *of (,with)* stinke af.
reel [ri:l] *s* rulle, trisse; (på fiskestang) hjul; (til film etc) spole // *v* vinde; spole (op); snurre; slingre, svaje; ~ *sth off* lire ngt af.
re-elect [ri:i'lɛkt] *v* genvælge; **re-election** *s* genvalg.
re-enter ['ri:'ɛntə*] *v* komme ind igen; **re-entry** *s* tilbagevenden.
re-establish [ri:i'stæbliʃ] *v* genoprette.
refer [ri'fə:*] *v:* ~ *to* henvise til; tilskrive; angå; omtale; hentyde til; *~ring to your letter* under henvisning til Deres brev.
referee [rɛfə'ri:] *s (sport)* dommer.
reference ['rɛfrəns] *s* henvisning; forbindelse; omtale; anbefaling; *(i ordbog etc)* opslagsord; *with ~ to* under henvisning til; *make ~ to* hentyde til; ~ **book** *s* opslagsbog; håndbog.
referendum [rɛfə'rɛndəm] *s (pl: referenda)* folkeafstemning.
referral [ri'fə:rəl] *s* henvisning.
refill *s* ['ri:fil] stift, patron; ny påfyldning // *v* [ri:'fil] efterfylde; sætte ny stift (,patron etc) i.
refine [ri'fain] *v* rense; (om olie, sukker) raffinere; forfine; **~d** *adj* forfinet; raffineret; **~ment** *s* forædling.
refinery [ri'fainəri] *s* raffinaderi.
refit [ri:'fit] *v* nyistandsætte.
reflect [ri'flɛkt] *v* genspejle, reflektere; kaste tilbage; tænke efter; ~ *on* tænke over; kaste skygge over.
reflection [ri'flɛkʃən] *s* genspejling; eftertanke, overvejelse; *on ~* ved nærmere eftertanke.
reflective [ri'flɛktiv] *adj* eftertænksom; refleks-.
reflector [ri'flɛktə*] *s* reflektor; refleks(mærke).
reflex ['ri:flɛks] *s* refleks, afspejling.
reflexive [ri:'flɛksiv] *adj (gram)* tilbagevisende, refleksiv.
reflux ['ri:flʌks] *s* tilbageløb.
reforestation ['ri:fɔrəs'teiʃən] *s* genplantning af skov.
reform [ri'fɔ:m] *s* reform // *v* reformere; forbedre.
re-form [ri:'fɔ:m] *v* omdanne; rekonstruere.
reformation [rɛfə'meiʃən] *s* reformation; forbedring.
reformer [ri'fɔ:mə*] *s* reformator.
reformist [ri'fɔ:mist] *adj* reformvenlig; reform-.
refract [ri'frækt] *v* (om lys) bryde.
refractory [ri'fræktəri] *adj* genstridig, stædig; ildfast; modstandsdygtig.
refrain [ri'frein] *s* omkvæd, refræn // *v:* ~ *from* afholde sig fra.
refresh [ri'frɛʃ] *v* forfriske; styrke; genopfriske; forny; **~er course** *s* genopfriskningskursus; **~ing** *adj* forfriskende; læskende; **~ment room** *s* buffet, restaurant; **~ments** *spl* forfriskninger.
refrigerator [ri'fridʒəreitə*] *s* køleskab.
refuel ['ri:'fjuəl] *v* tanke op; få brændstof på.
refuge ['rɛfju:dʒ] *s* tilflugt(ssted); (på gaden) helle; *take ~ in* søge ly i.
refugee [rɛfju'dʒi:] *s* flygtning.
refund *s* ['ri:fʌnd] refundering, godtgørelse // *v* [ri'fʌnd] refundere.
refurbish [ri:'fə:biʃ] *v* pudse op; renovere.
refusal [ri'fju:zl] *s* afslag; *have first ~ on sth* have forkøbsret til ngt; *meet with a flat ~* få et blankt afslag.
refuse *s* ['rɛfju:s] affald, skrald // *v* [ri'fju:z] nægte; afslå, afvise.
refuse ['rɛfju:z-] sms: ~ **chute** *s* affaldsskakt; ~ **collection** *s* renovation; ~ **collector** *s* skraldemand; ~ **disposal unit** *s* affaldskværn; ~ **dump** *s* losseplads.
refute [ri'fju:t] *v* gendrive.
regain [ri'gein] *v* få tilbage, genvinde;

nå tilbage til; ~ *consciousness* komme til bevidsthed.
regal [ri:gl] *adj* kongelig; prægtig; konge-.
regale [ri'geil] *v:* ~ *sby with sth* diske op med ngt for en.
regalia [ri'geiliə] *spl* kronregalier; *be in full* ~ være i fuld galla.
regard [ri'ga:d] *s* agtelse; hensyn; blik; *give my ~s to your wife* hils din kone fra mig; *with kindest ~s* med venlig hilsen; *hold sby in high* ~ have stor respekt for en; *in this* ~ hvad det angår; *with* ~ *to cars* hvad angår biler // *v* agte; angå; betragte, anse; *as ~s, ~ing* hvad angår, med hensyn til; **~less** *adj: ~less of* uden hensyn til, uanset.
regency ['ri:dʒənsi] *s* rigsforstanderskab; **Regency style** *s* eng. stil fra 1811-20, sv.t. empirestil.
regenerate [ri'dʒɛnəreit] *v* genskabe; regenerere.
regent ['ri:dʒənt] *s* regent; rigsforstander.
regime [rei'ʒi:m] *s* regime.
regimen ['rɛdʒimən] *s* diæt, kur.
regiment ['rɛdʒimənt] *s* regiment.
region ['ri:dʒən] *s* område, region; (skotsk, *adm)* sv.t. amt.
regional ['ri:dʒənəl] *adj* regional-, distrikts-, egns-; ~ **council** *s* sv.t. amtsråd; ~ **council district** *s* sv.t. amtskommune; ~ **development** *s* egnsudvikling.
register ['rɛdʒistə*] *s* register; liste; protokol; *the ~ of births, marriages and deaths* sv.t. folkeregistret // *v* registrere, vise; skrive ind; indskrive sig; *has it ~ed with John too?* er det også sivet ind hos John? **~ed** *adj* (ind)registreret; mønsterbeskyttet; (om brev) anbefalet.
registrar ['rɛdʒistra:*] *s* registrator; giftefoged; sv.t. vicedommer; (på sygehus) sv.t. reservelæge.
registration [rɛdʒi'streiʃən] *s* (ind)registrering; indskrivning; (også ~ *number)* bilregistreringsnummer.
registry ['rɛdʒistri] *s* indskrivningskontor; *(jur)* dommerkontor; ~ **office** *s* sv.t. folkeregister; *get married in a ~ office* blive borgerligt viet.
regression [ri'grɛʃən] *s* tilbagegang.
regret [ri'grɛt] *s* beklagelse; anger, sorg; *much to my* ~ til min store sorg; *send one's ~s* melde afbud // *v* beklage, fortryde; sørge over; **~fully** *adv* beklageligvis; beklagende; **~table** *adj* beklagelig.
regroup [ri:'gru:p] *v* omgruppere (sig).
regular ['rɛgjulə*] *s* stamkunde; fastansat // *adj* regelmæssig; fast; normal; regulær; ordinær; *a ~ bastard* (S) en rigtig lort.
regularity [rɛgju'læriti] *s* regelmæssighed.
regularly ['rɛgjuləli] *adv* regelmæssigt.
regulate ['rɛgjuleit] *v* regulere.
regulation [rɛgju'leiʃən] *s* regulering; reglement; bestemmelse.
rehabilitation ['ri:həbili'teiʃən] *s* rehabilitering; revalidering; genoptræning.
rehash ['ri:'hæʃ] *s* opkog // *v* (F) koge suppe på; give et opkog.
rehearsal [ri'hə:səl] *s* prøve; øvelse.
rehearse [ri'hə:s] *v* prøve; indstudere; holde prøve; øve (sig).
rehouse [ri:hauz] *v* genhuse.
reign [rein] *s* regering(stid) // *v* regere, herske; **~ing** *adj* regerende; førende.
reimburse ['ri:im'bə:s] *v* erstatte, refundere; **~ment** *s* tilbagebetaling, refusion.
rein [rein] *s* (til hest) tømme; (til barn) sele; *give a free ~ to sby* give en frie hænder; *keep a tight ~ on sby* holde en i stramme tøjler.
reindeer ['reindiə*] *s* rensdyr, ren.
reinforce ['ri:in'fɔ:s] *v* forstærke; bestyrke; **~d concrete** *s* jernbeton; **~ment** *s* forstærkning; armering.
reinstate [ri:in'steit] *v* genindsætte; genoprette.
reissue ['ri:'isju:] *v* genudsende; genoptrykke.
reiterate [ri:'itəreit] *v* gentage.
reject *s* ['ri:dʒɛkt] udskudsvare // *v* [ri'dʒɛkt] forkaste, vrage; kassere.
rejection [ri:'dʒɛkʃən] *s* forkastelse; afslag.

rejoice [ri'dʒɔis] *v* glæde (,fryde) sig *(at, in* over); ~ *in the name of John* lyde navnet John.
rejoin [ri'dʒɔin] *v* svare; stemme i; genforenes med.
rejuvenate [ri'dju:vəneit] *v* forynge; forfriske.
rekindle [ri:'kindl] *v* tænde igen; blusse op igen.
relapse [ri'læps] *s* tilbagefald // *v* falde tilbage; få tilbagefald.
relate [ri'leit] *v* berette; bringe i relation; ~ *to* angå, vedrøre; **~d** *adj* beslægtet *(to* med).
relating [ri'leitiŋ] *adj:* ~ *to* angående.
relation [ri'leiʃən] *s* beretning; forhold, forbindelse; slægtning; *in* ~ *to* i forhold til; **~ship** *s* forhold; slægtskab.
relative ['rɛlətiv] *s* slægtning // *adj* relativ; gensidig; ~ *to* vedrørende; **~ly** *adv* forholdsvis.
relax [ri'læks] *v* slappe af, slappe, løsne; slække på.
relaxation [rilæk'seiʃən] *s* (af)slappelse; afspænding, afslapning.
relay ['ri:lei] *s* stafetløb; hold; omgang; relæ; *work in ~s* arbejde i skift // *v* (re)transmittere; viderebringe.
release [ri'li:s] *s* løsladelse; befrielse; udløsning; (om gas etc) udslip; (om film etc) udsendelse; *(foto)* udløser; *press* ~ pressemeddelelse // *v* befri; løslade; udsende; slå fra (fx *the brake* bremsen); lade slippe ud; ~ *one's grip* slippe taget; ~ *the clutch* slippe koblingen.
relegate ['rɛligeit] *v* forvise; degradere, nedrykke; henvise.
relent [ri'lɛnt] *v* lade sig formilde; **~less** *adj* ubarmhjertig; uforsonlig.
relet ['ri:'lɛt] *v* fremleje.
relevance ['rɛləvəns] *s* relevans; ~ *to* tilknytning til.
relevant ['rɛləvənt] *adj* vedkommende, relevant.
reliability [rilaiə'biliti] *s* pålidelighed.
reliable [ri'laiəbl] *adj* pålidelig; driftsikker.
reliably [ri'laiəbli] *adv: it's ~ informed that...* det meddeles fra pålidelig kilde at...
reliance [ri'laiəns] *s* tillid; afhængighed.
relic ['rɛlik] *s* levn, minde; relikvie.
relief [ri'li:f] *s* befrielse; lindring; lettelse; hjælp; aflastning; *(mil)* afløsning; afløser; relief; ~ **bus** *s* ekstrabus.
relieve [ri'li:v] *v* befri; lindre; (af)hjælpe; fritage; afløse; *we were ~d to hear it* vi var lettede over at høre det; ~ *oneself* tisse.
religion [ri'lidʒən] *s* religion.
religious [ri'lidʒəs] *adj* religiøs.
relinquish [ri'liŋkwiʃ] *v* opgive; slippe; frafalde.
relish ['rɛliʃ] *s* velsmag; nydelse; *(gastr)* smagstilsætning; sovs; chutney // *v* give smag til; nyde; synes om; ~ *of* smage af.
reload ['ri:ləud] *v* omlade; lade igen.
relocate ['ri:ləu'keit] *v* (for)flytte.
reluctance [ri'lʌktəns] *s* modvillighed.
reluctant [ri'lʌktənt] *adj* modvillig, treven.
rely [ri'lai] *v:* ~ *on* stole på; være afhængig af.
remain [ri'mein] *v* være tilbage (,tilovers); blive; vedblive; forblive; restere, mangle; *that ~s to be seen* det vil tiden vise.
remainder [ri'meində*] *s* rest.
remaining [ri'meiniŋ] *adj* resterende.
remains [ri'meinz] *spl* rester, levninger.
remake ['ri:meik] *s (film)* nyindspilning // *v* lave om.
remand [ri'ma:nd] *s* varetægtsfængsling // *v:* ~ *sby into custody* varetægtsfængsle en.
remark [ri'ma:k] *s* bemærkning // *v* bemærke; ~ *on sth* udtale sig om ngt, kommentere ngt; **~able** *adj* bemærkelsesværdig; mærkelig.
remarry [ri:'mæri] *v* gifte sig igen.
remedial [ri'mi:diəl] *adj* hjælpe-; ~ **exercises** *spl* sygegymnastik.
remedy ['rɛmədi] *s* middel; lægemiddel // *v* afhjælpe; afbøde.
remember [ri'mɛmbə*] *v* huske, mindes; tænke på; ~ *me to your wife* hils din kone fra mig; *as far as I can* ~ så vidt jeg husker.

remembrance [ri'mɛmbrəns] *s* minde; erindringsgave.
remind [ri'maind] *v: ~ sby of sth* minde en om ngt; *~ sby to do sth* minde en om at han (,hun) skal gøre ngt; **~er** *s* påmindelse; rykkerskrivelse.
reminiscences [rɛmi'nisənsiz] *spl* minder, erindringer.
reminiscent [rɛmi'nisənt] *adj: be ~ of* minde om.
remiss [ri'mis] *adj* forsømmelig.
remission [ri'miʃən] *s* eftergivelse; *(med)* bedring.
remit [ri'mit] *v* eftergive; udskyde; henvise; sende (penge); betale; **~tance** *s* pengeforsendelse, anvisning.
remnant ['rɛmnənt] *s* (lille) rest.
remonstrate ['rɛmənstreit] *v* protestere.
remorse [ri'mɔ:s] *s* samvittighedsnag, anger; **~ful** *adj* angerfuld; **~less** *adj* ubarmhjertig; skrupelløs.
remote [ri'məut] *adj* fjern, afsidesliggende; utilnærmelig; *I haven't got the ~st* jeg har ingen anelse om det; **~ control** *s* fjernstyring; **~-control(led)** *adj* fjernstyret; **~ly** *adv* svagt, fjernt; *it's not ~ly like him* det ligner ham ikke spor (,det fjerneste).
remould ['ri:məuld] *s* slidbanedæk.
removable [ri'mu:vəbl] *adj* flytbar.
removal [ri'mu:vəl] *s* fjernelse; flytning; afskedigelse; **~ company** *s* flyttefirma.
remove [ri'mu:v] *v* flytte, fjerne; afskedige.
remover [ri'mu:və*] *s* farve- og lakfjerner; neglelakfjerner.
removers [ri'mu:vəz] *spl* flyttefirma.
remuneration [rimju:nə'reiʃən] *s* belønning; løn.
renaissance [ri'neisəns] *s* renæssance.
renal ['ri:nəl] *adj* nyre-.
rename [ri:'neim] *v* omdøbe.
rend [rɛnd] *v (rent, rent)* sønderrive, flænge; splittes.
render ['rɛndə*] *v* give; afgive; gøre; gengive; **~ing** *s* fortolkning, gengivelse.
rendez-vous ['rɔndivu:] *s* mødested // *v* mødes.
renegade ['rɛnigeid] *s* frafalden, desertør; overløber.
renew [ri'nju:] *v* forny; genoptage; **~able** *adj* som kan fornys; *~able energy* vedvarende energi.
renewal [ri'nju:əl] *s* fornyelse; forlængelse.
rennet ['rɛnit] *s* osteløbe.
renounce [ri'nauns] *v* frafalde; give afkald på; fornægte.
renovate ['rɛnəveit] *v* modernisere; renovere.
renovation [rɛnə'veiʃən] *s* istandsættelse.
renown [ri'naun] *s* ry; **~ed** *adj* berømt.
rent [rɛnt] *s* husleje; leje // *v* leje; udleje; (se også *rend).*
rental ['rɛntl] *s* leje; *(tlf)* abonnement.
renunciation [rinʌnsi'eiʃən] *s* frafald; opgivelse; fornægtelse.
reopen ['ri:'əupən] *v* genåbne; genoptage.
reorder ['ri:'ɔ:də*] *v* genbestille; omdanne.
reorganize [ri:'ɔ:gənaiz] *v* omorganisere.
rep [rɛp] *s* (F) repræsentant.
repair [ri'pɛə*] *s* reparation; vedligeholdelse; *in good (,bad) ~* godt (,dårligt) vedligeholdt; *it's beyond ~* den kan ikke repareres; *road ~s* vejarbejde; *put sth in for ~* sende ngt til reparation // *v* reparere; rette (fx *a mistake* en fejltagelse); **~ kit** *s* reparationsæske; lappegrejer; **~man** *s* reparatør; **~ shop** *s* reparationsværksted.
reparation [rɛpə'reiʃən] *s* erstatning; oprejsning.
repartee ['rɛpa:'ti:] *s* kvikt (gen)svar; pingpong med ord.
repatriate [ri:'pætrieit] *v* hjemsende.
repay [ri'pɛi] *v* betale tilbage; gengælde; **~ment** *s* tilbagebetaling.
repeat [ri'pi:t] *s* gentagelse; (i tv etc) genudsendelse // *v* gentage; fortælle videre; repetere; **~edly** *adv* gentagne gange, igen og igen; **~ order** *s* genbestilling.
repel [ri'pɛl] *v* slå tilbage; frastøde; sky.

repellent [ri'pɛlənt] *s: insect* ~ insektbeskyttelsesmiddel // *adj* -skyende; frastødende.
repent [ri'pɛnt] *v:* ~ *(of)* angre, fortryde; **~ance** *s* anger.
repercussion [ri:pə'kʌʃən] *s* genlyd, genklang; **~s** *spl* efterdønninger.
repertory ['rɛpətəri] *s* repertoire.
repetition [rɛpi'tiʃən] *s* gentagelse, repetition.
repetitive [ri'pɛtitiv] *adj* som gentager sig.
replace [ri'pleis] *v* lægge (,sætte etc) på plads; erstatte; afløse; udskifte; **~ment** *s* erstatning; udskiftning; reserve; **~ment part** *s* reservedel.
replay ['ri:plei] *s* gentagelse; omkamp.
replenish [ri'plɛniʃ] *v* fylde efter; supplere op.
replete [ri'pli:t] *adj* propfuld.
replica ['rɛplikə] *s* (tro) kopi, genpart.
replicate ['rɛplikeit] *v* kopiere.
reply [ri'plai] *s* svar; *in* ~ *to* som svar på // *v* svare.
report [ri'pɔ:t] *s* rapport; reportage; (om skud) brag; karakterbog // *v* rapportere; melde; indberette; aflægge beretning; ~ *to sby* melde sig hos en; ~ *sick* melde sig syg; *be* ~*ed missing* blive meldt savnet; *it is* ~*ed that* det forlyder at; **~er** *s* journalist.
repose [ri'pəuz] *s* hvile, ro // *v* hvile, ligge.
repository [ri'pɔzitəri] *s* opbevaringssted, lager; *be a* ~ *of knowledge* have et stort fond af viden.
reprehend [rɛpri'hɛnd] *v* dadle, klandre.
reprehensible [rɛpri'hɛnsibl] *adj* forkastelig.
represent [rɛpri'zɛnt] *v* forestille; fremstille; repræsentere; stå for; **~ation** [-'teiʃən] *s* fremstilling; repræsentation.
representative [rɛpri'zɛntətiv] *s* repræsentant // *adj* repræsentativ; karakteristisk.
repress [ri'prɛs] *v* holde nede; undertrykke; fortrænge.
repression [ri'prɛʃən] *s* undertrykkelse; fortrængning.
repressive [ri'prɛsiv] *adj* underkuende; repressiv.
reprieve [ri'pri:v] *s* henstand, udsættelse // *v: be* ~*d* blive benådet; få henstand.
reprimand ['rɛprima:nd] *s* reprimande, irettesættelse // *v* give en næse.
reprint *s* ['ri:print] genoptryk; særtryk // *v* [ri:'print] genoptrykke.
reprisal [ri'praizl] *s* gengældelse; repressalier.
reproach [ri'prəutʃ] *s* bebrejdelse; vanære // *v:* ~ *sby with sth* bebrejde en ngt; *beyond* ~ dadelfri; **~ful** *adj* bebrejdende.
reproduce [ri:prə'dju:s] *v* fremstille igen; formere sig; gengive, reproducere.
reproduction [ri:prə'dʌkʃən] *s* genfremstilling; gengivelse; formering; **reproductive** *adj* forplantnings-.
reproof [ri'pru:f] *s* irettesættelse.
reprove [ri'pru:v] *v* irettesætte.
reptile ['rɛptail] *s* krybdyr.
republican [ri'pʌblikən] *s* republikaner // *adj* republikansk.
repudiate [ri'pju:dieit] *v* afvise; ikke vedkende sig, fornægte.
repugnant [ri'pʌgnənt] *adj* frastødende.
repulse [ri'pʌls] *v* slå tilbage; afvise.
repulsion [ri'pʌlʃən] *s* væmmelse, afsky; tilbagestød.
repulsive [ri'pʌlsiv] *adj* frastødende.
reputable ['rɛpjutəbl] *adj* agtet, anerkendt.
reputation [rɛpju'teiʃən] *s* ry, omdømme; *have a* ~ *for being sth* have ord for at være ngt.
repute [ri'pju:t] *s* ry.
reputed [ri'pju:tid] *adj* anset; **~ly** *adv* efter sigende.
request [ri'kwɛst] *s* anmodning; *do sth at* ~ gøre ngt på opfordring // *v* anmode om, bede om; **~ programme** *s* ønskeprogram; **~ stop** *s* stoppested hvor der kun holdes når ngn skal af el. på.
require [ri'kwaiə*] *v* kræve; behøve, trænge til; påbyde; **~d** *adj* påbudt; ønsket; *if* ~*d* hvis det ønskes; **~ment** *s* krav; betingelse; behov.

requisite ['rɛkwizit] *s* fornødenhed; *toilet ~s* toiletsager // *adj* fornøden.
requisition [rɛkwi'ziʃən] *s* betingelse; krav // *v* rekvirere.
requital [ri'kwaitl] *s* gengældelse.
re-route ['ri:'ru:t] *v* omlægge (trafik).
re-run ['ri:'rʌn] *s* reprise.
resale ['ri:seil] *s* videresalg.
rescue ['rɛskju:] *s* redning; undsætning; *come to the ~* komme til undsætning // *v* redde; undsætte; **~ party** *s* redningsmandskab; **~r** *s* redningsmand.
research [ri'sə:tʃ] *s* forskning; undersøgelse // *v* foretage undersøgelser, forske; **~er** *s* forsker; **~ fellow** *s* forskningsstipendiat; **~ worker** *s* forsker.
resemblance [ri'zɛmbləns] *s* lighed.
resemble [ri'zɛmbl] *v* ligne.
resent [ri'zɛnt] *v* være krænket; ikke kunne lide; *he ~ed my having bought the car* han tog mig det ilde op at jeg havde købt bilen; **~ful** *adj* vred; fornærmet; bitter; **~ment** *s* krænkelse; vrede; bitterhed.
reservation [rɛzə'veiʃən] *s* pladsbestilling; forbehold; (på vej, også: *central ~*) midterrabat; reservat; *with certain ~s* med visse forbehold.
reserve [ri'zə:v] *s* reserve; reservat; forbehold // *v* reservere; holde tilbage; (forud)bestille; forbeholde sig; **~d** *adj* reserveret.
reservoir ['rɛzəvwa:*] *s* beholder, bassin, reservoir.
reset [ri:'sɛt] *v* indstille igen; nulstille.
reshuffle ['ri:'ʃʌfl] *s* (om kort) ny blanding; (også: *cabinet ~*) regeringsomdannelse.
reside [ri'zaid] *v* bo, residere.
residence ['rɛzidəns] *s* ophold; bopæl; beboelse; residens.
resident ['rɛzidənt] *s* beboer // *adj* fastboende; hjemmehørende.
residential [rɛzi'dɛnʃəl] *adj* bolig-, beboelses-; *~ area* beboelseskvarter; (ofte) villakvarter.
residual [ri'zidjuəl] *adj* resterende, rest-.
residue ['rɛzidju:] *s* rest.
resign [ri'zain] *v* opgive; sige op; gå af, træde tilbage; *~ oneself to sth* affinde sig med ngt.
resignation [rɛzig'neiʃən] *s* opsigelse; afgang; opgivelse; affindelse.
resigned [ri'zaind] *adj* resigneret.
resilience [ri'ziliəns] *s* elasticitet; ukuelighed; **resilient** *adj* fjedrende; ukuelig.
resin ['rɛzin] *s* harpiks.
resist [ri'zist] *v* modstå; gøre modstand (mod); kunne stå for.
resistance [ri'zistəns] *s* modstand; modstandskraft; modstandskamp.
resistant [ri'zistənt] *adj* modstandsdygtig; *be ~ to* (også) være modstander af.
resolute ['rɛzəlu:t] *adj* resolut, beslutsom.
resolution [rɛzə'lu:ʃən] *s* opløsning; *(tekn)* opløsningsevne; løsning; beslutsomhed; beslutning.
resolve [ri'zɔlv] *s* beslutsomhed // *v* beslutte; opløse(s); løse; **~d** *adj* fast besluttet.
resonant ['rɛzənənt] *adj* som giver genlyd, rungende.
resort [ri'zɔ:t] *s* tilholdssted; udvej; *as a last ~* som en sidste udvej; *in the last ~* i sidste ende; *holiday ~* feriested; *without ~ to force* uden at gribe til magtmidler // *v: ~ to* ty til, gribe til.
resound [ri'zaund] *v* genlyde *(with* af); runge; *a ~ing success* en bragende succes.
resource [ri'sɔ:s] *s* hjælpekilde, ressource; udvej; *he's a man of ~* han ved råd for alt; han er opfindsom; **~ful** *adj* opfindsom.
resources [ri'sɔ:siz] *spl* forråd; midler; *natural ~* naturrigdomme; *be left to one's own ~* blive overladt til sig selv.
respect [ri'spɛkt] *s* respekt; hensyn; henseende; *with ~ to* med hensyn til; *in this ~* i denne henseende; *I hold him in great ~* jeg har stor respekt for ham; *pay one's ~s to sby* gøre en sin opvartning; *give my ~s to him* hils ham; *without ~ to* uden

hensyn til, uanset; **~able** *adj* respektabel; **~ful** *adj* ærbødig.
respective [ri'spɛktiv] *adj* respektive; **~ly** *adv* henholdsvis.
respiration [rɛspi'reiʃən] *s* åndedræt.
respiratory [rɛ'spirətəri] *adj* åndedræts-; *the ~ tract* luftvejene.
respite ['rɛspait] *s* henstand; udsættelse.
resplendent [ri'splɛndənt] *adj* strålende.
respond [ri'spɔnd] *v* svare; reagere (*to* på).
response [ri'spɔns] *s* svar; reaktion; *in ~ to* som svar på.
responsibility [rispɔnsi'biliti] *s* ansvar; *accept ~ for* påtage sig ansvaret for.
responsible [ri'spɔnsibl] *adj* ansvarlig; ansvarsbevidst; *be held ~ for sth* blive gjort ansvarlig for ngt; *he was not ~ this time* det var ikke hans skyld denne gang.
responsive [ri'spɔnsiv] *adj* interesseret; lydhør; svar-.
rest [rɛst] *s* hvile; pause; læn, støtte; rest; *take a ~* holde hvil; *be at ~* hvile; ligge (,sidde etc) stille; *put her mind at ~* berolige hende; *come to ~* falde til ro; *the ~ of them* resten af dem, de andre; *and all the ~ of it* og alt det andet // *v* hvile (sig); støtte, læne; *~ on* hvile på; støtte sig til; *feel ~ed* føle sig udhvilet; *it ~s with him to...* det er op til ham at...; *~ assured that...* du kan være sikker på at...; **~ful** *adj* rolig; **~ home** *s* hvilehjem.
restitution [rɛsti'tju:ʃən] *s* tilbagegivelse; genoprettelse.
restive ['rɛstiv] *adj* urolig; utålmodig.
restless ['rɛstlis] *adj* urolig; hvileløs.
restoration [rɛstə'reiʃən] *s* restaurering; genoprettelse; tilbagegivelse.
restore [ri'stɔ:*] *v* restaurere; genoprette (fx *peace* freden); gengive.
restrain [ri'strein] *v* holde tilbage; betvinge, holde nede; *~ oneself* styre sig; *~ one's tears* holde tårerne tilbage; **~ed** *adj* behersket.
restraint [ri'streint] *s* tvang; tilbageholdenhed.
restrict [ri'strikt] *v* begrænse; **~ed area** *s (auto)* område med fartbegrænsning; *(mil)* forbudt område.
restriction [ri'strikʃən] *s* begrænsning; restriktion.
restrictive [ri'striktiv] *adj* indskrænkende.
result [ri'zʌlt] *s* resultat; *as a ~ of* som følge af, fordi // *v: ~ from* hidrøre fra; *~ in* resultere i, ende med.
resume [ri'zju:m] *v* tage igen; genoptage (fx *work* arbejdet); fortsætte.
resumption [ri'zʌmpʃən] *s* genoptagelse.
resurface ['ri:'sə:fis] *v* dykke (,dukke) op (igen), komme op til overfladen; give ny belægning.
resurgence [ri'sə:dʒəns] *s* genopståen; genopblomstring.
resurrection [rɛzə'rɛkʃən] *s* genopstandelse; genoplivelse.
resuscitate [ri'sʌsiteit] *v* genoplive.
resuscitation [risʌsi'teiʃən] *s* genoplivelse.
retail ['ri:teil] *s* (om salg) detail // *v* sælge en detail; bringe videre; **~er** *s* detailhandler; **~ price** *s* detailpris.
retain [ri'tein] *v* holde (på); bibeholde; beholde; **~er** *s* forskud; indskud; **~ing wall** *s* støttemur, -væg.
retaliate [ri'tælieit] *v* gøre gengæld.
retaliation [ritæli'eiʃən] *s* gengæld; repressalier.
retarded [ri'ta:did] *adj* forsinket; tilbagestående, retarderet.
retch [rɛtʃ] *v* gøre brækbevægelser.
retell ['ri:tɛl] *v* genfortælle.
retention [ri'tɛnʃən] *s* tilbageholdelse; bibeholdelse; hukommelse.
retentive [ri'tɛntiv] *adj: a ~ memory* en god hukommelse, en klæbehjerne.
reticence ['rɛtisns] *s* tilbageholdenhed.
reticent ['rɛtisnt] *adj* tilbageholdende; tavs; forbeholden.
retina ['rɛtinə] *s (anat)* nethinde (i øjet).
retinue ['rɛtinju:] *s* følge.
retire [ri'taiə*] *v* trække sig tilbage; tage sin afsked; gå i seng; **~d** *adj* pensioneret; forhenværende; **~ment** *s* pensionering; *early ~ment* førtidspensionering.

retort [ri'tɔ:t] *s* skarpt svar // *v* svare igen, give svar på tiltale.
retouch [ri'tʌtʃ] *v* retouchere.
retrace [ri'treis] *v: ~ one's steps* gå samme vej tilbage.
retract [ri'trækt] *v* trække tilbage, trække ind; tage tilbage.
retrain ['ri:'trein] *v* genoptræne; omskole.
retread ['ri:trɛd] *s* slidbanedæk.
retreat [ri'tri:t] *s* tilbagetog; tilflugtssted; *beat the ~* trække sig tilbage; *(fig)* trække i land // *v* trække sig tilbage, vige.
retrench [ri'trɛntʃ] *v* skære ned på; indskrænke.
retribution [rɛtri'bju:ʃən] *s* gengældelse; straf.
retrieval [ri'tri:vəl] *s* genfindelse; godtgørelse; *beyond ~* håbløs, uigenkaldelig.
retrieve [ri:tri:v] *v* få tilbage, genfinde; råde bod på.
retrorocket ['rɛtrəu,rɔkit] *s* bremseraket.
retrospect ['rɛtrəspɛkt] *s* tilbageblik; *in ~* når man ser tilbage.
retrospective [rɛtrə'spɛktiv] *adj* tilbageskuende, retrospektiv.
return [ri'tə:n] *s* tilbagevenden; tilbagelevering; betaling; gengæld; *(merk* etc) udbytte; beretning; (i sms) retur-; *in ~* til gengæld; *on his ~* da han kom tilbage; *we have reached the point of no ~* der er ingen vej tilbage; (se også *returns)* // *v* vende tilbage; returnere; gengælde; give fortjeneste; indberette; **~able** *adj* (om flaske etc) retur-; **~ match** *s* returkamp; **~s** *spl* returgods; overskud, udbytte; *tax ~s* selvangivelse; *many happy ~s!* til lykke (med fødselsdagen)! **~ ticket** *s* returbillet.
reunion [ri:'juniən] *s* genforening; møde.
reunite ['ri:ju:'nait] *v* genforene(s); mødes igen.
rev [rɛv] *s* (fork.f. *revolution) (auto)* omdrejning // *v: ~ (up)* speede motoren op; *the engine is ~ving* motoren er ved at varme op.
Rev. fork.f. *Reverend.*
revaluation [ri:vælju'eiʃən] *s* revaluering; omvurdering.
revamp [ri:'væmp] *v* pudse op, "shine" op.
reveal [ri'vi:l] *v* afsløre; røbe; **~ing** *adj* afslørende.
revel ['rɛvəl] *v: ~ in sth* svælge i ngt; nyde ngt i fulde drag.
revelation [rɛvə'leiʃən] *s* afsløring; åbenbaring.
revelry ['rɛvlri] *s* festen; sviren; svælgen.
revenge [ri'vɛndʒ] *s* hævn; hævnlyst; (i sport, spil etc) revanche // *v* hævne; **~ful** *adj* hævngerrig.
revenue ['rɛvənju:] *s* indtægter (se også: *Inland Revenue).*
reverberate [ri'və:bəreit] *v* genlyde.
revere [ri'viə*] *v* agte, ære.
reverence ['rɛvərəns] *s* ærefrygt; velærværdighed.
reverend ['rɛvərənd] *s* (om præst) ærværdig; *the Reverend (,Rev.) John Smith* pastor Smith.
reverent ['rɛvərənt] *adj* ærbødig.
reverie ['rɛvəri] *s* drømmeri.
reverse [ri'və:s] *s* det modsatte; bagside; vrang; (også: *~ gear)* bakgear; *it's quite the ~* det er lige modsat // *v* vende (om); ændre; slå 'om; *(jur)* omstøde; *(auto)* bakke, sætte i bakgear // *adj* modsat, omvendt; **~-charge call** *s (tlf)* opringning som modtageren betaler.
reversible [ri'və:sibl] *adj* vendbar; vende-.
revert [ri'və:t] *v: ~ to* komme tilbage til; vende tilbage til.
review [ri'vju:] *s* tilbageblik; overblik; anmeldelse (af bog etc); tidsskrift; revy // *v* gennemgå (igen); inspicere; anmelde; **~er** *s* anmelder.
revise [ri'vaiz] *v* gennemse, revidere; rette.
revision [ri'viʒən] *s* revision.
revisit [ri:'vizit] *v* besøge igen.
revival [ri'vaivəl] *s* genoplivelse; genoptagelse.
revive [ri'vaiv] *v* live (,leve) op igen; blomstre op igen; genoptage; genopfriske.

revoke [ri'vəuk] *v* kalde tilbage; tage tilbage.

revolt [ri'vəult] *s* oprør // *v* gøre oprør; væmmes; **~ing** *adj* frastødende; oprørende; oprørsk.

revolution [rɛvə'lu:ʃən] *s* revolution; omdrejning, omløb; **~ary** *s/adj* revolutionær; **~ counter** *s* omdrejningstæller.

revolutionize [rɛvə'lu:ʃənaiz] *v* revolutionere.

revolve [ri'vɔlv] *v* dreje; løbe rundt; **~r** *s* revolver.

revolving [ri'vɔlviŋ] *adj* roterende, dreje-; *~ door* svingdør; *~ stage* drejescene.

revue [ri'vju:] *s* revy.

revulsion [ri'vʌlʃən] *s* modvilje; væmmelse; afsky.

reward [ri'wɔ:d] *s* belønning, dusør // *v* belønne, lønne; **~ing** *adj* lønnende; lønsom; udbytterig.

rewind ['ri:'waind] *v* spole tilbage; (om ur) trække op.

rewire ['ri:'waiə*] *v: ~ a house* trække nye elektriske ledninger i et hus.

rhetoric ['rɛtərik] *s* talekunst, retorik.

rheumatic [ru:'mætik] *adj* reumatisk, gigt-.

rheumatism ['ru:mətizm] *s* reumatisme, gigt.

rhinoceros [rai'nɔsərəs] *s* næsehorn.

rhubarb ['ru:ba:b] *s* rabarber.

rhyme [raim] *s* rim, vers // *v* rime; skrive rim.

rhythm [riðm] *s* rytme; **~ic(al)** ['riθmikl] *adj* rytmisk.

rib [rib] *s (anat)* ribben; ribbensstykke; ribstrikning; ribbe // *v* lave sjov med; **~bed** [ribd] *adj* ribstrikket; ribbet, riflet.

ribbon ['ribn] *s* bånd; strimmel; farvebånd; *tear sth to ~s* rive ngt i stumper og stykker.

rib-cage ['ribkeidʒ] *s* brystkasse.

rice [rais] *s* ris; *ground ~* rismel; **~ paddy** *s* rismark; **~ pudding** *s* sv.omtr.t. risengrød.

rich [ritʃ] *adj* rig; værdifuld; righoldig; fed (fx *sauce* sovs); *that's a bit ~!* nej, den er for tyk! **~es** *spl* rigdomme.

rickets ['rikits] *s (med)* engelsk syge.

rickety ['rikiti] *adj* vaklevorn; leddeløs.

rid [rid] *v (rid, rid): ~ sby of sth* befri en for ngt; *get ~ of* blive af med; skille sig af med; **~dance** ['ridəns] *s* befrielse; *good ~dance!* godt af vi slap af med...!

ridden [ridn] *pp* af *ride* // *adj* plaget *(by* af); *doubt-~* naget af tvivl; *disease-~* sygdomsplaget.

riddle [ridl] *s* gåde // *v: ~ sby with bullets* gennemhulle en med kugler; *~d with mistakes* smækfuld af fejl.

ride [raid] *s* tur (til hest, i bil, på cykel etc); *take sby for a ~* tage en med på en tur; *(fig)* lave numre med en // *v (rode, ridden* [rəud, ridn]) ride; køre (på, i, med); sidde; *~ at anchor* ligge for anker; *~ out a storm* ride stormen af; *~ to hounds* drive rævejagt; *her skirt rode up* hendes nederdel gled op.

rider ['raidə*] *s* rytter; tillæg.

ridge [ridʒ] *s* ryg; højderyg, ås; bjergkam; næseryg; **~pole** *s* (i telt) overligger.

ridicule ['ridikju:l] *s* latterliggørelse // *v* gøre til grin.

ridiculous [ri'dikjuləs] *adj* latterlig.

riding ['raidiŋ] *s* ridning; **~ crop** *s* ridepisk; **~ habit** *s* ridedragt.

rife [raif] *adj* udbredt; fremherskende; *be ~ with* vrimle med.

riffle [rifl] *v* bladre i.

riffraff ['rifræf] *s* rak, pøbel.

rifle [raifl] *s* gevær, riffel // *v* røve, plyndre; *~ through* gennemrode; **~ range** *s* skudhold; skydebane.

rift [rift] *s* spalte, sprække.

rig [rig] *s (mar)* rig; udstyr; (også: *oil ~*) boretårn; boreplatform; antræk // *v* rigge til; *~ an election* lave valgsvindel; *~ out* maje (sig) ud; *~ up* rigge sammen; lave svindel med; **~ging** *s* rigning.

right [rait] *s* ret; rettighed; højre; *by ~s* egentlig; hvis det gik rigtigt til; *on the ~* på højre hånd; *be in the ~* have ret // *v* rette (til); ordne; gøre godt (igen) // *adj/adv* lige; rigtigt; helt; (til) højre; *be ~* have ret; være rigtig; *put sth* ~ bringe orden i ngt, ordne ngt; *(not)* ~ *now* (ikke) lige nu; ~ *against the wall* helt op mod muren; ~ *ahead* lige frem; ~ *away* straks, med det samme; ~ *in the middle* lige i midten; ~ *through* helt igennem; *turn* ~ dreje til højre; ~ *about turn! (mil)* højre om! ~ *you are!* godt! ok! *serves you* ~*!* det har du rigtig godt af! ~ **angle** *s* ret vinkel.

righteous ['raitʃəs] *adj* retfærdig.

right... sms: **~ful** *adj* retmæssig; **~-hand drive** *s (auto)* højrestyring; **~-handed** *adj* højrehåndet; **~-hand side** *s* højre side; **~ist** *s/adj* højreorienteret; **~-minded** *adj* retsindig; rettænkende; **~ of way** *s* forkørselsret; **~ wing** *s* højrefløj.

rigid ['ridʒid] *adj* stiv; streng, ubøjelig.

rigidity [ri'dʒiditi] *s* stivhed; usmidighed.

rigmarole ['rigmərəul] *s* lang remse; forvrøvlet sludder.

rigor mortis ['rigə'mɔ:tis] *s* dødsstivhed.

rigorous ['rigərəs] *adj* streng, hård.

rigour ['rigə*] *s* strenghed.

rig-out ['rigaut] *s* antræk.

rile [rail] *v* irritere, ærgre.

rim [rim] *s* rand; bræmme; (om briller) indfatning.

rime [raim] *s* rim(frost).

rimless ['rimləs] *adj* (om briller) uindfattet.

rimmed [rimd] *adj* kantet; indfattet.

rind [raind] *s* skræl; skal; (om bacon) svær; (om ost) skorpe.

ring [riŋ] *s* ring; kreds; klang; ringen; *give sby a* ~ ringe til en // *v (rang, rung* [ræŋ, rʌŋ]) ringe; ringe på; klinge, lyde; telefonere til; *it* ~*s true* det lyder sandt; ~ *the bell* ringe med klokken; ringe 'på; *that* ~*s a bell* det minder mig om ngt; ~ *off (tlf)* ringe af; ~ *out* lyde; ringe ud; **~ binder** *s* ringbind; **~leader** *s* anfører, hovedmand.

ringlet ['riŋlit] *s* slangekrølle.

rink [riŋk] *s* skøjtebane.

rinse [rins] *s* skylning; toning (af hår); skyllemiddel // *v* skylle; tone.

riot [raiət] *v* lave optøjer // *s: a* ~ *of colours* et farveorgie; *run* ~ løbe grassat; *he's a* ~ (F) han er enormt festlig; **~er** *s* urostifter.

riotous ['raiətəs] *adj* løssluppen.

riots ['raiəts] *spl* uroligheder, optøjer.

riot squad ['raiət ˌskwɔd] *s* (om politi) uropatrulje.

rip [rip] *s* flænge, rift // *v* rive, flå; trævle op; sprætte op; **~cord** *s* udløsersnor (i fx faldskærm).

ripe [raip] *adj* moden *(for* til); **~n** *v* modne(s); udvikle sig.

rip-off ['ripɔ:f] *s: it was a* ~ (F) det var ren(e) ågerpris(er).

ripple [ripl] *s* krusning; lille bølge // *v* kruse (sig); skvulpe.

rip-roaring ['rip'rɔ:riŋ] *adj* (F) løssluppen.

rise [raiz] *s* skråning; forhøjning; stigning; lønforhøjelse; rejsning; udspring; *give* ~ *to* fremkalde, give anledning til // *v (rose, risen* [rəuz, rizn]) rejse sig; stå 'op; stige, hæve sig; (om fisk) bide 'på; (om fugl) lette; stamme *(from* fra); ~ *above* være hævet over; ~ *to the bait* bide på krogen; ~ *to the occasion* være situationen voksen; ~ *in the world* komme frem i verden; **~r** ['raizə*] *s: be an early* ~*r* stå tidligt op.

rising ['raiziŋ] *s* opstand; stigning.

risk [risk] *s* risiko, fare; *take (,run) the* ~ *of* risikere at; *put sth at* ~ sætte ngt på spil; *be at* ~ være i fare; *let's* ~ *it* lad os tage chancen; *at one's own* ~ på egen risiko // *v* risikere; indlade sig på; **~y** *adj* risikabel, farlig.

risqué [ris'kei] *adj* vovet.

rissole ['rissəul] *s* sv.t. kroket, frikadelle.

rite [rait] *s* ceremoni; ritus; *the last* ~*s* den sidste olie.

ritual ['ritjuəl] *s* ritual // *adj* rituel.

rival [raivl] *s* rival; konkurrent // *v* rivalisere med; kappes med // *adj* konkurrerende; **~ry** *s* rivalisering, kappestrid.

river ['rivə*] *s* flod; strøm; *the* ~ *Thames* Themsen; **~bank** *s* flodbred; **~bed** *s* flodleje; **~side** *s* flod-

bred; *a ~side house* et hus ved floden.
rivet ['rivit] *s* nagle, nitte // *v* nitte, klinke; **~ing** *adj* fascinerende.
rivulet ['rivjulit] *s* bæk.
RN fork.f. *Royal Navy.*
road [rəud] *s* vej; *by ~* med bil; *along the ~* henad vejen (også *fig); he lives down the ~* han bor (længere) nede ad vejen; "*~ up*" "vejarbejde"; *one for the ~* en afskedsdrink; **~ accident** *s* trafikulykke; **~block** *s* vejspærring; **~hog** *s* motorbølle; **~ map** *s* vejkort; **~ safety** *s* trafiksikkerhed; **~side** *s* vejside, vejkant; **~sign** *s* vejskilt; færdselstavle; **~ surface** *s* vejbelægning; **~-test** *v* prøvekøre; **~ user** *s* trafikant; **~way** *s* vejbane, kørebane; **~works** *spl* vejarbejde; **~worthy** *adj* køredygtig; vejsikker.
roam [rəum] *v* strejfe om.
roar [rɔ:*] *s* brøl(en); vræl; buldren, larm // *v* brøle; vræle; buldre; bruse; drøne.
roaring ['rɔ:riŋ] *adj: ~ drunk* drønfuld; *a ~ fire* en buldrende ild; *a ~ success* en bragende succes; *a ~ trade* et strygende salg.
roast [rəust] *s* steg // *v* stege; riste // *adj* stegt; **~ chicken** *s* stegt kylling; **~ duck** *s* andesteg; **~ pork** *s* flæskesteg; **~ potatoes** *spl* bagte kartofler.
rob [rɔb] *v* røve; (ud)plyndre; *~ sby of sth* røve ngt fra en; berøve en ngt.
robber ['rɔbə*] *s* røver.
robbery ['rɔbəri] *s* røveri; udplyndring; *armed ~* væbnet røveri; *~ with violence* røverisk overfald.
robe [rəub] *s* (til fx dommer, præst) lang dragt, kjole; (også: *bath~*) badekåbe; gevandt // *v* iklæde.
robin ['rɔbin] *s* rødkælk.
robot ['rəubɔt] *s* robot.
robust [rə'bʌst] *adj* robust, solid.
rock [rɔk] *s* klippe; skær; bjergart; rokken; (S) ædelsten, diamant; rock; *on the ~s* (om drink) med isterninger; (om ægteskab) ved at lide skibbrud; *(økon)* konkurs // *v* vugge, gynge; ryste; vippe; **~-bottom** *s (fig)* lavpunkt.
rocker ['rɔkə*] *s* gyngestol; gænge; rocker; *be off one's ~* være skør.
rockery ['rɔkəri] *s* (i have) stenhøjsparti.
rocket ['rɔkit] *s* raket; skideballe, fur // *v: ~ (off)* (F) drøne af sted.
rock... ['rɔk-] sms: **~ face** *s* klippevæg; **~fall** *s* klippeskred; **~ing chair** *s* gyngestol; **~ing horse** *s* gyngehest.
rocky ['rɔki] *adj* klippefuld; klippe-; vaklende.
rod [rɔd] *s* kæp, stang; fiskestang; (i skole) spanskrør.
rode [rəud] *præt* af *ride.*
rodent ['rəudnt] *s (zo)* gnaver.
roe [rəu] *s* rogn; rådyr.
rogue [rəug] *s* skurk, slyngel; skælm.
roguish ['rəugiʃ] *adj* slyngelagtig; skælmsk.
role [rəul] *s* rolle.
roll [rəul] *s* rulle; rullen; liste; *(gastr)* sv.t. blødt rundstykke // *v* rulle, trille; tromle; valse; *~ by* (om tid) gå; *~ in* strømme ind; *~ one's eyes* rulle med øjnene; *he's better than Casanova and Don Juan ~ed into one* han er bedre end Casanova og Don Juan tilsammen; *~ over* vende sig; vælte; *~ up* rulle (sig) sammen; (om fx ærmer) smøge op; **~ call** *s* navneopråb, appel; **~ed gold** *s* gulddublé; **~ed oats** *spl* (valsede) havregryn; **~ed-up** *adj* sammenrullet; oprullet.
roller ['rəulə*] *s* valse, rulle; hårrulle; tromle; **~coaster** *s* rutschebane; **~ skates** *spl* rulleskøjter.
rollick ['rɔlik] *v* slå sig løs; **~ing** *adj* overstadig; hylende grinagtig.
rolling ['rəuliŋ] *adj* rullende; rulle-; (om landskab) kuperet, bølgende; *he's ~ in it* (F) han vælter sig i penge; **~ pin** *s* kagerulle; **~ stock** *s (jernb)* rullende materiel.
roll-neck ['rəulnɛk] *s* rullekrave.
roll-top desk ['rəultɔp,dɛsk] *s* jalousiskrivebord.
Roman ['rəumən] *s* romer // *adj* romersk; romer- (fx *numeral* tal); **~ Catholic** *s* katolik // *adj* romersk katolsk.

romance [rəu'mæns] *s* romantisk historie, romance; kærlighedsaffære // *v* fantasere; overdrive.

Romanesque [rəumə'nɛsk] *adj* (om stilart) romansk, rundbue-.

Romania [rəu'meiniə] *s* Rumænien; **~n** *s* rumæner // *adj* rumænsk.

romantic [rəu'mæntik] *adj* romantisk; eventyrlig.

romanticism [rəu'mæntisizəm] *s* (om kunst etc) romantik.

romp [rɔmp] *v:* ~ *(about)* boltre sig.

rompers ['rɔmpəz] *spl* kravledragt.

roof [ru:f] *s* tag; *the ~ of the mouth* ganen; *raise the ~ (fig)* få taget til at løfte sig; *go through the ~ (fig)* flyve helt op i loftet (af raseri); (om pris) blive skyhøj // *v* lægge tag på; tække; **~ garden** *s* tagterrasse; **~ing** *s* tagbeklædning; tag; **~ing felt** *s* tagpap; **~ rack** *s* tagbagagebærer.

rook [ru:k] *s* råge; (i skak) tårn.

room [ru:m] *s* værelse, rum; stue; plads; *men's ~* herretoilet; *ladies' ~* dametoilet; *make ~ for* gøre plads til; *there's plenty of ~* der er masser af plads; *~ to let* værelse til leje; *~ and board* kost og logi; **~mate** *s* værelsekammerat; **~s** *spl* (ung)karlelejlighed; *live in ~s* bo i (lejede) værelser; **~ temperature** *s* stuetemperatur.

roomy ['ru:mi] *adj* rummelig.

rooster ['ru:stə*] *s (zo)* hane.

root [ru:t] *s* rod; *(fig)* kerne; *square ~* kvadratrod; *take ~* slå rod // *v* slå rod; rode, rage; *~ about* rode rundt (i); *~ for sby* heppe en; *~ out* rykke op med rode; udrydde; **~crops** *spl* rodfrugter; **~ed** *adj: deeply ~ed* indgroet, *be ~ed in* have sine rødder i, komme fra; *~ed to the spot* (som) naglet til stedet.

rope [rəup] *s* reb, tov; *know the ~s* kende fiduserne; *give him more ~* give ham friere tøjler (, en længere snor); *be on the ~s* være ude i tovene // *v* binde med reb; indhegne med tove; *~ sby in* indfange (,kapre) en; **~ ladder** *s* rebstige.

rosary ['rəuzəri] *s (rel)* rosenkrans.

rose [rəuz] *s* rose; roset; (på vandkande) bruser // *præt* af *rise* // *adj* rosen-; **~bed** *s* rosenbed; **~bud** *s* rosenknop; **~hip** *s* hyben.

rosemary ['rəuzməri] *s* rosmarin.

rosewood ['rəuzwud] *s: (Brazilian) ~* palisander.

roster ['rɔstə*] *s* tjenesteliste, vagtskema.

rostrum ['rɔstrəm] *s* talerstol, podium; sejrsskammel.

rosy ['rəuzi] *adj* rosenrød.

rot [rɔt] *s* forrådnelse; råddenskab; sludder, vrøvl; *don't talk ~!* hold op med det sludder! *dry ~* (i hus etc) svamp; *oh ~!* pokkers også! // *v* rådne; mørne.

rota ['rəutə] *s* liste, turnus; *on a ~ basis* efter tur.

rotary ['rəutəri] *adj* roterende; rotations-.

rotate [rəu'teit] *v* rotere, dreje (sig); arbejde efter tur; skifte afgrøder; **rotating** *adj* roterende.

rotation [rəu'teiʃən] *s* rotation, omdrejning; skiften; *crop ~ (agr)* vekseldrift.

rote [rəut] *s: learn sth by ~* lære ngt udenad.

rotten [rɔtn] *adj* rådden; mørnet; korrumperet; (F) elendig, skidt; *feel ~* have det skidt.

rotter ['rɔtə*] *s* skidt fyr, lort.

rotund ['rəutʌnd] *adj* rund.

rouble [ru:bl] *s* rubel.

rough [rʌf] *s* bølle; rå diamant // *v* være grov; *~ it* leve primitivt // *adj* ru, grov, ujævn; hård, barsk; usleben; løselig (fx *calculation* beregning); *sleep ~* sove hvor det bedst kan falde sig; *cut up ~* blive grov.

roughage ['rʌfidʒ] *s* kostfibre.

rough copy ['rʌf 'kɔpi] *s* kladde.

rough customer ['rʌf 'kʌstəmə*] *s* ballademager.

rough draft ['rʌf 'dra:ft] *s* udkast.

roughen [rʌfn] *v* gøre (,blive) grov (,ru).

roughly ['rʌfli] *adv* groft; hårdhændet; cirka, omtrent.

Roumania [ru:'meiniə] *s* Rumænien.

round [raund] *s* kreds, ring; runde;

omgang; (om læge) sygebesøg; *(mus)* kanon; (om kød) skive, stykke; *go the ~s (med)* gå stuegang; (også:) gå en runde; *paper ~* avisrunde // *v* afrunde; runde; dreje (sig); *~ off* afrunde; slutte; *~ up* indkredse; omringe og fange; (om beløb) runde op // *adj* rund // *præp* rundt om; omkring; om // *adv* rundt; om(kring); uden om; *all the way ~* hele vejen rundt; *the long way ~* ad en omvej; *all the year ~* hele året (rundt); *~ the clock* døgnet rundt; *it's just ~ the corner* det er lige om hjørnet; *go ~* gå omkring; gå uden om; *go ~ to sby's house* gå hen og besøge en; *go ~ an obstacle* gå uden om en forhindring; *go ~ the back* gå ind ad bagindgangen; *go ~ a house* gå rundt i (,inspicere) et hus; *it's the other way ~* det er omvendt; *look ~ the house* se sig om i huset; **~about** *s* rundkørsel; karrusel // *adj* indirekte; *in a ~about way* ad omveje; **~ed** *adj* afrundet; fyldig; **~ly** *adv* rundt; ligefrem; i store træk; **~-shouldered** *adj* rundrygget; **~-the-clock** *adj* døgn-; **~ trip** *s* ud- og hjemrejse; **~up** *s* sammentrommen (af folk); sammenfatning; razzia.

rouse [rauz] *v* vække; vågne op; ruske op i; tirre.

rout [raut] *v* jage væk; flygte; rode (op i); *~ out* støve op; jage ud.

route [ru:t] *s* rute // *v* dirigere.

routine [ru:'ti:n] *s* rutine, arbejdsgang; formalitet // *adj* rutinemæssig; rutine-.

roux [ru:] *s (gastr)* opbagning.

rove [rəuv] *v* strejfe (om); flakke; *his eyes ~d the house* han lod blikket glide hen over huset; **roving** *adj* omstrejfende.

row [rəu] *s* række; (i strikning) pind, omgang; rotur; *in a ~* på rad // *v* ro; ro om kap med.

row [rau] *s* skænderi, ballade; *kick up a ~* lave en scene, skabe sig // *v* skælde ud; skændes.

rowan ['rəuən] *s: ~ (tree)* røn; **~berry** *s* rønnebær.

rowdy ['raudi] *s* bølle // *adj* bølleagtig, larmende.

rowing ['rəuiŋ] *s* roning; **~ boat** *s* robåd.

rowlock ['rɔlək] *s* åregaffel.

royal ['rɔiəl] *adj* kongelig; konge-.

royalty ['rɔiəlti] *s* kongelighed; kongelig(e) person(er); licensafgift; forfatterhonorar, royalty.

rpm (fork.f. *revs per minute)* omdrejninger pr. minut (o/m).

RSPCA (fork.f. *Royal Society for the Prevention of Cruelty to Animals)* sv.t. Foreningen til Dyrenes Beskyttelse.

RSPCC (fork.f. *Royal Society for the Prevention of Cruelty to Children)* kongeligt selskab til forebyggelse af børnemishandling.

RSVP (fork.f. *répondez s'il vous plaît)* svar udbedes (S.U.).

rub [rʌb] *s* (af)gnidning; ujævnhed; ulempe // *v* gnide, gnubbe; viske (med viskelæder); *~ down* strigle; frottere; slibe; vaske af; *don't ~ it in!* lad være med at tvære i det! *~ off on* smitte af på; *~ sby up the wrong way (fig)* stryge en mod hårene.

rubber ['rʌbə*] *s* gummi; viskelæder; (F) kondom; **~ band** *s* elastik, gummibånd; **~ dinghy** *s* gummibåd; **~ stamp** *s* gummistempel; **~-stamp** *v* stemple; godkende.

rubbery ['rʌbəri] *adj* gummiagtig.

rubbish ['rʌbiʃ] *s* affald, skrald; *(fig)* vrøvl; møg; *it's a load of ~* det er ngt værre vrøvl; **~ bin** *s* skraldebøtte; **~ chute** *s* affaldsskakt; **~ dump** *s* losseplads; **~ tip** *s* losseplads.

rubble [rʌbl] *s* murbrokker; grus.

rubicund ['ru:bikənd] *adj* rødmosset.

ruby ['ru:bi] *s* rubin; rubinrødt.

rucksack ['rʌksæk] *s* rygsæk.

ructions ['rʌkʃənz] *spl* ballade.

rudder ['rʌdə*] *s* (på fly el. skib) ror.

ruddy ['rʌdi] *adj* rødmosset; rødlig; (F) pokkers.

rude [ru:d] *adj* grov; uhøflig, ubehøvlet; uanstændig; **~ness** *s* uforskammethed.

rudimentary [ru:di'mɛntəri] *adj* elementær; rudimentær.

rudiments ['ru:dimənts] *spl* elementær viden (,kundskaber etc).
rueful ['ru:ful] *adj* bedrøvet; bedrøvelig.
ruff [rʌf] *s* pibekrave.
ruffian ['rʌfiən] *s* bandit; voldsmand.
ruffle [rʌfl] *s* flæse, rynket strimmel // *v* (om hår) pjuske, ugle; (om tøj) bringe i uorden; *(fig)* støde, krænke.
rug [rʌg] *s* lille tæppe.
rugged ['rʌgid] *adj* ujævn; forreven; (om ansigt) markeret; grov, knudret; barsk.
rugger ['rʌgə*] *s* (F) rugby(fodbold).
ruin ['ru:in] *s* ruin; undergang // *v* ruinere; ødelægge; **ruinous** *adj* ødelæggende.
rule [ru:l] *s* regel; målepind, lineal; styre, regering; *as a ~* som regel; *play by the ~s* overholde spillets regler // *v* styre, herske (over), regere; råde; *(jur)* afgive kendelse; liniere; *~ out* udelukke; **~d** *adj* (om papir) linieret.
ruler ['ru:lə*] *s* hersker, statschef; lineal.
ruling ['ru:liŋ] *s (jur)* kendelse // *adj* herskende, gældende.
rum [rʌm] *s* (om drik) rom // *adj* mærkelig, underlig.
Rumania [ru:'meiniə] *s* d.s.s. *Romania.*
rumble [rʌmbl] *s* rumlen, bulder // *v* rumle, buldre; knurre; **rumbling** *s* rumlen, buldren; murren.
ruminate ['ru:mineit] *v* tygge drøv (på).
rummage ['rʌmidʒ] *v* ransage, gennemsøge; rode *(for* efter).
rumour ['ru:mə*] *s* rygte // *v: it was ~ed that...* det rygtedes at...; man sagde at...
rump [rʌmp] *s* ende, rumpe, gump; *(gastr)* halestykke.
rumple [rʌmpl] *v* krølle; ugle.
rumpsteak ['rʌmpsteik] *s* bøf af tykstegen.
rumpus ['rʌmpəs] *s* (F) ståhej; ballade.
run [rʌn] *s* løb; løbetur; køretur; kørsel; strækning; efterspørgsel, run; *make a ~ for it* stikke af; *go for a ~* køre en tur; *break into a ~* sætte i løb; *in the long ~* i det lange løb; *in the short ~* på kort sigt; *be on the ~* være på flugt; *have the ~ of a place* have et sted til fri disposition // *v (ran, run)* løbe; strømme; deltage i løb; køre; gå; sejle; jage, drive; lede; stille op; *I'll ~ you to the station* jeg kører dig til stationen; *~ a bath* tappe vand i badekarret; *~ a risk* løbe en risiko; *it ~s in the family* det er ngt der ligger til familien; *~ a temperature* have feber; *~ about* løbe rundt; *~ across* løbe 'på, møde tilfældigt; *~ away* løbe væk; *~ down* løbe ned (ad); være udkørt; *~ for* løbe efter; *~ for it* løbe for at prøve at nå ngt; *~ for Parliament* stille op som kandidat ved parlamentsvalg; *~ into* støde ind i; løbe på; *~ off* stikke af, flygte; *~ out* løbe ud, udløbe; løbe tør; *~ out of* løbe tør for; *~ out on sby* svigte en; *~ over* køre over; *~ short of sth* være ved at løbe tør for ngt; *~ through* løbe igennem; bruge op; *~ up* løbe op; *~ up against* komme op imod; **~away** *adj* undsluppen, undvegen; (om hest) løbsk; *a ~away inflation* galoperende inflation; **~-down** *s* rapport; indskrækning // *adj* udkørt; faldefærdig.
rung [rʌŋ] *s* (på stige) trin; (i hjul) ege // *v pp* af *ring.*
runic ['ru:nik] *adj* rune- (fx *stone* sten).
runner ['rʌnə*] *s* løber; (på slæde etc) mede; (på skøjte) klinge; *(bot)* udløber; **~ bean** *s (bot)* pralbønne; **~-up** *s: be a ~-up* komme ind (i mål etc) som nummer to.
running ['rʌniŋ] *s* løb; drift; køreforhold // *adj* løbende, rindende; *a ~ start* en flyvende start; *six days ~* seks dage i træk.
runny ['rʌni] *adj* som løber (fx *nose* næse); rindende (fx *eyes* øjne).
runt [rʌnt] *s* kuld; (om person) lille gnom.
run-through ['rʌnθru:] *s* hurtig gennemgang.

run-up ['rʌnʌp] *s* opløb, slutspurt.
runway ['rʌnwei] *s (fly)* startbane; landingsbane.
rupture ['rʌptʃə*] *s* brud; sprængning; *(med)* brok // *v* sprænge(s), briste; ~ *oneself* få brok.
rural ['ruərəl] *adj* landlig, land-.
ruse [ru:z] *s* list, kneb.
rush [rʌʃ] *s (bot)* siv; strøm; tilstrømning; brusen; hast, jag; *be in a* ~ have travlt; *the Christmas* ~ juletravlheden // *v* bringe i en fart; storme, styrte (sig); jage, skynde sig; *don't* ~ *me!* lad være med at jage med mig! *be* ~*ed to hospital* blive kørt på hospitalet i en fart.
rushes ['rʌʃiz] *spl* siv, rør.
rush... ['rʌʃ-] sms: **~hour** *s* myldretid; **~ job** *s* hastesag; venstrehåndsarbejde; **~ order** *s* hasteordre.
rusk [rʌsk] *s* tvebak.
russet ['rʌsit] *adj* rødbrun.
Russia ['rʌʃə] *s* Rusland; **~n** *s* russer // *adj* russisk.
rust [rʌst] *s* rust; *green* ~ ir // *v* ruste.
rustic ['rʌstik] *adj* landlig; almue-.
rustle [rʌsl] *s* raslen, brusen // *v* rasle (med), knitre: ~ *up some tea* organisere ngt te.
rusty ['rʌsti] *adj* rusten.
rut [rʌt] *s* brunst; spor; fast skure.
ruthless ['ru:θlis] *adj* hensynsløs; ubarmhjertig; **~ly** *adv* med hård hånd.
rye [rai] *s (bot)* rug.

S

S, s [ɛs].
sabbath ['sæbəθ] *s* sabbat; søndag.
sabbatical [sə'bætikl] *adj:* ~ *(year)* sabbatår.
sable [seibl] *s* zobel.
sabotage ['sæbəta:ʒ] *s* sabotage // *v* sabotere.
sabre ['seibə*] *s* sabel // *v* nedsable.
sachet ['sæʃei] *s* pose; lille pakke.
sack [sæk] *s* sæk, pose; *get the* ~ blive fyret; *hit the* ~ (F) gå til køjs // *v* plyndre; afskedige, fyre; **~cloth** *s* sækkelærred; **~ing** *s* sækkelærred.
sacred ['seikrid] *adj* hellig; indviet.
sacrifice ['sækrifais] *s* offer; tab // *v* ofre.
sacrilege ['sækrilidʒ] *s* helligbrøde.
sacrosanct ['sækrəusæŋkt] *adj* fredhellig.
sad [sæd] *adj* bedrøvet, vemodig; sørgelig; **~den** *v* gøre (,blive) trist, bedrøve.
saddle [sædl] *s* sadel; *(gastr)* ryg (fx *of lamb* lamme-) // *v* sadle; *get* ~*d with sth* blive belemret med ngt, komme til at hænge på ngt; **~ horse** *s* ridehest.
sadly ['sædli] *adv* sørgeligt; desværre; ~ *he had to...* desværre skulle han....
sadness ['sædnis] *s* sorg, vemod; tungsindighed.
sae (fork.f. *stamped addressed envelope)* frankeret svarkuvert.
safe [seif] *s* pengeskab; boks // *adj* sikker; uskadt; ufarlig; pålidelig; forsigtig; ~ *from* i sikkerhed for; ~ *and sound* i god behold; *just to be on the* ~ *side* for en sikkerheds skyld; *play it* ~ gardere sig; ~ *journey!* god rejse! **~-conduct** *s* frit lejde; **~-deposit** *s* bankbox; **~guard** *s* værn, beskyttelse; sikkerhedsforanstaltning // *v* beskytte; sikre; **~keeping** *s* forvaring; **~ly** *adv* sikkert; *you can* ~*ly say that...* man kan roligt sige at...; *they got home* ~*ly* de kom godt hjem.
safety ['seifti] *s* sikkerhed; **~ belt** *s* sikkerhedsbælte (,-sele); **~ catch** *s* (på våben) sikring; **~ curtain** *s (teat)* jerntæppe; **~ pin** *s* sikkerhedsnål; **~ valve** *s* sikkerhesventil.
saffron ['sæfrən] *s* safran.
sag [sæg] *v* hænge; dale; synke.
sagacious [sə'geiʃəs] *adj* skarpsindig.
sage [seidʒ] *s* vismand; *(bot)* salvie // *adj* klog, vis.
Sagittarius [sædʒi'tɛəriəs] *s (astr)* Skytten.
said [sɛd] *præt* og *pp* af *say* // *adj: the* ~ ovennævnte, (tidligere) omtalte.
sail [seil] *s* sejl; sejltur; sejlads; *go for a* ~ tage ud at sejle; *set* ~ hejse sejl;

afsejle *(for* til) // *v* sejle; besejle; ~ *through one's exams* klare eksamen med bravur; **~cloth** *s* sejldug.

sailing ['seiliŋ] *s* sejlads; sejlsport; *go ~* tage på sejltur; *it's plain ~* det er lige ud ad landevejen; **~ boat** *s* sejlbåd; **~ ship** *s* sejlskib.

sailor ['seilə*] *s* sømand; matros; *he's a bad ~* (også) han lider af søsyge; *he's a good ~* han er søstærk.

saint [seint] *s* helgen; (om person) engel; sankt; *Saint George* St. Jørgen; *Saint Joan* Jeanne d'Arc; *Saint John* (evangelisten) Johannes; **saintly** *adj* helgenagtig; hellig.

sake [seik] *s: for the ~ of* for ... skyld; af hensyn til...; *for pity's ~* for Guds skyld.

salacious [sə'leiʃəs] *adj* liderlig.

salad ['sæləd] *s* salat; **~ bowl** *s* salatskål; **~ cream** *s* salatdressing; **~ days** *spl: his ~ days* hans grønne ungdom.

salaried ['sælərid] *adj* lønnet.

salary ['sæləri] *s* løn, månedsløn.

sale [seil] *s* salg; udsalg; *(up) for (,on)* til salg; *on ~ or return* med returret; *~s are up* salget er gået op; **~able** *adj* (let)sælgelig, til at sælge; **~room** *s* salgslokale; auktionslokale; **~s·man** *s* sælger; ekspedient; repræsentant; **~s·manager** *s* salgschef; **~s·manship** *s* salgsteknik; **~s·woman** *s* ekspeditrice.

salient ['seiliənt] *adj* fremspringende; fremtrædende.

saline ['seilain] *s* saltopløsning // *adj* saltholdig, salt-.

saliva [sə'laivə] *s* spyt.

salivary [sə'laivəri] *adj: ~ gland* spytkirtel.

salivate ['sæliveit] *v* savle.

sallow ['sæləu] *adj (bot)* pil; pilekvist // *adj* bleg, gusten.

salmon ['sæmən] *s* laks // *adj* laksefarvet; lakse-; **~ leap** *s* laksetrappe; **~ trout** *s* laksørred.

saloon [sə'lu:n] *s* (på skib) salon; *(auto)* sedan; **~ bar** *s* den fine afdeling af pub.

salt [sɔlt] *s* salt; *take it with a pinch of ~* tage det med et gran salt // *v* salte; komme salt på; **~cellar** *s* saltkar; **~petre** [-pi:tə*] *s* saltpeter; **~shaker** *s* saltbøsse.

salty ['sɔ:lti] *adj* saltagtig; salt.

salubrious [sə'lu:briəs] *adj* sund.

salutary ['sæljutəri] *adj* sund; gavnlig, nyttig.

salute [sə'lu:t] *s* hilsen; honnør; salut // *v* hilse; gøre honnør; salutere.

salvage ['sælvidʒ] *s* bjærgning; bjærgeløn // *v* redde, bjærge.

salvation [sæl'veiʃən] *s* frelse, redning; *the Salvation Army* Frelsens Hær.

salver ['sælvə*] *s* (metal)bakke.

salvo ['sælvəu] *s* (skud)salve; (klap)salve.

same [seim] *adj/pron* samme; *the ~* den (,det, de) samme; *treat them the ~* behandle dem ens; *all (,just) the ~* alligevel, ikke desto mindre; *it's all the ~ to me* det er mig det samme (,lige meget); *much the ~* ikke stort anderledes; *the ~ to you!* i lige måde!

sample [sa:mpl] *s* prøve; smagsprøve // *v* prøve; smage på.

sanctify ['sæŋktifai] *v* hellige; retfærdiggøre.

sanctimonious [saŋkti'məuniəs] *adj* skinhellig.

sanction ['sæŋkʃən] *s* sanktion; godkendelse // *v* godkende, stadfæste.

sanctuary ['sæŋktjuəri] *s* tilflugtssted; (dyre)reservat.

sand [sænd] *s* sand // *v* komme sand på (,i); slibe med sandpapir; **~bag** *s* sandsæk; **~blast** *v* sandblæse; **~castle** *s* sandslot; **~ dune** *s* klit.

sander ['sændə*] *s* slibemaskine.

sandpaper ['sændpeipə*] *s* sandpapir // *v* slibe (med sandpapir.

sandpit ['sændpit] *s* sandkasse.

sandwich ['sændwitʃ] *s* sandwich; *open ~* stykke smørrebrød // *v: ~ed between* klemt inde mellem; **~ course** *s* kursus med skiftevis teori og praktik.

sandy ['sændi] *adj* sandet; sand-; sandfarvet; rødblond.

sane [sein] *adj* sjæleligt sund; normal; fornuftig.

sang [sæŋ] *præt* af *sing.*
sanguine ['sæŋgwin] *adj* optimistisk; rødmosset.
sanitary ['sænitəri] *adj* sanitær, hygiejnisk; ~ **towel** *s* hygiejnebind.
sanitation [sæni'teiʃən] *s* sanitære installationer; sanitetsvæsen.
sanity ['sæniti] *s* tilregnelighed; (sund) fornuft.
sank [sæŋk] *præt* af *sink.*
Santa Claus ['sæntə,klɔ:z] *s* julemanden.
sap [sæp] *s* (plante)saft; livskraft // *v* underminere; tappe på livskraft.
sapling ['sæpliŋ] *s* ungt træ.
sapphire ['sæfaiə*] *s* safir; safirblåt.
sardine ['sa:di:n] *s* sardin; *be packed like ~s* stå som sild i en tønde.
sash [sæʃ] *s* skærf; vinduesramme; ~ **window** *s* skydevindue.
sat [sæt] *præt* og *pp* af *sit.*
satchel ['sætʃəl] *s* skuldertaske; skoletaske.
satellite ['sætəlait] *s* satellit; ~ **dish** *s* parabolantenne.
satire ['sætaiə*] *s* satire.
satirical [sə'tirikl] *adj* satirisk.
satiate ['seiʃieit] *v* mætte.
satisfaction [sætis'fækʃən] *s* tilfredsstillelse; tilfredshed; oprejsning.
satisfactory [sætis'fæktəri] *adj* tilfredsstillende.
satisfy ['sætisfai] *v* tilfredsstille; overbevise; **~ing** *adj* tilfredsstillende.
saturate ['sætʃəreit] *v* mætte; gennemvæde; **saturation** [-'reiʃən] *s* mætning.
Saturday ['sætədi] *s* lørdag; *on ~* på lørdag; *on ~s* om lørdagen, hver lørdag.
sauce [sɔ:s] *s* sovs; *have the ~ to say sth* være fræk nok til at sige ngt; **~boat** *s* sovseskål; **~pan** *s* kasserolle.
saucer ['sɔ:sə*] *s* underkop; *cup and ~* et par kopper; *flying ~* flyvende tallerken.
saucy ['sɔ:si] *adj* fræk.
Saudi ['sɔ:di] *s* saudiaraber // *adj* saudiarabisk.
saunter ['sɔ:ntə*] *v* slentre, drysse.
sausage ['sɔsidʒ] *s* pølse; ~ **dog** *s* (F) grævlingehund; ~ **meat** *s* pølsefars, rørt fars.
savage ['sævidʒ] *s* vild(mand) // *v* mishandle // *adj* vild; brutal; rasende.
savagery ['sævidʒəri] *s* grusomhed; vildskab.
save [seiv] *s* *(sport)* redning // *v* redde; spare op (,sammen); gemme; *God ~ the Queen* Gud bevare dronningen! // *præp* undtagen; på nær.
saving ['seiviŋ] *s* besparelse // *adj* frelsende; besparende.
savings ['seiviŋs] *spl* opsparing; ~ **bank** *s* sparekasse.
saviour ['seiviə*] *s* frelser.
savour ['seivə*] *s* (vel)smag; anstrøg // *v* smage; nyde.
savoury ['seivəri] *s* (let) anretning (ost etc) // *adj* velsmagende, lækker.
saw [sɔ:] *s* sav // *v (~ed, ~ed* el. *sawn)* save; *~ up* save i stykker // *præp* af *see;* **~dust** *s* savsmuld; **~horse** *s* savbuk; **~mill** *s* savværk.
sawn-off [sɔ:n'ɔf] *adj* (om gevær) oversavet.
saw-toothed ['sɔ:tu:θd] *adj* savtakket.
say [sei] *s: have one's ~* få sagt hvad man vil; *have a ~* have et ord at skulle have sagt // *v (said, said* [sɛd]) sige; udtale; *could you ~ that again?* hvad behager? *that's to ~...* det vil sige...; *to ~ nothing of* for ikke at tale om; *to ~ the least* mildest talt; *you can ~ that again!* ja det må du nok sige; *~ that...* lad os sige at...; *that goes without ~ing* det siger sig selv; *you don't ~!* det siger du ikke? **~ing** *s* talemåde; ordsprog; **~-so** *s* ordre.
scab [skæb] *s* skruebrækker; sårskorpe; *~ labour* uorganiseret arbejdskraft.
scabbard ['skæbəd] *s* skede (til sværd).
scabies ['skeibi:z] *s* fnat.
scaffold ['skæfəuld] *s* skafot; stillads; **~ing** *s* byggestillads.
scald [skɔ:ld] *v* skolde; **~ing** *adj* skoldende varm.
scale [skeil] *s* (om fisk etc) skæl; ska-

la; målestok; kedelsten; tandsten; *a pair of ~s* en (skål)vægt; *on a large ~* i stor målestok // *v* bestige; *~ down* formindske; *~ up* forstørre.
scallop ['skɔləp] *s* kammusling; *(gastr)* gratinskal.
scalp [skælp] *s* hovebund, skalp // *v* skalpere.
scamper ['skæmpə*] *v* løbe rundt, fare af sted.
scan [skæn] *s* (hurtig) gennemlæsning; *(med)* scanning // *v* studere nøje; kigge igennem; skanne.
scandal ['skændəl] *s* skandale; forargelse; sladder.
scandalize ['skændəlaiz] *v* forarge; bagtale.
scandalous ['skændələs] *adj* skandaløs.
Scandinavia [skændi'neiviə] *s* Skandinavien; **~n** *s* skandinav // *adj* skandinavisk, nordisk.
scant [skænt] *adj* kneben, knap; **~y** *adj* sparsom; mager; (om kjole) luftig.
scapegoat ['skeipgəut] *s* syndebuk.
scar [ska:*] *s* ar; *(fig)* skramme // *v* danne (,lave) ar; skramme.
scarce [skεəs] *adj* knap; sjælden; *money is growing ~* vi har snart ikke flere penge; *make oneself ~* stikke af; **~ly** *adv* næsten ikke, næppe, knap.
scarcity ['skεəsiti] *s* mangel, knaphed.
scare [skεə*] *s* skræk; panik; *give sby a ~* gøre en forskrækket; *bomb ~* bombetrussel // *v* skræmme; blive skræmt; **~crow** [-krəu] *s* fugleskræmsel; **~d** *adj: be (,get) ~d* blive forskrækket; **~monger** [-mɔŋgə*] *s* panikmager.
scarf [ska:f] *s (pl: scarves* [ska:vz]) (hals)tørklæde.
scarlet ['ska:lit] *adj* purpurrød; **~ fever** *s* skarlagensfeber.
scarper ['ska:pə*] *v* (F) stikke af, skride.
scarves [ska:vz] *spl* af *scarf.*
scary ['skεəri] *adj* (F) skræmmende; skræk-; frygtsom.
scathing ['skeiðiŋ] *adj* svidende; bidende.
scatter ['skætə*] *v* sprede(s); strø; **~brained** *adj* forvirret; glemsom; bims; **~ing** *s: a ~ing of...* enkelte..., nogle få spredte...
scatty ['skæti] *adj* (F) skør, bims.
scavenger ['skævindʒe*] *s* (om dyr) ådselæder; person der roder i og samler andres affald.
scenario [si'na:riəu] *s* drejebog; slagplan.
scene [si:n] *s* scene; sted; *the ~ of the crime* gerningsstedet; *that's not my ~* det er ikke rigtig mig; *behind the ~s* bag kulisserne; *set the ~ for sth* lægge op til ngt; *I need a change of ~* jeg trænger til luftforandring.
scenery ['si:nəri] *s* sceneri; dekoration; landskab.
scenic ['si:nik] *adj* scenisk; naturskøn.
scent [sεnt] *s* duft; spor; lugtesans; parfume; *pick up the ~* få færten; *put him off the ~* lede ham på vildspor // *v* lugte; vejre; parfumere.
sceptic ['skεptik] *s* skeptiker // *adj* skeptisk; **~al** *adj* skeptisk.
scepticism ['skεptisizm] *s* skepsis.
sceptre ['sεptə*] *s* scepter.
schedule ['ʃεdju:l] *s* (tids)plan; køreplan; program; tarif; liste; *on ~* som planlagt; *to ~* efter planen; *behind ~* forsinket // *v* fastslægge; *as ~d* planmæssigt.
scheme [ski:m] *s* plan; system, ordning; intrige // *v* planlægge; smede rænker.
scheming ['ski:miŋ] *adj* intrigant; beregnende.
schism [skizəm] *s* skisma; splittelse.
schizophrenia [skitsə'fri:niə] *s* skizofreni.
scholar ['skɔlə*] *s* videnskabsmand; lærd; stipendiat; **~ly** *adj* lærd; **~ship** *s* lærdom; stipendium.
school [sku:l] *s* skole; (fiske)stime; *go to ~* gå i skole; *leave ~* gå ud af skolen // *v* oplære, skole; **~book** *s* skolebog; **~days** *spl* skoletid; **~ing** *s* skolegang; skoling; **~-leaving age** *s* den alder hvor skolepligten ophører; **~marm** *s* (F, *spøg*) skolefrø-

ken; **~master** *s* lærer; **~mate** *s* skolekammerat; **~mistress** *s* lærerinde; **~ report** *s* karakterbog; **~room** *s* klasseværelse; **~teacher** *s* skolelærer; **~yard** *s* skolegård.
schooner ['sku:nə*] *s* skonnert; stort vinglas.
sciatica [sai'ætikə] *s* iskias.
science ['saiəns] *s* videnskab; naturvidenskab; **~ park** *s* forskerpark.
scientific [saiən'tifik] *adj* videnskabelig.
scientist ['saiəntist] *s* (natur)videnskabsmand.
sci-fi ['sai,fai] *s* (S) science fiction.
scintillating ['sintileitiŋ] *adj* glitrende, funklende.
scissors ['sisəz] *spl: a pair of ~* en saks.
scoff [skɔf] *v* (F) æde, drikke; håne; *~ at* kimse ad; spotte.
scold [skəuld] *v* skælde ud på; **~ing** *s* skældud, fur.
scone [skɔn] *s* slags tebolle.
scoop [sku:p] *s* øse, skovl; kup; godt stof // *v: ~ out* øse; *~ up* skovle.
scooter ['sku:tə*] *s* løbehjul; scooter.
scope [skəup] *s* rækkevidde; omfang; spændvidde; spillerum; *within the ~ of* inden for rammerne af.
scorch [skɔ:tʃ] *v* brænde, svide, branke, afsvide; **~er** *s* (F) brændende varm dag; **~ing** *adj* brændende, svidende.
score [skɔ:*] *s* regnskab; pointtal; *(mus)* partitur; snes; scoring; *keep the ~* tælle points; *what's the ~?* hvad står det? hvordan ser det ud? *settle a ~* afgøre et mellemværende; *by the ~* i massevis; *on that ~* hvad det angår; af den grund // *v* føre regnskab; kunne notere (fx *a success* en succes); få points, score; *~ a hit* blive en succes; *~ a bird* (S) få steg (dvs. en pige) på gaflen; *~ off (fig)* jorde; (om narkoman) fixe; **~board** *s* måltavle.
scorer ['skɔ:rə*] *s* regnskabsfører; målscorer.
scorn [skɔ:n] *s* foragt, hån // *v* foragte, håne; **~ful** *adj* hånlig.
Scorpio ['skɔ:piəu] *s (astr)* Skorpionen.
Scot [skɔt] *s* skotte.
Scotch [skɔtʃ] *s* (skotsk) whisky.
scotch *v* gøre det af med; sætte en stopper for.
scot-free ['skɔtfri:] *adj: get off ~* slippe godt fra det.
Scots [skɔts] *s/adj* skotsk // *spl* skotter.
Scottish ['skɔtiʃ] *adj* skotsk.
scoundrel ['skaundrəl] *s* skurk.
scour [skauə*] *v* skure; gennemsøge.
scourer ['skaurə*] *s* grydesvamp; skurepulver.
scourge [skə:dʒ] *s* svøbe, plage.
scout [skaut] *s* spejder // *v: ~ around* spejde, være på udkig.
scowl [skaul] *s* skulen // *v* skule; *~ at* se vredt på; se skævt til.
scrabble [skræbl] *s* kragetæer; kriblekryds // *v* kradse; *~ around* famle.
scraggy ['skrægi] *adj* tynd, afpillet.
scram [skræm] *v* stikke af; *~!* skrid!
scramble [skræmbl] *s* klatretur; vild kamp // *v* klatre; vade; *~ for* skubbes for at få fat i; løbe om kap efter; **~d eggs** *spl* røræg.
scrap [skræp] *s* stump; smule; slagsmål; glansbillede; skrot; *sell sth for ~* sælge ngt til ophugning // *v* kassere.
scrape [skreip] *s: get into a ~* komme i knibe // *v* skrabe, kradse; *~ through* hutle sig igennem; **~r** *s* skraber; spatel.
scrap... ['skræp-]sms: **~heap** *s* affaldsbunke; *(fig)* brokkasse; **~ iron** *s* skrot; **~ merchant** *s* skrothandler; **~ paper** *s* gen(brugs)papir.
scrappy ['skræpi] *adj* sammenbrokket; planløs.
scraps *spl* affald; udklip.
scrapyard ['skræpja:d] *s* bilkirkegård; skrotlager.
scratch [skrætʃ] *s* rift; kradsen; skratten; *start from ~* begynde helt forfra; *be up to ~* være i fin form; gøre fyldest // *v* kradse, rive; klø (sig).
scrawl [skrɔ:l] *s* kragetæer, skribleri // *v* kradse ned, skrible.
scrawny ['skrɔ:ni] *adj* tynd, splejset.
scream [skri:m] *s* skrig; *let out a ~* udstøde et skrig; *that's a ~* det er

hylende grinagtigt // *v* skrige.
screech [skri:tʃ] *s* skrig, hvin // *v* skrige, hvine.
screed [skri:d] *s* (F) lang smøre, "klamamse".
screen [skri:n] *s* skærm; *(film)* lærred // *v* skærme; afskærme; filmatisere; screene; skaffe oplysninger om; **~ing** *s (med)* kontrolundersøgelse, screening; **~play** *s* filmmanuskript.
screw [skru:] *s* skrue; *put the ~s on sby (fig)* sætte tommelskruerne på en // *v* skrue; dreje; presse; (V!) "knalde"; *have one's head ~ed on* have pæren i orden; *~ up* knibe sammen; forkludre; gøre skør; **~driver** *s* skruetrækker; **~ top** *s* skruelåg.
screwy ['skru:i] *adj* (F) skør.
scribble [skribl] *s* kradseri, skribleri // *v* skrible.
scrimmage ['skrimidʒ] *s* håndgemæng.
scrimp [skrimp] *v* spinke og spare.
script [skript] *s (teat* etc) manuskript; drejebog; håndskrevet dokument.
Scripture ['skriptʃə*] *s: the (Holy) ~* den hellige skrift, bibelen.
scriptwriter ['skriptraitə*] *s* tekstforfatter.
scroll [skrəul] *s* skriftrulle; snirkel.
scrounge [skraundʒ] *v* hugge; "redde" sig; *~ on sby* nasse på en.
scrounger ['skraundʒə*] *s* snylter, (F) nasserøv.
scrub [skrʌb] *s* skrubben; krat(bevoksning); (om person) lille skravl // *v* skrubbe, skure; annullere.
scruff [skrʌf] *s: by the ~ of the neck* i nakkeskindet; **~y** *adj* beskidt, lurvet.
scrumptious ['skrʌmʃəs] *adj* lækker.
scrunch [skrʌntʃ] *s* knasen // *v: ~ up* krølle sammen.
scruple [skru:pl] *s* skrupel; *~s* betænkeligheder.
scrupulous ['skru:pjuləs] *adj* omhyggelig, skrupuløs.
scrutinize ['skru:tinaiz] *v* granske, ransage; forske.
scrutiny ['skru:tini] *s* gransken, nøje undersøgelse; *it does not stand up under ~* det tåler ikke en nærmere undersøgelse.
scuba diving ['sku:bəˌdaiviŋ] *s* sportsdykning.
scuffle [skʌfl] *s* håndgemæng.
scullery ['skʌləri] *s* bryggers.
sculptor ['skʌlptə*] *s* billedhugger.
sculpture ['skʌlptʃə*] *s* skulptur, statue; billedhuggerkunst // *v* modellere.
scum [skʌm] *s* skum; afskum, udskud.
scupper ['skʌpə*] *s (mar)* spygat // *v* (F) sabotere.
scurrilous ['skʌriləs] *adj* grov, plat.
scurry ['skʌri] *v* smutte, pile.
scurvy ['skə:vi] *s* skørbug.
scuttle [skʌtl] *v* bore i sænk; fare, pile.
scythe [saið] *s* le // *v* meje.
SDP [ˌɛsdi:'pi:] fork.f. *Social Democratic Party.*
sea [si:] *s* hav; sø; *at ~* til søs; *be all at ~* være helt ude at svømme; *by ~* ad søvejen; *put to ~* stikke til søs, afsejle; **~bed** *s* havbund; **~bird** *s* havfugl; **~faring** *adj* søfarts-; **~food** *s* fisk (etc); "alt godt fra havet"; **~front** *s* strandpromenade; **~going** *adj* (om skib) søgående; **~gull** *s* måge.
seal [si:l] *s* sæl; sælskind; segl; plombe // *v* forsegle; besegle; lukke; *my lips are ~ed* min mund er lukket med syv segl; *~ up* forsegle; tætne.
sea level ['si:ˌlɛvl] *s* middelvandstand; *2000 feet above ~* 2000 fod over havets overflade.
seam [si:m] *s* søm; stikning; (om kul etc) åre, lag; *fall apart at the ~s (fig)* gå op i sømmene; **~less** *adj* sømløs.
seamstress ['sɛmstris] *s* syerske.
seamy ['si:mi] *adj* ulækker, smudsig.
seaplane ['si:plein] *s* flyvebåd.
seaport ['si:pɔ:t] *s* havn(eby).
sear [siə*] *v* brænde; ætse; svitse.
search [sə:tʃ] *s* søgen; eftersøgning; gennemsøgning; ransagning; *in ~ of* ude at lede efter; ude efter // *v* søge; gennemsøge; ransage; *~ me!* (F) det aner jeg ikke! **~ing** *adj* for-

skende; indgående; ~**light** *s* projektør, søgelys; ~ **party** *s* eftersøgningsmandskab; ~ **warrant** *s* ransagningskendelse.
searing ['siəriŋ] *adj* brændende; svidende.
sea... ['si:-] sms: ~**shell** *s* muslingeskal; ~**shore** *s* strandbred; ~**sick** *adj* søsyg; ~**sickness** *s* søsyge; ~**side** *s* kyst; ~**side resort** *s* badested.
season [si:zn] *s* årstid; sæson; *strawberries are in* ~ det er jordbærsæson; *be in* ~ (om dyr) være i løbetid (,brunst) // *v* krydre, smage til; ~**able** *adj* normal efter årstiden; belejlig; ~**ed** *adj* krydret; lagret; hærdet; ~**ing** *s* krydderi; lagring; ~ **ticket** *s* abonnementskort; buskort; togkort.
seat [si:t] *s* sæde; siddeplads; mandat; residens; (bukse)bag; *take a* ~! sid ned! *book a* ~ reservere plads // *v* sætte, anbringe; rumme, kunne bænke; ~ **belt** *s (auto)* sikkerhedssele; *(fly)* sikkerhedsbælte.
sea... ['si:-] sms: ~ **urchin** [-ə:tʃin] *s* søpindsvin; ~ **water** *s* havvand; ~**weed** *s* tang; alger; ~**worthy** [-wə:ði] *adj* sødygtig.
sec [sɛk] fork.f. *second(s)*.
secateurs ['sɛkətəz] *spl* beskæresaks.
secede [si'si:d] *v:* ~ *from the EEC* træde ud af EF.
secession [si'sɛʃən] *s* udtrædelse.
secluded [si'klu:did] *adj* isoleret; afsondret.
seclusion [si'klu:ʒən] *s* afsondrethed.
second ['sɛkənd] *s* sekund; *(sport)* nummer to; *(auto)* andet gear // *v* sekundere, støtte // *adj/adv* anden; næst-; *every* ~ *month* hver anden måned; *be* ~ *to none* ikke stå tilbage for ngn; *have* ~ *thoughts* ombestemme sig.
secondary ['sɛkəndəri] *adj* underordnet; sekundær; ~ **school** *s* skole for børn over 10 år.
second... ['sɛkənd-] sms: ~-**best** *adj* næstbedst; ~-**class** *adj* andenklasses; (om brev) B-forsendelse; ~**er** *s* en der støtter (et forslag etc); ~**hand** *adj* brugt // *adv* på anden hånd; ~ **hand** *s* (på ur) sekundviser; ~ **home** *s* fritidshus; ~-**in-command** *s* næstkommanderende.
secondly ['sɛkəndli] *adv* for det andet.
secondment [si'kɔndmənt] *s* forflyttelse.
second-rate ['sɛkəndreit] *adj* andenrangs.
second sight ['sɛkənd 'sait] *s: have* ~ være synsk.
second thoughts ['sɛkənd 'θɔ:ts] *spl: on* ~ ved nærmere eftertanke.
secrecy ['si:krəsi] *s* hemmeligholdelse; *in* ~ i hemmelighed.
secret ['si:krit] *s* hemmelighed; *the* ~ *service* efterretningstjenesten // *adj* hemmelig.
secretarial [sɛkri'tɛəriəl] *adj* sekretær.
secretary ['sɛkrətəri] *s* sekretær; *Secretary of State* minister; *(am)* udenrigsminister; ~ **general** *s* generalsekretær.
secrete [si'kri:t] *v* afsondre, udskille.
secretive ['si:krətiv] *adj* hemmelighedsfuld; tavs.
sect [sɛkt] *s* sekt.
sectarian [sɛk'tɛəriən] *adj* sekterisk.
section ['sɛkʃən] *s* snit; afdeling; del, sektion; udsnit // *v* dele (i sektioner).
sector ['sɛktə*] *s* afsnit; område; sektor.
secular ['sɛkjulə*] *adj* verdslig; ikkereligiøs.
secure [si'kjuə*] *v* sikre (sig) // *adj* sikker; tryg; forsvarlig; ~ *from* sikker mod; i sikkerhed for.
security [-'kjuəriti] *s* sikkerhed; kaution; *securities* værdipapirer; ~ **guard** *s* vægter; sikkerhedsvagt.
sedate [si'deit] *adj* sindig; adstadig // *v* give beroligende medicin; dølle (ned).
sedative ['sɛdətiv] *s* beroligende middel.
sedentary ['sɛdntri] *adj* fastboende; (stille)siddende.
sediment ['sɛdimənt] *s* bundfald; aflejring.
seduce [si'dju:s] *v* forføre; forlede.

seduction [si'dʌkʃən] *s* forførelse; tillokkelse.
seductive [si'dʌktiv] *adj* forførerisk; tillokkende.
see [si:] *v (saw, seen* [sɔ:, si:n]) se; indse; opleve; besøge; tale med; *we'll have to ~ about that* nu må vi se (ad); *you had better ~ a doctor* du må hellere gå til lægen; *~ sby to the door* følge en til døren; *go to ~ sby* tage hen og besøge en; *~ that he does it* sørge for at han gør det; *~ sby off* følge en (fx til toget); *~ sby out* følge en til døren; *I'll ~ myself out* jeg finder selv ud; *~ through* gennemskue; gøre færdig; *this money ought to ~ you through the holidays* du må klare dig med de her penge i ferien; *~ to* tage sig af; sørge for; *~ you!* farvel så længe! *I ~!* jeg forstår! nå, sådan!
seed [si:d] *s (bot)* frø; kerne; *(fig)* spire; *go to ~* gå i frø, forsumpe // *v* seede; *the second ~(ed)* (i tennis etc) nummer to på ranglisten.
seedbed ['si:dbɛd] *s* udklækningssted.
seedless ['si:dləs] *adj* uden kerner.
seedling ['si:dliŋ] *s* frøplante.
seedy ['si:di] *adj* lurvet; forsumpet.
seeing ['si:iŋ] *konj: ~ that...* i betragtning af at...
seek [si:k] *v (sought, sought* [sɔ:t]) søge (efter); forsøge; *~ out* opsøge.
seem [si:m] *v* synes; virke (som om); *there ~s to be...* der lader til at være...; **~ingly** *adv* tilsyneladende.
seemly ['si:mli] *adj* sømmelig.
seen [si:n] *pp* af *see.*
seep [si:p] *v* sive.
seersucker ['siəsʌkə*] *s* (om stof) bækogbølge.
seesaw ['si:sɔ:] *s* vippe; vippen.
seethe [si:ð] *v* syde, koge; *~ with anger* skumme af raseri.
see-through ['si:θru:] *adj* gennemsigtig.
segment ['sɛgmənt] *s* stykke; udsnit; del; (om appelsin) båd.
segregation [sɛgri'geiʃən] *s* (race)adskillelse; isolation.
seize [si:z] *v* gribe; bemægtige sig; pågribe; *~ (up)on* gribe ivrigt (efter); *my back has ~d up* jeg har vrøvl med ryggen; *the brake has ~d (up)* bremsen har sat sig fast; *the traffic has ~d up* trafikken er gået i stå.
seizure ['si:ʒə*] *s* pågribelse; *(med)* slagtilfælde; *(jur)* beslaglæggelse.
seldom ['sɛldəm] *adv* sjældent.
select [si'lɛkt] *v* (ud)vælge // *adj* udsøgt; eksklusiv.
selection [si'lɛkʃən] *s* udvælgelse; udvalg.
selective [si'lɛktiv] *adj* selektiv; kræsen.
selector [si'lɛktə*] *s* programvælger.
self [sɛlf] *s (pl: selves* [sɛlvz]) jeg; selv; *the ~* jeg'et; *my better ~* mit bedre jeg; **~-adhesive** [-əd,hi:siv] *adj* selvklæbende, klæbe-; **~-appointed** *adj* selvbestaltet; **~-assertive** *adj* selvhævdende; **~-assured** *adj* selvsikker; **~-catering** *adj* på egen kost; **~-centred** *adj* egocentrisk; **~-confidence** *s* selvtillid; **~-conscious** [-'kɔnʃəs] *adj* genert, forlegen; **~-contained** *adj* selvstændig; med egen indgang; **~-defence** *s* selvforsvar; **~-educated** *adj* selvlært, autodidakt; **~-effacing** *adj* selvudslettende; **~-employed** *adj* selvstændig; **~-esteem** *s* selvagtelse; **~-evident** [-'ɛvidənt] *adj* selvindlysende; **~-explanatory** *adj* som forklarer sig selv; **~-indulgent** *adj* som forkæler sig selv; nydelsessyg; **~-interest** *s* egenkærlighed.
selfish ['sɛlfiʃ] *adj* selvisk, egoistisk; **~ness** *s* egoisme.
self... sms: **~less** *adj* uselvisk; **~-pity** *s* selvmedlidenhed; **~-possessed** *adj* fattet, behersket; **~-preservation** *s* selvopholdelsesdrift; **~-righteous** [-'raitʃəs] *adj* selvretfærdig; **~-sacrifice** *s* selvopofrelse; *the* **~-same** den selvsamme; **~-satisfied** *adj* selvtilfreds; **~-seal** *adj* selvklæbende (fx kuvert); **~-service** *s* selvbetjening; **~-sufficient** *adj* selvtilstrækkelig; selvforsynende; **~-supporting** *adj* selvforsørgende; **~-taught** *adj* selvlært.

sell [sɛl] *v (sold, sold* [səuld]) sælge; blive solgt; ~ *off* udsælge; *he's sold on her* han er brændt varm på hende.
seller ['sɛlə*] *s* sælger.
selling price ['sɛliŋ prais] *s* salgspris.
sellout ['sɛlaut] *s* udsalg; forræderi; *it was a* ~ der blev udsolgt.
selvedge ['sɛlvidʒ] *s* ægkant (på stof).
selves [sɛlvz] *pl* af *self.*
semblance ['sɛmbləns] *s* skin; udseende; antydning.
semen ['si:mən] *s* sæd(væske); *(bot)* frø.
semi ['sɛmi] *s* d.s.s. *~detached house;* (F) d.s.s. *~-trailer;* **~-breve** [-bri:v] *s* helnode; **~circle** *s* halvcirkel; **~detached (house)** *s* halvt dobbelthus; **~finals** *spl* semifinale.
seminar ['sɛmina:*] *s* symposium; (fagligt) kursus.
seminary ['sɛminəri] *s* præsteseminarium.
semi... ['sɛmi-] sms: **~quaver** [-kweivə*] *s* sekstendedelsnode; **~skilled worker** *s* specialarbejder; **~-skimmed milk** *s* letmælk; **~-trailer** *s* anhænger (til lastvogn).
semolina [sɛmə'li:nə] *s* semulje(vælling).
senate ['sɛnit] *s* senat; *(univ)* konsistorium.
send [sɛnd] *v (sent, sent)* sende; ~ *word* sende besked; ~ *sby packing* give en løbepas; ~ *away* sende væk; ~ *away for* rekvirere; ~ *back* sende tilbage; ~ *down* (i skolen) bortvise; ~ *for* sende bud efter, skrive efter; ~ *off* afsende; *(sport)* udvise; ~ *out* udsende, sende ud; ~ *up* drive i vejret (fx *prices* priserne); sætte i fængsel; lade springe; **~er** *s* afsender; sender; **~-off** *s: a good ~-off* en god afskedsfest; en god start **~-up** *s* (F) parodi.
senile ['si:nail] *adj* senil.
senior ['si:niə*] *s* senior; *he's my ~ by five years* han er fem år ældre end jeg // *adj* senior-; ældre; **~ citizen** *s* pensionist; **~ consultant** *s* overlæge.
seniority [si:ni'ɔriti] *s* anciennitet.
sensation [sɛn'seiʃən] *s* følelse, fornemmelse; sensation; *cause a* ~ vække opsigt; **~al** *adj* sensationel; sensations-.
sense [sɛns] *s* sans; følelse; fornuft; betydning; *a ~ of humour* humoristisk sans; ~ *of duty* pligtfølelse; *make* ~ lyde fornuftig; være begribelig; *in the broadest ~ of the word* i ordets videste forstand; *come to one's ~s* komme til fornuft; *there is no ~ in...* der er ingen mening i at...; det kan ikke nytte at...; *in more ~ than one* i mere end én forstand; *anyone in his ~s* enhver der er ved sine fulde fem; *he had the ~ to phone* han var så fornuftig at ringe // *v* mærke; **~less** *adj* bevidstløs; meningsløs.
sensibility [sɛnsi'biliti] *s* følsomhed; følelse.
sensible ['sɛnsibl] *adj* fornuftig; mærkbar.
sensitive ['sɛnsitiv] *adj* følsom; ømfindtlig, sart.
sensitivity [sɛnsi'tiviti] *s* følsomhed, sensitivitet.
sensual ['sɛnʃuəl] *adj* sensuel; sanselig.
sensuous ['sɛnʃuəs] *adj* sensuel; sanselig.
sent [sɛnt] *præp* og *pp* af *send.*
sentence ['sɛntns] *s* sætning; *(jur)* dom; straf; *pass ~ on* afsige dom over // *v* dømme; ~ *sby to death* dømme en til døden.
sententious [sən'tɛnʃəs] *adj* salvelsesfuld.
sentiment ['sɛntimənt] *s* følelse; mening; synspunkt; sentimentalitet; **~al** [-'mɛntl] *adj* sentimental.
sentinel ['sɛntinəl] *s* skildvagt.
sentry ['sɛntri] *s* skildvagt, vagtpost; **~ box** *s* skilderhus.
separate *v* ['sɛpəreit] adskille; dele; skille sig ud; gå løs; skilles ad // *adj* ['sɛprit] adskilt; særskilt; *they went their ~ ways* de gik hver til sit; **~ly** *adv* hver for sig.
separation [ʃɛpə'reiʃən] *s* adskillelse; udskillelse; separation.
September [sɛp'tɛmbə*] *s* september.

septic ['sɛptik] *adj* septisk; (om sår) betændt.
septicaemia [sɛpti'si:miə] *s* blodforgiftning.
sepulchre ['sɛpəlkə*] *s* grav(sted).
sequel ['si:kwəl] *s* fortsættelse; følge, konsekvens.
sequence ['si:kwəns] *s* række(følge); sekvens.
sequin ['si:kwin] *s* paillet.
serene [si'ri:n] *adj* rolig; fredelig; skyfri.
serenity [si'rɛniti] *s* ro.
serf [sə:f] *s (hist)* livegen.
sergeant ['sa:dʒənt] *s* sergent; (om politi) sv.t. overbetjent.
serial ['siəriəl] *s* fortsat roman; tv-serie // *adj: ~ number* løbenummer; **~ize** [-aiz] *v* udsende som føljeton (,serie).
series ['siəri:s] *s* række; serie.
serious ['siəriəs] *adj* alvorlig; seriøs; vigtig; *are you ~?* mener du det (alvorligt)? *you can't be ~!* det mener du ikke! **~ly** *adv* alvorligt; *~ly though...* alvorligt talt...
sermon ['sə:mən] *s* prædiken.
serpent ['sə:pənt] *s* slange.
servant ['sə:vənt] *s* tjener; tjenestepige.
serve [sə:v] *v* tjene; servere; ekspedere; gøre tjeneste; afsone; (i tennis etc) serve; *it ~s him right* han har (rigtig) godt af det; *~ out (,up)* rette (maden) an.
server ['sə:və*] *s* bakke; serveringsske; *salad ~s* salatsæt.
service ['sə:vis] *s* tjeneste; servering; forbindelse; betjening; service; stel; (i tennis) serve(bold); *at your ~!* til tjeneste; *be of ~ to sby* være til nytte for en; *do sby a ~* gøre en en tjeneste; *put one's car in for ~* sende sin bil til service; *dinner ~* spisestel; *divine ~* gudstjeneste; **~able** *adj* anvendelig; **~ area** *s* (ved motorvej) rasteplads med benzintank, café, toiletter etc; **~man** *s* soldat; **~ station** *s* benzinstation (med værksted).
serving ['sə:viŋ] *s* portion.
servitude ['sə:vitju:d] *s* trældom.
sesame ['sɛsəmi] *s* sesam.
session ['sɛʃən] *s* møde; samling; skoleår; *be in ~* holde møde.
set [sɛt] *s* sæt; sortiment; apparat (fx *tv-~); (omgangs)kreds, gruppe, klike; *(teat* etc) dekoration; (om hår) fald // *v (set, set)* sætte, stille; indstille; angive; (om gelé etc) stivne; (om solen) gå ned; *~ to music* sætte musik til; *~ on fire* sætte ild til; *~ free* befri; *~ sth going* sætte ngt i gang; *~ sail* sætte sejl; *~ about* gå i gang med; *~ aside* sætte til side; se bort fra; *~ back* sætte (,stille) tilbage; *~ off* starte, tage af sted; affyre; sætte i gang; *~ out to* gå i lag med at; sætte sig for at; give sig ud for at; *~ up* etablere; nedsætte; installere // *adj* fast; foreskreven; parat; *be ~ on doing sth* være opsat på at gøre ngt; *be (dead) ~ against* være stærkt imod; *Denmark is ~ to become the summerland of the EEC* der er lagt op til at Danmark bliver EFs sommerland; **~back** *s* bagslag; nederlag; **~ square** *s* tegnetrekant.
settee [sɛ'ti:] *s* sofa.
setting ['sɛtiŋ] *s* ramme, baggrund; (til juvel) indfatning; miljø.
settle [sɛtl] *v* afgøre (fx *an argument* en diskussion); berolige; sætte (sig) til rette; slå sig ned; aflejres; *~ down* falde til; falde til ro; *~ for sth* affinde sig med ngt; *~ in* indrette sig; *~ to sth* finde sig til rette med ngt; *~ up with sby* afregne med en; **~ment** *s* afregning; dækning; ordning; koloni, bebyggelse, boplads.
settler ['sɛtlə*] *s* kolonist.
setup ['sɛtʌp] *s* ordning; situation; indretning.
seven [sɛvn] *num* syv.
seventeen ['sɛvnti:n] *num* sytten.
seventh ['sɛvənθ] *s* syvendedel // *adj* syvende.
seventy ['sɛvnti] *num* halvfjerds.
sever ['sɛvə*] *v* skille; dele; afskære.
several ['sɛvrəl] *adj* flere; *~ of us* flere af os; *they went their ~ ways* de gik hver sin vej.
severe [si'viə*] *adj* streng; alvorlig; slem.

severity [si'vɛriti] *s* strenghed, hårdhed.

sew [səu] *v (~ed, ~n)* sy; *~ up* sy sammen; *~ up a deal* få en aftale bragt på plads.

sewage ['su:idʒ] *s* kloakering; spildevand; **~ works** *s* rensningsanlæg.

sewer ['su:ə*] *s* kloak(ledning).

sewing ['səuiŋ] *s* syning, sytøj; **~ machine** *s* symaskine.

sewn [səun] *pp* af *sew.*

sex [sɛks] *s* køn; kønslivet, sex; *have ~ (with)* elske (med).

sexism ['sɛksizm] *s* kønsdiskriminering.

sexton ['sɛkstən] *s* kirketjener, graver.

sexual ['sɛksjuəl] *adj* kønslig, seksuel; *~ assault* voldtægtforsøg; *~ harassment* sexchikane; *~ intercourse* samleje; *~ maniac* sexgal person.

sexy ['sɛksi] *adj* sexet.

shabby ['ʃæbi] *adj* lurvet.

shack [ʃæk] *s* lille hytte; skur // *v: ~ up with sby* (F) flytte sammen (i parforhold) med en.

shackle [ʃækl] *s* lænke, kæde.

shade [ʃeid] *s* skygge; nuance; (lampe)skærm; *a ~ of* en anelse; *in the ~* i skyggen; *~s of blue* blå nuancer; *a ~ smaller* en anelse mindre // *v* skygge (for); afskærme; skravere.

shadow ['ʃædəu] *s* skygge; *be in sby's ~* stå i skyggen af en; *put a ~ on sby* lade en skygge // *v* skygge (en person).

shadowy ['ʃædəui] *adj* skyggefuld; *(am)* skummel.

shady ['ʃeidi] *adj* skyggefuld; lyssky; tvivlsom.

shaft [ʃa:ft] *s* (om fx spyd) skaft; (om fx mine) skakt; (om lys) stråle, stribe; *(auto* etc) aksel.

shaggy ['ʃægi] *adj* lodden; langhåret.

shake [ʃeik] *s* rysten; *give sth a ~* ryste ngt; *with a ~ of his head* med en hovedrysten // *v (shook, shaken* [ʃuk,ʃeikn]) ryste; ruske; få til at ryste; ryste sig; *~ hands with sby* give en hånden; hilse på en; *~ one's head* ryste på hovedet; *~ off* ryste af; vifte væk; *~ up* omryste; ryste op; **~-up** *s* rystetur; omvæltning.

shaky ['ʃeiki] *adj* rystende; vakkelvorn.

shale [ʃeil] *s* skifer(ler).

shall [ʃæl, ʃəl] *v (should* [ʃud]) skal; vil; *what ~ we do?* hvad skal vi gøre? *I ~ tell him* jeg siger (,vil sige) det til ham; *you ~ regret it* du vil komme til at fortryde det; *he should be here now* han burde være her nu.

shallot [ʃə'lɔt] *s* skalotteløg.

shallow ['ʃæləu] *adj* lavvandet; lav; *(fig)* overfladisk, "tyndbenet".

sham [ʃæm] *s* imitation; humbug; charlatan // *v* simulere, spille // *adj* forloren, imiteret, skin-.

shambles [ʃæmblz] *s* roderi, kaos; *the party was a ~* (F) der gik fuldstændig kage i festen.

shame [ʃeim] *s* skam; *for ~! ~ on you!* skam dig! *what a ~!* sikken en skam! det var synd! // *v* vanære; gøre skamfuld; gøre til skamme; **~faced** *adj* flov, skamfuld; **~ful** *adj* skammelig; **~less** *adj* skamløs, fræk.

shammy ['ʃæmi] *s* (også: *chamois)* vaskeskind.

shampoo [ʃæm'pu:] *s* hårvask; shampoo // *v* vaske (hår).

shamrock ['ʃæmrɔk] *s* kløverblad (Irlands nationalsymbol).

shank [ʃæŋk] *s* skaft; *~s pl* skinneben.

shan't [ʃa:nt] d.s.s. *shall not.*

shanty ['ʃænti] *s* hytte, skur; sømandssang; **~ town** *s* skurby (slumkvarter med blikskure).

shape [ʃeip] *s* form, facon; *in bad ~* i en dårlig tilstand; *get sth into ~* få sat skik på ngt; *in the ~ of* i form af; *take ~* få (,tage) form // *v* forme, danne; udforme; forme sig; *~ up* udvikle sig i en heldig retning; **~less** *adj* uformelig.

shapely ['ʃeipli] *adj* velskabt.

shard [ʃa:d] *s* skår.

share [ʃɛə*] *s* del, andel; aktie // *v* dele; deltage; *~ out* dele ud; deles om; **~holder** *s* aktionær.

shark [ʃa:k] *s* haj (også *fig).*

sharp [ʃa:p] *s (mus)* kryds; *C-~ major* cis-dur // *adj* skarp; spids; bidende; råkold; markeret; vaks, kvik // *adv* skarpt; præcis; *at 2 o'clock ~* præcis kl. 2; *look ~!* lad det nu gå lidt kvikt! *pull up ~* bremse pludseligt.

sharpen ['ʃa:pn] *v* hvæsse; spidse (fx *a pencil* en blyant); skærpe.

sharpener ['ʃa:pənə*] *s* blyantspidser.

sharp-eyed ['ʃa:paid] *adj* skarpsynet.

sharpshooter ['ʃa:pʃu:tə*] *s* skarpskytte.

sharp-witted ['ʃa:pwitid] *adj* skarpsindig, vågen.

shatter [ʃætə*] *v* knuse; smadre; splintre; blive knust; ødelægge; nedbryde; **~proof** *adj* (om glas) splintfri.

shave [ʃeiv] *s* barbering; *have a ~* barbere sig; *it was a close ~* (F) det var lige til øllet, det var på et hængende hår // *v* barbere (sig).

shaver ['ʃeivə*] *s* barbermaskine.

shaving ['ʃeiviŋ] *s* barbering; **~ brush** *s* barberkost; **~ cream** *s* barbercreme.

shavings ['ʃeiviŋz] *spl* (høvl)spåner.

shawl [ʃɔ:l] *s* sjal.

she [ʃi:] *pron* hun; den, det.

sheaf [ʃi:f] *s (pl: sheaves* [ʃi:vz]) neg, bundt.

shear [ʃiə*] *v (~ed, ~ed* el. *shorn* [ʃɔ:n]) klippe (fx *sheep* får); **~s** *spl* saks; hækkesaks.

sheath [ʃi:θ] *s* skede; (om kjole) hylster; kondom.

sheathe [ʃi:ð] *v* stikke i skeden; beklæde; armere.

sheaves [ʃi:vz] *spl* af *sheaf.*

shed [ʃɛd] *s* skur // *v (shed, shed)* fælde, kaste (af); udgyde (fx *tears* tårer); *~ light on* kaste lys over.

she'd [ʃi:d] d.s.s. *she had; she would.*

sheen [ʃi:n] *s* skin, glans.

sheep [ʃi:p] *s (pl: sheep)* får; **~dog** *s* fårehund.

sheepish ['ʃi:piʃ] *adj* flov; fåret.

sheepskin ['ʃi:pskin] *s* fåreskind.

sheer [ʃiə*] *adj* let; tynd, ren (og skær); meget stejl; *it's ~ nonsense* det er det rene vrøvl // *adv* helt.

sheet [ʃi:t] *s* lagen; ark; plade; flade; **~ing** *s* lærred; *plastic ~ing* plastovertræk; **~ metal** *s* metalplader.

shelf [ʃɛlf] *s (pl: shelves* [ʃɛlvz]) hylde; afsats; rev; revle.

shell [ʃɛl] *s* skal; konkylie; *(mil)* granat // *v* pille, afskalle; bælge; bombardere.

she'll [ʃi:l] d.s.s. *she shall; she will.*

shellfish ['ʃɛlfiʃ] *s* skaldyr.

shelter ['ʃɛltə*] *s* ly, beskyttelse; tilflugtssted; beskyttelsesrum // *v* skærme; give ly; søge læ (,ly).

sheltered ['ʃɛltəd] *adj* beskyttet; i læ; *~ accomodation* beskyttet bolig (for ældre); *~ housing* beskyttet boligbyggeri.

shelve [ʃɛlv] *v* lægge på hylden; skrinlægge; **~s** *spl* af *shelf.*

shepherd ['ʃɛpəd] *s* (fåre)hyrde; *~'s pie* pie af hakket kød med låg af kartoffelmos // *v* vogte; eskortere.

sherbet ['ʃə:bət] *s* sv.t. limonade med is; *(am)* sorbet-is.

sheriff ['ʃɛrif] *s* sherif; *(am)* sv. omtrt. politimeser; (skotsk) sv.t. fredsdommer.

she's [ʃi:z] d.s.s. *she has; she is.*

shield [ʃi:ld] *s* skjold; skærm // *v* skærme, værne *(from* imod).

shift [ʃift] *s* forandring; skiftehold; chemise // *v* flytte (rundt på); skifte; ændre; **~work** *s* skifteholdsarbejde.

shifty ['ʃifti] *adj* omskiftelig; flakkende.

shilling ['ʃiliŋ] *s* (indtil 1971 britisk mønt, *£1* sv.t. *20 ~s).*

shilly-shally ['ʃiliʃæli] *v* vakle, være usikker.

shimmer ['ʃimə*] *s* flimren // *v* glitre, flimre.

shin [ʃin] *s* skinneben.

shindig ['ʃindig] *s* (F) gilde; farlig ballade.

shine [ʃain] *s* skin; glans; *give sth a ~* pudse ngt; *come rain or ~* hvad enten vejret er godt el. dårligt // *v (shone, shone* [ʃɔn]) skinne, stråle; brillere; pudse.

shiner ['ʃainə*] *s* (F) blåt øje.

shingle [ʃingl] *s* tagspån; rullesten.

shingles [ʃinglz] *spl (med)* helvedesild.
shin guard ['ʃinga:d] *s (sport)* benbeskytter.
shiny ['ʃaini] *adj* blank, skinnende.
ship [ʃip] *s* skib; *abandon ~* gå i bådene // *v* sende (,transportere) med skib; indskibe (sig); (for)sende; **~broker** *s* skibsmægler; **~ment** *s* forsendelse, sending; **~owner** *s* skibsreder.
shipping ['ʃipiŋ] *s* søfart; forsendelse; **~ office** *s* rederikontor; spedition.
ship-shape ['ʃipʃeip] *adj* sømandsmæssig; i fineste orden.
shipwreck ['ʃiprɛk] *s* skibbrud // *v: be ~ed* lide skibbrud.
shipyard ['ʃipja:d] *s* skibsværft.
shire [ʃaiə*] (i sms: [-ʃə*] fx *York~* ['jɔ:kʃə*]) *s* grevskab; *out in the ~s* (også) ude i landområderne.
shirk [ʃə:k] *v* undgå; knibe udenom; pjække.
shirt [ʃə:t] *s* skjorte, skjortebluse; *keep your ~ on!* tag det med ro! **~-front** *s* skjortebryst.
shirty ['ʃə:ti] *adj* (F) knotten.
shit [ʃit] *s* (F) lort, skid; *be in the ~* (S) være på spanden; *tough ~!* (S) surt show! // *v (shit, shit)* (S) skide.
shiver ['ʃivə*] *s* rysten, gysen; *get the ~s* få kulderystninger // *v* ryste.
shoal [ʃəul] *s* stime; sandbanke; lavvandet sted.
shock [ʃɔk] *s* rystelse, stød; chok // *v* ryste; chokere; **~ absorber** *s* støddæmper.
shocking ['ʃɔkiŋ] *adj* chokerende; skandaløs.
shockproof ['ʃɔkpru:f] *adj* stødsikret.
shock wave ['ʃɔk ,weiv] *s* trykbølge.
shoddy ['ʃɔdi] *adj* dårlig; tarvelig.
shoe [ʃu:] *s* sko; *step into sby's ~s* træde i ens fodspor // *v (shod, shod* [ʃɔd]) sko; beslå; **~black** *s* skopudser; **~brush** *s* skobørste; **~lace** *s* snørebånd; **~ polish** *s* skocreme; **~ maker** *s* skomager; **~shine** *s* skopudsning; skopudser; **~string** *s (am)* snørrebånd; **~tree** *s* skolæst.
shone [ʃɔn] *præt* og *pp* af *shine.*
shoo [ʃu:] *v: ~ away* kyse væk.
shook [ʃuk] *præt* af *shake.*
shoot [ʃu:t] *s (bot)* skud; jagt; skydekonkurrence // *v (shot, shot* [ʃɔt]) skyde; affyre; gå på jagt; fare; *~ the lights* drøne over for rødt (lys); *~ in* fare ind; *~ one's mouth off* plapre ud med ngt; *~ up* skyde i vejret; fare op.
shooting ['ʃu:tiŋ] *s* skydning; jagt // *adj* skyde-; jagt-; *a ~ pain* et jag af smerte; **~ box** *s* jagthytte; **~ incident** *s* skudepisode; **~ range** *s* skydebane; **~ star** *s* stjerneskud.
shoot-out ['ʃu:taut] *s* skudopgør.
shop [ʃɔp] *s* forretning, butik; værksted; *set up ~* åbne forretning (,værksted) // *v* (også: *go ~ping)* gå på indkøb; *~ around for sth* se sig om efter ngt (man vil købe); **~ assistant** *s* ekspedient; **~ front** *s* butiksfacade; **~keeper** *s* butiksindehaver; handlende; **~lifter** *s* butikstyv; **~lifting** *s* butikstyveri; **~per** *s* en der går på indkøb; **~ping** *s* indkøb; **~ping bag** *s* indkøbstaske; **~ping centre** *s* butikscenter; **~ steward** *s* (på fabrik etc) tillidsmand; **~ window** *s* udstillingsvindue.
shore [ʃɔ:*] *s* kyst; land; *on ~* i land // *v: ~ up* stive af, forstærke.
shorn [ʃɔ:n] *pp* af *shear.*
short [ʃɔ:t] *adj* kort; kortvarig; for kort; kortfattet, studs; *be ~ of sth* mangle ngt; *~ of breath* forpustet; *I'm three ~* jeg mangler tre; *in ~* kort sagt; *be in ~ supply* være en mangelvare; *~ of* bortset fra; *everything ~ of...* alt undtagen...; *it is ~ for...* det er en forkortelse af...; *cut ~* afkorte; afbryde; *~ of* bortset fra, med undtagelse af; *fall ~ of* stå tilbage for; *be running ~ of sth* være ved at løbe tør for ngt; *make ~ work of sby* gøre kort proces med en; *stop ~* standse brat; *stop ~ of sth* ikke gå helt hen til ngt.
shortage ['ʃɔ:tidʒ] *s* mangel, knaphed.
short... ['ʃɔ:t] sms: **~bread** [-brɛd] *s* slags sprød mørdejskage; **~-change**

v give for lidt penge tilbage, snyde; **~-circuit** *s* kortslutning // *v* kortslutte; **~coming** *s* fejl, skavank; **~-crust pastry** *s* mørdej; **~cut** *s* genvej.

shorten ['ʃɔ:tn] *v* forkorte; blive kortere; **~ing** *s (gastr)* fedtstof (til bagning).

short... ['ʃɔ:t-] sms: **~fall** *s* underskud; **~hand** *s* stenografi; **~-handed** *adj* underbemandet; **~hand typist** *s* stenograf og maskinskriver; **~-lived** [-livd] *adj* kortvarig.

shortly ['ʃɔ:tli] *adv* kort; snart, inden længe.

short... ['ʃɔ:t-] sms: **~-range** *adj* kortrækkende; nær-; kortfristet; **~-sighted** *adj* nærsynet; kortsynet; **~-staffed** *adj* underbemandet; **~ story** *s* novelle; **~-tempered** *adj* irritabel; **~-term** *adj* korttids, kortfristet; **~wave** *s* kortbølge.

shot [ʃɔt] *s* skud; skytte; (F) forsøg; sprøjte; tår; foto; *have a ~ at sth* (F) forsøge sig med ngt; *he's a good ~* han er god til at skyde; *a big ~* (F) en stor kanon; *like a ~* hurtigere end lynet; **~gun** *s* haglgevær; **~putting** *s (sport)* kuglestød.

should [ʃud] *præt* af *shall; I ~ go now* jeg burde gå nu; *I ~ go if I were you* hvis jeg var dig ville jeg gå; *I ~ like to* jeg vil(le) gerne; *I ~ think so* det tror jeg nok; ja, mon ikke!.

shoulder ['ʃəuldə*] *s* skulder; *(gastr)* bov; (om vej) rabat; *rub ~s with sby* gnubbe sig op ad en // *v* tage over skulderen; *(fig)* tage på sine skuldre; **~-bag** *s* skuldertaske; **~ blade** *s* skulderblad; **~-length** *adj* skulderlangt; **~-strap** *s* skulderstrop.

shouldn't [ʃudnt] d.s.s. *should not.*

shout [ʃaut] *s* råb; *give sby a ~* kalde (,råbe) på en // *v* råbe; skråle; *~ sby down* overdøve en; *~ out* udstøde et skrig; **~ing** *s* råben.

shove [ʃʌv] *s* skub, puf // *v* skubbe, puffe; *~ sth in* (F) stoppe ngt ind (i); *~ off!* (F) skrid!.

shovel [ʃʌvl] *s* skovl // *v* skovle.

show [ʃəu] *s* skue; udstilling; forestilling, opvisning; skin; *steal the ~* stjæle billedet; *be on ~* være udstillet; *put up a good ~* klare sig fint; *~ of hands* håndsoprækning // *v (showed, shown* [ʃəun]) vise, udvise, fremvise; udstille; vise sig, kunne ses; *it just goes to ~* der kan man bare se; *does it ~?* kan det ses? *~ sby in* vise en ind; *the dress ~ed off her figure* kjolen fremhævede hendes figur; *~ off* vise sig, vigte sig; *~ sby out* vise en ud; *~ up* vise sig, dukke op; komme til sin ret; afsløre; **~ business** *s* underholdningsbranchen; **~case** *s* montre; udhængsskab; **~down** *s* styrkeprøve.

shower ['ʃauə*] *s* byge; regn; brusebad, bruser // *v* tage brusebad; *~ sby with* overøse en med; **~ cabinet** *s* brusekabine; **~ head** *s* bruser; **~proof** *adj* regntæt.

showery ['ʃauəri] *adj* byget; regnvejrs-.

showground ['ʃəugraund] *s* markedsplads; messeområde.

showing ['ʃəuiŋ] *s* forevisning.

showjumping ['ʃəudʒʌmpiŋ] *s* ridebanespringning.

showmanship ['ʃəumənʃip] *s* sans for PR.

shown [ʃəun] *pp* af *show.*

showpiece ['ʃəupi:s] *s* udstillingsgenstand; bravurnummer.

showplace ['ʃəupleis] *s* prestigebyggeri; turistattraktion.

showroom ['ʃəuru:m] *s* udstillingslokale.

showy ['ʃəui] *adj* prangende.

shrank [ʃræŋk] *præt* af *shrink.*

shrapnel ['ʃræpnəl] *s* granatsplint.

shred [ʃrɛd] *s* trævl; stump; smule; *be in ~s* hænge i laser; *(fig)* være ødelagt; *tear to ~s* rive i stykker // *v* rive (,skære) i strimler; **~der** *s* råkostmaskine; makuleringsmaskine.

shrew [ʃru:] *s* rappenskralde; *(zo)* spidsmus.

shrewd [ʃru:d] *adj* klog; fiffig, dreven.

shriek [ʃri:k] *s* skingrende skrig, hvin // *v* skrige, hyle.

shrill [ʃril] *adj* skringrende; skærende; skarp.

shrimp [ʃrimp] *s* reje; *(fig)* splejs.

shrine [ʃrain] *s* skrin; helligdom.

shrink [ʃriŋk] *s (am,* F) psykiater // *v (shrank, shrunk* [ʃræŋk, ʃrʌŋk]) krympe; vige tilbage; kvie sig *(at* ved).

shrinkage ['ʃriŋkidʒ] *s* krympning; svind.

shrinkproof ['ʃriŋkpru:f] *adj* krympefri.

shrink-wrap ['ʃriŋkræp] *v* (om vare) "krympe" (pakke i tæt plast).

shrivel [ʃrivl] *v: ~ (up)* skrumpe ind, visne; **~led** *adj* vissen; indskrumpen.

shroud [ʃraud] *s* svøb; dække; liglagen // *v: ~ed in mist* hyllet i tåge; *~ed in mystery* omgivet af mystik.

Shrovetide ['ʃrəuvtaid] *s* fastelavn.

shrub [ʃrʌb] *s* busk; **~bery** *s* buskads.

shrug [ʃrʌg] *s* skuldertræk // *v: ~ (one's shoulders)* trække på skuldrene; *~ sth off* slå ngt hen; ryste ngt af (sig).

shrunk [ʃrʌnk] *pp* af *skrink;* **~en** *adj* indskrumpen.

shudder ['ʃʌdə*] *s* gysen; skælven // *v* gyse; ryste; *I ~ to think of him* jeg gyser ved tanken om ham.

shuffle [ʃʌfl] *v* blande (kort); *~ one's feet* slæbe med fødderne, sjokke.

shun [ʃʌn] *v* undgå, sky.

shunt [ʃʌnt] *v* lede (ind på et sidespor); rangere; **~ing** *s* rangering.

shush [ʃʌʃ] *interj* tys, sch // *v* tysse på; tie stille.

shut [ʃʌt] *v (shut, shut)* lukke (sig); *~ down* lukke, nedlægge; *~ in* lukke inde; *~ off* lukke (af) for; spærre; *~ out* lukke ude; *~ up* lukke (inde); holde mund; lukke munden på; **~down** *s* lukning.

shutter ['ʃʌtə*] *s* skodde; *(foto)* lukker.

shuttle [ʃʌtl] *s* (i væv) skytte; fly i fast rutefart; *space ~* rumfærge; *~ service* pendultrafik, pendulfart; **~cock** *s* badmintonbold.

shy [ʃai] *adj* genert, sky; *fight ~ of sth* prøve at undgå ngt // *v: ~ away from* vige tilbage for, sky.

siblings *spl* søskende.

sick [sik] *s* bræk // *adj* syg; dårlig; sygelig; *be (,feel) ~* have kvalme; kaste op; *be ~ (and tired) of* være led og ked af; *be off ~* være sygemeldt; *be worried ~* være meget bekymret.

sicken [sikn] *v* blive (,gøre) syg; få (,give) kvalme; **~ing** *adj* kvalmende, ækel.

sickle [sikl] *s* segl.

sick leave ['sik,li:v] *s* sygeorlov.

sickly ['sikli] *adj* svagelig; vammel, kvalm.

sickness ['siknis] *s* sygdom; kvalme; **~ benefit** *s* sygedagpenge.

side [said] *s* side; parti; part; (om vej) rabat; (flod)bred; *have sth on the ~* lave et sidespring; *on either ~ of* på begge sider af; *this ~ of Easter* på denne side af påsken; *to be on the safe ~* for at være på den sikre side; *it's on the small ~* den er lidt for lille; *take ~s with* tage parti for, holde med // *v: ~ with sby* holde med en; **~board** *s* skænk; **~car** *s* sidevogn; **~ effect** *s* bivirkning; **~ issue** *s* biting; **~light** *s (auto)* parkeringslygte, sidelygte; **~line** *s (sport)* sidelinje; *(fig)* bibeskæftigelse; **~long** *adj* skrå, sidelæns; **~ plate** *s* sidetallerken, asiet; **~-splitting** *adj* hylende grinagtig; **~-step** *v* vige (til side); undgå; **~track** *v* føre (,komme) ind på et sidespor; distrahere(s); **~walk** *s (am)* fortov; **~ways** *adv* sidelæns.

sidle [saidl] *v: ~ up (to)* kante sig hen (til); liste sig hen (til).

siege [si:dʒ] *s* belejring; *lay ~ to* belejre.

sieve [si:v] *s* sigte, si // *v* sigte, si.

sift [sift] *v* si; strø; *(fig)* finkæmme.

sigh [sai] *s* suk; *heave a ~* drage et dybt suk // *v* sukke; (om vinden) suse.

sight [sait] *s* syn; seværdighed; sigte; *at first ~* ved første blik; *know sby by ~* kende en af udseende; *in ~* i syne; *lose ~ of* tabe af syne; *out of ~* ude af syne; *not by a long ~* ikke på langt nær, langt fra; *you look a ~!* sikken du ser ud; *a ~ better* me-

get bedre; *she has second* ~ hun er synsk // *v* få øje på; sigte.
sighted ['saitid] *adj* seende.
sighting ['saitiŋ] *s* iagttagelse.
sight-read ['saitri:d] *v* læse fra bladet.
sign [sain] *s* tegn; skilt; *there's no ~ of him* jeg (,vi) kan ikke se ham (nogen steder) // *v* gøre tegn; underskrive; signere; ~ *in* indskrive sig; stemple ind; melde sig; ~ *up* indmelde sig; *(mil)* lade sig hverve; ansætte; hverve, hyre.
signal ['signəl] *s* signal // *v* signalere, give tegn.
signature ['signətʃə*] *s* underskrift; ~ **tune** *s* kendingsmelodi.
signboard ['sainbɔ:d] *s* skilt.
significance [sig'nifikəns] *s* betydning.
significant [sig'nifikənt] *adj* betydningsfuld; talende (fx *look* blik).
signify ['signifai] *v* betegne, betyde; tilkendegive.
signpost ['sainpəust] *s* (vej)skilt; vejviser; **~ed** *adj* (om vej) afmærket.
silage ['sailidʒ] *s* ensilage; ~ **harvester** *s* grønthøster.
silence [sailns] *s* stilhed; tavshed // *v* lukke munden på.
silencer ['sailənsə*] *s* lyddæmper.
silent ['sailənt] *adj* stille, tavs; lydløs; *keep* ~ tie stille; ~ **movie** *s* stumfilm.
silicon ['silikən] *s (kem)* silicium.
silicone ['silikəun] *s* silikone.
silk [silk] *s* silke; *take* ~ blive *Queen's counsel;* **~lined** *adj* silkeforet.
silky ['silki] *adj* silkeagtig; silkeblød.
sill [sil] *s* vindueskarm; dørtrin.
silly ['sili] *adj* dum; *the ~ season* agurketiden.
silt [silt] *s* dynd, slam.
silver ['silvə*] *s* sølv; (sølv)mønter; sølvtøj; **~fish** *s* sølvkræ; ~ **foil** *s* sølvpapir; aluminiumsfolie; **~-plated** *adj* forsølvet; sølvplet-; **~smith** *s* sølvsmed; **~ware** *s* sølvtøj.
silvery ['silvəri] *adj* sølvskinnende.
similar ['similə*] *adj* lignende; *look ~ to* ligne.
similarity [simi'læriti] *s* lighed.
similarly ['similəli] *adv* ligeledes; på samme måde.
simmer ['simə*] *v* småkoge, snurre; ulme; ~ *down* hidse sig ned; fortage sig.
simper ['simpə*] *v* smiske; smile affekteret.
simple [simpl] *adj* enkel; simpel, ligetil; *pure and* ~ simpelthen; **~-minded** *adj* enfoldig, naiv.
simpleton ['simpltən] *s* tosse.
simplicity [sim'plisiti] *s* enkelhed, ligefremhed.
simplification [simplifi'keiʃən] *s* forenkling.
simplify ['simplifai] *v* forenkle.
simply ['simpli] *adv* simpelthen, kun.
simulate ['simjuleit] *v* foregive, efterligne; simulere.
simulation [simju'leiʃən] *s* efterligning; simulering.
simulcast ['siməlka:st] *s* samsending (mellem radio og tv).
simultaneous [siməl'teiniəs] *adj* samtidig, simultan.
sin [sin] *s* synd; ~ *of omission* undladelsessynd; *mortal* ~ dødssynd // *v* synde.
since [sins] *konj/præp* siden; da; eftersom; *long* ~ for længst; ~ *then* fra da af; siden da; *ever* ~ lige siden.
sincere [sin'siə*] *adj* oprigtig; ægte; *yours ~ly* (i brev) med venlig hilsen.
sincerity [sin'sɛriti] *s* oprigtighed.
sinecure ['sainikjuə*] *s: this job is no ~!* det her er ikke ngt hvilehjem!
sinew ['sinju:] *s* sene; **~s** *spl* kræfter, styrke.
sinful [sinful] *adj* syndig.
sing [siŋ] *v (sang, sung* [sæŋ, sʌŋ]) synge; ~ *sby's praises* rose en i høje toner; ~ *out* råbe (,tale) højt; lyde, høres.
singe [sindʒ] *v* svide.
singer ['siŋə*] *s* sanger.
singing ['siŋiŋ] *s* sang, syngen // *adj* syngende; sang-.
single [siŋgl] *s* enkeltbillet; enkeltværelse; single; *~s* single // *v: ~ out* udvælge, udtage // *adj* enkelt; alene, ene, ugift; ~ *parent* enlig forsørger; **~-breasted** *adj* enradet;

~ cream *s* sv.t. kaffefløde; **~ file** *s: in ~ file* i gåsegang; **~-handed** *adj* alene, på egen hånd; **~-minded** *adj* målbevidst; **~ness** *s: ~ness of purpose* målbevidsthed.

singlet ['siŋglit] *s* undertrøje; ærmeløs sportstrøje.

singly ['siŋgli] *adv* enkeltvis.

sing-song ['siŋsɔŋ] *s* fællessang // *adj* (monotont) syngende.

singular ['siŋgjulə*] *s (gram)* ental, singularis // *adj* enestående; mærkelig, sær.

sinister ['sinistə*] *adj* truende; uhyggelig; ond.

sink [siŋk] *s* køkkenvask // *v (sank, sunk* [sæŋk, sʌŋk]) synke; dale; sænke; *~ sth into sth* sænke ngt ned i ngt; *~ in* trænge ind; *it didn't ~ in* det gik ikke op for mig; *a ~ing feeling* et sug i maven, en forudanelse; *my heart sank* jeg mistede modet; *let sby ~ or swim* lade en klare sig som han bedst kan.

sinner ['sinə*] *s* synder.

sinuous ['sinjuəs] *adj* bugtet.

sinus ['sainəs] *s (anat)* bihule.

sinusitis [sainə'saitis] *s* bihulebetændelse.

sip [sip] *s* slurk; nip // *v* nippe (til).

siphon ['saifən] *s* sifon; hævert // *v* suge ud (,op).

sir [sə*] *s* hr.; *Sir* titel for *knight.*

siren ['saiərin] *s* sirene.

sirloin ['sə:lɔin] *s* mørbradssteg, tyksteg.

sissy ['sisi] *s* tøsedreng.

sister ['sistə*] *s* søster; (over)sygeplejerske; **~-in-law** *s* svigerinde.

sit [sit] *s (sat, sat)* sidde; have sæde; være samlet; *~ (for) an exam* gå op til eksamen; *~ back* læne sig tilbage; *~ down* sætte sig (,sidde) ned; *~ tight* blive siddende; *~ up* sidde (,sætte sig) op; sidde oppe.

site [sait] *s* byggeplads, grund; plads, sted; beliggenhed; *missile ~* raketbase.

sitting ['sitiŋ] *s* samling, møde; **~ duck** *s* let offer; **~ room** *s* dagligstue.

situated ['sitjueitid] *adj* beliggende; anbragt.

situation [sitju'eiʃən] *s* beliggenhed; situation; stilling; *~s vacant* ledige stillinger; *~s wanted* stillinger søges.

six [siks] *num* seks; *at ~es and sevens* i ét rod; kaotisk; **~-shooter** *s* seksløber.

sixteen ['siksti:n] *num* seksten.

sixth [siksθ] *s* sjettedel // *adj* sjette.

sixty ['siksti] *num* tres.

size [saiz] *s* størrelse; *be about the ~ of a cat* være omtrent på størrelse med en kat; *try sth on for ~* prøve ngt for at se om størrelsen passer; *what ~ shoes do you take?* hvad størrelse bruger du i sko? *cut sby down to ~* få en ned på jorden, pille en ned // *v: ~ sby up* se en an.

sizeable ['saizəbl] *adj* anselig.

sizzle [sizl] *s* syden // *v* syde.

skate [skeit] *s* skøjte; *(zo)* rokke // *v* løbe på skøjter; *~ over sth (fig)* skøjte hen over ngt; **~board** *s* rullebræt.

skater ['skeitə*] *s* skøjteløber.

skating ['skeitiŋ] *s* skøjteløb; **~ rink** *s* skøjtebane.

skedaddle [ski'dædl] *v* stikke af.

skein [skein] *s* (om garn) fed.

skeleton ['skɛlətən] *s* skelet; **~ key** *s* hovednøgle; **~ staff** *s* minimum af personale.

sketch [skɛtʃ] *s* skitse, udkast; sketch // *v* skitsere.

sketchy ['skɛtʃi] *adj* skitseret; flygtig, overfladisk.

skewer ['skju:ə*] *s* (grill)spid.

ski [ski:] *s* ski // *v* løbe på ski.

skid [skid] *s* udskridning // *v* skride (ud); **~mark** *s* bremsespor, skridspor.

skier ['ski:ə*] *s* skiløber.

skiing ['ski:iŋ] *s* skiløb.

ski jumper ['ski: ˌdʒʌmpə*] *s* skihopper; **ski jumping** *s* skihop.

skilful ['skilful] *adj* dygtig.

skillet ['skilit] *s* stegepande.

skill [skil] *s* dygtighed; færdighed; **~ed** *adj* faglært; dygtig.

skim [skim] *v* skumme (fx mælk); stryge hen over; kigge igennem skimme; *~ stones* slå smut; **~med**

milk *s* skummetmælk; **~mer** *s* hulske.
skimp [skimp] *v* være nærig (,fedtet).
skimpy ['skimpi] *adj* knap; stumpet.
skin [skin] *s* hud; skind; skræl; *get under sby's ~* gå en på nerverne; fascinere en; *by the ~ of one's teeth* på et hængende hår, med nød og næppe // *v* flå; pille; skrælle; *keep one's eyes ~ned for sth* holde skarpt udkig efter ngt; **~-deep** *adj* overfladisk; **~ diving** *s* svømmedykning; **~-flick** *s* (F) pornofilm; **~flint** *s* fedthas.
skinny ['skini] *adj* tynd, mager; **~-dip** *v* (F) bade nøgen.
skintight ['skintait] *adj* (om tøj) stramtsiddende.
skip [skip] *s* hop, spring; affaldscontainer // *v* hoppe, springe; sjippe; springe over.
skipping rope ['skipiŋrəup] *s* sjippetov.
ski resort ['ski:ri'zɔ:t] *s* vintersportssted.
skirmish ['skə:miʃ] *s* træfning; skærmydsel.
skirt [skə:t] *s* nederdel, skørt // *v* løbe langs med; gå uden om; **~ing board** *s* fodpanel.
ski-tow ['ski:təu] *s* skilift.
skittle [skitl] *s* kegle; **~s** *spl* keglespil.
skive [skaiv] *v* pjække.
skulk [skʌlk] *v* luske, snige sig.
skull [skʌl] *s* kranium; hovedskal.
skunk [skʌŋk] *s* stinkdyr.
sky [skai] *s* himmel; *praise sby to the skies* rose en til skyerne; **~-blue** *adj* himmelblå; **~diving** *s* frit fald (før faldskærmen udløses); **~-high** *adj* skyhøj; *blow sth ~-high* sprænge ngt i luften; *(fig)* ødelægge ngt fuldstændigt; **~jacker** *s* flypirat; **~lark** *s* lærke; **~line** *s* horisont; synskreds; **~rocket** *v* (om priser) ryge i vejret; **~scraper** *s* skyskraber.
slab [slæb] *s* plade (fx *of stone* sten-); flise; tavle.
slack [slæk] *adj* slap; træg; forsømmelig; *~ wind* svag vind; **~en** *v: ~en (off)* slappe(s); slække; løje af.
slag [slæg] *s* slagge.
slain [slein] *pp* af *slay*.
slam [slæm] *s* smæk(ken); smæld // *v* smække (fx *the door* døren); skælde ud; *~ on the brakes* hugge bremserne i.
slander ['slændə*] *s* bagvaskelse, sladder // *v* bagtale.
slant [sla:nt] *s* skråning, hældning; tendens; synsvinkel; **~ed** *adj* skrå; tendentiøs, som har slagside; **~ing** *adj* skæv, skrå.
slap [slæp] *s* slag, klask, smæk; *a ~ in the face* et slag i ansigtet; *(fig)* en afbrænder // *v* slå, klaske // *adv* lige, pladask; **~dash** *adj* forhastet, jasket; **~stick comedy** *s* falde på halen-komedie; **~-up** *adj: a ~-up meal* et lukullisk måltid.
slash [slæʃ] *s* snit; slag; skråstreg; nedskæring; *have a ~* (F om mand) slå en streg (dvs. tisse) // *v* flænge; slå; (om priser etc) nedskære drastisk.
slat [slæt] *s* liste; tremme.
slate [sleit] *s* skifer; tavle; *start with a clean ~* begynde et nyt liv.
slaughter ['slɔ:tə*] *s* slagtning; massakre // *v* slagte; slå ned; massakrere; **~house** *s* slagteri.
slave [sleiv] *s* slave, træl // *v: ~ (away)* slide og slæbe; **~ry** ['sleivəri] *s* slaveri.
Slavic ['slævik] *adj* slavisk.
slavish ['sleiviʃ] *adj* slavisk (fx *imitation* efterligning).
Slavonic [slə'vɔnik] *adj* slavisk.
slay [slei] *v (slew, slain* [slu:, slein]) (H) dræbe, slå ihjel.
sleazy ['sli:zi] *adj* snusket.
sledge [slɛdʒ] *s* slæde, kælk; **~hammer** *s* forhammer.
sleek [sli:k] *adj* (om hår etc) glat, glinsende; (om bil, båd etc) strømlinet, laber.
sleep [sli:p] *s* søvn; *go to ~* falde i søvn; *put to ~* få til at falde i søvn; lægge til at sove; bedøve; (om dyr) aflive // *v (slept, slept* [slɛpt]) sove; *the caravan ~s five* der er fem sovepladser i campingvognen; *~ around* gå i seng med alle og en-

hver; ~ *in* sove længe; sove over sig; ~ *it off* sove rusen ud; ~ *through the alarm clock* sove fra vækkeuret.

sleeper ['sli:pə*] *s* sovende person; sovevogn; jernbanesvelle; ørestik; *be a heavy* ~ sove tungt.

sleeping ['sli:piŋ] *adj* sovende; *have trouble* ~ have søvnbesvær; **~ bag** *s* sovepose; **Sleeping Beauty** *s* Tornerose; **~ policeman** *s* bump (i vejbane for at tvinge biler til at køre langsomt).

sleepless ['sli:plis] *adj* søvnløs.

sleepwalker ['sli:pwɔ:kə*] *s* søvngænger.

sleepy ['sli:pi] *adj* søvnig; søvndyssende.

sleet [sli:t] *s* slud, tøsne.

sleeve [sli:v] *s* ærme; (plade)omslag; *have sth up one's* ~ have ngt i baghånden; *be laughing up one's* ~ grine i skægget.

sleigh [slei] *s* slæde, kane // *v* køre i kane.

sleight [slait] *s:* ~ *of hand* fingerfærdighed.

slender ['slɛndə*] *adj* slank, tynd, spinkel.

slept [slɛpt] *præt* og *pp* af *sleep.*

sleuth [slu:θ] *s* detektiv.

slew [slu:] *præt* af *slay.*

slice [slais] *s* skive; plade; paletkniv; kageske // *v* snitte, skære i skiver.

slicer ['slaisə*] *s* osteskærer; pålægsmaskine.

slick [slik] *s* oliepøl (på vand) // *adj* glat, fedtet; smart.

slid [slid] *præt* og *pp* af *slide.*

slide [slaid] *s* gliden; skred; glidebane, rutschebane; lysbillede, dias; skydespænde // *v (slid, slid* [slid]) glide; rutsche; smutte; **~ mount** *s* diasramme; **~ rule** *s* regnestok.

sliding ['slaidiŋ] *adj* glidende; skyde- (fx *door* dør).

slight [slait] *s* fornærmelse // *v* negligere; støde, krænke // *adj* spinkel; skrøbelig; ubetydelig; let; *not the ~est* ikke det (,den) mindste; **~ly** *adv* let, lettere.

slim [slim] *v* slanke sig // *adj* slank; lille.

slime [slaim] *s* slim; slam.

slimmer ['slimə*] *s* person på slankekur.

slimming ['slimiŋ] *s* afmagring // *adj* slankende; slanke-.

slimy ['slaimi] *adj* slimet; ækel.

sling [sliŋ] *s* slynge; (skulder)rem; skråbind (fx til brækket arm); bæresele // *v (slung, slung* [slʌŋ]) slynge, kaste; **~backs** *spl* sko med hælrem; **~shot** *s (am)* slangebøsse.

slink [sliŋk] *v (slunk, slunk* [slʌŋk]) luske.

slinky ['sliŋki] *adj* (om kjole) tætsiddende.

slip [slip] *s* gliden; fejltrin; underkjole; pudebetræk; seddel; strimmel papir; *give sby the* ~ smutte fra en; *a ~ of the tongue* en fortalelse, en smutter // *v* glide; putte, smutte; liste; *it ~ped my mind* jeg glemte det, jeg har glemt det; *the shaver ~ped, so he lost his beard* barbermaskinen smuttede så han mistede skægget; ~ *away* smutte (,slippe) væk; ~ *off one's clothes* smutte ud af tøjet; ~ *out* liste (,smutte) ud; ~ *up* dumme sig, lave en brøler; **~ped disc** *s* discusprolaps.

slipper ['slipə*] *s* hjemmesko, sutsko.

slippery ['slipəri] *adj* glat, smattet.

slip... ['slip-] sms: **~ road** *s* tilkørselsvej, frakørselsvej (ved motorvej); **~shod** *adj* sjusket; udtrådt; **~-up** *s* dumhed, brøler; **~way** *s* bedding.

slit [slit] *s* sprække; flænge // *v (slit, slit)* skære (op); flænge; ~ *sby's throat* skære halsen over på en.

slither ['sliðə*] *v* glide; kure.

sliver ['slivə*] *s* splint; tynd skive.

slobber ['slɔbə*] *s* savl // *v* savle.

sloe [sləu] *s* slåen.

slog [slɔg] *s* hestearbejde, træls job (,tur) // *v* slå; ase, pukle; **~ger** *s* slider.

slop [slɔp] *v* sjaske, plaske; spilde.

slope [sləup] *s* skråning, skrænt; hældning // *v* skråne; stå skråt.

sloppy ['slɔpi] *adj* sjasket, sjusket; pløret; (om fx film) pladdersentimental.

slops [slɔps] *spl* spildevand; sprøjt.
slosh [slɔʃ] *v* slå; pjaske, skvulpe; **~ed** *adj* pløret.
slot [slɔt] *s* sprække, spalte; // *v: ~ in* stikke ind, passe ind i; gå i hak.
sloth [sləuθ] *s (zo)* dovendyr; dovenskab.
slot machine ['slɔtmə,ʃi:n] *s* automat.
slough [slʌf] *s (zo)* ham // *v* skifte ham.
slovenly ['slʌvənli] *adj* sjusket.
slow [sləu] *v: ~ (down, up)* sætte farten ned // *adj* langsom; sen; tungnem; *be ~* (om ur) gå for langsomt; *the ~ season* den stille årstid; *a ~ fire* en sagte ild; *~ off the mark* langsom i optrækket; **~coach** *s* smøl, drys; **~-witted** *adj* langsomt opfattende.
sludge [slʌdʒ] *s* mudder, slam.
slug [slʌg] *s (zo)* snegl; kugle; slurk, tår // *v* slå; **~gish** *adj* doven, ugidelig; træg.
sluice [slu:s] *s* sluse; skylning // *v* skylle, spule.
slum [slʌm] *s* slumkvarter.
slumber ['slʌmbə*] *s* slummer // *v* slumre.
slump [slʌmp] *s* pludseligt fald (i priser etc); krise // *v* falde; sidde sammenkrøben.
slung [slʌŋ] *præt* og *pp* af *sling.*
slunk [slʌŋk] *præt* og *pp* af *slink.*
slur [slə:*] *s* utydelig tale; ulæselig tekst; (skam)plet // *v* tale utydeligt.
slurp [slə:p] *v* slubre.
slush [slʌʃ] *s* tøsne, sjap; sentimentalt pladder.
slushy ['slʌʃi] *adj* sjappet; *(fig)* pladdersentimental.
slut [slʌt] *s* sjuske, tøs; mær.
sly [slai] *adj* snedig, snu; *on the ~* i smug.
smack [smæk] *s* smæk, klask; lussing; smag; anelse // *v* smække; *~ of* smage af; *~ one's lips* smække med læberne // *adv* lige; pladask.
small [smɔ:l] *adj* lille; smålig; *the ~ of the back* lænden; *in a ~ way* i det små; **~ ads** *spl* rubrikannoncer; **~ change** *s* småpenge; **~ fry** *s* småkravl; **~holder** *s* husmand.
smallish ['smɔ:liʃ] *adj* ret lille.
smallpox ['smɔ:lpɔks] *s (med)* kopper.
smalls [smɔ:lz] *spl* klatvask.
small-scale ['smɔ:lskeil] *adj* i mindre skala.
smalltalk ['smɔ:ltɔ:k] *s* småsnak.
smarmy ['sma:mi] *adj* slesk.
smart [sma:t] *s* svie, smerte // *v* svie; vride sig // *adj* sviende; rask; dygtig, smart; **~-aleck** *s* vigtigper; bedrevidende person.
smarten *v: ~ up* fikse (sig) op.
smash [smæʃ] *s* sammenstød, kollision; hårdt slag; brag // *v* smadre, slå i stykker; knuse; gå i stykker; *~ into* smadre ind i; *~ up* smadre.
smashed [smæʃd] *adj* døddrukken.
smasher ['smæʃə*] *s* flot fyr (,pige).
smash-hit ['smæʃhit] *s* kæmpesucces, -hit.
smashing ['smæʃiŋ] *adj* (F) strålende; dundrende; eddersmart.
smattering ['smætəriŋ] *s: a ~ of German* nogle få gloser på tysk.
smear [smiə*] *s* plet; *(fig)* tilsvining // *v* oversmøre; rakke ned; **~ campaign** *s* smædekampagne.
smell [smɛl] *s* lugt; lugtesans // *v (smelt, smelt)* lugte (til); dufte; snuse; *~ a rat* lugte lunten; *~ trouble* ane uråd; *~ sth out* opsnuse ngt; (F) hørme ngt til.
smelly ['smɛli] *adj* ildelugtende.
smile [smail] *s* smil; *be all ~s* være ét stort smil // *v* smile; *keep smiling!* hold humøret oppe! *~ at* smile ttil (,ad); *~ on* tilsmile.
smirch [smə:tʃ] *s* (smuds)plet // *v* tilsmudse, plette.
smirk [smə:k] *s* smørret grin // *v* grine smørret.
smith [smiθ] *s* smed.
smithereens [smiðə'ri:nz] *spl: smash to ~* slå i stumper og stykker.
smithy ['smiði] *s* smedje.
smitten [smitn] *adj: ~ with* (be)smittet med, ramt af.
smock [smɔk] *s* kittel, busseronne; smocksyning.
smog [smɔg] *s* tåge (blandet med røg).
smoke [sməuk] *s* røg; *have a ~* tage

sig en smøg // *v* ryge; ose; røge; **~less** *adj* røgfri.
smoker ['smǝukǝ*] *s* ryger; *(jernb)* rygekupé.
smokescreen ['smǝukskri:n] *s* røgslør.
smokestack ['smǝukstæk] *s* (fabriks)skorsten.
smoking ['smǝukiŋ] *s* rygning.
smoky ['smǝuki] *adj* rygende; røget; tilrøget; røgfarvet.
smooch [smu:tʃ] *v* (F) kysse og kramme; danse tæt.
smooth [smu:ð] *v* glatte (ud); udjævne // *adj* glat, jævn; blød; (om person) beleven.
smother ['smʌðǝ*] *v* kvæle(s); undertrykke; overvælde.
smoulder ['smǝuldǝ*] *v* ulme.
smudge [smʌdʒ] *s* (udtværet) plet, plamage // *v* plette; tvære.
smug [smʌg] *adj* selvglad.
smuggle [smʌgl] *v* smugle; **~r** *s* smugler.
smuggling ['smʌgliŋ] *s* smugleri.
smut [smʌt] *s* smuds; sjofelheder; **~ty** *adj* smudsig; sjofel.
snack [snæk] *s* bid mad, mellemmåltid; mundsmag.
snag [snæg] *s* hindring, vanskelighed.
snail [sneil] *s* snegl; *at a ~'s pace* med sneglefart.
snake [sneik] *s* slange; **~ charmer** *s* slangetæmmer.
snap [snæp] *s* smæld, klik; snap(pen); bid; *a cold ~* en pludselig indsættende kulde // *v* snappe; knække; klikke; *(foto)* knipse; *~ one's fingers* knipse med fingrene; *~ at* snappe efter; snerre ad; *~ open* smække (,springe) op; *~ shut* smække i; *~ off* brække af; *~ up* snuppe // *adj* lynhurtig; uoverlagt; **~ fastener** *s* tryklås.
snappy ['snæpi] *adj* bidsk; kvik; *make it ~!* se at få fart på!
snare [snɛǝ*] *s* snare // *v* fange i snare; forlokke.
snarl [sna:l] *s* snerren // *v* snerre; *~ up* lave kludder i; blive blokeret.
snatch [snætʃ] *s* snappen; stump; brudstykke; tyveri // *v* gribe; snappe, snuppe; stjæle.
snazzy ['snæzi] *adj* (F) smart.
sneak [sni:k] *v* snige sig, luske; liste.
sneakers ['sni:kǝz] *spl* gummisko.
sneaking ['sni:kiŋ] *adj* lumsk; snigende.
sneaky ['sni:ki] *adj* lusket.
sneer [sniǝ*] *s* vrængen, hånligt smil // *v* vrænge; spotte.
sneeze [sni:z] *s* nys(en) // *v* nyse; *not to be ~d at* ikke at kimse af.
snide [snaid] *adj* spydig.
sniff [snif] *s* snøft, snusen // *v* snøfte; snuse; sniffe; *~ at* rynke på næsen ad; *~ out* opsnuse.
sniffy ['snifi] *adj* storsnudet.
snigger ['snigǝ*] *s* fnisen // *v* fnise.
snip [snip] *s* klip; stump; røverkøb.
snipe [snaip] *s* sneppe // *v: ~ at* kritisere.
sniper ['snaipǝ*] *s* snigskytte.
snippet ['snipit] *s* bid, stump.
snivel [snivl] *s* snot // *v* snøfte; flæbe.
snobbish ['snɔbiʃ] *adj* snobbet.
snog [snɔg] *v* (F) kysse og kramme.
snooker ['snu:kǝ*] *s* slags billardspil.
snoop [snu:p] *v* snuse; spionere; *~ on sby* udspionere en.
snooty ['snu:ti] *adj* storsnudet.
snooze [snu:z] *s* lille lur // *v* snue.
snore [snɔ:*] *v* snorke.
snoring ['snɔ:riŋ] *s* snorken // *adj* snorkende.
snort [snɔ:t] *s* fnys(en) // *v* fnyse.
snorter ['snɔ:tǝ*] *s: a real ~* (F) ngt alle tiders, ngt dødlækkert; en hård nød at knække.
snotty ['snɔti] *adj* snottet; storsnudet.
snout [snaut] *s* snude.
snow [snǝu] *s* sne; snevejr; (S) kokain // *v* sne; drysse; *be ~ed under* være begravet (i arbejde etc); **~-bound** *adj* indesneet; **~-capped** *adj* med sne på toppen; **~drift** *s* snedrive; **~drop** *s (bot)* vintergæk; **~flake** *s* snefnug; **Snow White** *s* Snehvide.
snowy ['snǝui] *adj* snevejrs-; snedækket.
snub [snʌb] *v* bide 'af; give en næse; **~-nosed** *adj* med opstoppernæse.
snuff [snʌf] *s* snus(tobak) // *v* slukke;

snyde (et lys); kvæle; ~ *it* (S) kradse 'af.
snuffle [snʌfl] *v* snøfte.
snug [snʌg] *adj* hyggelig, rar; lun.
snuggle [snʌgl] *v* putte sig; smyge sig (ind til).
so [səu] *adv* så; sådan; derfor // *konj* derfor, altså; ~ *as to* for (,således) at; ~ *that* for at, sådan at; ~ *do I* det gør jeg også; *if* ~ i så fald; *you don't say ~!* det mener (,siger) du ikke! *I hope* ~ det håber jeg; *ten or* ~ ti el. der omkring, cirka ti; ~ *far* hidtil, foreløbig; ~ *long!* farvel (så længe)! *and* ~ *on* og så videre; ~ *what?* og hvad så?
soak [səuk] *v* gennembløde; lægge (,ligge) i blød; *be ~ed through* være helt gennemblødt; ~ *in* trænge (,sive) ind; ~ *up* opsuge; **~ing** *adj: ~ing (wet)* sjaskvåd.
so-and-so ['səuənsəu] *s* noksagt.
soap [səup] *s* sæbe; **~ dispenser** *s* sæbeautomat; **~flakes** *spl* sæbespåner; **~ powder** *s* vaskepulver; **~suds** *spl* sæbevand.
soapy ['səupi] *adj* sæbeagtig; glat; sentimental.
soar [sɔ:*] *v* flyve højt, svæve; (om priser etc) ryge i vejret.
sob [sɔb] *s* hulk // *v* hulke.
sober ['səubə*] *adj* ædru; nøgtern, sober; ~ *as a judge* pinligt ædru // *v:* ~ *down* falde til ro; ~ *up* blive ædru.
so-called ['səu,kɔ:ld] *adj* såkaldt.
soccer ['sɔkə*] *s* (afledt af *association football)* fodbold.
sociable ['səuʃəbl] *adj* omgængelig, selskabelig.
social ['səuʃəl] *s* selskabelig sammenkomst // *adj* social; samfunds-; selskabelig; **~ climber** *s* stræber; opkomling; **~ disease** *s* kønssygdom; **~ drinker** *s* en der kun drikker i selskab.
socialist ['səuʃəlist] *s* socialist // *adj* socialistisk.
socialize ['səuʃəlaiz] *v* socialisere; ~ *with* omgås.
social... ['səuʃəl-] sms: **~ science** *s* samfundsvidenskab; **~ security** *s* bistandshjælp; bistandskontor; **~ studies** *spl* samtidsorientering; **~ welfare** *s* socialforsorg; **~ worker** *s* socialrådgiver.
society [sə'saiəti] *s* samfund; selskab, forening; *high* ~ de højere kredse.
sock [sɔk] *s* sok; (F) slag; *pull your ~s up!* se nu at tage dig sammen! *put a ~ in it!* hold så kæft! // *v* smide; slå, gokke; ~ *him one* stikke ham en (på bærret).
socket ['sɔkit] *s* holder; *(anat)* (øjen)hule; (led)skål; *(elek)* stikdåse; (på lampe) fatning.
sod [sɔd] *s* græstørv; (F) svin, lort; *poor ~!* stakkels djævel! // *v:* ~ *it!* (F) forbandet lort!
sodden [sɔdn] *adj* gennemblødt.
sodding ['sɔdiŋ] *adj* (F) forbandet.
sodium ['səudiəm] *s (kem)* natrium; ~ *bicarbonate* tvekulsurt natron.
soft [sɔft] *adj* blød; dæmpet; mild, blid; dum; *have a ~ spot for* have en svaghed for; *a ~ drink* en alkoholfri drik; ~ *furnishings* boligtekstiler; *be ~ in the head* være blød i bolden; *be ~ on* være lun på; **~-boiled** *adj* blødkogt.
soften [sɔfn] *v* gøre (,blive) blød; dæmpe; formilde(s); **~er** ['sɔfnə*] *s* blødgøringsmiddel; skyllemiddel.
soft-pedal ['sɔftpɛdl] *v* (F) gå stille med dørene.
soft-spoken ['sɔftspəukn] *adj* med blid stemme.
software ['sɔftwɛə*] *s (edb)* programmel.
softy ['sɔfti] *s* skvat, tøsedreng.
soggy ['sɔgi] *adj* gennemblødt; klæg; vandet.
soil [sɔil] *s* jord(bund) // *v* snavse til; blive snavset.
sojourn ['sɔdʒə:n] *s* ophold // *v* opholde sig.
solace ['sɔlis] *s* trøst.
solar ['səulə*] *adj* solar-, sol-; **~ collector** *s* solfanger.
sold [səuld] *præt* og *pp* af *sell.*
solder ['səuldə*] *s* loddemetal // *v* lodde.
soldier ['səuldʒə*] *s* soldat, militær-

person // *v* være soldat; slide, kæmpe.

sole [səul] *s* sål; *(zo)* søtunge // *v* forsåle // *adj* eneste; ene-; **~ly** *adv* udelukkende.

solemn ['sɔləm] *adj* højtidelig.

solicitor [sə'lisitə*] *s* sagfører, advokat.

solicitous [sə'lisitəs] *adj* omsorgsfuld; ivrig.

solid ['sɔlid] *adj* fast, massiv; solid; grundig; *a ~ hour* en hel time.

solidify [sə'lidifai] *v* størkne; styrke.

solidity [sə'liditi] *s* fasthed, soliditet.

soliloquy [sə'liləkwi] *s* enetale, monolog.

solitary ['sɔlitəri] *adj* enlig; ensom; isoleret; afsides; **~ confinement** *s* isolationsfængsel.

solitude ['sɔlitju:d] *s* ensomhed.

soloist ['səuləuist] *s* solist.

solstice ['sɔlstis] *s* solhverv.

soluble ['sɔljubl] *adj* opløselig; til at løse.

solution [sə'lu:ʃən] *s* løsning; opløsning.

solve [sɔlv] *v* løse (fx *a puzzle* en gåde).

solvent ['sɔlvənt] *s* opløsningsmiddel // *adj* solvent.

sombre ['sɔmbə*] *adj* mørk, dyster.

some [sʌm] *adj/adv/pron* en el. anden; et el. andet; nogen, noget; en del; *~ day* engang; en skønne dag; *~ ten people* cirka ti personer; *~ (of it) was left* der blev ngt til overs; *will you have ~ tea?* vil du have en kop te?

somebody ['sʌmbədi] *pron* en el. anden; nogen; *~ else* en anden.

somehow ['sʌmhau] *adv* på en el. anden måde; af en el. anden grund.

someone ['sʌmwʌn] *pron* d.s.s. *somebody*.

somersault ['sʌməsɔ:lt] *s* saltomortale, kolbøtte // *v* slå saltomortaler.

something ['sʌmθiŋ] *pron* et el. andet; noget; *he's a teacher or ~* han er lærer el. sådan noget.

sometime ['sʌmtaim] *adj* tidligere, forhenværende // *adv* engang; *~ last month* engang i sidste måned.

sometimes ['sʌmtaimz] *adv* somme tider, til tider.

somewhat ['sʌmwɔt] *adv* ret; noget; lidt.

somewhere ['sʌmwɛə*] *adv* et el. andet sted; *~ else* andetsteds.

somnambulist [sɔm'næmbjulist] *s* søvngænger.

somnolent ['sɔmnələnt] *adj* søvnig, døsig; søvndyssende.

son [sʌn] *s* søn.

song [sɔŋ] *s* sang, vise; *buy sth for a ~* få ngt for en slik; *make a ~ and dance about sth* lave et stort nummer ud af ngt.

sonic ['sɔnik] *adj* lyd-; *~ barrier* lydmur; *~ boom* overlydsknald.

son-in-law ['sʌninlɔ:] *s* svigersøn.

sonorous ['sɔnərəs] *adj* klangfuld.

soon [su:n] *adv* snart; tidligt; *as ~ as...* så snart (som)...; *I'd just as ~ leave* jeg ville hellere gå; *be too ~* være for tidligt på den; **~er** *adv* snarere; tidligere; *I would ~er...* jeg ville hellere...; *the ~er the better* jo før jo bedre; *~er or later* før el. senere; *no ~er than...* knap ... før, aldrig så snart ... før.

soot [su:t] *s* sod.

soothe [su:ð] *v* berolige; lindre.

sop [sɔp] *s (fig)* "narresut"; pjok, vatnisse // *v: ~ up* opsuge; tørre op.

sophisticated [sə'fistikeitid] *adj* forfinet; raffineret.

sopping ['sɔpiŋ] *adj: ~ (wet)* dyngvåd.

soppy ['sɔpi] *adj* sentimental; smægtende.

sorcery ['sɔ:səri] *s* trolddom, hekseri.

sordid ['sɔ:did] *adj* beskidt, smudsig; smålig, luset.

sore [sɔ:*] *s* sår; ømt sted // *adj* øm; smertende; fornærmet; *have a ~ throat* have ondt i halsen; **~ly** *adv* svært, yderst.

sorrel ['sɔrəl] *s (bot)* skovsyre.

sorrow ['sɔrəu] *s* sorg, bedrøvelse; smerte.

sorry ['sɔri] *adj* sørgelig, trist; bedrøvelig; ked af det; ussel; *(so) ~!* undskyld! *feel ~ for sby* have medlidenhed med (,ondt af) en;

I'm ~ to say desværre; jeg beklager at; *say ~ to sby* sige undskyld til en.
sort [sɔ:t] *s* slags, sort, art; *he's a good ~* han er en rar fyr; *he's ~ of funny* han er ligesom lidt mærkelig; *be out of ~s* være gnaven; være sløj; *it's beer of a ~* det skal forestille øl; *you'll do nothing of the ~!* det kan der ikke være tale om! // *v: ~ (out)* sortere, ordne; *we must ~ it out* vi må se at finde ud af det.
so-so ['səusəu] *adv* så som så, nogenlunde.
sought [sɔ:t] *præt* og *pp* af seek; **~-after** *adj* efterspurgt.
soul [səul] *s* sjæl; ånd; *we didn't see a ~* vi så ikke en levende sjæl; *he's the ~ of kindness* han er venligheden selv; *bless my ~!* bevar mig vel! *poor ~* stakkel; **~-destroying** *adj* åndsfortærende; **~ful** *adj* sjælfuld; smægtende.
sound [saund] *s* lyd; *(geogr)* sund; *within ~ of* inden for hørevidde afr; *I don't like the ~ of it* det lyder ikke godt // *v* lyde; lade lyde; ringe med (,på); sondere; *~ the horn* tude i (,med) hornet; *~ the bell* ringe med (,på) klokken; *~ the alarm* slå alarm // *adj* sund; solid; god; dygtig; grundig; *of ~ mind* ved sine fulde fem; *safe and ~* i god behold // *adv: be ~ asleep* sove trygt; **~ barrier** *s* lydmur; **~ engineer** *s* lydtekniker; **~ings** *s(pl) (mar)* lodning; *(fig)* føler; **~ly** *adv* solidt, grundigt; **~proof** *adj* lydtæt // *v* lydisolere; **~-proofing** *s* lydisolering; **~track** *s (film)* tonebånd; lydspor.
soup [su:p] *s* suppe; *be in the ~* (F) være på spanden // *v: ~ up the car* tune (bil)motoren.
sour ['sauə*] *adj* sur; dårlig; *"it's ~ grapes" (fig)* "rønnebærrene er sure".
source [sɔ:s] *s* kilde; udspring.
south [sauθ] *s* syd // *adj* sydlig, syd- // *adv* sydpå, mod syd; *~ of London* syd for London; *he's gone ~* han er taget sydpå; **South Africa** *s* Sydafrika; **South America** *s* Sydamerika; **south-east** *s* sydøst.
southerly ['sʌðəli] *adj* sydlig, syd-;
southern ['sʌðən] *adj* sydlig; sydlandsk; syd-.
southerner ['sʌðənə*] *s* sydenglænder; sydlænding.
southward(s) ['sauθwədz] *adj* mod syd, sydpå.
south-west [sauθ'wɛst] *s* sydvest.
sovereign ['sɔvrin] *s* monark, hersker // *adj* suveræn, uovertruffen; **~ty** *s* overhøjhed, suverænitet.
sow [sau] *s* so.
sow [səu] *v (sowed, sown)* så.
soy [sɔi] *s: ~ (sauce)* soja(sovs).
sozzled ['sɔzəld] *adj* (F) fuld, pløret.
spa [spa:] *s* kurbad.
space [speis] *s* rum; plads; mellemrum; periode; *clear a ~ for sth* gøre plads til ngt; *take up a lot of ~* fylde meget // *v: ~ out* sprede, fordele; **~bar** *s* mellemrumstangent; **~craft** *s* rumfartøj; **~man** *s* rummand; **~ probe** *s* rumsonde; **~-saving** *adj* pladsbesparende; **~ship** *s* rumskib; **~ shuttle** *s* rumfærge; **~ suit** *s* rumdragt.
spacing ['speisiŋ] *s* mellemrum, afstand; *double ~* dobbelt linjeafstand.
spacious ['speiʃəs] *adj* rummelig.
spade [speid] *s* spade; (i kortspil) spar; *queen of ~s* spar dame; **~work** *s* forarbejde.
Spain [spein] *s* Spanien.
span [spæn] *s* tidsrum; spand (fx heste); spændvidde; brofag // *v* spænde over; omfatte; strække sig over; *præt* af *spin.*
spangle [spæŋgl] *s* paillet // *v* glitre; bestrø.
Spaniard ['spænjəd] *s* spanier.
Spanish ['spæniʃ] *s/adj* spansk.
spank [spæŋk] *v* give smæk; **~ing** *s* endefuld.
spanner ['spænə*] *s* skruenøgle; *adjustable ~* svensknøgle; *throw a ~ in the works* stikke en kæp i hjulet.
spare [spɛə*] *s* reservedel // *v* skåne, spare (for); spare på; undvære, afse; have tilovers; *he has a week's holiday to ~* han har en uges ferie tilovers; *can you ~ me a cigarette?*

kan du afse en cigaret til mig? // *adj* ekstra; reserve-; ~ **bed** *s* gæsteseng; ~ **part** *s* reservedel, løsdel; ~ **room** *s* gæsteværelse; ~ **time** *s* fritid; ~ **tyre** *s* reservedæk.

sparing ['spεəriŋ] *adj* sparsom; **~ly** *adv* med måde, med forsigtighed.

spark [spa:k] *s* gnist // *v* slå gnister; (om motor) tænde; *~ off* forårsage, udløse; vække; **~(ing) plug** *s* tændrør.

sparkle [spa:kl] *s* tindren; glitren; glimt, glans // *v* tindre, glitre, stråle.

sparkler ['spa:klə*] *s* stjernekaster.

sparkling ['spa:kliŋ] *adj* funklende; sprudlende; boblende.

sparrow ['spærəu] *s* spurv.

sparse [spa:s] *adj* sparsom; spredt; *~ly populated* tyndt befolket.

spartan ['spa:tən] *adj* spartansk.

spasm [spæzm] *s* krampe; jag (af smerte).

spat [spæt] *præt* og *pp* af *spit.*

spate [speit] *s* strøm.

spatial ['speiʃəl] *adj* rum-.

spats [spæts] *spl* gamacher.

spatter ['spætə*] *v* sprøjte.

spatula ['spætjulə] *s* spatel; *(gastr)* paletkniv.

spawn [spɔ:n] *s* rogn; yngel // *v* gyde (rogn el. æg); yngle.

speak [spi:k] *v (spoke, spoken* [spəuk, spəukn]) tale; sige; holde tale; *~ for yourself* tal for dig selv; *~ to sby of (,about) sth* tale med en om ngt; *~ out* tage bladet fra munden; *~ up* tale højere (,højt); sige sin mening; **~er** *s* taler; højttaler; *the Speaker* formanden i underhuset; *he's a native ~er of English* han er indfødt englænder.

speaking ['spi:kiŋ] *s* tale(n); *be on ~ terms* være på talefod.

spear [spiə*] *s* spyd, lanse // *v* spidde.

spec [spεk] *s: on ~* (F) i spekulationsøjemed; på lykke og fromme (se også *specs).*

special ['spεʃl] *s* ekstranummer; særudgave // *adj* speciel, særlig; special-; *take ~ care* være ekstra forsigtig; *today's ~* dagens ret; **Special Branch** *s* politiets efterretningstjeneste; **special delivery** *adj* ekspres-.

specialist ['spεʃəlist] *s* specialist.

speciality [spεʃi'æliti] *s* specialitet.

specialize ['spεʃəlaiz] *v: ~ (in)* specialisere sig (i).

specially ['spεʃəli] *adv* særligt, specielt.

species ['spi:ʃiz] *s* art, slags; *the origin of ~* arternes oprindelse; *the (human) ~* menneskeslægten.

specific [spε'sifik] *adj* speciel; specifik; konkret.

specify ['spεsifai] *v* specificere; beskrive nærmere.

specimen ['spεsimən] *s* eksemplar; prøve.

speck [spεk] *s* plet; smule; stænk.

speckled [spεkld] *adj* plettet; spættet.

specs [spεks] *spl* (F) d.s.s. **spectacles** ['spεktəkls] *spl* briller.

spectacular [spεk'tækjulə*] *adj* iøjnefaldende, flot.

spectator [spεk'teitə*] *s* tilskuer.

spectre [spεktə*] *s* spøgelse, genfærd.

speculate ['spεkjuleit] *v* spekulere.

sped [spεd] *præt* og *pp* af *speed.*

speech [spi:tʃ] *s* tale; taleevne; *make a ~* holde en tale; ~ **day** *s* skoleafslutning; **~less** *adj* målløs, stum.

speed [spi:d] *s* fart; hastighed; gear; (S) amfetamin; *at full (,top) ~* for (,i) fuld fart // *v (sped, sped* [spεd]) ile; køre (,gå etc) hurtigt; *~ up* fremskynde; sætte farten op; **~ing** *s (auto)* overskridelse af fartgrænsen; ~ **limit** *s* fartgrænse; ~ **skating** *s* hurtigløb på skøjter; ~ **trap** *s* fartfælde (hvor politiet holder med radar etc).

speedy ['spi:di] *adj* hurtig, snarlig.

spell [spεl] *s* periode; omgang; fortryllelse; *cast a ~ on sby* forhekse en; *dizzy ~s* svimmelhedsanfald // *v (~ed, ~ed* el. *spelt, spelt)* stave(s); betyde; *~ out* stave sig igennem; *(fig)* forstå, tyde; skære ud i pap.

spellbinding ['spεlbaindiŋ] *adj* fængslende; **spellbound** [-baund] *adj* tryllebundet.

spelling ['spɛliŋ] *s* stavning; stave-; ~ **dictionary** *s* retskrivningsordbog.
spelt [spɛlt] *præt* og *pp* af *spell*.
spend [spɛnd] *v* *(spent, spent)* (om penge) give ud, bruge; (om tid) tilbringe; udmatte; ~ *a penny (spøg)* gå på toilettet; **~ing money** *s* lommepenge; **~ing power** *s* købekraft.
spendthrift ['spɛndθrift] *s* ødeland, ødsel person.
spent [spɛnt] *præt* og *pp* af *spend* // *adj* opbrugt; udmattet.
sperm [spə:m] *s* sæd(celle); ~ **whale** *s* *(zo)* kaskelot.
spew [spju:] *v* udspy; brække sig.
sphere [sfiə*] *s* sfære; kugle, klode; felt, område.
spice [spais] *s* krydderi // *v* krydre.
spick-and-span ['spikən'spæn] *adj* flunkende ren; splinterny.
spicy ['spaisi] *adj* krydret; pikant, vovet.
spider ['spaidə*] *s* edderkop; **~'s web** *s* edderkoppespind.
spike [spaik] *s* pig, spids; nagle; spyd // *v* spidde; forpurre.
spill [spil] *v* *(~ed, ~ed* el. *spilt, spilt)* spilde; flyde (over); blive spildt; ~ *the beans* sladre, plapre ud med ngt.
spillage ['spilidʒ] *s* (olie)udslip.
spin [spin] *s* snurren, spin; lille (køre)tur // *v* *(spun* el. *span, spun* [spʌn]) spinde; snurre rundt; spinne; ~ *a yarn (fig)* spinde en ende, fortælle en historie; ~ *a coin* slå plat el. krone.
spinach ['spinitʃ] *s* spinat.
spinal [spainl] *adj* rygrads-, spinal-; ~ **cord** *s* rygmarv.
spindly ['spindli] *adj* tynd, ranglet.
spin-dryer ['spin,draiə*] *s* (tørre)centrifuge.
spine [spain] *s* rygrad, rygsøjle; torn, pig; bogryg; **~less** *adj* vattet, uden rygrad; uden torne.
spinning ['spiniŋ] *s* spinding, spinde-; skruning; ~ **wheel** *s* spinderok.
spin-off ['spinɔf] *s* biprodukt.
spinster ['spinstə*] *s* gammeljomfru.
spiral ['spaiərəl] *s* spiral; ~ **staircase** *s* vindeltrappe.
spire [spaiə*] *s* spir; tinde.
spirit ['spirit] *s* ånd, sjæl; mod; humør; spiritus; *he's in good ~s* han er i godt humør; *she's in low ~s* hun er nedtrykt // *v:* ~ *away* trylle væk; **~ed** *adj* livlig; åndrig; ~ **level** *s* vaterpas.
spirits ['spirits] *spl* sprit, spiritus.
spiritual ['spiritjuəl] *adj* åndelig; ånds-.
spit [spit] *s* (stege)spid; spyt // *v* *(spat, spat)* spytte; sprutte.
spite [spait] *s* ondskab; ond vilje; trods; *in ~ of* trods, skønt // *v* plage, chikanere; **~ful** *adj* ondskabsfuld.
spitfire ['spitfaiə*] *s* (om pige) hidsig trold.
spitroast ['spitrəust] *v* spydstege.
spitting ['spitiŋ] *adj: be the ~ image of sby* være som snydt ud af næsen på en.
spittle [spitl] *s* spyt.
spittoon [spi'tu:n] *s* spytbakke.
splash [splæʃ] *s* plask(en); sprøjt; stænk // *v* plaske; (over)sprøjte; ~ *money about* strø om sig med penge.
splatter ['splætə*] *s* sprøjt, stænk; plamage; klat // *v* sprøjte, stænke.
spleen [spli:n] *s* *(anat)* milt; *(fig)* humørsyge; *(gl)* livstræthed.
splendid ['splɛndid] *adj* strålende, storartet.
splendour ['splɛndə*] *s* pragt; glans.
splice [splais] *s* splejsning; fugning // *v* splejse.
splint [splint] *s* *(med)* benskinne.
splinter *s* flis, splint // *v* splintre(s), splitte(s); ~ **group** *s* udbrydergruppe.
split [split] *s* revne, spalte; splittelse; *do the ~s* gå ned i spagat // *v* *(split, split)* spalte, flække; splitte; revne; dele; ~ *up* (fx om par) gå hver til sit; (om møde) opløses; *a ~ second* en brøkdel af et sekund; *a ~ting headache* en dundrende hovedpine; **~-level** *adj* forskudt; **~peas** *s* tørrede (,gule) ærter.
splodge [splɔdʒ] *s* plamage.
splutter ['splʌtə*] *v* sprutte.
spoil [spɔil] *v* *(~ed, ~ed* el. *spoilt,*

spoilt) ødelægge(s); spolere; forkæle; **~s** *spl* bytte, rov; **~sport** *s* (om person) lyseslukker.

spoke [spəuk] *s* ege (i hjul); trin (på stige) // *præt* af *speak;* **~n** *pp* af *speak;* **~s·man** *s* talsmand.

sponge [spɔndʒ] *s* svamp // *v* vaske af (med svamp); ~ *on* nasse på; **~able** *adj* (om fx tapet) vaskbar; **~ bag** *s* toilettaske; **~ cake** *s* sv.t. sandkage.

sponger ['spɔndʒə*] *s* snylter, (F) nasserøv.

spongy ['spɔndʒi] *adj* svampet; blød.

sponsor ['spɔnsə*] *v* sponsorere.

spontaneous [spɔn'teiniəs] *adj* spontan.

spoof [spu:f] *s* parodi; fupnummer // *v:* ~ *sby* tage gas på en.

spooky ['spu:ki] *adj* uhyggelig.

spool [spu:l] *s* spole, rulle.

spoon [spu:n] *s* ske // *v:* ~ *up* øse op; **~-feed** *v* made (med ske); proppe (med); *(fig)* servere alt på et sølvfad; **~ful** *s* skefuld.

sport [spɔ:t] *s* sport; fornøjelse; sjov; flink fyr; *be a (good)* ~ være en flink fyr // *v* drive sport; optræde med; **~ing** *adj* sports-; jagt-; flink; *give sby a ~ing chance* give en en fair chance; **~s day** *s* idrætsdag; **~s·man** *s* sportsmand; jæger; lystfisker; **~s page** *s* (i avis) sportsside; **~s·wear** *s* sportebeklædning; **~y** *adj* sporty; flot.

spot [spɔt] *s* plet, prik; filipens; sted; smule, sjat; *a ~ of whisky* en sjat whisky; *on the* ~ på stedet; lige på pletten; *come out in ~s* få knopper; slå 'ud; *be in a tight* ~ være i knibe // *v* få øje på, opdage; finde; plette; **~ check** *s* stikprøve; **~less** *adj* pletfri; **~light** *s* projektør; spot(lys); søgelys; **~-on** *adj* (F) lige i øjet; helt rigtig; **~ted** *adj* plettet, spættet; **~ty** *adj* plettet; pletvis; med bumser.

spouse [spauz] *s* ægtefælle.

spout [spaut] *s* (på fx kande) tud; stråle; nedløbsrør // *v* sprøjte.

sprain [sprein] *s* forstuvning // *v* forstuve, forstrække (fx *one's ankle* anklen).

sprang [spræŋ] *præt* af *spring.*

sprat [spræt] *s* brisling.

sprawl [sprɔ:l] *v* ligge og flyde; brede sig.

spray [sprei] *s* sprøjt; sprøjtemiddel; spray; buket; kvist // *v* sprøjte, bruse, spraye; **~-gun** *s* sprøjtepistol.

spread [sprɛd] *s* udbredelse; spredning; *(gastr)* smørepålæg; opdækning // *v (spread, spread)* sprede, brede (ud); brede sig; strække sig; *(gastr)* smøre; **~-eagled** *adj* med spredte arme og ben.

spree [spri:] *s* soldetur.

sprig [sprig] *s* gren, kvist.

sprightly ['spraitli] *adj* livlig.

spring [spriŋ] *s* spring; fjeder; fjedren; forår; kilde // *v (sprang, sprung* [spræŋ, sprʌŋ]) springe; skyde op; ~ *from* stamme fra; ~ *a leak* springe læk; ~ *sth on sby* overraske en med ngt; ~ *up* (om problem etc) pludselig dukke op; **~board** *s* springbræt, trampolin; **~-clean(ing)** *s* forårsrengøring, hovedrengøring; **~ roll** *s (gastr)* forårsrulle; **~time** *s* forår(stid).

springy ['spriŋi] *adj* fjedrende, elastisk.

sprinkle [spriŋkl] *v* (over)drysse; (be)strø; stænke; ~ *with sugar* strø sukker på; *~d with (fig)* oversået med.

sprint [sprint] *s* spurt // *v* spurte.

sprout [spraut] *s* spire, skud; *Brussels ~s* rosenkål // *v* spire, skyde.

spruce [spru:s] *s* gran(træ) // *adj* smart, fiks // *v:* ~ *up* fikse op.

sprung [sprʌŋ] *pp* af *spring.*

spry [sprai] *adj* livlig, frisk.

spud [spʌd] *s* (F) kartoffel.

spun [spʌn] *præt* og *pp* af *spin.*

spur [spə:*] *s* spore; ansporelse; *on the ~ of the moment* på stående fod; impulsivt // *v:* ~ *(on)* anspore; tilskynde.

spurious ['spjuəriəs] *adj* uberettiget; falsk.

spurn [spə:n] *v* afvise hånligt.

spurt [spə:t] *s* stråle, sprøjt; kraftanstrengelse // *v* sprøjte; spurte.

sputter ['spʌtə*] *v* sprutte; hakke.
spy [spai] *s* spion // *v* få øje på; ~ *on* udspionere.
Sq, sq fork.f. *square.*
squabble [skwɔbl] *s* skænderi, kævl // *v* skændes.
squad [skwɔd] *s* hold; patrulje; ~ **car** *s* patruljevogn.
squadron ['skwɔdrən] *s (fly)* eskadrille; *(mil)* eskadron.
squalid ['skwɔlid] *adj* beskidt; ussel; gemen.
squall [skwɔ:l] *s* byge; uvejr; vræl.
squalor ['skwɔlə*] *s* smudsighed; elendighed.
squander ['skwɔndə*] *v* frådse med; ødsle; sprede(s).
square [skwεə*] *s* kvadrat, firkant; plads, torv; vinkellineal; *be back to ~ one* være tilbage hvor man begyndte // *v* gøre firkantet; kvadrere; opløfte til 2. potens; udligne; passe; ~ *one's account* afregne // *adj* firkantet; firskåren; afgjort; ærlig, fair; lige; *get a ~ deal* få en fair behandling; *a ~ meal* et ordentligt måltid mad; *get ~ with sby* ordne sit mellemværende med en; *two metres ~* to gange to meter; *one ~ metre* en kvadratmeter; ~ *root* kvadratrod; ~ *shoulders* brede skuldre; **~ly** *adv* lige.
squash [skwɔʃ] *s* mos; masen; *(bot)* courgette; *lemon (,orange) ~* citronsaft (,appelsinsaft) // *v* mase (sig); trykke flad; undertrykke.
squashy ['skwɔʃi] *adj* blød, splattet.
squat [skwɔt] *s* forladt (,BZ-)hus // *v* sidde på hug // *adj* lille og tyk; hugsiddende; **~ter** *s* husbesætter, BZ'er.
squawk [skwɔ:k] *s* hæst skrig; skræppen // *v* skræppe (op).
squeak [skwi:k] *s* hvin, piben // *v* hvine; knirke.
squeal [skwi:l] *v* hvine; ~ *(on)* (F) sladre (om).
squeamish ['skwi:miʃ] *adj* sart, pivet.
squeeze [skwi:z] *s* tryk, pres; knus; trængsel; klemme // *v* presse, klemme; omfavne.
squelch [skwεltʃ] *s* svuppen; gurglen // *v* svuppe; plaske; slubre.
squib [skwib] *s* kanonslag, kineser; *a damp ~* en fuser.
squid [skwid] *s* tiarmet blæksprutte.
squiggle [skwigl] *s* krusedulle.
squillion ['skwiljən] *s* (F) fantasillion.
squint [skwint] *s: have a ~* skele // *v* skele; skæve, skotte.
squire [skwaiə*] *s* godsejer.
squirm [skwə:m] *v* vride sig; krympe sig.
squirrel ['skwirəl] *s* egern.
squirt [skwə:t] *s* sprøjt(en); stråle // *v* sprøjte.
stab [stæb] *s* stød (med dolk etc); stikkende smerte, jag; (F) forsøg; *a ~ in the back* et bagholdsangreb // *v* stikke, dolke; **~bing** *s* knivstikkeri // *adj* jagende.
stability [stə'biliti] *s* stabilitet.
stabilize ['stæbilaiz] *v* stabilisere; **~r** *s* stabilisator.
stable [steibl] *s* (heste)stald // *adj* stabil, fast; varig.
stack [stæk] *s* stak; stabel, bunke // *v* stakke; stable; kunne stables.
stadium ['steidium] *s* stadion.
staff [sta:f] *s* stav; stang; stab, personale // *v* forsyne med personale; ~ **participation** *s* medarbejderindflydelse.
stag [stæg] *s* (kron)hjort.
stage [steidʒ] *s* scene; estrade, platform; stadium, trin; stadie; *go on the ~* gå til scenen; *in ~s* trinvis // *v* iscenesætte; foranstalte; opføre; ~ *a strike* arrangere en strejke; **~coach** *s* diligence; ~ **fright** *s* lampefeber; ~ **manager** *s* regissør; **~-struck** *adj* teatertosset.
stagger ['stægə*] *v* vakle; slingre; forbløffe, ryste; **~ing** *adj* forbløffende; overvældende.
stagnant ['stægnənt] *adj* stillestående.
stagnate [stæg'neit] *v* stå i stampe, stagnere.
stag party ['stæg,pa:ti] *s* mandfolkegilde; polterabend.
stagy ['steidʒi] *adj* teatralsk.
staid [steid] *adj* sat, adstadig.
stain [stein] *s* plet; farve, bejdse // *v* plette(s); farve, bejdse; **~ed** *adj*

plettet; **~ed glass (window)** *s* vindue med glasmaleri; **~less** *adj* pletfri; **~less steel** *s* rustfrit stål; **~ remover** *s* pletfjerner.

stair [stɛə*] *s* trappetrin; **~case** *s* trappe(gang); **~s** *spl* trappe; **~way** *s* trappe; **~well** *s* trappeskakt.

stake [steik] *s* stage, pæl; (i spil etc) indsats; aktiepost, andel; *be at ~* stå på spil; *be burned at the ~ (gl)* blive brændt på bålet // *v* risikere, satse; *~ a claim to sth* gøre krav på ngt.

stale [steil] *adj* gammel, overgemt; (om øl) doven; (om lugt) indelukket, hengemt; **~mate** *s* dødt punkt; hårdknude.

stalk [stɔ:k] *s (bot)* stængel; stok // *v* spankulere, skride; liste sig (ind på).

stall [stɔ:l] *s* bås; stand, stade; kirkestol // *v* køre fast; få motorstop; komme med udflugter; søge at vinde tid; holde en; **~s** *spl (teat)* parket.

stallion ['stæljən] *s* (avls)hingst.

stalwart ['stɔ:lwət] *adj* tro; kraftig; gæv.

stamina ['stæminə] *s* udholdenhed, styrke.

stammer ['stæmə*] *s* stammen // *v* stamme.

stamp [stæmp] *s* stampen; frimærke; stempelmærke; præg // *v* stampe, trampe; stemple; frankere; *~ed addressed envelope* adresseret (portofri) svarkuvert; **~ collector** *s* frimærkesamler; **~ duty** *s* stempelafgift.

stampede [stæm'pi:d] *s* voldsom tilstrømning; vild flugt.

stance [stæns] *s* (ind)stilling; holdning; positur.

stand [stænd] *s* holdt; stade, plads; tribune; stativ; *make a ~* holde stand; *take a ~* tage stilling; tage opstilling; *a one-night ~* (F) en engangsforestilling // *v (stood, stood* [stud]) stå; rejse sig; stille; gælde; holde til, tåle; *I can't ~ him* jeg kan ikke udstå ham; *he doesn't ~ a chance* han har ikke en chance; *I'll ~ you dinner* jeg giver en middag; *~ for Parliament* lade sig opstille til parlamentet; *it ~s to reason* det siger sig selv; *~ back* træde tilbage; holde sig på afstand; *~ by* være parat; vedstå; holde med; *~ down* trække sig tilbage; *~ for* betyde, repræsentere; finde sig i; *~ in for sby* være stedfortræder for en; *~ out* skille sig ud; holde ud; *~ up* stå op; rejse sig (op); *~ up for sby* forsvare en; *~ up to sth* klare (,tåle) ngt.

standard ['stændəd] *s* fane; standard; norm; stander // *adj* standard-; normal.

standardization [stændədai'zeiʃən] *s* standardisering.

standard lamp ['stændəd læmp] *s* standerlampe.

standards ['stændədz] *spl* moral.

stand-by ['stændbai] *s* reserve; **~ ticket** *s (fly)* afbudsbillet.

standing ['stændiŋ] *s* stilling; status; anseelse; *of long ~* mangeårig, langvarig // *adj* stående; løbende; **~ committee** *s* stående udvalg; **~ orders** *spl* reglement; **~ room** *s* ståplads.

stand-offish ['stænd'ɔfiʃ] *adj* afvisende; utilnærmelig.

standpoint ['stændpɔint] *s* standpunkt; synspunkt.

standstill ['stændstil] *s: be at a ~* ligge stille; være gået i stå; *come to a ~* gå i stå.

stank [stæŋk] *præt* af *stink.*

staple [steipl] *s* hækteklamme; hovednæringsmiddel; grundpille // *v* hæfte // *v* vigtigst, hoved-.

stapler ['steiplə*] ['steiplə*] *s* hæftemaskine.

star [sta:*] *s* stjerne // *v: ~ (in)* spille hovedrollen (i); præsentere i hovedrollen.

starboard ['sta:bəd] *s (mar)* styrbord.

starch [sta:tʃ] *s* stivelse // *v* stive.

stardom ['sta:dəm] *s* stjernestatus.

stare [stɛə*] *s* stirren // *v* stirre, glo.

starfish ['sta:fiʃ] *s* søstjerne.

stark [sta:k] *adj/adv* kras; barsk; utilsløret; grel; *~ naked* splitternøgen; *~ staring mad* bindegal.

starkers ['sta:kəz] *adj* (F) splitternøgen.

starling ['sta:liŋ]*s* stær.
starlit ['sta:lit] *adj* stjerneklar.
starry ['sta:ri] *adj* stjerneklar; **~-eyed** *adj* blåøjet, naiv.
star-studded ['sta:stʌdid] *adj (fig)* stjernespækket.
start [sta:t] *s* start, begyndelse; sæt, spjæt; *get off to a bad (,good) ~* få en dårlig (,god) start; *false ~* tyvstart; *for a ~* for et første // *v* begynde, starte; tage af sted; fare sammen; give et sæt; *~ing from Monday* fra på mandag af; *~ a family* stifte familie; *~ off* begynde, indlede; *~ up* fare op; *(auto)* starte; **~er** *s* startknap; forret; **~ing handle** *s* startsving; **~ing point** *s* udgangspunkt.
startle [sta:tl] *v* fare 'op; skræmme; **startling** *adj* chokerende, rystende.
starturn ['sta:'tə:n] *s* glansnummer; sensation.
starvation [sta:'veiʃən] *s* sult.
starve [sta:v] *v* sulte; dø af sult; lade sulte; udsulte; *I'm starving!* jeg er ved at dø af sult!
stash [stæʃ] *v: ~ away* (F) gemme.
state [steit] *s* tilstand; stat; stand, rang; pragt; *be in a ~* være ophidset; *be lying in ~* ligge på lit de parade; *the ~ of affairs* forholdene, tingenes tilstand; *~ of mind* sindstilstand // *v* erklære; konstatere; fastslå.
stated ['steitid] *adj* fastslået; foreskreven.
stately ['steitli] *adj* statelig, majestætisk.
statement ['steitmənt] *s* erklæring, meddelelse; udtalelse; *(jur)* forklaring; *bank ~* saldo.
stateroom ['steitru:m] *s* repræsentationslokale.
States: *the ~* Staterne (dvs. USA).
statesman ['steitsmən] *s* statsmand.
static ['stætik] *adj* statisk; stillestående.
station ['steiʃən] *s* station; stilling; rang; *(mil* etc) post // *v* stationere, postere.
stationary ['steiʃnəri] *adj* stillestående, stationær.
stationer ['steiʃənə*] *s* papirhandler; **~'s (shop)** *s* papirhandel.
stationery ['steiʃənəri] *s* papirvarer; brevpapir.
stationmaster ['steiʃən,ma:stə*] *s* stationsmester.
statistic [stə'tistik] *s* statistik // *adj* statistisk; **~al** *adj* statistisk; **~s** *spl* statistik (som videnskab).
statue ['stætʃu:] *s* statue.
statuesque [stætʃu'ɛsk] *adj* statueagtig; statelig.
stature ['stætʃə*] *s* statur; skikkelse, format.
status ['steitəs] *s* status; stilling; rang; *financial ~* økonomiske forhold.
statute ['stætʃu:t] *s* vedtægt; lov; statut.
statutory ['stætʃutəri] *adj* lovbestemt; lovmæssig.
staunch [stɔ:ntʃ] *adj* pålidelig; standhaftig, stærk // *v* standse.
stave [steiv] *s* stav; trin (på stige) // *v: ~ in* trykke (,slå) ind; *~ off* afværge.
stay [stei] *s* ophold // *v* blive; opholde sig, bo; *~ put* blive hvor man er; *~ with friends* besøge (og bo hos) venner; *~ the night* overnatte; *where are you ~ing?* hvor bor du? *the CD is here to ~* CD'erne er kommet for at blive; *~ behind* være bagud; *~ in* holde sig inde; *~ in bed* ligge i sengen; *~ on* blive; blive boende; *~ out* blive ude; *~ up* blive (,sidde) oppe; **~ing power** *s* udholdenhed.
stead [stɛd] *s: in his ~* i hans sted; *stand sby in good ~* komme en til nytte.
steadfast ['stɛdfa:st] *adj* fast, urokkelig.
steadily [stɛdili] *adv* sindigt, støt.
steady ['stɛdi] *s* (F) fast fyr (,pige) // *v* holde i ro; stabilisere; berolige // *adj* stabil, solid; sikker; rolig; støt; fast; bestandig; *go ~ with* komme fast sammen med; *~ now!* bare rolig!
steak [steik] *s* bøf; **~house** *s* bøfrestaurant.

steal [sti:l] *v (stole, stolen* [stəul, stəuln]) stjæle; snige sig; smutte; ~ *a glance at* kaste et stjålent blik på; ~ *up on* snige sig ind på.
stealth [stɛlθ] *s: by* ~ i smug.
stealthy ['stɛlθi] *adj* snigende; hemmelig.
steam [sti:m] *s* damp; dug (på rude etc); *get up* ~ sætte dampen op; *let off* ~ afreagere; *run out of* ~ køre træt; *under one's own* ~ for egen kraft // *v* dampe; dampkoge; ~ *along* dampe af sted; ~ *up* dugge (til); *be ~ed up* (om person) være ophidset; ~ **engine** *s* dampmaskine; damplokomotiv.
steamer ['sti:mə*] *s* damper.
steamiron ['sti:maiən] *s* dampstrygejern.
steamroller ['sti:mrəulə*] *s* damptromle // *v (fig)* tromle ned.
steamy ['sti:mi] *adj* fuld af damp; dampende; dugget.
steed [sti:d] *s* ganger.
steel [sti:l] *s* stål // *v: ~ oneself* gøre sig hård; samle mod.
steep [sti:p] *v* lægge i blød; lade stå og trække // *adj* stejl, brat; (om pris) skrap; **~ed** *adj: ~ed in sth* gennemsyret af; hensunket i ngt.
steeple [sti:pl] *s* spir; kirketårn; **~-chase** *s* forhindringsløb (til hest).
steer [stiə*] *s* tyrekalv; stud // *v* styre, lodse.
steering ['stiəriŋ] *s (auto)* styretøj; ~ **column** *s (auto)* ratsøjle; ~ **wheel** *s (auto)* rat.
stellar ['stɛlə*] *adj* stjerne-.
stem [stɛm] *s* (om træ etc) stamme; stilk; strå; (glas)stilk; *(mar)* stævn, forstavn // *v* dæmme op for, standse; stoppe; ~ *from* stamme fra; ~ **cutting** *s* stikling.
stench [stɛntʃ] *s* stank.
step [stɛp] *s* trin; skridt; fodtrin; *take ~s* træffe foranstaltninger; *watch one's* ~ være forsigtig, se sig for; *be in* ~ gå i takt; *be out of* ~ være ude af trit; *mind the ~!* pas på trinet! // *v* træde; komme; ~ *down* træde ned; træde tilbage; nedtrappe; ~ *forward* træde frem; ~ *in* gribe ind; ~ *off* komme ned fra; stå af; ~ *on it!* træd sømmet i bund! ~ *over* træde (,gå) over; ~ *up* optrappe; sætte(s) i vejret; **~father** *s* stedfar; **~ladder** *s* trappestige; **~mother** *s* stedmor; **~ped-up** *adj* øget, fremskyndet; **~ping-stone** *s* trædesten; *(fig)* springbræt; **~-up** *s* forfremmelse.
sterile ['stɛrail] *adj* steril.
sterilization [stɛrilai'zeiʃən] *s* sterilisering.
sterling ['stə:liŋ] *adj* sterling; ægte, lødig.
stern [stə:n] *s (mar)* agterstavn // *adj* streng, barsk.
stevedore ['sti:vdɔ:*] *s* havnearbejder.
stew [stju:] *s* ragout; gryderet; *be in a* ~ være ude af flippen // *v* småkoge; stuve; *~ed tea* te som har trukket for længe; *let sby* ~ lade en ligge som han har redt.
steward ['stju:əd] *s* hovmester; intendant; *(fly* etc) steward; **stewardess** *s* stewardesse, flyværtinde.
stick [stik] *s* stok, kæp; pind; stang; *take the* ~ (F) få klø (,på pelsen) // *v (stuck, stuck* [stʌk]) stikke; klæbe; lægge, putte; udstå; holde ud; sidde fast; forblive; ~ *around* blive, holde sig i nærheden; ~ *by sby* holde fast ved, fortsat støtte; ~ *out (,up)* stikke frem (,op); ~ *to* holde fast ved; klæbe til; ~ *together* holde sammen; ~ *up for* tage i forsvar.
sticker ['stikə*] *s* selvklæbende etiket; (om person) klæber.
sticking plaster ['stikiŋ ˌpla:stə*] *s* hæfteplaster.
stickleback ['stiklbæk] *s* hundestejle.
stickler ['stiklə*] *s: be a ~ for sth* holde (for) strengt på ngt.
stick-on ['stikɔn] *adj* klæbe-; **stick-up** *s* (F) holdup.
sticky ['stiki] *adj* klæbende; klæbrig; klistret; (om vejret) lummer; vanskelig.
stiff [stif] *s* (S) lig // *adj* stiv; svær, vanskelig; kold, streng; hård; *be bored* ~ dødkede sig.
stiffen ['stifn] *v* stivne; stive (af); gøre stiv; **~er** *s* stiver.

stiff-necked ['stifnɛkd] *adj* stædig, stejl.
stifle [staifl] *v* kvæle; undertrykke.
stifling ['staifliŋ] *adj* kvælende (fx *heat* varme).
stigma ['stigmə] *s* skamplet.
stile [stail] *s* stente.
stiletto [sti'lɛtəu] *s* stilethæl.
still [stil] *s* brændevinsbrænderi // *adj* stadig(væk); endnu; alligevel; stille, tavs // *v* berolige; **~born** *s* dødfødt; **~ life** *s* nature morte, stilleben.
stilt [stilt] *s* stylte; **~ed** *adj* opstyltet; påtaget.
stimulant ['stimjulənt] *s* opkvikkende middel; stimulans.
stimulate ['stimjuleit] *v* stimulere, kvikke op; **stimulation** [-'leiʃən] *s* stimulering.
stimulus ['stimjuləs] *s* spore, incitament.
sting [stiŋ] *s* stik; *(zo, bot)* brod // *v* *(stung, stung* [stʌŋ]) stikke; svie; såre.
stingy ['stindʒi] *adj* nærig, fedtet.
stink [stiŋk] *s* stank; *(fig)* ballade; *create a* ~ lave ballade // *v* *(stank, stunk* [stæŋk, stʌŋk]) stinke; være berygtet; *the idea ~s* det er en dødssyg idé; *it ~s to high heaven* det lugter langt væk (også *fig); **~ing*** *adj* (F) skide- (fx *drunk* fuld), sten- (fx *rich* rig).
stint [stint] *s* tørn.
stipend ['staipɛnd] *s* gage.
stipendiary [stai'pɛndiəri] *adj* (fast)lønnet.
stipulate ['stipjuleit] *v* fastsætte; stipulere.
stipulation [stipju'leiʃən] *s* betingelse, aftale.
stir [stə*] *s* røre, ståhej; omrøring // *v* røre (rundt i); sætte i bevægelse; vække; røre sig; ~ *in the sugar* røre sukkeret i; ~ *up* ophidse; hvirvle op; **~-fry** *v* (om mad) hurtigt vende på en (næsten) tør pande; **~ring** *adj* rørende, gribende.
stirrup ['stirəp] *s* stigbøjle.
stitch [stitʃ] *s* (i syning) sting; (i strikning etc) maske; sting i siden; *I haven't got a ~ to wear* jeg har ikke en trævl at tage på; *be in ~es* være ved at dø af grin // *v* sy, stikke.
stoat [stəut] *s* lækat, hermelin.
stock [stɔk] *s* forråd, lager; slægt; race; *(merk)* obligationer; *(agr)* (kreatur)besætning; *(gastr)* kraftsuppe, sky, fond; *~s and shares* børspapirer, fonde; *in* ~ på lager; *take* ~ foretage lageroptælling; *take ~ of sby* tage bestik af en // *v* have på lager; oplagre; fylde op // *adj* standard- (fx *reply* svar).
stockade [stɔ'keid] *s* palisade, pæleværk.
stock... ['stɔk-] sms: **~broker** *s* børsmægler; **~ cube** *s* bouillonterning; **~ exchange** *s* fondsbørs; **~holder** *s* aktionær.
stocking ['stɔkiŋ] *s* strømpe; *in one's ~ed feet* på strømpefødder; **~ stitch** *s* glatstrikning.
stockist ['stɔkist] *s* leverandør, forhandler.
stock... ['stɔk-] sms: **~ market** *s* børs; børskurser; **~pile** *s* (stort) lager; **~ phrase** *s* fast udtryk; **~-still** *adj* bomstille; **~taking** *s* *(merk)* lageropgørelse, status.
stocky ['stɔki] *adj* tætbygget, firskåren.
stoke [stəuk] *v* fyre (med brændsel); proppe i; **~r** *s* fyrbøder.
stole [stəul] *s* stola, sjal // *præt* af *steal;* **~n** *pp* af *steal.*
stolid ['stɔlid] *adj* upåvirket; upåvirkelig.
stomach ['stɔmək] *s* mave; mavesæk; appetit; *it turned my* ~ det fik det til at vende sig i mig // *v* finde sig i, tage; **~ ache** [-eik] *s* mavepine.
stone [stəun] *s* sten; *(pl: stone) (brit* vægtenhed: 6,348 kg) // *v* stene; udstene; **~-cold** *adj* iskold; *~-cold sober* pinligt ædru.
stoned ['stəund] *adj* (S) døddrukken; "skæv", "høj".
stone-deaf ['stəun,dɛf] *adj* stokdøv.
stonemason ['stəunmeisn] *s* stenhugger.
stonewall ['stəunwɔ:l] *v* stå benhårdt på ngt; lave obstruktion.

stoneware ['stəunwɛə*] *s* stentøj.
stony ['stəuni] *adj* stenet.
stood [stud] *præt* og *pp* af *stand*.
stooge [stu:dʒ] *s* stikirenddreng.
stool [stu:l] *s* skammel, taburet; afføring; ~ **pigeon** *s* lokkedue (også *fig*).
stoop [stu:p] *s* luden; bøjning // *v* lude; være rundrygget; bøje sig; ~ *to doing sth* nedlade sig til at gøre ngt.
stop [stɔp] *s* stop, standsning; (også: *full* ~) punktum; *put a* ~ *to* sætte en stopper for // *v* stoppe, standse; opholde sig, bo; ~ *at a hotel* tage ind på et hotel; ~ *by the office* kigge forbi kontoret; ~ *dead* standse brat op; ~ *it!* hold op! *he would* ~ *at nothing* han viger ikke tilbage for ngt; ~ *by sby* kigge indenfor hos en; ~ *off* gøre et kort ophold; ~ *over* gøre ophold; ~ *up* (til)stoppe); **~gap** *s* vikar; nødløsning; **~lights** *spl* stoplys; *(auto)* bremselygter; **~over** *s* kort ophold på rejse; *(fly)* mellemlanding.
stoppage ['stɔpidʒ] *s* afbrydelse; arbejdsnedlæggelse.
stopper ['stɔpə*] *s* prop; stopper.
stopwatch ['stɔpwɔtʃ] *s* stopur.
storage ['stɔ:ridʒ] *s* opbevaring; lagerrum; lagerafgift; *(edb)* lagring.
store [stɔ:*] *s* lager, forråd; depot; pakhus; varehus, stormagasin; *what is in* ~ *for us?* hvad mon der venter os? *set great* ~ *by sth* sætte stor pris på ngt // *v* opbevare; opmagasinere; ~ *up* opsamle, oplagre; **~room** *s* lagerlokale; pulterkammer.
storey ['stɔ:ri] *s* etage.
storm [stɔ:m] *s* uvejr; stærk storm // *v* (om vejr) rase; (om person, *mil)* storme; **~-beaten** *adj* stormomsust.
stormy ['stɔ:mi] *adj* stormende; hidsig, heftig.
story ['stɔ:ri] *s* historie; beretning; (i bog) handling; *short* ~ novelle; *her* ~ *is that*... hun hævder at...; *to cut a long* ~ *short* kort sagt; **~teller** *s* fortæller; løgnhals.
stout [staut] *s* stærkt øl (slags porter) // *adj* stærk, kraftig; kraftigt bygget.
stove [stəuv] *s* ovn; komfur; kamin.
stow [stəu] *v* anbringe; stuve; gemme væk; **~away** *s* blind passager.
straddle [strædl] *v* skræve (over); sidde overskrævs på.
strafe [streif] *v* beskyde.
straggle [strægl] *v* strejfe (,flakke) om; *~d along the coast* spredt langs kysten; **~r** *s* omstrejfer; efternøler; **straggling, straggly** *adj* (om hår etc) tjavset.
straight [streit] *adj/adv* lige; (om hår) glat; i orden; ærlig, oprigtig; (om drink) tør, ublandet; (F, om person) heteroseksuel; *keep a* ~ *face* holde masken; *put (,get)* ~ bringe i orden, ordne; ~ *ahead* ligeud, lige frem; ~ *away* lige, ligefrem; øjeblikkelig; ~ *off (,out)* ligefrem; *be* ~ *with sby* være ærlig overfor en; **~en** *v: ~en (out)* rette ud, glatte; ordne; **~-faced** *adv* uden at fortrække en mine; **~forward** *adj* direkte; ligetil; ærlig.
strain [strein] *s* belastning; (an)spændelse; forstrækning; anlæg; anstrøg; *be under* ~ være under pres // *v* stramme, spænde, anspænde; overanstrenge; forvride; si.
strained ['streind] *adj* (an)spændt; anstrengt.
strainer ['streinə*] *s* si, sigte.
strains [streinz] *spl* toner.
strait [streit] *s* (også: *~s) (geogr)* stræde; *be in dire ~s* være i en slem knibe, være på spanden; **~jacket** *s* spændetrøje; **~laced** *adj* snerpet.
strand [strænd] *s* snor, tråd; ranke // *v* strande; *be left ~ed* stå på bar bund.
strange [streindʒ] *adj* fremmed; ukendt; mærkelig; ~ *to say* mærkeligt nok; **~r** *s* fremmed.
strangle [stræŋgl] *v* kvæle; blive kvalt; *a ~d cry* et halvkvalt skrig; **~hold** *s* kvælertag.
strap [stræp] *s* strop; rem // *v* spænde med remme; slå med rem; ~ *up (med)* give hæfteplaster på; **~less** *adj* stropløs.

strapping ['stræpiŋ] *adj* stor og stærk; flot.
stratagem ['strætədʒəm] *s* krigslist.
strategic [strə'ti:dʒik] *adj* strategisk.
strategist ['strætədʒist] *s* strategiker.
strategy ['strætedʒi] *s* strategi.
stratified ['strætifaid] *adj* lagdelt; klassedelt.
stratum ['stra:təm] *s* *(pl: strata)* lag.
straw [strɔ:] *s* strå; sugerør; *the last ~* dråben der får bægeret til at flyde over.
strawberry ['strɔ:bəri] *s* jordbær.
stray [strei] *v* strejfe om; komme på afveje // *adj* omstrejfende; herreløs; spredt; *a ~ bullet* en vildfaren kugle.
streak [stri:k] *s* stribe; streg; anstrøg // *v* gøre stribet; slå streger; stryge; *~ past* stryge forbi.
streaky ['stri:ki] *adj* stribet (fx *bacon).*
stream [stri:m] *s* vandløb; strøm; (i skole etc) niveau // *v* strømme; (i skolen) niveaudele; **~er** *v* vimpel; serpentine; (på bus etc) klæbemærke; **~lined** *adj* strømlinet.
street [stri:t] *s* gade; *in (,on) the ~* på gaden; *it's right up his ~* det er lige hans speciale; *be ~s ahead* være langt forud; **~ lamp** *s* gadelygte.
strength [strɛŋθ] *s* styrke, kræfter; *turn out in ~* møde talstærkt op; *on the ~ of* i kraft af, i tillid til.
strengthen ['strɛŋθən] *v* styrke(s); forstærke(s).
strenuous ['strɛnjuəs] *adj* kraftig; ivrig; anstrengende.
stress [strɛs] *s* tryk; eftertryk; spænding, stress; *lay ~ on sth* lægge vægt på ngt // *v* betone; fremhæve; påvirke.
stretch [strɛtʃ] *s* strækning; stræk; periode; *at a ~* i ét stræk // *v* strække (sig); være elastisk; række; *~ a muscle* spænde en muskel; *~ out* række ud; strække sig (ud); *~ out for sth* række ud efter ngt.
stretcher ['strɛtʃə*] *s* båre.
stretchy ['strɛtʃi] *adj* elastisk.
strew [stru:] *v (~ed, ~ed* el. *~ed, ~n)* strø (ud); overså; *~n with* bestrøet med.
stricken [strikn] *adj* ramt; hjemsøgt.
strict [strikt] *adj* nøje; streng; *~ly confidential* strengt fortrolig; *~ly speaking* strengt taget.
stride [straid] *s* langt skridt; *take sth in one's ~* klare ngt med lethed; *get in your ~* komme (rigtigt) i gang, finde rytmen // *v* skride; skridte ud; skræve over.
strident [straidnt] *adj* skingrende, højrøstet.
strife [straif] *s* strid, ufred.
strike [straik] *s* slag; strejke; (om olie etc) fund; *(mil)* angreb; *come out on ~* gå i strejke // *v (struck, struck* [strʌk]) slå (på); ramme; stryge (fx *a match* en tændstik); slå 'til; strejke; *(fig)* have heldet med sig; gøre indtryk, virke; *~ the eye (fig)* springe i øjet; *~ the hour* (om ur) slå hel; *~ a note* anslå en tone; *~ oil* finde olie; *~ up (mus)* spille op; *~ up a friendship with* slutte venskab med; **~bound** *adj* strejkeramt, lammet af strejker; **~breaker** *s* strejkebryder.
striker ['straikə*] *s* strejkende.
striking ['straikiŋ] *adj* slående, påfaldende; meget smuk.
string [striŋ] *s* snor, bånd; række; *(mus)* streng; stryger; *a ~ of pearls* en perlekæde; *pull ~s (fig)* trække i trådene; *no ~s attached* uden betingelser; *the ~s* strygerne (i orkester) // *v (strung, strung* [strʌŋ]) trække på snor; sætte streng(e) på; **~ bag** *s* indkøbsnet; **~ bean** *s* snittebønne; **~(ed) instrument** *s* strygeinstrument, strengeinstrument.
stringent ['strindʒənt] *adj* stram, streng.
string vest ['striŋvɛst] *s* netundertrøje.
stringy ['striŋi] *adj* sej, senet; trævlet.
strip [strip] *s* strimmel; *comic ~* tegneserie // *v* klæde (sig) af; tage af; (også: *~ down)* skille ad, demontere; *~ sby of sth* ribbe en for ngt; *~ped to the waist* med nøgen overkrop.
stripe [straip] *s* stribe.
strip light ['striplait] *s* neonrør.
stripy ['straipi] *adj* stribet.

strive [straiv] *v (strove, striven* [strəuv, strivn]) stræbe *(to* efter at); kæmpe *(against* mod).
strode [strəud] *præt* af *stride.*
stroke [strəuk] *s* slag; tag; strøg; kærtegn; slagtilfælde; skråstreg; *at a* ~ med ét slag; *at the* ~ *of five* på slaget fem; *a* ~ *of genius* et genialt indfald; *a* ~ *of lightning* et lynnedslag; *a* ~ *of luck* et lykketræf; *put him off his* ~ bringe ham ud af fatning; distrahere ham; *a two-*~ *engine* en totaktsmotor // *v* slå streg; stryge, ae.
stroll [strəul] *s* spadseretur // *v* slentre (om).
strong [strɔŋ] *adj* stærk, kraftig; *they were fifty* ~ de var halvtreds mand høj; *still going* ~ i fuld vigør; fortsat i fuld funktion; **~-box** *s* pengekasse; **~hold** *s* borg.
strongly ['strɔŋli] *adv* stærkt, kraftigt; *I would* ~ *advise you to...* jeg vil på det kraftigste råde dig til at...
strongminded ['strɔŋmaindid] *adj* viljestærk.
strongroom ['strɔŋru:m] *s* bankhvælving; boksrum.
strove [strəuv] *præt* af *strive.*
struck [strʌk] *præt* og *pp* af *strike.*
structure ['strʌktʃə*] *s* konstruktion; struktur; bygning // *v* strukturere.
struggle [strʌgl] *s* kamp; *put up a* ~ sætte sig til modværge // *v* kæmpe; mase, bakse.
strum [strʌm] *v* klimpre (på).
strung [strʌŋ] *præt* og *pp* af *string.*
strut [strʌt] *s* stolpe // *v* spankulere.
stub [stʌb] *s* stump; træstub; (på billet etc) talon; skod // *v:* ~ *out a cigarette* slukke (,skodde) en cigaret.
stubble [stʌbl] *s* stub; skægstubbe.
stubborn ['stʌbən] *adj* stædig; genstridig.
stubby ['stʌbi] *adj* stumpet, kort.
stucco ['stʌkəu] *s* stuk.
stuck [stʌk] *præt* og *pp* af *stick // adj: be (,get)* ~ sidde fast; gå i stå; *be* ~ *for sth* stå og mangle ngt; *be* ~ *with sth* hænge på ngt; **~-up** *adj* (F) storsnudet.
stud [stʌd] *s* (bredhovedet) søm; dup; manchetknap; (heste)stutteri; (også: ~ *horse)* avlshest; ørestik; (S, om mand) tyr; **~ded** *adj:* ~*ded with* tæt besat med.
student ['stju:dənt] *s* studerende // *adj* studenter-.
studied ['stʌdid] *adj* bevidst, tilstræbt; raffineret.
studio ['stju:diəu] *s* atelier; *(tv)* studie.
studious ['stju:diəs] *adj* flittig; omhyggelig.
study ['stʌdi] *s* studium; studie; arbejdsværelse; udkast; *his face was a* ~ hans ansigtsudtryk var alle pengene værd // *v* studere, læse (på); undersøge.
stuff [stʌf] *s* sager, ting; ragelse; stof, materiale; ... *and* ~ *like that* ... og sådan ngt; *do you call this* ~ *whisky?* kalder du det her whisky? ~ *and nonsense* sludder og vrøvl; *know one's* ~ kunne sit kram; *that's the* ~*!* sådan skal det være! // *v* proppe, stoppe; udstoppe; *(gastr)* farsere; *get* ~*ed!* rend og hop!
stuffing ['stʌfiŋ] *s* fyld.
stuffy ['stʌfi] *adj* (om værelse) indelukket; *(fig)* forstokket; fornærmet.
stumble [stʌmbl] *v* snuble; ~ *on* finde ved et tilfælde, falde over; **stumbling block** *s* anstødssten.
stump [stʌmp] *s* (træ)stub; stump // *v* bringe ud af fatning, starte, vade.
stun [stʌn] *v* lamslå, chokere.
stung [stʌŋ] *præt* og *pp* af *sting.*
stunk [stʌŋk] *pp* af *stink.*
stunner ['stʌnə*] *s* (F) dødflot fyr (,pige), rigtig "steg".
stunning ['stʌniŋ] *adj* chokerende; overvældende; pragtfuld.
stunt [stʌnt] *s* kraftpræstation; kunststykke; stuntnummer // *v* hæmme (i væksten); være stuntman; **~ed** *adj* forkrøblet.
stupefy ['stju:pifai] *v* lamslå; gøre omtåget, bedøve.
stupendous [stju:'pɛndəs] *adj* vældig; fantastisk.
stupid ['stju:pid] *adj* dum; *be* ~ *at sth* være dum til ngt; *too* ~ *for words* dummere end man har lov at til at være.

stupidity [stju'piditi] *s* dumhed.
stupor ['stju:pə*] *s* døs; bedøvet tilstand.
sturdy ['stə:di] *adj* robust; stærk, beslutsom.
sturgeon ['stə:dʒən] *s* stør.
stutter ['stʌtə*] *s* stammen // *v* stamme.
sty [stai] *s* (svine)sti.
stye [stai] *s* bygkorn (på øjet).
style [stail] *s* stil; mode; maner; *do sth in* ~ gøre ngt med maner // *v* designe; forme.
stylish ['stailiʃ] *adj* smart, stilig.
stylized ['stailaizd] *adj* stiliseret.
stylus ['stailəs] *s* nål.
stymie ['staimi] *v* lægge hindringer i vejen for, hæmme.
suave [swa:v] *adj* (om person) åleglat, sleben.
sub... [sʌb-] sms: **~altern** ['sʌbltən] *s* underofficer; **~committee** [-kə,miti] *s* underudvalg; **~conscious** [-'kɔnʃəs] *adj* underbevidst; **~divide** [-divaid] *v* underinddele; **~division** [-di,viʒən] *s* underinddeling.
subdue [sʌb'dju:] *v* undertrykke; betvinge; dæmpe; **~d** *adj* kuet; dæmpet, spagfærdig.
subhuman [sʌb'hju:mən] *adj* umenneskelig, ukristelig.
subject *s* ['sʌbdʒikt] genstand; emne; (stats)borger; *(gram)* subjekt, grundled; *be* ~ *to* være udsat for; *change the* ~ skifte emne // *v* [səb'dʒɛkt]: ~ *to* udsætte for; *be* ~ *to* være underkastet; være pligtig at; være tilbøjelig til.
subjection [sʌb'dʒɛkʃən] *s* underkastelse; undertrykkelse.
subjective [sʌb'dʒɛktiv] *adj* subjektiv.
subject matter ['sʌbdʒikt ,mætə*] *s* stof, emne.
subjugate ['sʌbdʒugeit] *v* betvinge; underlægge sig.
subjunctive [səb'dʒʌŋktiv] *s (gram)* konjunktiv.
sublease [sʌb'li:s] *v* (selv) fremleje.
sublet ['sʌb'lɛt] *v* fremleje (til andre).
sublime [sə'blaim] *adj* storslået; sublim.
submarine ['sʌbmari:n] *s* undervandsbåd, ubåd.
submerge [sʌb'mə:dʒ] *v* sænke ned (i vand); dykke; oversvømme.
submission [sʌb'miʃən] *s* underkastelse; henstilling; **submissive** [-'misiv] *adj* underdanig.
submit [sʌb'mit] *v* forelægge; indsende; henstille; ~ *oneself* underordne sig.
subordinate [səb'ɔ:dinət] *s/adj* underordnet.
subpoena [səb'pi:nə] *s (jur)* indkaldelse af vidne // *v* indstævne som vidne.
subscribe [səb'skraib] *v* bidrage; abonnere *(to* på), subskribere; **~r** *s* bidragyder; abonnent.
subscription [-'skripʃən] *s* kontingent; abonnement; *take out a* ~ *for sth* tegne abonnement på ngt.
subsequent ['sʌbsikwɛnt] *adj* (efter)følgende, senere; **~ly** *adv* så, derpå; senere.
subservient [səb'sə:viənt] *adj* underdanig; nyttig, gavnlig; underkastet.
subside [səb'said] *v* synke ned; stilne af, lægge sig.
subsidence [səb'saidəns] *s* sammenskridning, nedsynkning.
subsidiary [səb'sidiəri] *s* hjælper // *adj* hjælpe-, bi-; ~ **company** *s* datterselskab.
subsidize ['sʌbsidaiz] *v* give støtte (,tilskud) til.
subsidy ['sʌbsidi] *s* (stats)støtte.
subsistence [sʌb'sistəns] *s* eksistens; underhold.
substance ['sʌbstəns] *s* stof; substans; væsen; indhold; vægt; *in* ~ faktisk, i realiteten; *a man of* ~ en velstående mand.
substandard [sʌb'stændəd] *adj* under lavmålet, ringe.
substantial [sʌb'stænʃəl] *adj* virkelig; håndgribelig; solid; væsentlig.
substantiate [sʌb'stænʃieit] *v* dokumentere, underbygge.
substitute ['sʌbstitju:t] *s* vikar, stedfortræder; erstatning // *v:* ~ *wine for beer* erstatte vin med øl; **substitution** [-'tju:ʃən] *s* indsættelse (i stedet for ngt andet); udskiftning.

subterfuge ['sʌbtəfju:dʒ] *s* nummer, kneb; udflugt.
subterranean [sʌbtə'reiniən] *adj* underjordisk.
subtitle ['sʌbtaitl] *s* undertitel; *(film, tv)* undertekst // *v* tekste.
subtle [sʌtl] *adj* fin; svag; spidsfindig; behændig; **~ty** *s* skarpsindighed; finhed; spidsfindighed.
subtract [səb'trækt] *v* trække fra.
subtraction [səb'trækʃən] *s* subtraktion.
suburb ['sʌbə:b] *s* forstad; *the ~s* omegnen; **suburban** [sə'bə:bən] *adj* forstads-.
suburbia [sə'bə:biə] *s* forstæderne.
subversive [səb'və:siv] *adj* undergravende; nedbrydende.
subway ['sʌbwei] *s* fodgængertunnel.
subzero ['sʌb'ziəreu] *adj* under frysepunktet, frost-.
succeed [sək'si:d] *v* lykkes, være heldig; efterfølge; *they ~ed in doing it* det lykkedes dem at gøre det; *~ to the throne* arve tronen; **~ing** *adj* (efter)følgende.
success [sək'sɛs] *s* held, succes; **~ful** *adj* heldig; vellykket.
succession [sək'sɛʃən] *s* rækkefølge; arvefølge.
successive [sək'sɛsiv] *adj* efterfølgende; i træk.
successor [sək'sɛsə*] *s* efterfølger.
succinct [sək'siŋkt] *adj* kortfattet, koncis.
succour ['sʌkə*] *v* komme til undsætning.
succulent ['sʌkjulənt] *s (bot)* sukkulent // *adj* saftig.
succumb [sə'kʌm] *v* bukke under *(to* for).
such [sʌtʃ] *adj/adv/pron* sådan, så; sådan ngt; *~ books* sådan nogle bøger; den slags bøger; *~ good books* så gode bøger; *~ as* såsom, sådan som; *as ~* som sådan(t); *~ and ~* den og den; det og det; de og de; *books and ~* bøger og sådan ngt; *there's no ~ thing as ufos* der findes ikke ufo'er; **~like** *pron* den slags.
suck [sʌk] *v* suge; sutte (på); patte.
sucker ['sʌkə*] *s* sugeskive; sugekop; (F) tosse.
suckle [sʌkl] *v* amme, give bryst.
suction ['sʌkʃən] *s* sug(en); sugning; **~ pad** *s* sugeskive.
sudden [sʌdn] *adj* pludselig; brat; *all of a ~* med ét; **~ly** *adv* pludselig.
suds [sʌdz] *spl* sæbevand.
sue [su:] *v* lægge sag an (mod), sagsøge.
suede [sweid] *s* ruskind.
suet ['suit] *s (gastr)* nyrefedt; oksetalg.
suffer ['sʌfə*] *v* lide *(from* af); tage skade; gennemgå; tåle; finde sig i; tillade; **~ing** *s* lidelse.
suffice [sə'fais] *v* være nok; slå 'til; tilfredsstille; *~ it to say that...* lad det være nok at sige at...
sufficient [sə'fiʃənt] *adj* tilstrækkelig, nok.
suffix ['sʌfiks] *s (gram)* endelse.
suffocate ['sʌfəkeit] *v* kvæle(s); **suffocation** [-'keiʃən] *s* kvælning.
sugar ['ʃugə*] *s* sukker // *v* komme sukker i (,på), søde; **~ basin** *s* sukkerskål; **~ beet** *s* sukkerroe; **~ cane** *s* sukkerrør; **~-coated** *adj* (sukker)glaseret; sukkerovertrukken; **~ed** *adj* sukkersød; **~ loaf** *s* sukkertop; **~ lump** *s* stykke sukker; **~ maple** *s* sukkerløn; **~y** *adj* sukkersød.
suggest [sə'dʒɛst] *v* foreslå; tyde på; antyde; lede tanken hen på.
suggestion [sə'dʒɛstʃən] *s* forslag; antydning; mindelse.
suggestive [sə'dʒɛstiv] *adj* tankevækkende; sigende.
suicide ['suisaid] *s* selvmord; selvmorder.
suit [su:t] *s* sæt tøj, habit; spadseredragt; (i kortspil) farve; (rets)sag; *follow ~* gøre ligeså // *v* passe (til); klæde; *~ yourself!* gør som du vil! **~able** *adj* passende; egnet.
suitcase ['su:tkeis] *s* kuffert.
suite [swi:t] *s* suite; møblement.
suitor ['su:tə*] *s* frier.
sulk [sʌlk] *v* surmule.
sulky *s* sulky // *adj* sur.
sullen ['sʌlən] *adj* trist, dyster.
sulphur ['sʌlfə*] *s* svovl.
sulphuric [sʌl'fjuərik] *adj: ~ acid* svovlsyre.

sultana [sʌl'ta:nə] *s* (lille) rosin.
sultry ['sʌltri] *adj* trykkende, lummer; sensuel, varm.
sum [sʌm] *s* sum; regnestykke; *in* ~ kortsagt // *v:* ~ *up* tælle sammen, opsummere; ~ *up a person* danne sig et indtryk af en person.
summarily ['sʌmərili] *adv* kortfattet; flygtigt; uden videre.
summarize ['sʌməraiz] *v* resumere.
summary ['sʌməri] *s* resumé, uddrag.
summer ['sʌmə*] *s* sommer // *adj* sommer-; ~ **camp** *s* sommerlejr; feriekoloni; ~ **holidays** *spl* sommerferie; ~**house** *s* (i have) lysthus; ~**school** *s* sommerkursus; ~**time** *s* sommertid.
summery ['sʌməri] *adj* sommerlig.
summit ['sʌmit] *s* (bjerg)top; højdepunkt; ~ *(conference)* topmøde.
summon ['sʌmən] *v* tilkalde; sammenkalde; stævne; ~ *up all one's strength* opbyde alle sine kræfter; ~**s** *s* stævning, tilsigelse.
sumptuous ['sʌmptjuəs] *adj* overdådig, luksuriøs; ødsel.
sun [sʌn] *s* sol; *catch the* ~ blive solskoldet; *a touch of the* ~ solstik; ~**bathe** *v* tage solbad; ~**beam** *s* solstråle; ~**bed** *s* solarium; ~**blind** *s* markise; persienne; ~**burnt** *adj* solbrændt; solskoldet.
sundae ['sʌndei] *s (gastr)* flødeis med frugt.
Sunday ['sʌndi] *s* søndag; *last* ~ i søndags; *on* ~ på søndag; *on* ~*s* om søndagen, hver søndag; *in one's* ~ *best* i stadstøjet.
sundial ['sʌndaiəl] *s* solur.
sundown ['sʌndaun] *s* (især *am)* solnedgang.
sundry ['sʌndri] *adj* forskellige; diverse; *all and* ~ alle og enhver; *sundries pl* diverse udgifter; ~ **shop** *s* blandet landhandel.
sunflower ['sʌnflauə*] *s* solsikke.
sung [sʌŋ] *pp* af *sing.*
sunglasses ['sʌngla:siz] *spl* solbriller.
sunk [sʌŋk] *pp* af *sink;* ~**en** *adj* sunket; indsunket.
sun... ['sʌn-] sms: ~**lamp** *s* højfjeldssol; ~**light** *s* sol(lys); ~**lit** *adj* solbeskinnet; ~**ny** ['sʌni] *adj* solrig; solskins-; glad; ~**rise** *s* solopgang; ~**roof** *s* soltag; ~**set** *s* solnedgang; ~**shade** *s* parasol; markise; ~**shine** *s* solskin; ~**stroke** *s* solstik; ~**tan** *s* solbrændthed; ~**tan oil** *s* sololie; ~**trap** *s* solkrog; ~-**up** *s* (især *am)* solopgang.
sup [sʌp] *v* spise middag.
super ['su:pə*] *adj* fin, glimrende; skøn; ~**annuation scheme** *s* pensionsordning.
superb [su'pə:b] *adj* storartet; fremragende, fortrinlig.
super... [su:pə-] sms: ~**cilious** [-'siliəs] *adj* overlegen, vigtig; ~**ficial** [-'fiʃəl] *adj* overfladisk, flygtig; ~**fluous** [su'pə:fluəs] *adj* overflødig; ~**human** [-'hju:mən] *adj* overmenneskelig; ~**impose** [-im'pəuz] *v:* ~*impose sth on sth* lægge ngt oven på ngt; ~**intendent** [-in'tɛndənt] *s* forstander; tilsynsførende; sv.t. politiinspektør.
superior [su:'piəriə*] *s* overordnet // *adj* højere; over-; overlegen; glimrende, fremragende.
superiority [su:piəri'ɔriti] *s* overlegenhed; overhøjhed.
super... [su:pə-] sms: ~**natural** [-'nætʃrəl] *adj* overnaturlig; ~**sede** [-'si:d] *v* afløse; fortrænge; ~**sonic** [-'sɔnik] *adj* overlyds-; ~**stition** [-'stiʃən] *s* overtro; ~**stitious** [-'stiʃəs] *adj* overtroisk; ~**vise** ['su:pəvaiz] *v* overvåge; føre opsyn med; ~**visor** ['su:pəvaizə*] *s* tilsynsførende; afdelingschef.
supine [su:pain] *adj* liggende; sløv, ligegyldig.
supper ['sʌpə*] *s* aftensmad; *the last* ~ den sidste nadver.
supplant [sə'pla:nt] *v* fortrænge.
supple [sʌpl] *adj* smidig, bøjelig.
supplement *s* ['sʌplimənt] tillæg, supplement // *v* [sʌpli'mɛnt] supplere; fylde op.
supplementary [sʌpli'mɛntəri] *adj* ekstra, supplerende.
supplicant ['sʌplikənt] *s* ansøger.
supplier [sʌ'plaiə*] *s* leverandør.
supply [sʌ'plai] *s* forsyning; forråd; ~

and demand udbud og efterspørgsel; *be in short* ~ være knap; *petrol is in short* ~ benzin er en mangelvare; ~ *teacher* lærervikar // *v* forsyne; levere; skaffe.

support [sə'pɔ:t] *s* støtte; underhold // *v* støtte; understøtte; bære; forsørge; **~er** *s* tilhænger; forsørger.

suppose [sə'pəuz] *v* antage, formode; *be ~d to* burde, skulle; *I ~ so* det tror (,antager) jeg; ~ *we did it?* hvad nu hvis vi gjorde det?

supposing [sə'pəuziŋ] *konj* hvis nu.

supposition [səpə'ziʃən] *s* antagelse; formodning.

suppress [sə'prɛs] *v* undertrykke; skjule, fortie.

suppression [sə'prɛʃən] *s* undertrykkelse.

supremacy [sə'prɛməsi] *s* overhøjhed.

supreme [sə'pri:m] *adj* højest, øverst; *rule* ~ være enerådende; ~ **court** *s* højesteret.

surcharge ['sə:tʃa:dʒ] *s* strafporto; ekstraafgift.

sure [ʃuə*] *adj* sikker, vis; ~ *enough* ganske rigtig; *know sth for* ~ vide ngt bestemt; *make* ~ sikre sig; *just to make* ~ bare for en sikkerheds skyld; *be ~ to remember!* sørg nu for at huske det! **~-fire** *adj* (F) *(fig)* bombesikker; **~ly** *adv* sikkert; da vel.

surety ['ʃuərəti] *s* sikkerhed; kaution.

surf [sə:f] *s* (om bølger) brænding.

surface ['sə:fis] *s* overflade; vejbelægning // *v* overfladebehandle; dukke op; ~ **mail** *s* alm. post (mods: luftpost).

surfboard ['sə:fbɔ:d] *s* bræt til surfriding; sejlbræt.

surfeit ['sə:fit] *s* overmål.

surge [sə:dʒ] *s* (stor) bølge; bølgen // *v* bruse, strømme.

surgeon ['sə:dʒən] *s* kirurg.

surgery ['sə:dʒəri] *s* kirurgi; konsultation(sværelse); konsultationstid; *undergo* ~ blive opereret; ~ **hours** *spl* konsultationstid.

surgical ['sə:dʒikl] *adj* kirurgisk; ~ **spirit** *s* hospitalssprit.

surly ['sə:li] *adj* sur, tvær.

surmise [sə:'maiz] *v* formode.

surmount [sə:'maunt] *v* overvinde.

surname ['sə:neim] *s* efternavn.

surpass [sə'pa:s] *v* overgå.

surplus ['sə:pləs] *s* overskud // *adj* overskuds-; overskydende.

surprise [sə'praiz] *s* overraskelse, forbavselse; *take sby by* ~ overraske en // *v* overraske, overrumple; **surprising** *adj* forbavsende.

surrender [sə'rɛndə*] *s* overgivelse; afståelse // *v* overgive (sig); opgive, afstå.

surreptitious [sʌrɛp'tiʃəs] *adj* stjålen, hemmelig.

surrogate ['sʌrəgeit] *s* erstatning, surrogat; ~ *mother* rugemor.

surround [sə'raund] *v* omgive, omringe.

surrounding [sə'raundiŋ] *adj* omgivende; **~s** *spl* omgivelser.

surtax ['sə:tæks] *s* særskat på høje indkomster.

surveillance [sə:'veiləns] *s* opsyn.

survey *s* ['sə:vei] overblik; oversigt; inspektion; opmåling // *v* [sə:'vei] overskue; bese, inspicere; kortlægge.

surveying [sə:'veiiŋ] *s* landmåling.

surveyor [sə:'veiə*] *s* tilsynsførende; landmåler.

survival [sə'vaivl] *s* overlevelse; levn.

survive [sə'vaiv] *v* overleve; leve videre.

survivor [sə'vaivə*] *s* overlevende.

susceptible [sə'sɛptibl] *adj* modtagelig *(to* for).

suspect *s* ['sʌspɛkt] mistænkt // *adj* mistænkelig, mistænkt // *v* [sə'spɛkt] mistænke.

suspend [sə'spɛnd] *v* ophænge; suspendere; standse; udsætte; **~ed sentence** *s* betinget dom.

suspender belt [sʌ'spɛndə ˌbɛlt] *s* strømpeholder.

suspenders [sʌ'spɛndəz] *spl* sokkeholder.

suspense [sə'spɛns] *s* udsættelse; spænding.

suspension [sə'spɛnʃən] *s* ophængning; affjedring; suspendering; frakendelse (fx af kørekort); ~ **bridge** *s* hængebro.

suspicion [sə'spiʃən] *s* mistanke; anelse.

suspicious [sə'spiʃəs] *adj* mistænksom; mistænkelig, suspekt.

suss [sʌs] *v:* ~ *sby out* føle en på tænderne; gennemskue en.

sustain [sə'stein] *v* støtte; opretholde; lide, tåle; **~ed** *adj* vedvarende; langvarig.

sustenance ['sʌstinəns] *s* næring(s-indhold).

svelte [svɛlt] *adj* slank; elegant.

swab [swɔb] *s* vatpind; tampon; *(med)* podning.

swagger ['swægə*] *v* spankulere; blære sig.

swallow ['swɔləu] *s (zo)* svale; mundfuld; slurk // *v* synke, sluge; *(fig)* æde i sig, sluge råt; *~ed up* (op)slugt.

swam [swæm] *præt* af *swim.*

swamp [swɔmp] *s* sump // *v* oversvømme; **~y** *adj* sumpet.

swan [swɔn] *s* svane // *v* (F) svanse, slentre.

swank [swæŋk] *v* blære sig // *adj* blæret; (over)smart.

swap [swɔp] *s* (bytte)handel // *v* bytte, udveksle; *I'll ~ you!* skal vi bytte?

swarm [swɔ:m] *s* sværm, vrimmel // *v* sværme, myldre.

swarthy ['swɔ:ði] *adj* mørklødet, sortsmudsket.

swat [swɔt] *s* fluesmækker // *v* smække, slå.

swathe [sweið] *v* svøbe, vikle ind.

sway [swei] *v* svaje, slingre; påvirke; *be ~ed by* lade sig påvirke af.

swear [swɛə*] *v (swore, sworn* [swɔ:*, swɔ:n]) sværge; bande; *~ at sby* lade ederne hagle ned over en; *~ by sth* sværge til ngt; sværge på ngt; *~ sby in* tage en i ed; *~ to sth* sværge på ngt; **~word** *s* bandeord.

sweat [swɛt] *s* sved; *in a ~* badet i sved // *v* svede; *~ it out* holde ud.

sweaty ['swɛti] *adj* svedig; møjsommelig.

Swede [swi:d] *s* svensker; **swede** *s* *(bot)* kålroe; **Sweden** ['swi:dən] *s* Sverige; **Swedish** ['swi:diʃ] *s/adj* svensk.

sweep [swi:p] *s* fejning; tag; fejende bevægelse; strækning; (også: *chimney ~)* skorstensfejer // *v (swept, swept* [swɛpt]) feje; stryge hen over; skride; strække sig; *~ away* rive bort; feje til side; *~ sby off his feet* feje fødderne væk under en; *~ past* stryge forbi; *~ sth under the rug* feje ngt ind under gulvtæppet (også *fig*); *~ up* feje op.

sweeper *s* gadefejer; fejemaskine; *(fodb)* sweeper.

sweeping ['swi:piŋ] *adj* fejende (fx *gesture* gestus); flot; omfattende; **~s** *spl* fejeskarn; *(fig)* bærme.

sweepstakes ['swi:psteiks] *spl* slags spil på heste.

sweet [swi:t] *s* dessert; bolsje etc; *~s pl* slik // *adj* sød; elskværdig; frisk (fx *milk* mælk); *have a ~ tooth* holde af søde sager; *be ~ on sby* (F) være lun på en; **~bread** *s (gastr)* brissel; **~corn** *s* sukkermajs.

sweeten [swi:tn] *v* søde; komme sukker i; forsøde; **~er** *s* sødemiddel.

sweetheart ['swi:tha:t] *s* kæreste, skat.

sweetly ['swi:tli] *adv* sødt, blidt.

sweet pea ['swi:tpi:] *s (bot)* latyrus.

sweet-shop ['swi:tʃɔp] *s* slikbutik.

swell [swɛl] *s* (om havet) dønning; (op)svulmen // *v (~ed, ~ed* el. *swollen* ['swəulən]) svulme (op); bugne // *adj* (F) alle tiders, mægtig(t); **~ing** *s* hævelse; bule.

sweltering ['swɛltəriŋ] *adj* (om varme) kvælende.

swept [swɛpt] *præt* og *pp* af *sweep.*

swerve [swə:v] *v* dreje (hurtigt) til siden; vige af.

swift [swift] *s (zo)* mursejler // *adj* hurtig, rap.

swig [swig] *s* slurk // *v* tylle, drikke.

swill [swil] *s* svineæde; affald // *v* bælge i sig, tylle; skylle af, spule.

swim [swim] *s* svømmetur; *in the ~* (F) orienteret // *v (swam, swum* [swæm, swʌm]) svømme (over); flyde; svæve; *my head ~s* jeg er

svimmel; **~mer** *s* svømmer; **~ming** *s* svømning; **~ming bath** *s* svømmehal; **~ming cap** *s* badehætte; **~ming costume** *s* badedragt; **~suit** *s* badedragt.
swindle [swindl] *s* svindelnummer // *v* svindle, fuppe; tilsvindle sig; **~r** *s* svindler.
swine [swain] *s* svin; (F) møgsvin.
swing [swiŋ] *s* gynge; gyngetur; sving(ning); swing; *get into the ~ of sth* blive grebet af ngt, gå op i ngt // *v (swung, swung* [swʌŋ]) gynge; svinge; dingle; blive hængt; påvirke, dreje; **~ing** *adj* rytmisk; som swinger.
swipe [swaip] *s* hårdt slag // *v* slå hårdt; knalde; (F) hugge.
swirl [swə:l] *s* hvirvel; hvirvlen // *v* hvirvle.
swish [swiʃ] *s* susen, hvislen // *v* suse; skvulpe; bruse.
Swiss [swis] *s* schweizer // *adj* schweizisk.
switch [switʃ] *s* kontakt, afbryder; omslag, skifte; *make a ~* bytte // *v* skifte; bytte; dreje, svinge; *~ off* slukke for; stoppe; *~ on* tænde for; starte; **~back** *s* rutschebane; **~board** *s (tlf)* omstillingsbord.
Switzerland ['switsələnd] *s* Schweiz.
swivel [swivl] *v: ~ (round)* dreje; **~ chair** *s* drejestol.
swollen ['swəulən] *pp* af *swell* // *adj* hævet; ophovnet.
swoon [swu:n] *s* besvimelse // *v* besvime.
swoop [swu:p] *s* lynangreb; razzia // *v* slå ned på.
sword [sɔ:d] *s* sværd, sabel.
swore [swɔ:*] *præt* af *swear;* **sworn** [swɔ:n] *pp* af *swear.*
swot [swɔt] *s* læsehest // *v* pukle, slide, terpe.
swum [swʌm] *pp* af *swim.*
swung [swʌŋ] *præt* og *pp* af *swing.*
syllable ['siləbl] *s* stavelse.
syllabus ['siləbəs] *s* pensum, program.
symbol ['simbl] *s* tegn *(of* på); symbol; **~ic(al)** [sim'bɔlik(l)] *adj* symbolsk.
symbolize ['simbəlaiz] *v* symbolisere.
symmetrical [si'mɛtrikl] *adj* symmetrisk.
symmetry ['simitri] *s* symmetri.
sympathetic [simpə'θɛtik] *adj* forstående, medfølende; *~ towards* velvilligt indstillet over for.
sympathize ['simpəθaiz] *v* sympatisere; have medfølelse; **~r** *s* sympatisør.
sympathy ['simpəθi] *s* sympati.
symphonic [sim'fɔnik] *adj* symfonisk.
symphony ['simfəni] *s* symfoni.
symptom ['simptəm] *s* symptom *(of* på).
synagogue ['sinəgɔg] *s* synagoge.
synchronize ['sinkrənaiz] *v* synkronisere.
syndicate ['sindikit] *s* konsortium; syndikat.
synonym ['sinənim] *s* synonym.
synonymous [si'nɔniməs] *adj* synonym.
synopsis [si'nɔpsis] *s (pl: synopses* [-si:z]) resumé, synopsis.
synthesis ['sinθəsis] *s (pl: syntheses* [-si:z]) syntese.
synthetic [sin'θɛtik] *adj* syntetisk, kunsig; kunst-; *synthetics pl* (om tekstiler) kunststoffer.
Syria ['siriə] *s* Syrien; **~n** *s* syrer // *adj* syrisk.
syringe ['sirindʒ] *s* (injektions)sprøjte.
syrup ['sirəp] *s* sød frugtsaft; sirup; *cough ~* hostesaft.
syrupy ['sirəpi] *adj* sødladen.
system ['sistəm] *s* system; metode; ordning.
systematic [sistə'mætik] *adj* ordnet; systematisk.
systems analyst ['sistimz ˌænəlist] *s (edb)* systemanalytiker.

T

T, t [ti:]; *it's him to a T* det ligner ham på en prik.
ta [ta:] *interj* (F) tak.
tab [tæb] *s* strop; skilt, mærke; *keep ~s on* holde øje med.
tabby cat ['tæbikæt] *s* stribet kat; hunkat.

table [teibl] *s* bord; tavle; tabel; *lay (,set) the* ~ dække bord(et); ~ *of contents* indholdsfortegnelse; *turn the* ~*s on sby (fig)* vende spillet // *v* stille op; fremsætte (fx *a motion* et forslag); **~cloth** *s* dug; **~ manners** *spl* bordskik; **~mat** *s* lunchserviet; bordskåner; **~spoon** *s* spiseske; **~spoonful** *s* spiseskefuld.

tablet ['tæblit] *s* tablet, pastil; tavle; stykke (fx sæbe); plade (fx chokolade).

tabletop ['teibltɔp] *s* bordplade.

tabloid ['tæblɔid] *s* avis i frokostformat; sensationsblad.

taboo [tə'bu:] *s/adj* tabu.

tacit ['tæsit] *adj* stiltiende; tavs.

taciturn ['tæsitə:n] *adj* fåmælt.

tack [tæk] *s* (tegne)stift; lille søm; risting; *be on the wrong* ~ *(fig)* være på vildspor // *v* fæste, ri.

tackle [tækl] *s* udstyr, grej(er); *(tekn)* talje; *(sport)* tackling // *v (fig)* gå løs på; tackle.

tacky ['tæki] *adj* klæbrig, klistret; tarvelig.

tact [tækt] *s* finfølelse, takt; **~ful** *adj* diskret.

tactical ['tæktikl] *adj* taktisk.

tactician [tæk'tiʃən] *s* taktiker.

tactics ['tæktiks] *spl* taktik.

tactless ['tæktlis] *adj* taktløs; indiskret.

tadpole ['tædpəul] *s* haletudse.

taffeta ['tæfitə] *s* taft.

tag [tæg] *s* etiket; prisskilt; stående udtryk; ettagfat // *v* traske; ~ *along with sby* hænge på hos en; ~ *on* hænge på (,ved).

tail [teil] *s* hale; (om kjole) slæb; bageste del, ende; (om person) skygge; *put a* ~ *on sby* skygge en; *turn* ~ stikke af// *v* følge, skygge; ~ *away* blive svagere, dø hen; ~ *off* ebbe ud, forsvinde; **~back** *s* bilkø; **~ end** *s* bagende; **~gate** *s* (på stationcar) bagklap; **~ light** *s* baglygte; **~-off** *s* afmatning, fald.

tailor ['teilə*] *s* skrædder; **~ing** *s* skræddersyning; snit; **~-made** *adj* skræddersyet (også *fig)*.

tails [teils] *spl* (F) kjolesæt; *heads or* ~ plat el. krone.

tailwind ['teilwind] *s* medvind.

tainted ['teintid] *adj* fordærvet; anløben; plettet.

take [teik] *s* (film)optagelse; bytte // *v (took, taken* [tuk, teikn]) tage; kræve; rumme; bringe; tage med; ledsage; *I* ~ *it that* jeg går ud fra at; ~ *sby for a walk* tage en med ud at gå tur; *be* ~*n ill* blive syg; *be* ~*n aback* blive overrasket (,paf); ~ *after sby* slægte en på; ~ *against sby* få ngt imod en; ~ *apart* skille ad; ~ *away* fjerne; trække fra; ~ *back* tage tilbage; tage i sig igen; ~ *down* nedrive (fx *a house* et hus); skrive (ned); ~ *in* narre; (op)fatte; omfatte; modtage; ~ *off* tage væk; tage af; imitere; (om fly) lette, starte; ~ *on* påtage sig; ansætte, antage; tage på; ~ *out* tage ud; skaffe sig; invitere ud; ~ *over* overtage; afløse; ~ *to* komme til at synes om; få smag for; ~ *up* tage op; genoptage; optage (fx *room* plads); indtage (fx *an attitude* en holdning); fylde; slå sig på; begynde på; ~ *sby up on sth* tage imod ens tilbud; **~away** *s* sv.t. grillbar // *adj* (om mad) ud af huset-; **~-home pay** *s* nettoløn; **~off** *s (fly)* start; *(fig)* parodi; **~over** *s* overtagelse.

takings ['teikiŋz] *spl (merk)* indtægt, indkomst.

talc [tælk] *s* talkum(pudder).

tale [teil] *s* fortælling, historie; *(neds)* løgnehistorie; *fairy* ~ eventyr.

talent ['tælənt] *s* talent, anlæg; **~ed** *adj* talentfuld.

talk [tɔ:k] *s* snak, tale(n); samtale; foredrag; *have a* ~ tale sammen; *give a* ~ holde et foredrag // *v* snakke, tale; *be* ~*ing sense* lyde fornuftig; ~*ing about money*... apropos penge...; *now you're* ~*ing!* det var ngt andet! ~ *back* svare igen; ~ *sby into doing sth* overtale en til at gøre ngt; ~ *sby out of doing sth* tale en fra at gøre ngt; ~ *shop* tale forretninger (,fag); ~ *sth over* diskutere ngt.

talkative ['tɔ:kətiv] *adj* snakkesalig.

talking book ['tɔ:kiŋ 'buk] *s* lydbog.

talking-to ['tɔ:kiŋtu] *s* omgang, overhaling.

tall [tɔ:l] *adj* høj, stor; (F) utrolig; *that's a bit ~!* (F) den er for langt ude! *a ~ story* en skrøne; **~boy** *s* høj kommode.
tallow ['tæləu] *s* talg.
tally ['tæli] *s* regnskab // *v: ~ (with)* stemme (med).
tame [teim] *v* tæmme // *adj* tam; mat, sagtmodig.
tamper ['tæmpə*] *v: ~ with* pille ved; manipulere med.
tan [tæn] *s* solbrændthed // *v* garve; gøre (,blive) solbrændt; *~ sby's hide* give en klø // *adj* gyldenbrun.
tang [tæŋ] *s* skarp lugt (,smag).
tangent ['tændʒənt] *s (mat)* tangent; *go off at a ~* komme væk fra emnet, køre ud ad et sidespor.
tangerine ['tændʒəri:n] *s* (om frugt) mandarin.
tangible ['tændʒəbl] *adj* håndgribelig.
tangle [tæŋgl] *s* sammenfiltret masse; vildnis; kaos; *get into a ~* komme i urede; få problemer // *v* sammenfiltres; *~ up* lave uorden i; *~ with* komme i karambolage med.
tangy ['tæŋi] *adj* (om smag el. lugt) skarp.
tank [tæŋk] *s* tank; beholder // *v: ~ up* tanke op; (S) drikke sig fuld.
tankard ['tæŋkəd] *s* ølkrus.
tanker ['tæŋkə*] *s* tankskib; tankvogn.
tanned [tænd] *adj* solbrændt; garvet.
tannic acid ['tænik ˌæsid] *s* garvesyre.
Tannoy ® ['tænɔi] *s* højtaleranlæg.
tantalizing ['tæntəlaiziŋ] *adj* meget fristende.
tantamount ['tæntəmaunt] *adj: ~ to* ensbetydende med.
tantrum ['tæntrəm] *s: throw a ~* få et raserianfald.
tap [tæp] *s* (let) slag; (vand)hane; *beer on ~* fadøl // *v* give et let slag; banke (let); tromme (med); tappe; aflytte; **~-dancing** *s* stepdans.
tape [teip] *s* bånd; bændel; klæbestrimmel, tape // *v* sætte tape på, tape; optage på bånd; *I've got him ~d* jeg ved godt hvad han er for en, jeg har luret ham; **~ measure** *s* målebånd.
taper ['teipə*] *s* kerte // *v* spidse til; *~ off* spidse til; ebbe ud.
tape recorder ['teipriˌkɔ:də*] *s* båndoptager.
tapestry ['tæpistri] *s* billedtæppe, gobelin.
tapeworm ['teipwə:m] *s* bændelorm.
taproom ['tæpru:m] *s* skænkestue.
tap water ['tæpwɔ:tə*] *s* ledningsvand.
tar [ta:*] *s* tjære // *v* tjære.
tardy ['ta:di] *adj* langsom, træg; forsinket.
target ['ta:git] *s* mål; skydeskive; målsætning // *v: ~ on* tage som mål, sigte på; **~ practice** *s* skydeøvelse.
tarmac ['ta:mæk] ® *s* (på vej) asfaltbelægning; *(fly)* startbane (med belægning) // *v* asfaltere.
tarnish ['ta:niʃ] *v* (om fx kobber) anløbe; falme; *(fig)* plette.
tarpaulin [ta:'pɔ:lin] *s* presenning.
tarragon ['tærəgən] *s (bot)* esdragon.
tart [ta:t] *s* (frugt)tærte; (F, *neds)* tøs; luder // *v: ~ oneself up* (F) maje sig ud; *~ sth up* (F) shine ngt op // *adj* skarp, besk.
tartan ['ta:tn] *s* skotskternet mønster, klantern // *adj* skotskternet.
tartar ['ta:tə*] *s* vinsten; tandsten; havgasse.
task [ta:sk] *s* hverv, opgave; pligt; *take sby to ~* gå i rette med en; **~ force** *s (mil)* kommandostyrke.
tassel ['tæsl] *s* kvast.
taste [teist] *s* smag; mundsmag; *in bad ~* smagløs; *in good ~* smagfuld; *each to his ~* enhver sin smag; *have a ~ for* have smag for; *have a ~ of sth* smage på ngt // *v* smage; **~ bud** *s* smagsløg; **~ful** *adj* smagfuld; **~less** *adj* smagløs; fad.
tasty ['teisti] *adj* velsmagende, lækker.
tat [tæt] *s* billigt skrammel (,kluns etc); *give tit for ~* give svar på tiltale, give igen af samme mønt.
tattered ['tætəd] *adj* laset; frynset.
tatters ['tætəz] *spl: in ~* i laser.
tattle [tætl] *s* sladder, sludder // *v* sladre, sludre.
tattoo [tæ'tu:] *s* tatovering; tattoo // *v* tatovere.
tatty ['tæti] *adj* nusset, tarvelig.

taught [tɔ:t] *præt* og *pp* af *teach.*
taunt [tɔ:nt] *s* spot; spydighed // *v* håne.
Taurus ['tɔ:rəs] *s (astr)* Tyren.
taut [tɔ:t] *adj* spændt; stram.
tavern ['tævən] *s (gl)* kro.
tawdry ['tɔ:dri] *adj* billig og smagløs.
tawny ['tɔ:ni] *adj* gyldenbrun.
tax [tæks] *s* skat; byrde // *v* beskatte; pålægge; sætte på prøve; bebrejde; ~ *sby with sth* beskylde en for ngt; bebrejde en ngt; **-able** *adj* skattepligtig; **-ation** [-'seiʃən] *s* beskatning; **~ bracket** *s* skatteklasse; **~ collector** *s* skatteopkræver; **~-deductible** *adj* fradragsberettiget; **~ dodge** *s* skattefidus; **~ evasion** *s* skattesnyderi; **~ exile** *s* person som lever i skattely; **~-free** *adj* skattefri; **~ haven** *s* skatteparadis.
taxi ['tæksi] *s* taxi, taxa // *v (fly)* køre på jorden, taxie.
taxidermist ['tæksidə:mist] *s* konservator; dyreudstopper.
taxidriver ['tæksidraivə*] *s* taxachauffør.
taxing ['tæksiŋ] *adj* anstrengende, krævende.
taxi rank *s* taxaholdeplads.
taxpayer ['tækspeiə*] *s* skatteyder; **tax return** *s* selvangivelse.
tea [ti:] *s* te; *have* ~ drikke te; *(high)* ~ eftermiddagsmåltid; aftensmad; **~ bag** *s* tepose, tebrev; **~ break** *s* tepause; **~ caddy** *s* tedåse; **~ cake** *s* rosinbolle.
teach [ti:tʃ] *v (taught, taught* [tɔ:t]) lære, undervise; ~ *sby to read* lære en at læse; ~ *history* undervise i historie; ~ *him a lesson* give ham en lærestreg.
teacher ['ti:tʃə*] *s* lærer.
teaching ['ti:tʃiŋ] *s* undervisning; *the ~s of Marx* Marx' lære; *go into* ~ blive lærer; **~ staff** *s* lærerstab.
tea cloth ['ti:klɔθ] *s* viskestykke.
tea cosy ['ti:kəuzi] *s* tevarmer.
teak [ti:k] *s* teaktræ.
tealeaf ['ti:li:f] *s* teblad.
team [ti:m] *s* hold; (om dyr) spand // *v:* ~ *up* slutte sig sammen; (om par) komme sammen; **~-mate** *s* holdkammerat.
teamster ['ti:mstə*] *s (am)* lastbilchauffør.
teamwork ['ti:mwə:k] *s* samarbejde.
teapot ['ti:pɔt] *s* tepotte.
tear [tiə*] *s* tåre; [tɛə*] flænge, rift; *be in ~s* græde; *bored to* ~ ved at kede sig ihjel; *burst into ~s* briste i gråd // *v* [tɛə*] *(tore, torn* [tɔ:*, tɔ:n]) flå, rive; revne; ~ *one's hair* rive sig i håret; ~ *along* fare (,drøne) af sted; *torn between* vaklende mellem; ~ *up* rive i stykker; **-ful** ['tiəful] *adj* tårevædet, grædende; **~ gas** ['tiəgæs] *s* tåregas; **tear-jerker** ['tiə,dʒə:kə*] *s* tåreperser.
tearoff ['tɛərɔf] *adj* afrivnings-.
tearoom ['ti:ru:m] *s* terestaurant.
tease [ti:z] *s* drilleri; (om person) drillepind // *v* drille; pirre; plage; (om hår) toupere.
teaser ['ti:zə*] *s* vanskeligt spørgsmål, hård nød at knække; drillepind.
tea... ['ti:-] sms: **-set** *s* testel; **--shop** *s* terestaurant; **-spoon** *s* teske; **~ strainer** *s* tesi.
teat [ti:t] *s* brystvorte; (på sutteflaske) sut.
tea towel ['ti:tauəl] *s* viskestykke.
technical ['tɛknikl] *adj* teknisk; **~ college** *s* teknisk skole.
technicality [tɛkni'kæliti] *s* teknisk detalje; formalitet.
technician [tɛk'niʃən] *s* tekniker; laborant.
technique [tɛk'ni:k] *s* teknik.
technologist [tɛk'nɔlədʒist] *s* teknolog.
technology [tɛk'nɔlədʒi] *s* teknologi.
teddy ['tɛdi] *s:* ~ *(bear* [bɛə]) bamse.
tedious ['ti:diəs] *adj* kedelig; trættende.
tedium ['ti:diəm] *s* kedsomhed.
teem [ti:m] *v* myldre, vrimle *(with* med); *it's ~ing down* det øser ned.
teens [ti:nz] *spl: be in one's* ~ være ung (under 20 år).
teenyweeny ['ti:ni'wi:ni] *adj* lillebitte.
teeter ['ti:tə*] *v* vakle.
teeth [ti:θ] *spl* af *tooth.*
teethe [ti:ð] *v* få tænder; *be teething* være ved at få tænder.
teething ['ti:ðiŋ] *s* tandfrembrud; ~

ring *s* bidering; ~ **troubles** *spl* ondt for tænder; begyndervanskeligheder.
teetotal ['ti:'təutl] *adj* totalt afholdende; afholds-; ~**ler** *s* afholdsmand.
telecast ['tɛlika:st] *s* fjernsynsudsendelse // *v* udsende i fjernsynet.
telegraph ['tɛligra:f] *s* telegraf; ~**ic** [-'græfik] *adj* telegrafisk.
telepathy [ti'lɛpəθi] *s* tankeoverføring, telepati.
telephone ['tɛlifəun] *s* telefon; *be on the* ~ have telefon; (være ved at) snakke i telefon; ~ **answering machine** *s* telefonsvarer; ~ **booth (,box)** *s* telefonboks; ~ **call** *s* telefonopringning; ~ **directory** *s* telefonbog; ~ **exchange** *s* telefoncentral; ~ **operator** *s* telefonist.
telephoto ['tɛlifəutəu] *s* telefoto; ~ **lens** *s* telelinse.
telescope ['tɛliskəup] *s* teleskop, kikkert.
televiewer ['tɛlivju:ə*] *s* (fjern)seer.
televise ['tɛlivaiz] *v* udsende i fjernsynet.
television ['tɛlivi3ən] *s* fjernsyn, tv; ~ **set** *s* fjernsyn(sapparat).
tell [tɛl] *v* (*told, told* [təuld]) fortælle; sige; give besked; afgøre, skelne; mærkes; ~ *sth from sth,* ~ *sth apart* skelne ngt fra ngt; ~ *on sby* sladre om en; *there's no ~ing* det er ikke til at vide (,sige); *be told to do sth* få besked på at gøre ngt; *be told off* få læst og påskrevet; ~ *me another!* (F) den må du længere ud på landet med! *I told you so!* det var jo det jeg sagde! ~**er** *s* stemmeoptæller; *(am)* kasserer.
telling ['tɛliŋ] *adj* rammende; sigende; *there's no* ~ det er ikke til at vide.
tell-off ['tɛlɔ:f] *s* overhaling, opsang.
telltale ['tɛlteil] *s* sladderhank // *adj* afslørende; forræderisk.
telly ['tɛli] *s* (F) fjernsyn.
temerity [ti'mɛriti] *s* dumdristighed.
temp [tɛmp] *s* (fork.f. *temporary)* kontorvikar // *v* arbejde som kontorvikar.
temper ['tɛmpə*] *s* sind; natur; humør; temperament; hidsighed; *be in a* ~ være gal i hovedet; *lose one's* ~ blive vred // *v* temperere; mildne; (om metal) hærde.
temperament ['tɛmprəmənt] *s* temperament; ~**al** [-'mɛntl] *adj* temperamentsfuld.
temperance ['tɛmpərəns] *s* mådehold; ædruelighed.
temperate ['tɛmpərət] *adj* moderat, mådeholdende; (om klima etc) tempereret.
temperature ['tɛmprətʃə*] *s* temperatur, feber; *have (,run) a* ~ have feber.
tempered ['tɛmpəd] *adj* hærdet.
tempest ['tɛmpist] *s* (stærk) storm.
tempestuous [tɛm'pɛstjuəs] *adj* stormfuld; storm-.
template ['tɛmplət] *s* skabelon.
temple [tɛmpl] *s* tempel; *(anat)* tinding.
temporal ['tɛmpərəl] *adj* verdslig; tidsmæssig, tids-.
temporarily ['tɛmprərəli] *adv* for øjeblikket; midlertidigt.
temporary *adj* midlertidig; provisorisk; kortvarig.
temporize ['tɛmpəraiz] *v* trække tiden ud, nøle.
tempt [tɛm(p)t] *v* friste, lokke.
temptation [tɛm'teiʃən] *s* fristelse.
tempting ['tɛmtiŋ] *adj* fristende.
ten [tɛn] *num* ti; *the upper* ~ de fine (i samfundet).
tenable ['tɛnəbl] *adj* holdbar, som kan forsvares.
tenacious [tə'neiʃəs] *adj* fast; sej; klæbrig; vedholdende.
tenacity [ti'næsiti] *s* fasthed; ihærdighed.
tenancy ['tɛnənsi] *s* leje; forpagtning.
tenant *s* lejer; forpagter; beboer.
tend [tɛnd] *v* passe, pleje; betjene; ~ *to* være tilbøjelig til at; gå i retning af, tendere imod.
tendency ['tɛndənsi] *s* tendens, tilbøjelighed.
tender ['tɛndə*] *s* plejer, passer; *(merk)* tilbud; *put out to* ~, *invite* ~*s* udbyde i licitation; *legal* ~ lovligt betalingsmiddel // *v* tilbyde // *adj* blød; (om mad) mør; sart, øm, kærlig.

tenderize ['tɛndəraiz] *v* gøre mør.
tenderloin ['tɛndəlɔin] *s* mørbradssteg.
tendon ['tɛndən] *s (anat)* sene.
tendril ['tɛndril] *s* slyngtråd; hårlok.
tenement ['tɛnəmənt] *s* udlejningsejendom; beboelseshus.
tenner ['tɛnə*] *s* 10-pundsseddel.
tennis ['tɛnis] *s* tennis; **~ court** *s* tennisbane; **~ racket** *s* tennisketsjer.
tenor ['tɛnə*] *s* tenor; hovedindhold; stil, ånd; forløb.
tenpin ['tɛnpin] *s* kegle; **~s** *s* bowling.
tense [tɛns] *s (gram)* tid // *adj* spændt, anspændt, nervøs; anspændende // *v: ~ up* blive (an)spændt, stivne.
tension ['tɛnʃən] *s* spænding; anspændthed.
tent [tɛnt] *s* telt // *v* ligge i telt.
tentacle ['tɛntəkl] *s (zo)* fangarm; *the ~s of the mafia* mafiaens kløer.
tentative ['tɛntətiv] *adj* prøvende; prøve-; foreløbig.
tenterhooks ['tɛntəhuks] *spl: be on ~* sidde som på nåle.
tenth [tɛnθ] *num* tiende // *s* tiendedel.
tenuous ['tɛnjuəs] *adj* fin, sart; svag; uholdbar.
tenure ['tɛnjə*] *s* embedstid; besiddelse, indehavelse.
tepid ['tɛpid] *adj* lunken.
term [tə:m] *s* termin, periode, frist; udtryk, vending; (i skole etc) semester; *~ of imprisonment* fængselsstraf; *in the long ~* i det lange løb; (se også *terms*) // *v* benævne, kalde.
terminal ['tə:minl] *s* endestation; terminal; (i batteri) pol // *adj* endelig; ende-; yder-; afsluttende; dødelig; døende.
terminate ['tə:mineit] *v* afslutte; ende; *~ in* ende med; munde ud i.
termination [tə:mi'neiʃən] *s* afslutning; ophævelse (af fx kontrakt); udløb; *~ (of pregnancy)* svangerskabsafbrydelse.
terminus ['tə:minəs] *s* endestation.
terms [tə:ms] *spl* betingelser, vilkår; *easy ~ (merk)* fordelagtige vilkår; *in ~ of* hvad angår..., når det gælder...; *be on good ~ with* stå på god fod med; *be on speaking ~ with* være på talefod med; *come to ~ with* komme til forståelse med; finde sit til rette med; *~ of reference* rammer; *~ of trade (økon)* bytteforhold.
terrace ['tɛrəs] *s* terrasse; husrække, rækkehuse; *the ~s* (på stadion) ståpladserne; **~d** *adj* terrasseformet; *~d houses* rækkehuse.
terrestrial [tə'rɛstriəl] *s* jordbo // *adj* land-; jordisk; jord-.
terrible ['tɛribl] *adj* frygtelig, skrækkelig.
terrific [tə'rifik] *adj* fantastisk; enorm.
terrify ['tɛrifai] *v* skræmme, gøre bange.
territorial [tɛri'tɔ:riəl] *adj* territoriel; *Territorial Army* hjemmeværn.
territory ['tɛritəri] *s* territorium, område.
terror ['tɛrə*] *s* skræk, rædsel; *he's a (real) ~* han er livsfarlig; **~ism** *s* terrorisme; **~ist** *s* terrorist.
terrorize ['tɛrəraiz] *v* terrorisere.
terror-stricken ['tɛrəstrikn] *adj* rædselslagen.
terry ['tɛri] *s: ~ (cloth)* frotté.
terse [tə:s] *adj* kort og klar; kort for hovedet.
test [tɛst] *s* prøve; undersøgelse; analyse; *put to the ~* sætte på prøve // *v* prøve, teste; undersøge; **~ ban** *s* (atom)prøvestop; **~ card** *s (tv)* prøvebillede; **~ flight** *s* prøveflyvning.
testify ['tɛstifai] *v* (be)vidne; attestere.
testimonial [tɛsti'məuniəl] *s* vidnesbyrd; attest.
testimony ['tɛstiməni] *s* vidneforklaring; bevis.
test... ['tɛst-] sms: **~ match** *s* (i cricket) landskamp; **~ paper** *s* skriftlig opgave; **~ tube** *s* reagensglas, prøverør; **~-tube baby** *s* reagensglasbarn.
testy ['tɛsti] *adj* irritabel.
tetanus ['tɛtənəs] *s* stivkrampe.
tetchy ['tetʃi] *adj* irritabel.
tether ['tɛðə*] *s: be at the end of one's ~* ikke kunne tage mere.

text [tɛkst] *s* tekst; **~book** *s* lærebog; *a ~book case* en sag lige efter (lære)bogen.

textile ['tɛkstail] *s* tekstil.

texture ['tɛkstʃə*] *s* vævning; struktur; konsistens; **~d** *adj* struktur-; struktureret.

Thai [tai] *s* thailænder // *adj* thailandsk; **Thailand** *s* Thailand.

Thames [tɛmz] *s: the ~* Themsen.

than [ðæn, ðən] *konj* end; *more ~* mere end; *rather ~* hellere end (at).

thank [θæŋk] *v* takke; *~ you (very much)!* (mange) tak! **~ful** *adj* taknemmelig; **~less** *adj* utaknemmelig; *~ God! ~ goodness!* Gud ske lov! *we have John to ~ for that* det kan vi takke John for; *~s to him* takket være ham; *it was no ~s to him* det var ikke hans fortjeneste; **~s·giving** *s* taksigelse.

that [ðæt, ðət] *pron (pl: those* [ðəuz]) den, det; de; der, som // *konj* at; fordi; så (,for) at // *adv* så; *~'s what he said* det sagde han; *~ is...* det vil sige...; *I can't work ~ much* jeg kan ikke arbejde så meget; *at ~* tilmed, oven i købet.

thatch [θætʃ] *s* stråtag; (om hår) manke // *v* tække; **~ed** *adj* stråtækt.

thaw [θɔ:] *s* tø(vejr) // *v* tø; optø; (om køleskab) afrime.

the [ðə, ði] den, det, de; jo, des(to); *~ sooner ~ better* jo før jo bedre; *so much ~ better* så meget des(to) bedre; *you're just ~* [ði:] *person I need* du er lige den jeg behøver.

theatre ['θiətə*] *s* teater; *operating ~* operationsstue; **~-goer** *s* teatergænger.

theatrical [θi'ætrikl] *adj* teatralsk; teater-.

thee [ði:] *pron (gl,* H) dig; jer.

theft [θɛft] *s* tyveri.

their [ðɛə*] *pron* deres; **~s** *pron* deres; *a friend of ~s* en af deres venner.

them [ðɛm, ðəm] *pron* dem, sig.

theme [θi:m] *s* tema; emne; (i skolen) stil; **~ park** *s* eventyrpark (sv.t. Danland, Fabuland etc); **~ song** *s* kendingsmelodi.

themselves [ðɛm'sɛlvz] *pron* sig; (sig) selv; *they did it ~* de gjorde det selv.

then [ðɛn] *adj/adv* da; dengang; daværende; så, derpå; *now and ~* nu og da; *from ~ on* fra da af; *by ~* på det tidspunkt; *till ~* indtil da.

thence [ðɛns] *adv (gl)* derfra.

theologian [θiə'ləudʒiən] *s* teolog.

theology [θi'ɔlədʒi] *s* teologi.

theoretical [θiə'rɛtikl] *adj* teoretisk.

theory ['θiəri] *s* teori; *in ~* teoretisk, i teorien.

therapist ['θɛrəpist] *s* terapeut.

therapy ['θɛrəpi] *s* behandling, terapi.

there [ðɛə*] *adv* der; derhen; *~, ~!* så, så! *~ you are!* værsgo! *~ he is* der er han; *he's not all ~* han er ikke rigtig velforvaret; *he's in ~* han er derinde; *he went ~* han gik (,tog) derhen; *~ now!* der kan du selv se! *~ you go again!* nu igen! **~abouts** *adv* deromkring; **~after** *adv* derefter; **~fore** *adv* derfor; **there's** d.s.s. *~ has, ~ is;* **~upon** *adv* derpå, så.

thermal ['θə:ml] *adj* varme-; termisk; termo-.

thermometer [θə'mɔmitə*] *s* termometer.

thermos ['θə:məs] ® *s* termoflaske.

thesaurus [θi'sɔ:rəs] *s* sv.t. synonymordbog; opslagsbog, leksikon.

these [ði:z] *pron (pl* af *this)* disse; *~ last few weeks* de sidste par uger; *I'm not seeing him ~ days* jeg ser ham ikke for tiden.

thesis ['θi:sis] *s (pl: theses* [-siz]) tese; disputats.

they [ðɛi] *pron* de; man; *~ say that...* de (,man) siger at...; *as ~ say* som man siger.

thick [θik] *adj* tyk; tæt; uklar; tykhovedet; *be ~ with sby* (F) være pot og pande med en; *that's a bit ~* det er altså for galt; *in the ~ of* midt i; *lay it on ~* smøre tykt på; *be as ~ as thieves* være pot og pande.

thicken ['θikn] *v* gøre (,blive) tyk; (om sovs) jævne; **~er** *s* jævning.

thicket ['θikit] *s* tykning, krat.

thickness ['θiknis] *s* tykkelse.

thickset ['θiksεt] *adj* (om person) tætbygget, firskåren.

thick-skinned ['θikskind] *adj* tykhudet.

thief [θi:f] *s (pl: thieves* [θi:vz]) tyv.

thieving ['θi:viŋ] *adj* tyvagtig.

thigh [θai] *s* lår; **~bone** *s* lårben; **~-length** *adj* lårkort.

thimble [θimbl] *s* fingerbøl.

thin [θin] *v* tynde ud; fortynde // *adj* tynd; spinkel; fin, let (fx *fog* tåge).

thine [ðain] *pron (gl,* H) din(e).

thing [θiŋ] *s* ting; tingest; sag; *for one ~* for det første; *the best ~ would be to* det bedste ville være at; *we'll do it first ~ tomorrow* vi gør det straks i morgen tidlig; *that's just the ~!* det er lige sagen! *it's a good ~ we didn't go* det var godt vi ikke gik derhen; *he did no such ~* det gjorde han slet ikke; *there is no such ~ as free love* fri kærlighed eksisterer ikke; *not feel quite the ~* ikke være helt oppe på mærkerne; *the ~ is that...* sagen er at...; *what with one ~ and another* det ene med det andet; *I've got this ~ about John* jeg kan ikke udstå John; jeg er helt vild med John; *poor ~!* den (,din) stakkel! **~s** *spl* sager; tøj, kluns.

thingummy ['θiŋəmi] *s* dims, duppedit, tingest.

thingy ['θiŋi] *s: I saw ~ in the street* (F) jeg mødte ham (,hende) du ved nok på gaden.

think [θiŋk] *v (thought, thought* [θɔ:t]) tænke; tro, mene; forestille sig; synes; *~ of sth* tænke på ngt; *what do you ~ of that?* hvad mener (,synes) du om det? *I'll ~ about it* jeg skal tænke over det; *I ~ so* det tror jeg (nok); *I ~ not* det tror jeg ikke; *~ nothing of* ikke regne det for noget; *~ for oneself* tænke selv; *just ~!* tænk bare! *~ well of* have høje tanker om; *~ up* finde på, udtænke; **~ing** *s* tænkning; *to my way of thinking* efter mine begreber; **~-tank** *s* tænketank.

thinner ['θinə*] *s* fortynder(væske).

third [θə:d] *s* tredjedel; *(mus)* terts; *(auto)* tredje gear // *num* tredje; **~-degree** *s* tredjegradsforhør; **~ly** *adv* for det tredje; **~ party insurance** *s* ansvarsforsikring; **~-rate** *adj* tredjerangs; *the* **Third World** *s* den tredje verden.

thirst [θə:st] *s* tørst // *v* tørste *(for* efter); **thirsty** *adj* tørstig.

thirteen ['θə:ti:n] *num* tretten.

thirty ['θə:ti] *num* tredive.

this [ðis] *pron (pl: these* [ði:z]) denne, dette; den (,det) her; de her, disse; *~ day week* i dag otte dage; *~ morning* i morges (,formiddags); *like ~* på denne måde, sådan her; *~ and that* dit og dat; *one of these days* en af dagene, en skønne dag.

thistle [θisl] *s* tidsel (skotsk nationalblomst).

thorn [θɔ:n] *s* torn; tjørn.

thorny ['θɔ:ni] *adj* tornet; *(fig)* tornefuld.

thorough ['θʌrə] *adj* grundig, omhyggelig; *(fig)* gennemført; **~bred** *adj* (om hest) fuldblods; (om person) dannet; **~fare** *s* vej, færdselsåre; *no ~fare* gennemkørsel forbudt; **~going** *adj* gennemgribende, dybtgående.

thoroughly ['θʌrəli] *adv* fuldkommen; til bunds; *he ~ agreed* han var helt enig.

those [ðəuz] *pl* af *that.*

thou [ðau] *pron (gl,* H) du.

though [ðəu] *adv* alligevel, dog // *konj* skønt, selv om; *as ~* som om; *even ~* selv om; *you have to do it, ~* du må alligevel gøre det.

thought [θɔ:t] *s* tanke; omtanke; overvejelse; tænkning; *at the ~ of* ved tanken om; *on second ~s* ved nærmere eftertanke; *she's a ~ better today* hun har det lidt bedre i dag; *that's a ~!* du siger noget! tænk bare! **~ful** *adj* tankefuld; betænksom; **~less** *adj* tankeløs; ubetænksom; **~-out** *adj* gennemtænkt; **~-provoking** *adj* tankevækkende; **~-reader** *s* tankelæser.

thousand ['θauzənd] *num* tusind; *~s of* tusindvis af; **thousandth** *s* tusindedel.

thrash [θræʃ] *v* tæve, slå; fægte; ~

about slå om sig; vælte sig; ~ *out* gennemdrøfte; **~ing** *s* omgang tæv.

thread [θrɛd] *s* tråd; *(tekn)* gevind // *v:* ~ *a needle* træde en nål; ~ *through the crowd* sno sig gennem mængden; **~bare** *adj* tyndslidt; luvslidt.

threat [θrɛt] *s* trussel; **~en** *v* true *(to* med at).

three [θri:] *num* tre; **~-piece suit** [-su:t] *s* sæt tøj med vest; **~-piece suite** [-swi:t] *s* sofagruppe (sofa og to lænestole).

thresh [θrɛʃ] *v (agr)* tærske; **~er, ~ing machine** *s* tærskeværk.

threshold ['θrɛʃəuld] *s* dørtrin; tærskel (også *fig).*

threw [θru:] *præt* af *throw.*

thrice [θrais] *adv (gl)* tre gange.

thrift [θrift] *s* økonomisk sans.

thrifty ['θrifti] *adj* økonomisk.

thrill [θril] *s* gys(en); spænding // *v* begejstre; gyse; *be ~ed with sth* være begejstret over ngt.

thriller ['θrilə*] *s* (om bog, film etc) gyser.

thrilling ['θriliŋ] *adj* spændende.

thrive [θraiv] *v (~d, ~d* el. *throve, thriven* [θrəuv, θrivn]) trives; have fremgang; ~ *on sth* stortrives ved ngt.

thriving ['θraiviŋ] *adj* blomstrende.

throat [θrəut] *s* hals, svælg; *clear one's* ~ rømme sig; *have a sore* ~ have ondt i halsen; *cut sby's* ~ skære halsen over på en.

throaty ['θrəuti] *adj* (om stemme) dyb, hæs.

throb [θrɔb] *s* (om hjerte) slag, banken; (om maskine) dunken // *v* banke, slå; dunke.

throne [θrəun] *s* trone.

throng [θrɔŋ] *s* trængsel; skare // *v* trænges, stimle sammen.

throttle [θrɔtl] *s (auto)* choker // *v* kvæle(s).

through [θru:] *adj/adv* igennem; (om tog, billet etc) gennemgående; færdig // *præp* gennem; ved; på grund af; ~ *and* ~ helt igennem; *be put* ~ *to sby (tlf)* blive stillet ind til en; *be* ~ være færdig; *be* ~ *with sby* være færdig med en; *no way* ~ blindgade; **~ flight** *s* direkte fly(vning); **~out** [θru'aut] *adv* helt igennem; over det hele // *præp* gennem hele; **~put** *s* kapacitet.

throve [θrəuv] *præt* af *thrive.*

throw [θrəu] *s* kast // *v (threw, thrown* [θru:, θrəun]) kaste, smide; ~ *a party* holde fest; ~ *away* smide væk; forspilde; ~ *in* give ekstra; indskyde; ~ *in one's hand* give op; ~ *off* skaffe sig af med; ryste af sig; ~ *open* smække op; ~ *up* kaste op; **~away** *adj* engangs-; **~-in** *s (sport)* indkast.

thrum [θrʌm] *v* klimpre, tromme.

thrush [θrʌʃ] *s* drossel.

thrust [θrʌst] *s* skub, puf; stød; udfald // *v (thrust, thrust)* skubbe; stikke; mase (sig); **~ing** *adj* dynamisk, driftig.

thud [θʌd] *s* bump, brag // *v* slå; stampe.

thug [θʌg] *s* bølle.

thumb [θʌm] *s* tommelfinger; *be all ~s* have ti tommelfingre; *give sby the ~s up* give en grønt lys // *v* bladre; ~ *a lift* blaffe; **~tack** *s (am)* tegnestift.

thump [θʌmp] *s* dunk; tungt slag // *v* dunke; dundre; hamre; **~ing** *adj* kæmpe, enorm.

thunder ['θʌndə*] *s* torden; buldren // *v* tordne; drøne, buldre; **~bolt** *s (fig)* tordenslag; **~clap** *s* tordenskrald.

thundering ['θʌndəriŋ] *adj* bragende.

thunderous ['θʌndərəs] *adj* tordnende.

thunderstorm ['θʌndəstɔ:m] *s* tordenvejr.

thunderstruck ['θʌndəstrʌk] *adj (fig)* som ramt af lynet.

Thursday ['θə:zdi] *s* torsdag; *on* ~ på torsdag; *~s* om torsdagen, hver torsdag.

thus [ðʌs] *adv* således; derfor; ~ *far* hidtil.

thwart [θwɔ:t] *v* forpurre; modarbejde; komme på tværs af.

thy [ðai] *pron (gl,* H) din(e).

thyme [taim] *s* timian.

thyroid ['θairɔid] *s* skjoldbruskkirtel.
tick [tik] *s* tikken; hak, mærke; *(zo)* skovflåt; *in a* ~ (F) om et sekund; *on* ~ (F) på kredit // *v* tikke; (F) fungere; ~ *off* checke af; ~ *sby off* give en en næse; *what makes him* ~*?* hvad foregår der inden i ham?
ticker ['tikə*] *s* (F) hjerte; ur.
ticket ['tikit] *s* billet; (mærke)seddel; bon; lånerkort; lodseddel; bøde; ~*s, please!* billettering! *that's the* ~*!* sådan skal det være! *get a (parking)* ~ få en parkeringsbøde // *v* sætte prismærker på; uddele parkingsbøde til; ~ **collector** *s* billettør; ~ **machine** *s* billetautomat; ~ **office** *s* billetkontor; ~ **window** *s* billetluge.
ticking ['tikiŋ] *s* bolster; ~**-off** *s: give sby a* ~*-off* give en en næse (,et møgfald).
tickle [tikl] *s* kilden // *v* kilde; more; smigre; glæde; *be* ~*d pink* fryde sig; føle sig virkelig smigret.
tickler ['tiklə*] *s* hård nød at knække; kilden sag.
ticklish ['tikliʃ] *adj* kilden.
tidal [taidl] *adj* tidevands-.
tiddly ['tidli] *adj* lillebitte; småsnalret; ~**winks** *s* loppespil.
tide [taid] *s* tidevand; *(fig)* tendens; strøm; *the* ~ *is in (,up)* det er højvande (,flod); *the* ~ *is out* det er lavvande (,ebbe); *go with the* ~ følge med strømmen // *v:* ~ *over* klare sig.
tidiness ['taidinəs] *s* orden; ordenssans.
tidings ['taidiŋs] *spl (gl)* budskab, nyhed(er).
tidy ['taidi] *v:* ~ *up* rydde op; nette sig // *adj* pæn, ordentlig; hæderlig; *it cost a* ~ *bit* det kostede en pæn sum penge.
tie [tai] *s* slips; bånd, snor; hæmsko; forbindelse; uafgjort kamp; *black* ~ (på indbydelse) smoking // *v* binde; ~ *down* binde (fast); ~ *sby down* være en klods om benet på en; ~ *in with* passe med; ~ *up* binde (sammen); klare, afslutte; båndlægge; *be* ~*d up* være ophængt, have travlt; ~ *up with* hænge sammen med; ~**-clasp,** ~**-pin** *s* slipsenål.
tier [tiə*] *s* lag; række; trin; ~**ed** *adj* lagdelt; ~*ed skirt* etagenederdel.
tiff [tif] *s* skænderi; kurre på tråden.
tiger ['taigə*] *s* tiger; vilddyr.
tight [tait] *adj* tæt; stram, snæver, trang; fast; (F) fuld, pløret; *be in a* ~ *spot* være i knibe; *a* ~ *bend* et skarpt sving; *sleep* ~*!* sov godt! ~**en** *v* stramme; spænde; blive stram; ~**-fisted** *adj* nærig; ~**rope** *s* line; *walk the* ~*rope between x and y* gå balancegang mellem x og y.
tights [taits] *spl* strømpebukser; trikot.
tile [tail] *s* tagsten; flise, kakkel; ~**d** *adj* tagstens-; flise-.
till [til] *s* pengeskuffe // *v* (op)dyrke // *præp* d.s.s. *until.*
tiller ['tilə*] *s* rorpind.
tilt [tilt] *s* hældning; *at full* ~ for fuld fart // *v* vippe; sætte på skrå, hælde.
timber ['timbə*] *s* tømmer; ~**yard** *s* tømmerplads.
time [taim] *s* tid; periode; tidspunkt; gang; takt; *any* ~ når som helst; ~ *and again* igen og igen; *for the* ~ *being* for øjeblikket, foreløbig; *from* ~ *to* ~ fra tid til anden, til tider; *in* ~ i tide, i rette tid; med tiden; *all in good* ~ det når sig nok; *in no* ~ på ingen tid, på et øjeblik; *five* ~*s five* fem gange fem; *what* ~ *is it?* hvad er klokken? *have a good* ~ more sig; have det godt; ~*'s up* så er tiden ude; *I've no* ~ *for that (fig)* det irriterer mig; *out of* ~ ude af takt // *v* tage tid; afpasse; vælge det rette øjeblik, time; ~ **bomb** *s* tidsindstillet bombe; ~**-consuming** *adj* tidkrævende, tidrøvende; ~ **lag** *s* tidsforskel; ~**less** *adj* evig, tidløs; ~ **limit** *s* frist; tidsbegrænsning; ~**ly** *adj* belejlig; i rette tid; ~**r** *s* minutur; ~**-saving** *adj* tidsbesparende; ~**table** *s* køreplan; (i skolen) skema; ~**worn** *adj* medtaget af tidens tand.
timid ['timid] *adj* frygtsom; sky; ængstelig.

timing ['taimiŋ] *s* tidtagning; valg af tidspunkt.
timorous ['timərəs] *adj* frygtsom, ængstelig.
timpani ['timpəni] *spl* pauker.
tin [tin] *s* tin; blik; (konserves)dåse; (bage)form; **~ foil** *s* aluminiumsfolie, sølvpapir.
tinge [tindʒ] *s* anstrøg; spor; skær.
tingle [tiŋgl] *v* prikke, snurre; dirre.
tin hat ['tinhæt] *s* stålhjelm.
tinker ['tiŋkə*] *s* bissekræmmer // flikke, lappe; rode med.
tinkle [tiŋkl] *s* ringen; klirren; *give me a* ~ (F) slå på tråden (til mig).
tinned [tind] *adj* på dåse, dåse- (fx *meat* kød).
tin opener ['tin,əupənə*] *s* dåseåbner.
tinsel ['tinsəl] *s* glimmer; lametta.
tint [tint] *s* farvetone; (om hår) toning; **~ed** *adj* tonet.
tiny ['taini] *adj* lillebitte.
tip [tip] *s* spids, top; dup; drikkepenge; losseplads; slaggebunke; tips, fidus // *v* vippe; vælte; give drikkepenge; tippe; læsse af; **~-off** *s* tip, fidus; **~ped** *adj* (om cigaret) med filter.
tipple [tipl] *s* (F) drink // *v* drikke, pimpe.
tipsy ['tipsi] *adj* bedugget.
tiptoe ['tiptəu] *s: on* ~ på tåspidserne // *v* gå på tå, liste.
tire [taiə*] *v* trætte, udmatte; blive træt; **~d** *adj* træt; *sick and ~d of* dødtræt af; **~less** *adj* utrættelig; **~some** *adj* trættende; kedelig.
tiring ['tairiŋ] *adj* trættende.
tissue ['tiʃu:] *s* stof, væv; renseserviet; papirslommetørklæde; **~ paper** *s* silkepapir.
tit [tit] *s (zo)* mejse; (F) brystvorte; ~*s* (V) patter; *give ~ for tat* give svar på tiltale; give igen af samme mønt.
titbit ['titbit] *s* godbid, lækkerbisken.
titillate ['titileit] *v* pirre, kildre.
title [taitl] *s* titel, navn; ret, krav; **~d** *adj* betitlet; **~ deed** *s (jur)* skøde; **~-holder** *s* titelindehaver.
titter ['titə*] *s* fnisen // *v* fnise.
tittle-tattle ['titl,tætl] *s* pladder, sludder; sladder.
tizzy ['tizi] *adj* ude af flippen.
to [tu, tə] *præp* at; for; til; *give it ~ me* giv mig den; *the key ~ the front door* nøglen til hoveddøren; *the main thing is to...* det vigtigste er at...; *go ~ England* tage til England; *go ~ school* gå i skole; *go ~ and fro* gå frem og tilbage; komme og gå; *come* ~ komme til sig selv igen.
toad [təud] *s* tudse; **~-in-the-hole** *s (gastr)* indbagt pølse; **~stool** *s (bot)* giftig svamp.
toady ['təudi] *adj* slesk.
toast [təust] *s* ristet brød; skål; *here's a ~ to us!* skål for os! // *v* riste; udbringe en skål (for); **~er** *s* brødrister; **~ rack** *s* holder til ristet brød.
tobacco [tə'bækəu] *s* tobak; **~nist** *s* tobakshandler.
to-be [tu'bi:] *adj* vordende, fremtidig.
toboggan [tə'bɔgən] *s* slæde, kælk // *v* kælke.
today [tə'dei] *s/adv* i dag.
toddler ['tɔdlə*] *s* rolling, kravlebarn.
to-do [tə'du:] *s* ståhej, postyr.
toe [təu] *s* tå; (om sko) snude; *keep sby on his ~s* holde en i ånde, sørge for at en er oppe på dupperne // *v: ~ the line* holde sig på måtten; **~hold** *s* fodfæste.
toffee ['tɔfi] *s* karamel; **~ apple** *s* kandiseret æble.
together [tə'gɛðə*] *adv* sammen, tilsammen; samtidig; i træk; **~ness** *s* det at komme hinanden ved.
togged [tɔgd] *adj: ~ out* klædt på, udstyret.
togs [tɔgs] *spl* (F) kluns, klude (dvs. tøj).
toil [tɔil] *s* slid, hårdt arbejde // *v* slide, mase.
toilet ['tɔilit] *s* toilet; toilette; *put sth down the* ~ skylle ngt ud i wc'et; **~ bag** *s* toilettaske; **~ bowl** *s* wc-skål; **~ paper** *s* toiletpapir.
toiletries ['tɔilətriz] *spl* toiletartikler.
toilet water ['tɔilit,wɔ:tə*] *s* eau de toilette.
toing ['tu:iŋ] *s: ~ and froing* faren (,bevægen) sig frem og tilbage, kommen og gåen.

token ['təukən] *s* tegn; mærke; bevis; kupon; polet; *in ~ of* som vidnesbyrd om; *get a ~ wage* få en rent symbolsk løn (dvs. ussel); *book ~* gavekort til bogkøb.

told [təuld] *præt* og *pp* af *tell; there were 25 people all ~* der var 25 personer i alt.

tolerable ['tɔlərəbl] *adj* tålelig; udholdelig; jævn; nogenlunde.

tolerant ['tɔlərənt] *adj* tolerant; modstandsdygtig.

tolerate ['tɔləreit] *v* tåle, tolerere; finde sig i.

toll [tʌul] *s* afgift; vejpenge; antal (ofre, sårede etc) // *v* (om klokke) ringe.

tomato [tə'ma:təu] *s* tomat.

tomb [tu:m] *s* grav; **~stone** *s* gravsten.

tome [təum] *s* tykt bind (af bog).

tomfoolery [tɔm'fu:ləri] *s* tossestreger.

tomorrow [tə'mɔrəu] *s/adv* i morgen; *the day after ~* i overmorgen; *~ morning* i morgen tidlig, i morgen formiddag.

ton [tɔn] *s* ton (1016 kg); *(mar* også: *register ~)* registerton (2,83 m^3); *come down on sby like a ~ of bricks* give en et ordentligt møgfald; *~s of* (F) masser af.

tone [təun] *s* tone, klang; stemning // *v* tone; stemme; harmonisere; *~ down* dæmpe(s); mildne(s); *~ in with sth* harmonere med ngt; *~ up* styrke; **~less** *adj* tonløs.

tongs [tɔŋz] *spl: a pair of ~* en tang.

tongue [tɔŋ] *s* tunge; sprog; *~ in cheek* uden at mene hvad man siger; *hold one's ~* holde mund; *loose one's ~* tabe mælet; *keep a civil ~ in one's head* tale ordentligt (,pænt); **~-tied** *adj* mundlam; **~-twister** *s* ord som er svært at udtale; halsbrækkende sætning.

tonic ['tɔnik] *s* styrkende middel; *(mus)* grundtone; (også: *~ water)* tonicvand // *adj* styrkende.

tonight [tə'nait] *s/adv* i aften; i nat.

tonne [tʌn] *s* ton.

tonsil ['tɔnsl] *s (anat)* mandel; *have one's ~s out* få fjernet mandlerne.

tonsillitis [tɔnsi'laitis] *s* halsbetændelse.

too [tu:] *adv* (alt) for; også; oven i købet; *~ much* for meget; *~ bad!* det var en skam! *me ~* også jeg (,mig); *all ~ soon* alt for hurtigt (,tidligt); *you can't do that! - I can ~!* det kan du ikke gøre! - Jo, 'det kan jeg!.

took [tuk] *præt* af *take.*

tool [tu:l] *s* redskab; stykke værktøj // *v* bearbejde; **~shed** *s* redskabsskur.

toot [tu:t] *v* tude.

tooth [tu:θ] *s (pl: teeth* [ti:θ]) tand; tak; spids; *have a ~ out* få trukket en tand ud; *have a sweet ~* være slikken; *fight ~ and nail* kæmpe med næb og kløer; *I'm fed up to the (back) teeth* det hænger mig langt ud af halsen; *he's lying through his teeth* det er løgn i hans hals; **~ache** [-eik] *s* tandpine; **~brush** *s* tandbørste; **~paste** *s* tandpaste; **~pick** *s* tandstikker.

top [tɔp] *s* top; øverste del; overdel; låg; tag; (på flaske) kapsel; *at the ~ of* øverst på; *at the ~ of one's voice* af fuld hals; *on ~ of* oven på; oven i; *come out on ~* vinde; *the job is getting on ~ of me* jeg drukner i arbejde; *be on ~ of the world* være ovenpå // *v* stå øverst (på); være førende; *~ped with sth* med ngt oven på; *~ up* fylde op (fx med benzin) // *adj* øverst; top-; bedst; *the ~ floor* øverste etage; *~ secret* strengt fortroligt; **~coat** *s* overfrakke; **~ hat** *s* høj hat; **~-heavy** *adj* tungest for oven.

topic ['tɔpik] *s* emne; **~al** *adj* aktuel.

top... ['tɔp-] sms: **~less** *adj* topløs; **~level** *s (pol* etc) topniveau; **~most** *adj* øverst, højest; **~-notch** *adj* førsterangs-; **~ping** *s* pynt (ovenpå) // *adj* helt fin, glimrende.

topple [tɔpl] *v* vakle, vælte.

topsy-turvy ['tɔpsi'tə:vi] *adj/adv* hulter til bulter; med bunden i vejret.

top-up ['tɔpʌp] *s* påfyldning.

torch [tɔ:tʃ] *s* fakkel; lommelygte; blæselampe; *carry the ~ for sby* være (hemmeligt) forelsket i en.

tore [tɔ:*] *pp* af *tear.*

torment *s* ['tɔ:mənt] pine, kval, plage // *v* [tɔ:'mɛnt] pine, plage.

torn [tɔ:n] *pp* af *tear // adj: ~ between* vaklende mellem.
tornado [tɔ:'neidəu] *s* hvirvelstorm.
torpid ['tɔ:pid] *adj* træg, apatisk.
torpor ['tɔ:pə*] *s* træghed, sløvhed.
torrent ['tɔrənt] *s* stærk strøm; skybrud.
torrential [tɔ'rɛnʃl] *adj* rivende; styrtende.
torrid ['tɔrid] *adj* brændende varm; *(fig)* glødende.
torsion ['tɔ:ʃən] *s* vridning, snoning.
tortoise ['tɔ:təs] *s* skildpadde; **~shell** *s* skildpaddeskjold; (om briller) horn-.
tortuous ['tɔ:tjuəs] *adj* snoet; forvreden; indviklet; omstændelig.
torture ['tɔ:tʃə*] *s* tortur; kval // *v* tortere; pine; fordreje.
Tory ['tɔ:ri] *s/adj* konservativ.
toss [tɔs] *s* kast; lodtrækning (ved plat og krone) // *v* kaste; smide; *~ one's head* slå med nakken; *~ the salad* vende salaten (i dressing); *~ a coin* slå plat og krone; *~ (up) for sth* trække lod om ngt; *~ and turn (in bed)* vride og vende sig (i sengen); **~-up** *s* tilfælde, "lotterispil".
tot [tɔt] *s* rolling; (F) tår, slurk.
total [təutl] *s* sum, facit // *v* beløbe sig til; udgøre; *~ up* tælle sammen.
totalitarian [təutəli'tɛəriən] *adj (pol)* totalitær.
totality [təu'tæliti] *s* helhed.
tote ['təut] *s* totalisator.
totter ['tɔtə*] *v* stavre, vakle.
touch [tʌtʃ] *s* berøring; kontakt; strøg; træk; anelse; stil; håndelag; *a ~ of* en anelse, en smule; *be in ~ with* have føling (,kontakt) med; *we'll be in ~ with you* du (,De) skal høre fra os; *get in ~ with* sætte sig (,komme) i kontakt med; *lose ~ with* miste forbindelsen med; *he's losing his ~* han er ved at miste håndelaget // *v* berøre, røre (ved); bevæge; måle sig med; *~ down* (om fly) lande; mellemlande; *~ sby for £50* slå en for £50; *~ on* komme ind på; angå; *~ up* fikse op på; pynte på; *~ upon* berøre; *~ wood* banke under bordet (af overtro); **~-and-go** *adj* uvis, usikker; *it was ~-and-go whether we did it* vi var lige ved ikke at gøre det; **~down** *s (fly)* landing; mellemlanding; (i rugby og *fig)* scoring.
touched ['tʌtʃt] *adj* rørt, bevæget.
touching ['tʌtʃiŋ] *adj* rørende // *præp* vedrørende.
touchline ['tʌtʃlain] *s (fodb)* sidelinje.
touchstone ['tʌtʃstəun] *s* prøvesten.
touch-typing ['tʌtʃtaipiŋ] *s* blindskrift (på skrivemaskine).
touchy ['tʌtʃi] *adj* sart; irritabel.
tough [tʌf] *s* gangster; hård negl // *adj* sej; skrap; hård, barsk; *get ~ with sby* blive grov mod en; *~ luck!* ærgerligt!
toughen ['tʌfn] *v* gøre (,blive) hård, sej etc.
tour [tu:ə*] *s* rejse; rundtur, turné; (i museum etc) omvisning // *v* rejse (,gå) rundt i; **~ing** *s* turisme; rejsen (rundt).
tourist ['tu:rist] *s* turist; **~ agency** *s* turistbureau; **~ board** *s* turistråd.
tournament ['tuənəmənt] *s* turnering.
tousled [tauzld] *adj* (om hår) uglet.
tout [taut] *s* (F) snushane; billethaj; bondefanger // *v* spionere, snuse; give staldtips; falbyde.
tow [təu] *s* slæb, bugsering; *take a car in ~* tage en bil på slæb // *v* bugsere, slæbe.
toward(s) [tə'wɔ:d(z)] *præp* (hen)imod; overfor; for at.
tow-bar ['təuba:*] *s (auto)* anhængertræk.
towel ['tauəl] *s* håndklæde; viskestykke; (også: *sanitary ~)* hygiejnebind // *v: ~ down* tørre (med håndklæde); **~ling** *s* frotté; frottering; **~ rail** *s* håndklædestang.
tower ['tauə*] *s* tårn // *v* hæve sig; knejse; **~ block** *s* højhus; **~ing** *adj* meget høj; imponerende.
towline ['təulain] *s* slæbetov; trosse.
town [taun] *s* by; *go to ~* tage til byen; *go (out) on the ~* tage ud at feste; **~ council** *s* byråd; **~ councillor** *s* byrådsmedlem; **~ hall** *s* rådhus; **~ planning** *s* byplanlægning.
towpath ['təupa:θ] *s* træksti (langs kanal etc).

towrope ['təurəup] *s* slæbetov; trosse.
toxic ['tɔksik] *adj* giftig.
toy [tɔi] *s* stykke legetøj // *v:* ~ *with* pusle med; lege med; ~ **shop** *s* legetøjsbutik.
trace [treis] *s* spor, mærke; sti; antydning; *without* ~ sporløst // *v* spore; mærke; skelne; tegne; ~ **element** *s* sporstof.
track [træk] *s* spor; aftryk; sti, bane; *keep* ~ *on* have føling med; have check på; *lose* ~ *of* miste følingen med; tabe af syne; miste overblikket over // *v* (efter)spore; ~ *down* støve op; forfølge og fange.
tracked [trækd] *adj (auto)* med larvefødder, bælte-.
tracksuit ['træksu:t] *s* træningsdragt; overtræksdragt.
tract [trækt] *s* egn, område; traktat; pjece; *the respiratory* ~ *(anat)* luftvejene.
traction ['trækʃən] *s* træk(kraft).
trade [treid] *s* handel; erhverv; håndværk; branche // *v* handle; udveksle, bytte; ~ *with (,in)* handle med; ~ *sth in* give ngt i bytte; ~ **fair** *s* handelsmesse; ~ **figures** *spl* handelstal; ~ **gap** *s* underskud på handelsbalancen; ~**-in (value)** *s* bytteværdi; ~**mark** *s* varemærke; firmamærke; ~**name** *s* varebetegnelse, varemærke; ~**r** *s* næringsdrivende; handelsskib; ~**s·man** *s* handlende; ~ **union** *s* fagforening; ~ **unionist** *s* medlem af (,forkæmper for) fagforening; ~ **wind** *s* passat.
trading ['treidiŋ] *s* handel; omsætning; ~ **stamps** *spl* rabatmærker.
tradition [trə'diʃən] *s* tradition; skik; ~**al** [-'diʃənl] *adj* traditionel.
traffic ['træfik] *s* trafik, færdsel; handel; samkvem // *v:* ~ *in sth* handle med ngt; ~ **island** *s* helle; ~ **jam** *s* trafikprop; ~ **lights** *spl* lyssignal, lyskurv; ~ **sign** *s* færdselsskilt; ~ **warden** *s* sv.t. parkeringsvagt.
tragedy ['trædʒədi] *s* tragedie; ulykke.
tragic ['trædʒik] *adj* tragisk.
trail [treil] *s* spor; sti; hale; stribe (fx *of smoke* røg) // *v* følge sporet efter; slæbe; slynge sig; ~ *behind* komme bagud; slæbe efter; ~**er** *s* påhængsvogn; anhænger; *(film)* trailer; ~**ing plant** *s* slyngplante.
train [trein] *s* tog; (på kjole etc) slæb; række, kolonne; følge; *his* ~ *of thought* hans tankegang; *be in* ~ være i gang.
train [trein] *v* uddanne (sig); oplære(s); træne; dressere; ~ *as sth* uddanne sig til ngt; ~**ed** *adj* uddannet; øvet; faglært.
trainee [trei'ni:] *s* praktikant; ~ *nurse* sygeplejeelev.
trainer ['treinə*] *s* træner; dressør; ~**s** *spl* træningssko.
training ['treiniŋ] *s* uddannelse; træning; ~ **college** *s* (lærer)seminarium.
train service ['trein,sə:vis] *s* tog(forbindelse).
train set ['trein,sɛt] *s* legetøjstog.
traipse [treips] *v* traske.
trait [treit] *s* karaktertræk; ansigtstræk.
traitor ['treitə*] *s* forræder.
trajectory [trə'dʒɛktəri] *s* bane; kurs.
tram [træm] *s* sporvogn.
tramp [træmp] *s* trampen; vagabond; luder // *v* trampe (på); traske; vagabondere; gennemstrejfe.
trample [træmpl] *v:* ~ *on* trampe på.
tramway ['træmwei] *s* sporvej.
tranquil ['træŋkwil] *adj* rolig, stille.
tranquillity [træŋ'kwiliti] *s* ro, stilhed.
tranquillizer ['træŋkwilaizə*] *s* beroligende middel, nervepille.
transaction [træn'zækʃən] *s* udførelse; forretning.
transcribe [træn'skraib] *v* skrive af; transkribere.
transcript ['trænskript] *s* genpart; udskrift; gengivelse.
transcription [træn'skripʃən] *s* omskrivning; transkription.
transept ['trænsɛpt] *s* (i kirke) tværskib.
transfer *s* ['trænsfə:*] overførsel; overføring; omstigning; overdragelse; overføringsbillede // *v* [træns'fə:*] overføre; overdrage; overflytte; stige om; ~ *the charges (tlf)* lade modtageren betale samtalen.

transfix [træns'fiks] *v* nagle fast; spidde; *stand ~ed* stå naglet til stedet.
transform [træns'fɔ:m] *v* omdanne; forandre; forvandle *(into* til).
transformation [trænsfə'meiʃən] *s* forandring; forvandling.
transformer [træns'fɔ:mə*] *s (elek)* transformator.
transfusion [træns'fju:ʒən] *s* overføring; transfusion.
transgress [træns'grɛs] *v* overtræde; overskride; synde.
transgression [træns'grɛʃən] *s* overtrædelse; synd.
transient ['trænziənt] *adj* forbigående; kortvarig.
transit ['trænsit] *s: in ~* på gennemrejse.
transition [træn'ziʃən] *s* overgang; **~al** [-'ziʃənəl] *adj* overgangs-.
transitory ['trænsitəri] *adj* kortvarig; flygtig.
translate [træns'leit] *v* oversætte; fortolke; overføre.
translation [træns'leiʃn] *s* oversættelse.
translator [træns'leitə*] *s* oversætter, translatør.
translucent [trænz'lu:snt] *adj* gennemsigtig; gennemskinnelig.
transmission [trænz'miʃən] *s* overføring; udsendelse, transmission.
transmit [trænz'mit] *v* sende, transmittere; meddele.
transparency [træns'pɛərənsi] *s* gennemsigtighed; transparent.
transparent [træns'pɛərənt] *adj* gennemsigtig; klar, tydelig.
transpire [træns'paiə*] *v* svede, transpirere; (om fx hemmelighed) sive ud, komme frem.
transplant *s* ['transpla:nt] omplantning; transplantation; transplantat // *v* [træns'pla:nt] omplante; transplantere.
transport *s* ['trænspɔ:t] transport; forsendelse; henrykkelse // *v* [træns'pɔ:t] transportere; henrykke.
transportation [trænspə'teiʃən] *s* transport(middel); deportation (af fanger).
transporter [træns'pɔ:tə*] *s* blokvogn.
transverse ['trænzvə:s] *adj* tvær-; transversal.
trap [træp] *s* fælde; (i rør) vandlås; *shut your ~!* klap i! // *v* fange (i en fælde); standse; *be ~ped* sidde i saksen; sidde fast; *be ~ped into doing sth* blive narret til at gøre ngt; **~door** *s* lem; faldlem.
trapeze [trə'pi:z] *s* trapez.
trappings ['træpiŋz] *spl* ydre tegn, staffage.
trash [træʃ] *s* bras, møg; *(am)* skrald, affald.
travel [trævl] *s* rejse // *v* rejse; bevæge sig; gennemrejse; **~ agency** *s* rejsebureau.
traveller ['trævlə*] *s* rejsende; **~'s checque** *s* rejsecheck.
travelling ['trævliŋ] *s* (det at) rejse // *adj* (om)rejsende; **~ exhibition** *s* vandreudstilling.
travel sickness ['trævl,siknis] *s* transportsyge.
travesty ['trævəsti] *s* parodi.
tray [trei] *s* bakke; brevbakke; plade.
treacherous ['trɛtʃərəs] *adj* forræderisk; lumsk.
treachery ['trɛtʃəri] *s* forræderi.
treacle [tri:kl] *s* sirup.
tread [trɛd] *s* trin; gang; skridt; (om dæk) slidbane // *v (trod, trodden* [trɔd, trɔdn]) træde; betræde; **~mill** *s (fig)* trædemølle.
treason [tri:zn] *s* (lands)forræderi.
treasure ['trɛʒə*] *s* skat // *v* sætte stor pris på; gemme på; bevare; **~ hunt** *s* skattejagt.
treasurer ['trɛʒərə*] *s* kasserer.
treasure trove ['trɛʒə,trəuv] *s* skat; guldgrube.
treasury ['trɛʒəri] *s* skatkammer; kasse; *the Treasury* sv.t. finansministeriet.
treat [tri:t] *s* (lille) gave; (dejlig) overraskelse; (lækkert) traktement; *it's my ~!* jeg giver! *it was a ~* det var en oplevelse // *v* behandle; traktere; *~ sby to sth* spendere ngt på en.
treatise ['tri:tiz] *s* afhandling.
treatment ['tri:tmənt] *s* behandling.
treaty ['tri:ti] *s* traktat.
treble [trɛbl] *s (mus)* diskant; (dren-

ge)sopran // *v* tredoble(s) // *adj* tredobbel; (om stemme) høj, skinger; ~ **clef** *s (mus)* diskantnøgle, G-nøgle.

tree [tri:] *s* træ; ~ **line** *s* trægrænse; **~-lined** *adj* omgivet af træer; ~ **trunk** *s* træstamme.

trefoil ['trɛfɔil] *s* kløver(blad).

trek [trɛk] *s* tur; vandring; *pony ~king* ferietur på pony // *v* tage på vandretur.

trellis ['trɛlis] *s* gitter(værk); tremmer.

tremble [trɛmbl] *v* ryste, skælve; vibrere.

trembling ['trɛmbliŋ] *s* rysten, dirren // *adj* rystende, bævende.

trembly ['trɛmbli] *adj* rystende, bævende, dirrende.

tremendous [tri'mɛndəs] *adj* enorm, kolossal; frygtelig.

tremor ['trɛmə*] *s* rysten, skælven.

tremulous ['trɛmjuləs] *adj* rystende; frygtsom.

trench [trɛntʃ] *s* grøft; udgravning; skyttegrav.

trend [trɛnd] *s* tendens; retning; mode; *upward (,downward) ~* stigende (,faldende) tendens.

trendy ['trɛndi] *adj* (om tøj etc) in; (om person) med på noderne.

trepidation [trɛpi'deiʃən] *s* frygt og bæven.

trespass ['trɛspa:s] *v: ~ on* trænge ind på; gøre indgreb i; *no ~ing* adgang forbudt; privat område.

trestle [trɛsl] *s* buk (til bord etc).

trial ['traiəl] *s* prøve; afprøvning; prøvelse; *(jur)* retssag; *be on ~* være på prøve; være anklaget; *by error and ~* ved at prøve sig frem; *put sby to the ~* sætte en på prøve; ~ **offer** *s* introduktionstilbud; ~ **run** *s* prøvekørsel.

triangle ['traiæŋgl] *s* trekant; *(mus* etc) triangel.

triangular [trai'æŋgjulə*] *adj* trekantet.

tribal ['traibəl] *adj* stamme-.

tribe [traib] *s* stamme; **~s·man** *s* stammemedlem.

tribunal [trai'bju:nl] *s* domstol; nævn.

tributary ['tribju:təri] *s* biflod // *adj* side-, bi-.

tribute ['tribju:t] *s* hyldest; skat; *pay ~ to* hylde.

trice [trais] *s: in a ~* på et øjeblik.

trick [trik] *s* kneb, trick; fidus; kunststykke; (i kortspil) stik; *a dirty ~* en grim streg; *play a ~ on sby* lave et nummer med en; *that should do the ~* det skulle kunne gøre det; *he's up to his ~s again* nu er han ude på numre igen // *v* snyde, narre; *~ out* maje ud; udstaffere, dekorere.

trickery ['trikəri] *s* fup; svindel.

trickle [trikl] *s* tynd strøm; piblen // *v* pible; sive; *~ in* (om personer) liste (,sive) ind.

trickster ['trikstə*] *s* svindler.

tricky ['triki] *adj* vanskelig; kilden, ømtålelig.

tricycle ['traisikl] *s* trehjulet cykel.

triennial [trai'ɛniəl] *adj* treårig; som sker hvert 3. år.

trifle [traifl] *s* bagatel, smule; *(gastr)* trifli // *v: ~ with* lege med.

trifling ['traifliŋ] *adj* ubetydelig.

trigger ['trigə*] *s* (om gevær etc) aftrækker; udløser // *v: ~ off* udløse, sætte i gang; **~-happy** *adj* skydegal.

trilateral [trai'lætərəl] *adj* tresidet; treparts-.

trilby ['trilbi] *s* (herre)filthat.

trill [tril] *s* trille // *v* trille; rulle.

trim [trim] *s* orden, stand; form; udstyr; (om hår) studsning; (på bil) pynteliste // *v* klippe, trimme, studse; gøre i stand, ordne; *~ back* beskære, skære ned; *~ down* skære ned på; studse; slanke sig; **~mings** *spl* pynt; udsmykning; *(gastr)* garnering, tilbehør; småkød.

Trinity ['triniti] *s: the ~* treenigheden.

trinket ['triŋkit] *s* nipsting; (billigt) smykke.

trip [trip] *s* rejse; udflugt; trippen, snublen; *be on a ~* være på rejse; (S) være høj // *v: ~ up* kludre; spænde ben for.

tripartite [trai'pa:tait] *adj* treparts- (fx *talks* drøftelser).

tripe [traip] *s (gastr)* kallun; *(neds)* møg, bras.

triple [tripl] *adj* tredobbel(t); *~ jump (sport)* trespring.

triplets ['triplits] *spl* trillinger.
triplicate ['triplikit] *s: in* ~ i tre eksemplarer.
tripod ['traipɔd] *s (foto)* stativ.
tripwire ['tripwaiə*] *s* snubletråd.
trite [trait] *adj* banal, fortærsket.
triumph ['traiʌmf] *s* triumf, sejr // *v* triumfere, hovere, sejre.
triumphal [trai'ʌmfl] *adj* sejrrig; triumf-.
triumphant [trai'ʌmfənt] *adj* sejrende; triumferende.
trivia ['triviə] *spl* bagateller.
trivial ['triviəl] *adj* ubetydelig; banal, triviel.
triviality [trivi'æliti] *s* ubetydelighed, bagatel.
trod [trɔd] *præt* af *tread;* **~den** [trɔdn] *pp* af *tread // adj* nedtrådt.
troll [trəul] *s* trold.
trolley ['trɔli] *s* trækvogn; indkøbsvogn; bagagevogn; sækkevogn; rullebord.
trollop ['trɔləp] *s (gl)* tøjte.
trombone ['trɔmbəun] *s* trækbasun.
troop [tru:p] *s* trop; flok, skare // *v* gå i flok; myldre; (se også *troops).*
trooper ['tru:pə*] *s* kavalerist.
trooping ['tru:piŋ] *s: ~ the colour* fanemarch.
troops ['tru:ps] *spl* tropper.
trophy ['trəufi] *s* trofæ.
tropic ['trɔpik] *s* vendekreds; *in the ~s* i troperne; *the Tropic of Cancer (,Capricorn)* krebsens (,stenbukkens) vendekreds.
tropical ['trɔpikl] *adj* tropisk; trope-.
trot [trɔt] *s* trav; travetur // *v* trave, traske; **~ter** *s* travhest; *pig's ~ters* grisetæer.
trouble [trʌbl] *s* besvær; vrøvl; bekymring(er); sygdom; *stomach ~* dårlig mave; *be in ~* have problemer, være i knibe; *make ~* lave ballade; skabe problemer; *go to the ~ of, take the ~ to* gøre sig den ulejlighed at; *that's the ~* det er det der er problemet; *it's no ~* det er ingen ulejlighed; *what's the ~?* hvad er der i vejen? *ask for ~* være ude på skrammer.
troubled ['trʌbld] *adj* bekymret, urolig.
trouble... sms: **~-free** *adj* problemfri; sorgløs; **~maker** *s* urostifter, ballademager; **~shooter** *s* fejlfinder; **~some** *adj* besværlig, vanskelig; **~ spot** *s* urocenter.
trough [trɔf] *s* trug; rende; *a ~ of low pressure* et lavtryksområde.
troupe [tru:p] *s* trup.
trousers ['trauzəz] *spl* bukser; *a pair of ~* et par bukser; **trouser suit** [-su:t] *s* buksedragt.
trousseau ['tru:səu] *s* brudeudstyr.
trout [traut] *s (pl: ~)* ørred, forel.
trowel [trauəl] *s* murske; planteske; *lay it on with a ~* smøre tykt på.
truant ['truənt] *s: play ~* pjække.
truce [tru:s] *s* våbenstilstand.
truck [trʌk] *s* lastvogn, lastbil; trækvogn; bagagevogn; **~ driver** *s* lastbilchauffør.
truckle bed ['trʌklbɛd] *s* rulleseng.
truckload ['trʌkləud] *s* vognlæs.
truculent ['trʌkjulənt] *adj* aggressiv.
trudge [trʌdʒ] *v* traske, trave.
true [tru:] *adj* sand; nøjagtig, tro; ægte; trofast; *be ~ to one's word* holde ord; *~ to life* vellignende, livagtig; *come ~* gå i opfyldelse.
truffle [trʌfl] *s* trøffel.
truly ['tru:li] *adv* sandt; virkelig; *yours ~* (i brev) Deres ærbødige.
trump [trʌmp] *s* trumf // *v* trumfe; overtrumfe.
trumped [trʌmpd] *adj: ~ up* falsk, opdigtet.
trumpet ['trʌmpit] *s* trompet; trompetist // *v* trompetere.
truncheon ['trʌntʃən] *s* politistav, knippel.
trundle [trʌndl] *v: ~ along* trille af sted.
trunk [trʌŋk] *s* (træ)stamme; krop; (elefant)snabel; *(am, auto)* bagagerum; (stor) kuffert; **~ call** *s (tlf)* udenbys samtale; **~ road** *s* hovedvej.
trunks [trʌŋks] *spl* bukser; badebukser.
truss [trʌs] *s* brokbind // *v* (om fjerkræ) opsætte; binde.
trust [trʌst] *s* tillid, tiltro; betroede midler; båndlæggelse; *(merk)* trust;

take sth on ~ tage ngt for gode varer; *be kept in* ~ være båndlagt, blive forvaltet // *v* stole på; betro; ~ *sth to sby,* ~ *sby with sth* betro (,overlade) en ngt.
trusted ['trʌstid] *adj* betroet.
trustee [trʌs'ti:] *s* formynder, værge; (i institution) bestyrelsesmedlem.
trusting ['trʌstiŋ] *adj* tillidsfuld.
trustworthy ['trʌstwə:ði] *adj* pålidelig.
trusty ['trʌsti] *adj* trofast.
truth [tru:θ] *s* sandhed; *to tell the* ~... for at sige det rent ud..., sandt at sige...; **-ful** *adj* sandfærdig; tro, sand.
try [trai] *s* forsøg, chance; *have a* ~ gøre et forsøg; *give it a* ~ prøve det; se hvordan det går; *worth a* ~ forsøget værd // *v (tried, tried)* prøve, forsøge; sætte på prøve; stille for retten, dømme; ~ *on* prøve (tøj); ~ *it on* (F) prøve at se om det går; ~ *it on for size* prøve om det passer; ~ *one's hand* forsøge sig; ~ *one's luck* prøve lykken; ~ *out* gennemprøve; *be tried for murder* blive anklaget for mord; **-ing** *adj* enerverende, ubehagelig.
tub [tʌb] *s* balje; bøtte; badekar.
tubby ['tʌbi] *adj* tyk.
tube [tju:b] *s* rør; tube; (i dæk) slange; *the* ~ (F) undergrundsbanen.
tubing ['tju:biŋ] *s* rørsystem; *valve* ~ ventilgummi.
TUC ['ti:ju:'si:] *s* (fork.f. *Trade Union Congress)* sv.t. LO.
tuck [tʌk] *s* (syet) læg; (F) guf, kræs // *v* putte, stoppe; proppe; ~ *away* gemme væk; ~ *in* (F) guffe i sig, lange til fadet; (om barn) putte, stoppe dynen ned om; ~ *up* putte (,stikke) op; smøge op; ~ **shop** *s* slikbutik.
Tuesday ['tju:zdi] *s* tirsdag; *on* ~ på tirsdag; ~*s* om torsdagen, hver torsdag.
tuft [tʌft] *s* dusk, tot; tue.
tug [tʌg] *s* træk; slæbebåd // *v* trække, slæbe; **~-of-war** *s* tovtrækning.
tuition [tju:'iʃən] *s* undervisning.
tulip ['tju:lip] *s* tulipan.
tulle [tju:l] *s* tyl.
tumble [tʌmbl] *s* fald; kolbøtte; rod, uorden // *v* falde; tumle (omkuld); rode op i; **~down** *adj* faldefærdig; forfalden; ~ **dryer** *s* tørretumbler.
tumbler ['tʌmblə*] *s* krus, glas.
tummy ['tʌmi] *s* (F) mave.
tumour ['tju:mə*] *s* svulst, tumor.
tumultuous [tju:'mʌltjuəs] *adj* stormende; tumultagtig.
tuna ['tju:nə] *s (pl:* ~*)* tunfisk.
tune [tju:n] *s* melodi; harmoni; *be in* ~ stemme; spille (,synge) rent; *be in* ~ *with* stemme med, være i harmoni med; *she calls the* ~ det er hende der giver tonen an (,bestemmer); *out of* ~ falsk; *to the* ~ *of...* på melodien...; til et beløb af... // *v* stemme (fx *the violin* violinen); afstemme; tune; ~ *in* indstille; ~ *up* stemme (instrument).
tuner ['tju:nə*] *s (radio)* tuner; (også: *piano* ~) klaverstemmer.
tunic ['tju:nik] *s* tunika, kjortel; gymnastikdragt.
tuning ['tju:niŋ] *s* (af)stemning, indstilling; ~ **fork** *s* stemmegaffel.
Tunisia [tju:'niziə] *s* Tunesien; **Tunisian** *s* tuneser // *adj* tunesisk.
tunnel [tʌnl] *s* tunnel; (mine)gang // *v* grave sig igennem.
tunny ['tʌni] *s* tunfisk.
tuppence ['tʌpəns] *s (gl)* to pence; *I don't care* ~ jeg er revnende ligeglad.
turbot ['tə:bət] *s (zo)* pighvar.
turbulence ['tə:bjuləns] *s* uro; voldsomhed.
turbulent ['tə:bjulənt] *adj* urolig; vild; omtumlet.
turd [tə:d] *s* (S) lort, skiderik.
tureen [tə'ri:n] *s* (suppe)terrin.
turf [tə:f] *s* græstørv; grønsvær; *the* ~ hestevæddeløb // *v:* ~ *out* smide ud.
turgid ['tə:dʒid] *adj* svulstig.
Turk [tə:k] *s* tyrk.
Turkey ['tə:ki] *s* Tyrkiet.
turkey ['tə:ki] *s* kalkun; *talk* ~ (F) gå lige til sagen.
Turkish ['tə:kiʃ] *s/adj* tyrkisk; ~ **delight** *s* sukkerovertrukket frugtkonfekt.

turmeric ['tə:mərik] *s* gurkemeje.
turmoil ['tə:mɔil] *s* oprør; uro.
turn [tə:n] *s* drejning; sving; tilbøjelighed; nummer; tur, omgang; *the ~ of the century* århundredskiftet; *do sby a good ~* gøre en en tjeneste; *a bad ~* en bjørnetjeneste; *it gave me quite a ~* jeg blev helt forskrækket; *no left ~* venstresving forbudt; *it's your ~* det er din tur; *in ~* skiftevis, efter tur; *take ~s* skiftes // *v* dreje; vende; forvandle; blive; forvride; (om mælk) blive sur; *without ~ing a hair* uden at fortrække en mine; *~ fifty* passere de halvtreds; *~ about* vende; *~ against* vende sig imod; *~ away* vende (sig) bort); *~ down* afvise; ombøje; skrue ned (for); *~ in* bukke om; angive, melde; (F) gå til køjs; *~ into* blive (,forvandles) til; *~ off* dreje 'af; slukke (for); stoppe; *~ on* tænde (for); starte; (F) vække interesse hos; gøre høj; *~ out* jage væk; slukke for; *~ out to be a singer* vise sig at være sanger; *~ up* dukke op, vise sig; skrue op (for); bukke op; smøge op; **~around** *s* kovending.
turning ['tə:niŋ] *s* (vej)sving; **~ point** *s* vendepunkt.
turnip ['tə:nip] *s* turnips, roe; kålrabi.
turnkey ['tə:n,ki:] *adj: a ~ house* et nøglefærdigt hus.
turn... ['tə:n-] sms: **~out** *s* fremmøde, mødeprocent; antræk; udrykning; rengøring; produktion; **~over** *s* omsætning; *(gastr)* sammenfoldet tærte; **~stile** [-stail] *s* tælleapparat; **~table** *s* pladetallerken; **~-up** *s* opslag.
turpentine ['tə:pəntain], **turps** [tə:ps] *s* terpentin.
turquoise ['tə:kwɔiz] *s* turkis // *adj* turkis(farvet).
turret ['tʌrit] *s* lille tårn.
turtle [tə:tl] *s* skildpadde; *mock ~* forloren skildpadde; **~neck (sweater)** *s* rullekravesweater.
tusk [tʌsk] *s* stødtand.
tussle [tʌsəl] *s* slagsmål.
tutor ['tju:tə*] *s* universitetslærer; huslærer // *v* undervise; give timer i.
tutorial [tju:'tɔ:riəl] *s* manuduktion(stime) // *adj* manuduktions-, undervisnings-; kursus- (fx *diskette* diskette).
tuxedo [tʌk'si:dəu] *s (am)* smoking.
TV ['ti:'vi:] *s* (fork.f. *television)* fjernsyn, tv; *on ~* i fjernsynet, i tv.
twang [twæŋ] *s* svirpen; knips; snøvlen // *v* knipse; anslå (en streng).
tweak [twi:k] *v* knibe, nappe.
tweet [twi:t] *v* kvidre.
tweezers ['twi:zəz] *spl: a pair of ~* en pincet.
twelfth [twɛlfθ] *num* tolvte // *s* tolvtedel; **Twelfth Night** *s* helligtrekongers aften.
twelve [twɛlv] *num* tolv.
twentieth ['twɛntiiθ] *num* tyvende // *s* tyvendedel.
twenty ['twɛnti] *num* tyve.
twerp [twə:p] *s* (F, om person) skid.
twice [twais] *adv* to gange; *~ a day* to gange om dagen; *~ as much* dobbelt så meget; *he's ~ her age* han er dobbelt så gammel som hun.
twiddle ['twidl] *v* dreje (på); trille (med); pille (ved).
twig [twig] *s* kvist, lille gren.
twilight ['twailait] *s* tusmørke, skumring.
twin [twin] *s* tvilling; **~ bed** *s* den ene af to ens senge (NB! ikke dobbeltseng); **~-bed** *adj* tosengs-.
twine [twain] *s* sejlgarn; snoning // *v* sno (sig); slynge (sig).
twinge [twindʒ] *s* jag, stik (af smerte).
twinkle [twiŋkl] *s* blink(en), glimt(en) // *v* blinke, tindre.
twin set ['twinsɛt] *s* cardigansæt.
twin town ['twin,taun] *s* venskabsby.
twirl [twə:l] *v* snurre (rundt); svinge (med).
twist [twist] *s* vridning, snoning; drejning // *v* sno (sig); vride (sig); forvride, forvrænge.
twisted ['twistid] *adj* forkvaklet, abnorm.
twit [twit] *s* skvat.
twitch [twitʃ] *s* trækning; ryk, spjæt // *v* rykke, spjætte; fortrække sig.
twitter ['twitə*] *v* kvidre.
two [tu:] *num* to; *put ~ and ~ toge-*

ther lægge to og to sammen; *he can put ~ and ~ together* han er ikke tabt bag af en vogn; *in ~s* to og to; *one or ~* et par (stykker); *just the ~ of us* kun os to; **~-edged** *adj* tveægget; **~-faced** *adj* (om person) falsk; **~fold** *adv: increase ~fold* vokse til det dobbelte; **~-piece (suit)** [-su:t] *s* spadseredragt; **~-piece (swimsuit)** *s* todelt badedragt; **~-seater** *s* topersoners bil; **~-stroke** *s* totakter // *adj* totakts-; **~-way** *adj* (om trafik) i begge retninger.

tycoon [tai'ku:n] *s* pamper.

type [taip] *s* type; forbillede, model; skrift; *small ~* små bogstaver // *v* skrive på maskine (,PC etc); **~script** *s* maskinskrevet manuskript; **~writer** *s* skrivemaskine; **~written** *adj* maskinskrevet.

typhoid ['taifɔid] *s* tyfus.

typhoon [tai'fu:n] *s* tyfon.

typical ['tipikl] *adj* typisk.

typing ['taipiŋ] *s* maskinskrivning; **~ error** *s* slåfejl.

typist ['taipist] *s* maskinskriver.

typographer [tai'pɔgrəfə*] *s* typograf.

tyranny ['tirəni] *s* tyranni.

tyrant ['tairənt] *s* tyran.

tyre [taiə*] *s* (om bil, cykel etc) dæk; **~ gauge** [-geidʒ] *s* trykmåler (til bildæk); **~ lever** *s* dækjern; **~ pressure** *s* dæktryk; **~ track** *s* bilspor.

U

U, u [ju:].

udder ['ʌdə*] *s* yver.

ugliness ['ʌglinis] *s* grimhed.

ugly ['ʌgli] *adj* grim, hæslig, styg.

UK ['ju:'kei] *s* (fork.f. *United Kingdom)* Storbritannien og Nordirland.

ulcer ['ʌlsə*] *s* mavesår.

ulterior [ʌl'tiəriə*] *adj: ~ motive* bagtanke.

ultimate ['ʌltimət] *adj* yderst; endelig; sidst; **~ly** *adv* til sidst, i sidste ende.

ultrasonic [ʌltrə'sɔnik] *adj* ultralyds-.

umbilical [ʌm'bilikl] *adj: ~ cord* navlestreng.

umbrage ['ʌmbridʒ] *s: take ~ at* tage anstød af.

umbrella [ʌm'brɛla] *s* paraply; *telescopic ~* taskeparaply; *under the ~ of the UN* under FN's auspicier.

umpire ['ʌmpaiə*] *s* voldgiftsmand; *(sport)* dommer // *v* være dommer.

umpteen ['ʌmpti:n] *adj: for the ~th time* for 117. gang.

UN ['ju:'ɛn] *s* (fork.f. *United Nations)* FN.

unabashed ['ʌnə'bæʃt] *adj* ufortrøden.

unabated ['ʌnə'beitid] *adj* usvækket.

unable [ʌ'neibl] *adj: ~ to* ude af stand til at.

unabridged ['ʌnə'bridʒd] *adj* uforkortet.

unaccompanied ['ʌnə'kɔmpənid] *adj* alene; uden akkompagnement.

unaccountable ['ʌnə'kauntəbl] *adj* uforklarlig; mystisk.

unaccustomed ['ʌnə'kʌstəmd] *adj* ikke vant *(to* til); uvant *(to* med).

unadulterated [ʌnə'dʌltəreitid] *adj* ren, uforfalsket.

unaffected ['ʌnə'fɛktid] *adj* upåvirket; ukunstlet.

unaided [ʌn'eidid] *adj* uden hjælp, på egen hånd.

unanimity [ju:nə'nimiti] *s* enstemmighed.

unanimous [ju:'nænimǝs] *adj* enstemmig.

unapproachable ['ʌnə'prəutʃəbl] *adj* utilnærmelig.

unarmed ['ʌn'a:md] *adj* ubevæbnet; forsvarsløs.

unashamed ['ʌnə'ʃeimd] *adj* uden at skamme sig, ugenert.

unasked [ʌn'a:skt] *adj* uopfordret; *~ for* uønsket.

unassisted ['ʌnə'sistid] *adj* uden hjælp, alene.

unassuming ['ʌnə'sju:miŋ] *adj* beskeden, fordringsløs.

unattached [ʌnə'tætʃt] *adj* uafhængig.

unattended ['ʌnə'tɛndid] *adj* (om barn etc) uden tilsyn (,opsyn); forsømt.

unattractive ['ʌnə'træktiv] *adj* ucharmerende; usympatisk.

unauthorized [ʌn'ɔ:θəraizd] *adj* uautoriseret; ubemyndiget.
unaware ['ʌnə'wɛə*] *adj: be ~ of* være uvidende om; ikke være klar over.
unawares ['ʌnʌ'wɛəz] *adv* uforvarende; uventet; *catch sby ~* overrumple en.
unbalanced [ʌn'bælənst] *adj* uligevægtig.
unbearable [ʌn'bɛərəbl] *adj* utålelig, uudholdelig.
unbeatable [ʌn'bi:təbl] *adj* uovervindelig.
unbeaten [ʌn'bi:tn] *adj* ubesejret.
unbecoming ['ʌnbi'kʌmiŋ] *adj* uklædelig; upassende.
unbelievable [ʌnbi'li:vəbl] *adj* utrolig, ufattelig.
unbend [ʌn'bɛnd] *v* slappe af, tø op; **~ing** *adj* ubøjelig.
unbiased [ʌn'baiəst] *adj* upartisk; saglig.
unbind [ʌn'baind] *v* binde op.
unborn ['ʌn'bɔ:n] *adj* ufødt.
unbreakable [ʌn'breikəbl] *adj* brudsikker; ubrydelig.
unbroken [ʌn'brəukn] *adj* ubrudt, hel; ubrydelig.
unburden [ʌn'bə:dn] *v: ~ oneself* lette sit hjerte.
unbutton [ʌn'bʌtn] *v* knappe op.
uncalled [ʌn'kɔ:ld] *adj* ukaldet.
uncalled-for [ʌn'kɔ:ldfɔ:*] *adj* malplaceret; uberettiget.
uncanny [ʌn'kæni] *adj* mystisk; uhyggelig.
uncared-for [ʌn'kɛədfɔ:*] *adj* forsømt.
uncaring [ʌn'kɛəriŋ] *adj* ufølsom; ligeglad.
uncertain [ʌn'sə:tn] *adj* usikker, uvis; omskiftelig.
uncertainty [ʌn'sə:tnti] *s* uvished; tvivl.
unchallenged [ʌn'tʃæləndʒd] *adj* uimodsagt; upåtalt.
uncharitable [ʌn'tʃæritəbl] *adj* fordømmende, streng.
uncle [ʌŋkl] *s* onkel.
unclothe [ʌn'kləuð] *v* klæde af.
uncoil [ʌn'kɔil] *v* rulle (sig) op (,ud).
uncomfortable [ʌn'kʌmfətəbl] *adj* ubekvem; ubehagelig; ilde til mode.
uncommon [ʌn'kʌmən] *adj* ualmindelig, usædvanlig.
uncompromising [ʌn'kɔmprəmaiziŋ] *adj* ubøjelig; kompromisløs.
unconcerned ['ʌnkən'sə:nd] *adj* ligeglad; ubekymret; ikke involveret.
unconditional [ʌnkən'diʃənl] *adj* betingelsesløs; ubetinget.
unconscious [ʌn'kɔnʃəs] *adj* bevidstløs; ubevidst; underbevidst; uvidende; **~ness** *s* bevidstløshed.
uncontrollable [ʌnkən'trəuləbl] *adj* ustyrlig, uregerlig.
uncooked [ʌn'kukt] *adj* rå.
uncork [ʌn'kɔ:k] *v* trække proppen op (af).
uncover [ʌn'kʌvə*] *v* afdække, afsløre.
unction ['ʌnkʃən] *s: extreme ~* den sidste olie.
unctuous ['ʌŋktʃuəs] *adj* fedtet; salvelsesfuld.
undamaged [ʌn'dæmidʒd] *adj* uskadt.
undaunted [ʌn'dɔ:ntid] *adj* uforfærdet, uforknyt.
undecided [ʌndi'saidid] *adj* ubeslutsom; uvis.
undeniable [ʌndi'naiəbl] *adj* ubestridelig; **undeniably** *adv* unægtelig.
under ['ʌndə*] *adv* nede; nedenunder // *præp* under; neden for; mindre end; *creep ~ sth* krybe ind under ngt; *be ~ the impression that* have det indtryk at; *be ~ threat of sth* være truet af ngt.
under-age [ʌndər'eidʒ] *adj* umyndig.
undercarriage ['ʌndəkæridʒ] *s* undervogn; landingsstel.
undercoat ['ʌndəkəut] *s* grundmaling.
undercover [ʌndə'kʌvə*] *adj* hemmelig, skjult.
undercut ['ʌndəkʌt] *s (gastr)* mørbrad(stykke) // *v* [ʌndə'kʌt] underbyde.
underdeveloped ['ʌndədi,vɛləpd] *adj* underudviklet.
underdone [ʌndʌ'dʌn] *adj (gastr)* ikke kogt (,stegt) nok.
underestimate [ʌndər'ɛstimeit] *v* undervurdere.
underexposed ['ʌndərikspəuzd] *adj*

(foto) underbelyst, undereksponeret.
underfed [ʌndə'fɛd] *adj* underernæret.
underfloor ['ʌndəflɔ:r] *adj* gulv-; ~ *heating* gulvvarme.
underfoot [ʌndə'fut] *adj* under fødderne.
undergo [ʌndə'gəu] *v* gennemgå, udstå.
undergraduate [ʌndə'grædjuit] *s* student; studerende.
underground ['ʌndəgraund] *s* undergrundsbane; modstandsbevægelse // *adv* [ʌndə'graund] under jorden.
undergrowth ['ʌndəgrəuθ] *s* bundvegetation.
underhand [ʌndə'hænd] *adj* lumsk; under hånden.
underlay ['ʌndəlei] *s* tæppeunderlag.
underlie [ʌndə'lai] *v* danne basis for; ligge til grund for.
underline [ʌndə'lain] *v* understrege.
underling ['ʌndʌliŋ] *s* *(neds)* underordnet; slave.
undermine [ʌndə'main] *v* underminere.
underneath [ʌndə'ni:θ] *adv* (neden)under; på bunden // *præp* under.
undernourished [ʌndə'nʌriʃt] *adj* underernæret.
underpaid [ʌndə'peid] *adj* underbetalt.
underpass ['ʌndəpa:s] *s* fodgængertunnel; (på motorvej) (vej)underføring.
underrate [ʌndə'reit] *v* undervurdere.
understaffed [ʌndə'sta:fd] *adj* underbemandet.
understand [ʌndə'stænd] *v* *(-stood, -stood)* forstå; indse; få at vide; opfatte; *make oneself understood* gøre sig forståelig; give klar besked; **~able** *adj* forståelig.
understanding [ʌndə'stændiŋ] *s* forståelse; forstand; opfattelse; *on the ~ that...* under den forudsætning at...; i den tro at... // *adj* forstående.
understatement [ʌndə'steitmənt] *s* underdrivelse.
understood [ʌndə'stud] *præt* og *pp* af *understand.*
understudy ['ʌndəstʌdi] *s* *(teat)* dubleant.
undertake [ʌndə'teik] v foretage; påtage sig.
undertaker ['ʌndəteikə*] *s* bedemand.
undertaking [ʌndə'teikiŋ] *s* foretagende; forpligtelse.
underthings ['ʌndəθiŋz] *spl* undertøj.
underwater ['ʌndəwɔ:tə*] *adj* undervands- // *adv* under vandet.
underwear ['ʌndəwɛə*] *s* undertøj.
underweight ['ʌndəweit] *adj* undervægtig.
undesirable [ʌndi'zaiərəbl] *adj* uønsket, mindre heldig.
undig [ʌn'dig] *v* grave op.
undisputed [ʌndis'pju:tid] *adj* ubestridt.
undo [ʌn'du:] *v* løse (op); knappe op; åbne; ødelægge.
undoubted [ʌn'dautid] *adj* utvivlsom; ubestridelig; **~ly** *adv* uden tvivl.
undreamt-of [ʌn'drɛmtɔv] *adj* uanet, som man ikke havde forestillet sig.
undress [ʌn'drɛs] *v* klæde (sig) af.
undue [ʌn'dju:] *adj* utilbørlig; upassende; unødig.
undulating ['ʌndjuleitiŋ] *adj* bølgende; kuperet.
unearned [ʌn'ə:nd] *adj: ~ income* arbejdsfri indtægt.
unearth [ʌn'ə:θ] *v* grave op; *(fig)* finde frem; **~ly** *adj* overnaturlig; ukristelig.
uneasy [ʌn'i:zi] *adj* ubekvem; generende; usikker; genert; urolig, bekymret.
uneducated [ʌn'ɛdjukeitid] *adj* ukultiveret; uuddannet.
unemployed [ˌʌnim'plɔid] *adj* arbejdsløs.
unemployment [ˌʌnim'plɔimənt] *s* arbejdsløshed; ~ **benefit** *s* arbejdsløshedsunderstøttelse.
unending [ʌn'ɛndiŋ] *adj* endeløs, uendelig.
unequal [ʌn'i:kwəl] *adj* ulige; ujævn; *feel ~ to sth* ikke kunne magte ngt; **unequalled** *adj* uovertruffen.
unerring [ʌn'ə:riŋ] *adj* ufejlbarlig; (usvigelig) sikker.

uneven [ʌn'i:vn] *adj* ujævn, ulige.
unexpected [ʌniks'pɛktid] *adj* uventet; uforudset.
unfailing [ʌn'feiliŋ] *adj* ufejlbarlig; unøjagtig.
unfair [ʌn'fɛə*] *adj* uretfærdig.
unfaithful [ʌn'feiθful] *adj* utro; uærlig; unøjagtig.
unfamiliar [ʌnfə'miliə*] *adj* fremmed; uvant; ukendt.
unfasten [ʌn'fa:sn] *v* løsne; lukke op.
unfeeling [ʌn'fi:liŋ] *adj* ufølsom, hård.
unfinished [ʌn'finiʃt] *adj* ufuldendt.
unfit [ʌn'fit] *adj* uegnet; ikke i form; *~ for* uanvendelig til; *~ to eat* uspiselig.
unfold [ʌn'fəuld] *v* folde (sig) ud; røbe, afsløre.
unforeseen [ˌʌnfɔ:'si:n] *adj* uforudset.
unforgettable [ˌʌnfə'getəbl] *adj* uforglemmelig.
unforgivable [ˌʌnfə'givəbl] *adj* utilgivelig; **unforgiving** *adj* hård, nådeløs.
unfortunate [ʌn'fɔ:tʃənət] *adj* uheldig; beklagelig; stakkels; **~ly** *adv* uheldigvis.
unfounded [ʌn'faundid] *adj* ubegrundet; uberettiget.
unfriendly [ʌn'frɛndli] *adj* uvenlig.
unfurl [ʌn'fə:l] *v* folde (sig) ud.
unfurnished [ʌn'fə:niʃt] *adj* umøbleret.
ungainly [ʌn'geinli] *adj* klodset; uskøn.
unguarded [ʌn'ga:did] *adj* ubevogtet; tankeløs.
unhappiness [ʌn'hæpinis] *s* ulykke; fortvivlelse; elendighed.
unhappy [ʌn'hæpi] *adj* ulykkelig; ked af det; uheldig.
unharmed [ʌn'ha:md] *adj* uskadt.
unhealthy [ʌn'hɛlθi] *adj* usund; skadelig; sygelig.
unheard-of [ʌn'hə:dɔv] *adj* uhørt; enestående.
unheeded [ʌn'hi:did] *adj: go ~* forblive upåagtet, blive overhørt.
unhinged [ʌn'hindʒd] *adj* sindsforvirret.
unhook [ʌn'huk] *v* tage krogen af; haspe af; tage af krogen.
unholy [ʌn'həuli] *adj* rædselsfuld; ukristelig.
unhurt [ʌn'hə:t] *adj* uskadt.
unicorn ['junikɔ:n] *s* enhjørning.
unidentified [ʌnai'dɛntifaid] *adj* uidentificeret; *~ flying object* flyvende tallerken, ufo.
uniform ['ju:nifɔ:m] *s* uniform // *adj* ensartet, jævn.
unify ['ju:nifai] *v* forene; samle; gøre ensartet.
unilateral [ju:ni'lætərəl] *adj* ensidig.
unimaginative [ʌni'mædʒinətiv] *adj* fantasiløs.
unimpaired [ʌnim'pɛəd] *adj* usvækket; uskadt.
unimportant [ʌnim'pɔ:tənt] *adj* uvigtig; uvæsentlig; uden betydning.
uninhabited [ʌnin'hæbitid] *adj* ubeboet.
uninhibited [ʌnin'hibitid] *adj* uhæmmet; hæmningsløs.
uninitiated [ˌʌni'niʃieitid] *adj* uindviet.
unintelligible [ˌʌnin'tɛlidʒibl] *adj* uforståelig.
unintentional [ʌnin'tɛnʃənəl] *adj* utilsigtet; ufrivillig.
uninvited ['ʌnin'vaitid] *adj* uindbuden.
union ['ju:niən] *s* union; forbund; forening; (også: *trade ~*) fagforbund.
unionize ['ju:niənaiz] *v* organisere sig (fagligt).
unique [ju'ni:k] *adj* enestående.
unison ['ju:nisn] *s: in ~* enstemmigt; i kor.
unit ['ju:nit] *s* enhed; (bygge)element; blok; gruppe, afdeling.
unite [ju'nait] *v* forene(s); samle(s); **~d** *adj* forenet; fælles; **United Kingdom** *s (UK)* Storbritannien og Nordirland; **United Nations** *s (UN, UNO)* Forenede Nationer (FN); **United States of America** *s (US, USA)* Forenede Stater (USA).
unity ['ju:niti] *s* enhed; enighed; helhed.
universal [ju:ni'və:sl] *adj* universel; almindelig, almen.
universe ['ju:nivə:s] *s* univers; verden.
university [ju:ni'və:siti] *s* universitet.
unjust [ʌn'dʒʌst] *adj* uretfærdig.

unkempt [ʌn'kɛmpt] *adj* uredt; usoigneret.
unkind [ʌn'kaind] *adj* uvenlig.
unknown [ʌn'nəun] *adj* ukendt; ubekendt.
unleash [ʌn'li:ʃ] *v* slippe løs.
unless [ʌn'lɛs] *konj* medmindre; hvis ikke; ~ *otherwise stated* medmindre andet angives.
unlicensed [ʌn'laisənst] *adj* som ikke har tilladelse til at sælge vin og spiritus.
unlike [ʌn'laik] *adj* uens; ulig; forskellig // *præp* i modsætning til; **~ly** *adj* usandsynlig.
unlimited [ʌn'limitid] *adj* ubegrænset, grænseløs.
unlisted [ʌn'listid] *adj: ~ phone number (am)* hemmeligt nummer.
unload [ʌn'ləud] *v* læsse af; losse; ~ *one's heart* lette sit hjerte.
unlock [ʌn'lɔk] *v* låse op.
unloose [ʌn'lu:s] *v* løsne.
unlucky [ʌn'lʌki] *adj* uheldig.
unmade [ʌn'meid] *adj (om seng)* uredt.
unmanageable [ʌn'mænidʒəbl] *adj* uhåndterlig; ustyrlig; vanskelig.
unmanned [ʌn'mænd] *adj* ubemandet.
unmarried [ʌn'mærid] *adj* ugift.
unmask [ʌn'ma:sk] *v* afsløre; lade masken falde.
unmatched [ʌn'mætʃt] *adj* uforlignelig, mageløs.
unmentionable [ʌn'mɛnʃənəbl] *adj* unævnelig.
unmistakable [ʌnmis'teikəbl] *adj* umiskendelig; ufejlbarlig.
unmitigated [ʌn'mitigeitid] *adj* absolut; rendyrket; forhærdet.
unnatural [ʌn'nætʃrəl] *adj* unaturlig; unormal.
unnecessary [ʌn'nɛsisri] *adj* unødvendig.
unnerve [ʌn'nə:v] *v* tage modet fra.
unnerving [ʌn'nə:viŋ] *adj* nedslående.
unnoticed [ʌn'nəutist] *adj* ubemærket.
UNO ['ju:nəu] *s* (fork.f. *United Nations Organization)* FN.
unobserved [ʌnəb'zə:vd] *adj* ubemærket.
unobtainable [ʌnəb'teinəbl] *adj* uopnåelig; *(tlf)* ikke til at træffe.
unobtrusive [ʌnəb'tru:siv] *adj* beskeden; upåagtet; diskret.
unoccupied [ʌn'ɔkjupaid] *adj* ubeboet (fx *flat* lejlighed); ubesat, ledig (fx *seat* plads).
unofficial [ʌnə'fiʃl] *adj* uofficiel; ~ *strike* ulovlig strejke.
unpack [ʌn'pæk] *v* pakke op (,ud).
unpaid [ʌn'peid] *adj* ulønnet; ~ *holiday* ferie uden løn.
unparallelled [ʌn'pærəlɛld] *adj* uden sidestykke, uden lige.
unpick [ʌn'pik] *v* sprætte op.
unpleasant [ʌn'plɛznt] *adj* ubehagelig; usympatisk.
unplug [ʌn'plʌg] *v* (om stik) trække ud; (om prop i vask etc) trække op.
unpopular [ʌn'pɔpjulə*] *adj* upopulær; ildeset.
unprecedented [ʌn'prɛsidəntid] *adj* eksempelløs, uhørt.
unpredictable [ʌnpri'diktəbl] *adj* uforudsigelig; uberegnelig.
unprejudiced [ʌn'prɛdʒudist] *adj* fordomsfri; upartisk.
unprepared [ʌnpri'pɛəd] *adj* uforberedt; improviseret.
unqualified [ʌn'kwɔlifaid] *adj* ukvalificeret; ubetinget.
unquestionable [ʌn'kwɛstʃənəbl] *adj* ubestridelig; utvivlsom.
unravel [ʌn'rævl] *v* udrede; bringe i orden; trevle(s) op.
unreal [ʌn'ri:əl] *adj* uvirkelig.
unreasonable [ʌn'ri:znəbl] *adj* urimelig; overdreven.
unrelenting [ʌnri'lɛntiŋ] *adj* uforsonlig; utrættelig; vedvarende.
unreliable [ʌnri'laiəbl] *adj* upålidelig; usikker.
unremitting [ʌnri'mitiŋ] *adj* utrættelig; stadig.
unrest [ʌn'rɛst] *s* uro.
unrivalled [ʌn'raivəld] *adj* uovertruffen.
unroll [ʌn'rəul] *v* rulle (sig) op (,ud); vikle ud.
unruly [ʌn'ru:li] *adj* uregerlig.
unsafe [ʌn'seif] *adj* farlig, usikker.
unsaid [ʌn'sɛd] *adj: leave sth ~* lade ngt være usagt.

unsatisfactory ['ʌnsætis'fæktəri] *adj* utilfredsstillende.
unsavoury [ʌn'seivəri] *adj* ulækker, ækel; usmagelig.
unscathed [ʌn'skeiðd] *adj* uskadt.
unscrew [ʌn'skru:] *v* skrue løs (,af).
unscrupulous [ʌn'skru:pjuləs] *adj* skrupelløs; forhærdet.
unseemly [ʌn'si:mli] *adj* upassende.
unseen [ʌn'si:n] *adj* uset; ubeset.
unsettled [ʌn'sɛtld] *adj* urolig; usikker; (om gæld etc) ikke betalt; uafgjort.
unshaven [ʌn'ʃeivn] *adj* ubarberet.
unsightly [ʌn'saitli] *adj* uskøn, hæslig.
unskilled [ʌn'skild] *adj* ukyndig; ~ *worker* ufaglært arbejder.
unsound [ʌn'saund] *adj* usund; dårlig; uholdbar; *of ~ mind* sindsforvirret, utilregnelig.
unsparing [ʌn'spɛəriŋ] *adj* rundhåndet; utrættelig; skånselsløs.
unspeakable [ʌn'spi:kəbl] *adj* ubeskrivelig; afskyelig.
unspoiled [ʌn'spɔild] *adj* ikke forkælet, ikke ødelagt; ufordærvet.
unspoken [ʌn'spəukən] *adj* uudtalt; tavs.
unstable [ʌn'steibl] *adj* ustabil; usikker.
unsteady [ʌn'stɛdi] *adj* ustadig; usikker; vaklende.
unstuck [ʌn'stʌk] *adj: come ~* gå løs (,op); slå fejl.
unsuccessful [ʌnsək'sɛsful] *adj* mislykket; forgæves; *be ~* ikke have held med sig; mislykkes.
unsuitable [ʌn'su:təbl] *adj* upassende; uegnet.
unsure [ʌn'ʃuə*] *adj* usikker.
unsurpassed [ʌnsə'pa:st] *adj* uovertruffen.
unsuspecting [ʌnsə'spɛktiŋ] *adj* intetanende; godtroende.
unswerving [ʌn'swə:viŋ] *adj* usvigelig.
unthinkable [ʌn'θiŋkəbl] *adj* utænkelig; utrolig.
untidy [ʌn'taidi] *adj* rodet; uordentlig, sjusket.
untie [ʌn'tai] *v* løse (,binde) op.
until [ən'til] *præp/konj* (ind)til; lige til; før(end); *not ~* ikke før, først (når); *~ then* indtil da.
untimely [ʌn'taimli] *adj* alt for tidlig (fx *death* død); uheldig, malplaceret.
unto [ʌn'tu:] *præp (gl)* til; ved.
untold [ʌn'təuld] *adj* uhørt; umådelig; utallig; *leave sth ~* lade ngt være usagt.
untoward [ʌntə'wɔ:d] *adj* uheldig; upassende; genstridig.
untrue [ʌn'tru:] *adj* usand; utro.
unusual [ʌn'ju:ʒuəl] *adj* usædvanlig; ualmindelig.
unveil [ʌn'veil] *v* afsløre, afdække.
unwanted [ʌn'wɔntid] *adj* uønsket.
unwarranted [ʌn'wɔrəntid] *adj* uberettiget, ubeføjet.
unwell [ʌn'wɛl] *adj* utilpas.
unwieldy [ʌn'wi:ldi] *adj* uhåndterlig, klodset.
unwilling [ʌn'wiliŋ] *adj* uvillig; modvillig; **~ly** *adv* nødig; mod sin vilje.
unwind [ʌn'waind] *v* vikle(s) op; spole af; rulle(s) ud; slappe af.
unwitting [ʌn'witiŋ] *adj* ubevidst; uden at vide det; **~ly** *adv* uforvarende.
unworthy [ʌn'wə:ði] *adj* uværdig *(of* til).
unwrap [ʌn'ræp] *v* pakke(s) ud.
unwritten [ʌn'ritn] *adj* uskrevet (fx *law* lov).
unzip [ʌn'zip] *v* lyne op.
up [ʌp] *adv/præp* op; oppe; op ad; hen; forbi; på færde; *go ~ a ladder* gå op ad en stige; *be ~ the mountain* være oppe på bjerget; *she went ~ to him* hun gik hen til ham; *time is ~* tiden er ude; *it is ~ to you* det må du om; det bliver din sag; det kommer an på dig; *what are you ~ to?* hvad har du for? hvad er du ude på? *he is not ~ to it* han kan ikke klare det; *be well ~ in sth* være godt inde i ngt; *~s and downs* svingninger; medgang og modgang; *~ yours!* (S) skråt op! **--and-coming** *adj* på vej frem, lovende.
upbringing ['ʌpbriŋiŋ] *s* opdragelse.
update [ʌp'deit] *v* ajourføre, opdatere.

up-end [ʌp'ɛnd] *v* stille på højkant.
up-front [ʌp'frɔnt] *adj* åben og ærlig // *adv* forud.
upgrade [ʌp'greid] *v* forfremme; forbedre; opvurdere.
upheaval [ʌp'hi:vl] *s* omvæltning; krise.
uphill ['ʌp'hil] *adj* op ad bakke.
uphold [ʌp'həuld] *v* opretholde; stadfæste.
upholstery [ʌp'həulstəri] *s* polstring; betræk; (i bil) indtræk.
upkeep ['ʌpki:p] *s* vedligeholdelse.
uplands ['ʌpləndz] *spl* højland.
upon [ə'pɔn] *præp* d.s.s. *on.*
upper ['ʌpə*] *adj* højere; øvre; øverst; over-; *gain the ~ hand* få overtaget; **~-case letters** *spl* store bogstaver.
uppermost ['ʌpəməust] *adj* øverst, højest.
uppity ['ʌpiti] *adj* (F) hovskisnovski.
upright *s* stolpe; opretstående klaver // *adj* lodret; opretstående; retskaffen.
uprising ['ʌpraiziŋ] *s* opstand; opgang, stigning.
uproar ['ʌprɔ:*] *s* tumult, råben og skrigen.
uproot [ʌp'ru:t] *v* rive op med rod; udrydde.
upset *s* ['ʌpsɛt] forstyrrelse, uorden; fald // *v* [ʌp'sɛt] vælte; forstyrre; gøre ked af det; bringe i uorden // *adj* [ʌp'sɛt] chokeret; ked af det; *have an ~ stomach* have dårlig mave.
upshot ['ʌpʃɔt] *s: in the ~* når det kommer til stykket, i sidste ende.
upside ['ʌpsaid] *s: ~ down* med bunden i vejret; *turn sth ~ down* vende op og ned på ngt.
upstairs [ʌp'stɛəz] *adj* ovenpå, på næste etage // *adv* op ad trappen; *there's no ~* der er ingen overetage.
upstanding [ʌp'stændiŋ] *adj (fig)* hæderlig, retskaffen.
upstart ['ʌpsta:t] *s* opkomling.
upstream ['ʌpstri:m] *adv* mod strømmen, op (,oppe) ad floden.
uptake ['ʌpteik] *s* optagelse; *quick on the ~* hurtig i optrækket, kvik.
uptight ['ʌptait] *adj* nervøs; snerpet; mopset.
up-to-date ['ʌptə'deit] *adj* ajour; moderne, tidssvarende.
upward ['ʌpwəd] *adj* opadgående; opadvendt; **upward(s)** *adv* opad; i vejret; foroven.
uranium [juə'reiniəm] *s* uran.
urban ['ə:bən] *adj* by-; bymæssig; **~ district** *s* bymæssig bebyggelse.
urbane [ə:'bein] *adj* kultiveret, beleven.
urchin ['ə:tʃin] *s* knægt, (lille) rod.
urge [ə:dʒ] *s* (stærk) trang, drift; lyst // *v: ~ sby to do sth* indtrængende anmode en om at gøre ngt; tilskynde en til at gøre ngt; *~ sby not to do sth* indstændigt fraråde en at gøre ngt; *~ on* drive frem, ægge.
urgency ['ə:dʒənsi] *s* pres; påtrængende nødvendighed; pågåenhed.
urgent ['ə:dʒənt] *adj* som haster, tvingende, presserende.
urinal ['juərinl] *s* pissoir.
urinate ['juərineit] *v* tisse.
US ['ju:'ɛs], **USA** ['ju:ɛs'ei] *s* (fork.f. *United States of America)* USA.
us [ʌs] *pron* os.
usage ['ju:zidʒ] *s* (skik og) brug; kutyme; behandling; *modern ~* moderne sprogbrug.
use *s* [ju:s] brug; skik; nytte; *in ~* i brug; *out of ~* gået af brug; ubenyttet; *it's no ~* det nytter ikke; *have the ~ of* kunne bruge // *v* [ju:z] bruge; benytte (sig af); behandle; *he ~d to do it* han plejede at gøre det; *be ~d to* være vant til; **~ful** *adj* nyttig; *come in ~ful* komme lige tilpas; **~less** *adj* nytteløs; ubrugelig.
user ['ju:zə*] *s* (for)bruger.
usher ['ʌʃə*] *s* dørvogter; kontrollør // *v* vise ind (,på plads); *(fig)* indvarsle.
usherette [ʌʃə'rɛt] *s* (i biograf) kvindelig kontrollør.
usual ['ju:ʒuəl] *adj* sædvanlig, almindelig; *as ~* som sædvanlig; **~ly** *adv* almindeligvis, i reglen, gerne.
usurp [ju:'zə:p] *v* bemægtige sig.
usury ['ju:ʒəri] *s* åger.
utensil [ju:'tɛnsl] *s* redskab.
utilitarian [ju:tili'tɛəriən] *adj* nyttemæssig; funktionel.

utility [ju:'tiliti] *s* nytte; (også: *public ~)* almennyttigt foretagende.
utilize ['ju:tilaiz] *v* udnytte.
utmost ['ʌtməust] *s/adj* det højeste (,yderste); *do one's ~* gøre sit yderste.
utter ['ʌtə*] *v* udtale; udstøde; udtrykke // *adj* fuldstændig, komplet.
utterance ['ʌtərəns] *s* ytring, udtalelse.
uvula ['ju:vjələ] *s* drøvel.

V

V, v [vi:].
v fork.f. *verse; versus; vide; volt.*
vac [væk] *s* (F) fork.f. *vacation; vacuum cleaner.*
vacancy ['veikənsi] *s* tomhed; tomrum; ledig stilling; ledigt værelse; *no vacancies* alt optaget.
vacant ['veikənt] *adj* tom; ledig; (om blik) udtryksløs.
vacate [və'keit] *v* fratræde; rømme, forlade.
vacation [və'keiʃən] *s* ferie.
vaccinate ['væksineit] *v* vaccinere.
vaccine ['væksi:n] *s* vaccine.
vacillate ['væsileit] *v* vakle; være usikker.
vacuous ['vækjuəs] *adj* tom, udtryksløs.
vacuum ['vækjuəm] *s* tomrum, vakuum // *v* støvsuge; ~ **cleaner** *s* støvsuger; ~ **flask** *s* termoflaske.
vagary ['veigəri] *s* lune.
vagina [və'dʒainə] *s* skede, vagina.
vagrant ['veigrənt] *s* vagabond // *adj* omstrejfende.
vague [veig] *adj* uklar, vag, ubestemt, svævende; **~ly** *adv* svagt.
vain [vein] *adj* forfængelig; forgæves; *in ~* forgæves.
valance ['væləns] *s* gardinkappe; omhæng.
valentine ['væləntain] *s* sv.t. gækkebrev (sendt til St. Valentins dag 14. feb).
valet ['vælit] *s* kammertjener; **~ing service** *s* (på hotel) presning etc af tøj.
valiant ['væliənt] *adj* tapper.
valid ['vælid] *adj* gyldig; effektiv.
validate ['vælideit] *v* godkende; erklære gyldig.
validity [væ'liditi] *s* gyldighed.
valley ['væli] *s* dal.
valour ['vælə*] *s* tapperhed, mod.
valuable ['væljuəbl] *adj* værdifuld; **~s** *spl* værdigenstande.
valuation [vælju'eiʃən] *s* vurdering.
value ['vælju:] *s* værdi; *get ~ for money* få ngt for pengene; *take sth at face ~* tage ngt for pålydende; *gold to the ~ of...* guld til en værdi af... // *v* vurdere; værdsætte; sætte pris på; **~-added tax** *s (VAT)* sv.t. moms; **valued** *adj* værdsat.
valve [vælv] *s* ventil; klap.
vamp [væmp] *s* vamp // *v: ~ sth up* piffe (,shine) ngt op.
van [væn] *s* varevogn; *(jernb)* godsvogn.
vandalism ['vændəlizm] *s* hærværk.
vandalize ['vændəlaiz] *v* øve hærværk, rasere.
vanguard ['vænga:d] *s* fortrop.
vanish ['væniʃ] *v* forsvinde; *~ into thin air* forsvinde ud i den blå luft; **~ing cream** *s* ansigtscreme, pudderunderlag; **~ing trick** *s* forsvindingsnummer.
vanity ['væniti] *s* forfængelighed; ~ **case** *s* kosmetikpung.
vanquish ['vænkwiʃ] *v* besejre.
vantage ['væntidʒ] *s* fordel; ~ **point** *s* fordelagtig stilling; udsigtspunkt.
vapid ['væpid] *adj* mat; fad.
vaporize ['veipəraiz] *v* (lade) fordampe.
vapour ['veipə*] *s* damp; em, dug; ~ **trail** *s (fly)* kondensstribe.
variable ['vɛəriəbl] *adj* foranderlig; variabel; skiftende.
variance ['vɛəriəns] *s: be at ~ (with)* være i strid med; være uenig med.
variation [vɛəri'eiʃən] *s* forandring, variation; *~s in opinion* meningsforskelle.
varicella [væri'sɛllə] *s* skoldkopper.
varicose ['værikəus] *adj: ~ veins* åreknuder.
varied ['vɛərid] *adj* afvekslende; varieret.

variegated ['vɛərigeitid] *adj* broget (også *fig).*
variety [və'raiəti] *s* afveksling, variation; slags, sort, type; afart; variant; *for a ~ of reasons* af mange grunde; ~ **show** *s* varietéforestilling.
various ['vɛəriəs] *adj* forskellige; adskillige; diverse.
varnish ['va:niʃ] *s* fernis; lak; glans // *v* fernisere; lakere.
varsity ['va:siti] *s (am)* universitets-.
vary ['vɛəri] *v* skifte, variere; forandre (sig).
vase [va:z] *s* vase.
vast [va:st] *adj* umådelig; vidtstrakt; enorm; *the ~ majority* det store flertal; **~ly** *adv* umådeligt, enormt.
VAT [vi:ei'ti:] (fork.f. *value added tax)* sv.t. moms.
vat [væt] *s* (vin)fad, stor tønde.
vault [vɔ:lt] *s* hvælving; gravkælder; (i bank) boksafdeling; spring // *v: ~ (over)* springe over.
vaunt [vɔ:nt] *v* rose i høje toner; prale af.
VCR ['vi:si:'a:*] *s* (fork. f. *video cassette recorder)* video.
VD ['vi:'di:] fork.f. *venereal disease.*
VDU fork.f. *visual display unit.*
veal [vi:l] *s* kalvekød; *roast ~* kalvesteg.
veer [viə*] *v* vende (sig); dreje, svinge.
veg [vɛdʒ] *s* d.s.s. *vegetable.*
vegetable ['vɛdʒitəbl] *s* grøntsag // *adj* plante-; grøntsags-; ~ **garden** *s* køkkenhave; ~ **marrow** *s* græskar.
vegetarian [vɛdʒi'tɛəriən] *s* vegetar // *adj* vegetarisk.
vegetate ['vɛdʒiteit] *v* vegetere.
vegetation [vɛdʒi'teiʃən] *s* vegetation, plantevækst.
vehemence ['vi:iməns] *s* voldsomhed.
vehement ['vi:imənt] *adj* heftig, voldsom.
vehicle [vi:kl] *s* køretøj, vogn; middel.
vehicular [vi'hikjulə*] *adj: no ~ traffic* kørsel forbudt.
veil [veil] *s* slør // *v* tilsløre.
vein [vein] *s* (blod)åre, vene; (på blad) streng; *(fig)* stemning.
velocity [vi'lɔsiti] *s* hastighed, fart.
velvet ['vɛlvit] *s* fløjl.
velveteen [vɛlvi'ti:n] *s* bomuldsfløjl.
velvety ['vɛlviti] *adj* fløjlsagtig; blød.
venal ['vi:nəl] *adj* korrupt, bestikkelig.
vending ['vɛndiŋ] *s: ~ machine* vareautomat.
vendor ['vɛndɔ:*] *s* sælger; *street ~* gadehandler.
veneer [və'niə*] *s* finering; *(fig)* fernis.
venerable ['vɛnərəbl] *adj* ærværdig.
venereal [vi'niəriəl] *adj: ~ disease (VD)* kønssygdom.
Venetian [vi'ni:ʃən] *adj* venetiansk; ~ **blind** *s* persienne.
vengeance ['vɛndʒəns] *s* hævn; *with a ~ (fig)* så det batter.
Venice ['vɛnis] *s* Venedig, Venezia.
venison ['vɛnisn] *s* (dyre)vildt.
venom ['vɛnəm] *s* gift; ondskab.
venomous ['vɛnəməs] *adj* giftig; ondskabsfuld.
vent [vɛnt] *s* lufthul; afløb; (i tøj) slids; *give ~ to* give frit afløb for // *v* lufte; *~ one's anger on sby* lade sin vrede gå ud over en.
ventilate ['vɛntileit] *v* udlufte; ventilere.
ventilation [vɛnti'leiʃən] *s* ventilation.
ventriloquist [vɛn'triləkwist] *s* bugtaler.
venture ['vɛntʒə*] *s* foretagende; satsning; vovestykke // *v* driste sig til; vove; satse; *~ on a journey* begive sig ud på en rejse; *~ out* vove sig ud.
venue ['vɛnju:] *s* mødested.
veracious [və'reiʃəs] *adj* sandfærdig; ærlig.
veracity [və'ræsiti] *s* sandhed; ærlighed.
verb [və:b] *s* udsagnsord, verbum.
verbal ['və:bl] *adj* verbal; mundtlig; ordret.
verbatim [və:'beitim] *adj/adv* ordret.
verbiage ['və:biidʒ] *s* ordskvalder, “blabla”.
verbose [və:'bəus] *adj* ordrig; vidtløftig.
verdict ['və:dikt] *s* kendelse, dom.
verdigris ['və:digri:s] *s* ir.
verge [və:dʒ] *s* kant, rand; *soft ~s* rabatten er blød; *on the ~ of* på randen af // *v: ~ on* grænse til.

verger ['və:dʒə*] *s* sv.t. kirketjener.
verification [vɛrifi'keiʃən] *s* bekræftelse; bevis.
verify ['vɛrifai] *v* bekræfte; verificere.
vermilion [və'miljən] *s* cinnoberrød.
vermin ['və:min] *spl* skadedyr, utøj.
vernacular [və'nækjulə*] *s* folkesprog; egnsdialekt // *adj* regional, egns-; folkellig.
versatile ['və:sətail] *adj* alsidig.
verse [və:s] *s* vers; **~d** *adj: ~d in* velbevandret i, velfunderet i.
version ['və:ʃən] *s* version; oversættelse; gengivelse.
versus ['və:səs] *præp* mod, kontra.
vertebra ['və:tibrə] *s (pl: vertebrae* [-'bri:]) ryghvirvel.
vertebrate ['və:tibrit] *s* hvirveldyr.
vertical ['və:tikl] *s* lodlinje // *adj* lodret; opretstående.
vertigo ['və:tigəu] *s* svimmelhed.
verve [və:v] *s* kraft(fuldhed); livfuldhed.
very ['vɛri] *adj/adv* meget; aller-; selv, selve; netop; *the ~ book I wanted* netop den bog jeg ville have; *at the ~ end* til allersidst; *the ~ last* den allersidste; *at the ~ least* i det mindste; *~ much* meget; *the ~ same day* den selvsamme dag.
vessel [vɛsl] *s* fartøj, skib; kar, beholder.
vest [vɛst] *s* undertrøje.
vested ['vɛstid] *adj* tilsikret, hævdvunden.
vestige ['vɛstidʒ] *s* spor; antydning.
vestments ['vɛstmənts] *spl* ornat.
vestry ['vɛstri] *s* sakristi.
vet [vɛt] *s* (fork.f. *veterinary)* dyrlæge // *v* undersøge grundigt.
veterinary ['vɛtrinəri] *s* dyrlæge // *adj* veterinær, dyrlæge-.
veto ['vi:təu] *s* veto // *v* nedlægge veto mod.
vex [vɛks] *v* ærgre, plage; oprøre.
vexation [vɛk'seiʃən] *s* ærgrelse; græmmelse.
vexed [vɛksd] *adj* ærgerlig, irriteret; omdiskuteret, omstridt.
viable ['vaiəbl] *adj* levedygtig; rentabel; brugbar; gennemførlig.
vial ['vaiəl] *s* lille flaske.
vibes [vaibz] *spl* (F) vibrationer.
vibrant ['vaibrənt] *adj* vibrerende, dirrende.
vibrate ['vaibreit] *v* vibrere, svinge; *~ with* genlyde af.
vibration [vai'breiʃən] *s* vibration, svingning; rystelse.
vicar ['vikə*] *s* sognepræst.
vicarage ['vikəridʒ] *s* præstegård.
vicarious [vi'kɛəriəs] *adj* indirekte; stedfortrædende.
vice [vais] *s* last, synd; *(tekn)* skruestik.
vice(-) [vais-] i sms: vice-; **~ chairman** *s* viceformand; **~ squad** *s* sædelighedspoliti.
vicinity [vi'siniti] *s* nærhed; nabolag.
vicious ['viʃəs] *adj* ondskabsfuld; voldsom.
vicissitude [vi'sisitju:d] *s* omskiftelse.
victim ['viktim] *s* offer; *fall ~ to* blive offer for.
victimize ['viktimaiz] *v* lade det gå ud over.
victor ['viktə*] *s* sejrherre.
Victorian [vik'tɔ:riən] *adj* viktoriansk (1837-1901).
victorious [vik'tɔ:riəs] *adj* sejrrig; sejrende.
victory ['viktəri] *s* sejr.
victuals ['vitlz] *spl* fødevarer; proviant.
vide ['vaidi] *v* se; *~ infra* se nedenfor.
video ['vidiəu] *s* video // *v* optage på video.
vie [vai] *v* kappes *(for* om).
Vienna [vi'ɛnə] *s* Wien; **Viennese** [viə'ni:z] *adj* wiener-.
view [vju:] *s* syn; udsigt; mening; *point of ~* synspunkt; *in ~ of* i betragtning af; *in my ~* efter min mening; *come into ~* komme til syne; *in full ~ of* lige for øjnene af; *in ~ of this...* med tanke på dette...; *have sth in ~* have ngt i syne; *on ~* (i fx museum) udstillet; *take a dim ~ of sth* ikke synes særlig godt om ngt; *with a ~ to* med henblik på // *v* bese; betragte, syne; **~data** *s* teledata.
viewer ['vju:ə*] *s (foto)* søger; *(tv)* seer.

viewfinder ['vju:faində*] *s (foto)* søger.
viewpoint ['vju:pɔint] *s* synspunkt.
vigil ['vidʒil] *s* (natte)vagt.
vigilance ['vidʒiləns] *s* årvågenhed.
vigilant ['vidʒilənt] *adj* vagtsom.
vigorous ['vigərəs] *adj* kraftig; frodig; energisk.
vigour ['vigə*] *s* (livs)kraft.
vile [vail] *adj* led, nederdrægtig; ækel; ussel; *a ~ temper* et rædsomt humør.
vilify ['vilifai] *v* tale ondt om, "svine til".
village ['vilidʒ] *s* landsby; ~ **hall** *s* forsamlingshus.
villager ['vilədʒə*] *s* landsbybo.
villain ['vilən] *s* skurk, bandit.
villainous ['vilənəs] *adj* ond; skurkagtig.
vim [vim] *s* kraft, energi.
vindicate ['vindikeit] *v* forsvare; retfærdiggøre.
vindictive [vin'diktiv] *adj* hævngerrig.
vine [vain] *s (bot)* vin; vinranke; slyngplante.
vinegar ['vinigə*] *s* eddike.
vine grower ['vaingrəuə*] *s* vinavler.
vineyard ['vinja:d] *s* vingård; vinmark.
vintage ['vintidʒ] *s* (om vin etc) årgang // *adj* årgangs-; klassisk; ~ **car** *s* veteranbil; ~ **wine** *s* årgangsvin.
viola [vai'əulə] *s (mus)* bratsch.
violate ['vaiəleit] *v* krænke; overtræde, bryde; voldtage.
violation [vaiə'leiʃən] *s* krænkelse; brud; voldtægt.
violence ['vaiələns] *s* vold; voldsomhed.
violent ['vaiələnt] *adj* voldsom; voldelig.
violet ['vaiələt] *s* viol // *adj* violet.
violin ['vaiəlin] *s* violin; **violinist** [-'linist] *s* violinist.
VIP ['vi:ai'pi:] *s* (fork.f. *very important person)* stor ping.
viper ['vaipə*] *s* hugorm; (om person) slange.
virgin ['və:dʒin] *s* jomfru; *the Blessed Virgin* den hellige jomfru, jomfru Maria // *adj* jomfruelig; uberørt.
virginity [və:'dʒiniti] *s* jomfruelighed.
virgin soil ['və:dʒin ˌsɔil] *s* uopdyrket jord.
Virgo ['və:gəu] *s (astr)* Jomfruen.
virile ['virail] *adj* mandlig; mandig, viril.
virility [vi'riliti] *s* manddom; mandighed.
virtual ['və:tjuəl] *adj* virkelig, faktisk; **~ly** *adv* praktisk talt.
virtue ['və:tʃu:] *s* dyd; fortrin; *by ~ of* i kraft af.
virtuoso [və:tʃu'əuzəu] *s* virtuos.
virtuous ['və:tʃuəs] *adj* dydig; retskaffen.
virulent ['virulənt] *adj* ondartet; giftig; dødelig.
virus ['vaiərəs] *s* virus.
visa ['vi:zə] *s* visum.
VISA (card) ['vi:zə(ka:d)] *s* hævekort, betalingskort.
viscount ['vaikaunt] *s* viscount (næstlaveste rang i brit. højadel).
visibility [vizi'biliti] *s* sigtbarhed; synlighed.
visible ['vizəbl] *adj* synlig; visibel.
vision ['viʒən] *s* syn; synsevne; udsyn; vision.
visionary ['viʒənəri] *adj* synsk; uvirkelig; med visioner.
visit ['vizit] *s* besøg; visit; ophold; *pay sby a ~* besøge en // *v* besøge; hjemsøge; **~ing card** *s* visitkort; **~ing hours** *spl* besøgstid; **~ing professor** *s* gæsteprofessor.
visitor ['vizitə*] *s* gæst; besøgende; tilsynsførende.
visor ['vaizə*] *s* visir; *(auto)* solskærm.
vista ['vistə] *s* udsigt; syn; fremtidsperspektiv.
visual ['viʒjuəl] *adj* synlig, syns-; ~ **aid** *s* visuelt hjælpemiddel; ~ **display unit** *s (VDU)* skærmterminal.
visualize ['viʒjuəlaiz] *v* se for sig, forestille sig; vente; visualisere.
vital [vaitl] *adj* livsvigtig; væsentlig, vital; livs-.
vitality [vai'tæliti] *s* vitalitet, energi.
vital statistics ['vaitl stə'tistiks] *spl* befolkningsstatistik; (F) personlige mål.
vitamin ['vitəmin] *s* vitamin; ~ **deficiency** *s* vitaminmangel.

vivacious [vi'veiʃəs] *adj* livlig, levende.
vivacity [vi'væsiti] *s* livlighed.
vivid ['vivid] *adj* livlig; levende.
viviparous [vi'vipərəs] *adj (zo)* som føder levende unger.
vixen ['viksən] *s* hunræv; (om kvinde) harpe.
viz [viz] *adv* nemlig.
V-neck ['vi:nɛk] *s* v-udskæring.
vocabulary [və'kæbjuləri] *s* ordforråd; ordliste.
vocal [vəukl] *s* sang // *adj* stemme-; sang-; vokal; højrøstet; ~ **cords** *spl* stemmebånd.
vocalist ['vəukəlist] *s* sanger.
vocation [vəu'keiʃən] *s* kald; erhverv.
vocational [və'keiʃənəl] *adj* erhvervs-; ~ *training* erhvervsrettet uddannelse.
vociferous [və'sifərəs] *adj* bralrende, højrøstet.
vogue [vəug] *s* mode; *in* ~ på mode.
voice [vɔis] *s* stemme, røst; mening; *at the top of one's* ~ af fuld hals; *with one* ~ enstemmigt // *v* udtrykke; (om sproglyd) stemme; **~-over** *s (film, tv)* kommentatorstemme.
void [vɔid] *s* tomrum // *adj* tom; forgæves; *null and* ~ ugyldig.
vol. fork.f. *volume.*
volatile ['vɔlətail] *adj* flygtig; livlig.
volcanic [vɔl'kænik] *adj* vulkansk.
volcano [vɔl'keinəu] *s* vulkan.
vole [vəul] *s* markmus.
volition [vɔ'liʃən] *s* vilje; *of one's own* ~ af egen fri vilje.
volley ['vɔli] *s* skudsalve; strøm, byge; *(sport)* flugtskud.
volt [vəult] *s* volt.
voltage ['vəultidʒ] *s (elek)* spænding.
voluble ['vɔljubl] *adj* veltalende; ordrig.
volume ['vɔlju:m] *s* (om bog) bind; rumfang, volumen; *turn down the* ~ skrue ned for lyden.
voluminous [vɔ'luminəs] *adj* omfangsrig; rummelig.
voluntary ['vɔləntəri] *adj* frivillig; forsætlig.
volunteer [vɔlən'tiə*] *s* frivillig // *adj* melde sig frivilligt; tilbyde.
voluptuous [və'lʌptʃuəs] *adj* vellystig; yppig.
vomit ['vɔmit] *s* opkast(ning), bræk // *v* kaste op, brække sig.
voracious [və'reiʃəs] *adj* grådig, glubende.
vote [vəut] *s* stemme; afstemning; stemmeret; ~ *of censure* mistillidsvotum; ~ *of no confidence* mistillidsvotum; ~ *of thanks* takkeskrivelse (,-tale); *have the* ~ have valgret // *v* stemme; vedtage.
voter ['vəutə*] *s* vælger.
voting ['vəutiŋ] *s* votering; (om)valg; ~ **booth** *s* stemmeboks; ~ **paper** *s* stemmeseddel.
vouch [vautʃ] *v:* ~ *for* garantere, indestå for.
voucher ['vautʃə*] *s* kupon; rabatkupon; polet; kvittering, bon; (også: *gift* ~) gavekort.
vouchsafe [vautʃ'seif] *v* forunde, værdige.
vow [vau] *s* (højtideligt) løfte, ed // *v* love, sværge.
vowel ['vauəl] *s* selvlyd, vokal.
voyage ['vɔiidʒ] *s* (sø)rejse.
voyager ['vɔiidʒə*] *s* rejsende.
VS fork.f. *versus.*
vulcanize ['vʌlkənaiz] *v* vulkanisere.
vulgar ['vʌlgə*] *adj* vulgær; tarvelig; grov.
vulnerable ['vʌlnərəbl] *adj* sårbar.
vulture ['vʌltʃə*] *s (zo)* grib; *(fig)* blodsuger, haj.

W

W, w ['dʌblju:].
wacky ['wæki] *adj* (F) skør, flippet.
wad [wɔd] *s* tot; klump; (om penge) seddelbundt; *he's got ~s of money* han vælter sig i penge.
wadding ['wɔdiŋ] *s* vattering; pladevat.
waddle [wɔdl] *v* vralte; sjokke.
wade [weid] *v* vade (over); ~ *in* kaste sig ud i det; blande sig; ~ *into sth* kaste sig over ngt; ~ *through (fig)* pløje sig igennem.
wader ['weidə*] *s* vadefugl.
wafer ['weifə*] *s* (tynd, sprød) vaffel; *(rel)* oblat.

waffle [wɔfl] *s* (blød) vaffel; (F) vrøvl, øregas // *v* ævle.
waft [wɔ:ft] *s* pust, vift // *v* vifte.
wag [wæg] *v* bevæge fra side til side; logre; vippe med; *let one's tongue ~* lade munden løbe.
wage [weidʒ] *s* (bruges oftes i *pl: ~s)* løn, hyre // *v: ~ war* føre krig; ~ **claim** *s* lønkrav; ~ **earner** *s* lønmodtager; ~ **freeze** *s* lønstop; ~ **packet** *s* lønningspose.
wager ['weidʒə*] *s* væddemål // *v* vædde.
waggle [wægl] *v* svinge; vrikke; logre.
wag(g)on ['wægən] *s* vogn; hestevogn; godsvogn; *be on the ~* (F) være på vandvognen.
wagtail ['wægteil] *s* vipstjært.
waif [weif] *s* hjemløst barn.
wail [weil] *s* jammer, hylen // *v* jamre, hyle; *the Wailing Wall* grædemuren.
wainscot ['weinzkət] *s* panel.
waist [weist] *s* talje, liv; **~band** *s* linning; **~coat** *s* vest.
waisted ['weistid] *adj* taljeret.
waistline ['weistlain] *s* talje; taljemål.
wait [weit] *s* venten; ventetid; *lie in ~ for* ligge på lur efter // *v* vente (på); varte op, servere; *I can't ~ to get there* jeg kan ikke komme hurtigt nok derhen; *just you ~!* du kan vente dig! bare vent og se! *~ one's turn* vente på sin tur; *~ behind* blive hjemme og vente; *~ for* vente på; *~ on* servere for, betjene.
waiter ['weitə*] *s* tjener.
waiting ['weitiŋ] *s* venten; *no ~* stopforbud.
waitress ['weitris] *s* serveringsdame.
waive [weiv] *v* give afkald på; opgive, frafalde; fravige; udsætte.
wake [weik] *s* kølvand; gravøl // *v* (*woke* el. *~d, woken* [wəuk, wəukn]) vække; vågne; *~ up* vække; vågne; **~ful** *adj* årvågen; søvnløs.
waken ['weikn] *v* d.s.s. *wake.*
walk [wɔ:k] *s* (spadsere)tur; gang, sti; *take (,go for) a ~* gå en tur; *10 minutes' ~ from* 10 minutters gang fra // *v* gå, spadsere; gå med; få til at gå; *~ the dog* gå tur med hunden; *~ the streets* gå rundt på gaden; (om luder) trække; *~ sby home* følge en hjem; *~ away with a prize* løbe af med en præmie; *~ in on sby* brase ind til en; *~ out on sby* lade en i stikken; **~about** *s* rundgang; **~away** *s: it was just a ~away (am)* det var en smal sag.
walker ['wɔ:kə*] *s* fodgænger, gående.
walking ['wɔ:kiŋ] *s* gang; føre // *adj* vandre-; omvandrende; ~ **shoes** *spl* spadseresko.
walkout ['wɔ:kaut] *s* arbejdsnedlæggelse.
walkover ['wɔ:kəuvə*] *s* (F) let sejr.
walkway ['wɔ:kwei] *s* gangbro.
wall [wɔ:l] *s* mur; væg; vold; *drive sby up the ~* gøre en skør; *go to the ~* bukke under; gå konkurs // *v: ~ in* omgive med mure; *~ up* mure til; ~ **bars** *spl (gymn)* ribber.
walled ['wɔ:ld] *adj* (om by) befæstet.
wallet ['wɔlit] *s* tegnebog.
wall-eyed ['wɔ:laid] *adj* skeløjet.
wallflower ['wɔ:lflauə*] *s (bot)* gyldenlak; *(fig)* bænkevarmer.
wallop ['wɔləp] *s* slag, bums // *v* slå, tæve; **~ing** *s* lag tæsk // *adj* enorm, kæmpe-.
wallow ['wɔləu] *v* vælte sig; *~ in* vade i.
wallpaper ['wɔ:lpeipə*] *s* tapet.
walnut ['wɔ:lnʌt] *s* valnød(detræ).
walrus ['wɔ:lrəs] *s (pl: ~* el. *~es)* hvalros.
waltz [wɔ:lts] *s* vals // *v* danse vals.
wan [wɔn] *adj* bleg, trist.
wand [wɔnd] *s* (trylle)stav.
wander ['wɔndə*] *v* strejfe om (i); (om tanke el. tale) ikke holde sig til sagen; være uopmærksom; *let one's mind ~* lade tankerne løbe.
wanderer ['wɔndərə*] *s* vandringsmand.
wane [wein] *s: be on the ~* være i aftagende // *v* tage af; svinde; blegne.
wangle [wæŋgl] *v* (F) luske sig til; sno sig.
want [wɔnt] *s* mangel; trang; fornødenhed; *for ~ of* af mangel på; i mangel af; *be in ~ of* trænge til //

v ønske (sig); mangle; behøve; gerne ville; søge; *you won't be ~ed any more* vi har ikke brug for dig længere; *your hair ~s cutting* dit hår trænger til at blive klippet; *be ~ed by the police* være eftersøgt af politiet; *he ~s in (,out)* (F) han vil ind (,ud); **~ing** *adj* mangelfuld; utilstrækkelig; *be ~ing* mangle, savnes; *he's ~ing in tact* han mangler finfølelse.

wanton ['wɔntən] *adj* kåd; letsindig; uansvarlig.

war [wɔ:*] *s* krig; *be at ~ with* være i krig med; *go to ~* gå i krig; *make ~ on* føre krig mod; *in times of ~* i krigstid.

warble [wɔ:bl] *v* kvidre.

war crime ['wɔ: kraim] *s* krigsforbrydelse.

war cry ['wɔ: krai] *s* krigshyl.

ward [wɔ:d] *s* (hospitals)afdeling, stue; *(jur,* om barn) myndling; formynderskab // *v: ~ off* afværge.

warden [wɔ:dn] *s* opsynsmand; bestyrer; (også: *traffic ~*) parkeringsvagt; (også: *church ~*) kirkeværge.

warder ['wɔ:də*] *s* fangevogter.

wardrobe ['wɔ:drəub] *s* klædeskab; garderobe.

warehouse ['wɛəhaus] *s* pakhus, lager.

wares [wɛəz] *spl* varer.

warfare ['wɔ:fɛə*] *s* krig(sførelse).

warhead ['wɔ:hɛd] *s (mil)* sprængladning.

warily ['wɛərili] *adv* forsigtigt.

warlike ['wɔ:laik] *adj* krigerisk, militant.

warm [wɔ:m] *v* varme; blive varm; *~ to sth* blive glad for ngt, få sympati for ngt; *~ up* varme op // *adj* varm; hjertelig; ivrig; *be ~* være (,have det) varm(t); **~-hearted** *adj* varmhjertet.

warmonger ['wɔ:mʌŋgə*] *s* krigsmager.

warmth [wɔ:mθ] *s* varme; begejstring.

warm-up ['wɔ:mʌp] *s* opvarmning.

warn [wɔ:n] *v* advare *(of* mod); formane; gøre opmærksom på; *~ sby that...* advare en om at...; *~ sby off sth* råde en til at holde sig fra ngt, advare en mod ngt.

warning ['wɔ:niŋ] *s* advarsel; varsel; meddelelse; *give ~* sige op; **~ light** *s* advarselslys.

warp [wɔ:p] *s* trend; slæbetov; skævhed (i træ); *(fig)* skavank; særhed // *v* (om træ) slå sig.

warped ['wɔ:pd] *adj* skæv, fordrejet.

war-paint ['wɔ:peint] *s* krigsmaling (også *fig).*

warpath ['wɔ:pa:θ] *s* krigssti.

warrant ['wɔrnt] *s (jur)* arrestordre; fuldmagt // *v* berettige (til); garantere.

warranty ['wɔrənti] *s* garanti.

warrior ['wɔriə*] *s* kriger.

Warsaw ['wɔ:sɔ:] *s* Warszawa.

warship ['wɔ:ʃip] *s* krigsskib.

wart [wɔ:t] *s* vorte.

wartime ['wɔ:taim] *s: in ~* i krigstid.

wary ['wɛəri] *adj* forsigtig.

was [wɔz] *præt* af *be.*

wash [wɔʃ] *s* vask; vasketøj; skvulpen; *give sth a ~* vaske ngt; *have a ~* vaske sig; *he could do with a ~* han trænger til at blive vasket; *your shirt is in the ~* din skjorte er lagt til vask // *v* vaske (sig); kunne vaskes; skylle, skvulpe; *that won't ~!* den går ikke! *~ away* vaske af; skylle(s) væk; *~ down* vaske, spule; skylle ned; *~ off* vaske af; *~ out* vaske væk; skylle; gå af i vask; *~ up* vaske op; *~ed up on the beach* skyllet i land på stranden; **~able** *adj* vaskeægte; vaskbar; **~-and-wear** [-wɛə*] *adj* strygefri; **~basin** *s* vaskekumme; håndvask; **~ed-out** *adj* udvandet; udkørt.

washer ['wɔʃə*] *s* vaskemaskine; *(tekn)* pakning.

washing ['wɔʃiŋ] *s* vask; vasketøj; **~ machine** *s* vaskemaskine; **~ powder** *s* vaskepulver; **~-up** *s* opvask.

washout ['wɔʃaut] *s* (F) fiasko.

washroom ['wɔʃru:m] *s* toiletter.

washstand ['wɔʃstænd] *s (gl)* servante.

wasn't [wɔznt] d.s.s. *was not.*

wasp [wɔsp] *s* hveps.

waspish ['wɔspiʃ] *adj* arrig.

wastage ['weistidʒ] *s* svind; spild; frafald; *natural* ~ naturlig afgang.
waste [weist] *s* ødemark; spild, ødslen; affald; *go to* ~ gå til spilde // *v* spilde; ødsle væk; ødelægge // *adj* øde; *lay* ~ lægge øde; **~bin** *s* skraldebøtte; **~ disposal unit** *s* affaldskværn; **~ful** *adj* ødsel; uøkonomisk; **~land** *s* øde område(r); **~-paper basket** *s* papirkurv; **~ pipe** *s* afløbsrør.
watch [wɔtʃ] *s* ur; vagt; *under* ~ under overvågning // *v* se på; overvære; holde udkig; våge; passe (på); holde øje med; ~ *it!* ~ *your step!* pas på! ~ *TV* se fjernsyn; ~ *out* passe på; **~dog** *s* vagthund; **~ful** *adj* påpasselig, årvågen; **~maker** *s* urmager; **~man** *s* vægter; **~strap** *s* urrem; **~tower** *s* vagttårn; **~word** *s* parole, løsen.
water ['wɔ:tə*] *s* vand; *fresh* ~ ferskvand; *in smooth* ~*s* i smult vande; *in British* ~*s* i britisk farvand; ~ *on the knee* vand i knæet; *get into deep* ~*s (fig)* komme ud hvor man ikke kan bunde; *hold* ~ være vandtæt; *pass* ~ (H) lade vandet; ~ *under the bridge* det er for sent at græmme sig over det nu; ~ *off a duck's back* det er som at slå vand på en gås // *v* vande; løbe i vand; ~ *down* fortynde; udvande; **~ biscuit** *s* (om kiks) cracker; **~colour** *s* vandfarve, akvarel; **~course** *s* vandløb; **~cress** *s* brøndkarse; **~fall** *s* vandfald; **~front** *s* havnefront; strandpromenade; **~ ice** *s (gastr)* sorbet.
watering ['wɔ:təriŋ] *s* vanding; **~ can** *s* vandkande.
water... ['wɔ:tə-] sms: **~ level** *s* vandstand; vandoverflade; **~lily** *s* åkande; **~line** *s* vandlinje; **~logged** *adj* gennemvåd, sumpet; **~ main** *s* hovedvandledning; **~mark** *s* (om papir) vandmærke; (i havn etc) vandstandsmærke; **~ meter** *s* vandmåler; **~proof** *s* regnfrakke, cottoncoat // *adj* vandtæt; **~-repellent** *adj* vandskyende; **~shed** *s (geol)* vandskel; *(fig)* skel; **~side** *s* kyst; **~ softener** *s* blødgøringsmiddel; **~splash** *s* sted hvor fx en bæk løber over vejen; **~spout** *s* skympumpe; nedløbsrør; **~ supply** *s* vandforsyning; **~ table** *s* grundvandsniveau; **~tight** *adj* vandtæt (også *fig); ~* **trap** *s* vandlås; **~-wings** *spl* svømmevinger; **~works** *spl* vandværk; *a ~works* et vandværk; *turn on the ~works (fig)* vande høns.
watery ['wɔ:təri] *adj* vandet; tynd; (om øjne) rindende.
wattage ['wɔtidʒ] *s (elek)* styrke i watt; watt-forbrug.
wattle [wɔtl] *s* risfletning; (på fx hane) hagelap.
wave [weiv] *s* bølge; vinken; *give sby a* ~ vinke til en; *have a natural* ~ have naturligt fald i håret // *v* vifte (med); vinke; bølge; **~length** *s* bølgelængde.
waver ['weivə*] *v* vakle; dirre; flakke.
wavy ['weivi] *adj* bølgende; slynget.
wax [wæks] *s* voks // *v* vokse; bone; (om ski) smøre; (om månen) tiltage.
waxen ['wæksn] *adj* voksagtig, bleg.
waxworks ['wækswə:ks] *spl* voksfigurer; vokskabinet.
way [wei] *s* vej; afstand; retning; måde; skik; vane; væsen; *all the* ~ hele vejen; *this* ~ denne vej; på denne måde; sådan her; *which* ~? hvilken vej? hvordan? *ask one's* ~ spørge om vej; *lead the* ~ føre an; *give* ~ vige, holde tilbage; ~ *back in 1648* helt tilbage i 1648; *by* ~ *of* via; som; *by the* ~ forresten; *by* ~ *of excuse* som (,til) undskyldning; *be in a bad* ~ have det dårligt; *be in the* ~ stå i vejen; *in a* ~ på en måde; *in some* ~*s* på en vis måde; *he's on his* ~ han er på vej; *out of the* ~ af vejen; *go out of one's* ~ *to (fig)* ulejlige sig med at; *keep out of sby's* ~ undgå en; *it is* ~ *out!* det er fantastisk; ~ *out* (også:) udgang; *there are no two* ~*s about it* der er ikke ngt at diskutere; *we'll do it my* ~ vi gør det på min måde; *the* ~ *things are* sådan som sagen stiller sig; *no* ~ *I'm doing it!* ikke ud af stedet om jeg gør det! *he has his lit-*

tle ~s han har sine små særheder (,nykker).
waylay [wei'lei] *v* ligge på lur efter; kapre.
way-out ['weiaut] *adj* excentrisk, udflippet.
wayside ['weisaid] *s* vejkant.
wayward ['weiwəd] *adj* uregerlig; egensindig.
we [wi:] *pron* vi; man; *it is ~* det er os.
weak [wi:k] *adj* svag, skrøbelig; (om fx te) tynd.
weaken ['wi:kn] *v* svække(s).
weakling ['wi:kliŋ] *s* svækling.
weakness ['wi:knis] *s* svaghed; skavank.
wealth [wɛlθ] *s* rigdom; righoldighed; *a man of considerable ~* en temmelig rig mand; **~ tax** *s* formueskat.
wealthy ['wɛlθi] *adj* rig, velhavende.
wean [wi:n] *v: ~ a baby* vænne et barn fra.
weapon ['wɛpən] *s* våben.
wear [wɛə*] *s* brug; slid; slitage; tøj; *look the worse for ~* se medtaget (,slidt) ud; *feel worse for ~* føle sig sløj; *~ and tear* slitage // *v (wore, worn* [wɔ:*, wɔ:n]) have på; bære; slide; holde (til); *~ away* slides (væk); (om tid) slæbe sig hen; *~ down* slide(s) ned (,op); *~ off* slide(s) af; fortage sig; *~ on* slæbe sig hen; *~ out* slide op; udmatte; *~ through* slide hul i.
weariness ['wiərinis] *s* træthed, lede.
weary ['wiəri] *v* blive træt; trætte // *adj* træt; nedslået; kedsommelig.
weather ['wɛðə*] *s* vejr; *be under the ~* være sløj (,uoplagt); *~ permitting* hvis vejret tillader det // *v* forvitre; klare sig igennem; overstå; *~ the storm (fig)* ride stormen af; **~-beaten** *adj* vejrbidt; forvitret; **~ chart** *s* vejkort; **~cock** *s* vejrhane.
weathered ['wɛðəd] *adj* vejrbidt.
weather forecast ['wɛðə,fɔ:ka:st] *s* vejrudsigt.
weatherproof ['wɛðəpru:f] *adj* vind- og regntæt.
weather vane ['wɛðəvein] *s* vejrhane.
weave [wi:v] *s* vævning // *v (wove, woven* [wəuv, 'wəuvn]) væve; flette; sætte sammen.
weaving ['wi:viŋ] *s* vævning.
web [wɛb] *s* væv; net; spind; *(zo)* svømmehud; **~bing** *s* (på møbler) gjord.
wed [wɛd] *v (~ded, ~ded)* gifte sig (med), ægte; vie; *the newly ~s* de nygifte.
we'd [wi:d] d.s.s. *we had; we would.*
wedding ['wɛdiŋ] *s* bryllup; **~ anniversary** *s* bryllupsdag; **~ dress** *s* brudekjole; **~ ring** *s* vielsesring.
wedge [wɛdʒ] *s* kile; (om lagkage etc) stykke kage // *v* kløve; fastkile; **~-heeled** *adj* (om sko) med kilehæl.
wedlock ['wɛdlɔk] *s* (H) ægtestand; *born out of ~* født uden for ægteskab.
Wednesday ['wɛdnzdi] *s* onsdag; *on ~* på onsdag; *on ~s* om onsdagen, hver onsdag.
wee [wi:] *adj* (især skotsk) lille; *a ~ bit* en lille smule // *v* (F) tisse.
weed [wi:d] *s* ukrudtsplante; (S) hash; skvat // *v* luge; rense (ud); **~-killer** *s* ukrudtsmiddel.
weedy ['wi:di] *adj* (F) skvattet.
week [wi:k] *s* uge; *a ~ today, this day ~* (i dag) om en uge, i dag otte dage; *Sunday ~* søndag otte dage; *last Sunday ~* i søndags for en uge siden; **~day** *s* hverdag; **~end motorist** *s* søndagsbilist; **~ly** *s* ugeblad; tidsskrift // *adj* ugentlig // *adv* en gang om ugen.
weep [wi:p] *s* tudetur // *v (wept, wept* [wɛpt]) græde, tude; *~ for joy* græde af glæde; *~ for sby* sørge over en.
weepy ['wi:pi] *s* tåreperser // *adj* tudevorn.
weft [wɛft] *s* islæt (i vævning).
weigh [wei] *v* veje; bedømme; *~ anchor* lette anker; *~ down* tynge ned; nedbøje; *~ in* blive vejet; få sin bagage vejet; blande sig.
weight [weit] *s* vægt; tyngde; byrde; *carry ~* have betydning; *pull one's ~* tage sin tørn; *put on ~* tage på i vægt; *throw one's ~ about* spille stor på den; gøre sin indflydelse gældende; *sale by ~* salg i løs vægt; **~less** *adj* vægtløs; **~lifter** *s* vægtløfter.

weighty ['weiti] *adj* tung, vægtig.
weird [wiəd] *adj* uhyggelig; overnaturlig; mærkelig.
weirdo ['wiədəu] *s* (F) skør person, sær snegl.
welcome ['wɛlkʌm] *s* velkomst; modtagelse // *v* hilse velkommen; tage imod // *adj* velkommen; *you're ~ to...* du må gerne...; *you're ~!* selv tak!
weld [wɛld] *s* svejsning // *v* svejse (sammen); **~er** *s* svejser; svejseapparat.
welfare ['wɛlfɛə*] *s* velfærd; *child ~* børneforsorg; *the public ~* det almene vel; **~ state** *s* velfærdsstat; **~ work** *s* socialt arbejde.
well [wɛl] *s* brønd; kilde // *v* strømme, vælde // *adj (better, best)* vel; rask; god // *adv* godt; ordentligt; nok; *as ~ as* såvel som; ligesom; *be ~* være rask, have det godt; *~ done!* godt (klaret)! *get ~ soon!* god bedring! *do ~* klare sig godt; *do ~ to* gøre klogt i at; *he may ~ have forgotten* han kan meget vel have glemt det; // *interj* nå! altså! *~, I never!* det siger du ikke! det må jeg nok sige!
we'll [wi:l] d.s.s. *we will; we shall.*
well... ['wɛl-] sms: **~advised** *adj* klog; **~behaved** *adj* velopdragen; **~-being** *s* velvære; vel; **~-bred** *adj* kultiveret; **~-connected** *adj* med gode (,fine) forbindelser; **~-defined** *adj* velafgrænset, skarp; **~developed** *adj* veludviklet; **~-disposed** *adj* positivt indstillet; **~-done** *adj* gennemstegt; **~-earned** *adj* velfortjent; **~-established** *adj* fast (fx *tradition);* **~-founded** *adj* velfunderet; **~-groomed** *adj* velplejet.
wellingtons ['wɛliŋtʌnz] *spl* gummistøvler.
well... ['wɛl-] sms: **~-kept** *adj* velholdt; **~-known** *adj* velkendt; **~-made** *adj* velskabt; **~-meaning** *adj* velmenende; **~-nigh** [-nai] *adj* så godt som; **~-off** *adj* velhavende; **~-preserved** *adj* velbevaret; **~-read** [-rɛd] *adj* belæst; **~-spoken** *adj* som taler et kultiveret sprog; **~-to-do** *adj* velhavende; **~-versed** *adj* velbevandret.
Welsh [wɛlʃ] *adj* walisisk; **~man** *s* waliser; **~ rarebit** *s (gastr)* ristet brød med smeltet ost.
wench [wɛntʃ] *s* pige(barn).
went [wɛnt] *præt* og *pp* af *go.*
wept [wɛpt] *præt* og *pp* af *weep.*
were [wə:*] *præt* af *be.*
we're [wiə*] d.s.s. *we are.*
weren't [wə:nt] d.s.s. *were not.*
werewolf ['wiəwulf] *s* varulv.
west [wɛst] *s* vest; vestlig del // *adj* vest-; vestlig // *adv* vestpå, mod vest.
westerly ['wɛstəli] *adj* vestlig, vestre.
western ['wɛstən] *s* cowboyfilm, western // *adj* vestlig, vest-.
west-facing ['wɛstfeisiŋ] *adj* vestvendt.
West-Indies ['wɛst 'indi:z] *spl: the ~* Vestindien.
westward(s) ['westwədz] *adv* vestpå, mod vest.
wet [wɛt] *s* regn; fugt; (F) vatnisse, skvat // *v* gøre våd; *~ one's pants* tisse i bukserne // *adj* våd; fugtig; regnfuld; *~ through* gennemblødt; *get ~* blive våd; *~ paint* (på skilt) nymalet; **~ blanket** *s (fig)* lysesluk-ker; **~lands** *spl* vådområder; **~nurse** *s* amme; **~ ones** *pl* (F) vådservietter; **~ suit** *s* våddragt.
we've [wi:v] d.s.s. *we have.*
whacking ['wækiŋ] *s* (F) tæv // *adj* (F) mægtig, kæmpe-.
whale [weil] *s* hval; *have a ~ of a time* more sig strålende; *a ~ of a car* en kæmpebil.
whaler ['weilə*] *s* hvalfanger(skib).
whaling ['weiliŋ] *s* hvalfangst.
wham [wæm] *interj* bang!
wharf [wɔ:f] *s (pl: wharves* [wɔ:vz]) brygge, kaj.
what [wɔt] *pron* hvad; hvilken; sikken; den (,det, de) der; hvad for; *~ are you doing?* hvad laver du? *~ has happened?* hvad er der sket? *~'s your name?* hvad hedder du? *~ a mess!* sikken et rod! *~ is it called?* hvad hedder det? *~ about (having) some tea?* hvad med en kop te? ~

about me? hvad med mig? *so ~?* og hvad så? *~'s that to you?* hvad kommer det dig ved?

whatever [wɔt'ɛvə*] *pron* hvad som helst; alt hvad; overhovedet; *~ book* lige meget hvilken bog; *do ~ you like* gør hvad du vil; *~ happens* uanset hvad der sker, hvad der end sker; *no reason ~* overhovedet ingen grund.

what-not ['wɔtnɔt] *s* dims, dippedut.

whatsoever [ˌwɔtsəu'ɛvə*] *adv: none ~* overhovedet (,slet) ingen.

wheat [wi:t] *s* hvede; **~germ** *s* hvedekim.

wheedle [wi:dl] *v: ~ sby into doing sth* overtale (,lokke) en til at gøre ngt.

wheel [wi:l] *s* hjul; rat, ror // *v* køre (med); trille; dreje; dreje rundt; **~barrow** *s* trillebør; **~chair** *s* kørestol.

wheeze [wi:z] *v* hvæse; hive efter vejret.

whelp [wɛlp] *s* hvalp (også *fig).*

when [wɛn] *adv/konj* hvornår; når; hvor; da; *on the day ~ I met him* den dag (hvor) jeg mødte ham; *say ~!* sig til! sig stop! *since ~?* siden hvornår?

whenever [wɛn'ɛvə*] *adv* når som helst; hver gang; hvornår; hvornår i alverden.

where [wɛə*] *adv/konj* hvor; hvorhen; der hvor; *this is ~* her er det; *she has gone to you know ~* hun er gået et vist sted hen.

whereabouts ['wɛərəbauts] *spl* opholdssted // *adv* hvor omtrent.

whereas [wɛər'æz] *adv* hvorimod.

whereupon [wɛərə'pɔn] *adv* hvorefter.

wherever [wɛər'ɛvə*] *adv* hvor ... end; hvor i alverden.

wherewithal [wɛəwi'ðɔ:l] *s* (økonomiske) midler.

whet [wɛt] *v* slibe, hvæsse; *(fig)* skærpe.

whether ['wɛðə*] *konj* om; hvorvidt; *it's doubtful ~...* det er tvivlsomt om...; *~ you go or not* hvad enten du går eller ej.

whey [wei] *s* valle.

which [witʃ] *pron* hvem; hvad; hvilken; som, der; *~ of you?* hvem af jer? *tell me ~ one you want* sig (mig) hvad for en du vil have; *I don't mind ~* jeg er ligeglad hvilken; *the book of ~ he was talking* den bog (som) han talte om; *after ~* hvorefter; *in ~ case* i hvilket fald.

whichever [wit'ʃɛvə*] *pron* hvilken (,hvilket) som helst; *take ~ book you prefer* tag hvilken bog du end foretrækker; *~ book you take* lige meget hvilken bog du tager.

whiff [wif] *s* pust; duft, luft; drag.

Whig [wig] *s (gl, pol)* medlem af det liberale parti.

while [wail] *s* tid, stund; øjeblik; *go away for a ~* rejse bort et stykke tid; *it's not worth the ~* det er ikke umagen værd; *all the ~* hele tiden // *v: ~ away the time* fordrive tiden // *konj* mens; selv om, skønt.

whilst [wailst] *konj* mens.

whim [wim] *s* lune, indfald; *at a ~* som det falder ham, (,hende etc) ind, efter en pludselig indskydelse.

whimper ['wimpə*] *s* klynken // *v* klynke.

whimsical ['wimzikl] *adj* lunefuld; excentrisk.

whimsy ['wimzi] *s* indfald, lune.

whine [wain] *s* jamren // *v* jamre.

whinge [windʒ] *v* beklage sig, jamre.

whinny ['wini] *v* vrinske.

whip [wip] *s* pisk; piskeslag; *(parl)* indpisker // *v* piske; fare; suse; snappe; **~lash** *s* piskesnert; **~ped cream** *s* flødeskum; **~-round** *s* (F) indsamling; **~stitch** *s* kastesting.

whirl [wə:l] *s* hvirvel; tummel; *my head is in a ~* jeg er helt rundt på gulvet // *v* hvirvle; snurre; svinge; **~pool** *s* strømhvirvel; malstrøm; **~wind** *s* hvirvelvind.

whirr [wə:*] *v* snurre; svirre.

whisk [wisk] *s* piskeris // *v* piske; viske; fare (af sted); snuppe; *~ sby away (,off)* bortføre en; *~ out* hive frem.

whisker ['wiskə*] *s* knurhår, børste; *by a ~* på et hængende hår, med kniberi; **~s** *spl* bakkenbarter.

whiskey ['wiski] *s* (irsk el. *am)* whisky; **whisky** *s* (skotsk) whisky
whisper ['wispə*] *s* hvisken; rygte; *speak in a* ~ hviske // *v* hviske.
whistle [wisl] *s* fløjte; fløjten; piben; *wet one's* ~ (F) skylle halsen, dyppe snabelen // *v* fløjte; pifte; pibe.
whit [wit] *s: not a* ~ ikke spor; *every* ~ *as good* mindst lige så god.
white [wait] *s* (ægge)hvide; hvid person // *adj* hvid; bleg; ren; ~ *tie* (på indbydelse) kjole og hvidt, selskabstøj; **~-coffee** *s* kaffe med mælk el. fløde; **~-collar job** *s* funktionærstilling; ~ **frost** *s* rimfrost; ~ **goods** *s* hårde hvidevarer.
Whitehall ['waithɔ:l] *s* (ofte =) regeringen.
white-hot ['wait'hɔt] *adj* hvidglødende.
whitening ['waitəniŋ] *s* hvidtning; kridting; hvidtekalk; skolekridt.
whitewash ['waitwɔʃ] *s* hvidtekalk // *v* hvidte, kalke; *(fig)* renvaske.
whither ['wiðə*] *adv (gl)* hvorhen.
Whitsun [witsn] *s* pinse.
whittle [witl] *v* snitte; ~ *away* reducere(s); svinde gradvis; ~ *down* reducere; forringe.
whiz(z) [wiz] *v* suse, fare; svirre; ~ **kid** *s* (F) vidunderbarn.
who [hu:] *pron* hvem; som, der; ~*'s speaking? (tlf)* hvem taler jeg med? **who'd** d.s.s. *who had; who would.*
whodunit [hu:'dʌnit] *s* (F) krimi.
whoever [hu:'ɛvə*] *pron* hvem der end; hvem i alverden; ~ *you marry* hvem du end gifter dig med; ~ *was that?* hvem i alverden var det?
whole [həul] *s* hele, helhed; *the* ~ *of the town* hele byen; *on the* ~, *as a* ~ i det store og hele, som helhed // *adj* hel (,helt, hele); velbeholden; **~foods** *spl* mad bestående af gode uforfalskede råvarer; **~-hearted** *adj* uforbeholden; **~meal** *s* fuldkornsmel; ~ **milk** *s* sødmælk; **~sale** *s* engrossalg // *adj* en gros-; *(fig)* masse-; **~saler** *s* grossist; **~some** *adj* sund; gavnlig.
wholly ['həuli] *adv* helt; fuldstændig.
whom [hu:m] *pron* (af *who*) hvem; som; ~ *did you meet?* hvem mødte du? *the boy* ~ *I told you about* den dreng (som) jeg fortalte dig om.
whoop [hu:p] *v* huje; hive efter vejret; **~ing cough** [-kʌf] *s* kighoste.
whoops [wups] *interj* hovsa.
whoosh [wu:ʃ] *v* suse.
whopper ['wɔpə*] *s* (F) fed løgn; ordentlig tamp, moppedreng.
whopping ['wɔpiŋ] *adj* (F) enorm, kæmpestor.
whore [hɔ:*] *s* (F, *neds)* hore, mær.
whorl [wə:l] *s* snoning; spiral.
whose [hu:z] *pron (gen* af *who* el. *which)* hvis; ~ *book is this?* hvis er denne bog? *the man* ~ *son you met* den mand hvis søn du mødte; ~ *is this?* hvis er den (,det) her?
Who's Who ['hu:z'hu:] *s* sv.t. Kraks Blå Bog.
why [wai] *adv* hvorfor; ~ *is it that...?* hvordan kan det være at...? *so that's* ~... nå, det var (,er) derfor...; *the reason* ~ grunden til at // *interj* nå da! ih! jah! jamen; ~, *here's John!* jamen der er jo John!
whyever [wai'ɛvə*] *adv* hvorfor i alverden.
wick [wik] *s* væge.
wicked ['wikid] *adj* ond; slem; ondskabsfuld; drilagtig.
wicker ['wikə*] *s* vidje; (også: ~*work)* kurvefletning.
wicket ['wikit] *s* låge, luge; (i cricket) gærde.
wide [waid] *adj* bred; udstrakt; vid, stor; ved siden af // *adv* vidt; ~ *open* på vid gab; *stare with* ~ *eyes* glo med store øjne; *shoot* ~ *(of the mark)* skyde (,ramme) langt ved siden af; **~-angle** *s (foto)* vidvinkel(objektiv); **~-awake** *adj* lysvågen; **~-eyed** *adj* med store øjne; naiv; **~ly** *adv* vidt (fx *different* forskellig); vidt og bredt; almindeligt (fx *known* kendt).
widen ['waidn] *v* udvide; øge(s); blive bredere.
widespread ['waidsprɛd] *adj* (almindeligt) udbredt; vidtstrakt.
widow ['widəu] *s* enke // *v: be* ~*ed* blive enke.

widower ['widəuə*] *s* enkemand.
width [widθ] *s* bredde; vidde; *(fig)* spændvidde.
wield [wi:ld] *v* håndtere; bruge; udøve.
wife [waif] *s (pl: wives* [waivz]) kone, hustru; ~ **battering** *s* hustruvold.
wig [wig] *s* paryk.
wiggle [wigl] *v* vrikke (med); sno sig.
wild [waild] *adj* vild; uopdyrket; øde; uregerlig; fantastisk; *a ~ guess* "et skud i mørket"; *run ~* gå for lud og koldt vand; gå amok; **~cat** *s* vildkat // *adj* vovelig, usikker; (om strejke) vild.
wilderness ['wildənis] *s* vildmark; vildnis.
wildfire ['waildfaiə*] *s: spread like ~* spredes som en løbeild.
wild-goose chase ['waildgu:s tʃeis] *s (fig)* forgæves forsøg.
wildlife ['waildlaif] *s* naturens verden; dyreliv.
wilds [waildz] *spl* ødemarker.
wiles [wailz] *spl* list, rænker, intrige.
wilful ['wilful] *adj* (om person) egenrådig; (om forbrydelse) overlagt, forsætlig.
will [wil] *s* vilje; testamente; *at ~* efter behag; hvis man vil; *work with a ~* arbejde med liv og lyst; *make a ~* skrive testamente // *v (præt: would* [wud]) vil; skal; (ofte ikke oversat); *(~ed, ~ed)* ville; tvinge til; *I ~ do it soon* jeg skal nok gøre det snart; *he ~ come* han kommer; *I ~ show you how* jeg skal (nok) vise dig hvordan; *he ~ed himself to go on* han tvang sig til at fortsætte; *he ~ watch football on the bedroom tv* han vil altid se fodbold i fjernsynet i soveværelset; *~ sby to do sth* få en til at gøre ngt; *men ~ be men* mænd er mænd.
willies se *willy.*
willing ['wiliŋ] *adj* villig; parat; *be ~ to* være villig til at; **~ly** *adv* gerne, med glæde; **~ness** *s* villighed.
willow ['wiləu] *s* pil(etræ).
willowy ['wiləui] *adj* slank, tynd.
willpower ['wilpauə*] *s* viljestyrke.
willy ['wili] *s* (F) tissemand; *he gives me the willies* han giver mig myrekryb; **~-nilly** *adj* hvad enten man vil el. ej.
wilt [wilt] *v* tørre hen, visne.
wily ['waili] *adj* snu, listig.
wimp [wimp] *s* skvat, tøsedreng.
win [win] *s* (i sport etc) sejr // *v (won, won* [wʌn]) vinde, sejre; nå; *~ sby over (,round)* få en over på sin side.
wince [wins] *v* krympe sig; *without wincing* uden at fortrække en mine.
winch [wintʃ] *s* håndsving, spil.
wind [wind] *s* vind; luftstrøm; fjert, prut; *get ~ of sth* få færten af ngt; *get the ~ up* blive bange; *get one's ~ back* få vejret; *the ~s (mus)* blæserne.
wind [waind] *v (wound, wound* [waund]) sno (sig); vikle; spole; (om ur) trække op; *~ back (,forward)* spole tilbage (,frem); *~ down* (om vindue) rulle ned; *(fig)* slappe af, koble af; *~ up* afslutte, afvikle.
wind... ['wind-] sms: **~bag** *s* (F) blærerøv; **~break** [-breik] *s* læhegn; **~cheater** *s* vindjakke; **~cone** *s* vindpose.
winded ['windid] *adj* forpustet.
windfall ['windfɔ:l] *s* nedfaldsfrugt; uventet held.
winding ['waindiŋ] *adj* snoet, bugtet; ~ **staircase** *s* vindeltrappe.
wind... ['wind-] sms: ~ **instrument** *s* blæseinstrument; **~lass** *s* (hejse)-spil; **~less** *adj* vindstille; **~mill** *s* vindmølle.
window ['windəu] *s* vindue; rude; ~ **box** *s* blomsterkasse; ~ **cleaner** *s* vinduespudser; **~-dresser** *s* (vindues)dekoratør; ~ **envelope** *s* rudekuvert; ~ **pane** *s* vinduesrude; ~ **seat** *s* vinduesplads; **~-shopping** *s: go ~-shopping* se på vinduer; **~sill** *s* vindueskarm.
wind... ['wind-] sms: **~pipe** *s (anat)* luftrør; **~screen** *s* vindskærm; *(auto)* forrude; *rear ~screen* bagrude; **~screen washer** *s (auto)* sprinkler; **~screen wiper** *s (auto)* vinduesvisker; **~swept** *adj* vindblæst; forblæst.
windy ['windi] *adj* (om vejret) blæsende; (om sted) forblæst.

wine [wain] *s* vin; vinrødt; ~ **cellar** *s* vinkælder; ~ **list** *s* vinkort; ~ **merchant** *s* vinhandler; ~ **tasting** *s* vinsmagning; ~ **waiter** *s* kyper.

wing [wiŋ] *s* vinge; (på hus) fløj; *on the* ~ i flugten; på farten; (se også *wings);* ~ **mirror** *s (auto)* sidespejl; ~ **nut** *s* vingemøtrik.

wings ['wiŋz] *spl* (også) kulisser.

wink [wiŋk] *s* blink(en); øjeblik; lur; *he did not sleep a* ~ han lukkede ikke et øje; *have forty* ~*s* få sig en lille lur (,en på øjet) // *v* blinke *(at* til).

winkle [wiŋkl] *v:* ~ *sby out* få en lempet ud; ~ *it out of him* lirke det ud af ham.

winner ['winə*] *s* vinder.

winning ['winiŋ] *adj* sejrende, vinder-; vindende; **~s** *spl* gevinst.

winter ['wintə*] *s* vinter; *in* ~ om vinteren // *v* overvintre; ~ **sports** *spl* vintersport.

wintry ['wintri] *adj* vinteragtig, kold.

wipe [waip] *s* aftørring // *v* tørre (af); ~ *the floor with sby* (F) jorde en; ~ *off* tørre væk; slette; ~ *out* slette; viske ud; udrydde; slå en streg over; ~ *up* tørre op.

wiper ['waipə*] *s* vinduesvisker.

wire [waiə*] *s* ståltråd; ledning; (F) telegram; *barbed* ~ pigtråd; *pull* ~*s (fig)* trække i trådene // *v* sætte ståltrådshegn om; trække ledninger i; (F) telegrafere; ~ **brush** *s* stålbørste; ~ **cutters** *s* bidetang.

wireless ['waiəlis] *s* trådløs telegrafi; radio(apparat).

wiretap ['waiətæp] *v* lave telefonaflytning.

wirewool ['waiəwu:l] *s* stålsvamp.

wiry ['waiəri] *adj* stiv, strittende; (om person) sej, senet.

wisdom ['wizdəm] *s* visdom, klogskab.

wise [waiz] *adj* klog; forstandig; vis; *get* ~ *to sth* få ngt at vide; *we're none the* ~*r* det blev vi ikke klogere af; *let's put him* ~ *to our plans* lad os indvi ham i vores planer.

-wise [-waiz] på ... vis; -mæssigt; *time*~ tidsmæssigt.

wisecrack ['waizkræk] *s* kvik bemærkning.

wish [wiʃ] *s* ønske; hilsen; *best* ~*es* (til jul etc) de bedste ønsker; *with best* ~*es* (i brev) med venlig hilsen; *give her my best* ~*es* hils hende fra mig; *make a* ~ ønske sig ngt // *v* ønske; ~ *sby goodbye* sige farvel til en; *he* ~*ed me well* han ønskede mig held og lykke; ~ *for* ønske sig; ~ *to (,that)* ønske at; gerne ville (have at); **~ful** *adj: it's* ~*ful thinking* det er ønsketænkning.

wishy-washy ['wiʃiwɔʃi] *adj* tynd; vandet; farveløs; slap.

wisp [wisp] *s* tjavs, tot; (om røg) stribe; *a* ~ *of hair* en hårtot.

wistful ['wistful] *adj* længselsfuld; tankefuld.

wit [wit] *s* forstand, intelligens; kvikhed, vid; *keep your* ~*s about you* hold hovedet koldt; *be at one's* ~*'s end* ikke ane sine levende råd; *scared out of one's* ~*s* skræmt fra vid og sans.

witch [witʃ] *s* heks; **~craft** *s* hekseri; **~hunt** *s* heksejagt.

with [wið, wiθ] *præp* med; af; trods; til; *bring the book* ~ *you* tag bogen med; *tremble* ~ *fear* ryste af skræk; ~ *all his kindness, he's (still) a dangerous man* trods al hans venlighed er han er farlig mand; *he took beer* ~ *his lunch* han drak øl til frokosten; *be* ~ *it (fig)* være med på noderne; *I'm* ~ *you there* det holder jeg med dig i.

withdraw [wið'drɔ:] *v (-drew, -drawn)* trække tilbage; inddrage; tage tilbage; ophæve; gå 'af.

withdrawal [wið'drɔ:əl] *s* tilbagetrækning; *(med)* abstinens.

wither ['wiðə*] *v* visne.

withered ['wiðəd] *adj* vissen; lammet.

withering ['wiðəriŋ] *adj* (om blik etc) dræbende, tilintetgørende.

withhold [wiθ'həuld] *v (-held, -held)* tilbageholde; nægte at give; ~ *sby from sth* hindre en i ngt; ~ *sth from sby* unddrage en ngt.

within [wið'in] *adv* indvendig; indenfor // *præp* inden for; inden i; in-

den; fra; ~ *sight* inden for synsvidde; ~ *a mile of* mindre end en *mile* fra; ~ *the week* inden ugens udgang; ~ *doors* inden døre.
without [wið'aut] *præp* uden (at); udenfor; *from* ~ udefra.
withstand [wið'stænd] *v (-stood, -stood)* modstå.
witness ['witnis] *s* vidne(udsagn); *be* ~ *to* overvære, være vidne til; *bear* ~ *to* bevidne; vidne om; *give* ~ vidne // *v* være vidne til, overvære; bevidne; ~ **box** *s* vidneskranke.
witticism ['witisizm] *s* vits, vittighed.
witty ['witi] *adj* vittig; åndrig.
wives [waivz] *spl* af *wife.*
wizard ['wizəd] *s* troldmand; *she's a* ~ *a maths* hun er en ørn til matematik.
wizardry ['wizədri] *s* trylleri.
wizened ['wizənd] *adj* indskrumpet.
wk fork.f. *week.*
wobble [wɔbl] *v* rokke; vakle.
wodge [wɔdʒ] *s* (F) bunke, bjerg.
woe [wəu] *s* sorg; smerte, kval; **~ful** *adj* sørgmodig; ynkelig.
woke [wəuk] *præt* af *wake;* **~n** *pp* af *wake.*
wolf [wulf] *s (pl: wolves* [wulvz]) ulv // *v* æde.
woman ['wumən] *s (pl: women* ['wimin]) kvinde; dame; kone; ~ **chaser** *s* skørtejæger; ~ **doctor** *s* kvindelig læge.
womanizer ['wumənaiz] *v* dyrke damer; **~r** *s* skørtejæger.
womanly ['wumənli] *adv* kvindelig.
woman-power ['wumənpauə*] *s* kvindelig arbejdskraft.
womb [wu:m] *s* livmor.
women ['wimin] *spl* af *woman; the* **~'s movement** *s* kvindebevægelsen; **~'s refuge** *s* kvindehus, krisecenter for kvinder.
won [wʌn] *præt* og *pp* af *win.*
wonder ['wʌndə*] *s* mirakel; (vid)under; undren; *work* ~*s* gøre underværker; *it's no* ~ *that...* det er ikke så mærkeligt at...; *do* ~*s* udføre mirakler; *a visit from him would work* ~*s* et besøg af ham ville være en mirakelkur // *v* undre sig; spekulere over; *I* ~ *whether (,if)* jeg gad vide om; ~ *at* undre sig over; **~ful** *adj* vidunderlig, dejlig.
wonky ['wɔŋki] *adj* vaklevorn; i uorden.
wont [wəunt] *adj: as is his* ~ som han plejer van; *be* ~ *to do sth* være vant til at gøre ngt.
won't [wəunt] d.s.s. *will not.*
woo [wu:] *v* gøre kur til; fri til.
wood [wud] *s* skov; (om materialet) træ; *touch* ~ banke under brodet; *the* ~*s (mus)* træblæserne; ~ **carving** *s* træskærerarbejde; **~cut** *s* træsnit.
wooded ['wudid] *adj* skovklædt.
wooden ['wudn] *adj* træ-; *(fig)* stiv.
wood... ['wud-] sms: **~land** *s* skov(område); **~pecker** *s (zo)* spætte; **~pulp** *s* træmasse; **~shed** *s* brændeskur; **~wind** [-wind] *s (mus)* træblæser; **~work** *s* trævarer; træværk; sløjd; **~worm** *s* træorm.
woody ['wudi] *adj* skovklædt; træagtig.
wool [wu:l] *s* uld; uldent tøj; uldgarn; *pull the* ~ *over sby's eyes (fig)* føre en bag lyset.
woollen ['wulən] *adj* ulden, uld-; **~s** *spl* uldvarer.
woolly ['wuli] *adj* ulden; uld-; uldhåret; *(fig)* blød og lækker; uklar, tåget.
word [wə:d] *s* ord; løfte; besked; *in other* ~*s* med andre ord; *break one's* ~ bryde sit løfte; *have a few* ~*s with sby* veksle et par ord med en, sludre lidt med en; *have* ~*s with sby* skælde en ud; skændes med en; *keep one's* ~ holde ord, holde sit løfte; *be as good as one's* ~ holde ord; *by* ~ *of mouth* mundtligt; *I'll take your* ~ *for it* jeg tror dig på ordet; *too stupid for* ~*s* ubeskriveligt dum; *send* ~ *that...* sende besked om at...; *it's the last* ~ *in stockings* det er sidste skrig i strømper; *my* ~*!* du godeste! **~ing** *s* ordlyd; ordvalg; ~ **processor** [-'prəusɛsə*] *s* tekstbehandlingsanlæg.
wordy ['wə:di] *adj* ordrig.
wore [wɔ:*] *præt* af *wear.*
work [wə:k] *s* arbejde, værk; *it's all in*

the day's ~ det må man tage med; *make short* ~ *of sth* gå let hen over ngt, ordne ngt i en ruf; *have one's* ~ *cut out to...* have nok at gøre med at...; *out of* ~ arbejdsløs; *get (,set) to* ~ gå i gang (med arbejdet); *a nasty piece of* ~ en led karl; *Minister of Works* minister for offentlige arbejder; (se også *works*) // *v* arbejde; fungere; virke; drive; bearbejde; udnytte; (op)dyrke; ~ *wonders* udrette mirakler, gøre underværker; ~ *loose* arbejde sig (,gå) løs; ~ *on sth* arbejde med ngt; udnytte ngt; ~ *out* udarbejde; løse; ordne; lave (hård) motionstræning; *it* ~*s out at £100* det beløber sig til £100; *get* ~*ed up* blive ophidset; **~able** *adj* gennemførlig.

workaholic [wə:kə'hɔlik] *s* arbejdsliderlig person.

work basket ['wə:k,ba:skit] *s* sykurv.

workbench ['wə:kbɛntʃ] *s* høvlebænk; arbejdsbord.

worker ['wə:kə*] *s* arbejder.

workforce ['wə:kfɔ:s] *s* arbejdsstyrke.

working ['wə:kiŋ] *adj* arbejdende; arbejds-; drifts-; *have a* ~ *knowledge of French* nogenlunde kunne begå sig på fransk; *in* ~ *order* funktionsdygtig; ~ **class** *s* arbejderklasse; ~ **environment** *s* arbejdsmiljø; ~ **man** *s* arbejder; ~ **party** *s* arbejdsudvalg.

workload ['wə:kləud] *s* arbejdsbyrde.

workman ['wə:kmən] *s* arbejder; **~ship** *s* håndværksmæssig dygtighed; kvalitet.

works [wə:ks] *s* fabrik, værk; *an iron*~ et jernværk; *get the* ~ gå hele møllen igennem; blive forkælet efter alle kunstens regler.

workshop ['wə:kʃɔp] *s* værksted; seminar.

worktop ['wə:ktɔp] *s* køkkenbord.

work-to-rule ['wə:ktə'ru:l] *s* arbejde efter reglerne-aktion.

world [wə:ld] *s* verden; folk; *all over the* ~ i hele verden; *go up in the* ~ blive til ngt; *think the* ~ *of* have meget høje tanker om; *out of this* ~ skøn, pragtfuld; *feel on top of the* ~ være ovenpå; have det strålende; *for all the* ~ *like* nøjagtig ligesom; *it will do him a* ~ *of good* han vil have mægtig godt af det; **~ly** *adj* verdslig, jordisk; **~-wide** *adj* verdensomspændende; verdens-.

worm [wə:m] *s* orm // *v:* ~ *sth out of sby* liste ngt ud af en; **~-eaten** *adj* ormædt.

worn [wɔ:n] *pp* af *wear* // *adj* slidt; ~ *out* udmattet; slidt op.

worried ['wʌrid] *adj* bekymret; plaget.

worry ['wʌri] *s* bekymring; ærgrelse // *v* bekymre sig; være urolig; plage; *don't* ~*!* lad være med at tage dig af det! tag det roligt! ~ *oneself sick over sth* være meget bekymret over ngt.

worse [wə:s] *s* det der er værre; *a change for the* ~ en forandring til det værre // *adj (komp* af *bad, ill)* værre, dårligere; *be the* ~ *for drink* være beruset; *be the* ~ *for wear* være slidt (,medtaget); *be none the* ~ *for* ikke have taget skade af; **worsen** *v* blive (,gøre) værre.

worship ['wə:ʃip] *s* dyrkelse; gudstjeneste; *your Worship* (titel for borgmester el. dommer) // *v* tilbede, dyrke; **~per** *s* tilbeder, dyrker.

worst [wə:st] *s: the* ~ det værste; *if the* ~ *comes to the* ~ i værste fald // *adj (sup* af *bad, ill)* værst, dårligst; ~ *of all* allerværst; *at* ~ i værste fald; *get the* ~ *of it* trække det korteste strå.

worsted ['wustid] *s* kamgarn.

worth [wə:θ] *s* værdi; *50p* ~ *of apples* for 50p æbler // *adj* værd; *he has brought the printout for all it's* ~ han har taget printudkørslen med, så må vi se om vi kan bruge den; *it's* ~ *it* det er det værd; **~less** *adj* værdiløs; uduelig.

worthwhile [wə:θ'wail] *adj* som er umagen værd; *a* ~ *book* en læseværdig bog.

worthy ['wə:ði] *adj* værdig; agtværdig; *be* ~ *of sth* fortjene ngt.

would [wud] *præt* af *will; he* ~ *have come* han ville være kommet; ~ *you like some tea?* vil du have lidt te? **~-be** *adj* vordende; såkaldt.

wouldn't [wudnt] d.s.s. *would not.*
wound [wu:nd] *s* sår // *v* såre; krænke.
wound [waund] *præt* og *pp* af *wind.*
wove [wəuv] *præt* af *weave;* **~n** *pp* af *weave.*
WPC *s* (fork.f. *woman police constable)* kvindelig politibetjent.
wrangle [ræŋgl] *s* skænderi // *v* skændes.
wrap [ræp] *s* sjal; kåbe; indpakning // *v* (også: ~ *up)* pakke ind; svøbe (ind); ~ *up a deal* (F) få en aftale på plads; **~-around, ~-over** *adj* (om nederdel etc) slå om-.
wrapper ['ræpə*] *s* indpakning; (om bog) (smuds)omslag.
wrapping paper ['ræpiŋ ,peipə*] *s* indpakningspapir.
wrath [rɔθ] *s* (H) vrede, rasen.
wreak [ri:k] *v* anrette; øve; stifte; ~ *havoc* anrette ødelæggelser, hærge; ~ *chaos* skabe kaos.
wreath [ri:ð] *s* krans; snoning.
wreathe [ri:ð] *v* kranse; sno sig.
wreck [rɛk] *s* vrag // *v* ødelægge; få til at forlise (,forulykke).
wreckage ['rɛkidʒ] *s* ødelæggelse; vragrester; murbrokker.
wren [rɛn] *s (zo)* gærdesmutte.
wrench [rɛntʃ] *s* ryk; vridning; smerte; skruenøgle, svensknøgle // *v* rykke; rive; vriste; forvride.
wrestle [rɛsl] *v* brydes, kæmpe; **wrestler** *s* bryder; **wrestling** *s* brydning.
wretch [rɛtʃ] *s* skrog, stakkel.
wretched ['rɛtʃid] *adj* elendig; ussel, sølle; (F) forbandet.
wrick [rik] *v* forvride.
wriggle [rigl] *s* vriden; vrikken // *v* vrikke (med); vride sig, sno sig.
wring [riŋ] *v (wrung, wrung* [rʌŋ]) vride; fordreje; ~ *his neck* dreje halsen om på ham; *it ~s my heart* det skærer mig i hjertet; **~ing** *adj: ~ing wet* drivvåd.
wrinkle [wiŋkl] *s* rynke; fold // *v* rynke; krølle; blive rynket.
wrist [rist] *s* håndled; **~ watch** *s* armbåndsur.
writ [rit] *s* skrivelse; *(jur)* stævning; *issue a ~ against sby* udtage stævning mod en.
write [rait] *v (wrote, written* [rəut, ritn]) skrive; ~ *down* skrive op (,ned); notere; ~ *off* afskrive; opgive; ~ *out* udfærdige; renskrive; ~ *up* skrive op; ajourføre; **~-off** *s* afskrivning; *the car is a ~-off* bilen er totalskadet.
writer ['raitə*] *s* forfatter, skribent.
writhe [raið] *v* vride sig.
writing ['raitiŋ] *s* skrift; skrivning; skriveri; *in ~* skriftligt; *put sth in ~* skrive ngt (ned); **~ desk** *s* skrivebord; **~ paper** *s* brevpapir.
written [ritn] *pp* af *write.*
wrong [rɔŋ] *s* uret; *be in the ~* have uret // *v* gøre uret; krænke // *adj* forkert // *adv* galt; *you are ~, you've got it ~* du tager fejl; *what's ~?* hvad er der i vejen? *it's all ~* det er helt forkert, *go ~* gå galt, mislykkes; komme i uorden; *don't get me ~!* misforstå mig ikke! **~-foot** *v* overrumple; **~ful** *adj* urigtig, uretfærdig; **~ side** *s* vrangside.
wrote [rəut] *præt* af *write.*
wrought [rɔ:t] *adj: ~ iron* smedejern; **~-up** *adj* afridset, frustreret.
wrung [rʌŋ] *præt* og *pp* af *wring.*
wry [rai] *adj* skæv; tør; besk.
wt. fork.f. *weight.*

X

X, x [ɛks].
Xerox ['ziərɔks] ® *s* fotokopi // *v* fotokopiere.
Xmas ['ɛksməs] *s* (fork.f. *Christmas)* jul.
X-ray ['ɛksrei] *s* røntgenstråle; røntgenbillede // *v* røntgenfotografere.

Y

Y, y [wai].
yacht [jɔt] *s* lystbåd; sejlbåd // *v* dyrke sejlsport; **~ing** *s* sejlsport; **~s·man** *s* sejlsportsmand; lystsejler.
yammer ['jæmə*] *v* jamre; hyle.
Yank [jæŋk] *s (neds)* yankee, amerikaner.

yank [jæŋk] *s* (F) ryk // *v* rykke, hive.
yap [jæp] *v* bjæffe, gø; (F) bralre op.
yard [ja:d] *s* gård, gårdsplads; (også: *ship~)* værft; yard (91,44 cm, *3 feet); the Yard* Scotland Yard; **~stick** *s (fig)* målestok.
yarn [ja:n] *s* garn, tråd; (F) (røver)historie.
yawn [jɔ:n] *s* gaben; *the film was a ~* (F) filmen var dødkedelig // *v* gabe; **~ing** *adj* gabende (også om afgrund etc).
yd fork.f. *yard(s).*
ye [ji:] *pron (gl)* I.
year [jiə*] *s* år; *~ by ~* år for år; *this ~* i år; *every ~* hvert år; *twice a ~* to gange om året; *for ~s* i årevis; *all the ~ round* året rundt; *it's going to take ~s* det kommer til at vare flere år; *that dress puts ~s on you* den kjole får dig til at se meget ældre ud; *young for one's ~s* ung af sin alder; **~-long** *adj* etårig; **~ly** *adj* årlig // *adv* en gang om året.
yearn [jə:n] *v: ~ for* længes efter; **~ing** *s* voldsom længsel.
year-round ['jiəraund] *adj* helårs-.
yeast [ji:st] *s* gær; *dry ~* tørgær; *brewer's ~* ølgær.
yell [jɛl] *s* hyl, skrål // *v* hyle.
yellow ['jɛləu] *adj* gul; (F) fej; *the ~ pages* sv.t. (telefon)fagbogen // *v* gulne; **~ish** *adj* gullig.
yelp [jɛlp] *s* bjæf; vræl // *v* bjæffe, hyle.
yes [jɛs] *s/interj* ja; jo; *~?* ja, og hvad så? virkelig? **~-man** *s* jasiger.
yesterday ['jɛstədi] *s* i går; *~ morning* i går morges (,formiddags); *the day before ~* i forgårs.
yet [jɛt] *adv* endnu; dog, alligevel; *as ~* endnu; *not ~* ikke endnu; *must you go just ~?* skal du allerede gå? *~ again* endnu en gang; *~ another* en til, endnu en; *the best ~* den hidtil bedste; *a few days ~* et par dage endnu; *and ~ we must go* og dog er vi nødt til at gå.
yew [ju:] *s (bot)* taks(træ).
Yiddish ['jidiʃ] *s/adj* jiddisch.
yield [ji:ld] *s* udbytte; ydelse // *v* give, yde; give efter *(to* for); overgive; **~ing** *adj* eftergivende.
YMCA ['waiɛmsi:'ei] *s* (fork.f. *Young Men's Christian Association)* KFUM.
yob [job] *s* (F) bølle; **yobbo** *s* d.s.s. *yob.*
yodel [jəudl] *v* jodle.
yog(h)urt ['jəugət] *s* yoghurt.
yoke [jəuk] *s* åg; (om okser) spand; (på kjole etc) bærestykke.
yokel ['jəukəl] *s* bondeknold.
yolk [jəuk] *s* æggeblomme.
yonder ['jɔndə*] *adv* derhenne; derovre.
yonks [jɔŋks] *spl: for ~, in ~* (S) i evigheder.
Yorkshire pudding ['jɔrkʃə 'pudiŋ] *s (gastr)* slags budding af pandekagedej (spises til oksesteg).
you [ju:] *pron* du; dig; De; Dem; I; jer; man; *~ never know* man kan aldrig vide; *you're a fool!* du er et fjols! *(and) so are ~!* det kan du selv være! det er du også!
you'd [ju:d] d.s.s. *you had; you would.*
young [jʌŋ] *s* (om dyr) unger; *the ~* de unge // *adj* ung; lille.
youngish ['jʌŋgiʃ] *adj* ret ung, yngre.
youngster ['jʌŋstə*] *s* ungt menneske.
your [jɔ:*] *pron* din, dit, dine; jeres; Deres.
you're [juə*] d.s.s. *you are.*
yours [jɔ:z] *pron* din, dit, dine; jeres; Deres; *is it ~?* er det din (,jeres, Deres)? *~ sincerely* din (,Deres) hengivne.
yourself [jɔ:'sɛlf] *pron (pl: yourselves* [-'sɛlvz]) du (,dig) selv; De (,Dem) selv; dig, Dem; selv; *did you do it ~?* gjorde du det selv?
youth [ju:θ] *s* ungdom; ung mand; **~ful** *adj* ungdommelig; **~ hostel** *s* ungdomsherberg; vandrerhjem.
you've [ju:v] d.s.s. *you have.*
yowl [jaul] *v* hyle.
Yugoslav ['ju:gəuˌsla:v] *s* jugoslav // *adj* jugoslavisk.
Yugoslavia [ju:gə'sla:viə] *s* Jugoslavien.
yuk [jʌk] *interj* bvadr!
yukky ['jʌki] *adj* (F) ækel, ulækker, klam.
yummy ['jʌmi] *adj* (F) lækker.

YWCA ['wai'dʌblju:si:'ei] *s* (fork.f. *Young Women's Christian Association)* KFUK.

Z

Z, z [zɛd].
zany ['zeini] *adj* skør, tosset.
zap [zæp] *v* (F) futte, fare, suse; *(spøg)* tage på kanalrundfart (i TV), zappe; ~ *sby* pløkke en; **~py** *adj* (F) smart, rap.
zeal [zi:l] *s* iver, nidkærhed.
Zealot ['zɛlət] *s* ivrig tilhænger, fanatiker.
zealous ['zɛləs] *adj* ivrig; begejstret; nidkær.
zebra ['zi:brə] *s* zebra; **~ crossing** *s* fodgængerovergang.
zero ['ziərəu] *s* nul; nulpunkt; *10 degrees below* ~ 10 graders frost // *v:* ~ *in on* sigte sig ind på; **~ growth** *s* nulvækst; **~ option** *s* nulløsning.
zest [zɛst] *s* veloplagthed; citronskal, appelsinskal; (F) fut, pif; ~ *for life* livslyst.
zigzag ['zigzæg] *s* siksak // *v* siksakke.
zinc [ziŋk] *s* zink.
zing [ziŋ] *s* (F) pift, pep.
zip [zip] *s* (også: ~ *fastener,* ~*per)* lynlås; (F) fart, go // *v* svirpe; suse; (også: ~ *up)* lyne; **~ code** *s* *(am)* postnummer; **~ped compartment** *s* lynlåsrum; **~per** *s* *(am)* lynlås.
zodiac ['zəudiæk] *s: the* ~ *(astr)* dyrekredsen.
zombie ['zɔmbi] *s* (F) sløv padde; robot.
zone [zəun] *s* område, zone.
zonked ['zɔŋkt] *adj* (F) dødtræt, helt flad; "skæv".
zoo [zu:] *s* zoo(logisk have).
zoological [zuə'lɔdʒikl] *adj* zoologisk.
zoologist [zu'ɔlədʒist] *s* zoolog.
zoology [zu'ɔlədʒi] *s* zoologi.
zoom [zu:m] *v* zoome; ~ *past* fare forbi; **~ lens** *s* zoomlinse.

DANISH–ENGLISH

A

à *præp: to æsker ~ 20 stk* two boxes of 20 each; *10 øller ~ 5 kr.* 10 beers at five kr. each; *det står ~ tre (fodb etc)* it is three all.

abdicere *v* abdicate.

abe *en* monkey; *(menneske~)* ape // *v: ~ efter* mimic, ape; **~gilde** *et* binge, rave-up; **~unge** *en* young monkey.

abnorm *adj* ab'normal.

abonnement *et* sub'scription; **~s·kort** *et* season ticket.

abonnent *en* sub'scriber.

abonnere *v* sub'scribe *(på* to).

aborre *en* perch.

abort *en (provokeret)* a'bortion; *(spontan)* mis'carriage; *få foretaget ~* have an a'bortion; **~ere** *v* have a mis'carriage.

abrikos *en* apricot.

absolut *adj* absolute; *skal du ~ se den film?* must you see that film? // *adv* absolutely; *(helt sikkert)* definitely; *~ ikke* definitely not; *skal du ~ besøge ham nu?* must you see him now? *hun ville ~ i biografen* she in'sisted on going to the cinema.

absorbere *v* ab'sorb; **~nde** *adj* ab'sorbent.

abstinenser *pl: have ~* have with'drawal symptoms.

abstrakt *adj* 'abstract.

absurd *adj* ab'surd.

acceleration *en* accele'ration.

accelerere *v* ac'celerate.

accent *en* 'accent; *tale med ~* speak· with an accent; *~ aigu* a'cute accent; *~ grave* grave accent.

acceptabel *adj* ac'ceptable.

acceptere *v* ac'cept.

a conto on ac'count.

ad *præp: hen ~ gaden* along the street; *gå ind ~ døren* come· in by (,through) the door; *op (,ned) ~ trappen* up (,down) the stairs; *le ~ en* laugh at sby; *spørge en ~* ask sby.

adel *en* no'bility; **adelig** *adj* noble.

adfærd *en* be'haviour; **~s·vanskelig** *adj* malad'justed.

adgang *en (tilladelse)* ad'mission; *(mulighed)* access; *~ forbudt* no ad'mittance; *gratis ~* ad'mission free; *få ~ til at gøre ngt* get· a chance (,oppor'tunity) to do sth; **~s·begrænsning** *en* re'stricted entry; **~s·eksamen** *en* entrance exami'nation; **~s·kort** *et* (entry) ticket; **~s·tilladelse** *en* per'mission to enter.

adjektiv *et (gram)* adjective.

adjunkt *en (i skolen)* schoolmaster; *(univ) sv.t.* lecturer.

adlyde *v* o'bey.

administration *en* administration.

administrere *v* manage; *~nde direktør* managing di'rector.

admiral *en* 'admiral.

adoptere *v* a'dopt.

adoption *en* a'doption.

adoptivbarn *et* a'dopted child.

addressat *en* addres'see.

adresse *en* ad'dress; *ubekendt efter ~n* un'known at this ad'dress; **~forandring** *en* change of address. **~kort** *et* dis'patch form.

addressere *v* ad'dress.

Adriaterhavet *s* the Adri'atic (Sea).

adræt *adj* agile; **~hed** *en* a'gility.

adskille *v* separate; *hvordan ~r en iraker sig fra en iraner?* how does an I'raqi differ from an I'ranian? **~lse** *en* sepa'ration.

adskillige *adj* various, several; *der var ~ der ikke kom* several people stayed away.

adskilligt *adv* a good deal, con'siderably.

adskilt *adj* separate; *leve ~* live a'part.

adsprede *v* a'muse; **~lse** *en* a'musement.

adspredt *adj* absent-minded.

adstadig *adj* se'date.

advare *v* warn *(mod* against); *~ en om at...* warn sby that...

advarsel *en* warning; *få en ~ (fodb)* get· booked; *slippe med en ~* be let off with a warning.

advarselstavle *en* warning sign.

advarselstrekant *en* warning triangle.

advent *en* Advent.

adventskrans *en* Advent wreath.
adverbium *et (gram)* 'adverb.
advokat *en* lawyer; **~fuldmægtig** *en sv.t.* trai'nee lawyer; **~praksis** *en* legal practice.
ae *v* stroke, ca'ress.
aerodynamisk *adj* aerody'namic.
aerogram *et* air letter.
af *præp (om materiale; del; dato)* of; *(om årsag)* of, with; *(ved passiv form)* by; *(væk fra)* off; *(om oprindelse, kilde; ud fra)* from; *(se også de enkelte ord som ~ forbindes med); lavet ~ jern* made of iron; *flere ~ dem* several of them; *dø ~ kræft* die of cancer; *bleg ~ skræk* pale with fear; *stiv ~ kulde* stiff with cold; *Deres brev ~ femte juni* your letter of June the fifth; *blive kørt over ~ en bil* be run over by a car; *et digt ~ Burns* a poem by Burns; *knappen er gået ~* the button has come off; *låne ngt ~ en* borrow sth from sby; *jeg ser ~ Deres brev at…* I see· from your letter that… // *adv (om ngt der fjernes)* off; *tage tøjet ~* take· off one's clothes; *~ og til* from time to time.
afbagning *en (gastr)* roux [ru:].
afbalancere *v* balance.
afbestille *v* cancel; **afbestilling** *en* cancel'lation.
afbetaling *en (rate)* in'stalment; *købe ngt på ~* buy· sth on hire purchase.
afbilde *v* picture.
afbleget *adj* bleached *(fx hår* hair); *(falmet)* faded.
afblæse *v (strejke etc)* call off.
afbryde *v* inter'rupt; *(standse helt)* stop; *(lukke for strøm etc)* switch off, turn off; *blive afbrudt (dvs. forstyrret)* be inter'rupted; *(tlf, elek)* be cut off.
afbrydelse *en* inter'ruption; stopping; stop; *(pause, ophold)* break; switching off, cutting off; *(standsning i strømforsyning etc)* cut-off; *uden ~ (dvs. uforstyrret)* uninter'rupted; *(dvs. uden pause)* non-stop.
afbryder *en (elek)* switch.
afbrænder *en: det var en ~* it was a slap in the face.
afbud *et: sende ~* send· one's a'pologies.
afbudsbillet *en* stand-by ticket.
afbøde *v: ~ et slag* ward off a blow.
afdeling *en (på sygehus, i firma, forretning)* de'partment; *(del)* part, section; *(mil)* unit; *det er ikke min ~* that's not my department.
afdelingschef *en* head of department.
afdelingssygeplejerske *en* (ward) sister.
afdrag *et* part-payment, in'stalment; *betale ngt i ~* pay· sth by instalments.
afdæmpet *adj (optræden)* re'strained; *(farve)* sub'dued.
afdød *adj* de'ceased; *min ~e mand* my late husband.
affald *et (skrald etc)* rubbish; *(køkken~)* garbage; *(som er smidt i naturen)* litter; *(kemisk ~, radioaktivt ~)* waste.
affalds... *sms:* **~depot** *et* waste dis'posal site; **~forbrænding** *en* incine'ration; *(anlæg)* in'cinerating plant; **~kurv** *en* litter bin; **~pose** *en* waste bag; *(til at sætte i stativ i køkkenet)* bin liner; **~skakt** *en* 'refuse chute; **~spand** *en* bin.
affarve *v (om hår etc)* bleach.
affekteret *adj* af'fected.
affinde *v: ~ sig med ngt* put· up with sth, come· to terms with sth.
affjedring *en (auto)* su'spension.
affolket *adj* de'populated.
affyre *v* fire; *(om missil)* launch.
affældig *adj* de'crepit; *(om person)* frail.
affærdige *v (problem etc)* brush a'side; *~ en* snub sby.
affære *en* business, af'fair; *tage ~* take· action; *(gribe ind)* inter'vene.
afføde *v* give· rise to.
afføring *en* bowel movement; *(ekskrementer)* stools *pl;* **~s·middel** *et* laxative.
afgang *en* de'parture; *(fra stilling)* resig'nation, re'tirement; *naturlig ~* natural wastage; **~s·bevis** *et* di'ploma; **~s·eksamen** *en (i skolen)* school leaving ex'am; **~s·hal** *en* de'parture hall; **~s·tid** *en* time of de'parture.

afghaner *en,* **afghansk** *adj* 'Afghan.
afgift *en* duty, tax; *(told)* customs duty; *(gebyr)* fee; *(i garderobe, toilet etc)* charge; *(vej~, bropenge)* toll; **~s·fri** *adj* duty-free.
afgive *v (afstå)* give· up; *(fremkomme med, fx rapport)* make·; *(udsende, fx lugt)* give· off; *~ bestilling på ngt* order sth; *~ sin stemme* vote; *~ vidneforklaring* give· evidence; **~lse** *en (afståelse)* sur'render; *(af rapport etc)* sub'mission; *(af ordre)* placing.
afgjort *adj (ordnet)* settled // *adv* definitely, de'cidedly.
afgrund *en* precipice; *(fig)* a'byss; *falde i ~en* fall· over the precipice; *på ~ens rand* on the edge of the precipice.
afgrænse *v (fig)* de'limit, de'fine; *marken er ~t af levende hegn* the field is bounded by hedgerows.
afgrøde *en* crop.
afgud *en* idol; **~s·dyrkelse** *en* i'dolatry.
afgøre *v (bestemme)* de'cide; *(fx en sag, strid)* settle; *(finde ud af)* make· out, tell·; *det er svært at ~* it is difficult to tell·.
afgørelse *en* de'cision; *(ordning)* settlement; *træffe en ~lse* make· (,come· to) a de'cision.
afgørende *adj* de'cisive; *(endelig)* final, con'clusive.
afgå *v (starte)* de'part, leave·; *~ ved døden* (H) pass away; **~ende** *adj (fx tog)* de'parting; **~et** *adj (fra stilling)* re'tired.
afhandling *en* treatise ['tri:tis]; *(disputats)* thesis, disser'tation.
afhente *v* fetch, col'lect; **afhentning** *en* col'lection.
afholde *v* hold·; *(fx koncert, selskab)* give·; *(betale)* pay·; *~ en fra at gøre ngt* pre'vent sby from doing sth; *regnen afholdt os fra at gå ud* the rain kept us from going out; *~ sig fra at gøre ngt* re'frain from doing sth; **~nde** *adj* ab'stemious.
afholdenhed *en* 'abstinence.
afholdsmand *en* tee'totaller.
afholdt *adj* popular.
afhopper *en (pol)* de'fector.
afhænge *v: ~ af* de'pend on; *det ~r af om han kommer* it de'pends on whether he's coming.
afhængig *adj* de'pendent *(af* on); **~hed** *en* de'pendence *(af* on).
afhøre *v (mistænkt)* question; **afhøring** *en* interro'gation.
afise *v* de'frost.
afkald *et: give ~ på ngt (dvs. opgive)* give· sth up; *(fx arv, trone)* re'nounce sth.
afkalke *v* de'calcify.
afklare *v* clarify; *(spørgsmål)* settle.
afklaring *en* clarifi'cation; *(af spørgsmål)* settlement.
afkom *et* offspring.
afkrog *en (om del af landet)* backwater.
afkræfte *v (gøre svag)* weaken; *(mods: bekræfte)* de'ny.
afkræftet *adj* weakened.
afkræve *v: ~ en ngt* de'mand sth from sby; *~ gebyr* charge a fee.
afkøle *v* cool, chill; *serveres ~t* serve chilled.
aflagt *adj: ~ tøj* cast-offs *pl.*
aflang *adj* oblong.
aflaste *v* re'lieve *(for* of).
aflastning *en* re'lief.
aflede *v (lede væk)* de'flect; *(adsprede)* dis'tract; *(om afstamning)* de'rive *(af* from); *~ ens opmærksomhed* dis'tract sby's attention.
afledning *en* de'flection; *(adspredelse)* di'version; *(af ens opmærksomhed)* dis'traction; *(af ord)* deri'vation; *(afledt ord)* de'rivative.
aflejre *v* de'posit; *~s* settle.
aflejring *en (lag)* de'posit; *(bundfald)* sediment.
aflevere *v* de'liver; *(opgive, give fra sig)* hand over, give· up; *(levere tilbage, fx lånt bog)* re'turn; *(fodb)* pass.
aflevering *en* de'livery; *(fodb)* pass.
aflive *v* kill; *(om dyr)* put· down.
aflivning *en* killing; *sende katten til ~* have the cat put down.
aflukke *et* cubicle; **~t** *adj* closed; *(aflåst)* locked.
aflyse *v* cancel, call off.

aflysning *en* cancel'lation.
aflyst *adj* cancelled, off.
aflytning *en (med skjult mikrofon)* bugging; *(tlf)* tapping; **aflytte** *v* bug; tap.
aflægge *v (fx ed, løfte)* make·; *(opgive fx vane)* drop; ~ *besøg hos en* call on sby; ~ *prøve* take· a test.
aflægger *en (bot)* cutting.
aflæse *v* read·.
aflæsse *v* un'load.
afløb *et* outlet; *(~s·rør)* drain; *få ~ (fig)* let· off steam; *få ~ for ngt* give· vent to sth; *hælde ngt ud i ~et* pour sth down the drain; **~s·rør** *et* drain, wastepipe; **~s·slange** *en* drain hose.
aflønne *v* pay·.
aflønning *en* pay, salary.
afløse *v (fx vagt)* re'lieve; *(erstatte)* re'place; *(følge efter)* suc'ceed; **~r** *en* re'lief; *(efterfølger)* suc'cessor.
afløsning *en (fx af vagt)* re'lief; *(erstatning)* re'placement; *(overtagelse)* suc'cession.
aflåst *adj* locked.
afmagring *en (ufrivillig)* loss of weight; *(med vilje)* slimming; **~s·kur** *en* slimming diet.
afmatning *en (økon)* re'cession.
afmærke *v* mark; *(med sedler, etiketter etc)* label.
afpasse *v* a'dapt *(efter* to); *(efter tiden)* time.
afpresning *en* blackmail.
afpresse *v: ~ en penge* blackmail sby.
afprøve *v* test, try (out).
afprøvning *en* test, trial.
afrakket *adj* shabby.
afreagere *v* let· off steam; ~ *på en* act it out on sby.
afregne *v: ~ med en* settle with sby.
afregning *en* settlement; *(skriftlig)* statement.
afrejse *en* de'parture.
Afrika *s* Africa; **afrikaner** *en,* **afrikansk** *adj* African.
afrime *v* de'frost.
afrive *v* tear· off.
afrivningskalender *en* tear-off calendar.
afruste *v* dis'arm.
afrustning *en* dis'armament.
afsats *en (på trappe)* landing; *(klippe~)* ledge.
afsavn *et: lide ~* suffer pri'vations.
afse *v* spare.
afsende *v* send· off, dis'patch; *(med posten)* post.
afsendelse *en* sending, dis'patch; posting.
afsender *en* sender; **~adresse** *en* re'turn ad'dress.
afsides *adj* out-of-the-way; *(fjern)* re'mote; *bo ~* live in a re'mote place; *gå ~ (dvs. på toilettet) (om kvinde)* go· and powder one's nose; *(om mand)* go· to the gents.
afsige *v: ~ en dom* pro'nounce a sentence; ~ *et abonnement* cancel a sub'scription.
afsindig *adj* mad, crazy // *adv* madly, terribly.
afskaffe *v* a'bolish.
afskaffelse *en* abo'lition.
afsked *en (fyring)* dis'missal; *(fratræden)* resig'nation; *(p.g.a. alder)* re'tirement; *(det at skilles)* parting; *(farvel)* leave; *tage ~ med en* take· leave of sby; *tage sin ~* re'sign; re'tire.
afskedige *v* dis'miss, sack.
afskedsansøgning *en* resig'nation.
afskedsfest *en* farewell party.
afskrift *en* copy.
afskrække *v* de'ter; **~nde** *adj* de'terrent; *(som fratager en lysten)* for'bidding, off-putting.
afsky *en* dis'gust, re'vulsion // *v* de'test, loathe.
afskyde *v* fire; *(om missil)* launch.
afskyelig *adj* dis'gusting.
afskære *v* cut· off; ~ *en fra at gøre ngt* pre'vent sby from doing sth.
afskåret *adj* cut off; *(om brød, pålæg)* sliced; *være ~ fra at gøre ngt* be un'able to do sth; ~ *fra omverdenen* cut off from the outside world; *afskårne blomster* cut flowers.
afslag *et* re'fusal; *(i pris)* 'discount; *få ~* be re'fused; *få ~ i prisen* get· a 'discount.
afslappet *adj* re'laxed; *(om påklædning)* casual.
afslutning *en* end, finish; *(måde hvor-*

på ngt ender, det at nå til ende) ending; *(skole~)* end-of-term (cele'bration).
afslutte *v* end; *(gøre helt færdig)* finish; *(gøre ende på)* terminate; **~nde** *adj* final, finishing.
afsløre *v (statue etc)* un'veil; *(røbe etc)* dis'close; *(åbenbare)* re'veal; *blive ~t* be found out; **~nde** *adj* re'vealing.
afsløring *en (af statue etc)* un'veiling; *(af hemmelighed etc)* dis'closure; *(åbenbaring)* reve'lation.
afslå *v* re'fuse, de'cline.
afsmag *en (grim smag, smag af ngt)* aftertaste; *(væmmelse)* dis'taste *(for* for).
afsnit *et* section; *(om tid)* period; *(af tekst)* passage; *(på side)* paragraph; *(af tv-serie)* episode.
afsondret *adj* isolated.
afsondring *en* iso'lation; *(udskillelse)* se'cretion.
afsone *v: ~ en straf* serve a sentence.
afsoning *en* im'prisonment; *~ af straf* serving of a sentence.
afspadsere *v* counter'balance overtime.
afspejle *v* re'flect.
afspille *v* play.
afspore *v* de'rail.
afsporing *en* de'railment.
afspænding *en (afslapning)* relax'ation; *(pol)* detente ['dei,ta:nt].
afspærre *v* close off, block; *(vejafsnit etc med afspærringscylindre)* cone off.
afspærring *en (fx brædder)* barrier; *(politi~)* cordon.
afstamning *en* de'scent, origin.
afstand *en* distance; *holde ~ (fx om biler)* keep· one's distance; *i en ~ af fem km* at a distance of five km; *på ~* at a distance; *det kan ses på lang ~* you can tell it a mile off; *tage ~ fra ngt* dis'sociate oneself from sth; **~s·måler** *en (foto, mil)* rangefinder; **~tagen** *en* dissoci'ation.
afsted *adv se sted.*
afstemning *en (valg)* voting, vote; *(hemmelig)* ballot; *(afpasning)* tuning, matching.
afstikker *en (lille tur)* trip; *(omvej)* detour.
afstraffe *v* punish; **~lse** *en* punishment.
afstøbning *en (det at støbe)* casting; *(det afstøbte)* cast.
afstå *v (opgive, afhænde)* give· up; *~ fra at kommentere ngt* ab'stain from com'menting on sth.
afsyre *v* acid-wash, strip; *~t eg* stripped oak.
afsyring *en* acid washing, stripping.
afsæt *et (før spring)* take-off.
afsætning *en (salg)* sale.
afsætte *v (sælge)* sell·; *(afskedige)* dis'miss; *(fx konge)* de'pose; *(sætte til side, reservere)* set· a'side.
afsættelse *en (fyring)* dis'missal; *(af konge etc)* depo'sition.
aftage *v (købe)* buy·; *(fjerne)* re'move; *(mindskes)* de'crease; *(om fx sygdom, blæst etc)* ease off; **~lig** *adj* de'tachable.
aftager *en* buyer.
aftale *en* ar'rangement; *(overenskomst)* a'greement, deal; *(møde~)* ap'pointment; *efter ~* as ar'ranged; *det er en ~!* that's a deal! *træffe ~ om at gøre ngt* a'gree to do sth // *v* ar'range; a'gree (on).
aftappe *v* bottle.
aften *en* evening, night; *god ~!* good evening! *i ~* to'night; *i (går) aftes* last night, yesterday evening; *i morgen ~* to'morrow night (,evening); *om ~en* in the evening, at night; *spise til ~* have supper; *hvad skal vi have til ~?* what are we having for supper? **~bøn** *en: bede ~bøn* say· one's evening prayers; **~kjole** *en* evening dress; **~kursus** *et,* **~skole** *en* evening classes *pl.*
aftensmad *en* supper.
aftjene *v: ~ sin værnepligt* do· one's military service.
aftrapning *en* de-escalation.
aftryk *et* im'pression; *(trykt)* reprint; *(foto)* print.
aftrækker *en* trigger.
afvande *v* drain.
afvanding *en* drainage.
afvej *s: komme på ~e* go· a'stray; **~e** *v* weigh.

afvejning *en* weighing.
afvekslende *adj* varied.
afveksling *en* va'riety; *til en ~* for a change.
afvente *v* a'wait, wait for; **~nde** *adj: forholde sig ~nde* wait and see.
afvige *v* deviate *(fra* from); *(være forskellig)* be different from; **~lse** *en* devi'ation; **~nde** *adj* different.
afviger *en* deviant; *(systemkritiker etc)* dissident.
afvikle *v (gennemføre)* con'clude; *(lukke fx firma)* wind· [waind] up; *(fx atomkraft)* phase out; *verdensmesterskaberne ~s i Italien* the World Championships are taking place in Italy.
afvikling *en* con'clusion; *(lukning)* winding ['waindiŋ] up.
afvise *v* turn down, re'fuse; *(forkaste)* re'ject; **~nde** *adj* negative.
afviserblink *en* flashing indicator.
afviserskilt *et* signpost.
afvisning *en* re'fusal, re'jection.
afvæbnende *adj* dis'arming.
afvænne *v: ~ en fra alkohol* cure sby of drinking.
afvænning *en (fra alkohol, stoffer etc)* treatment.
afværge *v* pre'vent.
agent *en* agent; **~film** *en* spy film.
agentur *et* agency.
agerbrug *et* agriculture.
agere *v* act, play.
agerhøne *en* partridge.
agern *et* acorn.
agression *en* ag'gression; **aggressiv** *adj* ag'gressive.
agitere *v: ~ for ngt* make· propa'ganda for sth, pro'mote sth, boost sth.
agt *en (hensigt)* in'tention, purpose; *give ~* look out; *'giv agt - højspænding!'* 'danger - high voltage!' *tage sig i ~* take· care, look out; *tage sig i ~ for ngt* be'ware of sth.
agte *v (respektere)* re'spect; *(have planer om)* in'tend *(at* to).
agtelse *en* re'spect, e'steem; *han steg i min ~* he rose in my esteem.
agter *adv (mar)* a'stern; **~ende, ~stavn** *en* stern; **~ud** *adv: sakke ~ud* fall· be'hind.
agtpågivende *adj* at'tentive; **agtpågivenhed** *en* at'tention.
agurk *en* cucumber; **~e·tid** *en (fig)* silly season.
ahorn *en (bot)* maple.
ajle *en* liquid ma'nure; **~beholder** *en* liquid-ma'nure tank.
ajour *adj: holde sig ~* keep· in'formed; *føre ngt ~* bring· sth up to date; **~føre** *v* update.
akademi *et* a'cademy; **~ker** *en* aca'demic.
akademisk *adj* aca'demic; *~ grad* uni'versity de'gree.
akavet *adj* awkward.
akillessene *en* A'chilles' tendon.
akklimatisere *v: ~ sig* become· ac'clima'tized.
akkompagnement *et* ac'companiment.
akkompagnere *v* ac'company.
akkord *en (mus)* chord; *arbejde på ~* do· piecework; *anslå en ~* strike· a chord; **~arbejde** *et* piecework; **~løn** *en* piece wages *pl.*
akkumulator *en* ac'cumulator.
akkumulere *v* ac'cumulate.
akkurat *adj (nøjagtig)* 'accurate // *adv (netop)* ex'actly, just.
akkuratesse *en* 'accuracy.
akrobat *en* 'acrobat.
akrobatik *en* acro'batics *pl.*
akryl *et* a'crylic.
aks *et (korn~)* ear; *(bot)* spike, shaft.
akse *en* axis.
aksel *en (i hjul)* axle; *(driv~)* shaft.
akt *en (handling; teat)* act; *(papir)* document; *sagens ~er* the dossier, the file.
aktie *en* share; **~børs** *en* stock ex'change; **~kapital** *en* share capital; **~majoritet** *en* ma'jority interest; **~post** *en* holding; **~selskab** *et (privat)* limited (lia'bility) company, Ltd.; *(offentligt)* public limited company, plc; *A/S Olsen og Jensen* Olsen and Jensen, Ltd.; **~udbytte** *et* 'dividend.
aktion *en* action; *gå i ~* take· action.
aktionær *en* shareholder.
aktiv *et (merk, fig)* asset // *adj* active.
aktivere, aktivisere *v* 'activate.

aktivist *en* 'activist.
aktivitet *en* ac'tivity.
aktualitet *en* relevance.
aktuar *en* actuary.
aktuel *adj* relevant; *(om emne, spørgsmål også)* topical; *(nuværende)* current; *hvis det skulle blive ~t* if the question should arise; *det bliver ikke ~t* it won't come up.
akupunktur *en* acupuncture.
akustik *en* a'coustics pl.
akut *adj* a'cute; *~ indlæggelse* e'mergency ad'mission.
akvarel *en* watercolour.
akvarium *et* a'quarium, fish tank.
al *adj* all; *(se også alle, alt).*
alarm *en* a'larm; *slå ~* sound the alarm; *for min skyld ingen ~* it is all right as far as I am con'cerned; **~beredskab** *et: i ~beredskab* on the a'lert.
alarmere *v* call; **~nde** *adj* a'larming.
alarmering *en* a'larm (call).
albaner *en* Al'banian; **Albanien** *s* Al'bania; **albansk** *adj* Al'banian.
albue *en* elbow; *have spidse ~er* have sharp elbows *(også fig) // v: ~ sig frem* use one's elbows; **~rum** *et* elbow-room.
aldeles *adv* com'pletely, quite; *~ ikke* not at all; *~ intet* nothing at all.
alder *en* age; *være stor af sin ~* be tall for one's age; *i en ~ af...* at the age of...; *i din ~* at your age; *være i sin bedste ~* be at the prime of one's life; *i en høj ~* at an ad'vanced age; *i en ung ~* at an early age; *hun er på hans ~* she is his age; *atomalderen* the a'tomic age.
alderdom *en* (old) age; **~s·hjem** *et* old people's home, rest home.
aldersforskel *en* difference in age.
aldersgrænse *en* age limit.
aldersklasse *en* age group.
aldrig *adv* never; *~ mere* never again, no more; *~ nogensinde* never ever; *jeg har ~ hørt magen!* well, I never! *~ i livet!* not on your life!
alene *adj* a'lone; *være ~ om ngt (også)* do· sth singlehanded *// adv* only; *~ det at...* the mere fact that...; *ene og ~* only; *~ tanken om det...* the mere thought of it...; *ikke ~ konen men også børnene* not only his wife but also his children; **~far** *en* single father; **~mor** *en* single mother.
alenlang *adj* mile-long, lengthy.
alf *en* fairy.
alfabet *et* alphabet.
alfabetisk *adj* alpha'betical.
alfons *en* pimp.
alfonseri *et* pimping.
alge *en* alga *(pl:* algae); (tang) seaweed.
algerier *en,* **algerisk** *adj* Al'gerian; **Algeriet** *s* Al'geria.
alibi *et* 'alibi.
alkohol *en* alcohol; *(som drikkes)* spirits *pl;* **~fri** *adj* 'non-alco,holic; *~fri drikke* non-alcoholic beverages, soft drinks; **~holdig** *adj* alco'holic.
alkoholiker *en* alco'holic; **alkoholisme** *en* alcoholism.
alkotest *en* breathalyzer.
alkove *en* 'alcove.
alle *pron* all; *(~ og enhver)* everybody; *(hvem som helst)* anybody; *~ bøgerne* all the books; *~ siger at...* everybody says that...; *~ andre* everybody else; *~ de andre* all the others; *~ andre end dig* everybody ex'cept you; *~ mennesker* everybody; *~ menneskene* all the people; *de kom ~ fire* all four of them came; *~ som én* to a man.
allé *en* avenue.
allehånde *s (krydderi)* allspice *// adj (alle slags)* all sorts of.
allerbedst *adj/adv* best of all; *de ~e vine* the very best wines.
allerede *adv* al'ready; *(selv, endog)* even.
allerflest *adj: i de ~e tilfælde* in the ma'jority of cases.
allerførst *adj* very first *// adv* first of all.
allergi *en* 'allergy; **~ker** *en* al'lergic.
allergisk *adj* al'lergic *(overfor* to).
aller... *sms:* **~helst** *adj: jeg vil ~helst have øl* I much pre'fer beer; **~helvedes** *adj: en ~helvedes larm* a hell of a noise; **~højst** *adj* at the utmost; **~mest** *adj* most of all; **~mindst**

adj: det er det ~mindste vi kan gøre it is the (very) least we can do // *adv* least of all; **-senest** *adj* very latest // *adv* at the very latest; **-sidst** *adj* very last, last of all; **-værst** *adj* worst of all.

allesammen *pron* all of them (,you, us), everybody; *de kom ~* they all came.

allevegne *adv* everywhere.

alliance *en* al'liance; **-fri** *adj (pol)* 'non-a,ligned.

alliere *v: ~ sig med en* join forces with sby; **-t** *en* ally // *adj* allied; *de ~de* the Allies.

alligevel *adv* still, yet, all the same; *(under alle omstændigheder)* anyway; *det var ~ dumt af dig* it was stupid of you, all the same; *du kan ~ ikke lide det* you don't like it anyway; *det blev solskin ~* it was sunshine after all.

almen *adj* common, general; *(for offentligheden)* public; **-gyldig** *adj* uni'versal; **-nyttig** *adj* non-profit making.

almindelig *adj (mods: sjælden)* common; *(som omfatter de fleste)* general; *(ordinær, sædvanlig)* ordinary; *(dagligdags)* plain; *det er ~ praksis* it is common practice; *~ brugt* in general use; *~e mennesker* ordinary people; *det er ngt ud over det ~e* it is sth out of the ordinary.

almindelighed *en: i ~* usually, generally.

almindeligvis *adv* generally, usually.

almue- *adj* peasant, rustic.

almægtig *adj* om'nipotent; *du ~e!* al'mighty God!

alpehue *en* 'beret.

Alperne *pl* the Alps.

alpeviol *en (bot)* 'cyclamen.

alpin *adj* 'alpine; *~e discipliner (i skisport)* alpine com'bined.

alrum *et* all-activity room.

alsidig *adj* versatile; *(omfattende)* allround; **-hed** *en* versa'tility.

alt *en (om stemme)* con'tralto // *adj/adv* all, everything; *(hvad som helst)* anything; *~ efter som...* ac'cording as...; *~ for* (far) too; *gøre ~ hvad man kan* do· everything one can; *skynde sig ~ hvad man kan* hurry as much as one can; *det er ~ for meget* it is far too much; *vi bliver 20 i ~* we will· be 20 in all; *~ i ~* altogether; *når ~ kommer til ~* after all; *hun er ~ andet end køn* she's anything but pretty.

altan *en* balcony; **-gang** *en* access balcony; **-kasse** *en* flower box.

alter *et* altar; *gå til ~s* take· Com'munion; **-gang** *en* Holy Com'munion; **-kalk** *en* chalice.

alternativ *et/adj* al'ternative.

altertavle *en* altarpiece.

altid *adv* always.

alting *pron* everything; *hvorom ~ er så...* however that may be...

altmuligmand *en* odd-job-man *(pl: ~ men).*

altomfattende *adj* 'all-em,bracing, global.

altsammen: *han tog det ~* he took· it all, he took· all of it.

altså *adv* so, therefore; *(dvs.)* that is; *(forstærkende)* really; *det er ~ for galt!* it is really too much! *du mener det ~? (også)* you mean· it then?

altædende *adj* om'nivorous.

aluminium *et* alu'minium.

alverden *s* all the world; *hvad i ~* what on earth; *hvorfor i ~* why on earth; *den koster ikke ~* it does not cost the earth; *han har ~s bøger og blade* he has all sorts of books and magazines.

alvidende *adj* om'niscient; *(neds)* know-all.

alvor *en* seriousness; *er det dit ~?* are you serious? *det er mit ~* I am serious; *for ~* seriously; *i ramme ~* in dead earnest; **-lig** *adj* serious // *adv* seriously; *~ligt talt* seriously (speaking).

amatør *en* 'amateur; **-agtig** *adj* 'amateurish.

ambassade *en* 'embassy.

ambassadør *en* am'bassador; *den danske ~ i Storbritannien* the Danish ambassador to Britain.

ambition *en* am'bition.

ambitiøs *adj* am'bitious.

ambolt *en* anvil.
ambulance *en* 'ambulance.
ambulant *adj: ~ behandling* outpatient treatment; *~ patient* outpatient.
ambulatorium *et* outpatients' clinic.
a-menneske *et* early riser.
Amerika *s* A'merica; **amerikaner** *en,* **amerikansk** *adj* A'merican; *amerikansk olie* castor oil.
amme *v* nurse, breastfeed·.
ammoniak *en* am'monia.
ammunition *en* ammu'nition.
amok *s: gå ~* run· a'muck.
amoralsk *adj* a'moral.
ampul *en* 'ampoule.
amputation *en* ampu'tation.
amputere *v* 'amputate.
amt *et sv.t.* county; *(i Skotland)* region; **~mand** *en sv.t.* prefect; **~s·kommune** *en sv.t.* county (,regional) district; **~s·råd** *et sv.t.* county (,regional) council.
amulet *en* charm.
analfabet *en* il'literate; **analfabetisme** *en* il'literacy.
analog *adj* a'nalogous; **~ computer** *en* analogue com'puter.
analyse *v* a'nalysis; **~re** *v* 'analyse.
analytiker *en* 'analyst.
ananas *en* pineapple.
anatomi *en* a'natomy; **anatomisk** *adj* ana'tomical.
anbefale *v* recom'mend; *(om brev)* register; **~t** *adj (om brev)* registered (R).
anbefaling *en* recommen'dation; *(ved jobansøgning)* reference.
anbringe *v* put·, place; *(om penge)* in'vest; *blive anbragt på institution* be sent to an insti'tution; **~lse** *en* putting, placing; in'vestment.
anciennitet *en* seni'ority; *efter ~* by seniority.
and *en* duck; *(avis~)* hoax (story).
andagt *en (i kirke)* prayers *pl; lytte med ~* listen with rapt at'tention; **~s·fuld** *adj* de'vout.
andejagt *en* duck-shooting.
andel *en* share, part; *have ~ i ngt* have a share in sth; **andels-** co'operative *(fx bevægelse* movement).
andelslejlighed *en* co'operative housing unit.
andemad *en (bot)* duckweed.
anden *pron* other; *en ~ (om person)* somebody else, an'other person; *(om ting)* an'other; *en el. ~* somebody; *en el. ~ ting* something or other; *den ene efter den ~* one after the other; *ingen ~ (om person)* nobody else; *(om ting)* no other; *(se også andet, andre) // num* second; *~ præmie* second prize; *den ~ maj* the second of May, May the second; *for det andet* secondly.
andenrangs *adj* second-rate.
anderledes *adj* different; *~ end* different from; *hvis ikke det kan være ~* if it must be // *adv* otherwise, differently; *(mere)* far more.
andesteg *en* roast duck.
andet *pron* other; *et ~ hus* an'other house; *alt ~ end* anything but; *blandt ~ (om mennesker)* among others; *(om ting)* among other things; *ikke ~* nothing else; *ikke ~ end* nothing but; *ngt ~* something else; anything else; *(se også anden, andre).*
andetsteds *adv* elsewhere; **~fra** *adv* from somewhere else; **~hen** *adv* somewhere else.
andre *pron* other; *alle ~ (om personer)* everybody else; *(om ting)* all others; *alle de ~* all the others; *ingen ~* nobody else; *de ~* the others, the rest of them; *vi ~* the rest of us.
andægtig *adj* de'vout; *(opmærksom)* at'tentive, rapt.
ane *en* ancestor.
ane *v* su'spect; *(mærke svagt)* sense; *(se svagt)* glimpse; *jeg ~r det ikke* I have not the faintest idea; *jeg ~r ikke hvad jeg skal gøre* I don't know what to do; *du ~r ikke hvad det koster* you have no idea what it costs.
anelse *en* su'spicion; *(smule)* touch; *have en ~ om at...* su'spect that...; *jeg har ingen ~ om det* I have not got a clue; *bange ~r* mis'givings.
anemone *en* a'nemone.
anerkende *v (berettigelsen af)* ac'knowledge; *(godkende)* recog-

nize; ~ *modtagelsen af et brev* acknowledge re'ceipt of a letter; **~lse** *en* ac'knowledgement; recog'nition; *(ros)* appreci'ation; **~nde** *adj* ap'preciative.

anerkendt *adj (godkendt)* ap'proved, recognized; *(kendt, med godt ry)* reputable; *almindelig* ~ generally ac'cepted.

anfald *et* at'tack; *(kort og pludseligt)* fit; *han fik et ~ over skrammen på bilen* he had a fit over the scratch on the car.

anføre *v* lead·; *(nævne)* mention; state.

anfører *en* leader; *(holdanfører, sport)* captain.

anførsel *en* leadership; *under ~ af* led by; **~s·tegn** *pl* quo'tation marks, in'verted commas.

anger *en* re'morse *(over* for).

angive *v (anføre, opgive)* give·, state; *(vise)* indicate; *(hævde, påstå)* pro'fess, claim; *(stikke, melde)* in'form on (,against); ~ *tidspunktet* state the time (of day); ~ *en til politiet* re'port sby to the po'lice; ~ *at være læge* claim to be a doctor.

angivelig(t) *adv* al'legedly.

angivelse *en* statement; *nøjere ~lse* specifi'cation.

angiver *en* in'former.

angre *v* re'gret; *(uden objekt)* re'pent.

angreb *et* at'tack; *(luft~)* raid; *gå til ~ på* make· an at'tack on; **~et** *adj: ~et af en sygdom* suffering from a dis'ease; **~s·spiller** *en (fodb)* forward; **~s·våben** *et* of'fensive weapon.

angribe *v* at'tack; *(voldsomt)* as'sault; **~r** *en* at'tacker; *(i krig)* ag'gressor

angst *en* fear; *(ængstelse)* an'xiety // *adj* a'fraid, anxious.

angå *v* con'cern; *hvad ~r* as to; *hvad ~r mig* for my part; *det ~r ikke dig* it is none of your business; **~ende** *præp* con'cerning, re'garding, about.

anholde *v* ar'rest; ~ *om ens hånd* ask for sby's hand in marriage; *være anholdt* be under arrest; **~lse** *en* ar'rest.

anhænger *en* trailer.

anis *en (krydderi)* aniseed.

anke *en (klage)* com'plaint; *(appel)* ap'peal // *v (klage)* com'plain *(over* of); *(appellere)* ap'peal.

ankel *en* ankle; **~sok** *en* sock.

ankenævn *et* board of ap'peal.

anker *et* anchor; *(tønde)* barrel; *lette* ~ weigh anchor; *kaste* ~ cast· (,drop) anchor; *ligge for* ~ lie· at anchor; **~plads** *en* anchorage.

anklage *en* accu'sation, charge // *v* ac'cuse, charge; ~ *en for ngt* ac'cuse sby of sth, charge sby with sth; *være under* ~ be on trial; **~bænk** *en* dock; **~myndigheden** *s* the prose'cution.

anklager *en* ac'cuser; *(i retten)* 'prosecutor.

anklageskrift *et* in'dictment [-'dait].

anklaget *adj: den anklagede* the ac'cused, the de'fendant.

ankomme *v* ar'rive *(til* at, in).

ankomst *en* ar'rival *(til* at, in); *ved ~en* on arrival; **~tid** *en* time of arriv-al.

ankre *v:* ~ *(op)* anchor.

anledning *en (lejlighed)* oc'casion; *(grund)* reason, cause; *(mulighed)* oppor'tunity; *i dagens* ~ in honour of the day; *give ~ til mistanke* give· cause for su'spicion; *få ~ til at gøre ngt* get· an opportunity to do sth; *i ~ af Deres skrivelse...* re'ferring to your letter...

anliggende *et* matter.

anlæg *et (fabrik etc)* plant, works; *(park)* park; *(have)* gardens; *(evne, talent)* talent.

anlægge *v (bygge etc)* build·; *(grundlægge)* found; *(have etc)* lay· out; ~ *sag* take· legal action; ~ *sag mod en* sue sby; ~ *skæg* grow· a beard.

anlægsarbejde *et* con'struction work.

anløbe *v (om skib)* call at; *(irre, blive sort)* be tarnished.

anløbsbro *en* jetty.

anmarch *en: være i* ~ approaching.

anmelde *v (til politiet etc)* re'port; *(bebude, annoncere)* an'nounce; *(deltagelse fx i konkurrence)* enter; *(som kritiker)* re'view.

anmeldelse *en* notifi'cation; *(til konkurrence etc)* entry; *(indtegning)* regi'stration; *(kritik)* re'view; **~s·blanket** *en* regi'stration form.
anmelder *en (kritiker)* critic, re'viewer; *(jur)* in'former.
anmode *v: ~ om* ask for; *~ en om at gøre ngt* ask sby to do sth.
anmodning *en* re'quest *(om* for); *efter ~* by request; *på ens ~* at sby's request.
anneks *s* an'nex.
annonce *en* ad'vertisement, (F) ad; **~kampagne** *en* advertising cam'paign.
annoncere *v* advertise; *~ et program (tv, radio)* an'nounce a programme.
annoncering *en* advertising; *(tv, radio)* an'nouncing.
annullere *v* cancel.
annullering *en* cancel'lation.
anonym *adj* a'nonymous; **~itet** *en* ano'nymity.
anorak *en* 'anorak.
anordning *en* de'vice.
anpartsselskab *et sv.omtr.t.* partnership.
anretning *en (opdækning)* table ar'rangement; *(ret mad)* course.
anrette *v (mad)* serve; *(forårsage)* cause *(fx skade* damage).
ansats *en* tendency; *(mus)* into'nation; *han har ~ til mave* he's beginning to develop a paunch.
anse *v: ~ for* con'sider (to be), re'gard as; *~ ngt for givet* take· sth for granted.
anseelse *en (godt ry)* repu'tation.
anselig *adj (ret stor)* con'siderable; *(om person)* notable.
anset *adj* di'stinguished, re'spected.
ansigt *et* face; *skære ~er* pull faces; *redde ~* save face; *tabe ~* lose· face; *sige ngt op i ens åbne ~* tell· sby sth to his face; *stå ~ til ~ med* come· face to face with; **~s·farve** *en* com'plexion; **~s·løftning** *en* facelift; **~s·maske** *en* face mask; **~s·træk** *pl* features; **~s·udtryk** *et* look.
ansjos *en* 'anchovy.
anskaffe *v: ~ sig ngt* get· oneself sth; **~lse** *en* acqui'sition, *(køb)* purchase.
anskuelse *en* view, o'pinion; *jeg er af den ~ at...* in my view...
anslag *et (på klaver etc)* touch; *200 ~ i minuttet sv.t.* 40 words per minute.
anslå *v (om streng etc)* strike·; *(vurdere)* estimate *(til* at).
anspændt *adj* tense // *adv* in'tently.
anstalt *en* insti'tution; *gøre ~er over ngt* fuss abouth sth.
anstandsdame *en* 'chaperone.
anstigende: *komme ~* show up.
anstrenge *v* strain; *(trætte)* tire; *~ sig for at gøre ngt* make· an effort to do sth; **~lse** *en* effort; *(stærk)* strain; **~nde** *adj* strenuous; *(trættende)* tiring.
anstrengt *adj (spændt)* tense; *(fx smil)* forced.
anstrøg *et* touch *(af* of).
anstændig *adj* decent; **~hed** *en* decency.
anstød *s: tage ~ af ngt* take· of'fence at sth; *vække ~* cause offence.
anstødelig *adj* of'fensive.
ansvar *et* responsi'bility; *(skyld)* blame; *på eget ~* on one's own responsi'bility; *blive draget til ~ for ngt* be held re'spon'sible for sth; *stå til ~ for ngt* be held re'sponsible for sth; **~lig** *adj* re'sponsible; **~s·forsikring** *en* personal lia'bility in'surance; *(auto)* third-party in'surance; **~s·fuld** *adj* re'sponsible; **~s·løs** *adj* irre'sponsible.
ansætte *v (i stilling)* em'ploy; *(i embede)* ap'point; *(vurdere, skønne)* estimate *(til* at); *(i skat)* as'sess; *være ansat i et firma* be with a firm; **~lse** *en* em'ployment; esti'mation; as'sessment; *tryghed i ~lsen* job se'curity.
ansøge *v* ap'ply *(om* for); **~r** *en* 'applicant *(til* for).
ansøgning *en* appli'cation *(om* for); **~s·skema** *et* application form.
antage *v (formode)* sup'pose; *(ansætte)* en'gage; *(godkende, acceptere)* ac'cept; *~ et nyt navn* a'dopt a new name.
antagelig *adj (god nok)* ac'ceptable; *(ret stor)* con'siderable // *adv (formentlig)* pre'sumably.

antagelse *en* as'sumption.
antal *et* number; *i et ~ af flere hundrede* several hundred in number.
Antarktis *s* the Ant'arctic.
antaste *v* ac'cost; *(ens rettigheder)* en'croach upon.
antenne *en* aerial.
antiatom- *adj* anti-nuclear.
antibiotika *pl* antibi'otics.
antibiotisk *adj* antibi'otic.
antik *adj* an'tique; **~ken** *s (hist)* An'tiquity.
antikvariat *et* second-hand bookshop.
antikvarisk *adj* second-hand.
antikveret *adj* obsolete.
antikvitet *en (som købes)* an'tique; *(fortidsminde)* an'tiquity; **~s·forretning** *en* an'tique shop; **~s·handler** *en* an'tique dealer.
antilope *en* 'antelope.
antipati *en* an'tipathy *(mod* to).
antisemitisk *adj* anti-se'mitic.
antiseptisk *adj* anti'septic.
antistatisk *adj* anti'static.
antistof *et* antibody.
antræk *et (påklædning)* get-up, outfit.
antyde *v* hint, sug'gest; *(tyde på)* indicate; *det tør svagt ~s!* you may say so!
antydning *en* hint, sug'gestion.
antænde *v* set· fire to; *~s* catch· fire; **~lse** *en* ig'nition.
anvende *v* use *(til* for); *(om tid)* spend; **~lig** *adj (nyttig)* useful; *(brugbar)* ap'plicable; **~lse** *en* use.
anvise *v (vise)* show; *(give, tildele)* as'sign; *~ beløbet til udbetaling* order the a'mount to be paid; *~ en plads* show sby to his (,her) seat.
anvisning *en (vejledning)* di'rections, in'structions *pl; (penge~)* money order.
anæmi *en* a'naemia.
aparte *adj* pe'culiar, odd.
apatisk *adj* apa'thetic.
apostel *en* a'postle.
apostrof *en* a'postrophe.
apotek *et* chemist's (shop), pharmacy; **~er** *en* pharmacist, di'spensing chemist.
apparat *et* de'vice, (F) con'traption; *(radio, tv)* set.
apparatur *et* appa'ratus.
appel *en* ap'peal; **~domstol** *en* court of ap'peal; **~lere** *v* ap'peal *(til* to); **~sag** *en* ap'peal case.
appelsin *en* orange; **~marmelade** *en* (orange) marmalade; **~skal** *en* orange peel.
appetit *en* 'appetite; **~lig** *adj* appetizing; **~vækker** *en* appetizer.
applikation *en (syning)* ap'pliqué.
applikere *v* ap'pliqué.
appretur *en* finish; *(selve midlet)* starch.
april *en* April; *den første ~* the first of April, April the first; *narre en ~* make· sby an April fool; **~s·nar** *en* April fool.
apropos *adv (for resten)* by the way; *~ penge, så har jeg ingen* talking of money, I don't have any.
ar *et* scar.
araber *en* 'Arab.
Arabien *s* A'rabia.
arabisk *et (sprog)* 'Arabic *// adj* 'Arab, A'rabian.
arbejde *et* work; *(hårdt, fysisk)* labour; *(beskæftigelse)* em'ployment; *få ~* get· a job, find· work; *gå på ~* go· to work; *han er rigtig kommet på ~* he's got his job cut out for him; *være i ~* be working; *være uden ~* be 'unem'ployed *// v* work; *(hårdt)* labour; *~ i en bank* be working in a bank; *~ med ngt* work at sth; *~ over* work overtime; *~ på at opnå ngt* work at a'chieving sth.
arbejder *en* worker; **~bevægelse** *en* labour movement; **~beskyttelse** *en* maintenance of in'dustrial health and safety; **~klassen** *s* the working class; **~parti** *et* labour party.
arbejds... *sms:* **~anvisning** *en sv.t.* job centre; **~besparende** *adj* labour-saving; **~byrde** *en* work load; **~dag** *en* working day; **~deling** *en* di'vision of labour; **~evne** *en* working ca'pacity; **~forhold** *pl* working con'ditions; **~formidling** *en sv.t.* job centre; **~giver** *en* em'ployer; **~giverforening** *en* em'ployers' fede'ration; **~gruppe** *en* team; **~indsats** *en* effort; **~kammerat** *en* 'colleague, workmate;

~klima *et* work climate; **~konflikt** *en* labour 'conflict; **~kraft** *en (arbejdere)* manpower; *(evne til at arbejde)* ca'pacity for work; **~krævende** *adj* 'labour-in,tensive; **~liderlig** *adj: han er ~liderlig* he is a work-a'holic; **~løn** *en* wages *pl.*

arbejdsløs *adj* 'unem'ployed, re'dundant; *blive ~* lose· one's job; **~hed** *en* 'unem'ployment, re'dundancy; **~hedskasse** *en* 'unem'ployment fund; **~hedunderstøttelse** *en* 'unem'ployment benefit; *få ~hedsunderstøttelse* (F) be on the dole.

arbejds... *sms:* **~marked** *et* labour market; **~medicin** *en* in'dustrial 'medicine; **~ministerium** *et* Ministry of Labour; **~moral** *en* work ethic; **~nedlæggelse** *en* walkout.

arbejdsom *adj* hard-working.

arbejds... *sms:* **~plads** *en* place of work; *færre ~pladser* fewer jobs; **~ret** *en sv.t.* in'dustrial tri'bunal; **~styrke** *en* workforce; **~søgende** *en* job hunter // *adj* job-hunting; **~tager** *en* employ'ee; **~tid** *en* working hours; *efter ~tid* after work; **~tilladelse** *en* work permit; **~tøj** *et* working clothes; **~udvalg** *et (parl)* drafting com'mittee; **~uge** *en* working week; **~ulykke** *en* in'dustrial accident; **~værelse** *et* study.

areal *et (område)* area; *(mål)* acreage.

arena *en* a'rena.

Argentina *s* the 'Argentine, Argen'tina; **argentiner** *en,* **argentinsk** *adj* Argen'tinian.

argument *et* 'argument; **~ere** *v* argue.

arie *en (mus)* aria.

aristokrat *en* a'ristocrat; **aristokrati** *et* ari'stocracy; **aristokratisk** *adj* aristo'cratic.

aritmetik *en* 'algebra.

ark *en: Noas ~* Noah's ark // *et* sheet *(fx papir* of paper).

arkitekt *en* 'architect; **~lampe** *en* anglepoise ® (lamp); **~tegnet** *adj* de'signed by an architecht.

arkitektur *en* 'architecture.

arkiv *et* 'archives *pl; (på kontor)* file; **~ar** *en* 'archivist; **~ere** *v* file.

Arktis *s* the Arctic; **arktisk** *adj* arctic.

arkæolog *en* arche'ologist; **arkæologi** *en* archae'ology.

arm *en* arm; *tage ngt i stiv ~* take· sth with'out flinching // *adj: ~e dig!* poor you! **~bevægelse** *en* gesture; **~bøjninger** *pl (gymn)* pushups; **~bånd** *et* bracelet; **~båndsur** *et* (wrist)watch.

armere *v* arm; *(pansre)* armour; *~t jernbeton* reinforced concrete.

armering *en* armament; *(panser)* armour.

armhule *en* armpit.

armlæn *et* armrest.

armring *en* bangle.

armstol *en* arm chair.

armsved *en* body odour.

aroma *en (smag)* flavour; *(lugt)* a'roma; **~tisk** *adj* aro'matic.

arrangement *et* ar'rangement.

arrangere *v* ar'range; *~ sig med en* make· an ar'rangement with sby.

arrangør *en* 'organizer.

arrest *en* custody; *(stedet)* prison; **~ere** *v* ar'rest; *være ~eret* be held in custody; **~ordre** *en* warrant.

arrig *adj* bad-tempered; **~skab** *en* bad temper.

arrivere *v* turn up.

arrogant *adj* 'arrogant.

arsenik *en* 'arsenic.

art *en (slags)* kind, sort; *(væsen, beskaffenhed)* nature.

arterie *en* 'artery.

artig *adj* good, 'well-be,haved.

artikel *en* 'article; *(videnskabelig også)* paper.

artilleri *et* ar'tillery.

artiskok *en* 'artichoke; **~bund** *en* arti'choke heart.

artist *en* ar'tiste.

arv *en* in'heritance; *(ved testamente)* 'legacy; *få ngt i ~* in'herit sth; *gå i ~ til en* pass on to sby.

arve *v: ~ sin onkel* be heir to one's uncle; *~ ngt efter en* get· sth after sby; **~afgift** *en* death duties *pl, (af formue)* in'heritance tax; **~anlæg** *et* he'reditary factor; **~følge** *en* line of suc'cession; **~lig** *adj* he'reditary; **~lighed** *en* he'redity; **~stykke** *et* heirloom.

arving *en (mand)* heir; *(kvinde)* heiress.
A/S *se aktieselskab.*
asbest *en* as'bestos.
asbestose *en* asbe'stosis.
ascorbinsyre *en* a'scorbic acid.
ase *v* struggle *(med* with).
asfalt *en* asphalt, tarmac; **~ere** *v* asphalt, tarmac.
asiat *en* Asian; **asiatisk** *adj* Asian.
asie *en: syltet ~ sv.t.* pickled pumpkin.
Asien *s* Asia.
asiet *en* (small) sideplate.
ask *en (bot)* ash.
aske *en* ashes *pl; (fra cigaret el. vulkan)* ash; **~bæger** *et* ashtray.
Askepot Cinde'rella.
askeskuffe *en* ash pan.
asketisk *adj* as'cetic.
asocial *adj* anti'social.
asparges *en* as'paragus; *fire ~* four stalks of asparagus; **~hoved** *et* as'paragus tip.
aspekt *et* 'aspect.
aspirant *en* candidate *(til* for); *(prøveansat) sv.t.* trai'nee.
assistance *en* as'sistance.
assistent *en* as'sistant.
assistere *v* as'sist *(ved* at); **~nde** *adj* as'sistant.
association *en* associ'ation.
assurance *en* in'surance.
assurandør *en (person)* in'surance man *(pl:* -men); *(selskab)* in'surance company.
asters *en (bot)* aster.
astma *en* asthma; **~tisk** *adj* asth'matic.
astrolog *en* a'strologist; **astrologi** *en* a'strology.
astronaut *en* 'astronaut.
astronom *en* a'stronomer; **astronomi** *en* a'stronomy; **astronomisk** *adj* astro'nomical.
asyl *et* a'sylum; *søge politisk ~* ap'ply for po'litical a'sylum; **~ansøger** *en (kan oversættes)* person ap'plying for po'litical a'sylum.
at *(foran infinitiv)* to; *prøv at gøre det* try to do it; *bogen er svær at læse* the book is difficult to read;
- *(infinitiv uden* to:) *få en til at græde* make· sby cry;
- *(ofte kan man vælge mellem* to + *infinitiv el.* -ing-*form:) han begyndte at løbe* he started to run, he started running;
- *(efter præp altid* -ing-*form:) de talte om at gøre det* they talked about doing it; *de gik uden at spise* they left without eating;
- *(foran sætning, udelades dog ofte)* that; *jeg ved at det er for sent* I know· (that) it is too late;
- *(andre forbindelser:) tale om at rejse til London* talk about going to London; *jeg kan ikke fordrage at se på det* I cannot stand watching it; *få en til at gøre ngt* make· sby do sth; *at du ikke skammer dig!* you ought to be a'shamed of your'self! *(tænk) at det skulle ske nu!* that it should happen now!
atelier *et* studio.
Athen *s* 'Athens.
Atlanterhavet *s* the At'lantic (Ocean).
Atlantpagten *s* the At'lantic Charter.
atlas *et* atlas.
atlet *en* 'athlete.
atletik *en* ath'letics; **atletisk** *adj* ath'letic.
atmosfære *en* 'atmosphere.
atom *et* 'atom; *(for sms se også kerne-);* **~affald** *et* nuclear waste; **~bombe** *en* a'tomic bomb, nuclear bomb; **~brændstof** *et* nuclear fuel; **~drevet** *adj* nuclear-powered; **~energi** *en* nuclear 'energy; **~forsøg** *et* nuclear test; **~fri** *adj: ~fri zone* de'nuclearized zone; **~fysik** *en* nuclear 'physics; **~fysiker** *en* nuclear 'physicist; **~kraft** *en* nuclear power; **~kraftværk** *et* nuclear power station (,plant); **~krig** *en* nuclear war; **~prøvestop** *et* test ban; **~sprængladning** *en* nuclear warhead; **~våben** *pl* nuclear weapons.
attachémappe *en* ex'ecutive case.
atten *num* eighteen; **~de** *adj* eighteenth.
attentat *et (forsøg)* assassi'nation at'tempt; *(mord)* assassi'nation; *begå ~ mod en* make· an attempt on sby's life.

atter *adv* a'gain, once more.
attest *en* cer'tificate; **~ere** *v* certify (to).
attraktion *en* at'traction.
attrap *en* dummy.
attråværdig *adj* de'sirable.
audiens *en* 'audience.
audiovisuel *adj* audio-visual.
auditorium *et* lecture hall; *(lille)* lecture room.
august *en* 'August; *den femte* ~ the fifth of August, August the fifth.
auktion *en* auction (sale); *sætte ngt på* ~ put· sth up for auction.
auktionarius *en* auctio'neer.
aula *en* as'sembly hall.
Australien *s* Au'stralia; **australier** *en*, **australsk** *adj* Au'stralian.
autentisk *adj* au'thentic.
autodidakt *adj* self-taught.
autograf *en* 'autograph.
autohandler *en* car dealer.
automat *en (salgs~)* vending ma'chine; *(spille~)* slot-machine; *(robot, fig)* au'tomaton.
automatisere *v* 'automate; **automatisering** *en* auto'mation.
automatisk *adj* auto'matic // *adv* auto'matically.
automekaniker *en* car me'chanic.
automobil *et* (motor) car; **~fabrik** *en* car factory; **~forhandler** *en* car dealer; **~forsikring** *en* motor (car) in'surance; **~værksted** *et* 'garage.
autorisation *en* authori'zation.
autorisere *v* authorize, licence.
autoritet *en* au'thority.
autoritær *adj* authori'tarian.
autovask *en* carwash.
autoværn *et* crash-barrier.
av *interj* ouch.
avance *en* profit; *med* ~ at a profit.
avancement *et* pro'motion.
avancere *v (blive forfremmet)* be pro'moted; *(rykke frem)* ad'vance; **~t** *adj* ad'vanced.
aversion *en* dis'like *(mod* of).
avertere *v* 'advertise *(efter* for); ~ *med ngt* 'advertise sth.
avis *en* paper, newspaper; **~kiosk** *en* newsstand; **~papir** *et* newsprint; **~udklip** *et* (press) cutting.
avl *en (høstudbytte)* crop; *(dyrkning)* growing; *(opdræt)* breeding.
avle *v (dyrke)* grow·; *(opdrætte)* breed·; *(få unger)* procreate; *(fig)* breed·.
avlsdyr *et* breeding animal.
avocado *en* avo'cado.

B

b *et:* ~ *for E (mus)* E flat.
baby *en* baby; **~lift** *en* carrycot; **~mad** *en (på glas el. dåse)* babymeal; **~sitter** *en: være ~sitter* babysit; **~udstyr** *et* lay'ette, baby things *pl.*
bacille *en* germ, bug.
bad *et (kar~)* bath; *(bruse~)* shower; *(i fri luft)* swim, bathe; *tage* ~ have a bath; *værelse med* ~ room with a private bath.
bade *v (inde)* have a bath; *(ude)* go· for a swim; *(~ fx øjne)* bathe; ~ *et barn* bath a child.
bade... *sms:* **~anstalt** *en* baths *pl;* **~bold** *en* beach ball; **~bro** *en* bathing jetty; **~bukser** *pl* bathing trunks; **~dragt** *en* bathing suit, swimsuit; **~hætte** *en* swimming cap; **~håndklæde** *et* bath towel; **~kar** *et* bath tub; **~kåbe** *en* bathrobe; **~salt** *et* bath salts *pl;* **~sted** *et* seaside re'sort; **~strand** *en* beach; **~vægt** *en* scales *pl;* **~værelse** *et* bathroom.
badminton *s* badminton; **~bold** *en* shuttlecock; **~ketsjer** *en* badminton racket.
badning *en* bathing.
bag *en (bagdel)* backside, bottom; *(bagside)* back // *adj/adv* be'hind; *gå* ~ *en* walk be'hind sby; ~ *i bilen* in the back of the car; ~ *på* on the back of; ~ *på huset (,bogen etc)* on the backside of the house (,book etc); *det kom* ~ *på os* it took us by sur'prise; ~ *ved* be'hind.
bagage *en* luggage, baggage; **~bærer** *en (på bil)* luggage rack; *(på cykel)* carrier; **~rum** *et (i bil)* boot; *(am)* trunk.
bagatel *en* trifle.
bagben *et* hindleg.

bagbord *s (mar)* port; **-s** *adj* port.
bagdel *en* backside, be'hind; *(ulempe, mods: fordel)* drawback.
bagdør *en* back door.
bage *v* bake; **-form** *en* baking tin.
bagefter *adv (senere)* afterwards; *(bagved)* be'hind; *mit ur er ~* my watch is slow; *være ~ med huslejen* be in ar'rears with the rent.
bage... *sms:* **-kartoffel** *en* baking po'tato; **-opskrift** *en* baking recipe ['rɛsipi]; **-ovn** *en* (baking) oven; **-papir** *et* non-stick paper; **-plade** *en* baking tray; **-pulver** *et* baking powder.
bager *en* baker; **-butik** *en* baker's.
bageri *et* bakery.
bagerist *en* wire rack.
bagest *adj* hindmost // *adv* at the back; *~ i salen* at the back of the hall.
bagfra *adv* from be'hind.
baggrund *en* background; *på ~ af* in the light of; **baggrunds-** background *(fx støj* noise).
baggård *en* backyard; **baggårds-** slum *(fx børn* children).
baghave *en* back garden.
baghjul *et* rear wheel; **-s·bremse** *en* rear-wheel brake; **-s·træk** *et* rear-wheel drive.
baghold *et* ambush; *falde i ~* be ambushed.
baghoved *et: have ngt i ~et* have sth at the back of one's mind.
baghus *et* back building.
baghånd *en (fx i tennis)* backhand; *have ngt i ~en* have sth up one's sleeve.
bagi *adv* in the back.
bagklap *en (auto)* hatch, tail-gate.
bagklog *adj: man kan altid være ~* it's easy to be wise after the e'vent.
baglomme *en* hip pocket.
baglygte *en* rear light, tail light.
baglæns *adj* backward // *adv* backwards.
baglås *s: gå i ~* jam.
bagmand *en (fig)* wire-puller; *~en* the man behind; **-s·politiet** *s* (F) the fraud squad.
bagning *en* baking.
bagom *adv* be'hind; *gå ~ (fx i forretning)* go· round the back.
bagover *adv* backwards; *falde (,gå) bagover* fall· backwards.
bagpå *adv* be'hind, on the back.
bag... *sms:* **-rude** *en* rear window; **-side** *en* back; **-slag** *et: give ~slag* backfire; **-smæk** *en (auto)* tail-board; **-stavn** *en (mar)* stern; **-sæde** *et* back seat; *(på motorcykel)* pillion; **-tale** *v* slander; **-tanke** *en* ul'terior motive; **-trappe** *en* back stairs *pl;* **-ud** *adv* to the rear; *(med betaling)* in ar'rears; *sakke ~ud* lag be'hind; **-ude** *adv* be'hind; **-vaskelse** *en* slander; **-ved** *adv* be'hind; **-vendt** *adj* turned the wrong way; *(fig)* awkward.
bagværk *et* pastry.
bajer *en: en ~* a beer, a lager.
bajersk *adj:* Ba'varian; *~ pølse* frankfurter.
bajonet *en* 'bayonet.
bakgear *et* re'verse gear.
bakke *en (i terrænet)* hill; *(til servering)* tray; *(til frugt og grønt)* punnet; *ned ad ~* downhill; *op ad ~* uphill // *v (gå, køre etc baglæns)* re'verse, back; *(ryge på pibe)* puff; *~ ham op* back him up; **-drag** *et* range of hills; **-t** *adj* hilly.
baklygte *en* re'versing lamp.
bakse *v: ~ med ngt* ma'noeuvre sth; *(slås med)* struggle with sth.
bakspejl *et* rear-view mirror.
bakterie *en* germ, bug.
bal *en (billardkugle)* ball // *et (dans)* dance; *(stort formelt)* ball.
balance *en* 'balance; *holde ~n* keep· one's balance; *ude af ~* off one's balance; **-gang** *en: gå ~gang mellem to alternativer* walk the tightrope between two alternatives; **-re** *v* 'balance; *få ngt til at ~re* 'balance sth.
balje *en (fx opvaske~)* bowl, basin; *(større kar)* tub.
balkon *en* 'balcony; *(teat)* (dress) circle.
ballade *en (halløj)* row [rau]; *(folkevise)* ballad; *få ~* get· into trouble; *lave ~* kick up a row; **-mager** *en* rowdy.

ballast *en* ballast.
balle *en (til varer)* bale; *give en en ~* give· sby a scolding.
ballet *en* 'ballet; **~danser** *en* 'ballet dancer; **~kjole** *en* 'tutu; **~sko** *en* 'ballet shoe.
ballon *en* bal'loon; **~gynge** *en* Ferris wheel; **~tyggegummi** *et* bubble gum.
balsam *en* balm; *(til håret)* hair con-'ditioner; **~ere** *v* em'balm.
baltisk *adj* Baltic.
bambus *en* bam'boo; **~skud** *et* bam-'boo shoot.
bamse *en* bear [bεə·]; *(som legetøj)* teddy bear.
banal *adj* ba'nal, trite; **~itet** *en* ba'nality; *(plat udtalelse)* 'platitude.
banan *en* ba'nana; *hård ~* tough guy **~klase** *en* bunch of bananas; **~skræl** *en* ba'nana skin; **~stik** *et* *(elek)* jack plug.
bandage *en* 'bandage.
bande *en* gang; *(på ishockeybane)* barrier.
bande *v* swear·, curse; *det kan du ~ på!* you can bet your life on it! *~ på at...* swear· that...; **~n** *en* swearing, cursing; **~ord** *et* swearword.
bandit *en* 'bandit, scoundrel; *(spøg)* rascal.
bandlyse *v* ban.
bane *en* track, course; *(jernb)* railway; *(papir, tæppe, stof)* length; *(om planet, rumskib)* orbit; *(sport, fx fodbold~)* pitch, ground; *(skyde~)* range; *(golf~)* course; *der er fri ~* the coast is clear; *mad i lange ~r* lots of food; *bringe ngt på ~* bring· sth up // *v* level, clear; *~ vej for ngt* pre'pare the way for sth; *~ sig vej* force one's way; **~brydende** *adj* pio'neering; **~dæmning** *en* (railway) em'bankment; **~gård** *en* railway station; **~legeme** *et* railway track; **~linje** *en* railway line; **~pakke** *en* railway parcel.
bange *adj* a'fraid, scared *(for* of); *gøre en ~* frighten sby; *jeg er ~ for at...* I am afraid that...; *er vi for sent på den? Ja, jeg er ~ for det!* are we late? Yes, I'm afraid so; *du skal ikke være ~, det går nok!* don't worry, it will be all right! **~buks** *en* coward.
bank *en (pengeinstitut)* bank; *sætte penge i ~en* de'posit (,put·) money in the bank; *sprænge ~en* break· the bank // *pl (klø)* beating; *få ~* get· a beating (,thrashing); **~assistent** *en* bank employ'ee; **~bog** *en* savings book; **~boks** *en* 'safe-de,posit box; **~direktør** *en* bank manager.
banke *en (bakke)* hill; *(fiske~)* bank; *(sand~)* bar // *v* knock, tap; *(om hjerte)* beat·; *(tæve)* beat·, thrash; *(slå i spil etc)* beat·; *det ~r* somebody is knocking; *~ på (døren)* knock (the door); **~kød** *et sv.t.* stewed beef; **~n** *en* knock(ing).
bankerot *en* bankruptcy // *adj* bankrupt; *gå ~* go· bankrupt.
banket *en* 'banquet.
bankier *en* banker.
bankkonto *en* bank ac'count; **banklån** *et* bank loan; **bankmand** *en* bank employ'ee.
bankospil *et* bingo.
bankrøver *en* bank robber; **bankrøveri** *et* bank robbery.
banner *et* banner.
bar *en* bar.
bar *adj* bare; *(nøgen)* naked; *(lutter)* sheer, pure; *med de ~e hænder* barehanded; *starte på ~ bund* start from scratch; *stå på ~ bund (fx om politi)* not have a clue; *gå på ~e fødder* walk barefoot; *(se også bare).*
barak *en* hut, shack.
barbarisk *adj* bar'baric.
barbenet *adj* bare-legged.
barber *en* barber; *(herrefrisør)* hairdresser; **~blad** *et* razor blade; **~creme** *en* shaving cream; **~e** *v: ~e (sig)* shave; **~ing** *en* shave; **~kniv** *en* razor; **~kost** *en* shaving brush; **~maskine** *en (elek)* e'lectric shaver; **~skum** *et* shaving foam; **~sprit** *et* after-shave (lotion); **~sæbe** *en* shaving soap.
bardun *en (til telt etc)* rope.
bare *adv* just, only // *konj* if only; *~ rolig!* take· it easy! don't worry! *du kan ~ vente dig!* you just wait! *det*

var ~ for sjov it was only for fun; *hvis ~ vi kan nå det* if only we can make it; *~ tanken om det...* the mere thought of it...; *(se også bar).*
barfodet *adj* barefoot(ed).
bark *en (på træ)* bark.
barm *en* bosom.
barmhjertig *adj* merciful; *(godgørende)* charitable; **~hed** *en* mercy; charity.
barn *et* child *(pl:* children); *få et ~ (med en)* have a child (by sby); *de skal have et ~* they are having a baby; *have kone og børn* have a wife and family; *som ~ var han ret stille* as a child he was rather quiet; **~agtig** *adj* childish.
barndom *en* childhood; *fra ~men* from childhood; *gå i ~* be in one's second childhood.
barne... *sms:* **~barn** *et* grandchild *(pl:* -children); **~billet** *en* half ticket; **~dåb** *en* christening; **~mad** *en* infant food; *(fig)* child's play; **~pige** *en* nanny; **~pleje** *en* child care; **~seng** *en* cot; **~stol** *en* child's chair; *(høj ~)* high chair; *(i bil)* (child's) safety seat; **~vogn** *en* pram.
barnlig *adj* childish; **~hed** *en* childishness.
barnløs *adj* childless.
barok *en/adj* ba'roque.
barometer *et* ba'rometer.
barre *en (guld etc)* bar; *(gymn)* 'parallel bars *pl; (forskudt ~)* un'even bars *pl.*
barriere *en* barrier.
barrikade *en* 'barricade; **~re** *v* 'barricade.
barsel *et* childbirth; **~s·orlov** *en* ma'ternity leave.
barsk *adj (klima etc)* rough; *(person)* hard, tough.
barsle *v* give· birth *(med* to).
bas *en (om sanger, guitar)* bass; *(kontra~)* double bass.
basar *en* ba'zaar.
base *en* base; **~re** *v* base.
basis *en* basis; *på ~ af* on the basis of.
baske *v* flap, flutter; *og det så det ~de!* and with a vengeance!
baskerhue *en* 'beret.
basse *en (wienerbrød)* Danish pastry; *det var en ordentlig ~!* it was a thumping big one! *han er en ordentlig ~* he's a real hunk.
bassin *et* pool; *(havne~ etc)* 'basin.
bassist *en* bass player.
bast *en* raffia.
bastant *adj (om fx mad)* sub'stantial; *(om person)* stout.
bastard *en* hybrid, crossbreed; (NB! bastard: *lort, dum skid).*
basun *en* trom'bone; **~ist** *en* trom'bone player; **~kinder** *pl* chubby cheeks.
batist *en* cambric.
batte *v: ~ ngt* have an ef'fect; *så det ~r* with a vengeance.
batteri *et* 'battery.
bautasten *en* standing stone.
bavian *en* ba'boon.
bearbejde *v* work; pre'pare; *(om fx manuskript)* a'dapt *(fx for tv* for television); *(presse en person)* try to persu'ade; **~lse** *en* working; prepa'ration; adap'tation; persu'asion.
bebo *v* live in, occupy.
beboelse *en* habi'tation, residence; **~s·hus** *et (etageejendom)* block of flats; **~s·kvarter** *et* resi'dential area.
beboer *en* occupant; *(lejer)* tenant; *(indbygger)* in'habitant; *(på hjem)* inmate.
beboet *adj* occupied, in'habited.
bebrejde *v: ~ en ngt* blame sby for sth; **~lse** *en* re'proach; **~nde** *adj* re'proachful.
bebude *v* an'nounce; **~lse** *en* an'nouncement.
bebygge *v* build· on; *(om byområde)* build· up, de'velop; **~lse** *en (det at bygge)* building; *(bygninger)* buildings *pl; (bebygget område)* built-up area; **~t** *adj* built-up.
bed *et (i have etc)* bed; *gå en i ~ene* poach on sby's premises.
bedding *en* slipway.
bede *v* ask; *(tigge)* beg; *(til gud)* pray; *man ~s...* please...; *~ en bøn* say· a prayer; *~ om* ask for; *~ en om at gøre ngt* ask sby to do sth; *~ en om forladelse* beg sby's pardon; *må jeg*

~ *om saltet?* could I have the salt please? *jeg be'r!* don't mention it!
bedemand *en* undertaker; funeral di'rector.
bedende *adj* en'treating.
bedrag *et* de'lusion; *(svindel)* fraud.
bedrage *v (snyde)* cheat, de'ceive; *(lave bedrageri mod)* swindle; *(lede på vildspor)* de'lude; *(i ægteskab)* be un'faithful to.
bedrager *en* swindler, im'postor.
bedrageri *et* de'ceit, swindling.
bedre *adj/adv* better; *det var ~!* that's better! *få det ~* get· better; *have det ~* be (,feel·) better; *det ville passe ~ i morgen* it would be better to'morrow; *i mangel af ~* for lack of sth better; *jeg kan ~ lide te* I pre'fer tea // *v: Gud ~ det* God help us.
bedrevidende *adj* know-all.
bedrift *en* a'chievement; *(firma)* con-'cern; *(fabrik)* factory; *(landbrug)* farm; **~s·læge** *en* works doctor.
bedring *en* im'provement; *god ~!* I wish you a speedy re'covery!
bedrøve *v* di'stress; **~lig** *adj* sad; **~lse** *en* sadness; **~t** *adj* sad.
bedst *adj* best; *i ~e fald* at best; *du gør ~ i at…* you had better…; *~ som…* just as…
bedste *et: det er til dit eget ~* it is for your own good; *til ens ~* for the benefit of sby; *til fælles ~* for the common good; **~far** *en* grandfather, (F) grandpa; **~forældre** *pl* grandparents; **~mor** *en* grandmother, (F) granny.
bedugget *adj* tipsy.
beduin *en* 'bedouin.
bedømme *v* as'sess, judge (about); **~lse** *en* as'sessment, judgement.
bedøve *v* an'aesthetize; *(med slag)* stun; *jeg er ~nde ligeglad* I could not care less; **~lse** *en* anaes'thesia; **~lsesmiddel** *et* anaes'thetic.
befale *v* order; *(give ordrer)* give· orders.
befaling *en* com'mand, order; *på ~* to order, under orders *(af* from); **~s·mand** *en* officer.
befinde *v: ~ sig* be; *(føle sig også)* feel·.
befippet *adj* per'plexed, baffled.
befolkning *en* popu'lation; *~en (også)* the in'habitants.
befordre *v (transportere)* con'vey; *(fremme)* pro'mote.
befordring *en* con'veyance; **~s·middel** *et* means of 'transport.
befri *v* free, re'lease; *~ en for ngt* free sby from sth; *det var helt ~ende* it was quite a relief; **~else** *en* libe'ration; *Befrielsen (1945)* the Libe'ration.
befrugte *v* fertilize.
befrugtning *en* fertili'zation; *kunstig ~* arti'ficial insemi'nation.
befærdet *adj* busy.
beføjelse *en* au'thority.
begavelse *en* gifts, talents *pl; han er en stor ~* he is very gifted (,talented); **begavet** *adj* gifted, talented.
begejstret *adj* enthusi'astic *(over* about); **begejstring** *en* en'thusiasm.
begge both; *vi kommer ~ to* we are both coming; *de er ~ to millionærer* both of them are millionaires, they are both millionaires; *~ dele* both.
begive *v: ~ sig til* go· to, set· out for.
begivenhed *en* e'vent; *(hændelse)* incident; **~s·rig** *adj* e'ventful.
begrave *v* bury; **~lse** *en* funeral; *(det at begrave en el. ngt)* burial.
begreb *et* i'dea, con'ception; *have ~ om ngt* know· about sth; *jeg har ikke ~ om det* I have no idea about it; *~et rigdom* the 'concept of wealth; *du gør dig ikke ~ om hvor…* you have no idea how…; *være med i ~ med at gøre ngt* be on the point of doing sth.
begribe *v* under'stand·, grasp; **~lig** *adj* compre'hensible.
begrundelse *en* reason; *med den ~ at…* for the reason that…
begrænse *v* limit; *(indskrænke)* re'duce; *~ sig til ngt* con'fine oneself to sth; **~t** *adj* limited.
begrænsning *en* limi'tation; re'duction.
begynde *v* start, be'gin·; *~ at løbe* start running, begin· to run; *han ~r at blive tyk* he is getting fat; *~ for sig selv* start one's own business;

til at ~ med to begin with; *~ med at gøre ngt* begin· by doing sth; *~ på at gøre ngt* start doing sth; **-lse** *en* be'ginning, start; *i ~lsen* at first; *i ~lsen af Januar* in the beginning of January; *han er i ~lsen af 50'erne* he is in his early fifties.

begynder *en* be'ginner; **-bakke** *en (til skiløb)* nursery slope; **-kursus** *et* ele'mentary course; **-vanskeligheder** *pl* teething troubles.

begær *et* de'sire; **-e** *v* de'sire; *(kræve)* de'mand; **-ing** *en* de'mand; *(ansøgning)* appli'cation; **-lig** *adj* eager *(efter* for; *efter at* to); *(grådig)* greedy.

begå *v* com'mit *(fx mord* murder); *~ en fejl* make· a mistake.

behag *et* pleasure; *efter ~* as you like; *smag og ~...* everyone to his taste; **-e** *v* please; *som man ~er* as you like it.

behagelig *adj* pleasant; *(rar, bekvem)* comfortable; *gøre sig det ~t* make· oneself comfortable; **-hed** *en* pleasantness; *(ngt rart)* comfort; *(fordel, gode)* ad'vantage.

behandle *v* treat; *(diskutere)* dis'cuss.

behandling *en* treatment; dis'cussion.

beherske *v (regere over)* rule over; *(kunne)* master; *(være fremtrædende)* dominate; *~ sig* con'trol oneself; **-lse** *en* con'trol; **-t** *adj* moderate.

behold *s: i god ~* safe (and sound).

beholde *v* keep·.

beholder *en* con'tainer.

beholdning *en (forråd)* sup'ply; *(lager)* stock.

behov *et* need; *have ~ for ngt* need sth; *efter ~* as re'quired.

behændig *adj* nimble, 'agile; **-hed** *en* nimbleness, a'gility.

behøve *v* need; *(være nødt til)* have to; *du ~r ikke at ringe* there is no need to call; *det ~s ikke* it is not necessary; *~r vi at gå?* must· we go? *hvis det ~s* if necessary.

bejdse *en/v* stain.

bejler *en* suitor.

bekende *v (indrømme)* ad'mit; *(tilstå)* con'fess; *~ kulør (fig)* show· one's hand; **-lse** *en* con'fession; *gå til ~lse* con'fess.

bekendt *en* ac'quaintance // *adj (kendt af alle)* well-known; *(som man er fortrolig med)* fa'miliar; *~ med* ac'quainted with; *(så vidt) mig ~* as far as I know; *som ~* as you know; *vi kan ikke være ~ at...* it won't do for us to...; *det kan du ikke være ~!* you ought to be a'shamed of yourself! *det måltid kan du godt være ~* that meal does you credit; **-gøre** *v* an'nounce; **-gørelse** *en* an'nouncement; **-skab** *et* ac'quaintance; *stifte ~skab med en* make· sby's ac'quaintance.

beklage *v (angre)* re'gret; *(have ondt af)* be (,feel·) sorry for; *~ sig over ngt* com'plain about sth; **-lig** *adj* un'fortunate; *(yderst ~lig)* de'plorable; **-ligvis** *adv* un'fortunately.

beklagelse *en* re'gret; *(medlidenhed)* pity; *(klage)* com'plaint; *det er med den største ~ at vi må...* much to our re'gret we have to...

beklæde *v (betrække, dække)* cover; *(med brædder)* board; *(en stilling)* hold·.

beklædning *en (påklædning)* clothes *pl; (betræk etc)* cover(ing); *(med brædder)* boarding; **-s·genstand** *en* garment.

bekneb *a: være i ~* be in a tight spot; *jeg er i ~ for penge* I'm rather short of money.

bekoste *v* pay· for; **-lig** *adj* costly.

bekostning *en* cost, ex'pense; *på ~ af* at the ex'pense of; *på min ~* at my ex'pense.

bekræfte *v (attestere etc)* certify; *(anerkende, bestyrke)* con'firm; **-lse** *en* certifi'cation; confir'mation; **-nde** *adj* af'firmative // *adv* in the af'firmative; *i ~nde fald* if so.

bekvem *adj (behagelig)* comfortable; *(praktisk)* handy, con'venient.

bekvemmelighed *en* comfort; con'venience; *moderne ~er* modern con'veniences; *(fork. i annonce)* mod cons; **-s·flag** *et* flag of con'venience.

bekymre *v* worry; *~ sig om ngt* worry

about sth; *(tage sig af)* con'cern oneself with sth; **~t** *adj* worried *(for, over* about).

bekymring *en* worry.

bekæmpe *v* fight·; *(nedkæmpe)* con'trol; *(sætte sig imod)* op'pose; *~ forureningen* fight pol'lution; *~ myndighederne* oppose the au'thorities; **~lse** *en* fight *(af* against).

belaste *v* put· weight on; *(anstrenge fx muskler)* strain; *(tynge på)* burden.

belastning *en (last)* load; *(fig)* strain; *(ngt graverende)* burden *(for* on).

belave *v: ~ sig på at gøre ngt* pre'pare oneself for doing sth.

belejlig *adj* con'venient; *snarest ~t* at your earliest con'venience, soonest possible; *det kom ~t* it came just at the right time; *det var ikke ~t* it was incon'venient.

belejre *v* be'siege.

belejring *en* siege; *være under ~* be be'sieged.

belemre *v: ~ en med ngt* en'cumber sby with sth.

Belgien *s* Belgium; **belgier** *en,* **belgisk** *adj* Belgian.

beliggende *adj* situated; **beliggenhed** *en* situ'ation.

bellis *en (bot)* daisy.

belyse *v (lyse på)* il'luminate; *(foto)* ex'pose; *(fig, kaste lys over)* throw· light on.

belysning *en (det at lyse på)* illumi'nation; *(elek, sol etc)* light; *(fig, af emne etc)* illu'stration; **~s·måler** *en (foto)* light meter; **~s·tid** *en (foto)* ex'posure time; **~s·væsenet** *s* the gas- and elec'tricity board.

belægge *v (dække)* cover; *(med lag af fx glasur)* coat; *(lægge beslag på, optage)* occupy; *~ med håndjern* handcuff; *~ med tæpper* carpet; *hotellet er fuldt belagt* the ho'tel is booked up.

belægning *en* cover(ing); coat(ing); *(ved fx kjolesyning)* facing; *(på vej)* surface.

belære *v: ~ en om ngt* teach· sby sth; **~nde** *adj* in'structive.

belæsse *v* load.

belæst *adj* well-read.

beløb *et* a'mount; *samlet ~* total amount; **~e** *v: ~e sig til* amount to.

belønne *v* re'ward.

belønning *en* re'ward; *få ngt i (, til) ~* get· sth as a reward.

belåne *v (om hus)* mortgage.

bemande *v* man; **bemanding** *en (mandskab)* crew; *(det at bemande)* manning.

bemyndige *v* authorize; **~lse** *en* authori'zation.

bemægtige *v: ~ sig ngt* take· pos'session of sth, seize sth.

bemærke *v (lægge mærke til)* notice; *(bide mærke i)* note; *(sige)* re'mark; *gøre sig ~t* draw· at'tention to oneself; *man bedes ~ at...* please note that...

bemærkelsesværdig *adj* re'markable; *(værd at bide mærke i)* noteworthy.

bemærkning *en* re'mark, 'comment; *komme med ~er om ngt* 'comment on sth.

ben *et* leg; *(knogle, fiske~, materialet)* bone; *(bijob)* sideline: *(biindtægt)* perk; *have ~ i næsen* be tough; *det er der ingen ~ i* that's child's play; *komme på ~ene* get· back on one's feet; *tage ~ene på nakken* take· to one's heels; *være på ~ene* be up and about; *spænde ~ for en* trip sby up; *jeg vil ikke sætte mine ~ i hans hus* I will not set· foot in his house; **~beskytter** *en* shin pad.

bene *v: ~ rundt* run· about.

ben... *sms:* **~ende** *en (i seng)* foot of the bed; **~fri** *adj* boneless; **~klæder** *pl* trousers; **~skade** *en* leg injury; **~skinne** *en* splint; **~varmere** *pl* leg warmers.

benytte *v* use, em'ploy; *~ sig af* make· use of; *~ lejligheden til at gøre ngt* take· the oppor'tunity to do sth.

benzin *en (til bil etc)* petrol; *(am)* gas(oline); *(rense~)* 'benzine; *løbe tør for ~* run· out of petrol; **~dunk** *en* petrol can; **~måler** *en* fuel gauge [gəidʒ]; **~tank** *en (tankstation)* petrol station; *(i bil)* petrol tank.

benægte *v* de'ny; **~lse** *en* de'nial;

~nde *adj* negative // *adv: svare ~nde* answer in the negative.
benåde *v* pardon; **benådning** *en* pardon.
beordre *v* order.
beplantning *en (det at plante)* planting; *(plantage)* plan'tation.
bereden *adj: ~t politi* mounted po'lice.
beredskab *et* readiness; *holde ngt i ~* have sth ready; *holde sig i ~* be on the standby (,alert); **~s·plan** *en* e'mergency plan.
beredt *adj* ready, pre'pared *(til* for, *til at* to).
beredvillig *adj* willing.
beregne *v* calculate; *(anslå)* estimate; *~t til (,på)* in'tended (,meant) for; *~t til (,på) at* intended to; *~ plads til en* leave· room for sby; *~ sig procenter* charge a per'centage; **~nde** *adj* calculating.
beregning *en* calcu'lation; *det gik efter ~en* it went as ex'pected; *uden ~* free of charge.
berejst *adj* widely travelled.
beretning *en* re'port; *(historie)* ac'count, story *(om* of); *aflægge ~ om ngt* make· a re'port on sth.
berette *v* tell· *(om* about).
berettige *v* en'title; **~lse** *en (myndighed)* au'thority; *(ret)* right; *(rimelighed)* justice; **~t** *adj* en'titled; *(rimelig)* just.
bero *v (henligge, være uafklaret)* be pending; *~ på (dvs. skyldes)* be due to; *(dvs. komme an på)* de'pend on.
berolige *v* calm (down), reas'sure; *(med medicin)* se'date; **~lse** *en* reas'surance; *til min ~lse sagde han at...* I was re'lieved to hear him say that...; **~nde** *adj* reas'suring; *(om medicin)* 'sedative; *et ~nde middel* a 'sedative.
beruse *v* in'toxicate; **~lse** *en* intoxi'cation; **~t** *adj* in'toxicated, drunk.
berygtet *adj* no'torious.
berømmelse *en* fame.
berømt *adj* famous; **~hed** *en (det at være berømt)* fame; *(person)* ce'lebrity.
berøre *v* touch; *(gøre indtryk på, påvirke, angå)* af'fect; *føle sig ilde berørt af ngt* feel· em'barrassed by sth; **berøring** *en* touch, contact.
besat *adj (om land; plads; hus)* occupied; *(om person)* pos'sessed; *fuldt ~* full up; *te sig som en ~* be'have like mad.
besejre *v* beat·, de'feat; *(fig)* over'come·.
besidde *v* pos'sess, have; **~lse** *en* pos'session; *~lser (dvs. ejendom, jord)* property; *komme i ~lse af ngt* get· hold of sth; *være i ~lse af ngt* be in posession of sth.
besk *adj* acrid.
beskadige *v* damage; *(såre)* injure; **~lse** *en* damage, injury.
beskatning *en* tax'ation; **beskatte** *v* tax.
besked *en* message; *(oplysning)* infor'mation; *(ordre)* in'struction; *få ~ om at...* be told that...; *få ~ på at gøre ngt* be told to do sth; *tage mod ~* take· a message; *vide ~ om ngt* know· about sth.
beskeden *adj* modest; **~hed** *en* modesty.
beskidt *adj* dirty, filthy.
beskikket *adj: ~ forsvarer sv.t.* Legal Aid counsel.
beskrive *v* de'scribe; **~lse** *en* de'scription.
beskylde *v: ~ en for ngt* ac'cuse sby of sth; **beskyldning** *en* accu'sation.
beskytte *v* pro'tect *(mod* from).
beskyttelse *en* pro'tection; **~s·hjelm** *en* pro'tective helmet; **~s·rum** *et* bomb shelter.
beskytter *en* pro'tector.
beskyttet *adj* pro'tected; sheltered *(fx bolig* accomo'dation; *værksted* workshop).
beskæftige *v (give arbejde, have ansat)* em'ploy; *(holde i gang med ngt)* keep· occupied; *~ sig med ngt (dvs. tage sig af, ordne)* deal· with sth; *(dvs. være optaget af)* be occupied with sth; *være travlt ~t med ngt* be very busy doing sth; **~lse** *en (arbejde)* em'ployment; *uden ~lse (dvs. arbejdsløs)* 'unem'ployed; *(dvs. uden ngt at tage sig til)* idle.

beskære *v* cut·; *(om træer)* prune; *(nedskære)* re'duce, cut·; **beskæring** *en* cutting; pruning; re'duction.

beslag *et (til pynt)* fitting; *(søm~)* studding; *lægge ~ på ngt (fx plads)* occupy sth; *(konfiskere)* 'confiscate sth; *lægge ~ på ens tid* take· up sby's time.

beslaglægge *v* 'confiscate; **~lse** *en* confi'scation.

beslutning *en* de'cision, reso'lution; *tage en ~ om ngt* make· a de'cision on sth; *vedtage en ~ (ved møde etc)* pass a reso'lution.

beslutsom *adj* 'resolute; **~hed** *en* reso'lution, resolve.

beslutte *v* de'cide; *(ved møde)* re'solve; *~ sig (til at)* make· up one's mind (to).

besparelse *en* cut, re'duction.

besparende *adj* cost-saving; *(økonomisk i brug)* eco'nomic.

bespise *v* feed·.

bespisning *en* feeding; *gratis ~* free meal(s).

bestalling *en: få ~ som advokat* be called to the bar; *blive frataget ~en* be dis'barred.

bestand *en (fx af hjorte)* popu'lation; *(af kvæg)* stock; **~del** *en* com'ponent, in'gredient.

bestandig *adv* con'tinual; *for ~* for good.

bestemme *v* de'cide; *(afgøre)* de'termine; *(fastsætte)* fix; *det må du ~* that's for you to de'cide; *~ sig* make· up one's mind; *~ sig for (, til) at...* de'cide to...; *~ over* con'trol.

bestemmelse *en* de'cision; *(vedtægt etc)* regu'lation; *(fastsættelse, fx af art, type)* determi'nation; *(skæbne)* 'destiny; *efter ~rne* ac'cording to regu'lations; *tage en ~* make· a de'cision; **~s·sted** *et* desti'nation.

bestemt *adj* definite; *(fig, viljefast etc)* de'termined, firm; *(speciel)* par'ticular, spe'cific; *(vis)* certain; *holde ~ på ngt* be very definite about sth; *nægte på det ~este* deny cate'gorically; *~ til* in'tended for; *~ til at* in'tended to // *adv (sikkert)* definitely; *(afgjort)* de'cidedly; *~ ikke* certainly not; **~hed** *en (vished, sikkerhed)* certainty; *(fasthed)* firmness.

bestige *v (fx bjerg)* climb; *(fx hest)* mount; *~ tronen* a'scend the throne.

bestik *et (spisegrej)* cutlery; *(tegne~)* drawing set; *tage ~ af ngt* size sth up.

bestikke *v* bribe; *lade sig ~* take· bribes; **~lse** *en* bribery; *tage imod ~lse* take· bribes.

bestille *v (gøre)* do·; *(reservere)* book, re'serve; *(afgive ordre på)* order; *~ billet* book (a ticket); *vi har meget at ~* we are very busy; *du skal få med mig at ~!* I'll be after you!

bestilling *en (arbejde)* work; *(stilling)* occu'pation, job; *(ordre)* order; *afgive ~ på ngt* place an order for sth; *gøre ngt på ~* do· sth to order; **~s·seddel** *en* order form.

bestride *v (nægte)* de'ny; *(gøre indsigelse mod)* dis'pute.

bestræbe *v: ~ sig på at...* en'deavour to...; **~lse** *en* effort.

bestråle *v* ir'radiate; **bestråling** *en* irradi'ation.

bestyre *v* be in charge of, manage.

bestyrelse *en* management; *(direktion)* board (of di'rectors); *(i forening)* com'mittee; *sidde i ~n* be on the board; **~s·medlem** *et* di'rector; *(i forening)* member of the com'mittee; **~s·møde** *et* board meeting; com'mittee meeting.

bestyrer *en* manager; *(af skole)* headmaster.

bestyrke *v* con'firm *(i* in).

bestyrtet *adj* dis'mayed, a'stonished.

bestøve *v* pollinate; **bestøvning** *en* polli'nation.

bestå *v (findes)* e'xist; *(vare ved)* last, en'dure; *(tage eksamen)* pass; *~ af* con'sist of; *~et (om eksamen)* passed; *ikke ~et (om eksamen)* failed.

besvare *v* answer; *(gengælde)* re'turn; **~lse** *en* answer; re'turn; *(af skoleopgave)* paper; *(i konkurrence)* entry; *i ~lse af Deres skrivelse...* in re'ply to your letter...

besvime *v* faint; **-lse** *en* faint.

besvær *et* trouble; *(anstrengelse)* effort; *(vanskelighed)* difficulty; ~ *med motoren* engine trouble; *vi havde et farligt ~ med dem* they gave us a lot of trouble; *gøre ngt med ~* do· sth with difficulty; *være til ~ for en* trouble sby, be a nuisance to sby.

besvære *v* trouble; ~ *sig over ngt* com'plain about sth.

besværlig *adj* troublesome; *(svær)* difficult; **-hed** *en* difficulty.

besynderlig *adj* odd, strange.

besyv *s: give sit ~ med* chip in.

besætning *en (mandskab)* crew; *(af kvæg)* livestock; *(pynt etc på tøj)* trimming.

besætte *v (om land etc)* occupy; *(om embede)* fill; **-lse** *en* occu'pation; *(af djævel og fig)* pos'session; *(af tomt hus)* squatting.

besøg *et* visit; *komme på ~ hos en* come· to see sby, visit sby; *have ~* have visitors; **-e** *v* visit; *(kort og uanmeldt)* drop in on; **-ende** *en* visitor; **-s·tid** *en (på sygehus etc)* visiting hours *pl.*

betage *v* thrill, im'press; **-lse** *en* thrill, ex'citement; **-nde** *adj* thrilling, im'pressive.

betakke *v: ~ sig for at* de'cline to; *jeg ~r mig!* thank you, but not for me!

betale *v* pay· *(for* for); *det skal du få betalt* you will have to pay· for that; ~ *sig* pay·, be worth it; ~ *af på ngt* pay· off on sth.

betaling *en (som man yder)* payment; *(som man får)* pay; *mod ~* for money; *tage ~ for ngt* charge for sth; *standse ~erne* su'spend one's payments; **-s·balance** *en* 'balance of payments; **-s·kort** *et* credit card.

betegne *v: ~ ngt som ngt* de'scribe sth as sth; **-lse** *en (navn)* name; *(angivelse)* indi'cation; **-nde** *adj* typical; *(vigtig)* sig'nificant.

betinge *v: ~ sig at...* make it a con'dition that...; ~ *sig ngt* re'serve the right to sth.

betingelse *en* con'dition; *gå ind på ens ~r* ac'cept sby's terms; *opfylde ~rne* ful'fil the demands; *på ~ af at...* on con'dition that...; *stille ~r* make· con'ditions; **-s·løs** *adj* uncon'ditional *(fx overgivelse* sur'render).

betinget *adj* con'ditional; ~ *af (dvs. nødvendiggjort af)* ne'cessitated by; *(dvs. afhængig af)* de'pendent on; *en ~ dom* a su'spended sentence.

betjene *v* serve; *(varte op)* wait on; ~ *sig af* use.

betjening *en* service; *(tjenere)* staff; *(af maskine)* ope'ration.

betjent *en* po'liceman *(pl:* -men), po'lice officer.

beton *en* concrete; *armeret ~, jern~* rein'forced concrete.

betone *v* stress, emphasize; **betoning** *en* emphasis.

betragte *v* look at; *(tænke over, anse)* con'sider; ~ *en som sin ven* con'sider sby (as) one's friend.

betragtning *en* conside'ration; *i ~ af at...* con'sidering that...; *tage ngt i ~* con'sider sth, take· sth into conside'ration; *komme i ~* be considered; *lade ngt ude af ~* ig'nore sth.

betro *v (give)* en'trust; *(fortælle)* con'fide; ~ *en sin bil* en'trust sby with one's car; ~ *en sine hemmeligheder* con'fide one's secrets to sby; ~ *sig til en* con'fide in sby; **-et** *adj: en ~et medarbejder* a trusted employ'ee.

betryggende *adj* reas'suring.

betræde *v* set· foot on; *græsset må ikke ~s* keep· off the grass.

betræk *et* cover *(også til dyne etc);* **-ke** *v* cover.

betyde *v* mean·; *hvad ~r det?* what does it mean? *hvad skal det ~?* what is that sup'posed to mean? ~ *ngt (dvs. være vigtig)* matter; *det ~r ikke ngt* it does not matter; **-lig** *adj* con'siderable; *(fremragende)* out'standing // *adv* con'siderably.

betydning *en* meaning, sense; *(vigtighed)* im'portance; *det er af ~* it is im'portant; *bruge et ord i en bestemt ~* use a word in a certain sense; *få ~ for en* be'come· im'portant to sby; *det er uden ~* it does not matter; **-s·fuld** *adj* im'portant.

betændelse *en* inflam'mation *(i* of); *der er gået ~ i såret* the wound has become in'flamed; **betændt** *adj* in'flamed.

betænke *v (tænke på, huske)* bear· in mind, re'member; *~ en i sit testamente* remember sby in one's will; *~ sig (dvs. tænke over det)* think· it over; *(dvs. ombestemme sig)* change one's mind; *(dvs. tøve)* hesitate *(på at* to); *uden at ~ sig* without hesitating; **~lig** *adj (risikabel)* dangerous, risky; *(bekymret, urolig)* un'easy; *finde ngt ~ligt* feel· doubtful about sth; **~lighed** *en* doubt.

betænkningstid *en* time to think.

betænksom *adj* thoughtful; **~hed** *en* thoughtfulness.

beundre *v* ad'mire; **~r** *en* ad'mirer; *(fan)* fan.

beundring *en* admi'ration; **~s·værdig** *adj* 'admirable.

bevare *v* keep·, pre'serve; *bevar mig vel!* dear me! *bevares (dvs. selvfølgelig)* by all means.

bevidne *v* testify; *(skriftligt)* certify.

bevidst *adj* conscious; *(gjort med vilje)* de'liberate; *være sig ngt ~* be conscious of sth; *ikke mig ~* not that I know of; **~hed** *en* consciousness *(om* of); *komme til ~hed* come· round; *miste ~heden* lose· consciousness; **~løs** *adj* un'conscious; **~løshed** *en* un'consciousness; *kunne ngt til ~løshed* know· sth ad nauseam.

bevilge *v* grant.

bevilling *en (af penge)* grant; *(tilladelse fx til handel med spiritus)* licence; *få ~* get· licenced.

bevirke *v* cause.

bevis *et* proof; *(retsligt)* evidence; *~ på* proof of, evidence of; *som ~ på* in proof of; **~e** *v* prove.

bevogte *v* guard; *~t jernbaneoverskæring* level crossing with barrier.

bevogtning *en* guard; *(overvågning)* sur'veillance.

bevokset *adj* over'grown.

bevoksning *en* growth.

bevæbne *v* arm; **bevæbning** *en* arming; *(våben)* weapons *pl.*

bevæge *v* move *(også fig); ~ sig* move; **~lig** *adj (som kan flyttes)* mobile.

bevægelse *en* movement, motion; *(sindsbevægelse)* e'motion; *sætte sig i ~* start moving; **~s·hæmmet** *adj* physically handicapped.

bevæget *adj (rørt)* moved; *(begivenhedsrig)* e'ventful.

bevæggrund *en* 'motive.

beværte *v* treat; *~ en med ngt* treat sby to sth.

beværtning *en (værtshus)* pub; *(mad og drikke)* food and drink.

beæret *adj: føle sig ~* feel· honoured.

bh *en* bra.

bi *en* bee // *adv: stå ~* stand· by; **~avl** *en* beekeeping.

bibeholde *v* keep·, re'tain.

bibel *en* bible; **bibelsk** *adj* biblical.

bibemærkning *en* a'side.

bibeskæftigelse *en* sideline.

bibliotek *et* library; **~ar** *en* li'brarian.

bid *en (stykke)* bit; *en ~ mad* a bite (to eat) // *et* bite; *få ~ (ved fiskeri)* get· a rise.

bide *v* bite·; *~ efter en* snap at sby; *~ i ngt* bite· sth; *~ mærke i ngt* make· a note of sth; *~ smerten i sig* bear· the pain; *~ tænderne sammen* clench one's teeth; *~ på (krogen)* rise· to the bait *(også fig);* **~nde** *adj* biting; *~nde koldt* bitterly cold; **~tang** *en* (pair of) wirecutters.

bidrag *et* contri'bution; *(til barn)* maintenance; *(til ægtefælle)* alimony; **~e** *v* con'tribute *(til* to); *~e med 100 kr.* con'tribute 100 kr.; **~yder** *en* con'tributor.

bidsel *et* bridle.

bidsk *adj* fierce.

bierhverv *et* sideline, extra job.

bifag *et* minor subject.

bifald *et* ap'plause; **~e** *v* ap'prove of; **~s·råb** *pl* cheers.

biflod *en* tributary *(til* of).

bigami *en* bigamy.

bihulebetændelse *en* sinu'sitis.

biks *en (butik)* shop // *et (møg)* rubbish.

bikse *v: ~ med ngt* fiddle with sth; *~ ngt sammen* con'coct sth; **~mad** *en sv.t.* hash.

bikube *en* beehive.

bil *en* car; *(taxa)* taxi; *køre ~* drive· a car; *køre i ~* go· by car; *tage en ~* take· a taxi.

bilag *et (vedr. udgifter)* voucher; *(vedlagt i brev)* en'closure.

bilde *v: ~ en ngt ind* make· sby be-'lieve sth; *~ sig ind at...* i'magine that...; *hvad ~r du dig ind?* who do you think you are?

bil... *sms:* **~dæk** *et* (car) tyre; *(på færge)* car deck; **~fabrik** *en* car factory; **~forsikring** *en* motor (car) in'surance; **~færge** *en* car ferry; **~ist** *en* motorist; **~kø** *en* tailback; **~kørsel** *en* motoring.

billard *et* billiards *pl;* **~bord** *et* billiard table.

bille *en* beetle.

billedbog *en* picture book.

billede *et* picture; *(foto)* photo-(graph); *(maleri)* painting; *stjæle ~t fra en* steal· the show from sby; *tage et ~* take· a photo.

billed... *sms:* **~hugger** *en* sculptor; **~huggerkunst** *en* sculpture; **~kunst** *en* visual art; **~lig** *adj* figurative; **~lotteri** *et* picture lottery; **~rør** *et (tv)* picture tube; **~skærerarbejde** *et* carving; **~tekst** *en* caption.

billet *en* ticket; *bestille ~ til Aïda* book for Aïda; *købe ~* buy· a ticket; **~automat** *en* ticket ma'chine; **~kontor** *et* booking office; *(teat)* box office; **~kontrollør** *en* ticket col'lector; **~pris** *en* ad'mission; *(for tog, skib etc)* fare.

billettere *v* col'lect fares; **billettering** *en* ticket con'trol.

billig *adj* cheap; **~bog** *en* paperback.

billige *v: ~ ngt* ap'prove of sth.

billigt *adv* cheap(ly); *købe ngt ~* buy· sth cheap.

bil... *sms:* **~lygte** *en (forlygte)* headlight; **~motor** *en* car engine; **~nummer** *et* regi'stration number; **~radio** *en* car radio; **~telefon** *en* car phone; **~tog** *et* car-train; **~tur** *en* drive; *tage på ~tur* go· for a drive; **~tyv** *en* car thief *(pl:* thieves); **~tyveri** *et* car theft; **~udlejning** *en* car hire; **~ulykke** *en* car accident; **~værksted** *et* re'pair shop, 'garage.

bilægge *v* settle.

bind *et (bandage)* 'bandage; *(hygiejne~)* (sanitary) towel; *(bog~)* cover, binding; *(del af bogværk)* volume; *gå med armen i ~* have one's arm in a sling; *have ~ om foden* have a bandaged foot; *have ~ for øjnene* be blindfolded.

binde *v* tie, bind·; *(klæbe)* stick·; *(sidde fast, fx om dør)* jam; *~ knude på ngt* tie a knot in sth; *~ an med ngt* tackle sth; *~ en bog ind* bind· a book; *~ snor om ngt* tie a piece of string round sth; *~ en knude op* un'tie a knot; *~ sig til at gøre ngt* com'mit oneself to doing sth; **~ord** *et* con'junction; **~streg** *en* hyphen.

binding *en* binding; **~s·værk** *et* half-timbering; **~s·værkshus** *et* half-timbered house.

bingo *et* bingo.

binyre *en* ad'renal gland.

biodynamisk *adj* biody'namic.

biograf *en* cinema; *gå i ~en* go· to the cinema.

biografi *en* bi'ography; **~sk** *adj* bio-'graphical.

biokemi *en* bio'chemistry; **~ker** *en* bio'chemist; **~sk** *adj* bio'chemical.

biolog *en* bi'ologist; **~i** *en* bi'ology; **~isk** *adj* bio'logical.

biord *et* 'adverb.

biprodukt *et* by-product.

birk *en* birch (tree).

birkes *pl* poppy seeds.

birolle *en* bit-part.

biskop *en* bishop.

bismag *en* after-taste.

bisp *en* bishop; **~e·dømme** *et* diocese.

bisse *en* rough, thug; *skrue ~n på* cut· up rough.

bistand *en* aid, as'sistance; *(social~)* social se'curity; **~s·hjælp** *en* social se'curity; **~s·kontor** *et* social se-'curity office.

bistik *et* bee sting.

bistå *v* aid, as'sist.

bisætning *en* sub'ordinate clause.

bisættelse *en* funeral.

bitter *en (drink)* bitters // *adj* bitter; **~hed** *en* bitterness.

bivej *en* secondary road.

bivirkning *en* side ef'fect.
bivoks *et* beeswax.
bjerg *et (bakke, mindre ~)* hill; *(højt ~, fjeld)* mountain; *bestige et ~* climb a mountain; *et ~ af bøger* a heap of books; **~art** *en* rock; **~bestiger** *en* mountai'neer; **~bestigning** *en* mountai'neering; **~kam** *en* (mountain) crest; **~kæde** *en* mountain range; **~landskab** *et* mountain scenery; **~pas** *et* mountain pass; **~rig** *adj* hilly, mountainous; **~ryg** *en* mountain ridge; **~skred** *et* landslide; **~top** *en* mountain peak; **~værk** *et* mine; **~værksdrift** *en* mining.
bjæffe *v* bark, yelp.
bjælde *en* bell.
bjælke *en* beam; *(i loftet)* rafter; **~hus** *et* timbered house; **~hytte** *en* log cabin.
bjærge *v* rescue; *(om skib)* salvage.
bjærgning *en* rescuing; *(om skib)* salvage.
bjørn *en* bear [bɛə·]; **~e·skindshue** *en* bearskin; **~e·tjeneste** *en* dis'service; **~e·unge** *en* bear's cub.
blad *et (på træ, i bog)* leaf *(pl: leaves); (tidsskrift etc)* magazine; *(avis)* paper; *(åre~, barber~ etc)* blade; *holde et ~* sub'scribe to a magazine (,paper); *spille (,synge) fra ~et* sight-read·.
blade *v: ~ i en bog* turn over the pages of a book; *~ et blad igennem* leaf through a magazine.
bladkiosk *en* newsstand.
blaffe *v* hitchhike; **~r** *en* hitchhiker.
blafre *v (om lys)* flicker; *(om flag etc)* flap.
blanchere *v* blanch.
blande *v* mix; *~ kortene* shuffle the cards; *~ ngt i dejen* mix sth into the dough; *~ sig i ngt* meddle (,inter'fere) in sth; *~ sig med* mingle with; *~ ngt sammen* mix sth; *(ikke kunne kende forskel)* mix sth up; *~ sig uden om* mind one's own business.
blandet *adj* mixed; *~ chokolade* as'sorted chocolates; *det var en ~ fornøjelse* it was a doubtful pleasure; *med blandede følelser* with mixed feelings; *~ ægteskab* mixed marriage.
blanding *en* mixture; *(det at blande)* mixing; *(sammenrod)* jumble; *en broget ~ af boghandlere* a medley of booksellers; **~s·batteri** *et* mixer tap.
blandt *præp* a'mong; *(ud af)* from among; *~ andet* among other things; *~ andet fordi han er sur* for one thing because he's cross; *~ andre* among others; *vi har fire veteraner (i) ~ os* we have four veterans among us.
blank *adj* shining, bright; *(glat også:)* shiny; *(med højglans)* glossy; *(tom, ubeskrevet)* blank; *et ~t afslag* a flat re'fusal; *være ~ (dvs. ikke kunne huske ngt)* have a mental block; *(dvs. ikke have penge)* be broke.
blanket *en* form; *udfylde en ~* fill in a form.
blankpoleret *adj* polished.
blankslidt *adj* (worn) shiny.
blafemi *en* 'blasphemy.
ble *en* nappy; **~bukser** *pl* nappy pants.
bleg *adj* pale; *blive ~* turn pale; **~e** *v* bleach; **~fed** *adj* pasty; **~hed** *en* paleness, pallor; **~ne** *v* turn pale; *(falme)* fade; **~næbbet** *adj* pale.
blender *en* liquidizer, blender.
blesnip *en* (dis'posable) nappy holder.
blid *adj* gentle, soft; *(rar, sød)* kind; **~hed** *en* gentleness, softness; kindness; **~t** *adv* gently, softly; kindly.
blik *et (metal)* tin; *(øjekast)* look, glance; *have ~ for ngt* have an eye for sth; *kaste et ~ på ngt* throw· a glance at sth; *sende en et ~* give· sby a look; *ved første ~* at first sight (,glance); **~dåse** *en* tin; **~fang** *et* eye-catcher.
blikkenslager *en* plumber; **~arbejde** *et* plumbing.
blikstille *adj* dead calm.
blind *adj* blind *(for* to); *blive ~* go· blind; *jeg er ikke ~ for hans fortrin* I'm not blind to his assets; *en ~* a blind person; *~ passager* stowaway; *~ vej* dead end; **~e** *s: i ~e* blindly, in the dark; **~e·buk** *en* blind man's

buff; **~gyde** *en (fig)* blind alley; **~e·skrift** *en* Braille [breil]; **~hed** *en* blindness; **~skrift** *en (på maskine etc)* touch-typing.

blindtarm *en* ap'pendix; **~s·betændelse** *en* appendi'citis.

blink *en (til fiskeri)* blinker // *et (lys~ etc)* flash, gleam; *(med øjnene)* wink; **~e** *v* flash, gleam; wink; *~e med en lygte* flash a light; **~lys** *et* flashlight; *(på bil)* indicator; *(på udrykningskøretøj)* flashing blue light.

blist *en* blister.

blitz *en (foto)* flash; **~pære** *en* flashbulb; **~terning** *en* flashcube.

blive *v* be; *(om ændring, overgang, efterhånden ~)* be'come·; *(foran adj også)* get·; *(lidt efter lidt ~)* grow·; *(pludseligt ~)* turn; *(forblive)* stay, re'main; *(vise sig at være)* be, turn out to be; *~ glemt* be for'gotten; *~ gift* get married; *han er blevet direktør* he has become a di'rector; *~ berømt* become· (,grow·) famous; *~ rig* get· rich; *han er blevet fed* he has grown fat; *~ vred* get· angry, go· mad; *~ rød i hovedet* turn red; *~ hjemme* stay at home; *de blev i en uge* the stayed for a week; *bogen blev en bestseller* the book was a bestseller; *det ~r 55p (om pris)* that will be 55p; *hun ~r 50 i maj* she will be 50 in May; *det ~r regnvejr* it is going to rain; *hvad blev der af ham?* what became of him? *det ~r der ikke ngt af* that won't happen; *~ af med en (,ngt)* get· rid of sby (,sth); *~ til (dvs. opstå)* come· into being; *(dvs. blive født)* be born; *~ til ngt (om person)* suc'ceed, get· somewhere; *(blive gennemført)* come· off; *det ~r ikke til ngt* nothing will come of it; *~ ved* go· on, con'tinue; *~ ved med at gøre ngt* go· on doing sth, con'tinue to do sth; *~ ved med at være ngt* re'main sth; *~ væk (dvs. holde sig væk)* stay away; *(dvs. forsvinde, gå tabt)* disap'pear, be lost.

blod *et* blood; *få ~ på tanden* de'velop a taste for it; *~et stivnede i mine årer* my blood froze; *han har det i ~et* it's in his blood; **~bad** *et* bloodbath, 'massacre; **~bank** *en* blood bank; **~bøg** *en* copper beech; **~donor** *en* blood donor; **~dråbe** *en* drop of blood; **~forgiftning** *en* blood poisoning.

blodig *adj (med blod på)* blood-stained; *(bloddryppende)* gory; *det er ~t alvor* it's dead serious.

blod... *sms:* **~kar** *et* blood vessel; **~legeme** *et* blood corpuscle; **~mangel** *en* a'naemia; **~omløb** *et* circu'lation; **~plet** *en* bloodstain; **~procent** *en* haemo'globin per'centage; **~prop** *en* blood clot; *~prop ved hjertet* coronary (throm'bosis); **~prøve** *en (selve prøven)* blood sample; *(analysen)* blood test; **~pøl** *en* a pool of blood; **~pølse** *en* black pudding; **~skam** *en* incest; **~skudt, ~sprængt** *adj* bloodshot; **~s·udgydelse** *en* bloodshed; **~sukker** *et* blood sugar; **~sænkning** *en (med)* sedimen'tation rate; **~tab** *et* loss of blood; **~transfusion** *en* blood trans'fusion; **~tryk** *et* blood pressure; *forhøjet ~tryk* hyper'tension; **~type** *en* blood group; **~tørstig** *adj* bloodthirsty; **~åre** *en* vein.

blok *en (klods, sko~, hus~, hejseværk etc)* block; *(skrive~ etc)* pad; *(pol, fx østblokken)* bloc.

blokade *en* bloc'kade; *lave ~ mod et firma* boycott a firm; **~vagt** *en* picket.

blokbogstaver *pl* block capitals.

blokdannelse *en (pol)* for'mation af blocs.

blokere *v (spærre)* block; *(firma etc)* bloc'kade; **blokering** *en* blocking; *(af hjul)* locking; *(psyk)* block.

blokfløjte *en* re'corder.

blokpolitik *en* joint policy.

bloktilskud *et* block grant.

blomkål *en* cauliflower.

blomme *en (bot)* plum; *(i æg)* yolk; *have det som ~n i et æg* be in clover; **~træ** *et* plum tree.

blomst *en* flower; *stå i ~* be in bloom; *afskårne ~er* cut flowers; *en buket ~er* a bunch of flowers.

blomster... *sms:* **~bed** *et* flowerbed; **~forretning** *en* florist's; **~frø** *et* flower seed; **~gødning** *en* fertilizer; **~handler** *en* florist; **~krans** *en* floral wreath; **~løg** *et* bulb.

blomstre *v* flower, be in flower; *(trives)* flourish; ~ *op* begin· to flourish; *(om person)* blossom out; **~nde** *adj* flowering; *(fig)* flourishing; **~t** *adj* flowered.

blomstring *en* flowering; *(fig)* bloom.

blond *adj* blonde, fair.

blonde *en* lace.

blondine *en* blonde.

blot *adj (bar, nøgen)* naked; *(alene)* mere, very; *med det ~te øje* with the naked eye; ~ *ved tanken om det...* at the mere thought of it... // *adv (kun)* only, simply, merely; *hvis* ~ if only; *når* ~ so long as.

blotte *v* un'cover; *(afsløre)* re'veal; *(røbe)* be'tray; ~ *hovedet* bare one's head; ~ *sig (dvs. dumme sig)* blunder; *(røbe sig)* give· oneself away; *(krænke blufærdigheden)* ex'pose oneself in'decently; **~lse** *en* ex'posure.

blotter *en* flasher.

blottet *adj (bar)* bare, naked; ~ *for* de'void of; *han er helt ~ for humoristisk sans* he has absolutely no sense of humour.

bluffe *v* bluff.

blufærdig *adj* modest; **~hed** *en* modesty; **~hedskrænkelse** *en* in'decent ex'posure.

blunde *v* doze.

blus *et (bål)* fire: *(ild)* blaze; *(gas~)* jet; *svagt ~ (på komfur)* low heat.

bluse *en* blouse; *(strik~)* jersey.

blusse *v (brænde)* blaze; *(rødme)* blush; ~ *op (om kampe etc)* flare up.

bly *et* lead [lɛd] // *adj* shy.

blyant *en* pencil; *skrive med ~* write· in pencil; **~spidser** *en* pencil sharpener; **~stift** *en* pencil lead [lɛd].

blyindfattet *adj* leaded ['lɛdid].

blæk *et* ink; **~hus** *et* inkpot; **~sprutte** *en* cuttlefish, squid; *(ottearmet)* octopus; *(til bagage)* luggage holder, spider.

blænde *v (med lys)* blind; *(imponere)* dazzle; *(dør, vindue)* cover (up); ~ *ned (om billygter)* dip the headlights; **~nde** *adj* dazzling.

blænder *en (foto)* 'aperture.

blære *en (anat)* bladder; *(vable)* blister; *(luft~)* bubble // *v:* ~ *sig* show off; **~betændelse** *en* cy'stitis; **~røv** *en* (S) swank; **~t** *adj(om person)* stuck-up.

blæse *v* blow·; *det ~r* it is windy; *vinduet blæste op* the window blew open; ~ *en ballon op* in'flate a bal'loon; ~ *være med det!* never mind! *det vil jeg ~ på* I could not care less; ~ *på horn (,trompet etc)* blow· the horn (,the trumpet etc); **~bælg** *en* bellows; **~instrument** *et* wind instrument; **~lampe** *en* blowtorch; **~nde** *adj* windy.

blæser *en (mus)* wind player; *(tekn)* blower; *~ne (i orkester)* the winds.

blæsevejr *et* windy weather.

blæst *en* wind.

blød *s: lægge ngt i ~* put· sth to soak; *lægge hovedet i ~* rack one's brains // *adj* soft; *(følsom)* sensitive; *(for ~, eftergivende)* weak; ~ *mand* new man; *gøre en ~* soften sby up; **~dyr** *et* mollusc.

bløde *v* bleed·; ~ *ngt op* steep sth.

bløder *en (med)* haemo'philiac; **~syge** *en* haemo'philia.

blødgøre *v* soften.

blødgøringsmiddel *et* softener.

blødhed *en* softness; *(eftergivenhed)* weakness.

blødkogt *adj* softboiled.

blødning *en* haemorrhage; *(menstruation)* period.

blødsøden *adj* soft.

blå *adj* blue; *~t mærke* bruise; *Blå Bog sv.t.* Who's Who; *~t øje* black eye, (S) shiner; **~bær** *et* bilberry; **~klokke** *en* bluebell; **~lig** *adj* bluish; **~mejse** *en* bluetit; **~musling** *en* mussel; **~øjet** *adj* blue-eyed; *(naiv)* naïve, simple.

BNP *(fork.f. bruttonationalprodukt)* GNP *(fork.f.* gross national product).

bo *et (konkurs~)* assets *pl; (døds~)* e'state; *(hjem)* home; *(dyrs ~)* nest, den; *sætte* ~ settle; *opgøre et* ~ wind· up an estate // *v* live; *(på besøg, kortere ophold)* stay; ~ *hos en* live (,stay) with sby.

boble *en/v* buble; **-hal** *en* air hall.

bod *en (bøde)* fine; *(handels~)* stall, booth; *(butik)* shop; *gøre* ~ do· penance; *råde* ~ *på ngt* make· sth good.

bog *en* book; *føre* ~ *over ngt* keep· a record of sth; **-bind** *et* cover, binding; **-binder** *en* bookbinder; **-finke** *en* chaffinch; **-føre** *v* enter; **-føring** *en* book-keeping.

boghandel *en (butik)* bookseller's; *(det at sælge bøger)* bookselling.

boghandler *en* bookseller.

bogholder *en* book-keeper.

bogholderi *et (afdeling)* book-keeping de'partment; *(det at føre bøger)* book-keeping.

boghvede *en* buckwheat.

boghylde *en* bookshelf *(pl:* -shelves).

bogmærke *et* book marker.

bogreol *en* bookcase, book shelves *pl.*

bogstav *et* letter, character; *små ~er* lower-case (,small) letters; *store ~er* upper-case (,capital) letters; *tale med store ~er til ham* give· him a piece of one's mind; **-e·lig** *adj* literal; *tage ngt ~e·ligt* take· sth literally, follow sth to the letter; *~e·lig talt* literally (speaking); **-orden** *en: i ~orden* alpha'betically.

bogstøtte *en* book end.

bogtrykker *en* printer.

bogtrykkeri *et* printer's, printing works.

boheme *en* bo'hemian.

boks *en* box; *(bank~)* safe-deposit (box); *(tlf)* (tele)phone booth.

bokse *v* box; **-handske** *en* boxing glove; **-kamp** *en* boxing match; **-r** *en* boxer *(også om hund);* **-ring** *en* ring; **boksning** *en* boxing.

bold *en* ball; *spille* ~ play ball; *spille ~en i hænderne på en* pass the ball to sby; **-bane** *en* playing field; **-dreng** *en (tennis)* ball boy; **-fornemmelse** *en (sport)* feel for the ball; **-spil** *et* ball game; **-træ** *et* bat.

bolig *en* residence; *(hus)* house; *(lejlighed)* flat; *skaffe* ~ pro'vide housing; **-anvisning** *en (kontor)* housing agency; **-blok** *en* block of flats; **-byggeri** *et* house building; **-forhold** *pl* housing con'ditions; **-haj** *en* slum landlord; **-hus** *et* furnishing house; **-indretning** *en* in'terior deco'ration; **-kvarter** *et* resi'dential area; **-mangel** *en* housing shortage; **-marked** *et* housing market; **-ministerium** *et* Ministry of Housing; **-nævn** *et* rent con'trol board; **-ret** *en* rent tri'bunal; **-selskab** *et* housing so'ciety; **-sikring** *en* housing al'lowance; **-søgende** *adj* flat-hunting; **-tekstiler** *pl* soft furnishings; **-udstyr** *et* furnishings *pl.*

bolle *en (af brøddej)* bun, muffin; *(kød~)* ball // *v* (V!) screw.

bolsje *et* sweet.

bolt *en* bolt; **-e** *v* bolt.

boltre *v:* ~ *sig* romp about; *han er ude at* ~ *sig (dvs. vifte med ørerne)* he's out 'gallivanting.

bolværk *et* wharf.

bom *en* bar; *(jernb)* gate; *(gymn)* beam.

bombardere *v* bom'bard; *(med bomber)* bomb.

bombe *en* bomb // *v* bomb; **-fly** *et* bomber; **-sikker** *adj (fig, helt sikker)* positive, dead certain.

bommert *en* blunder; *begå en* ~ make· a blunder, put· one's foot in it.

bomstille *adj* stock-still; *(tavs)* quite silent.

bomstærk *adj* strong as a horse.

bomuld *en* cotton; **-s·garn** *et* cotton (yarn); **-s·stof** *et* cotton (ma'terial).

bon *en* ticket, sales slip.

bonde *en* farmer; *(hist)* peasant; *(i skak)* pawn; **-fange** *v* con; **-fangeri** *et* confidence tricks *pl;* **-gård** *en* farm; **-kone** *en* farmer's wife *(pl:* farmers' wives*);* **-mand** *en* farmer; **-rose** *en (bot)* peony.

bone *v* polish; **-voks** *et* floor polish.

bonus *en* bonus.

boplads *en* settlement.

bopæl *en* ad'dress.

bor *et (tekn)* drill; *(kem)* boron.

bord *et* table; *dække* ~ lay· (,set·) the

table; *tage af ~et* clear the table; *rejse sig fra ~et* leave· the table; *gå fra ~e* go· a'shore; *gå om ~ i ngt (fig)* tackle sth; *falde over ~* fall· overboard; *gå til ~s* go· in to dinner (,lunch etc); *sidde til ~s* be at table; *koldt ~* smörgasbord; **-ben** *et* table leg; **-bøn** *en* grace; *bede ~bøn* say· grace; **-dame** *en* dinner partner.

borde *v (et skib)* board.

bordel *et* brothel.

bord... *sms:* **-ende** *en* head of the table; **-herre** *en* dinner partner; **komfur** *s* hob; **-kort** *et* place card; **-plade** *en* tabletop; **-plan** *en* seating plan; **-skåner** *en* (dish) mat; **-tennis** *et* table tennis, ping-pong®; **-vin** *en* table wine.

bore *v* bore, drill; *~ efter ngt* drill for sth; **-maskine** *en (elek)* power drill; **-platform** *en* oilrig; **-tårn** *et* derrick.

borg *en* castle, stronghold.

borger *en* citizen; **-krig** *en* civil war.

borgerlig *adj* civil; *(middelklasse-)* middle-class; *(neds)* bourgeois ['bu:rʒwa]; *(jævn)* plain; *de ~e partier* the non-socialist parties; *~ vielse* civil marriage.

borgerrepræsentation *en* town (,city) council.

borgerret *en* citizenship.

borgmester *en* mayor.

boring *en* boring, drilling; *(i fx kanon)* bore.

bornholmer *en* person from Bornholm; *røget ~* kipper from Bornholm; **-ur** *et* grandfather clock.

borsyre *en* boric acid.

bort *en* border; *(bånd)* ribbon.

bort *adj* away, off; *gå ~* go· away; *(dø)* pass away; *se ~ fra* leave· out of conside'ration; **-e** *adv* away, gone; *blive ~e* disap'pear; *(holde sig væk)* stay away; *langt ~e* far away.

bortforpagte *v* farm out.

bortføre *v* ab'duct; *(kidnappe)* kidnap; *~ et fly* hijack a plane; **-lse** *en* ab'duction; kidnapping; *(af fly)* hijacking; **-r** *en* ab'ductor; kidnapper; hijacker.

bortlede *v: ~ ens opmærksomhed fra ngt* di'vert sby's at'tention from sth.

bortrejst *adj* away, out of town.

bortset *adj: ~ fra* ex'cept for, a'part from; *~ fra at* ex'cept that.

bosiddende *adj* resident.

bosætte *v: ~ sig* settle; **-lse** *en* settlement.

botanik *en* 'botany; **-er** *en* 'botanist.

botanisk *adj* bo'tanical *(fx have* gardens).

bouillon *en* stock; **-terning** *en* stock cube.

bourgogne *en* 'burgundy.

bov *en (på dyr)* shoulder; *(mar)* bow.

boykotte *v* boycott.

bradepande *en* roasting pan.

brag *et* bang, crash; **-e** *v* crash; *~ende klapsalver* thunderous ap'plause; *~ende succes* smash hit.

brak *s: ligge ~* lie· fallow; *(fig)* be left unex'ploited; **-mark** *en* fallow field; **-tud** *en* snub nose; **-vand** *et* brackish water.

bramfri *adj* out'spoken, straight'forward.

branche *en* trade, line.

brand *en* fire; *stikke i ~* set· fire to; *komme i ~* catch· fire; **-alarm** *en* fire a'larm; **-bil** *en* fire engine; **-bælte** *et* fire break; **-dør** *en* fire door.

brandert *en: få sig en ~* get· drunk; *han gjorde det i en ~* he did· it under the influence; *sove ~en ud* sleep· it off.

brand... *sms:* **-fare** *en* danger of fire; **-farlig** *adj* in'flammable; **-forsikring** *en* fire in'surance; **-fælde** *en* firetrap; **-mand** *en* fireman *(pl:* -men); **-mur** *en* firewall; **-sikker** *adj* fireproof; **-sikring** *en* fire pre'cautions *pl;* **-slange** *en* fire hose; **-slukker** *en* fire ex'tinguisher; **-station** *en* fire station; **-stiftelse** *en* arson; **-sår** *et* burn; **-trappe** *en* fire e'scape; **-væsen** *et* fire bri'gade.

branke *v* burn·.

bras *et* rubbish, trash.

brase *v: ~ ind i stuen* barge into the

room; ~ *sammen* crash; ~ *kartofler* fry po'tatoes.
brasilianer *en*, **brasiliansk** *adj* Bra'zilian; **Brasilien** *s* Bra'zil.
brat *adj (stejl)* steep; *(pludselig)* sudden; *standse* ~ stop short.
bratsch *en* viola.
bravur *en: med* ~ with style; brilliantly; **~nummer** *et* star turn.
bred *en (af sø)* shore; *(af flod etc)* bank; *gå over sine ~der (om flod)* break· the banks // *adj* broad, wide.
bredde *en* breadth, width; *(geogr)* latitude; *i ~n* a'cross; **~grad** *en* de'gree of latitude; *på vore ~grader* in our parts.
brede *v* spread·; ~ *(ud)* spread; ~ *sig (dvs. fylde for meget)* take· up room; *(blive bredere)* broaden; *(blive udbredt, kendt)* spread·.
bredskuldret *adj* broad-shouldered.
bredt *adv* broadly, widely; *tale vidt og ~ om ngt* talk about sth in every detail.
bregne *en* fern, bracken.
bremse *en (zo)* horsefly; *(tekn)* brake // *v* brake; *(fig)* check; ~ *op* brake, ap'ply the brakes; **~belægning** *en* brake lining; **~lygte** *en* brake light; **~længde** *en* braking distance; **~pedal** *en* brake (pedal); **~spor** *et* skid marks *pl;* **~væske** *en* brake fluid; **bremsning** *en* braking.
Bretagne *s* 'Brittany.
brev *et* letter; *(kort ~)* note; *et ~ knappenåle* a packet of pins; *sende et ~ til en* send· sby a letter; **~bombe** *en* letter bomb; **~due** *en* carrier pigeon; **~hoved** *et* letterhead; **~kasse** *en (i hoveddør etc)* letterbox; *(på gaden)* post-box; *(i blad, avis)* letters to the editor; **~ordner** *en* file; **~papir** *et* notepaper; **~presser** *en* paperweight; **~porto** *en* postage; **~sprække** *en* letter-box; **~stemme** *en* postal vote; **~vægt** *en* letter scales.
brigade *en* bri'gade.
brik *en (i spil)* piece; *(bordskåner)* table mat; *(smørebræt)* platter.
briks *en (seng)* plank bed.
brillant *en* brilliant // *adj* splendid.
brilleetui *et* spectacle case; **brilleglas** *et* (spectacle) lens.
briller *pl* spectacles, glasses; *gå med ~* wear· spectacles (,glasses).
brilleslange *en* cobra.
brillestang *en* (spectacle) arm; **brillestel** *et* (spectacle) frame.
bringe *v (til den der taler)* bring·; *(væk fra den der taler)* take·; *(hente)* fetch; ~ *en til fornuft* bring· sby to his senses; ~ *varer ud* de'liver goods.
brint *en* hydrogen; **~overilte** *en* (hydrogen) per'oxide.
brise *en* breeze.
brissel *en* sweetbread.
briste *v* burst·; *(knække)* snap; *(gå galt)* fail; *det fik mit hjerte til at ~* it broke my heart; *vores håb ~de* our hopes were shattered; ~ *i gråd* burst· into tears.
brite *en* Briton; *~rne* the British.
britisk *adj* British.
bro *en* bridge; *(anløbs~)* jetty.
broche *en* brooch.
brochure *en* leaflet, pamphlet.
brod *en* sting.
broder *en se bror.*
brodere *v* em'broider.
broderi *et* em'broidery.
broder... *sms:* **~land** *et* sister country; **~parten** *s* the lion's share; **~skab** *et* brotherhood.
broget *adj (farverig)* colourful; *(plettet)* mottled; *(blandet)* motley; *(rodet)* con'fused; *en ~ forsamling* a motley crowd; *nu bliver det for ~!* that is too much!
brok *en* hernia; **~bind** *et* truss.
brokke *v: ~ sig over ngt* grumble about sth; *(klage)* com'plain about sth.
brolægning *en* paving.
brom *et (kem)* bromine.
brombær *et* blackberry; **~busk** *en* bramble.
bronkitis *en* bron'chitis.
bronze *en* bronze; **~alder** *en* bronze age.
bropenge *pl* bridge toll; **bropille** *en* pier.

bror *en* brother; *han er ~ til Susy* he is Susy's brother, he is a brother of Susy's.

brosten *en* cobble(stone).

brud *en* bride.

brud *et (hul, sprængning)* break *(på* in), bursting *(på* of); *(på rør også)* leak *(på* in); *(overtrædelse, fx af regler)* breach *(på* of); *(sten~, kalk~ etc)* quarry; *(knogle~)* fracture.

brude... *sms:* **~buket** *en* wedding bouquet; **~kjole** *en* wedding dress; **~par** *et* bride and groom; *(efter vielsen)* newlyweds *pl;* **~pige** *en* bridesmaid; **~slør** *et* bridal veil.

brudgom *en* bridegroom.

brudstykke *et* fragment.

brug *en* use; *gøre ~ af ngt* make· use of sth; *have ~ for ngt* need sth; *tage ngt i ~* start using sth; *være i ~* be in use; *klar til ~* ready for use; *til ~ for en* for the use of sby; *det er skik og ~* it is the custom; **~bar** *adj* us(e)able; *(til nytte)* useful.

bruge *v* use; *(gå med, fx briller)* wear·; *(penge, tid)* spend·; *~s inden... (på vare)* expi'ration date; *han ~r nr. 45 i sko* he takes a 45 in shoes; *~ mælk i teen* take· milk in one's tea; *~ ngt op* use sth up, finish sth; *smørret er brugt op* the butter is finished.

bruger *en* user; **~venlig** *adj* user-friendly.

brugs *en* co-op; **~anvisning** *en* di'rections for use *pl; (til maskine)* operating in'structions *pl;* **~forening** *en* co-'operative (con'sumer) so'ciety; **~genstand** *en* basic com'modity; *(redskab)* u'tensil; **~kunst** *en* com'mercial art.

brugt *adj* used, second-hand; **~vogn** *en* second-hand car.

brumme *v* hum; *(knurre)* growl, grumble.

brun *adj* brown; *(solbrændt)* tanned; **~e** *v* brown; *(om solen)* tan; *~ede kartofler* caramelled po'tatoes.

brunst *en (om han)* rut; *(om hun)* heat; **~ig** *adj* rutting, in heat; **~tid** *en* mating season.

brus *et* roar; *(i drik)* fizz; **~e** *v (om lyd)* roar; *(om drik)* fizz; *(med vand, sprøjte over)* spray; **~e·bad** *et* shower; **~e·kabine** *en* shower cubicle; **~e·niche** *en* shower cabinet; **~er** *en* shower.

brusk *en (i kød)* gristle; *(anat)* cartilage.

brutal *adj* brutal, cruel; **~itet** *en* bru'tality, cruelty.

bruttoløn *en* gross income; **bruttovægt** *en* gross weight.

Bruxelles *s* Brussels.

bryde *v* break·; *~ lyset* re'fract the light; *~ af* break off; *~ igennem* break through; *~ ind* break in; *~ ind i en samtale* inter'rupt a conver'sation; *~ løs* break out; *(om storm etc)* break; *~ op (dvs. tage af sted)* leave·; *~ en lås op* break· open a lock; *~ sammen* break· down; *~ ud* break· out; *~ sig om* like, care for; *(tage sig nær)* care about, mind; *(høre efter, tage notits af)* pay· at'tention to; *jeg ~r mig ikke om at gøre det* I don't like to do it; *jeg ~r mig ikke om hvad de siger* I don't care what they say; **~kamp** *en* wrestling match; **~r** *en* wrestler.

bryderi *et* trouble.

brydning *en* breaking; *(af kul etc)* mining; *(sport)* wrestling.

bryg *et* brew; **~ge** *v* brew; **~geri** *et* brewery; **~gers** *et* scullery; **~ning** *en* brewing.

bryllup *et* wedding; *holde ~ (dvs. gifte sig)* get· married; *(dvs. fejre ~)* have a wedding party; **~s·dag** *en* wedding anni'versary; **~s·rejse** *en* honeymoon.

bryst *et* breast; *(brystkasse)* chest; *give et barn ~* nurse a baby; **~barn** *et* breast-fed baby; **~holder** *en* bra, (H) brassiere; **~kasse** *en* chest; **~lomme** *en* breast pocket; **~mål** *et (om mand)* chest; *(om kvinde)* bust; **~svømning** *en* breaststroke; **~vorte** *en* nipple.

bræ *en* glacier.

brædder *pl* boards; **bræddevæg** *en* wooden wall.

bræge *v* bleat; **~n** *en* bleating.

bræk *s (opkast)* vomit; *(indbrud)* break-in; *lave et* ~ (S) pull a job.
brækjern *et* crowbar.
brække *v* break·; *(knække med et smæld)* snap; ~ *ngt op* break· sth open; ~ *sig* be sick, vomit.
brækning *en* vomiting.
brænde *et* (fire)wood // *v* burn·; *(være tændt)* be on; *(kaffe)* roast; *(keramik etc)* fire; *(lig)* cre'mate; ~ *et straffespark (fodb)* miss a penalty; ~ *en af (dvs. svigte aftale)* stand· sby up; *(dvs. ikke gifte sig med)* jilt sby; ~ *efter at* be dying to; ~ *inde* die in a fire; ~ *inde med ngt* be left sitting with sth; ~ *inde med et svar* not get· a chance to answer; ~ *ned* burn· down; ~ *op* be burnt; ~ *på (om mad)* be burnt; ~ *sammen (om bilmotor etc)* break· down; ~ *sig* burn· oneself; **-knude** *en* log; **-mærke** *v* brand; **-nde** *adj* burning; **-nælde** *en* (stinging) nettle; **-ovn** *en (til opvarmning)* stove; *(til keramik etc)* kiln; **-skur** *et* woodshed; **-vin** *en* spirits *pl.*
brænding *en (det at brænde)* burning; *(af keramik etc)* firing; *(om bølger)* surf.
brændpunkt *et* focus.
brændsel *et* fuel; **-s·olie** *en* fuel oil.
brændstof *et* fuel.
brændt *adj* burnt, burned; *lugte* ~ smell of sth burning.
bræt *et* board; *sætte alt på ét* ~ stake everything on one chance; **-sejlads** *en* windsurfing; **-spil** *et* board game.
brød *et* bread; *et* ~ a loaf *(pl:* loaves); *to* ~ two loaves; *smøre et stykke* ~ spread· a piece of bread; *ristet* ~ toast; *en skive* ~ a slice of bread; *gå som varmt* ~ sell· like hot cakes; *han er et ordentligt* ~ he's a big hunk.
brødebetynget *adj* guilty.
brød... *sms:* **-kasse** *en* bread bin; **-kniv** *en* bread knife *(pl:* knives); **-krumme** *en* breadcrumb; **-rister** *en* toaster; **-skorpe** *en* breadcrust.
brøk *en* fraction; **-del** *en* fraction; *på en ~del af et sekund* in a split second; **-streg** *en* fraction line.
brøl *et* roar; **-e** *v* roar; *(råbe)* shout; *(hyle, vræle)* howl; *(om ko)* low.
brøler *en* blunder, howler.
brønd *en* well; **-karse** *en* watercress.
bud *et (besked)* message; *(som bringer varer ud)* de'livery man *(pl:* men); *(som bringer besked)* messenger; *(tilbud)* offer; *de ti* ~ the ten com'mandments; *sende* ~ *efter en* send· for sby; *give et* ~ *på ngt* make· an offer for sth; *(ved auktion)* make· a bid for sth.
buddhist *en,* **buddhistisk** *adj* 'Buddhist.
budding *en* pudding.
budget *et* 'budget; *lægge* ~ draw· up a budget; *være på ~tet* be in the budget; **budget-** *(om billig vare etc)* af'fordable; **budgettere** *v* budget.
budskab *et* message; *(nyhed)* news.
bue *en (flits~, violin~ etc)* bow; *(tegnet, dannet)* curve; *(bygn)* arch // *v* arch, curve; **-gang** *en* ar'cade; **-skydning** *en* archery; **-skytte** *en* archer.
buffet *en (møbel)* sideboard; *(med servering)* 'buffet ['bufei].
bug *en (mave)* stomach, belly; *(underliv)* 'abdomen.
bugne *v* bulge; ~ *med* a'bound with.
bugserbåd *en* tug; **bugsere** *v* tow, tug; **bugsering** *en* towing.
bugspytkirtel *en* pancreas.
bugt *en* bay, gulf; *(mindre, vig)* creek; *(bugtning)* curve, bend; *få* ~ *med ngt* over'come· sth.
bugtaler *en* ven'triloquist.
bugte *v:* ~ *sig* wind·; **-t** *adj* winding.
buk *en (om ged)* billy goat; *(om hjort)* buck; *(støtte~, fx til bord)* trestle; *(gymn)* buck; *(hilsen)* bow; *springe* ~ play leapfrog.
buket *en (blomster)* bunch; *(vins duft)* bouquet; *(fig, fx spare~)* package.
bukke *v* bend·; *(hilse også)* bow *(for* to); ~ *ngt sammen* bend sth, double sth up; ~ *sig* bend down; ~ *under for* suc'cumb to.
bukse... *sms:* **-bag** *en* trouser seat; **-ben** *et* trouser leg; **-dragt** *en* trouser suit; **-lomme** *en* trouser pocket.
bukser *pl* trousers; *et par* ~ a pair of

trousers; *gå med* ~ wear· trousers; *tisse i* ~*ne* wet· one's pants.
buldre *v (banke på etc)* bang; *(larme)* rumble; ~ *på døren* bang the door.
bule *en (i panden)* bump; *(i bil etc)* dent; *(ngt der fylder)* bulge; *(beværtning)* joint // *v:* ~ *ud* bulge; **~t** *adj (om bil etc)* dented.
bullen *adj* swollen.
bumletog *et* local train.
bump *et (stød)* jolt; *(lyd)* thud; *(bule el. hul i vej)* bump; *(i gade for at nedsætte farten)* hump; **~e** *v* jolt; thud.
bums *en (filipens)* pimple; *(om person)* tramp.
bund *en* bottom; *i (,på)* ~*en af* in (,at) the bottom of; *i* ~ *og grund* throughly, utterly; *med* ~*en i vejret* upside down; *stå på bar* ~ *(om politiet)* not have a clue; *gå til* ~*s* go· down; *komme til* ~*s i ngt* get· to the bottom of sth.
bunde *v* touch bottom; ~ *i* be due to.
bunden *adj:* ~ *opgave* set subject; ~ *opsparing* com'pulsory saving.
bundfald *et* de'posit.
bundløs *adj* bottomless; *i* ~ *gæld* up to one's ears in debt.
bundrekord *en: sætte* ~ have reached an all-time low.
bundt *et* bundle; *(om blomster etc)* bunch; *hele* ~*et* the lot; *han er den bedste af hele* ~*et* he is the best of the bunch.
bunke *en* heap, pile; ~ *af* heaps of, lots of //*v:* ~ *sammen* heap up.
bunker *en* bunker.
buntmager *en* furrier.
bur *et* cage; *sætte et dyr i* ~ cage an animal.
burde *v* ought to; *det* ~ *du ikke gøre* you ought not to (,should not) do that.
bure *v:* ~ *sig inde* coop up.
bureau *et* office; **~krati** *et* bu'reaucracy; *(neds)* red tape.
burhøns *pl* battery hens.
burre *en (bot)* burdock; **~lukning** *en* velcro-fastening.
bus *en* bus; *(turistbus også)* coach; **~bane** *en* bus lane; **~chauffør** *en* busdriver.
busk *en* bush, shrub; *komme ud af* ~*en* come· out in the open.
buskads *et* shrubbery; *(tæt)* thicket.
busket *adj* bushy.
bussemand *en (i næsen)* bogey; *(som skræmmer)* bogeyman *(pl:* -men).
busseronne *en* smock.
buste *en* bust.
bustur *en* bus-ride.
butik *en* shop; *gå i* ~*ker* go· shopping; *se på* ~*ker* go· window-shopping; **~s·center** *et* shopping centre; **~s·indehaver** *en* shopkeeper; **~s·kæde** *en* chain of shops; **~s.medhjælper** *en* shop as'sistant; **~s·pris** *en* retail price; **~s·tyv** *en* shoplifter; **~s·vindue** *et* shopwindow.
butterdej *en* puff pastry.
butterfly *en* bow tie; *(svømning)* butterfly.
buttet *adj* plump.
by *en* town; *(storby)* city; *være i* ~*en* be out; *(på indkøb)* be shopping, *gå i* ~*en (på indkøb)* go· shopping; *(ud at more sig)* go· out; **~bud** *et* messenger; *(som bringer varer ud)* de'livery man *(pl:* -men).
byde *v (befale)* com'mand; *(tilbyde)* offer; *(komme med et bud)* bid· *(på* for); *(indbyde)* ask; ~ *en velkommen* bid· sby welcome; ~ *en indenfor* ask sby in; ~ *på ngt* offer sth; *(afgive bud på)* bid· for sth; ~ *ngt rundt* pass sth round.
bydel *en* part of town.
bydende *adj* com'manding; *(tvingende)* urgent; ~ *nødvendig* absolutely necessary.
bydreng *en* de'livery boy.
byg *en* barley.
byge *en* shower.
bygge *v* build·; ~ *om* re'build·; ~ *til* make· ad'ditions; **~grund** *en* building site; **~klodser** *pl* toy bricks; **~legeplads** *en* ad'venture playground; **~plads** *en* building site; **~ri** *et* building; **~sjusk** *et* jerry-building; **~sæt** *et* do-it-yourself kit; *(som legetøj)* building set; **~tilladelse** *en* building 'permit.
byggryn *pl* barley groats.

bygkorn *et (i øjet)* sty.
bygning *en* building; **~s·fejl** *en (i øjet)* a'stigmatism; **~s·håndværker** *en* builder; **~s·ingeniør** *en* con'struction engi'neer; **~s·værk** *et* building.
bykort *et* street plan.
byld *en* abscess.
bylt *en* bundle.
bymæssig *adj: ~ bebyggelse* built-up area; **byområde** *et* urban area; **byplanlægning** *en* town planning.
byrde *en* burden, load.
byret *en* city court; **byråd** *et* town council.
bytte *et (ombytning)* ex'change; *(røvet ~)* spoils *pl*, loot; *(dyrs ~)* prey; *få ngt i ~ for ngt* get· sth in ex'change for sth; *give ngt i ~ for ngt* trade sth in for sth; *være et let ~* be an easy prey // *v* change; *(udveksle)* ex'change; *~ ngt for ngt* change sth for sth; *~ om på ngt* change sth about; *~ (billeder af) popstjerner* swap pop stars; **~handel** *en* ex'change; **~penge** *pl* change.
byvåben *et* town (,city) arms.
bz'er *en* squatter.
bæger *et* cup.
bæk *en* brook; *~ og bølge (om stof)* seersucker.
bækken *et (anat)* pelvis; *(mus)* cymbal; *(til sengeliggende)* bedpan.
bælg *en (ærte~ etc)* pod; *(i harmonika, blæse~ etc)* bellows; **~e** *v: ~e ærter* shell peas; **~mørk** *adj* pitch-dark; **~øjet** *adj* wall-eyed.
bælle *v: ~ sig med ngt* swill sth (down).
bælte *et* belt; **~køretøj** *et* caterpillar vehicle.
bændel *et* tape; **~orm** *en* tapeworm.
bænk *en* bench, seat; **~e·varmer** *en* wallflower.
bær *et* berry.
bærbar *adj* portable *(fx computer* computer).
bære *v* carry; *(have på)* wear·; *(tåle, udholde)* bear·; *~ frugt* bear· fruit; *~ over med en* bear· with sby; *~ på ngt* carry sth; *~ sig ad med at...* manage to...; *sådan kan man ikke ~ sig ad* you can't carry on like that; *hvordan bar du dig ad med at...?* how did you manage to...? *det er ikke til at ~!* I can't bear· it! **~pose** *en* carrier bag; **~sele** *en* carrying sling; *(til baby)* baby sling; **~stykke** *et (på tøj)* yoke.
bærfrugt *en* soft fruit.
bæst *et* beast; *slide som et ~* work like a slave.
bæve *v* tremble, shake·; **~n** *en* trembling.
bæver *en* beaver.
bøddel *en* exe'cutioner.
bøde *en* fine; *få en ~ på 200 kr.* be fined 200 kr. // *v: ~ for ngt* pay· for sth; *~ på ngt* remedy sth.
bøf *en* steak [steik]; *(hakke~)* hamburger steak.
bøffel *en* buffalo.
bøg *en* beech; **~e·skov** *en* beech forest; **~e·træ** *et* beech; *(materialet)* beechwood.
bøje *en* buoy // *v* bend·, bow [bau]; *(gram)* in'flect; *~ af* turn off; *(give efter)* yield; *~ sig* bend·; *(give efter)* give· in: **~lig** *adj* flexible.
bøjle *en (til tøj)* hanger; *(til tænder)* brace.
bøjning *en* bow [bau]; *(gram)* in'flection; *(af verber)* conju'gation.
bølge *en* wave // *v* wave; **~blik** *et* corrugated iron; **~bryder** *en* breakwater; **~gang** *en* rough sea; **~længde** *en* wavelength; **~nde** *adj (om marker etc)* undulating; **~pap** *et* wellpaper.
bølle *en* thug; *(især fodb)* hooligan; **~hat** *en* sunhat; **~optøjer** *pl* hooliganism, riots.
bøn *en* prayer; *(anmodning)* re'quest *(om* for); *(indtrængende anmodning)* plea *(om* for); *bede en ~* say· a prayer; **~falde** *v* im'plore; **~høre** *v* hear·.
bønne *en* bean; **~spirer** *pl* bean sprouts.
bør *v* ought to; *man ~ ikke glemme at...* one should not forget that...; *(se også burde)*.
børne... *sms:* **~begrænsning** *en* birth con'trol; **~bidrag** *et* maintenance; **~bog** *en* children's book; **~børn** *pl*

grandchildren; **~have** *en* kindergarten; **~haveklasse** *en* nursery school; **~læge** *en* paedia'trician; **~mishandling** *en* child battering; **~rim** *et* nursery rhyme; **~sygdom** *en* children's dis'ease; **~sår** *et* im'petigo; **~tilskud** *et* family al'lowance; **~tøj** *et* children's wear; **~værelse** *et* nursery.

børs *en* ex'change; *på ~en* on the Ex'change; **~mægler** *en* stockbroker.

børste *en* brush; *rejse ~r (om dyr)* bristle; *(fig)* show fight // *v* brush; *~ tænder* brush one's teeth.

bøsse *en (til penge)* box; *(våben)* gun; *(homoseksuel)* gay; **~bar** *en*, **~værtshus** *et* gay place.

bøtte *en* bin; *(maler~)* pot; *hold ~!* shut up!

bøvl *et* trouble, bother.

bøvs *en* burp, belch; **~e** *v* burp, belch; *få en baby til at ~e* burp a baby.

båd *en* boat; *gå i ~ene* take· to the boats.

både *adv: ~ a og b* both a and b; *~ John, Peter og Bill kom* John, Peter and Bill all came.

både... *sms:* **~bygger** *en* boat-builder; **~havn** *en* boat harbour; **~hus** *et* boathouse.

bådshage *en* boathook.

bådsmand *en* boatswain [bəusn].

bål *et* fire; *(fx til St. Hans)* bonfire; *lave ~* build· a fire.

bånd *et* string; *(bændel)* tape; *(pynt~)* ribbon; *(til båndoptager)* tape; *optage ngt på ~* tape sth; **~e** *v* tape; **~kassette** *en* tape cas'sette; **~lægge** *v* tie up; **~optagelse** *en* tape re'cording; **~optager** *en* tape re'corder; **~salat** *en (fig)* spa'ghetti; **~sav** *en* band saw.

båre *en* stretcher; *(ved begravelse)* bier.

bås *en* stall, box; *(til parkering)* bay; *sætte en i ~ (om person)* label sby.

C

C *(fork.f. Celcius)* centigrade (C).

ca. *(fork.f. cirka)* ap'proximately, about.

cafeteria *s* cafe'teria.

camembert *en* 'camembert.

camouflere *v* 'camouflage; *(fig)* dis'guise.

campere *v* camp.

camping... *sms:* **~bus** *en* camper; **~plads** *en* camping ground, campsite; **~tur** *en: tage på ~tur* go· camping; **~vogn** *en* caravan.

canadier *en*, **canadisk** *adj* Ca'nadian.

cand. *i sms: ~ jur. sv.t.* Bachelor of Laws (LL.B); *~ mag. sv.t.* Bachelor of Arts (BA) *el.* Master of Arts (MA); *~ polit. sv.t.* Bachelor of Science (Econ.) (BSc); *~ scient. sv.t.* Master of Science (MSc); *~ theol. sv.t.* Bachelor of Di'vinity.

Caraibisk *adj: Det ~e Hav* the Carib'bean.

cayennepeber *et* cay'enne.

cedertræ *et* cedar.

celle *en* cell.

cellist *en* 'cellist.

cello *en* cello.

cellofan *et* 'cellophane ®.

celsius *s (C): 30 grader ~* 30 de'grees centigrade.

cembalo *et* harpsichord.

cement *en* ce'ment; *(beton)* 'concrete; **~ere** *v* ce'ment.

censor *en (ved eksamen)* ex'ternal ex'aminer; *(film etc)* censor.

censur *en* censorship.

censurere *v (ved eksamen)* mark; *(film etc)* censor.

center *et* centre.

central *en* central office; *(tlf)* ex'change // *adj* central; *et ~t spørgsmål* a crucial question; **~administration** *en* central admini'stration.

centralisere *v* 'centralize.

centralskole *en* district school (in the country).

centralvarme *en* central heating.

centrifuge *en* 'centrifuge; *(til tøj)* spin-drier; **~re** *v* 'centrifuge; *(om tøj)* spin-dry.

centrum *et* centre; *de bor i ~* they live in the City.

ceremoni *en* 'ceremony.

ceremoniel *adj* cere'monious, cere'monial.

certifikat *et* cer'tificate.
cerut *en* che'root.
chalotteløg *et* 'shallot.
chalup *en (mar)* barge.
champagne *en* cham'pagne [-'pein], (S) bubbly.
champignon *en* mushroom.
chance *en* chance; *(lejlighed)* oppor'tunity; *lad os tage ~n* let us risk it; *tage ~r* chance it, take· risks; *der er ikke store ~r for at de kommer* there is not much chance of their coming.
changere *v (om stof etc)* shimmer.
charkuteri *et* delica'tessen.
charme *en* charm // *v: ~ sig til ngt* use one's charm to obtain sth; **~re** *v* charm; **~rende** *adj* charming; **~trold** *en* charmer.
chartek *et* folder.
charterflyvning *en* charter flight; **chartre** *v* charter.
chatol *et* 'bureau.
chauffør *en* driver; *(privat~)* 'chauffeur; *(som kører varer ud)* de'livery man *(pl:* men).
check *en* cheque; *betale med ~* pay· by cheque; *hæve en ~* cash a cheque; *udstede en ~ på £500* make· out a cheque for £500 // *et (kontrol)* check; *have ~ på ngt* have sth under con'trol; *tage et ~ på en* check up on sby; **~e** *v* check; *~e efter* check up on; **~hæfte** *et* cheque book; **~konto** *en* cheque ac'count.
chef *en* head; *(arbejdsgiver)* em'ployer, (F) boss; **~kok** *en* chef; **~redaktør** *en* chief editor; **~sekretær** *en* personal secretary; **~stilling** *en* top po'sition.
chiffer *et* cipher, code.
chik *adj* smart.
chikane *en* ha'rassment; *(mobning)* bullying; **~re** *v* ha'rass; bully.
chilener *en,* **chilensk** *adj* 'Chilean.
chimpanse *en* chimpan'zee.
chok *et* shock, (F) turn; *jeg fik et helt ~* it gave me quite a turn.
choker *en (auto)* choke, throttle.
chokere *v* shock; *~t over ngt* shocked at sth.
chokolade *en* 'chocolate; **~mælk** *en* drinking chocolate.
ciffer *et* number, figure; *(taltegn)* digit; **-cifret** -digit; *et tocifret millionbeløb* tens of millions.
cigar *en* ci'gar.
cigaret *en* ciga'rette, (S) fag; *en pakke ~ter* a packet of cigarettes; **~skod** *et* ciga'rette end.
cigarkasse *en* ci'gar box; **cigarklipper** *en* ci'gar cutter.
cikorie *en* chicory.
cirka *adv* ap'proximately, about; **~pris** *en* ap'proximate price.
cirkel *en* circle; *en ond ~* a vicious circle; **~rund** *adj* circular.
cirkle *v* circle.
cirkulation *en* circu'lation; **cirkulere** *v* 'circulate.
cirkulære *et* 'circular.
cirkus *et* circus; **~artist** *en* circus ar'tiste; **~forestilling** *en* circus per'formance.
cisterne *en* 'cistern, tank.
citat *et* quo'tation; *~ begynder ... ~ slut* quote ... unquote.
citationstegn *pl* quo'tation marks, in'verted commas.
citere *v* quote.
citron *en* lemon; **~gul** *adj* lemon(-coloured); **~presser** *en* lemon squeezer; **~saft** *en* lemon juice; **~skal** *en* lemon peel; **~skive** *en* slice of lemon; **~syre** *en* citric acid.
civil *s: i ~* in plain clothes // *adj (mods: mil)* ci'vilian, 'civil; *(ikke i uniform)* in plain clothes; **~befolkningen** *s* the ci'vilian popu'lation; **~forsvar** *et* civil de'fence; **~ingeniør** *en* graduate engi'neer.
civilisation *en* civili'zation.
civilisere *v* 'civilize.
civilklædt *adj* in plain clothes.
clementin *en* 'clementine.
clips *en (papir~)* paper clip; *(øre~)* ear-clip; *(hår~)* hair-clip.
clou *et: festens ~* the climax (,highlight) of the party.
cognac *en* brandy; *(fransk)* cognac.
cola *en* (F) Coke®.
colibakterie *en* coli ba'cillus *(pl:* bacilli).

complet *s (om måltid)* conti'nental breakfast; *(om dragt)* suit, costume.
cottoncoat *en* waterproof.
courgette *en* squash.
cowboy... *sms:* **~bukser** *pl* jeans; **~film** *en* western; **~stof** *et* (blue) denim.
CPR-nummer *et* civil regi'stration number.
creme *en* cream; *(kage~)* custard; *(pudse~)* polish; **~fraiche** *en* sour cream.
crepe *et* crepe; **~nylon** *en* crepe nylon; **~papir** *et* crepe paper.
culotte *en (gastr) sv.t.* rumpsteak.
cyankalium *et* po'tassium cyanide.
cykel *en* bicycle, (F) bike; *køre på ~* ride· a bicycle; *trække cyklen* push the bike; **~bane** *en* cycle-racing track; **~handler** *en* bicycle dealer; **~kurv** *en* bicycle basket; **~lygte** *en* bicycle lamp; **~løb** *et* bicycle race; **~rytter** *en* racing cyclist; **~slange** *en* bicycle tube; **~smed** *en* (F) bike-mender; **~stativ** *et* bicycle stand; **~sti** *en* bicycle path; **~taske** *en* pannier.
cykle *v* cycle, ride a bicycle; (F) bike.
cyklist *en* cyclist.
cyklon *en* 'cyclone.
cyklus *en* cycle.
cylinder *en* 'cylinder; *en bil med 12 cylindre* a twelve-cylinder car.
Cypern *s* Cyprus.
cypriot *en*, **cypriotisk** *adj* 'Cypriot.
cølibat *et* celibacy; *leve i ~* be celibate.

D

da *adv* then, at that time // *konj (dengang ~)* when; *(lige idet)* (just) as; *(fordi)* since, as; *nu og ~* now and then; *fra ~ af* since then; *det var ~ godt de kom* I'm so glad they came; *ja, ja ~!* well, all right then! *~ du nu spørger* since you ask; *~ vi skulle til at gå* as we were leaving.
daddel *en (bot)* date.
dadel *en (kritik)* blame.
dadle *v* blame *(for* for).
dag *en* day; *en af ~ene* one of these days; *det går galt en ~* some day it will end in dis'aster; *god ~!* hello! *(formelt)* good morning (,afternoon, evening)! *komme for en ~ (fig)* come· to light; *~ens ret (på menu)* to'day's special; *i ~* to'day; *i ~ otte ~e* to'day week; *i vore ~e* nowadays; *i gamle ~e* in the old days; *om ~en* by day; *(i løbet af)* during the day; *flere gange om ~en* several times a day; *ved højlys ~* in broad daylight; *~ ud og ~ ind* day in, day out.
dagblad *et* (daily) newspaper.
dagbog *en* journal; *føre dagbog* keep· a diary.
dagdriver *en* idler.
dagdrømmer *et* daydreaming.
dagevis *adv: i ~* for days.
daggry *et* dawn; *ved ~* at dawn.
daginstitution *en* day-care insti'tution.
daglig *adj* daily; *(almindelig)* everyday; *~ påklædning* in'formal dress; *i ~ tale* in everyday language; *tjene til det ~e brød* earn a living // *adv* daily, a day; *til ~* normally; **~dags** *adj* everyday; **~stue** *en* living room; *(på institution, sygehus)* day room; **~vare** *en* everyday ne'cessity, basic com'modity.
dagpenge *pl (ved sygdom)* sickness benefit; *(ved arbejdsløshed)* unem'ployment benefit.
dagpleje *en (offentlig)* day care; *(privat)* child-minding; **~mor** *en* child-minder.
dags... *sms:* **~lys** *et* daylight; *ved ~lys* by daylight; **~orden** *en* a'genda; *(beslutning)* reso'lution; **~pressen** *s* the daily press.
dal *en* valley.
dale *v* fall·, go· down, sink·.
dam *en (lille sø)* pond // *et (spil)* draughts.
dame *en* lady; *(i kort)* queen; *(borddame etc)* partner; **~bekendtskab** *et* lady friend; **~brevkasse** *en* agony column, "Dear Jane"; **~cykel** *en* lady's bicycle; **~frisør** *en* (ladies') hairdresser; **~konfektion** *en* ladies' wear; **~sko** *pl* ladies' shoes; **~skrædder** *en* dressmaker.

damet *adj* ladylike; *(neds)* matronly.
dametaske *en* handbag.
dametoilet *et* ladies' (room), cloakroom.
dametøj *et* ladies' wear.
damp *en* steam; *for fuld ~* at full speed; *sætte ~en op* get· up steam; **~e** *v* steam; *(ryge)* smoke.
damper *en* steamer.
damp... *sms:* **~kedel** *en* boiler; **~koge** *v* steam; **~maskine** *en* steam engine; **~strygejern** *et* steam iron; **~tromle** *en* steamroller.
Danmark *s* Denmark; **danmarkskort** *et* map of Denmark; **danmarksmester** *en* Danish champion.
danne *v* form, shape; *(tildanne, skabe)* cre'ate; *~ sig en idé om ngt* get· an idea of sth.
dannebrog *et* the Dannebrog.
dannelse *en (opståen)* for'mation; *(kultur)* edu'cation; *(gode manerer)* good manners.
dannet *adj (kultiveret)* cultured; *(med gode manerer)* well-bred.
dans *en* dance; *(det at danse)* dancing; *gå til ~* take· dancing lessons.
danse *v* dance; *~ godt* be a good dancer; **~musik** *en* dance music.
danser *en* dancer.
danseskole *en* dancing school.
dansk *et/adj* Danish; *på ~* in Danish; *tale ~* speak· Danish; *~ vand* mineral water; **~er** *en* Dane; *hun er ~er* she is Danish; **~sproget** *adj* Danish-speaking.
dase *v* laze.
dask *et* slap; **~e** *v* slap; *hænge og ~e* flap.
data *pl* facts; *(edb)* data; **~base** *en* data base; **~behandling** *en* data processing; **~log** *en* com'puter scientist; **~logi** *en* com'puter science; **~lære** *en (i skolen)* com'puting; **~maskine, ~mat** *en* com'puter; **~skærm** *en* visual dis'play unit, VDU; **~styret** *adj* com'puterized; **~terminal** *en* data terminal.
datere *v* date; **datering** *en* dating; *(datoen)* date.
datid *en (gram)* the past tense, the preterite.
dativ *en (gram)* the dative.
dato *en* date; *af nyere ~* of recent date; *af ældre ~* of an earlier date; *dags ~* this day, to'day; *til ~* to date, so far; **~mærkning** *en* date stamp(ing).
datter *en* daughter; **~selskab** *et* sub'sidiary (company).
dav(s) *interj* hello! hi!
daværende *adj: den ~ statsminister* the prime minister at that time.
DDR *(Østtyskland)* the GDR.
de *pron (personligt)* they; *(demonstrativt)* those; *(bestemt artikel)* the; *De* you; *~ børn der kommer er søde* the children that are coming are nice; *~ børn er uartige* those children are naughty; *~ laver ballade* they make· trouble; *~ tilstedeværende* those present; *kan De sige mig...?* could you please tell me...?
debat *en* de'bate; *vække ~* be much dis'cussed; **~tere** *v* de'bate.
debitere *v: ~ en for ngt* charge sby for sth.
debitor *en* debtor.
debut *en* first ap'pearance, 'début; **~ere** *v* make· one's début; **~koncert** *en* first concert.
december *en* De'cember; *den 24. ~* the twenty-fourth of December, December the twenty-fourth.
dechifrere *v* de'cipher.
decideret *adv* de'cidedly.
decimal *en* 'decimal.
dedicere *v* 'dedicate.
defekt *en* 'defect, fault // *adj* de'fective.
defensiv *en: være i ~en* be on the de'fensive // *adj* de'fensive.
definere *v* de'fine; **definition** *en* defi'nition.
definitiv *adj* final; **~t** *adv* finally.
deform *adj* de'formed.
degenerere *v* de'generate.
degradere *v* de'grade; **degradering** *en* degra'dation.
dej *en (især gær~)* dough; *(især finere ~, fx til tærter)* pastry; *(flydende)* batter.
dejlig *adj* lovely; *(lækker)* de'licious; *det smager ~t* it is de'licious; *det*

var ~t vejr i går it was a lovely day yesterday; *her er ~ varmt* it is nice and warm here.

deklamere *v* re'cite.

deklaration *en* decla'ration; *(på vare)* (in'formative) labelling; *(om indholdet i fx madvarer)* (decla'ration of) 'contents.

deklarere *v* de'clare.

dekoration *en (pynt)* deco'ration; *(teat etc)* set.

dekoratør *en* 'decorator.

dekorere *v* 'decorate *(også med orden).*

dekret *et* de'cree; **dekretere** *v* de'cree.

del *en* part; *(andel)* share; *(afsnit)* section; *en ~ af sommeren* part of the summer; *jeg fik min ~ af pengene* I got my share of the money; *begge ~e* both; *en af ~ene* one or the other; *ingen af ~ene* neither; *største ~en af dem* most of them; *der er en (hel) ~ fejl i bogen* there are quite a few errors in the book; *han har en hel ~ bøger* he has quite a lot of books; *have ~ i ngt* have a share in sth; *til ~s* partly; *tage ~ i ngt* take· part in sth; **~agtig** *adj* in'volved; **~agtighed** *en (i ngt kriminelt)* com'plicity.

dele *v (i stykker, fordele)* di'vide; *(være fælles om)* share, split·; *~ ngt i otte stykker* divide sth into eight pieces; *vi delte udgifterne* we shared (,split) the ex'penses; *~ ngt op* divide sth; *~ ngt rundt* hand sth round; *~ sig* divide; *~ ud* dis'tribute, hand out.

delegeret *en* 'delegate // *adj* 'delegated.

delfin *en* dolphin.

delikat *adj (lækker)* de'licious; *(prekær)* 'delicate.

delikatesse *en* 'delicacy.

deling *en* di'vision; *(som man er fælles om)* sharing; *(mil)* pla'toon; *få ngt til ~* get· sth to share.

delle *en* roll of fat.

dels *adv* partly; *~ a ~ b* partly a partly b.

delt *adj* di'vided; *det kan der være ~e meninger om* that is a matter of o'pinion.

deltage *v* take· part, par'ticipate *(i* in); **~lse** *en* partici'pation; *(medfølelse)* sympathy.

deltager *en (i møde etc)* par'ticipant; *(i konkurrence)* com'petitor.

deltid *en* part-time; *arbejde på ~* work part-time; **~s·beskæftigelse** *en* part-time em'ployment.

delvis *adj* partial // *adv* partly, in part.

dem *pron* them; *~ der (,som) vi kender* the ones we know; *har De kedet Dem?* have you been bored?

dementere *v* de'ny.

dementi *et* de'nial.

demokrati *et* de'mocracy; *~ på arbejdspladsen* staff partici'pation; *(på fabrik)* in'dustrial de'mocracy; *økonomisk ~* eco'nomic de'mocracy.

demonstration *en* demon'stration; (F) demo; **demonstrativ** *adj* de'monstrative.

demonstrere *v* 'demonstrate.

den *pron (personligt)* it; *(demonstrativt)* that; *(om dyr ofte)* he, she; *jeg har set ~ film; ~ er god* I have seen that film; it is good; *~ idiot!* the fool! *der er en is til ~ der vinder* there is an ice cream for who'ever wins; *hun er nu ~ hun er* she is what she is; *~ sorte kat og ~ med pletter* the black cat and the one with spots.

denatureret *adj: ~ sprit* methylated spirits, (F) meths.

dengang *adv* at that time, then // *konj: ~ da* when.

denne *pron* this; *(sidstnævnte)* the latter, he, she; *den 31. ~s* the thirty-first of this month; *hans kollega og ~s kone* his colleague with wife.

dens *pron* its.

deodorant *en* de'odorant.

departementschef *en sv.t.* permanent secretary.

deponere *v* de'posit.

deportere *v (forvise)* de'port.

depositum *et* de'posit; *betale ~* put· down a deposit.

depot *et* 'depot; *(ved motorløb)* pit; *(affalds~)* dump.

depression *en* de'pression.
deprimeret *adj* de'pressed.
der *pron (om personer)* who; *(om andet)* which; *han ~ spiller er min fætter* it is my cousin who is playing; *den avis ~ kom i går* the newspaper which arrived yesterday // *adv* there; *de var ~ ikke* they were not there; *~ er min taske* there is my bag; *~ hvor vi kommer fra* where we come from; *det var ~ han faldt* that was where he fell; *~ er 42 km til Helsingør* it is 42 km to Elsinore; *hvem ~?* who is there? *~ flages i byen* they are flying flags in town; *~ blev gjort rent i huset* they cleaned the house; *ved du hvem ~ kommer?* do you know who is coming? *~ kan du se!* there you see! *hvad er ~?* what's wrong? what's the matter?
deraf *adv* of this, from this; *~ følger at...* hence it follows that...
derefter *adv* after that, afterwards; *(ifølge dette)* ac'cordingly; *vi handlede ~* we acted ac'cordingly; *resultatet blev ~* the re'sult was as might have been expected.
Deres *pron* your; *er det ~ hund?* it is your dog? *bogen er ~* the book is yours; *~ hengivne (i brev)* yours sin'cerely.
deres *pron* their; *(stående alene)* theirs; *det er ~ hus* it is their house; *huset er ~* the house is theirs.
derfor *adv (af den grund)* so, therefore; *(alligevel)* yet, all the same; *det var ~ de gik* that was why they left; *~ kan det jo godt passe* it may be true, all the same; and yet, it may be true.
derfra *adv* from there; from that; *de rejste ~* they left there; *~ trækkes moms* VAT will be de'ducted from that.
derhen *adv* there; **~ne** *adv* over there.
deri *adv* in that, there'in; **~gennem** *adv* through there; *(derved)* thus, so.
derimod *adv* on the other hand.
derind *adv* in there, into it; **~e** *adv* in there.
dermed *adv* with that; *(med disse ord)* so saying; *~ var sagen klar* that settled the matter; *~ være ikke sagt at...* that is not to say that...; *~ forlod han mødet* so saying, he left the meeting.
derned(e) *adv* down there.
deromkring *adv (i nærheden)* somewhere near there; *(cirka)* thereabouts.
derop(pe) *adv* up there.
derover *adv* over there; *(oven over)* a'bove (it); *folk på 67 år og ~* people of 67 plus.
derovre *adv* over there.
derpå *adv* then, after that; *~ sagde han...* then he said...; *dagen ~* the next day; *(efter fest)* the morning after.
dertil *adv* to that; *(hen til sted)* there; *(med det formål)* for that purpose; *(desuden)* be'sides; *~ kommer at han er rig* on top of that he's rich; *vi kom ~ om aftenen* we got there in the evening; *det skulle nødig komme ~* I hope it does not come to that.
derud *adv* out there; **~ad** *adv: det kører bare ~ad* it's running smoothly; **~e** *adv* out there.
derved *adv (ved hjælp af det)* in that way; *de bor nær ~* they live near there; *lad det blive ~* leave it at that.
Des: *være ~ med (kan oversættes:)* be on surname terms with.
des *adv* the; *jo mere ~ bedre* the more the better; *jo mere han råber, ~ værre bliver det* the more he shouts, the worse it gets.
desertere *v* de'sert; **desertør** *en* de'serter.
desinficere *v* disin'fect; *~nde middel* disin'fectant.
desorienteret *adj* con'fused.
desperat *adj* 'desperate.
desperation *en* despe'ration.
dessert *en* des'sert, sweet; *hvad skal vi have til ~?* what's for des'sert? (F) what's for afters?
destillation *en* distil'lation; **destillere** *v* di'stil.
desto *adv d.s.s. des.*

destruere *v* de'stroy.
destruktion *en* de'struction.
desuden *adv* be'sides, moreover.
desværre *adv* un'fortunately; *vi kan ~ ikke komme* un'fortunately we can't come, I'm sorry but we can't come; *vi må ~ meddele Dem at...* we re'gret to have to in'form you that...
det *pron (personligt)* it; *(refleksivt)* he, she, they; *(demonstrativt)* that; *(foran adj)* the; *har du set ~ hus? ~ er pænt!* have you seen that house? it is nice! *hvad er ~?* what is that? *~ er for sent nu* it is too late now; *hvem er ~?* who is it? *er ~ (der) din far?* is that your father? *~ mener du ikke!* you don't say!
detailhandel *en* retail trade; **detailhandler** *en* retailer.
detalje *en* detail; *gå i ~r* go· into detail; **~ret** *adj* detailed // *adv* in detail.
detektiv *en* de'tective; **~roman** *en* de'tective story.
detention *en* drying-out cell.
detonere *v* 'detonate.
dets *pron* its.
dette *pron* this; *(se også denne, disse).*
devaluere *v* de'value; **devaluering** *en* devalu'ation.
dia *et (foto)* slide.
diabetiker *en* dia'betic.
diagnose *en* 'diagnosis; *stille en ~* make· a diagnosis.
diagonal *en/adj* di'agonal.
diagram *et* 'diagram; *(kurve)* graph.
dialekt *en* 'dialect.
dialog *en* 'dialogue.
diamant *en* 'diamond.
diameter *en* di'ameter.
diametral *adj* dia'metrical; *~t modsat* dia'metrically op'posed.
diapositiv *et (foto)* slide.
diarré *en* diar'rhoea.
diasfremviser *en* slide pro'jector.
die *v* suck.
dieselmotor *en* diesel engine; **dieselolie** *en* diesel oil.
diffus *adj* dif'fuse.
dig *pron* you; *(refleksivt)* your'self; *nu skal jeg sige ~ ngt* I'll tell you sth; *morer du ~?* are you having fun? *keder du ~?* are you bored?
dige *et* dyke.
digt *et* poem; *(opspind)* fiction; **~e** *v (skrive vers)* write· poetry; *(opdigte)* in'vent.
digter *en* poet; *(forfatter)* writer.
digtning *en* writing; *(om poesi)* poetry.
digtsamling *en* col'lection of poems.
diktat *et (ordre)* 'dictate; *skrive efter ~* write· from dic'tation.
diktator *en* dic'tator; **diktatur** *et* dic'tatorship.
diktere *v* dic'tate.
dild *en* dill.
dilemma *et* di'lemma.
dilettant *en* 'amateur; *(neds)* dilet'tante.
dille *en* mania, craze; *han har en ~ med motorcykler* he's crazy about motorbikes.
dimension *en* di'mension, scale; *en sag af ~er* a very sizable matter.
dims *en* thingummy, whatsit.
din *pron* your; *(stående alene)* yours; *er det ~ bil?* is it your car? *denne bog er ~* this book is yours; *~ idiot!* you fool!
dingle *v* dangle; *(vakle, rave)* stagger; *~ med benene* dangle one's legs.
diplom *et* di'ploma.
diplomat *en* 'diplomat.
diplomati *et* di'plomacy.
diplomatisk *adj* diplo'matic.
dippedut *en* thingummy, whatsit.
direkte *adj (lige)* di'rect, straight; *(umiddelbar)* im'mediate; *(om person)* di'rect, blunt; *(komplet)* perfect // *adv* di'rectly, straight; *(ligefrem)* positively, downright; *gå ~ hjem* go· straight home; *udsende ~ (radio, tv)* trans'mit live; *~ valg* di'rect elections; *han var ~ grov* he was positively rude.
direktion *en* management.
direktør *en* manager, managing di'rector.
dirigent *en (mus)* con'ductor; *(ved møde)* chairman *(pl:* -men).
dirigere *v* con'duct; *(styre)* di'rect.
dirk *en* skeleton key; **~e** *v: ~e en lås op* pick a lock; **~e·fri** *adj* burglar-proof.

dirre *v* tremble.
dis *en (tåge)* mist.
disciplin *en* 'discipline.
diset *adj* misty.
disk *en* counter.
diskant *en (mus)* treble; **~blokfløjte** *en* treble re'corder.
diske *v (sport,* F) dis'qualify; *~ op med ngt* serve up sth; *(neds)* con'coct sth; *~ op for en* do· sby proud.
diskette *en (edb)* floppy (disk).
diskoskast *et (sport)* discus(-throwing).
diskotek *et* 'disco(theque).
diskret *adj* dis'creet.
diskretion *en* dis'cretion.
diskriminere *v* dis'criminate.
diskusprolaps *en* slipped disc.
diskussion *en* dis'cussion.
diskutere *v* dis'cuss.
diskvalificere *v* dis'qualify.
dispensation *en* dispen'sation.
dispensere *v* ex'empt.
disponent *en* sub-manager.
disponere *v* dis'pose; *~ over ngt* have sth at one's dis'posal; *være ~t for kræft* be predis'posed to cancer.
disponibel *adj* a'vailable, at dis'posal.
disposition *en (rådighed)* dis'posal; *(i stil etc)* plan, lay'out; *(beslutning)* ar'rangement; *have ngt til ~* have sth at one's dis'posal; *stå til ens ~* be at sby's dis'posal; *træffe sine ~er* make· one's ar'rangements.
disputats *en* thesis.
disse *en: ikke en ~* not a whit.
disse *pron* these; *(påpegende)* those; *(se også denne, dette).*
dissekere *v* dis'sect.
distance *en* 'distance; *stå ~n* go· the distance, see· it through; **~re** *v* out'distance.
distrahere *v* dis'tract.
distraktion *en* absent-mindedness.
distribuere *v* di'stribute.
distrikt *et* 'district, region; **~s·læge** *en sv.t.* medical officer of health; **~s·sygeplejerske** *en* 'district nurse.
distræt *adj* absent-minded.
dit *pron* your; *(stående alene)* yours; *det er ~ hus* it is your house; *huset er ~* the house is yours.
divan *en* couch.
diverse *adj* various.
dividende *en* 'dividend.
dividere *v* di'vide; *otte ~t med to er fire* eight di'vided by two makes four.
division *en (alle bet)* di'vision.
diæt *en* diet; *holde ~* be on a diet; **~er** *pl (dagpenge)* maintenance money; **~mad** *en* dietary food.
djævel *en* devil; **~sk** *adj* devilish; *det gør ~sk ondt* it hurts like hell.
dobbelt *adj* double // *adv* double, twice; *det koster det ~e* it costs twice as much; *~e vinduer* double glazing; *kvit eller ~* double or quits; **~billet** *en* re'turn ticket; **~bundet** *adj (om fx kuffert)* false-bottomed; *(fig)* am'biguous; **~dækker** *en (bus)* double-decker; **~gænger** *en* double; **~hage** *en* double chin; **~moral** *en* double standards; **~radet** *adj (fx jakke)* double-breasted; **~seng** *en* double bed; **~spil** *et* double game; **~stik** *et (elek)* two-way a'dapter; **~tydig** *adj* am'biguous; **~værelse** *et* double room.
doble *v: ~ op* double.
docent *en* reader.
docere *v* lecture.
dog *adv (alligevel)* how'ever, yet; *(imidlertid)* after all; *(sandelig)* really; *men ~!* dear me! *det er ~ for galt!* it is really too much! *sig det ~ bare* go on and say it; *gid jeg ~ var blevet i sengen* if only I had stayed in bed; *hvor er han ~ rar!* he really is nice! *hvad er der ~ i vejen?* what on earth is the matter?
dogmatisk *adj* dog'matic.
dogme *et* dogma.
dok *en* dock; *sætte skibet i ~* dock the ship.
doktor *en* doctor; **~afhandling** *en* thesis; **~grad** *en* doctorate.
dokument *et* 'document.
dokumentarfilm *en* docu'mentary.
dokumentation *en* documen'tation; **dokumentere** *v* 'document, prove.
dokumentmappe *en* briefcase.
dolk *en* knife *(pl:* knives); **~e** *v* stab.

dom *en* judgement; *(i kriminalsag)* sentence; *(fig)* verdict; *afsige ~* de'liver judgement, pro'nounce sentence; *~mens dag* the Day of Judgement; *betale i dyre ~me* pay· through the nose; **~hus** *et* court.
dominere *v* 'dominate; *(være fremherskende)* pre'dominate; **~nde** *adj* 'dominant; pre'dominant; *(neds om person)* domi'neering.
domkirke *en* ca'thedral.
dommedag *en* the Day of Judgement.
dommer *en (jur)* judge; *(fodb, boksning)* refe'ree; *(tennis, badminton)* umpire; **~kendelse** *en* warrant; **~komité** *en* jury.
domsmand *en sv.t.* juror.
domstol *en* court, law court; *gå til ~ene med en sag* take· a matter to court.
Donau *s* the Danube.
donkraft *en* jack; *hæve bilen med ~* jack up the car.
donor *en* donor.
dosere *v* measure out (into doses).
dosis *en* dose.
double *en (sport)* doubles *pl; herre~* men's doubles.
doven *adj* lazy; *(om øl etc)* flat, stale; **~dyr** *et (zo)* sloth; *(om person)* lazybones; **~skab** *en* laziness.
dovne *v* idle.
drab *et (det at dræbe)* killing; *(overlagt)* murder, homicide; *(uoverlagt)* manslaughter.
drabelig *adj (stor)* e'normous; *(frygtindgydende)* im'pressive.
drabsmand *en* killer.
drag *et: tømme flasken i ét ~* empty the bottle in one go; *nyde ngt i fulde ~* en'joy sth to the full.
drage *en (fantasidyr)* dragon; *(legetøj)* kite; *sætte en ~ op* fly· a kite.
drage *v (rejse)* go·; *(trække)* draw·, pull; *~ af sted* set· out; *~ omsorg for at…* see· to it that…; *~ en til ansvar for ngt* hold· sby res'ponsible for sth; **~flyvning** *en (sport)* hang gliding; **~r** *en* porter.
dragkiste *en* chest of drawers.
dragt *en (påklædning)* clothing, clothes *pl; (spadsere~)* suit; *(til udklædning)* costume; **~pose** *en* moth-proof bag.
dram *en* drink.
drama *et* drama; **~tiker** *en* 'dramatist; **~tisere** *v* 'dramatize; **~tisk** *adj* dra'matic.
dranker *en* drunkard.
drapere *v* drape; **draperi** *et* drapery.
drastisk *adj* drastic.
dreje *v* turn; *(sno)* twist; *(på tlf)* dial; *~ af* turn; *~ om hjørnet* turn the corner; *~ nøglen om* turn the key; *hvad ~r det sig om?* what is it about? *det ~r sig om at vinde* it is a question of winning; **~bog** *en (film)* script; **~bogsforfatter** *en* scriptwriter; **~bænk** *en* lathe; **~scene** *en (teat)* re'volving stage; **~skive** *en (tlf)* dial; *(til keramik)* potter's wheel; **~stol** *en* swivel chair.
drejning *en* turn(ing).
dreng *en* boy; *da han var ~* when he was a boy; **~e·streger** *pl* boyish pranks; **~et** *adj* boyish; **~e·tøj** *et* boys' clothes *pl.*
dressere *v* train.
dreven *adj* skilled; *(snedig)* shrewd.
drible *v* dribble.
drift *en (af virksomhed etc)* running; *(tilbøjelighed)* instinct, urge; *(tog~)* service; *i ~* running; *ude af ~* not working; *(edb)* down; *gøre ngt af egen ~* do· sth on one's own i'nitiative; *billig i ~* cheap to run; *der er 20 minutters ~ på ruten* there is a twenty-minute service on the line; **~sikker** *adj* re'liable; **~s·leder** *en* manager; **~s·omkostninger** *pl (i firma)* overheads; *(for maskine)* operating costs.
drik *en* drink; **~fældig** *adj* (F) on the bottle.
drikke *s: mad og ~* food and drink // *v* drink·; *hvad vil du have at ~?* what would you like to drink? *~ ens skål* drink to sby; *~ sig fuld* get· drunk; *~ af flaske* drink out of the bottle; *~ ud* empty one's glass (,cup); **~gilde** *et* drinking session; **~penge** *pl* tip; *give en ~penge* tip sby; **~ri** *et* drinking; **~vand** *et* drin-

king water; **~varer** *spl* beverages; *(kun om spiritus)* liqueur.

drilagtig *adj* teasing; *(om irriterende el. vanskelig ting)* tricky.

drille *v* tease; *motoren ~r* the engine is playing up; **~pind** *en* tease; **~ri** *et* teasing.

driste *v: ~ sig til at* dare to.

dristig *adj* bold; *(vovet)* daring; **~hed** *en* boldness; daring.

drive *en (sne~ etc)* drift // *v (jage, tvinge, tilskynde)* drive·; *(maskine, firma etc)* run·; *(~ af sted)* drift; *(dovne)* idle; *~ et hotel* run a hotel; *~ den af* loaf, laze; *~ til havs* drift out to sea; **~nde** *adj: ~nde våd* soaking wet.

drivhus *et* greenhouse, hothouse; **~effekt** *en* greenhouse effect.

drivkraft *en* drive *(også fig).*

drivtømmer *et* driftwood.

drivvåd *adj* soaking wet.

dromedar *en* 'dromedary.

dronning *en* queen.

droppe *v* drop, give· up.

drossel *en* trush.

drue *en* grape; **~klase** *en* bunch of grapes; **~saft** *en* grape juice; **~sukker** *et* 'glucose.

druk *s* drinking; **~ken** *adj* drunk; **~kenbolt** *en* alco'holic.

drukne *v (~ en el. ngt)* drown; *(~ selv)* be drowned; *være ved at ~ i arbejde* be up to one's ears in work; *~ i mængden* be lost in the crowd; **~ulykke** *en* drowning.

dryp *et* drip; *(dryppen)* dripping; **~pe** *v* drip; *(om steg)* baste; *~pe øjne (etc)* put· drops in one's eyes (etc); **~stenshule** *en* dripstone cave; **~tørre** *v* drip-dry.

drys *et* sprinkle; *(om person)* dawdler; **~se** *v (strø)* sprinkle; *(falde ned, fx om sne)* fall·; *(om juletræ)* shed· (it's needles); *(smøle)* dawdle; *~se sukker på kagen* sprinkle the cake with sugar; *~se aske på gulvet* drop ashes on the floor.

dræbe *v* kill; **~nde** *adj* deadly.

drægtig *adj* pregnant; **~hed** *en* pregnancy.

dræn *et* drain; **~rør** *et* drain pipe.

dræve *v* drawl; **~n** *en* drawl.

drøbel *en* uvula.

drøfte *v* di'scuss, de'bate; **~lse** *en* di'scussion, de'bate.

drøj *adj (som strækker langt)* eco'nomic; *(slidsom)* tough; *(grov)* coarse.

drøm *en* dream; *i ~me* in one's dreams.

drømme *v* dream·; *~ om at komme til London* dream of going to London; *jeg ville ikke ~ om at gøre det!* I would not dream of doing it!

drømmefyr *en* stunner; *hendes (,min) ~* the man of her (,my) dreams.

drømmeri *et* dreaming.

drømmeseng *en* camp bed, z-bed.

drøn *et* boom, roar; *for fuldt ~ (om lyd)* at full blast; *(om fart)* at full speed; **~e** *v* boom; *(køre larmende)* roar; *(køre hurtigt)* belt.

drønnert *en* oaf.

drøv *s: tygge ~* ruminate *(også fig).*

drøvel *en d.s.s. drøbel.*

drøvtygger *en* ruminant.

dråbe *en* drop; *en ~ vand* a drop of water; *en ~ i havet* a drop in the ocean; **~vis** *adv* drop by drop.

du *pron* you.

du *v* be good; *det ~er ikke* it is no good; *vise hvad man ~er til* prove one's worth.

dubleant *en* substitute; *(teat etc)* understudy.

dublere *v* double; substitute; understudy.

dublet *en* duplicate.

due *en* pigeon; *(fig, fx pol)* dove.

duel *en* 'duel.

duelig *adj* fit *(til* for).

duellere *v* duel.

dueslag *et* dovecot, pigeon loft.

duet *en* du'et.

duft *en* scent, smell; **~e** *v* smell· *(af* of); **~ende** *adj* fragrant.

dug *en (i græsset etc)* dew; *(på rude)* steam; *(bord~)* tablecloth; *der er ~ på ruden* the window is steamed up; *forsvinde som ~ for solen* vanish into thin air; **~dråbe** *en* dewdrop; **~ge** *v (om rude etc)* steam up, mist up.

dukke *en* doll; *(marionet)* puppet // *v*

(dyppe) duck; *(dykke)* dive; ~ *frem* e'merge; ~ *op (dvs. komme)* turn up; ~ *hovedet* duck one's head; ~ *sig* duck; **-dreng** *en (neds)* sissy; **-hus** *et* doll's house.
dukkert *en* dive; *give en en* ~ duck sby; *tage sig en* ~ *(dvs. springe i)* dive in; *(dvs. bade)* go· for a swim.
dukketeater *et* toy theatre; *(med marionetter)* puppet theatre; **dukketøj** *et* doll's clothes *pl;* **dukkevogn** *en* doll's pram.
duknakket *adj* stooping.
duks *en: være* ~ be top of the class.
dulle *en* doll; bird; *(neds)* tart.
dulme *v* ease, soothe; **-nde** *adj* soothing.
dum *adj* stupid, foolish; *det er slet ikke så* ~*t* it is not bad at all; *en* ~ *gås (om kvinde)* a silly goose; *spille* ~ act stupid; **-dristig** *adj* foolhardy; **-hed** *en* stu'pidity, foolishness; *lave* ~*heder* do· sth stupid.
dumme *v:* ~ *sig* make· a fool of oneself.
dump *adj* dull.
dumpe *v (falde)* fall·; *(til eksamen)* fail; *(smide affald)* dump.
dumpning *en (af affald)* dumping.
dumrian *en* fool, ass.
dun *et* down.
dundre *v* thunder; *(banke)* hammer; *en* ~*nde hovedpine* a splitting headache; **-n** *en* rumble, thunder; hammering.
dundyne *en* 'duvet, conti'nental quilt.
dunet *adj* downy.
dunk *en (beholder)* can // *et (slag)* knock; *(hårdt)* thump; **-e** *v* knock; *det* ~*er i mit hoved* my head is throbbing; ~*e en i ryggen* slap sby's back.
dunkel *adj* dark; *(utydelig)* dim; *(fig)* ob'scure.
duntæppe *et* quilt.
dup *en (på stok etc)* knob; *(på fodboldsko)* stud; *være oppe på* ~*perne* (F) be with it.
duplikere *v* 'duplicate.
duppe *v* dab.
dur *en (mus)* major; *as-dur* A flat major.
dus: *være* ~ *med en* be on first name terms with sby; *være* ~ *med ngt* be fa'miliar with sth.
dusin *et* dozen; *50p* ~*et* 50p a dozen.
dusk *en* tuft, wisp; *en dusk persille* a sprig of parsley.
dusør *en* re'ward; *udlove en* ~ offer a reward.
dvale *en* 'lethargy; *(vinterhi)* hiber'nation; *ligge i* ~ *(om dyr)* hibernate; *(fig)* lie· dormant.
dvask *adj* le'thargic.
dvs. *(fork.f. det vil sige)* that is, i.e.
dvæle *v* linger; *lad os ikke* ~ *ved det* let's not dwell on that.
dværg *en* midget, dwarf.
dy *v: kan du så* ~ *dig!* be'have your'self! *jeg kunne ikke* ~ *mig* I could not help myself; *vi kunne ikke* ~ *os for at gøre det* we could not re'sist doing it.
dyb *et* depth; *(afgrund)* a'byss // *adj* deep; ~*est set* basically; *i* ~*este hemmelighed* in the utmost secret; ~ *tallerken* soup plate; *i* ~ *søvn* fast a'sleep; *i* ~*e tanker* deep in thought; ~*t chokeret* deeply shocked; ~*t inde i skoven* deep in the forest; *bukke (,neje)* ~*t* bow (,curtsey) low.
dybde *en* depth; *gå i* ~*n med ngt* be thorough about sth, get· to the bottom of sth.
dybfrost *en* deep freeze; **-varer** *pl* frozen foods.
dybfryse *v* deep-freeze; **-r** *en* deep freeze.
dybhavs- deep-sea *(fx fiskeri* fisheries).
dybsindig *adj* pro'found; **-hed** *en (bemærkning)* pro'found re'mark.
dybtgående *et (om skib)* deep-draught // *adj (fig)* thorough.
dyd *en* virtue; **-ig** *adj* virtuous; **-s·mønster** *et* paragon (of virtue).
dygtig *adj* good; *(kvik)* clever; *(med godt håndelag)* skilful; *hun er* ~ *i skolen* she is doing well at school; *være* ~ *til sprog* be good at languages; **-hed** *en* cleverness, competence; skill.
dyk *et* dive; **-ke** *v* dive; ~*ke ned i ngt (fig)* delve into sth.

dykker *en* diver; **~dragt** *en* diving-suit; **~hjelm** *en* diver's helmet; **~udstyr** *et* diving e'quipment.

dykning *en* diving; *(sportsdykning)* skin-diving.

dynamik *en* dy'namic(s); **dynamisk** *adj* dy'namic.

dynamit *en* 'dynamite.

dynamo *en* dy'namo.

dynd *en* mud.

dyne *en* 'duvet, conti'nental quilt; *nu vil jeg se ~r!* (F) I'm going to hit the sack! *som at slå i en ~* like banging one's head against a brick wall; **~betræk** *et* duvet cover; **~frakke** *s* quilted coat.

dynge *en* heap, pile // *v: ~ ngt op* pile sth up.

dypkoger *en* im'mersion heater.

dyppe *v* dip.

dyppelse *en (gastr)* sauce; *(sky)* gravy.

dyr *et* animal; *vilde ~* wild animals; *(om rovdyr også)* wild beasts.

dyr *adj* ex'pensive; *betale i ~e domme* pay· through the nose; *det kommer til at koste dig ~t (fig)* you will have to pay for that; **~e·bar** *adj* precious.

dyre... *sms:* **~forsøg** *et* animal ex'periment; **~handel** *en* pet shop; **~have** *en* deer park; **~kredsen** *s (astr)* the zodiac; **~købt** *adj* hard-earned; **~kød** *et* venison; **~kølle** *en* haunch of venison; **~liv** *et* wildlife; **~passer** *en* (zoo-)keeper; **~riget** *s* the animal kingdom; **~ryg** *en (gastr)* saddle of venison.

dyrisk *adj* animal; *(fig)* bestial.

dyrke *v (op~)* cultivate; *(avle)* grow·; *(beskæftige sig med)* go· in for; *(tilbede)* worship; *~ jorden* cultivate the land; *~ kartofler* grow· potatoes; *~ sport* go· in for sports; *han ~r Mozart* he is keen on Mozart; **dyrker** *en* cultivator.

dyrkning *en* culti'vation; growing.

dyr... *sms:* **~læge** *en* vet, 'veterinary surgeon; **~plageri** *et* cruelty to animals; **~skue** *et* cattle show; **~tidsreguleret** *adj* with cost-of-'living ad'justment; **~tidstillæg** *et* cost-of-'living bonus.

dyse *en* nozzle.

dysse *en (hist)* dolmen // *v: ~ en i søvn* lull sby to sleep; *~ ngt ned* hush sth up.

dyster *adj* sombre.

dyt *et (om bilhorn)* honk; **~te** *v* honk.

dæk *et (bil~ etc)* tyre; *(skibs~)* deck; **~jern** *et* tyre lever.

dække *v* cover; *fjernsynet ~de kampen* they sent the match on television; *~ bord* lay· (,set·) the table; *~ op for en* do· sby proud; *~ over en* cover up for sby; *~ over ngt* hide· sth; *~ ngt til* cover sth up.

dækken *et* cloth, cover.

dækkeserviet *en* place mat; **dækketøj** *et* table linen.

dækning *en (ly)* cover, shelter; *(betaling)* payment; *gå i ~* seek· shelter; *der er ~ for checken* the cheque will be met; **~s·løs** *adj: en ~s·løs check* a rubber cheque.

dæksel *et* cover.

dæktryk *et* tyre pressure.

dæmme *v: ~ op for ngt* dam up sth; *(fig)* stem sth.

dæmning *en* dam.

dæmpe *v (om lyd)* muffle; *(mindske)* damp; *(undertrykke fx følelse)* sub'due; *(holde igen på)* curb; *~t belysning* sub'dued lighting; *~t musik* soft music; *tale med ~t stemme* speak· in a low voice; **~r** *en* damper; *(mus)* mute; *lægge en ~r på en* put· a damper on sth.

dæmre *v* dawn; *nu ~r det (for mig)* it is beginning to dawn (on me).

dæmring *en (om morgenen)* dawn; *(om aftenen)* twilight.

dø *v* die; *~ af kræft* die of cancer; *~ af sult* starve to death; *jeg er ved at ~ af sult* I'm starving; *ved at ~ af kedsomhed* bored to death; *hun var ved at ~ af grin* she nearly died laughing; *~ hen* die away; *~ ud* die out.

døbe *v* christen; **~font** *en* bap'tismal font.

død *en* death; *(dødsoffer)* dead; *~ og pine!* golly! *det er den visse ~* it is certain death; *det bliver min ~* it will be the death of me; *ligge for ~en* be dying; *der var over 20 ~e* there were over 20 dead; *dømme en til ~en* sentence sby to death // *adj* dead; *hvornår er hun ~?* when did she die? *hun har været ~ i et par år* she died a couple of years ago; *til minde om den ~e* in memory of the de'ceased; *falde ~ om* drop dead; *han var ~ på stedet* he died instantly; *mere ~ end levende* more dead than alive; *~t løb* dead heat; *nå et ~t punkt* reach a deadlock; *den ~e vinkel (i bil)* the blind spot; **~bider** *en* bore; **~bringende** *adj* deadly, lethal; **~drukken** *adj* dead-drunk.

dødelig *adj* mortal; *(som man dør af)* deadly, lethal; *~t forelsket* madly in love; *~t såret* fatally wounded; **~hed** *en* mor'tality.

dødfødt *adj* stillborn; *(fig)* doomed to failure.

dødkedelig *adj* deadly dull.

dødningehoved *et* skull.

døds... *sms:* **~annonce** *en* o'bituary (notice); **~bo** *et* e'state; **~dom** *en* death sentence; **~dømt** *adj* sentenced to death; *(om fx projekt)* doomed; **~fald** *et* death; **~fjende** *en* mortal enemy; **~fælde** *en* death trap; **~hjælp** *en* eutha'nasia; **~leje** *et* deathbed; **~offer** *et* victim; **~straf** *en* capital punishment; *få ~straf* be sentenced to death; **~stød** *et* deathblow; **~syg** *adj* mortally ill; *(fig,* F) rotten; **~synd** *en* mortal sin; **~årsag** *en* cause of death.

dødtræt *adj* tired to death.

dødvande *et* im'passe; *komme ind i et ~* reach an im'passe, come· to a dead end.

dødvægt *en* dead weight.

døgn *et* day and night, 24 hours; *rejsen varer tre ~* the journey takes three days and nights; *sove otte timer i ~et* sleep· eight hours a night; *~et rundt* day and night, round the clock; **~box** *en* night safe; **~drift** *en* round-the-clock work; **~radio** *en* round-the-clock programmes; **~åben** *adj* open round the clock.

døje *v: jeg kan ikke ~ ham* I can't stand him; *hun ~r med gigt* she is suffering from rheumatism.

døjt *en: ikke en ~* not a bit.

dømme *v* judge; *(idømme straf)* sentence; *(idømme bøde)* fine; *(ved fodboldkamp)* refe'ree; *efter alt at ~* to all ap'pearances; *~ om ngt* have an o'pinion on sth; *~ en til døden* sentence sby to death; *du kan selv ~* judge for your'self; **~kraft** *en* judgement.

dønning *en* swell; *(fig)* reper'cussion.

dør *en* door; *for lukkede ~e (jur)* in camera; *for åbne ~e* in public; *han stod i ~en* he was standing in the doorway; *komme ind ad ~en* come· in through the door; *holde sig inden ~e* stay indoors; *gå stille med ~ene (fig)* pussyfoot it; *smække med ~en* slam the door; *hun bor ~ om ~ med John* John is her next-door neighbour; *banke på ~en* knock the door; *ringe på ~en* ring the doorbell; *gå ud ad ~en* go· out of the door; **~hammer** *en* doorknocker; **~håndtag** *et* door handle; *(kugleformet)* doorknob; **~karm** *en* doorframe; **~klokke** *en* doorbell; **~lukker** *en* door spring; **~måtte** *en* doormat; **~slag** *et (sigte)* 'colander; **~spion** *en (kighul i dør)* peephole; **~trin** *et* doorstep; **~vogter** *en* doorkeeper; **~åbning** *en* doorway.

døs *en* doze; **~e** *v* doze; **~ig** *adj* drowsy.

døv *adj* deaf; *vende det ~e øre til ngt* turn a deaf ear to sth; *~ på det ene øre* deaf in one ear; **~hed** *en* deafness; **~stum** *adj* deaf-mute.

dåb *en* christening; **~s·attest** *en sv.t.* birth cer'tificate; **~s·kjole** *en* christening robe.

dåd *en* deed; *vågne op til ~* wake· up and get on with it.

dådyr *et* fallow dear.

dåne *v* faint.

dårlig *adj* bad; *(ringe)* poor; *(utilpas)* un'well; *(syg)* ill // *adv* badly; poorly; *(næppe)* hardly; *blive ~ (dvs. få kvalme)* get· sick; *(dvs. blive syg)* be taken ill; *du ser ~ ud* you don't look well; *vi har ~ tid* we are pressed for time; *(dvs. vi har travlt)* we are busy; *det er ~t vejr* the weather is bad; *vi kunne ~t kende ham igen* we hardly recognized him; **~ere** *v* worse; **~st** *adj* worst; *høre til de ~st stillede* be among those least well-off.

dåse *en* box; *(konserves~)* tin, can; *kød på ~* tinned meat; **~latter** *en* canned laughter; *(i tv-spil)* laugh track; **~mad** *en* tinned food; **~musik** *en (muzak)* piped music; **~øl** *en* canned beer; **~åbner** *en* tin-opener.

E

ebbe *en* low tide, ebb; *~ og flod* tide; *det er ~ (også)* the tide is out // *v: ~ ud* ebb away.

ed *en* oath; *aflægge ~* take· the oath *(på* on); *aflægge ~ på at…* swear· that…; *~er og forbandelser* cursing and swearing.

edb *s* edp, electronic data 'processing; **~anlæg** *et* com'puter system; **~styring** *en* com'puterizing.

edder… *sms:* **~dunsdyne** *en* eiderdown; **~kop** *en* spider; **~koppespind** *et* spider's web; **~smart** *adj* smashing; **~spændt** *adj* livid.

eddike *en* vinegar; **~sur** *adj (fig)* acid; **~syltet** *adj* pickled; **~syre** *en* a'cetic acid.

EF *s* the EEC.

efeu *en* ivy.

effekt *en* ef'fect; *få ~ (dvs træde i kraft; virke)* take· ef'fect; **~er** *pl (ting)* things; *(varer)* goods; *(værdipapirer)* se'curities.

effektiv *adj* ef'fective; *(om person)* ef'ficient; **~itet** *en* ef'ficiency.

efg *s sv.t.* vo'cational school, job-training classes.

efter *adv* after(wards), later; *dagen ~* the next (,following) day; *længe ~* a long time afterwards; *14 dage ~ sneede det* 14 days later it was snowing; *se ngt ~* go· over sth // *præp* after; *(ifølge)* ac'cording to; *(i retning mod)* at; *(for at hente etc)* for; *bruden ankom ~ brudgommen* the bride arrived after the bridegroom; *han er den dygtigste (næst) ~ John* he is the best after John; *det gik ~ planen* it went ac'cording to plan; *leveret ~ ordre* de'livered to order; *hun smed en tallerken ~ ham* she threw· a plate at him; *se ~ ngt (dvs. lede)* look for sth; *(dvs. passe på)* look after sth, keep· an eye on sth; *sende bud ~* send· for; *skrive ~* write· for; *en ~ en* one by one; *dag ~ dag* day after day; *~ min mening* in my o'pinion; *de er ude ~ ham* they are after him.

efterabe *v* mimic, imitate.

efterdønninger *pl (fig)* reper'cussions.

efterforske *v* in'vestigate; **efterforskning** *en* investi'gation.

efterfølge *v* suc'ceed; **~r** *en* suc'cessor; **~nde** *adj* subsequent, following.

eftergivende *adj* soft, com'pliant.

efterhånden *adv* gradually; *~ som* as; *man bliver ~ træt af det* it tends to get tiring.

efterkommer *en* de'scendant.

efterkrav *et: sende ngt pr. ~* send· sth cash on de'livery (,c.o.d.).

efterlade *v* leave· (be'hind); *han efterlod sig en formue* he left a fortune; *de efterladte* the be'reaved.

efterladenskaber *pl (om affald)* litter; *(om hundelort)* droppings.

efterligne *v* imitate, copy; **efterligning** *en* imi'tation.

efterlyse *v (ngt tabt)* advertise for; *(en savnet)* call a search for; *hun efterlyste lidt større interesse hos eleverne* she would like to see slightly more interest on behalf of the students; **efterlysning** *en (politi~)* search.

efterløn *en (efter fyring)* re'dundancy money; *(frivillig)* early re'tirement.

eftermiddag *en* after'noon; *i ~* this afternoon; *i går ~s* yesterday afternoon; *om ~en* in the afternoon; **~s·forestilling** *en* 'matinée; **~s·kaffe** *en sv.t.* (afternoon) tea.

efternavn *et* surname; *han hedder Smith til ~* his surname is Smith.

efternøler *en (alle bet)* latecomer.

efterret *en* second course; *(om dessert)* sweet; (F) afters.

efterretning *en* piece of infor'mation;

de seneste ~er the latest news; *tage ngt til ~* take· note of sth; **~s·væsen** *et* in'telligence service.
efterse *v* ex'amine; *(kontrollere)* check; *få vognen ~t* get· the car looked over.
eftersende *v* forward; *bedes eftersendt* please forward.
efterskole *en (kan oversættes)* boarding school (for lower secondary school pupils).
eftersom *konj* since.
efterspil *et* 'epilogue; *(fig)* sequel.
efterspore *v* track.
efterspurgt *adj* in de'mand; **efterspørgsel** *en* de'mand.
eftersyn *et (før auktion)* view; *(af fx bil)* overhaul; *ved nærmere ~* on closer in'spection.
eftersynkronisere *v* dub.
eftersøgning *en* search; **eftersøgt** *adj* wanted.
eftertanke *en: ved nærmere ~* on second thoughts.
eftertragtet *adj* in great de'mand, coveted.
eftertryk *et* emphasis; *lægge ~ på* emphasize; *~ forbudt* all rights re'served; **~kelig** *adj* em'phatic.
eftertænksom *adj* thoughtful.
eftervirkninger *pl* 'after-ef,fects.
efterår *et* autumn; *om ~et* in autumn; *til ~et* next autumn; **~s·agtig** *adj* au'tumnal; **~s·ferie** *en* autumn school holiday.
eg *en* oak.
egen *adj (eget, egne)* own; *(sær)* odd, strange; *(særskilt)* separate; *hun har ~ bil* she has a car of her own; *de bor i eget hus* they live in a house of their own; *han har sin ~ mening om tingene* he has his own o'pinion of things; *de har eget badeværelse* they have a separate bathroom.
egen... *sms:* **~art** *en* peculi'arity; **~hændig** *adj* personal // *adv* with one's own hands; **~navn** *et (gram)* proper name; **~sindig** *adj* headstrong, stubborn.
egenskab *en* characte'ristic, quality; *i ~ af* in the ca'pacity of.
egentlig *adj* real, actual; *(oprindelig, original)* proper // *adv* really; after all; *han er ~ helt rar* he is really quite nice; *hvad vil du ~ her?* what do you want here anyway? *hvad gør det ~?* after all, what does it matter? *i det ~e Skotland* in Scotland proper.
eger *en* spoke.
egern *et* squirrel.
eget *se egen.*
egetræ *et* oak tree; **~s·møbler** *pl* oak furniture.
egn *en* area, district, region, part of the country; *det er smukt her på ~en* it's beautiful in this part of the country; *jeg er ikke kendt her på ~en (dvs kender ikke ~en)* I'm not familiar with these parts.
egne *v: ~ sig til (,for) ngt* be suitable (,fit) for sth.
egnsudvikling *en* regional de'velopment.
egoisme *en* 'egoism, selfishness; **egoist** *en* 'egoist; **egoistisk** *adj* selfish, ego'istic.
Egypten *s* Egypt; **egypter** *en*, **egyptisk** *adj* E'gyptian.
ej *adv: hvad enten du vil eller ~* whether you want to or not.
eje *et: hans kæreste ~* his dearest pos'session // *v* own, pos'sess; *jeg vil hverken ~ eller have den* I would not have it as a gift.
ejendele *pl* be'longings, pos'sessions.
ejendom *en* property; *(hus)* house; *fast ~* real e'state; *bilen er min private ~* the car is my property.
ejendommelig *adj* strange, curious.
ejendoms... *sms:* **~ret** *en* ownership *(til* of); **~skat** *en* rates *pl;* **~kompleks** *et* block of flats; **~mægler** *en* e'state agent.
ejer *en* owner; *skifte ~* change hands; **~lejlighed** *en* owner-occupied flat, *(am)* condo.
ekko *et* echo; *give ~* echo, re'sound.
e.Kr. *(fork.f. efter Kristi fødsel)* AD.
eks- *(forhenværende) i sms:* ex- *(fx ~konge* ex-king).
eksakt *adj* ex'act.
eksamen *en* exami'nation, (F) ex'am; *dumpe til ~* fail the ex'am; *gå op til*

~ sit· (for) an ex'am; *tage* ~ pass an exami'nation; *(univ)* graduate; **-s·bevis** *et* di'ploma.
eksaminator *en* ex'aminer; **eksaminere** *v* ex'amine.
eksem *et* 'eczema.
eksempel *et* ex'ample *(på* of); *for* ~ for instance, for ex'ample *(fork.* e.g.); *følge ens* ~ follows sby's ex'ample; *statuere et* ~ set· an ex'ample.
eksemplar *et* specimen; *(af bog, blad etc)* copy; **-isk** *adj* ex'emplary.
eksercere *v* drill; **eksercits** *en* drill.
eksil *et* exile; *måtte gå i* ~ be exiled.
eksistens *en* ex'istence; **-minimum** *et* sub'sistence level.
eksistere *v* ex'ist.
ekskrementer *pl* faeces ['fi:si:z].
ekskludere *v (udelukke)* ex'clude; *(smide ud)* ex'pel.
eksklusiv *adj* ex'clusive; **-e** *adv* ex'clusive of *(fx moms* VAT).
ekskursion *en* (study) trip.
eksotisk *adj* ex'otic.
ekspandere *v* ex'pand.
ekspedere *v (kunder)* serve; *(ordne)* see· to, at'tend to; *(sende)* send· off, dis'patch; *(udføre)* carry out; *så blev det (,han)* ~*t* (F) that took care of that (,him).
ekspedient *en* shop as'sistant.
ekspedition *en (kontor)* office; *(af kunder)* service, at'tendance; *(forsendelse)* dis'patch; *(rejse)* expe'dition; **-s·tid** *en* office hours *pl.*
eksperiment *et* ex'periment; **-al** *adj* experi'mental; **-ere** *v* ex'periment.
ekspert *en* 'expert *(i* on, in).
ekspertise *en* 'expert knowledge.
eksplodere *v* ex'plode, blow· up; *(om dæk, ballon)* burst·.
eksplosion *en* ex'plosion; **eksplosiv** *adj* ex'plosive.
eksport *en* 'export(s *pl); **-ere** *v* ex'port; **-forbud** *et* 'export ban; **-fremstød** *et* 'export drive; **-tilladelse** *en* 'export licence; **-ør** *en* ex'porter.
ekspres *en (om tog)* ex'press // *adv* ex'press; **-brev** *et* special de'livery letter.
ekspropriere *v* ex'propriate.
ekstase *en* 'ecstasy; **ekstatisk** *adj* ecs'tatic.
ekstern *adj* ex'ternal.
ekstra *adj/adv* extra; *(reserve-, som er til overs)* spare *(fx værelse* room); **-arbejde** *et* extra work; **-fin** *adj* su'perior, choice; **-indtægt** *en* extra income; **-nummer** *et (af blad)* special (issue); *(ved koncert etc)* 'encore; **-ordinær** *adj* extra'ordinary; **-skat** *en* ad'ditional tax; **-tog** *et* special train; **-udgave** *en (af blad)* extra copy; *(af bog)* special e'dition.
ekstremist *en* ex'tremist; **-isk** *adj* ex'tremist.
el *en (bot)* alder; *(elek)* elec'tricity.
elastik *en* e'lastic; *(gummibånd)* rubber band; **elastisk** *adj* e'lastic, springy.
elefant *en* 'elephant; **-hue** *en* bala'clava; **-ordenen** *s* the Order of the Elephant.
elegance *en* 'elegance.
elegant *adj* 'elegant.
elektricitet *en* elec'tricity; **-s·måler** *en* (e'lectric) meter; *(for sms med* ~ *se også el-, fx elværk).*
elektriker *en* elec'trician.
elektrisk *adj* e'lectric; ~ *stød* e'lectric shock; ~ *udstyr* e'lectrical ap'pliances.
elektrode *en* e'lectrode.
elektron *en* e'lectron; **-blitz** *en* elec'tronic flash.
elektronik *en* elec'tronics; **-branchen** *s* the elec'tronics industry.
elektronisk *adj* elec'tronic.
element *et* 'element; *(elek)* cell, battery; *(del af køkken)* unit; **-hus** *et* prefab(ricated house); **-køkken** *et* (fully-)fitted kitchen.
elementær *adj* ele'mentary; *(grundlæggende)* basic.
elendig *adj* miserable, (F) rotten, lousy *(fx vejr* weather); **-hed** *en* misery; *(fattigdom)* poverty.
elev *en* pupil; *(studerende)* student; *(lærling)* ap'prentice.
elevator *en* lift; *(am)* 'elevator.
elevråd *et* pupils' council; **elevskole** *en (teat)* school of drama.

elfenben *et* ivory.
Elfenbenskysten *s* the Ivory Coast.
elg *en (zo)* elk, moose.
elite *en* é'lite; **~idræt** *en* com'petitive sport.
elkomfur *et* e'lectric cooker.
elkraft *en* e'lectric power.
elkøkken *et* e'lectric kitchen.
eller *konj* or; *enten a ~ b* either a or b; *hverken a ~ b* neither a nor b.
ellers *adv* or (else); *(hvis ikke)* if not; *(som regel)* generally, usually; *han er ~ meget rar* he is quite nice really; *hvis ~ du kan* that is if you can; *hvem ~?* who else? *var der ~ ngt?* anything else? *nej, ~ tak! (iron)* not for me, thank you!
elleve *num* e'leven.
ellevte *adj* e'leventh; **~del** *en* e'leventh.
ellipse *en* el'lipse; **~formet** *adj* el'liptic(al).
elm *en (bot)* elm; **~e·syge** *en* elm's dis'ease.
elmåler *en* (e'lectric) meter.
elske *v* love; *(have sex)* make· love *(med* to); **~lig** *adj* lovable.
elsker *en* lover; **~inde** *en* mistress.
elskov *en* love.
elskværdig *adj* kind, amiable ['ei-]; *vil De være så ~ at...?* would you kindly...?
elv *en* river.
elverfolk *pl* elves.
elværk *et* e'lectric power plant (,station).
em *en* vapour.
emalje *en* e'namel; **~maling** *en* e'namel paint; **~re** *v* e'namel.
emballage *en* packing; *(kasser etc)* con'tainer(s *pl).*
emballere *v* pack.
embede *et* post, office; *blive ansat i et ~* be ap'pointed to a post; *hans første år i ~et* his first year in office; *i embeds medfør* of'ficially.
embeds... *sms:* **~eksamen** *en* uni'versity de'gree; **~mand** *en* of'ficial; *(i ministerium)* civil servant; **~misbrug** *en* ab'use of one's po'sition; **~periode** *en* period of office.
emblem *et* badge.
emhætte *en* (ex'tractor) hood.
emigrant *en* 'emigrant.
emigrere *v* 'emigrate.
eminent *adj* 'eminent.
emne *et* subject; *(materiale)* ma'terial; *(om person)* candidate; *skifte ~* change the subject; **~uge** *en* feature week.
empirestil *en* French Empire.
emsig *adj* of'ficious; *en ~ person* a busybody.
en *(et) ubest. artikel:* a, *(foran vokal)* an; *(ubest. om tid, trykstærkt foran substantiv)* one; *(stående alene)* one, somebody, someone; *~ skønne dag* some day; *det er vel ~ to år siden at...* it is some two years ago since...; *~ efter ~* one by one; *hun snakkede i én køre* she talked con'tinuously; *hans ~e arm er brækket* one of his arms is broken; *~ gang for alle* once and for all; *han er ~ værre én* he is a bad one; *(rosende)* he is quite a guy; *~ eller anden* someone (or other); *vi ses ~ af dagene!* see you one of these days! *der var ~ der ringede* somebody called; *(se også et).*
enarmet *adj* one-armed; *~ tyveknægt* onearmed bandit.
encifret *adj: ~ tal* digit.
end *adv* -ever; *hvad du ~ siger* whatever you say // *konj* than; ex'cept, but; *han er større ~ sin bror* he is bigger than his brother; *hun er alt andet ~ dum* she is anything but stupid; *der var ikke andre ~ mig* there was no-one but me; *hvor gerne vi ~ ville* no matter how much we wanted to; *~ ikke* not even.
endda *adv* even; *(tilmed)* at that; *det var ikke så galt ~* it was not so bad after all; *hun er ~ kun 14 år* and she is only 14 at that; *det er galt nok ~* it is bad enough as it is; *han grinede ~* he even laughed.
ende *en (afslutning)* end; *(bagdel)* be'hind, bottom; *den øverste ~* the top; *den nederste ~* the bottom; *gøre en ~ på ngt* put· an end to sth; *i alle ~r og kanter* from top to bottom, inside out; *stå på den an-*

den ~ be on end; *der var ingen* ~ *på det* there was no end to it; *nå til vejs* ~ come· to the end of the road; *i sidste* ~... ultimately... // *v* end; *(fuldende)* finish; *det endte med at...* the outcome was that...; *vi endte med at blive hjemme* the end of it was that we stayed at home; *det* ~*r galt med dem* they will come to a bad end; *historien endte godt* the story had a happy ending.

endefuld *en* spanking.

endegyldig *adj* final.

endelig *adj* final; *træffe en* ~ *beslutning* make· a final de'cision // *adv* finally; *(langt om længe)* at last; *han kom* ~ he finally came, he came at last; *du må* ~ *blive* do stay; *vi må* ~ *ikke komme for sent* it won't do for us to be late.

endelse *en* ending.

endeløs *adj* endless.

endeskive *en (af brød)* end.

endestation *en* terminus *(pl:* termini).

endevende *v* turn upside down.

endnu *adv (stadig)* still; *(hidtil)* yet; *(ved komparativ)* even; *de er* ~ *ikke kommet* they have not ar'rived yet; *han kan nå det* ~ he can still make it; *hun bliver et par dage* ~ she is staying for another couple of days; ~ *bedre* even better; ~ *en gang* once more.

endog(så) *adv* even.

endsige *adv* not to mention.

endvidere *adv* moreover.

ene *adj* a'lone; *(kun)* only; ~ *og alene* only; *det er du ikke* ~ *om* you're not the only one.

enebarn *et: han er* ~ he is an only child.

eneboer *en* hermit.

enebær *et* juniper berry; **~busk** *en* juniper tree.

eneforhandler *en* sole agent.

enehersker *en* sole ruler, autocrat.

enemærker *pl* premises.

ener *en (om tal)* one; *(om person)* u'nique person; *han er en* ~ *(også)* he is sth out of the ordinary.

eneret *en* mo'nopoly *(på, til* of), ex'clusive rights *(på, til* to).

energi *en* 'energy; **~besparende** *adj* energy-saving; **~kilde** *en* energy source; **~krise** *en* energy crisis.

energisk *adj* ener'getic.

energispild *et* waste of energy.

enerverende *adj* 'enervating.

enes *v* a'gree *(om* on, about; *om at* to); *(forliges)* get· on *(med* with).

eneste *adj* only; single; *de* ~ *der kom* the only ones who came; *ikke en* ~ *ven* not a single friend; *hver* ~ *dag* every single day.

enestue *en (på sygehus)* private ward.

enestående *adj* u'nique.

enetime *en* private lesson.

enevælde *en* absolute monarchy.

enfamiliehus *et* one-family house.

enfoldig *adj* simple.

eng *en* meadow; *ude på* ~*en* (out) in the meadow.

engagement *et (ansættelse)* en'gagement; *(indblanding)* in'volvement.

engagere *v* en'gage; ~ *sig i ngt* engage in sth, com'mit oneself to sth.

engang *adv (i fortiden)* once; *(i fremtiden)* one day, some day; *der var* ~... *(i eventyr)* once upon a time...; *han har været gift* ~ he used to be married; *det vil du fortryde* ~ you will re'gret that some day; ~ *imellem* sometimes, from time to time; *ikke* ~ not even; *tænk* ~*!* (just) i'magine!

engangs... *sms:* **~bestik** *et* dis'posable cutlery; **~flaske** *en (uden pant)* 'non-re,turnable bottle; **~forestilling** *en* sole per'formance; *(fig)* one-off-affair; **~glas** *et* dis'posable glass; **~sprøjte** *en* dis'posable syringe.

engel *en* angel.

engelsk *et/adj* English; *på* ~ in English; *han taler flydende* ~ he speaks fluent English; *hvad hedder det på* ~*?* what is that in English? **~-dansk** *adj* Anglo-Danish; **~sindet** *adj* anglophile; **~sproget** *adj (om person)* English-speaking; *(om blad etc)* in English.

England *s* England; *(NB! gælder kun den del af Storbritannien der hedder England - ikke Skotland, Wales el. N-Irland).*

engleagtig *adj* an'gelic.
englænder *en* Englishman *(pl:* -men); *~ne* the English; *han (,hun) er ~* he (,she) is English.
en gros *adv* wholesale; **engrospris** *en* wholesale price.
enhed *en (helhed)* unity; *(del af system, flåde~ etc)* unit.
enhjørning *en* unicorn.
enhver *pron (alle)* every; *(stående alene)* everybody; *(af to el. af gruppe)* each; *(hvilken som helst)* any; *(hvem som helst)* anybody; *alle og ~* everybody, anybody; *~ andre end dig* anybody but you; *til ~ tid* any time.
enig *adj* u'nited; *(enstemmig)* u'nanimous; *blive ~e* a'gree *(om* on; *om at* to, that); *det er jeg ~ i* I a'gree with that; *de er ikke ~e* they don't a'gree.
enighed *en* a'greement; *(harmoni)* unity; *(enstemmighed)* una'nimity; *nå til ~* come· to an a'greement.
enke *en* widow; *blive ~* be widowed; **-dronning** *en* dowager queen.
enkel *adj* simple, plain; *vi kan ganske ~t ikke nå det* we simply can't make it; **-hed** *en* sim'plicity.
enkelt *adj (mods: dobbelt)* single; *(ukompliceret)* simple; *(særskilt)* indi'vidual; *der er kun en ~ fejl* there is only one error; *bare en ~* just one; *en ~ gang* once (in a while); *~e gange* oc'casionally; **-billet** *en* single (ticket), one-way ticket.
enkelthed *en* detail; *i de mindste ~er* in every detail.
enkeltvis *adv* one by one.
enkeltværelse *et* single room.
enkemand *en* widower.
enkepension *en* widow's pension.
enlig *adj* single; *~ forsørger* single parent; *de er ~e (om ægtepar)* they are childless.
enorm *adj* e'normous, huge; *det var ~t godt* (F) it was ter'rific.
enrum *et: i ~* in private.
ens *adj (helt ~)* i'dentical; *(omtrent ~)* a'like; *de er ~ af størrelse* they are the same size; *børnene er ~ klædt på* the children are dressed alike.
ensartet *adj* homo'genous.
ensbetydende *adj: det er ~ med at...* it means that..., that is to say...
ensfarvet *adj* plain.
ensformig *adj* mo'notonous; **-hed** *en* mo'notony.
ensidig *adj* uni'lateral; *(partisk)* one-sided, biassed *(fx syn* view); *~ kost* un'balanced food.
ensom *adj* lonely; *~t beliggende* solitary; **-hed** *en* loneliness; solitude.
ensrette *v* standardize; *ensrettet trafik* one-way traffic.
enstavelses- *adj* monosyl'labic.
enstemmig *adj* u'nanimous; *(mus)* in unison.
ental *et (gram)* the singular.
enten *adv* either; *~ a eller b* either a or b; *~ du el. jeg tager bussen* either you take the bus, or I do; *hvad ~ han vil eller ej* whether he wants to or not.
entré *en (gang)* hall; *(adgang)* ad'mission; *(adgangsbetaling)* entrance fee; *gratis ~* ad'mission free; **-dør** *en* front door.
entreprenør *en* building con'tractor.
entusiasme *en* en'thusiasm; **entusiastisk** *adj* enthusi'astic.
entydig *adj* clear, unam'biguous.
enzym *et* 'enzyme.
enægget *adj: enæggede tvillinger* i'dentical twins.
epidemi *en* epi'demic; **epidemisk** *adj* epi'demic.
epilepsi *en* 'epilepsy; **epileptisk** *adj* epi'leptic.
episode *en* 'episode; *(optrin)* incident.
epoke *en* epoch; **-gørende** *adj* epoch-making.
erantis *en (bot)* (winter) aconite.
eremit *en* hermit.
erfare *v (høre)* learn; *(opleve)* ex'perience.
erfaren *adj* ex'perienced.
erfaring *en* ex'perience *(u.pl); gøre sine ~er* learn by ex'perience; *tale af ~* talk from ex'perience.
ergoterapeut *en* occu'pational 'therapist; **ergoterapi** *en* occu'pational 'therapy.
erhverv *et (fag)* pro'fession; *(arbejde)*

occu'pation; *(del af ~s·livet)* industry.

erhverve *v:* ~ *(sig)* ac'quire.

erhvervs... *sms:* **~aktiv** *adj* working; **~arbejde** *et* paid work; **~drivende** *en* businessman *(pl:* -men); **~fiskeri** *et* in'dustrial fishing; **~hæmmet** *adj* partially dis'abled; **~liv** *et: ~s·livet* industry; *(forretningslivet)* business; **~orientering** *en* vo'cational guidance; **~praktik** *en* work ex'perience; **~sygdom** *en* occu'pational dis'ease; **~vejledning** *en* vo'cational guidance.

erindre *v* re'member.

erindring *en (hukommelse)* memory; *(minde)* souvenir; *til ~ om* in memory of; *udgive sine ~er* publish one's memoirs; **~s·forskydning** *en* lapse of memory.

erkende *v (indrømme)* ac'knowledge; *(tilstå)* ad'mit; *(indse)* recognize; *(blive klar over)* realize; *~ sig skyldig (i retten)* plead guilty; **~lse** *en* ac'knowledgement; *(det at indse)* recog'nition; *(det at blive klar over)* reali'sation.

erklære *v* de'clare; *~ krig mod* de'clare war on.

erklæring *en* decla'ration; *(udtalelse)* statement.

ernære *v* feed·, nourish; *~ sig som boghandler* make· a living as a bookseller.

ernæring *en* nu'trition; *(føde)* nourishment; *rigtig (,forkert) ~* a wrong (,proper) diet; **~s·ekspert** *en* nu'tritionist; **~s·tilstand** *en* state of nu'trition.

erobre *v* win·, conquer; *(indtage)* capture; *hun ~de verdensmesterskabet* she won the world championship; *~ ngt fra en* capture sth from sby.

erobring *en (alle bet)* conquest.

erotik *en* e'roticism; **erotisk** *adj* e'rotic.

erstatning *en (godtgørelse)* compen'sation; *(som man skal betale)* damages *pl; (surrogat)* substitute; *(som sættes i stedet)* re'placement; *betale ~* pay· damages; *slik er en dårlig ~ for mad* sweets are a bad substitute for food; **~s·krav** *et* claim for compen'sation (,damages).

erstatte *v* re'place; *(give erstatning for)* compensate for.

es *et (i kortspil)* ace; *være i sit ~* be in one's element.

eskorte *en,* **~re** *v* 'escort.

estisk *adj* Es'tonian; **Estland** *s* Es'tonia.

esdragon *en* tarragon.

et *se en; med ~* all of a sudden, suddenly; *det kommer ud på ~* it comes to the same thing; *under ~* altogether.

etablere *v* e'stablish; *~ sig* e'stablish oneself, set· up *(fx som bager* as a baker).

etage *en* floor, storey; *første ~* the first floor; *øverste ~* the top floor; *et hus med fire ~r* a four-storeyed house; **~ejendom** *en* block of flats; **~seng** *en* bunk bed.

etape *en* stage *(også i cykelløb).*

ethvert *se enhver.*

etiket *en* label; *sætte ~ på ngt* label sth.

Etiopien *s* Ethi'opia; **etiopier** *en,* **etiopisk** *adj* Ethi'opian.

etisk *adj* ethical.

etplanshus *et* bungalow.

ettal *et* one.

ettid *s: ved ~en* about one o'clock.

etui *et* case.

etværelses *adj* one-room.

etårig *adj (om plante)* annual; *se også -årig.*

Europa *s* Europe.

europamesterskab *et* Euro'pean championship.

Europaparlamentet *s* the Euro'pean Parliament; *medlem af ~* Euro-MP.

Europarådet *s* the Council of Europe.

europæer *en,* **europæisk** *adj* Euro'pean.

evakuere *v* e'vacuate; **evakuering** *en* evacu'ation.

evangelium *et* gospel; *Markusevangeliet* the Gospel ac'cording to St Mark.

eventuel *adj* possible; **~t** *adv (måske)* per'haps, possibly; *(om nødvendigt)*

if necessary; *jeg kunne ~t besøge dig* I might visit you; *hvis de ~t skulle dukke op* if they should turn up.
eventyr *et (oplevelse)* ad'venture; *(kærlighedsforhold)* af'fair; *(fortælling)* fairytale; *han er ude på ~* he is out looking for ad'venture; **~er** *en* ad'venturer; **~lig** *adj* fan'tastic; **~lyst** *en* thirst for ad'venture.
evig *adj* e'ternal; *(evindelig)* per'petual; *hver ~e dag* every single day; *~ sne* perpetual snow // *adv* for ever, e'ternally; *~ og altid* per'petually, always; *det tog en ~ tid* it took· ages.
evighed *en* e'ternity; *aldrig i ~* never ever; *for tid og ~* for ever; *det er ~er siden at…* it has been ages since…; *være en ~ om at…* take· ages to…; **~s·blomst** *en* everlasting flower.
evindelig *adj* e'ternal; *i det ~e* e'ternally, per'petually.
evne *en* a'bility; *(arbejds~)* ca'pacity; *han har gode ~r* he is talented; *han har en vis ~ til at sige det forkerte* he has a knack of saying the wrong thing; *leve over ~* live beyond one's means; *efter (bedste) ~* to the best of one's a'bility; *det overstiger mine ~r* it is beyond me.
evnesvag *adj* mentally handicapped.
excellere *v: ~ i ngt* ex'cel in sth.
excentrisk *adj* ec'centric.
exet *adj (om hjul)* buckled; *en smart bil gør ham helt ~* (F) a fancy car makes him go nuts.

F

fabel *en* fable; **~agtig** *adj* fabulous.
fable *v: ~ om (dvs. snakke om)* rave about; *(dvs. drømme om)* dream· of.
fabrik *en* factory, plant; *(tekstil~, papir~)* mill.
fabrikant *en* manu'facturer; *(som ejer ~)* in'dustrialist.
fabrikat *et (om vares art)* make, brand; *(om selve varen)* product.
fabrikation *en* manu'facture.
fabrikere *v* manu'facture, make·.
fabriks… *sms:* **~arbejder** *en* factory worker; **~by** *en* in'dustrial town; **~fremstillet** *adj* factory-made.
facade *en* front; *(fig)* fa'çade.
facet *en* 'facet.
faciliteter *pl* fa'cilities.
facit *et* re'sult, total; **~liste** *en* key.
facon *en (form)* shape; *(optræden)* manner; **~syet** *adj (om skjorte)* slimline, slimfit.
fad *et (serverings~)* dish; *(vaske~)* basin; *(tønde)* barrel // *adj (om smag)* in'sipid.
fadder *en* godfather, godmother.
fader *en d.s.s. far;* **~skab** *et* pa'ternity; **~vor** *et* the Lord's Prayer.
fadæse *en* blunder.
fadøl *et* draught beer.
fag *et (i undervisning)* subject; *(felt, område)* field; *(håndværk etc)* trade, pro'fession; *han er lærer af ~* he is a teacher by pro'fession; **~bevægelse** *en* (trade) union movement; **~blad** *et* peri'odical, journal; **~bog** *en* reference book; *(tlf) sv.t.* yellow pages; **~forbund** *et* fede'ration of trade unions; **~forening** *en* trade union.
faglig *adj* technical, pro'fessional; *(vedr. fagforening)* union.
fag… *sms:* **~litteratur** *en* non-fiction; **~lært** *adj* skilled; **~mand** *en* expert.
fagot *en* bas'soon; *spille ~* play the bassoon.
fagskole *en* technical college; **fagsprog** *et* technical language.
fagter *pl* gesticu'lation, gestures.
fakkel *en* torch.
faktisk *adj* real, actual // *adv* actually, as a matter of fact, in fact.
faktor *en* factor; *(på trykkeri)* supervisor.
faktum *et* fact.
faktura *en* invoice; **fakturere** *v* invoice.
fakultet *et* faculty.
fald *et* fall; *(brat, pludseligt)* drop; *(tilfælde)* case; *(hældning)* slope; *(tilbagegang)* de'cline; *have ~ i håret* have a natural wave; *i al ~* in any case, at any rate; *i bedste ~* at best; *i så ~* in that case; *i værste ~* at worst.

falde *v* fall·; *(om ting etc også)* drop; *(dale, fx om priser)* go· down; *lade ngt ~* drop sth; *~ af* fall· off; *~ for en* fall· for sby; *~ for fristelsen* give· in to the temp'tation; *~ fra (fx studier)* drop out; *~ i krigen* be killed in the war; *~ i søvn* fall· a'sleep; *~ i vandet* fall· into the water; *~ i øjnene* be con'spicuous; *det kunne ikke ~ mig ind* I would not dream of it; *hvor kunne det ~ dig ind?* how could· you? *det ~r ham let* he finds· it easy; *~ ned* fall· down; *~ ned af (,fra)* fall· off; *~ om* fall· down, drop; *~ død om* drop dead; *~ over ngt* fall· (,stumble) over sth; *(finde ngt tilfældigt)* come a'cross sth; *julen ~r på en søndag* Christmas falls on a Sunday; *~ på hovedet* fall· headfirst; *~ på ryggen* fall· on one's back; *~ sammen* col'lapse; *(om hustag etc)* fall· in; *~ til (dvs. vænne sig til)* settle down; *~ ud af vinduet* fall· out of the window.

faldefærdig *adj* ramshackle.

faldskærm *en* parachute; **~s·udspring** *et* parachute jump.

falk *en* falcon.

fallit *en* bankruptcy; *gå ~* go· bankrupt // *adj* bankrupt; (F) broke; **~erklæring** *en: det var en ~erklæring* it showed him (her, us, them etc) up.

falme *v* fade.

false *v* fold.

falset *en* fal'setto.

falsk *adj* false; *(forfalsket)* fake *(fx diamant* diamond), forged *(fx pengeseddel* banknote) // *adv* falsely; *(om musik)* out of tune.

falskmøntner *en* forger; **falskmøntneri** *et* forgery.

familie *en* family; *være i ~ med en* be re'lated to sby; *hun hører til ~n* she is one of the family; *~n Shaw* the Shaws; **~forsørger** *en* breadwinner; **~medlem** *et* member of the family; **~planlægning** *en* family planning; **~pleje** *en* family care; **~sammenføring** *en* family unifi'cation; **~vejledning** *en sv.t.* family counselling.

familiær *adj* family; *(tvangfri)* in'formal; *(neds)* fa'miliar.

famle *v* grope *(efter* for); *(fig og om tale)* hesitate.

fanatiker *en* fa'natic; **fanatisk** *adj* fa'natic.

fanatisme *en* fa'naticism.

fanden *en* the devil; *for ~!* damn! hell! *kan du for ~ ikke holde op!* can't you stop it, damn you! *hvem ~ siger det?* who the hell says so? *~ tage det!* blast it! *som bare ~* like hell; *(se også pokker).*

fandens *adj/adv* damned, bloody; *en ~ karl* one hell of a man; **~ mælkebøtte** *en* 'dandelion.

fane *en* flag; *(forenings~)* banner; *(mil)* colours *pl.*

fanfare *en* flourish.

fange *en* prisoner; *blive taget til ~* be taken prisoner // *v* catch·; *(pågribe)* capture; **~hul** *et* dungeon; **~lejr** *en* prison camp.

fangenskab *et* im'prisonment; *(om dyr)* cap'tivity.

fanger *en (eskimoisk)* sealer; *(hval~)* whaler.

fangevogter *en* gaoler.

fangst *en (det at gå på ~)* hunting, catching; *(bytte)* catch.

fantasere *v* fantasize, dream· *(om* about, of).

fantasi *en* imagi'nation; *(drøm)* fantasy; *en livlig ~* a lively imagination; *fri ~* pure in'vention; **~fuld** *adj* i'maginative; *(idérig også)* in'ventive; **~løs** *adj* uni'maginative.

fantastisk *adj* fan'tastic.

fantom *et* 'phantom.

far *en* father, (F) dad(dy); *han er ~ til John* he is John's father; *være ~ til tre børn* be the father of three children.

farbar *adj* passable; *ikke ~ (om vej)* closed to traffic.

farbror *en* (pa'ternal) uncle.

farce *en* farce.

fare *en* danger; *(risiko)* risk; *det er der ingen ~ for* there is no risk of that; *være i ~* be in danger; *han er i ~ for at miste højre arm* he is in danger of losing his right arm; *være uden for ~* be out of danger.

fare *v* rush; *(suse, køre hurtigt)* speed·;

~ *af sted* rush (,tear·) along; ~ *løs på en* fly· at sby; ~ *op* start up; *(blive vred)* fly· into a rage; ~ *rundt* dash around; ~ *sammen* start; ~ *vild* lose· one's way; **~signal** *et* danger signal; **~tillæg** *et* danger money; **~truende** *adj* ominous; menacing; **~zone** *en* danger zone (,area).

farfar *en* (pa'ternal) grandfather.

farlig *adj* dangerous; *(risikabel)* risky; *(skrækkelig)* awful; *et ~t spektakel* an awful noise; *hun ser ~ ud* she looks awful; *han er ~ for firmaet* he is a danger to the firm // *adv* dangerously; awfully.

farmaceut *en* pharmacist; **~isk** *adj* pharma'ceutical.

farmor *en* (pa'ternal) grandmother.

fars *en (kød~ til fyld)* forcemeat; *(fiske~) sv.t.* creamed fish; *rørt ~ sv.t.* sausage meat; **farsere** *v* stuff.

fart *en* speed; *(travlhed, hast)* hurry, rush; *bestemme ~en* set· the pace; *i en ~* in a hurry, quickly; *i fuld ~* at full speed; *være på ~en* be out and about; *have ~ på* be going fast; *(skulle skynde sig)* be in a hurry; *sætte ~en ned (,op)* re'duce (,in'crease) speed; **~begrænsning** *en* speed limit; **~fælde** *en (med politi, radar etc)* speed trap; **~måler** *en* spee'dometer; **~plan** *en* timetable; **~skriver** *en* tachograph.

fartøj *et* vessel.

farvand *et* water(s); *i dansk(e) ~(e)* in Danish waters; *være i ~et (fig)* be in the offing.

farve *en* colour; *(til farvning af tøj, hår etc)* dye; *(til fødevarer)* colouring // *v* colour; *(om tøj etc)* dye; **~blind** *adj* colour-blind; **~blyant** *en* crayon; **~bånd** *et* ribbon; **~film** *en* colour film; **~fjernsyn** *et* colour-TV; **~foto** *et* colour photo; **~handel** *en* paint shop; **~kridt** *et* crayon; *(til tavle)* coloured chalk.

farvel *et* good'bye // *interj* goodbye, bye-bye; ~ *så længe* see you (later).

farve... *sms:* **~lade** *en* paintbox; **~lægge** *v* colour; **~løs** *adj* colourless; *(bleg)* pale; **~rig** *adj* colourful *(også fig);* **~stof** *et* dye; *(til fødevarer)* colouring.

farvet *adj* coloured *(også om person); hun har ~t hår* her hair is dyed.

farveægte *adj* colourfast.

farvning *en* colouring; *(af tøj, hår etc)* dyeing.

fasan *en* pheasant.

fascinerende *adj* fascinating.

fascisme *en* 'fascism; **fascist** *en* 'fascist; **fascistisk** *adj* 'fascist.

fase *en* phase; **-faset:** -phase; *trefaset* three-phase.

fast *adj* firm; *(mods: flydende)* solid; *(mods: løs)* tight, firm; *(aftale etc)* fixed; *(varig)* permanent; *(tilbagevendende)* regular; ~ *ansættelse* permanent em'ployment; ~ *ejendom* real e'state; ~ *forbindelse (fx bro, tunnel)* fixed link; ~ *føde* solid food; *et ~ greb* a firm grip; ~ *kunde* regular customer; ~ *overbevisning* firm con'viction; *~e priser* fixed prices; *han er blevet sat ~* he has been taken into custody; *holde ~ ved ngt* stick· to sth; *(stædigt)* in'sist on sth; *sidde ~* be stuck; **~ansat** *adj* em'ployed on a regular basis.

faste *en* fast; **~lavn** *en* Shrovetide.

fastende *adj* fasting; *på ~ hjerte* on an empty stomach.

faster *en* (pa'ternal) aunt.

fastfryse *v* freeze *(også fig).*

fastgøre *v* fasten.

fasthed *en* firmness.

fastland *et (ikke ø)* mainland; *(kontinent)* continent; *(ikke hav)* dry land; **~s·klima** *et* conti'nental climate; **~s·sokkel** *en* conti'nental shelf.

fastlægge *v (om tid, pris, rækkefølge etc)* fix; *(afgøre)* de'termine.

fastlåse *v: situationen er blevet fastlåst* the situ'ation has reached a deadlock.

fastmaske *en* double crochet.

fastslå *v (erklære)* state; *(vise)* prove, e'stablish.

fastsætte *v* fix.

fat *adv: få ~ i ngt* get· hold of sth; *undskyld, det fik jeg ikke ~ i!* sorry, I didn't get that! *have ~ i ngt* have got hold of sth; *hvordan er det ~?* how are things? *tage ~ på ngt (dvs. gå i gang med)* get· down to sth.

fatal *adj* 'fatal.

fatning *en (ro)* com'posure; *(på lampe)* socket; *bevare (,tabe) ~en* main'tain (,lose·) one's composure; *blive bragt ud af ~* get· flustered.

fatte *v (begribe)* under'stand·, grasp; *~ sig i korthed* be brief; *~ mistanke til* be'come su'spicious of; **fattet** *adj* com'posed, calm.

fattig *adj* poor; *de ~e* the poor; *~ på ngt* lacking in sth; **-dom** *en* poverty; **-kvarter** *et* poor district.

favn *en* arms *pl; (mål)* fathom; *med ~en fuld af ngt* with an armful of sth; *holde ngt i ~en* hold· sth in one's arms.

favne *v: ~ vidt* be all-em'bracing.

favorisere *v* favour.

favorit *en* favourite.

favør *en: i ens ~* in sby's favour; **-pris** *en* special price.

fe *en* fairy.

feber *en* fever, temperature; *have ~* be running a temperature; **-fri** *adj* without a temperature.

febrilsk *adj* feverish.

februar *en* February; *den første ~* the first of February, February the first.

fed *et (garn)* skein; *(hvidløg)* clove.

fed *adj* fat; (S, *mægtig god)* great, smashing; *en ~ fest* a smashing party; *~ kost* fatty food; *blive ~* grow· fat; *det kan være lige ~t* it is all one (to me); *det skal ~t hjælpe!* a fat lot of good that's going to do! **-e** *v* fatten; *det ~er* it is fattening.

fedme *en* fatness; (H) o'besity.

fedt *et* fat; *(svine~)* lard; *(til smøring)* grease.

fedte *v* grease; *(være nærig)* be stingy; *~ for en* fawn on sby; **-røv** *en (slesk person)* bootlicker.

fedtet *adj* greasy; *(glat, fx omvej)* slippery; *(nærig)* mean, stingy.

fedtfattig *adj* low-fat; **fedtfri** *adj* nofat, fatfree.

fedtplet *en* grease spot.

fedtstof *et* fat; *(til bagning)* shortening.

fej *adj* cowardly.

feje *v* sweep·; *~ en af* snub sby; *~ ngt til side (fig)* brush sth a'side; **-bakke** *en* dustpan; **-kost** *en* broom; **-maskine** *en* sweeper.

fejhed *en* cowardice [-dis].

fejl *en (fejltagelse, ngt man har gjort forkert)* error, mis'take; *(mangel ved ngt)* fault, de'fect; *lave en ~* make· an error (,a mistake); *det er ikke min ~* it is not my fault // *adj* wrong *(fx adresse* address) // *adv* wrong(ly); *gå ~ af en* miss sby; *slå ~* go· wrong; *tage ~* be mis'taken, be wrong; *tage ~ af ngt* mis'take· sth; *tage ~ af a og b* mis'take· a for b; *det er ikke til at tage ~ af* it is unmis'takable; **-agtig** *adj* wrong.

fejle *v: hvad ~r du?* what is the matter with you? *ikke ~ ngt* be all right.

fejlfortolkning *en* misinterpre'tation.

fejlfri *adj* perfect.

fejlkilde *en* source of error.

fejltagelse *en* mis'take; *ved en ~* by mis'take.

fejltrin *et: begå et ~* make· a slip.

fejre *v* celebrate.

f.eks. *(fork.f. for eksempel, i skriftsprog)* e.g.

felt *et* field; **-flaske** *en* can'teen; **-råb** *et* password; **-seng** *en* campbed; **-tog** *et* cam'paign.

fem *num* five.

feminin *adj* feminine; *(om mand)* ef'feminate.

femininum *et (gram)* the feminine.

feminist *en* feminist; **-isk** *adj* feminist.

femkamp *en (sport)* pen'tathlon.

femkant *en* pentagon; **-et** *adj* pen'tagonal.

femlinger *pl* quin'tuplets, (F) quins.

femmer *en* five; *(pengestykke, -seddel)* fiver; *(bus etc)* number five.

femtal *et* five.

femte *adj* fifth; **-del** *en* fifth.

femten *num* fifteen; **-de** *adj* fifteenth.

femtid *en: ved ~en* (at) about five o'clock.

fennikel *en* fennel.

ferie *en* holiday(s); *(især am)* va'cation;

holde ~ be on holiday; *i* ~*n* during the holiday(s); *tage på* ~ go· on holiday; **~afløser** *en* holiday re'lief; **~job** *et (for studerende etc)* va'cation job; **~koloni** *en* holiday camp; **~penge** *pl* holiday al'lowance; **~re** *v* be on holiday; **~rejse** *en* holiday trip; **~sted** *et* holiday re'sort; **~tablet** *en* pep pill.
fernis *en* varnish; **~ere** *v* varnish.
fernisering *en (åbning af udstilling)* preview.
fersk *adj* fresh; *(om smag)* in'sipid; *gribe en på* ~ *gerning* catch· sby red-handed.
fersken *en* peach.
ferskvand *et* fresh water.
ferskvands- freshwater *(fx fisk* fish).
fest *en* party; *(by~, film~, musik~ etc)* festival; *holde* ~ throw· (,have) a party; *ved* ~*en* at the party; **~e** *v* have a party; *(fejre)* celebrate; **~forestilling** *en* gala per'formance; *det var en* ~*forestilling da de skulle tapetsere* it was a scream to see them hang the wallpaper.
festival *en* festival.
feta *en (ost)* Feta cheese.
festklædt *adj* in evening dress.
festlig *adj* festive; *(morsom)* very funny; *det var* ~*t* it was great fun; **~hed** *en* cele'bration.
festmiddag *en* banquet.
festspil *et* festival.
feteret *v* celebrated.
fiasko *en* failure, flop.
fiber *en* fibre; **~rig** *adj* high-fibre.
fidus *en (kneb)* trick; *(vink, råd)* tip; *(snyd)* fiddle; *ham har jeg ikke* ~ *til* I'm wary of him, I don't trust him.
fiffig *adj* smart; *(snu)* shrewd.
figen *en* fig; **~blad** *et* fig leaf *(pl:* leaves).
figur *en* figure; *i bar* ~ *(dvs. nøgen)* naked, in the nude; *(dvs. uden overtøj)* without a coat; *passe på* ~*en* watch one's figure.
figurere *v* figure.
figurløb *et (på skøjter)* figure skating.
fiks *adj* smart; *en* ~ *idé* an ob'session; ~ *på fingrene* dexterous.
fikse *v* fix; ~ *ngt op* do· sth up.
fiksere *v* fix; **fiksering** *en* fix'ation; **fiksersalt** *et* fixing salt.
fiksfakserier *pl* tricks, dodges.
fikstid *en* core time.
fil *en* file; **~e** *v* file.
filet *en* fillet; *rødspætte~* fillet of plaice; **filetere** *v* fillet.
filial *en* branch.
filipens *en* pimple, spot.
filippiner *en* Fili'pino; **filippinsk** *adj* Philippine; **Filippinerne** *pl* the Philippines.
film *en* film; *(især am)* movie; **~apparat** *et (optager)* cine camera; *(fremviser)* (film) pro'jector; **~atisere** *v* film; **~atisering** *en* film version; *(det at filme)* filming; **~fotograf** *en* cameraman *(pl:* -men); **~instruktør** *en* film di'rector; **~kamera** *et* film camera; *(til smalfilm)* cine camera; **~lærred** *et* (movie)screen; **~skaber** *en* film maker; **~stjerne** *en* filmstar.
filolog *en* phi'lologist; **filogi** *en* phi'lology.
filosof *en* phi'losopher; **filosofere** *v* phi'losophize *(over* about); **filosofi** *en* phi'losophy; **filosofisk** *adj* philo'sophical.
filt *en* felt.
filter *et* filter; *(på cigaret)* filter tip; *med* ~ filter-tipped.
filtre *v:* ~ *sig sammen* tangle, get· into a tangle.
filtrere *v* filter.
filtret *adj (om hår)* matted; *(om garn etc)* in a tangle.
fin *adj* fine; *(ekstra~)* choice; *(moderne, in)* fashionable; *(neds)* posh; ~*t!* great! fine! *have det* ~*t* feel· fine.
finale *en* fi'nale; *(sport)* final.
finanser *pl* finances.
finansiere *v* finance; **finansiering** *en* financing.
finans... *sms:* **~loven** *s* the Budget; **~ministerium** *et* Ministry of Finance; **~år** *et* fiscal year.
finde *v* find·; *(mene, synes)* think·; ~ *sted* take· place; ~ *vej* find one's way; ~ *tegnebogen frem* produce one's wallet; ~ *sig i ngt* put· up with sth; ~ *på ngt* think of sth; *(op-*

digte) make· sth up; ~ *ud af ngt (dvs. opdage)* dis'cover sth; *(dvs. forstå)* make· sth out; **~løn** *en* re'ward; **~s** *v* ex'ist.

finer *en* ve'neer.

finesse *en* fi'nesse, re'finement; *(trick)* trick; *(smart opfindelse, dims etc)* gadget.

finger *en* finger; *holde fingrene fra ngt* keep· one's hands off sth; *få fingre i ngt* get· hold of sth; *kunne ngt på fingrene* have sth at one's fingertips; *ikke røre en ~ for at hjælpe* not lift a finger to help; *krydse fingre for en* keep· one's fingers crossed for sby; *fingrene væk!* hands off! **~aftryk** *et* fingerprint; **~bøl** *et* thimble; *gemme ~bøl* hunt the thimble.

fingere *v* simulate; **~t** *adj* simulated, mock; *(falsk)* faked.

finger... *sms:* **~færdig** *adj* dexterous, nimble; **~færdighed** *en* dex'terity; **~nem** *adj* dexterous; **~peg** *et* hint; **~ring** *en* ring; **~spids** *en* fingertip.

finkæmme *v* comb.

Finland *s* Finland.

finmekaniker *en* pre'cision engi'neer.

finne *en (fra Finland)* Finn; *(på fisk)* fin.

finregn *en* drizzle.

finsk *et, adj* Finnish.

fintfølende *adj* sensitive; *(overfor andre)* tactful.

finvask *en (om tøjet)* delicates *pl.*

firben *et* lizard.

firdobbelt *adj* quadruple.

fire *num* four; *på alle ~* on all fours; **~personers** *adj (om bil)* fourseater.

firer *en* four; *(om bus etc)* number four.

firetaktsmotor *en* four-stroke engine.

firetiden *s: ved ~* (at) about four o'clock.

firhjulet *adj* four-wheel(ed); **firhjulstræk** *et* four-wheel drive.

firkant *en* square; *(aflang)* rectangle; **~et** *adj* square; rec'tangular; *(kluntet)* awkward.

firkløver *et* four-leaf clover.

firkort *s: spille ~* play happy families.

firlinger *pl* quadruplets, (F) quads.

firma *et* firm; **~bil** *en* company car; **~mærke** *et* trade mark.

firs *num* eighty; *han er født i ~erne* he was born in the eighties; *han er i ~erne* he is in his eighties

firskåren *adj* square-built.

firsporet *adj* four-lane.

firstemmig *adj* four-part.

firtal *et* four.

fis *en* fart; *lave ~ med en* (F) have sby on; **~e** *v* fart.

fisefornem *adj* stuck-up.

fisk *en* fish; *Fiskene (astr)* Pisces; *mange ~* lots of fish; *ti ~* ten fishes; *fange ~* catch· fish; *gå i ~* go· haywire; *hverken fugl el. ~* neither fish nor fowl; **~e** *v* fish; *tage ud at ~e* go· fishing; *~e sild* fish for herring; *~e efter ngt (fig)* fish for sth; *~e ngt op af lommen* pull sth out of one's pocket; **~e·banke** *en* fishing bank; **~e·ben** *et* fish bone; **~e·bolle** *en* fish ball; **~e·dam** *en (leg)* lucky dip; **~e·fars** *en sv.t.* creamed fish; **~e·filet** *en* fillet of fish; **~e·frikadelle** *en* fishcake; **~e·garn** *et* fishing net; **~e·handler** *en* fishmonger; **~e·kutter** *en* fishing boat; **~e·kvote** *en* fishing quota; **~e·net** *et* fishnet; **~e·plads** *en* fishing ground.

fisker *en* fisherman *(pl:* -men); *(sports~)* angler; **~båd** *en* fishing boat.

fiskeri *et* fishing; **~grænse** *en* fishing limit; **~havn** *en* fishing port; **~ministerium** *et* Ministry of Fisheries.

fiskerleje *et* fishing village.

fiskeskæl *et* fishscale.

fiskesnøre *en* fishing line.

fiskestang *en* fishing rod.

fisketur *en: tage på ~* go· fishing.

fjante *v* fool around; **~t** *adj* silly; *(pjattet, fnisende)* giggling.

fjeder *en* spring.

fjedre *v* be springy.

fjeld *et* mountain; *(klippegrund)* rock.

fjende *en* enemy.

fjendskab *et* enmity.

fjendtlig *adj (af indstilling)* hostile *(over for* to); *(som tilhører fjenden)* enemy *(fx soldat* soldier); **~hed** *en* hos'tility.

fjer *en* feather; *(stor hatte~)* plume;

have en ~ på (fig) be tipsy; **~bold** *en* shuttlecock.
fjerde *adj* fourth; **~del** *en* fourth, quarter; **~delsnode** *en* crotchet.
fjerkræ *et* poultry; **~avl** *en* poultry farming.
fjern *adj* distant, faraway; *(afsides)* re'mote; *(langt væk i tankerne)* far a'way; *Det Fjerne Østen* the Far East; *i en ~ fortid* in the distant past; *en ~ slægtning* a distant relative; *se ngt i det ~e* see· sth in the distance; **~betjening** *en* re'mote con'trol; **~e** *v* re'move; *~e sig* go· a'way; **~ere** *v* more distant, further (away); more re'mote; **~est** *adj* most distant, furthest; re'motest; *det betyder ikke det ~este* it does not make the least bit of difference; **~lys** *et (auto)* main beam; **~seer** *en* viewer; **~skriver** *en* telex; **~styret** *adj* re'mote-con'trolled; **~styring** *en* re'mote con'trol.
fjernsyn *et* television; *(om apparatet)* television set, (F) telly; *se ~* watch television; *være i ~et* be on television; *sende ngt i ~et* televise sth; **~s·antenne** *en* television aerial; **~s·apparat** *et* television set; **~s·licens** *en* television licence; **~s·narkoman** *en* television addict; **~s·program** *et* television programme; **~s·skærm** *en* television screen; **~s·udsendelse** *en* television programme.
fjernt *adv* far-off; *(fig)* distantly; *fjernt fra byens larm* far away from the hustle and bustle of the city.
fjernvarme *en* district (,mu'nicipal) heating.
fjoget *adj* foolish.
fjolle *v: ~ rundt* fool around; **~ri** *et* nonsense; **~t** *adj* silly.
fjols *et* fool.
fjor *s: i ~* last year; *i ~ sommer* last summer.
fjord *en* inlet; *(i Skotland)* firth; *(i Norden)* fjord.
fjorten *num* fourteen; *om ~ dage* in a fortnight; **~de** *adj* fourteenth; *hver ~de dag* every two weeks, once a fortnight.
fjumre *v: ~ med ngt* bungle sth; *~ rundt* fool around.
f.Kr. *(fork.f. før Kristi fødsel)* BC.
flabet *adj* cheeky; **~hed** *en* cheek; *(~ bemærkning)* cheeky re'mark.
flad *adj* flat; *(uden penge)* broke; *en ~ tallerken* a plate; *det var en ~ fornemmelse* it made me feel stupid.
flade *en (overflade)* surface; *(om landskab)* ex'panse.
flad... *sms:* **~fisk** *en* flatfish; **~lus** *en* crab louse *(pl:* lice); **~pandet** *adj* dumb; **~tang** *en: en ~tang* a (pair of) flat-nose pliers; **~trykt** *adj* flattened.
flag *et* flag; *hejse ~et* hoist the flag; *hejse ~et ned* lower the flag; *føre dansk ~* fly· the Danish colours; gå ned med ~et *(fig)* go· to pieces; *vise ~et* show the flag; **~dug** *en* bunting.
flage *en* flake; *(is~)* floe // *v* fly· a flag; *~ for kongens fødselsdag* fly the flags for the King's birthday; *~ et skib ud* flag out a ship.
flagermus *en* bat; **~lygte** *en* hurricane lantern.
flagre *v* flutter; *(baske)* flap.
flagskib *et* flagship *(også fig)*.
flagstang *en* flagpole.
flakke *v (om lys)* flicker; *(om øjne)* wander; *~ om* roam about.
flamberet *adj* flambée.
flamingo *en (zo)* fla'mingo; *(materiale)* ex'panded poly'styrene.
flamme *en* flame; *stå i ~r* be in flames // *v* flame, blaze.
flamsk *adj* Flemish.
flaske *en* bottle; *en ~ vin* a bottle of wine; *fylde ngt på ~r* bottle sth; *slå sig på ~n* (F) hit· the bottle // *v: ~ sig* work out; **~barn** *et* bottle-fed baby; **~beholder** *en (til genbrug)* bottle bank; **~gas** *en* bottled gas; **~hals** *en* bottleneck *(også fig)*; **~renser** *en* bottle-brush.
flatterende *adj* flattering.
fleksibel *adj* flexible *(også fig)*.
flekstid *en* flextime.
flere *adj* more; *(adskillige)* several; *(diverse, forskellige)* various; *~ end* more than; *~ og ~* more and more;

~ *tusind* several thousand; *har du ~ penge?* have you any more money? *regering og folketing med ~* government, parliament and others.

fleretages *adj* multi-storey.

flerstavelses *adj* polysil'labic.

flerstemmig *adj: ~ sang* part-song; *(det at synge...)* part-singing.

flertal *et* ma'jority; *(gram)* the plural; *vedtaget med stort ~* carried by a large majority; *være i ~* be in the majority.

flertydig *adj* am'biguous.

flest *adj* most; *de ~e* most; *(om personer)* most people.

fletning *en* plait [plæt]; *(det at flette)* plaiting.

flette *v* plait [plæt]; *~ fingre (med en)* hold· hands (with sby); *~ en krans* make· a wreath.

fletværk *et* wickerwork.

flid *en* diligence; *(arbejdsomhed)* industry; *(iver, vedholdenhed)* appli'cation.

flig *en* corner, snip.

flimmer *et* flicker; *~en (fjernsynet)* (F) the box.

flimre *v* flicker; **~n** *en* flicker.

flink *adj (rar)* nice; *(dygtig)* good, clever; *være ~ til ngt* be good at sth.

flintesten *en* flint(stone).

flintre *v: ~ af sted* belt along.

flip *en* collar; *stiv ~* starched collar; *være ude af ~pen* be flustered // *et* flop; *det var et ~* it was a flop.

flippe *v: ~ ud* freak out; **~r** *en* freak.

flippermaskine *en* pinball ma'chine.

flirte *v* flirt.

flis *en* splinter.

flise *en (på vej etc)* flagstone; *(væg~, gulv~)* tile; **~belægning** *en* tiling; **~bord** *et* tiletop table; **~gulv** *et* tiled floor; **~væg** *en* tiled wall.

flitsbue *en* bow [bəu].

flittig *adj* diligent; *(arbejdsom)* in'dustrious; *(travl)* busy.

flod *en* river; *(højvande)* high tide; *ned (,op) ad ~en* downstream (,upstream); *falde i ~en* fall· into the river; **~bred** *en* river side, river bank; **~bølge** *en* tidal wave; **~hest** *en* hippo'potamus; **~leje** *et* river bed; **~munding** *en* river mouth.

flok *en (af mennesker)* crowd; *(mindre)* group; *(om kvæg)* herd; *(om får, geder, fugle)* flock; *i samlet ~* in a body.

flokkes *v: ~ om* flock round.

flonel *et* flannel.

flor *et: i fuldt ~* in full bloom.

florere *v* be rampant.

flormelis *en* icing sugar.

floskel *en* empty phrase.

flosse *v* fray.

flot *adj (smart etc)* elegant; *(large)* generous; *(ødsel)* lavish; *(om ting)* fine; *en ~ fyr (,pige)* a good-looker; *hun har ~te ben* she has got smashing legs; *han har ~te vaner* he has got ex'pensive habits; *det var ~ klaret!* well done! **~hed** *en* elegance; gene'rosity; lavishness.

flotte *v: ~ sig med ngt* treat oneself to sth.

flov *adj (som skammer sig)* a'shamed; *(pinligt berørt, forlegen)* em'barrassed, awkward; *(om smag)* flat; *det var ~t for os* it was em'barrassing for us; **~e** *v: ~e sig* (F) be a'shamed; **~hed** *en* em'barrassment, awkwardness.

flue *en* fly; *han kunne ikke gøre en ~ fortræd* he would not hurt a fly; *slå to ~r med et smæk* kill two birds with one stone; **~fiskeri** *et* fly-fishing; **~papir** *et* fly-paper; **~smækker** *en* fly-swatter; **~svamp** *en* fly agaric; **~vægt** *en (sport)* flyweight.

flugt *en (det at flygte el. flyve)* flight; *(det at undslippe)* e'scape; *gribe ngt i ~en* catch· sth in the air; *på ~* on the run; *tage ~en* take· to one's heels, run· away; **~bilist** *en* hit-and-run driver.

flugte *v (være på højde)* be flush *(med* with); *(i tennis etc)* volley.

flugtstol *en* deck chair.

flugtvej *en* e'scape route.

fluor *en* fluorine; **~tandpasta** *en* fluoride toothpaste.

flute *et* French stick.

fly *et* aeroplane; **~billet** *en* plane ticket; **~bortførelse** *en* hijacking;

~bortfører *en* hijacker; **~forbindelse** *en* air service; *(se også flyve-)*.

flyde *v (svømme ovenpå)* float; *(rinde, løbe)* run·; *(om roderi)* be in a mess; *ligge og ~ (om ting)* be lying around; *(om person)* be lazing about; *gulvet flød med legetøj* the floor was littered with toys; *værelset ~r* the room is (in) a mess; *~ over* over'flow.

flydende *adj (om væske etc)* liquid, fluid; *(om sprog, tale)* fluent; *tale ~ engelsk* speak· fluent English.

flygel *et* grand piano.

flygte *v* run· a'way; *(undslippe)* e'scape.

flygtig *adj* passing; *(overfladisk)* casual; *(som let fordamper)* volatile; *en ~ berøring* a casual touch; *et ~t blik* a passing glance; **~t** *adj* casually; *se ~t på ngt* glance at sth.

flygtning *en* fugitive; *(p.g.a. krig, forfølgelse)* refu'gee.

Flygtningehjælpen *s (Dansk Flygtningehjælp)* the Danish Refu'gee Council.

flygtningelejr *en* refu'gee camp.

fly... *sms:* **~kaprer** *en* hijacker; **~kapring** *en* hijacking; **~katastrofe** *en* air dis'aster; **~rute** *en* air service; **~styrt** *et* plane crash.

flytning *en* re'moval.

flytte *v* move; *(fjerne)* re'move; *~ fra hinanden* split· up; *~ ting fra hinanden* move things a'part; *~ ind* move in; *~ om på ngt* move sth around; *~ sammen med en* move in with sby; *~ sig* move; *flyt dig lige!* move over, please! **~folk** *pl* re'moval men; **~kasse** *en* packing case; **~vogn** *en* furniture van.

flyve *v* fly·; *(suse, styrte)* dash, rush; **~base** *en* air base; **~billet** *en* plane ticket; **~båd** *en (med bæreplaner)* hydrofoil boat; *(luftpudebåd)* hovercraft; **~færdig** *adj* fully-fledged *(også fig)*; **~leder** *en* air-traffic con'troller; **~maskine** *en* aeroplane.

flyvende *adj* flying; *i ~ fart* at top speed; *~ tallerken* flying saucer; *~ tæppe* magic carpet.

flyveplads *en (lufthavn)* airport; *(mindre)* airfield.

flyver *en (maskine)* aeroplane; *(person)* pilot; **~certifikat** *et* flying cer'tificate; **~dragt** *en (til barn)* snowsuit.

flyvestævne *et* air show.

flyvetur *en* flight.

flyveulykke *en* plane crash.

flyvevåben *et* air force.

flyvning *en* flight; *(det at flyve)* avi'ation.

flyvsk *adj* volatile; *~e drømme* fancy dreams.

flæbe *v* snivel.

flække *en* small town // *v* split·.

flæng *s: i ~* at random.

flænge *en (i tøj, papir etc)* tear [tɛə*]; *(mindre sår)* scratch; *(større sår)* gash // *v* tear·; scratch; gash; *få bukserne ~t* tear· one's trousers.

flæse *en* frill.

flæsk *et (svinekød)* pork; *(bacon)* bacon; **~e·fars** *en* minced pork; **~e·steg** *en (kødstykke)* joint of pork; *(ret)* roast pork; **~e·svær** *en (spæklaget på svinekød)* bacon rind; *(sprød)* crackling.

fløde *en* cream; **~bolle** *en (slik) sv.omtr.t.* chocolate marshmallow; **~chokolade** *en* milk chocolate; **~farvet** *adj* cream; **~is** *en* ice cream; **~karamel** *en* toffee; **~skum** *et* whipped cream.

fløj *en* wing; **~dør** *en* double door.

fløjl *et* velvet; *(riflet)* corduroy; **~s·bukser** *pl* corduroys.

fløjt *et* whistle.

fløjte *en (tværfløjte)* flute; *(blokfløjte)* re'corder; *(legetøj, signalfløjte)* whistle; *direktøren spiller (på) ~* the manager plays the flute // *v* whistle; **~kedel** *en* whistling kettle; **~nist** *en* flute player.

flå *v (fx et dyr)* skin; *(rive i)* tear· [tɛə*]·; *blive ~et (i butik etc)* be fleeced.

flåde *en (samling af skibe)* fleet; *(tømmer~, redning~)* raft; *han er i ~n* he is in the navy; **~base** *en* naval base.

FM *(radio)* VHF.

FN *(fork.f. Forenede Nationer)* the UN *(fork.f.* United Nations).

fnat *en* scabies; **~tet** *adj (sølle)* lousy, measly.

fnise *v* giggle; *(hånligt)* snigger.

fnug *et* fluff; *(støv~)* speck; *(sne~)* flake; **~ge** *v* fluff; **~get** *adj* fluffy.

fnyse *v* snort *(ad* at).

fod *en* foot *(pl:* feet); *~ for ~* step by step; *få kolde fødder* get· cold feet *(også fig); have ømme fødder* have sore feet; *fryse om fødderne* have cold feet; *gå på bare fødder* walk barefoot; *på fri ~* free; *blive sat på fri ~* be re'leased; *stå på god ~ med en* be on good terms with sby; *på lige ~ med* on an equal footing with; *til ~s* on foot.

fodbold *en* football; *(om sportsgrenen også)* soccer; **~bane** *en* football ground (,pitch); **~hold** *et* football team; **~kamp** *en* football (,soccer) match; **~spiller** *en* football player, (F) footballer; **~træner** *en* (football) coach.

fodbremse *en* foot brake; *(på cykel)* pedal brake.

foder *et* feed; *(om hø etc)* fodder; **~bræt** *et* bird table; **~kage** *en* oil cake.

fodfolk *pl (mil)* infantry.

fodformet *adj* pediform; *(om meninger)* cut-and-dried.

fodfæste *et* foothold, footing; *miste ~t* lose· one's footing.

fodgænger *en* pe'destrian; **~område** *et* pe'destrian precinct; **~overgang** *en* pe'destrian crossing; *(med striber)* zebra crossing; **~tunnel** *en* subway.

fodklinik *en* chi'ropodist's.

fodnote *en* footnote.

fodpanel *et* skirting board.

fodre *v* feed·.

fodring *en* feeding.

fod... *sms:* **~spor** *et* footprint; *gå i ens ~spor* follow in sby's footsteps; **~støtte** *en* footrest; **~svamp** *en* athlete's foot; **~sved** *en: have ~sved* have sweaty feet; **~sål** *en* sole of the foot; **~trin** *et* (foot)step; **~tøj** *et* footwear.

foged *en (kongens ~) sv.t.* bailiff.

fok *en (mar)* foresail, jib.

fokus *et* focus; **~ere** *v* focus *(på* on).

fold *en (i tøj, papir etc)* fold; *(rynke)* wrinkle; *(presse~)* crease; *(indhegning)* pen; *lægge ngt i ~er* fold sth (up); *nederdel med ~er* pleated skirt.

folde *v* fold; *~ ngt sammen* fold sth up; *~ ngt ud* un'fold sth; *~ sig ud* un'fold; *(om person)* let· one'self go; **~kniv** *en* jackknife *(pl:* -knives).

folder *en* folder.

folie *en* foil.

folk *et* people; *(arbejdere)* men; *~et* the people; *hvad mon ~ vil sige?* I wonder what people will say.

folke... *sms:* **~afstemning** *en* refe'rendum; **~dans** *en (det at danse)* folk dancing; *(selve dansen)* folk dance; **~dragt** *en* national costume; **~eventyr** *et* folktale; **~højskole** *en* folk high school; **~kirke** *en* national church; **~lig** *adj* popular; *(jævn)* simple; **~musik** *en* folk music; **~mængde** *en (indbyggertal)* popu'lation; *(masse mennesker)* crowd; **~pension** *en* old age pension; **~pensionist** *en* old age pensioner, OAP ['əuei'pi:]; **~register** *et sv.t.* register of births, marriages and deaths; **~ret** *en* inter'national law; **~sagn** *et* legend; **~sanger** *en* folk singer; **~skole** *en* primary and lower secondary school (for children between 7 and 16), sv.omtr.t. mu'nicipal school; **~slag** *et* people; **~tinget** *s sv.t.* the parliament; **~tingsvalg** *et* general e'lection; **~tælling** *en* census; **~vandring** *en* mi'gration; **~vise** *en* ballad.

fond *et* fund; *(legat)* foun'dation; *(gastr)* stock; **~s·aktie** *en* bonus share; **~s·børs** *en* stock ex'change.

fondue *en* 'fondue.

fonetik *en* pho'netics.

for *et (i tøj)* lining.

for *præp (beregnet for; på grund af; om tid; som betaling for; i stedet for)* for; *(foran, i overværelse af)* be'fore, at, in front of; *(til beskyttelse mod)* from, to; *(med hensyn til)* to, from; *(foran at + infinitiv)* to, in order to; *(foran at + sætning)* so that, in order that; *(se også de enkelte ord som ~ forbindes med); den bog er ~*

børn that book is for children; *de lejede et værelse ~ en uge* they took· a room for a week; *han ville have 10.000 ~ bilen* he wanted 10,000 for the car; *takke en ~ ngt* thank sby for sth; *~ øjnene af børnene* in front of the children; *hele verden ligger ~ hans fødder* the whole world is at his feet; *han har hele livet ~ sig* he has his whole life before him; *søge ly ~ regnen* seek· shelter from the rain; *han var døv ~ hendes forklaringer* he was deaf to her expla'nations; *være ~ for ngt* be free from sth; *sætte sig ned ~ at spise* sit· down to eat; *~ ikke at glemme John* so as not to for'get John, not for'getting John; *gøre ngt ~ at forhindre krig* do· sth (in order) to pre'vent war; *~ at være sikker* (in order) to make sure; *~ at de ikke skulle komme for sent* so that they should not be late; *~ længe siden* a long time a'go; *~ et år siden* a year a'go; *være ngt ~ sig selv* be sth out of the ordinary; *hvad ~ ngt?* what? *hvad er det ~ en bog?* what book is that? // *adv (alt ~)* too; *spille ~ højt* play too loudly; *har du ngt ~ i dag?* are you doing anything today? *~ og imod* for and a'gainst // *konj (fordi)* be'cause, for; *hun råbte højt, ~ hun var vred* she yelled, for she was angry.

foragt *en* con'tempt.

foragte *v* de'spise; **~lig** *adj* con'temptible, de'spicable.

foran *præp* in front of; *(forud)* a'head *(for* of) // *adv* a'head; *(i spidsen)* in front; *vi standsede ~ pubben* we stopped in front of the pub; *han var langt ~ os* he was far a'head of us; *England var ~ med 3-0* England was leading by 3-0 (three goals to nil); *jeg vil sidde ~* I want to sit in front.

forandre *v* change; *~ sig* change *(til* into).

forandring *en* change; *til en ~* for a change.

foranstaltning *en* ar'rangement; *træffe ~er* make· arrangements, take· measures.

forarbejde *et* pre'liminary work; *han har lavet alt ~t (også)* he has paved the way.

forar'bejde *v* work, process; **forarbejdning** *en* working, processing.

forarge *v* shock, of'fend; *blive ~t over ngt* be shocked at sth; *~t over at...* shocked that... **~lse** *en* indig'nation; *vække ~lse* cause a scandal.

forbande *v* curse; **~lse** *en* curse.

forbandet *adj/adv* damned.

forbarme *v: ~ sig over en* take· pity on sby.

forbavse *v* sur'prise; **~lse** *en* sur'prise.

forbavset *adj* sur'prised; *~ over at...* sur'prised that... // *adv* in sur'prise.

forbedre *v* im'prove; *~ sig* im'prove; **forbedring** *en* im'provement.

forbehold *et* reser'vation; *tage ~* make· reservations; *uden ~* uncon'ditionally.

forbeholde *v: ~ sig ret til* re'serve the right to.

forbeholden *adj* re'served.

forben *et* foreleg.

forberede *v* pre'pare; *~ en (,sig) på (,til) ngt* pre'pare sby (,oneself) for sth; **~lse** *en* prepa'ration *(til* for); *under ~lse* in prepa'ration; **~nde** *adj* pre'liminary.

forbi *adv/præp (om bevægelse)* past; *(slut, ovre)* over; *(færdig)* finished; *gå (,køre etc) ~ ngt* walk (,drive· etc) past sth; *det er ~* it is over; **~er** *en* miss; **~fart** *en: i ~farten* (in) passing; **~gå** *v (ignorere)* over'look; *blive ~gået (ved forfremmelse)* be passed over; **~gående** *adj* passing, temporary.

forbillede *et* model, ex'ample; **forbilledlig** *adj* ex'emplary.

forbinde *v* con'nect *(med* with); *(sætte sammen)* join *(med* to); *(forene)* com'bine *(med* with); *(med bandage)* dress, bandage.

forbindelse *en* con'nection; *(rute)* service; *(forhold)* re'lationship; *(sammenhæng)* context; *(kemisk)* compound; *fast ~ (bro, tunnel)* fixed link; *få ~ med en* get· into touch with sby; *(tlf)* get· through to sby; *holde ~n ved lige* keep· in touch; *i denne ~* in this con'nection; *miste ~n med en* lose· touch with sby; *sætte sig i ~ med en* get· in touch with sby.

forbinding *en* bandage; *(det at forbinde)* bandaging, dressing; **forbindskasse** *en* first-aid box.

forbipasserende *en* passer-by *(pl:* passers-by).

forbitret *adj* bitter.

forbjerg *et* promontory, headland.

forblive *v* re'main; *(på stedet)* stay.

forbløde *v* bleed· to death.

forbløffe *v* a'maze, a'stonish; **~lse** *en* a'mazement, a'stonishment; **~nde** *adj* a'mazing.

forbogstav *et* i'nitial.

forbrug *et* con'sumption; **~e** *v* con'sume.

forbruger *en* con'sumer; **~råd** *et* con'sumers' ad'visory council; **~venlig** *adj* con'sumer-friendly.

forbrugsafgift *en* excise duty.

forbrugsgoder *pl* con'sumer goods; *varige ~* con'sumer durables.

forbryde *v: ~ sig mod en* com'mit an of'fence against sby; **~lse** *en* crime, of'fence; *begå en ~lse* com'mit a crime.

forbryder *en* criminal.

forbrænding *en* com'bustion, incine'ration; *(brandsår)* burn; **~s·anlæg** *et* incine'ration plant; **~s·ovn** *en* in'cinerator.

forbrændt *adj* burnt; *(af solen)* sunburnt.

forbud *et* prohi'bition *(mod* against), ban *(mod* on); *give en ~ mod at gøre ngt* for'bid· sby to do sth; *nedlægge ~ mod ngt* pro'hibit (,ban) sth; *ophæve et ~* lift a ban; **~s·tavle** *en* prohi'bition sign.

forbudt *adj* for'bidden, pro'hibited; *adgang ~* no ad'mittance; *~ for børn* for adults only.

forbund *et* union, league; *(stats~)* fede'ration; *(alliance)* al'liance.

forbundet *adj* con'nected; com'bined; joined; *(se forbinde); det var ~t med en vis risiko* it in'volved a certain risk.

forbunds... *sms:* **~fælle** *en* ally; **~kansler** *en* federal chancellor; **~republik** *en* federal re'public; **~stat** *en* federal state.

forbyde *v* for'bid·, pro'hibit, ban; *~ en adgang* forbid· sby to enter; *~ spiritus ved fodboldkampe* ban liquor from football matches.

forbøn *en: gå i ~ for en* inter'cede for sby.

force *en* strong point.

forcere *v* force.

fordampe *v* e'vaporate.

fordampning *en* evapo'ration.

fordel *en* ad'vantage; *have ~ frem for en* have an ad'vantage over sby; *til ~ for* in favour of; *til ens ~* to sby's ad'vantage.

fordelagtig *adj* advan'tageous; *(indbringende)* lucrative.

fordele *v* di'stribute; *(dele)* di'vide.

fordeling *en* distri'bution; di'vision.

fordi *konj* be'cause; *det er ikke ~ han er dum, men...* it is not that he is stupid, but...

fordoble *v* double.

fordobling *en* doubling.

fordom *en* prejudice *(mod* against); **~s·fri** *adj* unprejudiced.

fordrage *v: jeg kan ikke ~ det* I can't stand it; *jeg kan ikke ~ at gøre det* I hate to do it (,doing it).

fordre *v* de'mand; *(have krav på)* claim.

fordreje *v* dis'tort, twist: *med ~t ansigt* with a dis'torted face.

fordrejning *en* dis'torsion, twisting.

fordring *en* de'mand; *(jur, krav)* claim; *gøre ~ på ngt* claim sth; **~s·fuld** *adj* de'manding.

fordrive *v* drive· away; *~ tiden* pass the time.

fordrukken *adj: være ~* drink·.

fordufte *v* vanish.

fordybe *v: ~ sig i ngt* be'come· en'grossed in sth.

fordybning *en* hollow, de'pression; *(rille etc)* groove.

fordæk *et (på skib)* foredeck; *(på bil)* front tyre.

fordærv *et* ruin, dis'aster.

fordærve *v (om mad ec)* spoil·, ruin;

(om person) de'prave; **~lig** *adj: let ~lig* perishable.
fordærvet *adj (om mad)* bad; *(om person)* de'praved.
fordøje *v* di'gest; **~lig** *adj: let ~lig* di'gestible.
fordøjelse *en* di'gestion; *dårlig ~* indi'gestion.
fordømme *v* con'demn; **~lse** *en* condem'nation.
fordømt *adj* con'demned; *(pokkers)* damned.
fordør *en* front door.
fore *v* line; *~t kuvert* padded envelope, Jiffy bag.
forebygge *v* pre'vent; **~lse** *en* pre'vention; **~nde** *adj* pre'ventive; *(med)* prophy'lactic *(fx behandling* treatment).
foredrag *et* talk *(om* on); *(forelæsning)* lecture *(om* on); *holde ~ for* give· a talk (,lecture) to; **~s·holder** *en* lecturer.
foregangsmand *en* pio'neer *(for* of); *være ~ for ngt* pio'neer sth.
foregive *v* pre'tend, feign.
foregribe *v: ~ begivenhedernes gang* an'ticipate e'vents.
foregå *v* happen, go· on; *(finde sted)* take· place; *hvad ~r der?* what is happening? what is going on? *mødet ~r på rådhuset* the meeting is taking place at the town hall; *~ en med et godt eksempel* set· sby a good ex'ample.
foregående *adj* previous.
forehavende *et* under'taking, enterprise.
forekomme *v (ske)* happen; *(findes)* oc'cur; *(virke)* seem, ap'pear; *det ~r mig at...* it seems to me that...; **~nde** *adj (venlig)* courteous ['kə:tiəs].
forekomst *en* oc'currence.
forel *en* trout.
foreligge *v (findes)* be a'vailable; *der må ~ en misforståelse* there must be some mistake; **~nde** *adj* ex'isting; *i den ~nde situation* in the present situ'ation.
forelske *v: ~ sig i en* fall· in love with sby; **~lse** *en* love *(i* for).
forelsket *adj* in love.
forelægge *v* pre'sent; **~lse** *en* presen'tation.
forelæsning *en* lecture; *holde ~ om ngt* give· a lecture on sth; *gå til ~* at'tend a lecture.
foreløbig *adj* temporary // *adv (for en tid)* temporarily; *(indtil videre)* for the time being; *(hidtil)* so far; *~ går det fint* so far it is all right.
forene *v* com'bine, join; *(i en helhed)* u'nite; *De Forenede Nationer* the U'nited Nations; *De Forenede Stater* the U'nited States.
forenelig *adj* con'sistent *(med* with).
forening *en* so'ciety.
forenkle *v* simplify; **forenkling** *en* simplifi'cation.
foreskrive *v* pre'scribe; *(beordre)* order.
foreslå *v* sug'gest.
forespørge *v* en'quire; **forespørgsel** *en* en'quiry.
forestille *v (skulle være, gengive)* repre'sent; *(præsentere)* intro'duce; *hvad skal det ~?* what is that sup'posed to be? *~ sig ngt* i'magine sth; *du kan ikke ~ dig hvor skønt det var!* you have no i'dea how nice it was!
forestilling *en (teat etc)* per'formance; *(begreb, idé)* i'dea *(om* of).
forestå *v (lede)* be in charge of; *(nærme sig)* be near.
foretage *v* make·; *~ sig ngt* do· sth; *~ en rejse* make· a journey; *~ en operation* per'form an ope'ration.
foretagende *et* under'taking; *(firma)* business.
foretagsom *adj* enterprising; **~hed** *en* enterprise.
foretrække *v* pre'fer; *~ vin for øl* pre'fer wine to beer.
forevise *v* show; **forevisning** *en* showing.
forfald *et (ødelæggelse etc)* de'cay; *(udløb af frist)* settlement date.
forfalde *v (om hus)* fall· into disrepair; *(skulle betales)* fall· due.
forfalden *adj (i forfald)* di'lapidated, in disrepair; *(til betaling)* due.
forfalske *v (fx billeder, smykker)* fake;

(fx dokumenter) forge; *(penge)* counterfeit.

forfalskning *en (det at forfalske)* faking; forgery; counterfeiting; *(det forfalskede)* fake; forgery.

forfatning *en (grundlov)* consti'tution; *(tilstand)* state; **~s·stridig** *adj* unconsti'tutional.

forfatter *en* author, writer *(til* of); **~skab** *et (det en ~ har skrevet)* works *pl.*

forfinet *adj* so'phisticated.

forfjamsket *adj* flustered.

forfjor *s: i ~* the year before last.

forflytte *v* trans'fer.

forfra *adv (fra forsiden)* from in front; *(om igen)* a'gain, from the be'ginning.

forfremme *v* pro'mote; **~lse** *en* pro'motion.

forfriske *v* re'fresh; **~nde** *adj* re'freshing.

forfriskning *en* re'freshment.

forfrysning *en* frostbite.

forfædre *pl* ancestors.

forfængelig *adj* vain; **~hed** *en* vanity.

forfærdelig *adj* terrible, awful; *hun staver ~t* her spelling is awful // *adv* terribly, awfully; *det er ~ pænt af dig* it's awfully nice of you.

forfærdelse *en* horror, terror.

forfærdet *adj* shocked; *(stærkere)* horrified.

forfølge *v* persecute; *(løbe efter, jage)* pur'sue; *(genere, plage)* pester.

forfølgelse *en* perse'cution; pur'suit; chase; **~s·løb** *et* pur'suit race; **~s·vanvid** *et* perse'cution mania.

forføre *v* se'duce; **~lse** *en* se'duction.

forgifte *v* poison; **forgiftning** *en* poisoning.

forgive *v* poison.

forglemmelse *en* oversight; *ved en ~* by mis'take.

forglemmigej *en* for'get-me-not.

forgodtbefindende *et: efter ~* as one thinks fit.

forgrene *v: ~ sig* branch (off).

forgribe *v: ~ sig på ngt* misap'propriate sth; *~ sig på en* lay· hands on sby.

forgrund *en* foreground.

forgude *v* idolize; **~lse** *en* idoli'zation.

forgylde *v* gild; **forgyldt** *adj* gilt.

forgængelig *adj* perishable.

forgænger *en* predecessor.

forgæves *adj* vain; *et ~ forsøg* a vain at'tempt // *adv* in vain.

forgårs: *i ~* the day before yesterday.

forhadt *adj* hated.

forhal *en* hall.

forhale *v* de'lay.

forhandle *v* ne'gotiate; *(diskutere)* dis'cuss; *(sælge)* deal· in; *~ om en løsning* ne'gotiate (,dis'cuss) a so'lution.

forhandler *en* ne'gotiator; *(sælger)* dealer.

forhandling *en* negoti'ation; *(diskussion)* dis'cussion; *(om løn)* bargaining; *(salg)* sale; *indlede ~er med en* enter into negoti'ations with sby; **~s·partner** *en* ne'gotiating party; **~s·venlig** *adj* ready to ne'gotiate.

forhaste *v: ~ sig* be rash; **~t** *adj* rash, hasty; *(for tidlig)* premature.

forhekset *adj* be'witched.

forhenværende *adj* former, ex-.

forhindre *v* pre'vent; *~ en i et gøre ngt* pre'vent sby from doing sth.

forhindring *en (det at forhindre)* pre'vention; *(som spærrer etc)* obstacle; **~s·løb** *et* obstacle race.

forhippet *adj: ~ på at...* keen to...

forhistorisk *adj* prehi'storic.

forhjul *et* front wheel; **~s·træk** *et* front-wheel drive.

forhold *et (omstændighed, tilstand)* con'dition, circumstance; *(forbindelse, ~ mellem mennesker)* re'lationship; *(sag)* fact, matter; *(proportion)* pro'portion; *sociale ~* social con'ditions; *private ~* private af'fairs; *have et ~ til en (erotisk)* have an af'fair with sby; *have et godt ~ til en* be on good terms with sby; *i ~ til (dvs. sammenlignet med)* (as) com'pared to; *under de nuværende ~* under the present circumstances.

forholde *v: ~ sig* be; *det ~r sig sådan at...* the fact is that...; *~ sig roligt* keep· quiet; *vide hvordan man skal ~ sig* know· what to do.

forholdsmæssigt *adv* relatively.
forholdsord *et* prepo'sition.
forholdsregel *en* pre'caution, measure; *tage sine forholdsregler mod ngt* take· measures a'gainst sth.
forholdsvis *adv* relatively.
forhæng *et* curtain.
forhøje *v* raise, in'crease *(med* by); **-lse** *en* rise, 'increase.
forhøjning *en (i terrænet)* rise; *(i rum)* platform.
forhør *et* questioning, interro'gation; *(i retten)* exami'nation; *holde ~* hold· an in'quiry; *tage en i ~* in'terrogate sby; **-e** *v* question, in'terrogate; ex'amine; *~e sig* en'quire, ask.
forhåbentlig *adv* I hope, hopefully.
forhånd *en (i tennis etc)* forehand; *være i ~en (i kortspil)* have the lead; *på ~* in ad'vance, be'forehand.
forhåndenværende *adj (til at få fat i)* a'vailable; *(eksisterende)* ex'isting.
forjage *v* drive· away; **-t** *adj (stresset)* ha'rassed; *(for hurtig)* hasty.
forkalket *adj (om person)* senile.
forkaste *v* re'ject.
forkastning *en (geol)* fault.
forkert *adj* wrong; *(ved verber erstattes* wrong *ofte af:* mis-, *fx* misspell, miscalculate); *huske ~* be mis'taken; *uret går ~* the watch is wrong; *træde ~* stumble; *være ~ på den* be (in the) wrong.
forklare *v* ex'plain; *~ en ngt* explain sth to sby.
forklaring *en* expla'nation; *(vidne~)* evidence.
forkludre *v* bungle.
'forklæde *et* apron.
for'klæde *v* dis'guise.
forklædning *en* dis'guise.
forkorte *v* shorten; *(om tekst, bog)* a'bridge; **-lse** *en* abbrevi'ation.
forkromet *adj* chromium-plated.
forkrøblet *adj* crippled.
forkullet *adj* charred.
forkvaklet *adj* warped, mucked up.
forkvinde *en* chairwomen *(pl:* -women); *(for arbejdere)* forewoman *(sm. bøjn).*
forkynde *v (meddele)* pro'claim, an'nounce; *~ evangeliet* preach the gospel; **-lse** *en* procla'mation, an'nouncement; preaching.
forkæle *v* spoil·; *(neds)* pamper; *et ~t barn* a spoilt child.
forkæmper *en* advocate *(for* of).
forkærlighed *en* parti'ality; *have ~ for* be partial to.
forkøb *et: komme en i ~et (dvs. komme først)* an'ticipate sby; *(dvs. hindre)* fore'stall sby; **-s·ret** *en* first option *(til* on).
forkølelse *en* cold.
forkølet *adj: blive ~* catch· cold; *være ~* have a cold.
forkørselsret *en: have ~ for en* have the right of way over sby.
forlade *v* leave·; *(rømme)* de'sert; *(opgive)* a'bandon; *~ sig på ngt* de'pend on sth; **-lse** *en: om ~lse!* I'm sorry!
forladt *adj (øde, tom)* de'serted, desolate; *(opgivet)* a'bandoned.
forlag *et* publishing house; **-s·redaktør** *en* publishing editor.
forlange *v (bede om)* ask for; *(kræve)* de'mand; *(som sin ret)* claim; *(om pris)* ask, charge; *~ ngt af en* de'mand sth from sby; *det kan man ikke ~* that is too much to ask; *det er ikke for meget forlangt* it's not asking too much.
forlangende *et* de'mand.
forleden *adj: ~ dag* the other day.
forlegen *adj* shy, self-'conscious; **-hed** *en (generthed)* shyness, self-'consciousness; *(knibe)* difficulty; *være i ~hed* be in trouble.
forlig *et (aftale)* a'greement, deal; *slutte ~* come· to an agreement, (F) make· a deal; **-e** *v* reconcile; *~e sig med ngt* be'come reconciled to sth; **-es** *v* get· on; **-s·institutionen** *s sv.t.* ACAS ['eikəs] (Ad'visory, Concili'ation and Arbi'tration Service); **-s·mand** *en* mediator.
forlis *et* shipwreck; **-e** *v* be shipwrecked; *(fig)* fail.
forloren *adj* false; *~ hare sv.t.* meat loaf; *~ skildpadde* mock turtle; *forlorne tænder* false teeth.
forlove *v: ~ sig med en* get· en'gaged to sby.

forlovelse *en* en'gagement; **~s·ring** *en* en'gagement ring.
forlover *en (for brud)* he who gives away the bride; *(for brudgom)* best man *(pl:* men).
forlovet *adj* en'gaged *(med* to); *hendes forlovede* her fi'ancé; *hans forlovede* his fi'ancée.
forlyde *v: det ~r at...* it is re'ported that...; **~nde** *et* rumour.
forlygte *en* headlight.
forlystelse *en* a'musement, enter'tainment; **~s·syg** *adj* pleasure-seeking.
forlægge *v (så ngt bliver væk)* mis'lay·; *(flytte)* re'move; *~ residensen til* ad'journ to.
forlægger *en* publisher.
forlænge *v (udbygge etc)* ex'tend; *(gøre længere)* lengthen; *~t spilletid (fodb)* extra time; **~lse** *en* ex'tension; lengthening.
forlængerled(ning) *s* ex'tension.
forlængst *adv* long ago.
forlæns *adv* forward(s).
forløb *et* course; *efter ngn tids ~* after some time; *inden en måneds ~* with'in a month.
forløbe *v (om tid)* pass; *(foregå)* go·; *~ godt* go· well; *i den forløbne uge* during the past week; *~ sig* go· too far.
forløber *en* forerunner *(for* of).
form *en* form, shape; *(støbe~)* mould; *(bage~)* tin; *en ~ for smør* some sort of butter; *jeg er ikke i ~ til det* I'm not in form (,the shape) for it; *han er i fin ~* he is in very good shape; *i ~ af* in the shape of; *holde sig i ~* keep· fit; *holde på ~erne* stand· on ceremony.
formalitet *en* for'mality; *uden ~er* without any fuss; (H) in'formally.
formand *en (i forening etc)* president *(for* of); *(i bestyrelse)* chairman *(pl:* -men) *(for* of); *(arbejds~)* foreman *(pl:* -men); **~skab** *et* presidency; chairmanship.
formane *v* ad'monish; **formaning** *en* admo'nition, warning.
format *et* size; *(om bog, papir også)* format; *(om persons karakter)* standing; *en fest af ~* a grand party; *en person af ~* a person of standing; *i lille (,stort) ~* on a small (,large) scale.
formatere *v (edb)* format.
formation *en* for'mation.
forme *v* form, shape; *det ~de sig som...* it turned out to be...
formedelst *præp: ~ 100 kr.* a'gainst payment of 100 kr.
formel *en* formula; *~ 1-løb* formula one race // *adj* formal.
formentlig *adv* pre'sumably, I be'lieve.
formere *v: ~ sig* repro'duce, multiply; **formering** *en* repro'duction.
formgive *v* de'sign; **~r** *en* de'signer.
formgivning *en* de'sign.
formidabel *adj* 'formidable.
formiddag *en* morning; *i ~(s)* this morning; *i går ~s* yesterday morning; *i morgen ~* tomorrow morning; **~s·blad** *et (neds)* tabloid.
formidle *v (skabe, sørge for)* ar'range; *(give videre)* give·, con'vey; **~er** *en* mediator.
formidling *en* ar'rangement; *(udbredelse af viden om)* pro'motion.
formilde *v (berolige etc)* calm, soothe; *~nde omstændigheder* ex'tenuating circumstances.
formindske *v* re'duce, di'minish, lessen; **~lse** *en* de'crease.
formning *en* forming, shaping; *(i skolen)* art (class).
formode *v* sup'pose, pre'sume.
formodentlig *adv* pre'sumably, I sup'pose.
formodning *en* suppo'sition; *(gæt)* guess; *have ~ om at* su'spect that.
formssag *en: det er en ~* it's a matter of form.
formue *en* capital; *(stor)* fortune; **~nde** *adj* wealthy; **~skat** *en* wealth tax.
formular *en* form; *udfylde en ~* fill in a form.
formulere *v* ex'press, put· into words.
formulering *en (dvs. ordlyd)* wording.
formynder *en* guardian; **~skab** *et* guardianship.
formøble *v* squander, throw· away.
formørke *v* darken; **~lse** *en (om sol, måne)* e'clipse.

formå *v* be able *(at* to); *~ ham til at gøre ngt* in'duce him to do sth; **-en** *en* a'bility.

formål *et* purpose, aim; *have til ~ at* be in'tended to; *lavet til ~et* purpose-made; **~s·løs** *adj* pointless; **~s·tjenlig** *adj* suitable.

fornavn *et* Christian name, first name.

forneden *adv* be'low, at the bottom.

fornem *adj* di'stinguished.

fornemme *v* feel·, sense; **-lse** *en* feeling; *have på ~lsen at...* have a feeling that...

fornuft *en* reason; *det er sund ~* it is common sense; *tale en til ~* make· sby see reason; *tage imod ~* see· reason.

fornuftig *adj* sensible; *(rimelig)* reasonable.

forny *v* re'new; *(istandsætte)* renovate; *(udskifte)* re'place; *efter ~et overvejelse* after further conside'ration; **-else** *en* re'newal; reno'vation; re'placement.

fornægte *v* de'ny.

fornærme *v* of'fend, in'sult; **-lse** *en* in'sult *(mod* to); **-nde** *adj* in'sulting.

fornærmet *adj* of'fended; *(mopset)* miffed; *blive ~ over ngt* take· of'fence at sth; *blive ~ på en* be miffed with sby.

fornøden *adj* necessary; **-heder** *pl* necessaries.

fornøjelse *en* pleasure; *(forlystelse)* a'musement; *god ~!* have a good time! *med ~* with pleasure; *det er ikke for min ~s skyld* it is not for fun.

fornøjet *adj* pleased *(med* with).

forord *et* preface.

forordning *en* order, de'cree.

foroven *adv* a'bove, at the top.

forover *adv* forward.

forpagte *v* rent; *~ bort* lease.

forpagter *en* tenant.

forpagtning *en* tenancy, lease.

forpasse *v: ~ chancen* miss the oppor'tunity.

forpeste *v* poison.

forpjusket *adj* tousled.

forplante *v: ~ sig (om dyr)* repro'duce; *(om lyd etc)* spread·.

forplantning *en* repro'duction.

forplejning *en: inklusive ~* in'cluding meals.

forpligte *v: ~ sig til at gøre ngt* com'mit oneself to doing sth; *føle sig (,være) ~t til at gøre ngt* feel· (,be) o'bliged to do sth.

forpligtelse *en* com'mitment, obli'gation *(over for* towards; *til at* to).

forpligtende *adj* binding.

forpremiere *en* preview.

forpurre *v* thwart.

forpustet *adj* breathless; *blive ~* lose· one's breath.

forregne *v: ~ sig* mis'calculate.

forrest *adj* front, foremost // *adv* in front, first.

forret *en (gastr)* starter, first course; *(førsteret)* pri'ority.

forretning *en (firma etc)* business; *(butik)* shop; *(enkelt handel)* deal; *gøre en god ~* make· a bargain; *snakke ~er* talk shop; *gå i ~er* go· shopping; **~s·drivende** *en (med butik)* shopkeeper; *(i større stil)* businessman *(pl:* -men); **~s·forbindelse** *en* business con'nection; **~s·fører** *en* manager; **~s·gade** *en* shopping street; **~s·gang** *en* pro'cedure; **~s·mand** *en* businessman *(pl:* -men); **~s·mæssig** *adj* businesslike; **~s·rejse** *en* business trip.

forrige *adj* previous; *~ år* last year.

forringe *v* re'duce; *(i værdi)* de'preciate; **-lse** *en* re'duction; depreci'ation; **-s** *v* de'teriorate.

forrude *en (auto)* windscreen.

forrygende *adj* furious; *(fig)* wild, fan'tastic.

forrykt *adj* mad, crazy.

forræder *en* traitor.

forræderi *et* treachery.

forræderisk *adj* treacherous.

forråd *et* store, stock.

forråde *v* be'tray.

forrådnelse *en* de'cay, rot; *gå i ~* rot.

forsagt *adj* timid.

forsalg *et (af billetter)* ad'vance booking.

forsamle(s) *v* gather.

forsamling *en* meeting, gathering; *(publikum)* audience; *(menneskemængde)* crowd; **~s·hus** *et* village hall.
forsatsvinduer *pl* double glazing.
forse *v: ~ sig mod en* do· sby wrong; *~ sig på en (dvs. ikke kunne lide)* get· an'noyed with sby; *(dvs. falde for)* fall· for sby.
forseelse *en* of'fence.
forsegle *v* seal (up).
forsendelse *en (det at sende)* sending, dis'patch; *(hold varer)* shipment; *(pakke)* parcel.
forside *en* front; *(i avis, blad)* front page; **~stof** *et: blive ~stof* hit· the headlines.
forsigtig *adj* careful; *(blid)* gentle; *forsigtig! (på pakke etc)* handle with care! **~hed** *en* care, caution.
forsikre *v* in'sure; *(hævde, sværge på etc)* as'sure; *~ en om ngt* assure sby of sth.
forsikring *en* in'surance; *(hævdelse etc)* as'surance; **~s·agent** *en* insurance broker; **~s·police** *en* insurance policy; **~s·præmie** *en* insurance premium; **~s·selskab** *et* insurance company; **~s·tager** *en* policy holder.
forsinke *v* de'lay; **~lse** *en* de'lay.
forsinket *adj* late; *blive ~* be delayed; *(komme for sent)* be late; *bussen var 10 minutter ~* the bus was 10 minutes late.
forskanse *v: ~ sig (fig)* ensconce oneself.
forske *v* do· re'search *(i* into).
forskel *en* difference; *gøre ~ på* dis'tinguish be'tween; *kende ~ på John og Harry* tell· John from Harry: *han kan ikke se ~* he can't tell the difference; *der er ~ på piger* girls differ.
forskellig *adj* different *(fra* from); *~e (dvs. ikke ens)* different; *(dvs. diverse)* various; *det er meget ~t* it varies a lot.
forsker *en* re'searcher; *(naturvidenskabelig)* scientist; *(humanistisk)* scholar; **~park** *en* science park.
forskning *en* re'search *(i* into).
forskrift *en (reglement)* regu'lation; *(vejledning)* di'rections *pl.*
forskrække *v* frighten, scare; **~lse** *en* fright, scare.
forskræmt *adj* timid, scared.
forskubbe *v: ~ sig* move, shift.
forskud *et* ad'vance; *på ~* in ad'vance; *tage sorgerne på ~* an'ticipate e'vents; **~s·opgørelse** *en* estimate of next year's income.
forskærerkniv *en* carving knife *(pl:* knives).
forskærersæt *et* carving set, carvers *pl.*
forskønne *v (pynte (på))* em'bellish.
forskåne *v* spare; *forskån mig for detaljerne!* spare me the 'details!
forslag *et* pro'posal *(om* for); *(lov~)* bill; *(~ til afstemning ved møde)* motion; *komme med et ~* make· a proposal; *(ved møde)* put· a motion.
forslugen *adj* greedy.
forslået *adj* bruised.
forsmag *en* foretaste *(på* of).
forsone *v* reconcile; *~ sig med ngt* reconcile oneself to sth.
forsoning reconcili'ation.
forsorg *en* care, welfare.
forspil *et* prelude; *(om sex)* foreplay.
forspilde *v* waste; *~ sin chance* miss one's chance.
forspise *v: ~ sig* over'eat.
forspring *et* lead; *få et ~ (også fig)* get· a head start.
forstad *en* suburb; **~s** su'burban.
forstand *en (fornuft)* reason; *(tænkeevne)* intellect; *(intelligens)* in'telligence; *(sind)* mind; *gå fra ~en* go· mad; *er du fra ~en?* are you out of your mind? *i en vis ~* in a sense; *i den ~ at...* in the sense that...; *have ~ på ngt* know· about sth.
forstander *en (for skole)* headmaster; *(kvindelig)* headmistress; *(for institution etc)* di'rector.
forstavelse *en* prefix.
forstavn *en* bow.
forstenet *adj* petrified; *(om fossil)* fossilized.
forstening *en (af dyr el. plante)* fossil.
forstille *v: ~ sig* pre'tend, feign.
forstmand *en* forester.

forstoppe *v* block; *(med)* constipate.
forstoppelse *en (med)* consti'pation; *(om afløb etc)* block.
forstrække *v (fx muskel)* strain; *(give penge)* ad'vance.
forstue *en* hall.
forstuve *v* sprain.
forstuvning *en* sprain.
forstvæsen *et* forestry.
forstyrre *v* di'sturb; **-lse** *en* di'sturb-'ance.
forstyrret *adj* con'fused; *(skør)* crazy.
forstærke *v* strengthen; *(om lyd og fig)* in'crease.
forstærker *en (radio)* amplifier.
forstærkning *en* strengthening; *~er (mil)* rein'forcements.
forstørre *v* en'large.
forstørrelse *en* en'largement; **-s·glas** *et* magnifying glass.
forstøve *v* atomize.
forstøver *en* atomizer.
forstå *v* under'stand·; *(indse)* realize, see·; *hun forstod på ham at...* she under'stood from what he said that...; *han ~r at lave mad!* he knows how to cook! *~ mig ret* don't misunder'stand me; *lade en ~ at...* give· sby to under'stand that...; *er det ~et?* is that under'stood? *det skal ikke ~s bogstaveligt* it's not to be taken literally; *hvordan skal det ~s?* what do you mean by that? *~ sig på ngt* know· about sth; **-e·lig** *adj (dvs. til at begribe, tyde)* compre'hensible; *(dvs. som kan undskyldes)* under'standable; *gøre sig ~elig* make· oneself understood; *(give klar besked)* make· oneself clear; **-else** *en* under'standing; **-ende** *adj* under'standing.
forsuring *en* acidifi'cation.
forsvar *et* de'fence; *tage en i ~* stand· up for sby; *han er i ~et* he is in the army (,the Forces); **-e** *v* de'fend *(mod* a'gainst); *vi kan ikke ~e at lade ham lave maden* it would be too risky to let him do the cooking; **-er** *en* de'fender; *(jur)* counsel for the defence; **-lig** *adj* justifiable; *(sikker)* se'cure; **-s·løs** *adj* de'fenceless; **-s·ministerium** *et* Ministry of Defence; **-s·politik** *en* defence policy; **-s·udgifter** *pl* de'fence spending; **-s·våben** *et* de'fensive weapon.
forsvinde *v* disap'pear, vanish; *(blive væk også)* be (,get·) lost; *forsvind med dig!* get lost! scram! **forsvundet** *adj* lost; *(savnet)* missing.
forsyne *v: ~ en med ngt (dvs. levere ngt)* sup'ply sby with sth; *(dvs. udstyre en)* pro'vide sby with sth; *~ sig (med mad etc)* help one'self.
'forsynet *s* Providence.
forsyning *en* sup'ply.
forsæde *et (i bil)* front seat; *føre ~t (ved møde etc)* be chairman, chair.
forsæt *et* in'tention, purpose; *med ~* on purpose; **-lig** *adj* in'tentional, de'liberate.
forsøg *et (prøve)* test, trial; *(eksperiment)* ex'periment; *(bestræbelse)* at'tempt; *gøre et ~ på at...* make· an attempt to...; *det var ~et værd* it was worth a try; **-e** *v* try, at'tempt *(på at* to); **-s·dyr** *et* la'boratory animal; **-s·kanin** *en (fig)* guinea-pig; **-s·vis** *adv* as a trial.
forsømme *v (ikke passe på)* ne'glect; *(gå glip af, udeblive fra)* miss; *(være fraværende)* be absent; **-lig** *adj* negligent; **-lse** *en* ne'glect; absence; *~lser (i skolen)* absen'teeism; **forsømt** *adj* ne'glected.
forsørge *v* keep·, pro'vide for; *(økonomisk)* sup'port; **-lse** *en* sup'port.
forsørger *en* breadwinner; *enlig ~* single parent.
forsåle *v* sole; **forsåling** *en* soling.
fortabe *v* for'feit; *~ sig i ngt* get· lost in sth; **fortabt** *adj* lost; *føle sig fortabt* feel· lost; *give fortabt* give· up; *de er fortabt* they are done for.
fortage *v: ~ sig* wear· off; *(om lyd)* die down.
fortaler *en* spokesman *(pl:* -men) *(for* of).
fortalelse *en* slip (of the tongue).
fortand *en* front tooth *(pl:* teeth).
fortegnelse *en* list; *(systematisk)* record.
fortid *en* past; *(gram)* the past (tense).
fortie *v* hide·, con'ceal; *~ ngt for en* with'hold· sth from sby.

fortil *adv* in front.
fortilfælde *et* precedent.
fortjene *v* de'serve; *det har du fortjent* it serves you right.
fortjeneste *en (overskud)* profit; *(indtægt)* earnings *pl; (ngt man har opnået etc)* merit; *det er din ~ at...* it is thanks to you that...; *sælge ngt med ~* sell· sth at a profit.
fortjenstfuld *adj* de'serving.
fortjent *adj: gøre sig ~ til ngt* de'serve sth.
fortløbende *adj* con'secutive.
fortolde *v* de'clare; *(betale told af)* pay· duty on.
fortoldning *en* clearance; *(betaling)* payment of duty.
fortolke *v* in'terpret.
fortolker *en* in'terpreter.
fortolkning *en* interpre'tation.
fortov *et* pavement; **~s·restaurant** *en* pavement restaurant.
fortrin *et* ad'vantage.
fortrinlig *adj* excellent.
fortrinsret *en* pri'ority.
fortrinsvis *adv* preferably; *(især)* chiefly.
fortrolig *adj* confi'dential; *(som man kender godt)* fa'miliar; *blive ~ med ngt (dvs. lære at kende)* get· to know sth; *(dvs. sætte sig ind i)* make· one'self fa'miliar with sth; *en ~ ven* an intimate friend; **~hed** *en* confidence.
fortryde *v* re'gret; *det skal han komme til at ~* he will (live to) re'gret that; **~lig** *adj* an'noyed; *hun tog det ~ligt op* she re'sented it; **~lse** *en* an'noyance.
fortrylle *v* charm, be'witch; **~lse** *en* charm; *(trylleri)* spell; **~nde** *adj* charming.
fortræd *en* harm; *gøre en ~* harm (,hurt·) sby.
fortræffelig *adj* excellent.
fortrække *v (gå væk)* go· away; *(om ansigt etc)* dis'tort; *ikke ~ en mine* not turn a hair.
fortrænge *v* drive· away; *(udkonkurrere)* oust; *(psyk)* re'press.
fortrængning *en (psyk)* re'pression.
fortsat *adj* con'tinuous; *(historie, artikel)* con'tinued // *adv* still.
fortsætte *v* con'tinue, go· on; *~ med at gøre ngt* con'tinue to do sth, go· on doing sth; **~lse** *en* continu'ation.
fortvivle *v* de'spair; **~lse** *en* de'spair.
fortvivlet *adj* in de'spair, desperate.
fortynde *v* di'lute; **~r** *en (til maling etc)* thinner.
fortynding *en* di'lution.
fortælle *v* tell·; *hun fortalte at de var syge* she told me (,him, her, us, them) that they were ill; *~ en om ngt* tell· sby about sth; *vi har ladet os ~ at...* we have heard that...; **fortælling** *en* story.
fortænke *v: man kan ikke ~ ham i at han glemte det* you can't blame him for for'getting it.
fortøje *v* moor.
fortøjning *en* mooring; **~s·pæl** *en* bollard; *(ude i vandet)* dolphin.
fortørnet *adj* angry.
forud *adv* in ad'vance; *være ~ for en* be a'head of sby; **~bestilling** *en* reser'vation; *(af billetter)* ad'vance-booking.
forude *adv* a'head.
foruden *præp* be'sides.
forud... *sms:* **~gående** *adj (tidligere)* previous; **~indtaget** *adj* prejudiced; **~sat** *adj: ~sat at* pro'vided that; **~se** *v* fore'see·; **~sige** *v* pre'dict; **~sigelig** *adj* pre'dictable.
forudsætning *en* con'dition; *(antagelse)* as'sumption; *have ~er for at gøre ngt* be qualified to do sth; *ud fra den ~ at...* on the as'sumption that...
forudsætte *v (gå ud fra)* presup'pose; *(antage)* as'sume; *~ som givet at...* take· it for granted that...
forulykke *v (om bil, fly etc)* crash; *(om person)* have an accident; *(dvs. dø)* be killed in an accident.
forundret *adj* sur'prised *(over* at; *over at* that).
forundring *en* sur'prise.
forurene *v* pol'lute.
forurening *en* pol'lution; **~s·kilde** *en* pol'lutant.
forurolige *v* di'sturb; **~nde** *adj* di'sturbing.
forvalte *v* manage.

forvalter *en* manager; *(af landejendom)* (farm) bailiff.
forvaltning *en* admini'stration.
forvandle *v* change *(til* into); *~ sig* change.
forvandling *en* change.
forvaring *en* keeping; *(fængsel)* custody.
forvarsel *et* omen *(om* of).
forvask *en* prewash; **~et** *adj* washed-out.
forvejen *s: gå i ~* go· a'head; *gøre ngt i ~* do· sth be'forehand; *det var varmt nok i ~* it was al'ready warm e'nough.
forveksle *v* mix up; *~ a med b* mis-'take a for b, mix up a with b.
forveksling *en* mis'take; *de ligner hinanden til ~* they are hard to tell from one an'other.
forvente *v* ex'pect.
forventning *en* expec'tation; *mod ~* contrary to all expec'tations; *leve op til ~erne* come· up to expec'tations; *i ~ om...* ex'pecting; *over ~* be'yond expec'tation; **~s·fuld** *adj* ex'pectant.
forvirre *v* con'fuse.
exile**forvirring** *en* con'fusion.
forvise *v* ban; *(deportere)* de'port; *(landsforvise)* exile.
forvisning *en* depor'tation, exile.
forvisse *v: ~ sig om at...* make· sure that...
forvitre *v* dis'integrate.
forvolde *v* cause.
forvride *v* twist; *(forstuve)* sprain.
forvridning *en* twisting; spraining.
forvrænge *v* dis'tort; **forvrængning** *en* dis'tortion.
forvænt *adj* spoilt.
forværre *v* worsen, aggravate; *(syn, hørelse etc)* im'pair; **~s** *v* get· worse.
forværring *en* worsening; aggra'vation; im'pairment.
foryngende *adj* re'juvenating.
forældet *adj* out-'dated, obsolete.
forælder *en* parent; *enlig ~* single parent.
forældre *pl* parents; **~løs** *adj* orphaned; **~myndighed** *en* custody *(over* of); *fælles ~myndighed* joint custody.
forære *v* give·; *jeg har fået den ~nde* it was given to me (as a present).
foræring *en* gift, present.
forøge *v* in'crease *(med* by); **~lse** *en* in'crease.
forår *et* spring; *i ~et 1990* in the spring of 1990; *om ~et* in spring; *til ~et* next spring.
forårsage *v* cause, bring· about.
forårstid *en: ved ~* in springtime.
fos *en* waterfall.
fosfor *en* phosphorus.
fosse *v: ~ ud* gush out.
foster *et* embryo, foetus; **~vand** *et* amni'otic fluid; **~vandsprøve** *en* amniocen'tesis.
fostre *v* pro'duce.
foto *et* photo; **~graf** *en* pho'tographer; *(tv, film)* cameraman *(pl:* -men); **~grafere** *v* photograph; **~grafi** *et* *(billede)* photo(graph); *(det at fotografere)* pho'tography; **~grafiapparat** *et* camera; **~handler** *en* camera dealer, photo shop; **~kopi** *en* photocopy, Xerox ®; **~kopiere** *v* photocopy, Xerox ®; **~kopimaskine** *en* photocopier; **~stat** *en* photostat ®.
fr *(fru, frøken)* Ms.
fra *præp/konj* from; *(væk fra)* off; *(se også de enkelte ord som ~ forbindes med); de kommer ~ Skotland* they come· from Scotland; *holde sig ~ cigaretter* stay· off cigarettes; *fem ~ otte er tre* five from eight is three; *~ i dag af* from this day on; *hun har talt engelsk ~ hun var lille* she has been speaking English since she was a child // *adv* off; *tapetet er gået ~* the wallpaper has come off; *det gør hverken ~ el. til* it makes no difference.
fradrag *et (i selvangivelsen etc)* de-'duction; *(som skattevæsenet giver)* al'lowance; **~s·berettiget** *adj* 'tax-de'ductible.
fradømme *v: ~ en kørekortet* su'spend sby's driving licence, ban sby from driving.
frafald *et (fx fra kursus)* drop-out rate.
fragment *et* 'fragment.
fragt *en* freight; **~brev** *et* waybill; **~e**

v carry; **~gods** *et* goods *pl;* **~mand** *en* carrier; **~skib** *et* freighter.

frakke *en* coat; *tage ~n af* take· off one's coat; *tage ~n på* put· on one's coat; **~skåner** *en* dress guard.

frakørsel *en (fra motorvej)* exit, slip road.

fralandsvind *en* off-shore wind.

fralægge *v: ~ sig ansvaret* re'fuse to take responsi'bility.

frankere *v* stamp; **frankering** *en* stamping; *(porto)* postage.

Frankrig *s* France.

fransk *adj* French; *på ~* in French; *~e kartofler* po'tato crisps; **~brød** *et* white bread; **~mand** *en* Frenchman *(pl:* -men); *hun er ~mand* she is French; *~mændene* the French.

frarøve *v: ~ en ngt* rob sby of sth.

fraråde *v: ~ en at gøre ngt* ad'vise sby against doing sth.

frase *en* phrase.

fraseparereret *adj* separated.

frasige *v: ~ sig* re'nounce.

fraskilt *adj* di'vorced; *min ~e mand* my ex-husband.

frastødende *adj* re'pulsive.

fratage *v: ~ en ngt* de'prive sby of sth.

fratræde *v* re'sign; *(p.g.a. alder)* re'tire; **~lse** *en* resig'nation; re'tirement.

fravær *et* absence; *glimre ved sit ~* be con'spicuous by one's absence.

fraværende *adj* absent; *(distræt)* absent-minded.

fred *en* peace; *~ og ro* peace and quiet; *lade en være i ~* leave· sby a'lone; *slutte ~* make· peace.

fredag *en* Friday; *i ~s* last Friday; *om ~en* on Friday; *(hver ~)* on Fridays; *på ~* on Friday, next Friday.

frede *v* pro'tect, pre'serve.

fredelig *adj* peaceful.

fredet *adj* pro'tected, pre'served; *~ bygning (også)* listed building; *~ område* conser'vation area.

fredløs *adj* outlawed; *en ~* an outlaw.

fredning *en* preser'vation, conser'vation; **~s·nævnet** *s* the Conser'vation Board; **~s·tid** *en (for dyr)* close season.

freds... *sms:* **~aktivist** *en* peace activist; **~bevarende** *adj* peace-keeping *(fx styrker* forces); **~bevægelse** *en* peace movement; **~forhandlinger** *pl* peace talks; **~forslag** *et* peace bid; **~forstyrrer** *en* trouble-maker; **~prisen** *s* the Nobel Peace Prize; **~slutning** *en* peace a'greement; **~tid** *en: i ~tid* in times of peace.

fregat *en* frigate.

fregne *en* freckle; **~t** *adj* freckled.

frekvens *en* frequency.

frekventere *v* fre'quent.

frelse *en (redning)* rescue; *(åndelig)* sal'vation // *v* save, rescue.

Frelsens Hær the Sal'vation Army.

frelst *adj* saved, rescued; *(neds)* self-'righteous.

frem *adv (videre)* on; *(ud, til syne)* out; *(fremad)* forward(s); *~ for at sælge huset burde I leje det ud* rather than sell the house, you ought to let it; *træde ~* step forward; *komme ~ fra mørket* come· out of the dark; *tage ngt ~* take· sth out, pro'duce sth; *trave ~ og tilbage* walk up and down, walk to and fro.

fremad *adv* forward(s); *(videre)* on; *(ud i fremtiden)* a'head; **~stræbende** *adj* up-and-coming.

frembringe *v* pro'duce; **~lse** *en* pro'duction; *(det der frembringes)* product.

fremdatere *v* post'date.

fremfor *præp* be'fore, rather than; *~ alt* a'bove all.

fremgang *en* progress; *(held)* suc'cess.

fremgangsmåde *en* pro'cedure; *(metode)* method.

fremgå *v* ap'pear; *heraf ~r at...* from this it appears that...

fremherskende *adj* pre'vailing.

fremhæve *v* ac'centuate; *(lægge vægt på, understrege)* emphasize.

fremkalde *v* cause, e'voke; *(føre til)* bring· about; *(foto)* de'velop; *(sygdom)* in'duce; **~lse** *en (teat)* curtain call; *(foto)* de'velopment.

fremkalder *en (foto)* de'veloper.

fremkommelig *adj (om vej)* passable, practicable.

fremleje *v* sublet·.

fremlægge *v* pre'sent; *(til bedømmelse)* sub'mit.

fremme *s* ad'vancement // *v* pro'mote, further; *(bringe videre frem)* ad'vance, forward // *adv (foran)* in front; *(kommet frem, til at se)* out; *(i medierne etc)* in the news; *lade ngt ligge* ~ leave· sth lying about; *være langt* ~ *med ngt* be far a'head with sth; *vi er snart* ~ we will soon be there.

fremmed *en (ukendt person)* stranger; *(udlænding)* foreigner; *(gæst)* visitor // *adj (ukendt)* strange; *(fra udlandet)* foreign; *føle sig* ~ feel· a stranger; *være* ~ *for ngt* be a stranger to sth; ~ *valuta* foreign currency; **~arbejder** *en* immigrant worker; **~artet** *adj* strange, unfamiliar; *(eksotisk)* ex'otic; **~gørelse** *en* alie'nation; **~legeme** *et* foreign body; **~ord** *et* foreign word; **~politiet** *s* the aliens branch (of the po'lice); **~sprog** *et* foreign language.

fremmelig *adj (om barn)* pre'cocious.

fremmøde *et: et pænt* ~ quite a good at'tendance.

fremover *adv* forwards; *(for fremtiden)* in the future.

fremragende *adj* out'standing.

fremsende *v* forward; *vedlagt* ~*s...* en'closed you will find...

fremskaffe *v* pro'cure.

fremskridt *et* progress; *et* ~ a step forward; *gøre* ~ make· progress; **~s·venlig** *adj (også pol)* pro'gressionist.

fremskynde *v* speed up, hasten.

fremspring *et* pro'jection.

fremstille *v (lave)* make·, pro'duce, manu'facture; *(fortælle om)* de'scribe; *(afbilde, gengive)* repre'sent.

fremstilling *en* pro'duction, manu'facture; represen'tation; *(beretning)* ac'count; **~s·pris** *en* pro'duction price.

fremstød *et* venture; *(mil)* push; *(merk)* drive.

fremsynet *adj* far-sighted.

fremsætte *v (forslag)* pro'pose; *(klage, udtagelse)* make·.

fremtid *en* future; *for* ~*en* in future; *en gang i* ~*en* some time in the future; **~ig** *adj* future; **~s·udsigter** *pl* prospects.

fremtrædende *adj* prominent.

fremtvinge *v* force.

fremvise *v* show.

fremviser *en (til dias)* slide pro'jector; *(til film)* film pro'jector.

fremvisning *en* showing, presen'tation.

fri *v (bejle)* pro'pose *(til* to) // *adj* free; *vi får* ~ *kl. fire* we finish work (,school) at four; *holde* ~ take· time off; *slippe* ~ *fra ngt* e'scape sth; *jeg vil helst være* ~ I would rather not; *må vi så være* ~*!* now, that will do! *være* ~ *for ngt* be free from sth; *blive* ~ *for at gøre ngt* not have to do sth; *ude i det* ~ in the open air; **~billet** *en* free ticket; **~dag** *en* day off, holiday.

frier *en* suitor; **frieri** *et* pro'posal.

frifinde *v* ac'quit; **~lse** *en* ac'quittal.

frigear *et* neutral; *bilen er i* ~ the car is idling.

frigive *v* re'lease, set· free; *(gøre tilladt)* legalize; **~lse** *en* re'lease; legali'zation.

frigørelse *en* libe'ration.

frihandel *en* free trade.

frihavn *en* free port.

frihed *en* freedom, liberty; *tage sig den* ~ *at gøre ngt* take· the liberty of doing sth; **~s·berøvelse** *en (jur)* im'prisonment; **~s·bevægelse** *en* libe'ration movement; **~s·kamp** *en* struggle for freedom; *(modstandskamp)* re'sistance; **~s·kæmper** *en* freedom fighter; *(i modstandskamp)* re'sistance fighter; **~s·straf** *en* im'prisonment.

frihjul *s: køre på* ~ coast, freewheel.

frikadelle *en* meat cake, rissole; *(om person)* ham.

frikast *et* free throw.

frikende *v* ac'quit *(for* of); **~lse** *en* ac'quittal.

frikort *et (billet)* free pass; *(skattekort)* card showing how much you may earn without paying tax.

frikvarter *et* interval, break.

frilandsmuseum *et* open-air mu'seum.

frilufts... *sms:* **~forestilling** *en* open-air per'formance; **~liv** *et* outdoor life; **~menneske** *et* nature lover; **~teater** *et* open-air theatre.

friløb *et (på skøjter)* free skating.

frimodig *adj* frank, honest; **~hed** *en* frankness, honesty.

frimurer *en* freemason; **~loge** *en* ma'sonic lodge.

frimærke *et* stamp; **~automat** *en* stamp ma'chine; **~hæfte** *et* book of stamps; **~samling** *en* stamp col'lection.

friplads *en (i skole etc)* free place.

frisere *v* comb; *~ sig* comb (,do·) one's hair.

frisindet *adj* broad-minded.

frisk *adj* fresh; *(rask)* well; *(livlig)* lively; *begynde på en ~* start a'fresh; *en mundfuld ~ luft* a breath of fresh air; *~ frugt* fresh-picked fruit; **~bagt** *adj* freshly baked.

friske *v* freshen; *~ op (forfriske)* re'fresh; *~ sit engelsk op* brush up one's English.

frisklavet *adj* freshly made.

friskole *en* free school, private school.

frispark *et* free kick; *lave ~ mod en* foul sby.

frist *en (tidsrum)* period; *(tidspunkt hvor ngt skal ske)* deadline; *sidste ~* final date; *få en ~ til 1. maj* get· until May 1st; *overholde en ~* meet· a deadline.

fristad *en* freetown.

friste *v* tempt; **~lse** *en* temp'tation; **~nde** *adj* tempting.

fristil *en (i skolen)* essay.

frisure *en* hairdo, hairstyle.

frisør *en* hairdresser.

fritage *v* ex'cuse *(for* from); **~lse** *en* ex'emption.

fritid *en* leisure time, spare time; **~s·beskæftigelse** *en* hobby; **~s·center** *et* leisure centre; **~s·hjem** *et* after-school centre; **~s·hus** *et* holiday house, (F) getaway; **~s·tøj** *et* leisure wear.

fritstående *adj* free-standing; *(om hus)* de'tached.

fritte *v: ~ en ud* pump sby.

friturestege *v* deep-fry.

frivillig *en* volun'teer // *adj* voluntary; *melde sig som ~ til ngt* volun'teer for sth.

frodig *adj (om jord)* fertile; *(om kvinde)* buxom; **~hed** *en* fer'tility.

frokost *en* lunch; *spise ~* have lunch; *han er gået til ~* he is at lunch; *gå ud og spise ~* lunch out; **~pause** *en* lunchbreak.

from *adj* pious; *(blid)* gentle; *~ som et lam* meek as a lamb.

fromage *en sv.t.* cold soufflé.

fromhed *en* piety.

front *en* front.

frontal *adj* frontal; *~t sammenstød* head-on col'lision.

frossen *adj* frozen.

frost *en* frost; *ti graders ~* ten de'grees be'low zero; *få ~ i tæerne* get· frost-bitten toes; **~boks** *en (i køleskab)* freezing com'partment; **~vejr** *et* frosty weather; **~væske** *en (auto)* anti-freeze.

frotté *en* towelling; **~håndklæde** *et* towel.

frottere *v* rub.

frue *en (i huset)* mistress; *(hustru)* wife *(pl:* wives); *fru Hansen* Mrs Hansen; *javel, ~!* yes, madam! *hr. B. Pedersen og ~* Mr and Mrs B. Pedersen.

fruentimmer *et (neds)* female.

frugt *en* fruit; *bære ~* bear· fruit *(også fig);* **~avl** *en* fruit-growing; **~bar** *adj* fertile; **~barhed** *en* fer'tility; **~farve** *en* food colouring; **~grød** *en sv.t.* stewed fruit; **~plantage** *en* orchard; **~saft** *en* fruit juice; **~salat** *en* fruit salad; **~træ** *et* fruit tree.

frustreret *adj* 'frustrated.

fryd *en* joy, de'light.

fryde *v* de'light; *~ sig over ngt (dvs. glæde sig)* en'joy sth; *(dvs. hovere)* gloat over sth.

frygt *en* fear; *af ~ for* for fear of; *af ~ for at* for fear that.

frygte *v* fear, be a'fraid of, dread; *~ for ngt* fear (,dread) sth; *~ for at* fear that; **~lig** *adj* terrible, dreadful // *adv* terribly, dreadfully.

frygtindgydende *adj* terrifying.

frygtløs *adj* fearless.

frygtsom *adj* timid.
frynse *en* fringe; **~gode** *et* fringe benefit, perk.
fryse *v (om person)* be cold; *(nedfryse etc)* freeze; *det ~r* it is freezing; *det ~r 10 grader* it is 10 de'grees be'low zero; *~ ihjel* freeze to death; *~ om fingrene* have cold fingers; **~boks** *en* freezer; **~punkt** *et* freezing point; *under ~punktet* be'low zero; **~tørre** *v* freeze-dry.
fræk *adj* impudent, cheeky; *(dristig)* daring; *(uartig)* naughty; *han var ~ nok til at...* he had the cheek to...; **~hed** *en* impudence, cheek; daring; naughtiness.
fræse *v* mill; *~ af sted* belt along.
fræser *en* milling ma'chine.
frø *en* frog // *et* seed.
frøken *en* young lady, miss; *~ Jensen* Miss Jensen.
frømand *en* frogman; **~s·dragt** *en* wetsuit.
fråde *en* froth, foam // *v* foam; **~nde** *adj* foaming.
frådse *v* gorge; *(ødsle)* waste; *~ i ngt* gorge oneself with sth; **~ri** *et* gluttony; *(ødslen)* waste *(med* of).
fuge *en* joint; *gå op i ~rne* come· a'part at the seams // *v* joint.
fugl *en* bird; *det er hverken ~ el. fisk* it is neither here nor there; **~e·bur** *et* bird-cage; **~e·frø** *pl* birdseed; **~e·perspektiv** *et* bird's-eye-view; **~e·rede** *en* bird's nest; **~e·skræmsel** *et* scarecrow; **~e·unge** *en* young bird.
fugt *en* moisture; *(fx i hus, uønsket)* damp.
fugte *v* moisten; **fugter** *en* moistener.
fugtig *adj* moist, damp; **~hed** *en* hu'midity; dampness; **~hedscreme** *en* moisturizer; **~hedsmåler** *en* hy'grometer.
fuld *adj* full; *(om bus etc også)* crowded, packed; *(beruset)* drunk; *blive ~ (om person)* get· drunk; *~ af...* full of...; *køre for ~ kraft* go· at full steam; *køre i ~ fart* go· at full tilt; *~e navn* full name; *arbejde på ~ tid* work full time; *(se også fuldt)*.
fuldautomatisk *adj* fully auto'matic.
fuldblods- thoroughbred.
fuldende *v* com'plete, finish; **~lse** *en* com'pletion.
fuldendt *adj (hel)* com'plete; *(færdig)* finished; *(perfekt)* perfect.
fuldkommen *adj* perfect // *adv* perfectly, quite.
fuldkornsbrød *et* coarse wholemeal bread; **fuldkornsmel** *et* coarse wholemeal.
fuldmagt *en (skriftlig)* written au'thority; *(til at stemme for en)* proxy; *(jur)* power of at'torney.
fuldmægtig *en sv.t.* head clerk; *(i ministerium)* principal.
fuldmåne *en* full moon.
fuldskab *en* drunkenness; *i ~* while being drunk.
fuldskæg *et* (full) beard.
fuldstændig *adj* com'plete; *(perfekt)* perfect // *adv* com'pletely; perfectly.
fuldt *adv* com'pletely, fully; *tro ~ og fast på ngt* be'lieve firmly in sth; *have ~ op at gøre* have plenty to do; *gøre ngt ~ ud* do sth to the full; *~ ud tilfreds* perfectly satisfied.
fuldtallig *adj* com'plete.
fuldtids- full-time.
fuldtræffer *en* di'rect hit.
fumle *v* fumble, fiddle *(med* with).
fummelfingret *adj* fumble-fisted.
fund *et* find; *(billigt køb)* bargain.
fundament *et* foun'dation, base; *(fig)* basis.
fundamental *adj* funda'mental, basic; **~ist** *en* funda'mentalist.
fundere *v (spekulere)* ponder *(over* on).
fungere *v (handle)* act; *(virke)* work; *(om person)* function; **~nde** *adj* acting.
funktion *en* function; *(om maskine)* functioning; *i ~* working; *ude af ~* not working; **~s·dygtig** *adj* in working order; **~s·fejl** *en* mal'function.
funktionær *en (på kontor)* office worker; *(i det offentlige)* of'ficial.
fup *s* cheat, trickery; **~mager** *en* cheat; **~nummer** *et* trick; **~pe** *v* cheat, take· in.

fure *en (fx plov~)* furrow; *(rille)* groove; *(i ansigtet)* line.
furore *en: vække ~* cre'ate a sen'sation.
fuser *en* damp squib.
fusion *en (fys)* fusion; *(sammenslutning)* merger; **~ere** *v* merge.
fuske *v (kludre)* bungle; *~ med ngt* dabble in sth; **~ri** *et (kludder)* bungling; *(snyd)* cheating.
fut *s (liv)* go, pep; *sætte ~ i ngt* jazz sth up.
futte *v (om tog)* puff; *~ ngt af* burn· sth.
futteral *et* case.
fx *d.s.s. f.eks.*
fy *interj: ~ for pokker!* ugh! *~ skam dig!* you ought to be a'shamed of yourself!
fyge *v* drift, fly·.
fyld *et* filling; *(fx i fjerkræ, møbler)* stuffing.
fylde *v* fill; *(tage plads op)* take· up room; *(om fjerkræ etc)* stuff; *han ~r 20 i morgen* he will be 20 to'morrow; *~ tanken op (auto)* fill up the tank; *~ på* pour; *~ benzin på* fill up with petrol.
fyldepen *en* fountain pen.
fylderi *et (druk)* boozing.
fyldest *en: gøre ~* be satis'factory; *ske ~* be done; **~gørende** *adj* adequate.
fyldig *adj (om person)* plump; *(fig, omfangsrig)* copious; **~hed** *en* plumpness; copiousness.
fyldning *en* filling; *(i dør)* panel.
fyldt *adj* full *(med* of), filled *(med* with).
Fyn *s* Funen; **fynbo** *en* native of Funen; **fynsk** *adj* from Funen.
fyr *en (person)* chap, bloke; *(træ)* pine // *et (mar)* light; *(fyrtårn)* lighthouse; *(varme~)* boiler.
fyraften *en* closing time.
fyrbøder *en* stoker.
fyre *v (afskedige)* sack; *(tænde ild; afskyde)* fire; *(have ild i pejs el. kakkelovn)* have a fire; *(have tændt for varmeapparatet)* have the heating on; *~ en kanon af* fire a gun; *~ vittigheder af* crack jokes; *~ op* make· a fire; **~seddel** *en* notice (of dis'missal).
fyrfadslys *et* tea light.
fyrig *adj* fiery, ardent.
fyring *en (afskedigelse)* sacking, notice; *(optænding)* firing; *(opvarmning)* heating; **~s·olie** *en* fuel oil.
fyrre *num* forty; *han er født i ~rne* he was born in the forties; *han er i ~rne* he is in his forties.
fyrre... *sms:* **~skov** *en* pine forest; **~træ** *et* pine (tree); *(materialet)* pine(wood); **~træsmøbler** *pl* deal (,pine) furniture.
fyrretyvende *adj* fortieth.
fyrskib *et* lightship.
fyrste *en* prince; **~lig** *adj* princely.
fyrstendømme *et* princi'pality.
fyrstinde *en* prin'cess.
fyrtårn *et* lighthouse.
fyrværkeri *et* fireworks.
fyråb *pl* booing.
fysik *en* physics; *(kropsbygning)* phy'sique; **~er** *en* physicist.
fysiologi *en* physi'ology; **fysiologisk** *adj* physio'logical.
fysioterapeut *en* physio'therapist; **fysioterapi** *en* physio'therapy.
fysisk *adj* physical.
fæ *et* fool, ass.
fædreland *et* native country; **~s·sang** *en* patri'otic song.
fædrene *adj* pa'ternal; *på ~ side* on the father's side.
fægte *v (kæmpe)* fight·; *(sport)* fence; *~ med armene* ge'sticulate.
fægtning *en (sport)* fencing.
fæl *adj* nasty.
fælde *en* trap; *gå i ~n* fall· into the trap; *sætte en ~ for en* set· sby a trap; // *v (træ etc)* cut· down, fell; *(tabe hår)* shed·; *(tabe fjer)* moult; *~ en dom over en* pass sentence on sby; *~ en tåre* shed a tear; **~nde** *adj (fx bevis)* damning.
fælg *en (i hjul)* rim.
fælles *adj* common *(for* to), joint; *(ngt man deler)* mutual, shared; *have ngt til ~ med en* have sth in common with sby; *være ~ om ngt* share sth; *~ anstrengelser* joint effort; *ved ~ hjælp* be'tween us (,them, you); *vor ~ ven* our mutual friend.
fællesantenne *en* block aerial.

fælleseje *et* joint property.
fællesmarkedet *s* the Common Market; **fællesmarkeds-** Common Market, Com'munity.
fællesnævner *en* common de'nominator *(også fig)*.
fællesskab *et* com'munity; *gøre ngt i ~* do· sth to'gether.
fællesskole *en* coedu'cational school.
fællestillidsmand *en* senior shop steward.
fænge *v* catch· fire.
fængsel *et* prison, gaol [dʒeil]; *(~s·straf)* im'prisonment; **~s·betjent** *en* warder; **~s·straf** *en* im'prisonment.
fængsle *v* im'prison, put· in prison; *(fig, gribe, betage)* fascinate; **~nde** *adj* fascinating.
fængsling *en* im'prisonment.
fænomen *et* phe'nomenon; **~al** *adj* phe'nomenal.
færd *en: fra første ~* right from the be'ginning; *være i ~ med at gøre ngt* be doing sth; *hvad er der på ~e?* what is going on? *der er fare på ~e* there is danger brewing; *være tidligt på ~e* be (out) early.
færdes *v* move about; *(gå)* walk; *(i køretøj)* go·; *~ blandt de rige* mix with the rich.
færdig *adj* finished, done; *(parat)* ready; *gøre sig ~* get· ready; *er du snart ~?* when will you be finished? *jeg er ~ med ham* I've finished with him; *fiks og ~* cut-and-dried; **~gørelse** *en* finishing; **~hed** *en* skill, ac'complishment; **~pakket** *adj* prepacked; **~ret** *en* ready-to-serve meal; **~syet** *adj* ready-made, off-the-peg; *(om meninger etc)* cut-and-dried; **~varer** *pl* manu'factured goods.
færdsel *en* traffic; **~s·loven** *s* the Road Traffic Act; **~s·politi** *et* traffic po'lice; **~s·regler** *pl* traffic regu'lations; **~s·sikkerhed** *en* road safety; **~s·skilt** *et* traffic sign; **~s·uheld** *et* road accident; **~s·åre** *en (i by)* thoroughfare; *(på landet)* ar'terial road.
færge *en* ferry // *v* ferry; **~fart** *en* ferry service; **~leje** *et* ferry berth.
færing *en* Faro'ese.
færre *adj* fewer.
færrest *adj* fewest; *de ~e ved at...* few people know that..
Færøerne *pl* the Faroe Islands; **færøsk** *adj* Faro'ese.
fæstning *en* fortress.
fætter *en* cousin; *de er ~ og kusine* they are cousins.
føde *en* food; *(næring)* nourishment; *tage ~ til sig* take· nourishment; *tjene til ~n* earn one's living // *v (få barn, unge)* give· birth (to); *(forsørge, ernære)* sup'port; *hun har født tre gange* she has had three children; *hun er født i 1969* she was born in 1969; *fru Jensen født Hansen* Mrs Jensen née Hansen; **~afdeling** *en* ma'ternity ward; **~by** *en* native town; **~klinik** *en* ma'ternity clinic; **~kæde** *en* food-chain; **~sted** *et* place of birth; **~varer** *pl* foodstuffs.
fødsel *en* birth; *(nedkomst)* de'livery; *hun er engelsk af ~* she is English by birth; **~s·attest** *en* birth cer'tificate; **~s·dag** *en* birthday; **~s·dagsgave** *en* birthday present; *give en ngt i ~s·dagsgave* give· sby sth for his (,her) birthday; **~s·forberedelse** *en* antenatal exercises *pl;* **~s·kontrol** *en* birth con'trol; **~s·læge** *en* obste'trician; **~s·tal** *et* birthrate; **~s·veer** *pl* labour pains; **~s·år** *et* year of birth.
føje *v: ~ en* give· in to sby; *~ ngt sammen* join sth; *have ngt at ~ til* have sth to add; **~lig** *adj* com'pliant; *(eftergivende)* in'dulgent; **~lighed** *en* com'pliance; in'dulgence.
føjte *v* roam around; *være ude at ~* be out gallivanting.
føl *et* foal.
føle *v* feel·; *jeg ~r med dig* I feel· for you; *~ på ngt* feel· sth; *~ sig for* feel· one's way; *~ sig glad* feel· happy; *tæppet ~s varmt* the blanket feels warm; *~ en på tænderne* sound sby out; **~horn** *et* an'tenna *(pl:* antennae).
følelse *en* feeling; **~s·betonet** *adj* e'motional; **~s·løs** *adj* numb.

føler *en: sende en ~ ud* put· out a feeler.

følesans *en* sense of touch.

følge *en (resultat)* consequence; *(rækkefølge)* suc'cession; *få ~r* have consequences; *have til ~* re'sult in; *som ~ af* as a re'sult of; *han må tage ~rne* he will have to take the consequences // *et (ledsagelse)* escort // *v* follow; *(ledsage)* ac'company; *~ et råd* take· a piece of ad'vice; *~s ad* go· to'gether; *~ en hjem* see· sby home; *~ efter* follow; *~ med tiden* keep· up with the times; *~ en ud* see· sby out; *~ en til toget* see· sby to the station.

følgende *adj* following; *han skrev ~* he wrote as follows.

følgeseddel *en* de'livery note; **følgeskrivelse** *en* covering letter.

føling *en: have ~ med* be in touch with.

føljeton *en* serial story.

følsom *adj* sensitive; **~hed** *en* sensi'tivity.

føntørre *v* blow-dry.

før *adv/præp/konj* be'fore; *(tidligere)* earlier on; *(snarere, hurtigere, hellere)* sooner; *ikke ~ (dvs. først når)* not un'til; *(dvs. tidligst)* not be'fore; *har du set ham ~?* did you see him before? *nej, ikke ~ nu* no, not until now; *~ eller senere* sooner or later; *jo ~ jo bedre* the sooner the better; *næppe var vi kommet ~...* we had hardly ar'rived when...

føre *et: det er fint ~ (om veje)* the roads are fine; *(om sne)* the snow is fine; *det er dårligt ~ (om veje)* the roads are in a bad state; *(om sne)* the snow is bad.

føre *v (lede, føre an)* lead·, guide; *(transportere)* carry, take·; *(være i gang med, fx forhandlinger)* carry on; *~ bil* drive· (a car); *vejen ~r til stranden* the road leads to the beach; *~ en samtale* carry on a conver'sation; *~ norsk flag* fly· the Nor'wegian flag; *~ an* lead·; *~ det ind i journalen* enter it into the record; *~ med fem mål* lead· by five goals; *~ til* re'sult in, lead· to; *~ sin drøm ud i livet* realize one's dream; **~greb** *et* armlock; *tage ~greb på en* frogmarch sby; **~nde** *adj* leading.

fører *en (anfører)* leader; *(turist~)* guide; *(chauffør)* driver; **~bevis** *et* driving licence; **~hund** *en* guide dog; **~hus** *et* (driver's) cab; **~sæde** *et* driver's seat.

føring *en* lead; *have ~en* be in the lead; *tage ~en* take· the lead.

først *adj* first; *for det ~e* in the first place // *adv (i begyndelsen)* at first; *(ikke før)* not un'til; *komme ~* be first, come· first; *~ sagde hun ja* at first she said yes; *jeg så det ~ i går* I did not see it until yesterday; *~ og fremmest* first of all; *han er ~ i trediverne* he is in his early thirties; *~ lige* only just; *~ nu* not until now; *~ på måneden* in the be'ginning of the month.

første... *sms:* **~elsker** *en (film, teat)* leading man; *hun har smidt ~elskeren ud* she has sent her latest lover packing; **~hjælp** *en* first aid; **~hjælpskasse** *en* first-aid box; **~klasses** *adj* first-class, (F) A-1 ['ei'wʌn]; **~præmie** *en* first prize; **~rangs** *adj* first-rate; **~styrmand** *en* first mate.

førstkommende *adj* next.

førstnævnte *adj* the first mentioned; *(af to)* the former.

førtidspension *en* early re'tirement.

få *v (modtage)* get·, re'ceive, have; *(opnå)* ob'tain; *(mad el. drikke)* have; *~ et brev* get (ˌre'ceive) a letter; *~ en prop (fig)* have a fit; *du ~r pladen i morgen* you will get the record to'morrow; *~ vin til maden* have wine with one's meal; *~ bilen ordnet* have the car seen to; *få ngt gjort (af andre)* have sth done; *(dvs. selv gøre det)* get· sth done; *~ det overstået* get· it over with; *~ fat i ngt* get· hold of sth; *jeg fik ikke fat i navnet* I did not get the name; *~ en til at gøre ngt* make· sby do sth; *hun kunne ikke ~ sig til at gøre det* she could not bring herself to do it; *fik du ngt ud af det?* did it get you anywhere? *jeg kan ikke ~ pletten af* the spot won't go away; *jeg kan ikke ~ døren op* the door won't open.

få *adj* few; *(efter* in, only, not, no more than:) a few; *om ~ timer* in a few hours; *ikke så ~* quite a few; *nogle ~* a few; *vi har kun ~ penge* we only have a little money.

fåmælt *adj* taciturn.

får *et* sheep *(pl:* sheep); **~e·hyrde** *en* shepherd; **~e·kød** *et* mutton; **~e·syge** *en* mumps.

fåret *adj* sheepish.

fåtal *et: et ~* a mi'nority.

G

gab *et* mouth; *(afgrund etc)* chasm; *(gaben)* yawn; *døren stod på vid ~* the door was wide open.

gabe *v (åbne munden)* open one's mouth; *(være søvnig)* yawn; *(stå åben)* be wide open; *~ over for meget på en gang* bite· off more than one can chew.

gabestok *en: sætte en i ~ken (fig)* pillory sby.

gade *en* street, road; *gå hen (,ned) ad ~n* go· down the street; *gå over ~n* cross the street; *på ~n* in the street; *blive sat på ~n* be turned out; **~dør** *en* front door; **~dørsnøgle** *en* latchkey; **~fortegnelse** *en* street di'rectory; **~handler** *en* street vendor; **~hjørne** *et* street corner; **~kampe** *pl* street fighting *(u.pl);* **~kryds** *et* crossroads; *(om hund)* mongrel, crossbreed; **~kær** *et* village pond; **~lygte** *en* streetlamp; **~sanger** *en* street singer; **~skilt** *et* street sign; **~teater** *et* street theatre; **~uorden** *en* breach of the peace.

gaffel *en* fork; **~bidder** *pl* fillets of pickled herring; **~formet** *adj* forked; **~truck** *en* fork-lift truck.

gage *en* pay, salary; **~forhøjelse** *en* increment, rise.

gal *adj (vred)* angry; *(meget vred)* mad; *(forkert)* wrong; *(tosset)* crazy, mad; *blive ~* get· angry; *(dvs. blive sindssyg)* go· mad; *det er for ~t!* that's too much! *det er alt for ~t! (dvs. venligt)* you are too kind! *fare rundt som en ~* rush about like mad; *få ngt i den ~e hals* get· sth down the wrong way; *få ngt ~t i halsen (dvs. misforstå)* take· sth wrongly; *(se også galt).*

galakse *en* 'galaxy.

galant *adj* courteous ['kə:ʃəs].

galde *en (hos mennesker)* bile; *(hos dyr og fig)* gall; **~blære** *en* gallbladder; **~sten** *en* gallstone.

gale *v (om hane)* crow; *~ op (om person)* shout.

galej *en* galley.

galge *en* gallows.

galgenhumor *en* grim humour.

galionsfigur *en* figurehead.

gallaforestilling *en* gala per'formance.

galleri *et* gallery.

gallupundersøgelse *en* Gallup poll.

galoche *en* ga'losh.

galop *en* 'gallop; *i ~* at a gallop; **~bane** *en* racecourse.

galopere *v* gallop.

galopløb *et* horserace.

galskab *en (sindssyge)* madness; *(raseri)* rage; *det er den rene ~* it is sheer madness.

galt *adv* wrong(ly); *det gik ~* it went wrong; *der er ngt ~* there is sth wrong; *komme ~ af sted* get· into trouble; *(dvs. komme til skade)* get· hurt; *køre ~* have an accident.

gamacher *pl* leggings; *(korte, fx til kiltklædte)* spats.

gammel *adj* old; *(antik)* ancient; *(forhenværende)* former, old; *(brugt)* secondhand; *han er 80 år ~* he is 80 years old; *blive ~* grow· old; *i gamle dage* in the old days; *de er lige gamle* they are the same age; *alt er ved det gamle igen* everything is back to normal; *davs du gamle!* hello, old boy! **~dags** *adj* old-fashioned; *(som ikke længere bruges)* obsolete; **~jomfru** *en* old maid, spinster; **~klog** *adj* pre'cocious.

gane *en* palate; **~spalte** *en (med)* cleft palate.

gang *en (det at gå)* walk(ing); *(gangart)* gait; *(forløb)* course; *(om maskine etc)* running; *(om tidspunkt)* time; *(entré)* hall; *(have~)* path;

(passage, korridor) passage; *en ~ (i fortiden)* once; *(i fremtiden)* some day; *lad gå for denne ~* let· it pass for now; *tiden går sin ~* time passes on; *en ~ imellem* once in a while, sometimes; *alle gode ~e tre* third time lucky; *hver ~ vi ses* every time we meet·; *fire ~e fem er tyve* four times five makes twenty; *gøre ngt to ~e* do· sth twice; *for en ~s skyld* for once; *gå i ~ med arbejdet* set· to work; *motoren er i ~* the engine is running; *en ad ~en* one at a time; *lidt ad ~en* little by little; *på en ~* at once; *~ på ~* time after time; **~art** *en* gait; **~bar** *adj* current; **~besværet** *adj* dis'abled.

gange *v* multiply *(med* by); **~tegn** *et* multipli'cation sign.

gangsti *en* footpath.

gangtunnel *en* (pe'destrian) subway.

ganske *adv (fuldstændig)* absolutely, very; *(temmelig)* quite; *hun har det ~ godt* she is feeling quite well; *det var ~ forfærdeligt* it was absolutely awful; *~ vist* certainly; *~ vist... men* of course... but.

garage *en* garage.

garantere *v* guaran'tee; *(indestå for)* vouch for; *jeg ~r dig for at...* I promise you that...

garanti *en* guaran'tee; *(for lån)* se'curity; *der er et års ~ på maskinen* the machine has a year's guarantee; **~bevis** *et* guaran'tee slip.

garde *en* guard.

garder *en* guardsman *(pl:* -men).

gardere *v* guard *(sig imod* against).

garderobe *en* wardrobe; *(i restaurant etc)* cloakroom; **~skab** *et* wardrobe.

gardin *en* curtain; *(rulle~)* blind; **~kappe** *en* pelmet; **~stang** *en* curtain rail.

garn *et (strikke~)* yarn; *(sy~)* thread; *(uld~)* wool; *(bomulds~)* cotton; *(fiskenet)* net.

garnering *en (flæse etc)* trimming; *(gastr)* garnish.

garnison *en* garrison.

garniture *et* set; *(gastr om tilbehør)* garnish.

garnnøgle *et* ball of yarn (,wool, cotton).

gartner *en* gardener; *(på planteskole)* nurseryman *(pl:* -men).

gartneri *et (handelsgartneri)* market garden; *(planteskole)* nursery.

garvesyre *en* tannic acid.

garvet *adj (om skind)* tanned; *(om person)* hardened.

gas *en (også fig)* gas; *give den ~* put· one's foot down; *tage ~ på en* have sby on; **~apparat** *et* gas ring; **~beholder** *en (til camping etc)* gas cylinder; **~forgiftning** *en* gas poisoning; **~hane** *en* gas tap; **~kammer** *et* gas chamber; **~komfur** *et* gas cooker; **~ledning** *en* gas pipe; **~maske** *en* gas mask; **~måler** *en* gas meter; **~-og vandmester** *en* plumber; **~ovn** *en* gas oven; **~pedal** *en (auto)* ac'celerator (pedal).

gasse *v: ~ sig* snuggle up, feel· cosy; *(i solen)* bask (in the sun).

gastronomi *en* ga'stronomy; **gastronomisk** *adj* gastro'nomical.

gasvandvarmer *en* gas water heater.

gasværk *et: et ~* a gasworks.

gave *en* present, gift; *få ngt i ~* get· sth as a present (,gift); **~kort** *et* gift voucher; **~papir** *et* gift wrapping.

gavl *en* gable.

gavmild *adj* generous; **~hed** *en* gene'rosity.

gavn *en (nytte)* use, good; *(fordel)* benefit; *have ~ af ngt* benefit from sth; *gøre ~* be useful; *være til ~ for* be of benefit to.

gavne *v* be of use, be useful; *hvad skal det ~?* what is the good of that?

gavnlig *adj* useful; bene'ficial.

gaze *en* gauze; **~bind** *et* gauze bandage.

gear *et* gear; *første (,andet, tredje, fjerde) ~* bottom (,low, third, top) gear; **~e** *v: ~e op (,ned)* change up (,down); **~et** *adj: højt ~et (om person)* highly strung; **~kasse** *en* gearbox; **~stang** *en* gear lever ['li:və:].

gebis *et* denture, false teeth.

gebrokken *adj: tale ~t dansk* speak· broken Danish.

gebyr *et* fee.

gebærde *v: ~ sig* be'have.

ged *en* goat.
gedde *en* pike.
gede... *sms:* **~hams** *en* hornet; **~kid** *et* kid; **~ost** *en* goat's milk cheese.
gehør *et* ear; *spille efter ~* play by ear; *absolut ~* absolute pitch.
gejstlig *adj* clerical; *en ~* a clergyman (*pl:* -men); *de ~e* the clergy; **~hed** *en* clergy.
gelatine *en* 'gelatine.
gelé *en* jelly; *ål i ~* jellied eels.
geled *et* rank; *i række og ~* (drawn up) in ranks.
gelænder *et* railing; *(på trappe)* banister.
gemal *en* consort; **~inde** *en* consort.
gemen *adj* mean.
gemme *et* hiding place // *v (skjule)* hide·; *(lægge til side)* put· away; *(opbevare)* keep·; *(ikke bruge)* save; *~ sig for en* hide· from sby.
gemse *en* chamois (*pl: ~*).
gemyse *en (gastr)* vegetables *pl.*
gemyt *et (væsen)* dispo'sition; *(temperament)* temper; **~lig** *adj* jovial.
gen *et (biol)* gene.
genbo *en* opposite neighbour.
genbrug *en* re'cycling, re'use; **~e** *v* re'cycle, re'use; **~s·butik** *en* secondhand shop; **~s·flaske** *en* re'turnable bottle; **~s·papir** *et* re'cycled paper; **~s·tøj** *et* secondhand clothes *pl.*
gene *en* nuisance; *(forhindring)* im'pediment; *være til ~ for en* be a nuisance to sby.
general *en* general; **~direktør** *en* di'rector general; **~forsamling** *en* annual general meeting (a.g.m.).
generalieblad *et* po'lice record.
generalisere *v* generalize.
general... *sms:* **~konsul** *en* consul general; **~prøve** *en* re'hearsal; *(teat)* dress re'hearsal; **~sekretær** *en* secretary general; **~stabskort** *et* Ordnance Survey map; **~strejke** *en* general strike.
generation *en* gene'ration; **~s·kløft** *en* gene'ration gap.
generator *en* 'generator.
genere *v* bother; *(irritere)* an'noy; *(forstyrre)* di'sturb; *~ sig (dvs. være genert)* be shy (*over* about); *~ sig for at gøre ngt* be a'shamed to do sth; *~r det hvis jeg ryger?* do· you mind if I smoke?
generel *adj* 'general.
generobre *v* re'capture.
genert *adj* shy; *være ~ over ngt* be shy about sth; **~hed** *en* shyness.
generøs *adj* 'generous.
genetisk *adj* ge'netic.
genforening *en* re'union.
genforsikring *en* rein'surance.
genfortælle *v* re'tell·.
genfærd *et* ghost.
genfødt *adj* re'born.
genganger *en (ngt der kommer igen)* re'peat; *(spøgelse)* ghost.
gengive *v (give tilbage)* give· back; *(reproducere)* repro'duce; *(forestille)* picture, repre'sent; *(referere)* re'port; *(gentage)* re'peat; *~ ngt på engelsk* render sth in English; **~lse** *en* repro'duction; represen'tation; re'port; repe'tition.
gengæld *en* re'turn; *gøre ~* get· one's own back; *han er grim, men til ~ rar* he is ugly, but on the other hand he is nice; *jeg skal give dig ngt til ~* I'll give you sth in re'turn.
gengælde *v (gøre gengæld)* re'pay·; *(hævne sig)* pay· back; *(besvare fx følelser)* re'turn; *~ ondt med godt* re'turn good for evil; **~lse** *en (hævn)* retali'ation.
geni *et* genius (*pl:* geniuses); **~al** *adj* brilliant; *(om opfindelse etc)* in'genious; *en ~al idé* a stroke of genius.
genindføre *v* reintro'duce; *(importere igen)* reim'port.
genindkalde *v (soldater)* call up again.
genitiv *en (gram)* the genitive.
genkende *v* recognize; **~lse** *en* recog'nition.
genlyd *en: give ~ d.s.s.* **genlyde** *v* echo; *(runge etc)* re'sound (*af* with).
genne *v* chase (*væk* away).
gennem *d.s.s. igennem.*
gennemblødt *adj* soaked, wet through.
gennembore *v* pierce; **~nde** *adj (blik)* piercing.
gennembrud *et* breakthrough.

gennembryde *v* break· through.
gennemføre *v* carry through; **gennemførlig** *adj* feasible.
gennemgang *en (fx af pensum)* going through; *(kontrol)* going over; *(vej, passage)* passage.
gennemgribende *adj* thorough.
gennemgå *v (gennemleve)* go· through, under'go·; *(kontrollere)* go· over, check; *~ en operation* under'go· surgery.
gennemgående *adj (almindeligvis)* generally; *(om tog)* through.
gennemkørsel *en (vej, passage)* passage, thoroughfare; *~ forbudt* no thoroughfare.
gennemrejse *en* transit.
gennemsigtig *adj* trans'parent, (F) see-through; **~hed** *en* trans'parency.
gennemskue *v* see· through.
gennemslag *et (ved maskinskrivning)* carbon copy; **~s·papir** *et* copy paper.
gennemsnit *et* average; *i ~* on average; *over ~tet* above average; **~lig** *adj* average // *adv* on average.
gennemstegt *adj* well done.
gennemsyn *et: have ngt til ~* have sth on ap'proval.
gennemsyret *adj: ~ af* permeated with.
gennemsøge *v* search.
gennemtrumfe *v* force (,push) through.
gennemtræk *en* draught; *(om ansatte på arbejdsplads)* quick turnover.
gennemtrænge *v* pierce, penetrate; **~nde** *adj* piercing.
genopbygge *v* re'build·; **genopbygning** *en* recon'struction.
genopleve *v* re'live.
genoplive *v* re'vive, re'suscitate; **genoplivning** *en* re'vival; *(af fx druknet)* resusci'tation.
genoprette *v* re-e'stablish.
genoprustning *en* re'armament.
genopstå *v* rise· again; *~ fra de døde* rise· from the dead.
genoptage *v* re'sume; *(jur, om sag)* re'open.
genoptryk *et* reprint.
genoptræne *v* reha'bilitate; **genoptræning** *en* rehabili'tation.
genpart *en (kopi)* copy.
gense *v* see· again.
gensidig *adj* mutual.
genskabe *v* recre'ate.
genskin *et* re'flection.
genspejle *v* re'flect.
gensplejsning *en* ge'netic engi'neering.
genstand *en (ting)* object, thing; *(anledning, emne)* subject; *(mål)* object *(for* of); *(drink)* drink; *gøre ngt til ~ for diskussion* make· sth a subject for dis'cussion; *være ~ for beundring* be ad'mired; *være ~ for misundelse* be envied; **~s·led** *et (gram)* object.
genstridig *adj* obstinate.
gensyn *et* re'union, meeting (,seeing) again; *på ~!* see you (soon)! *~ med barndomshjemmet* re'turn to one's childhood home.
gentage *v* re'peat; *~ sig* be re'peated, happen again; *det gentog sig flere gange* it happened several times; **~lse** *en* repe'tition.
genudsendelse *en (radio, tv)* re'peat.
genvalg *et* re-e'lection.
genvej *en* short cut; *skyde ~* take· a short cut.
genvinde *v* re'gain; *(om jord, land)* re'claim.
genvordigheder *pl* troubles.
genvælge *v* re-e'lect.
genåbne *v* re'open.
geodætisk *adj* geo'desic.
geograf *en* ge'ographer.
geografi *en* ge'ography; **geografisk** *adj* geo'graphic(al).
geolog *en* ge'ologist.
geologi *en* ge'ology; **geologisk** *adj* geo'logical.
geometri *en* ge'ometry; **geometrisk** *adj* geo'metric(al).
germansk *adj* Ger'manic.
gerne *adv (som regel)* usually, generally; *(med glæde)* willingly, with pleasure; *vi sover ~ længe om søndagen* we usually have a long lie on Sundays; *jeg ville ~ gøre det hvis...* I should like to do it if...; *jeg vil ~*

have tre bananer (i forretning) three ba'nanas, please; *det vil jeg meget ~!* I should love to! *du må ~ være med* you may· join us if you like; *ja, så ~!* certainly! yes sir (,madam)!
gerning *en (handling)* action, act; *(virksomhed)* work; *blive grebet på fersk ~* be caught redhanded; **~s·manden** *s* the culprit; **~s·stedet** *s* the scene of the crime.
gerrig *adj (nærig)* stingy; *(havesyg)* ava'ricious; **~hed** *en* stinginess; avarice.
gesandt *en* envoy; **~skab** *et* le'gation.
gesims *en* cornice.
geskæftig *adj* of'ficious; *en ~ person (også)* a busybody.
gestikulere *v* ge'sticulate.
gestus *en* gesture.
gevaldig *adj* e'normous.
gevandt *et* robe; *(neds)* outfit.
gevind *et (på skrue)* thread; *gå over ~* get· out of control.
gevinst *en (udbytte)* profit; *(i lotteri)* prize; *(i spil)* winnings *pl.*
gevir *et* antlers *pl.*
gevær *et* rifle, shotgun; *præsentere ~* pre'sent arms.
ghetto *en* ghetto.
gib *et: det gav et ~ i mig* I started, I jumped.
gid *adv* I wish, if only; *~ han ville komme* I wish he would come, if only he would come; *~ det var så vel!* no such luck!
gide *v* take· the trouble to, be bothered to; *(have lyst til)* feel· like, like to; *han ~r ikke gå i skole* he can't be bothered to go to school; *det gad jeg nok se!* I should like to se that! *jeg gad vide om...* I wonder if...
gidsel *et* hostage; *tage en som ~* take· sby hostage; **~tager** *en* hostage-taker.
gift *en* poison; *give en ~* poison sby.
gift *adj* married; *blive ~* get· married; *være dansk ~* be married to a Dane.
gifte *v: ~ sig* marry, get· married; *hun ~de sig med ham for pengenes skyld* she married him for money; *vi skal ~s i morgen* we are getting married tomorrow.
giftermål *et* marriage.
giftfri *adj* non-poisonous; *(om kemikalier)* non-toxic.
giftgas *en* poison gas.
giftgrund *en* poison dump.
giftig *adj* poisonous; *(fig, om bemærkning)* venomous; *(om kemikalier, kemisk affald etc)* toxic.
giftmord *et* poisoning.
giftslange *en* poisonous snake.
giftstof *et* poison.
gigant *en* giant; **~isk** *adj* gi'gantic.
gigt *en* rheumatism; *(ledde~)* ar'thritis; **~feber** *en* rheu'matic fever.
gilde *et* party; *(orgie)* orgy; *holde ~* throw· (,hold·) a party; *betale ~t* foot the bill.
gine *en* dressmaker's dummy.
gips *en* plaster; **~bandage** *en* plaster cast; **~e** *v* plaster; **~figur** *en* plaster figure.
giraf *en* gi'raffe.
giro *en* giro; **~konto** *en* giro ac'count; **~kort** *et (til indbetaling)* giro inpayment form; *(til udbetaling)* giro cheque; **~nummer** *et* giro number.
gisp *et* gasp; **~e** *v* gasp, pant.
gitter *et* grille; *(til pynt, til planter etc)* lattice; **~port** *en* wrought-iron gate.
give *v* give·; *(yde, indbringe)* yield; *~ en hånden* shake· hands with sby; *~ en en hånd med* lend· sby a helping hand; *~ kort* deal· cards; *~r du en smøg?* can you spare me a fag? *~ efter* yield, give· (in); *~ ngt fra sig* give· sth up; *ikke ~ en lyd fra sig* not utter a sound; *~ igen (om penge)* give· change; *(give tilbage)* re'turn; *(hævne sig)* pay· back; *~ op* give· up; *~ penge ud på ngt* spend· money on sth; *~ sig (dvs. give op)* give· in; *(dvs. klage)* groan; *(være elastisk)* give·; *(om tøj)* stretch; *~ sig af med ngt* have to do with sth; *det ~r sig af sig selv* it goes without saying; *~ sig til at gøre ngt* start doing sth.
givet *adj: tage ngt for ~* take· sth for granted; *det er ~ at...* it is certain that...; *i ~ tilfælde* if oc'casion a'rises.

gjalde *v* re'sound.

gjord *en (i møbler)* webbing; *(til hest)* girth.

glad *adj* glad, happy; *(munter)* cheerful; *(henrykt)* de'lighted; *være ~ for ngt* be glad (,pleased) about sth; *være ~ for en* be fond of sby; *jeg er ~ for at se dig* I am glad to see you; *du kan sagtens være ~!* lucky you! *du ~e verden!* goodness me! *have en ~ aften* make· a night of it.

glans *en (om ngt blankt)* gloss, shine; *(som stråler)* sparkle; *(pragt)* splendour, glory; *bestå eksamen med ~* pass an exam with flying colours; *i al sin ~* in all one's glory; *tage ~en af ngt* rub the shine off sth; **~billede** *et* coloured scrap; **~nummer** *et: det er mit ~nummer* it is my specialty; **~papir** *et* glossy paper; **~rolle** *en* star part.

glarmester *en* glazier.

glas *et* glass; *(til syltetøj etc)* jar; *et ~ vand* a glass of water; **~dør** *en* glass door.

glasere *v* glaze; *(om kage etc)* ice.

glas... *sms:* **~fiber** *en* fibre glass; **~maleri** *et* stained-glass; **~puster** *en* glassblower; **~skår** *et* piece of broken glass; **~uld** *en* glass wool.

glasur *en* glazing; *(på kage)* icing.

glasværk *et: et ~* a glassworks.

glat *adj* smooth; *(smattet, som man glider på)* slippery; *(om hår)* straight; *det gik ~* it went smoothly; *give en det ~te lag* give· sby a piece of one's mind; **~barberet** *adj* clean-shaven.

glatførebane *en (for bilister)* skidpan.

glatis *en: være på ~ (fig)* be skating on thin ice.

glatstrikning *en* stocking stitch.

glatte *v: ~ ngt ud* smooth sth (out); *~ en skjorte (med strygejern)* iron a shirt.

glemme *v* for'get·; *(efterlade)* leave·; *jeg glemte paraplyen i bussen* I left my um'brella on the bus; *lad det nu være glemt* let· bygones be bygones; **~bogen** *s: gå i ~bogen* be for'gotten.

glemsel *en* ob'livion.

glemsom *adj* for'getful.

gletscher *en* glacier.

glide *v (jævnt)* glide, slide·; *(miste fodfæstet)* slip; *(om hjul)* skid; *~ fra hinanden (om par)* drift a'part; *~ i en bananskræl* slip on a ba'nana skin; *få ngt til at ~ ned* make· sth go down; *vi er gledet* (F) we're off; **~bane** *en* slide.

glimmer *et* tinsel.

glimre *v: ~ ved sit fravær* be con'spicuous by one's absence.

glimrende *adj* splendid, excellent.

glimt *et (af lys)* flash; *få et ~ af en (,ngt)* catch· a glimpse of sby (,sth).

glinse *v* glisten.

glip *s: gå ~ af ngt* miss sth; *du er ikke gået ~ af ngt* you didn't miss anything.

glippe *v (gå galt)* fail; *~ med øjnene* blink.

glo *v* stare *(på* at); *(måbe)* gape *(på* at).

globus *en* globe.

gloende *adj (glødende)* redhot // *adv: ~ varm* burning hot.

glorie *en* halo *(pl:* haloes).

glose *en* word; **~hæfte** *et* vo'cabulary.

glubende *adj* ravenous.

glubsk *adj* fe'rocious.

glæde *en* joy; *(fornøjelse, nydelse også)* pleasure; *græde af ~* weep· with joy; *have ~ af ngt* en'joy sth; *gøre ngt med ~* do· sth gladly (,with pleasure); *gøre en den ~ at...* do· sby the pleasure of... // *v* please; *(gøre glad også)* make· happy; *det ~r mig at høre det* I am glad to hear it; *~ sig over* be happy about; *~ sig til ngt* look forward to sth; **~lig** *adj* happy; *(behagelig)* pleasant; *en ~lig meddelelse* a piece of good news; *~lig jul!* merry Christmas! *~ligt nytår!* happy New Year! **~strålende** *adj* radiant.

glød *en* glow; *(i pejs, bål etc)* ember; *(fig)* ardour; **~e** *v* glow; **~e·tråd** *en (elek)* filament.

gnaske *v: ~ på ngt* munch sth.

gnave *v* gnaw; *(om sko etc)* chafe; *skoen har ~t hul i sokken* the shoe has worn a hole in the sock.

gnaven *adj* cross *(over* about; *på* with); *(irritabel)* fretful; *(sur og mut)* sulky.
gnaver *en (zo)* rodent.
gnide *v* rub; ~ *sig i hænderne* rub one's hands.
gnidning *en* rubbing; *(strid)* friction; **~s·løs** *adj* smooth.
gnidret *adj* cramped.
gnier *en* miser.
gnist *en* spark; *slå ~er* throw· sparks; *jeg har ikke en ~ forstand på biler* I don't know the first thing about cars.
gnom *en* gnome.
gnubbe *v* rub; ~ *sig op ad en* rub shoulders with sby.
gobelin *et* tapestry.
god *adj* good; *det er det ~e ved det* that is the good thing about it; *det vil gøre dig ~t* it will do you good; *hvad skal det gøre ~t for?* what is the use of that? *han har rigtig ~t af det!* it serves him right! *du har ikke ~t af salt* salt is not good for you; *så er det ~t!* that will do! *vær så ~!* here you are! *(dvs. maden er klar)* dinner (,lunch, tea etc) is ready; *sige ~ for en* vouch for sby; *være ~ ved en* be good to sby; *hun er ~ til at synge (,danse etc)* she is a good singer (,dancer etc); *have ngt til ~e* have sth coming; *hun har £10 til ~e hos John* John owes her £10; *gøre sig til ~e med ngt* tuck into sth; *(se også godt)*.
godartet *adj* be'nign.
goddag *interj* hello! good morning (,afternoon, evening)!
gode *et* ad'vantage; *det er et stort ~* it is a good thing; *nyde livets ~r* en'joy the good things in life; **~ste;** *du ~ste!* good God! dear me!
godgørende *adj* charitable; **godgørenhed** *en* charity.
godkende *v (tillade)* sanction; *(sige ja til)* ap'prove; **~lse** *en* sanction; ap'proval.
godmodig *adj* good-natured; **~hed** *en* good-naturedness.
godmorgen *interj* good morning!
godnat *interj* good night! **~lekture** *en* bedside reading.
gods *et (varer)* goods *pl; (ejendele)* property; *(herregård etc)* e'state; **~banegård** *en* goods station; **~ejer** *en* landowner; **~tog** *et* goods train; **~vogn** *en* goods waggon.
godt *adv* well; *(cirka, lidt over)* rather more than; *(knap)* just under; *det gik ~* it went well; *hav det ~!* take· care (of yourself)! *(dvs. mor dig)* have a good time! *vi har det ~* we are fine; *han har det ikke så ~* he is not well; *se ~ ud* look well; *(være smuk)* be goodlooking; *det kan ~ være at han kommer* he may· come, maybe he'll come; *så ~ man kan* as best one can; *der kom så ~ som ingen* hardly anybody came.
godte *v: ~ sig over ngt* gloat over sth.
godter *pl* sweets.
godtgørelse *en (erstatning)* compen'sation; *(betaling)* fee.
godtroende *adj* naïve.
godvilligt *adv* voluntarily.
gok *et* sock; *hun gav ham et ~* she socked him one.
gold *adj* barren.
golf... *sms:* **~bane** *en* golf course, golf links; **~kølle** *en* golf club; **~spiller** *en* golfer.
Golfstrømmen *s* the Gulf Stream.
gondol *en* 'gondola.
gonorré *en* gonor'rhea.
gorilla *en* go'rilla *(også fig)*.
gotisk *adj* gothic.
grab *en (på maskine)* bucket
graciøs *adj* graceful.
grad *en* de'gree; *(rang)* rank; *det er ti ~ers frost* it is ten de'grees below zero; *i den ~* to such an ex'tent; *i høj ~* ex'tremely; *i hvor høj ~?* to what ex'tent? *i nogen ~* to some ex'tent; *til en vis ~* to a certain ex'tent; **~bøjning** *en (gram)* com'parison.
graduere *v* graduate.
gradvis *adj* gradual // *adv* gradually.
grafiker *en* graphic artist (,de'signer); **grafisk** *adj* graphic.
gram *et* gramme; *100 ~ smør* a hundred grammes of butter.
grammatik *en* grammar; **grammatisk** *adj* gram'matical.

grammofon *en* gramophone, record player; **~optagelse** *en* (gramophone) re'cording; **~plade** *en* (gramophone) record.
gramse *v: ~ på ngt* paw sth.
gran *en* spruce // *et (smule)* bit.
granat *en (mil)* gre'nade, shell; *(ædelsten)* garnet; **~æble** *et* pome'granate.
granddanois *en* Great Dane.
grandonkel *en* great-uncle; **grandtante** *en* great-aunt.
grangivelig *adv* down to the last detail.
granit *en* granite; **~brud** *et* granite quarry.
grankogle *en* spruce cone.
granske *v* e'xamine; *(grundigt)* scrutinize.
granskov *en* spruce forest; **grantræ** *et* spruce.
grapefrugt *en* grapefruit.
gratiale *et* bonus.
gratin *en: blomkåls~* cauliflower au gratin; **~ere** *v* put· under the grill.
gratis *adj* free // *adv* free of charge; *få ngt ~* get· sth for nothing; *~ adgang* ad'mission free.
gratist *en* fare dodger.
gratulation *en* congratu'lation; **gratulere** *v* con'gratulate *(med* on).
grav *en* grave, tomb; *(udgravning)* pit; *(fx grøft)* ditch; *følge en til ~en* go· to sby's funeral; *være på ~ens rand* be near death.
grave *v* dig·; *~ ngt frem* dig· sth out; *~ ngt ned* bury sth; **~maskine** *en* excavator.
graver *en (på kirkegård)* gravedigger; *(ansat ved kirke)* sexton.
gravere *v* en'grave; **~nde** *adj* grave.
gravfund *et* grave find.
gravhund *en* dachshund.
gravhøj *en* burial mound; *(dysse)* barrow.
gravid *adj* pregnant.
graviditet *en* pregnancy.
gravko *en* excavator.
gravsted *et* burial place, tomb.
gravsten *en* gravestone.
gravøl *et* funeral feast.
greb *en* (pitch)fork // *et (tag)* hold, grip; *(dør~)* handle; *holde en i et fast ~* have a firm hold on sby; *slippe ~et i ngt* let· go of sth; *have et godt ~ om tingene* have a good grip on things; *stramme ~et* tighten one's hold.
grej *et* gear; **~e** *v (ordne)* manage; *(fatte)* grasp.
grel *adj* loud, glaring.
gren *en* branch; *(kvist)* twig; **~saks** *en* secateurs.
greve *en* count; **grevinde** *en* countess; **grevskab** *et* county.
grib *en* vulture.
gribe *v* catch·; *(med fast tag)* grasp, grip; *(rive til sig)* snatch, grab; *(pågribe)* catch·; *grib!* catch! *~ chancen* take· the oppor'tunity; *~ efter ngt* catch· (,grasp, snatch etc) at sth; *~ en i armen* grab sby by the arm; *~ en i at gøre ngt* catch· sby doing sth; *~ ind (dvs. skride ind)* inter'vene; *(dvs. forstyrre, blande sig)* inter'fere; *hvad skal vi ~ til?* what shall we do? *~ til våben* take· up arms; **~nde** *adj* moving.
grille *en: få ~r* get· ideas // *v* grill.
grillspid *et* skewer; **grillstegt** *adj* grilled.
grim *adj* ugly; *(ækel)* nasty; *(om person, ikke særlig køn)* plain.
grimasse *en* gri'mace; *skære ~r* make· faces.
grin *et* laugh; *få sig et billigt ~* have a good laugh; *gøre ~ med ngt* make· fun of sth; *blive til ~* make· a fool of oneself; *det er helt til ~* it is quite ri'diculous; *det er til at dø af ~ over* it is a scream; **~agtig** *adj* funny.
grine *v* laugh *(ad* at).
gris *en* pig; *en gammel ~ (om mand)* a dirty old man.
grise *v: ~ med ngt* mess with sth; *~ sig til* get· dirty; **~ri** *et* mess; **~sylte** *en* brawn; **~tæer** *pl* pig's trotters.
grisk *adj* greedy *(efter* for); **~hed** *en* greed.
gro *v* grow·; *~ sammen (om sår)* heal; *~ til (om have etc)* become· over'grown; *(om sø)* become· choked.
groft *adv* grossly; *(se grov).*
grosserer *en* wholesale dealer.

grotesk *adj* gro'tesque.
grotte *en* cave.
grov *adj* coarse; *(ru)* rough; *(uhøflig)* rude; *i ~e træk* roughly; *nej, det er for groft!* that's the limit! *på det ~este* grossly; *nu skal du ikke blive ~!* don't be rude now! **-brød** *et* wholemeal bread; **-hed** *en* coarseness, roughness, rudeness; *komme med ~heder* be rude; **-kornet** *adj (fig)* coarse; **-køkken** *et* scullery; **-smed** *en* blacksmith; **-æder** *en* glutton.
gru *en* horror; *han praler så det er en ~* he boasts something terrible.
grube *en* pit, mine; *(se også mine).*
gruble *v* ponder; *(melankolsk)* brood; *~ over ngt* ponder on (,over) sth.
grue *v: ~ for ngt* dread sth; **-lig** *adj* awful.
grufuld *adj* horrible.
grums *et* dregs *pl,* grounds *pl.*
grumset *adj* muddy.
grund *en (bund)* ground; *(grundlag)* foun'dation; *(lavvandet sted)* shoal; *(bygge~)* site; *(anledning, fornufts~)* reason; *(årsag)* cause; *sejle på ~* go· a'ground; *af gode ~e* for good reasons; *begynde fra ~en* start from the be'ginning; *han er i ~en rar* he is really rather nice; *på ~ af* be'cause of; *der er ingen ~ til at tro det* there is no reason to think so; *der er al mulig ~ til at tro det* there is every reason to think so; *brænde ned til ~en* burn· down; *gå til ~e* perish; *ligge til ~ for* under'lie·; *uden ~* for no reason.
grundbog *en* basic reader.
grunde *v (male første gang)* undercoat; *(gruble)* ponder *(over* on, over).
grundejer *en* house owner; *(af jord uden hus)* landowner.
grundforskning *en* funda'mental re'search.
grundfæstet *adj* e'stablished.
grundig *adj* thorough; *(gennemgribende)* radical; *tage ~t fejl* be quite mis'taken; **-hed** *en* care.
grunding *en (med maling)* undercoating.
grundkursus *et* basic course.
grundlag *et* foun'dation, basis; *på ~ af* on the basis of.
grundled *et (gram)* subject.
grundliggende *adj* under'lying.
grundlov *en* consti'tution; **-s·dag** *en sv.t.* national day; **-s·forhør** *et* pre'liminary questioning; **-s·stridig** *adj* unconsti'tutional.
grund... *sms:* **-lægge** *v* found; *(oprette)* e'stablish; **-læggelse** *en* foun'dation; e'stablishment; **-læggende** *adj* funda'mental, basic; **-lægger** *en* founder; **-maling** *en* undercoat; **-plan** *en* ground plan; **-skyld** *en* land tax; **-sten** *en* foun'dation stone; **-stof** *et* element; **-træk** *et: Skotlands historie i ~træk* Basic History of Scotland, An Outline of Scottish History; **-vand** *et* ground water; **-værdi** *en* land value.
gruopvækkende *adj* terrible.
gruppe *en* group; **-arbejde** *et* group work; **-billet** *en* group ticket; **-praksis** *en (om læger)* group practice; **-pres** *et* group pressure; **-rejse** *en* party tour; **-vis** *adv* in groups.
grus *et* gravel; *synke i ~* fall· into ruins; **-grav** *en* gravel pit.
grusom *adj* cruel *(mod* to); *(stor)* terrible; *han er ~t stor* he is terribly big; **-hed** *en* cruelty.
grusvej *en* gravel road.
gry *v* dawn; *dagen ~r* the day is dawning.
gryde *en* pot; *(kasserolle)* saucepan; *(stege~)* casserole; **-klar** *adj* oven-ready, ready for use; **-lap** *en* pot holder; **-låg** *et* lid; **-ret** *en* casserole; **-ske** *en* ladle; **-steg** *en* pot-roast; **-stegt** *adj* pot-roasted; **-svamp** *en* pan scrubber.
gryn *pl (i flager, fx havre~)* meal; *(som korn)* grits; **-et** *adj* gritty.
grynt *et* grunt; **-e** *v* grunt.
græde *v* cry, weep·; *~ af glæde* weep· for joy; *det er ikke ngt at ~ over* it is nothing to cry about; *få grædt ud* have a good cry; **-færdig** *adj* almost in tears.

Grækenland *s* Greece; **græker** *en* Greek.

græmme *v:* ~ *sig over ngt* be vexed at sth.

grænse *en (lande~)* frontier, border; *(naturlig)* boundary; *(~område)* border; *(fig)* limit; *køre over ~n* cross the frontier (,border); *der må være en ~* there must be a limit; *sætte en ~ for ngt* set· a limit to sth; *inden for visse ~r* within certain limits; *det var lige på ~n* it was a near thing // *v:* ~ *(op) til* border on; *det ~r til det utrolige* it is almost in'credible; **~egn** *en* border(land); **~løs** *adj* infinite; **~tilfælde** *et* borderline case; **~vagt** *en* frontier guard.

græs *et* grass; *bide i ~set* bite· the dust; *køerne er på ~* the cows are grazing; *slå ~* cut· (the) grass; **~enke** *en* grass widow; **~enkemand** *en* grass widower; **~gang** *en* pasture; *søge nye ~gange* be looking for new challenges; **~hoppe** *en* grasshopper.

græsk *et, adj* Greek; *Det Græske Øhav* the Greek Archi'pelago.

græskar *et* pumpkin.

græsplæne *en* lawn; *slå ~* mow the lawn.

græsrodsbevægelse *en* grassroots movement.

græsse *v* graze.

græsslåmaskine *en* lawn mower.

græsstrå *et* blade of grass.

græstørv *et* turf.

grævling *en* badger; **~e·hund** *en* dachshund.

grød *en (af gryn etc)* porridge; *(af frugt)* stewed fruit; **~et** *adj (om stemme)* thick; *(om væske etc)* mushy **~hoved** *et* oaf; **~is** *en* slush; **~ris** *pl* pudding rice.

grøft *en* ditch; *køre i ~en* go· into the ditch; **~e·kant** *en* roadside.

grøn *adj* green; *det ~ne køkken* vege'tarian cui'sine; *De Grønne (pol)* the Green; *give ~t lys for ngt* greenlight sth; *~ bølge (om trafiklys)* phased traffic lights; *i hans ~ne ungdom* in his early youth; **~kål** *en* kale, kail.

Grønland *s* Greenland.

grønlandsk *adj* Greenland, Green'landic; *~ slædehund* husky; **grønlænder** *en* Greenlander.

grønsager *pl* vegetables.

grønsagssuppe *en* vegetable soup.

grønskolling *en* puppy.

grønsvær *en* turf.

grønthandler *en* greengrocer.

grønthøster *en (agr)* silage harvester.

grønærter *pl* green peas.

grå *adj* grey; *det barn giver mig ~ hår i hovedet* that child makes my hair turn grey.

gråd *en (det at græde)* crying; *(tårer)* tears; *briste i ~* burst· into tears.

grådig *adj* greedy *(efter* for); **~hed** *en* greed.

grå... *sms:* **~håret** *adj* greyhaired; **~lig** *adj* greyish; **~sprængt** *adj* with a touch of grey; **~spurv** *en* sparrow; **~vejr** *et: det er ~vejr* it is overcast.

gud *en* god; *(Vorherre)* God; *~ ske lov!* thank God! *for ~s skyld* for God's sake; *~ ved om de kommer* God knows if they are coming; *det må ~erne vide* God knows; *ved ~* by Jove; *gu' vil jeg ej!* I'll be damned if I do! **~barn** *et* godchild *(pl:* -children); **~dommelig** *adj* di'vine; **~e·lig** *adj (from)* pious; *(neds)* sancti'monious; **~far** *en* godfather; **~frygtig** *adj* pious; **~inde** *en* goddess; **~mor** *en* godmother.

guds... *sms:* **~bespottelse** *en* blasphemy; **~forladt** *adj* 'godfor,saken; **~tjeneste** *en* service; *afholde ~tjeneste* hold· a service.

guf *et (slik)* sweets *pl; (noget lækkert)* goody; **~fe** *v: ~fe i sig* stuff oneself; *~fe kager i sig* scoff down cakes.

guirlande *en* fe'stoon.

guitar *en* gui'tar; *spille (på) ~* play the gui'tar; **~ist** *en* gui'tar player.

gul *adj* yellow; *der er ~t lys (i trafiklys)* the lights are amber; *~e ærter* pea soup.

guld *et* gold; *hun er ~ værd* she is worth her weight in gold; **~barre** *en* gold bar; **~bryllup** *et* golden wedding; **~fisk** *en* goldfish; **~grube** *en* gold mine; **~indfattet** *adj (om* *briller)* gold-rimmed; **~medalje** *en* gold medal; **~medaljevinder** *en* gold medallist; **~plombe** *en (i tand)* gold filling; **~randet** *adj* gilt-edged; **~regn** *en (bot)* la'burnum; **~smed** *en* goldsmith; *(zo)* dragonfly; **~vinder** *en* gold medallist.

gulerod *en* carrot; *reven ~* grated carrot.

gullasch *en* goulash.

gullig *adj* yellowish.

gulsot *en* jaundice.

gulv *et* floor; *gå i ~et* go· down; *tabe ngt på ~et* drop sth on the floor; *(fig)* bungle sth; *være helt rundt på ~et* be in a muddle; **~belægning** *en* flooring; **~bræt** *et* floor board; **~klud** *en* floorcloth; **~måtte** *en (lille tæppe)* mat; *(løber)* runner; **~skrubbe** *en* scrubbing brush; **~spand** *en* bucket; **~tæppe** *et* carpet; **~varme** *en* underfloor heating.

gumle *v* munch *(på ngt* sth).

gumme *en* gum.

gummi *et* rubber; *(kondom)* Durex, (S) rubber; **~bold** *en* rubber ball; **~båd** *en* rubber dinghy; **~bånd** *et (elastik)* rubber band; **~celle** *en* padded cell; **~ged** *en* loader tractor; **~slange** *en* rubber tube; **~støvle** *en* wellington, rubber boot; **~sål** *en* rubber sole.

gunst *en* favour; *til ~ for ham* in his favour; **~ig** *adj* favourable; *vælge et ~igt tidspunkt* pick a con'venient moment.

gurgle *v* gargle.

gurkemeje *en* turmeric.

guru *en* guru.

gusten *adj* sallow; *med ~t overlæg* in cold blood.

guvernante *en* governess.

guvernør *en* governor.

gyde *en (smal gade)* alley // *v (om fisk)* spawn.

gylden *en (hollandsk mønt)* guilder // *adj* golden; *den gyldne middelvej* the golden mean; *~t håndtryk* golden handshake.

gyldig *adj* valid; *med ~ grund* with good reason; **~hed** *en* va'lidity.

gylle *en* liquid ma'nure; **~tank** *en* liquid-ma'nure tank.

gylp *en (i bukser)* fly // *et (om ugle etc)* cast; **~e** *v: ~e (op)* vomit; *(om baby)* burp.

gymnasium *et sv.t.* grammar school, upper secondary school; *(am)* high school.

gymnastik *en (som sportsgren)* gym'nastics; *(øvelser, skolefag)* physical exercises, PE; *gøre ~* do· exercises; **~dragt** *en* gym suit, PE-suit; **~redskab** *et* gym'nastic appa'ratus; **~sal** *en* gym'nasium; **~sko** *en* gym shoe.

gynge *en* swing // *v* swing·; *(i gyngestol)* rock; *(om skib)* roll; *være på ~nde grund* be on thin ice; **~hest** *en* rocking horse; **~stol** *en* rocking chair.

gynækolog *en* gynae'cologist; **gynækologi** *en* gynae'cology.

gys *et (af frygt, kulde)* shiver, shudder; *(af fryd etc)* thrill; **~e** *v (af kulde etc)* shiver; *(af fryd)* be thrilled; *jeg ~er ved tanken* I shudder at the thought.

gyselig *adj (hæslig)* hideous; *(væmmelig)* a'trocious.

gyser *en (film, bog)* thriller.

gysser *pl* (F) brass.

gyvel *en (bot)* broom.

gæld *en* debt; *komme i ~* get' into debt; *stå i ~ til en* be in'debted to sby.

gælde *v (være gyldig)* be valid, be good; *(tælle med)* count; *(dreje sig om)* con'cern, ap'ply to; *billetten ~r ikke længere* the ticket is no longer valid; *det point ~r ikke* that point does not count; *nu ~r det!* this is it! *det ~r liv og død* it is a matter of life and death; *når det ~r penge, så spørg mig* when it comes to money, ask me; *det ~r om at få det gjort* the thing is to get it done; *hvad ~r det?* what is it about? **~nde** *adj (om billet etc)* valid; *(som er i kraft)* in force; *(eksisterende)* current, e'xisting; *ifølge ~nde lov* ac'cording to the existing laws; *gøre sig ~nde (om person)* as'sert oneself; *(om ting, fænomen)* have its ef'fect.

gældsbevis *et* IOU ['aiəu'ju:] *(dvs.* I owe you).

gældspost *en* item of a debt.
gælisk *adj* Gaelic.
gælle *en* gill; *ånde ved ~r* breathe by gills.
gænge *en (på gyngestol etc)* rocker; *være tilbage i den gamle ~* be back to normal.
gængs *adj* current; *(fremherskende)* pre'vailing; *(almindelig)* common.
gær *en* yeast.
gærde *et* fence; *(i kricket)* wicket.
gære *s: der er ngt i ~* there is sth brewing // *v* fer'ment.
gæring *en* fermen'tation.
gæsling *en* gosling; *(bot)* catkin.
gæst *en* visitor; *(indbudt)* guest; *vi får ~er til middag* we are having some people for dinner; *have liggende ~er* have people staying; **~e** *v* visit; **~e·arbejder** *en* immigrant worker; **~e·bog** *en* visitors' book; **~e·optræden** *en* guest per'formance; **~e·seng** *en* spare bed; **~e·toilet** *et* extra toilet; **~e·værelse** *et* spare bedroom.
gæstfri *adj* ho'spitable; **~hed** *en* hospi'tality.
gæt *et: et kvalificeret ~* an educated guess; **~te** *v* guess; *hun ~tede rigtigt* she guessed right; **~teri** *et* guessing; *det er det rene ~teri* it is pure guesswork.
gæv *adj* plucky.
gø *v* bark *(ad* at).
gøde *v* fertilize.
gødning *en (om midlet)* fertilizer; *(naturlig)* ma'nure; *(det at gøde)* fertili'zation; ma'nuring.
gøen *en* bark(ing).
gøg *en* cuckoo.
gøgler *en* buf'foon; *(som laver tricks)* juggler.
gør det selv- *adj* do-it-your'self.
gøre *v* do·; *(lave, foretage)* make·; *~ ondt* hurt·; *det gør mig ondt at høre det* I am sorry to hear it; *hvad skal det ~ godt for?* what is the good of that? *det gør ikke ngt* it does not matter; *hvor har du gjort af nøglen?* where did you put the key? *~ det af med en* dis'pose of sby; *han kan ikke ~ for det* he can't help it; *have at ~ med ngt* have to do with sth; *(beskæftige sig med)* deal· with sth; *~ kassen op* balance the cash; *~ en til anfører* make· sby the leader; *~ sig til af ngt* brag about sth; *hvad skal vi ~ ved det?* what shall we do about it?
gå *v* go·; *(på sine ben)* walk; *(om film etc, opføres)* be on; *(gå an)* do·; *(om maskine etc, køre)* run·; *(om tog, afgå)* leave·; *(om tiden)* pass; *være ude at ~* be out for a walk, be out walking; *Indiana Jones ~r i biografen* Indiana Jones is on at the cinema; *toget ~r kl. 16* the train leaves at 4 p.m.; *tiden ~r hurtigt* time passes quickly; *hvordan ~r det? (dvs. hvordan har du det)* how are you? *(dvs. hvordan glider tingene)* how are things? *det ~r godt (dvs. jeg har det godt)* I'm all right; *(dvs. tingene glider)* it is going all right;
~ af (løsne sig) come· off; *(fra stilling)* re'tire; *hvad ~r der af dig?* what is the matter (with you)?
~ an do·; *det ~r ikke an* that won't do;
~ (hen) efter ngt go· and get sth; *~ ngt efter* go· over sth;
~ for at være ngt pass for sth; *hvad ~r her for sig?* what is going on here?
~ fra (løsnes) come· loose; *~ fra en* leave· sby; *~ fra kone og børn* de'sert one's wife and family;
~ frem (dvs. gøre fremskridt) make· progress; *hvor ~r I hen?* where are you going?
~ i skole go· to school; *~ i vandet* bathe; *~ i stykker* go· to pieces, break·; *~ igennem byen* go· through the town; *han har ~et meget igennem* he has gone through a lot;
~ ind go· in, enter; *~ ind for ngt* go· in for sth;
~ med (om tøj, briller, hat) wear·; *(om stok)* use; *~ med til ngt* a'gree to sth;
~ ned go· down; *(om solen)* set·; *~ nedenom og hjem* go· to the dogs;
~ op go· up; *(åbne sig)* open; *(om*

snor) come· un'done; *(om regneopgave)* come· right; *(om kabale)* come· out; *det er ~et op for mig at…* I have realized that…; *~ over gaden* cross the street; *det ~r snart over* it will soon pass; *det ~r ham meget på* it is bothering him a lot; *~ på besøg* go· visiting; *~ på toilettet* go· to the bathroom; *~ rundt* go· round; *hvordan er det ~et til?* how did that happen? *her ~r det lystigt til* things are lively here; *pengene ~r til transport* the money is spent on transport; *~ til læge* see· a doctor; *~ ud* go· out; *(om træ, blomst)* die; *~ ud af døren* go· out of the door; *~ ud af stuen* leave· the room; *~ ud fra at…* as'sume that…; *det gik ud over børnene* it was the children who suffered; *hvad ~r det ud på?* what is it sup'posed to mean? *det ~r ud på at vinde* the thing is to win.

gåde *en* riddle; *(ngt mystisk)* mystery; *(ngt forvirrende)* puzzle; *løse en ~* solve a riddle; *det er mig en ~* it is a mystery to me, (F) it beats me; **~fuld** *adj* my'sterious.

gående *en* pe'destrian // *adj* going, walking; *holde den ~* keep· it up.

gåfelt *et* (pe'destrian) crossing.

gågade *en* pe'destrian street.

gåpåmod *et* go, drive; *(foretagsomhed)* enterprise.

går *s: i ~* yesterday; *i ~ aftes* last night, yesterday evening; *i ~ morges* yesterday morning.

gård *en (gårdsplads)* court(yard); *(skolegård)* playground; *(landejendom)* farm; *(herregård)* e'state; *køkkenet vender ud til ~en* the kitchen looks out on the courtyard; **~ejer** *en* farmer; **~have** *en* patio; **~mand** *en (som fejer gård etc)* caretaker; **~s·plads** *en* courtyard; *(på bondegård)* yard.

gås *en* goose *(pl:* geese); **~e·fjer** *en* goose feather; *(til at skrive med)* quill; **~e·gang** *en: gå i ~e·gang* walk in single file; **~e·hud** *en* gooseflesh; *det giver mig ~e·hud (også)* it gives me the creeps; **~e·leverpostej** *en* pâté de foie; **~e·steg** *en* roast goose; **~e·øjne** *pl* quo'tation marks, in'verted commas.

gåtur *en* walk.

H

h *(tone i musik)* B; *h-mol* B minor.

habil *adj* 'competent.

habit *en* suit.

had *et* hatred *(til* of); *nære ~ til en* hate sby; **~e** *v* hate; *(afsky også)* loathe; *jeg ~er at stå tidligt op* I hate getting up early.

hage *en (anat)* chin; *(krog)* hook // *v: ~ sig fast i* cling· to; **~kors** *et* swastika; **~smæk** *en* bib.

hagl *et (nedbør)* hail; *(til skydning)* shot; **~byge** *en* hail shower; **~bøsse** *en* shotgun.

hagle *v* hail; *sveden ~de af os* we were dripping with sweat.

haj *en* shark; **~tænder** *pl (på gade)* give-way markings.

hak *et* notch; *(i porcelæn)* chip; *ikke et ~* not a bit; *falde i ~* fall· into place; *få et ~ i tuden* get· a punch on the nose; *(fig)* be put· in one's place.

hakke *en (redskab)* hoe // *v (med ~)* hoe; *(med fx kniv)* hack; *(om fugl)* peck; *(om fx løg, purløg etc)* chop; *(om kød)* mince; *~ i det (om tale)* stammer; *(økon)* be hard up; *~ på en* nag sby; **~bræt** *et* chopping board; **~bøf** *en* hamburger steak; **~kød** *et* mince; **~maskine** *en* mincer; **~kniv** *en* chopper; **~orden** *en* pecking order.

hal *en* hall.

hale *en* tail; *(numse)* bottom // *v* pull; *(slæbe)* drag; *~ i ngt* pull at sth; *~ ind på en* gain on sby; **~stykke** *et (gastr)* rump; **~tudse** *en* tadpole.

hallo *interj* hello.

halløj *et* fun; *(ballade)* row [rau]; (F) hullaba'loo // *interj* hey.

halm *en* straw; **~strå** *et* straw.

hals *en* neck; *(det indre af halsen, svælget)* throat; *brække ~en* break· one's neck; *dreje ~en om på en* wring· sby's neck; *skære ~en over på en* cut· sby's throat; *af fuld ~* at the top of one's voice; *få ngt i den gale ~* get· sth down the wrong way; *få ngt galt i ~en (dvs. misforstå)* take· sth wrongly; *have ondt i ~en* have a sore throat; *falde om ~en på en* throw· one's arms around sby's neck; *over ~ og hoved* all of a sudden, in a rush; *skaffe en ngt på ~en* saddle sby with sth; *det hænger mig langt ud af ~en* I'm fed up with it; **~betændelse** *en* sore throat; **~brand** *en* heartburn; **~brækkende** *adj: i ~brækkende fart* at breakneck speed; **~bånd** *et (smykke)* necklace; *(til hund)* collar.

halse *v (gø)* bark; *~e af sted* pant along.

halshugge *v* be'head.

halshugning *en* be'heading.

halskæde *en* necklace.

halstørklæde *et* scarf; *(stort, uldent)* muffler.

halsudskæring *en* neckline.

halt *adj* lame.

halte *v* limp; *(fig)* halt; **~n** *en* limp.

halv *adj* half; *det ~e af det* half of it; *de glemte det ~e* they forgot half of it; *den koster kun det ~e* it only costs half; *det ~e København* half Copenhagen; *klokken er ~* it is half past; *den er fem minutter i ~* it is twenty-five (minutes) past; *tre en ~ dag* three and a half days; *en ~ time* half an hour; *om et ~t år* in six months.

halv... *sms:* **~anden** *adj* one and a half; *~andet år* a year and a half; **~cirkel** *en* semicircle; **~dagsarbejde** *et* half-time job; **~del** *en* half *(pl:* halves); *~delen af pengene* half of the money.

halvere *v* halve.

halveringstid *en (fys)* half-life.

halvfems *num* ninety; *han er født i ~erne* he was born in the nineties; *han er i ~erne* he is in his nineties.

halvfjerds *num* seventy; *i ~erne se halvfems.*

halvfærdig *adj* half-finished.

halvgammel *adj* elderly.

halvkreds *en* semicircle.

halvkugle *en (om Jorden)* hemisphere.

halvkvalt *adj* stifled.

halvlang *adj (om tøj)* half-length.

halvleg *en (fodb etc)* half; *(pausen mellem ~ene)* halftime, interval.

halvmørke *et* half-light.

halvmåne *en* half-moon.

halvnode *en (mus)* minim.

halvpension *en* half board.

halvrund *adj* semi'circular.

halvt *adv* half; *dele ngt ~ med en* go· halves with sby on sth; *~ om ~* half and half; *~ så meget* half as much.

halvtag *et* lean-to, shed.

halvtreds *num* fifty; *han er født i ~erne* he was born in the fifties; *han er i ~erne* he is in his fifties.

halvvej *s: på ~en* half-way.

halvvejs *adj: vi er ~* we have come half-way // *adv* half.

halvvoksen *adj (om barn)* ado'lescent; *(om dyr)* half-grown.

halvø *en* pen'insula.

halvår *et* six months; **~lig** *adj* half-yearly // *adv* every six months.

ham *en* slough; *skifte ~* shed· its skin.

ham *pron: det er ~* it is him; *det er ~ der kommer* it is he who is coming; *hun er ældre end ~* she is older than he; *~ du snakkede med* the one you spoke to.

hamburgerryg *en* smoked saddle of pork.

hamle *v: kunne ~ op med en* be a match for sby.

hammer *en* hammer; **~kast** *et (sport)* throwing the hammer.

hamp *en* hemp.

hamre *v* hammer; **~n** *en* hammering.

hamster *en* hamster.

hamstre *v* hoard; **hamstring** *en* hoarding.

han *en* male, he // *pron* he; *det sagde ~ selv* he said so himself.

handel *en* trade; *gøre en god ~* make· a bargain; *være i ~en* be on the market; **~s·balance** *en* balance of trade; **~s·flåde** *en* merchant navy; **~s·foretagende** *et* business (con'cern); **~s·gartner** *en* market gardener; **~s·højskole** *en* com'mercial college; **~s·ministerium** *et* Ministry of Commerce; **~s·partner** *en* trading partner; **~s·rejsende** *en* com'mercial traveller; **~s·skib** *et* merchant ship; **~s·skole** *en* com'mercial school; **~s·vare** *en* com'modity.

handicap *et* handicap; **~pet** *adj* handicapped; *(fysisk også)* dis'abled.

handle *v* act; *(drive handel)* trade, deal·; *(gå på indkøb)* go· shopping; *vi ~r i Brugsen* we shop at the Co-op; *~ med en* do· business with sby; *~ med ngt* deal· in sth; *det ~r om os* it is about us; *~ om prisen* bargain over the price.

handlekraft *en* energy; **~ig** *adj* ener'getic.

handlende *en* tradesman *(pl:* -men); *(detailhandler også)* shopkeeper.

handling *en* action; *(i bog etc)* story, plot; *(ceremoni etc)* ceremony; *skride til ~* take· action.

handske *en* glove; **~rum** *et* glove com'partment.

hane *en* cock; *(am)* rooster; *(vand~)* tap; **~gal** *et* cockcrow; **~kamp** *en* cockfight.

hangarskib *et* (aircraft) carrier.

hanhund *en* dog.

hank *en* handle; **~e** *v: ~e op i ngt* grab sth.

hankøn *et* male gender; *(gram)* the masculine; *af ~* male.

hans *adj* his; *bilen er ~* it is his car, the car be'longs to him.

hare *en* hare.

harem *et* harem.

hareskår *et (med)* harelip.

haresteg *en* roast hare.

harlekin *en* harlequin.

harmdirrende *adj* in'dignant.

harme *en* indig'nation; **~s** *v* feel in'dignant *(over* at).

harmløs *adj* harmless.

harmonere *v* harmonize, be in harmony.

harmoni *en* harmony.

harmonika *en* ac'cordion; *(lille)* concer'tina; **~sammenstød** *et* pile-up.

harmoniorkester *et* brass band.

harmonisere *v* harmonize.

harmonisk *adj* har'monious.

harpe *en (mus)* harp; *(neds, om kvinde)* harridan; **~nist** *en* harpist.

harpiks *en* resin.

harpun *en,* **~ere** *v* har'poon.

harsk *adj* rancid.

harve *en* harrow // *v* harrow.

has *s: få ~ på en* get· the upper hand over sby.

hasarderet *adj* rash.

hasardspil *et* gambling.

haspe *en (på vindue)* catch.

hasselnød *en* hazelnut.

hast *en* haste, hurry; *gøre ngt i ~* do· sth in a hurry; *det har ingen ~* there is no hurry; **~e** *v* hasten, hurry; *det ~er* it is urgent; *det ~er ikke* there is no hurry; **~e·sag** *en* urgent matter.

hastig *adj* quick; *(overilet)* hasty.

hastighed *en (fart)* speed; *køre med en ~ på 100 km i timen* go· at (a speed of) 100 km per hour; **~s·begrænsning** *en* speed limit.

hastværk *et* hurry; **~s·arbejde** *et* slapdash work.

hat *en* hat; *det tager jeg ~ten af for* I take· off my hat to that; *få så ~ten passer (dvs. blive skældt ud)* get· ticked off; **~temager** *en* hatter; **~tenål** *en* hatpin; **~teskygge** *en* hat brim.

hav *et* sea; *(ocean)* ocean; *et ~ af breve* heaps of letters; *være på ~et* be at sea; *de bor ved ~et* they live at the seaside.

havarere *v* be wrecked; *(om bil etc)* break· down.

havari *et (forlis)* shipwreck; *(skade)* damage, loss; *(om maskine)* breakdown; *lide ~ (om skib)* be shipwrecked; *(blive skadet)* break· down; *totalt ~* total loss.

havbugt *en* bay, gulf.

havbund *en* ocean bed, sea bed.

have *en* garden; *botanisk ~* bo'tanical gardens *pl; zoologisk ~* zoo.

have *v* have·, have got; *(om tilstand, levevilkår, form, farve)* be·; *han har kone og børn* he has a wife and family; *har du en tændstik?* have you got a match? *hvordan har I det?* how 'are you? *vi har det fint* we are fine;

~ *det varmt* be warm, feel· hot; *hvad farve har bilen?* what colour is the car? *hvad vil du ~?* what do you want? *han har det med at glemme* he has a tendency to for'get; *jeg vil gerne ~ et æble* I would like an apple, please; *har du noget imod at...?* do you mind if...? ~ *briller på* wear· spectacles; *det har ikke ngt på sig (fig)* there is nothing in it.
have... *sms:* **~arbejde** *et* gardening; **~arkitekt** *en* landscape gardener; **~fest** *en* garden party; **~forening** *en (med kolonihaver)* al'lotment so'ciety; **~gang** *en* garden path; **~låge** *en* gate; **~redskab** *et* gardening tool; **~saks** *en: en ~saks* a pair of garden shears; **~slange** *en* garden hose.
hav... *sms:* **~forskning** *en* maritime re'search; **~frue** *en* mermaid; **~mand** *en* merman *(pl:* -men); **~måge** *en* herring gull.
havn *en* harbour; *(stor, havneby)* port; *gå i ~* put· into harbour (,port).
havne *v (ende)* land, end up.
havnearbejder *en* docker.
havneby *en* port.
havnefoged *en* harbour master.
havre *en* oats *pl;* **~gryn** *pl* oatmeal; **~grød** *en* oatmeal porridge; **~suppe** *en* gruel.
havvand *et* seawater.
havørred *en* sea trout.
hebraisk *adj* Hebrew.
hed *adj (varm)* hot; *blive ~ om ørerne* get· the wind up.
hedde *v* be called; *hvad ~r du?* what is your name? *jeg ~r Liz* my name is Liz; *han ~r John* he's called John; *det ~r sig at...* it is said that...; *hvad ~r det på engelsk?* what is it called in English?
hede *en (~strækning)* moor, heath; *(varme)* heat; **~bølge** *en* heatwave.
hedensk *adj* heathen.
hedeslag *et* heatstroke.
hedning *en* heathen.
hedvin *en* des'sert wine.
heftig *adj* violent; *(af natur)* im'petuous.
hegn *et* fence; *levende ~* hedgerow; **~e** *v: ~e ngt ind* fence sth in.
hej *interj (ved møde)* hello! *(ved afsked)* see you!
hejre *en* heron.
hejse *v* hoist; **~værk** *et* hoisting appa'ratus.
heks *en* witch; *en gammel ~ (neds)* an old hag.
hekse *v* practise witchcraft; *jeg kan ikke ~* I can't work miracles; **~jagt** *en* witch hunt; **~ri** *et* witchcraft; **~skud** *et* lum'bago; **~sting** *et (i syning)* herringbone stitch.
hektar *en* hectare.
hektisk *adj* hectic.
hel *adj* whole; *(fuldstændig)* com'plete; *klokken slog ~* the clock struck the hour; *en ~ del* quite a few; *han tog det ~e* he took all of it; *det var det ~e, tak* that was all, thank you; *i det ~e taget* on the whole; *(overhovedet)* at all; *jeg har ondt over det ~e* I'm aching all over; *der var støvet over det ~e* it was dusty all over the place; *over ~e landet* all over the country; **~befaren** *adj (mar)* able-bodied.
helbred *et* health; *have et godt (,svagt) ~* have a strong (,weak) consti'tution; *det er godt for ~et* it is good for you; **~e** *v* cure; **~else** *en* cure; *(det at komme sig)* re'covery; **~s·attest** *en* health cer'tificate; **~s·tilstand** *en* (state of) health; **~s·undersøgelse** *en* medical.
held *et* luck; *have ~ med sig* be lucky; *ikke have ~ med sig* be un'lucky; *have ~ i kortspil* be lucky at cards; *det er et ~ at vi har bilen* we are lucky to have the car; *det var et ~!* what luck! *have ~ til at gøre ngt* suc'ceed in doing sth; *~ og lykke!* good luck! *til alt ~...* luckily...; *~ i uheld* a blessing in dis'guise.
heldagsarbejde *et* full-time job.
heldig *adj* lucky; *han er så ~ at have en ny bil* he is lucky in having a new car; *hvor er du ~!* lucky you! **~vis** *adv* fortunately, luckily.
heldækkende *adj: ~ tæppe* wall-to-wall carpet.
hele *et* whole; *(se også hel);* **~s** *v* heal up.

helgen *en* saint.
helhed *en* whole; *i sin* ~ in full; **~s·løsning** *en* overall so'lution.
helhjertet *adj* whole-hearted
helikopter *en* 'helicopter; **~landingsplads** *en (på jorden)* heliport; *(på fx boreplatform)* helipad.
hellang *adj (om kjole)* ankle length.
helle *en (trafik~)* traffic island; **~fisk** *en* halibut.
heller *adv: jeg kan ~ ikke gøre det* I can't do it either; *du må ~ ikke gøre det* you must not do it either; *det havde jeg ~ ikke tænkt mig* I was not planning to; *du har ~ aldrig tid!* you really never have the time, do you?
hellere *adv* rather; *vi må ~ skynde os* we had better hurry; *jeg vil ~ køre selv* I would rather drive my'self; *du skulle ~ gifte dig med ham* you'd better marry him; *jeg ville ~ end gerne gøre det* I should love to do it.
hellig *adj* holy; *(from)* pious; *(neds)* sancti'monious; *(indviet, fx bygning)* sacred; ~ *krig* holy war; **~brøde** *en* sacrilege; **~dag** *en* holiday; **~dom** *en* sanctuary.
hellige *v* de'vote, dedicate; ~ *sig arbejdet* de'vote oneself to work.
helligtrekongersaften *s* Twelfth Night.
helligånden *s* the Holy Spirit.
helnode *en (mus)* semibreve.
helpension *en* full board.
helsebutik *en* health food shop; **helsecenter** *et* health centre; **helsekost** *en* health food.
helsides *adj* full-page.
helsilke *en* pure silk.
Helsingør *s* Elsinore.
helskindet *adj: slippe ~ fra ngt* e'scape sth un'scathed.
helst *adj* preferably; *jeg vil ~ have te* I pre'fer tea; *du må ~ ikke gå* I would rather you did not go.
helt *en* hero *(pl:* heroes).
helt *adv* quite, com'pletely; *(ganske)* quite; *det er ~ forkert!* it is all wrong! *de kommer ~ fra Bornholm* they have come all the way from Bornholm; *han er ~ igennem pålidelig* he is thoroughly re'liable; *det er ngt ~ andet* that's quite an'other story.
heltemodig *adj* heroic.
heltids... *i sms:* full-time *(fx ~beskæftigelse* full-time employment).
heltinde *en* heroine.
helulden *adj* all-wook, pure-wool.
helvede *et* hell; *det er varmt som bare ~!* it is hot like hell! *for ~!* oh hell! *det går ad ~ til* (S) it's bloody awful.
helvedes *adj* damned, a hell of a // *adv* damned, like hell; *han tror han er en ~ karl* he thinks he is one hell of a man; *det er ~ varmt* it is damned hot.
helårshus *et (kan oversættes)* round-the-year house.
hemmelig *adj* secret; ~ *afstemning* secret vote; *~t nummer (tlf)* ex-di'rectory number; **~hed** *en* secret; *(det at holde ngt hemmeligt)* secrecy; *holde på en ~hed* keep· a secret; *i ~hed* in secret; *i dybeste ~hed* in the deepest secrecy; **~hedsfuld** *adj* secretive; *(mystisk)* my'sterious; **~stemple** *v* classify.
hen *adv: hvor skal du ~?* where are you going? ~ *ad vejen* along the road; *(fig, efterhånden)* as we go along; ~ *imod* to'wards; ~ *over engen* across the meadow; *gå ~ til en* go· up to sby; *kom ~ og se til mig* come· round and see me; *han gik ~ til døren* he went (over) to the door.
henad *præp: ~ aften* to'wards evening.
henblik *s: med ~ på (vedrørende)* con'cerning; *(for at)* with a view to.
hende *pron* her; *der er brev til ~* there is a letter for her; *det var ~ der sagde det!* it was she who said it; *han er ældre end ~* he is older than she; **~s** *pron* her; *(stående alene)* hers; *det er ~s bil* it is her car; *bilen er ~s* the car is hers.
henfald *et (radioaktivt)* de'cay.
hengiven *adj* de'voted; *Deres hengivne...* Yours sin'cerely...; *din hengivne...* Yours...; **~hed** *en* de'votion.

henhold *s: i ~ til* re'ferring to; *(ifølge fx regler)* ac'cording to.
henholde *v: ~ sig til* re'fer to; **~nde** *adj* stalling.
henholdsvis *adv* re'spectively.
henhøre *v* be'long *(under* under).
henimod *præp (om tidspunkt)* to'wards; *(om tal)* nearly.
henkastet *adj* casual.
henkoge *v* pre'serve.
henkogningsglas *et* pre'serving jar.
henlede *v: ~ ens opmærksomhed på ngt* draw· sby's at'tention to sth.
henlægge *v (lægge på hylden)* shelve; *(opgive)* drop; *(om forråd, gemme)* store; **~lse** *en* shelving; storage.
henne *adv: der ~* over there; *her ~* over here; *han er ~ hos bageren* he is at the baker's; *hvor er du ~?* where 'are you? *hvor har du været ~?* where have you been? *være 4 måneder ~* be four months gone.
henrette *v* execute; **~lse** *en* exe'cution.
henrivende *adj* lovely, charming.
henrykkelse *en* de'light.
henrykt *adj* de'lighted.
henseende *en* re'spect; *i den ~* in that re'spect; *i enhver ~* in every re'spect.
hensigt *en* in'tention; *(formål)* purpose; *i den ~ at gøre ngt* with the in'tention of doing sth; *gøre ngt i den bedste ~* do· sth with the best of in'tentions; *have til ~ at...* in'tend to...; *det var ikke ~en* it was not my in'tention; *hvad er ~en med det?* what is the purpose of that? **~s·mæssig** *adj* suitable; *(praktisk)* 'practical.
henstand *en* re'spite; *få ~ til 1. juni* get· until June 1st.
henstille *v (anbefale)* recom'mend; *(anmode)* re'quest.
henstilling *en* recommen'dation; re'quest; *rette ~ til en om at gøre ngt* ap'peal to sby to do sth.
hensyn *et* conside'ration; *af ~ til* be'cause of; *(om fx person)* for the sake of; *med ~ til* con'cerning, as re'gards; *tage ~ til* con'sider, show conside'ration for; *uden ~ til* re'gardless of; **~s·fuld** *adj* con'siderate; **~s·fuldhed** *en* conside'ration; **~s·løs** *adj* ruthless; **~s·løshed** *en* ruthlessness.
hente *v* fetch, get·; *(komme hen og ~)* come· for, col'lect; pick up; *~ børnene i børnehaven* fetch (,col'lect) the children from the kindergarten.
hentyde *v: ~ til* re'fer to; *(antyde)* hint at.
hentydning *en* reference; *(antydning)* hint.
henvende *v: ~ sig til en (dvs. tale til)* talk to sby; *(med forspørgsel etc)* ap'ply to sby; *~ sig ved skranken* en'quire at the counter; **~lse** *en (forespørgsel)* en'quiry; *(skriftlig)* letter; *(med bøn om ngt)* appli'cation.
henvise *v: ~ til* re'fer to.
henvisning *en* reference; *(til læge)* re'ferral; **henvist** *adj: være ~ til at* have to.
heppe *v* cheer.
her *adv* here; *~ og der* here and there; *kom ~!* come here! *er han ~ fra egnen?* is he from this area? *~ i huset* in this house.
heraf *adv* from this.
heraldik *en* heraldry.
herberg *et (kro etc)* inn; *(vandrehjem)* hostel.
herefter *adv (så)* after this, then; *(for fremtiden)* from now on.
herfra *adv* from here, from this; *de skal rejse ~* they are leaving here.
herhen *adv* here.
herhjemme *adv* here; *(her i landet)* in this country.
heri *adv* in this; *(på dette punkt)* on this point; **~blandt** *adv* in'cluding.
herind, herinde *adv* in here.
herkomst *en* origin.
herlig *adj* wonderful.
hermed *adv* with this; *(med disse ord)* so saying; *(således)* thus; *~ følger* en'closed please find.
hermelin *en* stoat; *(om perlsværk)* ermine.
hermetisk *adj: ~ lukket* her'metically sealed.
herned, hernede *adv* down here.
heroin *en* heroin.

heroisk *adj* he'roic.
herom *adv* about this; *(denne vej)* round here; **~kring** *adv* somewhere here, hereabouts; **~me** *adv* round here.
herop, heroppe *adv* up here.
herover, herovre *adv* over here.
herre *en (mand)* gentleman *(pl:* -men); *(hersker, chef)* master; *hr. Poulsen* Mr Poulsen; *javel, hr!* yes, sir! *der så ~ns ud* it looked awful; *være sin egen ~* be one's own master; *mine ~r!* gentlemen! *blive ~ over ngt* get· con'trol of sth; *være ~ over ngt* be master of sth, con'trol sth; **~bukser** *pl* men's trousers; **~cykel** *en* gentlemen's bicycle; **~double** *en* men's doubles; **~dømme** *et* con'trol *(over* of, over); *miste ~dømmet over ngt* lose· con'trol of sth; **~frisør** *en* men's hairdresser; **~gård** *en* manor (house); *det er ingen ~gård (dvs. ikke dyrt)* it does not cost the earth; **~kor** *et* male choir; **~løs** *adj* a'bandoned; *(om hund)* stray; **~mand** *en* squire; **~sko** *pl* men's shoes; **~skrædder** *en* tailor; **~toilet** *et* gents; **~tøj** *et* men's clothes.
herse *v: ~ med en* order sby around.
herskabelig *adj* lu'xurious.
herske *v (styre, regere)* rule; *(som monark)* reign; *(findes)* be·; *(være fremherskende)* pre'vail; *~ over ngt* rule sth, reign over sth; *der kan ikke ~ ngn tvivl om det* there can be no doubt about it.
hersker *en* ruler *(over* of); **~inde** *en* mistress *(over* of).
herskesyg *adj* domi'neering; *(ivrig efter magt)* greedy for power.
hertil *adv* here; *(til denne brug)* for this purpose; *~ kommer at...* add to this that...
hertug *en* duke; **~dømme** *et* duchy; **~inde** *en* duchess.
herud, herude *adv* out here.
herunder *adv* under here; *(inkluderet)* in'cluding.
herved *adv* by this, hereby; *~ meddeles at...* we hereby in'form you that...

hessian *en* hessian.
hest *en* horse; *(gymn)* vaulting horse; *til ~* on horseback; *spring over ~ (gymn)* horse vault; **~e·avl** *en* horse breeding; **~e·dækken** *et* horsecloth; **~e·hale** *en* horsetail; *(om frisure)* ponytail; **~e·kraft** *en (hk)* horsepower, hp; **~e·kød** *et* horseflesh, horsemeat; **~e·pære** *en* horse dropping; **~e·sko** *en* horseshoe; **~e·sport** *en* horseracing; **~e·stald** *en* stable; **~e·vogn** *en* horse cart; **~e·væddeløb** *et* horseracing; *(det enkelte løb)* horserace.
hetz *en* rabble-rousing (propa'ganda).
HFI-relæ *et (elek)* circuit breaker.
hi *et* lair; *gå i ~ (fig)* go· underground; *ligge i ~* hibernate.
hib *et* dig *(til* at), cutting re'mark *(til* to).
hidse *v: ~ en op* ex'cite sby; *(gøre vred)* make· sby angry; *~ sig op over ngt* get· ex'cited about sth; *hids dig ned!* don't get· ex'cited! calm down! *~e ngn op mod hinanden* set· sby on each other.
hidsig *adj* hot-headed; *blive ~* lose· one's temper; *et ~t gemyt* a hot temper; **~hed** *en* hot temper.
hidtil *adv* so far, up to now.
hierarki *et* hierarchy; **~sk** *adj* hie'rar'chic.
hik *et* hiccup.
hikke *en* hiccups *pl; have ~ke* have the hiccups // *v* hiccup.
hilse *v* say· hel'lo (,good morning, good afternoon, good evening); *(~ velkommen)* greet; *vil du ~ din kone?* give my re'gards to your wife! *jeg skal ~ fra familien* the family send· their re'gards; *~ ngt velkommen* welcome sth; *~ på en* say hello (etc) to sby.
hilsen *en* greeting; *(med nik)* nod; *med ~ fra køkkenchefen* with the compliments of the chef; *mange ~er (i brev)* best regards; *med venlig ~* yours sin'cerely.
himmel *en* sky; *(himmerig)* heaven; *det kom som sendt fra himlen* it was a godsend; *stjernerne på himlen* the stars in the sky; *for himlens skyld*

for heaven's sake; *under åben* ~ in the open (air); **-blå** *adj* azure; **-fart** *en: Kristi Himmelfartsdag* As'cension Day; **-henykt** *adj* over'joyed; **-legeme** *et* ce'lestial body; **-råbende** *adj* crying; **-seng** *en* four-poster.
himmelsk *adj* heavenly.
himmerig *et* Heaven.
hinanden *pron* one an'other; *i to dage efter* ~ for two days in suc'cession; *gå (,falde) fra* ~ go· (,fall·) to pieces; *være forelsket i* ~ be in love (with one another).
hind *en* hind.
hindbær *et* raspberry.
hinde *en* membrane; *(tyndt overtræk etc)* film.
hindre *v (standse, spærre for)* block, ob'struct; *(forhindre)* pre'vent; *(sinke)* hinder; ~ *en i at gøre ngt* pre'vent sby from doing sth.
hindring *en (som standser ngt)* obstacle, ob'struction; *(forhindring)* pre'vention; *(som sinker)* hindrance; *lægge hindringer i vejen for en* put· obstacles in the way of sby, ob'struct sby.
hingst *en* stallion.
hinke *v* skip; *(humpe)* limp; *(i hinkerude)* play hopscotch; **-rude, -sten** *en* hopscotch.
hinsides *præp* be'yond.
hip: *det kan være* ~ *som hap* it does not make any difference.
hirse *en* millet.
hist *adv:* ~ *og her* here and there.
historie *en (faget)* history; *(fortælling)* story; *(sag)* af'fair, business; *studere* ~ read· history; *læse en* ~ read· a story; *det er en længere* ~ it is a long story; *en pinlig* ~ an awkward business; *gå over i historien* go· down in history.
historiker *en* his'torian.
historisk *adj* historical.
hitliste *en* top of the pops.
hitte *v* find; ~ *rede i ngt* make· sth out; ~ *på ngt* think· of sth; *(digte)* think· up sth; ~ *ud af ngt* find· out about sth, make· sth out; **-barn** *et* foundling; **-gods** *et* lost property.
hive *v* pull; *(stærkt, pludseligt)* tug; ~ *efter vejret* gasp for breath; ~ *i snoren* pull the string; ~ *op i bukserne* hitch up one's trousers.
HIV-positiv *adj* in'fected with HIV.
hjelm *en* helmet.
hjem *et (alle bet)* home // *adv* home; *komme* ~ come· home; *invitere en* ~ ask sby home; **-ad** *adv* homeward; **-by** *en* home town; **-kalde** *v* re'call; **-komst** *en* homecoming; **-kundskab** *en (i skolen)* home eco'nomics; **-land** *et* native country; **-lig** *adj* do'mestic; *(rar, hyggelig)* cosy, homely; **-løs** *adj* homeless.
hjemme *adv* at home; *(kommet hjem)* home; *høre* ~ *et sted* be'long somewhere; *(bo)* live somewhere; *være* ~ be (at) home; *er han* ~*? (også)* is he in? *hun er* ~ *hos John* she's at John's place; **-arbejde** *et* homework; *~arbejdende husmor* housewife *(pl:* -wives); **-bagt** *adj* home-baked; **-bane** *en (sport)* home ground; *spille på ~bane* play at home; *føle sig på ~bane (fig)* feel· at home; **-boende** *adj* living at home; **-fra** *adv: rejse (,flytte) ~fra* leave· home; **-hjælp** *en* home help; **-hjælper** *en* home help; **-hørende** *adj: ~hørende i Danmark* a native of Denmark; *(bosat i)* resident in Denmark; **-kamp** *en (sport)* home match; **-lavet** *adj* home-made; **-marked** *et* do'mestic market; **-sejr** *en (sport)* home win; **-sko** *en* slipper; **-styre** *et* Home Rule; **-sygeplejerske** *en sv.t.* district nurse; **-værn** *et* terri'torial army.
hjemrejse *en* journey home; *på ~n mødte vi...* on our way home we met...
hjemsende *v* send· home; *(om tropper)* de'mobilize.
hjemsted *et* domicile.
hjemsøge *v: være hjemsøgt af ngt* be af'flicted by (,with) sth.
hjemve *en* homesickness; *have* ~ be homesick.
hjemvej *en* way home; *på ~en så vi kirken* we saw the church on our way home.

hjerne *en* brain; *(forstand)* brains *pl; få ngt på ~n* get· sth on the brain; **~arbejde** *et* brainwork; **~blødning** *en* cerebral haemorrhage; **~død** *en* brain death; **~rystelse** *en* con'cussion; *have ~rystelse* be con'cussed; **~skade** *en* brain injury; **~skadet** *adj* brain-damaged; **~skal** *en* skull; **~vask** *en* brainwashing.

hjerte *et* heart; *have dårligt ~* have a heart dis'ease; *have svagt ~* have a weak heart; *have ondt i ~t* have a pain in one's heart; *tung om ~t, med tungt ~* with a heavy heart, *have ngt på ~* have sth on one's mind; *af hele sit ~* with all one's heart; *der faldt en sten fra hans ~* it was a load off his mind; *hånden på ~t!* honest to God! **~anfald** *et* heart at'tack; **~banken** *en* palpi'tation; *(se også ~slag);* **~fejl** *en* or'ganic heart failure; **~kammer** *et* 'ventricle; **~klap** *en* heart valve **~lammelse** *en* heart failure; **~lig** *adj* hearty; *(dybfølt)* heartfelt; *(oprigtig)* sin'cere; *en ~lig latter* a hearty laugh; **~løs** *adj* heartless; **~musling** *en* cockle.

hjerter *en (i kort)* hearts; *~ dame* queen of hearts.

hjerteskærende *adj* heart-rending.

hjerteslag *et (om hjertets banken)* heartbeat; *(om hjertetilfælde)* heart failure.

hjertestop *et* heart failure.

hjertestyrkning *en* re'freshment.

hjertesygdom *en* heart dis'ease.

hjertetilfælde *et* heart at'tack.

hjertetransplantation *en* heart trans'plant.

hjord *en (om kvæg)* herd; *(om får)* flock.

hjort *en* deer; *to ~e* two deer.

hjortetaksalt *et* am'monium carbonate.

hjul *et* wheel; *(på rullebord etc)* castor; **~benet** *adj* bowlegged; **~damper** *en* paddle steamer; **~kapsel** *en* hub cap; **~pisker** *en* rotary beater; **~spor** *et (efter bil)* car track; *(efter anden vogn)* wheel track.

hjælp *en* help; *(assistance også)* as'sistance; *(undsætning)* rescue; *(understøttelse)* sup'port, aid; *(nytte)* use, help; *råbe om ~* cry for help; *komme en til ~* come· to sby's as'sistance (, rescue); *ved ~ af* by means of; *ved egen ~* single-handedly.

hjælpe *v* help; as'sist; rescue; sup'port, aid; be of use; *det ~r ikke (også)* it is no good; *hvad skal det ~?* what is the good of that? *~s ad* help one another; *~ en med at gøre ngt* help sby to do sth; *~ på ngt* im'prove sth; *~ til* give· a hand, help.

hjælpeløs *adj* helpless; **~hed** *en* helplessness.

hjælpemiddel *et* aid.

hjælper *en* helper, as'sistant.

hjælpepræst *en* curate.

hjælpsom *adj* helpful; **~hed** *en* helpfulness.

hjørne *et* corner; *gå om ~t* go· round the corner; *dreje om ~t* turn the corner; *på ~t af* at the corner of; **~spark** *et (fodb)* corner; **~tand** *en* eye tooth.

hob *en (bunke)* heap; *(mængde)* crowd; *(større mængde af ngt)* multitude; *~en* the masses; *alle til ~e* the whole lot of them.

hobe *v: ~ sig op* ac'cumulate, pile up.

hof *et* court; *ved ~fet* at Court; **~dame** *en* lady-in-waiting; **~leverandør** *en: kongelig ~leverandør* pur'veyor to His (,Her) Majesty the King (,Queen).

hofte *en* hip; **~ben** *et* hip bone; **~holder** *en* girdle; **~led** *et* hip joint; **~skål** *en* hip socket.

hold *et* team; *(mindre gruppe, selskab etc)* group, party; *(greb, tag)* hold, grasp; *(side, kant)* quarter; *(i ryg, nakke etc)* pain; *arbejde i ~* work in teams; *være med på ~et (sport)* be on the team; *på nært ~ af* close to.

holdbar *adj (stærk, solid)* durable; *(om mad)* non-perishable; *(om farve)* fast; *(om påstand)* tenable; **~hed** *en* dura'bility; *have lang ~hed (om mad)* keep· well.

holde *v* hold·; *(vedligeholde, bevare,*

underholde, overholde etc) keep·; *(abonnere på)* take·; *(standse)* stop; *(~ stille for kortere tid)* wait; *~ avis* take· a newspaper; *~ hund* keep· a dog; *~ af en* be fond of sby; *~ af at gøre ngt* like to do sth; *~ fast i ngt* hold· on to sth; *~ igen på ngt* hold· sth; *~ inde (med fx skydning)* cease; *(fx med at tale)* stop; *~ med en* side with sby; *~ en med tøj* keep· sby e'quipped; *~ en nede* keep· sby down; *~ op med at gøre ngt* stop doing sth; *hold nu op!* stop it now! *~ på (dvs. beholde)* hold· on to; *(dvs. hævde)* in'sist *(at* that); *(ved væddemål)* bet on; *~ sammen* stick· to'gether; *~ til et sted* live (,stay) in a place; *jeg kan ikke ~ til det mere* I can't stand it any longer; *~ tilbage* hold· back; *(i trafikken)* give· way; *~ ud (dvs. blive ved)* hold· out, keep· it up; *(dvs. udstå)* stand·; *~ sig (dvs. ikke blive dårlig)* keep·; *(dvs. forblive)* stay; *(dvs. ikke gå på toilettet)* con'tain one'self; *~ sig inde* stay indoors; *~ sig oppe (i vandet)* keep· a'float; *(ikke gå i seng)* stay up; *~ sig parat* keep· ready; *~ sig til reglerne* stick· to rules; *~ sig tilbage* hold· back.

holdeplads *en (for bus)* stop; *(for taxa)* taxi rank.

holder *en (til fx blyanter)* holder; *(til fx tape)* dis'penser.

holdning *en (af kroppen)* posture, bearing; *(måde at opføre sig på)* conduct; *(indstilling)* attitude; *(standpunkt)* po'sition; **~s·ændring** *en (fig)* change of attitude.

holdsammensætning *en (sport)* line-up.

holdt *et* halt.

Holland *s* Holland; **hollandsk** *adj* Dutch.

hollænder *en* Dutchman *(pl:* -men); *~ne* the Dutch; *hun er ~* she is Dutch.

homofil *adj* homophile.

homogen *adj* homo'geneous.

homoseksuel *adj* homo'sexual.

honning *en* honey; **~kage** *en sv.t.* gingerbread; **~melon** *en* honey dew melon.

honnør *en: gøre ~ for en* sa'lute sby.

honorar *et* fee; **honorere** *v (betale)* pay·; *(opfylde)* ful'fil.

hop *et* jump; *(stort)* leap; **~bakke** *en (til skihop)* ski jump.

hoppe *en (hest)* mare.

hoppe *v* jump; *(med store spring)* leap·; *~ af (tog etc)* jump off; *(pol)* de'fect; *~ over ngt* jump (over) sth; *(fig)* skip sth; *den ~r jeg ikke på* I won't buy that one; **~gynge** *en* baby bouncer.

hor *en (utroskab)* a'dultery; *begå ~* com'mit a'dultery; **~e** *en* whore // *v* fornicate.

horisont *en* ho'rizon; *ude i ~en* on the ho'rizon; **~al** *adj* hori'zontal.

hormon *et* 'hormone; **~mangel** *en* hormone de'ficiency; **~tilskud** *et* hormone supplement.

horn *et* horn; *(mus)* (French) horn; *(om brød)* croissant; *tude i ~et* blow· the horn; *spille (på) ~* play the horn; **~fisk** *en* garfish; **~hinde** *en (i øjet)* cornea; **~ist** *en* horn player; **~orkester** *et* brass band.

horoskop *et* horoscope; *få stillet sit ~* have one's horoscope cast.

hos *præp: være på besøg ~ en* be visiting sby; *bo ~ en ven* stay with a friend; *han er henne ~ bageren* he is at the baker's; *vil du sidde ~ mig?* will you sit by me? *her ~ os* in this house.

hospital *et* hospital; *komme på ~et* go· to hospital; *ligge på ~et* be in hospital; **~s·sprit** *en* surgical spirit.

hoste *en* cough; *(det at ~)* coughing; *have ~* have a cough // *v* cough; **~anfald** *et* fit of coughing.

hosten *en* cough(ing); **~saft** *en* cough mixture.

hotel *et* ho'tel; *bo på ~* stay at a hotel; **~platform** *en* accomo'dation rig; **~reservation** *en* room reser'vation; **~værelse** *et* ho'tel room; **~vært** *en* ho'tel keeper.

hov *en (på dyr)* hoof *(pl:* hooves) // *interj* hey! *hov, hov!* come, come!

hoved *et* head; *holde ~et koldt* keep· one's cool; *være kort for ~et* be ab'rupt, be curt; *få ngt i ~et* be hit on the head by sth; *have ondt i ~et* have a headache; *regne ngt i ~et* calculate sth in one's head; *sætte sig ngt i ~et* set· one's mind on sth; *falde på ~et ned ad trappen* fall· headfirst down the stairs; *ryste på ~et* shake· one's head; *springe på ~et i vandet* dive headfirst into the water; *stille ngt på ~et* stand· sth on its head, turn sth upside down; *slå det ud af ~et* put· it out of one's mind; *have ~ på (spøg)* have a hangover; **~banegården** *s* the central station; **~bestyrelse** *en* ex'ecutive com'mittee; **~bund** *en* scalp; **~bygning** *en* main building; **~dør** *en* front door; **~fag** *et* major subject; **~formål** *et* chief aim; **~gade** *en* main street; **~indgang** *en* main entrance; **~kontakt** *en (elek)* main switch; **~kontor** *et* head office; **~kulds** *adj* headlong // *adv* headfirst; **~kvarter** *et* headquarters, HQ; **~ledning** *en* main; **~nøgle** *en* master key; **~parten** *s* the greater part; *(de fleste)* the ma'jority; **~person** *en* central figure; **~pine** *en* headache; *have ~pine* have a headache; **~pude** *en* pillow; **~pudebetræk** *et* pillowcase, pillowslip; **~regning** *en* mental a'rithmetic; **~rengøring** *en* spring cleaning; **~rolle** *en* leading part; **~sagelig** *adj* mainly; **~sagen** *s* the main thing;**~spring** *et (ud i vandet)* header; **~stad** *en* capital; **~stads-** metro'politan; **~stød** *et (fodb)* header; **~sæde** *et* head office; **~telefoner** *pl* earphones, headset; **~trappe** *en* front stairs *pl;* **~træk** *s: i ~træk* in outline; **~tørklæde** *et* (head)scarf; **~vej** *en* main road, A-road.

hovere *v: ~ over ngt* gloat over sth; **~nde** *adj* gloating.

hovmester *en (på skib)* steward.

hovmod *et* arrogance; **~ig** *adj* arrogant.

hovne *v: ~ op* swell.

hr.: *~ Smith* Mr Smith.

hud *en* skin; *med ~ og hår* skin and all; *hård ~* callous skin; **~afskrabning** *en* a'brasion; **~farve** *en* colour (of the skin); **~løs** *adj* raw; **~løshed** *en* rawness; **~orm** *en* blackhead; **~pleje** *en* skin care; **~sygdom** *en* skin dis'ease.

hue *en* cap.

hug *et (med fx økse)* stroke; *sidde på ~* squat.

hugge *v (med økse etc)* cut·, chop; *(stjæle)* pinch; *(gribe)* catch·; *~ brænde* chop firewood; *~t sukker* lump sugar; *~ træer* fell trees; *~ ngt af* chop off sth; *~ bremserne i* slam on the brakes; *~ til* strike·; **~blok** *en* chopping block.

hugorm *en* viper.

hugtand *en (om slange)* fang; *(om andre dyr)* tusk.

huje *v* yell.

hukommelse *en* memory *(også edb); efter ~n* from memory; **~s·tab** *et* loss of memory.

hul *et* hole; *(sted hvor der mangler ngt)* gap; *(i fx vandrør)* leak; *stikke ~ i ngt* prick a hole in sth, puncture sth; *det er ~ i hovedet* it is madness; *få lavet ~ler i ørerne* have one's ears pierced; *der gik ~ på posen* there was a hole in the bag; *tage ~ på ngt* open sth; *(gå i gang med fx arbejde)* tackle sth.

hul *adj* hollow; *have en i sin ~e hånd* hold· sby in the hollow of one's hand.

hule *en* cave; *(om dyrs bo, om hybel)* den // *v: ~ ngt ud* hollow out sth; **~maleri** *et* cave painting.

huljern *et* gouge.

hulke *v* sob; **~n** *en* sobbing.

hullemaskine *en* punch.

hullet *adj* full of holes.

hulmur *en* cavity wall.

hulning *en* hollow.

hulrum *et* cavity.

hulske *en* skimmer.

hulspejl *et* con'cave mirror.

hulsøm *en* hemstich.

hulter *adv: ~ til bulter* pell-mell.

human *adj (god ved mennesker)* hu'mane; *(angående mennesker)* 'human.

humaniora *pl* the hu'manities.

humanisme *en* humanism; **humanistisk** *adj* huma'nistic.

himanitær *adj* humani'tarian.

humle *en* hop; **~bi** *en* bumblebee.

hummer *en* lobster // *et (værelse)* den.

humor *en* humour.

humorist *en* humorist; **~isk** *adj* humorous; *han har ~isk sans* he has (got) a sense of humour.

humpe *v* limp.

humpel *en* chunk.

humør *et* mood; *være i godt (,dårligt) ~* be in a good (,bad) mood; *være i ~ til at gøre ngt* be in the mood for doing sth; *op med ~et!* cheer up!

hun *en (om dyr)* female, she; *(om fugl)* hen // *pron* she; *det sagde ~ selv* she said· so her'self.

hund *en* dog; *have ~* keep· a dog; *lufte ~en* walk the dog; *føre en ~ i snor* have a dog on a leash; *slippe ~ene løs* un'leash the dogs; *gå i ~ene* go· to the dogs.

hunde... *sms:* **~angst** *adj* scared stiff; **~galskab** *en* rabies; **~halsbånd** *et* dog-collar; **~hus** *et* doghouse, kennel; **~hvalp** *en* puppy; **~kiks** *en* dog biscuit; **~kold** *adj* freezing cold; **~kulde** *en* freezing cold; **~lort** *en* dog shit, dog mess; **~pension** *en* boarding kennels; **~slæde** *en* dog sleigh; **~spand** *et* team of dogs; **~stejle** *en* stickleback; **~sulten** *adj* famished; **~syg** *adj: føle sig ~syg* feel· lousy; **~syge** *en* dis'temper; **~væddeløb** *et* dog racing, (F) the dogs.

hundrede *num* a hundred; *et ~* one hundred; *fem ~* five hundred; *der var ~r af mennesker* there were hundreds of people; *en ud af ~* one in a hundred; **~del** *en* hundredth.

hundredtusind *s* a hundred thousand; *~er* hundreds of thousands.

hundredvis *adv: i ~ af biler* hundreds of cars; *de kom i ~* they came· by the hundreds.

hundredårsjubilæum *et* cen'tenary.

hundse *v: ~ med en* bully sby.

hungersnød *en* famine.

hunhund *en* she-dog, bitch.

hunkøn *et* female sex; *(gram)* the feminine; *af ~* feminine.

hurra *interj* hur'rah, hur'ray; *(et ~råb)* cheer; *råbe ~ for en* cheer sby; *~ for det!* hurray for that! *det var ikke ngt at råbe ~ for* it was nothing to write home about; **~råb** *et* cheer.

hurtig *adj* quick; *(om bevægelse)* fast // *adv* quickly; *(snart)* soon; *(med stor fart)* fast; *kom så ~t du kan* come· as soon as you can; *så ~t som muligt* as quickly (,soon) as possible; **~løb** *et* sprinting; *(på skøjter)* speed skating; **~løber** *en* sprinter; **~tog** *et* fast train; **~virkende** *adj* quick-acting.

hus *et* house; *(bygning også)* building; *føre ~* keep· house; *holde ~ med ngt* e'conomize on sth; *her i ~et* in this house; *være i ~et (om ung pige)* be a mother's help; *have til ~e et sted* live somewhere; **~arrest** *en* house ar'rest; **~assistent** *en* housemaid, mother's help; **~behov** *et: kunne ngt til ~behov* do sth moderately well; **~bestyrerinde** *en* housekeeper; **~besætter** *en* squatter; **~blas** *en* gelatine; **~båd** *en* houseboat; **~dyr** *et* do'mestic animal.

huse *v* house; **~re** *v (være på spil)* be at work; *(hærge, rase)* ravage.

husgerning *en* housework; *(som skolefag)* do'mestic science.

hushjælp *en* maid; *(til rengøring)* charwoman, daily.

husholderske *en* housekeeper.

husholdning *en (det at føre hus)* housekeeping; *(familie, husstand)* household; **~s·penge** *pl* housekeeping money; **~s·regnskab** *et* household ac'counts; **~s·skole** *en* school of do'mestic science.

husjagt *en: være på ~* be house-hunting.

huske *v* re'member; *husk det nu!* don't for'get·! *~ galt* be mis'taken; *~ godt* have a good memory *hvis ikke jeg ~r meget galt* un'less I'm much mis'taken; *så vidt jeg ~r* as far as I (can) remember; *~ en på*

ngt re'mind sby of sth; **~seddel** *en* note; *(indkøbsliste)* shopping list.
husleje *en* rent; **~nævn** *et* rent tri'bu-nal; **~tilskud** *et* housing benefit.
huslig *adj* do'mestic; *~t arbejde* housework .
husly *et* shelter.
husmand *en* smallholder; **~s·sted** *et* smallholding; *(selve huset)* cottage.
husmor *en* housewife *(pl:* -wives); **~afløser** *en* home help.
husstand *en* household.
hustelefon *en (i firma)* inter-office telephone; *(ved gadedøren)* entry phone.
hustru *en* wife *(pl:* wives); **~bidrag** *et* alimony; **~mishandling, ~vold** *en* wife battering.
husundersøgelse *en* search (of a house).
husvild *adj* homeless.
hvad *pron* what; *~ siger du?* I beg your pardon? (F) what? *~ siger du til det?* what do you think of that? *~ hedder du?* what is your name? *~ hedder det på engelsk* what is it in English; *~ er der?* what is it? *gøre ~ der bliver sagt* do· as one is told; *~ gør det?* what is wrong with that? *~ skulle det være? (i forretning)* can I help you? *~ er det for ngt?* what is that? *~ for ngt?* what? *~ med en drink?* how about a drink? *og ~ så?* so what? *~ dag det skal være* any day.
hval *en* whale; **~fangst** *en* whaling.
hvalp *en* puppy; *få ~e* have pups; **~e·fedt** *et* puppy fat.
hvalros *en* walrus.
hvas *adj* sharp, keen.
hvede *en* wheat; **~brød** *et* white bread; *et ~brød* a white loaf; **~brødsdage** *pl* honeymoon; **~kim** *et* wheat germ; **~klid** *s* bran; **~mel** *et* wheat flour.
hvem *pron* who; *~ er det?* who is it? *~ af jer?* which (one) of you? *~ der bare havde en million!* if only I had a million! *~ som helst kan gøre det* anybody can do it; *~ har du sagt det til?* who did you tell (it to)?
hveps *en* wasp; **~e·rede** *en* wasps' nest; *(fig)* hornet's nest.
hver *pron (~ af alle)* every; *(~ af enkelte, af bestemt antal)* each; *~ dag* every day; *~ anden dag* every other (,second) day; *~ eneste dag* every single day; *~ og én* one and all; *~ for sig* separately; *de fik en cykel ~* they got a bike each; *~t øjeblik (det skal være)* any moment.
hverdag *en* weekday; *om ~en* (on) weekdays; *til ~* usually; **hverdags-** everyday- *(fx tøj* clothes).
hverken *konj: ~ a eller b* neither a nor b; *(efter nægtelse)* either a or b; *han kan ~ synge eller spille* he can neither sing nor play; *jeg har aldrig været ~ i London eller Liverpool* I have never been to either London or Liverpool.
hverv *et* task, as'signment; *blive pålagt et ~* be given an as'signment; *nedlægge sit ~* re'sign; **~e** *v (mil)* re'cruit, en'list; *(om stemmer)* canvass.
hvid *adj* white; *det koster det ~e ud af øjnene* it costs the earth.
hvide *en* (egg-)white; **~varer** *pl (om stoffer)* linen; *hårde ~varer* kitchen hardware.
hvidglødende *adj (af raseri)* livid.
hvidkål *en* cabbage; **~s·hoved** *et* head of cabbage.
hvidløg *et* garlic; **~s·presser** *en* garlic press.
hvidmalet *adj* painted white.
hvidte *v* whitewash.
hvidtning *en* whitewashing.
hvidtøl *en* low-alcohol beer.
hvidvin *en* white wine.
hvil *et* rest; *holde ~* take· a rest; *(fx under biltur)* make· a halt.
hvile *en* rest // *v* rest; *~ sig* rest, take· a rest; *lade ngt ~* let· sth be; *hvil! (mil)* at ease! **~løs** *adj* restless; **~pause** *en* rest, break.
hvilken, *hvilket, hvilke pron* what; *(ud af bestemt antal)* which; *på hvilket tidspunkt?* at what time? *hvilke af disse ting er dine?* which of these things belong to you? *der kom 50 af hvilke en del var udlændinge* 50 people came, some of whom were foreigners; *~ som helst* any.

hvin *et* shriek.
hvine *v* shriek; *(om bremser etc)* screech; *(om kugler)* whistle; **~nde** *adj* shrieking; *(om lyd også)* shrill.
hvirvel *en* whirl; *(lille ~ i vand)* eddy; *(ryg~)* vertebra *(pl:* vertebrae); *(i håret)* tuft; **~dyr** *et* vertebrate; **~storm** *en* tor'nado; **~søjle** *en* spinal column; **~vind** *en* whirlwind.
hvirvle *v* whirl; *~ støv op* raise dust.
hvis *pron* whose; *~ bil er det?* whose car is it? *den mand ~ bil vi har lånt* the man whose car we borrowed // *konj (dersom)* if; *~ bare* if only; *~ ikke* if not.
hviske *v* whisper.
hvisken *en* whisper(ing).
hvisle *v* hiss; *(om vind)* whistle.
hvor *adv (om sted)* where; *(om tid)* when; *(om grad, mængde etc)* how; *~ bor du?* where do you live? *en dag ~ vi har tid* some day when we have (got) time; *~ meget (koster det)?* how much (is it)? *~ er det rart!* how nice! *~ meget vi end arbejder...* no matter how much we work...; *~ kan det være at...?* how it is that...? (F) how come that...? *~ som helst* anywhere.
hvoraf *adv: ~ kommer det at...?* how is it that...? *100 passagerer ~ de 14 er børn* 100 passengers, 14 of whom (,which) are children.
hvordan *adv* how; *~ har du det?* how are you? *~ er han som lærer?* what is he like as a teacher? *~ kunne du gøre det?* how could you do it? *~ kan det være at...?* how is it that...?
hvorefter *adv* after which, whereupon.
hvorfor *adv* why; *~ kom du ikke?* why did you not come? *~ ikke?* why not? *~ det?* why? *~ i al verden?* why on earth?
hvorhen *adv* where; *~ fører denne vej?* where does this road lead.
hvori *adv* wherein, where.
hvorimod *konj* whereas.
hvornår *adv* when.
hvorom *adv: ~ alting er* how'ever that may be; *~ drejer det sig?* what is it about?
hvortil *adv (spørgende)* where ... to? *(dvs. hvor langt?)* how far? *(om formål)* what for? *(relativt)* to which, where; *~ kom vi?* how far did we get? *~ anvendes den?* what is it used for? *huset ~ de kom* the house which they came to.
hvorvidt *konj* whether.
hvælve *v: ~ sig* vault, arch.
hvælving *en* vault, arch.
hvæse *v* hiss.
hvæsen *en* hiss(ing).
hyacint *en* hyacinth.
hyben *et* (rose)hip; **~rose** *en* dog rose.
hybrid *en* 'hybrid.
hygge *en* cosiness, comfort // *v: ~ om en* make· sby feel at home; *~ sig* feel· cosy, have a nice time; **~krog** *en* cosy corner.
hyggelig *adj* cosy, comfortable; *(rar)* nice.
hygiejne *en* hygiene; **~bind** *et* sanitary towel.
hygiejnisk *adj* hy'gienic, sanitary.
hykler *en* hypocrite.
hykleri *et* hy'pocrisy.
hyklerisk *adj* hypo'critical.
hyl *et* howl, yell; *(om sirene)* wail; *(se også hyle)*.
hyld *en (bot)* elder.
hylde *en* shelf *(pl:* shelves); *lægge ngt på ~n* shelve sth; *lægge tobakken på ~n* give· up smoking // *v (med bifald)* ap'plaud; *(med hurraråb)* cheer.
hyldebær *et* elderberry.
hyldest *en* ap'plause, o'vation.
hyle *v* howl, yell; *(klagende)* wail; *blive ~t helt ud af det* get· flustered; *det var ~nde grinagtigt* it was a scream, it was screamingly funny.
hylen *en* howling, yelling; wailing.
hylster *et* case; *(pistol~)* holster.
hymne *en* hymn; *(nationalsang)* anthem.
hynde *en (sidde~)* cushion; *(ryg~)* bolster.
hypnose *en* hyp'nosis.
hypnotisere *v* hypnotize.
hypnotisk *adj* hyp'notic.
hypnotisør *en* hypnotist.
hypokonder *en* hypo'chondriac.

hypokondri *en* hypo'chondria.
hypotese *en* hy'pothesis.
hypotetisk *adj* hypo'thetical.
hyppig *adj* frequent; **~hed** *en* frequency.
hyrde *en (fåre~)* shepherd; **~hund** *en* sheepdog.
hyre *et (arbejde på skib)* job; *(løn for arbejde)* pay; *tage ~* sign on // *v* hire; **~vogn** *en* taxi.
hysse *v* hush.
hysteri *et* hy'sterics; *(begrebet)* hy'steria; **~anfald** *et: få et ~anfald* go· into hy'sterics.
hysterisk *adj* hy'sterical; *blive ~* go· into hy'sterics.
hytte *en* hut; *(lille hus)* cottage; **~fad** *et* well box; **~ost** *en* cottage cheese; **~sko** *en* moccasin.
hyæne *en* hy'ena.
hæder *en* honour; **~lig** *adj* honest; **~lighed** *en* honesty; **~s·gæst** *en* guest of honour; **~s·tegn** *et* medal.
hædre *v* honour.
hæfte *et (lille bog)* booklet; *(til at skrive op i)* notebook; *(stilebog)* exercise book; *(med frimærker, billetter, checks)* book(let); *(fængsel)* prison // *v (sætte fast)* fasten, fix; *(med ~maskine)* staple; *(være ansvarlig)* be re'sponsible; *~ ende (ved syning)* fasten off; *~ ngt sammen* fasten (,staple) sth together; *~ sig ved ngt* notice sth; **~klamme** *en* stapler; **~maskine** *en* stapler; **~plaster** *et* (sticking-)plaster.
hæftet *adj (om bog)* paperbound.
hæge *v: ~ om ngt* look well after sth.
hægte *en* hook; *komme til ~rne* re'cover // *v* hook; *~ ngt af (,op)* un'hook sth.
hæk *en* hedge; *(sport)* hurdle.
hækkeløb *et* hurdles *pl.*
hækkesaks *en:* pair of shears.
hækle *v* crochet; **~nål** *en* crochet hook.
hækling *en* crochet.
hækmotor *en* rear engine.
hæl *en* heel; *i ~ene på en* hard on sby's heels.
hælde *v (om væske, ~ op)* pour; *(skråne)* slope, slant; *(stå skråt, læne sig)* lean; *~ elskeren ud* chuck out one's lover.
hældning *en* slope; *(på tag)* pitch; *(om vejsving)* banking.
hæler *en* re'ceiver (of stolen goods).
hæmme *v (begrænse)* re'strict; *(gøre besværlig)* hamper; **~t** *adj (psyk)* in'hibited; *være ~t af ngt* be hampered by sth.
hæmning *en* re'straint; *(psyk)* inhi'bition; **~s·løs** *adj* unre'strained; *(uden skrupler)* un'scrupulous; **~s·løshed** *en (løssluppenhed)* a'bandon(ment).
hæmorroider *pl* haemorrhoids, piles.
hænde *v* happen.
hændelig *adj* acci'dental; *det er et ~t uheld* accidents 'will happen.
hændelse *en* oc'currence, incident.
hænge *v (uden obj)* hang·; *(med obj)* hang; *blive hængt* get· hanged; *~ fast* stick·, get· stuck; *~ i (dvs. slide)* work hard; *~ (og dingle) i ngt* hang· from sth; *~ vasketøj op* hang (up) the washing; *~ på den* be in for it; *~ sammen* stick· together; *nå, er det sådan det ~r sammen!* so that's how it is! *det ~r sådan sammen at...* the thing is that...; *~ en ud* ex'pose sby; *~ sig* hang oneself; *~ sig i småting* make· a fuss about details; **~bro** *en* su'spension bridge; **~køje** *en* hammock; **~lås** *en* padlock; *sætte ~lås for skabet* padlock the cupboard; **~mappe** *en* su'spension file; **~plante** *en* hanging plant; **~røv** *en (F, om person)* bore, geek; *have ~røv* have a sagging backside; *(om bukser)* be baggy; **~sofa** *en* garden hammock.
hængning *en* hanging.
hængsel *et* hinge.
hær *en* army; *gå ind i ~en* join the army.
hærde *v* harden, toughen; *~t glas* toughened glass.
hærdning *en* hardening, toughening.
hærge *v* ravage; *(om epidemi etc)* rage.
hærskare *en* host.
hærværk *et* vandalism; *begå ~* vandalize.
hæs *adj* hoarse.

hæsblæsende *adj* breathless; *(hurtig)* hurried // *adv* breathlessly, in a hurry.
hæshed *en* hoarseness.
hæslig *adj* ugly.
hætte *en* hood; *(låg)* top.
hævde *v (holde fast ved)* main'tain; *(stædigt)* in'sist (on); *(gøre krav på)* claim; ~ *sig* as'sert oneself; **~lse** *en* as'sertion.
hæve *v (løfte)* raise, lift (up); *(gøre højere)* raise; *(~ i bank)* draw·; *(om check)* cash; *(ophæve)* lift, cancel; *(om møde)* ad'journ; *(blive tykkere, svulme op)* swell; *(om dej)* rise·; ~ *priserne* put· up the prices; *føle sig ~t over ngt* be a'bove sth; *det er ~t over enhver tvivl* it is be'yond doubt; **~kort** *et* cash card; **~lse** *en* swelling.
hævert *en* siphon.
hævn *en* re'venge; *som hævn for ngt* in re'venge for sth; *tage ~ over en* re'venge oneself on sby; **~e** *v* re'venge; *~e sig* get· re'venge; **~gerrig** *adj* vin'dictive; **~gerrighed** *en* vin'dictiveness; **~tørstig** *adj* re-'vengeful.
hø *et* hay; *(fig)* trash; **~feber** *en* hay fever.
høflig *adj* po'lite; **~hed** *en* po'liteness, courtesy ['kə:təsi].
høg *en* hawk *(også fig)*.
høj *en* hill // *adj* high; *(om person og om høj og tynd ting)* tall; *(om lyd)* loud; *bjerget et 1000 m ~t* the mountain is 1000 metres high; *hvor ~ er du?* how tall are you? ~ *hat* top hat; *~e hæle* high heels; ~ *sne* deep snow; *det høje C (mus)* top C; *i en ~ alder* at an ad'vanced age; *(se også højt)*.
højde *en* height; *(niveau)* level; *(geogr, astr, fly)* altitude; *i stor ~* at a great height; *i ~ med taget* on a level with the roof; *han er på ~ med John* he is about the same height as John; *tage ~ for ngt* take· sth into ac'count; *være på ~ med situationen* be equal to the situ'ation; **~drag** *et* ridge, height; **~måler** *en* 'altimeter; **~punkt** *et* height, peak; *på ~punktet af hendes karriere* at the height (,peak) of her ca'reer; **~ryg** *en* ridge; **~spring** *et* high jump.
højere *adj* higher; taller; louder; *(se høj); ~!* louder! speak up!
højest *adj* highest; tallest; loudest.
højesteret *en* su'preme court.
høj... *sms:* **~fjeldssol** *en* sun lamp; **~forræderi** *et* high treason; **~halset** *adj* high-necked; **~hed** *en* highness; *Hans Kongelige Højhed* His Royal Highness; **~hus** *et* high-rise block; **~hælet** *adj* high-heeled; **~kant** *en: stå på ~kant* be on edge; *(fig, om satsning)* be at stake; **~konjunktur** *en* boom; **~land** *et* highland, up-land; **~lydt** *adj* loud // *adv* loudly; **~lys** *adj: ved ~lys dag* in broad daylight.
højre *et (pol)* the Right // *adj* right; *dreje til ~* turn right; *anden gade på ~ hånd* the second street on your right; *på ~ side af ngt* on the right hand side of sth.
højreb *et (gastr) sv.omtr.t.* wing rib, rib roast.
højre... *sms:* **~drejet** *adj (pol)* right-wing; **~kørsel** *en* traffic on the right hand side of the road; **~orienteret** *adj* right-wing; **~styring** *en* right-hand drive.
højrød *adj* scarlet.
højrøstet *adj* loud.
højrøvet *adj* stuck-up.
højskole *en* high school; *(folke~)* folk high school.
højslette *en* 'plateau.
højspænding *en* high voltage.
højst *adv (yderst, uhyre)* most, very, ex'tremely; *(ikke mere end)* at (the) most, not more than; *det er ~ sandsynligt* it is most likely; *det varer ~ 14 dage* it will be a fortnight at the most.
højsæson *en* peak season.
højt *adv* high; *(om grad)* highly; *(om lyd)* loudly; *sige ngt ~* say· sth a'loud; *læse ~* read· a'loud; *~ oppe* high up, far up; *(lystig etc)* in high spirits; *sige ngt ~ og tydeligt* say· sth loud and clear.
højtid *en* festival.

højtidelig *adj* solemn; *tage ngt ~t* take· sth seriously; **~hed** *en* ceremony; *(det at være ~)* so'lemnity.

højtryk *et* high pressure; *arbejde på ~* work flat out.

højtstående *adj* high(-ranking), (F) high-up.

højttaler *en* loudspeaker; **~anlæg** *et* public ad'dress system; *(i lufthavn etc)* Tannoy ®; *høre det i ~anlægget* hear· it over the Tannoy..

højvande *et* high tide; *det er ~ (også)* the tide is in.

høloft *et* hayloft.

hølæs *et* hayload.

høne *en* hen; *(gastr)* chicken; *have en ~ at plukke med en* have a bone to pick with sby; **høns** *pl* chickens.

hønse... *sms:* **~farm** *en* poultry farm; **~hus** *et* hen house; **~kødsuppe** *en* chicken soup; **~ri** *et* poultry farm; **~stige** *en* hen-coop ladder; **~tråd** *en* chicken wire.

hør *en* flax.

høre *v* hear·; *(lytte)* listen *(på* to); *~ dårligt* be hard of hearing; *lad os ~ ad* let· us ask; *~ efter børnene* keep· an ear on the children; *~ efter (hvad der bliver sagt)* listen (to what is said); *~ fra en* hear· from sby; *det ~r med!* that's part of it! *~ om ngt* hear· about sth; *~ til (dvs. være en del af)* be'long to; *(dvs. være en af)* be a'mong, be one of; **~apparat** *et* hearing aid; **~briller** *pl* hearing spectacles; **~sans** *en* sense of hearing; **~spil** *et* radio play; **~vidde** *en: inden (,uden) for ~vidde* within (,out of) earshot; **~værn** *et* hearing pro'tection.

hørfrø *et* linseed.

høring *en* hearing.

hørlig *adj* audible.

hørlærred *et* linen.

hørm *en* stench; **~e** *v* stink·.

høst *en* harvest; *(om udbyttet)* crop.

høstak *en* haystack.

høste *v* harvest; *(om korn)* reap; *(om frugt)* gather; *(fig)* gain, win·.

høstmaskine *en* reaper, harvester.

høtyv *en* hay fork.

høvding *en* chief(tain).

høvl *en* plane; **~e** *v* plane; **~e·bænk** *en* workbench; **~spån** *en* shaving.

håb *et* hope; *gøre sig ~ om ngt* hope for sth; *i ~ om at vejret bliver godt* hoping that the weather will be fine; *i ~ om at gøre karriere* hoping to make a ca'reer; **~e** *v* hope; *jeg ~er ikke de kommer!* I hope they don't come! *det ~er jeg!* I hope so! *det ~er jeg ikke!* I don't hope so! *~ på ngt* hope for sth.

håbløs *adj* hopeless; **~hed** *en* hopelessness.

hån *en* scorn.

hånd *en* hand; *give en ~en* shake· hands with sby; *give en en ~ med* lend· sby a hand; *have ngt for ~en* have sth to hand; *få ngt fra ~en* get· sth off one's hands; *sy (,skrive etc) i ~en* sew· (,write· etc) by hand; *holde en i ~en* hold· sby's hand; *de holder hinanden i ~en* they are holding hands; *gå ~ i ~* go· hand in hand; *få ngt i hænde (dvs. modtage)* re'ceive sth; *(dvs. få tilfældigt fat i)* get· hold of sth; *sidde med hænderne i skødet* sit· back and do· nothing; *på egen ~* single-handed; *lægge sidste ~ på ngt* put· the finishing touches to sth; *gå en til hånde* lend· sby a helping hand; *under ~en* confi'dentially; *have ngt ved ~en* have sth to hand.

hånd... *sms:* **~arbejde** *et (syning etc)* needlework; *skabet er ~arbejde* the cupboard is handmade; **~bagage** *en* hand luggage; *(fly)* carry-on luggage; **~bevægelse** *en* gesture; **~bog** *en* manual; **~bold** *en* handball; **~bremse** *en* handbrake; **~bruser** *en* hand shower; **~fast** *adj* firm; **~flade** *en* palm; **~fuld** *en* handful; **~gribelig** *adj* tangible; **~jern** *pl* handcuffs; **~klæde** *et* towel; **~kraft** *en: ved ~kraft* by hand; **~køb** *et (om medicin): i ~køb* without a pre'scription; **~langer** *en* helper; **~lavet** *adj* handmade; **~led** *et* wrist; **~plukket** *adj* hand-picked; **~skrevet** *adj* handwritten; **~skrift** *en* handwriting; **~s·rækning** *en: give en ~s·rækning* lend· sby a helping hand; **~sving** *et* crank; **~syet** *adj* hand-stitched; **~sæbe** *en* toilet soap; **~tag** *et* handle; **~taske** *en* bag; *(dametaske)* handbag.

håndtere *v* handle.

hånd... *sms:* **~tryk** *et* handshake; **~vask** *en* hand basin, wash basin; *(det at vaske hænder)* washing one's hands; **~værk** *et* craft; **~værker** *en* tradesman *(pl:* -men), craftsman *(pl:* -men).

håne *v* scorn; *(gøre nar af)* mock; *(kritisere voldsomt)* sneer at.

hånlatter *en* scornful laughter.

hånlig *adj* scornful; *med et ~t udtryk* with a sneer.

hår *et* hair; *rede sit ~* comb one's hair; *sætte ~et* do· one's hair; *få ~et ordnet* have one's hair done; *få klippet ~et* have a haircut; *~et rejste sig på hovedet af ham* his hair stood on end; *på et hængende ~* by the skin of one's teeth; **~balsam** *en* (hair) con'ditioner; **~bund** *en* scalp; **~børste** *en* hairbrush; **~bånd** *et* hair ribbon.

hård *adj* hard; *~ hud* callous skin; *~ modstand* strong re'sistance; *med ~ hånd* re'lentlessly; *(se også hårdt);* **~før** *adj* ro'bust; *(om plante)* hardy; **~hed** *en* hardness; **~hudet** *adj (fig)* thick-skinned; **~hændet** *adj* rough; **~knude** *en: gå i ~knude* get· stuck; **~kogt** *adj* hard-boiled *(også fig);* **~nakket** *adj (stædig)* stubborn; *(ihærdig)* per'sistent.

hårdt *adv* hard; *(slemt)* badly; *bremse ~ op* brake hard; *~ såret* badly wounded; *det var ~ for ham* it was hard on him; *slå ~ ned på (fig)* clamp down on.

håret *adj* hairy.

hår... *sms:* **~farve** *en* hair colour; *(middel som farver)* hair dye; **~fjerner** *en* hair re'mover; de'pilatory; **~klemme** *en* hair clip; **~lak** *en* hair spray; **~nål** *en* hairpin; **~nålesving** *et* hairpin bend; **~rejsende** *adj* hair-raising; **~sløjfe** *en* bow; **~spænde** *et* hair clip; *(skydespænde)* hair slide; **~tørrer** *en* hair-drier; **~vask** *en* sham'poo.

I

I *pron* you.

i *præp (om sted)* in; *(om afgrænset sted, punkt, adresse, institution)* at; *(hen til fx skole)* to; *(ind i, ned i, op i etc)* into; *(inde i)* in'side, in; *(om tidsrum)* at; *(i løbet af)* during; *(om varighed)* for; *(om klokkeslet)* to; *(se også de enkelte ord som ~ forbindes med); ~ Danmark* in Denmark; *~ avisen* in the newspaper; *de mødtes ~ skolen* they met at school; *stå af ~ Helsingør* get· off at Elsinore; *gå ~ skole* go· to school; *gå ~ seng* go· to bed; *gå ind ~ kirken* go· into the church; *gå op ~ badet* get· into the bath; *(inde) ~ bilen* in(side) the car; *ligge ~ sengen* be in bed; *~ foråret 1990* in the spring of 1990; *~ julen* at Christmas; *vi fik gjort huset rent ~ (løbet af) julen* we got the house cleaned up during Christmas; *de har boet her ~ fem år* they have been living here for five years; *klokken er fem minutter ~ to* it is five minutes to two; *tre ~ ni er tre* three into nine is three; *trække en ~ håret* pull sby's hair; *trække ~ tøjet* put· on one's things; *~ al fald* at any rate; *slå sig ~ hovedet* bang one's head; *skære sig ~ hånden* cut· one's hand.

iagttage *v (studere)* watch; *(overholde)* ob'serve; *(lægge mærke til)* notice; **~lse** *en* obser'vation.

ibenholt *et* ebony.

iberegnet *adj* in'cluded; *~ moms* in'clusive of VAT; *alt ~* everything in'cluded.

idag *se dag.*

idé *en* i'dea; *få en ~* get· an idea; *en genial ~* a stroke of genius; *der er ingen ~ i at invitere ham* there's no point in asking him; *du gør dig ingen ~ om hvor dum han var!* you can't i'magine how stupid he was!

ideal *et* i'deal // *adj* i'deal.

idealisme *en* i'dealism.

idealist *en* i'dealist.

idealistisk *adj* idea'listic.

ideel *adj* i'deal.
identificere *v* i'dentify.
identisk *adj* i'dentical *(med* with).
identitet *en* i'dentity; **~s·kort** *et* i'dentity card.
ideolog *en* ide'ologist.
ideologi *en* ide'ology.
ideologisk *adj* ideo'logical.
idérig *adj* in'ventive.
idet *konj* as; *vi mødtes ~ vi var på vej ud* we met as we were going out; *han kom ikke ~ han var syg* he did not come as he was ill.
idiot *en* idiot, fool; *din ~!* you fool! *John, den ~, har låst døren* that idiot John has locked the door.
idioti *en* idiocy.
idiotisk *adj* foolish, idi'otic.
idiotsikret *adj* foolproof.
ID-kort *et* i'dentity card.
idol *et* idol.
idræt *en* sports, ath'letics *pl; dyrke ~* go· in for sports; **~s·dag** *en* sports day; **~s·folk** *pl* athletes; **~s·gren** *en* discipline; **~s·hal** *en* sports centre; **~s·plads** *en* sports field.
idyl *en* idyll; **~lisk** *adj* i'dyllic.
idømme *v: ~ en en bøde* fine sby; *~ en fem års fængsel* sentence sby to five years' im'prisonment.
ifølge *præp* ac'cording to; *~ sagens natur* as is natural.
iføre *v: ~ sig ngt* put· sth on; *han var iført mørk habit* he wore· a dark suit.
igangsættelse *en* initi'ation.
igangsætter *en* i'nitiator.
igangværende *adj* ongoing.
igen *adv* a'gain; *(tilbage)* back; *(ofte bruges* re- *foran verbet, fx: læse en bog ~* reread· a book); *sig det ~!* say· that again! *få penge ~* get· money back; *give en ngt ~* give· sth back to sby; *kan du give ~? (om penge)* have you got change?
igennem *adv* through; *dagen (,natten) ~* all day (,night) long; *komme ~ parken* pass through the park.
igle *en* leech.
ignorere *v* ig'nore.
igår *adv* yesterday; *(se også går).*
ihjel *adv* to death; *ved at kede sig ~* bored to death; *slå en ~* kill sby; *blive slået ~* get· killed.
ihærdig *adj (ivrig, flittig)* ener'getic; *(vedholdende, stædig)* per'sistent; **~hed** *en* energy; per'sistence.
ikke *adv* not; *(foran komp. af adj)* no; *det var ~ ham der gjorde det* it was not he who did it, he did not do it; *du er ~ bedre end jeg* you are no better than I; *~ det?* really? *det håber jeg ~!* I hope not! *~ mere* no more; *(dvs. ikke længere)* no longer; *der kom ~ mindre end 20.000 til kampen* no less than 20,000 people watched the match; *her er ~ nogen* there is nobody here; *her er ~ nogen bøger jeg kan lide* there are no books here that I like; *der er ~ noget at se* there is nothing to see; *der var ~ noget øl tilbage* there was no beer left; *det mener du ~!* you don't say so! really! *det gør ~ ngt* it does not matter; *det er dejligt vejr, ~?* it's a lovely day, isn't it?
ikke-angrebspagt *en* 'non-ag'gression pact.
ikkeryger *en* non-smoker.
ikkevold *en* non-violence; **~e·lig** *adj* non-violent.
ild *en* fire; *der gik ~ i hans tøj* his clothes caught· fire; *har du ngt ~?* have you got a light? *have ~ i pejsen* have a fire (on); *sætte ~ til ngt* set· sth on fire; *der er ~ i trappen* the staircase is on fire; *puste til ~en (fig)* add fuel to the flames.
ilde *adv* badly; *føle sig ~ berørt* feel· un'comfortable; *være ~ stedt* be in trouble; *tage ngt ~ op* take· sth badly; **~befindende** *et* indispo'sition; **~brand** *en* fire; **~lugtende** *adj* evil-smelling; **~set** *adj* un'popular; un'welcome; **~varslende** *adj* ominous.
ildfast *adj* fireproof; *(som kan gå i ovnen)* ovenproof.
ildrager *en* poker.
ildrød *adj* burning red.
ildslukker *en* fire ex'tinguisher.
ildsted *et* fireplace.
ile *v* hurry.
ilgods *et* ex'press goods.

illegal *adj* il'legal.
illegitim *adj* ille'gitimate.
illoyal *adj* dis'loyal, un'fair.
illumination *en* illumi'nation.
illuminere *v* il'luminate.
illusion *en* il'lusion; *vi gør os ingen ~er om at vinde* we have no il'lusions about winning.
illusorisk *adj* il'lusory, vain.
illustration *en* illu'stration; **~s·tekst** *en* legend.
illustrator *en* illustrator.
illustrere *v* illustrate.
ilt *en* oxygen; **~e** *v* oxidize.
ilter *adj* fiery, hot.
iltmaske *en* oxygen mask.
image *et* image.
imaginær *adj* i'maginary.
imedens *adv d.s.s. imens.*
imellem *adv/præp* be'tween; *(blandt)* a'mong; *vi mødtes ~ stationen og rådhuset* we met be'tween the station and the town hall; *huset ligger ~ bjergene* the house stands among the mountains; *engang ~* from time to time, sometimes.
imens *adv* in the meantime // *konj* while; *(hvorimod)* where'as.
imidlertid *adv (dvs. dog)* how'ever; *(dvs. i mellemtiden)* in the meantime.
imitation *en* imi'tation.
imitere *v* imitate; **~t** *adj* imi'tation *(fx læder* leather).
immigrant *en* immigrant.
immigrere *v* immigrate.
immun *adj* im'mune *(mod* to, against); **~isere** *v* immunize; **~itet** *en* im'munity.
imod *adv/præp* a'gainst; *(hen ~)* to'wards; *(fig, over for)* to; *(se også de enkelte ord som ~ forbindes med); kæmpe ~ ngt* fight· (against) sth; *sige en ~* contra'dict sby; *~ vinden* against the wind; *køre ~ nord* drive· (towards the) north; *være rar ~ en* be nice to sby; *~ betaling af 50 kr.* on payment of 50 kr; *det er ikke ngt ~ hvad han gjorde* it is nothing com'pared to what he did.
imorgen *adv* to'morrow; *(se også morgen).*
imperativ *et (gram)* the im'perative.
imperfektum *s (gram)* the im'perfect (tense).
imperialisme *en* im'perialism; **imperialist** *en* im'perialist; **imperialistisk** *et* im'perialist.
imperium *et* empire.
impliceret *adj* in'volved.
imponere *v* im'press; *~t over* im'pressed by; **~nde** *adj* im'pressive.
import *en* import; **~afgift** *en* import duty; **~ere** *v* im'port; **~forbud** *et* import ban.
importør *en* im'porter.
impotens *en* impotence; **impotent** *adj* impotent.
impresario *en* impre'sario.
impressionisme *en* im'pressionism; **impressionist** *en* im'pressionist.
improvisation *en* improvi'sation; **improvisere** *v* improvise.
imprægneret *adj (vandtæt)* waterproof; *(brandsikker)* fireproof; *(mølsikret)* mothproof.
impuls *en* impulse; **impulsiv** *adj* im'pulsive.
imødekommende *adj* o'bliging.
ind *adv* in; *(se også de enkelte ~ som ~ forbindes med); ~ ad* in through, in at; *~ i* into; *lad os ikke komme ~ på politik* let's not go into politics. let's not dis'cuss politics; *~ til byen* into town; *~ under* under.
indad *adv* in, inward(s); *døren åbnes ~* the door opens inwards; **~til** *adv (i en person)* inwardly; *(i landet, firmaet etc)* in'ternally; **~vendt** *adj* introvert.
indbagt *adj* in a pastry crust.
indbefatte *v* in'clude; **~t** *adj* in'cluded.
indbegreb *et: han er ~et af en leder* he is the em'bodiment of a leader.
indberetning *en* re'port; **indberette** *v* re'port.
indbetale *v* pay· (in); *~s til bank* to be paid into a bank.
indbetaling *en* payment.
indbilde *v: ~ sig at…* i'magine that…; **indbildning** *en* imagi'nation.
indbildsk *adj* con'ceited; **~hed** *en* con'ceit.

indbildt *adj* i'magined.
indbinding *en* binding.
indblande *v: blive ~t i ngt* get· mixed up in sth; *være ~t* be in'volved.
indblanding *en* inter'vention; *(neds)* inter'ference.
indblik *et: få ~ i ngt* gain an insight into sth.
indbo *et* furniture.
indbringe *v* bring· in; *(indtjene)* fetch; *~ en sag for domstolene* take· a case to court; **~nde** *adj* lucrative.
indbrud *et* burglary; *begå ~ i et hus* burgle a house; **~s·tyv** *en* burglar; **~s·tyveri** *et* burglary, housebreaking.
indbudt *adj* in'vited.
indbyde *v: ~ en til ngt* in'vite (,ask) sby to sth; **~lse** *en* invi'tation; **~nde** *adj* tempting; *(lækker)* appetizing.
indbygger *en* in'habitant *(i* of); **~tal** *et* popu'lation.
indbygget *adj* built-in; *indbygget forældelse* planned obso'lescene.
indbyrdes *adj* mutual, re'ciprocal.
inddele *v* di'vide *(i* into).
inddeling *en* di'vision.
inddrage *v (omfatte, involvere)* in'volve; *(beslaglægge, konfiskere)* confiscate.
inddæmmet *adj* dyked; *~ land (også)* re'claimed land.
inde *adv* in, in'side; *(inden døre)* indoors; *holde sig ~* stay indoors; *holde ~ (dvs. tie)* stop talking; *holde ~ med skydningen* cease fire, stop shooting; *sidde ~ (i fængsel)* be in prison; *sidde ~ med ngt* be in pos'session of sth; be holding sth; *~ i* in'side; *langt ~ i skoven* deep in the wood; *tiden er ~ til at...* it is time to...
indebære *v* im'ply, in'volve.
indefra *adv* from within.
indefryse *v* freeze.
indehaver *en (ejer)* owner, pro'prietor; *(af fx pas)* holder.
indeholde *v* con'tain.
indeklima *et* indoor climate.
indeks *et* index; **~reguleret** *adj* index-linked.
indelukket *adj (om luft etc)* stuffy.
inden *adv/præp* be'fore; *(om tidsfrist)* with'in; *~ for* in'side; *~ i* in'side; *overhale ~ om* over'take· on the inside; *~ under* underneath.
indenad *adv: kunne læse ~* be able to read.
indenbys *adj* local.
indendørs *adj* indoor // *adv* indoors.
indenfor *adv* in'side; *kom ~!* come in!
indeni *adv* in'side.
indenlandsk *adj* do'mestic, inland.
indenom *adv* in'side; *overhale ~* over'take on the inside.
indenrigs... *sms:* **~fly** *et* do'mestic flight; **~ministerium** *et* Ministry of the In'terior; **~politik** *en* do'mestic policy.
indenunder *adv* under'neath.
inder *en* Indian; *han (,hun) er ~* he (,she) is an Indian.
inderbane *en (på flersporet vej)* inside lane.
inderkreds *en* inner circle.
inderlig *adj* deep, heartfelt // *adv* deeply; *jeg er ~ ligeglad* I could not care less.
inderlomme *en* inside pocket.
inderside *en* inside.
inderst *adj* inmost; *~ inde* deep down; *skifte fra ~ til yderst* change from top to toe.
indesluttet *adj* re'served.
indestængt *adj* pent-up *(fx vrede* anger).
indestå *v: ~ for* guaran'tee, vouch for; **~ende** *et (i bank)* de'posit.
indeværende *adj* this, the present; *~ måned* this month.
indfaldsvej *en* ap'proach.
indfaldsvinkel *en* ap'proach.
indfatning *en (på smykke)* setting; *(på briller)* rim; *(om ruder)* frame.
indfatte *v (ædelsten etc)* set·; *(vinduer)* frame.
indfinde *v: ~ sig (om person)* ap'pear, turn up; *(finde sted)* come·.
indflydelse *en* influence *(på* on); **~s·rig** *adj* influ'ential.
indflyvning *en* ap'proach.
indforstået *adj: være ~ med ngt* a'gree to sth; *et ~ blik* a knowing look.

indfri *v* re'deem, meet·.
indfødsret *en* citizenship; *have dansk ~* be a Danish subject; *få ~* become· naturalized.
indfødt *en, adj* native.
indføre *v* intro'duce; *(importere)* im'port; *jeg kunne ikke få et ord indført* I could not get a word in edgeways.
indføring *en* intro'duction *(i* to).
indførsel *en* import.
indgang *en* entrance, entry; *betale ved ~en* pay· at the door; **~s·dør** *en* entrance door.
indgreb *et (indblanding)* inter'ference; *(operation)* ope'ration; *foretage et ~ i ngt* inter'fere with (,in) sth.
indgroet *adj* ingrown; *(fig)* in'veterate *(fx ungkarl* bachelor).
indgå *v: ~ en aftale* make· an a'greement; *~ et forlig* make· a compromise; *~ et væddemål* make· a bet; *~ ægteskab* marry; *det ~r i vores planer* it is part of our plans; **~ende** *adj (grundig)* thorough; *(fx post, tog)* incoming.
indhegne *v* fence (off).
indhegning *en (hegn)* fence; *(det at indhegne)* fencing.
indhente *v* catch· up with; *(skaffe sig)* ob'tain; *~ oplysninger* gather infor'mation; *~ tilbud* in'vite offers, get· quo'tations.
indhold *et* contents *pl; (~ af en enkelt ting i et hele)* content; **~s·fortegnelse** *en* (table of) contents.
indhug *et: gøre ~ i ngt* draw· on sth.
indhylle *v: ~ i* wrap up in.
indianer *en* (Red) Indian.
indicium *et* circum'stantial evidence.
Indien *s* India.
indigneret *adj* in'dignant.
indirekte *adj* indi'rect // *adv* indi'rectly.
indisk *adj* Indian.
individ *et* indi'vidual.
individuel *adj* indi'vidual.
indkalde *v* summon; *(til militæret)* call up; *han er indkaldt (også)* he is doing military service; **~lse** *en* summons; *(mil)* calling up.
indkassere *v* col'lect.
indkast *et (fodb)* throw-in.
indkomst *en* income; **~gruppe** *en* income bracket; **~skat** *en* income tax.
indkvartere *v* ac'comodate, put· up; **indkvartering** *en* accomo'dation.
indkøb *et* purchase; *gøre ~, gå på ~* go· shopping; **~e** *v* buy·, purchase; **~s·net** *et* string bag; **~s·pris** *en* cost price; **~s·taske** *en* shopping bag; **~s·vogn** *en (taske på hjul)* shopping trolley; *(i supermarked)* supermarket trolley.
indkørsel *en* entrance, drive; *~ forbudt* no entry.
indlade *v: ~ sig med en* have to do with sby; *~ sig på ngt* en'gage in sth; *(om ngt risikabelt)* let· one'self in for sth; **~nde** *adj* willing; *(neds)* in'gratiating.
indlagt *adj (om møbel)* inlaid; *være ~ (på sygehus)* be in hospital.
indland *et: i ~et* in'side the country; **~s·fly** *et* do'mestic flight; **~s·is** *en* ice cap.
indlede *v* be'gin·, start (off); **~nde** *adj* intro'ductory; *de ~nde heats* the pre'liminary heats.
indledning *en (start)* be'ginning; *(forord, introduktion)* intro'duction.
indlemme *v* an'nex; **~lse** *en* anne'xation.
indlevere *v* hand in.
indlevering *en* de'livery.
indlysende *adj* obvious.
indlæg *et (tale)* speech; *(i sko)* (arch) sup'port.
indlægge *v* put· in; *(på sygehus)* send· to hospital; *blive indlagt* be ad'mitted to hospital; *~ elektricitet* in'stall elec'tricity; **~lse** *en (på sygehus)* ad'mission.
indløbe *v* ar'rive, come· in.
indløse *v (om check etc)* cash.
indlån *et* de'posit.
indmad *et (i dyr som spises)* offal; *(i fjerkræ)* giblets; *(i ting)* filling, in'sides.
indmeldelse *en* en'rolment, regi'stration; **~s·blanket** *en* regi'stration form.
indordne *v: ~ sig* a'dapt one'self; *~ sig under en* sub'mit to sby.

indpakning *en* wrapping; **~s·papir** *et* wrapping paper.
indprente *v:* ~ *en ngt* im'press sht on sby; ~ *sig ngt* make· a note of sth.
indramme *v* frame.
indramning *en* framing.
indre *et* in'terior // *adj* inner, in'terior; *(indenlandsk)* in'ternal; *den* ~ *by* the centre of town; *det* ~ *marked (EF)* the single market; *det* ~ *Mongoliet* Inner Mon'golia.
indregistrere *v* register.
indregistrering *en* regis'tration.
indrejse *en* entry *(i* into); **~tilladelse** *en* entry permit.
indretning *en* ar'rangement; *(af bolig)* deco'ration; *(dims, mekanisme)* con'traption, gadget; **~s·arkitekt** *en* in'terior decorator.
indrette *v* ar'range; *(om bolig)* decorate, furnish; ~ *sig efter en* a'dapt one'self to sby; ~ *sig på at...* pre'pare to...
indrykke *v:* ~ *en annonce* in'sert an ad'vertisement.
indrømme *v* ad'mit, con'fess; *(give, bevilge)* grant, al'low; **~lse** *en* ad'mission; con'fession; *give ~lser* make· con'cessions.
indsamling *en* col'lection.
indsats *en (som kan sættes ind i ngt)* inset; *(som man yder)* effort; *(i spil)* stake; *gøre en* ~ make· an effort; *med livet som* ~ at the risk of one's life.
indse *v* realize.
indsejling *en (havneløb)* entrance.
indsende *v* send· in, sub'mit.
indsigelse *en: gøre* ~ *mod ngt* ob'ject to sth.
indsigt *en* insight *(i* in).
indskrift *en* in'scription.
indskrive *v (i bog etc)* enter; *(bagage)* register; ~ *sig (på et hotel)* register (at a hotel).
indskrivning *en* entry; *(af bagage og på hotel)* regi'stration.
indskrænke *v (nedsætte, gøre mindre)* re'duce; *(begrænse)* limit; ~ *sig til* con'fine one'self to; **~t** *adj* limited; *(om person)* narrow-minded, stupid; **~t·hed** *en* stu'pidity.
indskrænkning *en (nedsættelse)* re'duction, cut; *(begrænsning)* limi'tation.
indskud *et (i bank)* de'posit; *(ved spil)* stake; **~s·borde** *pl* nest of tables.
indskyde *v (bemærke)* re'mark; *(penge)* pay· in; **~lse** *en* impulse; *få en ~lse* have an i'dea.
indskæring *en* in'cision, cut; *(vig, bugt)* bay.
indslag *et* element; *(tv etc)* feature.
indsmigrende *adj (neds)* fawning, in'gratiating.
indsnit *et (i tøj)* dart.
indsnævring *en* narrowing.
indspille *v (på bånd, plade)* re'cord; *(på film)* pro'duce.
indspilning *en (på bånd, plade)* re'cording; *(på film)* pro'duction.
indsprøjte *v* in'ject.
indsprøjtning *en* in'jection.
indstille *v (til en stilling)* nominate; *(standse)* stop; *(regulere)* ad'just; *(skarphed i kamera etc)* focus; ~ *radioen på en kanal* tune the radio to a channel; ~ *sig på ngt* pre'pare one'self for sth; *være fjendtligt ~t* be hostile; *være venligt ~t* be kind; *være ~t på at gøre det* be pre'pared to do it.
indstilling *en (til stilling)* nomi'nation; *(standsning)* stopping; *(justering)* ad'justment; *(af skarphed i kamera etc)* focusing; *(personlig holdning)* attitude *(til* to'wards).
indsætte *v* in'sert, put· in; *(i embede)* in'stall.
indsø *en* lake.
indtage *v* take· in; *(spise, drikke)* have, eat·, drink·; *(erobre)* take·; *(fylde, tage plads)* take· up, occupy; *(standpunkt)* a'dopt; **~lse** *en (erobring)* taking; **~nde** *adj* charming.
indtagning *en (i strikning, hækling)* de'crease.
indtaste *v (edb)* key in; type in.
indtegne *v* enter, register.
indtegning *en* regi'stration.
indtil *præp/konj* un'til, till; *(om afstand)* as far as, to; ~ *da* until then; ~ *nu* up un'til now; ~ *videre* so far.
indtjening *en* earnings *pl.*

indtryk *et* im'pression; *gøre ~ på en* make· an im'pression on sby, im'press sby.
indtræde *v* set· in; *~ i fællesmarkedet* join the Common Market.
indtræden *en (begyndelse)* com'mencement; *(det at indtræffe)* oc'currence; *~ i fællesmarkedet* entry into the Common Market.
indtræffe *v* oc'cur, take· place.
indtrængende *adj* urgent; *(om hær etc som trænger ind)* in'vading; *~ anmode en om at…* im'plore sby to…
indtægt *en* income; *~er* earnings; *en fast ~* a regular income.
industri *en* industry; **~el** *adj* in'dustrial; **~ferie** *en* annual holiday; **~område** *et* in'dustrial area; **~virksomhed** *en* industry.
indvandre *v* immigrate.
indvandrer *en* immigrant; **~politik** *en* immi'gration policy.
indvandring *en* immi'gration.
indvende *v* ob'ject *(mod* to); *har du ngt at ~?* do you have any ob'jection?
indvendig *adj* in'ternal, inside.
indvending *en* ob'jection *(mod* to, against).
indvi *v* consecrate; *(åbne)* open; *~ en i ngt (dvs. betro)* let· sby in on sth; *(dvs. forklare)* i'nitiate sby in sth; **~else** *en* conse'creation; opening; initi'ation.
indviklet *adj* complicated.
indvillige *v* a'gree *(i* to).
indvirke *v: ~ på* influence.
indvolde *pl* bowels.
indvortes *adj* in'ternal.
indædt *adj* grim; (stædig, bestemt) dogged.
indånde *v* breathe in.
indånding *en* breathing in; *tage en dyb ~* take· a deep breath.
infam *adj (pokkers)* damned.
infanteri *et* infantry.
infektion *en* in'fection; **~s·sygdom** *en* in'fectious dis'ease.
infernalsk *adj* in'fernal.
inficeret *adj* in'fected.
infiltration *en* infil'tration.
infiltrere *v* infiltrate.
infinitiv *en (gram)* the in'finitive.
inflation *en* in'flation.
influenza *en* influ'enza, (F) the flu.
information *en* infor'mation; *~er* infor'mation.
informere *v* in'form *(om at* that).
infrarød *adj* infra-red.
ingefær *en* ginger.
ingen *pron* nobody, no one // *adj* no; *(stående alene og foran* of) none; *der var ~ der kom* nobody came; *der var ~ andre end os* there was no one but us; *han har ~ penge* he has not got any money; *han har to børn, men hun har ~* he has got two children, but she has none; *~ af dem* none of them; *(af* to) neither of them.
ingeniør *en* engi'neer.
ingenmandsland *et* no-man's land.
ingenting *pron* nothing; *det er det rene ~* it is a mere trifle; *lade som ~* be'have as if nothing had happened.
ingrediens *en* in'gredient.
inhabil *adj* biassed, prejudiced; *blive erklæret ~* be con'sidered prejudiced.
inhalere *v* in'hale.
initialer *spl* i'nitials.
initiativ *et* i'nitiative; *tage ~et til at gøre ngt* take· the i'nitiative in doing sth; *han har ~* he has got enterprise; **~gruppe** *en* ginger group; **~rig** *adj* enterprising; **~tager** *en* i'nitiator.
injurie *en (mundtlig)* slander *(mod* of); *(skriftlig)* libel *(mod* against, on); **~sag** *en* action for slander; libel action.
inkarneret *adj* in'veterate.
inkasso *en* (debt) col'lection; **~sag** *en* (debt) re'covery suit.
inkludere *v* in'clude.
inklusive *adv* in'clusive of, in'cluding.
inkompetent *adj* in'competent.
insekt *et* 'insect; **~middel** *et* in'secticide.
insinuere *v* in'sinuate.
insistere *v* in'sist *(på* on, *på at* that).

inspektion *en* in'spection.
inspektør *en* in'spector.
inspicere *v* in'spect.
inspiration *en* inspi'ration.
inspirere *v* in'spire.
installation *en* instal'lation.
installatør *en* elec'trician.
installere *v* in'stall, put· in.
instans *en* instance; *i første* ~ in the first instance; *i sidste* ~ ultimately.
instinkt *et* instinct.
instinktiv *adj* in'stinctive.
institut *et* institute; **~ion** *en* insti'tution.
instruere *v* in'struct; *(teat, film)* di'rect.
instruktion *en* in'structions *pl;* di'rection; **~s·bog** *en* manual.
instruktør *en* in'structor; *(teat, film)* di'rector; *(tv)* pro'ducer.
instrument *et* instrument; **~bræt** *et (i bil)* dashboard.
instrumentere *v* orchestrate.
insulin *et* insulin; **~chok** *et* insulin shock.
intakt *adj* in'tact.
integreret *adj* integrated; *(om byggeri)* purpose-built; *~t kredsløb* integrated circuit.
intellektuel *adj* intel'lectual.
intelligens *en* in'telligence.
intelligent *adj* in'telligent.
intens *adj* in'tense; **~itet** *en* in'tensity.
intensiv *adj* in'tensive.
interessant *adj* interesting.
interesse *en* interest.
interessentskab *et* partnership.
interessere *v* interest; ~ *sig for ngt* be interested in sth, take· an interest in sth.
interiør *et* in'terior.
interimistisk *adj* temporary.
intern *adj* in'ternal.
international *adj* inter'national.
internere *v* in'tern.
internering *en* in'ternment.
interval *et* interval.
intet *pron* nothing // *adj* no; *(stående alene)* non; *han havde ~ at sige* he had nothing to say; ~ *mindre end* no less than; **~anende** *adj* unsu'specting; **~køn** *et (gram)* the neuter; **~sigende** *adj* meaningless; *(uvæsentlig)* insig'nificant.
intim *adj* intimate; **~itet** *en* intimacy.
intolerant *adj* in'tolerant.
intrige *en* in'trigue; *(handling i fx bog)* plot.
introducere *v* intro'duce.
introduktion *en* intro'duction.
intuition *en* intu'ition.
invalid *en* dis'abled person // *adj* dis'abled; **~e·pension** *en (p.g.a. fysisk handicap)* dis'ablement pension; *(p.g.a. sygdom)* inva'lidity pension; **~itet** *en* dis'ablement.
invasion *en* in'vasion.
inventar *et* furniture; *et stykke* ~ a fixture; *han er fast ~ her* he's part of the furniture.
investere *v* in'vest.
investering *en* in'vestment.
invitation *en* invi'tation.
invitere *v* in'vite, (F) ask; ~ *en indenfor* in'vite (,ask) sby in; ~ *en til middag* in'vite (,ask) sby to dinner; ~ *en på en kop te* offer sby a cup of tea.
involvere *v* in'volve; *blive ~t* get mixed up in sth.
involvering *en* in'volvement.
ir *en* verdigris.
Irak *s* I'raq; **iraker** *en,* **irakisk** *adj* I'raqi.
Iran *s* I'ran; **iraner** *en,* **iransk** *adj* I'ranian.
irer *en* Irishman; *han er* ~ he is an Irishman; *hun er* ~ she is Irish; *~ne* the Irish.
irettesættelse *en* reprimand.
Irland *s* Ireland.
ironi *en* irony.
ironisk *adj* i'ronical.
irrelevant *adj* ir'relevant.
irritabel *adj* irritable, edgy.
irritation *en* an'noyance, irri'tation.
irritere *v* an'noy, irritate; *~t over* annoyed by; *~t på* an'noyed with; **~nde** *adj* an'noying, irritating.
irsk *adj* Irish.
is *en* ice; *(til at spise også)* ice cream; **~afkølet** *adj* chilled, iced; **~bjerg** *et* iceberg; **~bjørn** *en* polar bear; **~blomster** *pl* frost patterns; **~bryder** *en* icebreaker.

iscenesætte *v* stage; **~lse** *en* pro'duction, staging; *(film)* di'rection.
isenkram *et* hardware.
isenkræmmer *en* ironmonger.
isflage *en* ice floe.
isglat *adj* icy.
Ishav *et: Det Nordlige ~* the Arctic Ocean; *Det Sydlige ~* the Antarctic Ocean.
iskage *en* ice cream.
iskias *en* sci'atica.
iskiosk *en* ice-cream booth.
iskold *adj* icy.
Islam *s* Is'lam.
islamisk *adj* Is'lamic.
Island *s* Iceland; **islandsk** *adj* Ice'landic.
islænder *en* Icelander; *(sweater)* Iceland sweater.
isnende *adj* icy.
isolation *en (ensomhed)* iso'lation; *(elek etc)* insu'lation; **~s·fængsel** *et* solitary con'finement.
isolere *v (afsondre)* isolate; *(elek etc)* insulate.
ispind *en* ice lolly.
Israel *s* Israel; **israeler** *en,* **israelsk** *adj* Isra'eli.
isse *en* top.
isslag *et* black ice.
istandsætte *v* re'pair; *(om lejlighed etc ofte)* re'decorate; **~lse** *en* re'pair; redeco'ration.
istap *en* icicle.
isterning *en* ice cube.
istid *en* Ice Age.
isvaffel *en* ice-cream cone; *(sprød kage)* wafer.
især *adv* e'specially; *hver ~* each.
Italien *s* Italy; **italiener** *en,* **italiensk** *adj* I'talian.
itu *adj/adv* broken, to pieces; *gå ~* go· to pieces; *slå ngt ~* break· sth.
iver *en* zeal, eagerness.
ivrig *adj* keen, eager; *~ efter at* keen to.
iværksætte *v* start.
iværksætter *en* i'nitiator.
iøjnefaldende *adj* striking.
ørefaldende *adj* catchy.

J

ja *interj* yes; *(~ vist)* certainly; *~, det tror jeg nok* yes, I think so; *sige ~ til ngt* ac'cept sth; *~, jeg ved ikke rigtig* well, I don't know.
jade *en* jade.
jag *et (hast)* hurry, rush; *(smerte)* twinge; *et værre ~* a terrible rush.
jage *v (haste)* hurry, rush; *(gå på jagt)* hunt, shoot·; *(forfølge)* chase; *~ en væk* chase sby away; *det ~r ikke* there is no hurry; *~ en nål i en* jab a needle into sby; *~ en på flugt* put· sby to flight.
jager *en (fly)* fighter; *(skib)* de'stroyer.
jagt *en* hunting, shooting; *(forfølgelse)* hunt, pur'suit *(på* of); *gå på ~* go· hunting *(efter* for); *~en på materielle goder* the pur'suit of ma'terial goods; **~e** *v* chase; **~gevær** *et* hunting rifle; **~hund** *en* pointer, re'triever; *(til rævejagt)* hound; **~hytte** *en* shooting lodge; **~ret** *en* shooting rights *pl;* **~tegn** *et* shooting licence.
jaguar *en* 'jaguar.
Jakel: *mester ~teater* Punch and Judy show.
jakke *en* jacket, coat; **~lomme** *en* coat pocket; **~sæt** *et* suit.
jalousi *en (følelse)* jealousy; *(til vindue)* (Ve'netian) blind; *(~dør i skab etc)* roll front.
jaloux *adj* jealous *(på* of).
jamen *interj: ~ er det dig!* well, if it is not you! *~ hør nu!* well, listen now! *~ så er det en aftale!* that's a deal then!
jammer *en (ynk)* misery; *(klagen)* moaning; **~lig** *adj* wretched, miserable; *(ynkelig)* pa'thetic.
jamre *v* moan, wail.
janitshar *en (mus)* per'cussionist.
januar *v* January; *den første ~* January the first, the first of January.
Japan *s* Ja'pan.
japaner *en,* **japansk** *adj* Japa'nese.
jas: *gamle ~* old boy.
jaske *v* be sloppy (in one's work); **~t** *adj* sloppy.

jasmin *en* 'jasmine.
jaså *interj* in'deed! I see!
javel *interj* yes! *(mil etc)* yes sir! *(mar)* aye-aye sir!
jeg *et* self, ego; *mit bedre* ~ my better self // *pron* I; ~ *så det selv* I saw· it my'self; *ja, det tror 'jeg!* I should· think so.
jer *pron* you; *(refleksivt)* your'selves; *jeg henter* ~ I'll pick you up; *morer I* ~*?* are you en'joying yourselves? *er han en ven af* ~*?* is he a friend of yours? *pas* ~ *selv!* mind your own business!
jeres *pron* your; *(stående alene)* yours; ~ *hus* your house; *huset er* ~ the house is yours.
jern *et* iron; *gammelt* ~ scrap iron; *være et* ~ *til ngt* be a wizard at sth; *smede mens* ~*et er varmt* strike· while the iron is hot.
jernalder *en: den ældre (,yngre)* ~ the early (,later) Iron Age; **~fund** *et* Iron-Age find.
jernbane *en* railway; *sende ngt med* ~*n* send· sth by railway; *(se også sms med tog-);* **~fløjl** *et* corduroy; **~færge** *en* train ferry; **~knudepunkt** *et* railway junction; **~linje** *en* railway line; **~overskæring** *en* level crossing; **~skinne** *en* rail; **~station** *en* railway station.
jern... *sms:* **~beton** *en* rein'forced concrete; **~malm** *en* iron ore; **~stang** *en* iron bar; **~støberi** *et* iron foundry; **~tæppe** *et (teat)* safety curtain; ~*tæppet (pol)* the Iron Curtain; **~værk** *s: et* ~*værk* an ironworks.
jetfly *et* jet plane.
jetjager *en* jet fighter.
jetmotor *en* jet engine.
jo *adv (som svar)* yes; *(forklarende)* you know; ~ *før* ~ *bedre* the sooner the better; *han er* ~ *min mand* he is my husband, you know; *du kan* ~ *ikke lide ham* you don't like him, do you?
job *et* job; *søge* ~ be looking for a job; *miste* ~*bet* lose· one's job; **~skabelse** *en* job cre'ation; **~søgning** *en* jobsearch.
jockey *en* 'jockey.
jod *en* iodine; *rød* ~ mer'curochrome.
jodle *v* yodel.
jogge *v* jog.
joggingdragt *en* track suit.
jogurt *en* yoghurt.
jokke *v (gå tungt)* tramp; *(træde på)* trample; ~ *en over tæerne* step on sby's feet; ~ *i spinaten* put· one's foot in it.
jolle *en* dinghy.
jomfru *en* virgin; *Jomfruen (astr)* Virgo; **~dom** *en* vir'ginity.
jomfruelig *adj* virgin.
jomfruhummer *en* Norway lobster.
jomfrunalsk *adj* old-maidish.
jomfrurejse *en* maiden voyage.
jonglere *v* juggle *(med* with).
jonglør *en* juggler.
jord *en (kloden, muld, elek)* earth; *(*~*overflade)* ground; *(*~*bund)* soil; *(*~*ejendom)* land; *her på Jorden* here on Earth; *lægge ngt på* ~*en* put· sth on the ground; *købe et stykke* ~ buy· a piece of land; *han ejer vidtstrakte* ~*er* he owns ex'tensive lands; *dyrke* ~*en* cultivate the land; *rejse Jorden rundt* travel round the world; *falde til* ~*en* fall· to the ground; *gå under* ~*en* go· underground; **~brug** *et* farming, agriculture; **~bund** *en* soil; **~bunden** *adj (negativt)* earthbound; *(positivt)* down-to-earth; **~bær** *et* strawberry.
jorde *v (begrave)* bury; *(slå ud, nedgøre): vi* ~*de dem* (F) we walked all over them.
jordejendom *en* land, landed property.
jordemor *en* midwife *(pl:* -wives); **~kaffe** *en* strong black coffee.
jordforbinde *v (elek)* earth; **~lse** *en* earth con'nection; *have* ~*lse (om person)* be down-to-earth; *miste* ~*lsen* lose· contact with re'ality.
jordisk *adj* earthly, worldly; *ikke have en* ~ *chance* not have an earthly (chance).
jord... *sms:* **~klode** *en* globe; **~ledning** *en (elek)* earth con'nection; *(kabel)* underground wire; **~nær** *adj* down-

to-earth; **~nød** *adj* peanut; **~nøddesmør** *et* peanut butter; **~- og betonarbejder** *en* navvy; **~skred** *et* landslide *(også fig);* **~skælv** *et* earthquake; **~slået** *adj* mouldy; **~stængel** *en* root-stock; **~varme** *en* geo'thermal heat.

journal *en* record; *(syge~)* medical record; *føre ~ over ngt* keep· a record of sth.

journalist *en* journalist, re'porter.

jovial *adj* jovial, jolly.

jubel *en (glædesråb)* cheers *pl; (begejstring)* en'thusiasm; *(munterhed)* hi'larity; *vække ~* arouse cheers.

jubilar *en* person celebrating an anni'versary.

jubilæum *et* jubilee, anni'versary; *50-års ~* fiftieth anniversary; *100-års ~* cen'tenary.

juble *v* cheer, shout with joy; *(grine)* roar with laughter.

jugoslav *en* Yougoslav; **Jugoslavien** *s* Yugo'slavia; **jugoslavisk** *adj* Yugoslav.

juks *et* trash.

jul *en* Christmas; *glædelig ~!* merry Christmas! *i ~en* at Christmas; *få ngt til ~* get· sth for Christmas.

jule *v* make Christmas prepa'rations; **~aften** *en* Christmas Eve; *lille ~aften* the 23rd of December; **~dag** *en: (første) ~dag* Christmas Day; *anden ~dag* Boxing Day; **~ferie** *en* Christmas holidays; **~frokost** *en (i firma etc)* Christmas party for the staff; *(i privathjem ~dag)* lunch on Christmas Day; **~gave** *en* Christmas present; **~kalender** *en* Advent Calendar; **~kort** *et* Christmas card; **~manden** *s* Father Christmas; **~pynt** *en* Christmas deco'rations *pl;* **~salat** *en (bot)* chicory; **~stjerne** *en (bot)* poin'settia; **~træ** *et* Christmas tree.

juli *en* Ju'ly; *den første ~* the first of July, July the first.

jumper *en* jumper.

jungle *en* jungle.

juni *en* June; *den femte ~* the fifth of June, June the fifth.

junta *en* junta.

jura *en* law, juris'prudence; *studere ~* read· (,study) law.

juridisk *adj* legal; *~ bistand* legal ad'vice; *~ kandidat* graduate in law; *~ rådgiver* legal ad'viser.

jurist *en* lawyer.

jury *en* jury; **~medlem** *et* juror.

justere *v (finindstille)* ad'just; *få ~t bremserne* have one's brakes ad'justed.

justits *en: holde ~* keep· discipline; **~ministerium** *et* Ministry of Justice; **~mord** *et* ju'dicial murder.

juvel *en* jewel; *(ædelsten)* gem.

juvelér *en (person)* jeweller; *(forretning)* jeweller's (shop).

jyde *en* Jutlander.

Jylland *s* Jutland.

jysk *adj* Jut'land(ic).

jæger *en* hunter; *(sports~)* sportsman *(pl:* -men); *(herregårdsskytte)* gamekeeper; **~korps** *et (mil)* com'mando troops *pl.*

jætte *en* giant; **~stue** *en* passage grave.

jævn *adj (plan)* even, level; *(glat)* smooth; *(om bevægelse, fart)* steady, even; *(nogenlunde)* moderate; *(ikke særlig god)* medi'ocre; *i ~t trav* at a steady trot; *almindelig ~ kost* plain food; *klare sig ~t (godt)* do· moderately (well); **~aldrende** *adj* of the same age; **~byrdig** *adj* equal; *en ~byrdig kamp* an even match; **~døgn** *et* equinox.

jævne *v* level, smooth; *(om sovs)* thicken; *blive ~t med jorden* be levelled with the ground.

jævnføre *v* com'pare.

jævning *en (gastr)* thickening, starch.

jævnlig *adj* frequent // *adv* frequently, often.

jævnstrøm *en* direct current.

jøde *en (mandlig)* Jew; *hun er ~* she is Jewish; **~dommen** *s* Jewry; **~forfølgelse** *en* anti-semitism, perse'cution of the Jews.

jødisk *adj* Jewish.

K

kabale *en* patience (game); *lægge ~* play patience.

kabaret *en* 'cabaret.
kabel *et* cable; **~-tv** *et* cable TV.
kabine *en (mar, fly)* cabin; **~scooter** *en* bubble car.
kabinet *et* 'cabinet.
kabliau *en* cod.
kadet *en* (naval) ca'det; *(færdiguddannet)* midshipman *(pl:* -men).
kafé *en* 'café.
kaffe *en* coffee; *en kop* ~ a cup of coffee; **~bar** *en* café; **~bønne** *en* coffee bean; **~filter** *et* coffee filter; **~fløde** *en* cream (with minimum 13% fat); **~grums** *et* coffee grounds *pl;* **~kande** *en* coffee pot; **~kop** *en* coffee cup; **~maskine** *en* coffee maker, percolator.
kage *en* cake; *(konditor~)* fancy cake; *(små~)* biscuit; *(lag af fx mudder)* cake; *mele sin egen* ~ feather one's nest; **~dåse** *en* biscuit tin; **~form** *en* baking tin; **~kone** *en* gingerbread woman; **~rulle** *en* rolling pin; **~spore** *en* pastry wheel; **~tallerken** *en* tea plate.
kagle *v* cackle.
kahyt *en* cabin; **~s·jomfru** *en* stewardess.
kaj *en* quay; *lægge til ved ~en* come· a'longside the quay.
kajak *en* kayak.
kajplads *en* moorage; *(for lystsejler)* (quay) berth.
kakadue *en* cacka'too.
kakao *en* cocoa; **~mælk** *en* drinking chocolate.
kakerlak *en* cockroach.
kaki *en* khaki.
kakkel *en* tile; **~bord** *et* tile-top table; **~ovn** *en* stove; *tænde op (,fyre) i ~ovnen* light the fire.
kaktus *en* cactus *(pl:* cacti).
kald *et (råb)* call; *(indre trang)* vo'cation; *(præste~)* living.
kalde *v* call; ~ *på en* call sby; *han blev kaldt John efter sin far* he was called John after his father; ~ *læge* call a doctor; *føle sig ~t til at gøre ngt* feel· called upon to do sth; *det ~r jeg held!* that's what I call luck! **~nummer** *et* dialling code
kaleche *en* hood.
kalender *en* calendar; **~år** *et* calendar year.
kaliber *en (om våben)* calibre, bore.
kalium *s (kem)* po'tassium.
kalk *en (jordarten)* lime; *(kem)* calcium; *(hvidte~)* whitewash; *(pudse~)* plaster; **~brud** *et* limestone quarry.
kalke *v (hvidte)* whitewash.
kalkere *v* trace.
kalkerpapir *et* carbon paper *(gennemsigtigt)* trading paper.
kalkgrube *en* lime pit.
kalkmaleri *et* wall painting, fresco.
kalktablet *en* calcium tablet.
kalkulation *en* calcu'lation.
kalkulere *v* calculate.
kalkun *en* turkey; *stegt* ~ roast turkey.
kalorie *en* calorie; *tomme ~r* junk food; **~fattig, ~let** *adj* low-calorie, (F) low-cal.
kalot *en (jødisk)* skullcap.
kalv *en* calf *(pl:* calves); *(om kødet)* veal; **~e·knæet** *adj* knock-kneed; **~e·kotelet** *en* veal cutlet; **~e·kød** *et* veal; **~e·lever** *en* calf's liver; **~e·skind** *et* calfskin; **~e·steg** *en* roast veal.
kam *en* comb; *(på bølge)* crest; *(gastr, fx svine~)* loin, back; *skære alle over én* ~ lump everybody together.
kamel *en* camel; **~uld** *en* camel hair.
kamera *et* camera.
kamfer *en* camphor.
kamgarn *et* worsted ['wustid].
kamille *en* camomile; **~te** *en* camomile tea.
kamin *en* fireplace; **~hylde** *en* mantelpiece; **~gitter** *et* fender.
kammer *et (værelse)* room; *(hjerte~, grav~, pol)* chamber.
kammerat *en* friend; (F) buddy, chum; *~ Jeltsin (pol)* Comrade Yeltsin; **~lig** *adj* friendly, chummy; **~skab** *et* comradeship.
kammermusik *en* chamber music.
kammertjener *en* valet.
kammertonen *s* the concert pitch.
kamp *en* fight, struggle *(om* for); *(mil)* combat, action; *(sport)* match, game; *han har aldrig været i* ~ he's

never seen battle; *tage ~en op* give· battle; *en ~ på liv og død* a fight to the death.

kampagne *en* cam'paign.

kampesten *en* (granite) boulder.

kamp... *sms:* **~fly** *et* fighter; **~dommer** *en (tennis)* umpire; **~leder** *en (i boksning)* refe'ree; **~skrift** *et* broadsheet; **~valg** *et* con'tested e'lection; **~vogn** *en* tank.

kanal *en (kunstig)* ca'nal; *(naturlig, tv og fig)* channel; *Kanalen (geogr)* the Channel; **~rundfart** *en* tour of the ca'nals; *tage på ~rundfart* (S, *tv)* graze; **~tunnelen** *s* the Channel tunnel; *(spøg)* the Chunnel; **~vælger** *en (tv)* channel selector.

kanariefugl *en* ca'nary.

kande *en* can, jug; *(kaffe~, te~)* pot.

kandidat *en* candidate; *(som har bestået eksamen)* graduate.

kandis *en* candy.

kandiseret *adj* candied.

kane *en* sleigh, sledge; *køre i ~* go· sleighing, sleigh; *hoppe i ~n (fig)* hit· the sack.

kanel *en* cinnamon; *stødt ~* powdered cinnamon; *det er hverken skidt el. ~* it is neither here nor there.

kanin *en* rabbit; **~foder** *et (iron, om råkost)* rabbit feed.

kannibal *en* cannibal.

kano *en* ca'noe; *ro i ~* go· ca'noeing.

'kanon *en (mus)* round // **ka'non** *en* gun; *som skudt ud af en ~* like a shot; *han er en stor ~ (fig)* he is a big shot.

kanonade *en* canno'nade, barrage.

kanonfuld *adj* dead drunk, stoned.

kanonkugle *en* cannon ball.

kanonslag *et* ma'roon.

kant *en* edge, border; *(på glas, kop etc)* rim; *(på stof)* selvage; *(egn)* region; *falde ud over ~en* fall· over the edge; *i alle ender og ~er* inside (and) out, from top to bottom; *komme på ~ med en* fall· out with sby; *de kom fra alle ~er* they came· from all over the place; *jeg er født på de ~er* I was born in those parts; *der må være en ~!* there must be a limit!

kantarel *en (bot)* chante'relle.

kante *v* edge, border; *~ sig* edge; *~ sig ind* get· in edgeways; **~bånd** *et* edging.

kantet *adj* edged; *(fig)* awkward.

kantine *en* can'teen, staff restaurant.

kantsten *en* kerb.

kanyle *en* hypo'dermic needle.

kaos *et* chaos.

kaotisk *adj* cha'otic.

kap *et (forbjerg)* cape, headland; *Kap Det Gode Håb* the Cape (of Good Hope); *løbe (, køre) om ~* race *(med en* sby).

kapacitet *en* ca'pacity; *han er en ~ på sit område* he is an expert within is field.

kapel *et* chapel; *(lig~)* mortuary; *(orkester)* orchestra.

kapellan *en* curate.

kapelmester *en* con'ductor.

kapers *pl* capers.

kapital *en* capital; **~anbringelse** *en* in'vestment; **~flugt** *en* capital flight.

kapitalisme *en* capitalism.

kapitalist *en* capitalist; **~isk** *adj* capitalist, *adj* capitalist.

kapitalstærk *adj* fi'nancially strong.

kapitel *et* chapter; *det er et ~ for sig* that's a story all in it'self.

kapitulation *en* capitu'lation.

kapitulere *v* ca'pitulate, sur'render.

kapløb *et* race.

kappe *en* cloak, mantle; *(dommer~ etc)* gown; *(til hovedet)* cap; *(gardin~)* pelmet // *v* cut·.

kappes *v: ~ om ngt* com'pete for sth.

kappestrid *en* compe'tition.

kapre *v* capture, get· hold of; (F) pinch; *han har ~t min plads* he has pinched my seat; *~ et fly* hijack a plane.

kaprifoleum *en (bot)* honeysuckle.

kaproning *en* boat race; **~s·båd** *en* racing boat.

kapsejlads *en* re'gatta.

kapsel *en* capsule; *(til flaske)* top, cap; **~åbner** *en* bottle opener.

kaptajn *en* captain.

kar *et* vessel; *(stort)* vat; *(bade~)* tub.

karaffel *en* ca'rafe; *(med prop)* de'canter.

karakter *en* character; *(i skolen etc)* mark; **~bog** *en* school re'port; **~egenskab** *en* characte'ristic; **~fast** *edj* firm, de'termined.
karakterisere *v* characterize.
karakteristisk *adj* characte'ristic *(for* of).
karakterstyrke *en* strength of character, (F) guts.
karamel *en* caramel; *(fx fløde~)* toffee; **~rand** *en* caramel pudding; **~sovs** *en* caramel sauce.
karantæne *en* quarantine; *(sport) fodboldspilleren fik seks ugers* ~ the football player was banned for six weeks.
karat *en* carat.
karate *en* ka'rate.
karavane *en* caravan.
karbad *et* bath; *(om karret)* bathtub.
karbonade *en (gastr)* meat rissole.
karbonpapir *et* carbon paper.
karburator *en (auto)* carburettor.
kardanaksel *en (auto)* pro'peller shaft.
kardemomme *en* cardamom.
karet *en* coach.
karikatur *en* caricature.
karklud *en* dishcloth, dishrag.
karl *en (på gård)* farmhand; *(fyr)* chap, bloke; *han tror han er en farlig* ~ he thinks he is one hell of a man.
Karlsvognen *s (astr)* the Great Bear.
karm *en* frame; *(vindues~ hvor man stiller planter etc)* windowsill.
karneval *et* carnival; *(mindre, indendørs)* fancydress ball; **~s·dragt** *en* fancydress.
karotte *en* baby carrot.
karré *en* block of flats.
karriere *en* ca'reer; *gøre* ~ make a career for oneself; **~ræs** *et* ca'reerism.
karrosseri *et* bodywork.
karrusel *en* merry-go-round.
karry *en* curry; *boller i* ~ meat balls in curry sauce; *høns i* ~ curried chicken.
karse *en* cress; **~hår** *et* crewcut.
kartoffel *en* po'tato; *han er en heldig* ~ he's a lucky devil; *franske kartofler* potato crisps; *bagt* ~ (oven)-baked potato; *en varm* ~ *(også fig)* a hot potato; **~mel** *et* po'tato starch; **~mos** *en* mashed po'tatoes, (F) mash; **~salat** *en* po'tato salad; **~skræl** *en* po'tato peel; **~skræller** *en (om kniv)* po'tato peeler.
karton *en (materialet)* cardboard; *(emballage)* cardboard box; *en* ~ *cigaretter* a carton of ciga'rettes.
kartotek *et* card index, file; **~s·kort** *et* index card.
kaserne *en* barracks *pl.*
kasket *en* cap.
kaskoforsikring *en* third party fire and theft in'surance.
kasse *en* box, case; *(pak~)* packing case; *(i forretning)* cash desk; *den film gav* ~ that film was a box office hit; *give en et par på ~n* bash sby on the head; **~apparat** *et* cash register; **~bon** *en* sales slip; **~dame** *en* ca'shier; **~kredit** *en* cash credit.
kassere *v (smide væk)* throw· away, chuck out; *(ved session)* re'ject.
kasserer *en* ca'shier; *(i forening)* treasurer.
kasserolle *en* saucepan.
kassette *en* cas'sette; **~bånd** *et* cas'sette tape; **~båndoptager** *en* cas'sette (tape) re'corder.
kassevogn *en (auto)* box van.
kast *et* toss, throw; *(vindstød)* gust; *give sig i* ~ *med ngt* tackle sth.
kastanje *en* chestnut; **~brun** *adj* chestnut.
kaste *v* throw·; *(voldsomt)* fling·; ~ *med sten* throw· stones *(efter* at); ~ *op* be sick, vomit; ~ *sig om halsen på en* throw· one's arms around sby's neck; ~ *et blik på ngt* throw· a glance at sth; ~ *sig over en* throw oneself on sby; *de ~de sig over de billige hatte* they pounced on the cheap hats; ~ *sig ud i ngt* plunge into sth; **~spyd** *et* javelin; **~vind** *en* gust (of wind).
kastrere *v* castrate.
kasus *et (gram)* case.
kat *en* cat; *han gør ikke en* ~ *fortræd* he wouldn't hurt a fly; *her er ikke en* ~ there is not a soul here; *det*

var ~tens! well, I'll be damned! *av for ~ten!* ouch! *gå som ~ten om den varme grød* beat· around the bush; *købe ~ten i sækken* buy· a pig in a poke.

katalog *et* catalogue, list *(over* of).

katalogisere *v* catalogue, list.

katalysator *en* catalyst.

katar *en* ca'tarrh.

katastrofal *adj* di'sastrous, cata'strophic.

katastrofe *en* ca'tastrophe, di'saster; **~alarm** *en* e'mergency a'larm; **~område** *et* di'saster area.

kateder *et (i skole)* teacher's desk.

katedral *en* ca'thedral.

kategori *en* category.

kategorisk *adj* cate'gorical; *~ benægtelse* flat re'fusal; *nægte ~ at...* absolutely re'fuse to...

katolik *en* Roman Catholic.

katolsk *adj* Catholic.

katte... *sms:* **~grus** *et* cat litter; **~killing** *en* kitten; **~musik** *en* cats' concert; **~pine** *en: være i en slem ~pine* be in a fix; **~øje** *et (på cykel)* re'flector.

kaution *en* guaran'tee, se'curity; *(jur)* bail; *løsladt mod ~* (re'leased) on bail; *stille ~* put· up bail.

kautionere *v* guaran'tee, sign for.

kautionist *en* guarantor.

kavaleri *et* cavalry.

kavalkade *en* caval'cade.

kaviar *en* caviar.

ked *adj: være ~ af ngt (dvs. træt af)* be tired of sth; *(dvs. bedrøvet over)* be sorry about sth; *være ~ af det* be un'happy, be sad; *jeg er ~ af at måtte sige det* I'm sorry to have to say it; *være led og ~ af en* be fed up with sby; *er du ~ af at flytte dig lidt?* would you mind moving over? *han er rigtignok ikke ~ af det!* he's got a nerve!

kede *v* bore; *~ sig (ihjel)* be bored (stiff, to death); *~ sig over ngt* be bored by sth.

kedel *en* kettle; *sætte kedlen over* put· the kettle on; **~dragt** *en* boiler suit.

kedelig *adj* boring; *(trættende)* tiresome, tedious; *(trist)* dreary; *(ærgerlig)* an'noying; *(pinlig)* awkward; *det var ~t at du ikke kom* what a pity that you didn't come.

kedelsten *en* fur, scale.

kedsomhed *en* boredom.

kegle *en (mat)* cone; *(i spil)* (nine)pin, skittle; *et spil ~r* a game of skittles; *tage ~r (fig)* make· a hit; **~bane** *en* skittle alley; **~formet** *adj* conical.

kejser *en* emperor; **~dømme** *et* empire; **~inde** *en* empress; **~snit** *et* cae'sarian.

kejtet *adj* clumsy, awkward.

kejthåndet *adj* left-handed.

keltisk *adj* Celtic.

kemi *en* chemistry.

kemikalie *et* chemical.

kemiker *en* chemist.

kemisk *adj* chemical; *~ rensning* drycleaning; *~ krigsførelse* chemical warfare.

kemoterapi *en (med)* chemo'therapy.

kende *en (smule, anelse)* trifle, bit; *give sig til ~* dis'close one's i'dentity; *(om følelser, sygdom etc)* show· it'self // *v* know·; *(genkende)* recognize; *~r du John?* do you know John? *kan du ~ ham igen?* do you recognize him? *jeg kan ~ ham på skægget* I know (,recognize) him by his beard; *~ den ene tvilling fra den anden* tell· one twin from the other; *~ til ngt* know about sth; *han blev kendt skyldig* he was found· guilty.

kendelse *en (jur)* de'cision; *(nævninge~)* verdict.

kendeord *et (gram)* article.

kender *en (om fx mad, vin)* 'connoisseur.

kendetegn *et* characte'ristic; **~e** *v* be characte'ristic of.

kendingsbogstav *et (auto)* regi'stration letter.

kendingsmelodi *en* signature tune.

kendsgerning *en* fact.

kendskab *en* knowledge *(til* of).

kendt *adj (berømt)* well-known, famous; *(velbekendt)* fa'miliar; *han blev en ~ mand* he be'came· famous; *han er ~ fra fjernsynet* he is known from television; *hun er ~ med alle* she knows everybody; *jeg er ikke ~*

her på stedet I am a stranger here.
kennel *s: en* ~ a kennels *(NB!* a kennel: *et hundehus).*
keramik *en* pottery; *(tekn)* ce'ramics *pl.*
keramiker *en* potter; ce'ramic artist.
kerne *en (i nød)* kernel; *(i æble etc)* pip; *(i korn)* grain; *(fig)* core, seed; *sagens* ~ the heart of the matter; *den hårde* ~ the hard core; **~familie** *en* nuclear family; **~fysik** *en* nuclear physics; **~hus** *et* core; **~kraft** *en* nuclear power; **~sund** *adj* as sound as a bell; **~våben** *et* nuclear weapon; *(se også atom...).*
ketchup *en* ketchup.
ketsjer *en (sport)* racket; *(til fiskeri)* landing net.
KFUK *(fork.f. Kristelig Forening for unge Kvinder)* YWCA *(fork.f.* Young Women's Christian Asso-ci'ation).
KFUM *(fork.f. Kristelig Forening for unge Mænd)* YMCA *(fork.f.* Young Men's Christian Associ'ation).
kid *et* kid.
kidnappe *v* kidnap.
kig *et* peep; *få* ~ *på ngt* catch· sight of sth; *have* ~ *på ngt (dvs. være ude efter)* be after sth.
kigge *v* look, glance, peep; ~ *ind ad nøglehullet* peep through the keyhole; *vi ~de lige inden for hos dem* we just looked in on them.
kighoste *en* whooping cough.
kighul *et* peephole.
kikke *v d.s.s. kigge.*
kikkert *en (lang)* telescope; *(mindre, tøjet)* bi'noculars *pl,* field glasses *pl; (teater~)* opera glasses *pl; have ngt i ~en* have one's eye on sth.
kiks *en* biscuit, cracker; *(fejlskud etc)* miss.
kikse *v* miss *(fx et mål* a goal); **~r** *en* miss.
kilde *en* spring; *(også fig)* source // *v* tickle.
kilden *adj* ticklish; *(penibel)* delicate.
kildeskat *en* Pay-As-You-Earn tax (PAYE).
kildevand *et* spring water.
kile *en* wedge; *(i tøj)* gusset; **~hæl** *en* wedged heel.
killing *en* kitten.
kilo(gram) *et* kilogram(me).
kilometer *en* kilometre; *han kørte 120 ~ i timen* he went at 120 kilometres per hour; **~tæller** *en sv.t.* mileage indicator.
kim *et* germ, seed.
kime *v* ring·; *(om kirkeklokke)* peal; **kimen** *en* ringing; peal.
kimplante *en* seedling.
kimse *v:* ~ *ad* sniff at.
Kina *s* China.
kinakål *en* Chi'nese cabbage.
kind *en* cheek; **~ben** *et* cheekbone; **~e·rødt** *s* blusher; **~skæg** *et* whiskers *pl;* **~tand** *en* molar.
kineser *en* Chi'nese; *(om fyrværkeri)* firecracker; *du store ~!* Great Scott! **~tråd** *en* button thread.
kinesisk *adj* Chi'nese.
kinin *en (med)* quinine.
kiosk *en* kiosk; *(blad~)* newsstand.
kirke *en* church; *(katolsk, frikirke)* chapel; *gå i* ~ go· to church (,chapel); **~bog** *en* parish register; **~bøsse** *en* offertory box; **~gænger** *en* church-goer; **~gård** *en (ved kirken)* churchyard; *(større, ikke ved kirken)* cemetary; **~klokke** *en* church bell; **~lig** *adj* church; **~ministerium** *et* Ministry of Ecclesi'astical Af'fairs; **~musik** *en* church music; **~skib** *et (bygn)* nave; **~stol** *en* pew; **~tid** *en* service time; **~tjener** *en sv.t.* sexton; **~tårn** *et* church tower; **~værge** *en* churchwarden.
kiropraktor *en* osteopath.
kirsebær *et* cherry; **~likør** *en* cherry brandy.
kirtel *en* gland; *hævede kirtler* swollen glands; **~syge** *en* glandular dis'ease.
kirurg *en* surgeon.
kirurgi *en* surgery.
kirurgisk *adj* surgical.
kisel *en* silicon.
kissejag *et* rush.
kissemisseri *et (kys og kram i krogene)* hanky-panky.
kiste *en* chest; *(lig~)* coffin; **~bund** *en: have penge på ~bunden* have put money by; **~glad** *adj* as pleased as Punch.

kit *en* putty // *et* kit; **~te** *v* putty.
kittel *en (dame~)* smock; *(arbejds~)* overall; *(læge~)* coat.
kiv *en* quarrel; *yppe ~* pick a quarrel; **~es** *v* quarrel.
kjole *en* dress, frock; *(lang)* gown; *(herre~)* dress coat; *lang ~* evening gown; *~ og hvidt* tails, evening dress; **~stof** *et* dress ma'terial, fabric; **~syning** *en* dressmaking; **~sæt** *et* dress suit.
kjortel *en* tunic.
kladde *en* draft; **~hæfte** *et* notebook.
klage *en (anke)* com'plaint; *(jamren)* wailing, la'ment; *indsende en ~ over en* lodge a com'plaint about sby // *v* com'plain; *(jamre)* wail, moan; *~ over ngt* com'plain about sth; *~ sig* wail; *(af smerte)* groan, moan; **~ret** *en (jur)* a Danish court of ap'peal; **~skrivelse** *en* written com'plaint; **~skrig** *et* wail, moan.
klam *adj* cold and damp; *han er en ~ fyr* (F) he is yukky; *en ~ fidus* a damp squib.
klamme *en* bracket.
klammeri *et* quarrel.
klamphugger *en* bungler; **klamphuggeri** *et* bungling.
klamre *v: ~ sig til* cling· to.
klang *en* sound, ring; **~fuld** *adj* sonorous; **~løs** *adj* toneless, dull; *(om stemme)* flat.
klap *en* flap; *(i hjertet etc)* valve; *(for øjet)* patch; *der gik en ~ ned for mig (,ham, hende etc)* I (,he, she etc) had a mental block // *et (på kinden etc)* pat; *give en et ~ på skulderen* give· sby a pat on his (,her) shoulder; *det har du ikke et ~ forstand på* you don't know the first thing about it; **~bord** *et* folding table.
klappe *v* clap; *(bifalde)* ap'plaud; *(på kinden)* pat; *(gå godt)* go· smoothly; *~ ad en* ap'plaud sby; *~ i hænderne* clap one's hands; ap'plaud; *~ i* shut· up; *~ sammen (dvs. folde sammen)* fold up.
klappen *en (bifald)* ap'plause.
klapperslange *en* rattlesnake.
klapre *v* rattle, clatter; *(om tænder)* chatter.
klaps *et* slap.
klapsalve *en* round of ap'plause.
klapstol *en* folding chair.
klapsæde *et (i bil)* folding seat.
klaptræ *et (film)* clapperboard.
klapvogn *en* pushchair.
klar *adj* clear; *(lys)* bright; *(tydelig)* plain, evident; *(parat)* ready; *blive ~ over* realize; *være ~ over* be a'ware of; *gøre sig ngt ~t* realize sth; *gøre sig ~* get· ready; *det er ~t at han lyver* he is evidently lying; *sige ngt ~t og tydeligt* spell sth out.
klare *v (ordne, overkomme)* manage, cope with; *han ~r sig godt* he is doing well; *~ op (om vejret)* clear up; *~ skærene* pull through, make· it; *~ sig* manage, cope; *kan du ~ dig med 50 kr?* can you manage with 50 kr? *~ sig ud af en knibe* get· out of a fix; *~ sig uden ngt* do· with'out sth.
klarhed *en* clarity; *(om lys)* brightness; *komme til ~ over ngt* get· sth in the clear.
klarinet *en* clari'net; *spille ~* play the clarinet.
klase *en* bunch; *en ~ vindruer* a bunch of grapes.
klask *et* slap, smack; **~e** *v* slap, smack.
klasse *en* class; *(højere skoleklasse)* form; *rejse på første ~* travel first-class; *første ~s kvalitet* first-rate quality; **~kammerat** *en* classmate; **~kamp** *en* class struggle; **~værelse** *et* classroom.
klassificere *v* classify.
klassiker *en* classic.
klassisk *adj* classic(al).
klat *en (klump)* lump; *(plet)* stain, blot; *(smule)* handful; *en ~ smør* a knob of butter; **~maleri** *et* daubing; **~papir** *et* blotting paper.
klatre *v* climb; *~ ned ad ngt* climb down sth; *~ op ad et bjerg* climb a mountain; *~ op i et træ* climb a tree; *~ over en mur* climb a wall; **~plante** *en* climber.
klatte *v* blot, stain; *~ sine penge væk* fritter away one's money; squander one's money.

klatvask *en: ordne (,vaske) ~en* wash one's smalls.
klatøjet *adj* bleary-eyed.
klaver *et* pi'ano; *spille ~* play the pi'ano; **~stemmer** *en* pi'ano tuner.
klejnsmed *en* locksmith.
klem *et: give en et ~* give· sby a hug; *med fynd og ~* ener'getically; *døren stod på ~* the door was a'jar.
klemme *en (knibe)* tight spot, fix; *(tøj~)* clothes peg; *(hår~)* hair clip; *(stykke mad) sv.t.* sandwich; *få foden i ~ i døren* get one's foot caught· in the door; *have en ~ på en* have a hold on sby // *v* squeeze; *(om sko)* pinch; *(få i ~)* get· caught, jam; *~ på en pakke* squeeze a package; *~ på med ngt* work away at sth; *klem bare på!* just get on with it!
klemte *v* peal, clang.
kleptoman *en* klepto'maniac.
kliché *en (til trykning)* block; *(frase etc)* cliché.
klid *et* bran.
klient *en* client.
klientel *et* clientèle.
klik *et* click, snap; *slå ~* fail; *(om pistol etc)* mis'fire.
klike *en* clique, set.
klikke *v (om lyd)* click; *(slå fejl)* fail; *(om pistol etc)* mis'fire.
klima *et* climate; **~anlæg** *et* air-conditioning.
klimaks *et* climax.
klimpre *v: ~ på* strum, twang.
klinge *en* blade; *gå en på ~n* press sby hard // *v* sound, ring·; **~nde** *adj* sonorous *(fx stemme* voice).
klinik *en* clinic; *(mindre sygehus)* nursing home; **~assistent, ~dame** *en (hos tandlæge)* as'sistant; *(hos læge)* re'ceptionist.
klinisk *adj* clinical.
klink *en: han ejer ikke en ~* he hasn't got a penny to his name; *spille ~* play pitch and toss.
klinke *en (på dør)* latch; *(flise)* clinker // *v (reparere)* rivet; *(skåle)* touch glasses; *jeg skal ikke have ngt ~t* I'd rather stay out of it.
klint *en* cliff.
klip *et* cut; *(på billet)* punch; *der er fire ~ tilbage på billetten* the ticket can be used four times more; **~fisk** *en* dried cod; **~ning** *en* cutting, clipping; *(om hår)* haircut.
klippe *en* rock // *v* cut·, clip; *(om billet)* punch; *få håret ~t* have a haircut; *~ ens hår* cut· sby's hair; *~ negle* cut· one's nails; **~blok** *en* rock, boulder; **~kort** *et* punch ticket; **~væg** *en* rock wall; **~ø** *en* rocky island.
klirre *v* rattle; *(med nøgler, mønter)* jingle; *(med glas)* clink; *(om ruder)* rattle.
klister *et* paste; **~mærke** *et* sticker.
klistre *v* paste; *(hænge fast)* stick·; *~ sig op ad en* cling· to sby; **~t** *adj* sticky.
klit *en* dune.
klo *en* claw; *(skrift)* scrawl; *slå en ~ i ngt* grab sth; *forsvare sig med næb og kløer* de'fend oneself tooth and nail.
kloak *en* sewer; **~afløb** *et* drain.
kloakering *en* sewerage.
klode *en* globe; *~n rundt* all over the globe.
klodrian *en* bungler.
klods *en* block; *(legetøj)* toy brick; *(om person)* big lump, bungler; *købe ngt på ~* (F) buy· sth on tick.
klodset *adj* clumsy.
klodsmajor *en* clumsy fool.
klog *adj* clever, in'telligent; *(forsigtig)* prudent; *(fornuftig)* wise, sound; *(snedig)* shrewd; *blive ~ på ngt* make· sth out; *gøre ~t i at* be wise to; *er du rigtig ~?* are you out of your mind? *han er ikke rigtig ~* he is not quite right in the head; *vi er stadig lige ~e* we are no wiser for that; *gå til en ~ kone (,mand)* see· a healer; *(neds)* see· a quack; **~skab** *en* cleverness, in'telligence; prudence; wisdom, soundness; shrewdness.
klokke *en* bell; *de kom ~n syv* they ar'rived at seven; *~n er ni nu* it is nine o'clock now; *hvad er ~n?* what's the time? *ringe med (,på) ~n* ring the bell; *han ved hvad ~n er*

slået he knows· what the score is // *v:* ~ *i det* bungle; **~r** *en* bellringer; **~slag** *et* stroke of a bell; **~slæt** *et: på ~slæt* on the stroke; **~spil** *et* carillon; **~tårn** *et* belfry.

klor *en* chlorine; **~vand** *et* chlorine water.

klos *adv:* ~ *op ad ngt* close to sth.

kloster *et (munke~)* monastery; *(nonne~)* convent; *gå i ~ (om mand)* become· a monk; *(om kvinde)* take· the veil; **~kirke** *en* abbey; **~skole** *en* convent school.

klov *en* hoof *(pl:* hoofs *el.* hooves).

klovn *en* clown; *(klodrian)* bungler.

klub *en* club.

klud *en* rag; *(vaske~ etc)* cloth; *~e* (F, *om tøj)* things, rags; *sætte liv i ~ene* liven things up.

kludder *et* mess, muddle; (F) balls-up.

kludedukke *en* rag doll.

kludetæppe *et* rag rug.

kludre *v* bungle, mess up; ~ *med ngt* bungle sth; ~ *i det* mess things up.

klukke *v (om høne)* cluck; *(le)* chuckle; *(om bæk etc)* gurgle.

kluklatter *en* chuckle.

klump *en* lump; *der er ~er i sovsen* the sauce is lumpy; *få en ~ i halsen* get· a lump in one's throat; **~e** *v* clot; *~e sig sammen (om personer)* mass to'gether; **~et** *adj* lumpy; **~fod** *en* club foot.

klunker *pl* tassels; (V!) balls.

kluns *et* gear, things *pl.*

kluntet *adj* clumsy.

klynge *en* cluster; *(menneske~)* group // *v:* ~ *sig til en* cling· to sby.

klynke *v* whimper, cry·; **~ri** *et* whining.

klæbe *v* stick·, cling·; *malingen ~r* the paint sticks; ~ *plakater op* stick· up posters; **~bånd** *et,* **~strimmel** *en* ad'hesive tape.

klæbrig *adj* sticky.

klæde *et* cloth; *~r pl* clothes // *v* dress, clothe; *(passe til)* suit; ~ *(sig) af* un'dress; ~ *(sig) på* dress; ~ *sig om* change; ~ *om til middag* dress for dinner; *klædt ud som klovn* dressed up as a clown; *dårligt klædt* badly dressed; *pænt klædt* well-dressed; *klædt i hvidt* dressed in white; ~ *en af til skindet* strip sby naked; *(fig)* fleece sby; *rødt ~r dig* red suits you; **~bøjle** *en* coat-hanger; **~børste** *en* clothes brush; **~dragt** *en* clothing.

klædning *en* clothing; **~s·stykke** *et* garment.

klæg *adj (om brød etc)* pasty; *(om jord)* sticky.

klækkelig *adj: en ~ sum penge* a handsome sum of money.

klø *pl* beating; *en ordentlig gang ~* a sound beating // *v (uden obj)* itch; *(med obj)* scratch; *(slå, tæve)* beat·; *det ~r i fingrene på mig efter at...* my fingers are itching to...; *min næse ~r* my nose is itching (,tickles); ~ *sig i nakken* scratch one's neck.

kløe *en* itch(ing).

kløft *en* cleft; *(i klippe)* ra'vine, cre'vasse; *(i hagen)* dimple; *(fig)* gap; *der er en ~ imellem dem* there is a gap between them.

klør *en (i kort)* clubs *pl; en ~* a club; ~ *dame* queen of clubs.

kløve *v* split; ~ *brænde* chop wood.

kløver *en* clover; **~bladsudfletning** *en* cloverleaf *(pl:* -leaves).

km *(fork.f. kilometer): han kørte 100 km/t* he went at 100 km/h (kilometres per hour).

knage *en* peg // *v* creak.

knageme *adv: han er ~ ikke rigtig klog* he is jolly mad; *den er ~ god* it is jolly good.

knald *et* bang; *(om skud)* crack; *(om prop)* pop; *(abegilde)* beano; (V! *samleje)* screw; *han har ~ i låget* he has got bats in the belfry; *det var ~ el. fald* it was touch-and-go.

knalde *v* bang; crack; *(slå i stykker)* smash; *(gå i stykker)* break·; (V! *have samleje)* screw, have it off; *hun ~ede ham en lussing* she socked him one; *~e døren i* slam the door; *~e røret på (tlf)* slam down the re'ceiver.

knaldhætte *en* cap.

knaldroman *en* thriller.

knaldrød *adj* bright red.
knallert *en (køretøj)* moped; *(fyrværkeri)* cracker; **~fører** *en* moped driver.
knap *en* button; *(på radio etc)* knob; *trykke på ~pen* press the button; *tælle på ~perne* be in two minds.
knap *adj/adv* scarce, scanty; *(næppe)* hardly, scarcely; *(kun lige)* barely; *han var ~ inde før...* he was barely in'side when...; *vi kender ham ~ nok* we hardly know· him; *i ~t et år* for almost a year; *det varer ~ ti minutter* it will be about ten minutes.
knaphul *et* buttonhole.
knappe *v* button (up); *~pe op* un'button; **~nål** *en* pin.
knase *v (uden obj)* crackle; *(med obj)* crunch; *~nde sprød* crunchy, crisp.
knast *en* knot.
knastør *adj* bone-dry.
kneb *et (fif)* trick; *alle ~ gælder* it is a free-for-all.
kneben *adj* scarce, narrow; *her er ~ plads* it is cramped here; *vinde med et ~t flertal* win· by a narrow ma'jority.
kneble *v* gag.
knebre *v (om stork)* clatter; *(snakke)* prattle, blether.
knejpe *en* joint.
knejse *v (rage op)* tower; *(kro sig)* strut; *(holde hovedet højt)* hold· one's head high.
knibe *en* fix, tight spot; *være i ~* be in a tight spot (,fix) // *v* pinch; *(klemme)* squeeze; *nu ~r det vist for ham* he is in trouble now; *det ~r for ham at nå det* he has trouble making it; *~ sig i armen* pinch one's arm; *~ munden sammen* tighten one's lips; *~ øjnene sammen* screw up one's eyes; *det ~r med smør* we are short of butter.
knibtang *s: en ~* a pair of pincers.
kniple *v* make· lace.
knipling *en* lace.
knippel *en (politi~)* truncheon.
knippel- jolly, thumping *(fx god* good).
knipse *v* flick; *(om fx guitarstreng)* pluck; *(foto)* snap; *~ med fingrene* snap one's fingers.
knirke *v* creak; *deres ægteskab ~r* they are having trouble in their marriage.
knitre *v (om ild etc)* crackle; *(om papir etc)* rustle.
kniv *en* knife *(pl:* knives); *der er krig på ~en mellem dem* they are at daggers drawn; *stikke en ned med ~* knife sby; **~s·blad** *et* knife blade; **~skarp** *adj* razor-sharp; **~spids** *en* knife point; *(som mål)* pinch; **~stik** *et* stab; **~stikkeri** *et* knifing.
kno *en* knuckle.
knob *en/et* knot.
knofedt *et* elbow grease.
knogle *en* bone; **~brud** *et* bone fracture; **~marv** *en* bone marrow; **~skørhed** *en (med)* brittle-bone dis'ease.
knojern *et* knuckle-duster.
knokle *v* slave away.
knold *en* clod; *(høj)* knoll; *(hoved)* nob; *(bot)* bulb.
knop *en* knob; *(bot)* bud; *(bums etc)* pimple, spot; *han giver mig røde ~per* he makes me come out in spots; *skyde ~per* bud; **~skydning** *en* budding.
knotten *adj* grumpy.
knubs *pl* blows *(også fig).*
knude *en* knot; *(svulst etc)* lump, tumour; *(frisure)* bun; *slå ~ på en snor* tie a knot in a string; *løse en ~ (op)* untie a knot; *gøre ~r* make· trouble; **~punkt** *et* junction.
knudret *adj* knotty, gnarled; *(indviklet, uklar)* intricate.
knuge *v* squeeze, press; *(omfavne)* hug; *(tynge)* op'press; *føle sig ~t* feel op'pressed.
knurhår *pl* whiskers.
knus *et: give en et ~* give· sby a hug; **~e** *v* break·, smash; *(omfavne)* hug; *det ~te hans hjerte* it broke his heart; **~ende** *adj: han tog det med en ~ende ro* he did not turn a hair; *et ~ende nederlag* a shattering de'feat.
knyst *en* bunion.
knytnæve *en* fist.

knytte *v* tie· *(sammen* up); *være ~t til en* be at'tached to sby; *et ~t tæppe* a knotted carpet; *~ en forbindelse* e'stablish a con'nection.

knæ *et* knee; *falde på ~* go· down on one's knees; *ligge på ~* be on one's knees, be kneeling; *stå i vand til ~ene* be knee-deep in water; **~beskytter** *en* kneepad; **~bukser** *pl* breeches; **~bøjning** *en* knee bend, (H) genu'flection.

knægt *en* boy, lad; *(i kort)* jack; *hjerter ~* jack of hearts.

knæhase *en* hollow of the knee.

knæk *et* crack; *(på rør etc)* bend; *(ombøjning)* fold; *der lød et ~* there was a crack; *han fik et ~* he had a blow; **~brød** *et* crispbread.

knække *v* break·, crack; *(med et smæld)* snap; *~ nødder* crack nuts; *~ midt over* break· in two; *~ sammen af grin* double up laughing; *~ sig* (F) be sick.

knækort *adj* knee-length.

knæle *v* kneel· *(for en* to sby).

knæ... *sms:* **~skade** *en (akut)* knee injury; *(længerevarende, ældre)* bad knee; **~skal** *en* kneecap; **~strømpe** *en* knee sock.

ko *en* cow; *der er ingen ~ på isen* there is no danger.

koagulere *v* co'agulate.

koalition *en* coa'lition.

kobber *et* copper; **~stik** *et* copperplate; *(om billedet)* print.

koble *v* couple; *~ ngt sammen* couple sth; *~ fra* discon'nect; *~ til* con'nect; *~ af (fig)* re'lax.

kobling *en* coupling; *(auto)* clutch; *slippe ~en* re'lease the clutch; *træde på ~en* de'press the clutch.

koboltblå *adj* cobalt(blue).

kode *en* code; **~lås** *en* combi'nation lock; **~ord** *et* code word.

kodriver *en (bot)* primrose.

kofanger *en (auto)* bumper.

koffein *en* caffeine; **~fri** *adj* de'caffeinated.

kog *s: komme i ~* come· to the boil; *holde i ~* keep· boiling.

koge *v* boil; *(lave mad)* cook; *kedlen ~r* the kettle is boiling; *~ suppe* make· a soup; *lade ngt ~ op* parboil sth; *~ over* boil over; **~bog** *en* cookery book; **~grejer** *pl* cooking u'tensils; **~kunst** *en* cooking, cui'sine; **~plade** *en* (e'lectric) cooker; **~pose** *en: ris i ~pose* boil-in-the-bag rice; **~punkt** *et* boiling point; **~sektion** *en* hob; **~ægte** *adj: dugen er ~ægte* the cloth may be boiled; **~ø** *s* central (cooking) island.

kogle *en* cone.

kogning *en* boiling; *(madlavning)* cooking.

kogsalt *et* cooking salt.

kok *en* cook; *(køkkenchef)* chef.

kokain *en* co'caine, (F) snow.

kokasse *en* cow-pat, cow dropping.

koket *adj* flir'tatious; **~tere** *v* flirt; *~tere med ngt* play upon sth; **~teri** *et* flir'tation.

kokkepige *en* cook.

kokos... *sms:* **~mel** *et* desiccated coconut; **~måtte** *en* coconut mat; **~nød** *en* coconut; **~palme** *en* coconut palm.

koks *pl* coke; *der er gået ~ i det* (F) it has gone haywire; **~e** *v* (F) go· bunkers; *~e i det* bungle; **~grå** *adj* charcoal (grey).

kolbe *en* flask; *(på gevær)* butt; *(majs~)* cob.

kolbøtte *en* somersault; *slå en ~* (do· a) somersault.

kold *adj* cold; *slå ~t vand i blodet* keep· one's head; *vise en den ~e skulder* give· sby the cold shoulder; *det ~e bord* smorgasbord; **~blodig** *adj* cool, com'posed; **~blodighed** *en* cool, com'posure; **~brand** *en* gangrene.

kolibri *en* humming bird.

kolik *en* colic.

kollega *en* colleague.

kollegium *et (studenterbolig)* hall of residence.

kollektion *en (mode~)* col'lection *(vare~)* as'sortment.

kollektiv *et* commune // *adj* col'lective; *~ aftale* col'lective a'greement; *~ trafik* public transport; **~hus** *et* commune.

kollidere *v* col'lide.

kollision *en* col'lision.
kolon *et* colon.
koloni *en* colony.
kolonialhandel *en* grocer's shop.
kolonihave *en* al'lotment.
kolonisere *v* colonize.
kolonne *en* column; *(arbejds~)* gang.
kolos *en* co'lossus.
kolossal *adj* e'normous; **~t** *adv: ~t stor* e'normously big.
kombination *en* combi'nation; **~s·lås** *en* combi'nation lock.
kombinere *v* com'bine.
komedie *en* comedy, play; *(halløj)* row; *(forstillelse)* play-acting; **~spil** *et* play-acting.
komet *en* comet; **~agtig** *adj: en ~agtig karriere* a mete'oric ca'reer.
komfortabel *adj* comfortable.
komfur *et* cooker, kitchen range; *elektrisk ~* e'lectric cooker; *gas~* gas cooker; *bord~* hob.
komik *en* comedy, comic; *kan du se ~ken?* do you see· the joke? **~er** *en* co'median.
komisk *adj* comic(al), funny.
komité *en* com'mittee; *sidde i en ~* be on a com'mittee.
komma *et* comma; *(i tal)* point; *5,75* five point seven five (NB! *skrives på eng:* 5.75); *i løbet af nul ~ fem* in no time.
kommandere *v* com'mand; *~ med en* order sby around.
kommanditselskab *et* limited partnership.
kommando *en* com'mand; *gøre ngt på ~* do· sth on command; *have ~en over* be in command of; **~bro** *en (mar)* bridge; **~tropper** *pl* com'mando troops; **~vej** *en: gå ~vejen* go· through the proper channels.
kommandør *en* com'mander.
komme *et* ap'proach, coming // *v* come·; *(ankomme)* ar'rive; *(om bevægelse, rejse, følelse)* get·; *(putte)* put·; *(hælde)* pour; *kom nu!* come on! *vi ~r nu!* (we are) coming! *han ~r kl. 5* he is coming (,ar'riving) at 5; *de kom for sent* they were (too) late; *~ sig (dvs. blive bedre)* im'prove; *(dvs. blive rask)* re'cover *(af* from); *hvordan ~r man til lufthavnen?* how do you get to the airport? *~ sukker i teen* put· sugar in the tea; *~ mælk i koppen* pour milk into the cup; *det ~ af at...* it is because...; *det ~r an på dig* it de'pends on you, it is up to you; *han kom efter bilen* he came for the car; *~ frem (dvs. ~ videre)* get· on; *(nå frem)* get· through; *(blive afsløret)* be re'vealed; *han kom hen til mig* he came up to me; *(dvs. hen i mit hus)* he came round to my place; *~ igen* come· back, re'turn; *~ ind* get· in; *~ ind i* enter; *~ ind på en sag* touch on a matter; *må jeg ~ med?* may· I come along too? *de kom med vinen* they brought· the wine; *hun kom med en undskyldning* she came up with an excuse; *~ sammen* meet·, get together; *hun ~r sammen med en fyr* she is going steady with a bloke; *kan du ~ til?* can you manage? *~ til at gøre ngt* do· sth by accident (,mis'take); *det ~r du til at lave om* you will have to do that again; *lad nu mig ~ til!* let· me have a go; *~ til kræfter* re'cover; *kom du ngt til?* did· you get hurt? *~ tilbage* come· back, re'turn; *de ~r godt ud af det sammen* they get· on well together; *~ ud for ngt* meet· with sth; *det ~r ud på ét* it comes to the same thing; *det er ikke til at ~ uden om* there is no getting away from it; *det ~r ikke dig ved* it is none of your business; *hvad ~r det dig ved?* what business is that of yours?
kommen *pl (bot)* caraway seeds.
kommen *en: ~ og gåen* comings and goings, toing and froing.
kommende *adj* coming, future; *i den ~ tid* in future, from now on; *de ~ to år* the next two years.
kommentar *en* 'comment.
kommentator *en* commentator.
kommentere *v* 'comment on.
kommerciel *adj* com'mercial.
kommis *en* shop as'sistant.
kommission *en* com'mission, board.
kommissær *en* com'missioner; *(politi~ sv.t.)* superin'tendent.

kommode *en* chest of drawers.
kommunal *adj* mu'nicipal.
kommunalbestyrelse *en* town council; **~s·medlem** *et* town councillor.
kommunalvalg *et* local e'lection.
kommune *en* munici'pality, local au'thority; **~bibliotek** *et* mu'nicipal library; **~skat** *en* local tax; **~skole** *en* mu'nicipal school; *(sv. ofte t.)* local school.
kommunikation *en* communi'cation; **~s·middel** *et* means of communi'cation.
kommunikere *v* com'municate.
kommunist *en,* **~isk** *adj* 'communist.
kompagni *et* company; **~skab** *et* partnership; *gå i ~skab med en* enter into partnership with sby.
kompagnon *en* partner.
kompakt *adj* compact.
kompas *et* compass; *efter ~set* by the compass.
kompensation *en* compen'sation.
kompensere *v* compensate.
kompetence *en* competence; *have ~ til at* have the au'thority to, be competent to; *overskride sin ~* ex'ceed one's au'thority; **~givende** *adj* qualifying.
kompetent *adj* competent, qualified.
kompleks *et* complex; *(bygn)* block of houses // *adj (sammensat)* complex.
komplet *adj* com'plete; *(negativt)* sheer, utter; *det er ~ spild af kræfter* it is sheer waste of energy; *~ åndssvag* utterly stupid; **~tere** *v* com'plete; *(supplere)* supplement.
kompliceret *adj* complex, complicated.
komplikation *en* compli'cation.
kompliment *en* compliment; **~ere** *v* compliment; *må jeg ~ere dig for dit arbejde?* may I compliment you on your work?
komplot *et* con'spiracy, plot.
komponent *en* com'ponent.
komponere *v* com'pose.
komponist *en* com'poser.
kompostbunke *en* compost heap.
kompot *en* stewed frut.
kompres *et* compress.
komprimere *v* com'press.
kompromis *et* compromise; *indgå ~* (make· a) compromise.
komsammen *et* get-together.
koncentration *en* concen'tration; **~s·lejr** *en* concen'tration camp.
koncentrere *v* concentrate *(sig om* on).
koncern *en* firm, combine, group.
koncert *en* concert; *(om musikstykke, fx violin~)* con'certo; **~flygel** *et* concert grand; **~mester** *en* (orchestra) leader; **~sal** *en* concert hall.
kondemnere *v (om hus)* con'demn.
kondensator *en* con'denser.
kondensere *v* con'dense.
kondensstribe *en (fly)* vapour trail, (F) contrail.
kondens(vand) *et* conden'sation.
kondi *en* fitness, con'dition; *holde ~en i orden* keep· fit; **~cykel** *en* exercise bike; **~løb** *et* jogging; **~rum** *et* exercise room; **~sko** *pl* trainers; **~tion** *en* con'dition.
konditor *en* con'fectioner; **konditori** *et* con'fectioner's; *(om lokalet)* tearoom; **konditorkage** *en* fancy cake.
konditræning *en* fitness training.
kondolere *v: ~ en* offer one's con'dolences to sby.
kondom *et* condom, sheath.
konduktør *en (i bus, sporvogn)* con'ductor; *(i tog)* ticket col'lector.
kone *en (hustru)* wife *(pl:* wives); *(kvinde)* woman *(pl:* women); *(hushjælp)* char(woman) *(sm.bøjn); han har ~ og børn* he has a wife and family; *hun er ~n i huset* she is the mistress of the house; *hils din ~!* re'member me to your wife!
konet *adj* matronly.
konfekt *en* chocolates *pl; lakrids~* liquorice allsorts; *dobbelt ~* the same thing twice over.
konfektion *en* ready-made clothing; **~s·syet** *adj* ready-made.
konference *en* conference, congress; *han er til ~* he is at a conference.
konferencier *en* 'compere; *være ~ ved en forestilling* 'compere a show.
konferere *v (sammenligne)* com'pare; *(forhandle)* con'fer.
konfetti *en* con'fetti.

konfirmand *en* young person due for confir'mation.
konfirmation *en* confir'mation.
konfiskere *v* confiscate, seize.
konflikt *en* conflict; **~e** *v* conflict, go· (,be·) on strike; **~ramt** *adj (ved strejke)* strikebound.
konfrontation *en* confron'tation.
konfrontere *v* con'front.
konfus *adj* con'fused; **konfusion** *en* con'fusion.
konge *en* king; **~blå** *adj* royal blue; **~dømme** *et* kingdom; **~familie** *en* royal family; **~lig** *adj* royal; *de ~lige* the royal family; *Det Kongelige Teater* The Royal Theatre; **~loge** *en (teat etc)* royal box; **~par** *et* royal couple; **~rige** *et* kingdom; *~riget Danmark* the Kingdom of Denmark; **~skib** *et* royal yacht; **~slot** *et* royal palace; **~tro** *adj* royalist; **~ørn** *en* golden eagle.
kongres *en* congress, conference.
konjunktion *en (gram)* con'junction.
konjunktiv *en (gram)* the sub'junctive.
konjunktur *en* eco'nomic situ'ation; *dårlige ~er, lav~* de'pression; *høj~* boom; **~stigning** *en* boom.
konkav *adj* con'cave.
konkludere *v* con'clude.
konklusion *en* con'clusion.
konkret *adj (ikke abstrakt)* concrete; *(bestemt)* definite; *få en ~ aftale* get· a definite a'greement.
konkurrence *en* compe'tition; **~deltager** *en* com'petitor; **~dygtig** *adj* com'petitive; **~evne** *en* com'petiveness.
konkurrent *en* com'petitor, rival.
konkurrere *v* com'pete; *~ med en om ngt* com'pete with sby for sth; *~ en ud* oust a com'petitor.
konkurs *en* bankruptcy // *adj* bankrupt; *gå ~* go· bankrupt, (F) go· bust; **~bo** *et* bankrupt's e'state; *(om aktieselskab)* winding-up e'state; **~ramt** *adj* bankrupt.
konkylie *en* conch, shell.
konsekvens *en (følge)* consequence; *(fornuft)* con'sistency; *tage ~en* take· the consequences.
konsekvent *adj* con'sistent.
konservativ *adj* con'servative; *de ~e (pol)* the Con'servative Party.
konservator *en (som udstopper dyr)* taxi'dermist; *(som reparerer kunst etc)* re'storer.
konservatorium *et* a'cademy of music.
konservere *v* pre'serve.
konservering *en* preser'vation; **~s·middel** *et* pre'servative.
konserves *en* tinned food; **~dåse** *en* tin, *(am)* can.
konsistens *en* con'sistency; **~fedt** *et* grease.
konsonant *en* consonant.
konsortium *et* syndicate.
konspirere *v* con'spire.
konstant *en, adj* constant.
konstatere *v* find·; *(påvise)* e'stablish, demonstrate; *(fastslå)* state, note; *(indse)* realize; *~ gift i vinen* demonstrate poison in the wine; *der er ~t tilfælde af mund- og klovsyge på egnen* cases of foot-and-mouth disease have been re'corded in the region.
konstitueret *adj* acting, temporary.
konstitution *en* consti'tution.
konstruere *v* con'struct.
konstruktion *en* con'struction.
konstruktiv *adj* con'structive.
konstruktør *en* con'structor, de'signer; *(tekn)* engi'neer.
konsul *en* consul; **~at** *et* consulate.
konsulent *en* ad'viser, con'sultant; *min juridiske ~* my legal adviser.
konsultation *en* consul'tation; *(læges)* surgery; *(tandlæges)* clinic; **~s·tid** *en (læges)* surgery hours.
konsultere *v* con'sult; *~ en læge* (F) see· a doctor.
konsument *en* con'sumer.
konsumere *v* con'sume.
konsumvarer *pl* con'sumer goods.
kontakt *en* contact; *(elek)* switch; *(fig)* touch; *komme i ~ med in* get· in touch with sby; make· contact with sby; *miste ~en med en* lose· contact with sby; **~annoncer** *pl* personal column.
kontakte *v* 'contact, get· in touch with.

kontaktlim *en* 'contact ad'hesive.
kontaktlinse *en* 'contact lens.
kontant *adj* cash; *(fig, ligefrem)* straightforward; *(håndgribelig)* concrete; *købe ~* buy· for cash; *mod ~ betaling* on cash payment; *betale ~* pay· cash; *et ~ svar* a straightforward answer; **~rabat** *en* cash discount.
kontinent *et* continent.
kontinental *adj* conti'nental.
kontingent *et* sub'scription.
kontinuerlig *adj* con'tinual.
konto *en* ac'count; *sæt det på min ~* charge it to my ac'count; *åbne en ~* open an ac'count *(hos* with); **~kort** *et* credit card.
kontor *et* office; *hun er på ~et* she is in (,at) the office; **~artikler** *pl* office e'quipment; **~assistent** *en* typist; **~chef** *en (i ministerium) sv.t.* permanent undersecretary; *(øvrige) sv.t.* head of de'partment; **~hus** *et* office block; **~ist** *en* clerk; **~personale** *et* office staff; **~tid** *en* office hours *pl.*
kontoudtog *et* bank statement.
kontrabas *en* double bass.
kontrakt *en* contract, a'greement; *skrive ~ med en* make· up an a'greement (,contract) with sby; *hæve en ~* cancel a contract; *i henhold til ~en* under the a'greement (,contract); **~ansat** *adj* ap'pointed on a contract basis; **~brud** *et* breach of contract; **~mæssig** *adj* con'tractual.
kontra... *sms:* **~ordre** *en* counterorder; **~punkt** *et (mus)* counterpoint; **~spionage** *en* counterespionage.
kontrast *en* 'contrast; *stå i ~ til* con'trast with.
kontrol *en* con'trol; *(opsyn)* super'vision; *(~sted)* con'trol, checkpoint; *føre ~ med ngt* keep· con'trol on sth, supervise sth; *få bolden under ~* get· the ball under con'trol; *gå til ~ hos lægen* go· for a medical check-up; **~anordning** *en* con'trol de'vice; **~foranstaltning** *en* con'trol measure.
kontrollere *v* con'trol; *(holde øje med)* supervise; *(undersøge)* check.
kontrollør *en* in'spector, supervisor; *(af billetter)* ticket col'lector; *(teat)* at'tendant; *(ved fodboldbane)* gateman *(pl:* -men).
kontroltårn *et (fly)* con'trol tower.
kontrolur *et* time clock.
kontroversiel *adj* contro'versial.
kontur *en* outline.
konveks *adj* con'vex.
konversation *en* conver'sation; **~s·leksikon** *et* encyclo'paedia.
konversere *v* con'verse (with), speak· (with).
konvertere *v* con'vert; *(blive omvendt)* be con'verted.
konvoj *en* convoy, escort.
konvolut *en* envelope.
kooperation *en* co-operation.
kooperativ *et, adj* co-operative.
koordinere *v* co-'ordinate.
kop *en* cup; *et par ~per* a cup and saucer; *en ~ te* a cup of tea.
kopi *en* copy; *et brev med en (,to) kopier* a letter in duplicate (,triplicate); **~ere** *v* copy; *(efterligne)* imitate; **~maskine** *en* photocopier.
kopper *pl (med)* smallpox.
koppevaccination *en* smallpox vacci'nation.
kor *et (alle bet)* choir; *synge (,råbe) i ~* sing· (,cry·) in chorus; *hun synger i et ~* she is singing in a choir.
koral *en* coral; *(mus)* cho'rale; **~rev** *et* coral reef; **~ø** *en* a'toll.
Koranen *s* the Ko'ran.
kordegn *en sv.t.* churchwarden; **~e·kontor** *et sv.t.* parish office.
korende *en* currant.
koreograf *en* chore'ographer; **koreografi** *en* chore'ography.
kork *en* cork; **~prop** *en* cork.
kormusik *en* choral works *pl.*
korn *et* corn; *(om kerne etc)* grain; **~avl** *en* culti'vation of grain; **~blomst** *en* cornflower.
kornet *en (mus)* cornet.
kornmagasin *et* granary.
kornmark *en* cornfield.
kornsort *en* cereal.
korporlig *adj* corporal, bodily.

korps *et* corps, body.
korpulent *adj* stout.
korrekt *adj* cor'rect; *(nøjagtig)* accurate.
korrektur *en* proof; *læse ~ på en bog* read· the proofs for a book; **~læser** *en* proofreader.
korrespondance *en* corre'spondence.
korrespondent *en* corre'spondent.
korrespondere *v* corre'spond *(med* with).
korridor *en* corridor.
korrigere *v* cor'rect.
korrupt *adj* cor'rupt.
korruption *en* cor'ruption.
kors *et* cross; *lægge armene over ~* fold one's arms; *med benene over ~* with crossed legs; *krybe til ~et* eat· humble pie; *~, hvor er han dum!* God, how stupid he is!
korsang *en* choral singing; *(om sangen)* part song.
korse *v: ~ sig over ngt* be ap'palled at sth.
korset *et* corset; *(hofteholder)* girdle.
korsfæste *v* crucify; **~lse** *en* cruci'fixion.
korssting *et* cross stitch.
korstog *et* cru'sade.
kort *et* card; *(land~, bil~)* map; *(post~)* postcard; *et ~ over London* a map of London; *skal vi tage et slag ~?* shall we play a game of cards? *vil du give ~?* will you deal·? // *adj* short; *(kortfattet)* brief; *om ~ tid* shortly, soon; *for ~ tid siden* recently, a short time ago; *~ efter* shortly after; *~ sagt* in short; *~ for hovedet* curt.
kortbølge *en* short-wave; **~behandling** *en* short-wave 'diathermy.
kortege *en* cortège.
kort... *sms:* **~fattet** *adj* brief, con'cise; **~fristet** *adj* short-term; **~hed** *en* shortness; briefness; *(se kort); fatte sig i ~hed* be brief; *sagt i al ~hed* to be brief; **~håret** *adj* short-haired; **~kunster** *spl* card tricks; **~lægge** *v* map; **~sigtet** *adj* shortterm; **~slutning** *en* short circuit; **~slutte** *v* short-circuit; **~spil** *et* card game; *(om selve kortene)* pack of cards; **~varig** *adj* brief, transitory.
kosmetik *en* cos'metics *pl.*
kosmetisk *adj* cos'metic.
kosmisk *adj* cosmic.
kost *en (feje~)* broom; *(barber~ etc)* brush; *(sømærke)* shallows marker.
kost *en (føde)* food, diet; *en alsidig ~* a balanced diet; *have en på ~* have sby as a boarder; *betale for ~ og logi* pay· for board and lodging; *det er skrap ~!* it is heavy stuff!
kostald *en* cowshed.
kostbar *adj* valuable, precious; *(dyr)* ex'pensive; *gøre sig ~* need to be persu'aded; **~hed** *en* preciousness; *(~ ting)* treasure.
koste *v* cost·; *hvad ~r den bog?* how much is that book? *den ~r alt for meget* it is far too ex'pensive; *det ~de ham livet* it cost· him his life; *~ hvad det ~ vil* at all costs, cost· what it may.
kostelig *adj* priceless.
kosteskab *et* broom cupboard.
kosteskaft *et* broomstick.
kostskole *en* boarding school.
kostume *et* costume; **~bal** *et* fancy-dress ball; **~tegner** *en* costume de'signer.
kotelet *en* chop, cutlet.
kovending *en (pol etc)* turnaround.
koøje *et (mar)* porthole.
kr. *(fork.f. kroner)* crowns, Dkr.
krabat *en* fellow, bloke.
krabbe *en* crab.
kradse *v* scratch; *(skrabe)* scrape; *(irritere)* irritate; *(om tøj)* be scratchy; *~ sig på maven* scratch one's stomach; *den trøje ~r* that cardigan is scratchy; *~ 'af* (F) kick the bucket; *~ ngt ned* jot sth down.
kraft *en* strength, force; *(elek etc)* power; *(gyldighed)* force; *brug dine kræfter* use your strength; *køre for fuld ~* run· at full steam; *for egen ~* under one's own steam; *samle kræfter* build· up one's strength; *komme til kræfter* re'cover one's strength; *af alle kræfter* with all one's might; *i ~ af* by virtue of; *træde i ~* come· into force; *sætte ud af ~* an'nul, cancel; **~anstrengelse** *en* e'xertion; **~idiot** *en* blithering idiot.

kraftig *adj* strong, powerful; *(energisk)* vigorous; *(om person)* stout, heavy; *~t bygget* strongly built; *(tyk)* heavy; *advare en på det ~ste* give· sby a strong warning.
kraftudtryk *et* oath, swearword.
kraftværk *et* power station (,plant).
krage *en* crow; **-tæer** *pl (fig)* scrawl.
krak *et (på børsen etc)* crash.
krakilsk *adj* quarrelsome, cussed.
krakke *v* crash, (F) go· bust.
kram *et* stuff, things *pl; kunne sit ~* know· one's stuff; *det passer i mit ~* it suits me down to the ground; *få ~met på en* get· the upper hand over sby.
kramme *v (klemme)* squeeze, crush; *(gramse på)* paw; *(kæle for)* cuddle; *~ ngt sammen* crumple sth up; *kysse og ~* kiss and cuddle; *~ ud med ngt* come· out with sth.
krampagtig *adj* forced.
krampe *en* con'vulsions *pl; (mindre trækning)* spasm; *(i foden etc)* cramp; **-anfald** *et* con'vulsive fit; **-latter** *en* hy'sterical laughter; **-trækning** *en* spasm.
kran *en* crane; **-fører** *en* crane driver.
kraniebrud *et* fractured skull.
kranium *et* skull.
krans *en* wreath; **-e** *v* wreathe; *(omgive)* sur'round; **-e·kage** *en* almond cake.
kranvogn *en* breakdown truck.
krat *et* scrub, brushwood.
krater *et* crater.
krav *et* de'mand; *(jur)* claim; *(ved eksamen, stillingsbesættelse)* re'quirement; *gøre ~ på* claim; de'mand; *stille et ~* make· a demand.
krave *en* collar; **-ben** *et* collar bone; **-knap** *en* (collar) stud.
kravle *v* crawl; **-barn** *et* toddler; **-dragt** *en* rompers *pl;* **-gård** *en* playpen.
kreativ *adj* cre'ative.
kreatur *et* head of cattle; *~er pl* cattle, livestock.
krebinet *en (gastr)* meat rissole.
krebs *en* crab, crayfish; *Krebsen (astr)* Cancer; *Krebsens vendekreds* the Tropic of Cancer.
kredit *en* credit; **-ere** *v* credit; **-kort** *et* credit card; **-køb** *et* credit buying; **-oplysningsbureau** *et* credit rating agency; **-or** *en* creditor; **-værdighed** *en* credit rating.
kreds *en* circle, ring; *(distrikt)* district; *(omgangs~)* set, circle; *(valg~)* con'stituency; *sidde i ~* sit· in a circle; *i venners ~* among friends; *i politiske ~e* in po'litical circles; *kendt i vide ~e* widely known.
kredse *v* circle; *~ om ngt (fig)* re'volve around sth.
kredsløb *et (anat, med, fig)* circu'lation; *(elek)* circuit; *(om rumskib etc)* orbit.
krematorium *et* crema'torium.
kremere *v* cre'mate.
Kreml *s (i Moskva)* the Kremlin.
krepere *v* (F) kick the bucket; *(ærgre)* an'noy.
kreperlig *adj* annoying.
krible *v* prickle; *det ~r i mine fingre efter at...* my fingers are itching to...
kridt *et* chalk; *købe på ~* (F) buy· on tick; **-e** *v* chalk; *~e skoene (og stå fast)* dig· in one's heels; **-hus** *et: være i ~et hos en* be in sby's good books; **-pibe** *en* clay pipe.
krig *en* war; *(krigsførelse)* warfare; *erklære ~ mod* de'clare war on; *føre ~* wage war *(også fig); gå i ~* go· to war; *gå i ~ med ngt (fig)* tackle sth; *han faldt i ~en* he was killed in the war; *under ~en* during the war.
kriger *en* warrior; **-isk** *adj* bel'ligerent.
krigs... *sms:* **-dans** *en* wardance; **-erklæring** *en* decla'ration of war; **-fange** *en* prisoner of war; **-forbrydelse** *en* war crime; **-forbryder** *en* war criminal; **-førelse** *en* warfare; **-førende** *adj: de ~førende lande* the countries at war; **-humør** *et: være i ~humør* be on the warpath; **-indsats** *en* war effort; **-invalid** *en* dis'abled soldier; **-maling** *en (også fig)* warpaint; **-ret** *en: blive stillet for en ~ret* be court-'martialled; **-råd** *et* council of war; **-skib** *et* warship;

~**sti** *en: være på ~stien* be on the warpath; ~**tid** *en* wartime; *i ~tid* in times of war.
krimi *en* (F) who'dunit.
kriminal... *sms:* ~**assistent** *en sv.t.* de'tective in'spector; ~**betjent** *en* de'tective constable; ~**film** *en* de'tective film; ~**forsorg** *en* penal system; ~**itet** *en* crime; ~**politi** *et* criminal po'lice; ~**roman** *en* de'tective story, (F) who'dunit.
kriminel *adj* criminal; *den ~le lavalder* the age of criminal responsi'bility.
krimskrams *et* scrawl; *tegne ~* doodle.
kringle *en* pretzel // *v: han forstår at ~ den* (F) he knows· how to fix it.
kringlet *adj* intricate.
krinkelkroge *pl* nooks and crannies.
krise *en* crisis *(pl:* crises) ~**plan** *en* e'mergency plan;; ~**ramt** *adj* de'pressed *(fx område* area); ~**tid** *en* de'pression.
kristen *adj* Christian; ~**dom** *en* Christi'anity.
kristtorn *en (bot)* holly.
Kristus *s* Christ; *før Kristi fødsel (f.Kr.)* be'fore Christ (BC); *efter Kristi fødsel (e.Kr.)* anno Domini (AD).
kritik *en* criticism; *(anmeldelse)* re'view; *bogen fik god ~* the book got good reviews; the book was well re'ceived; ~**er** *en* critic; *(anmelder)* re'viewer.
kritisere *v* criticize.
kritisk *adj* critical; *(afgørende)* crucial; *det ~e punkt* the crucial point.
kro *en (hotel)* inn; *(værtshus)* pub; *(hos fugle)* crop // *v: ~ sig* strut; ~**ejer** *en* innkeeper.
krog *en (tekn)* hook; *(hjørne)* corner; *(haspe etc)* catch; *bide på ~en (også fig)* rise· to the bait; *trænge en op i en ~* corner sby; ~**et** *adj* crooked, bent.
kroket *s (spil)* croquet; *(gastr)* cro'quette.
krokodille *en* crocodile.
krokone *en* landlady *(pl:* -ladies).
krokus *en (bot)* crocus.
krom *s (kem)* chromium.
kromand *en* innkeeper.
kromosom *et* chromosome; ~**tælling** *en* chromosome count.
kronblad *et (bot)* petal.
krone *en (også om mønt)* crown; *(lyse~)* chande'lier; *(træ~)* top; *få sat ny ~ på en tand* have a tooth crowned; *han har ikke en ~ tilbage* he has not got a penny left; *plat eller ~* heads or tails; *slå plat og ~ om* toss up for // *v* crown.
kronhjort *en* red deer; *(om hannen)* stag.
kronik *en* feature article.
kroning *en* coro'nation.
kronisk *adj* chronic; *~ syg* chronically ill; *~ dranker* chronic alco'holic.
kronjuveler *pl* crown jewels.
kronologisk *adj: i ~ orden* in chrono'logical order.
kronprins *en* crown prince.
krop *en (legeme)* body; *(kroppen alene)* trunk; *hun rystede over hele ~pen* she was trembling all over; *hun har ikke en trævl på ~pen* she has not got a stitch on; ~**s·bevidst** *adj* body-conscious; ~**s·bygning** *en* build; ~**s·lig** *adj* physical; ~**s·nær** *adj* clinging, close-fitting *(fx kjole* dress); ~**s·visitation** *en* search, (F) frisking.
krostue *en* taproom.
krovært *en* innkeeper; *(på værtshus)* publican.
krucifiks *et* crucifix.
krudt *et* (gun)powder; *(fut)* go, pep; *skyde med løst ~* fire blanks; *spare på ~et* save one's energy; *han har ikke opfundet ~et* he is not e'xactly a genius.
krukke *en* jar, pot; *(om person)* af'fected person; ~**ri** *et* affec'tation; ~**t** *adj* af'fected.
krum *adj* crooked, bent; ~**bøjet** *adj* bent, stooping.
krumme *en* crumb; *der er ~r i den dreng* that boy has got guts // *v* bend·, bow; *~ sig sammen* double up, bend over; *~ ryg (om kat etc)* arch one's back; *~ tæer (fig)* feel· a'shamed, cringe.

krumning *en (på vej, bane etc)* bend; *(det at krumme)* bending.
krumspring *pl* capers.
krumtap *en (tekn)* crank.
krus *et* mug; *(om hår)* frizzle.
kruse *v (om hår)* frizzle; *(om vand)* ruffle, ripple.
krustade *en (gastr)* patty shell.
kryb *et* creepy-'crawly; *(om person)* vermin.
krybbe *en* crib; *(jule~)* manger.
krybdyr *et* reptile.
krybe *v (kravle)* crawl; *(klatre)* climb; *(snige sig)* creep·; *(fig)* cringe; *(om tøj)* shrink·; *~ for en* fawn on sby, crawl to sby; *~ op i sofaen* crawl onto the set'tee; *~ sammen* huddle; **~kælder** *en* service space; **~spor** *et (på motorvej)* slow lane.
krybskytte *en* poacher.
krybskytteri *et* poaching.
krydder *en sv.t.* big rusk.
krydderi *et* spice; *sætte ~ på tilværelsen* add a bit of spice to life, spice it up.
kryddernellike *en* clove.
kryddersild *en* pickled herring.
krydderurt *en* herb.
krydre *v* season; **~t** *adj* spicy, seasoned.
kryds *et* cross; *(mus)* sharp; *(gade~ etc)* crossing, crossroads; *(~togt)* cruise; *sætte ~ ved ngt* put· a cross against sth; *over (,på) ~* crosswise; *~ og bolle (leg)* noughts and crosses; *~ for A (mus)* A sharp; *på ~ og tværs* this way and that.
krydse *v* cross; *(mar)* tack; *(sejle omkring)* cruise; *~ navne af* tick off names; *~ fingre for en* cross one's fingers for sby.
krydsermissil *et* cruise missile.
krydsfiner *en* plywood.
krydsforhør *et* 'cross-exami,nation; **~e** *v* 'cross-e,xamine.
krydsild *en* cross-fire.
krydsning *en (om dyr)* cross-breed, hybrid.
kryds-og-tværs, krydsord *en* crossword puzzle.
krydstogt *et* cruise.
krykke *en* crutch; *gå med ~r* walk on crutches.
krymmel *en (farvet)* hundreds and thousands.
krympe *v* shrink·; *(pakke i tæt plast)* shrink-wrap; *~ sig ved at gøre ngt* shrink· at doing sth; **~fri** *adj* non-shrink.
krympning *en* shrinking.
krypt *en (i kirke)* crypt.
kryptisk *adj* cryptic.
krysantemum *en* chry'santhemum.
krystal *en* crystal; **~glas** *et* crystal (glass); **~klar** *adj* crystal(-clear); **~lisere** *v* crystallize; **~sukker** *et (hugget sukker)* lump sugar.
kryster *en* coward.
kræft *en* cancer; **~behandling** *en* cancer therapy; **~fremkaldende** *adj* carcino'genic; **~svulst** *en* (cancer) tumour.
kræmmerhus *et (af papir)* screw of paper; *(gastr)* cone.
krænge *v (mar, hælde)* heel (over); *(fly)* bank; *(vende vrangen ud)* turn inside out; *~ en skjorte af* strip off a shirt; *~ en strømpe på* roll on a sock.
krænke *v* of'fend; *(såre)* hurt·; *(overtræde, bryde)* violate, break·; *hun blev dybt ~t* she was deeply hurt; *blive ~t over ngt* be of'fended at sth; *~ loven* break· the law; **~lse** *en* of'fence; breach; vio'lation.
kræs *et* delicacies *pl,* goodies *pl;* **~e** *v: ~e op for en* do· sby proud.
kræsen *adj* par'ticular; *(meget ~)* squeamish.
kræve *v (forlange)* de'mand, re'quire; *(~ som sin ret)* claim; *(nødvendiggøre)* re'quire, call for; *~ erstatning* claim damages; *~ ind* be de'manding; *~ penge ind* col'lect money; *~ en til regnskab* call sby to ac'count; *dette ~r stor omhu* this calls for e'xactitude; **~nde** *adj* de'manding.
krøbling *en* cripple.
krøl *et* curl, frizzle; *have ~ i håret* have curly hair; **~fri** *adj* crease-re'sistant.
krølle *en* curl; *(slange~)* ringlet; *have naturlige ~r* have a natural curl; *grisen slog ~ på halen* the pig curled up its tail // *v (om hår)* curl; *(om*

papir, tøj) crumple, crease; ~ *papir sammen* crumple up paper; ~ *sig sammen* curl up; **~jern** *et* curling iron.
krøllet *adj (om hår)* curly; *(om tøj)* creased.
krønike *en* chronicle.
kråse *en (hos fugl)* gizzard.
kube *en* hive.
kubikmeter *en* cubic metre.
kubikrod *en* cube root.
kue *v* in'timidate.
kuffert *en* suitcase; *(stor)* trunk; *(weekend~)* bag; *pakke sin* ~ pack one's suitcase; *pakke ~en ud* un'pack.
kugle *en* ball, globe; *(gevær~ etc)* bullet; *spille ~r* play marbles; *skyde sig en ~ for panden* blow· one's brains out; **~hoved** *et (til skrivemaskine)* golf-ball; **~leje** *et* ball bearing; **~pen** *en* ballpoint (pen); **~stød** *et (sport)* shot-putting.
kujon *en* coward; **~ere** *v* bully.
kuk *et: ikke et* ~ not a word; **~ke** *v (om gøg)* call; *sidde og ~ke* sit· all alone, mope; **~ker** *en (gøg)* cuckoo; **~ur** *et* cuckoo clock.
kul *et* coal; *(træ~, tegne~)* charcoal; *(kem)* carbon; *lægge ~ i ovnen* put· coal on the fire; **~brinte** *en (kem)* hydro'carbon.
kuld *et (om dyr)* litter; *(om fugle)* brood; *et ~ studenter* the students of the year.
kulde *en* cold; *det er 10 graders* ~ it is 10 degrees be'low zero; *dø af* ~ freeze· to death; **~gys(ning)** *en* shiver; *få ~gysninger* get· the shivers.
kuldioxid *en* carbon di'oxide.
kuldskær *adj* sensitive to cold.
kuldslået *adj* tepid.
kulhydrat *s* carbo'hydrate.
kulilte *en* carbon mo'noxide.
kulinarisk *adj* culinary.
kuling *en* wind, breeze; *stiv* ~ strong breeze; *hård* ~ moderate gale.
kulisse *en (teat)* wing; *(dekoration)* set piece; *der foregår ngt i ~rne* there is sth going on be'hind the scenes.
kulkasse *en* coal box.
kulkælder *en* coal cellar; *han er helt nede i ~en* he is really de'pressed.
kuller *en (fisk)* sort of cod; *få* ~ go· crazy, go· round the bend.
kulmine *en* coal-mine; **~arbejder** *en* coal-miner.
kulminere *v* culminate, top.
kulos *en* soot.
kulravende *adv:* ~ *mørk* pitch-dark.
kulret *adj* crazy.
kul... *sms:* **~sort** *adj* pitch-black; **~spand** *en* coal scuttle; **~stof** *et (kem)* carbon; **~støv** *et* coaldust; **~syre** *en (kem)* car'bonic acid; *(som luftart)* carbon di'oxide; *(i sodavand)* fizz.
kult *en* cult.
kultiveret *adj* cultivated.
kultur *en* culture; **~center** *et* cultural centre.
kulturel *adj* cultural.
kulturhistorie *en* history of civili'zation.
kulturministerium *et* Ministry of Cultural Af'fairs.
kultveilte *en (kem)* carbon di'oxide.
kulør *en* colour; *(til sovs)* browning; *sætte ~ på foretagendet* jazz things up; *bekende ~ (i kortspil)* follow suit; *(fig)* show one's hand.
kulørt *adj* coloured *(også om person); ~e blade* glossy magazines; **~vask** *en* coloureds *pl.*
kumme *en (vaske~)* (wash)basin; *(wc~)* (toilet) bowl; **~fryser** *en* chest freezer.
kun *adv* only; *(~ lige)* just; *(udelukkende)* merely; *der er ~ lidt te tilbage* there is only a little tea left; *drengen er ~ seks år* the boy is only six; *pigen er ~ lige ti år* the girl is just ten; *hun er ~ et barn* she is a mere child.
kunde *en* customer; **~kreds** *en* customers *pl,* clien'tele; **~service** *en (i stormagasin)* service de'partment.
kundgøre *v* an'nounce; **~lse** *en* an'nouncement.
kundskab *en (viden)* knowledge; *(kendskab)* infor'mation; *~er* knowledge; *vi har fået ~ om at...* we have been in'formed that...

kunne *v (være i stand til)* be able to; *(forstå, kende)* know·; *(om mulighed, tilladelse)* may·; *(om vane)* will·; *jeg kan ikke lide ham* I do· not like him; *han kan løbe 20 km på en time* he can run· 20 km in an hour; *jeg kan tale engelsk* I can speak· English; *vi ~ ikke finde hende* we could· not find her; *han ~ godt komme* he was able to come; *hun kan sine lektier* she knows· her lessons; *han kan tysk* he understands (,speaks) German; *de kan komme når som helst* they may· be here any time; *det kan da godt være* that may· (well) be; *vi ~ måske besøge ham* we might visit him; *du kan godt gå nu* you may· go now; *han kan sidde og se tv i timevis* he will sit watching the telly for hours; *de kan ikke med hinanden* they do not get on; *kan du så holde op!* will you stop it! do stop it! *så kan det være nok!* that will do!

kunnen *en* a'bility; *(dygtighed)* com-petence; *(viden)* knowledge.

kunst *en* art; *(dygtighed)* skill; *(~styk-ke)* trick; *han samler på ~* he col-'lects art; *~en at stave* the art of spelling; *det er ingen ~* that is a piece of cake; *efter alle ~ens regler* thoroughly; *de skønne ~er* the fine arts; **~akademi** *et* art school; **~art** *en* art; **~færdig** *adj* in'genious; *(kompliceret)* e'laborate; **~genstand** *en* objet d'art; **~gødning** *en* arti'fi-cial fertilizer; **~handler** *en* art dealer; **~historie** *en* history of art; **~håndværk** *et* (handi)craft.

kunstig *adj* arti'ficial; *(syntetisk også)* man-made; *(neds)* false, imi'tation; *~e tænder* false teeth; *~t åndedræt* arti'ficial respi'ration; *~t fremstillet* imi'tation, man-made *(fx læder* leather); *~t lys* arti'ficial light.

kunst... *sms:* **~industri** *en* ap'plied art; **~læder** *et* imi'tation leather; **~ma-ler** *en* artist, painter; **~museum** *et* art gallery.

kunstner *en* artist; **~isk** *adj* ar'tistic; **~kittel** *en* smock.

kunst... *sms:* **samler** *en* col'lector (of art); **~silke** *en* arti'ficial silk; **~skøj-teløb** *et* figure skating; **~stykke** *et* trick; **~værk** *et* work of art.

kup *et* coup; *(fig)* scoop; *(stats~)* coup d'état; *gøre et ~ (fig)* make· a good haul.

kupé *en* com'partment.

kuperet *adj (om terræn)* hilly; *(om hund)* docked.

kupforsøg *et* at'tempted coup.

kupon *en* coupon.

kuppel *en* dome; *(mindre)* cupola; *(til lampe)* globe.

kur *en* cure, treatment; *(ved hoffet)* court; *hun er på ~* she is under-'going treatment; *(om slankekur)* she is on a diet; *gøre ~ til en* court sby.

kure *v* slide·.

kurér *en* 'courier.

kurere *v (helbrede)* cure; *nu er han vist ~t (iron)* I think· he has had it now.

kuriositet *en* curio, curi'osity.

kurre *en: en ~ på tråden* a tiff // *v (om due og fig)* coo.

kurs *en (retning)* course; *(om penge)* rate of ex'change; *(om værdipapi-rer)* going rate; *sætte ~en mod England* set· out for England; *have ~ mod ngt* be heading for sth; *kom-me ud af ~* get· off one's course; *være i høj ~* be high; *(fig, populær)* be popular; **~gevinst** *en* profit.

kursiv *en (om skrift)* i'talics *pl;* **~ere** *v* print in italics.

kurstab *et* loss.

kursted *et* health re'sort.

kursus *et* course *(i* on).

kursværdi *en* market value.

kurv *en* basket; *give en en ~* send· sby packing.

kurve *en* curve; *(om vej)* bend; **~kuf-fert** *en* wicker trunk; **~møbler** *pl* wicker furniture; **~stol** *en* basket chair.

kusine *en* (female) cousin; *de er fæt-ter og ~* they are cousins.

kusk *en* driver.

kusse *en* (V!) cunt.

kustode *en* at'tendant.

kutter *en* cutter.

kutyme *en: det er ~ at...* it is the custom to...
kuvert *en (konvolut)* envelope; *(ved bordet)* cover; *foret ~* padded (,Jiffy) envelope; **~brød** *et* roll.
kuvøse *en* incubator.
kvadrat *en* square; **~isk** *adj* square; **~meter** *en* square metre; **~rod** *en* square root.
kvadrere *v* square.
kvaj *et* ass, clot; **~e** *v: ~e sig* make· a gaffe, step in it; **~hoved, ~pande** *en* ass.
kvaksalver *en* quack.
kvaksalveri *et* quackery.
kval *en* agony, anguish; *have ~er med ngt* have trouble with sth.
kvalificere *v: ~ sig til ngt* qualify for sth.
kvalifikation *en* qualifi'cation; **~s·kamp** *en (sport)* qualifying match.
kvalitet *en* quality; **~s·bevidst** *adj* quality-conscious.
kvalm *adj (om luft)* stifling; *(om smag)* sickening.
kvalme *en* nausea; *have ~* feel· sick; *jeg får ~ af det* it makes· me sick.
kvante *et* quantum *(pl:* quanta).
kvantitet *en* quantity.
kvantum *et* quantity.
kvark *en* quarg.
kvart *en* quarter; *(mus)* fourth; *klokken er ~ i (,over) et* it is a quarter to (,past) one // *adj* quarter of.
kvartal *et* quarter, three months; **~s·vis** *adv* quarterly.
kvarter *et (om tid)* quarter (of an hour); *(bydel)* district; *(mil)* quarters; *klokken er et ~ i (,over) fire* it is a quarter to (,past) four; *om tre ~* in three quarters of an hour, in forty-five minutes; *et ~s tid* a quarter of an hour.
kvartet *en (mus)* quar'tet.
kvartfinale *en (sport)* quarterfinals *pl.*
kvarts *en* quartz; **~ur** *et* quartz watch (,clock).
kvas *et (grene, kviste)* brushwood.
kvase *v* crush.
kvast *en* tassel; *(pudder~)* puff.
kvidder *et (om fugle)* chirping, twitter; *jeg forstår ikke et ~* I do· not under'stand a word.
kvidre *v* chirp, twitter.
kvie *en (ung ko)* heifer // *v: ~ sig ved ngt* shrink· (back) from sth.
kvik *adj (opvakt)* bright; *(rask)* well; *(hurtig)* quick; *han er et ~t hoved* he is bright; *lad det nu gå lidt ~t!* hurry up now!
kvikke *v: ~ (op) (dvs. opmuntre)* cheer up; *kaffe ~r* coffee is stimulating.
kviksand *et* quiksands *pl.*
kviksølv *et* mercury.
kvindagtig *adj* ef'feminate.
kvinde *en* woman *(pl:* women); **~bevægelse** *en* women's (,feminist) movement; **~frigørelse** *en* women's lib; **~hader** *en* woman-hater; **~hus** *et* women's refuge; **~kønnet** *s* the female sex; **~lig** *adj* female, woman; *(feminin)* feminine, womanly; *~lig læge* woman doctor; **~lighed** *en* femi'ninity; **~litteratur** *en* women's literature; **~læge** *en* gynae'cologist; **~menneske** *et (neds)* female; **~sagen** *s* feminism; **~sagskvinde** *en* feminist, women's libber; **~sygdom** *en* women's dis'ease; **~tække** *et: han har ~tække* he is a lady-killer.
kvint *en (mus)* fifth.
kvintet *en (mus)* quin'tet.
kvist *en (på gren)* twig; *(på hus)* attic; **~lejlighed** *en* attic (flat); **~vindue** *et* dormer.
kvit *adj: så er vi ~* that makes us quits; *blive en ~* get· rid of sby; *~ el. dobbelt* double or quits; *få ngt ~ og frit* get· sth free of debt.
kvitte *v* give· up, (F) quit.
kvittere *v (skrive under)* sign; *(gøre gengæld)* re'pay·.
kvittering *en* re'ceipt.
kvota *en* quota.
kvotient *en* quotient.
kvæg *et* cattle; *10 stk. ~* ten head of cattle; **~avl** *en* cattle breeding; **~besætning** *en* livestock; **~flok** *en* herd of cattle; **~race** *en* breed of cattle.
kvæk *et (om frø)* croaking; *ikke et ~* not a word; **~ke** *v* croak.
kvæle *v* choke; *(med reb etc)* strangle;

(af mangel på luft) suffocate, stifle; *(ved tilstopning af luftvejen)* smother; *han blev kvalt i en mundfuld kød* he choked on a piece of meat; *hun kvalte ham med en pude* she stifled him with a cushion; *~ en gaben* stifle a yawn; *~ ngt i fødslen* nip sth in the bud; *det er ~nde varmt* it is stifling hot; **-nde** *adj* stifling.

kvælerslange *en* boa con'strictor.

kvælertag *et* stranglehold.

kvælstof *et* nitrogen.

kværn *en* (grinding) mill; **-e** *v* grind·; *(snakke)* gabble.

kværulant *en* grumbler.

kværulere *v* grumble, grouse *(over* about).

kvæste *v* injure, bruise; *der var mange ~de* many people were injured; *han er helt ~t (fig)* he has got a bad hangover; **-lse** *en* injury, bruise.

kyle *v* fling·.

kylling *en* chicken; *stegt ~* roast chicken; **-e·gryde** *en (gastr)* chicken casserole.

kyndig *adj (dygtig)* skilled; *(vidende)* knowledgeable; **-hed** *en* skill; knowledge.

kynisk *adj* cynical.

kys *et* kiss; *(let, fx på kinden)* peck.

kyse *en* bonnet.

kysk *adj* chaste; **-hed** *en* chastity.

kysse *v* kiss; *(let)* peck; *~ hinanden, ~s* kiss; **-tøj** *et* (F) kisser.

kyst *en* coast; *(strand)* shore; *(feriested)* seaside; *langs ~en* along the coast; *gå i land på ~en* go a'shore; *tage ud til ~en* go· to the seaside; *byen ligger ved ~en* the town is on the coast (,at the seaside); **-banesocialist** *en sv.t.* cham'pagne socialist; **-fiskeri** *et* inshore fishing; **-klima** *et* maritime climate; **-linje** *en* coastline; **-vagt** *en* coastguard.

kysægte *adj* kissproof.

kæbe *en* jaw; **-ben** *et* jawbone; **-hulebetændelse** *en* ma'xillary sinu'sitis; **-stød** *et* hook to the chin.

kæde *en* chain *(også om bjerge) // v: ~ sammen* link up; **-brev** *et* chain letter; **-forretning** *en* chain store; **-kasse** *en (på cykel)* chain guard; **-reaktion** *en* chain re'action; **-ryger** *en* chain smoker; **-sting** *et* chain stitch.

kæft *en: hold ~!* shut· up! *der kom ikke en ~* (S) not a soul turned up; **-e** *v: ~e op* shout.

kæk *adj* brave, bold; **-hed** *en* bravery, boldness.

kælder *en* cellar; *(~etage)* basement; **-lejlighed** *en* basement flat; **-rum** *et* cellar.

kæle *v: ~ for en* ca'ress sby; *~ for sit arbejde* take· pains over one's work; **-barn** *et* pet; **-dyr** *et* pet.

kælen *adj (om barn etc)* af'fectionate; *(forelsket)* amorous; *(om stemme)* languishing.

kælenavn *et* pet name.

kæleri *et* cuddling; *(seksuelt)* necking.

kælk *en* sledge, to'boggan; **-e** *v* sledge.

kælling *en* old woman *(pl:* women); *en gammel ~ (neds)* an old hag; *hun er en dum ~* she is a bitch; **-e·knude** *en* granny knot.

kælve *v* calve.

kæmpe *en* giant // *v* fight·; *(hårdt)* struggle; *(konkurrere)* com'pete; *~ sig frem* struggle along; *~ mod ngt* fight· (against) sth; *~ om guldet* com'pete for the gold; **-høj** *en* barrow // *adj* giant; **-mæssig** *adj* giant; **-stor** *adj* gi'gantic.

kænguru *en* kanga'roo.

kæntre *v* cap'size.

kæp *en* stick; *stikke en ~ i hjulet for en* throw· a spanner in the works for sby; **-hest** *en* hobbyhorse *(også fig)*; **-høj** *adj* pert, fresh.

kær *et* pond, pool; *(sump)* marsh // *adj (elsket)* dear, be'loved; *(sød)* sweet, dear; *~e hr NN* dear Mr NN; *~e ven!* my dear (friend)! *er det ikke en ~ unge?* isn't that a darling child? *er hun ikke ~?* isn't she a dear?

kæreste *en (mandlig)* fi'ancé, boy friend; *(kvindelig)* fi'ancée, girl friend; **-brev** *et* love letter; **-sorg** *en* lovesickness.

kærkommen *adj* welcome.

kærlig *adj* af'fectionate, loving; *~ hilsen fra... (i brev)* love from...

kærlighed *en* love, af'fection; *kaste sin ~ på en* fall· in love with sby; *det er hans store ~* it is his passion; *erklære en sin ~* de'clare one's feelings to sby; *han skal få ~en at føle* he'll catch it; *~ ved første blik* love at first sight; **~s·erklæring** *en* decla'ration of love; **~s·forhold** *et* love af'fair; **~s·roman** *en* love story.
kærne *en (smør~)* (butter)churn // *v* churn; **~mælk** *en* buttermilk.
kærre *en* cart.
kærte *en* candle.
kærtegn *et* ca'ress; **~e** *v* ca'ress.
kætter *en* heretic; **kætteri** *et* heresy.
kø *en* queue; *(billard~)* cue; *(bil~)* tailback; *stå i ~* queue up.
køb *et* purchase; *(det at købe ngt)* buying; *(handel)* bargain; *~ og salg* buying and selling; *gøre et godt ~* make· a bargain; *oven i ~et* into the bargain; *få ngt med i ~et* get· sth thrown in.
købe *v* buy·, purchase; *~ ngt af en for 50p* buy· sth off sby at 50p; *~ ind* go· shopping; *~ ngt op* buy· sth up; *~ en ud* buy· sby out; **~dygtig** *adj* with money to spend; **~kort** *et* credit card; **~kraft** *en (om kunde)* spending power; *(om penge)* purchasing power.
København *s* Copen'hagen; **københavner** *en* Copen'hagener; **københavnsk** *adj* Copen'hagen.
køber *en* buyer, purchaser.
købesum *en* purchase price.
købmand *en* grocer; *(grosserer)* merchant; *gå til ~en* go· to the grocer's; **~s·forretning** *en* grocer's, general store; **~s·skole** *en* com'mercial school.
købslå *v* bargain *(om* for).
købstad *en* borough.
kød *et (på levende væsen; fiske~ og frugt~)* flesh; *(som mad)* meat; *~ og blod* flesh and blood; *hakket ~* mince; *stegt ~* roast meat; *gå alt ~ets gang* go· the way of all flesh; *der var ikke meget ~ på den historie* it was not much of a story; **~ben** *et* bone; **~bolle** *en* meat ball.
kødelig *adj (mods: åndelig)* bodily; *(sanselig)* carnal; *han er min ~e fætter* he is my first cousin.
kødfars *en* forcemeat; *(færdigrørt)* sausage meat.
kødgryde *en* stewpan; *blive hjemme ved ~rne* stay· home in the kitchen.
kødhakkemaskine *en* mincer.
kødhammer *en* (meat) tenderizer.
kødrand *en* moulded meat ring; *(om tilskuere)* crowd.
kødsuppe *en* soup, meat broth.
kødædende *adj* car'nivorous.
køje *en (på skib etc)* berth; *(i hus)* bunk; *gå til køjs* turn in, (F) hit· the sack; **~seng** *en* bunk bed.
køkken *et* kitchen; *(om kogekunst)* cui'sine; **~adgang** *en: værelse med ~adgang* room with access to kitchen; **~bord** *et* kitchen table; *(overside af ~element)* worktop; **~dør** *en* back entrance; **~have** *en* vegetable garden; **~maskine** *en* kitchen ap'pliance; **~rulle** *en* kitchen roll; **~salt** *et* cooking salt; **~trappe** *en* backstairs *pl;* **~udstyr** *et* kitchenware; *(hårde hvidevarer)* kitchen hardware; **~vask** *en* kitchen sink.
køl *en (mar)* keel; *(køling)* chilling; *på ret ~* on an even keel; *lægge vinen på ~* chill the wine.
køle *v* cool, chill; *regnen ~r* the rain is cooling; *~ ngt af* chill sth; **~bil** *en* re'frigerated van; **~disk** *en* re'frigerated counter.
køler *en (auto)* radiator; **~gitter** *et* radiator grille; **~hjelm** *en* bonnet; **~væske** *en* anti-freeze.
køleskab *et* re'frigerator, (F) fridge; **~s·kold** *adj* straight from the fridge.
køletaske *en* insulated bag.
kølevand *et* cooling water.
kølevogn *en (jernb)* re'frigerator van; *(lastbil)* re'frigerator lorry.
kølig *adj* cool; *(ubehageligt ~)* chilly; *det er ~t vejr* the weather is chilly; **~hed** *en* coolness; chill.
kølle *en* club; *(gastr)* leg.
Køln *s* Co'logne.
kølvand *et* wake; *med kone og børn i ~et* with wife and kids in his wake.

køn *et* sex; *(gram)* gender; *det modsatte* ~ the opposite sex.

køn *adj* pretty, nice; *en* ~ *udsigt* a pretty view; *du er en* ~ *en!* you are a nice one! *det er en* ~ *redelighed!* it is a pretty mess!

køns... *sms:* **~celle** *en* ga'mete; **~dele** *pl* private parts; **~diskriminerende** *adj* sexist; **~liv** *et* sex life; **~moden** *adj* sexually ma'ture; **~organ** *et* sexual organ; **~rolle** *en* sex role; **~sygdom** *en* ve'nereal dis'ease, VD.

køre *en: ud i én* ~ non-stop // *v* drive·, go·; *(motorcykel, cykel)* ride·; *(afgå)* leave·; ~ *bil* drive· (a car); ~ *en hjem* drive· (,take·) sby home; *bussen* ~*r kun på lørdage* the bus is running only on Saturdays; ~ *med toget* go· by train; *han* ~*r på cykel til arbejde* he rides his bike to work; ~ *ind i en mur* run· into a wall; ~ *forkert* take· the wrong road; ~ *frem for rødt* drive· through the red lights; ~ *galt* have an accident; ~ *ind til siden* pull in to the side; *må jeg* ~ *med?* can you give me a lift? ~ *en ned* run· sby over; *blive kørt over* be run over; ~ *en tur* go· for a drive; **~bane** *en* roadway; *(spor på motorvej)* lane; **~klar** *adj (i orden)* in running order; *(parat)* ready to start; **~kort** *et* driving licence; *han blev frataget* ~*kortet* he had his licence su'spended; **~lejlighed** *en* lift; **~lærer** *en* driving in'structor; **~plan** *en* timetable; **~prøve** *en* driving test; **~stol** *en* wheelchair; **~tur** *en* ride; *(i egen bil)* drive, run; **~tøj** *et* vehicle.

kørsel *en* driving; *(transport)* haulage; *(edb)* run; *der er to timers* ~ *til byen* it is two hours' drive into town; *farlig* ~ dangerous driving; **~s·retning** *en* di'rection of travelling.

kørvel *en* chervil.

køter *en* cur.

kåbe *en* coat; *(fig)* cloak.

kåd *adj* playful; *(tankeløs)* wanton; **~hed** *en* playfulness; wantonness; *i* ~*hed* for fun.

kål *en (især hvid~, rød~)* cabbage; *(grøn~)* kale; *gøre* ~ *på en* get· the better of sby; **~hoved** *et* head of cabbage; **~orm** *en* caterpillar; **~rabi, ~roe** *en* swede.

kår *pl* circumstances; *trange* ~ poor circumstances.

kårde *en* rapier.

kåre *v* choose·, se'lect.

kåring *en* e'lection, se'lection.

L

lab *en* paw; *suge på* ~*ben* tighten one's belt.

laban *en* rascal.

labbe *v:* ~ *ngt i sig* lap sth up.

laber *adj* (F) super; *en* ~ *larve* (S) an eyeful, a bird.

laborant *en* lab(oratory) tech'nician.

laboratorium *et* la'boratory, (F) lab.

labskovs *en* stew.

lad *et (på bil)* platform // *adj* lazy; *ligge på den* ~*e side* be idle.

lade *en* barn.

lade *v* let·, al'low to; *(foregive)* pre'tend; *lad os vente og se* let us wait and see; *lad hende være (i fred)* leave· her alone; ~ *som om man er ung* pre'tend to be young; *lad være (med det)!* don't (do that)! *hun kunne ikke* ~ *være med at grine* she could not help laughing; ~ *som ingenting* be'have as if nothing had happened; *det* ~*r til at være i orden* it seems to be in order; ~ *sig narre* be fooled; *det* ~*r sig ikke gøre* it can't be done.

lade *v (et gevær etc)* load; *(et batteri)* charge.

ladning *en* load; *(om skib)* cargo; *(elek)* charge.

lag *et* layer; *(maling, lak etc)* coat; *gå i* ~ *med ngt* tackle sth; *et* ~ *maling* a coat of paint.

lage *en (gastr)* pickle; *lægge agurker i* ~ pickle cucumber.

lagen *et* sheet.

lager *et* store; *(i forretning og fig)* stock; *have ngt på* ~ keep· sth in stock.

lagkage *en* layer cake.

lagre *v* store; *(lægge til modning)*

ma'ture; *en ~t ost* a ma'tured cheese.

lagring *en* storage; ma'turing.

lak *en (fernis)* lacquer, varnish; *(maling)* e'namel; *(til møbler, negle)* polish, varnish.

lakej *en (neds)* lackey.

lakere *v* varnish.

lakfjerner *en* lacquer re'mover; *(til negle)* nail varnish re'mover.

lakrids *en* liquorice; **~konfekt** *en* liquorice allsorts.

laks *en* salmon *(pl: ~)*.

laksko *en* patent leather shoe.

laksørred *en* sea trout.

lalle *v* drivel; *~nde idiot* blithering idiot.

lam *et* lamb // *adj* paralyzed.

lamel *en (i træbund)* slat; *(på champignon etc)* gill.

lametta *en* tinsel.

lamhed *en* pa'ralysis.

lamme *v* paralyse; *stå som lammet* be petrified *(af skræk* with fear).

lammekød *et* lamb.

lammelse *en* pa'ralysis.

lammesteg *en* roast lamb.

lammeuld *en* lambswool.

lampe *en* lamp; **~feber** *en* stage fright; **~skærm** *en* lampshade.

lampet *en* wall bracket.

lamslået *adj* dumb'founded.

lancere *v* launch.

land *et* country; *(jord)* land(s); *gå i ~* go· a'shore; *trække i ~ (fig)* backtrack; *længere inde i ~et* further inland; *rejse over ~ (,til ~s)* go· by land; *ude på ~et* in the country; *den må du længere ud på ~et med!* you can tell that to the ma'rines! *tage på ~et* go· into the country; *her til ~s* in this country; **~arbejder** *en* farm worker; **~befolkningen** *s* the rural popu'lation.

landbrug *et* farming; *(faget)* agriculture; *(landejendom)* farm; **~er** *en* farmer; **~s·jord** *en* farmland; **~s·ministerium** *et* Ministry of Agriculture; **~s·skole** *en* agri'cultural school.

lande *v* land; *(om fly også)* touch down.

landevej *en* country road; *lige ud ad ~en (om person)* straightforward; *(om ngt nemt)* simple; *på ~en* on the road; **~s·løb** *et (cykling)* road race.

landflygtig *adj* exiled; **~hed** *en* exile.

landgang *en* landing; **~(s·bro)** *en* gangway; **~s·brød** *et (gastr)* huffer.

landhandel *en* general store; *blandet ~* sundry shop.

landing *en* landing; *(om fly også)* touch-down; **~s·bane** *en* runway; **~s·stel** *et* landing gear.

land... *sms:* **~jorden** *s: på ~jorden* on dry land; **~kort** *et* map; **~krabbe** *en (neds)* landlubber; **~lig** *adj* rural; **~mand** *en* farmer; **~måler** *en* sur'veyor; **~måling** *en* sur'veying; **~område** *et* territory.

lands... *sms:* **~by** *en* village; **~bykirke** *en* village church; **~del** *en* part of the country; **~dækkende** *adj* nationwide; **~forræder** *en* traitor; **~forræderi** *et* treason; **~forvisning** *en* exile; **~hold** *et: det engelske ~hold* the English inter'national team, the English e'leven.

landskab *et* landscape, scenery; **~e·lig** *adj* scenic.

landskamp *en* inter'national (match).

landskinke *en* ham.

landsmand *en* fellow countryman *(pl:* -men); *hvad ~ er du?* what natio'nality are you?

landsomfattende *adj* nationwide.

landsret *en sv.t.* high court and court of ap'peal.

land... *sms:* **~sted** *et* country seat; **~tange** *en* isthmus; **~vin** *en* local wine; **~vinding** *en* (major) a'chievement; **~æg** *et* barn egg.

lang *adj* long; *(høj)* tall; *hele natten ~* all night long; *få en ~ næse* be disap'pointed; *falde så ~ man er* fall· flat; *i ~ tid* for a long time; *blive ~ i ansigtet* pull a long face; *(se også langt)*; **~distance** long-range; **~drag** *s: trække i ~drag* go· on and on.

lange *v (række)* hand; *~ ud efter ngt* reach out for sth; *~ ud efter en* hit· out at sby.

lang... *sms:* **~fart** *en* long voyage; **~finger** *en* middle finger; *(om per-*

son) pickpocket; **~fredag** *en* Good Friday; **~fristet** *adj* longterm *(fx lån* loan); **~håret** *adj* long-haired; **~rend** *et (på ski)* cross-country skiing.

langs *adv/præp* along; *~ med* along; *på ~* lengthwise; *ligge på ~* be in bed.

langsigtet *adj* longterm.

langsom *adj* slow; *uret går for ~t* the watch (,clock) is slow; *~t men sikkert* slowly but surely; *~t virkende* slow-acting.

langstrakt *adj* lengthy.

langsynet *adj* long-sighted.

langt *adv* far; *(+ superlativ)* by far; *~ fra* far from; *~ væk* far away; *der er ~ til stationen* it is a long way to the station; *hun er ~ henne (om gravid)* she is far gone; *~ inde i skoven* deep in the forest; *~ om længe* at long last; *~ ud på natten* late in the night; *det er lidt ~ ude (fig)* it is a bit far out (,far-fetched); *ikke på ~ nær* not by a long chalk; *~ den bedste* by far the best.

langtids... *sms:* **~holdbar** *adj* with a long shelf-life; **~ledig** *adj* long-term unemployed; **~parkering** *en* long-term parking.

lang... *sms:* **~trukken** *adj* pro'longed; **~turschauffør** *en* long-distance lorry driver; **~varig** *adj* lengthy, pro'longed; **~vejs** *adv: ~vejs fra* from far away.

lanse *en* lance.

lanterne *en* lantern.

lap *en (på tøj etc)* patch; *(stykke papir)* piece of paper; *(se også same).*

lappe *v* patch, mend; *~ cykel* mend a puncture; **~grejer** *pl* (bicycle) re'pair outfit.

laps *en* dandy; **~et** *adj* foppish.

larm *en* noise; *byens ~* the hustle and bustle of the city; **~e** *v* make· a noise; **~ende** *adj* noisy.

larve *en (zo)* caterpillar; (F, *om pige)* bird; **~fødder** *pl* caterpillar tracks.

las *en* rag.

laserstråle *en* laser beam.

laset *adj* tattered.

lasket *adj* flabby.

lasso *en* lasso.

last *en (uvane, synd)* vice; *(byrde)* weight, load; *(ladning)* cargo; *(lastrum)* hold; **~bil** *en (åben)* truck; *(lukket)* van; *(stor, tung)* lorry.

laste *v (tage om bord)* load; *(bebrejde)* blame.

lastrum *et (mar)* hold.

lastvogn *en d.s.s. ~bil;* **~s·tog** *en* lorry and trailer, (F) juggernaut.

latin *et* Latin; **latinsk** *adj* Latin.

latter *en* laughter; *(~anfald, måde at le på)* laugh; *slå en høj ~ op* burst· into a loud laugh; *vække ~* be the laughing stock; **~gas** *en* laughing gas; **~krampe** *en: få ~krampe* go· into fits of laughter; **~lig** *adj* ri'diculous.

latyrus *en (bot)* sweet pea.

laurbær *pl: hvile på sine ~* rest on one's laurels; **~blad** *et* bay leaf *(pl:* leaves); **~krans** *en* laurel wreath.

lav *en (bot)* lichen // *et (håndværker~)* guild.

lav *adj (ikke høj)* low; *(gemen)* mean; *(om vand)* shallow.

lava *en* lava.

lavalder *en: den kriminelle ~* the age of criminal responsi'bility.

lave *s: af ~* out of order; *(om fx verden)* out of joint; *gå i ~* go· right // *v (fremstille)* make·; *(gøre)* do·; *(reparere)* mend, re'pair; *hvad ~r du?* what are you doing? *~ mad* cook, pre'pare a meal; *~t af* made of; *~ ngt om* change sth; *~ om på ngt* alter sth; *~ til* pre'pare; *~ cykel* mend one's bike; *få ~t låsen (også)* have the lock seen to.

lavement *et* e'nema.

lavendel *en* lavender.

lavine *en* avalanche.

lavkonjunktur *en* de'pression.

lavland *et* lowland.

lavmål *et: under ~et* below par.

lavprisvarehus *et* dis'count store.

lavtlønnet *adj* low-paid; **lavtlønstillæg** *et* supplement for low-paid workers.

lavtryk *et (om vejret)* de'pression.

lavvande *et (ebbe)* low water (,tide); **~t** *adj* shallow.

le *en* scythe.

le *v* laugh *(ad* at); ~ *af glæde* laugh with joy.

led *en (retning)* di'rection; *på den lange* ~ lengthwise // *et (anat)* joint; *(i kæde)* link; *(låge)* gate; *gå af* ~ be dislocated; *være af* ~ be out of joint; *være et* ~ *i ngt* be part of sth.

led *adj (ækel)* dis'gusting; *være* ~ *og ked af ngt* be fed up with sth; *en* ~ *karl* a nasty piece of work, a bastard.

leddelt *adj* ar'ticulated.

leddeløs *adj (om fx stol)* rickety; *(fig, om person)* weak.

lede *en* dis'gust; *føle* ~ *ved* be dis'gusted by // *v (føre)* lead·; *(vejlede)* guide; *(stå for)* manage; *(søge)* look; *(grundigt)* search; *(elek etc)* con'duct; ~ *et møde* chair a meeting; ~ *en på sporet* give· sby a clue; ~ *efter en* look for sby; ~ *huset igennem* search the house.

ledelse *en* management; *(vejledning)* guidance; *under* ~ *af (mus)* con'ducted by; *under* ~ *af hr. Pedersen (om møde)* chaired by Mr. Pedersen.

ledende *adj* leading.

leder *en* leader; *(elek)* con'ductor; *(artikel)* leading article.

ledetråd *en* lead.

ledig *adj (ubesat)* vacant, un'occupied; *(arbejdsløs)* ,unem'ployed; *(fri)* free; **~gang** *en* idleness; **~hed** *en* ,unem'ployment.

ledning *en (elek)* wire; *(til lampe etc)* lead; *(rør)* pipe; **~s·vand** *et* tap water.

ledsage *v* ac'company; *(som beskyttelse)* e'scort; **~r** *en* com'panion, 'escort.

ledtog *s: stå i* ~ *med* be an ac'complice of.

leg *en* play; *(spil etc efter regler)* game; *det går som en* ~ it is going on wheels; *holde op mens* ~*en er god* stop while the going is good.

legal *adj* legal.

legalisere *v* legalize.

legat *et (studie~)* scholarship; *(fra staten)* grant.

legation *en* le'gation.

lege *v* play; *(foregive)* pre'tend; ~ *sørøvere* play at pirates; ~ *med ngt* play with sth; *(ens følelser etc)* trifle with; *(pille ved)* toy with sth; *må jeg* ~ *med?* may· I join you? **~gade** *en* play street; **~kammerat** *en* playmate.

legeme *et* body.

legems... *sms:* **~del** *en* part of the body; **~størrelse** *en: i* ~*størrelse* life-size; **~vægt** *en* (body)weight; **~øvelser** *pl (i skolen)* physical edu'cation.

legendarisk *adj* legendary.

legende *en* legend.

legeplads *en* playground.

legering *en* alloy.

legesyg *adj* playful.

legetøj *et* toys *pl; et stykke* ~ a toy; **~s·butik** *en* toyshop.

legitimation *en (bevis, kort)* identifi'cation papers.

legitimere *v:* ~ *sig* i'dentify oneself.

lejde *et: få frit* ~ get· a safe-conduct.

leje *et* bed; *(færge~)* berth.

leje *en (lejemål)* lease; *(betaling)* rent; *værelse til* ~ room for hire; *bo til* ~ rent a room (,flat, house); *bo til* ~ *hos en* lodge with sby // *et* bed // *v* rent; *(for kort tid også)* hire; ~ *en bil* hire (,rent) a car; ~ *ngt ud (om hus, lejlighed)* let· sth; *(om fx bil, båd)* hire sth out; **~kontrakt** *en (for hus)* lease; *(for fx bil)* hire contract; **~morder** *en* hired killer; **~mål** *et* lease.

lejer *en (af bolig)* tenant; *(for lang tid)* leaseholder; *(af værelse)* lodger; *(af bil)* hirer.

lejesoldat *en* mercenary.

lejlighed *en (bolig)* flat; *(gunstig* ~*)* chance, oppor'tunity; *(anledning)* oc'casion; *leje en* ~ rent a flat; *benytte* ~*en* take· the opportunity; *få* ~ *til at* get· a chance to; *ved* ~ some day; *ved en senere* ~ later; *han dyrker damer ved enhver* ~ any time he gets the chance, he's after the ladies.

lejlighedsvis *adv* oc'casionally.

lejr *en* camp; *ligge i* ~, *slå* ~ camp; **~bål** *et* campfire.

lejre *v: ~ sig (dvs. slå sig ned)* settle down.
lejrskole *en* camp school.
lejrsport *en* camping.
leksikon *et (konversations~)* encyclo'paedia; *(ordbog, mindre ~)* dictionary.
lektie *en* lesson; *lave ~r* do· one's homework; **~hjælp** *en* (private) coaching.
lektion *en* lesson.
lektor *en (univ)* senior lecturer; *(i gymnasium)* senior teacher.
lekture *en* reading matter.
lem *en (dør)* hatch; *(klap)* shutter; *vi må se at komme ud af ~men* we'd better get a move on; // *et (legemsdel)* limb; *det mandlige ~* the male member; *risikere liv og ~mer* risk one's life.
lemlæste *v* mutilate.
lempe *s: fare med ~* go· easy // *v (flytte, lette)* ease; *(tilpasse)* a'dapt; *~ kontrollen* re'lax con'trol; **~lig** *adj* gentle; *(om fx betingelser)* easy; **~lse** *en (i krav etc)* slackening.
leopard *en* leopard ['lɛpəd].
ler *en* clay; **~due** *en* clay pigeon; **~et** *adj* clayey; **~varer** *pl* pottery, earthenware.
lesbe *en,* **lesbisk** *adj* lesbian.
let *adj (ikke tung)* light; *(nem)* easy; *(svag)* slight // *adv* lightly; easily; slightly; *gå ~ hen over ngt* pass lightly over sth; *have ~ ved ngt* do· sth easily; *en ~ forkølelse* a slight cold; *det er ~tere sagt end gjort* it is easier said than done; *~ påklædt* lightly dressed; **~fattelig** *adj* easily under'stood; **~fordærvelig** *adj* perishable; **~fordøjelig** *adj* di'gestible.
lethed *en (om vægt)* lightness; *(nemhed)* ease; easiness; *med ~* easily.
letkøbt *adj* cheap.
Letland *s* Latvia.
letmælk *en* low-fat milk, semi-skimmed milk.
letsindig *adj (uansvarlig)* irre'sponsible; *(ligeglad)* careless; *(for hurtig, uoverlagt)* rash; **~hed** *en* irresponsi'bility; carelessness; rashness.
lette *en* Latvian.
lette *v (om vægt)* lighten; *(gøre nemmere)* make· easier; *(om fly)* take· off; *(om tåge)* lift; *~ anker* weigh anchor; *~ sit hjerte* un'burden oneself; *det ~de!* what a re'lief! *~ en i hans arbejde* make· sby's job easier for him; *~ ben (om hund)* cock a leg.
lettelse *en* re'lief.
lettet *adj* re'lieved; *ånde ~t op* breathe again.
lettilgængelig *adj* ac'cessible; *(let at forstå)* easily under'stood.
lettisk *s/adj* Latvian.
letvægt *en (sport)* lightweight; **letvægts-** lightweight *(fx suit* habit).
leve *et: udbringe et ~ for en* give· three cheers for sby // *v* live; *(være i live)* be a'live; *~ af grønsager* live on vegetables; *~ for sit arbejde* live for one's work; *~ for 500 kr. om ugen* live on 500 kr. a week; *han ~r og ånder for musik* music is his whole life; *~ med i ngt* take· a strong interest in sth; *~ op til* live up to; *~ sammen med en* live with sby; *de ~r sammen* they live to'gether.
levebrød *et* livelihood; *(stilling)* job.
levefod *en* standard of living.
levende *adj* living; *(efter verbum)* a'live; *(foran substantiv, ikke om person)* live; *(livlig)* lively; *i ~ live* (while) a'live; *slippe ~ fra ngt* e'scape sth alive; *~ lys* candle; *jeg kan ~ forestille mig at...* I can very well i'magine that...; *være ~ interesseret i ngt* take a lively interest in sth; *~ hegn* hedgerow.
leveomkostninger *pl* cost of living.
lever *en* liver; *tale frit fra ~en* speak· freely, (F) let· fly.
leverance *en* de'livery.
leverandør *en* sup'plier.
leverbetændelse *en* hepa'titis.
levere *v (aflevere, merk)* de'liver; *(forsyne)* sup'ply; *(fremstille)* pro'duce; *(fremskaffe)* pro'vide; *~ ngt tilbage* re'turn sth.
levering *en* de'livery; *(forsyning)* sup'ply; *til ~ i uge 9* for de'livery in week 9; *betales ved ~en* payable on

delivery; **~s·betingelser** *pl* terms of de'livery; **~s·dygtig** *adj* able to de'liver; **~s·tid** *en* date of de'livery; *14 dages ~s·tid* to be de'livered within 14 days.

leverpostej *en* liver pâté.

levertran *en* cod liver oil.

leve... *sms:* **~råb** *pl* cheers; **~standard** *en* standard of living; **~tid** *en* lifetime, life (*pl:* lives); **~vej** *en* ca'reer; job; **~vis** *en* way of life.

levn *et* relic; **~e** *v* leave·.

levned *et* life (*pl:* lives); **~s·middel** *et* foodstuff.

levning *en (også fortids~)* relic; **~er** *pl (om mad)* left-overs, leavings; *(ruiner)* remnants.

libaneser *en,* **libanesisk** *adj* Leba'nese; **Libanon** *s* Lebanon.

liberal *adj* liberal; **~isme** *en* liberalism.

licens *en* licence; *betale fjernsyns~* pay· the TV licence fee.

licitation *en: udbyde ngt i ~* in'vite tenders for sth.

lide *v* suffer *(af* from); *~ nød* suffer depri'vation; *~ nederlag* be de'feated; *~ tab* suffer losses.

lide *v: kunne ~* like; *jeg kan bedre ~ den ost* I pre'fer that cheese; *jeg kan ikke ~ ham* I don't like him.

lidelse *en* suffering; *(sygdom)* dis'ease; *(elendighed)* misery; *den guitar er en ~ at høre på* it is agony to listen to that gui'tar; **~s·fælle** *en* fellow-sufferer; **~s·historien** *s (rel)* the Passion.

lidenskab *en* passion.

lidenskabelig *adj* passionate.

liderlig *adj* randy; *(neds)* lecherous.

lidet *adv* not very, little; *~ tilfredsstillende* not very satis'factory.

lidt *adj* little // *adv* a little, slightly; *kun (,bare) ~* just a little; *~ af hvert* a bit of everything; *vi har set ~ af hvert* we've seen all sorts of things; *hun har prøvet ~ af hvert (dvs. levet livet)* she's been around; *vil du have ~ te?* would you like some tea? *vent ~!* wait a minute! *~ efter* a little later; *~ efter ~* little by little; *om ~* in a minute; *for ~ siden* a moment ago; *den er ~ i et (om klokken)* it's almost one o'clock; *han er ikke så ~ blæret* he's too arrogant by half.

lift *en (baby~)* carrycot; *(tekn)* lift // *et: få et ~* get· a lift; **~e** *v* hitchhike.

lig *et* dead body; *(jur, med)* corpse; *ligne et ~* look like death; *det bliver over mit ~!* over my dead body.

lig *adj (lignende)* like; *(~ med)* equal to; *to og to er ~ fire* two and two equals (,is) four.

liga *en* league.

ligbrænding *en* cre'mation.

lige *en: uden ~* un'paralleled // *adj (ikke skæv)* straight; *(direkte)* di'rect; *(jævnbyrdig)* even; *(ligeberettiget)* equal; *i ~ linje* in a straight line; *(om nedstamning)* in di'rect line; *~ for ~* fair is fair // *adv (ikke skævt)* straight; *(direkte)* di'rectly; *(ligeligt)* equally; *(jævnt)* evenly; *(netop)* just; *~ før han kom* just be'fore he came; *det er ~ meget* it does· not matter; *de er ~ gamle* they are the same age; *køre ~ frem* drive· straight on; *de er ~ store* they are the same size; *han er ~ så tyk som hun* he is just as fat as she is; *~ nu* just now, this minute; *kør bare ~ ud* just drive· straight on; *vi bor ~ ved søen* we live close to the lake; *han var ~ ved at falde* he almost fell; *~ et øjeblik* just a moment; *det skete ~ foran kirken* it happened right in front of the church.

ligeberettigelse *en* equal rights *pl.*

ligefrem *adj* straightforward, plain; *han var meget ~* he was quite straight'forward // *adv (simpelthen)* simply; *(bogstavelig talt)* literally; *det er ikke ~ nemt* it is not e'xactly easy; *han var ~ venlig* he was positively friendly.

ligeglad *adj (uinteresseret)* in'different; *(sjusket)* careless; *jeg er ~* I don't care; *han er ~ med båden* he does not care about the boat.

ligegyldig *adj (uden betydning)* unim'portant; *(uinteresseret)* in'different; *(sjusket)* careless; *~ hvad du gør* no matter what you do; *det er*

ret ~t it does· not really matter; **~hed** *en* in'difference.
ligeledes *adv* also, as well.
ligelig *adj* equal; *(retfærdig)* fair.
ligeløn *en* equal pay.
ligemand *en* equal.
ligesindet *adj* like-minded.
ligesom *adv* sort of; *(noget)* a little; *det er ~ lidt sært* it is sort of odd; *det går ~ bedre* it is kind of better // *konj* like; *(idet)* just as; *hun er blond ~ du* she is blonde just like you; *gør ~ jeg* do· as I do·; *~ om* just as if; *~ vi skulle til at gå...* just as we were leaving...
ligestillet *adj* equal; **ligestilling** *en* equal oppor'tunities.
ligeså(dan) *adj* the same; *gøre ~* do· the same.
ligetil *adj: det er ganske ~* it is quite simple.
ligeud *adv (om retning)* straight on; *sige det ~* put· it bluntly.
ligevægt *en* balance; *bevare ~en (dvs. ikke vælte)* keep· one's balance; *(dvs. ikke blive ophidset)* re'main calm; *tabe ~en (dvs. vælte)* lose· (one's) balance; *(dvs. blive ophidset)* lose· one's head; *bringe en ud af ~* throw· sby off his (,her) balance; **~ig** *adj* well-balanced, calm.
ligge *v* lie·; *(om hus etc)* stand·; *lade ngt ~* let· sth lie; *(fig)* leave· sth alone; *~ for døden* be dying; *det ~r lige for* it is obvious; *det ~r ikke for ham* he has no aptitude for it, (F) he was not made for it; *~ i sengen (dvs. være syg)* be in bed; be ill in bed; *~ inde med ngt* hold· sth; *~ stille* lie still; *(om produktion etc)* be at a standstill; *~ under for* be the victim of; *huset ~r ved skoven* the house stands· by the forest; **~nde** *adj* lying (down; *blive ~* stay; *have ~nde gæster* have people staying.
liggestol *en* deck chair.
liggesår *et* bedsore.
liggevogn *en (jernb)* cou'chette.
lighed *en* simi'larity; *(stærkere)* likeness; *(ligeret)* e'quality; *i ~ med* like; **~s·punkt** *et* simi'larity; **~s·tegn** *et* equals sign.
ligkiste *en* coffin.
ligne *v (af ydre)* look like; *(af væsen)* be like; *~ sine forældre (også)* take· after one's parents; *~ en på en prik* look e'xactly like sby; *hvor det ~r dig!* how very like you! *ikke det der ~r* not a bit.
lignelse *en* parable.
lignende *adj* similar; *og ~* and the like; *jeg har aldrig set ngt ~* I never saw anything like it.
ligning *en (mat)* e'quation; *(i skat)* as'sessment.
ligtorn *en* corn.
likvidation *en* liqui'dation.
likvidere *v (merk)* wind· up; *(dræbe)* liquidate.
likør *en* li'queur.
lilje *en* lily; **~konval** *en* lily-of-the-valley.
lilla *adj* purple.
lille *adj* small; *(kort)* short; *~ bitte* tiny; *da han (,hun) var ~* when he (,she) was a little boy (,girl); *fra ~ af* from childhood; *en ~ uges tid* just under a week; *hun venter en ~* she is ex'pecting (a baby); *blive den ~* get· the worst of it.
lille... *sms:* **~bror** *en* little brother, younger brother; **~finger** *en* little finger, (F) pinkie; **~juleaften** *en* the evening be'fore Christmas Eve; **~put** *en* midget; **~skole** *en* small private school; **~søster** *en* little sister, younger sister; **~tå** *en* little toe.
lim *en* glue; **~e** *v* glue; *~e ngt fast på ngt* stick· sth onto sth; **~farve** *en* dis'temper.
limning *en* gluing; *gå op i ~en* come· un'stuck; *(fig)* fall· a'part.
limonade *en* lemo'nade.
limstift *en* glue stick.
lind *en (træ)* lime // *adj (blød)* soft; **~e·træ** *et* lime tree.
lindre *v* re'lieve, ease.
lindring *en* re'lief.
line *en* line; *gå på ~* walk the tightrope.
lineal *en* ruler.
linedanser *en* tightrope walker.
lingeri *et* underwear.

linje *en* line; *i store ~r* in broad outline; *bevare den slanke ~* keep· one's figure; *ny ~ (i diktat)* new paragraph; *over hele ~n* all along the line; *køre med ~ ti* go· by number ten; *det er på ~ med hvad John sagde* it's in line with what John said; **~afstand** *en* line spacing; **~dommer** *en (tennis)* linesman *(pl:* -men).

linjere *v* rule.

linjeskriver *en (edb)* line printer.

linjevogter *en (sport)* linesman *(pl:* -men).

linned *et* linen.

linning *en (på nederdel etc)* waistband; *(ærme~)* wrist-band; *(hals~)* neckband.

linoleum *et* li'noleum; **~s·snit** *et* linocut.

linolie *en* linseed oil.

linse *en (bot)* lentil; *(optisk)* lens.

lire *v: ~ et vers af* reel off a poem.

lirekasse *en* barrel organ.

lirke *v: ~ ngt ud af en* wangle sth out of sby; *~ ved ngt* pick at sth; *~ sig frem* feel· one's way.

list *en* trick; *(snedighed)* cunning.

liste *en (af træ etc)* strip (of wood etc); *(til pynt)* trim; *(fortegnelse)* list; *skrive sig på en ~* put· one's name down on a list.

liste *v* creep·, tiptoe; *(neds)* sneak; *~ sig væk* steal· away; *~ sig til ngt* wangle sth.

listig *adj* sly, cunning; **~hed** *en* slyness, cunning.

Litauen *s* Lithu'ania; **litauer** *en* Lithu'anian; **litauisk** *s/adj* Lithu'anian.

lit de parade *en: ligge på ~* lie· in state.

liter *en* litre; **~mål** *et* litre measure; **~vis** *adv* by the litre.

litteratur *en* literature; **~historie** *en* history of literature; **~søgning** *en* infor'mation re'trieval.

litterær *adj* literary.

liv *et* life *(pl:* lives); *(overdel på kjole etc)* bodice, top; *(talje)* waist; *det drejer sig om ~ el. død* it is a matter of life and death; *hans ~s chance* the chance of a lifetime; *miste ~et* lose· one's life; *nyde ~et* en'joy life; *tage ~et af en* kill sby; *tage sit eget ~* take· one's own life; *en ven for ~et* a friend for life; *være i ~e* be a'live; *aldrig i ~et* over my dead body; *føre ngt ud i ~et* put· sth into ef'fect; *med ~et i hænderne* with one's heart in one's mouth; *sætte ~ i en fest* liven up a party; *true en på ~et* threaten sby's life; *sætte en bøf til ~s* con'sume a steak.

livagtig *adj* vivid, lifelike.

livgarden *s* the Royal Life Guards.

livlig *adj* lively; *det gik ~t til* things were lifely.

livløs *adj* lifeless; *(død)* dead.

livmoder *en* womb; *få fjernet ~en* have a hyster'ectomy.

livredder *en (på strand)* lifeguard; *(fig)* rescuer.

livrem *en* belt; *spænde ~men ind* tighten one's belt.

livret *en* favourite dish.

livs... *sms:* **~anskuelse** *en* phi'losophy (of life); **~betingelser** *pl* living conditions; **~fare** *en* mortal danger; *være i ~fare* be in danger of one's life; *(om patient)* be in a critical con'dition; *være uden for ~fare* be out of danger; **~farlig** *adj* highly dangerous; *den dreng er ~farlig (iron)* that boy is a menace; **~forsikring** *en* life in'surance; **~glad** *adj* happy; **~historie** *en* life-story; **~kraftig** *adj* vigorous; **~kvalitet** *en* quality of life; **~nødvendig** *adj* vital; **~stil** *en* lifestyle; **~tegn** *et* sign of life; *give ~tegn fra sig* show· signs of life; **~tid** *en: fængsel på ~tid* prison for life, life sentence; **~varig** *adj* lifelong, for life; *få ~varigt fængsel* get· a life sentence; **~vigtig** *adj* vital.

livvagt *en* bodyguard.

livvidde *en* waist.

lod *en (skæbne)* fate; *(andel)* share // *et (i lotteri)* lot; *(til vægt el. ur)* weight; *(mar)* lead [lɛd]; *trække ~ om ngt* draw· lots for sth; *være i ~ (tekn)* be plumb.

lodde *v (om metal)* solder; *(mar)*

sound; ~ *stemningen* test the atmosphere; **~kolbe** *en* soldering iron.
lodden *adj* hairy; *(om stof)* fleecy.
loddetin *et* solder.
lodret *adj* vertical; *(i krydsord)* down; *en ~ løgn* a downright lie.
lods *en* pilot; **~e** *v* pilot.
lodseddel *en* (lottery) ticket.
lodtrækning *en* draw.
loft *et (i stue etc og fig)* ceiling; *(~rum)* loft; *(pulterkammer)* attic; *ryge helt op i ~et (fig)* hit· the ceiling; *lægge ngt på ~et* put· sth in the attic; *lægge ~ over ngt (fig)* put· a ceiling on sth; **~s·lampe** *en* ceiling fitting.
logbog *en* log book.
loge *en (teat)* box; *(frimurer~)* lodge.
logere *v* lodge; **~nde** *en* lodger.
logi *et* lodgings; *(for kort ophold)* accomo'dation.
logik *en* logic.
logisk *adj* logical.
logre *v (om hund)* wag the tail; *(om person)* crawl *(for* to).
lok *en* lock; *gyldne ~ker (dvs. krøller)* golden ringlets.
lokal *adj* local; *~ 334 (tlf)* ex'tension 344; **~bedøvelse** *en* local anaes'thetic; **~befolkningen** *s* the locals.
lokale *et* room; *(sal)* hall.
lokalisere *v (finde)* lo'cate.
lokal... *sms:* **~nummer** *et (tlf)* ex'tension; **~plan** *en* district plan; **~radio** *en* local radio; **~samfund** *et* local com'munity; *(på landet)* rural so'ciety; **~tog** *et* local train.
lokke *v (friste)* tempt; *(forlokke)* se'duce; *(besnakke)* coax; *~ en i en fælde* lead· sby into a trap; *~ ngt ud af en* get· sth out of sby; **~due** *en* 'decoy; **~mad** *en* bait.
lokomotiv *et* engine; **~fører** *en* engine driver.
lokum *et (udendørs)* privy; (F, *om wc)* loo.
lomme *en* pocket; *have penge på ~n* be flush; be in the money; *putte ngt i ~n* put· sth into one's pocket; pocket sth; *være i ~n på en* be in sby's pocket; *tage ngt op af ~n* take· sth out of one's pocket; **~bog** *en* notebook; **~kalender** *en* a'genda; **~kniv** *en* pocket knife *(pl:* knives); **~lygte** *en* torch; **~lærke** *en* hipflask; **~penge** *pl* pocket money; **~regner** *en* pocket calculator; **~smerter** *pl: have ~smerter* be broke; **~tyv** *en* pickpocket; **~tørklæde** *et* handkerchief; **~ur** *et* watch.
loppe *en* flea // *v: ~ sig* scratch oneself; **~marked** *et* jumble sale; **~spil** *et* tiddlywinks; **~tjans** *en* jammy job; **~torv** *et* flea market.
lort *et* (V) shit, crap; *(om person)* bastard.
los *en (zo)* lynx // *et: et ~ i røven* (F) a kick in the pants // *adj: hvad er der ~?* what's going on?
losse *v (skib el. vogn)* un'load; **~plads** *en* rubbish dump.
lotteri *et* lottery; **~gevinst** *en* prize; **~spil** *et: det er lidt af et ~spil* it's a bit of a gamble.
lov *en* law; *(tilladelse)* per'mission; *ifølge ~en* ac'cording to law; *gældende ~* the e'xisting legis'lation; *bestemt ved ~* statutory; *få ~ til at* be al'lowed to; *bede om ~* ask permission; *give en ~ til at gøre ngt* al'low (,permit) sby to do sth.
love *v* promise; *jeg skal ~ for at det var koldt!* you bet it was cold! *jeg har ~t det* I promised; *Gud være ~t!* thank God!.
lovende *adj* promising.
lovforslag *et* bill; *vedtage et ~* pass a bill.
lovgivning *en* legis'lation.
lovlig *adj* legal; *(tilladt også)* lawful; *en ~ undskyldning* a le'gitimate ex'cuse // *adv (lidt for)* rather, a bit too; *han er ~ fræk* he is a bit too cheeky.
lovord *pl* praise.
lovovertrædelse *en* of'fence.
lovpligtig *adj* com'pulsory.
lovstridig *adj* il'legal.
lovændring *en* a'mendment.
loyal *adj* loyal *(mod* to).
loyalitet *en* loyalty.
LP, lp *en* LP(-record), album.
lud *en: gå for ~ og koldt vand* be ne'glected; **~doven** *adj* bone-lazy.
luder *en* prostitute, (S) tart, pro.

ludfattig *adj* destitute.
ludo *et* ludo.
lue *en* flame; *stå i lys* ~ be a'blaze.
luffe *en (vante)* mitten; *(zo)* flipper.
luft *en* air; *(~art)* gas; *trække frisk* ~ get· some fresh air; *en mundfuld frisk* ~ a breath of fresh air; *få* ~ *for ngt* give· vent to sth; *i fri* ~ in the open (air); *springe (,sprænge) i ~en* blow· up; *forsvinde ud i den blå* ~ vanish into thin air; *det er grebet ud af ~en* it's pure in'vention; **~alarm** *en* air-raid warning; **~art** *en* gas; **~bøsse** *en* airgun.
lufte *v* air; ~ *hunden* take· the dog for a walk; ~ *ud* air, ventilate; *det ~r* there is a slight breeze.
luft... *sms:* **~fart** *en* avi'ation, flying; **~forandring** *en* change of air; **~forsvar** *et* air de'fence; **~forurening** *en* air pol'lution; **~fugtighed** *en* hu'midity; **~havn** *en* airport; **~hul** *et (fly)* air pocket.
luftig *adj* airy; *(om tøj)* light.
luft... *sms:* **~kølet** *adj* air-cooled; **~madras** *en* airbed, lilo®; **~maske** *en* chain-stitch; **~post** *en* air mail; **~pudebåd** *en* hovercraft; **~rum** *et* airspace; **~rør** *et (anat)* windpipe; **~spejling** *en* 'mirage; **~tom** *adj: ~tomt rum* vacuum; **~tæt** *adj* airtight // *adv* her'metically; **~våben** *et* air force.
luge *en* hatch // *v* weed; **~jern** *et* hoe.
lugt *en* smell; *(duft)* scent.
lugte *v* smell· *(af* of); ~ *til ngt* smell· sth; **~sans** *en* sense of smell.
lukke *v* shut·; *(~ af, spærre)* close; ~ *en virksomhed* close down a business; ~ *en ind* let· sby in, ad'mit sby; ~ *en inde* lock sby up; ~ *op for vandet* turn on the water; ~ *op for fjernsynet* switch on the television; ~ *hunden ud* let· out the dog; ~ *en ude* shut· sby out.
lukker *en (foto)* shutter.
lukket *adj* closed, shut; *(om person)* re'served; ~ *afdeling* locked ward; *for lukkede døre (jur)* closed to the public; *~vej* dead end.
lukketid *en* closing time; *efter* ~ after hours.
lukning *en* shutting; closing; *(på nederdel etc)* fastening; *(se lukke)*.
luksuriøs *adj* lu'xurious.
luksus *en* luxury.
lummer *adj (om vejr, luft)* close, sultry.
lumpen *adj* mean.
lumsk *adj* treacherous; *(bedragerisk)* de'ceitful; *(snedig)* cunning; *have en ~ mistanke* have a hunch.
lumskeri *et* treachery; cunning; *(kunster, tricks)* tricks *pl.*
lun *adj* warm; *(rar)* snug, cosy; *(om person)* humorous; *være* ~ *på en* have a crush on sby.
lund *en* grove.
lune *et* mood; *(humor)* humour; *(indfald)* whim // *v (varme op)* warm; *det ~de!* that was nice! **~fuld** *adj* unpre'dictable, fickle; *(om vejr)* changeable.
lunge *en* lung; **~betændelse** *en* pneu'monia [nju-]; **~kræft** *en* lung cancer.
lunken *adj* lukewarm; *(fig)* half-hearted.
luns *en* chunk.
lunte *en* fuse; *lugte ~n* smell· a rat // *v:* ~ *af sted* trot along.
lup *en* magnifying glass.
lur *en* nap; *(mus)* lur(e); *stå på* ~ lie· in wait *(efter* for).
lure *v (lytte)* eavesdrop; *(kigge)* peep; *(narre)* take· in; ~ *en kunsten af* pick up the trick from sby; *jeg har ~t ham* I'm onto him; ~ *på en chance* watch for a chance.
lurvet *adj* shabby; *(gemen)* mean.
lus *en* louse *(pl:* lice); *(om person)* creep; **~et** *adj* lousy; *(ussel)* measly.
luske *v (snige sig)* sneak; ~ *af* slink· away; ~ *rundt* hang· around; ~ *sig til ngt* wangle sth; **~peter** *en* sneak.
luskeri *et* hanky-panky.
lusket *adj: der er ngt* ~ *ved det* there is sth fishy about it.
lussing *en* slap on (,in) the face; *give ham en* ~ *(også)* box his ear; (F) sock him one.
lut *en* lute; **~spiller** *en* lutenist.
lutter *adj* sheer; *være* ~ *venlighed* be all kindness.

luv *en* pile, nap; **~slidt** *adj* threadbare.

ly *et* shelter; *søge ~* seek· shelter; *i ~ af* under cover of.

lyd *en* sound; *(støj)* noise; *ikke give en ~ fra sig* not make· a sound; *slå til ~ for ngt* advocate sth; *skrue ned for ~en* turn down the volume; **~bog** *en* talking book; **~bølge** *en* soundwave; **~dæmper** *en* silencer.

lyde *v* sound; *(klinge)* ring· (out); *der ~r musik* music is heard; *det ~r godt* that sounds good; *det ~r som om han mener det* it sounds as if he means it; *han ~r rar* he sounds nice; *~ navnet Pedersen* answer to the name of Pedersen.

lydhør *adj (fintmærkende)* sensitive; *(opmærksom)* at'tentive, ob'servant; *(positiv)* sympa'thetic *(over for)* to.

lydig *adj* o'bedient; **~hed** *en* o'bedience.

lyd... *sms:* **~isolering** *en* soundproofing; **~kulisse** *en (film, tv)* sound ef'fects *pl;* **~løs** *adj* silent, soundless; **~mur** *en* sound barrier; **~potte** *en (auto)* silencer; **~skrift** *en* pho'netics *pl;* **~spor** *et (film, tv)* sound track; **~styrke** *en* volume.

lydt *adj: huset her er meget ~* you hear every sound in this house.

lydtæt *adj* soundproof.

lygte *en (gade~, bil~)* light; *(cykel~)* lamp; *(lomme~)* torch; **~pæl** *en* lamp post.

lykke *en* happiness; *(held)* (good) luck; *gøre ~* be a suc'cess; *prøve ~n* try one's luck; *have ~n med sig* be lucky; *(se også tillykke);* **~lig** *adj* happy *(over* about); *(heldig)* fortunate; *prise sig ~lig* count oneself lucky.

lykkes *v* suc'ceed; *det lykkedes os at gøre det* we suc'ceeded in doing it.

lykkestjerne *en* lucky star.

lykketal *et* lucky number.

lykketræf *et* stroke of luck.

lykønske *v* con'gratulate *(med* on); **lykønskning** *en* congratu'lation.

lymfe *en* lymph; **~kirtel** *en* lymph gland.

lyn *et* lightning; *som et ~ fra klar himmel* like a bolt from the blue; *som ramt at ~et* thunderstruck; *med ~ets fart* at lightning speed; *~et slog ned i tårnet* the tower was struck by lightning; **~afleder** *en* lightning con'ductor.

lynche *v* lynch.

lyne *v* flash; *det ~r* it is lightening; *~ op (om lynlås)* zip up; *~ ned (om lynlås)* un'zip.

lynfrossen *adj* quick-frozen.

lyng *en* heather.

lyn... *sms:* **~hurtig** *adj* like lightning; **~kursus** *et* crash course; **~lås** *en* zip(per); **~nedslag** *et* flash of lightning; **~tog** *et* high-speed train; **~visit** *en* flying visit.

lyrik *en* (lyric) poetry.

lyrisk *adj* lyric; *(sentimental)* lyrical.

lys *et* light; *(belysning)* lighting; *(stearin~)* candle; *tænde (,slukke) ~et* switch on (,off) the light; *han er ikke ngt ~* he is not very bright; *føre en bag ~et* pull the wool over sby's eyes; *der gik et ~ op for mig* it dawned on me; *en 60-~ pære* a 60-watt bulb // *adj* light; *(lysende, klar)* bright; *(om farve)* fair, pale; *når det bliver ~t* at dawn; *de ~e nætter* the light summer nights; *~t øl* light beer; *se ~t på tingene* have a bright outlook.

lysbilledapparat *et* (slide) pro'jector.

lysbillede *et* slide.

lyse *v* shine·; *~ op* shine·; *(fig)* brighten up; **lyse-** *(om farver)* pale, *fx:* **~blå** *adj* pale blue; **~dug** *en* (table) mat; **~krone** *en* chande'lier; **~rød** *adj* pink; **~slukker** *en (om person)* spoilsport; **~stage** *en* candlestick.

lysglimt *et* flash.

lyshåret *adj* fair.

lyske *en (anat)* groin.

lyskurv *en* traffic light(s *pl).*

lysmåler *en (foto)* light meter.

lysne *v* grow· light; *(om daggry)* dawn; *(om vejret)* brighten (up); *det ~r forude* things are beginning to look brighter.

lysnet *et (elek)* mains *(pl).*

lysning *en (i skov)* clearing; *(bedring)* im'provement.

lys... *sms:* **~pen** *en (edb)* light pen; **~punkt** *et: øjne et ~punkt* see· a ray of hope; **~reklame** *en* neon sign; **~signal** *et* light signal; *(ved fodgængerovergang etc)* traffic lights *pl;* **~sky** *adj* shady; **~stofrør** *et* fluo'rescent tube; **~styrke** *en* lumi'nosity; *(om elek pære)* wattage.

lyst *en (ønske, tilbøjelighed)* incli'nation; *(begær)* de'sire; *(glæde)* joy, pleasure; *have ~ til ngt (dvs. ville have)* want sth; *(dvs. føle trang til)* feel· like sth; *miste ~en til ngt* go· off sth; *kom hvis du har ~* come along if you like; *få sin ~ styret* have enough; *enhver sin ~* everyone to his taste; **~båd** *en* yacht; **~bådehavn** *en* yachting harbour; **~fisker** *en* angler; **~fiskeri** *et* fishing, angling; **~hus** *et* summerhouse.

lystig *adj* merry, jolly.

lystre *v* o'bey.

lystspil *et* comedy.

lystyacht *en* yacht.

lysvågen *adj* wide a'wake.

lysægte *adj* non-fade.

lytte *v* listen; *(lure)* eavesdrop.

lytter *en* listener.

lyve *v* lie *(for* to); *nej, nu ~r du!* no, kidding!

læ *et* shelter; *søge ~* seek· shelter; *stå i ~ af et træ* be sheltered by a tree.

læbe *en* lip; *ikke kunne få et ord over sine ~r* be struck dumb; **~pomade** *en* lip balm; **~stift** *en* lipstick.

læder *et* leather; **~varer** *pl* leather goods.

læg *en (anat)* calf *(pl:* calves) // *et (fold)* pleat; *lægge stoffet i ~* pleat the ma'terial // *adj* lay.

læge *en* doctor; *(mediciner)* phy'sician; *(kirurg)* surgeon; *almenpraktiserende ~* general prac'titioner, GP; *kvindelig ~* woman doctor; *tilkalde ~n* call the doctor; *læse til ~* read· medicine // *v* heal, cure; *(om sår)* heal up.

læge... *sms:* **~attest** *en* medical cer'tificate; **~hus** *et* health centre; **~kittel** *en* (doctor's) white coat; **~middel** *et* drug, medicine; **~plante** *en* me'dicinal plant; **~sekretær** *en* doctor's secretary; **~undersøgelse** *en* medical (exami'nation); **~vagt** *en* medical e'mergency service; **~videnskab** *en* medicine.

lægge *v* put·, lay·; *~ sig ned* lie· down; *gå ind og ~ sig* go· to bed; *~ frakken* take· off one's coat; *~ æg* lay· eggs; *~ sag an mod en* sue sby; *~ an på en* be courting sby; *~ fra (land) (om båd)* set· out; *~ en kjole ned* let· down a dress; *~ op til ngt* set· the stage for sth; *der er lagt op til at Sverige skal blive medlem før år 2000* Sweden is set to be'come a member be'fore 2000; *~ tal sammen* add up figures; *~ tøj sammen* fold up clothes; *~ til ved en ø (om båd)* call at an island; *~ ngt til side* put· sth a'side; *~ en bluse ud* let· out a blouse; *~ sig ud* put· on weight; *~ sig ud med en* fall· out with sby.

lægget *adj* pleated.

lægmand *en* layman *(pl:* -men).

læhegn *et* windbreak.

læk *en* leak *(også fig)* // *adj* leaky; *springe ~* spring· a leak.

lækage *en* leak.

lække *v* leak *(også fig).*

lækker *adj* de'licious; (F, *fx om bil)* smashing; (F, *om fyr)* dishy; *han kommer i aften. - Lækkert!* he's coming to'night. - Super! *gøre sig ~ for en* make· up to sby.

lækkerbisken *en* delicacy, titbit.

lækkerier *pl* delicacies.

lækkersulten *adj: være ~* feel· like sth good to eat.

lænd *en* loin; **lænde-** lumbar *(fx smerter* pain).

læne *v* lean·; *~ sig op ad ngt* lean· against sth; *~ sig tilbage* lean· back; **~stol** *en* easy-chair.

længde *en* length; *(geogr)* longitude; *stuen er syv meter i ~n* the room is seven metres long; *det går ikke i ~n* it won't do in the long run; **~grad** *en* de'gree of longitude; **~spring** *et (sport)* long jumping.

længe *en* wing // *adv* long, for a long time; *for ~ siden* a long time ago; *det er ~ siden sidst* it has been a long time; *hvor ~ varer det?* how long will it be (,take)? *inden ~* be'fore long; *endelig langt om ~* at long last; *være ~ oppe* stay up late; *så ~ han ikke er rejst…* as long as he has not left…; *farvel så ~!* see you (later)! *der er ~ til ferien* it's a long time until the holidays.

længere *adj* longer; *(om sted)* farther, further // *adv* any longer; *kør lidt ~* go· a little further on; *ikke ~* not any longer; *nu gider vi ikke ~* we can't be bothered any more.

længes *v* long; *~ efter ngt* long for sth; *~ hjem* be homesick; *~ efter at…* long to…

længsel *en* longing; **~s·fuld** *adj* longing.

længst *adj/adv* longest; *(om sted)* farthest; *for ~* long ago.

lænke *en* chain // *v* chain; **~hund** *en* watchdog.

lærd *adj* learned ['lə:nid].

lærdom *en* learning.

lære *en (anskuelse, teori)* doctrine; *(uddannelse, ~plads)* ap'prenticeship; *(lærestreg)* lesson; *(forkyndelse)* teachings *pl; stå i ~ hos en* serve one's ap'prenticeship with sby; *lad det være dig en ~!* let that be a lesson to you! *bibelens ~* the teachings of the Bible; *tage ved ~* learn· *(af* from) // *v (undervise)* teach·; *(lære af andre)* learn·; *~ at læse* learn· to read; *hvem har lært dig engelsk?* who taught you English? *~ en at kende* get· to know sby; *jeg skal ~ dig!* I'll teach you! **~bog** *en* textbook; *~bøger (fagligt)* edu'cational books; **~midler** *pl* teaching aids; **~nem** *adj* quick to learn; **~plads** *en* po'sition as an ap'prentice.

lærer *en* teacher; **~kræfter** *pl* teaching staff; **~studerende** *en* student teacher; **~værelse** *et* staff room.

lærestreg *en* lesson; *give en en ~* teach· sby a lesson.

lærk *en (om træ)* larch.

lærke *en* lark.

lærling *en* ap'prentice; **~e·tid** *en* ap'prenticeship.

lærred *et* linen; *(om maleri)* canvas; *(biograf~)* screen; **~s·sko** *en* canvas shoe.

læs *et* load.

læse *v* read·; *(studere også)* study; *~ lektier* do· one's homework; *~ højt for en* read· (aloud) to sby; *~ op af en bog* read· from a book; *~ til eksamen* pre'pare for an exam(i'nation); *~ til læge* study medicine; **~bog** *en* reader; **~briller** *pl* reading glasses; **~hest** *en (i skolen)* swot; *(som elsker at læse)* bookworm.

læselig *adj* legible.

læser *en* reader; **~brev** *et* letter to the editor.

læsesal *en* reading room.

læsestof *et* reading matter.

læseværdig *adj (om bog)* worth reading.

læsion *en* lesion, injury.

læske *v (om tørst)* quench; *(forfriske)* re'fresh; **~drik** *en* soft drink.

læskur *et* shelter.

læsning *en (det at læse)* reading; *(det at læsse)* loading.

læspe *v* lisp.

læspen *en* lisp(ing).

læsse *v* load; *~ af* un'load; *~ på* load; **~vis** *adv: i ~vis af* loads of.

løb *et* run; *(det at ~e)* running; *(kap~)* race; *(enkelt ~ i sportskonkurrence etc)* heat; *(flod~, tid)* course; *(sejl~ etc)* channel; *(gevær~)* barrel; *dødt ~* dead heat; *i ~et af dagen* during the day; *i det lange ~* in the long run; *i tidens ~* in the course of time; *sætte i ~* start running; *hun vandt andet ~* she won the second heat; *give tårerne frit ~* let· one's tears flow.

løbe *v* run·; *~ sin vej* run· away; *vandhanen ~r* the tap is running; *~ af med sejren* come· out the winner; *~ fra sit ansvar* shirk one's responsi'bility; *~ ind i en på gaden* come· across sby in the street; *det løb mig koldt ned ad ryggen* it sent a chill down my spine; *~ om kap med en* race sby; *badekarret løb over* the bath over'flowed; *få det til at ~ rundt (økon)* make· ends meet; ~

tør for benzin run· out of petrol; *farverne ~r ud* the colours run·; *~ ud i sandet* come· to nothing.
løbegang *en (i tøj)* casing.
løbehjul *et* scooter.
løbende *adj* current *(fx forhandlinger* negoti'ations).
løbenummer *et* serial number.
løbepas *et: give en ~* send· sby packing; *(afskedige)* sack sby.
løber *en (sport, bord~, tæppe~)* runner; *(i skak)* bishop.
løbetid *en (frist)* term; *(om dyr)* rutting season.
løbsk *adj* runaway; *løbe ~* run· away; *en ~ fantasi* an un'bridled imagi'nation.
lødig *adj* high-quality; **~hed** *en (om metal* purity; *(fig)* high quality.
løfte *et* promise; *aflægge et ~* make· a promise *(om at* to); *holde et ~* keep· a promise; *bryde et ~* break· a promise // *v* lift; *(hæve fx glasset)* raise; **~raket** *en* booster; **~stang** *en* lever.
løftet *adj: i ~ stemning* (slightly) tipsy.
løg *et* onion; *(blomster~)* bulb.
løgn *en* lie; *det er ~* it is a lie; *være fuld af ~* be a born liar; *man skulle tro det var ~* you would not be'lieve it; *for at det ikke skulle være ~* to make quite sure; **~agtig** *adj* lying.
løgnehistorie *en* pack of lies.
løgner *en* liar.
løjer *pl* fun; *nu skal du se ~!* now you'll see!
løjerlig *adj* odd, funny.
løjpe *en* ski run.
løjtnant *en* lieu'tenant.
løkke *en* loop; *(på lasso)* noose.
lømmel *en* lout.
løn *en* wage(s *pl); (gage)* salary; *hvad får du i ~?* what is your salary? (F) how much do you get paid? **~aftale** *en* wage a'greement; **~forhandlinger** *pl* wage negoti'ations; **~forhøjelse** *en* pay in'crease; **~indtægt** *en* earned income; **~krav** *et* wage claim; **~modtager** *en* wage earner; **~modtagerfradrag** *et sv.t.* earned income re'lief.
lønne *v* pay·; *(belønne)* re'ward; *det ~r sig* it is worth it; *det ~r sig ikke* it does· not pay.
lønning *en d.s.s. løn;* **~s·dag** *en* pay day; **~s·pose** *en* pay packet.
løn... *sms:* **~seddel** *en* pay slip; **~skala** *en* wage scale; **~stop** *et* wage freeze; **~tillæg** *et* al'lowance, bonus.
lørdag *en* Saturday; *i ~s* last Saturday; *om ~en* on Saturdays; *på ~* on Saturday.
løs *adj/adv* loose; *(aftagelig)* de'tachable; *(om ansættelse)* temporary; *(slap)* slack; *(vag)* vague; *(skønnet)* rough; *knappen er gået ~* the button has come loose; *nu går det ~!* here we go! *gå ~ på en* go· for sby; *pludre ~* chat away; *et ~t rygte* a groundless rumour; *et ~t skøn* a rough estimate.
løse *v (gåde etc)* solve; *(slippe fri)* let· loose; *(løsne)* loosen; *(knude)* un'tie; *~ billet* book (a ticket); **~lig** *adj* rough; **~penge** *pl* ransom.
løslade *v* re'lease, set· free; **~lse** *en* re'lease.
løsne *v* loosen; *(fx stram snor)* slacken; *(greb)* re'lax; *(skud)* fire; *~ sig* work loose.
løsning *en (af gåde etc)* so'lution; *(det at løsne)* loosening; slackening.
løsrive *v: ~ sig* break· away; *(om land)* se'cede; **~lse** *en* de'tachment; se'cession.
løssluppen *adj (fx fest)* wild.
løstsiddende *adj (om fx kjole)* loose-fitting.
løv *et* foliage, leaves *pl.*
løve *en* lion; **~unge** *en* lion cub.
løvsav *en* fretsaw.
løvskov *en* de'ciduous forest.
løvstikke *en (bot)* lovage.
løvtræ *et* de'ciduous tree.
låg *et* lid; *(stort)* cover.
låge *en (i stakit etc)* gate; *(i skab etc)* door.
lågfad *et* covered dish.
lån *et* loan; *få et ~* ob'tain (,get·) a loan; *tak for ~ af blyanten* thank you for lending me your pencil; *have ngt til ~s* have sth on loan.

låne *v (~ af en)* borrow; *(~ ud til en)* lend·; *~ ngt af en* borrow sth from sby; *~ en ngt* lend· sby sth; *~ i en bank* get· a loan from a bank; *må jeg ~ din blyant?* may I borrow your pencil?

låner *en* borrower; **~kort** *et* library card.

lår *et* thigh; *(gastr, om kød)* leg; **~ben** *et* thighbone; **~kort** *adj* mini- *(fx nederdel* skirt).

lås *en* lock; *(hænge~)* padlock; *(på taske etc)* catch; *sætte ~ for ngt* lock sth up; *under ~ og slå* under lock and key.

låse *v* lock; *~ huset af* lock up the house; *~ en inde* lock sby up; *~ døren op* un'lock the door; *~ en ud* let· sby out; *~ en ude* lock sby out; **~smed** *en* locksmith.

M

mad *en* food; *(en ~)* sandwich; *lave ~* cook, pre'pare the meal; *smøre ~* spread· sandwiches; *hvornår er ~en færdig?* when will the meal be ready? *give hunden ~* feed· the dog; *uden ~ og drikke* without food and drink; *tak for ~! (bruges ikke men man kan sige:)* that was a lovely meal; *varm ~* a hot meal.

madbestråling *en* irradi'ation of foodstuff.

maddike *en* maggot.

madding *en* bait.

made *v* feed·.

mad... *sms:* **~forgiftning** *en* food poisoning; **~kasse** *en* lunch box; **~kurv** *en* picnic basket; **~lavning** *en* cooking; *(finere)* cui'sine; **~lede** *en: hun har ~lede* she has gone off food; **~opskrift** *en* recipe; **~pakke** *en* packed lunch; **~papir** *et* greaseproof paper.

madras *en* mattress.

mad... *sms:* **~rester** *pl* bits of food; *(som genbruges)* leftovers; **~ro** *en: kan vi så få ~ro!* let us eat in peace! **~sminke** *en* cos'metic additives *pl;* **~sted** *et: et godt ~sted* a place where they serve good food; **~varer** *pl* food; *(om råvarer)* foodstuffs; **~æble** *et* cooking apple.

mag *s: i ro og ~* at one's leisure.

magasin *et (lager)* warehouse; *(stor~)* de'partment store; *(i våben og om tidsskrift)* magazine.

mage *en (sidestykke)* match; *(ligemand)* equal; *(del af par)* fellow; *(om fugl)* mate; *(om ægtefælle)* husband, wife *(pl:* wives); *min kjole er ~n til din* my dress is e'xactly like yours; *jeg har aldrig set ~(n)* I never saw· the like of it; *nej, nu har jeg aldrig kendt ~(n)!* well, I never!

magelig *adj (om fx stol)* comfortable; *(om person)* leisurely; *~t anlagt* easygoing; *der kan ~t være fire i bilen* the car easily seats four; *gøre sig det ~t* make· oneself comfortable.

mageløs *adj (enestående)* u'nique.

mager *adj (om person)* thin; *(om kød)* lean; *(ringe)* poor, meagre.

magi *en* magic.

magisk *adj* magic.

magister *en (humanistisk) sv.t.* Master of Arts (MA); *(naturvidenskabelig) sv.t.* Master of Science (MSc).

magistrat *en* mu'nicipal au'thorities *pl.*

magnet *en* magnet; **~bånd** *et* mag'netic tape.

magnetisk *adj* mag'netic.

magnetisme *en* 'magnetism.

magnetlås *en* mag'netic catch.

magnettavle *en* mag'netic board.

magnumflaske *en* magnum (bottle).

magt *en* power; *af al ~* with all one's might; *have ~en* be in con'trol; *(pol)* be in power; *have en i sin ~* have power over sby; *have ~ til at gøre ngt* have the power to do sth; *vanens ~* the force of habit; *stå ved ~* be in force; *tage ~en* seize power; **~balance** *en* balance of power; **~beføjelser** *pl* au'thority.

magte *v* manage, cope with; *mere end vi kan ~* more than we can cope with; **~s·løs** *adj* powerless.

magtfuld *adj* powerful.

magthaver *en* ruler; *~ne* those in power.

magtkamp *en* power struggle.
magtmidler *pl* instruments of power.
magtovertagelse *en* takeover.
magtpåliggende *adj: det er os ~ at...* it is im'portant to us to...; *det var ham ~ at blive holdt ajour* it mattered a great deal to him to be kept in'formed.
mahogni *en* ma'hogany.
maj *en* May; *den femte ~* the fifth of May, May the fifth.
maje *v: ~ sig ud* (F) doll (,tart) one-self up.
majestæt *en* majesty; *Deres Majestæt* Your Majesty.
majestætisk *adj* ma'jestic.
majonæse *en* 'mayonnaise.
major *en* major.
majoritet *en* ma'jority.
majroe *en* turnip.
majs *en (som plante)* maize; *løse ~* corn; **~kolbe** *en* corn cob; **~mel** *et* cornflour.
makaber *adj* ma'cabre; *(bloddryppende)* gory.
makaroni *en* maca'roni.
makeup *en* make-up.
makke *v: ~ ret* be'have; *(om ting)* work.
makker *en* partner, mate.
makrel *en* mackerel.
makron *en* maca'roon; *gå til ~erne* get· down to it.
maksimal- maximum.
makværk *et (om ngt mislykket)* botch-up; *(om bog, film etc)* trash.
malaria *en* ma'laria.
male *v (med farver, maling)* paint; *(på kværn)* grind·; *(på mølle)* mill; *~ med oliefarver* paint in oil; *~ sig (dvs. med sminke)* make· up, (F) paint one's face; **~nde** *adj: en ~nde beskrivelse* a vivid de'scription.
maler *en* painter *(også kunstmaler).*
maleri *et* painting.
malerisk *adj* pictu'resque.
maler... *sms:* **~kost** *en* paintbrush; **~kunst** *en* painting; **~mester** *en* (master) painter; **~pensel** *en* paint-brush.
malerulle *en* (paint) roller.
maling *en* paint.
malke *v* milk; **~ko** *en* milking cow; **~maskine** *en* milking ma'chine.
malle *en (til hægte)* eye.
malm *en* ore.
malplaceret *adj* out of place.
malt *en* malt.
maltraktere *v* ill-treat.
man *pron (inkl. en selv)* one; *(inkl. den tiltalte)* you; *(andre mennesker)* they; *(ofte omskrives, fx:) ~ sendte bud efter lægen* the doctor was sent for; *~ bedes benytte bagdøren* please enter by the back door; *~ skulle tro at...* one would think that...; *~ siger at der bliver valg* they say· there is going to be an e'lection; *~ kan aldrig vide* you never can tell.
manchet *en* cuff; **~knapper** *pl* cuff links.
mand *en* man *(pl:* men); *(ægte~)* husband; *han er ~ for at gøre det* he is the sort of man who can do it; *han gjorde det ene ~* he did· it single-handed; *~ mod ~* man to man; *~en i huset* the master of the house; *han tog det som en ~* he took it like a man; *se dig dog for ~!* watch where you are going, man! *en øl pr. ~* one beer per head.
mandag *en* Monday; *i ~s* last Monday; *på ~* next Monday; *om ~en* (on) Mondays.
mandarin *en* 'mandarin.
mandat *et* authori'zation; *(i folketinget)* seat; *nedlægge sit ~* re'sign one's seat.
manddom *en* manhood.
manddrab *et* manslaughter.
mande *v: ~ sig op* pull oneself to'gether; **~bevægelsen** *s* the men's movement.
mandel *en* almond; *(anat)* tonsil.
mandfolk *et* man *(pl:* men); *han er et rigtigt ~* he is a real man.
mandig *adj* virile.
mandlig *adj* male *(fx sygeplejerske* nurse); *(typisk for mænd)* mascu-line.
mandschauvinist *en* male chauvinist (pig).
mandsdomineret *adj* male dominated.

mandskab *et* men *pl; (på skib, fly)* crew; *(hold)* team.
mandsperson *en (neds)* male.
mandssamfund *et* male-dominated so'ciety.
mane *v: ~ til eftertanke* give· food for thought; *~ til forsigtighed* call for caution.
manege *en (i cirkus)* ring.
manér *en (måde)* manner, way; *(vane)* trick; *gøre ngt på sin egen ~* do· sth in one's own way; *han har gode ~er* he has got good manners.
mange *adj* a lot, (a great) many; *(foran brit entalsord)* much; *~ tak!* thank you very much! *der er ~ blomster i haven, men ikke ret ~ træer* there are lots of flowers in the garden but not very many trees; *~ penge* much money, lots of money; *de har ~ møbler* they have lots of furniture.
mangedobbelt *adj* multiple.
mangel *en* lack; *(fejl)* fault, de'fect; *(knaphed)* shortage; *af ~ på* for lack of; *i ~ af bedre* for want of sth better; *~ på B-vitamin* lack of vitamin B; **~fuld** *adj (med fejl)* de'fective; *(ikke god nok)* in'adequate; **~vare** *en* scarce com'modity; *gode redaktører er en ~vare* good editors don't grow on the trees.
mangemillionær *en* multi-millionaire.
mangeårig *adj* long-standing.
mangfoldig *adj* multiple; *~e gange* many a time; **~gøre** *v* multiply; **~hed** *en* va'riety.
mangle *v* lack; *(trænge til)* need; *(ikke være til stede)* be absent; *(være forsvundet, savnes)* be missing; *vi ~r smør* we are short of butter; *vi ~r kun at slå græsset* we only have to cut the grass; *vi ~r meget endnu* we still have a lot to do; *det ~de bare!* by all means! *det var lige det der ~de* that was all we needed.
mani *en* mania.
manipulere *v: ~ (med)* ma'nipulate; fiddle.
manke *en* mane.
mannequin *en* model; *(voks~)* dummy; **~opvisning** *en* fashion show.
manuel *adj* manual.
manufakturhandel *en* draper's (shop).
manuskript *et* manuscript.
manøvre *en* ma'nouvre; **~dygtig** *adj* in working order; *(skib, fly etc)* navigable.
manøvrere *v* ma'nouvre.
mappe *en* briefcase; *(omslag)* file.
maratonløb *et* marathon race; **~er** *en* marathoner.
march *en* march; **~ere** *v* march; **~hastighed** *en (auto, fly)* cruising speed; **~ordre** *en* marching orders.
marcipan *en* marzipan; **~brød** *et* marzipan bar.
marengs *en* me'ringue.
mareridt *et* nightmare.
margarine *en* margarine, (F) marge.
margen *en* margin.
marginal *adj* marginal; **~jorder** *pl* marginal land.
mariehøne *en* ladybird.
marinade *en* mari'nade; *(til salat)* dressing.
marine *en* navy; **~blå** *adj* navy blue.
marinere *v* marinate; *~t sild* pickled herring.
marinesoldat *en* ma'rine.
marionet *en* puppet; **~teater** *et* puppet theatre.
mark *en* field; *gøre studier i ~en* do· fieldwork.
markant *adj* pro'nounced.
marked *et* market; *(forlystelses~, messe)* fair; *det indre ~ (EF)* the single market; *på det frie ~* in the open market; *sende ngt på ~et* put· sth on the market; **~s·analyse** *en* market a'nalysis; **~s·andel** *en* market share; **~s·føre** *v* market; **~s·føring** *en* marketing; **~s·undersøgelse** *en* market survey.
markere *v* mark; *(betegne)* show; *~ sig* make· an image for oneself.
markering *en* marking *(også fodb)*.
marketenderi *et* can'teen.
markise *en* awning; *(foran butik)* sunblind.
marmelade *en (citrus~)* marmalade; *(fx jordbær~)* jam.

marmor *en* marble.
marokkaner *en,* **marokkansk** *adj* Mo'roccan; **Marokko** *s* Mo'rocco.
Mars *s* Mars; **~boer** *en* Martian.
marsk *en* marsh(land), fen.
marskandiser *en* second-hand dealer; **~butik** *en* second-hand shop.
marsvin *et (hvalart)* porpoise; *(gnaver)* guinea pig.
marts *en* March; *den femte ~* the fifth of March, March the fifth.
martyr *en* martyr.
martyrium *et* martyrdom.
marv *en* marrow; *(i træ)* pith.
mas *et* trouble; *vi havde et værre ~ med ham* we had an awful lot of trouble with him; *det var et værre ~ at få billetterne* it was a bit of a hassle getting the tickets.
mase *v (ase)* strive·; *(knuse)* crush; *(presse)* press, squeeze; *~ med ngt* struggle with sth; *~ sig frem* push on, squeeze through.
maske *en (for ansigtet)* mask; *(i strikning etc)* stitch; *(i net)* mesh; *holde ~n* keep· a straight face; *han tabte ~n* his face fell·; *tabe en ~ (i strikning)* drop a stitch; *der er løbet en ~ i strømpen* there is a ladder in my (,your, her) stocking.
maskerade *en* masque'rade.
maskere *v* dis'guise.
maskinarbejder *en* me'chanic, ma'chine ope'rator.
maskine *en* ma'chine; *(fx damp~, motor)* engine; *(skrive~)* typewriter; *sy på ~* use a sewing machine; *skrive på ~* type.
maskineri *et* ma'chinery; *(edb)* hardware.
maskin... *sms:* **~fabrik** *en: en ~fabrik* an engi'neering works; **~gevær** *et* ma'chine gun; **~ist** *en* engi'neer; **~læsbar** *adj (edb)* ma'chine-readable; **~mester** *en* chief engi'neer; **~pistol** *en* submachine gun; **~rum** *et* engine room; **~skade** *en* engine trouble; **~skrevet** *adj* typewritten; **~skrivning** *en* typing; **~syning** *en* ma'chining, ma'chine stitching; **~værksted** *et* ma'chine shop.
maskot *en* mascot.
maskulin *adj* masculine.
maskulinum *s (gram)* the masculine (gender).
masochist *en* masochist.
masonit(plade) *en* hardboard.
massage *en* massage; **~klinik** *en* massage parlour.
massakre *en* massacre; **~re** *v* massacre.
masse *en (stof)* mass; *en ~* lots, a lot; *en ~ mennesker* lots of people; *~r af* lots of; *en hel ~* a whole lot; **~drab** *et* mass murder; *(på fx jøder)* holocaust; **~medier** *pl* mass media; **~produceret** *adj* 'mass-pro'duced; **~produktion** *en* 'mass pro'duction.
massere *v* massage; *cremen ~s ind i huden* rub the cream into the skin.
massevis *adv: i ~* in large numbers; *i ~ af* lots of.
massiv *adj (fast, ren etc)* solid; *~ modstand* massive re'sistance.
massør *en* mas'seur; **massøse** *en* mas'seuse.
mast *en* mast; *(elek)* pylon.
mat *adj (svag)* weak; *(glansløs)* dull; *(om foto)* mat; *(om rude)* frosted; *(i skak)* mated.
matador *en (om person)* kingpin; *(om spil)* Mo'nopoly ®.
matematik *en* mathe'matics; (F, *i skolen)* maths; **~er** *en* mathema'tician.
matematisk *adj* mathe'matical.
materiale *et* ma'terial.
matiné *en* matinée.
matrone *en* matron.
materialist *en sv.t.* druggist; *(om forretningen)* drugstore.
materie *en (pus)* pus; *(fig)* matter.
materiel *et* e'quipment, sup'plies *pl; (edb)* hardware; *rullende ~ (jernb)* rolling stock // *adj* ma'terial.
matros *en* sailor; **~tøj** *et* sailor suit.
mattere *v (fx overflade)* give· a matt finish to; *(glas)* frost.
mave *en* stomach; *(underliv)* abdomen; (F) tummy; *(vom)* paunch; *have ondt i ~n* have a stomach ache; *have dårlig ~* have stomach trouble, have indi'gestion; *hård ~* consti'pation; *tynd ~* diar'rhoea; *ligge på ~n for en* cringe to

sby; *på tom* ~ on an empty stomach; *hans* ~ *rumler (af sult)* his stomach is growling (with hunger); *han er ved at få* ~ he's de'veloping a paunch; *slå* ~ di'gest // *v:* ~ *sig af sted* worm one's way forward.

mave... *sms:* **~bælte** *et (på cigar)* band; *(til kjolesæt etc)* sash; **~dans** *en* belly dancing; **~katar** *en* 'gastroente'ritis; **~kneb** *et* colic; **~landing** *en* belly landing; **~pine** *en* stomach ache; **~plaster** *et* belly flop; **~syre** *en* gastric acid; **~sæk** *en* stomach; **~sår** *et* (gastric) ulcer; **~-tarmkanal** *en* gastro-in'testinal tract; **~ur** *et (spøg)* tummy clock; **~tilfælde** *et* up'set stomach.

mayonnaise *en* mayonnaise.

med *præp* with; *(om transportmiddel)* by; *(om måde)* with, in; *(indbefattet)* in'cluding; *(iklædt)* in, wearing; *tage* ~ *toget* go· by train; *gøre ngt* ~ *forsigtighed* do· sth with care; *tegne* ~ *blæk* draw· in ink; *skrive* ~ *blokbogstaver* print; *til at begynde* ~ to be'gin with; *gange (,dividere)* ~ multiply (,di'vide) by; ~ *andre ord* in other words; *er momsen* ~*?* is the VAT in'cluded? ~ *tiden* in time // *adv* along with (me, you, etc); *tager du børnene* ~*?* are you taking the children (along with you)? *kommer du* ~*?* are you coming (along)? *vil du køre* ~*?* can I give you a lift? *må jeg være* ~*?* may I join you? *være* ~ *til at gøre ngt* help to do sth; *er du* ~*? (dvs. har du forstået)* you see? get it?

medalje *en* medal; **~vinder** *en* medallist.

medaljon *en* me'dallion; *(smykke)* locket.

medansvar *et: have et* ~ bear· one's share of the responsi'bility.

medarbejder *en (kollega)* colleague; *(ansat i firma)* staff member; **~demokrati** *et* staff partici'pation.

medbestemmelse *en* partici'pation.

medborger *en* co-citizen.

medbringe *v (hertil)* bring· (along); *(væk herfra)* take· (along).

meddelagtig *adj* implicated; **~hed** *en* com'plicity *(i* in).

meddele *v (lade vide)* in'form; *(en ngt* sby of sth); *(bekendtgøre)* an'nounce; *(om avis etc)* re'port; *han meddelte os at...* he told· us that...; *herved* ~*s at... (i brev)* we hereby in'form you that...

meddelelse *en* message; *(bekendtgørelse)* an'nouncement; *(brev)* letter; *(i avis)* re'port; *skriftlig* ~ written message.

mede *en* runner.

medejer *en* joint owner.

medens *konj (om tid)* while; *(hvorimod)* whereas.

medfødt *adj* in'nate, in'herent; *(om sygdom)* con'genital.

medfølelse *en* sympathy.

medfør *s: i embeds* ~ of'ficially.

medføre *v* im'ply; *(have til følge)* re'sult in; *det* ~*r en vis risiko* it im'plies a certain risk.

medgang *en* suc'cess; *i* ~ *og modgang* in good times and bad.

medgørlig *adj* o'bliging, friendly.

medhjælper *en* as'sistant.

medhold *s: få* ~ meet· with ap'proval.

medicin *en* medicine; *(medikament også)* drug; *han studerer* ~ he is studying (,reading) medicine.

medicinalfirma *et* drug company.

medicinalvarer *pl* pharma'ceuticals.

mediciner *en (studerende)* medical student; *(læge, mods: kirurg)* phy'sician.

medicinglas *et* medicine bottle.

medicinmisbrug *en* drug ab'use.

medicinsk *adj* medical; ~ *afdeling* de'partment of (in'ternal) medicin.

medicinskab *et* medicine cupboard.

medie... *sms:* **~begivenhed** *en* media e'vent; **~bevidst** *adj* media-conscious; **~dækning** *en* media coverage; **~forskning** *en* media re'search; **~tække** *et: have* ~*tække* be media'genic.

medikament *et* drug, pharma'ceutical.

medindehaver *en* joint owner.

medisterpølse *en* frying-sausage.

meditere *v* meditate.

medlem *et* member; **~skab** *et* mem-

bership; **~s·kontingent** *et* sub'scription; **~s·kort** *et* membership card.
medlidenhed *en* pity, com'passion; *have ~ med en* feel· sorry for sby; **~s·drab** *et* eutha'nasia.
medlyd *en* consonant.
medmenneske *et* fellow (human) being; **~lig** *adj* charitable.
medmindre *konj* un'less.
medregne *v* in'clude.
medskyldig *en* ac'complice // *adj* ac'cessary *(i* to).
medspiller *en* fellow player.
medtaget *adj (træt, syg etc)* ex'hausted, worn out; *(beskadiget)* damaged.
medvind *en* tail wind; *(fig)* luck.
medvirke *v* take· a part *(til, i* in), col'laborate *(i* on); *(bidrage)* con'tribute *(til* to); **~n** *en* co-ope'ration; *under ~n af* with the as'sistance of; **~nde** *en* par'ticipant; *(film, teat)* cast.
medynk *en* pity *(med* on).
meget *adj* a lot, a good deal; *(især nægtende og spørgende samt efter* too, so, as) much; *hvor ~ koster det?* how much is it? *de fik ~ at spise* they had a lot to eat; *de fik for ~ at drikke* they had too much to drink; *det er jeg ikke ~ for* I am not very keen on that; *det er mig lige ~* it's all the same to me // *adv* very; *(i komparativ)* much; *(temmelig)* quite; *han er ~ syg* he is very ill; *hun er ~ stærkere* she is much stronger; *de har rejst ~* they have travelled a lot; *bogen er ~ omdiskuteret* the book has been much dis'cussed; *det kan være meget godt, men...* that's all very well, but...; *den film var da ~ sjov* that film was quite funny; *så ~ desto bedre* so much the better; *så ~ mere som...* the more so as...
meje *v* mow.
mejeri *et* dairy; **~produkt(er)** *s(pl)* dairy produce.
mejetærsker *en* combine (harvester).
mejse *en (fugl)* tit.
mejsel *en* chisel; **mejsle** *v* chisel.
mekanik *en* me'chanics; *(maskineri)* mechanism.
mekaniker *en* me'chanic; **~værksted** *et (auto)* garage.
mekanisk *adj* me'chanical.
mekanisme *en* mechanism.
mel *et* flour; *(fuldkorns~)* meal.
melankoli *en,* **melankolsk** *adj* melancholy.
melde *v* re'port; *(meddele ngt til personer)* in'form; *~ fra* ex'cuse oneself; *~ en til politiet* re'port sby to the po'lice; *~ sig* re'port *(hos* to); *(til konkurrence)* enter; *(til fx politiet)* give oneself up; *~ sig ind i en klub* join a club; *~ sig syg* re'port sick; *~ sig ud* withdraw· (from).
melding *en* re'port.
meleret *adj* mixed.
melet *adj* mealy.
melis *en* sugar; *stødt ~* granulated sugar.
mellem *d.s.s. imellem.*
Mellemamerika *s* Central A'merica.
mellemdistanceraket *en* inter'mediate-range bal'listic missile.
Mellemeuropa *s* Central Europe.
mellemfolkelig *adj* inter'national.
mellemgulv *et (anat)* diaphragm.
mellemlanding *en (fly)* touchdown.
mellemliggende *adj: i den ~ tid* in the interval.
mellemlægsserviet *en* doily.
mellemmad *en* snack.
mellemmand *en* inter'mediary; *(neds)* go-between.
mellemrum *et* space; *(stort)* gap; *(i tid)* interval; *med ~* at intervals; *med to timers ~* with two hours' interval.
mellemstor *adj* medium.
mellemstørrelse *en* medium size.
mellemtid *en: i ~en* in the meantime.
mellemting *en: en ~ (mellem)* something in between.
mellemvægt *en* middleweight.
mellemværende *et (uenighed)* difference; *(gæld)* debt.
mellemørebetændelse *en* inflam'mation of the middle ear.
Mellemøsten *s* the Middle East; **mellemøstlig** *adj* Middle-East.
melodi *en* melody; *(om sang, vise etc)* tune; *til ~en af...* to the tune of...

melodisk *adj* me'lodious.
melon *en* melon.
memo *et* memo; **~rere** *v* memorize.
men *et* injury; *han har stadig ~ af ulykken* he is still suffering from the 'after-ef'fects of the accident.
men *konj* but; *~ alligevel...* but still...; *skøn fest, ikke? - Jo, ~ lidt vild!* great party, don't you think? - Yes, a bit wild though; *~ John dog!* really John! *~ dog!* dear me!
mene *v (tænke, tro)* think·, be'lieve; *(sigte til, agte at, tænke på)* mean·; *hvad ~r du om ham?* what do you think of him? *hvad ~r du med det?* what do you mean by that? *jeg forstår ikke hvad du ~r* I don't under'stand· what you mean; *jeg ~r det alvorligt* I am serious; *han ~s at være blevet dræbt* he is thought to have been killed.
mened *en* perjury.
menig *en* private (soldier) // *adj* ordinary, common.
menighed *en (trossamfund)* church; *(kirkegængerne)* congre'gation; *(beboerne i sogn)* pa'rishioners *pl;* **~s·hus** *et* parish hall; **~s·råd** *et sv.t.* church council.
menigmand *s* the man in the street.
mening *en (anskuelse)* o'pinion; *(betydning, hensigt)* meaning, i'dea; *(fornuft)* sense; *efter min ~* in my opinion; *der er ingen ~ i at gøre det* there is no sense in doing it; *hvad er ~en?* what is the idea? *det var min ~ at...* I meant to...; *det er ~en at vi skal diskutere det* we are sup'posed to dis'cuss it; *sige sin ~* speak· one's mind; *skifte ~* change one's mind; *gøre ngt i den bedste ~* do· sth with the best of in'tentions; **~s·forskel** *en* difference of o'pinion; **~s·fyldt** *adj* meaningful; **~s·løs** *adj (dum)* senseless; *(uden mening)* pointless; **~s·måling** *en* o'pinion poll.
menisk *en (anat)* me'niscus.
menneske *et* person; *(som fænomen, mods: dyr)* human being; *~ne* man'kind; *~t (som begreb)* man; *alle ~r* everybody; *vi så ikke et ~* we did not see a soul; *føle sig som et nyt og bedre ~* feel· like a different person; *han bliver aldrig ~ igen* he will never be a man again; *jeg er kun et ~!* I'm only human! *der var mange ~r* there were lots of people; **~abe** *en* anthropoid; **~alder** *en* gene'ration; *(levetid)* lifetime; **~heden** *s* man'kind, hu'manity; **~kærlig** *adj* charitable, hu'mane.
menneskelig *adj* human; *(~kærlig)* hu'mane; *(som opfører sig ordentligt)* decent; *det er ikke ~t muligt* it is not humanly possible.
menneskeliv *et: ulykken kostede fire ~* four lives were lost in the accident.
menneskemængde *en* crowd.
menneskerettighederne *pl* the human rights.
menneskeskæbne *en* life *(pl:* lives).
menneskétom *adj* de'serted.
menneskeæder *en* cannibal.
mens *d.s.s. medens.*
menstruation *en* period; *hun har ~* she has got her period.
mental *adj* mental.
mentalitet *en* men'tality.
mentalundersøgelse *en* psychi'atric exami'nation.
mentol *s* 'menthol.
menu *en* menu *(også edb);* **~kort** *et* menu.
mere *adj/adv* more; *aldrig ~* no more, never again; *ikke ~ (end)* no more (than); *jeg holder ~ af te* I pre'fer tea; *vil du have ~ te?* would you like some more tea? *~ og ~* more and more; *meget ~* much more; *~ end nok* more than e'nough.
mergelgrav *en* marl pit.
merian *en (bot)* marjoram.
merindkomst *en* ex'cess earnings *pl.*
merudgift *en* ad'ditional ex'penditure.
messe *en (i kirke)* Mass; *(salgs~ etc)* fair; *(mil, mar)* mess(room) // *v* chant; **~hagel** *en* chasuble.
messing *en* brass; **~blæserne** *pl (mus)* the brass; **~suppe** *en* brass-band music.

mest *adj/adv* most; *(for det meste, især)* mostly, mainly; *det ~e af indholdet* most of the contents; *for det ~e* mostly, generally; *~ af alt* most of all; *~ af alle* more than anyone else; *jeg holder ~ af salat* I like salad best; *han er ~ kendt for...* he is best known for...

mester *en* master *(i, til* at); *(sport)* champion; *øvelse gør ~* practice makes perfect; **~lig** *adj* masterly; **~skab** *et* mastery; *(sport)* championship; **~skytte** *en* marksman *(pl:* -men); **~stykke** *et* masterpiece.

mestre *v* master.

metal *et* metal; **~lisk** *adj* me'tallic; **~træthed** *en* metal fa'tigue; **~tråd** *en* wire.

metastase *en (med)* me'tastasis.

meteor *en* meteor.

meteorolog *en* meteo'rologist; **~isk** *adj: ~isk institut sv.t.* the Met Office.

meter *en* metre; **~mål** *et: sælge ngt i ~mål* sell· sth by the metre; **~systemet** *s* the metric system; *gå over til ~systemet* go· metric; **~varer** *pl* fabrics.

metode *en* method.

metodisk *adj* me'thodical.

midaldrende *adj* middle-aged.

middag *en (tidspunkt midt på dagen)* noon; *(måltid)* dinner; *i går ~s* yesterday at noon; *sove til ~* take· a nap; *spise til ~* have dinner, dine; *invitere en til ~* ask sby to dinner; *hvad skal vi have til ~?* what are we having for dinner? **~s·bord** *et* dinner table; **~s·lur** *en* nap; **~s·mad** *en* dinner; **~s·selskab** *et* dinner party; **~s·tid** *en: ved ~s·tid* at noon; *(tidspunkt for måltidet)* at dinner time.

middel *et* means *pl; (læge~)* remedy; *midler (dvs. penge)* re'sources; *de offentlige midler* the public funds // *adj: over (,under) ~* a'bove (,be'low) the average.

Middelalderen *s* the Middle Ages *pl.*

middelalderlig *adj* medi'eval.

Middelhavet *s* the Mediter'ranean.

middelmådig *adj* medi'ocre, (F) middling.

mide *en* mite.

midlertidig *adj* temporary // *adv* temporarily.

midnat *en* midnight; **~s·forestilling** *en* midnight show; **~s·sol** *en* midnight sun; **~s·tid** *en: ved ~s·tid* around midnight.

midsommer *en* midsummer.

midt *adv: ~ for* right in front of; *~ i* in the middle of; *~ i maj måned* in mid-May; *~ imellem Esbjerg og Harwich* halfway between Esbjerg and Harwich; *~ om natten* in the middle of the night; *knække ~ over* break· in two; *~ på marken* in the middle of the field; *~ under koncerten* in the middle of the concert.

midtbane *en (fodb)* midfield.

midte *en* middle; *(lige i ~n)* centre; *på ~n* in the middle.

midter... *sms:* **~linje** *en (fodb)* halfway line; **~parti** *et (pol)* centre party; *(midterste del af ngt)* central part; **~rabat** *en (på motorvej)* central reser'vation.

midtpunkt *et* centre.

mig *pron* me; *(refleksivt, undtagen efter præp)* my'self; *kan du se ~?* can you see me? *jeg har slået mig* I have hurt myself; *det var ikke ~ der gjorde det* 'I did not do it; *jeg skal skynde ~* I'm in a hurry.

migræne *en* migraine.

mikro... *sms:* **~bølgeovn** *en* microwave oven; *retten kan tilberedes i ~bølgeovn (også)* the dish is microwaveable; **~datamat** *en* micro com'puter; **~fon** *en* microphone, (F) mike; **~skop** *et* microscope; **~skopisk** *adj* micro'scopic.

mikse *v* mix.

mild *adj (om fx vejr)* mild; *(om person, stemme etc)* gentle; *for at sige det ~t* to put it mildly; *du ~e!* goodness me!

mildne *v* re'lieve.

milepæl *en* milestone; *(fig også)* landmark.

milevidt *adv* for miles *(omkring* around).

militær *et* army; *~et* the army // *adj* military; **~nægter** *en* con'scientious ob'jector; **~tjeneste** *en* military service.

miljø *et* en'vironment; **~aktivist** *en* environ'mentalist, (F) greenster; **~beskyttelse** *en* environ'mental pro'tection; **~bevidst** *adj* environ'mental, eco-conscious; **~forurening** *en* environ'mental pol'lution; **~ministerium** *et* Ministry of the En'vironment; **~skadet** *adj (om fx barn)* malad'justed; **~venlig** *adj* eco-friendly, ˌnon-pol'luting; *~venlige affaldsposer* 'photode'gradable bin liners; *~venligt vaskepulver* biode'gradable wash'ing powder; **~ødelæggelse** *en* ecocide.

milliard *en* billion.

millimeter *en* millimetre.

million *en* million; *fem ~er indbyggere* five million in'habitants; *~er af mennesker* millions of people; **~bøf** *en* minced beef stew.

millionær *en* millio'naire.

milt *en* spleen.

mimik *en (ansigtsudtryk)* facial ex'pression; **~er** *en* mime (artist).

mimose *en* mi'mosa.

mimre *v* quiver; **~kort** *et* OAP travel pass.

min *pron* my; *(stående alene)* mine; *det er ~ bil* it is my car; *bilen er ~* the car is mine.

minarine *en* low-fat margarine.

minde *et (erindring)* memory; *(~s·mærke)* me'morial; *(souvenir)* souvenir; *til ~ om en* in memory of sby; *ikke i mands ~* not within living memory // *v: ~ en om at gøre ngt* re'mind sby to do sth; *det ~r mig om ngt* it re'minds me of sth; **~højtidelighed** *en* commemo'ration.

mindes *v (huske)* re'member; *(fejre ~t om)* com'memorate.

mindesmærke *et* me'morial.

mindesten *en* monument.

mindeværdig *adj* memorable.

mindre *adj (om størrelse)* smaller; *(mods: mere, om mængde)* less; *(ubetydelig)* minor; *(yngre)* younger; *han er ~ end sin søn* he is smaller than his son; *~ støjende* less noisy; *en ~ forseelse* a minor of'fence; *ikke desto ~* neverthe'less; *der kom ikke ~ end 500 personer* no less than 500 people came; *det varede ~ end fire timer* it took· less than four hours; *med ~* un'less; **~bemidlet** *adj* low-income; **~tal** *et* mi'nority; **~værdskompleks** *et* inferi'ority complex; **~årig** *adj* under age; *en ~årig* a minor.

mindske *v* re'duce, di'minish.

mindst *adj (om størrelse)* smallest; *(mods: mest, om mængde)* least; *(yngst)* youngest // *adv* least; *(ikke under)* at least; *i det ~e* at least; *ikke ~* not least, e'specially; *ikke den ~e smule* not the least bit; *det ~ mulige* the smallest (,least) possible.

mindsteløn *en* minimum wage.

mine *en (grube)* mine, pit; *(mil)* mine; *(ansigtsudtryk)* look; *gøre ~ til at* make· a move to; **~arbejder** *en* miner; **~distrikt** *et* mining district; **~drift** *en* mining.

mineral *et* mineral; **~vand** *en* mineral water.

minespil *et* facial ex'pressions *pl.*

minestryger *en (mar)* minesweeper.

minesøger *en* mine de'tector.

miniature *en* 'miniature.

mini... *sms:* **~cykel** *en* folding bike; **~datamat** *en* mini (com'puter); **~golf** *s* crazy golf; **~mal** *adj* minimal; **~mum** *et* minimum; **~skørt** *et* mini skirt.

minister *en* minister *(for* of), secretary *(for* for).

ministerium *et* ministry; *(regering)* cabinet.

ministerpræsident *en* prime minister.

mink *en* mink.

minoritet *en* mi'nority.

minus *et (tegnet)* minus; *(underskud)* deficit; *(fig)* drawback // *adv* minus, less; *ti ~ fire er seks* ten minus four is six; *~ seks grader* six de'grees below zero; **~dage** *pl* off-days.

minut *et* minute; *den er fem ~ter i ti* it is five minutes to ten; *den er fem ~ter i halv* it is twenty-five past; *den er fem ~ter over halv* it is thirty-five past; **~viser** *en* minute hand.

minutiøs *adj* detailed, scrupulous.
mirakel *et* miracle.
mirakuløs *adj* mi'raculous.
mis *en (om kat)* pussycat; *som en ~* like a shot.
misbillige *v* disap'prove (of); **~lse** *en* disap'proval.
misbrug *en (med vilje)* a'buse; *(forkert brug)* mis'use; **~e** *v* abuse; misuse.
misdannelse *en* malfor'mation.
misdannet *adj* de'formed.
misfornøjelse *en* dis'pleasure.
misfornøjet *adj (utilfreds)* dis'pleased; *(gnaven)* cross.
misforstå *v* misunder'stand·; **~else** *en* misunder'standing.
mishandle *v* ill-treat.
mishandling *en* ill-treatment; *(af børn, hustru, dyr)* cruelty *(af* to).
miskmask *et* mishmash.
mislyd *en* discord.
mislykkes *v* fail; *det mislykkedes for os* we failed; *dømt til at ~* doomed to failure.
mislykket *adj* unsuc'cessful; *være mislykket* be a failure.
misse *v (med øjnene)* blink.
missil *et* missile.
mission *en* mission; *(mil opgave etc)* as'signment, task; **~ere** *v* do· missionary work; *(fig)* preach.
missionær *en* missionary.
mistanke *en* su'spicion; *have ~ om at* su'spect that; *have ~ til en* su'spect sby; *vække ~* arouse su'spicion.
miste *v* lose·.
mistelten *en* mistletoe.
mistillid *en* mis'trust, dis'trust *(til* of); *have ~ til en* mis'trust (,dis'trust) sby; **~s·votum** *et* vote of censure.
mistro *en, v* mis'trust, dis'trust; **~isk** *adj* su'spicious.
mistænke *v* su'spect; *~ en for at gøre ngt* su'spect sby of doing sth; *han er mistænkt for at være spion* he is a su'spected spy; **~lig** *adj* su'spicious.
mistænksom *adj* su'spicious.
misunde *v* envy.
misundelig *adj* envious *(på* of); *være ~ på ens karriere* envy sby his (,her) ca'reer.
misundelse *en* envy.
misvisende *adj* mis'leading.
misvækst *en* crop failure.
mit *se min.*
mixer *en* mixer.
mjave *v* miaow.
mobbe *v* bully.
mobil *adj* mobile.
mobilisere *v* mobilize.
mobilisering *en* mobili'zation.
mobning *en* bullying.
mod *et* courage; *miste ~et* lose· courage; *tage ~ til sig* take· heart; *frisk ~!* cheer up! *have ~ på at gøre ngt* have a mind to do sth; *ilde til ~e* ill at ease // *præp d.s.s. imod.*
modangreb *et* counterattack.
modarbejde *v* op'pose.
modbydelig *adj* dis'gusting.
mode *en* fashion; *være på ~* be in fashion; *det er på ~ nu* it is the thing now; *gået af ~* out of fashion; *komme på ~* come into fashion; **~bevidst** *adj* fashion-conscious; **~blad** *et* fashion magazine; **~butik** *en* fashion shop, bou'tique; **~farve** *en: hvidt er sommerens ~farve* white is the thing this summer; **~hus** *et* fashion house.
model *en* model; *gå ~ (om mannequin)* model; *stå ~ (for kunstner)* sit· for an artist; *stå ~ til ngt (fig)* stand· for sth; **~lere** *v* model; **~lervoks** *et* plasticine ®.
moden *adj (om frugt etc)* ripe; *(om person, vin, ost etc)* ma'ture; *blive ~* ripen; *(om person, vin, ost)* ma'ture; *være ~ til* be ready for; **~hed** *en* ripeness; ma'turity.
moder *en d.s.s. mor.*
moderat *adj* moderate.
moder... *sms:* **~kage** *en* pla'centa; **~lig** *adj* motherly; **~løs** *adj* motherless; **~mælk** *en* breast milk; **~mælkserstatning** *en* breast milk substitute; **~mærke** *et* birthmark.
moderne *adj (nutids)* modern, con'temporary; *(på mode)* fashionable, in.
modernisere *v* modernize; *(om hus)* renovate; **modernisering** *en* moderni'zation; reno'vation.
moder... *sms:* **~selskab** *et* parent

company; **~skab** *et* motherhood; **~s·mål** *et* native language.
modeskaber *en* fashion de'signer.
modevarer *pl* millinery.
modgang *en* bad luck; *(nød)* hardship.
modgift *en* antidote.
modig *adj* brave, cou'rageous.
modkørende *adj* oncoming.
modlys *et (foto etc)* contre-jour; **~blænde** *en (foto)* lens hood.
modløs *adj* de'spondent.
modne(s) *v* ripen; *(om person, vin)* ma'ture.
modpart *en* op'ponent.
modsat *adj* opposite; *i ~ fald* otherwise; *~ ham besøger hun faktisk forældrene* un'like him she actually visits their parents // *adv* the other way round.
modsige *v* contra'dict; **~lse** *en* contra'diction.
modspil *et* re'sponse; *(modstand)* oppo'sition; *det er rart med et kvalificeret ~* it's nice to get an in'telligent re'sponse.
modstand *en* re'sistance; *(forsvar)* oppo'sition; *gøre ~ mod ngt* re'sist sth; **~er** *en* op'ponent; **~s·bevægelse** *en* re'sistance movement; **~s·kamp** *en* re'sistance; **~s·kraft** *en* (power of) re'sistance.
modstrid *en* contra'diction; *være i ~ med ngt* be contrary to sth, be in conflict with sth; **~ende** *adj* conflicting.
modstræbende *adj* re'luctant.
modstykke *et* counterpart.
modstå *v* re'sist; *ikke til at ~* irre'sistible.
modsætning *en* contrast; *(forskel)* difference; *i ~ til* contrary to, un'like.
modsætte *v: ~ sig* op'pose; *(fysisk)* re'sist.
modtage *v (få)* get·, re'ceive; *(sige ja til)* ac'cept; *(ved toget etc)* meet·; *(hilse velkommen)* welcome; *blive godt ~t* be well re'ceived; **~lig** *adj (påvirkelig)* sus'ceptible *(for* to).
modtagelse *en* re'ception; *(af ting, vare)* re'ceipt; *(accept)* ac'ceptance.
modtager *en (radio)* re'ceiver.
modul *et* 'module.
modvilje *en* an'tipathy, a'version; *(stærk)* re'vulsion.
modvillig *adj* re'luctant.
modvind *en* headwind; *komme i ~ (fig)* meet· oppo'sition.
modvirke *v* counter'act.
modvægt *en* 'counterbalance; *danne ~ til* counter'balance.
mol *s (mus)* minor; *sangen står i a-~* the song is in A-minor.
mole *en* pier, jetty.
molekyle *et* molecule.
molevitten *s: hele ~* the whole ca'boodle (,lot).
moment *et* factor.
moms *en* value-added tax, VAT; **~fri** *adj* e'xempt from VAT.
mon *adv* I wonder; *hvem ~ han er?* I wonder who he is? *ja, ~ ikke* I sup'pose so; *(dvs. det kan du tro)* you bet!
monarki *et* monarchy.
monolog *en* 'monologue.
monopol *et* mo'nopoly *(på* on).
monoton *adj* mo'notonous.
monstrum *et* monster; *(stor, klodset ting)* mon'strosity.
montage *en (installation)* instal'lation; *(film)* montage.
montere *v (installere)* in'stal; *(anbringe)* mount, fit; *(samle)* as'semble.
montre *en* showcase.
montør *en* fitter; *(elek)* elec'trician.
monument *et* 'monument.
monumental *adj* monu'mental.
mopset *adj* miffed, in a huff.
mor *en* mother; (F) mummy, ma; *hun er ~ til tre børn* she is the mother of three children; *blive ~* be a mother; *hun skal være ~* she is going to be a mother.
moral *en (etik)* ethics; *(livsførelse)* morals *pl; (kampånd etc)* mo'rale; *prædike ~* moralize.
moralsk *adj* moral.
morbror *en* (ma'ternal) uncle.
mord *et* murder, killing; *begå ~* com'mit murder; *~et på Palme* the murder of Palme, the Palme murder.
morder *en* murderer, killer.

morderisk *adj* murderous.
mordforsøg *et* at'tempted murder.
mordlysten *adj* bloodthirsty.
more *v* a'muse; *(underholde også)* enter'tain; *det ~r ham ikke at vaske op* he does· not en'joy doing the dishes; *~ sig* en'joy oneself, have fun; *~ sig over ngt* en'joy sth, be a'mused at sth.
morfar *en* (ma'ternal) grandfather, (F) granddad.
morfin *en* morphia; **-base** *en* morphine base.
morgen *en* morning; *god ~!* good morning! *fra ~ til aften* all day long; *i ~* to'morrow; *i ~ eftermiddag* to'morrow after'noon; *i ~ tidlig* to'morrow morning; *i morges* this morning; *i går morges* yesterday morning; *jeg betaler på mandag! - Ja, god ~!* I'll pay you on Monday! - Tell that to the ma'rines! **-avis** *en* morning paper; **-bord** *et* breakfast table; **-brød** *et* (fresh rolls etc for breakfast); **-frue** *en (bot)* marigold; **-gry** *et* dawn; **-kåbe** *en* dressing gown; **-mad** *en* breakfast; **-mand** *en* early riser; **-post** *en* morning post; **-sko** *en* slipper.
mormor *en* (ma'ternal) grandmother, (F) granny.
morsealfabet *et* Morse code.
morskab *en* fun.
morsom *adj* funny, a'musing; *(underholdende)* enter'taining; *hvor ~t!* how funny! *skal du være ~?* are you trying to be funny? *det var ~t at hilse på Dem* it was nice to meet you; **-hed** *en* joke.
morter *en* mortar.
mortér *en (mil)* mortar.
mos *et (bot)* moss // *en (gastr)* mash.
mosaik *en* mo'saic.
mose *en* bog // *v* mash; **-fund** *et* bog find; *(iron om person)* mu'seum piece; **-konebryg** *et* ground mist.
moské *en* mosque.
moskito *en* mo'squito.
moskus *en* musk.
Moskva *s* Moscow.
most *en (æble~ etc)* juice; *han kan ikke tåle ~en (fig)* it's too much for him.
moster *en* (ma'ternal) aunt.
motel *et* mo'tel.
motion *en* exercise; *få ~* take· exercise; **-ere** *v* exercise; **-s·cykel** *en* exercise bike; **-s·gymnastik** *en* exercises *pl.*
motiv *et* subject; *(bevæggrund)* motive; *(kunst, foto)* mo'tif; **-ere** *v (begrunde)* give· reasons for; *(give stødet til)* motivate.
motor *en* engine; **-bølle** *en* roadhog; **-båd** *en* motor boat; **-cykel** *en* motor cycle, (F) motor bike; **-hjelm** *en (auto)* bonnet; **-iseret** *adj* motorized; **-køretøj** *et* motor vehicle; **-skade** *en* engine trouble; **-sport** *en* motoring; **-stop** *et* engine failure; **-vej** *en* motorway.
motto *et* motto *(pl:* -es).
mousserende *adj* sparkling.
mudder *et* mud; **-pøl** *en* puddle.
mudret *adj* muddy.
muffe *en* muff; *være ved ~n* be in the money.
mug *en* mould; **-gen** *adj* mouldy; *(sur)* sulky; *(mystisk)* fishy.
mugne *v* go· mouldy.
muhamedaner *en,* **muhamedansk** *adj* Muslim.
muk *et: ikke forstå et ~ (af det hele)* not understand· a word (of it all); **-ke** *v* grumble.
mulat *en* mu'latto *(pl:* -es).
muld *en (jordlag)* top soil; **-jord** *en* humus.
muldvarp *en* mole *(også fig);* **-e·skud** *et* molehill.
mule *en* muzzle; **-pose** *en* nosebag.
mulig *adj* possible; *hvis det er ~t, om ~t* if possible; *samle på alt ~t* col'lect all sorts of things; *det er meget ~t* that's quite possible; *på alle ~e måder* in every possible way; *mest ~* as much as possible; *snarest ~* as soon as possible; *arven gjorde det ~t for os at...* the in'heritance en'abled us to...
mulighed *en* possi'bility, chance; *(lejlighed)* oppor'tunity; *(en af to ~er)* al'ternative; *der er ingen ~ for at...*

there is no chance of...; *der er ingen anden* ~ there is no al'ternative; *have gode ~er (dvs. evner)* have a good po'tential; *(dvs. udsigter)* have good prospects.
muligvis *adv* possibly, per'haps.
multinational *adj* multi'national.
multiplicere *v* multiply.
multiplikation *en* multipli'cation.
mumie *en* mummy.
mumle *v* murmur; *(utydeligt)* mumble.
mund *en* mouth; *bruge* ~ shout; *(groft)* be rude; *holde* ~ keep· quiet; *tage bladet fra ~en* speak· up; *tale en efter ~en* say· what sby wants to hear; *hold så ~!* be quiet! shut up! **~aflæsning** *en* lip-reading.
munde *v:* ~ *ud i (om flod)* flow into; *(om vej)* join; *(fig)* end in.
mundfuld *en* mouthful.
mundharmonika *en* mouth organ.
mundhuggeri *et* quarrel, row.
munding *en* mouth.
mundkurv *en* muzzle.
mund- og klovsyge *en* foot-and-mouth dis'ease.
mundstykke *et* mouthpiece; *(på cigaret)* tip.
mund til mund-metoden *s* the kiss of life.
mundtlig *adj* oral.
mundvig *en* corner of the mouth.
munk *en* monk; **~e·kloster** *et* monastery; **~e·kutte** *en* cowl; **~e·orden** *en* mo'nastic order.
munter *adj* cheerful, merry; *(livlig)* lively; **~hed** *en* cheerfulness; *(latter)* laughter.
muntre *v:* ~ *en op* cheer sby up; ~ *sig* have fun.
mur *en* wall; **~brokker** *pl* rubble.
mure *v* build·; *(lægge mursten)* do· bricklaying; ~ *ngt inde (i væggen)* wall sth up.
murer *en* bricklayer; **~mester** *en* master bricklayer; **~svend** *en* journeyman bricklayer.
mursten *en* brick.
murværk *et* masonry.
mus *en* mouse *(også edb) (pl:* mice).
muse *en* muse.
musefælde *en* mousetrap.
musehul *et* mousehole.
musestille *adj* as quiet as a mouse.
museum *et* mu'seum; **~s·genstand** *en* mu'seum piece.
musik *en* music; *sætte ~ til ngt* set· sth to music; *for fuld* ~ with flying colours; *være ngt ved ~ken* be in with the high-ups.
musikalsk *adj* musical.
musiker *en* mu'sician.
musikhandel *en* music shop.
musikinstrument *et* musical instrument.
musikkonservatorium *et* a'cademy of music.
musikkorps *et* band.
musikstykke *et* piece of music.
muskat(nød) *en* nutmeg.
muskel *en* muscle; **~kraft** *en* physical strength.
muskuløs *adj* muscular.
muslimsk *adj* Muslim.
musling *en* mussel; *(kam~)* scallop; **~e·skal** *en* shell.
musvit *en* great tit.
mut *adj* sulky.
muzak *en* piped music.
myg *en* midge, mo'squito; **~ge·balsam** *en* mo'squito re'pellant; **~gestik** *et* mo'squito bite.
mylder *et* crowd, swarm.
myldre *v* swarm; *byen ~r med turister* the city is teeming with tourists; *eleverne ~de ind i klassen* the pupils flocked into the classroom; **~tid** *en* rush hour.
München Munich.
mynde *en* greyhound.
myndig *adj (bestemt)* au'thoritative; *(jur)* of age; *blive* ~ come· of age; **~hed** *en* au'thority; *(jur)* ma'jority; *~hederne* the au'thorities.
myrde *v* murder.
myre *en* ant; **~flittig** *adj* in'dustrious; **~kryb** *s: han giver mig ~kryb* he gives· me the creeps; **~sluger** *en* anteater; **~tue** *en* anthill.
myrte *en (bot)* myrtle.
mysterium *et* mystery.
mystik *en* mystery.
mystisk *adj* my'sterious, (F) fishy.

myte *en* myth.
mytologi *en* my'thology.
mytteri *et* mutiny; *gøre* ~ mutiny.
mæcen *en* patron.
mægle *v* mediate.
mægler *en (i forlig)* mediator; *(vare~)* broker.
mægling *en* medi'ation; **~s·forslag** *et* draft settlement; **~s·mand** *en* mediator.
mægtig *adj (magtfuld)* powerful; *(stor)* huge, tre'mendous // *adv (meget)* tre'mendously; ~ *godt* jolly good.
mælk *en* milk; **~e·bøtte** *en (bot)* dandelion; **~e·flaske** *en* milk bottle; **~e·junge** *en* milk can; **~e·karton** *en* milk carton; **~e·mand** *en* milkman *(pl:* -men); **~e·pulver** *et* powdered milk; **~e·spand** *en* milk pail; **~e·syre** *en* lactic acid; **~e·tand** *en* milk tooth *(pl:* teeth); **~e·vej** *en (astr)* galaxy; *Mælkevejen* the Milky Way.
mængde *en* quantity; *(tællelig)* number; *(utællelig)* a'mount; *en* ~ a lot, lots; *der var en* ~ *folk* there was a lot of people, there were lots of people; *i tilstrækkelig* ~ suf'ficiently; *i rigelige* ~*r* in large quantities; *en hel* ~ a whole lot (of); **~tal** *et* cardinal number.
mænge *v:* ~ *sig med* mix with.
mær *en* bitch.
mærkat ® *s* sticker.
mærkbar *adj* noticeable.
mærke *et (tegn)* sign, mark; *(etiket)* label; *(varesort)* brand, make; *bide* ~ *i ngt* make· a note of sth; *lægge* ~ *til ngt* notice sth; *sætte* ~ *ved ngt* put· a mark against sth; *sætte* ~*r på ngt (dvs. plette)* stain sth; *være oppe på* ~*rne* be on the a'lert // *v (føle)* feel·; *(bemærke)* notice; *(sætte* ~*)* mark; *ikke lade sig* ~ *med ngt* be'have as if nothing had happened; *man kan* ~ *at de sidder hårdt i det* you can tell that they are hard up; *jeg har ikke* ~*t ngt* I did not notice anything; **~dag** *en* red-letter day.
mærkelig *adj* strange, odd; ~*t nok* strangely e'nough; *det var da* ~*t* how odd.
mærkeseddel *en* label; *(som bindes på)* tag.
mærkevare *en* pro'prietary article.
mærkværdig *adj* odd; **~hed** *en* oddity.
mæske *v:* ~ *sig* stuff oneself.
mæslinger *pl* measles.
mæt *adj* full(-up), satisfied; *spise sig* ~ eat· one's fill; *er du* ~*?* have you had enough to eat? **~te** *v* satisfy; *(fys)* saturate; *ris er meget* ~*tende* rice is very filling; *have mange munde at* ~*te* have many mouths to feed.
møbel *et* piece of furniture; *købe møbler* buy· furniture; *de har mange møbler* they have lots of furniture; **~arkitekt** *en* furniture de'signer; **~handler** *en* furniture dealer; **~polstrer** *en* up'holsterer; **~snedker** *en* cabinet-maker; **~stof** *et* furnishing fabric.
møblere *v* furnish.
mødding *en* dunghill; *kaste ngt på* ~*en* scrap sth.
møde *et* meeting; *(kort, tilfældigt)* en'counter; *(aftalt)* ap'pointment; *gå en i* ~ go· to meet sby; *holde* ~ be at a meeting, be in conference; *på* ~*t besluttede vi at...* at the meeting we de'cided to... // *v* meet·; *(tilfældigt)* come· a'cross; *vi mødte en demonstration* we came across a demonstration; ~ *til tiden* be on time; ~ *op (i retten)* ap'pear (in court); **~lokale** *et* conference room; **~protokol** *en* minutes *pl.*
mødes *v* meet·; *vi mødtes på gaden* we met in the street.
mødom *en* vir'ginity.
mødrene *adj* ma'ternal; *på* ~ *side* on his (,her) mother's side.
møg *et (agr)* ma'nure; *(snavs)* dirt; *(bras)* trash, rubbish; **~beskidt** *adj* filthy; **~fald** *et: give en et* ~*fald* take· sby to the laundry; **~vejr** *et* lousy weather.
møjsommelig *adj* la'borious.
møl *et* moth; **~kugle** *en* mothball.
mølle *en* mill; *det er lige vand på min* ~ it is right up my street; **~hjul** *et* mill wheel.

møller *en* miller.
møllesten *en* millstone.
møl... *sms:* **~pose** *en* moth bag; *lægge ngt i ~pose (også fig)* mothball sth; **~tæt** *adj* mothproof; **~ædt** *adj* motheaten.
mønje *en* red lead [lɛd].
mønster *et* pattern *(også snitmønster); (tegning, plan)* de'sign; *være et ~ på ngt* be a model of sth; **~beskyttet** *adj* registered.
mønstre *v* in'spect, e'xamine; *~ på (,af) (mar)* sign on (,off).
mønt *en* coin; *(valuta)* currency; *i fremmed ~* in foreign currency.
møntet *adj: det var ikke ~ på dig* it was not aimed at you.
møntfod *en* monetary standard.
møntrenseri *et* self-service cleaners.
mønttelefon *en* pay phone, callbox.
møntunion *en* monetary union.
møntvaskeri *et* launde'rette.
mør *adj (smuldrende)* crumbling; *(om kød)* tender; *(om grønsager)* done; *(udmattet)* ex'hausted; **~banket** *adj* (beaten) black and blue.
mørbrad *en* tenderloin; **~steg** *en* sirloin.
mørdej *en* rich shortcrust pastry.
mørk *adj* dark; *blive ~t* grow· dark.
mørke *et* darkness; *efter ~ts frembrud* after dark; *i ~* in the dark; *i nattens mulm og ~* in the dead of night; **~blå** *adj* dark blue; **~kammer** *et (foto)* darkroom; **~rød** *adj* dark red.
mørklægge *v* black out; *(en sag)* classify.
mørklægning *en* blackout.
mørkning *en* twilight.
mørtel *en* mortar.
møtrik *en* nut.
må *s: på ~ og få* at random.
måbe *v* gape.
måde *en* way; *(henseende)* re'spect; *i lige ~!* the same to you! *med ~* moderately; *over al ~* be'yond measure; *der må være ~ med galskaben* e'nough is e'nough; *på en ~* in a way; *på en el. anden ~* some way or other; *på alle ~r* in every possible way; *på den ~* that way; *på ingen ~* by no means.
mådehold *et* mode'ration; **~en** *adj* moderate.
mådelig *adj* medi'ocre.
måge *en* seagull.
mål *et (formål)* purpose; *(som man stræber efter)* aim; *(som man sigter på)* target; *(i boldspil)* goal; *(i løb etc)* finishing-line; *(størrelse)* measurement; *lave ~ (fodb)* score (a goal); *det er hans ~ at blive præsident* he aims to be president; *rejsens ~ er London* the desti'nation is London; *sigte på et ~* aim at a target; *~ og vægt* weights and measures; *få taget sine ~* have one's measurements taken; *syet efter ~* made· to measure; *kunne stå ~ med* measure up to; *tage ~ af hinanden (fig)* size one an'other up; *nu er ~et fuldt!* that is the limit! **~bevidst** *adj* de'termined.
måle *v* measure; *kunne ~ sig med en* measure up to sby; *~ ngt op* measure sth; **~bånd** *et* tape measure.
måler *en (gas~, el~ etc)* meter; **~aflæser** *en* meter man *(pl:* men).
målestok *en* scale; *efter dansk ~* by Danish standards; *i stor ~* on a large scale.
målfelt *et (sport)* goal area.
målgruppe *en* target group.
måling *en (det at måle)* measuring; *(måleresultat)* measurement.
mål... *sms:* **~kast** *et (sport)* goal-throw; **~linje** *en (fodb etc)* goal-line; *(i løb)* finishing-line; **~løs** *adj (stum)* speechless; *(sport)* goalless; **~mand** *en* goalkeeper; **~rettet** *adj* purposeful; **~scorer** *en* scorer; **~scoring** *en* score; **~spark** *et* goal kick; **~stolpe** *en* goalpost; **~streg** *en (fodb etc)* goal-line; *(i løb)* finishing-line; **~sætning** *en* ob'jective; **~tavle** *en* scoreboard.
måltid *et* meal.
måne *en* moon; *(skaldet plet)* bald spot.
måned *en* month; *i juli ~* in (the month of) Ju'ly; *sidst på ~en* to'wards the end of the month; *hun er i sjette ~* she is six months gone;

~lig *adj* monthly; *tre gange ~lig* three times a month; **~s·blad** *et* monthly; **~s·løn** *en* monthly income; **~s·tid** *en: om en ~s·tid* in a month or so; **~s·vis** *adv* monthly; *~s·vis betaling* pay by the month; *i ~s·vis* for months.

måneformørkelse *en* lunar e'clipse.

måneskin *et* moonlight; **~s·arbejde** *et* moonlighting.

mår *en (zo)* marten.

måske *adv* per'haps, maybe; *~ bliver det sent* it may· be late.

måtte *en* mat; *holde sig på ~ten* go· easy.

måtte *v (have lov til)* be al'lowed to; *(om ønske)* might·; *(nødvendigvis skulle)* must·; *du må godt gå nu* you may· go now; *må jeg låne din blyant?* may I borrow your pencil? *gid du ~ komme med* I wish you might come; *vi må hellere gå nu* we had better go now; *du må være gal!* you must be mad! *jeg må altså gå nu* I must go now; *det ~ jo ske* it was bound to happen; *det må du om* it is for you to de'cide; *ja, det må du nok sige!* you may well say so.

N

nabo *en* neighbour; *han er inde hos ~en (også)* he is next door; **~lag** *et* neighbourhood; **~overvågning** *en (mod indbrud etc)* neighbourhood watch.

nadver *en: den hellige ~* Holy Com'munion.

nag *s* grudge; *bære ~ til en over ngt* bear· sby a grudge for sth.

nage *v: det ~r mig* it is preying on my mind.

nagle *en* rivet // *v* rivet; *stå ~t til stedet* freeze (in one's tracks).

naiv *adj* naïve; **~itet** *en* naïvety.

nakke *en* (back of the) neck; *klø sig i ~n* scratch one's head; *slå med ~n* toss one's head; *have øjne i ~n* have eyes at the back of one's head; *være på ~n af en* be after sby; *tage benene på ~n* take· to one's heels; *tage sig selv i ~n* pull one'self to'gether; **~kam** *en (gastr)* neck *(fx* of pork, of lamb); **~pølle** *en (slags pude)* neck roll; **~støtte** *en (i bil etc)* headrest.

nap *et (kniben)* nip, pinch; *(arbejdsindsats)* effort, go; *give et ~ med* lend· a hand; **~pe** *v (knibe)* nip, pinch; *(bide)* snatch.

Napoli *s* Naples.

nar *en* fool; *gøre ~ af* make· a fool of.

narko *en* drugs *pl;* **~forhandler** *en* drug pusher; **~man** *en* drug addict; **~mani** *en* drug ad'diction.

narkose *en: være i ~* be under a general anaes'thetic.

narkotika *pl* drugs; **~handel** *en* drug peddling; **~misbrug** *et* drub ab'use.

narre *v* fool; *(snyde)* cheat; *~ en for ngt* cheat sby out of sth; *lade sig ~ af ngt* be taken in by sth; **~streger** *pl* tricks; *lave ~streger* play tricks; **~sut** *en* dummy.

narv *en* grain.

nas *s: leve på ~* scrounge; **~se** *v* sponge *(på* on).

nasset *adj* messy.

nat *en* night; *god ~!* good night! *hele ~ten* all night; *i ~ (dvs. foregående)* last night; *(dvs. kommende)* to'night; *(i løbet af natten)* during the night; *om ~ten* at night; *blive ~ten over* stay the night; *ud på ~ten* late in the night; *~ten til den femte maj* the night of May the fourth; *ved ~* by night; **~arbejde** *et* nightwork; **~bord** *et* bedside table; **~dragt** *en (til barn)* sleeping suit; **~hold** *et* night shift.

nation *en* nation.

national *adj* national; **~bank** *en* central bank; **~dragt** *en* national costume.

nationalisere *v* nationalize.

nationalisme *en* nationalism.

nationalist *en* nationalist.

nationalistisk *adj* nationalist.

nationalitet *en* natio'nality; **~s·mærke** *et (på bil)* natio'nality plate.

nationalsang *en* national anthem.

naionaløkonomi *en* eco'nomics.

natkjole *en* nightgown, (F) nightie.

natklub *en* night club.

natlogi *et* accomo'dation (for the night).
natmad *en* snack.
natostilling *en (for tilskadekomne)* re'covery po'sition.
natrium *et* sodium.
natron *et* sodium bi'carbonate.
natskjorte *en* nightshirt.
natsværmer *en* moth.
nattefrost *en* night frost.
natteravn *en (person)* night owl.
nattergal *en* nightingale.
nattero *en: må vi så få ~!* let us get some sleep!
nattesjov *et: holde ~* keep· late hours.
nattesøvn *en* night's sleep.
nattevagt *en* night watch; *(person)* night watchman; *have ~* be on night duty.
nattog *et* night train.
nattøj *et* night clothes *pl.*
natur *en* nature; *(landskab)* scenery; *den fri ~* the open nature; *ængstelig af ~* anxious by nature; *~ens orden* the course of nature; *ifølge sagens ~* naturally; **~fag** *s (i skolen)* general science; **~folk** *pl* primitive people; **~forhold** *pl* nature; **~fredning** *en* nature con'servancy; **~fænomen** *et* natural phe'nomenon; **~gas** *en* natural gas; *(i Brit ofte)* North-Sea gas; **~katastrofe** *en* natural di'saster; **~kraft** *en* natural force; **~kræfterne** *pl* the forces of nature.
naturlig *adj* natural; *(enkel)* simple; *i ~ størrelse (om portræt)* lifesize; *(vedr. ting)* full-scale; **~vis** *adv* naturally, of course.
naturmedicin *en* herbal medicine (,remedies).
naturmindesmærke *et* natural monument.
naturreservat *et* nature re'serve.
natursilke *en* natural silk.
naturstridig *adj* un'natural.
natursvin *et* litter lout.
naturtalent *et (om person)* natural prodigy.
naturvidenskab *en* (natural) science; **~s·mand** *en* scientist.
nav *et (i hjul)* hub.
navigation *en* navi'gation.
navigere *v* 'navigate.
navle *en* navel; **~snor** *en* um'bilical chord.
navn *et* name; *give en ~* name sby; *fulde ~* full name; *kendte ~e* di'stinguished people, VIP's; *hvad var Deres ~?* what was the name? *kende en af ~* know· sby by name; *i lovens ~* in the name of the law; *hvorfor i himlens ~...?* why on earth...? *lægge ~ til ngt* lend· one's name to sby; *under ~et...* under the name of...; *sætte sit ~ under ngt* sign sth; *en mand ved ~ Smith* a man called (,named) Smith.
navne... *sms:* **~bog** *en (tlf)* telephone di'rectory; **~forandring** *en* change of name; **~fælle** *en* namesake; **~opråb** *et* roll call; **~ord** *et* noun; **~skilt** *et* nameplate.
navngive *v* name.
navnlig *adv* e'specially.
navnløs *adj* nameless; *(ubeskrivelig)* un'speakable.
nazist *en* Nazi; **~isk** *adj* Nazi.
ned *adv* down; *solen går ~ i vest* the sun sets· in the west; *~ ad trappen* down the stairs, downstairs; *op og ~ ad gaden* up and down the street; *~ fra* down from, off; *~ med krigen!* down with the war! *~ over* down.
nedad *adv* down(wards).
nedarvet *adj* he'reditary.
nedbrudt *adj* broken down.
nedbrydelig *adj* decom'posable.
nedbør *en* precipi'tation; *(om regn)* rainfall; *(om sne)* snowfall.
neddykket *adj (om ubåd)* sub'merged.
nede *adv* down, be'low; *~ på gaden* down in the street; *han er langt ~* he is de'pressed; *længere ~ ad vejen* further down the road; *han er der ~* he is down there.
neden *adv: fra ~* from be'low; *anden linje fra ~* the second line from the bottom.
nedenfor *adv* be'low.
nedennævnt *adj* mentioned be'low.
nedenom *adv* round be'low; *gå ~ og hjem* go· to the dogs.
nedenunder *adv* be'low; *(i hus)* downstairs.

nederdel *en* skirt.
nederdrægtig *adj/adv* beastly.
nederlag *et* de'feat; *lide* ~ suffer de'feat; *tilføje en et* ~ de'feat sby.
Nederland *s* the Netherlands *pl.*
nederlandsk *adj* Dutch.
nederst *adj* lowest, bottom // *adv* at the bottom; *fra øverst til* ~ from top to bottom; *stå* ~ *på listen* be at the bottom of the list; *~e etage* the bottom floor.
nedfald *et (radioaktivt)* fallout; **~s·frugt** *en* windfalls *pl.*
nedfryse *v* freeze·.
nedgang *en* de'cline; *(om fx solen)* setting; *(fald i fx priser)* fall, de'crease; *(vælgertab etc også)* climb-down; **~s·tid** *en* de'pression.
nedgroet *adj* ingrowing.
nedkaste *v (fra fly)* drop.
nedkomme *v* give· birth *(med* to); **nedkomst** *en* de'livery.
nedkøle *v* chill.
nedlade *v:* ~ *sig til at* stoop to; **~nde** *adj* patronizing.
nedlægge *v (lukke ned)* close (down); *(opgive)* re'sign; *(dræbe)* kill; *(lægge fra sig)* lay· down; *(konservere)* pickle; ~ *arbejdet* stop work; *(strejke)* go· on strike; ~ *forbud mod ngt* ban sth; ~ *protest imod ngt* pro'test against sth; ~ *våbnene* lay· down arms; **~lse** *en (lukning)* closure; *(af arbejde)* strike.
nedløbsrør *et* drainpipe.
nedprioritere *v* downgrade.
nedre *adv* lower.
nedringet *adj (om fx kjole)* low-cut.
nedrive *v (fx hus)* knock down, de'molish; **nedrivning** *en* demo'lition.
nedrustning *en* dis'armament.
nedrykning *en:* ~ *til 2. division (sport)* rele'gation to the second di'vision.
nedsat *adj* re'duced; *til ~te priser (også)* at cut prices.
nedskæring *en* cut; *blive ramt af ~er* (F) get· the axe.
nedslag *et (i pris)* re'bate; *(om projektil etc)* impact.
nedslidt *adj* worn out *(fx dæk* tyre).
nedslående *adj* dis'couraging.
nedslået *adj* dis'couraged, down-hearted.
nedsmeltning *en (fys)* meltdown.
nedstamme *v:* ~ *fra* be de'scended from.
nedstemme *v (ved afstemning)* vote down.
nedstryger *en* hacksaw.
nedsætte *v (formindske)* re'duce; *(udnævne, fx udvalg)* ap'point; ~ *priserne* re'duce (,cut·) the prices; ~ *sig som læge* set· up as a doctor; **~lse** *en* re'duction; ap'pointment; *(bogudsalg)* sale; **~nde** *adj* de'rogatory.
nedtrapning *en* de-escalation; *(fra medicin, stoffer)* with'drawal.
nedtrappe *v* de-escalate; *(fra stoffer)* with'draw· from drugs.
nedtrykt *adj* de'pressed.
nedtur *en (tilbagegang)* de'cline; *(depression)* de'pression.
nedtælling *en* count-down.
nedværdige *v:* ~ *sig* de'grade oneself; ~ *sig til at gøre ngt* stoop to doing sth; **~nde** *adj* hu'miliating.
neg *et* sheaf *(pl:* sheaves).
negativ *et, adj* negative.
neger *en* black; *(neds)* negro; *han er* ~ he is black.
negl *en* nail; *bide (,klippe) ~e* bite· (,cut·) one's nails; *en hård* ~ a tough guy.
negle *v* (F) pinch.
negle... *sms:* **~børste** *en* nailbrush; **~bånd** *et* cuticle; **~fil** *en* nailfile; **~klipper** *en* nail clippers *pl;* **~lak** *en* nail varnish; **~lakfjerner** *en* nail varnish re'mover; **~renser** *en* nail-cleaner; **~saks** *en* nailscissors.
negligere *v* ig'nore.
nej *et* no; *få et* ~ be re'fused // *interj* no; *(overrasket)* oh! *~!* oh no! ~ *hør nu!* now, now! ~, *se bare!* oh, look! *sige* ~ *til ngt* re'fuse sth; ~ *tak* no thanks.
neje *v* curtsy *(for* to).
nejstemme *en* no *(pl:* -es).
nekrolog *en* o'bituary.
nellike *en (blomst)* car'nation; *(krydderi)* clove.

nem *adj* easy; *(lethåndterlig)* handy; *(omgængelig)* easy to get on with; *(om barn)* easy; ~ *mad* easy cooking; *slippe ~t fra ngt* have an easy job of sth; *have ~t ved ngt* do· sth easily; **-hed** *en* ease; *for ~heds skyld* for the sake of sim'plicity.

nemlig *adv (forklarende)* that is, you see; *vi var tre, ~ Ole, Hans og mig* we were three, that is Ole, Hans and me; *han var ~ ret fuld* he was rather drunk, you see; *er det forstået? ~!* is that understood? right (you are)!

neon *s* neon; **-lys** *et* neon light.

nerve *en* nerve; *have dårlige ~r* have bad (,weak) nerves; *han går mig på ~rne* he gets on my nerves; **-pille** *en* tranquillizer; **-pirrende** *adj* thrilling; **-sammenbrud** *et* nervous breakdown; **-sygdom** *en* nervous dis'order; **-system** *et* nervous system; **-vrag** *et* nervous wreck.

nervøs *adj* nervous *(for* about).

nervøsitet *en* nervousness.

net *et* net; *(vej~, blodkar~ etc)* system; *(bære~)* string bag; *(spind og fig)* web; **-hinde** *en (i øjet)* retina; **-melon** *en* netted melon.

netop *adv* just; *(akkurat)* e'xactly; *det var ~ hvad jeg tænkte* it is e'xactly what I thought; *det er ~ mit speciale* it happens to be my specialty; *hvorfor ~ her?* why here of all places? *hvorfor ~ mig?* why me of all people? *ja, ~!* e'xactly! *~ nu* just now; *vi er ~ kommet hjem* we only just came· home.

netto *adv: tjene 10.000 ~* make· 10,000 net; **-fortjeneste** *en* net profit; **-pris** *en* net price; **-vægt** *en* net weight.

neurokirurg *en* neurosurgeon.

neurolog *en* neu'rologist.

netundertrøje *en* string vest.

neurose *en* neu'rosis.

neurotisk *adj* neu'rotic.

neutral *adj* neutral; *holde sig ~* re'main neutral.

neutralisere *v* neutralize.

neutralitet *en* neu'trality.

nevø *en* nephew.

ni *num* nine.

niche *en* niche *(også fig)*.

nidkær *adj* zealous ['zɛ-].

niende *adj* ninth; **-del** *en* ninth.

nier *en* nine; *(om bus)* number nine.

nik *et* nod; **-ke** *v* nod; *~ke med hovedet* nod one's head; *~ke en en skalle* smash one's head into sby's face; *~ke til bolden* head the ball; **-kedukke** *en* yes-man *(pl:* -men).

nikkel *et* nickel.

nikotinforgiftning *en* nicotine poisoning.

nip *et (af drik)* sip; *være på ~pet til at gøre ngt (dvs. ngt risikabelt)* be with'in an inch of doing sth; *(lige skulle til at)* be on the point of doing sth.

nippe *v (tage små bidder)* nibble; *(tage små slurke)* sip; *(knibe)* nip; *~pe til maden* pick at one's food.

nips *et* bric-a-brac; **-e·nål** *en* pin with coloured head.

nipsgenstand *en* knick-knack; *(om pige)* doll.

niptang *en* pliers *pl.*

nisse *en* goblin.

nital *en* nine.

nitiden *s: ved ~* about nine o'clock.

nitrat *et* nitrate.

nitte *en* rivet; *(i lotteri)* blank // *v* rivet.

nitten *num* nineteen; **-de** *adj* nineteenth.

nive *v* pinch; *~ en i bagen* pinch sby's bottom.

niveau *et* level; *i ~ med* on a level with; *på højt ~* on a high level.

nivellere *v* level.

nobel *adj (af ydre)* di'stinguished; *(ædel)* noble.

nobelprisen *s* the No'bel prize; **nobelpristager** *en* No'bel prize winner.

node *en* note; *~r* music; *spille efter ~r* play from music; *spille uden ~r* play by heart; *være med på ~rne* be with it; **-papir** *et* music paper; **-skrift** *en* musical no'tation; **-stativ** *et* music rest.

nogen *pron (en eller anden)* somebody, someone; *(~ som helst af per-*

soner) anybody; *(brugt som adj: et vist antal)* some; *(~ som helst om andet end personer)* any; *~ af dem* some of them; *ikke ~ af dem* none of them; *der er ~ der har taget tasken* somebody took the bag; *er der ~ der har set den?* did anybody see it? *vil du have ~ kager?* would you like some cakes? *er der ~ breve til mig?* are there any letters for me? *uden ~ problemer* with'out any problems.

nogenlunde *adv* fairly; *det gik ~* it was not too bad; *vi klarede os ~ godt* we managed to scrape through.

nogensinde *adv* ever; *aldrig ~* not ever.

noget *pron (et eller andet)* something; *(~ som helst)* any; *(stående alene)* anything; *(en vis mængde)* some; *er der ~ i vejen?* is something the matter? *er der ~ mælk?* is there any milk? *har du købt ~?* did you buy· anything? *der er ~ mad til overs* there is some food left over // *adv (temmelig)* rather, a bit; *det varer ~* it will be some time; *vi blev ~ skuffede* we were somewhat disap'pointed.

nogle *pron* some; *~ mennesker* some people; *~ få* a few; *~ og tres* sixty odd.

nok *adj/adv* e'nough; *(sandsynligvis)* probably; *have fået ~ af ngt* have had enough of sth; *de kommer ~ (dvs. sikkert)* they are sure to come; *(dvs. måske)* they will probably come; *du kan ~ forstå...* you can i'magine...; *det skal ~ gå!* it's going to be all right! *det må jeg ~ sige!* well, I say! *det må du ~ sige!* you may well say so! *det tænkte jeg ~!* I thought so! *nu er det ~!* that's enough!

nomade *en* nomad.

nominere *v* nominate.

nonne *en* nun; **~kloster** *et* convent.

nopret *adj* nobbly.

nord *en, adv* north; *vinden er i ~* the wind is in the north; *vende mod ~* face north; *~ for* north of; *mod ~* north(wards).

Nordamerika *s* North America.

nordbo *en* Scandi'navian.

Norden *s* Scandi'navia.

nordenvind *en* north wind.

Nordeuropa *s* Northern Europe.

nordfra *adv* from the north.

nordisk *adj* Nordic, Scandi'navian; *Nordisk Råd* the Nordic Council.

nordlig *adj* northern; *i det ~e Norge* in the north of Norway; *vinden er ~* the wind is in the north; **~ere** *adj* further north *(end* than); **~st** *adj* northernmost.

nordlys *et* northern lights.

nordmand *en* Nor'wegian.

Nordpolen the North Pole.

nordpå *adv* north; *(oppe ~)* in the north; *flytte længere ~* move further north.

nordre *adj* northern.

Nordsøen *s* the North Sea.

nordsøolie *en* North Sea oil.

nordvest *en* north west; **~lig** *adj* north western; *det ~lige Skotland* the north west of Scotland.

nordøst *en* north east; **~lig** *adj* north eastern; *~lig vind* north easterly wind.

Norge *s* Norway.

norm *en* standard.

normal *en, adj* normal; *over (,under) ~en* a'bove (,be'low) normal; **~løn** *en* standard wage; **normalt** *adv* normally.

norsk *et, adj* Nor'wegian.

nosser *pl* (V) balls.

nostalgisk *adj* no'stalgic.

notat *et* note; *tage (,gøre) ~er* take· notes.

note *en* note; *(i bog)* anno'tation; **~re** *v: ~re sig ngt* make· a note of sth; *~re ngt ned* take· sth down; *blive ~ret af politiet* be re'ported by the po'lice.

notesbog *en* notebook.

notits *en* notice; *(i avis)* paragraph; *tage ~ af ngt* take· notice of sth.

notorisk *adj: en ~ løgner* a no'torious liar.

nougat *en* nougat; *blød ~ sv.omtr.t.* fudge.

novelle *en* short story.

november *en* no'vember.
nr. *(fork.f. nummer)* No., no.
nu *et (øjeblik)* moment, instant; *~et* the present; *i samme ~* that instant (,moment) // *adv* now; *kom ~!* come on! *fra ~ af* from now on; *hvad ~?* what now? *indtil ~* up to now; *~ til dags* nowadays; *det har jeg ~ aldrig sagt* now, I never said that.
nuance *en* shade; **~ret** *adj* varied.
nudler *pl* noodles.
nul *et* zero, nought; *(om person)* nobody; *(i fodbold)* nil; *(i tennis)* love; *~ plus 2 er 2* nought and two makes two; *mit lokalnummer er 300* my ex'tension is 300 ['θri:dʌbl'əu].
nulevende *adj* con'temporary.
nullermænd *pl* fluff.
nulløsning *en* zero option.
nulpunkt *et* zero; *på ~et* at zero.
nulvækst *en* zero growth.
nummer *et* number; *(i tøj, sko)* size; *(af blad)* issue; *(på program el. liste)* item; *(trick)* trick; *fortsættes i næste ~* to be con'tinued in the next issue; *han bruger ~ 45 i sko* he takes· size 45 in shoes; *blive ~ ét* come· first; *lave numre med en* play tricks on sby; *det er ikke lige mit ~* it's not my cup of tea; *gøre et stort ~ ud af ngt* make· a lot of fuss about sth; **~oplysningen** *s (tlf)* di'rectory en'quiries *pl;* **~plade** *en (auto)* number plate.
numse *en* bottom, bum.
nuppe *v* pinch.
nusse *v: ~ med ngt* fiddle with sth; *~ rundt* potter a'round.
nusset *adj (snavset)* tatty; *(uordentlig)* un'tidy.
nutid *en* present (day); *(gram)* the present (tense); *~ens ungdom* young people of to'day; **~ig** *adj* con'temporary.
nutidskunst *en* modern art.
nutildags *adv* nowadays.
nuværende *adj* present.
ny *s: i ~ og næ* on and off // *adj* new; *hvad ~t?* what's the news? *det er ikke ngt ~t* that is nothing new; *af ~ere dato* of recent date; *føle sig som et ~t menneske* feel· like a new person; *hvad ~t?* what's the news? *det ~este ~e* the latest; *på ~* once more; **~ankommen** *s* newcomer // *adj* newly ar'rived; **~anskaffelse** *en* new purchase; **~bagt** *adj (om brød)* freshly baked; *(om fx far)* new; **~begynder** *en* novice; **~bygger** *en* settler.
nyde *v (med velbehag)* en'joy; *(mad og drikke)* take·, have; *(med skadefryd)* gloat over; *(modtage)* re'ceive; *jeg ~r ikke spiritus* I don't take alcohol; *~ godt af ngt* have the benefit of sth; *tak, jeg skal ikke ~ ngt!* I'm not having any, thank you!
nydelig *adj* pretty, nice; *du er en ~ en!* you are a nice one!
nydelse *en* pleasure; *det var en ~ at...* it was sheer pleasure to...; **~s·middel** *et* stimulant.
nyfødt *adj* newborn.
nygift *adj* newly married; *de ~e* the newly-weds.
nyhed *en (ngt nyt)* novelty; *(efterretning etc)* news *pl; en ~* a piece of news; *dårlige ~er* bad news; *det er ingen ~* that is no news; *have ~ens interesse* be a novelty; **~s·bureau** *et* news agency; **~s·udsendelse** *en (radio)* news broadcast; *(tv)* television news.
nykker *pl: få ~ (om person)* be in one of one's moods; *(om fx bil)* play up.
nylagt *adj (om æg)* freshly laid.
nylavet *adj* freshly made.
nylig *adj/adv: for ~* recently; *først for ~* only recently.
nymalet *adj* freshly painted; *(om kaffe)* freshly ground.
nymalket *adj: ~ mælk* milk straight from the cow.
nymåne *en* new moon; *det er ~* there is a new moon.
nynne *v* hum.
nyre *en* kidney; *kunstig ~* kidney ma'chine; **~sten** *en* kidney stone; **~transplantation** *en* kidney transplant.
nys *et: få ~ om ngt* get· the wind of sth.
nys(en) *s* sneeze.

nyse *v* sneeze.
nysgerrig *adj* curious *(efter at* to); **~hed** *en* curi'osity.
nyt *se ny.*
nytte *en* use, usefulness; *(fordel)* benefit; *gøre ~* be of use; *til hvad ~ er det?* what's the use of it? *ingen ~ til* no use; *have ~ af ngt* benefit from sth // *v* be of use; *det ~r ikke* it is no use; *hvad ~r det?* what's the use of it? **~have** *en* kitchen garden; **~løs** *adj* useless; **~plante** *en* useful plant.
nyttig *adj* useful.
nytår *et* New Year; *glædeligt ~!* happy New Year! **~s·aften** *en* New Year's Eve; **~s·dag** *en* New Year's day.
næb *et (buet)* beak; *(lige)* bill; *hænge med ~bet* be down in the mouth; *med ~ og kløer* tooth and nail.
næbbet *adj* pert.
nægte *v (benægte)* de'ny; *(afslå)* re'fuse; *~ en ngt* deny sby sth; *~ at gøre ngt* refuse to do sth; *det kan ikke ~s* it can't be denied; *han ~r sig ikke ngt* he does not deny himself anything; **~lse** *en* de'nial; re'fusal; *(gram)* ne'gative.
nælde *en* nettle; **~feber** *en* nettle rash.
nænne *v: hvor kan du ~ det!* how can you do it! *jeg kan ikke ~ at…* I have not got the heart to…
nænsom *adj* gentle; **~hed** *en* gentleness.
næppe *adv* hardly, scarcely; *han havde ~ sagt det før…* he had hardly said it when…; *undgå ngt med nød og ~* have a narrow e'scape.
nær *adj* near, close // *adv* near; *(næsten)* nearly, almost; *~e slægtninge* close relatives; *i ~ fremtid* in the near future; *~ ved huset* close to (,near) the house; *tage sig ngt ~* take· sth to heart; *alle kom på ~ John* everybody came ex'cept John; *det er ngt ~ alt han kan* that is about all he can; *ikke på langt ~ nok* far from e'nough // *præp* near, close to; *være døden ~* be dying; *være ~ de 50* be close on 50; **~betjent** *en* local po'liceman *(pl:* -men); **~billede** *et* close-up; **~butik** *en* corner shop; **~demokrati** *et* local de'mocracy.
nære *v (føle)* have, feel·; *(give næring)* feed·; *(~ sig)* be'have; *~ kærlighed til* love; *~ afsky for* de'test; *~ interesse for* take· an interest in; *kan du så ~ dig!* do be'have! *vi kunne ikke ~ og for at gøre det* we could not re'sist doing it; *han kunne ikke ~ sig for kløe* he could not bear the itching.
nærende *adj* nourishing.
nærgående *adj (om spørgsmål)* tactless; *nu skal du ikke blive ~ (mod mig)!* don't get fresh (with me)!
nærhed *en* pro'ximity; *i ~en af* close to, near; *han bor et sted her i ~en* he lives somewhere a'round here.
nærig *adj* stingy; **~hed** *en* stinginess.
næring *en (føde)* nourishment, food; *(erhverv)* business, trade; *give ilden ~* feed· the fire; **~s·brev** *et* licence (to trade); **~s·drivende** *en* tradesman *(pl:* -men); **~s·liv** *et* trade; **~s·middel** *et* foodstuff; **~s·stof** *et* nutrient; **~s·vej** *en* trade; *(om person)* pro'fession; *(om stat)* industry.
nærkamp *en* close combat.
nærliggende *adj* nearby; *(fig)* obvious.
nærlys *et* dipped headlights *pl.*
nærme *v: ~ sig* come· closer, ap'proach, draw· near; *ferien ~r sig* the holidays are drawing near; *din opførsel ~r sig det uartige* your be'haviour verges on rudeness.
nærmere *adj* nearer, closer; *afvente ~ besked* a'wait further orders; *ved ~ eftertanke* on second thoughts; *det er ~ ad denne vej* this way is shorter // *adv: angive ngt ~* specify sth; *~ betegnet* to be spe'cific; *se ~ på ngt* take· a closer look at sth; *undersøge ngt ~* e'xamine sth more closely.
nærmest *adj* nearest, closest; *i den ~e omegn* in the im'mediate neighbourhood; *i den ~e fremtid* in the near future // *adv* nearest; *(temmelig)* rather; *(næsten)* almost; *hun var ~ ked af det* she was almost

sorry // *præp* nearest to, next to; *enhver er sig selv* ~ it is every man for him'self.

nærsynet *adj* short-sighted, my'opic; **~hed** *en* short-sightedness, my'opia.

nærtrafik *en* local traffic.

nærved *adv (i nærheden)* nearby, close by; *(næsten)* almost.

nærværelse *en* presence; *i vidners* ~ be'fore witnesses.

nærværende *adj (til stede)* present; *(nuværende)* e'xisting; *samtlige* ~ all those present.

næs *et* foreland; *(stejlt)* headland.

næse *en* nose; *(irettesættelse)* reprimand; *pille* ~ pick one's nose; *pudse* ~ blow· one's nose; *få en lang* ~ be disap'pointed; *stikke sin* ~ *i ngt* poke one's nose into sth; *være som snydt ud af ~n på en* be the spitting image of sby; *smække døren i for ~n af en* slam the door in sby's face; *han snuppede den lige for ~n af mig* he just beat· med to it; *bogen ligger lige for ~n af dig* the book is right under your nose; *falde på ~n* fall· flat on one's face; *blive taget ved ~n* be taken in.

næse... *sms:* **~blod** *et* nosebleed; *have ~blod* have a nosebleed; **~bor** *et* nostril; **~horn** *et* rhi'noceros, (F) 'rhino; **~tip** *en* nosetip.

næst *adv:* ~ *efter* next to, after; **~bedst** *adj* second best.

næste *en* neighbour // *adj* next; *(følgende)* following; *til* ~ *år* next year; *fortsættes på* ~ *side* con'tinued over'leaf; *værsgo,* ~*!* next, please! **~kærlighed** *en* charity.

næsten *adv* nearly, almost; ~ *aldrig* almost never; ~ *altid* nearly always; ~ *ikke* hardly; ~ *ingen* hardly anybody; ~ *intet* hardly anything; *jeg synes* ~ *at...* I'm in'clined to think that...; *det er* ~ *synd for ham* one almost feels sorry for him.

næst... *sms:* **~formand** *en* vice-president; **~kommanderende** *en* second in com'mand; **~sidst** *adj* last but one; **~ældst** *adj* second oldest; **~øverst** *adj* second from the top.

næsvis *adj* im'pertinent; **~hed** *en* im'pertinence.

næve *en* fist; *knytte ~rne* clench one's fists.

nævenyttig *adj* of'ficious.

nævn *et* board; *sidde i et* ~ be on a board.

nævne *v (sige navnet på)* name; *(omtale)* mention; ~ *en ved navn* call sby by name; **~lse** *en: med navns ~lse* by name.

nævner *en (i brøk)* de'nominator.

nævneværdig *adj* worth mentioning.

nævning *en* juror; *~ene* the jury; **~e·sag** *en* trial by jury.

nød *en (bot)* nut; *en hård* ~ *at knække* a tough nut to crack; *give en et gok i ~den* bash sby on the head // *en (vanskeligheder)* di'stress; *(fattigdom)* need; *lide* ~ suffer hardships; *der er stor* ~ *i landet* there is ex'treme poverty in the country; *komme i* ~ get· into trouble; *undslippe med* ~ *og næppe* have a narrow es'cape; *vi klarer det til* ~ we can just about manage; **~bremse** *en* e'mergency brake.

nøddeknækker *en* nutcracker.

nøddeskal *en* nutshell; *det er sagen i en* ~ that is it in a nutshell.

nøde *v (tvinge)* force; *(overtale)* press, urge.

nødhjælp *en* first aid.

nødig *adv (mods: gerne)* re'luctantly; *vi gør det* ~ we hate to do it; *jeg vil* ~ *forstyrre* I don't like to di'sturb; *jeg ville* ~ *være ham* I would not like to be in his shoes; *det skulle* ~ *komme så vidt* I hope it won't come to that.

nød... *sms:* **~landing** *en* e'mergency landing; **~lidende** *adj* di'stressed; *(fattig)* needy; **~løgn** *en* white lie; **~saget** *adj: være ~saget til at* be forced to; **~signal** *et* di'stress signal; **~spor** *et (langs motorvej etc)* hard shoulder; **~stedt** *adj* in di'stress; **~s·tilfælde** *et* e'mergency; *i ~s·tilfælde* in an e'mergency.

nødt: *være* ~ *til* have to.

nød... *sms:* **~telefon** *en* e'mergency telephone; **~tvungent** *adv* of ne'cessity, per'force; **~tørft** *en: forrette sin ~tørft* answer the call of nature; **~udgang** *en* e'mergency exit.

nødvendig *adj* necessary; *kun det ~ste* only the es'sentials; *ikke mere end strengt ~t* no more than strictly necessary; **~hed** *en* ne'cessity; *af største ~hed* of the utmost ne'cessity; **~vis** *adv* necessarily.

nødværge *s* 'self-de,fence.

nøgen *adj* naked, nude; *vi badede nøgne* we went swimming in the nude; **~badning** *adj* nude bathing; **~hed** *en* nakedness, nudity.

nøgle *en* key; *(mus)* clef; *(garn~)* ball; **~barn** *et* latchkey child; **~ben** *et* collarbone; **~hul** *et* keyhole; **~klar** *adj (om hus)* ready for moving into; *(fabrik)* keys-in-hand; **~knippe** *et* bunch of keys; **~ord** *et* keyword; **~person** *en* key person; **~stilling** *en* key po'sition.

nøgtern *adj* sober, down-to-earth.

nøjagtig *adj* accurate; *(præcis)* e'xact, pre'cise; *en ~ kopi* an exact copy; *være meget ~* be very precise // *adv* e'xactly, pre'cisely; *sig mig helt ~...* tell me exactly...; *hvad er klokken ~?* what is the e'xact time? **~hed** *en* accuracy; e'xactness, pre'ciseness.

nøje *adj (omhyggelig)* careful; *(nær)* close; *ved ~re eftersyn* on close in'spection; *en ~ efterligning* a careful copy; *efter ~ overvejelse* after careful conside'ration // *adv* carefully; closely; *(nøjagtigt)* e'xactly; *~ overholde reglerne* keep· strictly to the rules; *det tager vi ikke så ~* we are not par'ticular about that; **~regnende** *adj* par'ticular.

nøjes *v: ~ med* be con'tent with; *kan du ~ med kold mad?* will it do with cold food?

nøjsom *adj (som ikke kræver meget)* undemanding; *(beskeden)* modest; **~hed** *en* modesty.

nøle *v* hesitate; *(trække tiden ud)* play for time; *uden at ~* with'out de'lay; **nølen** *en* hesi'tation; de'lay.

nå *v* reach, get· to; *(komme i tide til)* be in time for; *(om tog, bus etc)* catch·; *(indhente)* catch· up with; *(opnå)* a'chieve; *få ~et ngt* get· sth done; *han ~ede det lige* he just made it; *kan vi ~ det?* can we make it? *vi ~ede ikke bussen* we missed the bus.

nå *interj* well! *~ sådan!* oh, I see! *~, hvad siger du så!* well, what do you say now? *~, ~!* come, come!

nåde *en (barmhjertighed)* mercy; *(rel)* grace; *(gunst)* favour; *lade ~ gå for ret* be merciful; *bede om ~* beg for mercy; *tage en til ~* for'give· sby // *v: Gud ~ dig!* God help you!

nådig *adj* merciful, gracious.

nål *en* needle; *(knappe~, sikkerheds~)* pin; *sidde som på ~e* be like a cat on hot bricks; **~e·pude** *en* pincushion; **~e·skov** *en* co'niferous forest; **~e·træ** *et* conifer.

når *konj* when; *~ bare* if only; *~ først de kommer* once they come; *~ som helst* when'ever, anytime.

O

oase *en* o'asis *(pl:* oases).

obduktion *en* autopsy, post-'mortem.

oberst *en* colonel ['kə:nl].

objekt *et* object.

objektiv *et (linse)* lens // *adj* ob'jective.

obligation *en* bond; **~s·kurs** *en* bond quo'tation.

obligatorisk *adj* com'pulsory.

obo *en* oboe; *spille ~* play the oboe; **~ist** *en* oboe player, oboist.

observans *en (synspunkter)* views *pl.*

observation *en* obser'vation.

observatorium *et* ob'servatory.

observatør *en* ob'server.

observere *v* ob'serve.

ocean *et* ocean.

Oceanien *s (geogr)* the Pa'cific Islands.

od *en (spids)* point.

odde *en* land tongue, point.

odder *en* otter; *(om person)* oaf.

offensiv *en, adj* of'fensive; *gå i ~en* take· the offensive.
offentlig *adj* public; *det ~e* the au'thorities *pl; en ~t ansat* a public servant; *det er en ~ hemmelighed* it's an open secret // *adv* in public; *~ tilgængelig* open to the public.
offentliggøre *v* publish; **-lse** *en* publi'cation.
offentlighed *en* pu'blicity; *~en (dvs. folk)* the (general) public; *det er i ~ens interesse* it is in the public interest.
offer *et* sacrifice; *(person som det går ud over)* victim; *bringe et ~* make· a sacrifice; *blive ~ for ngt* be the victim of sth.
officer *en* officer.
officiel *adj* of'ficial.
ofre *v* sacrifice; *(give ud, bruge)* spend·; *~ sig for en sag* de'vote oneself to a cause; *~ tid på ngt* spend· time on sth.
ofte *adv* often, frequently; **-re** *adv* more often; *lad det ikke ske ~re* don't let it happen a'gain; **-st** *adv (som regel)* usually, as a rule.
og *konj* and; *vi skal ud ~ købe ind* we are going shopping; *gå hjem ~ sov* go· home and sleep.
også *adv* also, too; *hun kan ~ køre bil* she can· also drive, she can· drive too; *det er da ~ irriterende!* how an'noying! *han spiller guitar og det gør hun ~* he plays the gui'tar and so does she; *mener du nu ~ det?* are you sure you mean that? *ikke ~?* don't you think?
okkupere *v* occupy.
okse *en* ox *(pl:* oxen); *(kød af ~)* beef *(ubøj)*; **-bryst** *et* brisket (of beef); **-filet** *en* fillet of beef; **-hale** *en* oxtail; **-kød** *et* beef *(ubøj)*; **-kødssuppe** *en* (beef) broth; **-steg** *en (rå)* joint of beef; *(stegt)* roast beef.
oktantal *et* octane number (,rating); *med højt ~* high-octane.
oktav *en (mus)* octave; *(format)* oc'tavo.
oktober *en* Oc'tober; *den første ~* the first of October, October the first; **-ferie** *en* autumn school holiday.
OL the O'lympic Games; *ved ~ i Montreal* at the Montreal Olympics.
oldefar *en* great-grandfather; **oldemor** *en* great-grandmother.
oldfrue *en* matron.
olding *en* old man.
oldnordisk *adj* Old Norse; *(fig)* antedi'luvian.
oldtid *en (klassisk)* an'tiquity; *Danmarks ~* early Danish history; **-s·fund** *et* prehistoric find; **-s·kundskab** *en* classical civili'zation.
olie *en* oil; *finde ~* strike· oil; *bore efter ~* drill for oil; **-farve** *en* oil colour; *male med ~farver* paint in oils; *den sidste ~* ex'treme unction; **-felt** *et* oilfield; **-forekomst** *en* oil de'posit; **-fyr** *et* oil-burner; **-kilde** *en* oil well; **-kridt** *et* crayon; **-maling** *en* oil-based paint; **-målepind** *en (auto)* dipstick; **-pøl** *en (på vandet)* oil slick; **-raffinaderi** *et* oil re'finery; **-selskab** *et* oil company; **-skift** *et (auto)* oil change; **-stand** *en* oil level; **-udslip** *et* oil slip; *(ved et uheld)* oil leak.
oliven *en* olive; **-grøn** *adj* olive; **-olie** *en* olive oil; **-træ** *et* olive (tree).
olympiade *en (OL)* O'lympic Games, O'lympics *pl.*
olympisk *adj: ~ mester* O'lympic champion.
om *præp (rundt ~)* about, (a)round; *(angående)* about, on, of; *(om tid)* in, on; *(pr.)* a; *(se også de enkelte ord som ~ forbindes med); han bor lige ~ hjørnet* he lives just round the corner; *dreje ~ hjørnet* turn the corner; *spørge en ~ ngt* ask sby about sth; *bede en ~ ngt* ask sby for sth; *filmen handler ~ krigen* the film is about the war; *~ en time (,uge etc)* in an hour (,a week etc); *arbejde ~ natten* work at night; *flere gange ~ dagen* several times a day; *~ morgenen* in the morning; *~ søndagen* on Sundays; *(om bestemt søndag)* on Sunday; *falde ~* fall· over; *gøre ngt ~* do· sth again; *bygge huset ~* re'build· the house // *konj* if,

whether; *jeg ved ikke ~ de kommer* I don't know whether they will come; *~ jeg så må sige* if I may say so; *som ~* as if; *kan du lide ham? - ja, om!* do you like him? - you bet I do.

omadressere *v* forward.

omarbejde *v* alter, re'vise.

ombestemme *v: ~ sig* change one's mind.

ombord *adv* on board.

ombudsmand *en* ombudsman *(pl:* -men).

ombygning *en* re'building; *under ~* being re'built.

ombæring *en (af post og fig)* de'livery; *det må blive i næste ~* it will have to wait till next time.

omdanne *v* change, con'vert *(til* into); *(ordne om)* re'organize; *(om regering)* re'shuffle; **~lse** *en* change, con'version; reorgani'zation; re'shuffle.

omdele *v* di'stribute.

omdiskuteret *adj* much di'sputed; *(omstridt)* contro'versial.

omdrejning *en* revo'lution, ro'tation; *... ~er i minuttet ...* revolutions per minute.

omdømme *et* repu'tation.

omegn *en* neighbourhood, sur'roundings *pl; København og ~* Copenhagen and its en'virons; *de bor i ~en af København* they live on the outskirts of Copenhagen; **~s·kommune** *en* su'burban munici'pality.

omelet *en* 'omelette.

omfang *et (størrelse)* size; *(udstrækning)* ex'tent; *(omkreds)* cir'cumference; *(rækkevidde, ~ af arbejde, undersøgelse etc)* scope; *i stort ~* on a large scale; *i fuldt ~* com'pletely.

omfangsrig *adj (stor, tyk)* vo'luminous; *(rummelig)* spacious; *(om viden, interesser etc)* wide.

omfart(svej) *en* by-pass.

omfatte *v (inkludere)* in'clude; *(angå)* af'fect; **~nde** *adj (vidtgående)* ex'tensive; *(som rummer meget)* compre'hensive; *(grundig)* thorough.

omfavne *v* em'brace; **~lse** *en* em'brace.

omflakkende *adj* un'settled; *(om vagabond etc)* vagrant.

omformer *en (elek)* con'verter.

omgang *en (runde)* round; *(det at omgås)* dealings *pl (med* with); *(måde at bruge ngt på)* handling *(med* of); *pleje ~ med en gruppe* mix with a group; *en skrap ~* tough going; *en dyr ~* an ex'pensive af'fair; *give en en ordentlig ~* take· sby to the laundry; *i denne ~* this time; *i første ~ (dvs. først)* at first; *(dvs. først og fremmest)* first of all; *på ~* by turns; *gå på ~* pass round.

omgangskreds *en* ac'quaintances *pl,* friends *pl.*

omgive *v* sur'round; **~lser** *pl* sur'roundings, en'virons; *(miljøet)* en'vironment.

omgående *adj* im'mediate // *adv* im'mediately.

omgås *v (personer)* mix with; *(ting)* handle, deal· with; *vi ~ formelt* we see each other formally; *nem at ~* easy to get on with; *~ ngt med forsigtighed* handle sth with care.

omhu *en* care.

omhyggelig *adj* careful *(med* about).

omkamp *en (sport)* replay.

omklædning *en* changing (one's clothes).

omklædningsrum *et* changing room; *(med skabe til tøj etc)* locker room.

omkomme *v* die, get· killed; *være ved at ~ af grin* nearly die laughing.

omkostninger *pl* costs, ex'penses.

omkreds *en* cir'cumference; *i miles ~* for miles around.

omkring *adv/præp* about, (a)round; *(cirka)* about; *de bor her ~* they live around here; **~liggende** *adj* sur'rounding.

omkuld *adv* over, down; *vælte ~* fall· down; *vælte en ~* knock sby down.

omkvæd *et* chorus.

omkørsel *en* di'version.

omlægge *v (dvs. ændre)* change, re'organize; *(om vej)* relocate; *(om trafik)* redirect.

omløb *et* circu'lation; *sætte ngt i* ~ 'circulate sth; *være i* ~ be circu'lating; *have* ~ *i hovedet* be bright.
omme *adv (forbi)* over; *da tiden var* ~ when the time was up; ~ *bag træet* be'hind the tree; *den står der* ~ it is back there.
omplante *v* trans'plant; *(potteplante)* repot.
omregne *v* con'vert *(til* into); **omregning** *en* con'version.
omrejsende *adj* travelling, i'tinerant *(fx teater* theatre).
omrids *et* outline; *tegne et* ~ *af ngt* outline sth; *i korte* ~ in brief outline.
omringe *v* sur'round.
område *et* area, region; *(som tilhører en stat)* territory; *(fig, felt)* field; *(fig, gren)* branch; *på fjendens* ~ in enemy territory; *det ligger uden for mit* ~ it is out of my field; **~nummer** *et (tlf)* area code.
omsider *adv* finally, at last.
omskiftelig *adj* changeable; *(om vejr)* changing.
omskole *v* retrain.
omskoling *en* retraining.
omskæring *en* circum'cision.
omslag *et (til papirer etc)* cover; *(med, fx varmt* ~*)* compress; *(skift, ændring)* (sudden) change.
omsonst *adj* futile // *adv* in vain.
omsorg *en* care; ~ *for de ældre* eldercare; *drage* ~ *for* take· care of; **~s·arbejde** *et* social work; **~s·fuld** *adj* careful; *(af indstilling)* so'licitous.
omstigning *en* change; **~s·billet** *en* transfer ticket.
omstille *v (produktion, tv, radio etc)* switch over *(til* to); *(tlf)* put· through *(til* to); ~ *sig til ngt nyt* a'dapt to sth new.
omstilling *en (af produktion etc)* switch-over, change-over; **~s·bord** *et (tlf)* switchboard.
omstrejfende *adj* vagrant; *(om fx hund)* stray.
omstridt *adj* contro'versial, dis'puted.
omstændelig *adj* e'laborate; *(langtrukken)* long-winded.
omstændighed *en* circumstance; *(kendsgerning)* fact; ~*er (formaliteter)* fuss; *efter* ~*erne går det godt* it goes as well as can be ex'pected; *alt efter* ~*erne* ac'cording to circumstances; *nærmere* ~*er* further details; *være i* ~*er (dvs. gravid)* be ex'pecting; *under alle* ~*er (dvs. alligevel)* at any rate; *(dvs. for enhver pris)* at all costs; *under ingen* ~*er* under no circumstances.
omsværmet *adj: han (,hun) er* ~ he (,she) is very popular with the girls (,boys).
omsvøb *et: lave* ~ beat· around the bush; *uden* ~ straight out.
omsætning *en (handel)* trade, business; *(merk, fx et års* ~*)* turnover; *(om penge, cirkulation)* circu'lation.
omsætte *v (sælge)* sell·; *de har omsat for 100 millioner i første halvår* they have had a turnover of 100 millions for the first six months.
omtale *en* mention; *jeg kender ham af* ~ I know· him by name; *få god* ~ *(dvs. anmeldelse)* get· a good mention // *v* mention; *omtalte politiker*... the said poli'tician...
omtanke *en: vise* ~ show conside'ration; *vælge ngt med* ~ choose· sth with care.
omtrent *adv* about; *(næsten)* almost; *(cirka)* ap'proximately; *den kostede* ~ *100 kroner* it was almost 100 kroner; *sådan* ~ *100 kroner* 100 kroner or so; ~ *sådan her* something like this; **~lig** *adj* ap'proximate.
omtåget *adj* dazed; *(af alkohol)* muzzy.
omvej *en* detour; *(fig)* roundabout way; *gå en* ~ *(med vilje)* make· a detour; *(ufrivilligt)* go· the long way round; *ad* ~*e (fig)* indi'rectly.
omvende *v* con'vert; **~lse** *en* con'version.
omvendt *adj (om rækkefølge)* re'verse; *(modsat)* opposite, the other way round; *blive* ~ *til islam* con'vert to Islam // *adv* the other way round; *(på hovedet)* upside down; *han elsker hende og* ~ he loves her and vice versa; *billedet hænger* ~ the picture is upside down.

omvisning *en* con'ducted tour.
omvæltning *en (drastisk ændring)* radical change; *(pol etc)* revo'lution.
onanere *v* masturbate.
onani *en* mastur'bation.
ond *adj* wicked, evil; *(slem)* bad, nasty; *en ~ ånd* an evil spirit; *få ~t* get· a pain; *gøre ~t* hurt·; *det gør ~t i såret* the wound hurts; *det gør mig ~t at høre det* I am sorry to hear it; *have ~t af en* feel· sorry for sby; *have ~t i halsen* have a sore throat; *have ~t i maven (,hovedet)* have a stomachache (,headache); *tale ~t om en* say· bad things about sby, vilify sby; *der er ikke ngt ~t i at prøve* there is no harm in trying.
ondartet *adj (om person)* vicious, nasty; *(om sygdom)* serious; *(om svulst)* ma'lignant.
onde *et* evil; *et nødvendigt ~* a nevessary evil.
ondsindet *adj* ma'licious.
ondskab *en* wickedness, evil.
ondskabsfuld *adj* ma'licious; **~hed** *en* malice; *(bemærkning)* spiteful remark.
onkel *en* uncle.
onsdag *en* Wednesday; *i ~s* last Wednesday; *om ~en* on Wednesdays; *på ~* next Wednesday.
op *adv/præp* up; *(i hus)* up'stairs; *(se også de enkelte ord som ~ forbindes med); gå ~ (om kabale)* come· out; *køre ~ ad bakke* drive· uphill; *klatre ~ ad et bjerg* climb a mountain; *~ ad trappen* up the stairs, up'stairs; *lukke døren ~* open the door; *hun er ~ imod de 80* she is getting on for eighty; *tage ngt ~ af lommen* take· sth out of one's pocket; *~ med humøret!* cheer up! *gå til eksamen* sit· an e'xam.
opad *adv* up, upwards; **~til** *adv* at the top *(på* of).
oparbejde *v (firma etc)* build· up; *(atomaffald)* re'process.
oparbejdningsanlæg *et* re'processing plant.
opbagning *en (gastr)* roux [ru:].
opbakning *en* sup'port, backing.
opbevare *v* keep·.
opbevaring *en* keeping, storage; *(i sikkerhed)* safekeeping.
opbremsning *en* braking.
opbrud *et* de'parture.
opbud *et: et stort ~ af pressefolk* an im'posing ar'ray of re'porters.
opbygning *an* building up; *den militære ~* the military build-up.
opdage *v* dis'cover; *(finde ud af)* find· out; *(få øje på)* spot.
opdagelse *en* dis'covery; *gå på ~lse* go· ex'ploring; **~s·rejse** *en* expe'dition.
opdager *en* dis'coverer; *(detektiv)* de'tective.
opdele *v* di'vide up.
opdeling *en* di'vision.
opdigtet *adj* in'vented.
omdrage *v (om barn)* bring· up; *(uddanne)* educate; *(om fx hund)* train; *dårligt ~t* ill-bred; *godt ~t* well-bred; **~lse** *en* upbringing; edu'cation; training.
opdrive *v* get· hold of, find·; *ikke til at ~* im'possible to get hold of.
opdræt *et* breeding; **~te** *v* breed·.
opdyrke *v* cultivate.
opdyrkning *en* culti'vation.
opdækning *en (kuvert)* setting; *(fodb)* marking.
opefter *adv* upwards.
opera *en* opera; **~sanger** *en* opera singer.
operation *en* ope'ration; *gennemgå en ~ (også)* under'go· surgery; **~s·bord** *et* operating table; **~s·stue** *en* operating theatre.
operatør *en* operator; *(om kirurg)* surgeon.
operere *v* operate; *~ en* operate on sby; *blive ~t* be operated on, under'go surgery.
operette *en* ope'retta.
opfange *v* catch·.
opfarende *adj* violent-tempered.
opfatte *v (forstå)* under'stand·; *(mærke)* per'ceive; *(få fat i, opfange)* catch·, get·; *(betragte, anse)* re'gard; *(tyde)* in'terpret, take· *(som* as); *jeg ~de ikke meningen* I did not get the meaning; *~ ngt som ren politik* re'gard sth as sheer politics; *~ ngt forkert* misunder'stand sth.

opfattelse *en* under'standing; per'ception; *(mening)* o'pinion, view; *(idé)* idea, concept; *efter min* ~ in my o'pinion (,view); *langsom i ~n* slow on the uptake.

opfinde *v* in'vent; **~lse** *en* in'vention.

opfinder *en* in'ventor.

opfindsom *adj* in'ventive; *(fantasifuld)* i'maginative; **~hed** *en* inge'nuity.

opfordre *v* ask, in'vite *(til at* to).

opfordring *en* re'quest; *på ens* ~ at sby's request.

opfostre *v* bring· up.

opfylde *v* fill; *(udføre, indfri, holde fx løfte)* ful'fil, carry out; *(rette sig efter)* com'ply with, meet·; *få sit ønske opfyldt* have one's wish; ~ *hans ønske* carry out his wish.

opfyldelse *en* ful'filment; *gå i* ~ come· true, be ful'filled.

opfølgning *en* follow-up.

opføre *v (bygge)* build·; *(spille fx koncert)* per'form; *(indskrive på liste)* enter; ~ *sig godt (,dårligt)* be'have well (,badly).

opførelse *en (bygning)* building; *(teat, mus)* per'formance; *under* ~ in con'struction.

opførsel *en* be'haviour.

opgang *en (trappe~)* staircase; *(stigning)* rise; *(vækst)* increase, growth; *solens* ~ sunrise.

opgave *en* task, job; *(formål)* purpose; *(i skolen, øvelse)* exercise; *(regne~)* problem; *(gåde)* puzzle; *det er ikke din ~ at...* it is not your job to...; *regne ~r* do· sums; *skriftlig* ~ written exercise; *stille en en* ~ set· sby a task.

opgive *v* give· up; *(angive, meddele)* give·, state; ~ *at gøre ngt* give· up doing sth; **~lse** *en* giving up; statement.

opgør *et (strid)* clash, scene; *de havde et ~ (også)* they had it out.

opgøre *v (om regnskab)* make· up, settle; *(anslå)* estimate; **~lse** *en* statement.

ophavsmand *en* instigator, o'riginator *(til* of).

ophavsret *en* copyright *(til* on).

ophidse *v* ex'cite, up'set·; **~lse** *en* ex'citement.

ophidset *adj* ex'cited, up'set; *blive* ~ get· ex'cited; *(blive vred)* get· angry.

ophold *et (kortere)* stay; *(fast)* residence; *(pause)* stop, break; *(forsinkelse)* wait, de'lay; *tjene til livets* ~ earn one's living; *gøre et ~ (under arbejdet)* have a break; *(på rejse)* stop; *køre uden* ~ go non-stop.

opholde *v (forsinke)* de'lay; ~ *sig* stay; *(fast)* live *(hos* with).

opholdssted *et* whereabouts; *(fast)* residence.

opholdsstue *en* living room; *(i virksomhed etc)* recre'ation room.

opholdstilladelse *en* residence permit.

opholdsvejr *et* dry weather.

ophugning *en: sende bilen til* ~ send· the car to the breakers.

ophæve *v (gøre ugyldig)* a'bolish; *(om lov)* re'peal; *(om kontrakt)* cancel, an'nul; *(om forlovelse)* break· off; *(hæve fx blokade)* lift; **~lse** *en* abo'lition; re'peal; cancel'lation, an'nulment.

ophør *et* end(ing), ces'sation; *(om forretning etc)* closing down.

ophøre *v* stop, cease; close down; ~ *med at gøre ngt* stop doing sth.

ophørsudsalg *et* clearance sale.

opinion *en* public o'pinion; **~s·undersøgelse** *en* o'pinion poll.

opkald *et (tlf)* call.

opkalde *v: ~ en efter hans onkel* name sby after his uncle.

opkast *et* vomit; **~ning** *en* vomiting.

opklare *v* clear up, solve.

opklaring *en (af gåde etc)* so'lution; *(om vejret)* clearing up.

opkog *et: give ngt et ~ (om mad)* boil sth up again; *(dvs. blanchere)* parboil sth.

opkomling *en* upstart.

opkræve *v* col'lect.

opkrævning *en* col'lection; *(postopkrævning)* cash-on-de'livery.

opkvikkende *adj* stimulating.

opkøb *et (af virksomhed)* buyout, takeover.

oplade *v (batteri)* charge.

oplag *et (af bog)* im'pression; *(af varer)* stock.
oplagre *v* store (up).
oplagring *en* storing.
oplagt *adj (dvs. i form)* in form, fit *(til* for, *til at* to); *(indlysende)* evident, obvious; *ikke være ~ til at arbejde* not feel· like working.
opland *et* back-up area; *(for skole, sygehus)* catchment area.
opleve *v* ex'perience; *(gennemleve)* go· through; *(komme ud for)* have, meet· with; *~ en masse i ferien* have an e'ventful holiday; *~ ngt rart (,væmmeligt)* have a pleasant (,nasty) ex'perience; *tænk at jeg skulle ~ det med!* I never thought I'd live to see that! *jeg har aldrig ~t ngt lignende!* I never saw the like! **~lse** *en* ex'perience.
oplukker *en (dåse~)* tin opener; *(flaske~)* bottle opener.
oplyse *v (belyse)* light· (up); *(meddele)* de'clare, state; *(uddybe, forklare)* ex'plain; *~ en om ngt* in'form sby of sth; **~nde** *adj* in'formative.
oplysning *en (med lys)* lighting; *(åndeligt stade)* en'lightenment; *(undervisning)* edu'cation; *(besked)* infor'mation; *~en (tlf)* Infor'mation; *give en ~ om ngt* in'form sby of sth; *nærmere ~er* further details; *indhente ~er* make· en'quiries.
oplyst *adj (med lys)* lit-up; *(fig)* en'lightened, educated.
oplæg *et* intro'duction; *(forslag)* pro'posal.
opløb *et (af folk)* crowd; *(ved løb, spurt)* final spurt; *standse ngt i ~et* nip sth in the bud.
opløfte *v: ~ et tal til 3. potens* raise a number to the third power.
opløftende *adj (opmuntrende)* en'couraging; *(lovende)* promising; *(moralsk belærende)* edifying; *et ~ syn* an im'pressive sight.
opløse *v* dis'solve; *~s* dis'solve; **~lig** *adj* soluble; *let ~lig* readily soluble.
opløsning *en* disso'lution; *(færdig ~, fx sukker~)* so'lution; *gå i ~* dis'integrate; *(om lig)* decom'pose.
opløsningsmiddel *et* solvent.
opmagasinere *v* store.
opmuntre *v* en'courage *(til at* to); *(live op)* cheer up; **~nde** *adj* en'couraging.
opmuntring *en* en'couragement.
opmærksom *adj* at'tentive; *(som ser alt)* ob'servant; *(hensynsfuld)* con'siderate *(mod* towards); *gøre en ~ på ngt* draw· sby's at'tention to sth; *blive ~ på ngt* be'come· a'ware of sth; **~hed** *en* at'tention; *(lille gave)* token (gift); *henlede ~heden på ngt* draw· at'tention to sth; *det er undgået min ~hed* it has e'scaped my attention; *vække ~hed* at'tract attention.
opnå *v* get·, obtain; *(resultat, mål)* a'chieve; *(vinde)* gain; *~ at* manage to; *ikke ~ ngt* a'chieve nothing.
opnåelig *adj* ob'tainable.
opofrende *adj* self-'sacrificing.
oppe *v: ~ sig* pull one'self to'gether // *adv* up, above; *(~ i huset)* up'stairs; *(~ af sengen)* up; *være længe ~* stay up late; *der ~* up there; *her ~* up here; *være tidligt ~* be up early; *være ~ til eksamen* sit· for an exami'nation; *helt ~ på bjerget* right on top of the mountain; *højt ~* high up; *være højt ~ (fig)* be in high spirits.
oppefra *adv* from above.
opposition *en* oppo'sition.
oppustelig *adj* in'flatable.
oppustet *adj (om ballon el. priser)* in'flated; *(om fed person)* bloated; *(blæret)* stuck-up.
oprejsning *en: få ~* get· satis'faction.
oprejst *adj* upright; *hun kunne næsten ikke holde sig ~* she was ready to drop.
opretholde *v* main'tain; *(forbindelse, kontakt)* keep· up; *(vedligeholde)* sus'tain; *~ livet* keep· alive; **~lse** *en* maintenance, upkeep.
opretstående *adj* upright *(fx klaver* piano).
oprette *v (grundlægge)* e'stablish, found; *(indgå, fx kontrakt)* make·; **~lse** *en* e'stablishment, foun'dation; making.
oprindelig *adj* o'riginal.

oprindelse *en* origin.
opringning *en (tlf)* call.
oprustning *en* armament.
oprydning *en* clearing-up; *(i hjemmet)* tidying-up.
oprykning *en (sport)* pro'motion.
oprør *et* re'volt, re'bellion, uprising; *(uro, røre)* tumult; *gøre ~* re'volt; *være i ~ (også fig)* be in a turmoil.
oprørende *adj* out'rageous.
oprører *en* rebel.
oprørsk *adj* re'bellious; *(om barn)* un'ruly.
oprørt *adj (om hav etc)* rough; *(om person)* in'dignant *(over* at, *over at* that).
opråb *et* ap'peal; *(navne~)* call-out.
opsamlingsheat *et (sport)* inter'mediate heat.
opsamlingslejr *en* re'ception camp.
opsang *en: hun gav ham en ordentlig ~* she gave· him a piece of her mind; *(stærkere)* she read· him the riot act.
opsat *adj: ~ på at gøre ngt* set· on doing sth, keen to do sth; *have ~ hår* have one's hair up.
opsige *v (kontrakt etc)* terminate; *(abonnement)* cancel; *(fyre)* dis'miss; *~ en lejer* give· sby notice (to quit); *~ sin lejlighed* give· in notice for one's flat; *~ sin stilling* give· in one's notice.
opsigelse *en* termi'nation; cancel'lation; dis'missal; *få sin ~* be given notice; *have en måneds ~* have a month's notice.
opsigt *en: vække ~* cause a sen'sation.
opsigtsvækkende *adj* sen'sational.
opskrift *en (strikke~)* pattern; *(mad~)* recipe *(på* for).
opslag *et (ærme~)* cuff; *(bukse~)* turn-up; *(revers)* la'pel; *(plakat)* poster; *(bekendtgørelse)* notice.
opslagsbog *en* reference book.
opslagstavle *en* notice board.
opslugt *adj: ~ af* ab'sorbed in.
opslå *v (stilling)* advertise.
opsnappe *v* inter'cept.
opsnuse *v* ferret out.
opsparing *en (beløbet)* savings *pl; (det at spare)* saving up; *tvungen ~* com'pulsory saving.
opspind *et* fabri'cation, in'vention.
opspore *v* track down.
opstand *en* uprising, re'volt.
opstandelse *en (uro)* com'motion; *(fra de døde)* resur'rection.
opstille *v* put· up; *(kontrakt, budget etc)* make·, draw· up; *(selv ~ til valg)* run· *(til* for); *(~ en til valg)* nominate; *(~ på række etc)* line up.
opstilling *en* putting up; *(af kontrakt, budget etc)* making, drawing up; *(til valg, om en selv)* running; *(til valg om en anden)* nominating; *(på række etc)* lining up.
opstoppernæse *en* snub nose.
opstrammer *en (drink)* pick-me-up.
opstød *et* burp; *surt ~* acid regurgi'tation; *(om person)* sourface.
opstå *v* a'rise·, come· into being; *ilden opstod ved en kortslutning* the fire was caused by a short circuit.
opsummere *v* sum up.
opsving *et (økon)* boom.
opsvulmet *adj* swollen.
opsyn *et (overvågning)* super'vision *(med* of); *(med person)* sur'veillance; *(med børn)* care *(med* of); *(kontrollør)* at'tendant; *holde ~ med ngt* supervise sth, be in charge of sth.
opsynsmand *en* at'tendant.
opsætning *en* setting up; *(af forestilling)* pro'duction.
opsøge *v (besøge)* call on; *(finde)* seek· out; *~nde arbejde* fieldwork.
optage *v (tage op; opsuge)* take· up; *(som medlem, elev etc)* ad'mit *(i* to); *(på liste)* in'clude; *(foto)* take· (a photo of); *(film)* film, shoot·; *(på plade, bånd)* re'cord; *~ meget plads up* take up space; *~ et lån* raise a loan; *det ~r ham meget* it interests him very much.
optagelse *en* taking up; *(af medlem, elev etc)* ad'mission *(i* to); *(på liste)* in'clusion; *(foto)* photo; *(film)* filming, shooting; *(på plade, bånd)* re'cording.
optagelsesprøve *en* entrance exami'nation.
optager *en* re'corder.
optaget *adj (om person)* busy; *(om toilet, tlf, siddeplads)* en'gaged; ~

af at gøre ngt busy doing sth; ~ *af en bog* ab'sorbed in a book; *alt* ~ full up; **~tone** *en (tlf)* en'gaged signal (,tone).
optakt *en: det var ~en til en krig* it marked the beginning of a war.
optegnelse *en* note, record.
optik *en* optics; *(på kamera)* lens system.
optiker *en* op'tician.
optimisme *en* 'optimism.
optimist *en* 'optimist; **~isk** *adj* opti'mistic.
option *en: have ~ på ngt* have the first option on sth.
optisk *adj* optical; ~ *bedrag* optical il'lusion; ~ *læser (edb)* optical character reader.
optog *et* pro'cession, pa'rade.
optrapning *en* esca'lation.
optrappe *v* escalate.
optrin *et* scene.
optryk *et* reprint.
optræde *v (vise sig, ses)* ap'pear *(som* as); *(som kunstner etc)* per'form; *(forekomme)* oc'cur; *(opføre sig)* be'have; *(handle)* act; ~ *på ens vegne* act for sby; ~ *høfligt* be courteous; *de ~nde* the per'formers.
optræden *en* ap'pearance; *(som kunstner etc)* per'formance; *(forekomst)* oc'currence; *(opførsel)* be'haviour.
optræk *et: der er ~ til ballade* there is trouble brewing; *der er ~ til regn* it looks like rain; *langsom i ~ket* slow in the uptake.
optælle *v* count.
optælling *en* count.
optændingsbrænde *et* firewood.
optøjer *pl* riots.
opvarme *v* heat.
opvarmning *en* heating; *(sport)* warming-up.
opvarte *v (om tjener)* wait on, serve.
opvartning *en* service, at'tendance.
opvask *en* washing-up; *tage ~en* do· the dishes; **~e·balje** *en* washing-up bowl; **~e·børste** *en* washing-up brush; **~e·maskine** *en* dishwasher; **~e·middel** *et* washing-up liquid; **~e·stativ** *et* dish rack; **~e·vand** *et* dishwater.
opveje *v (fig)* make· up for; ~ *hinanden* balance one a'nother.
opvisning *en* show.
opvækst *en* childhood, youth.
orakel *et* oracle.
orange *en* orange; **~marmelade** *en* (orange) marmalade.
orangutang *en* orang-u'tan.
ord *et* word; *så er det et ~* that is settled then; *sige ngt med rene ~* say· sth straight out; *ikke et ~ mere om det* not another word about it; *jeg kunne ikke få et ~ indført* I couldn't get a word in edgeways; *det har jeg ikke hørt et ~ om* I never heard anything about it; *han har ~et* it is his turn to speak; *han har også et ~ at skulle have sagt* he has a say too; *have ~ for at være ngt* have a repu'tation for being sth; *holde sit ~* keep· one's word; *med andre ~* in other words; *tage ~et* start speaking; *(i forsamling)* take· the floor; *tage en på ~et* take· sby at his word; *komme til ~e* get· a chance to speak.
ordblind *adj* dys'lexic; **~hed** *en* dys'lexia.
ordbog *en* dictionary; *slå ngt op i en ~* look sth up in a dictionary.
orden *en* order *(også om udmærkelse); holde ~* keep· things tidy; *det er helt i ~* it is quite all right; *for en ~s skyld* as a matter of form; *er bilen i ~?* is the car working? *få ngt bragt i ~* settle sth.
ordens... *sms:* **~duks** *en* monitor; **~magten** *s* the po'lice; **~menneske** *et* tidy person; **~politiet** *s* the uniformed po'lice; **~regler** *pl* regu'lations; **~tal** *et* ordinal (number).
ordentlig *adj (som holder orden)* tidy, orderly; *(regelret, korrekt)* regular, cor'rect; *(pæn, anstændig)* decent, nice; *(rigtig)* proper, real; *opføre sig ~t* be'have (properly); *en ~ omgang (tæv)* a sound beating.
ordforråd *et* vo'cabulary.
ordfører *en* spokesman *(pl:* -men).
ordinere *v (præst)* or'dain; *(foreskrive)* pre'scribe.
ordinær *adj* ordinary; *(simpel)* common, vulgar; *~t medlem* full member.
ordkløveri *et* quibbling.

ordknap *adj* taciturn.
ordlyd *en: brevet har følgende* ~ the letter reads as follows.
ordne *v* ar'range; *(bringe i orden)* put· in order; *(rydde op)* tidy (up); *(sortere)* sort out; *(klare)* manage, settle; *det ~r sig nok* it will sort it'self out, it's going to be all right.
ordning *en* ar'rangement; *(aftale om fx betaling)* settlement; *(system)* system.
ordre *en* order; *efter* ~ by order; *(om varelevering)* to order; *afgive en ~ på ngt* place an order for sth; *få ~ til at* be ordered to; **~seddel** *en* order form.
ordret *adj/adv* ver'batim, literal.
ordspil *et* pun.
ordsprog *et* proverb.
ordstyrer *en* chairman *(pl:* -men).
organ *et* organ.
organisation *en* organi'zation.
organisere *v* organize; *blive ~t (i fagforening)* unionize; *~t arbejdskraft* union labour.
organisk *adj* or'ganic.
organisme *en* 'organism.
organist *en* organ player, 'organist.
orgasme *en* 'orgasm.
orgel *et* organ.
orgie *et* orgy.
orientalsk *adj* ori'ental.
Orienten *s* the East.
orientere *v* in'form; ~ *en* put· sby in the picture; ~ *sig* get· one's bearings; *ikke kunne ~ sig* have lost one's bearings.
orientering *en* infor'mation; *(som skolefag) sv.t.* general sciences; **~s·løb** *et* orien'teering.
original *en* o'riginal; *(om person)* ec'centric // *adj* o'riginal; *(om person)* ec'centric; *en ~ Turner* a genuine Turner; **~udgave** *en (af bog)* first e'dition.
orkan *en* hurricane.
orke *v* be able to; *jeg ~r ikke mere* (F) I'm all in; *jeg ~r ikke at se ham nu* I can't be bothered to see him now.
orkester *et* 'orchestra; **~plads** *en (teat)* stall.
orkidé *en* orchid.
orlogsværft *et* naval shipyard.
orlov *en* leave; *have* ~ be on leave.
orm *en* worm; **~ædt** *adj* worm-eaten.
ornament *et* 'ornament.
ornat *et* vestments *pl.*
orne *en* boar.
ornitolog *en* orni'thologist; **ornitologi** *en* orni'thology.
ortodoks *adj* 'orthodox.
ortopædisk *adj* ortho'paedic.
ortopædkirurgi *en* ortho'paedic surgery.
os *en (røg)* smoke; *(stank)* reek.
os *pron* us; *(refleksivt)* our'selves; *(efter præp)* us; *han så* ~ he saw· us; *vi morede* ~ we had a good time, we had fun; *vi glæder ~ til at...* we are looking forward to...; *til ~ selv* for our'selves; *mellem ~ sagt* be'tween our'selves; *det bliver mellem* ~ it will go no further; *en ven af* ~ a friend of ours.
ose *v (ryge)* smoke; *(stinke)* reek.
ost *en* cheese.
oste... *sms:* **~anretning** *en* cheeseboard; **~klokke** *en* cheese cover; **~mad** *en* cheese sandwich; **~skorpe** *en* cheese rind; **~skærer** *en* cheese slicer.
osv. *(fork.f. og så videre)* etc. *(fork.f.* etcetera).
otium *et* re'tirement.
otte *num* eight; *om ~ dage* in a week; *i dag ~ dage* today week.
ottende *adj* eighth.
ottendedel *en* eighth; **~s·node** *en* quaver.
otter *en* eight; *(om bus)* number eight.
ottetal *et* eight.
ottetiden *s: ved* ~ about eight o'clock.
ottetimers- eight-hour.
oval *en, adj* oval.
oven *adv:* ~ *for* a'bove; *fra* ~ from above; ~ *i hinanden* on top of one another; *(lige efter hinanden)* in suc'cession; ~ *i købet* into the bargain; ~ *over* above; ~ *på* on top of; *(i hus)* up'stairs; *de bor ~ på os* they live up'stairs from us // *præp:* ~ *senge* up and about; ~ *vande* above water.

ovenfor *adv* a'bove.
ovenfra *adv* from a'bove.
oveni *adv* on top (of).
ovenlysvindue *et* skylight.
ovennævnt *adj* a'bove(-mentioned).
ovenover *adv* a'bove.
ovenpå *adv* a'bove; *(i hus)* up'stairs; *(siden, bagefter)* afterwards; *svømme ~* float; *være ~ (dvs. den stærkeste)* have the upper hand; *(dvs. glad, i fin form)* be on top of the world.
ovenstående *adj* the a'bove.
ovenud *adv: ~ lykkelig* be'side oneself with joy.
over *præp/adv* over; *(oven ~)* above; *(tværs ~, fx gade)* across; *(mere end)* over, above, more than; *(om klokkeslæt)* past; *(på grund af)* at, of; *(via)* by, via; *hoppe ~ en pyt* jump over a puddle; *have magt ~ en* have power over sby; *det tog ~ tre timer* it lasted over (,more than) three hours; *fem grader ~ frysepunktet* five de'grees above zero; *klokken er ~ ti* it is past ten o'clock; *glæde sig ~ ngt* be pleased about sth; *være vred ~ ngt* be angry at (,about) sth; *tage til Exeter ~ Reading* go to Exeter via (,by) Reading; *elske en ~ alt (i verden)* love sby more than anything (in the world); *det går ~ min forstand* it is beyond me.
overalt *adv* everywhere; *jeg har søgt ~* I have been looking all over (,everywhere); *~ i verden* all over the world; *~ hvor man kommer* wher'ever you go.
overanstrenge *v: ~ sig (med arbejde)* over'work; *(fysisk)* over'strain one-'self; **~lse** *en* overe'xertion; strain.
overarbejde *et* overtime; *have ~* work overtime.
overbalance *en: få ~* lose· one's balance.
overbefolket *adj* over'populated.
oberbelastet *adj (om person)* over-'taxed; *(om fx tlf, elek)* over'loaded.
overbevise *v* con'vince *(om* of, *om at* that); *være overbevist om at...* be convinced that...
overbevisning *en* con'viction; *være ngt af ~* be sth by con'viction; *efter min bedste ~* to the best of my be'lief.
overblik *et: få ~ over ngt* get· a general i'dea of sth; *miste ~ket* lose· track of things; *et ~ over aftenens program* a survey of to'night's programmes.
overbyde *v* out'bid·
overbygning *en* superstructure.
overbærende *adj* in'dulgent *(mod* to).
overbærenhed *en* in'dulgence.
overdel *en* top; *(på kjole)* bodice.
overdosis *en* overdose; *tage en ~* (F) OD ['əu'di:].
overdrage *v* trans'fer; *(betro)* en'trust; *(ansvar)* give·; *(opgave)* as'sign; *(hus, ejendom)* make· over; *~ ngt til en* en'trust sby with sth; **~lse** *en* 'transfer; trusting; giving; as'signment; making over.
overdreven *adj* e'xaggerated.
overdrive *v* e'xaggerate; *(drive det for vidt)* over'do· it, go· too far; **~lse** *en* exagge'ration; *man kan uden ~lse sig at...* it is no exagge'ration to say that...
overdøve *v* drown; *(skaffe sig ørenlyd)* make· oneself heard above.
overdådig *adj* opulent, lu'xurious; **~hed** *en* opulence, lu'xuriance.
overens *adv: komme ~ om ngt* a'gree on sth; *stemme ~* tally *(med* with).
overenskomst *en* a'greement; *slutte ~* make· an agreement; **~forhandlinger** *pl* (col'lective) wage nego-ti'ations; **~stridig** *adj* contrary to the agreement.
overensstemmelse *en* a'greement; *være i ~ med* a'gree (,tally) with.
overfald *et* at'tack, as'sault *(på* on); *(på gaden også)* mugging *(på* of).
overfalde *v* at'tack, as'sault; mug; *~ en bank* raid a bank; *~ en med spørgsmål* bom'bard sby with questions.
overfart *en* crossing.
overflade *en* surface; *komme op til ~n* surface.
overfladisk *adj* super'ficial.
overflod *en* a'bundance *(af* of); *(velstand)* affluence; *blomster i ~* plenty

of flowers, an a'bundance of flowers; **~s·samfund** *et* affluent so'ciety.

overflødig *adj* su'perfluous.

overfor *adv* opposite.

overfyldt *adj* full, packed, crowded.

overfølsom *adj (sart)* over'sensitive *(for* to); *(allergisk)* al'lergic *(for* to); **~hed** *en* oversensi'tivity; 'allergy.

overføre *v* trans'fer; *(om sygdom)* trans'mit.

overføring *en (bro)* flyover.

overførsel *en* 'transfer; *(om sygdom)* trans'mission.

overført *adj (om betydning)* figurative.

overgang *et (sted hvor man går over)* crossing; *(tid)* time; *(skift, ændring)* tran'sition; *(elek)* leak; *det er kun for en ~* it is only for a time; *hans stemme er gået i ~* his voice is breaking; **~s·alder** *en* cli'macteric; *~s·alderen (også)* the change of life; **~s·løsning** *en* interim so'lution; **~s·sted** *et* crossing; **~s·tid** *en* tran'sitional period; *(mellem årstiderne)* in-between season.

overgive *v* hand over; *(betro)* en'trust with; *(udlevere)* give· up; *~ sig* sur'render; **~lse** *en* sur'render.

overgreb *et* in'fringement; *(overfald)* as'sault.

overgå *v (være bedre end)* sur'pass; *(yde mere end)* out'do·; *(ske)* happen to; *(ændres, skifte)* change *(til* into); *~ sig selv* sur'pass oneself; *~ til statseje* be'come· state property.

overhale *v (indhente)* over'take·, pass.

overhaling *en* over'taking, passing; *(grundig istandsættelse etc)* overhaul; *(skældud)* ticking-off; **~s·bane** *en* fast lane.

overholde *v (fx regler)* ob'serve, keep·.

overhoved *et* head.

overhovedet *adv* at all; *~ ikke* not at all; *har du ~ tænkt dig om?* did you think at all? *det har ~ ingen betydning* it has no im'portance whatso'ever.

overhuset *s (brit)* the House of Lords.

overhængende *adj: ~ fare* imminent danger.

overhøre *v (ikke høre)* not hear, miss; *(komme til at høre)* over'hear·.

overhånd *en: få ~* gain the upper hand; *tage ~* get· out of hand.

overilet *adj* rash, hasty.

overiset *adj* iced up.

overkant *en* top, upper edge; *det er i ~en* it is a bit much.

overklasse *en* upper classes *pl;*

overklasse- upper-class.

overkomme *v* manage; *(kunne betale)* af'ford; **~lig** *adj* feasible; *(håndterlig)* manageable.

overkrop *en* upper part of the body; *med nøgen ~* stripped to the waist.

overkæbe *en* upper jaw.

overkøje *en* upper berth.

overlade *v (lade få, give)* let· have; *(betro)* en'trust *(en ngt* sby with sth); *(låne)* lend·; *det vil jeg ~ til dig at bestemme* I'll leave· that for you to de'cide; *være overladt til sig selv* be left to one'self; *~ en til hans skæbne* a'bandon sby to his fate.

overlagt *adj (om forbrydelse)* wilful, pre'meditated.

overlapning *en* 'overlap.

overlappe *v* over'lap.

overlegen *adj (storsnudet etc)* super'cilious; *(bedre end)* su'perior; *være en ~* be su'perior to sby; *en ~ sejr* a con'vincing victory; **~hed** *en* super'ciliousness; superi'ority.

overleve *v* sur'vive; *(leve længere end)* out'live *(med to år* by two years); *den bil har ~t sig selv* that car has had its day; **~nde** *en* sur'vivor // *adj* sur'viving.

overlevering *en (aflevering)* de'livery; *(skreven)* record; *(tradition)* tra'dition.

overligger *en (i mål)* crossbar.

overlyds- super'sonic.

overlæbe *en* upper lip.

overlæsset *adj (om pynt)* over'decorated, or'nate.

overlæg *s: med ~* on purpose, de'liberately.

overlæge *en* senior con'sultant.

overmagt *en* superi'ority.

overmand *en* su'perior; *møde sin ~* meet· one's match.

overmande *v* over'come·; *blive ~t af ngt* be over'come by sth.
overmorgen *s: i ~* the day after to'morrow; *i ~ aften* the day after to'morrow in the evening.
overmund *en (om protese)* upper denture.
overnatning *en* staying over'night.
overnatte *v* stay the night *(hos en* with sby).
overnaturlig *adj* super'natural.
overordentlig *adj* extra'ordinary // *adv* ex'tremely.
overordnet *s/adj* su'perior; *den overordnede målsætning* the overall ob'jective.
overraske *v* sur'prise; *(overrumple også)* take· by surprise; *~ en i at gøre ngt* catch· sby doing sth; *blive ~t over ngt* be surprised at sth; *blive ~t af et tordenvejr* be caught in a storm; **-lse** *en* sur'prise; *til min store ~lse* much to my surprise.
overrendt *adj* over'run *(af* by); *(plaget)* pestered *(af* by).
overrumple *v: ~en* take· sby by sur'prise, catch· sby off his (,her) guard.
overrække *v: ~ en ngt* pre'sent sby with sth.
overse *v (se ud over)* sur'vey; *(ikke se)* over'look, miss; *~ at...* over'look the fact that...
oversigt *en* 'survey *(over* of); *(tabel)* table *(over* of).
overskride *v* cross; *(fig)* ex'ceed; *~ grænsen for det anstændige* go· beyond what is decent.
overskrift *en* heading; *(avis~)* headline.
overskrævs *adv: ~ på ngt* a'stride sth.
overskud *et* surplus *(af* of); *(fortjeneste)* profit; *give ~* yield a profit; *have ~ til at gøre ngt* have strength enough to do sth; **~s·deling** *en* gain-sharing; **~s·lager** *et* surplus stock.
overskue *v* sur'vey; *det er ikke til at ~ hvor længe* it is im'possible to tell how long; **~lig** *adj* clear; *(til at klare)* manageable; *inden for en ~lig fremtid* in the fore'seeable future.
overskydende *adj* surplus.
overskyet *adj* overcast.
overskæg *et* mou'stache.
overskæring *en (jernb)* (level) crossing.
overslag *et* estimate *(over* of).
overspændt *adj* highly-strung.
overstadig *adj* hi'larious; *(vild)* boisterous.
overstige *v* ex'ceed, go· be'yond.
overstrømmende *adj* ef'fusive; *(neds)* gushing.
overstå *v* get· through, get· over; *få det ~et* get· it over with; *godt det er ~et!* thank God it is over.
oversvømme *v* flood; *~et af turister* over'run by tourists; **~lse** *en* flooding.
oversygeplejerske *en* senior nursing officer.
oversætte *v* trans'late; *~ fra dansk til engelsk* trans'late from Danish into English; **~lse** *en* trans'lation.
oversætter *en* trans'lator.
oversøisk *adj* overseas.
overtag *et: få ~et* get· the upper hand.
overtage *v* take· over; *(påtage sig)* take· on; *(købe)* buy·; *~ kommandoen efter en* take· over com'mand from sby; *~ ens vaner* a'dopt sby's habits; **~lse** *en* takeover; *(det at overtage)* taking over.
overtal *et: være i ~* be in the ma'jority; *(være for mange)* be su'perior in number.
overtale *v: ~ en til at gøre ngt* persu'ade sby to do sth; **~lse** *en* persu'asion.
overtro *en* super'stition; **~isk** *adj* super'stitious.
overtræde *v (fx regler)* break·; **~lse** *en* of'fence *(af* against), breach *(af* of).
overtræk *et* cover; *(på konto)* overdraft; **~ke** *v* cover; *(med chokolade, lak etc)* coat; *(om konto)* over'draw·.
overtræt *adj* over'tired.
overtøj *et* outdoor things *pl,* coat.
overveje *v* con'sider, think· about; *jeg skal ~ det* I'll think about it; *~ ngt igen* recon'sider sth; *~ at tage*

til Kina con'sider going to China; *~ for og imod* weigh the pros and cons; **~lse** *en* conside'ration, thought; *efter nærmere ~lse* on closer exami'nation; *tage ngt op til ~lse* look into sth.

overvejende *adv* mainly, chiefly; *det er ~ sandsynligt at de kommer* most likely they will come; *~ tørt vejr* mainly dry.

overvidde *en (om kvinde)* breast; *(om mand)* chest.

overvinde *v* de'feat; *(fig)* over'come·; *~ sig til at gøre ngt* bring· oneself to do sth; **~lse** *en* over'coming; *det kostede mig stor ~lse* it took· me a lot of will power.

overvurdere *v* over'estimate.

overvægt *en* overweight; *der er ~ af udlændinge* there is a pre'dominance of foreigners.

overvægtig *adj* overweight.

overvælde *v* over'whelm; *blive ~t af ngt* be over'whelmed with sth, be over'come by sth; **~nde** *adj* over'whelming.

overvære *v* be present at, at'tend; *(se)* see·; *~ en fodboldkamp* watch a football match; **~lse** *en: i ~lse af* in the presence of, be'fore.

overvåge *v (holde opsyn med)* super'vise; *(observere, fx om patient)* watch, ob'serve; *(en mistænkt)* keep· under sur'veillance; *(med måleapparatur)* monitor *(fx stråling* radi'ation).

overvågning *en (opsyn)* super'vision; *(observation af fx patient)* obser'vation; *(af mistænkt)* sur'veillance; *(med måleudstyr)* monitoring.

overøse *v: han overøste hende med gaver* he showered presents on her.

ovn *en (bage~)* oven; *(varme~)* stove; *(til brænding af fx keramik)* kiln; **~fast** *adj* ovenproof; **~klar** *adj* oven-ready.

ovre *adv* over; *der ~* over there; *her ~* over here.

oxyd *en* oxide.

oxydere *v* oxidize.

ozon *et* ozone; **~laget** *s* the ozone layer.

P

pace *v: ~ en frem* drive· (,push) sby (on); **~maker** *en* pacemaker.

pacificere *v* pacify.

pacifist *en* 'pacifist; **~isk** *adj* 'pacifist.

padde *en* am'phibian; *sløv ~ (fig)* slowcoach; *(langsomt opfattende)* dimwit.

paddehat *en* toadstool; *(spiselig)* mushroom.

padderokke *en (bot)* horsetail.

padle *v* paddle.

paf *adj* flappergasted.

pagaj *en* paddle.

pagt *en* pact, treaty.

paillet *en* sequin.

pakhus *et* warehouse.

pakistaner *en,* **pakistansk** *adj* Paki'stani.

pakkasse *en* case; *(stor)* crate.

pakke *en* parcel, package; *(lille, fx ~ cigaretter)* packet // *v (fx kuffert)* pack; *~ ind* pack up; *(i papir)* wrap up; *~ op* un'pack; *(om papirspakke)* un'wrap; *~ sammen* pack up; *~ ud d.s.s. ~ op;* **~løsning** *en* package so'lution; **~nelliker** *pl* odds and ends; **~post** *en* parcel post.

pakning *en (i emballage etc)* packing; *(til vandhane)* gasket.

palads *et* palace.

palet *en* pa'lette; **~kniv** *en (gastr)* spatula; **~ske** *en (gastr)* fish slice.

palisander *et* (Bra'zilian) rosewood.

palle *en* pallet.

palme *en* palm; **~søndag** *en* Palm Sunday.

palmin *en* vegetable fat.

palæ *et* palace; *(fint hus)* mansion.

Palæstina *s* 'Palestine; **palæstinenser** *en,* **palæstinensisk** *adj* Pale'stinian.

pamper *en* ty'coon.

pande *en (anat)* forehead; *(stege~)* pan; *rynke ~n* frown; *løbe ~n mod en mur* run· one's head against a brick wall.

pandebånd *et (til sportsfolk etc)* sweat-band.

pandehulebetændelse *en* sinu'sitis.

pandehår *et* fringe.
pandekage *en* pancake; **~dej** *en* batter.
panel *et* panelling; *(om personer)* panel; **~diskussion** *en* panel discussion.
panere *v* bread.
panik *en* panic; *der gik ~ i dem* they panicked; **~slagen** *adj* panic-stricken.
panisk *adj* panic.
panser *et* armour; **~bil** *en* armoured car; **~dør** *en* steel door; **~glas** *et* armoured glass.
pansre *v* armour; *~t bil* armoured car.
pant *et* se'curity; *(i ejendom)* mortgage; *(for fx flaske)* de'posit; *(symbol, tegn)* token; *sætte ngt i ~* give· sth as a se'curity; *sætte ~ i huset* mortgage the house; **~e·brev** *et* mortgage deed; **~e·foged** *en* bailiff; **~e·låner** *en* pawnbroker.
pantomine *en* mime; *(i Tivoli)* com'media dell'arte.
panter *en* panther.
pantsætte *v* pawn; *(om hus)* mortgage.
pap *et* cardboard; *skære ngt ud i ~* (F) spell sth out.
papegøje *en* parrot.
papir *et (materialet)* paper; *(brev~, skrive~)* stationery; *(værdi~)* se'curity; *have ~ på ngt* have sth in writing; *få sin afsked på gråt ~* get· sacked; **~affald** *et* wastepaper; **~fabrik** *en* paper mill; **~kniv** *en* paper knife *(pl:* knives); **~kurv** *en* wastepaper basket; **~løs** *adj: ~løs samlever* common-law wife (,husband); *~løst samliv* cohabi'tation; *leve ~løst sammen* co'habit, (F) live together; **~nusseri** *et* paperpushing; **~serviet** *en* paper napkin; **~s·lommetørklæde** *et* paper hankie; **~s·pose** *en* paper bag.
papmælk *en* milk in cartons.
paprika *en* paprika.
paptallerken *en* paper plate, dis'posable plate.
papvin *en* wine in cartons.
papæske *en* cardboard box.
par *et (to ting etc der hører sammen)* pair; *(gifte, forlovede etc)* couple; *et ~ (dvs. nogle få)* a couple of, a few; *et ~ kopper* a cup and saucer; *et ~ gange* a couple of times; *hun er et ~ og fyrre* she is forty-odd.
parabolantenne *en* satellite dish.
parade *en* pa'rade.
paradis *et* paradise; *hoppe ~* play hopscotch; **~æble** *et* crab apple.
paradoks *et* paradox; **~al** *adj* para'doxical.
paraffin *s* 'paraffin; **~olie** *en* 'paraffin oil.
paragraf *en (i lov etc)* section; *(i kontrakt etc)* clause; *klare ~ferne* sort things out.
parallel *en, adj* parallel *(med* to).
paranød *en* Bra'zil nut.
paraply *en* um'brella; *slå ~en op (,ned)* put· up (,down) one's umbrella; **~klapvogn** *en* stroller.
parasit *en* parasite.
parasol *en* sunshade.
parat *adj* ready; *~ til at gøre ngt* ready to do sth; *gøre sig ~* get· ready; *holde maden ~* have the meal ready.
parcelhus *et* de'tached house.
parentes *en* pa'renthesis, bracket; *i ~ bemærket* by the way, inci'dentally; *sætte ngt i ~* put· sth in brackets.
parfait *en (is)* ice cream (with bits of fruit, chocolate etc).
parforhold *et* couplehood; *leve i ~* live together as husband and wife.
parfume *en* perfume, scent; **~re** *v* scent; **~ri** *et* per'fumery.
park *en* park.
parkere *v* park.
parkering *en* parking; *~ forbudt* no parking; **~s·billet** *en* parking slip; **~s·bøde** *en* parking ticket; **~s·hus** *et* (multi-storey) car park; **~s·lys** *et* parking light; **~s·plads** *en (til én bil)* parking space; *(til flere biler)* car park; **~s·skive** *en* parking disc; **~s·vagt** *en sv.t.* traffic warden.
parket *et (teat)* stalls; *(gulvbelægning)* parquet (flooring); **~gulv** *et* parquet floor.
parkometer *et* parking meter.

parlament *et* parliament; *(om det brit ~)* Parliament.
parlamentarisk *adj* parlia'mentary.
parlamentere *v* ne'gotiate, di'scuss.
parlamentsmedlem *et* member of parliament, MP.
parlamentsvalg *et* e'lection.
parløb *et (på skøjter)* pair-skating; *(på cykel)* partner race.
parlør *en* phrase book.
parodi *en* parody *(på* of*)*.
parodiere *v* parody; im'personate.
parre *v (om dyr)* mate; *(om ting)* pair; *~ sig (om dyr)* mate.
parring *en* mating; **~s·tid** *en* mating season.
part *en (del)* part; *(andel)* share; *den anden ~ i sagen* the other party; *have ~ i en forretning* have an interest in a business; *det er bedst for alle ~er* it is the best for everybody con'cerned.
partere *v* cut· up.
partering *en* cutting up.
parthaver *en* partner.
parti *et (pol)* party; *(del)* part; *(om varer)* lot; *(kortspil)* game; *(ægteskab)* match; *tage ~ for en* take· sby's side; **~formand** *en* party leader; **~fælle** *en* fellow party member; **~ledelse** *en* party com'mittee; **~politik** *en* party politics.
partisk *adj* partial, bias(s)ed.
partitur *et (mus)* score.
partner *en* partner.
parvenu *en* upstart.
parvis *adv* in couples, in pairs.
paryk *en* wig; *(spøg om hår)* mop of hair; *gå med ~* wear· a wig.
pas *et (rejse~)* passport; *(bjerg~)* pass; *melde ~* give· up.
pasform *en* fit.
pasfoto *et* passport photo.
paskontrol *en* passport con'trol.
pasning *en (pleje)* care; *(i fodbold)* pass.
passage *en* 'passage.
passager *en* passenger; *blind ~* stowaway; **~fly** *et* airliner; **~skib** *et* (passenger) liner.
passant: *en ~* by the way.
passe *v (pleje)* nurse; *(tage sig af)* take· care of, look after; *(~ i målene, fx om tøj)* fit; *(være rigtig)* be true (,right); *(være belejlig)* suit, be con'venient; *skoene ~r godt* the shoes fit well (,are a good fit); *~ sin lillesøster* look after one's little sister; *~ sit arbejde* at'tend to one's work; *det ~r mig fint* it suits me fine; *~ tiden* keep· check on the time, (F) mind the time; *~ en op* waylay· sby; *~ på (tage sig af)* take· care of; *(være forsigtig)* take· care, be careful; *pas på!* look out! take care! *~ sammen* go· well to'gether, be a good match;; *~ sammen med (i farver etc)* go· well with.
passende *adj* suitable; *(belejlig)* con'venient; *(sømmelig)* decent, proper.
passer *en* compasses *pl; en ~* a pair of compasses.
passere *v (komme forbi)* pass (by); *(komme igennem)* pass through; *(komme over)* cross; *(ske)* happen.
passioneret *adj* keen, de'voted.
passiv *adj* passive; *~t medlem sv.t.* as'sociate member; *~ rygning* passive smoking.
passus *en* passage.
pasta *s (fx tand~)* paste; *(spaghetti etc)* pasta.
pastel(farve) *en* pastel.
pasteuriseret *adj* 'pasteurized.
pastil *en* lozenge.
pastinak *en* parsnip.
pastor *en: ~ A. Jensen (i omtale)* the Reverend A. Jensen; *(i tiltale)* Mr. Jensen; *~en* the vicar.
pâté *en* 'pâté.
patent *et* patent; *have ~ på ngt* hold· a patent for sth; *tage ~ på ngt* take· out a patent for sth; **~anmeldt** *adj* patent pending; **~beskyttet** *adj* patented.
patentere *v* patent.
patentløsning *en* pana'cea.
patient *en* patient; *ambulant ~* out-patient.
patina *en* patina.
patologisk *adj* patho'logical.
patriot *en* 'patriot; **~isk** *adj* patri'otic.
patron *en (til våben)* cartridge; *(til*

pen) refill; **~hylster** *et* cartridge case.
patrulje *en* pa'trol; **~re** *v* pa'trol; **~vogn** *en* pa'trol car.
patte *en (om dyr)* teat; *~r* (V, *neds om bryster)* tits // *v* suck; *~ på ngt* suck sth; **~barn** *et* baby; **~dyr** *et* mammal; **~gris** *en* suckling pig.
pauker *pl (mus)* timpani.
paukist *en* timpanist.
pause *en* pause; *(teat)* interval; *(i arbejde etc)* break; *holde ~* take· a break; **~signal** *et* interval sign.
pave *en* pope; *stolt som en ~* proud as a peacock; **~dømme** *et* papacy.
pavillon *en* pa'vilion.
peber *en* pepper; **~bøsse** *en* pepper pot; **~frugt** *en* pepper; **~korn** *et* peppercorn; **~kværn** *en* pepper mill; **~mynte** *en* peppermint; **~mø** *en* spinster; **~nødder** *pl* (F, *om småpenge)* peanuts; **~rod** *en* horseradish; **~svend** *en* bachelor.
pebret *adj (krydret)* peppery; *(dyr)* ex'pensive; *(om pris)* stiff.
pedal *en* pedal; *træde i ~erne* (pedal (along).
pedant *en* pedant; **~isk** *adj* pe'dantic.
peddigrør *et* cane.
pedel *en* janitor.
pege *v* point; *~ i retning af, ~ mod* point to; *~ på ngt* point at sth; *(påpege)* point sth out; **~finger** *en* index finger, forefinger; **~pind** *en* pointer.
pejle *v* get· the bearings of; **~vogn** *en* de'tector van.
pejs *en* open fireplace; **~e·sæt** *et* fire irons.
pekingeser *en* peki'nese, (F) peke.
pelargonie *en* ge'ranium.
pelikan *en* pelican.
pels *en* fur; *redde ~en* save one's skin; *vove ~en* risk one's skin; **~dyr** *et* furred animal; **~dyravl** *en* fur farming; **~foret** *adj* fur-lined; **~handler** *en* furrier; **~krave** *en* fur collar; **~værk** *et* furs *pl.*
pen *en* pen; *skrive med ~ og blæk* write· in pen and ink.
penalhus *et* pencil case.
pendant *en* match, counterpart.
pendle *v (om fly, tog)* shuttle; *(om person)* com'mute.
pendul *et* pendulum; **~fart** *en* commu'tation; *køre i ~fart* shuttle, com'mute.
penge *pl* money *(singularis); han har mange ~* he has got lots of money; *i rede ~* in cash, in ready money; *tjene ~* make· money; *få ngt for ~ne* get· one's money's worth; *det var alle ~ne værd* it was priceless; **~afpresning** *en* blackmail; **~automat** *en (ved bank etc)* cash dis'penser, cashpoint; **~institut** *et* fi'nancial insti'tution; **~kasse** *en* money box; **~nød** *en: være i ~nød* be hard up; **~pung** *en* purse; **~sager** *pl* money matters, fi'nances; **~seddel** *en* bank note; **~skab** *et* safe; **~stykke** *et* coin; **~stærk** *adj* fi'nancially strong.
penicillin *et* peni'cillin.
penneven *en* pen pal.
pensel *en* (paint) brush.
pension *en* pension; *(kost)* board; *(pensionat)* boarding house, pension; *gå af med ~* re'tire with a pension.
pensionat *et* boarding house, pension.
pensioneret *adj* re'tired.
pensionist *en* (old-age) pensioner, OAP.
pensionsalder *en* re'tirement age.
pensionsberettiget *adj* en'titled to a pension.
pensionsbidrag *et* contri'bution to a pension fund.
pensionskasse *en* pension fund.
pensionsordning *en* pension scheme.
pensionær *en* boarder.
pensle *v* paint; *~ en i halsen* paint sby's throat.
per *præp (fork. pr.)* per; *(i adresse)* near; *der er tre ~ person* there are three per head; *overskud ~ 31. december* balance as of December 31st.
perfekt *adj* 'perfect.
perfektionist *en* per'fectionist.
perfektum *s (gram)* the perfect tense; *~ participium* the past participle.

perforere *v* perforate.
pergament *et* parchment; **~papir** *et (til madpakke etc)* grease-proof paper.
periferi *en* pe'riphery; *(omegn)* suburbs *pl,* outskirts *pl;* **~udstyr** *et (edb)* pe'ripherals *pl.*
periode *en* period.
periodisk *adj* peri'odic.
periskop *et* periscope.
perle *en (ægte)* pearl; *(af glas, træ etc)* bead; *(dråbe)* drop; **~høne** *en* guinea fowl; **~kæde** *en* string of pearls (,beads); **~løg** *et* pearl leek; **~mor** *en* mother-of-pearl; **~musling** *en* pearl oyster; **~strikning** *en* moss stitch.
permanent *en* perm // *adj* permanent; **~e** *v* perm.
perpleks *adj* be'wildered.
perron *en* platform; **~billet** *en* platform ticket.
persianer *en* Persian lamb.
persienne *en* (Ve'netian) blind.
persille *en* parsley; **~kværn** *en* parsley mincer; **~rod** *en* parsley root.
persisk *adj* Persian.
person *en* person; *(i bog, skuespil etc)* character; *en firepersoners bil* a four-seater; *møde i egen* ~ ap'pear personally; *præsidenten i egen høje* ~ the president in person.
personale *et* staff; **~chef** *en* personnel manager.
personlig *adj* personal; ~ *samtale (tlf)* personal call // *adv* personally; *kende en ~t* know· sby personally; **~hed** *en* perso'nality; *(væsen, natur)* character; *være en ~hed* be a character.
person... *sms:* **~nummer** *et* civil regis'tration number; **~søger** *en (bipper)* bleeper; **~tog** *et* passenger train; **~vogn** *en* car; **~vægt** *en* scales.
perspektiv *et* per'spective; **~plan** *en* blueprint.
pertentlig *adj* me'ticulous; *(neds)* per'nickety.
peruaner *en,* **peruansk** *adj* Pe'ruvian.
pervers *adj* per'verted; ~ *person* 'pervert; **perversitet** *en* per'version.
pessar *et* diaphragm.
pessimist *en* pessimist; **~isk** *adj* pessi'mistic.
pest *en* plague; *hade ngt som ~en* hate sth like poison.
pestilens *en* 'pestilence.
petitesse *en* trifle; *gå op i ~r* be a stickler for details.
petroleum *en* paraffin, kerosene; **~s·apparat** *et* paraffin (cooking) stove; **~s·ovn** *en* paraffin heater.
pianist *en* 'pianist, pi'ano player.
pibe *en* pipe; *ryge* ~ smoke a pipe // *v (fløjte)* pipe, whistle; *(om hund etc)* whine; *(klynke)* whimper; **~hoved** *et* pipe bowl; **~kradser** *en* pipe-bowl scraper.
piben *en* piping; whistling; whining; whimper(ing); *(se pibe).*
piberenser *en* pipe cleaner.
piberyger *en* pipe smoker.
pibetobak *en* smoking to'bacco.
piccolo *en (på hotel)* bellboy; **~fløjte** *en* piccolo.
piedestal *en* pedestal.
piffe *v:* ~ *op* spruce up.
pift *et* whistle; **~e** *v* whistle; *~e en cykel* let· down the tyre(s) of a bike.
pig *en (på pindsvin etc)* spine; *(på plante, busk etc)* prickle; *(af metal)* spike; **~dæk** *et* studded tyre.
pige *en* girl; *(tjeneste~)* maid; **~navn** *et (dvs. før ægteskab)* maiden name; **~skole** *en* girls' school; **~spejder** *en* girl guide; **~værelse** *et* maid's room.
pighvar *en (fisk)* turbot.
pigkrøllejern *et* curling brush.
pigtråd *en* barbed wire.
pik *en* (V) prick, cock.
pikant *adj* 'piquant; *(dristig, fx historie)* racy.
pil *en (bot)* willow; *(til bue og på skilt)* arrow; *(kaste~)* dart.
pile *v:* ~ *af sted* dash along.
pilespids *en* arrowhead.
piletræ *et* willow (tree).
pilgrim *en* pilgrim; **~s·rejse** *en* pilgrimage.
pilk *en* jig; **~e** *v: ~e torsk* fish cod.
pille *en (tablet)* pill; *(søjle)* pillar; *(bro~)* pier; *(på hængebro)* pylon //

v pick; *(skrælle etc)* peel; ~ *næse* pick one's nose; *ikke* ~*!* don't touch! ~ *en ned* cut· sby down to size; ~ *ved ngt* touch sth, fiddle with sth; **~arbejde** *et* niggling work; **~kartofler** *pl* po'tatoes to be cooked in their jackets; **~sikret** *adj* fiddle-proof.

pilot *en* pilot.

pilotere *v* pile; **pilotering** *en* piling.

pilotprojekt *et* pilot scheme.

pilsner *en* lager.

pimpe *v* booze.

pimpsten *en* pumice ['pʌmis] (stone).

pincet *en: en* ~ a pair of tweezers.

pind *en* stick; *(strikke~)* needle; *(række masker i strikning)* row; *stiv som en* ~ stiff as a rod; *jeg forstår ikke en* ~ *af det hele* I don't understand a word of it; *stå på* ~*e for en* wait on sby hand and foot.

pinde *v:* ~ *ngt ud for en* spell sth out for sby.

pindebrænde *et* firewood.

pindemad *en* canapé.

pindsvin *et* hedgehog.

pine *en* pain; *(stærk* ~*)* agony; *det var en* ~ *at høre på* it was agony to listen to; *død og* ~*!* good God! // *v (smerte)* pain; *(tortere, volde smerte)* torture, tor'ment; *det* ~*r ham at hun vandt* it irks him that she won.

ping *en (om person)* bigwig, mandarin.

pingvin *en* penguin.

pinlig *adj (ubehagelig)* painful, awkward; *(flov)* em'barrassing; *(omhyggelig)* me'ticulous; *det var vel nok* ~*t!* how em'barassing! *føle sig* ~*t berørt* feel· em'barrassed; ~*t ædru* stone cold sober; ~ *orden* me'ticulous order.

pinse *en* Whitsun; **~dag** *en: første* ~*dag* Whit Sunday; *anden* ~*dag* Whit Monday; **~lilje** *en* (white) nar'cissus.

pioner *en* pio'neer.

pip *et (fugle~)* chirp; *det tog* ~*pet fra os* it dis'couraged us; *få* ~ go· nuts; *det er det rene* ~ it is com'pletely crazy.

pipette *en* pi'pette.

pippe *v (om fugl)* chirp.

pirat *en* pirate; **~kopi** *en (af plade, edb-program etc)* pirated version; **~sender** *en* pirate radio (,station).

pirre *v* tickle; *(ophidse)* ex'cite; **~lig** *adj* irritable.

pirring *en* stimu'lation, exci'tation.

pis *et* (V) piss; *det er ngt værre* ~ it's a load of crap; *tage* ~ *på en* take· the piss out of sby.

pisk *en* whip; *(en omgang* ~*)* whipping.

piske *v (med pisk)* whip; *(om æg)* whisk; *(om fløde)* whip; *regnen* ~*de ned* the rain was pelting down; *være* ~*t til at gøre ngt* be forced to do sth.

piskefløde *en* double cream.

piskeris *et* whisk.

pisse *v* (V) piss; **~fuld** *adj* pissed; **~åndssvag** *adj* bloody stupid.

pissoir *et* urinal.

pistol *en* pistol; **~hylster** *et* holster.

pive *v (jamre)* whimper; *(beklage sig)* whine.

pivet *adj* soft, wet.

pjalt *en* rag; *slå sine* ~*er sammen (dvs. gifte sig)* get· spliced; *(dvs. slå sig sammen)* com'bine forces.

pjank *et* nonsense; *(flirten)* hanky'panky; **~e** *v* fool around; **~et** *adj* silly.

pjask *et (plask)* splash; *(tynd te etc)* slush; **~e** *v* splash; **~våd** *adj* dripping wet.

pjat *et d.s.s. pjank;* **~te** *v d.s.s.* pjanke; **~tet** *adj: han er hel* ~*tet med Mozart* (F) he is crazy about Mozart.

pjece *en* pamphlet, leaflet.

pjok *et* sissy.

pjusket *adj (om hår etc)* tousled; *(om udseende)* ruffled.

pjække *v:* ~ *fra skole* play truant; ~ *fra arbejde* shirk one's work.

pjækkeri *et (fra skole)* truancy; *(fra arbejde)* absen'teeism.

placere *v* place.

placering *en* placing, placement; *(beliggenhed)* situ'ation; *(sport)* ranking.

pladask: *falde* ~ fall· flat (on one's face).

pladder *et (pløre)* slush; *(vrøvl)* nonsense; **~sentimental** *adj* soppy, slushy; **~våd** *adj* sopping wet.

plade *en* plate; *(tynd ~, metal~)* sheet; *(rund ~)* disc; *(LP etc)* record; *(bord~)* top; *(lille løgn)* fib; *en ~ chokolade* a bar of chocolate; *lægge en ~ på* put· on a record; *stikke en en ~* tell· sby a fib; **~omslag** *et* cover, sleeve; **~optagelse** *en* re'cording; **~spiller** *en* record player; **~tallerken** *en* turntable.

pladre *v (plaske)* splash; *(snakke)* prattle.

plads *en (sted)* place; *(torv)* square; *(sidde~)* seat; *(~ til ngt)* room; *(stilling)* job, po'sition; *er der ~ til en til?* is there room for one more? *bestille ~ (fx i teat)* book a seat; *(på hotel)* book a room; *jeg kan ikke få ~ til skålen* I can't find room for the bowl; *gøre ~ for en* make· room for sby; *der er god ~* there is plenty of room; *lægge ngt på ~* put sth in its place; *sætte en på ~* put· sby in his right place; *tage ~* take· a seat, sit· down; **~besparende** *adj* space-saving; **~billet** *en* seat reser'vation; **~hensyn** *et: af ~hensyn* to save space; **~mangel** *en* lack of space.

plage *en (gene)* nuisance; *(pine)* 'torment // *v (genere)* plague; *(irritere)* irritate; *(om børn der tigger)* pester; *(pine)* torture; *~ livet af en* worry sby to death; *(med plagerier)* pester sby to death.

plageri *et (tiggeri)* pestering.

plageånd *en* pest.

plagiat *et* plagiarism.

plagiere *v* imitate.

plaid *en* travelling rug; *(i hjemmet)* (wollen) blanket.

plakat *en (opslag med oplysninger etc)* notice; *(med billeder)* poster; *sætte et stykke på ~en (teat)* bill a play; **~søjle** *en* advertising column.

plamage *en* blotch, smudge.

plan *en* plan; *(kort over ngt)* map; *gå efter ~en* go· ac'cording to plan; *lægge ~er* make· plans; *have ~ om at gøre ngt* plan to do sth // *et (niveau)* level; *i (det) samme ~* on the same level; *på højeste ~* at top level // *adj (jævn)* even; *(vandret)* level; *(flad)* flat.

planere *v* level.

planche *en (billedside)* plate.

planering *en* levelling.

planet *en* planet.

planetarium *et* plane'tarium.

planke *en* plank; **~værk** *et* hoarding, fence.

planlægge *v* plan *(at* to); *~ at tage til Frankrig* con'sider going to France.

planlægning *en* planning.

planmæssig *adj (efter køreplanen etc)* scheduled.

plantage *en* plan'tation; **~ejer** *en* planter.

plante *en* plant // *v* plant; **~fiber** *en* vegetable fibre; **~margarine** *en* vegetable margarine; **~skole** *en* nursery; **~vækst** *en* vege'tation.

plantning *en* planting.

plapre *v: ~ op* prattle away; *~ ud med ngt* let· sth out.

plask *et* splash; **~e** *v* splash; **~våd** *adj* dripping wet.

plaster *et* (sticking-)plaster; *som et ~ på såret* by way of conso'lation.

plastic *en* plastic; **~maling** *en* e'mulsion paint.

plastikkirurgi *en* plastic surgery.

plastpose *en* plastic bag.

plat *s: slå ~ og krone* toss a coin; *~ el. krone?* heads or tails? // *adj* vulgar.

platan(træ) *en/et* plane (tree).

plateau *et* 'plateau.

platfodet *adj* plat-footed.

platform *en* platform.

platin *et* 'platinum; **~blond** *adj* platinum blonde.

pleje *en* care; *(af syge el. børn også)* nursing; *have et barn i ~* foster a child // *v (passe)* take· care of, nurse; *vi ~r at gøre det* we usually do it; *~ sin hud* take· care of one's skin; *vi ~r ikke at glemme* we don't usually for'get; *gør som du ~r* do· as you are used to; **~barn** *et* foster child; **~forældre** *pl* foster parents; **~hjem** *et (for børn)* foster home; *(for ældre)* nursing home.

plet *en (mindre ~, sted)* spot; *(større*

~, *fx blod~)* stain; *(sølv~)* silver plate; *møde på ~ten* be there one the spot; *sætte ~ter på ngt* stain sth; *ikke røre sig ud af ~ten* not budge; *ramme ~* hit· the bull's eye; **~fjerner** *en* 'stain-re,mover; **~fri** *adj* spotless; **~rensning** *en* spot-cleaning; **~skud** *et* bull's-eye.

plette *v* spot, stain; **~t** *adj* spotted; *(spættet)* speckled; *(snavset)* stained.

pletvis *adj* in places; in spots.

pligt *en* duty; *gøre sin ~* do· one's duty; *han har ~ til at gøre det* it is his duty to do it; **~følelse** *en* sense of duty.

pligtig *adj: ~ til* under an obli'gation to.

pligtopfyldende *adj* consci'entious.

pligtskyldigst *adv* dutifully.

plisseret *adj* pleated.

plombe *en (segl)* lead [lɛd] seal; *(i tand)* filling; **~re** *v (forsegle)* seal; *(om tand)* fill.

plov *en* plough; **~fure** *en* furrow.

pludre *v (snakke)* chat; *(om barn)* babble.

pludselig *adj* sudden // *adv* suddenly, all of a sudden; *standse ~t (også)* stop short.

plukke *v (blomster etc)* pick, gather; *(fjerkræ)* pluck; *(udplyndre)* fleece; *have en høne at ~ med en* have a bone to pick with sby.

plump *et/interj* splash // *adj* rude, course.

plumpe *v* plump; *~ i vandet* go· splash into the water; *~ i (dvs. dumme sig)* make· a gaffe; *~ ud med det hele* spill the beans.

plus *et* plus; *(fordel)* ad'vantage // *adv: to ~ to er fire* two plus two makes four; *~ tre grader* three de'grees above zero.

plyndre *v* loot; *(om by også)* plunder; *(ved overfald på person)* rob; *(flå for penge)* fleece.

plyndring *en* looting; fleecing.

plys *et* plush; **~klippet** *adj* crew-cut; **~se** *v* crew-cut.

plæne *en* lawn; *slå ~* mow the lawn; **~klipper** *en* lawn-mower.

pløje *v* plough; *~ sig igennem ngt* plough one's way through sth; **~mark** *en* ploughed field.

pløjning *en* ploughing.

pløk *en* peg.

pløkke *v: ~ en ned* (F) plug sby.

pløre *et* mud; **~t** *adj* muddy; (F, *fuld)* stoned.

pochere *v (gastr)* poach.

pode *v* graft.

podium *et* platform; *(med talerstol)* rostrum.

poesi *en* poetry; **~bog** *en* autograph book.

poetisk *adj* po'etic.

point *et* point; *vinde på ~s* win· on points.

pointe *en (i historie)* point; *(i vittighed)* punchline; **~re** *v* emphasize.

pokal *en* cup; **~finale** *en (sport)* cup final; **~kamp** *en* cup-tie.

pokker *s* the devil; *hvad ~ mener du?* what the hell do you mean? *det var som ~!* well, I'll be damned! *bo ~ i vold* live miles from anywhere; *give ~ i ngt* not give· a damn about sth.

pokkers *adj* damned, blasted; *~!* damn! *en ~ karl* one hell of a man.

pol *en* pole.

polak *en* Pole; *paven er ~* the Pope is Polish.

polarcirkel *en* polar circle; *den nordlige (, sydlige) ~* the Arctic (,Ant'arctic) Circle.

polarforsker *en* arctic (,ant'arctic) ex'plorer.

polarklima *et* arctic climate.

Polarstjernen *s* the Pole Star.

Polen *s* Poland.

polere *v* polish, shine; **polering** *en* polish(ing).

polet *en* token.

police *en* policy.

poliklinik *en* out-patients' de'partment.

polio *m* polio.

politi *et* po'lice; *tilkalde ~et* call the police; **~afspærring** *en* police cordon; **~assistent** *en sv.t.* police in'spector; **~beskyttelse** *en* police pro'tection; **~betjent** *en* po'liceman *(pl:* -men), constable; *(kvindelig)* po'licewoman *(pl:* -women); **~bil** *en* police car; **~folk** *pl* po'licemen; *6 ~folk blev såret (også)* six po'lice were injured; **~fuldmægtig** *en sv.t.* as'sistant chief constable; **~inspektør** *en sv.omtr.t.* chief superin'tendent.

politik *en* politics; *(speciel ~)* policy.

politiker *en* poli'tician.

politi... *sms:* **~kommissær** *en sv.omtr.t.* po'lice superin'tendent; **~mand** *en* po'lice officer; **~mester** *en sv.t.* po'lice constable; **~skilt** *et* po'liceman's badge; **~station** *en* po'lice station; **~stav** *en* truncheon; **~styrke** *en* po'lice force.

politur *en* polish.

pollen *s* pollen; **~tal** *et* pollen count.

polsk *adj* Polish; *leve på ~* co'habit.

polstret *adj (om møbel)* up'holstered; *hun er godt ~* she's well-padded.

polstring *en* up'holstery.

polterabend *en (for brudgom)* bachelor's night, stag party; *(for brud)* hen party.

polyp *en* 'polyp; *have ~per (i næsen)* have 'adenoids.

pomade *en* hair-cream.

pomerans *en* bitter orange.

pommes frites *pl (brit)* po'tato chips; *(am)* French fries.

pompøs *adj* grandiose.

ponton *en* pon'toon.

pony *en* pony.

popgruppe *en* pop group.

poplin *et* poplin.

popmusik *en* pop music.

poppel *en* poplar.

popsanger *en* pop singer.

popularitet *en* popu'larity.

populær *adj* popular *(hos* with).

porcelæn *et* 'porcelain; *(ting af ~)* china; *kongeligt ~* Royal Copenhagen; **~s·fabrik** *en* porcelain factory; **~s·figur** *en* china figurine.

pore *en* pore.

porno *en* porn; **~blad** *et* porno magazine; **~film** *en* porn movie; **~grafi** *en* por'nography; **~grafisk** *adj* porno'graphical.

porre *en* leek.

portal *en* portal.

port *en* gate; *smide en på ~en* send· sby packing.

porter *en (øl)* stout.

portier *en* (hall) porter.

portion *en (om mad)* helping; *(part)* part; *(mængde)* a'mount; lot; *i små ~er* little by little; *en ~ til* a second helping; *der skal en god ~ frækhed til* it takes a fair amount of cheek.

portner *en* caretaker.

porto *en* postage; **~fri** *adj* free of charge.

portræt *et* 'portrait; **~tere** *v* por'tray.

Portugal *s* Portugal.

portugiser *en,* **portugisisk** *adj* Portu'guese.

portvin *en* port.

portør *en (på sygehus)* hospital porter; *(jernb)* railwayman *(pl:* -men).

porøs *adj* porous.

pose *en* bag // *v (om bluse etc)* puff out; *(om bukser)* bag; **~dame** *en* bag lady.

posere *v* pose.

poset *adj (om kjole etc)* baggy.

position *en* po'sition; *skabe sig en ~* e'stablish a po'sition for oneself; *parkering i anden ~* double-parking; **~s·lys** *en* parking lights.

positiv *adj (velvillig)* sympa'thetic; *(bekræftende)* positive; *være ~t indstillet over for ngt* have a positive attitude to'wards sth.

positur *en* posture.

post *en (~væsen, forsendelser)* post, mail; *(vandpumpe)* pump; *(vandhane)* tap; *(stilling)* post; *(i regnskab)* entry; *(på liste)* item; *sende ngt med ~en* post sth, send· sth by mail; *er der ~ til os?* is there any mail for us? *blive på sin ~* re'main at one's post; *være på sin ~* be on one's guard *(overfor* against); **~anvisning** *en* postal order; **~bil** *en* mail van; **~boks** *en* post-office box, PO-box; **~bud** *et* postman *(pl:* -men); **~distrikt** *et* postal 'district.

poste *v (sende)* post; *(om vand etc)* pump.

postej *en* pâté; *(portions~)* patty.

postevand *et* tap water.

post... *sms:* **~hus** *et* post office; **~kas-**

se *en (offentlig)* post-box; *(privat)* letter box; **~kort** *et* postcard; **~mester** *en* postmaster; *(kvindelig)* postmistress; **~nummer** *et (brit)* postcode; *(am)* zip code; **~ombæring** *en* mail de'livery; **~ordre** *en* mail order; **~pakke** *en* parcel; *sende ngt som ~pakke* send· sth by parcel post; **~stempel** *et* postmark; **~takst** *en* postal charges *pl;* **~væsen** *et* mail services *pl.*

postyr *et (opstandelse)* fuss; *(uro)* com'motion.

potaske *en* potash.

pote *en* paw; *give ~ (om hund)* shake· hands; *(fig, lønne sig)* pay· off.

potens *en (mat)* power; *(seksuel)* potency; *to i anden ~* the square of two; *ni i tredje ~* the cube of nine; *opløfte et tal til anden (,tredje) ~* square (,cube) a figure; *i højeste ~ (fig)* to the highest de'gree.

potent *adj* potent.

potte *en* pot; *(til barn)* pottie; *så er den ~ ude* that takes care of that // *v: ~ om* repot; **~mager** *en* potter; **~mageri** *et* pottery; **~plante** *en* potted plant.

poulard *en sv.t.* broiler.

p-pille *en: ~n* the pill; *hun tager ~r* she is on the pill.

pr. *d.s.s. per.*

Prag *s* Prague.

pragt *en* splendour; **~eksemplar** *et* beauty; *(om dyr, mand)* fine specimen; **~fuld** *adj* splendid, mag'nificent.

praj *et* hail; *give mig lige et ~* give· me a hint; **~e** *v* hail.

prakke *v: ~ en ngt på* palm sth off on sby.

praksis *en* practice; *i ~* in practice; *føre ngt ud i ~* put· sth into practice.

praktik *en* practice; *(under uddannelse)* trai'nee service; *(i skolen)* work ex'perience.

praktikant *en* trai'nee.

praktikplads *en* trai'nee job.

praktisere *v* practise; *~nde læge* general prac'titioner, GP.

praktisk *adj* practical // *adv* practically; *~ talt* so to speak.

prale *v* boast; *(skryde)* brag; *~ med sin bil* show· off one's car; **~ri** *et* boasting, bragging.

pralhals *en* braggart.

pram *en* barge.

prangende *adj* sumptuous, showy.

prelle *v: ~ af på* glance off on; *dine ord ~r af på ham* your words are lost on him.

premiere *en* first night, opening night.

premierminister *en* prime minister.

pres *et* pressure; *lægge ~ på en* put· pressure on sby; *være under stærkt ~* be under a lot of pressure; *lægge ngt i ~* press sth.

presenning *en* tar'paulin.

presning *en* pressing.

presse *en (presseanordning)* press; *(aviser, blade)* news media; *(pressefolk)* newsmen *pl* // *v* press; *(om frugt etc)* squeeze; *~ en til at gøre ngt* press sby to do sth; *~ penge af en* blackmail sby; *få sit tøj ~t* have one's clothes pressed; **~bureau** *et* news agency; **~fold** *en* crease; **~folk** *pl* newsmen; **~fotograf** *en* press pho'tographer; **~kampagne** *en* press cam'paign; **~konference** *en* press 'conference; **~meddelelse** *en* press re'lease.

presserende *adj* urgent.

pression *en* pressure; **~s·gruppe** *en* pressure group.

prestige *en* pre'stige.

prik *en* dot; *(plet)* spot; *(stik)* prick; *ligne ngt på en ~* be com'pletely like sth; *til punkt og ~ke* to the letter; *~ken over i'et (fig)* the finishing touch.

prikke *v* prick; *~ hul i ngt* puncture sth; *~ til en* get· at sby.

primitiv *adj* primitive.

primtal *et* prime number.

primus *en*® primus stove; **~ motor** *en* leading figure.

primær *en* primary.

princip *et* principle; *af ~* on principle; *i ~pet* in principle.

principiel *adj: af ~le grunde* on grounds of principle; *vi er enige i det ~le* we a'gree in principle; **~t** *adv* in principle.

prins *en* prince.
prinsesse *en* prin'cess.
prinsgemal *en* prince consort.
prioritere *v (give forret)* give pri'ority to; *(om ejendom)* mortgage; ~ *ngt højt* give· sth a high priority; *~t til op over skorstenen* mortgaged to the rooftop.
prioritet *en (forret)* pri'ority; *(i ejendom)* mortgage; *have første* ~ have top pri'ority.
pris *en* price; *(billet~, i bus etc)* fare; *(betaling som kræves også)* charge; *(præmie)* prize; *tage for høje ~er* charge too much; *han måtte betale ~en* he had to pay the price; *opgive ~en på ngt* quote the price for sth; *for enhver* ~ at all costs; *sætte* ~ *på ngt* ap'preciate sth, set· great store by sth; *til en* ~ *af...* at a price of...; *til halv* ~ at half price; **~belønnet** *adj* prize-winning; **~belønning** *en* a'ward; **~bevidst** *adj* price-conscious; **~billig** *adj* inex'pensive; **~dyk** *et* sudden drop in prices.
prise *v* praise; ~ *sig lykkelig* count oneself lucky.
pris... *sms:* **~fald** *et* fall in price(s); **~forskel** *en* difference in price(s); **~givet** *adj: være ~givet en* be at the mercy of sby; **~idé** *en* sug'gested price; **~klasse** *en* price range; **~nedsættelse** *en* price cut; *(udsalg)* sale; **~niveau** *et* price level; **~skilt** *et* price label, tag; *(i vindue etc)* show card; **~stigning** *en* price increase; **~stop** *et* price freeze; **~tal** *et* price index; **~talsreguleret** *adj* index-linked; **~uddeling** *en* prize-giving; **~vinder** *en* prizewinner; **~værdig** *adj* laudable.
privat *adj* private // *adv* privately, in private; **~bane** *en* private railway; **~chauffør** *en* 'chauffeur; **~detektiv** *en* private de'tective, (F) private eye; **~ejet** *adj* on private hands; **~hospital** *et* private hospital.
privatisere *v* privatize.
privatklinik *en* private clinic.
privatsag *en* private matter.
privatsekretær *en* private secretary.
privatskole *en* private school.
privilegeret *adj* privileged.
privilegium *et* privilege.
problem *et* 'problem.
problematisk *adj* proble'matic.
problemfri *adj* problem-free.
procedure *en* pro'cedure.
procent *en* per cent (p.c.); *(~del)* per'centage; *betale 10* ~ *rente* pay· a 10 per cent interest; *få ~er* get· a 'discount; **~del** *en* per'centage; **~vis** *adj/adv* per'centage.
proces *en* 'process; *(retssag)* case; *gøre kort* ~ *med en* make· short work of sby.
procession *en* pro'cession.
producent *en* pro'ducer, manu'facturer.
producere *v* pro'duce, manu'facture.
produkt *et* 'product.
produktion *en* pro'duction, manu'facture; **~s·middel** *et* means of pro'duction; **~s·sted** *et* place of manu'facture (,pro'duction).
produktiv *adj* pro'ductive.
profession *en* pro'fession; *(om håndværk)* trade; *han er gartner af* ~ he is a gardener by trade.
professionel *en* pro'fessional, (F) pro // *adj* pro'fessional.
professor *en* pro'fessor; *hun er* ~ *i fysik ved universitetet* she holds· a chair of physics at the uni'versity; **~at** *et* pro'fessorship.
profet *en* prophet.
profetere *v* prophesy.
profeti *en* prophecy.
profil *en* 'profile; *(fig)* image; *holde en lav* ~ keep· a low profile.
profit *en: sælge ngt med* ~ sell· sth at a profit.
prognose *en* pre'diction; *(vejr~)* forecast; *(ved sygdom)* prog'nosis.
program *et* programme; *(edb)* program; *stå på ~met* be on the programme; **~erklæring** *en* mani'festo.
programmel *et (edb)* software.
programmere *v* 'program; *være ~t til ngt (ikke om edb)* be geared to sth.
programmør *en* 'programmer.
programoversigt *en* to'day's (,to'night's) programme.

progressiv *adj* pro'gressive.
projekt *et* 'project; *(plan også)* plan.
projektere *v* pro'ject; plan.
projektgruppe *en* 'project team.
projektør *en (til belysning af bygning etc)* floodlight; *(teat)* spot(light); *(på politibil etc)* searchlight; **~lys** *et* floodlight; spotlight.
projicere *v* pro'ject.
proklamere *v* pro'claim.
prokura *s: have ~ for et firma* sign for a firm.
prolog *en* 'prologue.
promenade *en* 'promenade; **~vogn** *en* pushchair.
promenere *v* stroll.
promille *en* per thousand; *(spiritus~)* alcohol level; **~kørsel** *en* drunken driving.
prominent *adj* prominent.
prompte *adv* promptly
pronomen *et (gram)* pronoun.
prop *en (til flaske)* cork; *(af glas, gummi etc)* stopper; *(til badekar etc)* plug; *(sikring)* fuse; *få en ~* have a fit.
propaganda *en* propa'ganda.
propagandere *v* propagate *(for* for).
propel *en* pro'peller.
propfuld *adj* crammed, packed.
proportion *en* pro'portion.
proportional *adj: omvendt ~ med* in in'verse pro'portion to.
proportionsforvrængning *en: det er ~* it is out of all pro'portion.
proppe *v (stoppe fuld)* cram; *~ flasker til* cork bottles; *~ sig med mad* stuff oneself with food; *ngt i sig* scoff down sth.
proptrækker *en* corkscrew.
prosa *en* prose; **~isk** *adj* pro'saic.
prosit *interj* bless you!
prostata *en* prostate (gland).
prostitueret *en/adj* 'prostitute.
prostitution *en* prosti'tution.
protein *et* 'protein.
protese *en (arm, ben etc)* arti'ficial limb; *(tand~)* denture.
protest *en* 'protest; *nedlægge ~ mod ngt* make· a protest against sth.
protestant *en* 'Protestant; **~isk** *adj* 'Protestant.
protestere *v* pro'test *(mod* against, about).
protestmøde *et* 'protest meeting.
protestskrivelse *en* letter of 'protest.
protokol *en (navneliste; skole~)* register; *(regnskabs~)* ledger; *(møde~)* minutes *pl; (rets~)* transcript.
prototype *en* prototype.
proviant *en* pro'visions *pl;* **~ere** *v* pro'vision.
provins *en* 'province; *ude i ~en* out in the provinces; **~by** *en* pro'vincial town.
provinsiel *adj* pro'vincial, small-town.
provision *en* com'mission.
provisorisk *adj* temporary.
provokation *en* provo'cation.
provokere *v* pro'voke; **~nde** *adj* pro'voking.
provst *en* dean.
pruste *v* snort.
prut *en* fart; **~te** *v (om pris)* haggle; *(fjerte)* fart.
pryd *en* ornament; **~busk** *en* orna'mental bush.
pryde *v (pynte)* 'decorate; *(være en ~ for)* a'dorn.
prygl *pl* hiding, beating.
prygle *v* beat·, thrash; **~straf** *en* corporal punishment.
præcis *adj* e'xact, pre'cise; *(punktlig)* punctual // *adv* e'xactly, pre'cisely; punctually; *kom klokken to ~* come· at two o'clock sharp; *klokken er ~ halv* it is e'xactly half past; *være ~* be punctual; **~ere** *v* de'fine; *(specificere)* specify.
præcision *en* pre'cision; *(punktlighed)* punctu'ality.
prædike *v* preach.
prædiken *en* sermon; *(neds)* lecture.
prædikestol *en* pulpit.
præfabrikeret *adj* pre'fabricated, 'prefab.
præg *et (udseende)* look; *(egenskab)* character; *(på mønt)* strike; *sætte sig ~ på ngt* leave· one's stamp on sth; *bære ~ af* have a look of; *(være mærket)* be marked by.
præge *v (om mønt)* strike·; *(sætte ~*

på) mark, stamp; *(påvirke)* influence; *(karakterisere)* characterize; **-maskine** *en* label maker.
prægtig *adj* fine.
præke *v* preach.
præliminær *adj* pre'liminary.
præmie *en (belønning)* re'ward; *(gevinst)* prize; *(forsikrings~)* premium; *vinde første ~* win· the first prize; **-konkurrence** *en* prize 'contest; **-obligation** *en* premium bond.
præmiere *v* give· an award to.
præmieuddeling *en* prize giving.
præparat *et* prepa'ration.
præparere *v (behandle)* pre'pare; *(påvirke)* work on.
præposition *en (gram)* prepo'sition.
prærie *en* prairie; **-ulv** *en* coy'ote; **-vogn** *en* prairie wagon.
præsens *s (gram)* the present (tense).
præsentation *en* presen'tation; *(af personer for hinanden)* intro'duction.
præsentere *v* pre'sent; *(~ personer for hinanden)* intro'duce; *må jeg ~ min kone for Dem?* (H) allow me to intro'duce my wife!; (F) this is my wife; *~ sig* intro'duce oneself; *~ en for ngt* intro'duce sby to sth; *~ gevær* pre'sent arms.
præservativ *et (kondom)* contra'ceptive sheath, (F) rubber.
præservere *v* pre'serve.
præserveringsmiddel *et* pre'servative.
præsident *en* president; **-kandidat** *en* presi'dential candidate; **-valg** *et* presi'dential e'lection.
præsidere *v (ved møde)* pre'side *(ved* over).
præst *en* clergyman *(pl:* -men); *(sogne~)* vicar, rector; *(i frikirke)* minister; *(katolsk)* priest; *gå til ~* go to confir'mation classes.
præstation *en* a'chievement, per'formance.
præstebolig *en* vicarage, rectory; *(katolsk)* presbytery.
præstekald *et* living.
præstekjole *en* (minister's) gown.
præstere *v (udføre)* per'form; *(opnå)* a'chieve; *han ~de at ødelægge to biler* he managed to ruin two cars.
præstinde *en* priestess.
prævention *en* contra'ception.
præventiv *adj (mod sygdom etc)* prophy'lactic; *~t middel (mod svangerskab)* contra'ceptive.
prøjsisk *adj* Prussian.
prøve *en* test, trial; *(på koncert etc)* re'hearsal; *(vare~, smags~)* sample *(på* of); *(eksamen)* ex'am, test; *have ngt på ~* have sth on trial; *sætte ngt på en ~* put· sth to the test // *v (forsøge)* try; *(undersøge)* test; *~ en kjole* try on a dress; *~ sig frem* feel· one's way; *du kan bare ~ på det!* you just try! **-ballon** *en: opsende en ~ballon* put· out a feeler; **-billede** *et (tv)* testcard; **-boring** *en* test drilling; **-flyvning** *en* test flight; **-klud** *en* guineapig; **-køre** *v* try out; *(om bil)* test-drive·.
prøvelse *en (lidelse)* trial.
prøveløsladelse *en* con'ditional re'lease.
prøverum *et (i fx tøjbutik)* fitting booth.
prøvesprængning *en (af a-våben)* nuclear test.
prøvestop *et (for atomforsøg)* test ban.
prøvetid *en* trial period.
pseudonym *et* pseudonym.
p-skive *en* parking disc.
psyke *en (sind)* men'tality; *(ånd)* mind.
psykiater *en* psy'chiatrist; **psykiatri** *en* psy'chiatry.
psykisk *adj* mental, psycho'logical // *adv* mentally; *~ handicappet* mentally dis'abled.
psykoanalyse *en* psychoa'nalysis.
psykoanalytiker *en* psycho'analyst.
psykolog *en* psy'chologist; **-isk** *adj* psycho'logical.
psykopat *en* psychopath.
psykose *en* psy'chosis *(pl:* psychoses).
psykoterapi *en* psycho'therapy.
psykotisk *adj* psy'chotic.
pubertet *en* puberty; **-s·alder** *en* age of puberty.
publicere *v* publish.
publikation *en* publi'cation.

publikum *et (tilskuere, tilhørere)* audience; *(offentligheden)* the public.
publikumstække *et: have* ~ be popular, draw· crowds.
puddel(hund) *en* poodle.
pudder *et* powder; **-dåse** *en* powder box; *(til at have i tasken)* powder compact; **-kvast** *en* powder puff; **-sukker** *et* brown sugar; **-underlag** *et* foun'dation (cream).
pude *en (sofe~ etc)* cushion; *(hoved~)* pillow; **-betræk** *et* cushion cover; *(til hoved~)* pillowcase.
pudre *v: ~ (sig)* powder.
puds *en (på mur)* plaster; *spille en et* ~ play a trick on sby.
pudse *v (polere)* polish; *(rense)* clean; *(væg, mur)* plaster; *~ næse* blow· one's nose; *~ sølvtøj* polish the silver; *~ hunden på en* set· the dog on sby; **-creme** *en* polish; **-klud** *en* polishing cloth.
pudsig *adj* funny.
puf *et* push; **-fe** *v* push; *~fe til en* push sby.
pufærme *et* puff sleeve.
pukkel *en* hump; *(overskud)* surplus; *få på puklen* catch· it; *slide sig en ~ til* work like a slave; **-rygget** *adj* hunchbacked.
pukle *v* slave.
puld *en (på hat)* crown.
pulje *en (alle bet)* pool.
puls *en* pulse; *føle en på ~en (fig)* sound sby out.
pulse *v (ryge)* puff.
pulsere *v* throb.
pulsåre *en* artery.
pult *en* desk.
pulterkammer *et* box room; *(loft)* attic.
pulver *et* powder; **-fløde** *en* powdered cream.
pulverisere *v* pulverize; *(smadre)* smash up.
pulverkaffe *en* instant coffee.
pulverslukker *en* dry-powder ex'tinguisher.
puma *en* mountain lion.
pumpe *en* pump // *v* pump; *(~ op, fx om dæk)* in'flate, pump up.
pund *et* pound; *tre ~ kartofler* three pounds of po'tatoes.
pung *en (til penge)* purse; *(til tobak etc)* pouch; *(anat)* scrotum; **-dyr** *et* mar'supial.
punge *v: ~ ud* (F) fork out, pay· up.
punkt *et* point; *(prik)* dot; *(henseende)* re'spect; *(stadium)* stage; *nå et dødt ~* reach a deadlock; *det springende ~* the crucial point; *vi har nået det ~ hvor...* we have reached the stage where...; *du har ret på det ~* you are right on that point; *på nogle ~er går det godt* in some re'spects things are all right; *til ~ og prikke* to the letter.
punktere *v* puncture; *(med et brag)* burst; *hans bil (,cykel) er ~t* he has a puncture.
punktering *en* puncture.
punktlig *adj* punctual.
punktstrejke *en* pinpoint strike.
punktum *et* full stop, period; *sætte ~* put· a full stop; *sætte ~ for ngt* put· an end to sth.
pupil *en* pupil.
puppe *en* pupa *(pl:* pupae).
puré *en* 'purée; **purere** *v* cream.
puritaner *en* Puritan; **puritansk** *adj* Puritan.
purløg *pl* chives.
pus *en (materie)* pus // *et (barn)* darling.
pusle *v (rumstere)* move about; *(passe, pleje)* nurse; *(om baby)* change; *~ med ngt* fiddle with sth; **-bord** *et* baby's changing table; **-spil** *et* jigsaw (puzzle); *lægge ~spil* do· a jigsaw.
pust *en (ånde)* breath; *miste ~en* get· out of breath // *et (af vind)* breath of air; *(pause)* breather.
puste *v* blow·; *(hvile)* breathe; *~ og stønne* pant; *~ en ballon op* in'flate a bal'loon; *~ sig op* puff oneself up; *~ på ngt* blow· on sth; *~ til ilden (fig)* add fuel to the fire; *~ ud* breathe; *~ et lys ud* blow· out a candle; **-rum** *et* breathing space; **-rør** *et* pea-shooter.
putte *v (anbringe)* put·; *(et barn)* tuck in; *~ ngt i lommen* put· sth into one's pocket, pocket sth; *~ sig (under dynen etc)* snuggle down (in bed).

pyjamas *en* py'jamas *pl; hvor er min ~?* where are my pyjamas?
pylre *v: ~ om en* mollycoddle sby.
pylret *adj* soft.
pynt *en (næs)* point; *(ngt fint)* finery; *(dekoration)* ornament, deco'ration; *(besætning fx på kjole)* trimming; *klare ~en (fig)* weather the storm.
pynte *v (udsmykke)* decorate; *(være pæn)* look nice; *~ juletræ* decorate the Christmas tree; *~ sig* smarten oneself up; *~ på historien* em'bellish the story; *~ på regnskaberne* doctor the ac'counts.
pyramide *en* 'pyramid.
pyroman *en* pyro'maniac; **~brand** *en* arson.
pyt *en (regn~)* puddle // *interj: ~ med det!* never mind!
pædagog *en* teacher, edu'cationalist.
pædagogik *en* edu'cation.
pædagogisk *adj* edu'cational.
pæl *en* stake; *(stor stolpe)* post; *(tlf etc)* pole; *stå på gloende ~e* be on end.
pæn *adj* nice; *det var ~t af dig* it was nice of you; *han tog det ~t* he was very nice about it; *have ~t tøj på* be nicely dressed; *klare sig ~t* do· quite well; *spise ~t* have good table manners.
pære *en (bot)* pear; *(elek)* bulb; (F, *hjerne)* brains *pl; han har ~n i orden* he has got brains; **~dansk** *adj* typically Danish; **~let** *adj* dead easy; **~træ** *et* pear tree; **~vælling** *en (fig)* hotchpotch.
pøl *en* puddle; *(svømme~)* pool.
pølse *en* sausage; *bajersk ~* frankfurter; *~r og kartoffelmos* (F) bangers and mash; **~mad** *en* sandwich with sausage; **~vogn** *en* sausage stand.
pønse *v: ~ på ngt* plan sth; *(ngt ondt)* be up to sth.
på *adv/præp* on; *(i, i løbet af, om sprog, om måde, om gader, bydele etc)* in; *(om sted el. punkt, om sted hvor ngt sker, om adresse, virksomhed, bygning)* at; *(beskrivelse, tilhørsforhold)* of; *(se også de enkelte ord som ~ forbindes med); ~ mandag* on Monday; *sidde ~ gulvet* sit· on the floor; *han er ~ på sit værelse* he is in his room; *vi gjorde det ~ to timer* we did it in two hours; *sige det ~ engelsk* say· it in English; *vi bor ~ Nygade* we live in Nygade; *han bor ~ Fyn* he lives in Funen; *~ balletskolen* in the school of ballet; *~ hjørnet* at the corner; *~ det tidspunkt* at that time; *han er ~ posthuset* he is at the post office; *en pige ~ otte år* a girl of eight; *en lejlighed ~ fire værelser* a flat of four rooms; *taget ~ bilen* the top of the car; *(andre sammenhænge) se ~ en (,ngt)* look at sby (,sth); *tabe ngt ~ gulvet* drop sth on the floor; *tage ~ landet* go· into the country; *gå ~ besøg* go· visiting; *være vred ~ en* be angry with sby; *lægge låget ~* put· the lid on; *tage sweater ~* put· on a jersey.
påbegynde *v* be'gin·.
påberåbe *v: ~ sig* re'fer to; *(hævde retten til)* claim.
påbud *et* order.
påbudt *adj* pre'scribed.
pådrage *v: ~ sig* in'cur; *(en sygdom)* catch·.
pådutte *v: ~ en ngt (dvs prakke på)* palm (,foist) sth (off) on sby; *(give skylden for)* a'scribe sth to sby.
påfaldende *adj* striking.
påfugl *en* peacock.
påfund *et (idé)* idea; *(lune)* whim; *(ngt opdigtet)* fabri'cation.
påfylde *v: ~ benzin* fill up with petrol.
pågribe *v* catch·; *(anholde)* ar'rest.
pågældende *adj: den ~ (person)* the person in question (,con'cerned).
pågående *adj* ag'gressive, pushy.
påholdende *adj* stingy.
påhæng *et (om familie etc)* ap'pendages *pl.*
påhængsmotor *en* outboard motor.
påhængsvogn *en* trailer.
påhør *s: i ens ~* in front of (,be'fore) sby.
påklædning *en (det at klæde sig på)* dressing; *(dragt)* dress, clothes *pl; tvangfri ~* in'formal dress; *festlig ~* evening dress; **~s·dukke** *en* paper doll, cutout.

påklædt *adj* dressed.
påkrævet *adj* re'quired; *(nødvendig)* necessary.
påkøre *v* run· into.
påkørsel *en* col'lision.
pålandsvind *en* onshore wind.
pålidelig *adj* re'liable; *fra ~ kilde* from a re'liable source.
pålydende *et* denomi'nation; *tage ngt for ~* take· sth at face value.
pålæg *et (på brød)* (slices of) sausage, vegetables, ham etc for open sandwiches; *(smøre~)* spread; *(befaling)* order *(om at* to); *(løn~)* rise.
pålægge *v (befale)* order *(at* to); *(lægge på)* put· on.
pålægschokolade *en* thin chocolate wafers for open sandwiches.
pålægsforretning *en* delica'tessen (shop).
påmindelse *en* re'minder.
påpasselig *adj* careful.
påpege *v* point out.
pårørende *en* relative.
påsat *adj: ilden var ~* the fire had been set, it was arson.
påse *v: ~ at* see· to it that.
påsejling *en* col'lision.
påske *en* Easter; *i ~en* at Easter; **-bryg** *en* strong light beer brewed for Easter; **-dag** *en: første ~dag* Easter Sunday; *anden ~dag* Easter Monday; **-ferie** *en* Easter holidays *pl;* **-lilje** *en* daffodil; **-æg** *et* Easter egg.
påskud *et* pretext, ex'cuse; *under ~ af at* on the pretext that.
påskønne *v* ap'preciate.
påstand *en (krav, hævdelse)* claim.
påstå *v (kræve, hævde)* claim, al'lege; *(erklære)* de'clare; *(holde fast ved)* in'sist; **-e·lig** *adj* stubborn.
påstået *adj* al'leged.
påsyn *et: i ens ~* in front of (,before) sby.
påtage *v: ~ sig ansvaret* take· on the responsi'bility; *~ sig at gøre ngt* take· upon oneself to do sth.
påtaget *adj* af'fected; *~ navn* as'sumed name.
påtale *v* com'plain about.
påtrængende *adj (om person)* in'sistent, pushing; *(om nødvendighed)* urgent.
påtvinge *v: ~ en ngt* force sth on sby.
påtænke *v* plan.
påvirke *v* influence; *han lader sig ikke ~ af dem* he is unaf'fected by them; **-lig** *adj: let ~lig* easily influenced.
påvirket *adj (beruset)* under the influence (of drink).
påvirkning *en* influence.
påvise *v* show·; *(bevise)* prove; **-lig** *adj* demonstrable.

R

rabalder *et* din, racket.
rabarber *en* rhubarb; **-kompot** *en* stewed rhubarb.
rabat *en (om pris)* 'discount *(på* on); *(vej~)* shoulder, side; *(havebed)* border; *der er 10% ~ på sko* there is a 10 per cent discount on shoes; *give ~* give· a discount; *~ten er blød (på vejskilt)* soft shoulder; **-kort** *et (til bus etc)* re'duced-rate ticket.
rabies *en* rabies.
rable *v: ~ ngt af sig* reel sth off; *nu ~r det for ham* he is cracking up; **-nde** *adj: ~nde sindssyg* stark staring mad.
race *en* race, breed; **-blanding** *en (om dyr)* crossbreed; *(om mennesker)* mixture of races; **-diskrimination** *en* racial discrimi'nation; **-fordom** *en* racial prejudice; **-hest** *en* thoroughbred; **-optøjer** *pl* race riots.
racerbil *en* racer (car).
racerbåd *en* powerboat.
racercykel *en* racing bike.
raceuroligheder *pl* race riots.
racisme *en* 'racism.
racist *en* 'racist; **-isk** *adj* 'racist.
rad *en (række)* row, line; *(fyr, karl)* fellow, bloke; *stille op på ~ (og række)* line up; *stå i ~* stand· in a row; *gå ~en rundt* go· the rounds.
radar *en* radar; **-station** *en* radar station.
radbrække *v* maim; *(fx et sprog)* murder; *jeg er helt ~t* I am aching all over.

radere *v (slette)* e'rase; *(et billede)* etch.
radering *en* etching.
radialdæk *et* radial (tyre).
radiator *en* 'radiator.
radikal *adj* radical; *(pol)* liberal.
radio *en* radio, wireless; *høre ngt i ~en* hear· sth on the radio; *det blev udsendt i ~en* it was broadcast·; **~aktiv** *adj* radio'active; **~aktivitet** *en* radioac'tivity; **~antenne** *en* aerial; **~avis** *en* news; **~bil** *en (i tivoli etc)* bumper car, dodgem; **~fyr** *et* radio beacon; **~graf** *en* radi'ographer; **~licens** *en* radio licence fee; **~log** *en* radi'ologist; **~modtager** *en* radio set; **~program** *et* radio programme; **~sender** *en* radio trans'mitter; *(sendestation)* radio station; **~styret** *adj* radio-con,trolled; **~telegrafist** *en* wireless operator; *(på skib,* F) sparks; **~udsendelse** *en* radio programme.
radise *en* radish; *Radiserne (tegneserie)* Peanuts.
radius *en* radius *(pl:* radii); *i en ~ af 10 km* within a radius of 10 km.
radmager *adj* skinny.
raffinaderi *et* re'finery.
raffineret *adj (udspekuleret)* so'phisticated; *(spidsfindig)* subtle; *(smart)* smart; *(renset, fx om olie)* re'fined.
rafle *v* throw· dice *(om* for).
rage *v: ~ frem* pro'trude; *~ op* rise·; *(om bygning etc)* tower; *~ uklar med en* fall· out with sby; *~ i skufferne* rummage in the drawers; *~ ngt til sig* grab (,snatch) sth; *hvad ~r det dig?* mind your own business! *det ~r mig en fjer!* I could not care less! **~kniv** *en* razor.
ragelse *et* junk, rubbish.
ragout *en* stew.
raket *en* rocket; *(som våben)* missile; *affyre en ~* fire a rocket; *opsende en ~ til Mars* launch a rocket for Mars; **~base** *en* missile base; **~våben** *et* missile.
rakke *v: ~ ned på en* run· down sby, 'denigrate sby; *~ rundt* knock about.
rakle *en* catkin.
ralle *v* rattle.
ram *s: få ~ på en* get· at sby // *adj (om lugt etc)* acrid; *det er hans ~me alvor* he is in dead earnest.
ramaskrig *et: opløfte et ~* raise an outcry.
ramle *v (falde)* fall·; *~ sammen (dvs. falde sammen)* fall· (,tumble) down; *(støde sammen)* col'lide; *(slås)* fight·.
ramme *en* frame; *(omgivelser)* setting; *(grænser)* limits *pl; sætte et billede i ~* frame a picture; *inden for ~rne af...* within the limits of...; *sprænge ~rne for ngt* go· be'yond the scope of sth // *v (træffe)* hit·; *(berøre)* af'fect; *~ ind* frame; *bolden ramte overliggeren* the ball hit· the bar; *den bemærkning ramte* that remark went home; *blive ramt af sygdom* be taken ill; *føle sig ramt* feel· stung; *~ ved siden af* miss; *~ en pæl ned* ram in a stake.
rammende *adj (om bemærkning etc)* apt; *(om parodi)* lifelike, pre'cise.
rampe *en (skråning)* ramp; *(affyrings~)* launching pad; **~lys** *et (fig)* limelight.
• **ramponeret** *adj* battered, damaged.
rand *en (kant)* edge; *(bræmme)* border; *(på glas, kop etc)* rim; *(fig)* verge, brink; *fyldt til ~en* brimful; *sorte ~e under øjnene* dark rings under the eyes; *glasset lavede ~e på bordet* the glass left rings on the table; *på afgrundens ~* on the brink of the precipice; *være på gravens ~* have one foot in the grave; *være på sammenbruddets ~* be on the verge of a breakdown
rang *en* rank; *første ~s* first rate; *gøre en ~en stridig* challenge sby's po'sition.
rangerbanegård *en* marshalling yard.
rangere *v (jernb)* shunt; *(i rang)* rank; **rangering** *en* shunting.
rangle *en* rattle.
ranglet *adj* lanky.
rangstige *en* hierarchy.
rank *adj* e'rect.
ranke *en (bot)* vine // *v: ~ ryggen* straighten up.
ransage *v* search.

ransagning *en* search.
rap *et (slag)* rap; *de fik tre sønner i ~* they had three sons in rapid suc'cession // *adj (hurtig)* quick; *(næsvis)* pert; *(smart)* smart, racy; (S) zappy; **~kæftet** *adj: være ~kæftet* have a big mouth.
rappe *v (om and)* quack.
rappenskralde *en* shrew; *(om hustru)* nagging wife.
rapport *en* re'port; *aflægge ~ om ngt* make· a report on sth; **~ere** *v* re'port.
raps *en (bot)* rape.
raptus *en* crazy i'dea.
rar *adj* nice; *her er ~t at være* it is nice to be here; *det var ~t at høre* I am glad to hear it; *det ville være ~t med en drink (,et bad)* I could do with a drink (,a bath); *vær nu lidt ~!* do be good now!
rase *v* rage; *(være vanvittig)* rave; *få ~t ud* let· off steam.
rasende *adj* furious *(på* with); *(vanvittig)* mad; *blive ~ på en* get· furious (,mad) with sby; *i ~ fart* at a furious rate // *adv* furiously, madly.
rasere *v (hærge)* ravage, play havoc; *(barbere)* shave.
raseri *et* rage, fury; **~anfald** *et* fit of rage.
rask *adj (sund)* healthy, sound; *(hurtig)* quick, rapid; *(kæk)* brave; *blive ~* re'cover; *lad det nu gå lidt ~!* get a move on! *tage en ~ beslutning* make· a quick de'cision // *adv* quickly, rapidly; *~ væk* just like that.
rasle *v* rattle; *(om tallerkener etc)* clatter; *(om papir, blade, skørter)* rustle; *(om mønter, nøgler)* jingle; *~ med ngt* rattle (,clatter, rustle, jingle) sth; *pundet ~de ned* the pound slumped.
raslen *en* rattling, rattle; *(om tallerkener etc)* clatter(ing); *(om papir, blade etc)* rustling; *(om mønter, nøgler)* jingling, jingle.
rasp *en (tekn)* rasp; *(gastr)* breadcrumbs *pl; vende fisken i ~* bread the fish.
rast *et: holde ~* stop, take· a break.
raste *v* rest; **~plads** *en* lay-by; *(ved motorvej også)* picnic area.
rastløs *adj* restless; **~hed** *en* restlessness.
rat *et* (steering) wheel; *ved ~tet* at the wheel.
rate *en* in'stalment; *betale i ~r* pay· by in'stalments.
ratgear *et* column (gear) shift.
ration *en* ration.
rationalisere *v* 'rationalize.
rationalisering *en* rationali'zation.
rationel *adj* rational.
rationere *v* ration.
rationering *en* rationing.
ratlås *en* steering(-wheel) lock.
ratslør *et* play.
ratsøjle *en* steering column.
rav *et* amber; *lave ~ i den* stir things up.
rave *v (vakle)* stagger, reel.
ravn *en* raven.
razzia *en* raid; *foretage ~ på et værtshus* raid a pub.
reagensglas *et* test tube; **~barn** *et* test-tube baby.
reagere *v* re'act *(på* to).
reaktion *en* re'action *(mod, på* to).
reaktionær *adj* re'actionary.
reaktor *en* re'actor.
realisere *v (gennemføre)* carry out; *(sælge)* sell·; *~ sig selv* ful'fil oneself.
realisme *en* realism.
realistisk *adj* rea'listic.
realitet *en* re'ality; *i ~en* in reality; **~s·sans** *en: have ~s·sans* have a sense of reality.
realløn *en* real wages *pl.*
reb *et* rope; **~e** *v: ~e sejlene* reef the sails; **~stige** *en* rope ladder.
rebus *en* picture puzzle, riddle.
recept *en* pre'scription; *fås kun på ~* only on pre'scription; *skrive ~ på ngt* make· out a pre'scription for sth.
reception *en (i hotel etc)* re'ception desk; *(sammenkomst)* re'ception.
receptpligtig *adj* a'vailable only on pre'scription.
reck *en (gymn)* hori'zontal bar.

redaktion *en (det at redigere)* editing; *(kontoret)* edi'torial office; *(personalet)* edi'torial staff; **~el** *adj* edi'torial; **~s·chef** *en* chief sub-editor; **~s·sekretær** *en* sub-editor.

redaktør *en* editor.

redde *v* save, rescue; *(bjærge)* salvage; *~ ansigt* save face; *~ en fra ngt* save sby from sth; *~ sig en forkølelse* catch· a cold; *prøve at ~ stumperne (fig)* pick up the broken pieces; *~ sig ud af ngt* get· out of sth.

rede *en* nest; *gøre ~ for ngt* ex'plain sth; *(stå til regnskab)* ac'count for sth; *få ~ på ngt (dvs. ordne)* get· sth straight; *(dvs. erfare)* find· out sth; *det er ikke til at hitte ~ i* (F) I can't make head nor tail of it; *holde ~ på* keep· track of.

rede *v: ~ sit hår* comb one's hair; *~ op til en* make· up a bed for sby; *~ seng* make· the bed.

rede *adj (parat)* ready, pre'pared; *være ~ til at* be pre'pared to; *holde sig ~* be ready; *~ penge* ready money; *have svar på ~ hånd* not be at a loss for an answer.

redegørelse *en* re'port *(for* of); *(beretning)* ac'count *(for* of).

redekam *en* comb.

redekasse *en* nesting box.

redelig *adj* honest; *ærligt og ~t* honestly; **~hed** *en* honesty; *(rod)* mess; *sikken en ~hed!* what a mess!

reder *en* shipowner.

rederi *et* shipping company.

redigere *v* edit.

redning *en (frelse)* sal'vation; *(bjærgning)* rescue; *(udvej)* re'sort; *(om målmand)* save; **~s·arbejde** *et* rescue work; **~s·bælte** *et* lifebelt; **~s·båd** *en* lifeboat; **~s·flåde** *en* life-raft; **~s·korps** *et* rescue service; **~s·mand** *en* rescuer; **~s·vest** *en* life jacket.

redskab *et* tool; *(instrument)* 'instrument; *(køkken~)* u'tensil; **~s·skur** *et* tool shed; **~s·øvelser** *pl (gymn)* appa'ratus gym'nastics.

reducere *v* re'duce *(med* by); *holdet ~de til 2-1 (fodb)* the team brought down the score to 2-1.

reduktion *en* re'duction.

reel *adj (virkelig)* real; *(god)* genuine; *(om person)* re'liable; **~t** *adv* really; *(ærligt)* honestly.

referat *et* re'port *(af* on).

reference *en* 'reference.

referere *v* re'port; *(genfortælle)* re'peat; *~ til* re'fer to.

refleks *en (genskin)* re'flection; *(som kaster refleks)* re'flector; *(med, fx i benet)* 'reflex; **~bånd** *et* luminous strip.

reflektere *v* re'flect; *~ på en annonce* re'ply to an ad'vertisement.

reform *en* re'form.

reformation *en* refor'mation.

reformere *v* re'form.

reformvenlig *adj* re'formist.

refræn *et* re'frain, chorus.

refundere *v* reim'burse.

refusion *en* reim'bursement.

regel *en* rule; *(forskrift)* regu'lation; *følge reglerne* stick· to the rules; *efter alle kunstens regler* thoroughly; *en undtagelse fra reglen* an ex'ception to the rule; *i reglen, som ~* as a rule; **~mæssig** *adj* regular.

regent *en* ruler, sovereign; **~par** *et* royal couple.

regere *v (styre)* rule, govern; *(som konge, dronning)* reign; *(støje, herse)* carry on; *~ med en* boss sby around; **~nde** *adj: ~nde dronning* reigning queen.

regering *en* government; *danne ~* take· office; *sidde i ~en* be a member of the government; **~s·avis** *en* government paper; **~s·chef** *en* head of government; **~s·forslag** *et* government bill; **~s·krise** *en* government crisis; **~s·magt** *en: overtage ~s·magten* come· into office; **~s·parti** *et* governing party; **~s·tid** *en (om monark)* reign; *(om valgt regering)* term of office.

regi *en (iscenesættelse)* pro'duction; *i FN's ~* under the auspices of the UN.

regime *et* re'gime.

regiment *et* 'regiment; **~s·chef** *en* com'manding officer.

region *en* region.

regional *adj* regional; **~radio** *en* regional radio (station); **~tog** *et* local train.

regissør *en* stage manager.

register *et (indholdsfortegnelse)* table of contents; *(alfabetisk)* index; *(orgel~)* stop.

registrere *v* 'register; *(lægge mærke til)* note.

registrering *en* regi'stration *(også om bil)*; **~s·nummer** *et* licence number.

reglement *et* regu'lations *pl.*

reglementeret *adj* pre'scribed.

regn *en* rain; *det ser ud til ~* it looks like rain; **~bue** *en* rainbow; **~bue-hinde** *en (i øjet)* iris; **~byge** *en* shower; **~dråbe** *en* raindrop.

regne *v (om regn)* rain; *(med tal)* calculate; *(tælle)* count; *(anse)* con'sider; *det ~r stærkt* it is raining hard; *~ regnestykker* do· sums; *højt ~t* at the outside; *rundt ~t* a'round; *han ~s for en god dirigent* he is con'sidered a good con'ductor; *~ med at* ex'pect that, take· it for granted that; *~ med en* count on sby; *~ ngt med* in'clude sth; *~ sammen* add up; *~ ngt ud* work sth out; *(udtænke)* figure out sth; **~ark** *et (edb)* spreadsheet; **~fejl** *en* miscalculation; **~maskine** *en* calculator; **~opgave** *en* sum; **~stok** *en* slide rule; **~stykke** *et* sum; *~stykket går ikke op* it won't work out.

regnfrakke *en* mac(kintosh), waterproof.

regning *en (fag)* a'rithemetic; *(beregning)* calcu'lation; *(nota)* bill, invoice; *må jeg bede om ~en?* can I have the bill please? *for egen ~* on one's own ac'count; *det er på min ~* it is on me; *en stor ~* a heavy bill.

regnmåler *en* rain gauge [geidʒ].

regnorm *en* earthworm.

regnskab *et* ac'count(s); *føre ~* keep· an account; *gøre ~ for ngt* ac'count for sth; *gøre ~et op* settle the account; *kræve en til ~* call sby to account; *stå til ~ for* answer for; **~s·chef** *en* chief ac'countant; **~s·år** *et* fiscal year.

regn... *sms:* **~skov** *en* rain forest; **~skyl** *et* downpour; **~slag** *et* waterproof cape; **~tid** *en* rainy season; **~tæt** *adj* showerproof; **~tøj** *et* rainwear; **~vand** *et* rainwater; **~vejr** *et* rain, rainy weather; *det bliver ~vejr* it is going to rain.

regulerbar *adj* ad'justable.

regulere *v* 'regulate; *(indstille)* ad'just; **regulering** *en* regu'lation; ad'justment.

regulær *adj* regular; *(rigtig)* proper.

rehabilitere *v* reha'bilitate; **rehabilitering** *en* rehabili'tation.

reje *en v (fjord~)* shrimp; *(større, fx nordsø~)* prawn; *pille ~r* shell shrimps; *ikke en rød ~* not a penny; *tage ud og fiske ~r* go· shrimping; **~mad** *en* open sandwich with shrimps.

rejse *en (mindre)* trip; *(større)* journey; *(til søs)* voyage; *god ~!* pleasant journey! *være på ~* be travelling, be on a trip // *v (tage af sted)* leave·, set· out; *(rejse fra et sted til et andet)* go·; *(være på ~)* travel; *~ til England* go· to England; *de rejste i går* they left yesterday; *vi ~r til London i morgen* we are leaving for London tomorrow; *~ med tog* go· by train; *~ med fly* go· by air; *~ væk* go· away.

rejse *v (om bygning etc)* put· up, e'rect; *(et spørgsmål, penge etc)* raise; *~ ngt op* stand· sth upright; *~ sag mod en* sue sby; *~ sig* get· up, stand· up; *(bygges, rage op, gøre oprør, blæse)* rise·; *~ sig fra bordet* leave· the table; *der rejste sig en storm af protester* a storm of ob'jections arose.

rejse... *sms:* **~arrangør** *en* tour operator; **~bureau** *et* travel agency; **~check** *en* traveller's cheque; **~fører** *en* guide; **~gilde** *et* topping-out ceremony; **~gods** *et* luggage; **~holdet** *s (politiets) sv.t.* the Flying Squad; **~leder** *en* 'courier; **~mål** *et* desti'nation; **~nde** *en* traveller, passenger; **~selskab** *et (på charterrejse)* party; **~skrivemaskine** *en* portable typewriter.

rejsning *en (det at rejse ngt op)* raising; *(holdning)* carriage; *(erektion)* e'rection.

reklamation *en (klage)* com'plaint.

reklame *en (som begreb)* pu'blicity; *(annonce etc)* ad'vertisement; *(det at gøre ~)* 'advertising; *(i tv)* com'mercial; *gøre ~ for ngt* 'advertise sth, (F) boost sth; **~afdeling** *en* pu'blicity de'partment; **~bureau** *et* advertising agency; **~film** *en* com'mercial; **~indslag** *et* com'mercial break.

reklamere *v (gøre reklame)* advertise; *(klage)* com'plain *(over* about).

reklameskilt *et* advertising sign.

reklametegner *en* com'mercial artist.

reklametrick *et* sales trick.

rekognoscere *v* recon'noitre; **rekognoscering** *en* re'connaissance.

rekonstruere *v* recon'struct; **rekonstruktion** *en* recon'struction.

rekonvalescens *en* conva'lescence; **rekonvalescent** *en* conva'lescent.

rekord *en* 'record; *han har ~en i tennis på græs* he holds· the record for lawn tennis; *slå en ~* break· a record; *sætte en ~* set· up a record; *det slår alle ~er* that beats everything; **~indehaver** *en* record-holder; **~tid** *en: på ~tid* in record time.

rekreation *en* conva'lescence; **~s·hjem** *et* conva'lescent home.

rekreere *v: ~ sig* re'cuperate.

rekrut *en* re'cruit; **~tere** *v* re'cruit; **~tering** *en* re'cruitment.

rektangel *et* rectangle.

rektangulær *adj* rect'angular.

rektor *en (ved skole) (mandlig)* headmaster; *(kvindelig)* headmistress; *(ved universitet)* vice-chancellor.

rekvirere *v* order, requi'sition.

rekvisit *en* 'requisite; *~ter* e'quipment; *(teat)* props.

rekvisition *en* requi'sition.

relation *en* re'lation.

relativ *adj* relative.

relevant *adj* relevant.

relief *et* re'lief.

religion *en* re'ligion; *(tro)* faith; *(som skolefag)* re'ligious in'struction; **~s·frihed** *en* re'ligious freedom.

religiøs *adj* re'ligious.

relikvie *et* relic.

relæ *et (elek)* re'lay.

rem *en* strap; *(liv~)* belt.

remedier *pl* tools, e'quipment.

remoulade *en* remoulade.

remse *en* string of words; *(børne~)* jingle // *v: ~ ngt op* reel off sth.

ren *en (rensdyr)* reindeer.

ren *adj (mods: snavset)* clean; *(ublandet)* pure; *(~ og skær)* sheer; *(kun)* mere; *gøre ~t* clean up (the house); *gøre ngt ~t* clean sth; *synge ~t* sing· in tune; *det var et ~t tilfælde* it was pure accident; *det ~e vanvid* sheer madness; *han er et ~t barn* he is a mere child; *~t ud sagt* quite frankly; *jeg sagde det til ham ~ ud* I told him plainly; *vi har ~t glemt det* we have clean forgotten.

rend *et* run(ning); *der var et værre ~* there was a coming and going all the time; *stikke i ~* start running.

rende *en (rille)* groove; *(grøft)* ditch; *(sejl~)* channel // *v* run·; *(være utæt)* leak; *~ fra sit ansvar* shirk one's responsi'bility; *~ sin vej* run· away; *rend og hop!* get· stuffed! **~sten** *en* gutter.

rendyrket *adj* thorough.

rengøring *en* cleaning; **~s·assistent** *en* cleaner; **~s·dille** *en* housework mania; **~s·kone** *en* char(woman) *(pl:* -women); **~s·selskab** *et* cleaning service.

renhed *en* cleanliness; *(ublandethed, ægthed)* purity.

renlig *adj* cleanly; **~hed** *en* cleanliness.

renommé *et* repu'tation.

renovation *en* garbage col'lection; **~s·vogn** *en* dust cart.

rense *v* clean; *(grundigt)* cleanse [klɛns]; *(fx luft)* purify; *(for mistanke etc)* clear; *(skylle)* rinse; **~creme** *en* cleansing cream; **~middel** *et* cleansing agent.

renseri *et* (dry-)cleaners.

renseserviet *en* cleansing tissue.

renskrive *v: ~ ngt* write· out a fair copy of sth.

rensning *en* cleaning; **~s·anlæg** *et* purifi'cation plant.

rent *adv se ren.*
rentabel *adj* profitable.
rente *en* interest *(af* on); *give ~r* bear· interest; *tage 12% i ~ af ngt* charge (a) 12 per cent interest on sth; **~fod** *en* rate of interest; **~fri** *adj* free of interest; **~sats** *en* rate of interest.
renvasket *adj* clean.
renæssance *en* re'naissance.
reol *en* bookcase, book shelves *pl.*
reorganisere *v* re'organize.
reparation *en* re'pair(s *pl); (mindre, fx af tøj)* mending; **~s·værksted** *et* re'pair shop; *(auto også)* garage.
reparere *v* re'pair; *(tøj etc)* mend.
repertoire *et* 'repertory.
repetere *v (gentage)* re'peat; *(læse igen)* re-read·.
repetition *en* repe'tition.
replik *en (svar)* re'ply; *(teat etc)* line(s).
reportage *en (tv etc)* re'port.
repos *en (på trappe)* landing.
reprimande *en* 'reprimand.
reprise *en* re'peat.
reproducere *v* repro'duce.
reproduktion *en* repro'duction.
repræsentant *en* repre'sentative; *(for firma også)* agent; **~skab** *et* board.
repræsentation *en (selskabelighed)* enter'tainment.
repræsentere *v* repre'sent; *(være)* be.
republik *en* re'public.
republikansk *adj* re'publican.
reservat *et (fx for indianere)* reser'vation.
reservation *en* reser'vation; *(tilbageholdenhed)* re'serve.
reserve *en* re'serve; *have ngt i ~* have sth in reserve; **~del** *en* spare part; **~hjul** *et* spare wheel; **~lager** *et* e'mergency stock; **~læge** *en* registrar; **~officer** *en* re'serve officer.
reservere *v* re'serve; *(bestille forud)* book; **~t** *adj* re'served.
reservetank *en* re'serve tank.
reservoir *et* 'reservoir.
residens *en* 'residence; *forlægge ~en til* ad'journ to.
residere *v* re'side.
resignere *v (opgive)* give· up; *(affinde sig)* re'sign oneself; **~t** *adj* re'signed.
resolut *adj* de'termined.
resonans *en* 'resonance; *give ~* re'sound.
respekt *en* re'spect, re'gard; *have ~ for en* re'spect sby; *sætte sig i ~* make· oneself re'spected.
respektabel *adj* re'spectable.
respektere *v* re'spect.
respektindgydende *adj* awe-inspiring.
respektiv *adj* re'spective.
respektive *adv* re'spectively.
respektløs *adj* disre'spectful.
respirator *en* 'respirator.
ressourcer *pl* re'sources.
rest *en* re'mainder; *(som er levnet)* remnant; *~en* the rest; *~er* re'mains, leavings; *(madrester)* leftovers; *den sidste ~ af ngt* the last bit of sth; *de sørgelige ~er* the sad remnants; *for ~en (dvs. apropos)* by the way, inci'dentally; *(dvs. for den sags skyld)* for that matter; *(dvs. desuden)* be'sides; *blive til ~* be left (over).
restance *en: være i ~ med ngt* be in ar'rears with sth.
restaurant *en* 'restaurant.
restauratør *en* 'restaurant pro'prietor.
restaurere *v* re'store; **restaurering** *en* resto'ration.
restere *v* re'main; *det ~nde* the re'mainder.
restgæld *en* re'maining debt.
restlager *et* re'maining stock.
restskat *en* under'payment of tax.
resultat *et* re'sult; *(bedrift, ngt som opnås)* a'chievement; *(virkning)* ef'fect; *give ~* have an effect; *(dvs. være vellykket)* come· off, be a success.
resultere *v* re'sult *(i* in).
resumé *et* summary.
ret *en (mad)* dish; *(mods: uret, rettighed)* right; *(domstol)* (law)court; *dagens ~* to'day's special; *vi fik tre ~ter mad* we had three courses; *få ~* prove right; *give en ~* a'gree with sby; *det har du ~ i* you are right (there); *have ~ til ngt* have a right to sth; *med ~te* rightly; *gå ~tens*

vej go· to court; *finde sig til ~te (dvs. vænne sig til ngt, slå sig til ro)* settle down; *sætte sig til ~te* settle oneself; *tale en til ~te* reason with sby.

ret *adj (lige)* straight; *(rigtig)* right; *strikke ~* knit plain; *komme i ~te tid til ngt* be in time for sth; *i en ~ vinkel* at right angles // *adv (lige)* straight; *(rigtig)* rightly; *(temmelig)* rather; *det blev ~ sent* it was rather late; *jeg har det ikke ~ godt* I don't feel very well; *kender jeg ham ~, så har han glemt det* if I know him, he has for'gotten; *stå ~* stand· at at'tention.

retarderet *adj* re'tarded, backward.

retfærdig *adj* just.

retfærdiggøre *v* justify.

retfærdighed *en* justice; *lade ~en ske fyldest* let· justice be done.

retmaske *en* plain stitch.

retmæssig *adj* lawful, rightful.

retning *en* di'rection; *(henseende)* re'spect; *(tendens)* 'tendency; *i alle ~er (dvs. henseender)* in all re'spects; *køre i ~ af York* drive· to'wards York; *ngt i ~ af* something like; *eller ngt i den ~* or something like that; **~s·linjer** *pl* guidelines.

retræte *en* re'treat.

retsforfølge *v* sue.

retsgyldig *adj* valid.

retshjælp *en* legal aid.

retskaffen *adj* honest, upright.

retskrivning *en* spelling; **~s·ordbog** *en* spelling dictionary.

retslig *adj* legal; *~ undersøgelse* ju'dicial in'quiry.

retsmedicin *en* fo'rensic medicine; **~er** *en* fo'rensic doctor.

retspleje *en* admini'stration of justice.

retssag *en* case; *(kriminal~)* trial; *(civil)* law suit.

retsvidenskab *en* juris'prudence.

retsvæsen *et* ju'dicial system.

rette *v (korrigere)* cor'rect; *(stile)* di'rect; *(henvende)* ad'dress; *(gøre lige)* straighten (out); *~ stile* mark essays; *~ sig* straighten up; *(få det bedre)* get· better; *~ sig efter en* com'ply with sby; *(adlyde)* o'bey sby; *~ på slipset* ad'just one's tie; *~ ngt til* ad'just sth; **~blæk** *et* cor'rection fluid.

rettelse *en (af fejl)* cor'rection; *(tilretning)* ad'justment.

rettere *adv: eller ~ (sagt)...* or rather...

rettesnor *en (fig)* guiding principle.

rettidigt *adv* on time; *(tids nok)* in time.

rettighed *en* right.

retur *en* re'turn; *være på ~ (dvs. i aftagende)* be de'clining // *adv* back; *lade ngt gå ~* re'turn sth; *tage ngt ~* take· sth back; **~billet** *en* return ticket; **~flaske** *en* re'turnable bottle.

returnere *v* re'turn.

rev *et* reef.

revalidering *en* rehabili'tation; *(omskoling)* re-edu'cation.

revanche *en* re'venge; *få (,tage) ~* have (take·) one's re'venge.

revet *adj (på rivejern)* grated.

revers *et (på jakke etc)* la'pel.

revidere *v* re'vise.

revision *en* re'vision; *(af regnskaber)* audit.

revisor *en* auditor; *statsautoriseret ~ sv.t.* chartered ac'countant.

revle *en* sandbank.

revne *en (i væg etc)* crack; *(i klippe)* crevice; *(i huden)* chap; *(i tøj)* tear; *slå ~r* crack; *(fig)* crack up // *v* crack; *(sprænges)* burst, be bursting; *være ved at ~* be ready to burst.

revnende *adv: jeg er ~ ligeglad* (F) I don't give a damn.

revolution *en* revo'lution.

revolutionere *v* revo'lutionize; **~nde** *adj* revo'lutionary.

revolutionær *adj* revo'lutionary.

revolver *en* re'volver.

revy *en (teat)* re'vue, show; *(tidsskrift)* re'view; *(mil)* re'view; *passere ~ (fig)* pass in re'view.

Rhinen *s* the Rhine.

rhinskvin *en* hock.

ri *v* baste, tack.

ribbe *en (i blad etc)* rib; *(gymn)* wall bar // *v (udplyndre)* rob, strip; *(om fx bønner)* string.

ribben *et* rib; **~s·steg** *en* rib roast; **~s·stykke** *et* spare rib.
ribbort *en* ribbing.
ribs *et* red currant.
ribstrikket *adj* ribbed.
ribstrikning *en* rib stitch.
ridder *en* knight; *udnævne en til ~* make· sby a knight.
ride *v* ride·; *~ en tur* go· for a ride; *~ stormen af (fig)* weather the storm; **~bane** *en* (riding) a'rena; **~bane-springning** *en* show jumping; **~bukser** *pl* riding breeches; **~hest** *en* saddle-horse, mount.
ridende *adj* on horseback; *~ politi* mounted police.
ride... *sms:* **~pisk** *en* riding crop; **~skole** *en* riding school; **~sport** *en* (horse-)riding; **~sti** *en* bridle-path; **~stævne** *et* horse show; **~støvle** *en* riding-boot.
ridning *en* riding; *gå til ~* take· riding lessons.
ridse *en* scratch // *v* scratch; *~ ngt op* sketch sth; *~ en steg* score a roast.
ridt *et* ride.
riffel *en* rifle.
rift *en* scratch; *(flænge)* cut, tear [tɛə:]; *der er rift om det* there is a great de'mand for it.
rig *adj* rich; *(velhavende også)* wealthy; *blive ~* grow· rich; *have ~ lejlighed til at* have ample oppor'tu-nity to; *~ på* rich in.
rigdom *en* riches *pl; (velstand)* wealth; *(formue)* fortune; *(rigelighed)* a'bundance *(på* of).
rige *et* realm; *(konge~)* kingdom.
rigelig *adj (stor)* ample; *(mere end nok)* plenty of; *(lidt for stor)* on the big side; *i ~e mængder* a'bundantly // *adv* amply; *have ~ tid* have plenty of time.
righoldig *adj* rich.
rigmand *en* rich man *(pl:* men).
rigning *en (mar)* rigging.
rigs... *sms:* **~advokat** *en* head of pub-lic prose'cution; **~arkiv** *et* public record office; **~dag** *en* parliament; **~dansk** *et (om sproget)* standard Danish; **~våben** *et* national arms.
rigtig *adj* right; *(sand)* true; *(passende)* proper; *(virkelig)* real // *adv* right; properly; *(i høj grad)* very; *(helt)* quite; *det er ~t* that's right; *det er ~ koldt* it's really cold; *ganske ~* quite right; *de kom ganske ~* they came· right e'nough; *en ~ dame* a real lady; *det er ngt af det ~e* that is something like it; *han er ikke ~ klog* he is out of his mind.
rigtignok *adv* certainly; *han er ~ ikke ked af det!* he has got a nerve!
rille *en* groove; *(i jorden)* furrow.
rim *et (i vers)* rhyme; *(~frost)* hoar-frost, rime.
rime *v* rhyme; *(passe sammen)* a'gree; *der er ngt der ikke ~er* it does not make sense.
rimelig *adj* reasonable // *adv* fairly *(fx god* good), reasonably *(fx til-freds* satisfied); **~hed** *en* reasonable-ness; *inden for ~hedens grænser* with'in reason; **~vis** *adv* probably.
rimfrost *en* hoarfrost.
rimtåge *en* frosty mist.
rindende *adj: ~ vand* running water.
ring *en* ring; *(kreds også)* circle; *(bil~)* tyre; *gå med ~* wear· a ring; *køre i ~* drive· in a circle; **~bind** *et* ring binder.
ringe *v (om klokke)* ring·; *(telefonere)* phone, call; *~ med en klokke* ring· a bell; *~ en op, ~ til en* phone (,call) sby; *~ på* ring· (the bell) // *adj (lille)* small; *(dårlig)* poor; *(beske-den)* humble; *i ~ grad* little; *en ~ ulejlighed* a small trouble; *efter min ~ mening* in my humble o'pinion; *ingen ~re end* no less than; *ikke det ~ste* not the least.
ringeklokke *en* bell-push.
ringetone *en (tlf)* ringing tone.
ringfinger *en* ring finger.
ringforlovet *adj* formally en'gaged.
ringmærke *v* ring.
ringning *en* ringing.
ringridning *en* riding at the ring.
ringvej *en* ring road, orbital road.
rippe *v: ~ op i ngt* stir up sth.
ris *en* rice *(pl: ~); ~ i kogepose* boil-in-the-bag rice // *et (kviste)* twigs *pl; (til afstraffelse)* rod.
risengrød *en* rice pudding.

risikabel *adj* risky.
risikere *v* risk; ~ *at miste sit arbejde* risk losing one's job.
risiko *en* risk; *der er ~ for at...* there is a risk that...; *løbe en ~* run· a risk; *på egen ~* at one's own risk (,peril).
risle *v* trickle; *(om lyden)* murmur; *det ~de mig koldt ned ad ryggen* it sent a chill down my spine.
rislen *en* trickle; *(om lyden)* murmur.
rismark *en* paddy field.
rismel *et* rice flour.
rispapir *et* rice paper.
rist *en* grating; *(stege~)* grill.
riste *v (på pande, i ovn)* roast; *(på grill)* grill; *(om brød)* toast; *~t brød* toast.
ritråd *en* tacking thread.
ritual *et* ritual; **rituel** *adj* ritual.
rival *en* rival.
rivalisere *v* rival, com'pete.
rive *en* rake // *v (kradse)* scratch; *(flænge)* tear·; *(med rive)* rake; *(på rivejern)* grate; *(~ til sig)* snatch; *~ sig* get· scratched; *~ hul i bukserne* tear· one's trousers; *~ vittigheder af sig* crack jokes; *~ løg* grate onions; *~ ngt løs* tear· sth off; *~ sig løs fra ngt* break· loose from sth; *~ et hus ned* knock down a house; *~ en side ud af bogen* tear· a page out of the book; **~gilde** *et* (F) rough-house; **~jern** *et* grater.
rivende *adj (hurtig)* rapid; *(om flod etc)* tearing; *i ~ fart* at a tearing speed; *den er ~ gal* it is all wrong; *en ~ udvikling* a rapid de'velopment.
ro *en (fred)* peace; *(hvile)* rest; *(stilhed)* quiet; *(sindsro)* calm; *fred og ~* peace and quiet; *få ~ til sit arbejde* be al'lowed to work in peace; *holde sig i ~* keep· quiet; *(uden at arbejde)* take· a break; *i ~ og mag* at one's ease; *gå til ~* re'tire; *tag den med ~!* take· it easy! *falde til ~* calm down.
ro *v* row; *tage ud at ~* go· rowing.
robot *en* 'robot.
robust *en* ro'bust.
robåd *en* rowing boat.
rod *en (om plante)* root; *(bølle)* thug; *(uorden)* dis'order, mess; *slå ~* take· root; *værelset var ét ~* the room was a com'plete mess; **~behandling** *en* root treatment.
rode *v (lave uorden)* make· a mess; *(søge)* rummage; *(i jorden)* root; *~ sig ind i ngt* get· in'volved in sth; *~ med ngt* mess around with sth; *~ tingene sammen* mix things up; **~butik** *en* mess; **~hoved** *et* un'tidy person, clutterer; **~kontor** *et* tax col'lector's office.
rodet *adj* un'tidy.
rodfrugter *pl* root crops.
rodløs *adj* rootless.
roe *en* beet.
roer *en* oarsman *(pl:* -men).
roesukker *et* beat sugar.
rogn *en* roe.
rokere *v: ~ om på ngt* change sth around, rear'range sth.
rokke *v* rock; *(ryste, svække)* shake·; *(flytte)* move.
rolig *adj* quiet, calm; *(jævn, uden vaklen)* steady // *adv* quietly, calmly; steadily; *sidde (,stå etc) ~t* sit· (,stand· etc) still; *en ~ bydel* a quiet part of town; *~e vindforhold* calm weather; *han var helt ~* he was quite calm; *tag det ~t!* take· it easy! *du kan ~t tage familien med* it's no problem if you want to bring your family.
rolle *en* part, role; *det spiller ingen ~* it does not matter; *det spiller en stor ~* it is very im'portant; **~liste** *en* cast.
Rom Rome.
rom *en (drik)* rum.
roman *en* novel; **~forfatter** *en* novelist.
romansk *adj (om kunst etc)* roma'nesque; *~ stil (brit)* Norman style.
romantik *en (stilart)* Ro'manticism; *(kærlighed)* ro'mance.
romer *en* Roman; **~riget** *s* the Roman Empire.
romersk *adj* Roman; **~-katolsk** *adj* Roman 'Catholic.
romertal *et* Roman numeral.
Romtraktaten *s* the Treaty of Rome.

roning *en* rowing.
ror *et* rudder; *(rat)* wheel; *stå til ~s* be at the helm; **~pind** *en* tiller.
ros *en* praise; *det tjener til din ~* it does you credit.
rose *en (bot)* rose // *v* praise; *~ sig af ngt* boast of sth.
rosen... *sms:* **~knop** *en* rosebud; **~krans** *en (rel)* rosary; **~kål** *pl* Brussel(s) sprouts; **~rød** *adj* rosy; **~træ** *et (om materialet)* rosewood.
rosin *en* raisin; *som ~en i pølseenden* as a re'ward.
roskildesyge *en* gastroente'ritis.
rosmarin *en (bot)* rosemary.
rosport *en* rowing.
rotation *en* ro'tation.
rotere *v* ro'tate; **~nde** *adj* re'volving.
rotte *en* rat; *han er en gammel ~* he knows· all the tricks // *v: ~ sig sammen* gang up *(mod* against); **~fælde** *en* rat trap; **~gift** *en* rat-poison; **~haler** *pl (om frisure)* pig-tails; **~ræs** *et* ratrace.
rotur *en: tage på ~* go· rowing.
rouge *en* rouge.
roulade *en (om kage)* Swiss roll.
roulet *en* rou'lette.
rov *et (plyndring)* pillage; *(bytte)* spoils; *gå på ~ (om dyr)* go· in search of prey; **~drift** *en* exploi'ta-tion; *drive ~drift på ngt* ex'ploit sth; **~dyr** *et* beast of prey; **~fisk** *en* 'predator; **~fugl** *en* bird of prey; **~mord** *et* robbery with murder.
ru *adj (ujævn)* rough; *(hæs)* hoarse.
rubin *en* ruby.
rubrik *en (i spørgeskema etc)* space; *(i avis etc)* section; *(længere)* article; **~annonce** *en* small ad.
rude *en* (window) pane; **~kuvert** *en* window envelope.
ruder *en (i kort)* diamonds *pl; ~ konge* king of diamonds.
rudevasker *en (auto)* windscreen washers *pl.*
rug *en* rye; **~brød** *et* brown rye bread.
ruge *v (også om person)* brood; *(ruge ud)* hatch; **~høne** *en* sitting hen; **~maskine** *en* incubator; **~mor** *en* surrogate mother.
rugmel *et* rye flour.
rugning *en* brooding; *(i maskine)* incu'bation.
ruin *en* ruin; *ligge i ~er* be in ruins; *det blev hans ~* it ruined him.
ruinere *v* ruin.
rulle *en* roll; *(valse)* roller; *(til at rulle ngt om)* reel; *(til håret)* curler; *(film~)* reel; *(til tøj)* mangle; *(kage~)* rolling-pin // *v* roll; *~ med øjnene* roll one's eyes; *~ gardinet ned* draw· the blind; *~ gardinet op* pull up the blind; *~ rundt* roll (over); *~ sig sammen* curl up; *~ dej ud* roll out pastry (,dough); *~ sig ud (udfolde sig)* prove one's worth; *(slå sig løs)* let· one's hair down; *(blive vred)* let· oneself go.
rulle... *sms:* **~bord** *et* tea trolley; **~gardin** *et* roller blind; **~håndklæde** *et* roller-towel; **~krave** *en* polo-neck; **~pølse** *en* sausage made of rolled and pressed meat; **~sele** *en (auto)* (i'nertia reel) seatbelt; **~skøjte** *en* roller skate; **~sten** *en (lille)* pebble; *(stor)* cobble; **~stol** *en* wheelchair; **~trappe** *en* escalator.
rum *et (værelse)* room; *(verdensrum)* space; *(i skab, taske etc)* com'part-ment // *adj: i ~ sø* in the open sea; *en ~ tid* quite some time; **~dragt** *en* spacesuit.
rumfang *et* volume.
rumfart *en* spacetravel.
rumforskning *en* space re'search.
rumfærge *en* space shuttle.
rumle *v* rumble.
rumme *v* con'tain; *(indebære)* im'ply.
rummelig *adj* spacious, roomy.
rumpe *en* be'hind, bottom.
rumpilot *en* astronaut.
rumraket *en* space rocket.
rumrejse *en* space flight.
rumskib *et* spaceship.
rumsonde *en* space probe.
rumstere *v* rummage.
rumæner *en* Ro'manian; **Rumænien** *s* Ro'mania; **rumænsk** *adj* Ro'manian.
rund *adj* round; *med ~ hånd* gene-rously.
rundbordssamtale *en* round-table conference.

runddel *en (rund plads)* circus.
runde *en* round; *(tur)* stroll // *v (gøre ~)* round; *(sejle rundt om)* double; *(være rund)* curve; ~ *af* round off.
rundfart *en* tour *(i* of).
rundhåndet *adj* generous; **-hed** *en* gene'rosity.
runding *en (det at gøre rund)* rounding; *(krumning)* bending.
rundkirke *en* round church.
rundkreds *en* circle.
rundkørsel *en* roundabout.
rundpind *en* circular needle.
rundrejse *en* tour *(i* of).
rundrygget *adj* stooping.
rundsav *en* circular saw.
rundskrivelse *en* circular.
rundspørge *et* o'pinion poll.
rundstrikning *en* circular knitting.
rundstykke *et* roll.
rundt *adv* round, about, around // *præp* round; *hele året* ~ all the year round; ~ *regnet* about; *gå* ~ *i huset* walk around (in) the house; *finde* ~ *i London* find· one's way around London; *være helt* ~ *på gulvet* be in a muddle.
rundtosset *adj* giddy.
rundtur *en* tour *(i* of).
rundvisning *en* con'ducted tour *(i* of).
rune *en* runic character, rune; **-indskrift** *en* runic in'scription; **-sten** *en* rune-stone.
runge *v* re'sound; **-nde** *adj* ringing, re'sounding.
rus *en (beruselse)* intoxi'cation; *(fig)* ecstasy; *sove ~en ud* sleep· it off.
ruse *en* fish trap.
rusgift *en* drug.
ruske *v* shake·; *(trække)* pull; ~ *en i armen* shake· sby by the arm; ~ *en i håret* pull sby's hair.
ruskind *et* suede.
Rusland *s* Russia.
russer *en,* **russisk** *adj* Russian.
rust *en* rust; *(på biler etc)* cor'rosion; **-beskyttelse** *en* anti-rust treatment; **-beskytter** *en* rust-proofer.
ruste *v (blive rusten)* rust; cor'rode; *(opruste)* arm (oneself); *(forberede sig)* pre'pare (oneself); **-n** *adj* rusty; *en ~n stemme* a hoarse voice.
rustfri *adj* stainless.
rustning *en (harnisk)* armour; *(oprustning)* armament; **-s·kapløb** *et* arms race.
rustrød *adj* russet; *(om hår)* auburn.
rustvogn *en* hearse.
rute *en* route; *(forbindelse, fx bus~)* service, run; **-bil** *en* coach; **-fart** *en* regular service; **-fly** *et* airliner.
rutine *en* rou'tine; *få ~ i ngt* get· ex'perienced in sth; **-arbejde** *et* rou'tine work; **-mæssig** *adj* rou'tine.
rutineret *adj* ex'perienced.
rutsche *v* slide·; **-bane** *en* switchback; *(på legeplads)* slide.
ry *et* repu'tation; *have ~ for at være ngt* have a repu'tation for being sth.
rydde *v* clear; ~ *en (,ngt) af vejen* get· rid of sby (,sth); ~ *op* tidy (up); ~ *op i stuen* tidy up the room; **-lig** *adj* tidy.
rydning *en* clearing.
ryg *en* back; *(bjerg~)* ridge; *vende ~gen til en* turn one's back on sby; *det løb mig koldt ned ad ~gen* it sent a shiver down my spine; *have ondt i ~gen* have a backache; *skyde* ~ arch one's back; **-dækning** *en* backing.
ryge *v* smoke; *(fare, styrte)* rush; *(falde)* fall·; *må man ~ her?* is smoking al'lowed here? *han ~r pibe, hun ~r cigaretter* he smokes a pipe, she smokes cigarettes; *der røg den fridag!* bang goes that holiday! *hun røg ned ad trapperne* she fell down the stairs; *sikringerne er røget* the fuses have blown; **-kupé** *en* smoker; **-pause** *en* smoking break.
ryger *en* smoker; *ikke-ryger* non-smoker.
ryghvirvel *en* vertebra *(pl:* vertebrae).
ryghynde *en* bolster.
ryglæn *et* back(-rest).
rygning *en* smoking; ~ *forbudt* no smoking.
rygrad *en* spine.
rygsmerter *pl* backache.
rygstød *et* back(-rest).
rygsvømning *en* backstroke.
rygsæk *en* rucksack.

rygte *et* rumour; *(ry, omdømme)* repu'tation; *der går ~r om at...* rumour has it that...; *det er bare løse ~r* it is just vague rumours.

rygtes *v* be rumoured; *(blive kendt)* get· about.

ryk *et (træk)* pull; *(hurtigt)* jerk; *(spjæt)* start; *det gav et ~ i ham* he started.

rykke *v (trække)* pull; *(flytte)* move; *~ for svar* press for an answer; *~ frem mod* ad'vance on; *~ ned i 2. division* be relegated to the second di'vision; *~ nærmere* ap'proach; *~ op i 1. division* move up to the first di'vision; *~ planter op* pull up plants; *~ ud (fx om politi)* turn out; *~ ud med ngt* come· out with sth.

rykker(skrivelse) *en* re'minder.

rynke *en (i hud etc)* wrinkle; *(i stof)* gather // *v* wrinkle; *(fx skørt)* gather; *~ panden* frown; *~ på næsen ad ngt* turn up one's nose at sth; **~t** *adj* wrinkled; *en ~t nederdel* a gathered skirt.

ryste *v* shake·; *~ på hovedet* shake· one's head; *~ over det hele* be shaking all over.

rystelse, rysten *en* shaking; *(jordskælv)* tremor; *(fig)* shock.

rystet *adj* shaken; *(chokeret)* shocked.

rytme *en* rhythm.

rytmik *en* rhythmics.

rytmisk *adj* rhythmical.

rytter *en* rider, horseman *(pl:* -men).

rytteri *et* cavalry.

rytterstatue *en* e'questrian statue.

ræb *et* belch; **~e** *v* belch; **~en** *en* belching.

ræd *adj* scared.

ræddike *en* (black) radish.

rædsel *en (frygt)* horror, terror; *(om fx hus)* mon'strosity; *(om fx hat, person)* fright; **~s·fuld** *adj* terrible, awful; **~slagen** *adj* terrified.

rædsom *adj* awful.

række *en* row; *(geled)* line; *(serie)* series; *(antal)* number; *stille op på ~* line up; *en ~ år* a number of years; *en ~ forelæsninger* a series of lectures; *komme i første ~* have pri'ority // *v (give)* hand; *(give videre)* pass; *(nå, række ud efter)* reach; *(strække)* stretch; *~ hånden frem (,ud)* hold· out one's hand; *~ en ngt* hand sby sth; *pengene ~r ikke langt* the money does not go very far; **~følge** *en* suc'cession, order; *i ~følge* in order (of succession); *(efter tur)* by turns; *i omvendt ~følge* in re'verse order; **~hus** *et* terraced house; **~vidde** *en* reach; *(om skud, lyd etc)* range; *(betydning)* scope.

rækværk *et* parapet; *(gelænder)* railing.

ræling *en* railing; *(i åben båd)* gunwale [gʌnl].

ræs *et* (F) race, rush; *et værre ~* an awful rush; *stå af ~et* opt out.

ræv *en* fox; *(hunræv)* vixen; *(pelskrave)* fox fur; *en klog gammel ~ (om person)* a sly old fox; **~e·grav** *en* fox's den; **~e·hale** *en* fox's tail; **~e·jagt** *en* fox-hunt(ing); **~e·saks** *en* foxtrap.

røbe *v (afsløre)* be'tray, re'veal; *(vise)* show·; *~ sig* give· oneself away.

rød *adj* red *(også pol); (stærkt ~)* scarlet; *blive ~ i hovedet (af anstrengelse el. vrede)* flush; *(af generthed)* blush; *Det Røde Hav* the Red Sea; *~e hunde* German measles; *Røde Kors* the Red Cross; *~ numse (om baby)* nappy rash; *køre over for ~t* jump the lights; *standse for ~t* stop at red; **~bede** *en* beetroot; **~brun** *adj* chestnut; **~glødende** *adj* red-hot; **Rødhætte** *en* Little Red Ridinghood; **~håret** *adj* redhaired; *en ~håret person* a redhead; **~kælk** *en (zo)* robin; **~kål** *en* red cabbage; **~lig** *adj* reddish; **~løg** *et* red onion.

rødme *en* blush // *v* blush.

rød... *sms:* **~mosset** *adj* ruddy; **~randet** *adj* red-rimmed; **~spætte** *en* plaice; **~spættefilet** *en* fillet of plaice; **~strømpe** *en* redstocking; **~vin** *en (generelt)* red wine; *(bordeaux)* claret; *(bourgogne)* 'burgundy.

røg *en* smoke; **~bombe** *en* smoke bomb; **~e** *v* smoke.

røgelse *en* incense.

røgeri *et* smokehouse.
røget *adj* smoked *(fx sild* herring).
røg... *sms:* **~forgiftning** *en* asphyxi'ation; **~fri** *adj* smokeless; *~frit område* no-smoking area; **~fyldt** *adj* smoky; **~sky** *en* cloud of smoke; **~slør** *et* smokescreen; **~tobak** *en* smoking to'bacco.
rømme *v (flygte)* run· away; *(desertere)* de'sert; *(forlade)* leave·; *(rydde, tømme)* clear; *(evakuere)* e'vacuate; *~ sig* clear one's throat.
rømning *en (flugt)* es'cape; *(desertering)* de'sertion; *(tømning)* clearing; *(evakuering)* evacu'ation.
røn *en* rowan.
rønnebær *et* rowan berry; *~rene er sure!* sour grapes.
røntgen *s* X-rays *pl;* **~afdeling** *en* radio'logical de'partment; **~behandling** *en* radio'therapy; **~billede** *et* radiograph, X-ray; **~fotografere** *v* X-ray; **~læge** *en* radi'ologist; **~undersøgelse** *en* X-ray (exami'nation).
rør *et (vand~, lednings~)* pipe; *(tv-~, stål~ etc)* tube; *(tlf)* re'ceiver; *(bot)* reed; *lægge ~et på (tlf)* put· down the re'ceiver.
røre *et* com'motion // *v (berøre)* touch; *(bevæge)* move; *(~ rundt)* stir; *(gribe, vække medfølelse)* move, touch; *ikke ~!* don't touch! *det ~r mig ikke* I don't care; *~ benene* stretch one's legs; *~ rundt i sovsen* stir the sauce; *~ mel ud i mælk* mix flour with milk; *~ på sig* move; *~ sig* move; *~ ved ngt* touch sth.
rørelse *en* e'motion.
røremaskine *en* mixer.
rørende *adj* touching; *det er vi ~ enige om* we could not a'gree more.
røreskål *en* mixing bowl.
rørfletning *en* wickerwork.
rørformet *adj* tubular.
rørhøne *en (zo)* moorhen.
rørig *adj* active.
rørledning *en* pipeline.
rørstrømsk *adj* mushy, sloppy.
rørsukker *et* cane sugar.
rørt *adj (bevæget)* moved, touched; *dybt ~* deeply moved (,touched).
røræg *s* scrambled eggs *pl.*
røst *en* voice; *med høj ~* in a loud voice.
røv *en* (V) arse; *være helt på ~en* be on one's arse; *rend mig i ~en!* get stuffed! *tage ~en på en* (V) take· the piss out of sby.
røve *v* rob, steal·; *~ en bank* rob a bank; *~ ngt fra en* rob sby of sth, steal sth from sby.
røver *en* robber; *(spøg)* rascal; *lege ~e og soldater* play cops and robbers; **~historie** *en* yarn.
røveri *et* robbery; **~forsøg** *et* at'tempted robbery.
røverkøb *et* bargain.
røvhul *et* (V) arse-hole; *(om person)* bastard.
røvrende *v: ~ en* do· the dirty on sby; *(fuppe)* (V) take· the piss out of sby.
rå *adj* raw, crude; *(grov)* course; *(brutal)* 'brutal, rough; *sluge ngt ~t* swallow sth hook, line and sinker.
råb *et* call, shout; **~e** *v* shout, call out, cry; *~e efter (,på) en* call sby, shout for sby; *~e om hjælp* shout for help; *~e op* shout; *~e navne op* call names.
råbåndsknob *et* reef knot.
råd *et (vejledning)* ad'vice; *(middel)* remedy; *(forsamling)* council, board; *give en et ~* give· sby a piece of advice; *følge ens ~* take· sby's advice; *spørge en til ~s* ask sby's advice; *have ~ til ngt* be able to af'ford sth; *vi har ikke ~ til bil* we cannot af'ford a car.
rådden *adj* rotten; *behandle en som et ~t æg* handle sby with kid gloves; **~skab** *en* rottenness; *(i hus, træværk etc)* rot.
råde *v (give råd)* ad'vise; *(regere)* reign; *(herske over)* com'mand; *(bestå)* pre'vail; *~ en fra at gøre ngt* ad'vise sby against doing sth; *~ over ngt* have sth at one's dis'posal; *~ en til at gøre ngt* recom'mend sby to do sth.
rådgiver *en* ad'viser.
rådgivning *en* ad'vising, con'sultancy.
rådhus *et* town hall.
rådighed *en* dis'posal; *have ~ over*

ngt have sth at one's dis'posal; *stå til ~ for en* be at sby's dis'posal.
rådne *v* rot, de'cay; *(om organiske stoffer, fx lig)* decom'pose.
rådvild *adj* at a loss, be'wildered.
rådyr *et* roe (deer); *(kød af ~)* venison.
rågummi *en (til såler)* crepe rubber.
råkold *adj* raw.
råkost *en* raw vegetables and fruit; **~jern** *et* grater, shredder.
råolie *en* crude oil.
råvare *en* raw ma'terial.

S

sabbat *en* Sabbath; **~år** *et* sab'batical (year).
sabel *en* sabre; *rasle med ~en (fig)* rattle the sabre.
sable *v: sable en ned* butcher sby; *(med kritik)* take· to pieces.
sabotage *en* 'sabotage.
sabotere *v* 'sabotage.
sadel *en* saddle; **~mager** *en* saddler; *(møbelpolstrer)* up'holsterer; **~taske** *en (på cykel)* tool-bag.
sadisme *en* 'sadism; **sadist** *en* 'sadist; **sadistisk** *adj* sa'distic.
sadle *v* saddle (up); *~ om (fig)* change one's policy.
safir *en* 'sapphire.
safran *en* 'saffron.
saft *en* juice; *(i fx træ)* sap; *(sukker-syltet)* syrup.
saftig *adj* juicy; *(fx bemærkning)* racy.
saftpresser *en* juice ex'tractor.
sag *en (anliggende)* matter; *(emne)* subject; *(ting)* thing; *(rets~)* case; *(som man er optaget af, fx en god ~)* cause; *~en er den at...* the thing is that...; *det er en anden ~* that is a different matter; *det er ingen ~* it is easy; *det er lige ~en* it's just the thing; *det må blive hans ~* that's up to him, that's his headache; *som ~erne står* as things are; *for den ~s skyld* for that matter; *gå til ~en* get· on with it; *gå lige til ~en* get· straight to the point; *lægge ~ an mod en for ngt* sue sby for sth.
saga *en* saga.
sagesløs *adj* innocent.
sagfører *en se advokat.*
sagkyndig *adj* expert *(i* on).
saglig *adj (nøgtern)* matter-of-fact; *(upartisk)* ob'jective; **~hed** *en* matter-of-factness; objec'tivity.
sagn *et* legend.
sags... *sms:* **~anlæg** *et* legal action; **~behandler** *en (på bistandskontor etc)* caseworker; **~behandling** *en* casework; **~omkostninger** *pl* legal costs.
sagsøge *v* sue.
sagsøger *en* plaintiff.
sagsøgte *s* the de'fendant.
sagte *adj (om lyd, dæmpet)* soft, low; *(svag)* slight, faint; *(let, mild)* gentle; *(om varme, ild)* slow.
sagtens *adv (let)* easily; *vi kan ~ nå det* we can· easily make it; *du kan ~!* lucky you! *du kan ~ snakke* it's all very well for you to talk.
sagtne *v: ~ farten* slow down.
sakke *v: ~ bagud* fall· be'hind.
saks *en: en ~* (a pair of) scissors; *må jeg låne ~en?* may I borrow the scissors? *sidde i ~en* be trapped.
sal *en* hall; *(etage)* floor; *bo på anden ~* live on the second floor.
salamander *en* newt.
salat *en (bot)* lettuce; *(som ret)* salad; **~fadet** *s* Black Ma'ria; **~hoved** *et* (head of) lettuce; **~olie** *en* salad oil; **~slynge** *en* salad washer; *(mekanisk)* salad spinner; **~sæt** *et* salad servers *pl.*
saldo *en* balance.
salg *et* sale; *(det at sælge)* selling; *til ~* for sale; *sætte ngt til ~* put· sth up for sale; **~s·betingelser** *pl* con'ditions of sale; **~s·chef** *en* sales manager; **~s·dag** *en: sidste ~s·dag* sell-by date; **~s·fremstød** *et* sales drive; **~s·kampagne** *en* sales cam'paign; **~s·pris** *en* retail price.
salig *adj* blessed; *(lykkelig)* blissful; **~hed** *en* bliss.
salme *en* hymn; *(i bibelen)* psalm; **~bog** *en* hymn book.
salmiakspiritus *en* (liquid) am'monia.
salon *en (stue)* drawing room; *(på skib)* sa'loon; *(frisør~)* 'salon.

salpeter *en* 'saltpetre; **~syre** *en* nitric acid.
salt *et/adj* salt; *han ejer ikke ~ til et æg* he has not got a penny to his name; **~bøsse** *en* salt shaker.
salte *v* salt; *(nedsalte fx kød)* cure; *(nedsalte grønsager)* pickle.
saltholdig *adj* salty.
saltindhold *et* saltiness; *med lavt ~* low-salt.
saltkar *et* salt cellar.
saltlage *en* brine.
saltomortale *en* somersault; *lave en ~* do· a somersault.
saltsyre *en* hydro'chloric acid.
saltvand *et* salt water; **~s·indsprøjtning** *en (fig)* boost.
salut *en* sa'lute; **~ere** *v* sa'lute.
salve *en (creme)* ointment; *(skud~)* volley.
salvelsesfuld *adj* unctuous.
salvie *en (bot)* sage.
salær *et* fee.
samarbejde *et* co-ope'ration // *v* co-'operate.
samarbejdsudvalg *et (på arb.plads)* works com'mittee.
sambeskatning *en* joint ta'xation.
sameksistens *en* co-e'xistence.
samfund *et* so'ciety; *(fællesskab)* com'munity; *~et* so'ciety; **~s·fag** *et* social studies, civics *pl;* **~s·klasse** *en* social class; **~s·mæssig** *adj* social; **~s·tjeneste** *en* com'munity service; **~s·videnskab** *en* social sciences *pl;* **~s·økonomi** *en* eco'nomics *pl.*
samfærdsel *en* traffic, communi'cation.
samhandel *en* trade.
samkvem *et: have ~ med* mix with; **~s·ret** *en* visiting rights *pl; have ~s·ret med (også)* have access to.
samkøre *v* co'ordinate; **samkøring** *en* coordi'nation.
samle *v* gather; *(~ på)* col'lect; *(løse dele)* as'semble; *~ kræfter* gather strength; *~ ind til ngt* collect (money) for sth; *~ op* pick up; *~ på ngt* collect sth; *~ sig (dvs. samles)* gather; *(dvs. tage sig sammen)* pull oneself to'gether; **~bånd** *et* as'sembly line; *på ~bånd (fig)* non-stop.
samleje *et* (sexual) intercourse; *have ~ med en* (F) have sex with sby.
samler *en* col'lector; **~mani** *en* collecto'mania; **~objekt** *et* col'lector's item.
samlesæt *et* kit.
samlet *adj (fælles)* joint; *(hel)* total; *(forsamlet)* as'sembled // *adv* jointly.
samlever *en* common-law husband (,wife), (F) cohab.
samling *en (af ting)* col'lection; *(ophobning)* accumu'lation; *(af løsdele)* as'sembly; *(forsamling)* gathering, as'sembly.
samliv *et* living to'gether; *(papirløst)* cohabi'tation; *(i ægteskab)* married life.
samme *adj* the same; *i det ~* just then; *med det ~* at once; *det kan være det ~* never mind; *jeg har kun den ~* I've only got the one; *de bor i ~ hus* they live in the same house.
sammen *adv* to'gether; *(i forening)* jointly; *alt ~* all (of it); *bo ~* live together; *de kommer ~ (dvs. ses)* they see each other; *(dvs. som par)* they are going steady; *lægge ~ (dvs. folde ~)* fold up; *(om tal)* add up; *tale ~* talk.
sammenbidt *adj* grim, de'termined.
sammenbrud *et* breakdown, col'lapse.
sammendrag *et* summary.
sammenfatte *v* summarize.
sammenhold *et* soli'darity.
sammenhæng *en* con'nection, con'nexion; *(i tekst)* context; *sagens rette ~* the facts (of the case); **~ende** *adj* co'herent; *(uafbrudt)* con'tinuous; *(i træk)* con'secutive; *(indbyrdes forbundne)* con'nected.
sammenkalde *v* call (to'gether).
sammenklappelig *adj* col'lapsible *(fx bord* table); folding *(fx cykel* bike).
sammenkogt *adj: ~ ret* 'casserole.
sammenkomst *en* gathering, (F) get-together.
sammenlagt *adj* put together; *(om tøj)* folded; *(om beløb)* total; *det bliver ~ £8* it is £8 in all.

sammenligne *v* com'pare *(med* with); *det kan ikke ~s* there is no com-'parison.
sammenligning *en* com'parison; *det tåler ikke ~ med* it does not com-'pare with; *i ~ med* com'pared with (,to); *uden ~ den bedste* by far the best.
sammenlægning *en (af tal)* ad'dition; *(af firmaer)* merger.
sammensat *adj* 'compound; *(indvik-let)* 'complex.
sammenskudsgilde *et* Dutch party, *sv.omtr.t.* bottle party.
sammenslutning *en* union; *(fusion)* merger; *(forening)* associ'ation.
sammenspist *adj* cliquey.
sammenstød *et* col'lision; *(skænderi)* row.
sammensvorne *pl* con'spirators.
sammensværge *v: ~ sig* con'spire; **~lse** *en* con'spiracy.
sammensætning *en* compo'sition; *(gram)* 'compound.
sammensætte *v* put· together.
sammentræf *et* co'incidence.
sammesteds *adv* in the same place; **~fra** *adv* from the same place; **~hen** *adv* to the same place.
samordne *v* co-'ordinate; **samord-ning** *en* co-ordi'nation.
samråd *et* consul'tation; *i ~ med* after con'ferring with.
samsending *en (radio, tv)* hook-up.
samspil *et (mus)* en'semble playing; *(fig)* inter'action; *(samarbejde)* teamwork.
samt *konj* and, plus.
samtale *en* conver'sation; *(uformel)* talk; *(tlf)* call; *føre en ~* have a con-ver'sation (,talk); **~anlæg** *et* inter-com; **~emne** *et* topic.
samtid *en: ~en (dvs. nu)* our time; *(dvs. tidligere)* that age.
samtidig *adj* con'temporary *(med* with); *(på én gang)* simul'taneous // *adv* at the same time, simul-'taneously; *(på den anden side)* on the other hand; *~ med at...* at the same time as...
samtidsorientering *en* modern studies *pl.*
samtlige *adj* all (of).
samtykke *et* con'sent; *give sit ~ til ngt* (give one's) con'sent to sth // *v* con'sent *(i* to).
samvittighed *en* conscience; *have ngt på ~en* feel· guilty about sth; *have dårlig ~* have a bad conscience, feel· guilty; **~s·fuld** *adj* consci'en-tious; *(omhyggelig også)* pains-taking; **~s·nag** *en* pangs of con-science; **~s·spørgsmål** *et* matter of conscience.
samvær *et* company; *selskabeligt ~* get-together.
sand *et* sand; *løbe ud i ~et* come· to nothing // *adj* true; *det er ~t, vi skal jo vaske op!* by the way, we have to do the dishes! *det er da ikke ~t!* it can't be true! *det er for godt til at være ~t* it is too good to be true; *du så det, ikke ~t?* you saw it, didn't you? *~t at sige* to tell the truth.
sandal *en* 'sandal.
sandblæse *v* sandblast.
sandbund *en* sandy bottom.
sandelig *adv* in'deed, really.
sandfærdig *adj* truthful; **~hed** *en* truthfulness.
sandhed *en* truth; *tale ~* tell· the truth; *~en er at* to tell the truth.
sand... *sms:* **~jord** *en* sandy soil; **~kage** *en sv.t.* sponge cake; **~kasse** *en* sandpit; **~papir** *et* sandpaper; **~sten** *en* sandstone; **~strand** *en* sandy beach.
sandsynlig *adj* likely, probable; **~hed** *en* proba'bility; *efter al ~hed* in all proba'bility; **~vis** *adv* probably.
sandsæk *en* sandbag.
sanere *v (om bydel etc)* rede'velop; *(om fx økonomi)* reha'bilitate.
sanering *en* rede'velopment; *(økon)* rehabili'tation; **~s·hus** *et* con-'demned house.
sang *en* song; *(syngen)* singing; *gå til ~* take· singing lessons; **~bog** *en* songbook.
sanger *en* singer.
sangfugl *en* song-bird.
sangkor *et* choir.
sangleg *en* singing game.

sangstemme *en* singing voice; *(node, del af musikstykke)* vocal part.
sankt *s* Saint, St.; **~hansaften** *en* Midsummer's Eve; **~hansbål** *et* Midsummer's Eve bonfire.
sanktion *en* sanction; **~ere** *v* sanction.
sans *en* sense; *have ~ for ngt* have a sense of sth; *(værdsætte)* ap'preciate sth; *gå fra ~ og samling* take· leave of one's senses.
sanse *v (opfatte)* per'ceive; *de ~de ingenting* they did not feel a thing; *de kunne hverken ~ el. samle* they did not know whether they were coming or going; *han ~de kun hende* he sensed only her.
sanselig *adj* sensuous; *(erotisk)* sensual; **~hed** *en* sensu'ality.
sanseløs *adj* blind, frantic.
sardin *en* 'sardine.
sarkasme *en* 'sarcasm.
sarkastisk *adj* sar'castic.
sart *adj (følsom)* sensitive; *(svag)* delicate; *(pivet)* squeamish; *(som let bliver stødt)* touchy.
sat *adj* se'date.
satan *en* Satan; *for ~!* damn it! oh hell! *det var ~s!* well, I'll be damned! *(se også pokker);* **satanisk** *adj* sa'tanic.
satellit *en* 'satellite.
satire *en* 'satire *(over* on).
satirisk *adj* sa'tirical.
sats *en (tarif etc)* rate; *(typ)* type; *(mus)* movement.
satse *v: ~ på ngt* bet on sth; *(stile efter)* aim at sth; *~ alt på ngt* stake everything on sth; *vi ~r på at han kommer* we as'sume that he'll come; *vi ~r på at tage til London* we are counting on going to London.
saudi-araber *en* Saudi; **Saudi-Arabien** *s* Saudi A'rabia; **saudi-arabisk** *adj* Saudi (A'rabian).
sauna *en* sauna.
sav *en* saw; **~buk** *en* sawhorse.
save *v* saw; *~ ngt over* saw through sth; *(i to dele)* saw sth in two.
savl *et* sa'liva.
savle *v* dribble; *~ over ngt* slobber over sth.
savn *et (mangel)* want; *(behov)* need; *det er et stort ~* it is a great loss.
savne *v* miss; *(mangle, ikke have)* lack, want; *(trænge til)* need; *vi har ~t dig* we missed you; *være ~t* be missed; *(dvs. forsvundet)* be missing.
savsmuld *en* sawdust; **~s·tapet** *et* wood-chip paper.
savtakket *adj* ser'rated.
savværk *et* sawmill.
saxofon *en* 'saxophone.
scene *en* scene; *(teat)* stage; *lave en ~* create a scene; *gå til ~en* go· on stage; *sætte ngt i ~* stage sth; *(teat, film)* pro'duce sth; **~instruktør** *en* pro'ducer, di'rector; **~mester** *en* stage manager.
sceneri *et* setting.
scenograf *en* set-designer.
scepter *et* sceptre.
Schweiz *s* Switzerland; **schweizer** *en,* **schweizisk** *adj* Swiss.
schæfer(hund) *en* al'satian.
score *v* score *(også fig S)*.
se *v (kunne se, få øje på)* see·; *(bruge øjnene, se på ngt)* look; *(være tilskuer til, overvære)* watch; *kan du ~ ham?* do you see him? *~ fjernsyn* watch television; *~ her!* look here! *~s* meet·; *vi ~s!* see you! *kan det ~s, kan man ~ det?* does it show? *~ sig for* look where one is going; *~ sig om* look around; *(dvs. rejse)* travel around; *~ sig om efter ngt* look around for sth; *jeg skal ~ ad* I'll see; *~ bort fra ngt* ig'nore sth; *~ efter (dvs. lede)* look for; *(dvs. holde øje)* look after; *~ ngt efter* look sth over; *~ frem til* look forward to; *~ ned på en* look down on sby; *~ op til en* look up to sby; *~ på ngt* look at sth; *(som tilskuer)* watch sth; *~ til (som tilskuer)* look on, watch; *~ til at taget bliver lavet* see· to it that the roof is mended; *~ en del til en* see· quite a lot of sby; *~ sig tilbage* look back; se (to it) that...; *~ ud (af ydre)* look; *(virke)* seem; *hvordan ~r hun ud?* what does she look like; *~ ud af vinduet* look out of the window; *det ~r ud som om* it looks as if; *det ~r ikke ud*

af ret meget it is not much to look at; *det ~r ud til regn* it looks like rain.
seddel *en (penge~, besked etc)* note; *(papir~)* slip (of paper); *(mærke~)* label; *4000 kr. i store sedler* 4,000 kr. in large denomi'nations; **~penge** *pl* paper money.
seer *en (tv)* viewer; **~tal** *et* ratings *pl.*
segl *et* seal; *(høstredskab)* sickle.
segne *v* drop; **~færdig** *adj* ready to drop.
sej *adj* tough; *(fig, stædig)* dogged; **~hed** *en* toughness; doggedness.
sejlads *en (det at sejle)* navi'gation; *(sejltur)* sail; *(sørejse)* voyage.
sejlbræt *et* windsurfer.
sejlbåd *en* sailing boat.
sejldug *en* canvas.
sejle *v* sail; *(som sport)* yacht; *(i robåd)* row; *(i kano)* go· ca'noeing; *lade en ~ i sin egen sø* leave· sby to his own de'vices; *hele huset ~de (fig)* the house was one big mess; *~ med Englandsbåden* go· on the boat to England; *~ over Kanalen* cross the Channel; *tage ud at ~* go· sailing.
sejl... *sms:* **~garn** *et* string; **~klub** *en* sailing club; **~rende** *en* fairway; **~skib** *et* sailing ship; **~sport** *en* sailing, yachting; **~tur** *en* sail.
sejr *en* victory; (F) win; *vinde ~* gain the victory; *en ~ på 3-1 over Tyskland* a 3-1 win over Germany.
sejre *v* win·; *~ over en* win· over sby; *(i sport)* beat· sby.
sejrherre *en* victor, winner; *blive ~* come· out the winner.
sejrrig *adj* vic'torious.
sejrsskammel *en (sport)* winner's stand.
sekret *et* se'cretion.
sekretariat *et* secre'tariat.
sekretær *en (person)* 'secretary; *(møbel)* 'bureau.
seks *num* six; **~dagesløb** *et* six-day race; **~er** *en* six; *(om bus etc)* number six; **~kant** *en* hexagon; **~kantet** *adj* he'xagonal; **~løber** *en* six-shooter; **~tal** *et* six.
seksten *num* sixteen.
sekstet *en (mus)* sex'tet.
sekstiden *s: ved ~* about six o'clock.
seksualitet *en* sexu'ality.
seksualoplysning *en* sex edu'cation; *give en ~* teach· sby the facts of life.
seksuel *adj* sexual; **~t** *adv* sexually.
sekt *en* sect.
sektion *en* section.
sektor *en* sector.
sekund *et* second.
sekundant *en* second.
sekundere *v* second.
sekundviser *en* second hand.
sekundær *adj* secondary.
sekvens *en* sequence.
sele *en* strap; *(auto, fly)* seat belt; *(gå~ til barn)* reins *pl; (bære~ til barn)* carrying sling; *~r (til bukser etc)* braces; *lægge sig i ~n for at gøre ngt* make· a real effort to do sth; **~tøj** *et* harness.
selleri *en (rod~)* ce'leriac; *(blad~)* 'celery.
selskab *et (fest; rejse~ etc)* party; *(forening)* so'ciety; *(handels~ etc)* company; *(det at være sammen med ngn)* company; *han er godt ~* he is good company; *komme i dårligt ~* get· into bad company; *holde et ~* have a party; *holde en med ~* keep· sby company; **~e·lig** *adj* social; *(om person)* sociable; **~e·lighed** *en (som man selv afholder)* enter'taining; *(som man går ud til)* parties *pl.*
selskabs... *sms:* **~kjole** *en* evening gown; **~leg** *en* parlour game; **~rejse** *en* con'ducted tour; **~skat** *en* corpo'ration tax.
selv *pron singularis:* my'self (,your'self, him'self, her'self, it'self, one'self); *pl:* our'selves (,your'selves, them'selves); *jeg gjorde det ~* I did it myself; *hun så det ~* she saw it herself; *de syr ~ deres tøj* they make· their own clothes; *det må I ~ om* that's up to you; *det kan du ~ være!* the same to you! *du ligner dig ~* you have not changed; *gøre ngt af sig ~* do· sth of one's own ac'cord; *det begynder af sig ~* it starts auto'matically; *være ngt for sig ~* be sth out of the ordinary;

komme til sig ~ re'cover; *(efter besvimelse)* come· round // *adv* even; ~ *chefen tog fejl* even the boss was wrong.

selvangivelse *en* (income) tax re'turn.

selvbeherskelse *en* 'self-con,trol.

selvbestaltet *adj* 'self-ap,pointed.

selvbetjening *en* self-service.

selvbevidst *adj* 'self-as,sured; *(neds)* con'ceited.

selvbiografi *en* autobi'ography.

selvbrunende *adj:* ~ *creme* de'veloper.

selvdisciplin *en* self-'discipline.

selve *adv: i* ~ *huset* in the house it'self; *under* ~ *krigen* during the actual war; ~*ste kongen* the king him'self.

selveje *et* freehold; **~nde** *adj (om institution)* inde'pendent.

selverhvervende *adj (selvstændig)* 'self-em,ployed; *(om hustru)* working.

selvforsvar *et* 'self-de,fence.

selvforsynende *adj* 'self-suf,ficient.

selvfølge *en* matter of course; *det er en* ~ it goes without saying; *tage ngt som en* ~ take· sth as a matter of course.

selvfølgelig *adj (naturlig)* natural; *(indlysende)* obvious // *adv* naturally, of course; *mon han kommer?* ~ *gør han det!* I wonder if he's coming. Of course he is! **~hed** *en (ngt naturligt)* naturalness; *(ngt indlysende)* obviousness.

selvglad *adj* self-'satisfied.

selvhjulpen *adj (som klarer sig selv)* 'self-re,liant; *(selvforsynende)* 'self-sup,porting.

selvhøjtidelig *adj* pompous.

selvisk *adj* selfish; **~hed** *en* selfishness.

selvjustits *en: øve* ~ take· the law into one's own hands.

selvklæbende *adj* 'self-ad,hesive.

selvkritik *en* self-criticism.

selvlyd *en (vokal)* vowel.

selvlysende *adj* luminous.

selvmodsigende *adj* contra'dictory.

selvmord *et* suicide; *begå* ~ com'mit suicide; **~er** *en* suicide; **~s·forsøg** *et* at'tempted suicide.

selvmål *et (sport)* own goal.

selvom *konj (skønt)* (even) though; *(også hvis)* even if.

selvopofrende *adj* self-'sacrificing.

selvoptaget *adj* self-centred.

selvportræt *et* self-portrait.

selvrespekt *en* self-respect.

selvrisiko *en* own lia'bility.

selvsikker *adj* 'self-as,sured; **~hed** *en* 'self-as,surance.

selvskreven *adj: være* ~ *til ngt* be the obvious choice for sth.

selvstyre *et* au'tonomy.

selvstændig *adj* inde'pendent; *(særskilt)* separate; *(egen)* of one's own will; *blive* ~ *(med eget firma)* set· up on one's own; ~ *erhvervsdrivende* self-employed person; **~hed** *en* inde'pendence.

selvtilfreds *adj* com'placent, smug; **~hed** *en* com'placency, smugness.

selvtillid *en* self-'confidence.

selvvalg *et (tlf)* direct dialling.

selvvalgt *adj* 'self-e,lected; *(tlf)* self-dialled.

semester *et* se'mester; *(især am)* term.

semifinale *en* semifinal(s *pl)*.

semikolon *et* semi'colon.

seminar *et (møde)* 'seminar.

seminarium *et* teacher training college.

sen *adj* late; *(langsom)* slow; *(forsinket)* be'lated; *i en* ~ *alder* late in life; *for* ~*t* too late; *komme for* ~*t til ngt* be late for sth; *komme for* ~*t til toget* miss the train; ~*t på dagen* late in the day; *vi er* ~*t på den* we are late; *så* ~*t som i mandags* only last Monday; *bedre* ~*t end aldrig* better late than never.

senat *et* 'senate.

senator *en* 'senator.

sende *v* send·; *(merk)* dis'patch, forward; *(med skib el. fly)* ship; *(i radio)* broadcast; *(i tv)* trans'mit; ~ *bud efter en (,ngt)* send· for sby (,sth); **~bud** *et* messenger.

sender *en (radio)* trans'mitter.

sendetid *en (i tv)* airtime.

sending *en (parti)* shipment.
sene *en* sinew.
senere *adj* later; *(fremtidig)* future // *adv* later; *(bagefter)* afterwards; ~ *på dagen* later in the day; *i de ~ år* in recent years; *i den ~ tid* lately; *før el.* ~ sooner or later.
senest *adj* latest; *(langsomst)* slowest // *adv* at the latest; ~ *1. maj* on May the first at the latest, not later than May the first; *i den ~e tid* recently.
seng *en* bed; *holde ~en* stay· in bed; *gå i ~* go· to bed; *gå i ~ med en* sleep· with sby; *gå i ~ med alle og enhver* sleep· around; *ligge i ~en* be in bed; *(være syg)* be ill in bed; *rede ~* make· the bed; **~e·hest** *en* bed guard; **~e·kant** *en* bedside; **~e·liggende** *adj* bedridden; **~e·tid** *en* bedtime; **~e·tæppe** *et* bedspread; **~e·tøj** *et* bed linen.
senil *adj* 'senile; **~itet** *en* se'nility.
sennep *en* mustard.
sensation *en* sen'sation; *skabe ~* cre'ate a sen'sation.
sensationel *adj* sen'sational.
sensibel *adj* sensitive.
sentimental *adj* senti'mental, soppy; **~itet** *en* sentimen'tality.
separat *adj* 'separate.
separation *en* sepa'ration; **~s·bevilling** *en* sepa'ration order.
september *en* Sep'tember; *den første ~* Sep'tember the first, the first of Sep'tember.
septiktank *en* septic tank, cesspit.
serenade *en* 'serenade.
sergent *en* 'sergeant.
serie *en* series; *(merk)* batch; *(tv)* serial; **~fremstillet** *adj* 'mass-pro,duced.
seriøs *adj* serious.
serv *en (i tennis etc)* service.
serve *v* serve.
servere *v* serve; *(varte op)* wait at table; *~ for en* wait on sby; *middagen er ~t* dinner is served.
servering *en* service; **~s·dame** *en* waitress.
service *et (porcelæn etc)* service // *en* service; *sende bilen til ~* take· the car in for service; **~station** *en* petrol station; **~ydelse** *en* service.
serviet *en* napkin; *(rense~)* tissue.
servitrice *en* waitress.
servostyring *en (auto)* power(-assisted) steering.
set *adj* seen; *bilen ~ fra siden (,forfra, bagfra)* side (,front, rear) view of the car; *sådan ~* in a way.
seværdighed *en* sight.
sex *s* sex; **~et** *adj* sexy.
sexistisk *adj* 'sexist.
sfære *en* sphere.
sgu *interj: det er ~ sjovt!* it's damned funny! *det er ~ møgvejr igen!* it's bloody awful weather again! *jeg mener det ~!* I mean it, damn you! *han er ~ genial!* he's a bloody genius!
shampoo *en* sham'poo.
si *en* sieve; *(te~)* strainer; *(dørslag)* 'colander // *v (om væske)* strain; *(om fx mel)* sift.
sidde *v* sit·; *(være anbragt)* be; *(om tøj)* fit; *de sad og spiste* they were eating; *den sad!* that hit home! *der ~r en flue på lampen* there is a fly on the lamp; *kjolen ~r godt* the dress is a nice fit; *~r du godt?* are you comfortable? *~ efter (i skolen)* have de'tention; *~ fast* be stuck; *dit slips ~r skævt* your tie is not straight; *~ i møde* be at a meeting, be in conference; *~ i et udvalg* be on a com'mittee; *~ inde (i fængsel)* do· time; *~ inde med ngt* hold· sth; *~ ned* be sitting (,seated); *(sætte sig)* sit· down; *~ til bords* be at table; **~nde** *adj* sitting, seated; *(om regering etc)* present; *blive ~nde* re'main seated; *(sidde fast)* be· stuck; *bliv bare ~nde!* please don't get up! **~plads** *en* seat; *der er 400 ~pladser i salen (også)* the hall seats 400.
side *en* side; *(i bog etc)* page; *(ngt typisk)* point; *det er ikke hans stærke ~* it is not his strong point; *en anden ~ af sagen* a different matter; *de kom fra alle ~r* they came from all sides; *der lød protester fra alle ~r* all parties pro'tested; *vise sig fra*

sin bedste ~ show· oneself at one's best; *se det fra den lyse* ~ look at it from the bright side; *køre i højre (,venstre)* ~ *(af vejen)* drive· on the right (,left) hand side (of the road); *se næste* ~ see· over'leaf, see· next page; *få en over på sin* ~ get· sby on one's side; *på den anden* ~ *(fig)* on the other hand; *på den anden* ~ *af gaden* on the opposite side of the street; *se til* ~*n* look a'side; *til alle* ~*r* on all sides; *lægge ngt til* ~ put· sth a'side; *ved* ~*n af* be'side, next to; *det er helt ved* ~*n af* it is quite be'side the point; *de bor inde ved* ~*n af* they live next door.

sideblik *et* sidelong glance.

sidebygning *en* wing.

sidegade *en* side street.

sidelinje *en (fodb)* touchline; *(tennis)* sideline.

sidelæns *adv* sideways.

sideløbende *adj* 'parallel.

sidemand *en: min* ~ the person next to me.

siden *adv* since; *(derefter)* afterwards; *(om lidt)* presently; *før el.* ~ sooner or later; *det er flere år* ~ *vi sås* it's been several years since we met; *det var for tre år* ~ it was three years a'go; *det er længe* ~ it is a long time a'go; *for længe* ~ a long time a'go // *præp/konj* since; ~ *du nu vil have det* since you want it; ~ *sidst* since last time.

sideskift *et (sport)* changeover.

sidespejl *et (auto)* side-view mirror.

sidespor *et* side track; *komme ind på et* ~ get· sidetracked.

sidespring *et (fig)* di'gression; *et* ~ *(i ægteskabet)* a bit on the side.

sidesting *et* stitch.

sidestykke *et (fig)* 'parallel.

sidevej *en* side road.

sidevind *en* crosswind.

sidevogn *en (på motorcykel)* side car.

sidst *adj* last; *(senest)* latest // *adv* last; *komme* ~ be last; *(i mål)* come· in last; ~*e nyt* the latest news; *hvornår sås vi* ~*?* when did we meet last? *den tredje* ~*e* the last but two; *han er* ~ *i tresserne* he is in his late sixties; ~ *på måneden* at the end of the month; *til* ~ *(dvs. endelig)* at last; *(dvs. til slut)* finally.

sidstnævnte *s* the last-mentioned; *(ud af to)* the latter.

sig *pron (efter v:)* one'self (,him'self, her'self, it'self, them'selves); *(efter præp:)* him, her, it, them; *hun morede* ~ she en'joyed herself; *de slog* ~ they hurt themselves; *de så* ~ *omkring* they looked about them; *(ofte oversættes* ~ *ikke, fx) hun satte* ~ she sat down; *de giftede* ~ they married; *få* ~ *en øl* have a beer, *gøre ngt af* ~ *selv (dvs. automatisk)* do· sth auto'matically; *(dvs. frivilligt)* do· sth of one's own ac'cord.

sige *v* say·; *(fortælle, give besked)* tell·; *hvad* ~*r du til det?* what do· you say to that? *han sagde farvel* he said good'bye; *jeg skal* ~ *dig ngt* I will tell you sth; *kan du* ~ *mig hvad klokken er?* can you tell me what time it is? *det* ~*s at vi får valg* they say there will be an e'lection; *hun sagde at de skulle vaske sig* she told them to wash; ~*r det dig ngt?* does it (,that) ring a bell? ~ *en imod* contra'dict sby; ~ *op* give· notice; *hvad* ~*r du til at gå i teatret?* how would you like to go to the theatre? *hvad* ~*r du til det?* what do you think of that? *der er ikke ngt at* ~ *til at de gik* you can't blame them for leaving; *sig til når du er færdig* tell me when you are finished.

sigende *s: efter* ~ *er det den bedste bil* it is said to be the best car // *adj (om blik)* meaning.

signal *et* signal; *give en* ~ *til at standse* signal sby to stop.

signalement *et* de'scription.

signalere *v* signal.

signalflag *et* signal flag.

signatur *en* signature.

signere *v* sign.

sigt *et* sight; *(sigtbarhed)* visi'bility; *på kort (,langt)* ~ in the short (,long) run; **~barhed** *en* visi'bility.

sigte *en* sieve; *(til væske)* strainer // *et (ngt man stræber efter, formål)* aim; *(~korn på våben)* sight; *få ngt* *i* ~ catch· sight of sth; *tabe ngt af* ~ lose· sight of sth // *v (si)* sift; *(tage ~)* take· aim; *(anklage)* charge *(for* with); ~ *efter ngt* aim at sth; ~ *imod at* aim to; *hvad ~r du til?* what are you getting at?

sigtelse *en* charge *(for* with).

sigøjner *en* gipsy.

sikke(n) *pron* what a; *sikken en larm!* what a noise! *sikke varmt det er!* so warm it is! // *adv* how; *sikken han ser ud!* how he looks! *sikken de ter sig!* what a way to be'have!

sikker *adj* certain, sure; *(stensikker)* positive; *(sikret, stærk nok, i sikkerhed)* safe; *(selv~)* confident; *en ~ sejr* certain victory; *på ~ afstand* at a safe distance; *det er helt ~t* it is absolutely certain; *er du ~?* are you sure? *ja, jeg er helt ~!* yes, I'm positive; *jeg er ikke* ~ I'm not sure *(på at* that); *være ~ på ngt* be sure about sth; *for at være på den sikre side* to be on the safe side; *(se også sikkert).*

sikkerhed *en* safety; *(sikring for fremtiden, tryghed)* se'curity; *(selv~)* confidence; *(dygtighed)* skill; *(garanti, kaution)* se'curity, guaran'tee; *for en ~s skyld* to be on the safe side; *bringe ngt i* ~ save sth; *komme i* ~ save oneself; *stille ~ for ngt* offer se'curity for sth; *som en ~ mod pirater* as a safeguard against pirates; *være i* ~ be safe; **~s·bestemmelser** *pl* safety regu'lations; **~s·bælte** *et* seat belt; **~s·lås** *en* safety lock; **~s·net** *et* safety net; **~s·nål** *en* safety pin; **~s·politik** *en* se'curity policy; **~s·repræsentant** *en* safety steward; **Sikkerhedsrådet** *s (i FN)* the Se'curity Council; **~s·sele** *en* seat belt; **~s·tropper** *pl* se'curity troops; **~s·vagt** *en* se'curity man *(pl:* men); *(livvagt)* bodyguard; **~s·ventil** *en* safety valve.

sikkert *adv (sandsynligvis)* probably, no doubt; *(utvivlsomt)* un'doubtedly; *(helt ~)* certainly; *(uden fare el. risiko)* safely; *han glemmer ~ nøglen* he is sure to for'get· the key; *han vil ~ også med* he is sure to want to come too.

sikre *v* make· sure; *(garantere)* guaran'tee; *(få fat i)* se'cure, get·; *(beskytte)* safeguard, pro'tect; ~ *sig* make· sure; *(skaffe sig)* se'cure, get· hold of; ~ *sig mod ngt* pro'tect one'self against sth.

sikring *en* pro'tection; *(elek)* fuse; *(på skydevåben)* safety catch; *sprænge ~erne* blow· the fuses.

siksak *en: i* ~ zigzag; **~ke** *v* zigzag.

sild *en* herring; *røget* ~ smoked herring; *som ~ i en tønde* like sardines in a tin; **~e·anretning** *en* as'sorted herring dishes; **~e·postej** *en* smoked herring pâté; **~e·salat** *en* salad of herring, beetroot etc; *(iron om ordener etc)* fruit salad.

sile *v (om regn)* pour down.

silhuet *en* silhou'ette.

silke *en* silk; **~orm** *en* silkworm; **~papir** *et* tissue paper.

silo *en* silo.

simili *s* imi'tation; **~smykker** *pl* paste jewellery.

simpel *adj (enkel)* simple, plain; *(ren og skær)* mere; *(ufin)* common; **~hed** *en* sim'plicity, plainness; commonness.

simpelt *adv: ganske ~t* quite simply.

simpelthen *adv* simply.

simre *v* simmer.

simulere *v* feign, pre'tend (to be).

sin, *sit, sine pron* his, her; *(stående alene)* hers, its, one's; *han bor i sit hus, hun i sit* he lives in his house, she in hers; *glemme sin paraply* for'get· one's um'brella; *gøre sit til at...* do one's best to...; *de fik hver sin gave* they got a present each; *de har hver sit værelse* they have separate rooms; *~e steder* in places.

sind *et* mind; *(temperament)* temper, dispo'sition; *have i ~e at* in'tend to; *i sit stille* ~ secretly.

sinde: *nogen* ~ ever; *aldrig nogen* ~ not ever.

-sindet dis'posed; *venlig~* friendly; *dansk~* pro-Danish.

sindig *adj* steady.

sindrig *adj* in'genious.

sinds... *sms:* **~bevægelse** *en* e'motion; *(ophidselse)* ex'citement;

~forvirret *adj* mentally con'fused; **~oprivende** *adj* nerve-racking, most up'setting; **~ro** *en* calmness; *med største ~ro* quite calmly; **~stemning** *en* mood; **~syg** *adj* mentally ill; *(skør)* mad, crazy; **~syge** *en* mental illness; **~tilstand** *en* state of mind.

singularis *s (gram)* the singular.

sinke *en* mentally re'tarded person // *v* de'lay, de'tain.

sippet *adj* prudish; *(overpertentlig)* fussy.

sirene *en* siren.

sirlig *adj* neat; *(pertentlig)* me'ticulous.

sirup *en (lys)* syrup; *(mørk)* treacle.

sisal *en* sisal.

sit *se sin.*

situation *en* situ'ation; *en vanskelig ~* a difficult po'sition; *være ~en voksen* rise· to the oc'casion.

siv *pl* rushes.

sive *v* ooze; *(om lys og fig)* filter; *(forlade stedet lidt efter lidt)* trickle out (,away); *~ ind (dvs. blive forstået)* sink· in; *lade ngt ~ ud* leak sth; **~brønd** *en* cesspool.

sjal *et* shawl.

sjap *et* slush; **~pet** *adj* slushy.

sjask *et* slush; **~e** *v* splash; **~et** *adj* sloppy.

sjat *en* drop, spot; *en ~ te* a drop of tea; *jeg skal kun have en ~ vin* I just want a spot of wine.

sjette *adj* sixth; **~del** *en* sixth.

sjipning *en* skipping.

sjippe *v* skip; **~tov** *et* skipping rope, jump-rope.

sjofel *adj (uanstændig)* dirty; *(led)* filthy; **~hed** *en* dirty trick; *(historie etc)* dirty story (,joke etc); *(~t ord)* ob'scenity.

sjofle *v: sjofle en* treat sby like dirt; *sjofle ngt* ne'glect sth.

sjokke *v* scuffle.

sjov *s* fun; *det er kun for ~* it is only for fun; *lave ~* have fun; *lave ~ med en* have sby on // *adj* fun; *(morsom)* funny; *det er ~t* it is fun(ny); *det er ~t at lege* it is fun to play; *se ~ ud* look funny; *~t nok* strangely e'nough.

sjover *en* bastard.

sjus *en* whisky-and-soda.

sjusk *et* bungling; *(ligegyldighed)* carelessness; **~e** *v* be careless, be slovenly; **~eri** *et* bungling; **~et** *adj* slovenly; *(rodet, ~ i tøjet)* un'tidy.

sjæl *en* soul; *af hele min ~* with all my heart; *lægge sin ~ i ngt* put· one's heart (and soul) into sth.

sjælden *adj* rare; *(bemærkelsesværdig)* re'markable; *i ~ grad* ex'ceptionally; *en ~ gang imellem* at rare intervals; **~hed** *en* rarity; *det hører til ~hederne* it is a rare thing.

sjældent *adv (ikke ofte)* rarely; *(specielt)* re'markably.

sjæleliv *et* inner life.

sjælemesse *en (rel)* requiem mass.

Sjælland *s* Zealand; **sjællandsk** *adj* Zealand.

skab *et* cupboard; *(klæde~)* wardrobe.

skabagtig *adj* af'fected.

skabe *v* cre'ate, make·; *(give anledning til)* cause; *~ sig (dvs. være krukket)* be af'fected; *(tage på vej)* make· a fuss *(over* about); *(give problemer, fx om motor)* play up; *(te sig dumt)* play the fool; *~ sig et navn* make· a name for oneself; *(se også skabt).*

skabelon *en* template; *(form)* shape.

skabelse *en* cre'ation, making; *~n* the Cre'ation.

skaber *en* cre'ator, maker.

skaberi *et* affec'tation.

skabning *en* creature.

skabt *adj* cre'ated, made; *han er flot ~* he is well-made; *være som ~ til at være ngt* be cut out to be sth.

skade *en (zo)* magpie; *(beskadigelse)* damage; *(fortræd)* harm; *(legemlig)* injury; *(maskin~)* trouble; *tage ~ (om ting)* be damaged; *komme til ~ (om person)* get· hurt; *(blive såret etc)* be injured; *det tager han ingen ~ af* it won't harm him; *det er ingen ~ til at prøve* there is no harm in trying // *v (om ting)* damage; *(om person, kvæste etc)* injure; *(lettere)* hurt·; *(om helbred)* harm; *det ~r ikke* there is no harm in it; *spil-*

leren er ~t (sport) the player is injured; **~dyr** *et* pest; **~fro** *adj* gloating; *være ~fro over ngt* gloat over sth; **~fryd** *en* gloating; **~lig** *adj* harmful; *(alvorligere)* damaging.

skadesløs *adj: holde en ~* in'demnify sby.

skadestue *en* e'mergency (,casualty) ward.

skaffe *v (få fat i)* get· (hold of); *(ved særlig indsats)* pro'cure; *(om penge)* raise, find·; *(levere)* pro'vide, sup'ply; *~ sig af med ngt* get· rid of sth.

skafot *et* scaffold.

skaft *en (på fx pande, hammer etc)* handle; *(på spyd, stang)* shaft; *(på strømpe, støvle)* leg; *(på kost)* stick.

Skagen *s* the Skaw.

Skagerak *s* the Skagerak.

skak *et* chess; *et parti ~* a game of chess; *holde en i ~* stall sby; **~brik** *en* chessman *(pl:* -men); **~bræt** *et* chessboard; **~mat** *adj* checkmate; **~spil** *et (om delene)* chessboard and chessmen; *(om spillet)* game of chess; **~spiller** *en* chessplayer.

skakt *en* shaft; *(til affald)* chute.

skal *en* shell; *(på frugt)* skin, peel; *(på korn)* husk; *(hjerne~)* skull; (F, *om hovedet)* nut.

skala *en* scale.

skaldet *adj* bald; *(sølle)* measly; **~hed** *en* baldness.

skaldyr *et* shellfish.

skalle *en: nikke en en ~* smash one's head into sby's face // *v: ~ af (om maling etc)* peel off; *(om hud)* peel.

skalotteløg *et* shallot.

skalp *en* scalp; **skalpere** *v* scalp.

skam *en* shame, dis'grace; *det er en ~* it is a pity; *gøre en til ~me (dvs. overgå)* put· sby in the shade // *adv* really, you know; *det er ~ ikke let* it is not easy, you know; *han gjorde det ~* he really did it.

skamfere *v (beskadige)* damage; *(vansire)* dis'figure.

skamfuld *adj* a'shamed *(over* of; *over at* that).

skamløs *adj* shameless.

skamme *v: ~ sig* be a'shamed *(for at* to; *over* of); *du skulle ~ dig!* you ought to be ashamed of yourself; **~krog** *en: blive sat i ~krogen* be put in the corner.

skammel *en* stool.

skammelig *adj* dis'graceful.

skandale *en* 'scandal; *lave ~* cause a scandal; **~pressen** *s* the gutter press.

skandaløs *adj* 'scandalous.

skandinav *en* Scandi'navian; **Skandinavien** *s* Scandi'navia; **skandinavisk** *adj* Scandi'navian.

skank *en* leg.

skanse *en* en'trenchment; *holde ~n (fig)* hold the fort.

skare *v* crowd, flock.

skarlagensfeber *en* scarlet fever.

skarn *et (snavs)* dirt; *(affald)* rubbish; *(møg)* dung.

skarp *adj* sharp; *(fig om fx hørelse)* keen; *skyde med ~t* shoot· with live ammu'nition; *(fig)* let· fly; *se ~t på en* look keenly at sby; *indstille kameraet ~t* bring· the camera into focus; **~hed** *en* sharpness; keenness; *(foto)* focus; **~ladt** *adj* loaded with live ammu'nition.

skarpsindig *adj* a'cute; *(nøgtern)* shrewd.

skat *en (kostbar ting)* treasure; *(om person)* darling, dear; *(stats~)* tax; *(kommune~)* local tax; *(ejendoms~)* rates *pl; (afgift)* duty; *betale ~ af ngt* pay· tax on sth; *gider du tænde lyset, så er du en ~?* switch on the light, there's a dear!.

skatte... *sms:* **~borger** *en* tax-payer; **~fidus** *en* tax dodge; **~fradrag** *et (på selvangivelse)* de'duction; *(som myndighederne giver)* al'lowance; **~fri** *adj* tax-free; **~frihed** *en* tax e'xemption; **~lettelse** *en* tax re'lief; **~ly** *et* tax haven; **~paradis** *et* tax haven; **~pligtig** *adj (om person)* liable to pay tax; *~pligtig indkomst* taxable income; **~snyd** *et* tax e'vasion; **~væsen** *et* tax au'thorities *pl; ~væsenet* (F) the taxman; **~yder** *en* tax-payer; **~år** *et* fiscal year.

skavank *en* fault; *(mindre)* flaw; *(fysisk)* disa'bility.

ske *en* spoon.

ske *v* happen; *(foregå, finde sted)* take· place; *hvad er der ~t?* what (has) happened? *det kan godt ~ at han har ret* he may· be right; *nu er det ~t med os* we are done for now; *det ~te i påsken* it happened (,took place) at Easter.

skede *en* sheath; *(vagina)* va'gina.

skefuld *en* spoonful.

skel *et (adskillelse)* barrier; *(mellem grunde)* boundary.

skele *v* squint *(til* at); **skelen** *en* squint.

skelet *et* 'skeleton; *(i bygning og fig)* framework.

skelne *v* make· out; *(kende forskel på)* di'stinguish; *~ mellem rødt og grønt* di'stinguish between red and green, tell· red from green.

skeløjet *adj* cross-eyed.

skema *et (skole~ etc)* timetable; *(plan)* schedule; *(diagram)* 'diagram; **~tisk** *adj* sche'matic.

skepsis *en* sceptisism.

skeptisk *adj* sceptical *(over for* of).

ski *en* ski; *stå (,løbe) på ~* ski, go· skiing.

skib *et* ship; *(kirke~)* nave; *(side~ i kirke)* aisle; *sende ngt med ~* send· sth by ship; **~brud** *et* shipwreck; *lide ~brud* be shipwrecked; *(fig, om sag el. person)* fail.

skibs... *sms:* **~bygger** *en* shipbuilder; **~fart** *en (som erhverv)* shipping; *(det at sejle)* navi'gation; **~mægler** *en* shipbroker; **~reder** *en* shipowner; **~rederi** *et* shipping company; **~værft** *et* shipyard.

skid *en* (V) *(fjert)* fart; *(om person)* shit, turd; *slå en ~* fart; *have en ~ på* (V) be pissed.

skide *v* (V) shit·; *~ på ngt* not give a damn about sth; **skide-** (V) bloody; *~ god* bloody good; **~balle** *en: give en en ~balle* take· sby to the laundry; **~fuld** *adj* (V) pissed; **~rik** *en* bastard.

skidragt *en* ski suit.

skidt *et (snavs)* dirt, filth; *(fig, fx om bog)* trash; *~ med det!* never mind! *hele ~et* the whole lot // *adj* bad // *adv* badly; *det går ~* it is not going well; *have det ~* feel· bad; *en ~ fyr* a nasty piece of work.

skifer *en* slate.

skift *et* shift; *(ændring)* change; *arbejde i ~* do· shiftwork; *på ~* in turns; *gøre ngt på ~* take· turns at doing sth.

skifte *et (ændring)* change; *(jur)* di'vision of an e'state // *v* change; *(flytte rundt på)* shift; *(veksle)* alternate; *~ dæk* change a tyre; *~ ble på den lille* change the baby's nappy; *~ mening* change one's mind; *~ tøj* change; *~ ngt ud (med ngt andet)* re'place sth (with sth else); **~holdsarbejde** *et* shiftwork.

skiftende *adj* changing, varying.

skiftenøgle *en* monkey wrench.

skifteramme *en* clip-on picture frame.

skifteret *en (jur)* pro'bate court.

skiftes *v* take· turns; *~ til at gøre ngt* take· turns at doing sth.

skiftetøj *et* a change of clothes.

skiftevis *adv* alternately.

skihop *et* ski jumping; *(hopbakke)* ski jump.

skik *en* custom; *det er ~ og brug* it is customary; *få ~ på ngt* get· sth into shape.

skikkelig *adj* harmless.

skikkelse *en* shape, form; *(tilstand)* state; *(person)* figure; *han har en flot ~* he is well-made; *i ~ af* in the shape of.

skilderhus *et* sentry box.

skildpadde *en* tortoise; *(hav~)* turtle; *forloren ~* mock turtle.

skildre *v (i ord)* de'scribe; *(udmale, afbilde)* de'pict.

skildring *en* de'scription; picture.

skildvagt *en* sentry.

skille *v* separate; *(dele)* di'vide; *(om mælk, sovs etc)* curdle; *blive skilt* be di'vorced; *lade sig ~ fra en* di'vorce sby; *~ ngt ad* separate sth; *(pille fra hinanden)* take· sth to pieces; *~ sig af med ngt* get· rid of sth; **~rum** *et* par'tition.

skilles *v* separate; *(blive skilt)* be di'vorced; *(om ting)* come· a'part; *deres veje skiltes* they went their separate ways.

skillevej *en* crossroads.
skillevæg *en* par'tition (wall).
skilling *en: ikke eje en ~* not have a penny; *tjene ~er (dvs. mange penge)* make· a packet.
skillinge *v: ~ sammen* club together.
skilning *en* parting.
skilmisse *en* di'vorce; *søge ~* ap'ply for a di'vorce; **~barn** *et* child from a broken home.
skilt *et (butiks~)* signboard; *(reklame~)* ad'vertisement board; *(trafik~)* sign; *(vej~)* signpost; *(navne~)* nameplate; *(politi~)* badge.
skilte *v: ~ med ngt* show sth off.
skiltning *en (i trafikken)* signage.
skiløb *et* skiing; **~er** *en* skiier.
skimmel *en (om hest)* grey; *(mug)* mould.
skin *et* light; *(ubehageligt, grelt)* glare.
skind *et* skin; *(huder)* hide; *(om pelsdyr)* coat; *(pelsværk)* fur; *(læder)* leather; *dit ~!* poor thing! *holde sig i ~et* re'strain oneself; *våd til ~et* wet through; *være ved at gå ud af sit gode ~* be be'side one'self; **~handske** *en* leather glove.
skindød *adj* in a state of ap'parent death.
skinger *adj* shrill, highpitched.
skingre *v* shrill; **~nde** *adj* shrill; *~nde skør* raving mad.
skinke *en* ham; *røget ~* smoked ham, gammon.
skinne *en (jernb etc)* rail; *(ben~ etc)* splint; *få sagen sat på ~r (fig)* get· things going.
skinne *v (lyse)* shine·; *lade ngt ~ igennem* hint at sth.
skinneben *et* shin.
skinnebus *en* rail bus.
skinnende *adj* bright, shining; *~ ren* spotless, spick and span.
skinsyg *adj* jealous *(på* of); **~e** *en* jealousy.
skipper *en* skipper.
skisport *en* skiing; **~s·sted** *et* ski(ing) re'sort.
skistav *en* ski stick.
skistøvle *en* ski boot.
skitse *en* sketch; *(til plan)* draft; **~re** *v* sketch; *(fig)* outline.
skive *en (kød, brød, ost etc)* slice; *(rund plade)* disc; *(ur~, tlf)* dial; *(skyde~)* target; *skære brød i ~r* slice bread; **~bremse** *en* disc brake.
skjold *et* shield; *(våben~)* coat of arms; *(plamage, plet)* blotch.
skjoldbruskkirtel *en* thyroid gland.
skjorte *en* shirt; **~bluse** *en* shirt-blouse; **~bryst** *et* shirtfront; **~ærmer** *pl* shirtsleeves.
skjul *et (gemmested)* hiding place; *(ly)* cover; *i ~ (af)* under cover (of); *krybe i ~* seek· shelter; *lege ~* play hide-and-seek; *ikke lægge ~ på ngt* make· no secret of sth.
skjule *v* hide·; *(dække over)* cover up; *~ sig* hide· *(for* from); **~sted** *et* hiding place.
skjult *adj* hidden; *holde ngt ~t* hide· sth; *i det ~e* secretly.
sko *en* shoe; *gå i for små ~ (fig)* be petty-minded // *v (om hest)* shoe; **~børste** *en* shoe brush; **~creme** *en* shoe polish.
skod *et (cigaret~)* fag-end.
skodde *en* shutter.
skodde *v (en cigaret)* stub out; *(med årerne)* back (the oars).
skohorn *et* shoehorn.
skolde *v* scald; *(om solen)* scorch.
skoldkopper *pl* chicken pox.
skole *en* school; *i ~n* at school; *gå i ~* go· to school; *gå ud af ~n* leave· school; *klare sig godt (,dårligt) i ~n* do· well (,badly) at school; *danne ~* be'come· the ac'cepted thing // *v* school, train; **~bestyrer** *en (mand)* headmaster; *(kvinde)* headmistress; **~blad** *et* school magazine; **~bog** *en* schoolbook; **~eksempel** *et* classic e'xample *(på* of); **~elev** *en* pupil; **~gang** *en* schooling; *tvungen ~gang* com'pulsory schooling; **~gård** *en* playground; **~kammerat** *en* school friend; **~køkken** *et (som fag)* do'mestic science; **~lærer** *en* schoolteacher; **~penge** *pl* school fees; **~ridning** *en* dressage; **~skema** *et* timetable; **~skib** *et* training ship; **~taske** *en* school bag; **~tid** *en* school hours; *(dengang man gik i ~)* shooldays; **~træt** *adj* tired of

school; **~vogn** *en* learner car; **~væsen** *et* edu'cation au'thorities *pl;* **~år** *et* school year.
skomager *en* shoemaker.
skopudser *en* shoeblack.
skorpe *en (på brød, jord etc)* crust; *(på ost)* rind; *(på sår)* scab.
skorpion *en* scorpion; *Skorpionen (astr)* Scorpio.
skorsten *en* chimney; *(på skib)* funnel; **~s·fejer** *en* chimney-sweep.
skostiver *en* shoe tree.
skosværte *en* shoe polish.
skotsk *adj* Scottish; *(om person og sprog)* Scots; *(om whisky)* Scotch; **~ternet** *adj* tartan.
skotte *en* Scot(sman *pl:* -men); *hun er ~* she is Scottish (,Scots).
skotøj *et* footwear; **~s·forretning** *en* shoe shop; **~s·æske** *en* shoe box.
skov *en (stor)* forest; *(mindre)* wood; *gå tur i ~en* walk in the woods (,the forest); *det er helt i ~en!* it's neither here nor there! *i ~ og mark* in woods and fields; **~arbejder** *en* forestry worker; **~bevokset** *adj* woody; **~brand** *en* forest fire; **~brug** *et* forestry; **~bund** *en* forest floor; **~døden** *s* the global de'struction of the forests (due to pollution).
skove *v* cut· down trees.
skovfoged *en* ranger.
skovgrænsen *s* the timber line.
skovhugger *en* lumberjack.
skovjordbær *et* wild strawberry.
skovl *en* shovel; *(lille)* scoop; *(på gravemaskine)* bucket; *få ~en under en* get· sby where you want him (,her); **~e** *v* shovel, scoop; *~e penge ind* make· loads (of money); *~e (mad) i sig* scoff down (food).
skovrider *en* forester.
skovskade *en (fugl)* jay.
skovsnegl *en* black slug.
skovstrækning *en* woodland.
skovsvin *et* litter lout.
skovtur *en (med madkurv)* picnic; *(uden madkurv)* walk in the woods.
skrabe *v* scrape; *(kradse)* scratch; *~ østers* dredge for oysters.
skraber *en* scraper.
skrabet *adj (om fx budget)* cut (down), re'duced; *brød med ~ smør* bread and scrape.
skrabeæg *et* free-range egg.
skrald *et (om torden etc)* clap, crash; *(om trompet, eksplosion etc)* blast; *(affald)* rubbish; *(køkkenaffald)* garbage.
skralde *en* rattle // *v (runge)* peal.
skraldebøtte *en* dustbin, rubbish bin.
skraldemand *en* garbage man *(pl:* -men).
skraldepose *en (lille)* bin liner.
skramle *v* rattle; *~ med ngt* rattle sth; **~kasse** *en (om bil)* banger; **skramlen** *en* rattling.
skramme *en* scratch; *være ude på ~r* be asking for it // *v* scratch.
skrammel *et* junk, rubbish; **~legeplads** *en* ad'venture playground.
skrammet *adj* scratched.
skranke *en (disk)* counter; *(barriere)* barrier, bar.
skrante *v* be ailing, be sickly; **~nde** *adj* ailing, sickly.
skrap *adj (hård, streng)* hard; *(anstrengende, vanskelig)* tough; *(urimelig, ubehagelig)* stiff; *(dygtig)* smart; *(om ord, tale)* sharp; *(om smag)* strong; *det er vel nok ~t!* it is a bit stiff (,thick)! *det var en ~ omgang* it was tough going; *være ~ til ngt* be a wizard at sth.
skratte *v* rattle; *(skurre)* grate; *(om pen, negl)* scratch.
skravere *v* hatch; **skravering** *en* hatching.
skred *et (jord~, også fig)* landslide; *(lavine)* avalanche; *komme i ~ (om bil)* go· into a skid; *(fig, komme i gang)* get· going.
skribent *en* writer.
skride *v (glide)* slip; *(om bil etc)* skid; *(gå sin vej)* bugger off; *skrid!* get lost! *~ frem (om arbejde etc)* make· progress; *~ ind mod ngt* take· action against sth; *~ ud (om bil)* skid.
skridsikker *adj* non-skid.
skridt *et* step; *(i bukser og anat)* crotch; *med raske ~* at a brisk pace; *tage det første ~ (fig)* take· the first step, make· the first move; *på syv*

~s afstand at a distance of seven paces; *holde en tre ~ fra livet* keep· sby at arm's length.
skrift *en* writing; *(hånd~)* handwriting // *et (publikation)* publi'cation; *(afhandling, artikel)* paper; *hans samlede ~er* his col'lected works.
skrifte *v* con'fess; **~mål** *et* con'fession; **~stol** *en* con'fessional.
skriftlig *adj* written, in writing.
skriftsprog *et* written language.
skrig *et (råb, kalden)* cry; *(højt)* scream; *(hyl)* yell; *give et ~* cry out, scream; *det er sidste ~* it is the latest.
skrige *v (råbe, kalde)* cry; *(højt)* scream; *(hyle)* yell; *~ op* cry out; yell; **~n** *en* crying; screaming; yelling; **~nde** *adj* crying; *(om farve)* loud.
skrin *et (lille)* box; *(større)* chest; *hun stak ham en på ~et* she landed him one; **~lægge** *v* shelve.
skrive *v* write·; *(på maskine)* type; *~ ngt af* copy sth; *~ efter ngt* write· for sth; *~ med blyant (etc)* write· in pencil (etc); *NATO ~s med store bogstaver* NATO is written in capital letters; *~ ngt ned (,op)* write· sth down; *blive skrevet op til ngt* have one's name put down for sth; *~ til en* write· sby; *~ ngt under* sign sth; *i ~nde stund* at writing; **~blok** *en* writing pad; **~bord** *et* desk; **~hjul** *et (på printer etc)* daisy wheel, print wheel.
skrivelse *en* letter.
skrivemaskine *en* typewriter; *skrive på ~* type.
skrivepapir *et* notepaper.
skriveunderlag *et* blotting pad.
skrivning *en* writing.
skrog *et (af skib)* hull; *(af fly)* fuselage; *(af æble)* core; *(af kylling etc)* carcase; *(om stakkel)* poor thing.
skrot *et* scrap (iron); **~te** *v* scrap.
skrubbe *en (fisk)* flounder; *(børste)* scrubber // *v* scrub; *skrub af!* get lost! scram!
skrubtudse *en* toad; *have en ~ i halsen* have a frog in one's throat.
skrue *en* screw; *han har en ~ løs* he is not all there // *v* screw; *~ ngt fast* screw sth up; *~ ngt løs* un'screw sth; *~ ned for radioen* turn down the radio; *~ op for gassen* turn up the gas; **~blyant** *en* pro'pelling pencil; **~brækker** *en* scab; **~is** *en* pack ice; **~låg** *et* screw top; **~nøgle** *en* spanner; **~stik** *en* vice; **~trækker** *en* screwdriver; **~tvinge** *en* clamp.
skrummel *et* mon'strosity.
skrumpe *v: ~ (ind)* shrink·.
skrupel *en* scruple; *have skrupler* have scruples; **~løs** *adj* un'scrupulous.
skrupforvirret *adj (kronisk)* scatter-brained; *(akut)* flustered.
skrupgrine *v* laugh one's head off.
skrupskør *adj* nuts.
skrupsulten *adj* famished.
skryde *v (om æsel)* bray; *(prale)* brag.
skrædder *en* tailor; *(dame~)* dress-maker; **~kridt** *et* tailor's chalk; **~saks** *en* tailor's shears *pl;* **~stilling** *en: sidde i ~stilling* sit· cross-legged; **~syet** *adj* tailored; *(fig)* tailor-made; **~syning** *en (til herrer)* tailoring; *(til damer)* dressmaking.
skræk *en (frygt)* fear; *(rædsel)* terror; *(pludseligt chok)* fright, scare; *den unge er en ~* that kid is a menace; *af ~ for* for fear of; *af ~ for at* for fear that; *til min ~ kom han* to my great horror he came; *være ved at dø af ~* be scared stiff; *ryste af ~* tremble with fear; *jage en en ~ i livet* give· sby a fright; **~indjagende** *adj* terrifying.
skrækkelig *adj* terrible, awful // *adv* terribly, awfully.
skrækslagen *adj* terror-stricken.
skræl *en* peel; *(på banan)* skin.
skrælle *v* peel; **~kniv** *en* paring knife *(pl:* knives).
skræmme *v* frighten, scare; *du skræmte mig* you gave me a fright; **~skud** *et* warning shot.
skrænt *en* slope.
skræppe *v (om and)* quack; *~ op* cackle.
skræve *v* straddle; *~ over ngt* stride· over sth; *(sidde overskrævs på)* straddle sth.
skrøbelig *adj* fragile; *(om person)* frail; **~hed** *en* fra'gility; frailty.

skrøne *en* fairytale.
skrå *en (tobak)* chewing to'bacco // *v* chew to'bacco; *~ over gaden* cross the street // *adj* slanting, sloping; *på ~* o'bliquely; *klippe stof på ~* cut· material on the bias; *lægge hovedet på ~* cock one's head; *~t op!* (F) stuff it! **-bånd** *et* bias strip; *(i metermål)* bias binding.
skrål *et* bawl, yell; **-e** *v* bawl, yell.
skråne *v* slant, slope.
skråning *en* slope.
skråplan *et (fys)* in'clined plane; *komme ind på et ~ (fig)* leave· the straight and narrow.
skråstreg *en* slash.
skråtobak *en* chewing to'bacco.
skub *et* push; *sætte ~ i ngt* get· sth moving.
skubbe *v* push; *~ til en* push sby.
skud *et* shot; *(af plante)* shoot; *han måtte stå for ~* he came· under fire; *~ på mål (fodb)* goal kick; *et ~ i tågen* a shot in the dark.
skude *en* ship, boat.
skudhold *s: på (,uden for) ~* with'in (out of) range.
skudsikker *adj* bulletproof; *(fig)* cast-iron.
skudt *adj: være ~ i en* have a crush on sby.
skudår *et* leap year.
skuespil *et* play; **-forfatter** *en* playwright, dramatist.
skuespiller *en (mand)* actor; *(kvinde)* actress.
skuffe *en* drawer // *v (gøre skuffet)* disap'point; *~ sne* shovel snow; *~ havegangen* weed the garden path; *blive ~t over ngt* be disap'pointed at (,in) sth; *~t over en* disap'pointed with sby; **-jern** *et* (Dutch) hoe.
skuffelse *en* disap'pointment.
skulder *en* shoulder; *trække på ~en* shrug; **-blad** *et* shoulder blade; **-bredde** *en (mål)* shoulders; **-strop** *en* shoulder strap **-taske** *en* shoulder bag.
skule *v* scowl *(til* at); **skulen** *en* scowl.
skulle *v (være nødt til)* have to, must·; *(have ordre til)* must·, be to; *(burde)* ought· to; *(råd man giver)* should·; *(siges at være)* is (,are) said to be; *jeg skal altså nå det til tiden!* I must make it in time! *jeg skal tisse* I have to pee; *jeg skal møde ham på stationen* I am to meet him at the station; *de ~ være her nu* they ought to be here now; *det ~ du have sagt før* you should have said that be'fore; *han skal være en god læge* he is said to be a good doctor; *hvad skal vi gøre?* what are we (going) to do? *skal jeg komme?* do· you want me to come? *skal du ngt i morgen?* are you doing anything to'morrow? *hvad ~ det være? (i butik)* can I help you? *hvad skal det være? (dvs. forestille)* what is that sup'posed to be? *vi skal af næste gang* we are getting off at the next stop; *hvor skal vi hen?* where are we going? *hvad skal vi her?* what are we doing here? *vi ~ lige til at gå* we were just leaving; *han skal til at gå i skole* he is starting school; *der skal mere til for at...* it takes more to...; *vi skal ud i aften* we are going out to'night.
skulptur *en* 'sculpture.
skum *et* foam; *(på øl)* froth; **-bad** *et* foam bath; **-gummi** *en* foam rubber.
skumme *v* foam; froth; *(~ fløde af mælk etc)* skim.
skummel *adj* sinister; *(mørk, dyster)* gloomy; *vi omgås med skumle planer om at...* we are secretly planning to...
skummetmælk *en* skimmed milk.
skumring *en* twilight.
skumslukker *en* foam ex'tinguisher.
skumsprøjt *et* spray.
skur *et* shed; *(neds om hus)* shack.
skure *v* scrub; **-børste** *en* scrubbing brush, scrubber; **-pulver** *et* scouring powder.
skurk *en* scoundrel; *(teat etc)* villain; *din lille ~!* you little rascal!
skurre *v* jar; *~ i ørerne* jar on the ear; **skurren** *en* jarring.
skurvogn *en sv.t.* building workers' hut.
skvadderhoved *et* fool, twit.
skvadre *v* blether.

skvat *et* softy, sissy.
skvatte *v* fall·.
skvattet *adj* wet.
skvulpe *v (om bølger)* lap; *(plaske)* splash; *~ over* splash over.
skvæt *et: et ~ maling (,kaffe etc)* a spot of paint (,coffee etc).
sky *en* cloud; *(kødsaft)* gravy; *(stivnet kødsaft)* jelly; *han var helt oppe i ~erne* he was on cloud nine; *rose en til ~erne* praise sby to the skies // *adj* shy; **~brud** *et* cloudburst.
skyde *v (med våben)* shoot·; *(puffe)* push; *(gro, spire; ~ på mål)* shoot·; *~ genvej* take· a short cut; *~ af* fire; *~ efter en* shoot· at sby; *~ forbi* miss; *blive skudt ned* be gunned down; *(om fly)* be shot down; *~ på ngt* shoot· at sth; *~ skylden på en* put· the blame on sby; *jeg vil ~ på at...* my guess is that...; *~ 50 kr. til* con'tribute 50 kr.; *~ ngt ud (dvs. skubbe)* push sth out; *(dvs. udsætte)* put· sth off; **~bane** *en* shooting range; **~dør** *en* sliding door.
skyder *en (våben)* gun, shooter; *(slå)* slide.
skyderi *et* shooting.
skydeskive *en* target.
skydespænde *et* hair slide.
skydevindue *et (i typisk brit stil)* sash window.
skydevåben *et* firearm.
skydning *en* shooting, fire; *(typ)* leading ['lɛdiŋ].
skydække *et* cloud ceiling.
skyet *adj* cloudy.
skyfri *adj* cloudless, clear.
skygge *en* shadow; *(mods: sol)* shade; *(på hat)* brim; *30 grader i ~n* thirty de'grees in the shade; *ikke ~n af et bevis* not the slightest proof; *kaste en ~ over ngt* cast· a shadow on sth // *v* shade; *(udspionere)* tail; *~ for ngt* shade sth; *~ for en* stand· in sby's light; **~fuld** *adj* shady; **~kabinet** *et* shadow 'cabinet; **~side** *en (om måne etc)* dark side; *på livets ~side* on the dark side of life.
skyld *en (skyldfølelse; det at være skyldig)* guilt; *(fejl)* fault; *(ansvar)* blame; *få ~ for ngt* get· the blame for sth; *det er ikke min ~* it is not my fault; *give en ~en for ngt* blame sby for sth; *det er din egen ~* you have only your'self to blame; *for din ~* for your sake; *(på grund af dig)* be'cause of you; *for fredens ~* for the sake of peace; *for en gangs ~* for once; *for en ordens ~* as a matter of form; *for en sikkerheds ~* to be on the safe side; *for sjovs ~* for fun; *være ~ i ngt* be guilty of sth; **~bevidst** *adj* guilty.
skylde *v* owe; *du ~r mig at gøre det* you owe it to me to do it; *~ en 500 kr.* owe sby 500 kr.
skyldes *v* be due to; *(stamme fra)* stem from.
skyldig *adj* guilty; *erkende sig ~* plead guilty *(i* of); *ikke ~* not guilty *(i* of); *det ~e beløb* the a'mount owing; *der bliver jeg dig svar ~* there you have me.
skylle *en (af regn)* downpour // *v (vasketøj, hår etc)* rinse; *(i wc'et)* flush; *~ i land* be washed a'shore; *det ~de ned* it was pouring down; *~ væk* be washed away; **~middel** *et (ved vask)* con'ditioner, softener.
skynde *v: ~ på en* urge sby to hurry up; *~ sig* hurry; *skynd dig!* hurry up! *~ sig at gøre ngt* hasten to do sth.
skympumpe *en* waterspout.
skyskraber *en* skyscraper.
skysovs *en* gravy.
skyts *et* guns *pl; tungt ~* heavy ar'tillery; *køre frem med det tunge ~ (fig)* bring· up one's big guns; **~engel** *en* guardian angel; **~helgen** *en* patron saint.
skytte *en (person der skyder)* rifleman *(pl: -*men), shot; *(ansat, fx på gods)* gamekeeper; *han er en god ~* he is a good shot; *Skytten (astr)* Sagit'tarius; **~grav** *en* trench.
skæbne *en* fate; *~n* fate; *(tilfældet)* chance; *~n ville at de tabte slaget* they were destined to lose the battle; *det var skæbnens ironi at...* by a curious irony...
skæbnesvanger *adj* di'sastrous, fatal.
skæg *et* beard; *(over~)* mou'stache;

(kind~) whiskers *pl; (sjov)* fun; *få ~, lade ~get stå* grow· a beard (ˌmou'stache); *~ og ballade* fun and games; *lave ~ med en (dvs. drille)* have sby on; *(have det sjovt med)* have fun with sby // *adj* funny; *det var mægtig ~* it was great fun; **~get** *adj* bearded; *(med skægstubbe)* un'shaven; **~stubbe** *pl* stubble.

skæl *et (på fisk etc)* scale; *(i håret)* dandruff.

skælde *v* scold; *~ en ud for ngt* call sby sth; *~ en ud over ngt* scold sby for sth; *~ ud over ngt* be angry about sth.

skældsord *et* swearword ['swɛə-].

skældud *s* scolding.

skælve *v* tremble, shake· *(af* with); *(af kulde el. gys)* shiver; **~n** *en* trembling, shaking; shivering.

skæmme *v* blemish; *(stærkt, vansire)* dis'figure.

skæmt *en* jest; **~e** *v* jest.

skænd *s: få ~* be scolded; *give en ~* give· sby a scolding.

skænde *v (skælde ud)* scold; *(voldtage)* violate; *(helligt sted etc)* desecreate.

skænderi *et* argument, row [rau].

skændes *v* argue, have a row [rau]; *hold op med at ~!* stop arguing! *komme op at ~* start a row; *~ med en om ngt* quarrel with sby about sth.

skændig *adj* dis'graceful.

skændsel *en* dis'grace.

skænk *en (møbel)* sideboard; *(i restaurant)* buffet; *(drink)* drink.

skænke *v (give)* give·; *(hælde op)* pour; *~ en ngt* give· sby sth (as a present); *han ~de det aldrig en tanke at…* it never oc'curred to him that…; *~ sin formue væk* give· away one's fortune; *~ teen* pour the tea; *~ for en* pour sby a drink (etc); *~ i koppen* fill the cup; **~stue** *en* taproom, bar.

skær *et (klippe~)* rock; *(lys~)* gleam; *(glød)* glow; *(stærkt, grelt lys)* glare; *(nuance, anstrøg)* touch; *klare ~ene (fig)* pull through // *adj (ren)* pure; *(klar)* clear; *ren og ~ indbildning* sheer imagi'nation; *~t kød* low-fat meat with no bones.

skære *v* cut·; *~ ansigt* pull faces; *(af væmmelse)* make· a wry face; *~ tænder* grit one's teeth; *~ af* cut· off; *~ for* carve; *~ i ngt* cut· sth; *~ ngt i skiver* slice sth; *~ ngt i stykker* cut· sth; *~ ned på forbruget* cut· down on the con'sumption; *~ halsen over på en* cut· sby's throat; *~ sig* cut· oneself; *~ sig i fingeren* cut· one's finger; **~brænder** *en* cutting torch; **~bræt** *et (til brød)* breadboard; *(til steg)* carving board.

skærende *adj* cutting; *(om stemme)* shrill; *(om lys etc)* glaring.

skærgård *en* archi'pelago.

skæring *en (nummer fra LP)* cut.

skærm *en* screen; *(edb)* monitor, dis'play; *(på bil, cykel)* mudguard; **~e** *v (beskytte)* pro'tect *(mod* from).

skærmterminal *en (edb)* visual dis'play unit, VDU.

skærpe *v* sharpen; *(gøre skrappere)* tighten; *~ appetitten* whet one's appetite; *~ reglerne* tighten rules; *~nde omstændigheder* aggravating circumstances; **~lse** *en* sharpening; tightening.

skærsilden *s* purgatory.

skærtorsdag *en* Maundy Thursday.

skæv *adj* o'blique, slanting; *(om fx næse)* crooked; *(ulige)* un'equal; *(ensidig)* lopsided; *(påvirket af stoffer)* high; *et ~t smil* a wry smile; *~e øjne* slanted eyes; *(se også skævt);* **~benet** *adj* crooked-legged.

skæve *v: ~ til en* look at sby out of the corner of one's eye.

skævhed *en* crookedness; *(fejl)* fault; *(ulighed)* ine'quality.

skævt *adv* a'wry; *(på skrå)* a'slant; *(forkert)* wrongly; *(ulige)* un'equally; *billedet hænger ~* the picture is not straight; *gå ~* go· wrong; *se ~ til en* look a'skance at sby.

skød *et* lap, knee; *(fig)* bosom; *sidde på ~et hos en* sit· on sby's lap; *sidde med hænderne i ~et* sit· back (and take it easy).

skøde *et (jur)* deed.

skødehund *en* lap-dog.
skødesløs *adj (om person)* careless; *(forsømmelig)* negligent; *~ påklædning (ikke neds!)* casual wear.
skøjte *en* skate; *løbe på ~r* skate, be skating; **-bane** *en* skating rink; **-løb** *et* skating; **-løber** *en* skater.
skøn *et (vurdering)* estimate; *(mening)* o'pinion; *danne sig et ~ over ngt* make· an estimate of sth; *handle efter bedste ~* act to the best of one's judgement // *adj (smuk, dejlig)* lovely, beautiful; *vi har det ~t (dvs. vi nyder det)* we are having a good time; *(dvs. vi har det godt)* we are fine; *en ~ne dag* one day; *(ud i fremtiden)* one of these days; *de ~ne kunster* the fine arts.
skønhed *en* beauty; **-s·fejl** *en* blemish, flaw; **-s·klinik** *en* beauty parlour; **-s·plet** *en* mole; **-s·præparat** *et* cos'metic.
skønlitteratur *en* fiction.
skønne *v (vurdere)* estimate; *(mene)* judge; *(efter undersøgelse)* find·; *så vidt man kan ~* to all ap'pearances; *~ om ngt* estimate sth; *(danne sig en mening)* judge sth; *~ på ngt* ap'preciate sth.
skønsmæssig *adj* estimated; **-t** *adv* on an estimate.
skønt *konj* (al)though.
skør *adj (skrøbelig)* fragile; *(tosset)* crazy *(med* about); *blive ~* go· crazy.
skørbug *en* scurvy.
skørt *et (nederdel)* skirt; *(under~)* underskirt, slip; **-e·jæger** *en* womanizer.
skål *en* bowl, basin; *(en ~ for en)* toast; *udbringe en ~ for en* drink· to sby; *~ for os!* here's to us! **-e** *v* touch glasses *(med* with); *~e for en* drink· to sby.
skåne *v* spare; *(passe godt på)* be careful about; *skån mig for dine kommentarer!* spare me your comments! **-kost** *en* light diet.
skånsom *adj* gentle; **-hed** *en* gentleness.
skår *et (hak)* clip; *(i fx tallerken)* chip; *(fx glas~)* broken piece; *et skår i glæden* a fly in the ointment; *et sejt ~* (F, *om pige, fyr)* a crumpet; **-et** *adj (om fx tallerken)* chipped.
sladder *en* gossip; **-hank** *en* telltale; **-kælling** *en* gossip.
sladre *v (snakke)* gossip; *(angive)* tell· tales *(om* about); *~ om en* tell· on sby; *du må ikke ~ om det!* don't tell! mum's the word!
slag *et (enkelt ~ fx med hånden)* blow; *(med kølle, ketsjer, om ur)* stroke; *(psykisk)* blow, shock; *(cape)* cape; *(i krig)* battle; *(i kortspil)* game; *et ~ i luften* an empty gesture; *på ~et syv* at 7 o'clock sharp; *det var et ~ i ansigtet* it was a slap in the face; *~et på Reden* the Battle of Copenhagen; **-bas** *en* stringbass; **-bor** *et* per'cussion drill; **-fast** *adj* shock-proof.
slagger *pl (af kul etc)* cinders.
slagkraftig *adj* powerful.
slagmark *en* battlefield.
slagord *et* buzzword, slogan.
slagplan *en* plan of action.
slags *en* sort, kind; *han er en ~ guru* he is a kind of guru; *den ~ ting* that sort of thing; *hvad ~ bil har du?* what sort of car do you have? *i al ~ vejr* in all sorts of weather.
slagside *en: få ~* take· a list; *(fig)* get· out of pro'portion.
slagskib *et* battleship.
slagsmål *et* fight; *komme i ~* start fighting.
slagte *v* slaughter, kill; *(brutalt)* butcher; **-kvæg** *et* beef cattle.
slagter *en* butcher.
slagteri *et* slaughterhouse.
slagtesvin *et* porker.
slagtilfælde *et* stroke.
slagtning *en* slaughter(ing).
slagtøj *et (mus)* per'cussion; **-spiller** *en* per'cussionist.
slalom *en* slalom; *stor~* giant slalom.
slam *et* mud; *(kloak~)* sludge.
slange *en (zo)* snake; *(af gummi, plast etc)* tube; *(i bil, cykel)* inner tube; *(have~, støvsuger~)* hose // *v: ~ sig* sprawl; **-bøsse** *en* catapult; **-krøller** *pl* corkscrew curls; **-skind** *et* snakeskin.
slank *adj* slim; *bevare den ~e linje* keep· one's figure.

slanke *v: ~ sig (dvs. blive tyndere)* grow· thinner; *(dvs. ved diæt)* slim; *fiberkost ~r* a high-fibre diet is slimming; **~kost** *en* slimming diet; **~kur** *en* slimming regimen.
slap *adj* slack, loose; *(kraftløs)* limp; *(fig)* slack; **~hed** *en* slackness, looseness; limpness.
slappe *v* slacken, loosen; *(afslappe)* re'lax; *~ af* re'lax.
slapper *en (pol)* dove.
slapsvans *en* weakling, softy.
slaske *v* flap.
slatten *adj* limp.
slave *en* slave *(af* to); **~arbejde** *et (fig, fx om jobbet)* drudgery; **~handel** *en* slave trade.
slaveri *et* slavery.
slavisk *adj (nøjagtig)* slavish; *(om folk, sprog)* Slavic.
slem *adj* bad; *være ~ ved en* be hard on sby; *være ~ til at glemme* have a tendency to for'get.
slentre *v* stroll; **~n** *en* strolling.
slesk *adj (krybende)* grovelling, fawning; **~e** *v: ~e for en* grovel be'fore sby, fawn on sby.
slet *adj (dårlig)* bad; *(ond)* wicked // *adv* badly, wickedly; *~ ikke* not at all; *~ ingen* nobody at all; *~ ingen penge* no money at all; *~ intet* nothing at all.
slette *en* plain // *v* strike· out; *(med viskelæder)* rub out; *(på bånd og edb)* e'rase; *(annullere)* cancel; **~bånd** *et* cor'rection tape.
slev *en* ladle.
slibe *v (gøre skarp)* sharpen; *(polere)* polish; *(tildanne)* grind·; **~maskine** *en* grinding ma'chine; **~sten** *en* grindstone; **~stål** *et (til knive)* sharpening steel.
slibning *en* sharpening; grinding; polishing *(se slibe).*
slibrig *adj* lewd.
slid *et (mas)* hard work, toil; *(på ting)* wear; **~bane** *en (på dæk)* tread.
slide *v (arbejde)* work hard, toil; *(ved brug)* wear·; *~ i det* slave away; *~ op* wear· out; *~ sig ihjel* work oneself to death.
slider *en* hard worker; *(læsehest)* swot.
slidgigt *en* ar'throsis.
slids *en (i tøj)* slit; *(i jakke, frakke)* vent.
slidstærk *adj* hard-wearing.
slidt *adj* worn; *(luv~)* threadbare; *~ op* worn out.
slik *et* sweets *pl; købe ngt for en ~* buy· sth for a song; **~butik** *en* sweet shop.
slikke *v* lick; *(spise slik)* eat· sweets; *~ solskin* bask in the sun; *~ på ngt* lick sth.
slikken *adj være ~* have a sweet tooth.
slikkepind *en* lollipop.
slim *et* slime; *(i næse, hals)* mucus; *(opspyt)* phlegm.
slimet *adj* slimy.
slimhinde *en* mucous membrane.
slingre *v (om bil etc)* sway; *(om hjul)* wobble; *(om fuld person)* reel; **slingren** *en* swaying; wobble; reeling.
slip *et (pause)* pause; *give ~ på ngt* let· go of sth.
slippe *v (~ ngt)* let· go of; *(tabe)* drop; *(give slip)* let· go; *(~ fri for)* get· off; *~ af med* get· rid of; *~ af sted* get· away; *~ for ngt* e'scape sth; *(undgå med vilje)* a'void sth; *~ fra en* get· away from sby; *~ godt fra ngt (dristigt el. frækt)* get· away with sth; *(fra ulykke etc)* have a lucky e'scape; *~ en ind* let· sby in; *~ løs* break· loose; *~ ngt løs* let· sth loose; *~ med en bøde* get· off with a fine; *~ op* come· to an end; *benzinen er sluppet op* we have run out of petrol; *~ ud* get· out; *(om hemmelighed etc)* leak out; *~ en ud* let· sby out.
slips *et* tie; **~e·nål** *en* tie pin, tie clasp.
slitage *en* wear (and tear).
slot *et* castle; *(kongeligt)* palace; *(herregård)* manor house; **~s·plads** *en* palace square; **~s·ruin** *en* ruined castle.
slubbert *en* scoundrel; *(om barn)* rascal.
slubre *v* slurp; *(om sko)* flap.
slud *en* sleet.
sludder *et* nonsense, rubbish; *(samtale)* chat; *sige ngt ~* talk nonsense; ~

og vrøvl rubbish; *slå en* ~ *af med en* have a chat with sby.

sludre *v* chat; *(vrøvle)* talk nonsense; **~hoved** *et* blabber, chatterbox.

sluge *v* swallow; *(æde grådigt)* gulp down; *(forbruge)* con'sume *(fx benzin* petrol); ~ *en bog* de'vour a book; ~ *maden* gulp down one's food; ~ *ngt råt (fig)* swallow sth hook, line and sinker.

slughals *en* glutton.

slugt *en* gorge.

slukke *v (om ild)* put· out; *(om lys, radio etc)* turn off; ~ *tørsten* quench one's thirst.

slukning *en* putting out; *(om brandvæsen)* fire-fighting; **~s·apparat** *et* fire-ex'tinguisher.

slukøret *adj* down in the dumps, with one's tail between one's legs.

slum(kvarter) *et* slum (district).

slump *s: på* ~ at random.

slumrende *adj* dormant; *væk ikke den* ~ *løve* let· sleeping dogs lie.

slumstormer *en* squatter.

slurk *en* swallow, gulp.

sluse *en* sluice; *(til at sejle igennem)* lock // *v:* ~ *folk ind* let· people in.

slut *s* end // *adj* over; *(færdig)* finished, at an end; *til* ~ finally; **~fase** *en* final stages *pl*, **~kamp** *en (sport)* final.

slutning *en* end; *(afslutning)* con'clusion; *(i bog, film)* ending; *i ~en af tyverne* in the late twenties; *mod ~en af ngt* to'wards the end of sth.

slutopgørelse *en* final settlement.

slutresultat *et* final re'sult.

slutrunde *en (sport)* final(s).

slutte *v* end, finish; *(indgå, fx forlig)* enter into; *(konkludere)* con'clude; ~ *fred* make· peace; ~ *af med at gøre ngt* finish up by doing sth; ~ *sig sammen* u'nite; *(om firmaer)* merge; ~ *sig til en* join sby; ~ *sig til hvad en siger* go· a'long with sby; ~ *en lampe til* con'nect a lamp.

sluttet *adj: i* ~ *trop* in a body.

slynge *en* sling // *v* sling·, fling·; ~ *sig* wind·; *(om å, flod)* me'ander; ~ *om sig med ngt* bandy sth about.

slyngel *en* scoundrel.

slyngplante *en* climber.

slæb *et (på kjole)* train; *(arbejde)* hard work; *(besvær)* trouble; *have en på* ~ have sby in tow.

slæbe *v (med besvær)* drag; *(bugsere)* tow; *(arbejde hårdt)* work hard; ~ *på fødderne* drag one's feet; ~ *sig af sted* drag along; **~båd** *en* tug.

slæbende *adj (om fødder)* shuffling; *(om stemme)* slow.

slæbetov *et* towrope.

slæde *en* sledge; *(kælk)* to'boggan; *køre i* ~ go· sledging; **~hund** *en* husky.

slægt *en* family; *være i* ~ *med en* be re'lated to sby; ~ *og venner* kith and kin; **~e** *v: ~e en på* take· after sby.

slægtning *en* relative.

slægtsforskning *en* gene'alogy.

slægtskab *et* re'lationship; *(samfølelse, beslægtethed)* af'finity.

slægtsnavn *et* family name.

slække *v* slacken; ~ *på reglerne* re'lax the rules.

slæng *et* crowd, set; **~e** *v* throw·, fling·.

sløj *adj (ikke rask)* un'well, poorly; *(ringe)* poor.

sløjd *en* woodwork.

sløjfe *en* bow; *(fig, om linje etc)* loop // *v (nedrive)* de'molish; *(nedslægge, afskaffe)* a'bolish; *(udelade)* leave· out.

slør *et* veil; *(i bilrat)* play; *(i hjul)* wobble; *løfte ~et for ngt* re'veal sth; **~e** *v* blur; *(om lys)* dim; *med ~et stemme* in a husky voice.

sløse *v (ødsle)* waste; *(sjuske)* be slovenly; **~ri** *et* negligence.

sløv *adj (om person, forestilling etc)* dull; *(ligeglad)* apa'thetic; *(søvnig, døsig)* drowzy; *(om kniv)* blunt.

sløve *v* dull; **~nde** *adj (om arbejde)* dulling; *pillerne kan virke ~nde* the pills may make you drowzy.

sløvhed *en* 'lethargy; *(om kniv)* bluntness.

slå *en* bolt; *skyde ~en for* bolt the door; *skyde ~en fra* un'bolt the door.

slå *v* beat·; *(enkelt slag)* hit·; *(om ur)*

strike·; *(~ hårdt)* knock; *(støde imod så det gør ondt)* hurt·; *(gøre indtryk på)* strike·; *~ fejl* go· wrong; *~ græsplænen* mow the lawn; *~ igen* hit· back; *~ igennem (om fx kunstner)* get· known; *~ en ihjel* kill sby; *~ med nakken* toss one's head; *~ en med en kæp* hit· sby with a stick; *~ en ned* knock sby down; *~ et oprør ned* sup'press a re'bellion; *~ blikket ned* cast· down one's eyes; *det slog ned i mig at...* it suddenly oc'curred to me that...; *lynet slog ned* the lightning struck; *~ om (om vejr)* change; *(om vind)* shift; *~ bogen op* open the book; *~ ngt op i ordbogen* look sth up in the dictionary; *~ op med en* break· with sby; *~ liggestolen op* fold up the deckchair; *~ til (dvs. slå hårdt)* hit· out; *(dvs. være nok)* be suf'ficient; *(dvs. gå i opfyldelse)* come· true; *morderen har ~et til igen* the killer has struck again; *~ ud (dvs. få udslæt)* come· out in a rash; *~ en ud* knock sby out; *(besejre)* beat· sby; *~ sig* hurt· oneself; *planken har ~et sig (dvs. er skæv)* the plank is warped; *~ sig ned (sætte sig)* sit· down; *(i by etc)* settle down; *~ sig på flasken* hit· the bottle.

slåen *en (bot)* sloe.

slående *adj (om lighed)* striking; *(om fx argument)* con'vincing.

slåfejl *en (i ngt maskinskrevet)* typing error.

slåmaskine *en* mower.

slå om-nederdel *en* wrap-around skirt.

slås *v* fight·; *~ med en* fight· (with) sby; *~ med ngt* struggle with sth; *~ om ngt* fight· over sth.

smadre *v* smash (up).

smag *en* taste; *(let, lækker ~)* flavour; *enhver sin ~* everyman to his taste; *det er ikke min ~* it is not my cup of tea; *det er lige efter min ~* it is e'xactly to my taste; *få ~ for ngt* ac'quire a taste for sth; *falde i ens ~* be to sby's taste.

smage *v* taste; *det ~r af citron* it tastes of lemon; *~ på ngt* taste sth; *~ til med krydderier* add spices to taste.

smagfuld *adj* in good taste.

smagløs *adj* in bad taste.

smagsprøve *en* sample.

smagssag *en: det er en ~* it is a matter of taste.

smagsstof *et* flavouring; *tilsat kunstigt ~* arti'ficial flavouring added.

smal *adj* narrow; *det er en ~ sag* it is quite simple; **~film** *en* cine-film; **~filmskamera** *et* cine-camera; **~sporet** *adj (om person)* narrow-minded.

smaragd *en* emerald.

smart *adj* smart; *lige lovlig ~* too clever by half.

smaske *v* eat· noisily.

smattet *adj* slippery.

smed *en (grov~)* blacksmith; *(klejn~)* locksmith; **~e** *v* forge; *~e mens jernet er varmt* strike· while the iron is hot; **~e·jern** *et* wrought iron.

smedje *en* smithy.

smelte *v* melt; *~ ngt om* melt sth down; **~ost** *en* 'processed cheese; **~punkt** *et* melting point; **~vand** *et* melt-water.

smeltning *en* melting.

smerte *en* pain; *have ~r* be in pain; *have mange ~r* be in a lot of pain; *have ~r i ryggen* have a pain in one's back // *v (gøre ondt)* ache; *(bedrøve)* grieve; **~fri** *adj* painless; **~fuld** *adj* painful; **~lig** *adj (ubehagelig)* painful; *(sørgelig)* sad; **~stillende** *adj* pain-killing; *~stillende middel* painkiller.

smide *v* throw·, (F) chuck; *(let, overlegent, fx om bold)* toss; *(voldsomt)* fling·; *~ med sten* throw· stones; *~ sig ned* fall· down flat; *~ en ud* throw· sby out; *~ ngt ud (,væk)* throw· sth away, (F) chuck sth out.

smidig *adj* supple; *(om materiale)* plastic; *(fig, som kan indrette sig)* flexible; **~hed** *en* supplenes; pla'sticity; flexi'bility.

smiger *en* flattery.

smigre *v* flatter; **~nde** *adj* flattering.

smil *et* smile.

smile *v* smile; ~ *ad (,over, til)* smile at; **-hul** *et* dimple.
sminke *en* make-up // *v:* ~ *(sig)* make up, paint (oneself).
sminkning *en (det at sminke)* making-up; *(resultatet)* make-up.
sminkør *en* make-up artist.
smitsom *adj* con'tagious, in'fectious.
smitstof *et* germs *pl.*
smitte *en* in'fection // *v* in'fect; *(fig)* be con'tagious; ~ *en med forkølelse* pass one's cold on to sby; *blive ~t med influenza* catch· the flu; *blive ~t af en* catch· it off sby; ~ *af på* come· off on; *(fig)* in'fect; **-fare** *en* danger of in'fection; **-farlig** *adj* con'tagious; **-kilde** *en* source of in'fection.
smittende *adj (fx latter)* catching.
smoking *en* dinner jacket; *(på indbydelse)* black tie.
smuds *en* dirt; **-blad** *et (om avis)* dirt rag.
smudsig *adj* dirty; *(ufin)* sordid.
smudslitteratur *en* trash; *(porno)* por'nography.
smudsomslag *et (på bog)* dust jacket.
smug *s: i* ~ secretly.
smugle *v* smuggle.
smugler *en* smuggler.
smugleri *et* smuggling.
smuglervarer *pl* contraband.
smuk *adj* beautiful; *(om mand)* handsome; *(køn)* good-looking; *(ædel)* noble; *det var ~t af dig* that was very good of you.
smuldre *v* crumble.
smule *en* bit; *(af væske)* drop; *en* ~ a little, a bit; *ikke en* ~ nothing at all, not a bit.
smut *et (lille tur)* trip; *jeg kom lige et ~ forbi* I'm just dropping in for a minute; *slå* ~ *(med sten)* play ducks and drakes; **-hul** *et* hiding place; *(fig)* loophole.
smutte *v (hurtigt)* nip, pop; *(gå ubemærket; kikse)* slip; *nu ~r jeg* I'm off; ~ *over og se til en* pop over to see sby; ~ *i tøjet* slip into one's clothes; ~ *fra en* give· sby the slip; *barbermaskinen ~de så han skar sig* the shaver slipped so he cut himself; ~ *mandler* blanch almonds.
smutter *en (fejl)* slip.
smuttur *en* trip.
smutvej *en* short cut.
smykke *et (ægte)* piece of jewellery; *(ikke kostbart)* trinket; *~r* jewellery // *v* decorate; **-skrin** *et* jewel box.
smægtende *adj* languishing; ~ *sange om kærlighed (neds)* soppy love-songs.
smæk *et (lyd)* snap; *(stærkt)* bang; *(slag)* slap; *(hage~, bukse~)* bib; *få* ~ be spanked; *give en* ~ give· sby a spanking; **-fornærmet** *adj* miffed.
smække *v (om lyd)* snap; bang, slam; *(slå)* slap; *(give endefuld)* spank; ~ *med døren* slam the door; ~ *døren op* throw· the door open; ~ *røret på (tlf)* bang down the re'ceiver; ~ *sig ude* lock oneself out.
smækkys *et* smacker.
smæklås *en* latch; *slå ~en fra* leave· the door on the latch.
smæld *et* click, snap; *(stærkt)* bang; *slå* ~ *med tungen* click one's tongue; **-e** *v* crack, snap.
smøg *en* (F) fag; *trænge afsindigt til en* ~ be dying for a fag.
smøge *en (gyde)* alley, passage // *v:* ~ *ngt af sig* slip sth off; ~ *ærmerne op* turn up one's sleeves.
smøl *et* slowcoach; **-e** *v* dawdle *(med* over).
smør *et* butter; *komme ~ på brødet* butter the bread; **-blomst** *en* buttercup.
smøre *v* smear; *(gnide ind)* rub; *(om brød)* spread·; *(med smør)* butter; *(med olie)* oil; *(med fedtstof)* grease; **-bræt** *et* platter; **-grav** *en* grease pit; **-kande** *en* oil can; **-kniv** *en* spreading knife *(pl:* knives).
smørelse *en* lubricant.
smøreolie *en* lubricating oil.
smøreost *en* cheese spread.
smøreri *et (om skriveri)* scribbling; *(om maleri)* daubing.
smørkniv *en* butter knife *(pl:* knives).
smørkrukke *en* butter jar.
smørrebrød *et* open sandwiches *pl; et stykke* ~ an open sandwich; **-s·bord** *et* smorgasbord; **-s·papir** *et* grease-proof paper.

smørret *adj: et ~ grin* a silly grin.
smørskål *en* butter dish.
smørsovs *en* melted butter.
små *adj* small, little; *(knap, ca.)* just under; *de ~* the children; *gøre ngt i det ~* do· sth in a small way; *så ~t* gradually; *vi har ~t med tid* we are short of time; **~borgerlig** *adj (neds)* petty bourgeois; **~børn** *pl* young children, infants; **~kage** *en* (sweet) biscuit; **~koge** *v* simmer; **~kød** *et: hakket ~kød* mince.
smålig *adj (for nøjeregnende)* petty; *(fedtet)* stingy; *(snæversynet)* narrow-minded; **~hed** *en* pettiness; stingyness; narrow-mindedness.
småpenge *pl* (small) change; *det er kun ~* (F) it is only peanuts.
småregne *v* drizzle.
småsløjd *en sv.t.* handicrafts *pl.*
småternet *adj* small-checked.
småting *pl* small things; *(ligegyldige)* trifles; **~s·afdeling** *en (med sysager)* haber'dashery de'partment; *det hører til ~s·afdelingen* it is a mere trifle.
småtosset *adj* batty.
småtterier *pl* trifles.
snabel *en* trunk; *(næse)* conk.
snage *v: ~ i ngt* pry into sth.
snak *en (samtale)* talk; *(sludder)* nonsense; *(sladder)* gossip; *der er ngt om ~ken* there is sth in it; *løs ~* gossip; *sikke ngt ~!* what nonsense! *få sig en ~* have a chat; *komme i ~ med en* get· into conver'sation with sby.
snakke *v* talk, chat; *(vrøvle)* talk nonsense; *(sladre)* gossip; *du kan sagtens ~!* it's all very well for you to talk! *~ med en* talk to sby; *~ om ngt* talk about sth; *~ udenom* beat· about the bush; **~salig** *adj* talkative.
snappe *v* snatch; *(bide)* snap *(efter* at); *~ efter vejret* gasp for breath.
snaps *en* snaps.
snarere *adv* rather; *(nærmest)* if anything; *(hurtigere)* sooner; *vi er ~ for tidligt på den* we are too early, if anything.
snarest *adv (så hurtigt som muligt)* as soon as possible; *(nærmest)* if anything.
snarlig *adj* early; *(nært forestående)* ap'proaching.
snart *adv* soon, shortly; *(kort efter)* soon, shortly after(wards); *(næsten)* almost, nearly; *det er ~ for sent* it will soon be too late; *det er ~ på tide* it is about time; *så ~ (som)* as soon as.
snavs *et* dirt, filth.
snavse *v: ~ ngt til* dirty sth; *~ sig til* get· dirty.
snavset *adj* dirty; *(meget beskidt)* filthy.
snavsetøj *et* washing, laundry; **~s·kurv** *en* laundry basket.
sne *en* snow; *høj ~* deep snow; *slås med ~* throw· snowballs // *v* snow; *det ~r* it is snowing; *~ inde* be snowed up; *(om bil)* get· stuck in the snow; **~bold** *en* snowball; **~briller** *pl* snowgoggles.
snedig *adj* cunning; *(neds: snu)* sly; *(snild)* clever; **~hed** *en* cunning; slyness; cleverness.
snedker *en (bygnings~)* joiner; *(tømrer)* carpenter; *(møbel~)* cabinet-maker.
snedkerere *v* do· woodwork.
snedrive *en* snowdrift.
snefnug *et* snowflake.
snegl *en* snail; *(uden hus)* slug; *(øre~)* earpiece; *en sær ~* an odd fish.
snegle *v: ~ sig af sted* crawl along; *(tage lang tid)* drag on; **~fart** *en: i ~fart* at a snail's pace; **~hus** *et* snail-shell.
sne... *sms:* **~hvid** *adj* snow-white; **Snehvide** Snow White; **~kastning** *en* snow shovelling; **~kæde** *en* snow chain; **~mand** *en* snowman *(pl:* -men); **~plov** *en* snowplough.
snerpe *v: ~ munden sammen* purse one's lips; **~ri** *et* prudery; **~t** *adj* prudish.
snerre *v* growl *(ad* at).
snerydning *en* snow clearing.
snes *en* score; *en halv ~* about a dozen; **~e·vis** *adv: i ~e·vis* in scores.
sne... *sms:* **~scooter** *en* snowcat;

~sjap *et* slush; **~skred** *et* avalanche; **~storm** *en* snowstorm, blizzard; **~vejr** *et* snow.
snuffe *v* sniff.
snige *v:* ~ *sig* steal·, creep· *(ind på en* up on sby); **~nde** *adj* sneaking, creeping.
snigmord *et* assassi'nation.
snigskytte *en* sniper.
snild *adj* handy.
snilde *et* skill.
snip *en* corner; *(ble~)* nappy holder.
snit *et* cut; *(tvær~, ud~)* section; *se sit ~ til at* see· one's chance to; *i ~ (dvs. gennemsnit)* on (an) average; **~mønster** *en* pattern; **~sår** *et* cut; *(dybt)* gash.
snitte *en (smørrebrød)* open sandwich, canapé // *v (skære i stykker, skiver)* cut· (up), slice; *(skære i strimler)* shred; **~bønne** *en* French bean.
sno *v* twist; ~ *sig* twist; *(om å, vej)* wind·; *(i trafikken)* weave.
snob *en* snob; **~beri** *et* snobbery; **~bet** *adj* snobbish.
snoet *adj* twisted; *(om vej)* winding.
snog *en* grass snake.
snoning *en (det at sno sig)* twisting; *(bugtning)* winding; *(i strikning)* cable stitch.
snor *en* string; *(tlf, elek)* cord; *(tøj~)* line; *(hunde~)* leash; *have hunden i ~* have the dog on a leash; *hun holder ham i en stram ~ (fig)* she's got him on a string; *binde en ~ om ngt* tie sth up (with string).
snorke *v* snore; **~n** *en* snore, snoring.
snot *et* snot; **~klud** *en* (V!) snotrag; **~tet** *adj* snotty.
snu *adj* sly.
snuble *v* stumble *(over* over).
snude *en (på dyr)* nose; *(på person, neds)* snout; *(på sko)* toe; *stikke sin ~ i ngt* poke one's nose into sth.
snue *en* cold.
snuppe *v* snatch; *(stjæle)* pinch; *blive ~t (af politiet)* (F) get· done, get· pulled.
snurre *v (om bevægelse)* spin, whirl; *(om lyd)* whirr; *(småkoge)* simmer; *det ~r i min fod* I have pins and needles in my foot.
snurren *en (om bevægelse)* spinning, whirling; *(om lyd)* whirring; *(om gryde)* simmering.
snurrig *adj* funny, quaint.
snuse *v* sniff; *(bruge snus)* snuff; ~ *rundt* nose around.
snushane *en* nosy-parker.
snusket *adj (snavset, ulækker)* dirty; *(fig)* sordid.
snustobak *en* snuff.
snyde *v* cheat; ~ *næse* blow· one's nose; ~ *en for ngt* cheat sby out of sth; ~ *i kortspil* cheat at cards; ~ *i skat* fiddle one's income tax; *være som snydt ud af næsen på en* be the spitting image of sby.
snyder *en* cheat.
snyderi *et* cheating.
snylte *v (om person)* sponge *(på* on).
snylter *en* parasite.
snære *v* be too tight.
snæver *adj (smal)* narrow; *(om tøj etc)* tight; *i en ~ vending* at a pinch; **~synet** *adj* narrow-minded.
snævre *v:* ~ *ind* narrow.
snøft *et* sniff; **~e** *v* sniff; *(pruste)* snort.
snøre *en* line // *v* lace up; **~bånd** *et* (shoe)lace; **~sko** *en* lace-up shoe.
snøvle *v* speak· through one's nose.
so *en* sow.
sober *adj* sober.
social *adj* social; *~t boligbyggeri sv.t.* council housing; **~arbejder** *en* social worker; **~demokratiet** *s* the Social Demo'cratic Party, the SDP; **~forsorg** *en* social welfare (services *pl); ~***hjælp** *en* social se'curity.
socialisme *en* 'socialism; **socialist** *en,* **socialistisk** *adj* 'socialist.
socialkontor *et* social se'curity (office).
socialministerium *et* Ministry for Social Af'fairs.
socialrådgiver *en* social worker.
sociolog *en* soci'ologist; **sociologi** *en* soci'ology.
sod *en* soot.
soda *en* soda.
sodavand *en (hvid)* soda water; *(farvet)* fizzy soft drink; **~s·is** *en* ice lolly.

sofa *en* sofa; *(mindre)* set'tee; **~bord** *et* coffee table; **~vælger** *en* non-voter.

sogn *et* parish; **~e·kirke** *en* parish church; **~e·præst** *en* vicar; *(i katolsk sogn)* parish priest.

soiré *en* soirée.

soja *en* soy; **~bønne** *en* soy bean; **~sovs** *en* soy sauce.

sok *en* sock.

sokkel *en (til fx mur)* plinth; *(til søjle)* base; *(til elek pære)* holder.

sol *en* sun; *~en skinner* the sun is shining; *~en går ned* the sun is setting; *~en står op* the sun is rising; *tage ~* go· to the sun centre.

solarium *et* so'larium.

sol... *sms:* **~bad** *et: tage ~bad* sunbathe; **~batteri** *et* solar battery; **~briller** *pl* sunglasses; **~brændt** *adj* suntanned; **~brændthed** *en* suntan; **~bær** *et* black currant; **~celle** *en* solar cell; **~creme** *en* suntan lotion.

soldat *en* soldier; *være ~* be in the army; *være inde som ~* do· military service.

solde *v: ~ pengene op på ngt* throw· one's money away on sth; *være ude at ~ (dvs. drikke)* be out on the booze.

solderi *et (ødslen)* waste; *(druk)* boozing.

sole *v: ~ sig* sit· (,lie· etc) in the sun; **~klar** *adj* crystal-clear.

sol... *sms:* **~energi** *en* solar energy; **~fanger** *en* solar col'lector (,panel); **~filter** *et (i creme)* sunblock; **~formørkelse** *en* solar e'clipse; **~hungrende** *adj: de ~hungrende* the sun-seekers; **~hverv** *et* solstice.

solid *adj* solid; *(holdbar, modstandsdygtig)* ro'bust; *(om måltid)* sub'stantial; *(til at stole på)* re'liable.

solidarisk *adj* solidary; *være ~ med* show soli'darity with.

solidaritet *en* soli'darity.

solist *en* soloist.

sollys *et* sunlight.

solnedgang *en* sunset.

solo *en/adj* solo; **~danser** *en* leading dancer; *(kvindelig)* prima balle'rina.

sol... *sms:* **~olie** *en* suntan oil; **~opgang** *en* sunrise; **~sikke** *en* sunflower; **~skin** *et* sunshine; **~skinsdag** *en* sunny day; **~skoldet** *adj* sunburnt; **~sort** *en* blackbird; **~stik** *et* sunstroke; **~stråle** *en* sunbeam; *(astr)* sunray; **~system** *et* solar system; **~tag** *et (i bil)* sunshine roof; **~ur** *et* sundial; **~varme** *en* solar heat.

som *pron (om person, som subjekt)* who; *(som objekt)* whom; *(efter præp)* whom; *(om alt andet end personer)* which; *den dame ~ kommer i morgen* the lady who is coming to'morrow; *den mand ~ du bad feje gården* the man (whom) you asked to sweep the yard; *det brev ~ kom i går* the letter which arrived yesterday; *det samme ~ vi fik i går* the same as we had yesterday // *konj (indledende en sætning; i egenskab af)* as; *(ikke indledende en sætning; lige som)* like; *(så som)* such as; *lige ~ vi kom* just as we ar'rived; *~ forventet* as ex'pected; *gør ~ jeg siger* do· as I tell you; *efterhånden ~* as; *få ngt ~ belønning* get· sth as a re'ward; *opføre sig ~ en gal* be'have like a madman; *kæledyr ~ hamstre og marsvin* pets like hamsters and guinea pigs; *~ det dog regner!* how it rains! *~ om* as if; *sort ~ kul* as black as coal; *~ sådan* as such.

sommer *en* summer; *i ~ (dvs. sidste)* last summer; *(dvs. kommende)* this summer; *om ~en* in summer; *til ~* next summer; **~dag** *en* summer's day; **~ferie** *en* summer holidays *pl;* **~fugl** *en* butterfly; **~hus** *et* holiday house, cottage; **~lejr** *en* holiday camp; **~tid** *en* summertime.

sommetider *adv* sometimes, from time to time.

sonate *en* so'nata.

sonde *en* probe; *(til flydende ernæring)* tube.

sondere *v* probe; *~ terrænet (fig)* see· how the land lies.

sondre *v: ~ imellem* di'stinguish be'tween.

sonet *en* 'sonnet.

soppe *v* paddle; **~bassin** *et* paddling pool.

sopran *en* so'prano.
sordin *en (mus)* mute.
sorg *en* grief; *(beklagelse)* re'gret; *(bekymring)* worry; *bære ~* be in mourning; *en ~ens dag* a sad day; *det er med ~ at vi må meddele Dem at...* we re'gret to have to in'form you that...
sorgløs *adj* carefree.
sort *en (art)* sort, kind; *(mærke)* brand.
sort *adj* black; *arbejde ~* do· moonlighting; *~ kaffe* black coffee; *komme på den ~e liste* be blacklisted; *se ~ på tingene* look on the dark side of things; *have det ~ på hvidt* have it in black and white; **~børs** *en* black market.
Sortehavet *s* the Black Sea.
sorteper *en: blive ~ (fig)* be left holding the baby; *lade ~ gå videre* pass the buck.
sortere *v* sort; *~ fra* sort out; *det ~r under ham* that's his responsi'bility.
sortering *en* sorting; *(finhed, kvalitet etc)* quality, grade; *andensorterings* second grade.
sortie *en* exit.
sortiment *et* as'sortment.
sortseer *en* pessimist, gloomster; *(tv)* licence dodger.
sortsmudsket *adj* dark, swarthy.
souschef *en* deputy head.
souvenir *en* 'souvenir.
sove *v* sleep·, be a'sleep; *sov godt!* sleep well! *~ godt* be fast asleep; *han ~r let* he is a light sleeper; *~ længe* have a long lie; *~ over sig* over'sleep·; *~ på det* sleep· on it; *~ rusen ud* sleep· it off; **~briks** *en* plank bed; **~by** *en* dormitory town; **~kammerøjne** *pl* (F) come-to-bed eyes; **~pille** *en* sleeping pill; **~pose** *en* sleeping bag; **~sal** *en* dormitory; **~sofa** *en* bed set'tee; **~vogn** *en* sleeping car, sleeper; **~værelse** *et* bedroom.
sovjetisk *adj* 'Soviet.
Sovjetunionen *s* the 'Soviet Union, the USSR.
sovs *en* sauce; *(sky~)* gravy; **~e·skål** *en* sauceboat.
spade *en* spade.
spadsere *v* walk; *(slentre)* stroll; **~dragt** *en* suit; **~tur** *en* walk; stroll.
spagat *s: gå i ~* do· the splits.
spagfærdig *adj* meek.
spaghetti *pl* spa'ghetti.
spalte *en* crack; *(større, fx klippe~)* crevice; *(i bog, avis)* column // *v* split· (up); *(om brænde)* chop.
spaltning *en* splitting (up); *(om atomer)* fission.
spand *en* pail; *(større)* bucket; *(neds om bil)* banger; *være på ~en* be in a fix (,jam, tight spot) // *et (om heste)* team.
Spanien *s* Spain; **spanier** *en* Spaniard; **spansk** *adj* Spanish.
spanskrør *et* cane.
spar *en (i kort)* spades; *~ konge* king of spades.
spare *v (~ op, ikke bruge)* save; *(skåne)* spare; *(være sparsommelig)* e'conomize; *spar mig for detaljerne!* spare me the details! *~ op* save up; *~ på saltet (dvs. ikke spise for meget)* go· easy on the salt; *~ på strømmen* e'conomize on the current; *~ på kræfterne* save one's strength; *~ sig ulejligheden* save oneself the trouble; **~bøsse** *en* savings box; **~gris** *en* piggy bank; **~kasse** *en* savings bank; **~kniv** *en: blive ramt af ~kniven* get· the axe; **~penge** *pl* savings.
spark *et* kick; *få et ~ bagi* get· a kick in the pants.
sparke *v* kick; *~ en over skinnebenet* kick sby's shin; *~ til ngt* kick sth; **~bukser** *pl* (pair of) rompers.
sparsom *adj (spredt)* sparse; *(tynd)* thin.
sparsommelig *adj* eco'nomical; **~hed** *en* e'conomy.
spartansk *adj* spartan.
spartel *en* spatula; *(kitte~)* putty knife *(pl:* knives); **~masse** *en* stopping.
spartle *v* fill; *(kitte)* putty.
spastiker *en* spastic; **spastisk** *adj* spastic.
speaker *en (tv, radio)* an'nouncer.
specialarbejder *en* semi-skilled worker.

specialbygget *adj* purpose-built.
speciale *et* specialty; *(afhandling)* disser'tation; *(i skolen)* term paper.
specialisere *v:* ~ *sig i* specialize in; **specialisering** *en* speciali'zation.
specialist *en* specialist.
specialitet *en* specialty.
speciallæge *en* specialist.
speciel *adj* special.
specielt *adv* e'specially; *(udtrykkelig)* specially.
specificere *v* specify; *(om regning)* itemize.
specifik *adj* spe'cific.
specifikation *en* specifi'cation.
spedalsk *s: en* ~ a leper; **-hed** *adj* leprosy.
speditør *en* shipping agent.
speedbåd *en* speedboat.
speede *v:* ~ *op* speed up.
speeder *en (i bil)* ac'celerator.
speedometer *et* spee'dometer.
spegepølse *en* sa'lami.
spegesild *en* salted herring.
speget *adj (indviklet)* complicated; *(rodet sammen, forvirret)* muddled.
spejde *v* look out *(efter* for).
spejder *en (pige~)* girl guide; *(drenge~)* boy scout.
spejl *et* mirror; *se sig i ~et* look in the mirror; **-billede** *et* re'flection.
spejle *v:* ~ *sig (dvs. se sig i ~et)* look in the mirror; *(dvs. genspejles)* be re'flected; ~ *æg* fry eggs.
spejlglas *et* mirror glss; *(vindue)* plate glass.
spejlglat *adj* slippery.
spejlreflekskamera *et* reflex camera.
spejlvendt *adj* the wrong way round.
spejlæg *et* fried egg.
spektakel *et* noise; *spektakler (dvs. uro, optøjer)* riots.
spektrum *et* spectrum.
spekulation *en* specu'lation.
spekulere *v* think· *(over, på* about); *(fx over problem)* puzzle *(over, på* about); *(være bekymret)* worry *(over, på* about); ~ *i ngt (økon)* speculate in sth; ~ *på at gøre ngt* think· of doing sth.
spencer *en* pinafore dress.
spendere *v* spend·; ~ *ngt på en* treat sby to sth.
spid *et* spit; *sætte ngt på* ~ spit sth; **-de** *v* pierce.
spids *en (skarp)* point; *(yderste ende)* tip; *(øverste ende)* top; *gå i ~en* lead· the way; *gå op i en* ~ (F) get· into a flap *(over* about); *stå i ~en for ngt* be at the head of sth // *adj (også fig)* pointed, sharp; **-belastning** *en* peak (load).
spidse *v* sharpen *(fx en blyant* a pencil); ~ *ører* prick up one's ears.
spidsfindig *adj* subtle.
spidskål *en* spring cabbage.
spidstege *v* spitroast; *spidstegt lam* spitroasted lamb.
spil *et* play; *(efter regler, fx kort, tennis)* game; *(skuespillers ~)* acting; *(musikers ~)* playing; *(hejseværk)* winch; *have frit* ~ have a free rein; *et ~ kort (dvs. selve kortene)* a pack of cards; *(dvs. spillet)* a game of cards; *have en finger med i ~let* have a hand in it; *sætte ngt på* ~ put· sth at stake; *stå på* ~ be at stake; *være på ~ (om person etc)* be at work; *gå til* ~ take· music lessons.
spild *s* waste; *(affald)* refuse; *det er ~ af tid* it is a waste of time; *lade ngt gå til ~e* waste sth; *gå til ~e* be wasted.
spilde *v* spill·; *(ødsle væk)* waste; ~ *sovs på skjorten* spill· sauce on one's shirt; ~ *tid(en)* waste time; **-vand** *et* wastewater; *(kloakvand)* sewage.
spildolie *en* waste oil; *(på stranden)* oil pol'lution.
spile *v:* ~ *ngt ud* dis'tend sth.
spiler *en (mar)* spinnaker.
spille *v* play; *(opføre)* per'form; *(om rolle)* act; ~ *helt* act the hero; ~ *klaver* play the piano; ~ *kort* play cards; *det ~r ingen rolle* it does not matter; ~ *syg* pre'tend to be ill; ~ *med i et spil* join a game; ~ *om ngt* play for sth; ~ *op til en* make· up to sby; **-automat** *en* slot ma'chine; **-dåse** *en* music box; **-film** *en* feature film; **-fugl** *en* gambler; **-hal** *en* (a'musement) ar'cade; **-kasino** *et* (gambling) ca'sino; **-kort** *et* playing card; **-lærer** *en* music teacher.

spiller *en* player; *(i hasardspil)* gambler.
spilopper *pl* fun.
spinat *en* spinach; *jokke i ~en* put· one's foot in it.
spinde *v* spin·; *(om kat)* purr.
spindelvæv *et* spider's web, cobweb.
spinderi *et* spinning mill.
spinderok *en* spinning wheel.
spinkel *adj* slight; *(skrøbelig)* delicate, frail; *(slank)* slender; *et ~t flertal* a narrow ma'jority.
spion *en* spy *(pl:* spies).
spionage *en* espionage.
spionere *v* spy.
spir *et* spire.
spiral *en* spiral; *(mod graviditet)* coil, IUD.
spire *en* shoot; *(bønne~)* sprout; *(fig)* germ // *v (om frø)* germinate; *(om plante, løg etc)* sprout; *(fig)* be'gin·.
spiring *en* sprouting, germi'nation.
spiritus *en* alcohol; *(om drikke)* drink, liquor, (F) booze; **~beskatning** *en* alcohol duty; **~bevilling** *en* licence (to sell alcoholic beverages); **~kørsel** *en* drunken driving; **~prøve** *en (med spritballon)* breathalyzer; *(med blodprøve)* blood alcohol test; **~påvirket** *adj* under the influence (of alcohol).
spise *v* eat·, have; *~ (til) middag* have dinner; *hvornår skal vi ~?* when do we eat? *blive spist af med ngt* be fobbed off with sth; *~ op* eat· up; *~ ude* eat· out; **~bord** *et* dining table; **~kammer** *et* larder; **~kort** *et* menu; **~krog** *en* dining area; **~køkken** *et* kitchen-dining room; **~lig** *adj (dvs. ikke giftig)* edible; *(dvs. værd at spise)* eatable; **~olie** *en* salad oil; **~pinde** *pl* chopsticks; **~rør** *et* gullet; **~ske** *en* tablespoon; **~sted** *et* eating place; **~stel** *et* dinner service; **~stue** *en* dining room; **~tid** *en* mealtime; **~vogn** *en (jernb)* dining car; *(kun med let servering)* buffet (car); **~æble** *et* eating apple.
spisning *en* eating; *(lettere bespisning)* re'freshments *pl.*
spjæld *et (i ovn, kamin)* (flue) damper; *sidde i ~et* (F) be in the nick.
spjæt *et* start; **~te** *v* twitch; *(med fødderne)* kick.
splejs *en* shrimp.
splejse *v* splice; *(deles om udgifter)* club to'gether *(til ngt* to buy sth).
splid *en* conflict; *så ~* make· trouble.
splint *en* splinter; *(flis)* fragment.
splinterny *adj* brand-new.
splintfri *adj: ~t glas* safety glass.
splintre *v* splinter.
splitflag *et* swallow-tailed flag.
splitte *v* split·, di'vide; *(sprede fx folkemængde)* scatter; *~ ngt ad (dvs. sprede)* scatter sth; *(dvs. pille fra hinanden)* take· sth to pieces.
splittelse *en* split; *(opløsning)* split-up.
splitternøgen *adj* stark naked, starkers.
splitterravende *adj* stark staring.
splittet *adj* di'vided; *(om person)* split.
spole *en* spool, reel; *(til symaskine)* bobbin // *v (om garn)* spool, wind·; *(om film)* reel; *~ frem (på båndoptager)* wind· forwards; *~ tilbage* re'wind·.
spolere *v* spoil·, ruin.
sponsor *en* sponsor; **~ere** *v* sponsor.
spontan *adj* spon'taneous; **~itet** *en* sponta'neity.
spor *et (fod~)* footprint, track; *(hjul~)* wheel track; *(jernb, sti)* track; *(mærke efter ngt)* mark, trace; *ikke ~ (dvs. ingenting)* nothing at all; *(dvs. slet ikke)* not at all; *bære ~ af* show· traces of; *følge i ens ~* follow in sby's footsteps; *løbe af ~et (om tog)* be de'railed; *komme på ~et af ngt* get· onto sth.
spore *en* spur // *v (om hest)* spur; *(mærke, opsnuse)* trace.
-sporet *(om vej)* -lane; *(jernb)* -track.
sporløst *adv* without (a) trace.
sporskifte *et* points *pl.*
sporstof *et* trace element.
sport *en* sports *pl; dyrke ~* go· in for sports.
sports... *sms:* **~begivenhed** *en* sporting e'vent; **~folk** *pl* sportsmen, athletes; **~forretning** *en* sports shop; **~gren** *en* sport; **~hal** *en* sports centre; **~lig** *adj* sporting; **~mand** *en*

athlete; **~plads** *en* sports ground; **~siderne** *pl (i avis)* the sports pages; **~strømpe** *en* knee-stocking; **~stævne** *et* sports meeting; **~trænet** *adj* ath'letic; **~tøj** *et (i forretning)* sportswear; *(antræk)* sports clothes; **~udstyr** *et* sports e'quipment; **~vogn** *en (auto)* sports car; **~udsendelse** *en* sportscast; **~ånd** *en* sportsmanship.

sporvogn *en* tram.

spot *en* mockery, ridicule; **~pris** *en: til ~pris* for a song.

spotte *v* mock (at); *(med hånlige bemærkninger)* sneer at; *(være ugudelig)* blas'pheme; **~tende** *adj* mocking.

spraglet *adj* colourful, brightly coloured; *(neds, alt for ~)* loud.

sprede *v* spread·; *(splitte, ~ vidt og bredt)* scatter; *~ sig* spread; scatter.

spredning *en* spreading; scattering; *(statistisk)* dis'persion; *(fig)* vari'ation.

spredt *adj* scattered; *~e byger* scattered showers; *~ bifald* spo'radic ap'plause.

spring *et* jump; *(stort)* leap; *~ over hest (gymn)* horse vault; *stå på ~ til at...* be ready to...; *vove ~et* take· the plunge; **~bræt** *et* springboard.

springe *v* jump; *(større ~)* leap; *(om kilde)* spring·; *(om springvand)* play; *(~ i stykker)* burst·; *(om fx streng)* snap; *(eksplodere)* ex'plode, blow· up; *der er sprunget en sikring* a fuse has blown; *~ af toget* jump off the train; *~ fra ngt (fig)* back out of sth; *~ i luften* blow· up, ex'plode; *døren sprang op* the door flew open; *~ over ngt* jump sth; *~ ngt over* skip sth; *(udelade)* leave· sth out; *(glemme)* miss sth; *~ ud (om blomst etc)* come· out; *(i vandet)* dive in; *~ ud ad vinduet* jump out of the window.

springer *en* jumper; *(i skak)* knight.

springform *en* springform.

springkniv *en* flick knife *(pl:* knives).

springmadras *en* spring mattress.

springvand *et* fountain.

sprinkler *en* sprinkler; *(auto)* windscreen washers *pl;* **~anlæg** *et* sprinkler system.

sprit *en* alcohol, spirit; *(spiritus)* spirits *pl;* **~apparat** *et* spirit stove; **~bilist** *en* drunken driver; **~kørsel** *en* drunken driving.

spritte *v: ~ ngt af* clean sth with spirit.

sprog *et* language; *(måde at tale på)* speech; *være god til ~* be good at languages; **~brug** *en* usage; **~forskning** *en* lin'guistic re'search; **~kundskaber** *pl* language skills; **~kursus** *et* language course; **~lig** *adj* lin'guistic; **~lære** *en* grammar.

sprosse *en (i vindue)* bar.

sprudle *v* bubble; *~ frem* well out; **~nde** *adj* bubbling; *(om fx vin)* sparkling.

sprukken *adj (om stemme)* rough; *(om hud)* chapped; *(om væg etc)* cracked.

sprut *en* (F) booze; **~te** *v* splutter; *(om stegepande etc)* sputter.

sprække *en (revne)* crack; *(fx klippe~)* crevice; *(møntindkast)* slot // *v* crack, burst·.

sprælle *v* kick about; *(med kroppen)* wriggle; **~mand** *en* jumping jack.

sprælsk *adj* lively.

sprænge *v* burst·; *(eksplodere)* blow· up; *(ved eksplosion)* blow· up; *(om bombe)* ex'plode; *(åbne med magt)* break· (,force) open; *(opløse fx møde)* break· up; *~ banken* break· the bank.

sprænges *v* burst·; *(om fx regering)* split·.

sprængfarlig *adj* ex'plosive.

sprængladning *en* ex'plosive charge; *(i missil)* warhead.

sprængning *en* bursting; ex'plosion; breaking open (,up); splitting; **~s·eksperter** *pl* bomb dis'posal squad.

sprængstof *et* ex'plosive; *(fig)* dynamite.

sprængt *adj (om kød)* salted, pickled.

sprætte *v: ~ ngt op (om tøj)* un'stitch sth; *(om kuvert)* slit· sth open; *(om bog)* cut· the pages of sth.

sprød *adj* brittle; *(om mad)* crisp, crunchy.

sprøjt *et* splash; *(neds, fx om tynd te)* dishwater; *(om dårlig vin)* plonk.

sprøjte *en (til indsprøjtning)* syringe; *(brand~)* fire engine; *(neds om avis)* rag; *få en ~ (fx vaccination)* get· a jab; *være på ~en* be on the needle // *v* spray; *(indsprøjte)* in'ject; *(stænke)* spatter; *(plaske)* splash; **-male** *v* spray (paint); **-pistol** *en* spray-gun; **-pose** *en* sa'voy bag.

sprøjtning *en* spraying.

spule *v* wash down.

spurt *en* spurt; **-e** *v* spurt.

spurv *en* sparrow.

spyd *et* spear; *(sport)* javelin.

spydig *adj* sar'castic; **-hed** *en* sar'castic re'mark; *(det at være spydig)* 'sarcasm.

spydkast *et (sport)* throwing the javelin.

spyflue *en* bluebottle.

spyt *et* spittle, sa'liva; **-kirtel** *en* salivary gland; **-slikker** *an* bootlicker.

spytte *v* spit·.

spæd *adj (lille)* tiny; *(fin, sart)* tender; *en ~ stemme* a frail voice; *da han var ~* when he was a baby; **-barn** *et* baby, infant.

spæk *et (svine~)* bacon fat; *(hval~)* blubber.

spække *v (gastr)* lard; *~t med (dvs. fuld af)* bristling with; **-bræt** *et* trencher.

spænde *et* clasp; *(på fx sko)* buckle; *(hår~)* (hair) slide // *v (stramme)* tighten; *(udspænde)* stretch; *(om bælte)* clasp; *(om rem)* strap; *hvordan spændte det af?* how did it go? *~ ben for en* trip sby up; *~ livremmen ind* tighten one's belt; *~ vidt (fig)* cover a wide field.

spændende *adj* ex'citing, thrilling.

spændetrøje *en* straitjacket.

spænding *en (ngt spændende)* ex'citement; *(elek)* voltage; *(stramning)* tightening; *(det at være spændt el. stram, social ~ etc)* tension.

spændstig *adj* e'lastic; *(smidig)* supple; **-hed** *en* ela'sticity; suppleness.

spændt *adj (nysgerrig, interesseret)* curious; *(anspændt)* tense; *(ivrig)* anxious; *(strammet)* tight; *være ~ på ngt* be curious to see sth.

spændvidde *en (fig)* scope.

spæne *v* bolt, run·.

spær *et* rafter.

spærre *v* bar, block; *vejen er ~t* the road is closed; *~ en gade af* close a street; *(om politiet)* cordon off a street; *~ for en* ob'struct sby; *~ en inde* shut· sby up; *(i fængsel)* lock sby up; *~ øjnene op* stare.

spærring *en* barring, blocking, closing; *(ved ind- el. udgang)* barrier; *(vej~)* road block; *(politi~)* cordon.

spætte *en* woodpecker.

spættet *adj* speckled.

spøg *en* joke; *for ~* for fun; *det var kun min ~* I was only joking; *forstå ~* have a sense of humour; *~ til side* joking a'part.

spøge *v* joke; *(gå igen)* haunt; *~ med ngt* make· a joke of sth; *det er ikke ngt at ~ med* it is no joking matter; *det ~r på slottet* the castle is haunted; **-fugl** *en* joker; **-fuld** *adj* playful; *(humoristisk)* humorous.

spøgelse *et* ghost; **-s·historie** *en* ghost story.

spøgeri *et* haunting.

spørge *v* ask; *(høfligt, formelt)* in'quire; *(bydende, krævende)* de'mand; *~ en (ad)* ask sby; *~ efter en* ask for sby; *~ om ngt* ask (,in'quire) about sth; *~ hvad det koster* ask the price; *~ en om vej* ask sby the way; *~ til en* ask after sby; *~ en ud* question sby.

spørgende *adj* in'quiring.

spørgeskema *et* question'naire.

spørgsmål *et* question; *(sag)* matter; *stille en et ~* ask sby a question; *det er ~et* that is the question; *et ~ om liv og død* a matter of life and dead; *det er et ~ om vi når det* the question is whether we can make it; **-s·tegn** *et* question mark; *sætte ~s·tegn ved ngt (fig)* question sth.

spå *v* fore'tell·; *(forudsige ud fra viden)* pre'dict; *(profetere)* prophesy; *blive ~et* have one's fortune told; *~ i kort* tell· the future from cards; **-kone** *en* fortuneteller.

spån *en* chip; *(høvl~)* shaving; **-plade** *en* chipboard.

stab *en* staff.
stabel *en (bunke)* pile *(fx bøger* of books); *(større, fx brænde~)* stack; *løbe af ~en (også fig)* be launched; **~afløbning** *en* launching; **~stole** *pl* stacking chairs.
stabil *adj* steady; *(mods: usikker)* stable.
stabilisere *v* 'stabilize.
stabilitet *en* sta'bility.
stable *v: ~ op* pile (,stack) up.
stade *et (salgs~)* stall; *(på messe)* stand; *(bi~)* hive; *(trin)* stage, level.
stadfæste *v* con'firm, ratify; **~lse** *en* confir'mation, ratifi'cation.
stadig *adj (uforandret)* constant; *(om vejr)* settled; *(uafbrudt)* steady // *adv* constantly; *(endnu)* still; *~ bedre* better and better; *han er ~ direktør* he is still a director; **~hed** *en* steadiness; *til ~hed (dvs. permanent)* permanently; *(dvs. altid)* constantly.
stadigvæk *adv* still.
stadion *et* stadium.
stadium *et* stage; *på et sent (,tidligt) ~* at an ad'vanced (,early) stage; *det er et overstået ~* it be'longs to the past.
stads *en (ngt fint)* finery; *(ngt skidt)* rubbish, trash; *gøre ~ af en* make· a fuss about sby; *være i ~en* be wearing one's Sunday best.
stafetløb *et* 'relay (race).
staffeli *et* easel.
stage *en (stang)* pole, stake; *(til lys)* candlestick // *v (om båd)* punt.
stagnere *v* stagnate.
stak *en* stack; *(bunke)* pile, heap.
stakit *et* fence, paling.
stakkel *en* poor thing; *din ~!* poor you!
stakkels *adj* poor; *~ hende (,ham)!* the poor thing!
stakåndet *adj* breathless.
stald *en* stable; *(ko~)* cowshed.
stamgæst *en* regular.
stamme *en (træ~)* trunk; *(ord~)* stem; *(folke~)* tribe // *v (om talefejl)* stutter, stammer; *~ fra* come· from; *(skyldes)* be due to, o'riginate in.
stammen *en* stutter, stammer.
stampe *s: stå i ~* make· no progress, be at a standstill // *v* stamp (one's foot).
stamtavle *en* pedigree.
stamtræ *et* family tree.
stand *en (tilstand)* con'dition, state; *(om fx hus)* (state of) re'pair; *(samfundsklasse)* class, rank; *(bod etc på udstilling)* stand; *være i ~ til at* be able to; *være ude af ~ til at* be un'able to; *gøre ngt i ~* put· sth in order; *(reparere)* re'pair sth; *gøre sig i ~ (dvs. vaske sig etc)* clean up; *(dvs. klæde sig på)* dress; *gøre huset i ~ (dvs. gøre rent)* clean the house; *(dvs. male etc)* re'decorate (the house); *huset er i god ~* the house is in good re'pair; *lave ngt i ~ (dvs. reparere)* mend (,re'pair) sth.
standard *en* standard; *(niveau)* level.
standardisere *v* 'standardize.
standerlampe *en* standard lamp.
standhaftig *adj* steadfast.
standpunkt *et (synspunkt)* point of view; *(holdning)* attitude; *(stadium)* stage; *(niveau)* level; *(i kundskaber)* pro'ficiency.
standse *v* stop; *(om fx bil også)* pull up; *~ for rødt* stop at red; *~ op* stop short; *de er ikke til at ~* there's no stopping them.
standsning *en* stopping, stop; *(i trafikken)* hold-up; *(afbrydelse)* inter'ruption.
stang *en* bar; *(fiske~)* rod; *(telt~, flag~)* pole; *(cykel~)* crossbar; *en ~ chokolade* a chocolate bar; *flage på halv ~* fly· the flag at half mast; *holde en ~en* hold· sby at bay.
stangdrukken *adj* dead drunk; sozzled.
stange *v* butt; *~ tænder* pick one's teeth; *~ ål* spear eels.
stangspring *et* pole vaulting.
stangtøj *et* off-the-peg clothes.
stank *en* stink, stench.
stankelben *et (zo)* daddy-long-legs.
stanniol *en* tinfoil.
start *en* start, be'ginning; *fra ~en* from the beginning; *få en flyvende ~* get· off to a flying start; **~bane** *en* runway; *(lille)* airstrip.

starte *v* start; **-r** *en* starter.
startforbud *et: få ~ (om fly)* be grounded; *(sport)* be banned.
starthul *et: se at komme ud af ~lerne* get· off the marks.
startkapital *en* i'nitial capital.
startklar *adj* ready to start.
startlinje *en* starting line.
startnøgle *en* ig'nition key.
startsignal *et* starting signal.
startskud *et* starting signal.
stat *en* state; *~en* the State.
statelig *adj* im'posing.
station *en* station; **-car** *en* e'state car.
stationere *v* station.
stationsforstander, stationsmester *en* station-master.
stationær *adj* stationary.
statisk *adj* static.
statist *en* extra.
statistik *en* sta'tistics; **statistisk** *adj* sta'tistical.
stativ *et* stand, rack; *(foto)* tripod.
stats... *sms:* **-advokat** *en* public prosecutor; **-autoriseret** *adj sv.t.* chartered; **-bane** *en* state railway; **-borger** *en* citizen; **-borgerskab** *et* citizenship; **-chef** *en* head of state; **-ejet** *adj* state-owned; **-forbund** *et* confede'ration; **-garanti** *en* state guarantee; **-gæld** *en* national debt; **-kassen** *s sv.t.* the Ex'chequer; **-kirke** *en* state church; **-kundskab** *en* po'litical science; **-kup** *et* coup d'état; **-lig** *adj* state(-), national; **-lån** *et* government loan; **-mand** *en* statesman *(pl:* -men); **-minister** *en* prime minister; **-støtte** *en* state subsidy; **-støttet** *adj* state-subsidized; **-tilskud** *et* government grant; **-videnskab** *en* po'litical science.
statue *en* statue.
statuette *en* statu'ette.
status *en: gøre ~* make· out the balance sheet; *(fig)* take· stock; **-symbol** *et* status symbol.
statut *en* 'statute.
staude *en* pe'rennial; **-bed** *et* her'baceous border.
stav *en* stick; *(politi~)* truncheon; *falde i ~er* be lost in thought.
stave *v* spell·; *hvordan ~s det?* how do you spell it? *~ til 'squeegee'* spell squeegee; **-fejl** *en* mis'spelling.
stavelse *en* syllable.
stavlygte *en* torch.
stearinlys *et* candle.
sted *et* place; *(lille ~, plet)* spot; *finde ~* take· place, happen; *alle ~er* everywhere, all over the place; *et el. andet ~* somewhere; *et andet ~* some place else, some other place; *vi går ingen ~er* we are not going anywhere; *komme galt af ~ (dvs. til skade)* get· hurt; *lad os se at komme af ~* let's get started; *tage af ~* start, leave· *(til* for); *i ~et for* in'stead of; *vi tog bussen i ~et* we took the bus in'stead; *i dit ~ ville jeg gå* if I were you I'd walk; *på ~et* on the spot; *være til ~e* be present *(ved* at); *komme til ~e* ap'pear; *de rørte sig ikke ud af ~et* they did not move; *ikke ud af ~et om jeg gør det!* no way I'm going to do it!.
stedbarn *et* stepchild *(pl:* -children).
stedfader *en* stepfather.
stedfortræder *en* substitute.
stedkendt *adj: være ~* know· one's way around.
stedlig *adj* local.
stedmoder *en* stepmother; **-blomst** *en* pansy.
stednavn *et* place name.
stedord *et* pronoun.
stedsans *en* sense of di'rection.
stedse *adv: for ~* for good, for ever; **-grøn** *adj* evergreen.
stedvis *adj* local // *adv* in places.
steg *en* roast.
stege *v (i ovn el. gryde)* roast; *(på pande)* fry; *(på rist)* grill; *stegt kalkun* roast turkey; *stegt fisk* fried fish; **-fedt** *et* dripping; **-flæsk** *et* pork loin; **-gryde** *en* stewpan.
stegende *adj: ~ varm* baking hot.
stegepande *en* frying pan.
stegespid *et* skewer.
stegning *en (i ovn el. gryde)* roasting; *(på pande)* frying.
stejl *adj* steep; *(om person)* stubborn.
stejle *v (om hest)* rear; *~ over ngt (også fig)* bridle at sth.

stel *et* frame; *(spise~ etc)* set, service.
stemme *en* voice; *(ved valg)* vote; *med høj ~* in a loud voice; *med 50 ~r mod 48* by 50 votes to 48 // *v (et instrument)* tune; *(passe)* be cor'rect, be right; *(ved valg)* vote; *det ~r!* that's right! *~ for ngt* vote for sth; *~ imod ngt* vote against sth; *~ ned* vote down; *~ om ngt* put· sth to the vote; *~ overens med* a'gree with; *~ på en* vote for sby; **~berettiget** *adj* en'titled to vote; **~bånd** *et* vocal chord; **~gaffel** *en* tuning fork; **~jern** *et* chisel; **~ret** *en* the vote; **~seddel** *en* ballot paper; **~tal** *et* poll; **~urne** *en* ballot box.
stemning *en (sinds~)* mood; *(på et sted)* atmosphere; *(af instrument)* tuning; *er der ~ for en drink?* what about a drink? *i løftet ~* in high spirits; *være i ~* be in a good mood; **~s·fuld** *adj* full of atmosphere.
stempel *et* (rubber) stamp; *(i motor)* piston; **~mærke** *et* revenue stamp; **~pude** *en* (ink) pad.
stemple *v* stamp; *~ en som forbryder* brand sby as a criminal.
stemt *adj (om instrument)* in tune; *(om sproglyd)* voiced; *være ~ for ngt* be in favour of sth; *venligt ~* well dis'posed *(over for, mod* to).
sten *en* stone; *(lille)* pebble; *(kampesten)* boulder; *sove som en ~* sleep· like a log; **~alder** *en* Stone Age; **~brud** *et* quarry; **Stenbukken** *s (astr)* Capricorn; **~dysse** *en* dolmen.
stene *v* stone; **~t** *adj* stony.
stenhugger *en* stone mason.
stenhøj *en (i have)* rockery.
stenhård *adj* (as) hard as rock.
stenografere *v* do· shorthand.
stenografi *en* shorthand.
stenrig *adj* (F) filthy rich.
stensikker *adj* positive, dead certain.
stentøj *et* stoneware.
step(dans) *en* tap-dancing.
steppe *en (slette, prærie)* steppe // *v* tap-dance.
stereo(anlæg) *et* stereo (system).
stereotyp *adj* stereotype.
steril *adj* sterile.
sterilisere *v* sterilize.
sterilisering *en* sterili'zation.
sterilitet *en* ste'rility.
stetoskop *et* 'stethoscope.
stewardesse *en (fly)* air hostess, stewardess.
sti *en* path.
stift *en (søm)* nail; *(tegne~ etc)* tack; *(til pladespiller)* stylus; *(til blyant)* lead [lɛd]; *(kirkeligt)* diocese.
stifte *v (grundlægge)* found, e'stablish; *(fremkalde, fx uro)* cause, stir up; *~ bekendtskab med* get· to know; *~ familie* start a family; *~ fred* make· peace; *~ gæld* in'cur debts.
stiftelse *en* foun'dation.
stiftende *adj: ~ generalforsamling* statutory general meeting.
stifter *en* founder.
stigbøjle *en* stirrup.
stige *en* ladder // *v* rise·, go· up; *(om pris også)* in'crease; *(vokse)* grow·; *~ af bussen* get· off the bus; *~ i ens agtelse* rise· in sby's e'steem; *~ i løn* get· a rise; *~ i pris* go· up; *priserne er steget med 5 procent* the prices have gone up by 5 per cent; *~ om (fx til anden bus)* change; *~ op i badekarret* climb into the tub; *~ på (fx bus)* get· on; *~ ud* get· off; *~ ud af badet* get· out of one's bath.
stigning *en* rise; *(vækst)* 'increase.
stik *et (med nål, søm etc)* prick; *(med kniv)* stab; *(af fx myg)* bite; *(af bi)* sting; *(jag af smerte)* twinge; *(elek kontakt, tlf-stik)* point; *(~prop)* plug; *(i kortspil)* trick; *holde ~* hold· good, prove to be right; *lade en i ~ken* leave· sby in the lurch // *adv: ~ imod* dead against; *(fig)* di'rectly contrary to; *~ modsat* di'rectly opposite; *~ syd* due south; **~dåse** *en (elek)* socket.
stikirenddreng *en* errand boy.
stikke *v (med nål, søm etc)* stick·, prick; *(med kniv)* stab; *(anmelde)* in'form on; *(om myg)* bite·; *(om bi)* sting·; *(putte, anbringe)* put·; *(række)* hand; *(sy)* stitch; *stik mig lige smørret!* hand me the butter, please! *hun stak ham en* she socked him one; *~ af* clear out; *(flygte)*

bolt, beat· it; *~ frem* stick· out; *(dvs. række frem)* put· out; *~ i ngt* prod sth; *~ ild i ngt* set· fire to sth; *~ ngt i lommen* put· sth into one's pocket; *(for at hugge det)* pocket sth; *~ ngt ind i ngt* put· sth into sth; *~ en ned* stab sby; *~ op* stick· up; *~ til en (fig)* get· at sby; *~ til maden* toy with one's food; *~ ud* stick· out; *~ sig på ngt* prick oneself on sth.

stikkelsbær *et* gooseberry.

stikkende *adj* pricking; *(om smerte)* shooting; *~ øjne* piercing eyes.

stikker *en* in'former.

stikkesting *et* backstitch; *sy ~* backstitch.

stikkontakt *en* socket, point.

stikling *en* cutting.

stikning *en (søm)* seam; *(det at sy ~)* stitching.

stikord *et (i ordbog)* headword; *(skuespillers etc)* cue.

stikpille *en (med)* sup'pository; *(hib)* gibe.

stikprop *en* plug.

stikprøve *en* spot test.

stil *en* style; *(i skolen)* essay; *i den ~* along those lines; *i ~ med* something like; *i stor ~* on a large scale; **-art** *en* style.

stile *v* ad'dress *(til* to); *~ efter at gøre ngt* aim to do sth; *~ mod (om retning)* make· for; *(fig)* aim at.

stilebog *en* exercise book.

stilethæl *en* sti'letto heel.

stilfærdig *adj* quiet, gentle; **-hed** *en* quietness, gentleness.

stilhed *en* quiet, calm; *(tavshed)* silence; *i al ~* quietly; *(tavst)* silently.

stilk *en* stalk; *(blomster~, ~ på glas)* stem; *deres øjne stod på ~e* their eyes were popping out of their heads.

stillads *et (bygge~)* scaffolding.

stille *v (anbringe)* put·, place; *(møde op)* ap'pear, turn up; *(indstille fx ur)* set·; *(tørst)* quench; *(sult)* satisfy; *~ en et spørgsmål* ask sby a question; *~ uret* set· the watch; *være dårligt (,godt) ~t* we badly (,well) off; *blive ~t for en dommer* be brought be'fore a judge; *~ sig i række* line up; *~ ind på en kanal* tune into a channel; *~ sig op (rejse sig)* get· up; *~ om til (tlf)* put· through to; *(i formation)* take· up one's po'sition; *(om flere personer)* line up; *hvad skal vi ~ op?* what are we going to do? *der er ikke ngt at ~ op* there is nothing we can do; *~ op til folketingsvalget* stand· for parliament; *blive ~t over for ngt* be con'fronted with sth; *~ sig på tå* stand· on tip-toe; *hvordan ~r du dig til sagen?* what do· you think of the matter?

stille *adj (rolig)* quiet, calm; *(ubevægelig)* still; *(tavs)* silent; *ganske ~* quietly; *holde ~* be standing still; *(standse)* stop, come· to a halt; *ligge ~* lie· still; *stå ~* stand· still; *tie ~* be quiet; *være nu ~!* be quiet now!

Stillehavet *s* the Pa'cific Ocean.

stilling *en* po'sition; *(indstilling)* attitude; *(arbejde også)* job; *(erhverv)* occu'pation; *(situation)* situ'ation; *(i sportskamp)* score; *søge ~* ap'ply for a job; *tage ~ til ngt* make· up one's mind about sth; *(dvs. udtale sig)* give· one's o'pinion on sth.

stilmøbler *pl* period furniture.

stilne *v: ~ af* calm down.

stilstand *en* standstill.

stiltiende *adj* tacit.

stime *en* shoal.

stimle *v: ~ sammen* crowd.

stimmel *en* crowd.

stimulans *en* stimulant.

stimulere *v* stimulate.

sting *et* stitch; *få ~ (i siden)* get· a stitch; *få ~ene taget* have the stitches taken out.

stinkdyr *et* skunk.

stinke *v* stink·, reek.

stipendiat *en* scholarship holder.

stipendium *et* scholarship.

stirre *v* stare; *(begejstret, drømmende)* gaze; *~ tomt ud i luften* be staring into space.

stirren *en* staring; gazing; *(blik)* stare.

stiv *adj* stiff; *blive ~ (om fx budding)* set·; *(om person, stivne)* stiffen; *~*

af skræk scared stiff; *tage ngt i ~ arm* not bat an eyelid; *se stift på en* look fixedly at sby; *nej, det er for stift!* that's the limit! (F) that takes the cake! *han er ikke ~ i latin* he is not very strong in Latin; *en ~ whisky* a stiff whisky.

stive *v* starch; *~ ngt af* prop sth up; *~de skørter* starched skirts.

stivelse *en* starch.

stiver *en (i fx krave)* stiffener; *(i paraply)* rib; *(støttebjælke)* brace.

stivfrossen *adj* frozen stiff.

stivhed *en* stiffness.

stivkrampe *en* tetanus.

stivne *v* stiffen; *(om budding, gelé)* set·.

stjerne *en* star; **~billede** *et* constel'lation; **~himmel** *en* starry sky; **~klar** *adj* starry; **~skruetrækker** *en* Phillips ® screwdriver; **~skud** *et* shooting star.

stjæle *v* steal·, (F) pinch.

stodder *en* beggar; (F, *fyr)* bloke.

stof *et (tøj)* ma'terial, fabric; *(fys)* matter; *(emne)* subject; *(fig, fx til artikel, bog)* ma'terial; *~fer (narko)* drugs; *~ til eftertanke* food for thought.

stofmisbrug *en* drug ab'use; **~er** *en* drug addict.

stofprøve *en* sample.

stofskifte *et* me'tabolism.

stoftryk *et* textile printing.

S-tog *et* su'burban train.

stok *en* stick.

stokdøv *adj* stone deaf.

stokkonservativ *adj* 'arch-con,servative.

stokrose *en* hollyhock.

stol *en* chair; *(på strygeinstrument)* bridge; *sætte sig mellem to ~e* fall· be'tween two chairs.

stola *en* stole.

stole *v: ~ på en (dvs tro på)* trust sby; *(dvs regne med)* re'ly on sby, count on sby; *det kan du ~ på!* you can take my word for it! **~ryg** *en* back of a chair; **~sæde** *et* seat.

stolpe *en* post; *snakke op og ned ad ~r om ngt* talk endlessly about sth.

stolt *adj* proud *(af* of); *(flot, pragtfuld)* grand; **~hed** *en* pride.

stop *et* stop; *sige ~* call a halt; **~forbud** *et (skiltetekst)* no waiting; **~fuld** *adj* crammed *(af* with); *(om bus etc)* packed; **~lygte** *en* stop-light.

stopning *en* stuffing; *(i sok etc)* darning.

stoppe *v (standse)* stop; *(fylde, proppe)* fill, cram; *(putte)* tuck; *(tilstoppe)* block; *(reparere, fx sok)* darn, mend; *(give forstoppelse)* be constipating; *~ ngt i sig* scoff sth down; *~ skjorten ned i bukserne* tuck one's shirt into one's trousers; *~ op* stop; **~garn** *et* darning wool; **~nål** *en* darning needle.

stopper *en: sætte en ~ for ngt* put· a stop to sth.

stoppested *et* stop, halt.

stopsignal *et* stop signal.

stopur *et* stopwatch.

stor *adj* big, large; *(høj)* tall; *(fin, god, mægtig)* great; *blive ~* grow· (big); *(dvs. blive voksen)* grow· up; *en ~ mand (af størrelse)* a tall man; *(fig)* a great man; *et ~t hus* a big house; *i det ~e og hele* on the whole; *de er lige ~e* they are the same size; *han er dobbelt så ~ som hun* he's twice as big as she is; *Danmark skrives med ~t* Denmark is written with a capital D; *~t set* on the whole; *gøre ~e øjne* be all eyes; *være ~ på den* be hoity-toity, be snooty; *se ~t på ngt* not be very par'ticular about sth; *ikke ~t bedre* not much better.

storartet *adj (glimrende)* splendid; *(skøn)* gorgeous.

Storbritannien *s* Great Britain.

storby *en* big city, me'tropolis.

storebror *en* big brother.

storesøster *en* big sister.

storetå *en* big toe.

storhed *en* greatness; *(pragt etc)* glory; **~s·tid** *en* days of glory; **~s·vanvid** *et* megalo'mania.

stork *en* stork; **~e·rede** *en* stork's nest.

storm *en (om vejret)* gale; *(med sne, regn etc også)* storm; *(angreb)* as'sault; *stilhed før ~en* calm be'fore the storm.

stormagasin *et* de'partment store.

stormagt *en* great power.
storme *v (fare, suse af sted)* rush; *(angribe)* as'sault; *det ~r* there is a gale blowing; **~nde** *adj* stormy; *~nde bifald* a storm of ap'plause.
storm... *sms:* **~flod** *en* storm tide, flood; **~fuld** *adj* stormy; **~lygte** *en* hurricane lantern; **~skader** *pl* storm damage *(u.pl);* **~varsel** *et* gale warning; **~vejr** *et* stormy weather.
stor... *sms:* **~ryger** *en* heavy smoker; **~sejl** *et* mainsail; **~slalom** *en* giant slalom; **~slået** *adj* mag'nificent; **~snudet** *adj* snooty; **~snudethed** *en* arrogance; **~stilet** *adj* large-scale; **~vask** *en* wash(ing); *holde ~vask* do· the washing; *(fig)* have a clean-up; **~vildt** *et* big game.
strabadser *pl* strain.
straf *en* punishment; *(dom)* sentence; *til ~* as a punishment; *den unge er en ~* (F) that kid is a menace; **~arbejde** *et* hard labour; **~bar** *adj: en ~bar handling* a criminal of'fence.
straffe *v* punish *(for* for); *han har været ~t* he has been con'victed; **~anstalt** *en* penal insti'tution; **~boks** *en (sport)* penalty box; **~fange** *en* convict; **~ret** *en (jur)* criminal law; **~spark** *et* penalty kick; **~sparkfelt** *et* penalty area.
strafporto *en* ex'cess (postage).
straks *adv* im'mediately, at 'once; *(lige ~, om lidt)* presently, in a minute; *jeg kommer ~* I won't be a minute; *vil du ~ holde op!* will you stop it im'mediately! *det er ~ midnat* it is close on midnight; *~ da han startede, punkterede han* the moment he started, he had a puncture; *~ i morgen tidlig* first thing to'morrow morning.
stram *adj* tight; *(om person)* stiff, se'vere.
stramaj *et* canvas.
stramhed *en* tightness; *(fig)* stiffness, se'verity.
stramme *v (gøre stram, fx snor)* tighten; *(være for ~, genere)* be too tight; *~ reglerne* tighten rules.
strammer *en (pol)* hawk.
stramning *en* tightening; *(nedskæring)* cut.
stramtsiddende *adj* tight-fitting.
strand *en* beach; *på ~en* on the beach; **~bred** *en* beach.
strande *v* be stranded; *(fig, slå fejl)* fail.
stranding *en (forlis)* wreck.
strandtøj *et* beachwear.
strateg *en* strategist.
strategi strategy.
strategisk *adj* stra'tegic.
streg *en* line; *(stribe)* streak; *(tanke~)* dash; *(gavtyve~, nummer)* trick; *gå over ~en* over'step the mark; *slå en ~* draw· a line; *det var en ~ i regningen for him* it thwarted his plans; *hun er en ~ i luften* she's as thin as a rake; *slå en ~ over ngt (fig)* for'get· sth; *(opgive)* drop sth; *sætte ~ under* under'line.
strege *v (slette)* strike· out, de'lete; *~ under* under'line.
stregkode *en* bar code.
strejfe *v (flakke rundt)* roam; *(om hund)* stray; *(røre let ved)* brush against, touch; *(nævne i forbifarten)* touch on.
strejke *en* strike // *v* (be on) strike, come· out (on strike); *køleskabet ~r* the fridge has packed up; *motoren ~r* the engine is playing up; **~bryder** *en* scab; **~kasse** *en* strike fund; **~ramt** *adj* strikebound; **~vagt** *en* picket; **~varsel** *et* strike notice.
streng *en (på instrument el. bue)* string // *adj* strict; *(hård)* se'vere; *(af ydre og væsen)* stern; *~t arbejde* hard work; *~t forbudt* strictly for'bidden; *~t nødvendig* absolutely necessary; *~e regler* strict rules; *~ straf* se'vere punishment; *være ~ ved en* be strict with sby; *nej, det er for ~t!* no, that is too much! *~t taget* strictly speaking; **~hed** *en* strictness, se'verity; sternness.
stresset *adj (om person)* under stress, stressed.
stribe *en* stripe; *(lys~)* streak; *en hel ~ af nye love* a whole series of new laws; *de faldt om på ~* they went down like ninepins; *stille op på ~* line up.

stribet *adj* striped; streaky.
strid *en (uenighed)* argument, dis'pute; *(kamp)* fight; *det er i ~ med reglerne* it is against the rules; *komme i ~* get· into an argument; *(i kamp)* start fighting // *adj (stiv)* stiff, hard; *(om flod etc)* rapid; *hun er en ~ kælling* she is a bit of a bitch; *det regner i ~e strømme* it is pelting down; *øllet flød i ~e stømme* there were oceans of beer; **~bar** *adj* pug'nacious.
stride *v (kæmpe)* fight·; *(slide, mase)* struggle, toil; **~s** *v (være uenige)* argue *(om* about); *(kæmpe)* fight· *(om* over).
stridigheder *pl* quarrels; *(kampe)* fighting.
stridsspørgsmål *et* matter of dis'pute.
stridsøkse *en: begrave ~n* bury the hatchet.
strigle *en* currycomb; *(kælling)* bitch // *v* groom.
strikke *en* rope // *v* knit; **~garn** *et* knitting yarn; *(af uld)* knitting wool; **~opskrift** *en* knitting pattern; **~pind** *en* knitting needle; **~tøj** *et* knitting.
strikning *en* knitting.
striks *adj* strict.
strikvarer *pl* knitwear.
strimmel *en* strip; *(lang ~ af papir el. stof)* tape; *(film~)* reel; *skære salat i strimler* shred lettuce.
strisser *en* (F) cop; (S) bizzy.
stritte *v (fx om hår)* bristle; *(om ører)* pro'trude; *~ imod* struggle (against); *(fig)* dig· in one's heels; *~ med fingrene* stick· out one's fingers; **~nde** *adj* bristly; *(om ører etc)* pro'truding.
strop *en* strap; *(fx i jakke)* hanger; **~løs** *adj* strapless.
strube *en* throat; **~hoved** *et* larynx.
struds *en* ostrich.
struktur *en* structure.
strukturere *v* structure.
struma *en* goitre.
strutte *v (stritte)* bristle; *(bule ud)* bulge; *(om skørt)* be full; *~ af sundhed* be bursting with health; **~nde** *adj (om skørt)* flouncy.
stryge *v (med strygejern)* iron; *(med hånden)* stroke; *(strege, slette)* strike· out, de'lete; *(aflyse)* cancel; *(suse, fare)* run·, shoot·; *~ en af listen* take· sby off the list; *~ rejer* shrimp; *~ en tændstik* strike· a match; **~bræt** *et* ironing board; **~fri** *adj* non-iron; **~jern** *et* iron; **~kvartet** *en* string quar'tet.
stryger *en (som spiller strygeinstrument)* string player; *~ne (i orkester)* the strings.
strygning *en* ironing; stroking; striking; cancel'lation *(se stryge).*
stryknin *en* 'strychnine.
stræbe *v: ~ efter (dvs. have som mål)* aim at; *(dvs. anstrenge sig for)* strive· for; *~ efter at* aim (,strive·) to.
stræben *en* striving, efforts *pl; (ærgerrighed)* aspi'ration.
stræber *en* swot.
stræbsom *adj* hardworking.
stræde *et (smal gade)* lane, alley; *(smalt sund)* straits.
stræk *et (~behandling)* traction; *læse en bog i ét ~* read· a book at one go.
strække *v* stretch; *(få til at slå til)* make· go further; *~ hånden ud efter ngt* reach out for sth; *lønnen ~r ikke langt* the pay does not go far; *det ~r lige til* it is just e'nough; *~ sig* stretch oneself; *(om fx skov, marker)* stretch (out); *~ sig over tre uger* last (for) three weeks.
strækning *en (det at strækkes)* stretching; *(stykke land, skov)* stretch; *(vejlængde)* distance.
stræknylon *en* stretch nylon.
strø *v* strew, sprinkle; *~ sukker på en kage* sprinkle a cake with sugar; *~ om sig med penge* throw· money about.
strøg *et (område)* stretch; *(let berøring)* touch; *(pensel~, bue~)* stroke.
strøget *adj: en ~ teskefuld* a level teaspoonful.
strøm *en (elek, hav, luft etc)* current; *(å, flod etc)* stream; *en ~ af gæster* a stream of visitors; *~men er gået* the elec'tricity is off; **~afbrydelse** *en*

power cut; **-førende** *adj* live; **-linet** *adj* streamlined.

strømme *v* stream, pour; *(om fx flod)* flow; *regnen ~de ned* the rain was pouring down; *folk ~de til* people flocked to the place.

strømning *en* current; *(fig også)* trend.

strømpe *en (lang)* stocking; *(kort)* sock; **-bukser** *pl* tights, pantyhose; **-holder** *en* su'spender belt; **-sokker** *pl: gå på ~sokker* walk in one's stockinged feet.

strømstyrke *en* strength of the e'lectric current; *(om fx elek pære)* wattage.

strømsvigt *et* power failure.

strå *et* straw; *være højt på ~* be top brass; *trække det korteste ~* get· the worst of it; **-hat** *en* straw hat.

stråle *en* ray; *(tyk lysstråle)* beam (of light); *(af vand, gas etc)* jet // *v* shine·; *(glitre)* sparkle.

strålende *adj (af glæde)* beaming, radiant; *(glitrende)* sparkling; *han har det ~* he is fine; *i ~ humør* in high spirits; *~ oplyst* a'blaze with light.

strålesyge *en* radi'ation sickness.

stråling *en* radi'ation.

stråtag *et* thatched roof.

stråtækt *adj* thatched.

stub *en (træ~)* stump; *(korn~, skæg~)* stubble.

stud *en* bullock; *(om person)* boor; *~.jur.* law student; *~.med.* medical student; *~.polit.* student of po'litical science; *~.polyt.* student of engi'neering; *~.theol.* student of di'vinity.

student *en (som har taget eksamen)* post'graduate; *(som studerer)* (uni'versity) student.

studenterforening *en* students' union.

studentereksamen *en sv.t.* GCSE (General Cer'tificate of Secondary Edu'cation).

studenterkammerat *en* fellow student.

studere *v* study; *~ til læge (også)* read· medicine; **-nde** *en* student.

studie *et (atelier, radio~ etc)* studio; **-kreds** *en* study circle; **-lån** *et* student loan; **-rejse** *en* study trip; **-vært** *en (tv)* (television) host.

studium *et* study.

studse *v (klippe)* trim; *(blive forbavset)* be sur'prised; *~ over ngt* be'gin· to wonder about sth.

stue *en* room; *(daglig~)* drawing room; *(på sygehus)* ward; *(~etage)* ground floor; **-antenne** *en* indoor aerial; **-etage** *en* ground floor; **-gang** *en (på sygehus)* rounds *pl; gå ~gang* go· the rounds; **-hus** *et* farmhouse; **-pige** *en (på hotel)* chambermaid; **-plante** *en* house plant, potted plant; **-temperatur** *en* room temperature; **-ur** *et* clock.

stuk *en* stucco.

stum *adj* dumb, mute; *jeg blev helt ~* I was speechless; **-film** *en* silent movie.

stump *en (smule)* piece, bit; *(af glas)* fragment; *(rest af træ, af amputeret ben etc)* stump; *(lille barn)* little darling; *slå ngt i ~er og stykker* smash sth to pieces // *adj: en ~ vinkel* an ob'tuse angle.

stumpe *v (om fx skørt)* be too short.

stumtjener *en* hat stand.

stund *en: i samme ~* at the same moment; *om en ~* in a while; *i stille ~er* in moments of peace; *nu om ~er* nowadays.

stutteri *et* stud farm.

stuve *v: ~de grønsager* boiled vegetables in a white sauce, vegetable casserole; *~ ngt sammen* pack sth; *~nde fuld* packed.

styg *adj (uartig)* naughty; *(væmmelig)* bad, nasty; *(grim)* ugly.

stykke *et* piece, bit; *(skive fx af brød)* slice; *(del)* part; *(skuespil)* play; *et ~ brød (dvs. en bid el. humpel)* a piece of bread; *(dvs. en skive)* a slice of bread; *et ~ mad* a sandwich; *et par ~r* one or two; *koste tre kr. ~t* cost· three kr. each (,a piece); *et ~ vej* some distance; *rive ngt i ~r* tear· sth to pieces; *slå ngt i ~r* smash sth; *bilen er i ~r* the car is out of order, (F) the car has packed up; *når det kommer til ~t* after all.

stylte *en* stilt.
styr *et (på cykel)* handlebars *pl; have ~ på ngt* be in con'trol of sth; *holde ~ på ngt* con'trol sth; **~bord** *et* starboard.
styre *et (regering)* government; *(ledelse)* management // *v (regere)* govern, rule; manage; *(lede)* manage; *(om skib)* steer; *(om bil)* drive·; *(holde styr på)* con'trol; *børnene er svære at ~* the children are difficult to cope with; *~ sig* re'strain oneself; *have fået sin lyst ~t* have had e'nough.
styrelse *en* admini'stration; *(ledelse)* management; *(bestyrelse)* board.
styring *en (ledelse)* management; *(kontrol)* con'trol; *(vejledning)* guidance.
styrke *en* strength; *(om lyd)* volume; *(om fx briller)* power; *~r (dvs. tropper)* forces // *v (gøre stærkere)* strengthen; *(opkvikke)* re'fresh.
styrkelse *en* strengthening.
styrkeprøve *en* trial of strength; *(af materiale)* test of strength.
styrmand *en* mate; *(i robåd)* cox(swain); *første ~* chief officer; *anden ~* second officer; *uden ~ (om kaproningsbåd)* coxless.
styrt *et* fall; *(med fly)* crash; **~dyk** *et* nosedive; **~dykke** *v (om fx dollarkurs)* slump.
styrte *v* fall· down; *(~ ned fx om fly)* crash; *(falde om)* fall· down; *(fare, suse)* rush; *~ regeringen* bring· down the government; *~ ind i stuen* come· bursting into the room; *~ ned (om fly)* crash; *(om regn)* be pouring down; *~ sammen* col'lapse; *(om jord, klipper etc)* fall· in; **~nde** *adj: ~nde rig* filthy rich; *have ~nde travlt* be terribly busy.
styrthjelm *en* crash helmet.
styrtløb *et (på ski)* downhill (racing).
stædig *adj* stubborn; **~hed** *en* stubbornness.
stængel *en* stem.
stænk *et* splash; *(plet)* spot; *(lille smule, fx parfume)* dash; *(fig, antydning)* touch.
stænke *v (sprøjte)* splash; *(lettere, også om tøj)* sprinkle; **~lap** *en (auto)* mud flap.
stær *en (zo)* starling; *(om øjensygdom:) grå ~* cataract; *grøn ~* glau'coma.
stærk *adj* strong; *(om lyd)* loud; *med ~ fart* at (a) high speed; *~e farver* bright colours; *en ~ kikkert* a powerful telescope; *~e verber* strong verbs.
stærkt *adv* strongly; loudly; *(hurtigt)* fast; *(meget ~)* heavily; *det blæser ~* it is blowing hard; *løbe ~* run· fast; *det ser ~ ud til at der bliver krig* it is ex'tremely likely that there will be a war, everything seems set for war.
stævne *et* meeting; *sætte en ~* make· an ap'pointment with sth; **~møde** *et* date.
stævning *en (jur)* summons.
støbe *v* cast; *sidde som støbt* fit like a glove; **~jern** *et* cast iron.
støberi *et* foundry.
støbning *en* casting; *(fig)* cast.
stød *et (skub)* push; *(elek)* shock; *(med dolk)* stab; *(i bil ved huller i vejen)* bump; *(i trompet, horn)* blast; *(i sprog)* glottal stop; *give ~et til ngt (dvs. sætte i gang)* i'nitiate sth; *(dvs. være årsag til)* be the cause of sth; *være i ~et* be in form; **~dæmper** *en* shock ab'sorber.
støde *v (skubbe)* push; *(findele, knuse)* pound; *(bumpe)* jolt; *(beskadige, slå)* hurt·; *(såre, fornærme)* of'fend; *~ foden* hurt· one's foot; *~ imod ngt* hit· sth, bump against sth; *~ ind i ngt* col'lide with sth; *~ op til* ad'join; *~ på en (dvs. træffe)* come· a'cross sby; *~ sammen* col'lide; **~nde** *adj* of'fensive.
stødpude *en* buffer.
stødt *adj (findelt, fx peber)* ground; *(om fx æble)* bruised; *(om person)* of'fended *(over* at).
stødtand *en* tusk.
støj *en* noise; *lave ~* make· a noise; **~dæmper** *en* silencer.
støje *v* make· a noise; **~nde** *adj* noisy.
støjforurening *en* noise pol'lution.
støjfri *adj* quiet; *(lydløs)* silent.

støjsender *en (radio)* jamming station.

støn *et* groan; **~ne** *v (gispe)* pant; *(give sig, jamre)* groan; **~nen** *en* panting; groaning.

størkne *v* harden; *(om blod)* clot, co'agulate.

større *adj* bigger, greater; *(højere)* taller.

størrelse *en* size; *(højde)* height; *(mængde)* quantity; *(omfang)* ex'tent; *hvilken ~ bruger du?* what size do you take? *hun bruger ~ 42 i bluser* she takes a size 16 in blouses; *hun er på min ~* she is my size.

størrelsesorden *en* magnitude; *ngt i den ~* sth like that, sth to that ef'fect.

størst *adj* biggest, greatest; *(højest)* tallest.

størstedelen *s* the greater part; *(de fleste)* the ma'jority; *~ af eleverne* most of the pupils.

støtte *en* sup'port; *(statue)* 'statue; *(søjle)* pillar; *(økonomisk ~, tilskud)* subsidy // *v* sup'port; *kommunen ~r skolen* the council subsidizes the school; *~ sig til ngt* lean· on sth; **~ben** *et (til cykel)* kick stand; **~bind** *et (elastisk)* crepe sup'port; **~pille** *en* buttress; **~punkt** *et* (point of) sup'port; *(mil)* base.

støv *et* dust; *tørre ~ af ngt* dust sth; **~bold** *en (bot)* puffball; **~drager** *en (bot)* stamen.

støve *v* raise dust; *~ ngt af* dust sth; *~ ngt igennem* search sth; *~ ngt op* dig· sth out; **~klud** *en* duster; **~t** *adj* dusty.

støvfnug *et* speck of dust.

støvle *en* boot; **~knægt** *en* bootjack; **~skaft** *en* bootleg.

støv... *sms:* **~regn** *en* drizzle; **~regne** *v* drizzle; **~sky** *en* cloud of dust; **~suge** *v* vacuum-clean, (F) hoover; **~suger** *en* vacuum cleaner, (F) hoover®; **~sugerslange** *s* hose.

stå *s: gå i ~* stop // *v* stand·; *(dvs. befinde sig)* be; *~ fast (på mening etc)* be firm; *~ stille* stand· still; *der ~r en statue uden for* there is a statue out'side; *det ~r 3-1 til Danmark* the score is 3-1 (three to one) in favour of Denmark; *de stod og ventede* they were waiting; *~ af (fx bussen)* get· off; *hvad ~r X for?* what does X stand for? *~ for indkøbene* be in charge of the shopping; *hun kunne ikke ~ for den taske* she could not re'sist that bag; *det ~r i avisen (,bogen etc)* it is in the paper (,the book); *~ ngt igennem* get· through sth; *~ op* stand·; *~ op (af sengen)* get· up; *solen ~r op* the sun is rising; *~ over for* face; *~ på (fx bussen)* get· in, get· on; *hvad ~r menuen på?* what is on the menu? *det stod på i fire uger* it lasted (for) four weeks; *hvis det stod til mig...* if you asked me...; *~ ud (af bil etc)* get· out; *~ ved sit løfte* stand· by one's promise.

stådreng *en: have ~* (V) have a hard-on.

stående *adj* standing; *blive ~ (dvs. ikke flytte sig)* re'main standing; *(dvs. standse)* stop; *lade ngt blive ~* let· sth stand; *på ~ fod (dvs. straks)* im'mediately; *(dvs. uden forberedelse)* off the cuff.

ståhej *en* fuss; *stor ~* a lot of fuss.

stål *et* steel; **~børste** *en* wire brush; **~tråd** *en* (steel) wire; **~trådshegn** *et* wire fence; **~uld** *en* steel wool; **~værk** *et: et ~værk* a steelworks.

ståplads *en* standing room.

subjekt *et (gram)* subject; *(om person)* sot.

subjektiv *adj* sub'jective.

subsistensløs *adj* destitute.

subskribere *v: ~ på* sub'scribe to.

subskription *en* sub'scription.

substantiv *et (gram)* noun.

subtropisk *adj* sub'tropical.

succes *en* suc'cess; *have ~* be a success; *have ~ med ngt* be suc'cessful in sth.

sufflere *v* prompt.

sufflør *en* prompter.

sug *et* suck; *(af fx drink)* sip, (F) swig; *(af cigaret)* puff.

suge *v* suck; *~ ngt op* ab'sorb sth; *~ på labben* tighten one's belt; **~mærke** *et* love bite; **~rør** *et* (drinking) straw; **~skive** *en* suction pad.

sugning *en* suction.
suk *et* sigh; *jeg forstår ikke et* ~ I don't under'stand· a word of it; *drage et dybt* ~ heave a deep sigh; *drage et lettelsens* ~ heave a sigh of relief.
sukat *en* candied peel.
sukke *v* sigh; **-n** *en* sighing.
sukker *et* sugar; *hugget* ~ lump sugar; *et stykke* ~ a lump of sugar; *komme* ~ *i ngt* put· sugar in sth; **-fabrik** *en* sugar mill; **-fri** *adj* no-sugar, un'sweetened; **-overtræk** *et* sugar coating; **-roe** *en* sugar beet; **-rør** *et* sugar cane; **-skål** *en* sugar basin; **-syge** *en* dia'betes; **-sygediæt** *en* dia'betic diet; **-sød** *adj* sugary.
sulfosæbe *en* de'tergent.
sult *en* hunger; *dø af* ~ die of star'vation; *være ved at dø af* ~ be starving.
sulte *v* starve.
sulten *adj* hungry; *meget* ~ (F) famished, starving.
sultestrejke *en* hunger strike.
sum *en* sum, total; *en stor* ~ *penge* a large sum of money.
summe *v (om bi)* hum, buzz.
summen *en* humming, buzzing.
summetone *en (tlf)* dialling tone.
sump *en* swamp; *(i motor)* sump; **-et** *adj* swampy.
sund *et* sound; *Sundet* the Sound.
sund *adj (rask)* sound; *(god for helbredet)* healthy; *(fornuftig)* sound; *fibre er* ~*t for maven* roughage is good for your stomach; ~ *fornuft* common sense.
sunde *v:* ~ *sig* col'lect oneself, re'cover.
sundhed *en* health; **-s·apostel** *en* health freak; **-s·farlig** *adj* damaging to health; **-s·ministerium** *et* Ministry of Health; **-s·pleje** *en* hygiene; **-s·plejerske** *en* (infant) health visitor; **-s·sektoren** *s* the health sector; **-s·væsen** *et* health au'thorities *pl.*
superb *adj* su'perb, splendid.
superlativ *en (gram)* the su'perlative.
supermagt *en* superpower.
supermarked *et* supermarket.
suppe *en* soup; *klar* ~ consommé; **-gryde** *en* soup pot; **-høne** *en* boiling fowl; **-ske** *en* soup spoon; *(opøseske)* ladle; **-terning** *en* stock cube; **-terrin** *en* tu'reen; **-urter** *pl* vegetables.
suppleant *en* substitute.
supplement *et* supplement.
supplere *v* supplement; **-nde** *adj* supple'mentary.
supplering *en* supplementing; *(af lager)* re'plenishment.
sur *adj* sour; *(syreholdig)* acid; *(om person)* cross; *(om vejr)* dull; *blive* ~ *(om person)* get· cross; *(om mælk)* turn (sour); *være* ~ *over ngt* be cross about sth; *være* ~ *på en* be cross with sby // *løbe* ~ *i det* get· it all mixed up; **-dej** *en* leaven; **-hed** *en* sourness, a'cidity; crossness; **-mule** *v* sulk.
surre *v (binde fast)* se'cure; *(om fx bi)* buzz, hum.
surrogat *et* substitute.
suse *v (om blæst)* whistle; *(fare af sted)* rush, tear·.
susen *en* whistling; rushing.
suspekt *adj* su'spicious.
suspendere *v* su'spend.
sut *en (på flaske)* teat; *(narre~)* dummy; *(sko)* slipper; *(dranker)* drunken sot.
sutte *v* suck *(på ngt* sth); **-flaske** *en* (feeding) bottle.
suveræn *adj* sovereign; *(overlegen)* su'perior.
svag *adj* weak; *(meget ~, afkræftet)* feeble; *(let)* faint, slight; *min* ~*e side* my weak point; ~ *vind* light breeze; *en* ~ *hvisken* a faint whisper; *blive* ~*ere* weaken.
svagelig *adj* delicate.
svaghed *en* weakness.
svagt *adv* weakly, feebly; faintly; *det tør* ~ *antydes!* I should say so!
svaj *et (fx i bukser)* flare; **-e** *v* sway, swing·; **-rygget** *adj* sway-backed.
sval *adj* cool.
svale *en* swallow // *v* cool; ~ *ngt af* cool sth (down); **-skab** *et* chiller cupboard.
svamp *en (bot, spiselig)* mushroom; *(bot, giftig)* toadstool; *(i træværk*

etc) dry-rot; *(bade~)* sponge; *(fod~)* athlete's foot.
svampet *adj* spongy.
svane *en* swan; **~unge** *en* cygnet.
svang *en (på foden)* arch; *gå i ~* be rampant.
svangerskab *et* pregnancy; **~s·afbrydelse** *en* termi'nation of pregnancy; **~s·forebyggelse** *en* contra'ception.
svanse *v* (F) swan *(af sted* along).
svar *et* answer, re'ply; *give en ~ på ngt* give· sby an answer to sth; *få ~ på tiltale* get· one's own back; *som ~ på Deres skrivelse* in reply to your letter; *blive ~ skyldig* be at a loss for an answer.
svare *v* answer, re'ply; *jeg ~r ikke for følgerne* I won't answer for the consequences; *~ igen* answer back; *~ på ngt* answer sth; *~ sig* pay·; *~ til ngt* corre'spond to sth; *(passe til)* match sth.
svarkuvert *en* stamped ad'dressed envelope, s.a.e.
svarskrivelse *en* (written) re'ply.
sved *en* sweat [swɛt].
svede *v* per'spire, sweat; *~ ngt ud (dvs. glemme)* for'get· sth.
sveden *adj (om mad etc)* burnt; *et ~t grin* a mischievous grin.
svedig *adj* sweaty.
svejse *v* weld.
svejsning *en* welding.
Svejts *s* Switzerland.
svelle *en (jernb)* sleeper.
svend *en (håndværker)* journeyman *(pl:* -men); *(fyr)* fellow.
svendeprøve *en* exami'nation to become a journeyman.
svendestykke *et* journeyman's piece.
svensk *adj* Swedish; **~er** *en* Swede.
svensknøgle *en* ad'justable spanner.
Sverige *s* Sweden.
sveske *en* prune.
svide *v* singe, scorch; *(om mad)* burn·.
svie *en* pain // *v* sting·.
sviger... *sms:* **~datter** *en* daughter-in-law; **~far** *en* father-in-law; **~forældre** *pl* parents-in-law, (F) 'in-laws; **~inde** *en* sister-in-law; **~mor** *en* mother-in-law; **~søn** *en* son-in-law.
svigte *v (~ en)* let· down; *(løfte etc)* break·, go· back on; *(om kræfter, mod, mekanik etc)* fail; *motoren ~de* the engine broke down; *modet ~de ham* his courage failed; *føle sig ~t* feel· let down, feel· be'trayed.
svimlende *adj* dizzy; *(meget stor)* e'normous.
svimmel *adj* dizzy, giddy; **~hed** *en* dizziness, giddiness.
svin *et (zo)* pig; *(om kødet)* pork; *(om person)* swine, pig; *et dumt ~* a bastard.
svind *et* waste, loss.
svinde *v (mindskes)* de'crease, de'cline; *(forsvinde)* vanish; *(om tid)* pass; *~ hen* waste away.
svindel *en* swindle; *(bedrageri)* fraud; *(det at svindle)* swindling.
svindle *v* swindle; *~ med ngt (dvs. forfalske)* fiddle sth; **svindler** *en* swindler; fraudster.
svine *v: ~ ngt til* dirty sth, mess up sth; **~fedt** *et* lard; **~held** *et* fat luck; **~kam** *en* neck of pork; **~kotelet** *en* pork chop; **~kød** *et* pork; **~lever** *en* pig's liver; **~læder** *et* pigskin.
svineri *et* filth, mess.
svinesti *en* pigsty.
sving *et (drejning)* turn; *(vej~)* bend, turning; *(svingning)* swing; *sætte ngt i ~* set· sth going; *være i fuldt ~* be in full swing; **~dør** *en* swing door; *(som drejer rundt)* re'volving door.
svinge *v (dreje)* turn; *(om pendul etc)* swing·; *(svinge med, vifte med)* wave; *(skifte ustadigt)* change, fluctuate; *~ med ngt* wave sth; *humøret er ~nde* the mood changes; *~ om hjørnet* turn the corner; *~ sig* swing.
svingning *en (drejning)* turn; *(vibration)* vi'bration; *(skiften)* changing, fluctu'ation.
svinsk *adj* filthy, dirty.
svip *et: få ~* go· nuts; *det er til at få ~ af* it's e'nough to drive· you up the wall.
svipse *v* go· wrong, fail.
svipser *en: det var en ~* it was a flop.
sviptur *en* trip; *vi tog en ~ til Paris i weekenden* we nipped over to Paris for the weekend.

svire *v* booze.
svirre *v* whirr; *(om møl etc)* buzz.
svoger *en* brother-in-law.
svovl *et* sulphur; **~syre** *en* sul'phuric acid.
svulme *v* swell; **~nde** *adj* swelling; *(om kvinde)* buxom; *(om bryst)* ample.
svulst *en* growth; *(med)* tumour.
svulstig *adj* pompous; **~hed** *en* pompousness.
svække *v* weaken; **~lse** *en* weakening; *(det at være svækket, svagelig)* frailty, weakness.
svækling *en* weakling.
svælg *et (hals)* throat; *(slugt etc)* a'byss.
svælge *v (synke)* swallow; *~ i ngt* revel in sth.
svær *en (flæske~)* rind; *(sprød)* crackling // *adj (tung)* heavy; *(tyk, kraftig)* stout; *(stærk)* strong, solid; *(vanskelig)* difficult, hard; *lide ~e tab* suffer heavy losses; *(se også svært).*
sværd *et* sword.
sværge *v* swear· *(på* to; *på at* that); *~ til ngt* swear by sth.
sværhed *en (se svær);* heaviness; stoutness; difficulty.
sværindustri *en* heavy industry.
sværm *en* swarm; *(af folk)* crowd.
sværme *v (om insekter)* swarm; *~ for en* have a crush on sby; *~ for ngt* be very fond of sth.
sværmeri *et (lidenskab)* passion; *(drømmeri)* dreaming.
svært *adv (tungt)* heavily; *(meget)* very, most; *(alvorligt)* seriously *(fx kvæstet* injured); *(tykt, kraftigt)* heavily, stoutly; *have ~ ved at gøre ngt* have trouble doing sth, find· it difficult to do sth; *det var ~ hyggeligt* it was very nice.
sværte *en (tryk~)* ink; *(sko~)* polish // *v (om sko)* black; *(med tryk~)* ink; *(gøre sort)* blacken; *(bagtale)* smear.
sværvægt *en* heavyweight.
svæve *v* float; *(om fugl)* hover; *(om fly)* glide; **~bane** *en* cable railway; **~fly** *et* glider; **~flyvning** *en* gliding.
svøbe *v* wrap; *~ ngt ind* wrap sth up.
svømme *v* swim·; *de ~r i penge* they are rolling in money; *~ ovenpå* float; *~ over Kanalen* swim· the Channel; *være ude at ~ (dvs. føle sig usikker)* be all at sea; **~bassin** *et* swimming pool; **~bælte** *et* swimming belt; **~dykker** *en* skin-diver; **~dykning** *en* skin-diving; **~fugl** *en* swimming bird; **~fødder** *pl (zo)* webbed feet; *(til mennesker)* flippers; **~hal** *en* swimming bath.
svømmer *en* swimmer; *(tekn)* float.
svømmetag *et* stroke.
svømmetur *en* swim; *tage en ~* go· for a swim.
sweater *en* jersey; *(kraftig)* sweater.
sy *v* sew; *~ sit eget tøj* make· one's own clothes; *få ~et en dragt* have a suit made; *~ på maskine* ma'chine(-stitch); *~ knapper i* sew on buttons; *~ ngt sammen* sew sth up.
syd *en* south; *i ~en* in the south; *~ for* south of; *rejse mod ~* go· south; *stuen vender mod ~* the room faces south.
Sydafrika *s* South Africa.
Sydamerika *s* South A'merica.
Syddanmark *s* Southern Denmark.
syde *v* seethe.
Sydeuropa *s* Southern Europe.
sydfra *adv* from the south.
Sydfrankrig *s* the South of France.
sydfrugt *en (citron, appelsin etc)* citrus fruit.
Sydhavet *s* the South Sea.
sydlig *adj* southern; *(om vind)* south; *den ~e vendekreds* the Tropic of Capricorn; **sydligere** *v* more southern, further south; **sydligst** *adj* southernmost.
Sydpolen *s* the South Pole.
sydpolsekspedition *en* Ant'arctic expe'dition.
sydpå *adv* south, towards the south; *(nede sydpå)* in the south.
sydvendt *adj* facing south.
sydvest *en (om regnhat)* sou'wester // *adj* south-west.
sydøst *adj* south-east.
syerske *en* seamstress; *(dameskrædder)* dressmaker.

syfilis *en* syphilis.

syg *adj* ill; *(foran substantiv)* sick; *(om del af kroppen, fx ben)* bad; *han er syg* he is ill; *en ~ mand* a sick man; *blive ~* be taken ill; *jeg bliver ~ af at se på det* it makes me sick to look at it; *være ~* be ill; *(sygemeldt)* be off sick; *være ~ efter at gøre ngt* be dying to do sth; *være ~ med ngt* be crazy about sth.

sygdom *en* illness, sickness; *(om bestemt sygdom)* dis'ease.

syge *en* dis'ease; **~besøg** *et: gå på ~besøg (generelt)* visit a patient; *(om læge)* do· one's rounds; **~dage** *pl* days off due to illness; **~dagpenge** *pl* sickness benefit; **~forsikring** *en* health in'surance; **~hjælper** *en* as'sistant nurse; **~hus** *et* hospital; **~lig** *adj (svagelig)* sickly; *(pervers)* sick; **~melding** *en* notifi'cation of illness; **~meldt** *adj: være ~meldt* be off sick; **~orlov** *en* sick leave; **~pleje** *en* nursing; **~plejeelev** *en* student nurse; **~plejer** *en* male nurse; **~plejerske** *en* nurse; **~sikring** *en* (national) health in'surance.

sygne *v: ~ hen* waste away.

syl *en* awl.

sylespids *adj* sharp as a needle.

sylte *en (gastr)* brawn // *v* pre'serve; *(lave saft)* make· juice; *(lave syltetøj)* make· jam; *~ en sag* shelve a case; **~tøj** *et* jam; **~tøjsglas** *et* jam jar.

syltning *en* pre'serving.

symaskine *en* sewing ma'chine; *sy på ~* ma'chine.

symbol *et* 'symbol *(på* of).

symbolisere *v* 'symbolize.

symbolsk *adj* sym'bolic.

symfoni *en* 'symphony; **~orkester** *et* 'symphony 'orchestra.

symmetri *en* 'symmetry.

symmetrisk *adj* sym'metrical.

sympati *en* 'sympathy, liking; *have ~ med en* 'sympathize with sby.

sympatisk *adj* nice, pleasant.

sympatistrejke *en* sympathy strike // *v* come· out in sympathy.

symptom *et* 'symptom *(på* of).

syn *et (synsevne)* eyesight, vision; *(det man ser)* sight; *(anskuelse)* view; *(bilkontrol)* MOT(-test); *have et svagt ~* have bad eyesight; *se ~er* see· things; *det var et sørgeligt ~* it was a sorry sight; *komme til ~e* ap'pear; *forsvinde af ~e* disap'pear; *for et ~s skyld* for the sake of ap'pearances; *ved ~et af ham* at the sight of him.

synagoge *en* 'synagogue.

synd *en* sin; *det var ~ du ikke så det!* what a pity you didn't see it! *det er ~ for dig!* I feel· sorry for you! poor you! *det ville være ~ hvis...* it would be a shame if...; *det er ~ og skam* it's a crying shame.

synde *v* sin; **~buk** *en* scapegoat; **~fuld** *adj* sinful.

synder *en* sinner; *~en (dvs. den skyldige)* the culprit.

synderegister *et* record.

syndflod *en* deluge; *Syndfloden* the Flood.

syndig *adj* sinful; *et ~t rod* an awful mess.

syndsforladelse *en* abso'lution.

syne *v* in'spect; *det ~r ikke af meget* it is not very im'pressive.

synes *v (mene)* think·; *(virke)* seem; *hvad ~ du?* what do you think? *jeg ~ den er pæn* I think it's nice; *det ~ som om...* it seems as if...; *gør det, hvis du ~!* do it if you like! *~ om ngt* like sth; *hvad syntes du om bogen?* how did you like the book?

synge *v* sing·; *~ med* join 'in.

syning *en (det at sy)* sewing, stitching; *(søm)* seam; *(håndarbejde)* needlework; *(af sår)* stitches *pl.*

synke *v (sluge)* swallow; *(dale)* sink·; *(om skib)* go· down; *(om temperatur)* fall·, go· down; *~ ned i ngt* sink· into sth; *jeg var ved at ~ i jorden af skam* I wished the ground would swallow me up; *~ sammen* col'lapse.

synkron *adj* synchronous.

synkronisere *v* synchronize; *(film)* dub.

synlig *adj* visible; *(åbenbar)* obvious.

synonym *et* 'synonym // *adj* sy'nonymous *(med* with).

syns... *sms:* **~bedrag** *et* optical il'lusion; **~forstyrrelser** *pl* visual di'sturbances; **~kreds** *en* ho'rizon; **~prøve** *en* eye test; **~punkt** *et* point of view; **~vidde** *en: inden for ~vidde* with'in sight; *uden for ~vidde* out of sight; **~vinkel** *en (fig)* aspect.

syntese *en* 'synthesis.

syntetisk *adj* syn'thetic, man-made *(fx sål* sole).

synål *en* sewing needle.

syre *en* acid.

syren *en* lilac.

syrer *en* Syrian.

syreregn *en* acid rain.

Syrien *s* Syria; **syrisk** *adj* Syrian.

syrlig *adj* sour, acid.

sysilke *en* sewing silk.

sysle *v: ~ med ngt* be doing sth; *(pille, nusse)* fiddle with sth.

system *et* 'system; *"Systemet"* the E'stablishment; *sætte ngt i ~* systematize sth; **~analytiker** *en* 'systems 'analyst.

systematisk *adj* syste'matic.

systemchef *en* 'systems 'manager.

sytråd *en* sewing thread.

sytten *num* seventeen.

sytøj *et* sewing.

syv *num* seven; *de klarer sig fint, ~, ni, tretten!* they are doing well, touch wood! *det varede ~ lange og ~ brede* it took ages.

syvende *adj* seventh; *til ~ og sidst* in the upshot; **~del** *en* seventh.

syver *en* seven; *(om bus etc)* number seven.

syvtal *et* seven.

syæske *en* sewing box.

sæbe *en* soap; *et stykke ~* a cake of soap; *brun ~* soft soap // *v: ~ ngt af* wash sth with soap; **~automat** *en* soap di'spenser; **~boble** *en* soap bubble; **~pulver** *et* soap powder; **~skum** *et* lather; **~spåner** *pl* soapflakes; **~vand** *et* soapy water.

sæd *en* seed; *(sperma)* semen; **~celle** *en* sperm cell.

sæde *et* seat; *have ~ i parlamentet* have a seat in Parliament.

sædelighed *en* mo'rality; **~s·forbrydelse** *en* sex crime; **~s·politi** *et* vice squad.

sædvane *en* custom; *efter ~* ac'cording to custom; *imod ~* contrary to custom.

sædvanlig *adj* usual; *(vant)* customary; *som ~* as usual; *han er ngt ud over det ~e* he is sth out of the ordinary.

sædvanligvis *adv* usually.

sæk *en (mindre)* bag; *(større)* sack.

sækkelærred *et* sackcloth.

sækkepibe *en* bagpipe.

sækkestol *en* bean-bag chair.

sæl *en* seal; **~fangst** *en* sealing.

sælge *v* sell·; *grunde ~s* land for sale.

sælger *en* seller; *(om jobbet)* salesman *(pl:* -men).

sælskind *et* sealskin.

sænke *v* lower; *(om skib)* sink·; *~ sig (om mørket)* fall·; **~køl** *en* centreboard.

sænkning *en* lowering; *(af skib)* sinking; *(i landskabet)* de'pression, hollow; *(med)* sedimen'tation rate.

sær *adj (mærkelig)* odd, pe'culiar; *(sur)* cross.

særbehandling *en: få ~* get· special treatment.

særdeles *adv* ex'tremely, very; **~hed** *en: i ~hed* e'specially.

særeje *et* sepa'ration of property; *huset er mit ~* the house is my separate property.

særhed *en (se sær);* oddity, peculi'arity; crossness.

særlig *adj* special, par'ticular; *(særskilt)* separate // *adv* specially; *(især, specielt)* e'specially; *ikke ~ rar* not very nice; *det var ikke ngt ~t* it was nothing special.

særling *en* ec'centric.

sær... *sms:* **~nummer** *et* special (issue); **~præg** *et* characte'ristic, peculi'arity; **~præget** *adj (mærkelig)* pe'culiar; **~skilt** *adj* separate, indi'vidual; **~syn** *et* rarity; **~tog** *et* special train; **~tryk** *et* reprint.

sæson *en* season; *det er ~ for jordbær* strawberries are in season.

sæt *et (sammenhørende ting)* set; *(ryk)* start, jump; *et ~ byggeklodser* a set of toy bricks; *et ~ tøj* a suit; *et ~ undertøj* a set of underwear; *det gav et ~ i ham* he jumped (,started).

sætning *en (gram)* sentence; *(typ)* type-setting.

sætte *v (anbringe)* put·, place, set·; *(antage)* sup'pose; *(typ)* set·; ~ *sig (ned)* sit· down; ~ *sig for at holde op med at ryge* de'cide to stop smoking; ~ *sig ind i ngt* get· ac'quainted with sth; ~ *sig til at læse* start reading; *sæt nu at han har glemt det* sup'posing he has forgotten; ~ *penge af til ngt* set· a'side money for sth; ~ *en af på vejen hjem* drop sby on the way home; ~ *ngt fast* fasten sth; ~ *en fast* ar'rest sby; ~ *en i fængsel* put· sby in prison; ~ *farten ned* re'duce speed; ~ *farten op* in'crease speed; ~ *tapet op* hang· wallpaper; ~ *håret op* put· up one's hair; ~ *vand over* put· the kettle on; ~ *ngt sammen* put· sth to'gether, as'semble sth; ~ *ngt til (dvs. miste)* lose· sth; ~ *ngt til livs* con'sume sth; *motoren satte ud* the engine failed; ~ *en lejer ud* turn out a tenant; ~ *sit navn under ngt* sign sth.

sættemaskine *en* type-setter.

sættevogn *en* semi-trailer.

sø *en (indsø)* lake; *(bølge, hav)* sea; *(pyt)* pool; *i rum* ~ on the open sea; *lade ham sejle i sin egen* ~ leave· him to his own de'vices; *til ~s* at sea; **~bred** *en* lakeside.

sød *adj (om smag etc)* sweet; *(rar, pæn)* nice; *(artig)* good; *(nuttet)* cute; *hvor er det ~t af dig!* how nice of you! *~e sager* sweets; *det smager ~t* it tastes sweet; *vi sov ~t* we slept soudly; *gå nu, så er du ~!* go now, there's a dear!

søde *v* sweeten; *(komme sukker i også)* sugar; **~middel** *et* sweetener.

sødladen *adj* sugary.

sødlig *adj* sweetish.

sødme *en* sweetness.

sødmælk *en* whole milk.

sø... *sms:* **~dygtig** *adj* seaworthy; **~farende** *en* sailor, seaman *(pl:* -men); **~fart** *en* navi'gation; *(som fag)* shipping; **~folk** *pl* sailors, seamen; **~gang** *en* sea; *høj ~gang* heavy sea.

søge *v (lede)* look, search; *(lede efter)* look for; *(ansøge)* ap'ply *(om* for); ~ *at gøre ngt* try to do sth; ~ *hjælp* ask for help; ~ *job* be looking for a job; ~ *ly* seek· shelter; ~ *læge* see· a doctor; ~ *efter ngt* look for sth, search for sth; ~ *om ngt* ap'ply for sth; **~lys** *et* searchlight; *være i ~lyset* be in the limelight.

søgen *en* search(ing).

søger *en (foto)* viewfinder.

søgning *en* search *(også edb); (kunder)* custom.

søgt *adj (populær)* 'popular; *(om vare)* in de'mand; *(kunstig, affekteret)* af'fected.

søhelt *en* naval hero.

søhest *en* sea horse.

søjle *en* column, pillar; **~gang** *en* colon'nade.

søkort *et* (nautical) chart.

søle *et* mud.

sølle *adj* poor, measly.

sølv *et* silver; **~bryllup** *et* silver wedding; **~kræ** *et (zo)* silver fish; **~mærke** *et* hallmark; **~papir** *et (stanniol)* tinfoil, alu'minium foil; **~plet** *s* silverplate; **~smed** *en* silversmith; **~tøj** *et* silverware.

søløve *en* sea lion.

søm *en (syning)* seam; *(ombøjet, fx forneden på kjole)* hem; *sy en* ~ stitch a seam (,hem); *gå op i ~mene* burst· at the seams // *et* nail; *(stift)* tack; *slå* ~ *i* drive· in nails.

sømand *en* sailor, seaman *(pl:* -men); **~s·skole** *en* sea training school.

sømil *en* nautical mile.

sømløs *adj* seamless.

sømme *v (slå fast)* nail; *(sy)* stitch; ~ *sig* be proper.

sømmelig *adj* decent, proper; **~hed** *en* decency, pro'priety.

sømmerum *et (i tøj)* seam al'lowance.

sømærke *et* maritime signal; *(bøje)* buoy.

søn *en* son; *være* ~ *af en* be the son of sby, be sby's son.

søndag *en* Sunday; *i ~s* last Sunday; *om ~en* on Sundays; *på* ~ on Sunday, next Sunday; **~s·bilist** *en* Sunday driver; **~s·skole** *en* Sunday school; **~s·tøj** *et* Sunday clothes *pl.*

sønder *adv: ~ og sammen* to bits (and pieces).
Sønderjylland *s* the South of Jutland.
sønderknust *adj (fig)* heartbroken.
sønderlemmende *adj* devastating.
søndre *adj* southern.
søofficer *en* naval officer; **~s·skole** *en* naval college.
søpindsvin *et* sea urchin.
søredningstjeneste *en* air-sea rescue (service).
sørejse *en* voyage; *(overfart)* crossing.
søret *en (domstol)* maritime court.
sørge *v* grieve; *(over afdød også)* mourn; *~ for ngt* take· care of sth, look after sth; *~ for at...* see· to it that...; *sørg for at lukke vinduerne!* be sure to shut the windows! *~ over en* mourn for sby; *de ~nde* the mourners; **~dragt** *en* mourning.
sørgelig *adj* sad; *(ynkelig)* pitiful; *i en ~ tilstand* in a sorry state.
sørgmodig *adj* sad; **~hed** *en* sadness.
sørøver *en* pirate; **sørøveri** *et* piracy.
søskende *pl* brother(s) and sister(s).
søslag *et* naval battle.
søspejder *en* sea scout.
søster *en* sister; **~datter** *en* niece; **~søn** *en* nephew.
sø... *sms:* **~stjerne** *en* starfish; **~stærk** *adj: hun er ~stærk* she is a good sailor; **~syg** *adj* seasick; **~syge** *en* seasickness; **~sætning** *en* launching; **~sætte** *v* launch; **~tunge** *en (fisk)* sole.
søvn *en* sleep; *falde i ~* fall· a'sleep; *gå i ~e* sleepwalk; *tale i ~e* talk in one's sleep; **~dyssende** *adj* sopo'rific; *(kedelig)* mo'notonous; **~gænger** *en* sleepwalker.
søvnig *adj* sleepy; **~hed** *en* sleepiness.
søvnløs *adj* sleepless; **~hed** *en* in'somnia.
søværnet *s* the Navy.
så *v (lægge frø)* sow.
så *adv/interj (om tid, derpå, da etc)* then; *(derfor)* so; *(så meget, i den grad)* so; *(i så fald)* then; *(andre sammenhænge, se eksempler); hun blev vred, og ~ gik han* she got angry and then he left; *det er sent, ~ vi må gå* it is late, so we must leave; *det er ~ koldt at...* it is so cold that...; *hvis du er syg, ~ må du hellere gå hjem* if you are ill, then you had better go home; *kom ~ skal du se* come and see; *~ dum kan man da ikke være!* how stupid can you get! *gør det nu, ~ er du sød!* do it now, there's a dear! *så, så!* come, come! *det var ~ det* that was that, then; *det var ~ som ~* it was so so; *~ gør det da!* (well) do it then!.
sådan *adj* such, like that // *adv (så meget)* so much; *(således)* like this, like that; *han er ~ en idiot* he is such a fool; *~ en stor mand* such a big man, a big man like that; *hvorfor siger du ~?* why do you say that (,so)? *~!* that's it! *~ noget* that sort of thing, stuff like that; *nå, ~!* I see! *~ set* in a way; *~ som du kører* the way you drive.
sågar *adv* even.
såfremt *konj* in case.
såkaldt *adj* so-called.
sål *en* sole.
således *adv* like this, like that.
såmænd *adv (egentlig)* really; *det gik ~ meget godt* it really went quite well; *det skal ~ nok gå* I'm sure it will be all right.
sår *et* wound; *(kronisk, fx mave~)* ulcer; *forbinde et ~* dress a wound; **~bar** *adj* vulnerable.
såre *v* hurt, injure, wound; *blive ~t (i krig etc)* get· wounded; *(ved ulykke)* get injured; *(fig)* get· hurt; *hårdt ~t* seriously wounded (,injured); **~nde** *adj (om bemærkning etc)* hurtful.
såsom *adv* such as.
såvel *adv: ~ a som b* both a and b.

T

tab *et* loss; *lide et ~* suffer a loss; *store ~ (i krig og økon etc)* heavy losses; *sælge ngt med ~* sell· sth at a loss.
tabe *v* lose·; *(ud af hånden)* drop; *de tabte kampen (i krig etc)* they lost the battle; *(i sport)* they were beaten; *han tabte glasset på gulvet* he dropped the glass on the floor; *give*

tabt give· it up; *gå tabt* be lost; *uret har tabt fem minutter* the watch has lost five minutes; ~ *i vægt* lose· weight.

tabel *en* table.

taber *en* loser; *social* ~ social loser; *være en god* ~ be gracious in de'feat.

tabgivende *adj* loss-making.

tablet *en* 'tablet, pill.

tabu *et* ta'boo.

taburet *en* stool; *(om ministers)* office.

tackle *v* tackle; **tackling** *en* tackle.

taft *en* taffeta.

tag *et (på hus etc)* roof; *(greb)* hold, grip; *(håndelag)* knack; *(svømning, roning)* stroke; *få* ~ *i ngt* get· hold of sth; *have godt* ~ *på at gøre ngt* have the knack of doing sth; *miste* ~*et* lose· one's hold (,grip); *slippe* ~*et i ngt* let· go of sth; **~antenne** *en* roof aerial; **~bagagebærer** *en* roof rack; **~beklædning** *en* roofing.

tage *v* take·; *(tåle, udholde)* stand·, take·; *(rejse, begive sig)* go·; *tag det roligt!* take it easy! *jeg kan ikke* ~ *den fyr* I can't stand that chap; ~ *af (om tøj)* take· off; *(mindskes)* de'crease; *(i vægt)* lose· weight; ~ *tøjet af (også)* un'dress; ~ *af bordet* clear the table; ~ *af sted* leave·, start; ~ *for sig (af retterne)* help oneself; ~ *£10 for en bog* charge £10 for a book; ~ *ngt frem* take· sth out, pro'duce sth; ~ *imod ngt (dvs. modtage)* re'ceive sth; ~ *imod en ved toget* meet· sby at the station; ~ *imod fornuft* listen to reason; ~ *ind (i strikning)* de'crease; ~ *ind på et hotel* put· up at a hotel; ~ *med bussen* go· by bus; *han tog hende med ud (i byen)* he took her out; ~ *ngt op (fra gulvet)* pick sth up (from the floor); ~ *ngt op af lommen* take· sth out of one's pocket; ~ *plads op* take· up room; ~ *på (om tøj)* put· on; ~ *tøjet på (også)* get· dressed; ~ *på i vægt* put· on weight; *det tog hårdt på ham* it was hard on him; *de er* ~*t på landet* they have gone into the country; *hun tog sig et bad* she had a bath; ~ *sig af* take· care of, look after; *(være bekymret over)* worry about; *det skal du ikke* ~ *dig af!* don't worry about that! ~ *sig sammen* pull oneself to'gether; ~ *til (øges)* in'crease; ~ *til London* go· to London; ~ *en til fange* take· sby prisoner; ~ *ud* take· out; *(udvælge)* pick (out); *(i strikning)* in'crease; *(af bordet)* clear the table.

tagetage *en* top floor.

tagfat *en: lege* ~ play tag.

taghave *en* roof garden.

tagkammer *et* attic room.

tagpap *en* roofing felt, asphalt paper.

tagrende *en* gutter.

tagselvbord *et* 'buffet.

tagskæg *et* eaves *pl.*

tagsten *en* tile.

tagterrasse *en* roof terrace.

tagvindue *et* skylight.

tak *en (spids)* point, jag; *(på sav)* tooth; ~*ker (på hjort)* antlers.

tak *en* thanks, (F) ta; *mange* ~*!* thank you very much! *ja* ~*!* yes, please! *nej* ~*!* no, thanks! no thank you! *selv* ~*!* don't mention it! *nej, nu skal du snart have* ~*!* now, look here! ~ *for brevet* thank you for the letter; ~ *i lige måde* the same to you; *jeg er ham* ~ *skyldig* I owe him; *tage til* ~*ke med ngt* make· do with sth.

takke *v* thank; ~ *en for ngt* say· thank you to sby for sth; *vi kan* ~ *ham for at det gik* it went well thanks to him; *ikke ngt at* ~ *for!* don't mention it! ~*t være* thanks to; **~skrivelse** *en* letter of thanks.

taknemmelig *adj* grateful *(for* for); *(tilfredsstillende)* worthwhile; *jeg er ham meget* ~ I am very grateful to him; **~hed** *en* gratitude.

taks *en (bot)* yew (tree).

taksere *v:* ~ *til* estimate at, value at.

takst *en* charge, rate; *(i bus, tog etc)* fare; **~zone** *en* fare stage.

takt *en* time; *(mus)* measure; *(finfølelse)* tact; *holde* ~*en* keep· time; *gå i* ~ walk in step; *slå* ~ beat· time; *ude af* ~ out of time; *en fire*~*s motor* a four-stroke engine; **~fast** *adj* measured // *adv* in time; **~fuld** *adj* dis'creet.

taktik *en* 'tactics *pl,* policy; **~er** *en* tac'tician.

taktisk *adj* 'tactical.

taktløs *adj* indi'screte; **~hed** *en* indi'scretion.

taktslag *et* beat.

taktstok *en* baton.

tal *et (antal)* number; *(~tegn)* figure; *(i flercifret ~)* digit; *lige (,ulige) ~* even (,odd) number; *holde ~ på ngt* keep· count of sth.

tale *en* speech; *(samtale)* talk; *holde en ~* make· a speech; *det hus der er ~ om* the house in question; *har du hørt ~ om ham?* have you heard of him? *der er ~ om et større beløb* it in'volves a fair a'mount of money; *det kan der ikke være ~ om* that is out of the question; *komme på ~* be con'sidered; (F) come· up // *v* speak·, talk; *~ engelsk* speak· English; *~ forretninger* talk business; *ærligt talt* frankly, honestly; *~ ens sag* plead for sby; *det ~r for sig selv* that speaks for it'self; *der er meget der ~r for det* there is a lot to be said for it; *~ en fra at gøre ngt* talk sby out of doing sth; *~ i telefon* be on the telephone; *~ med en* talk to sby; *hvem ~r jeg med? (tlf)* who is speaking? *De ~r med Ms Johnson (tlf)* this is Ms Johnson speaking; *~ om ngt* talk about sth; *ikke ngt at ~ om* nothing to speak of; *~ sammen* talk; *~ til en* talk (,speak) to sby; *~ ud* finish (speaking); *~s ved* talk.

tale... *sms:* **~boble** *en* bal'loon; **~fejl** *en* speech im'pediment; **~fod** *en: være på ~fod med en* be on speaking terms with sby; *de er ikke på ~fod* they are not on speaking terms; **~gaver** *pl* eloquence; **~måde** *en (udtryk)* phrase, turn of speech.

talende *adj* talking, speaking; *(udtryksfuld)* meaning, sig'nificant; *den ~* the speaker; *meget ~* talkative.

talent *et* talent, gift; *have ~ for at gøre ngt* have a talent for doing sth; **~fuld** *adj* talented; **~løs** *adj* un'talented; **~spejder** *en* talent spotter.

taler *en* speaker; **~stol** *en* platform, rostrum.

talerør *et (fig om person)* spokesman *(pl:* -men) *(for* for)

talesprog *et* spoken language.

talestemme *en* speaking voice.

talg *en* tallow.

talje *en (midje)* waist; *(mål)* waistline; *(tekn)* tackle.

talkum *en* talc(um powder).

tallerken *en* plate; *dyb ~* soup plate; *flad ~* plate; *flyvende ~* flying saucer; *en ~ gullasch* a plate(ful) of goulash.

talløs *adj* in'numerable, countless.

talon *en (på check)* counterfoil.

talord *et* numeral.

talrig *adj* numerous.

talsmand *en* spokesman *(pl:* -men); *gøre sig til ~ for ngt* 'advocate sth.

tam *adj (mods: vild)* tame; *(om husdyr)* do'mesticated.

tamburmajor *en* drum major; *(i pigegarde)* majo'rette.

tamp *en* rope end; *en ordentlig ~ (om mand)* a big hunk; *(om ting)* a thumping big one.

tampon *en* 'tampon; *(til at tørre af med)* swab.

tamtam *en* (F, *fest etc)* do.

tand *en* tooth *(pl:* teeth); *børste tænder* brush one's teeth; *få tænder* cut· one's teeth; *bide tænderne sammen* set· one's teeth; *skære tænder* grit one's teeth; *vise tænder (om dyr)* bare one's teeth; *det får tænderne til at løbe i vand* it makes your mouth water; **~beskytter** *en (sport etc)* mouthpiece; **~byld** *en* gumboil; **~børste** *en* toothbrush; **~hjul** *et* cogwheel; **~krus** *et* tooth mug; **~kød** *et* gum; **~læge** *en* dentist; **~løs** *adj* toothless; **~pasta** *en* toothpaste; **~pine** *en* toothache; **~sten** *pl* tartar; **~stikker** *en* toothpick; **~tekniker** *en* dental tech'nician; **~tråd** *en* dental floss; **~udtrækning** *en* ex'traction (of tooth).

tang *en (værktøj)* (pair of) tongs; *(med)* forceps; *(vandplante)* seaweed.

tange *en (som forbinder landområde)* isthmus; *(næs)* tongue (of land).

tangent *en (på klaver, skrivemaskine etc)* key.

tangere *v* touch (on); *(fig)* border on; *~ verdensrekorden* equal the world record.

tank *en* rank; *(~station)* petrol station; **-bil** *en* tanker.

tanke *en* thought; *(indfald, idé)* i'dea; *(hensigt)* in'tention; *gå i sine egne ~r* be lost in thought; *hun skænkede ham ikke en ~* she did not give him a thought; *jeg skænkede det ikke en ~ (også)* it did not cross my mind; *komme i ~ om ngt* come· to think of sth; *komme på bedre ~r* think· better of it; *hun fik den ~ at…* it oc'curred to her that…; *ved ~en om det* at the thought of it; *jeg bliver dårlig bare ved ~n om det* the mere thought of it makes me sick // *v: ~ op* fill up; *(om fx olietank også)* re'fuel; **-fuld** *adj* pensive, thoughtful; **-gang** *en* mind; *(tænkemåde)* way of thinking; **-læser** *en* mind-reader; **-læsning** *en* mind-reading; **-løs** *adj* thoughtless; **-streg** *en* dash; **-torsk** *en* blunder; **-vækkende** *adj* worth a thought.

tankpasser *en* petrol station at'tendant.

tankskib *et* tanker.

tankstation *en* petrol (,filling) station.

tankvogn *en (jernb)* tank wagon.

tante *en* aunt.

tap *en (som ngt drejer om)* pivot; *(hane)* faucet, tap.

tapet *et* wallpaper; *sætte ~ op* hang· wallpaper, (re)paper; *være på ~et* be on the order of the day.

tapetsere *v* hang· wallpaper, (re)-paper; **tapetsering** *en* paper-hanging.

tapning *en* tapping, drawing off; *(af tlf)* tapping.

tappe *v* tap, draw·; *~ på flasker* bottle; *~ en for penge* drain sby of money.

tapper *adj* brave; **-hed** *en* courage.

tarif *en* rate; *(gebyr)* charge.

tarm *en* in'testine; *~ene (også)* the bowels; **-katar** *en* ente'ritis; **-slyng** *et* volvulus.

tartelet *en* patty shell.

tarvelig *adj (beskeden)* simple, frugal; *(dårlig)* in'ferior, poor; *(gemen)* mean; *hvor er du ~!* how mean you are! **-hed** *en* sim'plicity, fru'gality; inferi'ority, poorness; meanness.

taske *en* bag; *(hånd~)* handbag; *(mappe)* (brief)case; **-tyv** *en* bag-snatcher.

tastatur *et* keyboard.

taste *en* key // *v: ~ (ind)* keyboard; **-apparat** *et (tlf)* push-button telephone; **-operatør** *en* keyboard operator.

tatovere *v* tat'too; **tatovering** *en* tat'too(ing).

tavle *en* board; *(i skole)* blackboard; *(opslags~)* notice board.

tavs *adj* silent; *(uudtalt)* tacit, mute; *det ~e flertal* the silent ma'jority; *forholde sig ~* re'main silent.

tavshed *en* silence; *forbigå ngt i ~* pass over sth in silence; **-s·pligt** *en* pro'fessional secrecy.

taxa *en* taxi; *ringe efter en ~* call a taxi; **-chauffør** *en* taxi driver; **-holdeplads** *en* taxi rank; **-meter** *et* taximeter.

te *en* tea; *en kop ~* a cup of tea; *det var en tynd kop ~ (fig)* it was old hat // *v: ~ sig* carry on.

teaktræ *et* teak.

teater *et* theatre; *gå i teatret* go· to the theatre; *spille ~* playact; **-billet** *en* theatre ticket; **-direktør** *en* theatre manager; **-forestilling** *en* (the'atrical) per'formance; **-kikkert** *en* opera glasses *pl;* **-stykke** *et* play; **-tosset** *adj* stage-struck.

teblad *et* tea-leaf *(pl:* -leaves).

tebolle *en sv.omtr.t.* muffin, scone.

tebrev *et* tea bag.

tedåse *en* tea caddy.

tegl *en (til mur)* brick; *(til tag)* tile; **-værk** *s: et ~værk* a tileworks.

tegn *et* sign; *(typ)* character; *være ~ på ngt* be a sign of sth; *vise ~ på* show signs of; *som ~ på* as an indi'cation of; *give ~ (i trafik etc)* signal; *gøre ~ til en* signal to sby.

tegne *v* draw·; *(let)* sketch; *~ et hus (om fx barn)* draw· a house; *(om ar-*

kitekt) de'sign a house; ~ *abonnement på et blad* take· out a sub'scription for a magazine; ~ *en forsikring* take· out an in'surance; *det ~r godt* it looks promising; *det ~r til at blive godt vejr* it looks like a fine day; **-blok** *en* drawing pad; **-bog** *en (til penge etc)* wallet; **-film** *en* car'toon.

tegner *en (kunstner)* artist; *(teknisk)* draughtsman *(pl:* -men).

tegneserie *en* comic strip.

tegnestift *en* drawing pin, thumbtack.

tegnestue *en* 'architect's office (,studio).

tegning *en* drawing; *(af aktier, abonnement etc)* sub'scription.

tegnsprog *et* sign language.

tegnsætning *en* punctu'ation.

tehætte *en* tea cosy.

tekande *en* tea pot.

teint *en* com'plexion.

teknik *en* tech'nique; *(som videnskab)* tech'nology; **-er** *en* tech'nician, engi'neer.

teknisk *adj* technical; ~ *skole sv.t.* poly'technic; ~ *uheld* technical hitch.

teknologi *en* tech'nology; **teknologisk** *adj* techno'logical.

tekst *en* text; *(til musik)* words *pl; (til fx popmelodi)* lyrics *pl; (til illustration)* caption; *(under~ i tv)* subtitles *pl; komme videre i ~en* get· on with it; **-behandling** *en* word 'processing; **-behandlingsanlæg** *et* word 'processor.

tekste *v (om film)* subtitle.

tekstil *et* 'textile; *(stof)* fabric; **-varer** *pl* textiles.

tekøkken *et* kitche'nette.

teledata *s* viewdata.

telefax *en* telefax; **-e** *v* fax.

telefon *en* telephone, (F) phone; *have ~* be on the telephone; *tale i ~* be on the telephone; *tage ~en* answer the telephone; *der er ~ til dig* you are wanted on the telephone; **-besked** *en* telephone message; **-bog** *en* telephone di'rectory (,book); **-boks** *en* phone booth; **-bombe** *en* bomb scare; **-bruser** *en* hand shower; **-central** *en* telephone ex'change.

telefonere *v* telephone, (F) phone, call; *han ~r hele dagen* he is on the phone all day (long); ~ *til en* call (,phone) sby.

telefonforbindelse *en* (telephone) con'nection.

telefonist *en* (telephone) operator.

telefon... *sms:* **-møde** *et* link-up; **-nummer** *et* (tele)phone number; **-opringning** *en* (telephone) call; **-rør** *et* re'ceiver; **-samtale** *en* (telephone) call; **-selskab** *et* telephone company; **-svarer** *en* answering ma'chine; **-vækning** *en* wake-up service; **-væsen** *et* telephone service.

telegraf *en* telegraph; **-ere** *v* cable, wire; *~ere til en* cable sby.

telegrafist *en* telegraph operator; *(på skib)* wireless operator, (F) sparks.

telegram *et* telegram, cable; **-blanket** *en* telegram form; **-bureau** *et* news agency.

telekommunikation *en* 'telecommuni,cation.

teleobjektiv *et* telephoto lens.

telepati *en* te'lepathy.

teleskop *et* telescope.

telex *en* telex; **-e** *v* telex.

telt *et* tent; *(stort, fx til havefest)* mar'quee; *ligge i ~* camp; **-dug** *en* canvas; **-lejr** *en* camp; **-pløk** *en* tent peg; **-stang** *en* tent-pole; **-underlag** *et* ground sheet.

tema *et (emne)* subject, topic.

temmelig *adv* rather, fairly; *der var ~ mange mennesker* there was quite a lot of people; ~ *længe* quite a long time; *de spiste ~ meget* they ate rather a lot.

tempel *et* temple.

temperament *et* temper; *have ~* have a temper; **-s·fuld** *adj* tempera'mental.

temperatur *en* 'temperature; *have ~* run· a temperature.

tempo *et (mus)* tempo; *(fart)* pace, speed; *i roligt ~* at a steady pace.

tendens *en* 'tendency; *(moderetning*

etc) trend; *have ~ til at* have a tendency to.
tendentiøs *adj* biased.
tennis *en* tennis; *(på græs)* lawn tennis; **~bane** *en* tennis court; **~bold** *en* tennis ball; **~ketsjer** *en* tennis racket; **~sko** *pl* tennis shoes; **~spiller** *en* tennis player; **~stjerne** *en* tennic ace.
tenor *en* 'tenor; **~sax** *en (mus)* tenor saxophone.
teolog *en* theo'logian.
teologi *en* the'ology, di'vinity.
teologisk *adj* theo'logical.
teoretiker *en* theorist.
teoretisk *adj* theo'retic(al).
teori *en* theory; *i ~en* in theory.
tepause *en* tea break.
tepotte *en* tea pot.
terapeut *en* 'therapist.
terapi *en* 'therapy.
termin *en (frist)* deadline; *betale ~en (om husejer etc)* pay one's mortgages.
terminal *en (edb)* data terminal; *(fly)* air terminal.
terminologi *en* termi'nology.
teminsprøve *en sv.t.* mock exam.
termo... *sms:* **~flaske** *en* thermos ® flask; **~kande** *en* vacuum jug; **~meter** *et* ther'mometer; **~rude** *en* double glazing; **~stat** *en* thermostat.
tern *en* check pattern.
terne *en (firkant)* square; *(fugl)* tern.
ternet *adj* checkered; *(skotsk~)* tartan.
terning *en* die *(pl:* dice); *(mat)* cube; *spille ~er* throw· dice; *skære ngt i ~er* cut· sth into cubes.
terpe *v* swot, cram.
terpentin *en* turpentine, (F) turps; *(mineralsk)* white spirit.
terrarium *et* vi'varium.
terrasse *en* 'terrace; *(i have også)* patio.
terrin *en* tu'reen.
territorialfarvand *et* terri'torial waters *pl.*
territorium *et* 'territory.
terror *en* terror; **~balance** *en* balance of terror.
terrorisere *v* 'terrorize.
terrorist *en* 'terrorist.
terrorregime *et* reign of terror.
terræn *et* country, ground; *vinde ~* gain ground; *sondere ~et* see· how the land lies; **~gående** *adj (om bil etc)* cross-country; **~løb** *et* cross-country race.
terts *en (mus)* third.
tesi *en* tea-strainer.
teske *en* teaspoon; **~fuld** *en* teaspoonful.
testamente *et* will; *lave ~* make· a will; *Det Ny (,Gamle) Testamente* the New (,Old) Testament.
testamentere *v* be'queath *(til* to).
teste *v* test.
testikel *en* 'testicle.
tevarmer *en* tea-cosy.
teæg *et* tea ball.
Themsen *s* the Thames.
ti *num* ten; *køre med linje ~* go· by number ten; *spar ~* ten of spades.
tid *en* time; *(tidspunkt også)* moment, hour; *(tidsalder)* age; *(aftalt ~, fx hos læge)* ap'pointment; *(gram)* tense; *~en går* time passes; *hele ~en* all the time; *har du ~ et øjeblik?* have you got a minute? *vi har god ~* we have got plenty of time; *vi har ikke ~ til det* we don't have the time for it; *det tager lang ~* it takes a long time; *(nu) for ~en* at present, these days; *i disse ~er* nowadays; *prøve at vinde ~* play for time; *i ~e* in time; *fra ~ til anden* from time to time; *følge med ~en* move with the times; *om en uges ~* in a week or so; *om kort ~* shortly, soon; *nu er det på ~e at gå* it is time to leave now; *på Christian den Fjerdes ~* at the time of Christian the Fourth; *gæsterne kom til ~en* the guests ar'rived on time; *det må ~en vise* that re'mains to be seen; *det vil ~en vise* time will· show; *til sin ~* in due course; *somme ~er, til ~er* at times, sometimes.
tidevand *et* tide; **tidevands-** tidal *(fx bølge* wave).
tidlig *adj/adv* early; *vi er for ~ på den* we are early; *to timer for ~t* two

hours early; *~t på dagen* early in the day; *i morgen ~* to'morrow morning; *for ~t født* premature; **-ere** *adj* earlier; *(forudgående)* previous; *(forhenværende)* former, ex- // *adv* earlier; formerly; previously; *som ~ere nævnt* as previously mentioned; *han er ~ere statsminister* he is an ex-prime minister; *min ~ere mand* my ex-husband.

tidligst *adj* earliest // *adv* at the earliest; *vi spiser ~ kl. 6* we eat at 6 at the earliest.

tidløs *adj* timeless; *(om fx kjole)* classic.

tidnød *en: være i ~* be pressed for time.

tids *adv: ~ nok* in time; *komme ~ nok til ngt* be in time for sth.

tidsalder *en* age, era.

tidsbegrænset *adj* limited; **tidsbegrænsning** *en* time limit.

tidsfæste *v* date.

tidsbesparende *adj* time-saving.

tidsel *en* thistle.

tids... *sms:* **-fordriv** *et* pastime; *til ~fordriv* to pass the time; **-frist** *en* time limit; **-indstillet** *adj: ~indstillet bombe* time bomb; **-krævende** *adj* 'time-con,suming; **-plan** *en* timetable, schedule; **-punkt** *et* time, moment; *på det ~punkt* at that time; *på dette ~punkt (dvs. nu)* at the moment; *på et el. andet ~punkt* (at) some time (or other); **-regning** *en (kalender)* calendar; *(epoke)* era; *efter vor ~regning* anno Domini, AD; *før vor ~regning* before Christ, BC; **-rum** *et* period; **-skrift** *et* peri'odical, journal; **-spilde** *en* waste of time; **-spørgsmål** *et* question of time; **-svarende** *adj* up-to-date.

tie *v: ~ stille (være tavs)* be silent; *(holde mund)* stop talking; *ti så stille!* be quiet! (F) shut up! *få en til at ~ stille* silence sby.

tiende *s (gl, kirkeskat)* tithe.

tiende *num* tenth; **-del** *en* tenth.

tier *en (mønt)* ten-kroner (piece); *(bus etc)* number ten; *(kort)* ten.

tiger *en* tiger; **-unge** *en* tiger cub.

tigge *v* beg; *~ en om ngt* beg sth of sby; *~ en om at gøre ngt* beg sby to do sth.

tigger *en* beggar.

tikamp *en (sport)* de'cathlon.

tikke *v* tick.

tik-tak *(om ur)* tick-tock.

til *præp* to; *(efter:* arrive, arrival) at, in; *(bestemt for, om bestemmelsessted)* for; *(om tid, indtil)* until, till; *(om tid, senest)* by; *(om tidspunkt)* at; *(førstkommende)* next; *(om tidspunkt for møde, fest etc)* for; *(om pris etc)* at; *(se også de ord hvormed ~ forbundes); sige ngt ~ til en* say· sth to sby; *tage ~ England* go· to England; *ankomme ~ stationen* ar'rive at the station; *ankomme ~ Danmark* ar'rive in Denmark; *blomsterne er ~ dig* the flowers are for you; *vi skal have fisk ~ middag* we are having fish for dinner; *tage af sted ~ Jylland* leave· for Jutland; *vent ~ i aften* wait until this evening; *fra morgen ~ aften* from morning till night; *I må prøve at være her ~ klokken otte* you must try to be here by eight; *de kommer ~ sommer* they are coming next summer; *jeg har inviteret dem ~ klokken syv* I asked them for seven o'clock; *mødet er aftalt ~ i morgen* the meeting has been ar'ranged for to'morrow morning; *maleriet er vurderet ~ 500.000* the painting has been valued at 500,000; *(andre eksempler) have tid ~ at...* have time to...; *være god ~ ngt* be good at sth; *drikke øl ~ maden* have beer with one's meal; *tage ~ (dvs. øges)* in'crease // *adv (ekstra, yderligere)* more; an'other; *gøre ngt en gang ~* do· sth once more; *vil du have en kop te ~?* would you like another cup of tea?

tilbage *adv* back; *(bagude)* be'hind; *(baglæns)* backward(s); *(tilovers)* left (over); *de rejste ~ til London* they went back to London; *han fik tegnebogen ~* he got his wallet back; *hun blev ~ med børnene* she stayed behind with the children; *gå to skridt* ~ take· two steps backwards; *der blev ngt mad* ~ there was some food left over; *han er lidt* ~ he is a bit backward.

tilbagebetale *v* pay· back.

tilbageblik *et* retrospect; *(i film etc)* flashback.

tilbagefald *et* re'lapse.

tilbagegang *en* fall, de'cline.

tilbageholde *v* hold· back; *(om politiet)* de'tain; *han kunne ikke* ~ *et smil* he could not help smiling; *med tilbageholdt åndedræt* with bated breath; **~nde** *adj* re'served; *(forsigtig)* cautious; *(beskeden)* modest.

tilbageholdenhed *en* re'serve.

tilbagekalde *v* call back; *(hjemkalde)* re'call; *(et løfte)* re'tract; *(om vare)* call in.

tilbagekomst *en* re'turn.

tilbagelægge *v* cover *(fx en afstand* a distance).

tilbagerejse *en* re'turn journey.

tilbageskridt *et* step backwards.

tilbageslag *et* rebound; *(om gevær etc)* recoil; *(fig)* reper'cussion.

tilbagestrøget *adj (om hår)* swept-back.

tilbagestående *adj* backward, re'tarded.

tilbagetog *et* re'treat; *være på* ~ be in the re'treat.

tilbagetræden *en* resig'nation.

tilbagetrækning *en* with'drawal.

tilbagevej *en: på ~en* on the way back.

tilbagevirkende *adj: med* ~ *kraft fra 1. januar* retro'spective to the 1st of January.

tilbede *v* a'dore; *(rel)* worship; **~lse** *en* ado'ration; worship.

tilbeder *en (beundrer)* ad'mirer; *(rel)* worshipper.

tilbehør *et* ac'cessories *pl.*

tilberede *v* pre'pare, make·; *(om mad også)* cook.

tilberedning *en* prepa'ration, making; cooking.

tilbringe *v* spend·; ~ *natten med at diskutere ordbøger* spend· the night dis'cussing dictionaries.

tilbud *et* offer; *(om pris)* quo'tation; *(overslag)* estimate; *dagens* ~ today's special (offer); *kjolen var på* ~ the dress was a special offer; ~ *og efterspørgsel* sup'ply and de'mand.

tilbundsgående *adj* thorough, ex'haustive.

tilbyde *v* offer; ~ *sig* volun'teer.

tilbygning *en* ex'tension.

tilbøjelig *adj:* ~ *til (villig til, med tendens til)* in'clined to; *(med hang til)* given to; *jeg er* ~ *til at give dig ret* I'm in'clined to a'gree with you; **~hed** *en* incli'nation; tendency.

tildele *v* give·; *(præmie etc)* a'ward; *(titel etc)* be'stow.

tildeling *en* al'lotment; *(af præmie etc)* a'ward; *(af titel etc)* be'stowal.

tilegne *v* dedicate *(fx en en bog* a book to sby); ~ *sig ngt (fx viden)* ac'quire sth; *(fx et sprog)* pick up sth; *(tage med sig)* ap'propriate sth; **~lse** *en* dedi'cation.

tilflugt *en* refuge; *søge* ~ *hos en* seek· refuge with sby; *tage sin* ~ *til (fig)* re'sort to.

tilflugtssted *et* refuge.

tilflytter *en* newcomer.

tilfreds *adj (fornøjet)* con'tented, pleased; *(som har fået nok)* satisfied; ~ *med ngt* satisfied (,happy) with sth; *han er svær at stille* ~ there's no pleasing him, he's hard to please; *give sig* ~ be con'tent; *stille en* ~ satisfy (,please) sby; **~hed** *en* con'tent; satis'faction; **~stille** *v* satisfy, please; **~stillende** *adj* satis'factory; *lidet ~stillende* less than satis'factory.

tilfælde *et* case; *(lykketræf)* chance; *(sammentræf)* co'incidence; *(hændelse)* oc'currence; *(anfald)* fit; *~t (skæbnen)* chance; *et* ~ *af influenza* an at'tack of flu; *hun fik et* ~ she had a fit; *i alle* ~ at any rate, in any case; *i* ~ *af at han glemmer det* in case he forgets; *hvis det er ~t* if that is the case; *i hvert* ~ at any rate, anyway; *ved et* ~ by accident; *det er et rent* ~ *at...* it is sheer co'incidence that...; *for alle ~s skyld* just in case.

tilfældig *adj (ved et tilfælde)* acci'dental, chance; *(lejlighedsvis)* oc'casional; *vi opdagede det helt ~t* we found out by mere chance; *et ~t bekendtskab* a chance ac'quaintance; *~t valgt* chosen at random; **-hed** *en* chance; *(sammentræf)* co'incidence.

tilfældigvis *adv* by chance, acci'dentally; *(for resten)* inci'dentally; *vi kom ~ forbi* we happened to pass by; *du har vel ikke ~ en cigaret?* do you by any chance have a cigarette?

tilfælles *adv* in common.

tilføje *v (lægge til)* add; *(volde)* in'flict *(fx en et sår* a wound on sby); cause *(fx skade* damage); **-lse** *en* ad'dition; *(tillæg)* ap'pendix.

tilføre *v (skaffe)* sup'ply; *(om fx luft)* let· in.

tilførsel *en* sup'ply; *(om luft etc)* intake.

tilgang *en (forøgelse)* increase; *(af personer)* intake *(fx af studerende* of students).

tilgift *en: give (,få) ngt i ~* give· (,get·) sth into the bargain.

tilgive *v* for'give·; **-lse** *en* for'giveness.

tilgodehavende *et* credit; *hans ~ (også)* the a'mount due to him.

tilgodese *v* con'sider.

tilgroet *adj* over'grown.

tilgængelig *adj* ac'cessible; *(til at få fat i)* a'vailable; *offentligt ~* open to the public.

tilholdssted *et* haunt, re'sort.

tilhænger *en* sup'porter, (F) fan; *være ~ af ngt* be'lieve in sth.

tilhøre *v* be'long to; *han ~r familien* he is one of the family; *~ et etnisk mindretal* be one of (,part of) an ethnic mi'nority; **-nde** *adj* be'longing (to); *(tilsvarende)* matching.

tilhører *en* listener; *~ne (også)* the audience; *mange ~e* a large audience.

tilintetgøre *v* de'stroy; *(ved massakre etc)* ex'terminate; **-lse** *en* de'struction; extermi'nation.

tilkalde *v (til hjælp)* call (in); *~ lægen (, politiet)* call (,send· for) the doctor (,the po'lice).

tilkaldevagt *en: have ~* be on call.

tilkendegive *v (vise)* show·; *(ytre)* ex'press; **-lse** *en* manife'station; ex'pression.

tilknytning *en (forbindelse)* con'nection, associ'ation; *i ~ til* in con'nection with; *(dvs. efter)* following.

tilknyttet *adj* con'nected with.

tilkomme *v: det ~r ikke dig at...* it is not for you to...

tilkommende *adj: hans ~* his future wife, his fi'ancée; *hendes ~* her future husband, her fi'ancé.

tilkæmpe *v: ~ sig ngt* win· sth.

tilkøre *v (bil)* run· in.

tilkørsel(svej) *en* ap'proach.

tillade *v* al'low, per'mit; *~er De?* ex'cuse me! may I? *~ en ngt* al'low (,per'mit) sby (to do) sth; *~ sig at gøre ngt* take· the liberty to do sth; *det kan man ikke ~ sig* that is not done; *~r du virkelig det?* do· you al'low that? *hvis vejret ~r det* weather per'mitting.

tilladelse *en* per'mission; *(officiel, fx til indrejse)* 'permit; *bede om ~ til at...* ask per'mission to...; *give ~ til ngt* per'mit sth.

tilladt *adj* al'lowed, per'mitted; *er det ~ at parkere (,ryge) her?* is parking (,smoking) allowed here? *det burde ikke være ~* it ought to be for'bidden.

tillid *en* confidence, trust, faith; *have ~ til en* have confidence in sby, trust sby; *miste ~en til en* lose· confidence in sby.

tillidsbrud *et* breach of confidence.

tillidsfuld *adj* confident; *(om barn)* trustful.

tillidshverv *et* honorary office.

tillidskvinde, tillidsmand *en* shop steward.

tillige *adv* too, as well; *(desuden)* in ad'dition.

tillykke *adv: ~!* congratu'lations! *~ med fødselsdagen!* many happy re'turns! *ønske en ~ med ngt* con'gratulate sby on sth.

tillæg *et (til blad etc)* supplement; *(tilføjelse)* ad'dition; *(i løn)* rise; *(til pris)* extra charge.

tillægge *v* add; ~ *en ngt* a'scribe sth to sby; ~ *ngt stor betydning* at'tach great im'portance to sth.
tillægsmåde *en (gram)* participle.
tillægsord *et (gram)* adjective.
tilløb *et (til spring)* run-up; *(begyndelse)* ap'proach; *(forsøg)* at'tempt.
tilløbsstykke *et (teat)* box office at'traction; *(fig)* draw.
tilmelde *v* en'rol; *(konkurrence)* enter; ~ *sig et kursus* put· one's name down for a course.
tilmelding *en* en'rolment, regi'stration *(til* for).
tilnavn *et* epithet; *(øgenavn)* nickname; *med ~et* nicknamed.
tilnærmelse *en* ap'proach; *gøre ~r (til kvinde)* make· ad'vances; *(neds)* take· liberties *(til* with).
tilnærmelsesvis *adj* ap'proximate, (F) rough *(fx skøn* estimate) // *adv* ap'proximately; *ikke ~ så god* not nearly so good.
tilovers *adv (til rest)* left (over); *(som ikke bruges)* spare; *føle sig ~* feel· left out; *ham har vi ikke ngt ~ for* we have not got much time for him.
tilpas *adj* right // *adv* suf'ficiently; *(om tid)* at the right moment; ~ *stegt* done just right; *gøre en ~* please sby; *han er umulig at gøre ~* there is no pleasing him; *føle sig dårligt (,godt) ~* feel· rotten (,fine); *er det ~?* is that all right? *det er lige ~* it is just right; **-ning** *en* ad'justment, adap'tation.
tilpasse *v* ad'just, a'dapt; *(om mønster, tøj)* fit; ~ *sig til ngt* a'dapt (oneself) to sth.
tilredt *adj: ilde ~* in a bad state; *(mørbanket)* badly bruised.
tilregnelig *adj* sane.
tilrejsende *en* visitor.
tilrettelægge *v* organize; *(forberede)* pre'pare; *(fx for tv)* a'dapt; **tilrettelægning** *en* organi'zation, ar'rangement; *(tv)* adap'tation.
tilrøget *adj* smoky; *(om pibe)* seasoned.
tilråb *et* call; *komme med ~ (dvs. opmuntre)* cheer; *(dvs. øvråb)* boo.
tilråde *v* recom'mend *(en ngt* sth to sby; **-lig** *adj* to be recom'mended.
tilsammen *adv (om sum)* in all; *(i fællesskab)* be'tween us (,them); *det blev 100 kr. ~* it was 100 kr. in all; *vi havde ~ 100 kr.* we had 100 kr. between us; *han er bedre end Poul og Peter ~* he is better than Poul and Peter rolled into one.
tilse *v* at'tend to, see·.
tilsidesætte *v* ne'glect.
tilsigelse *en* summons.
tilsigtet *adj* in'tentional; *den tilsigtede virkning* the de'sired ef'fect.
tilskadekommen *adj* injured.
tilskud *et* contri'bution; *(offentligt)* subsidy, grant; *give ~ til ngt* con'tribute to sth; *(om det offentlige)* subsidize sth.
tilskudsberettiget *adj* en'titled to a subsidy.
tilskuer *en* onlooker; *~ne (teat etc)* the audience; *(til fodbold)* the crowd; *være ~ til* watch; *(tilfældigt overvære)* witness; **~pladserne** *pl* the seats; *(på stadion)* the grandstand.
tilskynde *v* en'courage; **-lse** *en (opmuntring)* in'centive; *(stærk)* urge.
tilskæring *en (at lave mønster)* cutting out; *(tilpasning af tøj)* fitting.
tilslutning *en (støtte)* sup'port; *(samtykke)* con'sent, ap'proval; *(tilhængere)* following; *(elek, trafik etc)* con'nection; *give sin ~ til ngt* en'dorse sth; *i ~ til mødet* in con'nection with the meeting; *vinde ~* meet· with approval.
tilslutte *v* con'nect; ~ *sig (dvs. støtte)* go· a'long with; *(gå med i)* join.
tilsløre *v* veil; *(fig)* dis'guise.
tilstand *en* con'dition, state; *huset var i en elendig ~ (også)* the house was in very bad re'pair.
tilstedeværelse *en* presence.
tilstedeværende *adj* present; *de ~* those present.
tilstoppet *adj (om afløb)* blocked.
tilstrækkelig *adj* suf'ficient, e'nough; *han er ~ dum til at gøre det* he is stupid e'nough to do it; *der er ~ med brød* there is enough bread; *i ~ mængde* in suf'ficient quantities.

tilstrømning *en (af folk)* rush; *der er stor ~ til filmen* the film draws· large audiences.
tilstøde *v: der er tilstødt dem en ulykke* they have had an accident; *der er tilstødt komplikationer* there are compli'cations; **-nde** *adj* ad'joining *(fx værelser* rooms); ad'jacent *(fx hus* house).
tilstå *v* ad'mit; *(bekende)* con'fess; *~ en forbrydelse* con'fess to a crime; *jeg må ~ at jeg har glemt det* I must con'fess that I have for'gotten.
tilståelse *en (bekendelse)* con'fession; *aflægge ~* make· a confession, con'fess.
tilsvarende *adj* corre'sponding; *(lignende)* similar.
tilsyn *et (overvågning)* super'vision; *(undersøgelse)* in'spection; *(person)* supervisor, in'spector; *føre ~ med ngt* be in charge of sth; *(holde øje med)* look after sth.
tilsyneladende *adj* ap'parent // *adv* ap'parently.
tilsynsførende *en se tilsyn.*
tilsynsværge *en (for kriminel)* pro'bation officer.
tilsætning *en* ad'dition; *(krydderi)* seasoning; *(til kaffe)* chicory.
tilsætningsstof *et* additive; *fri for ~fer* free of additives.
tilsætte *v* add.
tiltag *et* i'nitiative.
tiltage *v (vokse)* in'crease, grow·; *(om månen)* wax; **-nde** *adj* in'creasing, growing.
tiltale *en (henvendelse)* ad'dress; *(i retten)* charge; *rejse ~ mod en for ngt* charge sby with sth; *få svar på ~* get· one's own back; *give ham svar på ~* give· him tit for tat // *v (henvende sig til)* ad'dress, speak· to; *(i retten)* prosecute; *(behage)* please; *han er tiltalt for manddrab* he has been charged with manslaughter; *føle sig tiltalt af et sted* take· to a place.
tiltalende *adj (af ydre)* at'tractive; *(af væsen)* nice.
tiltro *en* confidence, faith; *have ~ til en* have faith in sby // *v: ~ en ngt* be'lieve sby capable of sth; *det ~r jeg ham gerne* I would not put it past him.
tiltræde *v (stilling)* take· up; *(acceptere)* ac'cept.
tiltrække *v* at'tract, draw·; *~ sig opmærksomhed* at'tract at'tention; **-nde** *adj* at'tractive.
tiltrækning *en* at'traction.
tiltrænges *v* be needed; *være hårdt tiltrængt* be badly (,much) needed.
tiltænke *v: ~ en ngt* in'tend sth for sby.
tilvalgsfag *et* optional subject.
tilvækst *en* in'crease, growth *(i* in).
tilvænning *en* habitu'ation; *(til stoffer)* ad'diction.
tilværelse *en* e'xistence, life *(pl:* lives).
time *en* hour; *(undervisnings~)* lesson; *en halv ~* half an hour; *halvanden ~* an hour and a half; *for en ~ siden* an hour ago; *hver ~* every hour; *det varer en ~s tid* it takes about an hour; *tre gange i ~n* three times an hour; *køre 60 miles i ~n* drive· at 60 miles per hour; **-løn** *en: få ~løn* be paid by the hour; **-plan** *en* timetable; **-vis** *adv: i ~vis* for hours.
timian *en (bot)* thyme.
tin *et (grundstoffet)* tin; *(materialet)* pewter.
tinde *en* peak, pinnacle.
tinding *en* temple; *han er ved at blive grå i ~erne* he has got greying temples; *han er ved at få høje ~er* his hairline is re'ceding.
tindre *v* sparkle.
ting *en* thing; *(genstand også)* object; *(sag)* matter; *en ~ ad gangen* one thing at a time; *passe sine ~* see to one's business; *det er en anden ~* that is a'nother matter; *pas du dine egne ~!* mind your own business! *~ene glider* things are coming a'long.
tinge *v: ~ om* bargain about.
tingest *en* thing, gadget; (F) thingummy.
tinglyse *v (ejendom)* register.
tip *et: give en et ~* tip sby off.
tipning *en* the pools; *vinde 10.000 i ~*

win· 10,000 on the pools.
tipolde- great-great-grand... *(fx -mor* -mother).
tippe *v (vippe; give et tip)* tip; *(i tipning)* do· the pools; *jeg vil ~ på at han kommer i aften* I bet you he's coming to'night.
tipsgevinst *en* win on the pools.
tipskupon *en* pools coupon.
tipsresultater *pl sv.t.* football re'sults.
tipvogn *en* tipper wagon.
tirre *v* irritate; *(drille)* tease.
tirsdag *en* Tuesday; *i ~s* last Tuesday; *på ~* on Tuesday; *om ~en* (on) Tuesdays.
tis *et* pee.
tisse *v* pee, piddle; *~ i bukserne* wet one's pants; *jeg skal ~* I need to pee; **~mand** *en* willie.
tit *adv* oten; *~ og ofte* time and time again.
tital *et* ten; **~systemet** *s* the decimal system; *gå over til ~systemet* go· decimal.
titel *en* title; *en bog med titlen "It"* a book en'titled "It"; **~blad** *et* title page; **~kamp** *en (i boksning)* title match; **~melodi** *en* theme tune.
titiden *s: ved ~* at about ten o'clock.
titte *v* peep.
titulere *v* ad'dress.
tivoli *et* funfair; *Tivoli (i Kbh)* the Tivoli Gardens.
tiår *et* decade.
tjavs *en* wisp; **~et** *adj* wispy.
tjekker *en,* **tjekkisk** *adj* Czech.
Tjekkoslovakiet *s* Czechoslo'vakia.
tjene *v (gøre tjeneste)* serve; *(indtjene)* earn; *det her kan du ikke være tjent med* you are ill-served with this; *hun ~r godt* she has a good income; *han tjente £100 på handelen* he made £100 on the deal; *~ til at* serve to.
tjener *en (i restaurant)* waiter; *(privattjener)* man-servant *(pl:* menservants); *(fig)* servant.
tjeneste *en* service; *(vagt etc)* duty; *(hjælp)* favour; *han gjorde ~ i marinen* he served in the navy; *han har ~ i aften* he is on duty to'night; *fritaget for ~* e'xempt from duty; *gøre en en ~* do· sby a favour; **~bolig** *en* of'ficial residence; **~folk** *pl* servants; **~fri(hed)** *s* leave; **~mand** *en* of'ficial; *(i ministerium)* civil servant; **~rejse** *en* business trip.
tjenstgørende *adj* on duty.
tjenstlig *adj* of'ficial.
tjenstvillig *adj* helpful.
tjære *en* tar // *v* tar.
tjørn *en* hawthorn.
to *num* two; *~ og ~ er fire* two and two make four; *gå ~ og ~* walk in twos; *de kommer begge ~* they are both coming; *I ~ er også inviteret* you two (,the two of you) have also been in'vited; *han kan lægge ~ og ~ sammen (fig)* he can put two and two to'gether.
tobak *en* to'bacco; **~s·dåse** *en* to'bacco tin; **~s·handler** *en* to'bacconist; **~s·pung** *en* to'bacco pouch; **~s·rygning** *en* to'bacco smoking; **~s·røg** *en* to'bacco smoke.
tocifret *adj* two-digit; *et ~ millionbeløb* tens of millions.
todelt *adj* in two parts; *(om tøj)* two-piece.
toer *en* two; *(om bus etc)* number two.
toetages *adj (om hus)* two-storeyed; *(om bus)* double-decker.
tog *et* train; *tage med ~et* go· by train; *nå ~et* catch· one's train; *han nåede ikke ~et* he missed his train; *de mødtes i ~et* they met on the train; **~forbindelse** *en* train con'nection (,service); **~fører** *en* chief guard; **~kiosk** *en* 'buffet; **~konduktør** *en* ticket col'lector; **~kort** *et* season ticket; **~plan** *en* timetable; **~rejse** *en* railway journey; **~sammenstød** *et* train crash; **~ulykke** *en* railway accident.
toilet *et* toilet, (F) loo; *(i restaurant etc) (dame~)* ladies' (room); *(herre~)* men's (room); *gå på ~tet* go· to (,use) the bathroom; **~artikler** *pl* toiletries; **~bord** *et* dressing table; **~papir** *et* toilet paper; **~taske** *en* sponge bag, toilet bag.
toilette *et: gøre ~* dress.
told *en (afgift)* (customs) duty; *~en*

(om sted) the customs; *betale ~ af ngt* pay· duty on sth; **~betjent** *en* customs officer; **~eftersyn** *et* customs check.

tolder *en* customs officer.

toldfri *adj* duty-free.

toldpligtig *adj* dutiable.

toldunion *en* customs union.

toldvæsen *et* customs au'thorities *pl.*

tolerance *en* 'tolerance.

tolerant *adj* 'tolerant; *(for ~)* per'missive.

tolerere *v* 'tolerate.

tolk *en* in'terpreter; **~e** *v* in'terpret.

tolkning *en* interpre'tation.

tolv *num* twelve; **~er** *en* twelve; *(bus etc)* number twelve.

tolvte *adj* twelfth; **~del** *en* twelfth.

tolvtiden *s: ved ~* at about twelve o'clock.

tom *adj* empty; *(om udtryk)* blank, vacant; *huset står ~t* the house is empty; *glo ~t ud i luften* stare into empty space.

tomat *en* to'mato; **~ketchup** *en* to'mato ketchup; **~puré** *en* to'mato paste.

tombola *en* tom'bola.

tomgang *en* idling; *gå i ~* idle.

tomhed *en (se tom)* emptiness; vacancy; blankness.

tomhændet *adj* empty-handed.

tommelfinger *en* thumb; *rejse på ~en* hitch-hike; *have ti tommelfingre* be all thumbs; *trille tommelfingre* twiddle one's thumbs.

tommestok *en (sammenklappelig)* folding rule.

tomotorers *adj* twin-engine.

tomrum *et* vacuum.

tomt *en (grund)* site.

ton *et (1000 kg)* ton, tonne.

tone *en (lyd, klang)* sound, tone; *(enkelt ~)* note; *(~højde)* pitch; *(farve~)* shade, tone; *(opførsel)* tone; *det er ikke god ~* it is not done // *v (klinge)* sound; *(farve)* tint; *~t glas* tinted glass; *~ frem* ap'pear; **~angivende** *adj* leading; *(m.h.t. mode)* trendsetting; **~art** *en* key; **~fald** *et* tone of voice; **~hoved** *et (i båndoptager)* re'cording head.

top *en* top; *(bjerg~)* summit, peak; *(paryk)* hairpiece; *(overdel)* top; *fra ~ til tå* from top to bottom; *ligge i ~pen* be (at the) top // *interj: top!* done!

topersoners *adj: ~ bil* two-seater.

top... *sms:* **~hastighed** *en* top speed; **~hue** *en* pixie cap; **~løs** *adj* topless; **~møde** *et* summit (meeting); **~nøgle** *en (tekn)* box spanner; **~pakning** *en (i motor)* 'cylinder head gasket.

toppe *v* culminate.

toppes *v* bicker *(om* about, over), quarrel *(om* about, over).

top... *sms:* **~præstation** *en* first-rate per'formance; **~punkt** *et* summit; *(fig)* zenith; **~skefuld** *en* heaped spoonful; **~stilling** *en* top po'sition; **~stykke** *et (i motor)* 'cylinder head.

torden *en* thunder; *det trækker op til ~* it looks like thunder; *som lyn og ~* like lightning; **~skrald** *et* clap of thunder; **~vejr** *et* thunderstorm.

tordne *v* thunder.

torn *en* thorn; *det er mig en ~ i øjet* it is a thorn in my flesh; *(om ngt grimt)* I find· it an eyesore.

tornebusk *en* briar.

Tornerose *s* the Sleeping Beauty.

torpedere *v* tor'pedo.

torpedo *en* tor'pedo; **~jager** *en (mar)* de'stroyer.

torsdag *en* Thursday; *i ~s* last Thursday; *om ~en* (on) Thursdays; *på ~* next Thursday.

torsk *en (fisk)* cod(fish); *(person)* fool.

torskedum *adj* thick, dense.

torskelever *en* cod liver.

torskerogn *en* cod roe.

tortere *v* torture.

tortur *en* torture; *det var en ~ at høre ham synge* it was agony to hear him sing.

torv *et (plads i by)* square; *(marked)* market; *gå på ~et* go· to the market.

tosidet *adj* two-sided; *(om aftale etc)* bi'lateral.

tosporet *adj (om vej)* two-lane.

tosproget *adj* bi'lingual.

tosse *en* fool // *v: ~ rundt* fool around.

tosseri *et* nonsense.
tosset *adj* foolish; *(skør)* crazy, (F) nuts; *blive ~* go· crazy; *det er til at blive ~ af* it is e'nough to drive you crazy; *være ~ efter en* be crazy about sby; *det ser ikke så ~ ud* it does not look so bad.
tot *en* tuft, wisp; *en ~ vat* a wad of cottonwool.
totakter *en (motor)* two-stroke engine.
total *et (tallet 2)* two.
total *adj* total.
totalitær *adj* totali'tarian.
totalskade *en* total loss; *bilen blev ~t* the car was a write-off.
totalt *adv* com'pletely; *det var ~ mislykket* it was a com'plete failure.
totiden *s: ved ~* at about two o'clock.
toupere *v (om hår)* backcomb.
tov *et* rope; **~bane** *en* cable railway; *(stolelift)* chair lift; **~trækkeri** *et (fig);* **~trækning** *en* tug-of-war; **~værk** *et* ropes *pl.*
toværelses *adj* two-room.
tradition *en* tra'dition; *~en tro* in keeping with tradition; *ifølge ~en* true to tradition, tra'ditionally.
traditionel *adj* tra'ditional.
traditionsbundet *adj* bound by tra'dition.
traditionsrig *adj* rich in tra'dition.
trafik *en* 'traffic; *stærk ~* heavy traffic.
trafikant *en* road-user.
trafikere *v* use; *stærkt ~t* busy.
trafik... *sms:* **~fly** *et* airliner; **~forbindelser** *pl* communi'cations; **~lys** *et* traffic lights *pl;* **~ministerium** *et* Ministry of Transport; **~prop** *en* traffic jam; *(bilkø)* tailback; **~sikkerhed** *en* road safety; **~ulykke** *en* road accident.
tragedie *en* tragedy.
tragisk *adj* tragic // *adv* tragically.
tragt *en* funnel; *(tlf)* mouthpiece.
tragte *v (kaffe etc)* filter; *(si)* strain; *~ efter ngt* a'spire to sth.
traktat *en* treaty.
traktere *v: ~ en på ngt* treat sby to sby; *jeg ~r!* it is on me!
traktor *en* tractor; **~fører** *en* tractor-driver.
trampe *v (i gulvet etc)* stamp; *(~ ned)* trample; *~ med fødderne* stamp one's feet.
trampen *en* stamping; trampling.
trampolin *en (sport)* 'trampoline.
tran *en* whale oil.
tranchere *v* carve.
tranchersaks *en* poultry shears *pl.*
tranchersæt *et* carving set.
trane *en* crane.
tranebær *et* cranberry.
trang *en (behov)* need *(til* for); *(lyst)* de'sire; *(nød)* want; *føle ~ til at sige ngt* feel· a desire to speak, want to speak // *adj (kneben)* narrow; *(stram)* tight; *~e tider* hard times.
transaktion *en* trans'action.
transformator *en* trans'former.
transfusion *en* trans'fusion.
transistor *en* tran'sistor; **~radio** *en* tran'sistor (radio).
transit *en* 'transit.
translatør *en* in'terpreter.
transmission *en* trans'mission; *(i tv, radio)* broadcast.
transmittere *v* trans'mit; broadcast·.
transparent *en (skilt med slagord etc)* banner // *adj* trans'parent.
transpiration *en* perspi'ration.
transpirere *v* per'spire.
transplantation *en* 'transplant, transplan'tation; *hjerte~* heart transplant.
transplantere *v* trans'plant.
transport *en* 'transport; *(forsendelse)* shipment.
transportabel *adj* movable; *(bærbar)* portable.
transportbånd *et* con'veyer belt.
transportere *v* carry; *(sende)* ship.
transportmiddel *et* means of transport.
transportsyge *en* motion sickness.
transportvogn *en* truck; *(varevogn)* van.
transvestit *en* trans'vestite.
trapez *en* tra'peze.
trappe *en* staircase, stairs *pl; (udvendig)* steps *pl; gå ned ad ~n* go· down'stairs; *gå op ad ~n* go· up'stairs // *v: ~ ned* de-'escalate; *(om narko, medicin)* with'draw·; *~ op*

escalate; **~afsats** *en* landing; **~opgang** *en* staircase; **~sten** *en* doorstep; **~stige** *en* step ladder; **~trin** *et* step.

traske *v* plod, trudge.

trauma *et* trauma; **~tisk** *adj* trau'matic.

trav *et (gangart)* trot; *(sport)* trotting; *i rask ~* at a brisk trot; **~bane** *en* trotting course.

trave *v* trot.

traver *en: det er en gammel ~r* that's old hat.

travesko *en* walking shoe.

travetur *en* hike.

travhest *en* trotting horse.

travkusk *en* sulky driver.

travl *adj* busy; *have meget ~t (dvs. meget at lave)* be very busy; *(dvs. skulle skynde sig)* be in a hurry; *have ~t med ngt* be busy doing sth; **~hed** *en (hast, jag)* hurry; *der var stor ~hed på kontoret i dag* we had a lot to do at the office today.

travløb, travsport *s* trotting.

tre *num* three; *alle gode gange ~* third time lucky; *gæt ~ gange* you can have three guesses; **~cifret** *adj* three-digit; **~dimensional** *adj* 'three-di,mensional.

tredive *num* thirty; *han er i ~rne* he is in his thirties; *han er født i ~rne* he was born in the thirties; **tredivte** *adj* thirtieth.

tredje *adj* third; *for det ~* thirdly; *den ~ verden* the Third World **~del** *en* third; ⅔ two thirds; **~grads** *adj* 'third-de,gree; **~rangs** *adj* third-rate.

tredobbelt *adj* triple.

treer *en (om bus etc)* number three; *(om kort)* three.

treetages *adj* three-storey.

trefaset *adj* three-phase.

trehjulet *adj: ~ cykel* tricycle.

trekant *en* triangle; **~et** *adj* tri'angular.

trekvart *adj* three quarters.

tremme *en (i stakit etc)* slat; *(i vindue og bur)* bar; *han er bag ~r* he is be'hind bars; **~kalv** *en* battery calf *(pl:* calves); **~seng** *en* cot; **~værk** *et* lattice.

trend *en (i vævning)* warp; *(tendens, mode)* trend.

tres *num* sixty; *han er i ~serne* he is in his sixties; *han er født i ~serne* he was born in the sixties.

trestjernet *adj* three-star.

tresporet *adj (om vej)* three-lane.

tretal *et* three.

tretiden *s: ved ~* at about three o'clock.

tretten *num* thirteen; **~de** *adj* thirteenth.

treven *adj* un'willing; *(langsom)* slow.

treværelses *adj* three-room.

tribune *en* platform; *(tilskuer~)* stand.

trikot *et* tights *pl.*

trikotage *en* hosiery; *(om strikvarer)* knitwear; **~handler** *en* hosier.

trille *en (i sang etc)* trill; *(om fugl)* warble; *slå ~r* trill; warble // *v (rulle)* roll; *(langsomt, fx om tåre)* trickle; *(med ngt på hjul, fx barnevogn)* wheel; *(slå ~r)* trill; warble.

trillebør *en* wheelbarrow.

trilling *en* triplet.

trimme *v* trim.

trimning *en* trimming.

trin *et (fod~, trappe~)* step; *(stadium)* stage; *(niveau)* level; **~bræt** *et* footboard; *(lille station)* halt; **~vis** *adv* step by step.

trio *en* trio.

trippe *v* trip; *(om lyden)* patter; *stå og ~* shuffle one's feet; *(utålmodigt, nervøst)* fidget.

trisse *v (til garn)* reel; *(hejseværk)* pulley // *v: ~ rundt* potter about.

trist *adj* sad; *(deprimerende)* de'pressing, dreary; *(kedelig)* boring; *~ vejr* dreary weather; *i ~ humør* gloomy; **~hed** *en* sadness; de'pression, dreariness.

trit *et: holde ~ med en* keep· pace with sby; *ude af ~* out of step.

triumf *en* 'triumph; *fejre ~er* be a great suc'cess.

triumfere *v* 'triumph; *(skadefro)* gloat; **~nde** *adj* tri'umphant.

trivelig *adj* plump.

trives *v (have det rart)* be happy; *(vokse etc)* thrive *(ved* on).

trivialitet *en* trivi'ality, ba'nality; *(om bemærkning)* commonplace.

triviel *adj* 'trivial, ba'nal.
trivsel *en* well-being; *(vækst)* growth; *~ på arbejdspladsen* job satis'faction.
tro *en* be'lief; *(stærkere; rel)* faith; *(tillid)* confidence; *i god ~* in good faith; *lad dem blive i ~en* don't rob them of their il'lusions; *miste ~en på en (ngt)* lose· faith in sby (,sth); *i den ~ at* thinking that; *erklæring på ~ og love* affi'davit.
tro *v (mene)* think·; *(være sikker på)* be'lieve; *(stole på)* trust; *(rel)* be'lieve *(på* in); *jeg ~r ikke de kommer* I don't think they are coming; *nej, det kan du ~ (de ikke gør)!* you bet (they are not)! *man skulle ~ at...* you would think that...; *hvem skulle have ~et det?* who would have thought it? *du kan ~ det var rart* you have no idea how nice it was; *jeg kunne knapt ~ mine egne øjne* I could hardly believe my eyes; *det kan jeg ikke ~ om ham* I can't be'lieve that of him; *det ~r jeg gerne* I can (well) be'lieve that; *~ på spøgelser* be'lieve in ghosts; *~ på en* trust sby.
tro *adj (trofast)* faithful, loyal *(mod* to); *(nøjagtig)* accurate.
trods *en* de'fiance; *gøre ngt på ~* do· sth in sheer de'fiance; *til ~ for at...* in spite of the fact that..., de'spite the fact that... // *præp* in spite of, de'spite; *~ alt* in spite of everything; *(dog, alligevel)* after all.
trodse *v* de'fy.
trodsig *adj* de'fiant; *(om barn)* difficult.
trofast *adj* faithful, loyal *(mod* to); **~hed** *en* faithfulness, loyalty.
trofæ *en* 'trophy.
trold *en* goblin; *(i eventyr)* troll; **~dom** *en* magic; **~mand** *en* ma'gician, wizard.
troløs *adj* dis'loyal; **~hed** *en* dis'loyalty.
tromle *en* roller; *(tønde)* drum // *v* roll; *~ en ned* bulldoze sby.
tromme *en* drum; *spille ~* play the drum; *slå på ~ for ngt (fig)* beat· the drum for sth // *v* drum; *~ i bordet* drum the table; **~hinde** *en* eardrum; **~slager** *en* drummer; **~stik** *en* drumstick.
trompet *en* trumpet; *spille ~* play the trumpet; *støde i ~en* blow· the trumpet.
trompetist *en* trumpet player.
tronarving *en* heir to the throne.
trone *en* throne; *komme på ~n* come· to the throne; *frasige sig ~n* abdicate, re'nounce the throne // *v* sit· in state.
tronfølger *en* heir to the throne.
trop *en* troop, squad; *følge ~* keep· up; *(se også tropper).*
troperne *pl* the tropics.
tropisk *adj* tropical.
troppe *v: ~ op* turn up.
tropper *pl* troops, forces.
trosbekendelse *en* creed.
troskab *en* faithfulness *(mod* to).
troskyldig *adj* innocent, naïve.
troværdig *adj (pålidelig)* re'liable; *(sandsynlig)* credible; **~hed** *en* relia'bility; credi'bility.
true *v* threaten *(med* with; *med at* to); *~de skove* en'dangered woods; **~nde** *adj* threatening; *(overhængende)* imminent.
trug *et* trough [trɔf].
trummerum *en: den daglige ~* the daily grind.
trusseindlæg *et* panty liner.
trussel *en* threat *(mod* to).
trusser *pl (til herrer)* briefs; *(til damer)* panties.
trut *et (i bilhorn)* hoot; *(i horn)* toot; *give et ~ i (bil)hornet* honk, sound the horn; **~mund** *en* pout; *lave ~mund* pout.
trutte *v (om bil)* hoot, honk; *(om horn)* toot.
tryg *adj* safe, se'cure; *føle sig ~* feel· safe; *det kan du ~t stole på* you can safely re'ly on that; **~hed** *en* safety; se'curity.
trygle *v* beg, im'plore; *~ en om ngt* beg sby for sth.
tryk *et (pres)* pressure; *(typ)* print; *udøve et ~ på en* put· pressure on sby; *sætte ngt på ~* put· sth in print; *gå i ~ken* go· to press; *~ket*

ligger på første stavelse the stress is on the first syllable; **-bølge** *en* shock wave; **-fejl** *en* misprint; **-fod** *en (på symaskine)* presser foot; **-kabine** *en* pressurized cabin.

trykke *v* press; *(klemme)* squeeze; *(på knap, skubbe)* push; *(typ)* print; ~ *en i hånden* shake· hands with sby; *er der ngt der ~r dig?* do· you have sth on your mind? ~ *af (på gevær etc)* pull the trigger; ~ *på en knap* press a button; **-nde** *adj (om luft)* close, heavy; *(fig)* op'pressive.

trykkeri *et* printing works, printer's.

trykket *adj (utilpas)* op'pressed; *(nedtrykt)* de'pressed; *føle sig* ~ feel· ill at ease; *en* ~ *stemning* an un'pleasant atmosphere.

tryk... *sms:* **-knap** *en* pushbutton; **-koger** *en* pressure cooker; **-luft** *en* com'pressed air; **-luftbor** *et* pneu'matic drill; **-lås** *en* press-stud; **-ning** *en* printing; **-sag** *en* printed matter; **-stærk** *adj* stressed; **-svag** *adj* un'stressed; **-sværte** *en* printer's ink.

trykt *adj* printed; *~e bogstaver* print; *(skrevet i hånden)* block letters.

trylle *v* conjure *(frem* up); *jeg kan ikke* ~ *(fig)* I can't work miracles; **-kunst** *en* conjuring trick; **-kunstner** *en* conjurer, ma'gician.

trylleri *et* magic.

tryllestav *en* magic wand.

tryne *en* snout.

træ *et (som vokser)* tree; *(materialet)* wood; *af* ~ wooden; *gode tenorer hænger ikke på ~erne* good tenors don't grow on trees; **-bevokset** *adj* wooded; **-blæseinstrument** *et* woodwind (instrument).

træde *v (gå)* step; *(trampe)* tread·; *(stærkere)* trample; ~ *frem* step forward; ~ *i ngt* step on sth; ~ *i pedalerne* pedal hard; ~ *i kraft* come· into force; ~ *i spinaten* put· one's foot in it; ~ *i stedet for en* take· sby's place; ~ *et dyr ihjel* trample an animal to death; ~ *ind (i)* enter, step into; ~ *ned fra ngt* step down from sth; ~ *ngt ned* tread· sth down; ~ *nærmere* ap'proach; ~ *en over tæerne* step on sby's toes; ~ *på ngt* step (,tread) on sth; ~ *tilbage* stand· back; *(fra stilling)* re'sign.

trædepude *en (zo)* pad.

træf *et (tilfælde)* co'incidence; *(møde)* get-together; *et heldigt* ~ a stroke of luck.

træffe *v (møde)* meet·, come· a'cross; *(ramme)* hit·; *(foretage)* make· *(fx foranstaltninger* ar'rangements); *~r jeg direktøren?* can I see the di'rector, please? *lægen ~s efter kl. 11* you can see the doctor after 11; *føle sig truffet* feel· stung; **-nde** *adj (om bemærkning)* apt; *(om lighed)* striking.

træffer *en (om skud etc)* hit.

træffes *v* meet·.

træffetid *en (på kontor)* office hours *pl; (hos læge)* surgery hours *pl.*

træfpunkt *et (tlf) sv.t.* chatline.

træfsikker *adj* accurate.

træg *adj (langsom)* slow; **-hed** *en* slowness; *(fig, fys)* in'ertia.

trægrænsen *s* the timber line.

træhus *et* wooden house.

træk *en (i skorsten, hus)* draught; *(ryk)* pull; *(ansigts~)* feature; *(egenskab)* trait; *(om fugle)* mi'gration; *(i skak og fig)* move; *fire gange i* ~ four times running; *i ét* ~ at a stretch, at one go; *i korte* ~ briefly; *i store* ~ broadly.

trækasse *en* wooden box.

trækbasun *en* trom'bone.

trækfugl *en* migratory bird.

trække *v (rykke, hale)* pull; *(slæbe)* drag; *(bugsere)* tow; *(om fugle)* migrate; *(om skorsten og te)* draw·; *(om luder)* be on the game; *det ~r her* there is a draught here; ~ *lod om ngt* draw· lots for sth; ~ *cyklen* wheel the bike; ~ *(gardinerne) for* draw· the curtains; ~ *(gardinerne) fra* draw· back the curtains; ~ *fra (i regning)* sub'tract; ~ *10% fra* de'duct 10 per cent; ~ *i ngt* pull at sth; ~ *en i ørerne* pull sby's ears; ~ *ned* pull down; ~ *rullegardinet ned* lower the blind; ~ *uret op* wind· the clock (,watch); ~ *proppen op* draw· the cork; *det ~r op til torden* it looks like thunder; *vagtparaden ~r op* they are changing the guard; *~ på skuldrene* shrug; *~ ngt tilbage* with'draw· sth; *~ sig tilbage* re'tire; *~ ud* pull out; *(om fx møde)* drag on; *~ tiden ud* play for time.

trækkes *v: ~ med ngt* have to put up with sth.

trækning *en (i ansigtet)* twitch; *(krampe~)* spasm; *(lod~)* draw.

trækningsliste *en* list of winners.

trækpapir *et* blotting paper.

trækprocent *en* (income) tax rate.

trækrude *en* 'ventilator.

trækul *et* charcoal.

trækvind *en* draught.

trækvogn *en* handcart.

træl *en* slave; **~dom** *en* bondage.

træls *adj* la'borious; *(kedelig)* tiresome.

træne *v* train *(til* for); *(øve sig i)* exercise.

træner *en* trainer; *(sport)* coach.

trænge *v (være i trang)* suffer hardship; *(presse)* force; *~ frem* ad'vance; *~ igennem ngt* penetrate sth; *~ ind (fig)* sink· in; *~ ind i et hus* force one's way into a house; *~ en op i et hjørne* corner sby; *~ til ngt* need sth; *han ~r til at blive vasket* he could do with a wash; *~ sig ind på markedet* muscle in on the market; *~ sig på hos en* im'pose on sby.

trængende *adj (fattig)* needy; *være ~ (dvs. skulle tisse)* need (to go to) the bathroom.

trænges *v (stimle sammen)* crowd.

trængsel *en (af folk)* crowd; *(modgang)* hardship; *der er ~ i butikken* the shop is crowded; **trængsler** *pl* hardship(s).

træning *en* training; *(øvelse)* practice; *være i ~* be in practice; *være ude af ~* be out of practice; **~s·dragt** *en* track suit; **~s·sko** *pl* trainers.

træ... *sms:* **~rod** *en* tree root; **~sko** *en* clog; **~skæreri** *et* wood carving; **~sløjd** *en* woodwork; **~snit** *et* woodcut; **~sort** *en* (kind of) wood; **~sprit** *en* wood alcohol; **~stamme** *en* tree trunk; **~stub** *en* tree stump.

træt *adj* tired; *blive ~* get· tired; *blive ~ af ngt (dvs. ked af)* be fed up with sth; *køre ~* be run down; **~hed** *en* tiredness; *(udmattelse; metaltræthed)* fa'tigue.

trætop *en* treetop.

trætte *v (gøre træt)* tire; *(kede)* bore; **~nde** *adj* tiring; *(kedelig)* tiresome.

trættes *v (blive træt)* tire; *(strides)* quarrel.

trævarer *pl* wooden articles.

trævl *en* thread; *(las)* rag; *uden en ~* without a stitch on.

trævle *v (om stof)* fray; *~ ngt op* un'ravel sth; **~si** *en (i vaskemaskine)* fluff trap.

træværk *et* woodwork; *(paneler også)* panelling.

trøffel *en* truffle.

trøje *en* jacket; *(strikket)* cardigan; *(strikket jumper)* jersey.

trøst *en* comfort; *få ~* be comforted; *det er da en ~ at...* it is always sth that...

trøste *v* comfort; *jeg kan ~ dig med at...* it may comfort you to know that...; **~s·løs** *adj (trist)* dreary, de'pressing; *(håbløs)* hopeless.

trøstpræmie *en* conso'lation prize.

tråd *en* thread; *(snor)* string; *trække i ~ene* pull (the) strings *(også fig); få taget ~ene (om sår)* have the stitches taken out.

tråde *v: ~ en nål* thread a needle.

-trådet *(om garn)* -ply; *3-trådet uld* 3-ply wool.

trådkurv *en* wire basket.

trådnet *et* wire netting.

trådretning *en (i stof)* lenghtwise grain.

trådudløser *en (foto)* cable re'lease.

tuba *en* tuba; **tubaist** *en* tuba player.

tube *en* tube.

tuberkulose *en* tubercu'losis, TB.

tud *en (på kande etc)* spout; *(næse)* (F) hooter; **~brøle** *v* howl.

tude *v* howl; *(om ugle)* hoot; *(om bil)* honk; *(græde)* cry.

tudegrim *adj* ugly as sin.

tudehorn *et* horn.

tudse *en* toad.

tue *en* mound; *(af græs)* tuft.

tulipan *en* tulip.

tumle *v (boltre sig)* romp (about); *(falde)* tumble; *(styre, klare)* manage; *~ med ngt (om besværlig ting)* struggle with sth.

tummel *en* tumult, turmoil.

tumpet *adj* dim, dumb.

tumult *en (optøjer etc)* riot; *(larm)* uproar.

tuneser *en* Tu'nisian; **Tunesien** *s* Tu'nisia; **tunesisk** *s/adj* Tu'nisian.

tunfisk *en* tuna.

tung *adj* heavy; *(besværlig)* hard; *det ligger ~t med penge* money is scarce; *tage ~t på ngt* take· sth hard.

tunge *en* tongue; *række ~ ad en* stick· one's tongue out at sby; *holde ~n lige i munden* watch one's step; *jeg har det lige på ~n* it is on the tip of my tongue.

tunghør *adj* hard of hearing.

tungnem *adj* slow-witted.

tungsindig *adj* 'melancholy.

tunnel *en* tunnel; *(fodgænger~)* subway.

tur *en (spadsere~)* walk; *(køre)* ride, drive; *(udflugt)* outing; *(rejse)* trip; *(sørejse)* voyage; *(omgang)* turn; *gå en ~* go· for a walk; *køre en ~* go· for a drive; *cykle en ~* go· for a ride; *vi skal en ~ til London* we are going on a trip to London; *hvis ~ er det nu?* who's next? *nu er det din ~* it is your turn now; *stå for ~* be next; *gøre ngt efter ~* do· sth in turns.

turde *v* dare; *vi tør ikke gøre det* we daren't do it, we are a'fraid to do it; *de tør godt gøre det* they are not a'fraid to do it; *det tør siges!* I should say so! ... *om man tør spørge* ... if I may ask.

turisme *en* 'tourism.

turist *en* 'tourist; **~bureau** *et* tourist agency; **~bus** *en* coach; **~forening** *en* tourist associ'ation; **~plakat** *en* travel poster.

turkis *en/adj* 'turquoise.

turné *en* tour; *en ~ i England* a tour of England; *være på ~* be on a tour, be touring.

turnering *en* 'tournament.

tusch *en* Indian ink.

tusind *s/num* a thousand; *tre ~ mennesker* three thousand people; *flere ~ mennesker* several thousand people; *det er ~ gange værre* it is a thousand times worse; **~ben** *et* millipede.

tusindedel *en* thousandth.

tusindvis *adv: i ~* by the thousand; *i ~ af børn* thousands of children.

tusmørke *et* twilight, dusk.

tusse *en (filtpen)* marker, felt tip // *v: ~ rundt* potter around.

tv *et* 'television, TV; *på ~* on TV; *se ~* watch TV.

tvang *en* com'pulsion; *gøre ngt under ~* do· sth under com'pulsion; *bruge ~ mod en* e'xert pressure on sby; **~fri** *adj (om person)* casual; *(om tøj)* informal; **~s·arbejde** *et* forced labour; **~s·auktion** *en* com'pulsory sale; **~s·fodre** *v* force-feed·; **~s·indlægge** *v* com'mit to mental hospital; **~s·tanke** *en* ob'session.

tv-avisen *s* the 'television news.

tvebak *en* rusk.

tvetydig *adj* am'biguous; **~hed** *en* ambi'guity.

tvilling *en* twin; *Tvillingerne (astr)* Gemini.

tvinge *v* force, com'pel; *~ en til at gøre ngt* force sby to do sth; *~ ngt igennem* force sth through; *føle sig tvunget til at gøre ngt* feel· forced to do sth; **~nde** *adj: ~nde nødvendig* absolutely necessary.

tvist *en (strid)* dis'pute *(om* over); *(pudse~)* cotton waste.

tvivl *en* doubt; *være i ~ om ngt* doubt about sth; *der er ingen ~ om at han mener det* there is no doubt that he means it; *uden ~* no doubt; *det er hævet over enhver ~* it is be'yond doubt.

tvivle *v* doubt; *~ om (,på)* doubt; *jeg ~r på at han kommer* I doubt whether he will come; *det ~r jeg ikke på* I don't doubt it; **~nde** *adj* doubting; *(som tvivler)* doubtful; *stille sig ~nde over for ngt* have one's doubts about sth.

tvivlrådig *adj* in doubt.

tvivlsom *adj* doubtful, dubious.
tvivlsspørgsmål *et* matter of dis'pute.
tvivlstilfælde *et: i ~* when in doubt, in case of doubt.
tvungen *adj* forced, com'pelled; *(påbudt)* com'pulsory.
tvære *v: ~ ngt ud (mase)* crush sth; *(smøre)* smear sth; *(blæk etc)* smudge sth; *lad nu være med at ~ i det!* don't rub it in!
tværfløjte *en* trans'verse flute.
tværgående *adj (fx trafik)* cross.
tværpolitisk *adj* all-party; *(parl)* cross-bench.
tværs *adv: ~ igennem* right through; *på ~ af* a'cross; *(fig)* in oppo'sition to; *gå ~ over gaden* cross the street; *der er kommet ngt på ~* sth has up'set my (,our) plans.
tværsnit *et* cross section.
tværstribet *adj* cross-striped.
tværtimod *adv* on the contrary.
tværvej *en* crossroad.
tyde *v (tolke)* in'terpret; *(om skrift, tegn etc)* make· out; *~ på* sug'gest, indicate; *det ~r godt (,dårligt)* it is a good (,bad) sign.
tydelig *adj* clear, di'stinct; *(ligefrem, forståelig)* plain; *tale ~t* speak· di'stinctly; *skrive ~t* write· clearly; *jeg kan ~ huske at...* I di'stinctly re'member that...
tyfon *en* ty'phoon.
tyfus *en* typhoid fever.
tygge *v* chew; *~ på ngt* chew sth; *(fig)* think· about sth; **~gummi** *et* chewing gum.
tygning *en* chewing.
tyk *adj* thick; *(om person)* fat; *han er blevet ~* he has grown fat; *et ~t gulvtæppe* a thick carpet; *følge en i ~t og tyndt* follow sby through thick and thin; *det et for ~t! (fig)* that's a bit much! *smøre ~t på (fig)* lay· it on thick; **~hovedet** *adj* fat-headed; **~hudet** *adj* thick-skinned *(også fig).*
tykkelse *en* thickness; *(diameter)* di'ameter; *(omfang)* cir'cumference.
tykmælk *en sv.t.* junket.
tyksteg *en (gastr)* rump steak.
tyktarm *en* colon.
tyktflydende *adj* thick, viscous.
tyl *et* tulle [tju:l].
tylle *v: ~ (i sig)* swig, knock back.
tynd *adj* thin; *(slank)* lean; *(mager)* thin, skinny; *(knap, sparsom)* sparse; *blive ~* grow· thin; *en ~t befolket ø* a sparsely in'habited island.
tynde *v: ~ ud (i)* thin (out).
tyndslidt *adj* threadbare *(også fig).*
tyndtarm *en* small in'testine.
tyndtflydende *adj* thin, runny.
tyngde *en* weight; *(fys)* gravity; **~kraft** *en* gravi'tation; *~kraften* gravity; **~punkt** *et* main point.
tynge *v (være tung)* be heavy; *(med objekt)* weigh down; *(fig)* weigh on; *~t af ansvar* loaded down with responsi'bility; *hvad er det der ~r dig?* what's on your mind? **~nde** *adj* heavy.
type *en* type; **~hus** *et* standard house.
typisk *adj* typical *(for* of).
typograf *en* ty'pographer; **typografi** *en* ty'pography; **typografisk** *adj* typo'graphical.
tyr *en* bull; *Tyren (astr)* Taurus.
tyran *en* tyrant.
tyranni *et* tyranny; **~sere** *v* bully.
tyrannisk *adj* ty'rannical.
tyrefægtning *en* bullfight.
tyrk(er) *en* Turk; **Tyrkiet** *s* 'Turkey; **tyrkisk** *et/adj* Turkish.
tysk *et/adj* German; **tysker** *en* German; **Tyskland** *s* Germany.
tysse *v: ~ på en* hush sby up, shush sby.
tyttebær *et* cowberry.
tyv *en* thief *(pl:* thieves); *(indbruds~)* burglar.
tyve *num* twenty; *han er i ~rne* he is in his twenties; *han er født i ~rne* he was born in the twenties.
tyvende *adj* twentieth; **~del** *en* twentieth.
tyveri *et* theft; *(indbruds~)* burglary; **~alarm** *en* burglar a'larm; **~forsikring** *en* burglary in'surance.
tyvstarte *v (sport)* jump the gun.
tæge *en* bug.
tække *v (om tag)* thatch; **~s** *v: ~s en* make· up to sby.

tælle *v* count; *dine dage er talte* your days are numbered; *~ efter* check; *~ ngt med* in'clude sth; *de ~r ikke (med)* they don't count; *~ sammen* add up; *~ til ti* count up to ten; **~apparat** *et (ved indgang)* turnstile.
tæller *en (til el etc)* meter; *(i brøk)* numerator.
tælling *en* counting; *måtte tage ~ (om bokser)* go· down for a count.
tæmme *v* tame; *(følelse, begær)* curb; *(gøre til husdyr)* do'mesticate.
tæmning *en* taming; domesti'cation.
tænde *v* light·; *(radio, lys etc)* switch (,put·) on; *(om motor)* ig'nite; *~ for gassen* light the gas; *~ et lys* light a candle; *lyset er tændt (dvs. det elektriske)* the light is on; *~ ild i ngt* set· fire to sth; *~ op* light· a fire.
tænder *en* lighter.
tænding *en* lighting; *(om motor)* ig'nition; **~s·nøgle** *en* ig'nition key.
tændrør *et* spark(ing) plug.
tændstik *en* match; *tænde en ~* strike· a match; *en æske ~ker* a box of matches; **~æske** *en* matchbox.
tænke *v* think·; *(agte, ville)* in'tend *(at* to); *tænk bare!* just i'magine! just think! *tænk at det skulle ske!* to think that this should happen! *det tænkte jeg nok!* I thought so! *jeg havde tænkt mig at gå klokken fem* I was planning to leave at five; *jeg kunne godt ~ mig en kop te* I would not mind a cup of tea; *kunne du ~ dig at gå i biografen?* would you like to go to the cinema? *~ ngt igennem* think sth over; *~ sig om* think; *~ over ngt* think about sth, con'sider sth; *~ på ngt* think of (,about sth; *~ på at gøre ngt ved det* in'tend to do sth about it; *vi kom til at ~ på at...* it oc'curred to us that...
tænkelig *adj: det er meget ~t* it's quite possible; *det værst ~e resultat* the worst possible result.
tænksom *adj* thoughtful.
tænkt *adj* i'maginary *(fx linje* line); *det var ~ som en gave* it was meant to be a present.
tæppe *et (gulv~)* carpet; *(mindre)* rug; *(uld~)* blanket; *(vat~)* quilt; *(væg~)* tapestry; *(teat)* curtain; *ægte ~r* Ori'ental carpets; **~banker** *en* carpet-beater; **~belægning** *en* carpeting; **~maskine** *en* carpet-sweeper.
tære *v (om metal)* cor'rode; *~ på formuen* eat· into one's fortune; *~s hen* waste away.
tæring *en (af metal)* cor'rosion; *(gl, med)* con'sumption.
tærske *v* thresh.
tærskel *en* threshold.
tærskemaskine *en* threshing ma'chine.
tærskning *en* threshing.
tærte *en* pie, tart; *(med frugt også)* flan.
tæsk *pl* thrashing.; *en omgang ~* a good trashing.
tæske *v* thrash; *~ i klaveret* thump the pi'ano.
tæt *adj* close, near; *(mods: utæt)* tight // *adv* close(ly); tight(ly); *~ besat (med folk)* packed; *holde ~* keep· tight; *(tie stille)* keep· one's mouth shut; *~ op ad ngt* close to sth; *det var ~ på!* it was a near thing! *gå ~ på en* question sby closely; *sidde ~ sammen* be sitting close together; *de bor ~ ved* they live nearby; *huset ligger ~ ved skoven* the house stands close to (,near) the forest; **~bebygget** *adj* densely built-up; **~befolket** *adj* densely populated; **~hed** *en* closeness; tightness; *(fys)* density; **~klippet** *adj* close-cropped.
tætning *en* tightening; *(af sprækker)* sealing; **~s·liste** *en* draught strip, seal.
tætpakket *adj* packed.
tætsiddende *adj* close-set *(fx øjne* eyes); *(om tøj)* clinging.
tætsluttende *adj* close-fitting.
tætte *v* make· tight; *(om sprækker etc)* seal (up); *(om hus, isolere)* insulate.
tæv *pl* beating; *en omgang ~* a thorough beating.
tæve *en (hunhund)* bitch.
tæve *v* thrash, beat· up.
tø *en* thaw // *v* melt, thaw; *det ~r* it is thawing.

tøffel *en* slipper; *være under ~en* be henpecked.

tøj *et (stof)* ma'terial; *(klæde)* cloth; *(klæder)* clothes *pl*, clothing; *lægge ~et (dvs. overtøjet)* take· off one's coat (,jacket etc); *(dvs. klæde sig af)* un'dress; *skifte ~* change; *tage ~et på (dvs. overtøjet)* put· on one's coat (,jacket etc); *(dvs. klæde sig på)* dress, get· dressed; *pæn i ~et* nicely dressed; *et sæt ~* a suit; **~dyr** *et* fluffy animal; **~klemme** *en* clothes-peg.

tøjle *en* rein; *få frie ~r* get· a free hand; *stramme ~rne* tighten the reins // *v (fig)* curb; *~ sig* re'strain oneself.

tøjlesløs *adj* un'bridled.

tøjre *v* tether.

tøjsnor *en* clothesline.

tømme *en* rein // *v* empty; *~s* empty.

tømmer *et* timber; **~flåde** *en* raft; **~mænd** *pl* hangover.

tømning *en* emptying; *(om postkasse, skraldebøtte etc)* col'lection.

tømre *v* make·, build·.

tømrer *en* carpenter.

tønde *en (af træ)* barrel; *(af metal)* drum; *som sild i en ~* like sardines in a tin.

tør *adj* dry; *(om fx whisky)* neat; *løbe ~ for benzin* run· out of petrol; *give den lille ~t på* change the baby's nappy; **~dok** *en* dry dock; **~gær** *en* dry yeast; **~hed** *en* dryness.

tørke *en* drought; **~ramt** *adj* drought-stricken.

tørklæde *et* scarf *(pl:* scarves).

tørlægge *v* drain; *(for øl, sprut)* make· dry.

tørmælk *en* dried milk.

tørn *en* turn; **~e** *v: ~e ind i* run· into; *~e sammen* col'lide.

tørre *v* dry; *~ ngt af* wipe sth; *~ af efter opvasken* dry the dishes; *~ hænderne* wipe one's hands; *hænge vasketøj til ~* hang· up the washing; *~ ud* dry out; *~ sig* wipe oneself; **~hjelm** *en* hairdrier; **~skab** *et* drying cupboard; **~snor** *en* clothes-line; **~tumbler** *en* tumbler drier.

tørring *en* drying; wiping.

tørskoet *adj* dry-shod.

tørst *en* thirst *(efter* for).

tørste *v* be thirsty; *~ efter ngt* crave for sth, thirst for sth.

tørstig *adj* thirsty.

tørv *en* peat; *(græs~)* turf.

tørvejr *et* dry weather; *stå i ~* take· cover; *det er blevet ~* it has stopped raining.

tørvemose *en* peat bog.

tørvestrøelse *en* garden peat.

tøs *en* girl, lass; *(neds)* broad; *(luder)* tart.

tøsedreng *en* sissy, poofter.

tøsne *en* sleet, slush.

tøve *v* hesitate *(med at* to).

tøvejr *et* thaw.

tøven *en* hesi'tation; *uden ~* with'out de'lay.

tå *en* toe; *fra top til ~* from top to bottom; *træde en over tæerne* step on sby's toes; *på ~* on tiptoe.

tåbe *en* fool.

tåbelig *adj* foolish, stupid; **~hed** *en* foolishnes, stu'pidity.

tåge *en* fog; *(dis)* mist; *et skud i ~n (fig)* a shot in the dark; **~dis** *en* mist; **~horn** *et* foghorn; **~lygte** *en* fog light.

tåget *adj* foggy; *(let)* misty; *(uklar)* dim, vague.

tåle *v (finde sig i)* put· up with, take·; *(udholde)* stand·, bear·; *(lide)* bear·, suffer; *jeg kan ikke ~ den fyr* I can't stand that chap; *han kan ikke ~ hvidløg* garlic doesn't a'gree with him; *man må ~ meget* one has to put· up with a lot; *~r ikke varme (om vare)* keep away from heat, store in a cool place.

tålelig *adj* tolerable; *(så nogenlunde)* passable.

tålmodig *adj* patient; **~hed** *en* patience; *tabe ~heden* lose· patience *(med* with).

tånegl *en* toe nail.

tår *en* drop; *en ~ øl* a drink (,drop) of beer.

tåre *en* tear; **~gas** *en* tear gas; **~persende** *adj* weepy; **~vædet** *adj* tearful *(fx blik* look).

tårn *et* tower; *(med spir)* steeple;

(klokke~) belfry; *(i skak)* rook, castle.
tårne *v: ~ sig op* pile up.
tårnfalk *en* kestrel.
tårnhøj *adj (fig)* sky-high *(fx pris* price).
tårnspring *et (i svømning)* high diving.
tårnur *et* tower clock.
tåspids *en* tip of the toe; *på ~erne* on tiptoe.

U

uadskillelige *adj* in'separable.
uafbrudt *adj (uden pause)* con'tinuous, constant; *(som stadig gentages)* con'tinual // *adv* constantly; con'tinually; *~ i otte timer* for eight hours on end.
uafgjort *adj* un'settled; *(sport)* drawn; *kampen endte ~* the match ended in a draw.
uafhængig *adj* inde'pendent *(af* of); **~hed** *en* inde'pendence.
uafklaret *adj* un'clarified; unde'cided.
uafladelig *adj* constant // *adv* constantly.
uagtsom *adj: ~t manddrab* homicide by misad'venture; **~hed** *en* negligence.
ualmindelig *adj* un'usual, ex'ceptional.
uanet *adj* un'dreamt of.
uanfægtet *adj* unaf'fected *(af* by).
uanmeldt *adj* unin'vited.
uanselig *adj* insig'nificant; *(om person)* ordinary; *(lille)* small.
uanset *præp* re'gardless of; *~ hvordan (,hvor, hvem etc)* no matter how (,where, who etc); *~ om det regner* whether it is raining or not.
uanstændig *adj* in'decent; **~hed** *en* in'decency.
uansvarlig *adj* irre'sponsible; **~hed** *en* irresponsi'bility.
uantastet *adj* un'challenged.
uanvendelig *adj* useless.
uappetitlig *adj* un'savoury.
uarbejdsdygtig *adj* un'fit for work.
uartig *adj* naughty; *(uhøflig, grov)* rude; *(sjofel)* dirty; *være ~ mod en* be naughty to sby; **~hed** *en* naughtiness; rudeness.
ubarberet *adj* un'shaven.
ubarmhjertig *adj* merciless, pitiless; **~hed** *en* mercilessness, pitilessness.
ubeboelig *adj* unin'habitable.
ubeboet *adj* unin'habited.
ubegavet *adj* unin'telligent.
ubegribelig *adj (umulig at forstå)* incompre'hensible; *(ufattelig)* incon'ceivable.
ubegrundet *adj* un'founded.
ubegrænset *adj* un'limited.
ubehag *et (fysisk)* dis'comfort; *(ved ngt man ikke kan lide)* dis'like *(ved* of, for).
ubehagelig *adj* un'pleasant; *~t til mode* ill at ease, un'easy; **~hed** *en* un'pleasantness; *~heder* trouble; *få ~heder* get· into trouble.
ubehersket *adj* uncon'trolled; *opføre sig ~* show lack of 'self-con,trol.
ubehjælpsom *adj* clumsy; **~hed** *en* clumsiness.
ubehøvlet *adj* rude.
ubekendt *adj* un'known; *være ~ med ngt* be a stranger to sth.
ubekvem *adj* un'comfortable.
ubelejlig *adj* incon'venient.
ubemidlet *adj* without means.
ubemærket *adj* un'noticed; **~hed** *en: i ~hed* un'noticed.
ubenyttet *adj* un'used.
uberegnelig *adj* unpre'dictable; **~hed** *en* unpredicta'bility.
uberettiget *adj* un'warranted; *(uden grund)* un'founded, groundless.
uberørt *adj* unaf'fected *(af* by); *~ natur* virgin nature.
ubesat *adj* vacant.
ubeset *adj: købe ngt ~* buy· sth without seeing it first.
ubeskrivelig *adj* inde'scribable; *(neds)* un'speakable // *adv* inde'scribably; un'speakably.
ubeslutsom *adj* ir'resolute, hesitant; **~hed** *en* hesitancy.
ubestemmelig *adj* inde'terminable; *(neds)* 'nonde,script.
ubestemt *adj* in'definite; *på ~ tid* in'definitely.
ubesvaret *adj* un'answered; *hun lod*

hans tilnærmelser være ~ she did not re'act to his ad'vances.

ubetinget *adj* uncon'ditional, absolute // *adv* absolutely.

ubetydelig *adj* insig'nificant; **-hed** *en* insig'nificance; *(lille smule)* trifle.

ubetænksom *adj* thoughtless; *(uovervejet)* rash.

ubevidst *adj* un'conscious.

ubevogtet *adj* un'guarded; ~ *jernbaneoverskæring* level crossing without barrier.

ubevæbnet *adj* un'armed.

ubevægelig *adj* motionless; *(ikke til at bevæge)* im'mobile; **-hed** *en* immo'bility.

ublu *adj* shameless; *(om pris)* stiff.

ubodelig *adj* ir'reparable *(fx skade* damage).

ubrugelig *adj* useless.

ubøjelig *adj* in'flexible; *(hård)* re'lentless; *(stiv)* rigid.

ubønhørlig *adj* re'lentless.

ubåd *en* submarine.

uciviliseret *adj* un'civilised; *(vild)* savage.

ud *adv* out; *(se også de enkelte ord som* ~ *forbindes med); (se også ude); gå* ~ go· out; *gå (,køre etc) lige* ~ go· (,drive· etc) straight on; *tale* ~ finish speaking; *få talt* ~ *med en* have it out with sby; *en* ~ *af ti* one in ten; *parkere* ~ *for kirken* park opposite the church; ~ *ad døren* out of the door; *komme* ~ *af det* get· con'fused; *komme godt* ~ *af det med en* get· along with sby; *komme* ~ *for ngt* meet· with sth, ex'perience sth; ~ *fra* from; *kunne ngt* ~ *og ind* know· sth inside out; *hverken vide* ~ *el. ind* be all at sea; *punge* ~ *med 50 kr.* pay· out 50 kr.; *vende* ~ *mod* look out on, face; ~ *over* over, more than; *(foruden)* be'sides; *(undtagen)* ex'cept; ~ *på dagen* late in the day; *ugen* ~ to the end of the week.

udad *adv* outwards.

udadtil *adv* outwardly.

udadvendt *adj* extrovert.

udarbejde *v* pre'pare, make· *(fx en rapport* a report); **-lse** *en* prepa'ration, making; *under* ~*lse* being pre'pared, in the making.

udarte *v* de'generate *(til* into); *(komme ud af kontrol)* get· out of hand.

udbasunere *v:* ~ *ngt* shout sth from the rooftops.

udbede *v:* ~ *sig ngt* ask for sth; *svar* ~*s* please answer; *(på indbydelse)* RSVP.

udbedre *v (om mindre skade)* mend; *(om større skade)* re'pair.

udbedring *en* mending; re'pair.

udbetale *v* pay· (out); *få udbetalt en check* cash a cheque.

udbetaling *en* payment; *(på afdragskøb)* down payment; *betale 500 kr. i* ~ pay 500 kr. down.

udblæsning *en (auto)* ex'haust; *for fuld* ~ at full blast.

udblæsningsrør *et (auto)* ex'haust pipe.

udbrede *v* spread· (out); ~ *sig om ngt (i tale el. skrift)* en'large on sth; **-lse** *en (almindelig)* 'prevalence; *(om sygdom)* incidence; *(af skriftligt el. trykt materiale)* circu'lation; *(fordeling)* distri'bution.

udbredt *adj (almindeligt)* widespread; *(fremherskende)* 'prevalent, pre'vailing.

udbringe *v (varer, post)* de'liver; ~ *et leve for en* call for (three) cheers for sby; ~ *en skål for en* pro'pose a toast for sby.

udbringning *en* de'livery.

udbrud *et (start)* outbreak *(fx af krig* of war); *(om vulkan)* e'ruption; *(udråb)* excla'mation; *komme til* ~ break· out; *(om vulkan)* e'rupt.

udbryde *v (sige)* ex'claim, cry; *(om krig etc)* break· out.

udbrændt *adj (om hus og fig)* burnt-out.

udbud *et* sup'ply; ~ *og efterspørgsel* sup'ply and de'mand.

udbyde *v:* ~ *til salg* offer for sale; ~ *i licitation* in'vite tenders (for).

udbygge *v* en'large; *(forklare nærmere)* e'laborate.

udbygning *en (udvidelse, tilbygning)* ex'tension; *(udhus)* outhouse; *(forbedring)* de'velopment.

udbytte *et (fortjeneste)* profit; *(af høst)* yield; *få ~* get· a profit; *have ~ af ngt* profit from sth // *v* ex'ploit; **~deling** *en* profit-sharing; **~rig** *adj* profitable.

uddanne *v* educate, train; *~ sig til læge* study medicine; *han ~r sig til lærer* he is training to become a teacher; *hun er ~t sygeplejerske* she is a qualified nurse.

uddannelse *en* edu'cation, training; **~s·stilling** *en* trainee job; **~s·politik** *en* edu'cational policy; **~s·støtte** *en* study grant.

uddele *v* di'stribute; *(dele rundt også)* hand out; *~ præmier* a'ward prizes.

uddeling *en* distri'bution; *(delen rundt)* handing out; *(af post)* de'livery.

uddrag *et* 'extract; *(fx af artikel)* abstract; *lave ~ af ngt* ex'tract sth.

uddybe *v (fig)* e'laborate.

uddø *v* be'come ex'tinct.

uddød *adj* ex'tinct.

ude *adv* out; *(udenfor)* out'side; *(udendørs)* out (of doors); *(forbi)* up, at an end; *være ~ af sig selv af skræk* be be'side oneself with fear; *være ~ at køre (,gå, etc)* be out driving (,walking etc); *~ at rejse* travelling; *spise ~ (på restaurant)* eat· out; *(i det fri)* eat· out'side; *være ~ efter en (,ngt)* be after sby (,sth); *nu er det ~ med ham* he is done for now; *du var selv ~ om det* you were asking for it; *~ på landet* in the country; *være ~ på ngt* be up to sth.

udearbejdende *adj* working.

udebane *en (sport)* away ground; *kamp på ~* away match.

udeblive *v* stay away, not turn up; *(ikke ske)* not happen; **~lse** *en* absence; *(pjæk)* absen'teeism.

udefra *adv* from the outside; *(fra udlandet)* from a'broad.

udekamp *en* away match.

udelade *v* o'mit, leave· out; **~lse** *en* o'mission.

udelt *adj* undi'vided // *adv: ikke ~ begejstret* not wholly enthusi'astic.

udelukke *v* ex'clude; *(vise bort)* ex'pel; *man kan ikke ~ at han har været i god tro* you can't ig'nore the fact that he may have been in good faith; **~lse** *en* ex'clusion; ex'pulsion.

udelukkende *adv* ex'clusively, en'tirely.

udelukket *adj: det er ~* it is out of the question.

uden *præp* with'out; *(ikke inkluderet)* ex'cluding; *~ at ane det* without knowing it; *~ moms* ex'clusive of VAT; *~ for huset* out'side the house; *~ for Danmark* out of Denmark; *~ om* round; *man kan ikke komme ~ om at...* there is no de'nying that...; *~ på* on the outside of, out'side.

udenad *adv* by heart.

udenbords *adv* outboard *(fx motor* engine); *(over bord)* over'board.

udenbys *adj/adv* out of town; *han er ~ fra* he is from out of town; *~ telefonsamtale* trunk call.

udendørs *adj* outdoor // *adv* out of doors.

udenfor *adv* out'side; *føle sig ~* feel· left out; *holde sig ~ ngt* keep· out of sth.

udenforstående *en* out'sider.

udenlands *adv* a'broad; **udenlandsk** *adj* foreign.

udenom *adv: gå ~ ngt* go· round sth; *der er ingen vej ~* there is no getting around it; *man kan ikke komme ~ at ...* there's no getting away from the fact that...

udenomsbekvemmeligheder *pl* con'veniences.

udenpå *adv* out'side.

udenrigs... *sms:* **~handel** *en* foreign trade; **~korrespondent** *en* foreign corre'spondent; **~ministerium** *et* Ministry of Foreign Af'fairs; **~politik** *en* foreign politics.

udesejr *en (sport)* a'way win.

udfald *et (resultat)* re'sult, issue.

udfaldsvej *en* ar'terial road.

udfletning *en (af motorvej)* motorway inter'section.

udflugt *en (tur)* outing, ex'cursion; *(med madkurv)* picnic; *(snakken*

udenom) e'vasion; *komme med ~er* beat· about the bush.
udflåd *et (med)* discharge.
udfolde *v: ~ sig (om person)* show· what one is worth; *(komme i gang)* get· going; *(slå sig løs)* let· one's hair down.
udfordre *v* challenge; **~nde** *adj* pro'vocative.
udfordring *en* challenge.
udforme *v* form, structure, shape; *~ sig* de'velop *(til* into).
udformning *en* shaping; structure.
udforske *v* ex'plore.
udforskning *en* explo'ration.
udfylde *v (tomt rum)* fill up; *(skema)* fill in; *(stilling)* fill.
udfyldning *en* filling up (,in).
udfærdige *v* make· out *(fx en regning* an invoice); draw· up *(fx et testamente* a will); **~lse** *en* prepa'ration.
udføre *v (gøre)* carry out, do·; *(fremføre)* per'form; *(eksportere)* ex'port; *~ en ordre* carry out an order; *~ sit arbejde* do· one's work; *~ en kunst* per'form a trick; **~lse** *en* carrying-out; per'formance; *(om kvaliteten af ngt)* workmanship; *(om arten af ngt)* version; *bringe ngt til ~lse* carry sth out; *under ~lse* in the making.
udførlig *adj* e'laborate, detailed // *adv* in detail.
udførsel *en* 'export, expor'tation; **~s·forbud** *et* em'bargo; **~s·tilladelse** *en* export licence.
udgang *en* exit, way out; *(resultat)* issue; *stuen har ~ til terrasse* the room opens on to a patio; *ved årets ~* at the end of the year; **~s·dør** *en* exit; **~s·forbud** *et* curfew; **~s·punkt** *et* starting point; **~s·tilladelse** *en* per'mission to go out; *(mil)* pass.
udgave *en* e'dition.
udgift *en* ex'pense; *faste ~er* regular outlays; *diverse ~er* sundries; **~s·bilag** *et* ex'penditure voucher; **~s·post** *en* item of ex'penditure.
udgive *v (bog, avis etc)* publish; *~ sig for ngt* pre'tend to be sth; pose as sth; **~lse** *en* publi'cation.
udgiver *en* publisher.
udgravning *en* exca'vation; *(arkæologisk)* dig.
udgøre *v (danne, være)* make· up; *(repræsentere)* make· out; *(beløbe sig til)* a'mount to.
udgå *v (ikke blive inkluderet)* be left out, be o'mitted; *(stamme)* come· *(fra* from).
udgående *adj* outgoing *(fx post* mail).
udgået *adj (om vare)* out of stock; *(om træ)* dead; *være ~ for ngt* be out of sth.
udholdende *adj* en'during.
udholdenhed *en* en'durance.
udhule *v* hollow out.
udhus *et* outhouse.
udhvilet *adj* rested.
udhængsskab *et* showcase.
udkant *en* outskirts *pl; i ~en* on the outskirts.
udkast *et* sketch.
udkig *et: holde ~ efter* be on the look-out for.
udklip *et* cutting; *(fra avis)* press cutting.
udklække *v (æg)* hatch; *(plan)* cook up.
udklækning *en* hatching; **~s·sted** *et (fig)* seedbed *(for* of).
udkomme *v (om bog etc)* ap'pear, be published.
udkæmpe *v* fight·.
udkørsel *en (vej ud)* exit, way out; *(det at køre varer etc ud)* de'livery; *(edb)* run.
udkørt *adj* ex'hausted, worn out.
udlandet *s* the foreign countries; *fra ~* from a'broad; *i ~* a'broad; *tage til ~* go· a'broad.
udlede *v (slutte)* de'duce *(af* from); *(fx spildevand)* let· out.
udlejning *en* letting, hiring out; **~s·bil** *en* hired car; **~s·ejendom** *en* tenement house.
udlevere *v (aflevere)* de'liver; *(afstå)* give· up; *(uddele)* di'stribute; *(om forbryder, der sendes til et andet land)* extradite; *~ en (dvs. gøre til grin, afsløre)* compromise sby.
udlevering *en* de'livery; *(uddeling)* distri'bution; *(af forbryder)* extra'dition.

udligne *v (forskelle; i sport)* equalize; *(opveje)* counter'balance.
udligning *en* equali'zation; *(merk)* settlement; **~s·mål** *et (sport)* equalizer.
udluftning *en* airing.
udlæg *et* outlay; *gøre ~ i ngt* di'strain upon sth.
udlægge *v* lay· out; *(tyde, tolke)* in'terpret.
udlægning *en* laying out; *(fortolkning)* interpre'tation.
udlænding *en* foreigner.
udlært *adj* trained, skilled.
udløb *et (af flod)* mouth; *(af frist etc)* expi'ration, ex'piry; *inden månedens ~* be'fore the end of the month; **~e** *v (om frist)* ex'pire.
udløber *en (af plante)* runner; *(fig)* offshoot.
udløse *v (starte)* start, trigger off; *~ en bombe* re'lease a bomb; *~ spændingen* re'lieve the tension.
udløser *en (foto)* shutter re'lease.
udløsning *en* re'lease; *(for vrede etc)* outlet; *(seksuelt)* satis'faction.
udlån *et* loan; *(på biblioteket)* lending; **~e** *v* lend·.
udmale *v* de'pict.
udmatte *v* ex'haust; **~lse** *en* ex'haustion.
udmeldelse *en (af skole)* with'drawal; *(af forening)* resig'nation; *~ af EF* se'cession from the EEC.
udmunde *v: ~ i (om flod)* flow into; *(fig)* end in.
udmunding *en (om flod)* mouth.
udmærke *v: ~ sig* di'stinguish oneself; **~lse** *en* di'stinction; *(orden)* deco'ration.
udmærket *adj* excellent; *det er ~!* that is fine! *vi har det ~* we are fine // *adv* very well; *det kan ~ være at han kommer* he may· very well come.
udnytte *v (bruge)* utilize; *(misbruge)* ex'ploit; *~ ens viden* draw· on sby's knowledge; **~lse** *en* utili'zation; exploi'tation.
udnævne *v* ap'point; *~ en til direktør* ap'point sby di'rector; **~lse** *en* ap'pointment *(til* as).
udpege *v* point out; *(udnævne)* ap'point.
udpluk *et* se'lection
udplyndre *v* rob.
udplyndring *en* robbery.
udpræget *adj* pro'nounced, di'stinct.
udpumpning *en: sende en til ~ (med)* send· sby to have his (,her) stomach pumped.
udredning *en (forklaring)* expla'nation; *(undersøgelse)* a'nalysis.
udregne *v* calculate.
udregning *en* calcu'lation.
udrejse *en (af et land)* de'parture; **~tilladelse** *en* exit permit.
udrensning *en (af personer el. politiske grupper)* purge.
udrette *v (udføre)* a'chieve.
udrikkelig *adj* un'drinkable, un'fit for con'sumption.
udringet *adj* low-cut.
udruge *v* hatch.
udruste *v* e'quip; *(med* with); *godt ~t* 'well-e'quipped.
udrustning *en* e'quipment, outfit.
udrydde *v* wipe out, ex'terminate; **~lse** *en* extermi'nation.
udrykning *en* turn-out; **~s·horn** *et* siren, (S) hee-haw; **~s·vogn** *en* ambulance; fire engine; po'lice car.
udråb *et* excla'mation; *(råb)* cry; **~s·ord** *et* inter'jection; **~s·tegn** *et* excla'mation mark.
udsagn *et* statement; **~s·ord** *et* verb.
udsalg *et* sale; *(butik)* shop; **~s·pris** *en* retail price; *(under nedsættelse)* sale price.
udsat *adj* ex'posed *(for* to); *(udskudt, fx om møde)* put· off, post'poned.
udse *v: ~ sig ngt* pick out sth; *han havde allerede ~t sig et offer* he al'ready had his eye on a victim.
udseende *et* look, ap'pearance; *kende en af ~* know· sby by sight; *dømme efter ~t* go· by ap'pearances; *give det ~ af at ...* make· it look as if...
udsende *v* send· out; *(udgive)* publish; *(i tv, radio)* broadcast·; *~ stormvarsel* send· out a gale warning; **~lse** *en* sending out; publi'cation; broadcasting; *(enkelt ~lse)* programme.

udsending *en* envoy; *(delegeret)* 'delegate.
udsigt *en* view; *(fig)* prospect; *(om vejr)* forecast; *det er en flot ~ fra taget* there is a fine view from the roof; *der er ~ til byger* showers may be ex'pected; *have ~ til at arve ngt* have good prospects of in'heriting sth; *stille en ngt i ~* promise sby sth; *det har lange ~er* that is a distant project.
udskejelse *en* ex'cess.
udskifte *v* change *(med* for), re'place *(med* by).
udskiftning *en* change, re'placement; *(fodb)* substi'tution.
udskille *v* separate; *(fjerne)* move; *(afsondre)* se'crete; *~ sig fra ngt* separate from sth; **~lse** *en* sepa'ration; re'moval; se'cretion.
udskrabning *en (med)* cu'rettage, C and D.
udskrift *en (afskrift)* transcript; *(edb)* printout.
udskrive *v (en check etc)* write· out, make· out; *(skat etc)* levy; *(fra sygehus)* dis'charge; *~ valg* call an e'lection.
udskrivning *en* writing out; *(af skatter)* levying; *(fra sygehus)* dis'charge; *(af soldater)* con'scription; *(udgift)* ex'pense.
udskud *et (om person)* scum, pariah.
udskyde *v* post'pone, put· off; **~lse** *en* post'ponement.
udskænkning *en* serving (of drinks).
udskænkningstilladelse *en* licence.
udskæring *en* cutting out; *(på møbler)* carving; *(stykke kød)* cut; *(af kød)* carving.
udskåret *adj (møbel etc)* carved; *(kjole etc)* low-cut.
udslag *et (resultat)* re'sult, ef'fect *(af* of); *(tegn)* symptom *(af* of); *(om viser på fx vægt)* de'flection; *give sig ~ i* be re'flected in; *(resultere i)* re'sult in; **~givende** *adj* de'cisive.
udslette *v* wipe out; *(tilintetgøre også)* an'nihilate; **~lse** *en* oblite'ration; annihi'lation.
udslidt *adj* worn out.
udslip *et* leak(age).
udslukt *adj* ex'tinct.
udslæt *et* rash; *få ~ (også)* come· out in spots.
udsmykke *v* decorate.
udsmykning *en* deco'ration.
udsolgt *adj* sold out; *(teat)* full house.
udsovet *adj: være ~* have had a good night's sleep.
udspekuleret *adj* sly, cunning.
udspil *et (forslag)* pro'posal; *(initiativ)* i'nitiative; *du har ~let* it is your move; *komme med et ~* make· a pro'posal.
udspilet *adj* di'lated.
udpille *v: ~ sig* take· place.
udspionere *v* spy on.
udsprede *v* spread· (out).
udspring *et (om svømmer)* dive, plunge; *(som sportsgren)* diving; *(om flod)* source; *(i faldskærm)* jump.
udspringe *v (om flod)* rise·.
udspørge *v* question.
udstationere *v* station.
udsted *et (grønlandsk)* (small) settlement.
udstede *v* issue; *~ en recept* write· out a pre'scription; *~ et pas* issue a passport; **~lse** *en* issue; making out.
udstille *v* ex'hibit, show.
udstilling *en* exhi'bition, show; **~s·genstand** *en* ex'hibit; **~s·vindue** *et* show window.
udstoppe *v* stuff.
udstrakt *adj (strakt ud)* out'stretched; *(vid, omfattende)* ex'tensive; *ligge ~ (om person)* lie· prone; *(om landskab)* stretch.
udstrækning *en* ex'tension; *(omfang)* ex'tent; *i vid ~* to a large ex'tent.
udstråling *en* radi'ation; *(om person)* aura.
udstykke *v* parcel out.
udstykning *en* parcelling out; *(til byggeri)* de'velopment.
udstyr *et* e'quipment; *(tilbehør)* ac'cessories *pl; (brude~)* trousseau; *(baby~)* lay'ette; *(møbler)* furnishings *pl; (køkken~)* u'tensils *pl.*
udstyre *v* e'quip; *(med* with); *(forsyne)* pro'vide *(med* with).
udstøde *v (forstøde, udvise)* ex'pel;

(suk, råb etc) give·, utter; ~ *et suk* heave a sigh; **-lse** *en* ex'pulsion.
udstødning *en (auto)* ex'haust.
udstå *v (holde ud)* stand·, bear·; *(lide, gennemgå)* under'go·, suffer; *(straf, lære)* serve; *jeg kan ikke ~ ham* I can't stand him.
udstående *adj (om ører, øjne etc)* pro'truding.
udsvævende *adj* dissipated.
udsætte *v (udskyde, opsætte)* post'pone, put· off; *(udlove fx dusør)* offer; *(sætte på gaden)* e'vict; ~ *en for ngt* ex'pose sby to sth; *blive udsat for at blive glemt* run· the risk of being for'gotten; *have ngt at ~ på ngt* find· fault with sth; *nationalsangen udsat for hornorkester* the national anthem ar'ranged for brass band; ~ *vagtposter* post sentries; **-lse** *en* post'ponement; e'viction; *(af frist)* re'spite; *(af militærtjeneste)* de'ferment; *(af musik)* ar'rangement.
udsøge *v: ~ sig* pick, se'lect.
udsøgt *adj (af bedste kvalitet)* choice; *(særlig lækker el. fin)* exquisite.
udtage *v* se'lect *(til* for); **-lse** *en* se'lection.
udtale *en* pronunci'ation // *v* pro'nounce; *(sige)* say·; *h ~s ikke foran v* the h is silent in front of v; ~ *ngt forkert* mispro'nounce sth; ~ *sig om ngt* give· one's o'pinion on sth; ~ *sig til en* speak· to sby; **-lse** *en* pro'nouncement; *(bemærkning)* re'mark, comment; *(anbefaling ved stillingsansøgning)* reference; *komme med en ~lse* make· a pro'nouncement.
udtog *et* 'extract, 'excerpt; *(sammenfatning)* summary; *(konto~)* statement; *(mus)* ar'rangement.
udtryk *et* ex'pression; *(vending, talemåde også)* phrase; *(bevis)* token *(for* of), sign *(for* of); *(ord også)* term; *give ~ for ngt* ex'press sth; *komme til ~* show (,ex'press) itself.
udtrykke *v* ex'press; ~ *sig* ex'press oneself.
udtrykkelig *adj* ex'plicit.
udtryksfuld *adj* ex'pressive.
udtryksløs *adj* ex'pressionless; *(om ansigt også)* blank.
udtrykt *adj: være ens ~e billede* be the spitting image of sby.
udtræde *v: ~ af* with'draw (,re'sign) from; ~ *af EF* se'cede from the EEC; **-lse** *en* with'drawal, resig'nation; se'cession.
udtræk *et (af urter etc)* extract; *(i kogende vand)* in'fusion.
udtrække *v* ex'tract.
udtrækning *en* ex'traction.
udtræksbord *et* ex'tension table.
udtrådt *adj (om sko)* well-worn.
udtænke *v* think· up (,out).
udtømmende *adj* ex'haustive; in-depth.
udtørret *adj* dried-up.
uduelig *adj* in'competent; **-hed** *en* in'competence.
udvalg *et (som man kan vælge fra)* se'lection; *(komité)* com'mittee; *sidde i et ~* be on a com'mittee; *nedsætte et ~* set· up a com'mittee; *et stort ~ af ngt* a large se'lection of sth.
udvalgt *adj* se'lected; *(særlig fin)* choice.
udvandre *v (emigrere)* emigrate; *(fra møde etc)* walk out.
udvandrer *en* emigrant.
udvandring *en* emi'gration; walk-out.
udvej *en* way (out); *som en sidste ~* in a last re'sort; *på ~en* on the way out.
udveksle *v* ex'change.
udveksling *en* ex'change; **~s·studerende** *en* ex'change student.
udvendig *adj* outside, ex'ternal // *adv* on the outside, ex'ternally; *det ~e af huset* the outside (,ex'terior) of the house.
udvide *v (gøre større)* en'large; *(om firma etc)* ex'pand; *(om fx bukser, sko)* stretch; *(forøge)* in'crease; ~ *sig* ex'pand; **-lse** *en* en'largement; ex'pansion; stretching.
udvikle *v* de'velop *(sig til* into).
udviklet *adj (om barn)* ma'ture; *tidligt ~t* pre'cocious.
udvikling *en* de'velopment; *(biol)* evo'lution; **~s·hjælp** *en* de'velopment aid, foreign aid; **~s·land** *et* de'veloping country.

udvinde *v* ex'tract.
udvinding *en* ex'traction.
udvise *v (vise)* show, dis'play; *(sende ud af landet)* ex'pel; *(ved sportskamp)* send· off.
udvisning *en* ex'pulsion; *(sport)* sending-off; **~s·bænk** *en* penalty bench.
udvortes *adj: kun til ~ brug* for ex'ternal use only.
udvælge *v* choose·, se'lect; **~lse** *en* choice, se'lection.
udødelig *adj* im'mortal; **~hed** *en* immor'tality.
udørk *en* 'desert.
udøve *v* exercise; *(sport etc)* practise; *~nde kunstner* practising artist.
udånding *en* expi'ration.
uegennyttig *adj* un'selfish.
uegnet *adj* un'fit *(til* for).
uendelig *adj* infinite; *(endeløs)* endless; *i det ~e* in'definitely, endlessly // *adv* infinitely; *~ mange...* no end of...; **~hed** *en* in'finity; *i én ~hed* endlessly.
uenig *adj: blive ~e* fall· out (with one an'other); *være ~e* disa'gree; *være ~ i ngt* disa'gree with sth; **~hed** *en* disa'greement.
uerstattelig *adj (om ting)* irre'placeable; *(om fx skade, tab)* ir'reparable.
ufaglært *adj* unskilled.
ufarlig *adj* harmless, safe.
ufattelig *adj* incon'ceivable // *adv* incon'ceivably; *~ dum* in'credibly stupid.
ufin *adj* tactless.
ufo *en* UFO.
uforanderlig *adj (som ikke kan ændres)* un'changeable; *(som ikke ændrer sig)* in'variable.
uforbederlig *adj* in'corrigible.
uforbeholden *adj* unre'served, wholehearted (fx *støtte* sup'port).
uforbindende *adj (om svar)* non-com'mittal; *(om tilbud etc)* with no strings at'tached.
ufordøjelig *adj* indi'gestible.
uforenelig *adj* incom'patible *(med* with); *(i modstrid med)* incon'sistent *(med* with).
uforfalsket *adj* genuine.
uforglemmelig *adj* unfor'gettable.
uforholdsmæssig *adj* dispro'portionate; *~t stor* out of all pro'portion.
uforklarlig *adj* inex'plicable.
uformel *adj* in'formal.
uformelig *adj* shapeless.
uformindsket *adj* undi'minished.
ufornuftig *adj* un'wise.
uforpligtende *adj (fx svar)* 'non-com'mittal; *(om tilbud etc)* with no strings at'tached.
uforrettet *adj: med ~ sag* with'out having a'chieved anything.
uforsigtig *adj* careless; *(uovervejet)* rash.
uforskammet *adj* impudent, im'pertinent; *en ~ pris* an out'rageous price; **~hed** *en* impudence, im'pertinence; *en ~hed* an insult.
uforsonlig *adj* irrecon'cilable.
uforstyrret *adj* undi'sturbed.
uforståelig *adj* unin'telligible.
uforstående *adj* unsympa'thetic *(over for* to); *se ~ ud* look blank.
uforsvarlig *adj* irre'sponsible; *~ kørsel* reckless driving.
uforudset *adj* unfore'seen, 'unex,pected.
ufremkommelig *adj* im'practicable.
ufri *adj* not free; *(hæmmet)* con'strained.
ufrivillig *adj* unin'tentional.
ufrugtbar *adj* barren; *(fig om fx møde)* fruitless.
ufuldendt *adj* un'finished.
ufuldkommen *adj* im'perfect; **~hed** *en* imper'fection.
ufuldstændig *adj* incom'plete.
ufærdig *adj* un'finished.
ufølsom *adj* in'sensitive *(over for* to); **~hed** *en* insensi'tivity.
uge *en* week; *i sidste ~* last week; *i denne ~* this week; *i næste ~* next week; *om en ~* in a week; *i dag om en ~* to'day week; *flere gange om ~n* several times a week; **~blad** *et* weekly; **~dag** *en* day of the week, weekday.
ugenert *adj (ikke genert)* ,unem'barrassed; *(hæmningsløs)* ,unin'hibited; *(uforstyrret)* undi'sturbed.
ugentlig *adj/adv* weekly, a week; *tre gange ~* three times a week.

ugepenge *pl* weekly al'lowance.
ugevis *adv: i* ~ for weeks.
ugidelig *adj* lazy.
ugift *adj* single, un'married.
uafgjort *adj: ikke lade ngt* ~ leave· nothing un'done.
ugle *en* owl // *v:* ~ *sit hår* tousle one's hair; **~set** *adj* un'popular *(af* with).
ugunstig *adj* un'favourable.
ugyldig *adj* in'valid; **~hed** *en* inva'lidity.
uhelbredelig *adj* in'curable.
uheld *et* accident; *(mods: held)* bad luck; *held i* ~ a blessing in disguise; *have* ~ *i spil (,kærlighed)* be un'lucky at cards (, in love); *sidde i* ~ be out of luck; *være ude for et* ~ have an accident; *teknisk* ~ technical hitch; *ved et* ~ by accident.
uheldig *adj (mods: heldig)* un'lucky; *(beklagelig)* un'fortunate; *(som ikke lykkes)* unsuc'cessful; *(skadelig)* bad; *det var da også ~t!* what a shame! bad luck! **~vis** *adv* un'fortunately.
uheldsvanger *adj* ominous.
uhjælpelig *adv:* ~ *fortabt* irre'trievably lost.
uholdbar *adj (fx situation)* in'tolerable; *(som ikke holder længe)* not durable; *(om madvarer)* perishable.
uhumsk *adj* filthy; **~hed** *en* filthiness; *(skidt)* filth.
uhygge *en (som fremkalder frygt)* horror; *(mods: hygge)* dis'comfort; *(dårlig atmosfære)* dismal atmosphere.
uhyggelig *adj (som fremkalder frygt)* sinister, frightening; *(ubehagelig)* un'comfortable; *(mystisk)* un'canny; ~ *til mode* un'easy.
uhygiejnisk *adj* in'sanitary.
uhyre *et* monster, beast // *adj* huge, e'normous // *adv* e'normously, vastly.
uhyrlig *adj* monstrous; **~hed** *en* mon'strosity.
uhæderlig *adj* dis'honest.
uhæmmet *adj* unre'strained; *(hensynsløs, grov)* reckless.
uhøflig *adj* rude.
uhøjtidelig *adj* in'formal.
uhørt *adj* un'heard of, in'credible // *adv* in'credibly.
uhåndgribelig *adj* in'tangible.
uhåndterlig *adj* un'wieldy.
uigenkaldelig *adj* irre'vocable // *adv* irre'vocably.
uigennemførlig *adj* im'practicable.
uigennemsigtig *adj* o'paque.
uigennemskuelig *adj* im'penetrable.
uimodståelig *adj* irre'sistible.
uimodtagelig *adj* insus'ceptible *(for* to); *(for sygdom)* im'mune *(for* to).
uindbudt *adj* unin'vited.
uindbundet *adj* un'bound.
uindfattet *adj (om briller)* rimless.
uindskrænket *adj* un'limited.
uindviet *adj* uni'nitated.
uinteressant *adj* un'interesting.
uinteresseret *adj* un'interested.
ujævn *adj* un'even, rough; *(om hullet vej)* bumpy; **~hed** *en* un'evenness, roughness; *(på vej)* bump.
ukendt *adj* un'known; *(uvant)* unfa'miliar; *være* ~ *med ngt* not be fa'miliar with sth.
uklar *adj (utydelig)* vague, indi'stinct; *(diset)* hazy; *(om væske)* muddy; *(svær at forstå)* ob'scure; *(forvirret)* con'fused; *rage* ~ *med en* fall· out with sby; *det er ~t hvornår* it is not clear when; **~hed** *en* vagueness; haziness; muddiness; ob'scurity; con'fusion.
uklog *adj* un'wise.
ukristelig *adj* un'godly // *adv* awfully; *et ~t tidspunkt* an un'godly hour; *en* ~ *masse* an awful lot.
ukrudt *et (enkel plante)* weed; *(generelt)* weeds *pl; luge* ~ weed.
ukrudtsmiddel *et* weedkiller.
ukuelig *adj* in'domitable.
uland *et* de'veloping country; **~s·hjælp** *en* de'velopment aid, foreign aid.
ulastelig *adj* im'maculate.
uld *én* wool.
ulden *adj* woollen; *(fig, tåget)* vague.
uldgarn *et* wool.
uldtæppe *et* woollen blanket.
uldvarer *pl* woollens.
ulejlige *v* trouble, bother; ~ *sig med*

at gøre ngt take· the trouble to do sth; *du behøver ikke ~ dig* you needn't bother.
ulejlighed *en* trouble, bother; *gøre ~* give· trouble; *gør dig ingen ~!* don't bother! *gøre sig den ~ at* take· the trouble to; *komme til ~* come· at an incon'venient time; *undskyld ~en!* I'm sorry to di'sturb you! ex'cuse me! *det er ikke ~en værd* it is not worth the trouble.
ulempe *en* drawback.
ulidelig *adj* un'bearable.
ulige *adj* un'equal; *(tal)* un'even, odd; *~ numre* odd numbers; *det er ~ bedre* it is far better; *~ fordeling* un'even distri'bution.
uligevægtig *adj* un'balanced.
ulighed *en (socialt etc)* ine'quality.
ulme *v* smoulder *(også fig)*.
ulogisk *adj* il'logical.
ulovlig *adj* il'legal; **~hed** *en* un'lawfulness; *(forbrydelse)* of'fence.
ultimatum *et* ulti'matum; *stille en et ~* give· sby an ulti'matum.
ultimo: *~ august* at the end of August.
ultralyd *en* ultrasound; **~scanning** *en* (ultrasound) scan.
ulv *en* wolf *(pl:* wolves); **~e·unge** *en* wolf cub *(også om spejder)*.
ulydig *adj* diso'bedient *(mod* to); *være ~* diso'bey; **~hed** *en* diso'bedience.
ulykke *en (ulykkestilfælde)* accident; *(katastrofe)* dis'aster; *(mangel på held)* mis'fortune; *han blev dræbt ved en ~* he was killed in an accident; *det var hans ~ at…* it was his mis'fortune that…; *komme i ~* get· into trouble; *lave ~r* make· mischief.
ulykkelig *adj (ked af det)* un'happy *(over* about); *(uheldig)* un'fortunate; *(beklagelig)* de'plorable; *være ~t stillet* be in di'stress; **~vis** *adv* un'fortunately.
ulykkes… *sms:* **~forsikring** *en* accident in'surance; **~fugl** *en (som bringer uheld)* bird of ill omen; *(som altid kommer galt af sted)* accident-prone person; **~stedet** *s* the scene of the accident; **~tilfælde** *et* accident.
ulyksalig *adj* un'fortunate.
ulækker *adj* un'appetizing; *(fig)* un'savoury; (S) yukky.
ulæselig *adj* il'legible.
ulønnet *adj* un'paid.
uløselig *adj* in'soluble.
umage *en* trouble, pains *pl; gøre sig ~ for at…* take· pains to…; *gøre sig ~ med ngt* take· pains over sth; *det er ikke ~n værd* it is not worth the trouble // *adj (ikke ens)* odd; *to ~ sokker* two odd socks.
umedgørlig *adj* difficult.
umenneskelig *adj* in'human.
umiddelbar *adj* im'mediate, 'direct; *(om person)* straightforward; *i ~ nærhed af stationen* in the im'mediate vi'cinity of the station; **~hed** *en* sponta'neity.
umiddelbart *adv* im'mediately, di'rectly; *(i begyndelsen)* at first.
umindelig *adj: det er ~e tider siden vi sås* it's been donkey's years since we met.
umoden *adj* un'ripe; *(om person)* immature; **~hed** *en* un'ripeness; imma'turity.
umoderne *adj* old-fashioned, outdated.
umoralsk *adj* im'moral.
umotiveret *adj* un'called for, un'founded.
umulig *adj* im'possible; *det kan ~t passe* it can't possibly be true; *det er mig ~t at komme* it is im'possible for me to come; *han er ~ til regning* he is hopeless at a'rithmetic; **~hed** *en* impossi'bility.
umyndig *en* minor // *adj* under age; **~gøre** *v: ~gøre en* (legally) inca'pacitate sby.
umærkelig *adj* imper'ceptible.
umættelig *adj* in'satiable.
umøbleret *adj* un'furnished.
umådelig *adj* im'mense.
unaturlig *adj* un'natural.
unddrage *v: ~ en ngt* with'hold· sth from sby; *~ sig* e'vade.
unde *v (ønske, håbe på)* wish; *(forunde)* give·; *jeg ~r dig det gerne* I'm de'lighted for you; *jeg ~r hende ikke den triumf* I grudge her that triumph; *det er ham vel undt* I don't

grudge him that; *han ~r sig ingen ro* he gives himself no peace.
under *et* wonder; *det er ikke ngt ~ at...* no wonder that...; *det er et Guds ~ at...* it is a miracle that...
under *præp (mods: over; mindre end; dækket af)* under; *(neden under, lavere end)* be'low; *(i løbet af)* during *(fx krigen* the war); *~ al kritik* be'neath con'tempt; *~ ti år* under ten; *temperaturen er ~ nul* the temperature is below zero; *~ bæltestedet* be'low the belt.
underarm *en* forearm.
underbelyst *adj (foto)* underexposed.
underbemandet *adj* short-staffed.
underbetalt *adj* under'paid.
underbevidst *adj* sub'conscious; **-hed** *en* sub'consciousness; *~heden* the sub'conscious.
underbo *en* downstairs neighbour.
underbukser *pl* pants; *(trusser)* briefs.
underdanig *adj* sub'missive; **-hed** *en* sub'missiveness.
underdanigt *adv* humbly.
underdel *en* lower part.
underentreprenør *en* 'subcontractor.
underernæret *adj* under'nourished.
underernæring *en* malnu'trition.
underforstået *adj* tacit; *~ at...* im'plying that...
underfundig *adj (bemærkning, smil)* enig'matic.
undergang *en* de'struction, ruin; *verdens ~* the end of the world.
undergrave *v* under'mine; *adj: ~nde virksomhed* sub'version; *~nde kræfter* sub'versive elements.
undergrund *en* subsoil; **-s·bane** *en* underground, (F) tube.
underhold *et (for andre)* maintenance; *(for en selv)* sub'sistence, living.
underholde *v (more)* enter'tain; *(forsørge)* sup'port.
underholdning *en* enter'tainment; **-s·musik** *en* light music.
underholdsbidrag *et (til hustru)* alimony; *(til børn)* maintenance.
underhuset *s (brit)* the House of Commons.
underjordisk *adj* subter'ranean; *(fig)* underground.
underkant *en: i ~en* not quite good enough.
underkaste *v: ~ en forhør* sub'ject sby to interro'gation; *~ sig en* sub'mit to sby; *være ~t ngt* be subject to sth.
underkende *v (beslutning etc)* over'rule.
underkjole *en* slip.
underkop *en* saucer.
underlag *et* foun'dation; *(i telt)* groundsheet.
underlagscreme *en* foun'dation cream.
underlegen *adj* in'ferior; **-hed** *en* inferi'ority.
underlig *adj* strange, odd; (F, *ofte)* funny; *han er en ~ en* he is a strange one; *føle sig ~t tilpas* feel· funny; *~t nok* strangely enough; *det er ikke så ~t at...* (it is) no wonder that...
underliv *et* abdomen.
underlæbe *en* lower lip.
underminere *v* under'mine.
undermund *en (om gebis)* lower denture.
underneden *adv* under'neath.
underordne *v: ~ sig en (,ngt)* sub'mit to sby (,sth).
underordnet *adj (af lavere rang)* sub'ordinate; *(ligegyldig, ikke af betydning)* secondary.
underretning *en* infor'mation *(u.pl); få ~ om ngt* be in'formed of (,about) sth; *give en ~ om ngt* in'form sby of sth.
underrette *v* in'form, notify *(om* of; *om at* that); *holde en ~t* keep· sby in'formed.
underskrift *en* signature; *sætte sin ~ under ngt* sign sth.
underskrive *v* sign.
underskud *et* deficit, loss; *et ~ på 0,5 million* a deficit of 0.5 million; *forretningen gav ~* the shop ran at a loss.
underskørt *et* underskirt, slip.
underskål *en (til potteplante)* drip saucer.
underslæb *et* em'bezzlement; *begå ~* em'bezzle.

underst *adj* lowest, bottom; *(af to)* lower // *adv* at the bottom.
understel *et (fly)* undercarriage; *(auto)* 'chassis.
understrege *v* under'line; *(fig)* emphasize.
understregning *en* under'lining; emphasis.
understøtte *v* sup'port.
understøttelse *en* sup'port; *(fra det offentlige som legat etc)* grant; *(til arbejdsløse)* benefit; *være på* ~ (F) be on the dole.
understå *v:* ~ *sig i at gøre ngt* have the nerve to do sth.
undersøge *v* e'xamine; *(gennemsøge)* search; *(afprøve)* test; *(efterforske)* in'vestigate; ~ *en sag* look into a matter; *blive undersøgt hos lægen* have a medical check-up; **-lse** *en* exami'nation; search; test; investi'gation; *ved nærmere* ~*lse* on closer examination.
undersøisk *adj* underwater.
undertegne *v* sign; ~*de* the undersigned.
undertekst *en (film, tv)* subtitle.
undertiden *adv* from time to time, now and then.
undertrykke *v (holde nede)* op'press; *(slå ned)* sup'press; ~ *en gaben* stifle a yawn; **-lse** *en* op'pression; sup'pression.
undertrøje *en* vest.
undertøj *et* underwear.
undervandsbåd *en* submarine.
undervejs *adv* on the way; *pakken er* ~ the parcel is on its way.
undervise *v* teach·; ~ *i ngt* teach· sth; ~ *en i historie* teach· sby history.
undervisning *en* in'struction; *(timer)* lessons *pl; (generelt)* edu'cation; *(som lærer giver)* teaching; *give* ~ *i ngt* teach· sth; *få* ~ *i programmering* take· programming lessons; **-s·midler** *pl* teaching aids; **-s·ministerium** *et* Ministry of Edu'cation; **-s·pligt** *en* com'pulsory edu'cation.
undervognsbehandle *v: få bilen* ~*t* have the car undersealed.
undervurdere *v* under'estimate.
undgå *v* a'void; *(slippe godt fra)* e'scape; *ikke hvis jeg kan* ~ *det* not if I can help it; ~ *ngt med nød og næppe* narrowly e'scape sth; *det er* ~*et min opmærksomhed* it has e'scaped my attention; *vi kunne ikke* ~ *at høre det* we could not a'void hearing it; *(dvs. vi kom til at)* we could not help hearing it.
undlade *v:* ~ *at gøre ngt (dvs. afstå fra at)* re'frain from doing sth; *(dvs. glemme at)* fail (,ne'glect) to do sth; ~ *at stemme* ab'stain.
undre *v* sur'prise; ~ *sig* wonder; ~ *sig over ngt* be sur'prised at sth; *det* ~*r mig at de kom* I am sur'prised that they came; *det skulle ikke* ~ *mig* I shouldn't wonder.
undren *en* sur'prise, wonder.
undskylde *v* ex'cuse; *(bede om undskyldning)* a'pologize *(for* for); *undskyld!* sorry! *(dvs. tillader De)* ex'cuse me! *undskyld at jeg kommer for sent!* I'm sorry I'm late; *det må du meget* ~*!* I'm terribly sorry! ~ *sig* make· ex'cuses; **-nde** *adj (fx smil)* apolo'getic.
undsætning *en* rescue; *komme en til* ~ come· to sby's rescue.
undtage *v* ex'cept.
undtagelse *en* ex'ception; *med* ~ *af* ex'cept; *uden* ~ with'out exception; *en* ~ *fra reglen* an ex'ception to the rule; **-s·tilstand** *en* state of e'mergency; **-s·vis** *adv* for once.
undtagen *præp* ex'cept; ~ *hvis* un'less; *alle* ~ *John* everybody but John.
undulat *en* budgerigar, (F) budgie.
undvigende *adj* e'vasive.
undvære *v* do· with'out; *(afse)* spare.
ung *adj* young; *som* ~ *var han en flot fyr* when he was young, he was a goodlooker; *de* ~*e* the young.
ungarer *en* Hun'garian; **Ungarn** *s* 'Hungary; **ungarsk** *adj* Hun'garian.
ungdom *en* youth; ~*men (dvs. de unge)* the young (people); *i min* ~ when I was young.
ungdommelig *adj* youthful; *se* ~ *ud* look young.
ungdomsforbryder *en* young of'fender.
unge *en* young one; *(barn)* kid; *(~ af*

hund, løve, tiger, ræv) cub; *få ~r* have young ones.
ungkarl *en* bachelor.
uniform *en* 'uniform.
uniformere *v* dress in uniform; **~t** *adj* in uniform.
union *en* union.
univers *et* 'universe.
universal *adj* uni'versal; **~arving** *en* sole heir; **~middel** *et* pana'cea; **~nøgle** *en (hovednøgle)* master key; *(skruenøgle)* uni'versal spanner.
universel *adj* uni'versal.
universitet *et* uni'versity; *læse ved ~et* be at uni'versity; **~s·center** *et* uni'versity centre; **~s·lærer** *en* uni'versity teacher.
unormal *adj* ab'normal.
unyttig *adj* useless.
unægtelig *adv* unde'niably.
unødvendig *adj* un'necessary.
unøjagtig *adj* in'accurate; **~hed** *en* in'accuracy.
unåde *en* dis'grace; *komme i ~ hos en* fall· into dis'grace with sby.
uopdragen *adj* ill-mannered; **~hed** *en* bad manners *pl.*
uopfindsom *adj* uni'maginative.
uopfordret *adv* with'out being asked.
uopmærksom *adj* inat'tentive; **~hed** *en* inat'tention.
uopslidelig *adj* im'perishable.
uorden *en* dis'order; *(rod)* mess; *i ~ (dvs. ude af funktion)* out of order; *(dvs. rodet)* in a mess, un'tidy.
uordentlig *adj* dis'orderly; *(rodet)* un'tidy; *(sjusket)* slovenly.
uorganiseret *adj* un'organized; *~ arbejdskraft* non-union labour.
uorganisk *adj* inor'ganic.
uoverenstemmelse *en* dis'crepancy; *(uenighed)* disa'greement.
uoverkommelig *adj* insur'mountable.
uoverskuelig *adj (ikke til at forudse)* unfore'seeable; *(umådelig)* im'measurable; *(mængde)* im'mense; *(rodet)* con'fused.
uovervindelig *adj* in'vincible.
upartisk *adj* un'biased, im'partial; **~hed** *en* imparti'ality.
upassende *adj* im'proper; *(uheldig, fx bemærkning)* ill-timed.
upersonlig *adj* im'personal.
uplejet *adj (om person)* un'tidy; *(om fx have)* ne'glected.
upopulær *adj* un'popular *(hos* with).
upraktisk *adj* un'practical; *(om besværlig ting)* awkward.
upålidelig *adj* unre'liable; *(om vejr)* un'settled; **~hed** *en* unrelia'bility; un'settledness.
upåvirkelig *adj* in'different *(af* to).
upåvirket *adj* unaf'fected *(af* by), in'different *(af* to).
ur *et (stort, fx væg~, tårn~)* clock; *(armbånds~)* watch; *hvad er klokken på dit ~?* what is the time by your watch? *have ~ på* wear· a watch; *med ~et* clockwise; *mod ~et* anti-clockwise.
uran *et* u'ranium.
uredt *adj* un'kempt; *(om seng)* un'made.
uregelmæssig *adj* ir'regular; **~hed** *en* irregu'larity.
uregerlig *adj* un'ruly.
uren *adj* un'clean; *(blandet)* im'pure; *(om hud)* bad; **~hed** *en* im'purity.
uret *en* wrong, in'justice; *gøre en ~* do· sby an in'justice; *have ~* be wrong.
uretfærdig *adj* un'fair, un'just *(mod* to); **~hed** *en* in'justice.
urigtig *adj* wrong; *(usand)* un'true.
urimelig *adj* un'reasonable, ab'surd; *(uretfærdig)* un'fair; *(grov, fx pris)* ex'orbitant; **~hed** *en* un'reasonableness, ab'surdity; *(uretfærdighed)* in'justice.
urin *en* urine.
urinere *v* urinate.
urinprøve *en* urine specimen.
urinvejene *pl* the urinary system.
urmager *en* watchmaker, clockmaker.
urne *en* urn.
uro *en (nervøsitet)* agi'tation; *(rastløshed)* restlessness; *(angst)* an'xiety; *(politisk, social)* un'rest; *(røre)* com'motion; *(mobile)* 'mobile.
urokkelig *adj* un'shakable; *(rolig)* imper'turbable; *(stædig)* stubborn.
urolig *adj* troubled; *(nervøs)* nervous *(over* about; *(om vejr)* windy, rough; *(rastløs)* restless; *(bange)*

anxious; *være ~ for (,over) ngt* worry about sth.
uroligheder *pl* di'sturbances; *(optøjer)* riots.
uropatrulje *en* riot squad.
urostifter *en* troublemaker.
urrem *en* watch strap.
urskive *en* dial.
urskov *en* jungle.
urt *en* herb; *(grønsag)* vegetable.
urtepotte *en* flowerpot; **~skjuler** *en* (flower) con'tainer, (F) planter.
urtete *en* herbal tea.
urviser *en* hand.
urværk *et* clockwork.
urørlig *adj (uden at røre sig)* motionless; *(som ikke kan røres)* in'violable.
urørt *adj* un'touched; *lade ngt stå ~* leave· sth un'touched.
uråd *s: ane ~* smell· a rat; *ikke ane ~* su'spect nothing.
usammenhængende *adj* inco'herent.
usand *adj* un'true; **~hed** *en* un'truth, lie.
usandsynlig *adj* un'likely; *~ dum* in'credibly stupid; **~hed** *en* improba'bility.
uselvisk *adj* un'selfish; **~hed** *en* un'selfishness.
usikker *adj (i tvivl)* doubtful, un'certain; *(farlig)* un'safe, risky; *(ikke til at stole på)* unre'liable; *(ustabil, vaklende)* un'steady, shaky; *isen er ~* the ice is not safe; *være ~ om ngt* be doubtful (,un'certain) about sth; **~hed** *en (tvivl)* doubt, un'certainty; *(risko)* risk, danger.
uskadelig *adj* harmless.
uskadt *adj* un'harmed, safe.
uskarp *adj (om foto etc)* blurred.
uskik *en* bad habit.
uskyld *en* innocence; *miste sin ~* lose· one's vir'ginity.
uskyldig *adj* innocent *(i* of); **~hed** *en* innocence.
usmagelig *adj* un'savoury.
uspiselig *adj* in'edible, un'fit for con'sumption.
ussel *adj* miserable, wretched; *(led)* mean; **~hed** *en* wretchedness; meanness.
ustabil *adj* un'stable.
ustadig *adj* un'steady; *(om vejr)* changing.
udstandselig *adv* constantly.
ustraffet *adj* un'punished.
ustyrlig *adj* un'ruly; *det var ~ morsomt* it was a scream.
usund *adj* un'healthy; *det er ~t for dig (også)* it is not good for you.
usympatisk *adj* un'pleasant; *(frastødende)* re'pulsive.
usynlig *adj* in'visible; **~hed** *en* invisi'bility.
usædelig *adj* in'decent.
usædvanlig *adj* un'usual; *(mærkelig)* extra'ordinary.
utaknemmelig *adj* un'grateful *(mod* to); **~hed** *en* in'gratitude.
utal *et: et ~ af...* countless..., vast numbers of...
utallig *adj* countless, in'numerable; *~e gange* in'numerable times, hundreds of times.
utid *s: i ~e* at the wrong moment; *(dvs for tidligt)* prema'turely; *i tide og ~e* time and again.
utidig *adj (ikke i form)* not up to it; *(om barn)* fretful.
utilfreds *adj* dis'satisfied; **~stillende** *adj* unsatis'factory.
utilgivelig *adj* unfor'givable.
utilgængelig *adj* inac'cessible *(for* to).
utilladelig *adj* inad'missible; *(chokerende, grov)* out'rageous.
utilnærmelig *adj* unap'proachable.
utilpas *adj* indi'sposed, un'well; *(fig)* un'easy *(ved* about); **~hed** *en* indispo'sition.
utilsigtet *adj* unin'tentional.
utilsløret *adj* un'veiled, open.
utilstrækkelig *adj* insuf'ficient; **~hed** *en* insuf'ficiency.
utraditionel *adj* uncon'ventional, un'orthodox.
utro *adj* un'faithful *(mod* to).
utrolig *adj* in'credible // *adv* in'credibly.
utroskab *en* un'faithfulness; *begå ~ (i ægteskabet)* com'mit a'dultery.
utryg *adj* inse'cure *(ved* about); **~hed** *en* inse'curity.
utrættelig *adj* un'tiring.
utrøstelig *adj* incon'solable.

utvivlsomt *adv* un'doubtedly.
utvungen *adj* free, 'unre'strained; *(ikke kunstig)* unaf'fected; **~hed** *adj* sponta'neity, ease.
utydelig *adj* indi'stinct.
utænkelig *adj* un'thinkable.
utæt *adj* leaky; **~hed** *en (hul)* leak.
utøj *et* vermin.
utålelig *adj* in'tolerable // *adv* in'tolerably.
utålmodig *adj* im'patient; **~hed** *en* im'patience.
uudholdelig *adj* in'tolerable.
uudslettelig *adj* in'delible.
uundgåelig *adj* in'evitable.
uundværlig *adj* indi'spensable.
uvane *en* bad habit.
uvant *adj* unac'customed *(med* to).
uvedkommende *en* trespasser, in'truder; *~ forbydes adgang* no trespassing // *adj* ir'relevant; *det er sagen ~* it is ir'relevant.
uvejr *et* storm.
uven *en* enemy; *blive ~ner med en* fall· out with sby; *være ~ner med en* have fallen out with sby.
uvenlig *adj* un'kind, un'friendly *(mod* to); **~hed** *en* enmity.
uventet *adj* unex'pected.
uvidende *adj* ignorant *(om* of).
uvidenhed *en* ignorance.
uvildig *adj* im'partial.
uvilje *en (tøven)* re'luctance; *(modvilje)* a'version *(mod* to).
uvilkårlig *adv* in'voluntarily.
uvillig *adj* un'willing; **~hed** *en* re'luctance; un'willingness.
uvis *adj* un'certain; *~t hvorfor* for some un'known reason; **~hed** *en* un'certainty; *hun holdt ham hen i ~hed* she kept him in su'spense.
uvurderlig *adj* in'valuable.
uvægerligt *adv* in'variably; *(uundgåeligt)* in'evitably.
uægte *adj (kunstig)* imi'tation, arti'ficial; *(forfalsket)* false, fake; *~ barn* ille'gitimate child.
uændret *adj* un'changed.
uærlig *adj* dis'honest; **~hed** *en* dis'honesty.
uønsket *adj* un'wanted, unde'sirable.
uøvet *adj* un'practised.

V

vable *en* blister.
vaccination *en* vacci'nation *(mod* against).
vaccine *en* 'vaccine.
vaccinere *v* vaccinate, in'oculate.
vade *v* wade; *~ i ngt (dvs. have masser af)* be rolling in sth; **~fugl** *en* wader; **~hav** *et* (tidal) flats *pl;* **~sted** *et* ford.
vaffel *en (sprød kage)* wafer; *(blød, bagt i jern)* waffle; *(kræmmerhus)* cone; **~jern** *et* waffle iron.
vag *adj* vague.
vagabond *en* tramp.
vager *en (mar)* marker buoy.
vagt *en* guard, watch; *(tjeneste)* duty; *have ~ (fx om læge)* be on duty; *holde ~* keep· watch; *være på ~ over for en* be on one's guard against sby; **~havende** *adj* on duty; **~hund** *en* watchdog; **~parade** *en sv.t.* changing of the guards; **~post** *en* sentry; **~selskab** *et* se'curity corps.
vagtsom *adj* vigilant.
vakkelvorn se *vaklevorn.*
vakle *v (om stol etc)* wobble, shake·; *(om person)* totter; *(være i tvivl)* hesitate, falter; **vaklen** *en* wobble, shaking; hesi'tation, faltering.
vaklevorn *adj* rickety.
vaks *adj* bright.
vakuum *et* vacuum; **~pakket** *adj* vacuum-packed.
valdhorn *et* French horn.
valen *adj (af kulde)* numb; *et ~t svar* a vague answer.
valfarte *v* go· on a pilgrimage.
valg *et* choice; *(mellem to ting)* al'ternative; *(folketings~)* e'lection; *træffe sit ~* make· one's choice; *vi havde ikke ngt ~* we had no al'ternative; *få frit ~* be given a free choice; *udskrive ~* call a general e'lection; **~bar** *adj* eligible; **~fri** *adj* optional; **~fusk** *s* ballot-rigging; **~kamp** *en* e'lection cam'paign; **~kreds** *en* con'stituency; **~ret** *en: have ~ret* have the vote; **~sprog** *et* motto; **~urne** *en* ballot box.

valle *en* whey.
valmue *en* poppy.
valnød *en* walnut.
vals *en* waltz; *danse* ~ waltz.
valse *en* roller; *(på skrivemaskine)* platen; **~værk** *et* rolling mill.
valuta *en (pengesort)* currency; *(værdi)* value; *fremmed* ~ foreign currency; *få* ~ *for pengene* get· value for one's money; **~kurs** *en* ex'change rate; **~slange** *en (i EF)* currency snake.
vammel *adj* sickly; **~hed** *en* sickliness.
vampyr *en* 'vampire.
vand *et* water; *rindende* ~ running water; *lade ~et* urinate; *det er lige ~ på min mølle* it is right up my street; *træde ~e* tread· water; *gå i ~et* bathe, go· swimming; *øjnene løber i* ~ the eyes water; *have* ~ *i knæet* have water on the knee; *sætte* ~ *på* put· on the kettle; *til ~s* by sea; *(ude på vandet)* at sea; *stå under* ~ be flooded; *ved ~et* by the sea; **~bad** *et: koge i ~bad* cook in a bain-marie; **~beholder** *en* water tank; **~cykel** *en* 'pedalo; **~damp** *en* steam; **~dråbe** *en* drop of water.
vande *v* water; *(overrisle)* irrigate.
vandet *adj* watery; *(om vittighed)* thin.
vand... *sms:* **~fad** *et* wash basin; **~fald** *et* waterfall; **~farve** *en* watercolour; *male med ~farve* paint in watercolour; **~fast** *adj* waterproof; **~forsyning** *en* water sup'ply; **~hane** *en* tap; **~hul** *et* pool.
vanding *en* watering; *(overrisling)* irri'gation.
vand... *sms:* **~kande** *en* watering can; **~kanon** *en* water cannon; **~kraft** *en* water-power; **~kraftværk** *et* 'hydro-e'lectric power station; **~ladning** *en* uri'nation; **~løb** *et* stream; **~lås** *en* (odeur) trap; **~mand** *en (zo)* jellyfish; *Vandmanden (astr)* A'quarius; **~melon** *en* water melon; **~mølle** *en* water-mill; **~pistol** *en* water pistol; **~plante** *en* a'quatic plant; **~post** *en* pump; **~pyt** *en* puddle.
vandre *v* walk; *være ude at* ~ be hiking; **~hjem** *et* youth hostel.
vandrer *en (som er på ~tur)* hiker.
vandreservoir *et* 'reservoir.
vandret *adj* hori'zontal; *(i krydsord)* a'cross; *ligge* ~ *i luften (af travlhed)* work flat out.
vandretur *en* hike.
vandring *en* walk.
vand... *sms:* **~rutschebane** *en* aquatube; **~rør** *et* waterpipe; **~skel** *et* watershed; **~ski** *en* water-ski; **~skyende** *adj* 'water-re'pellent; **~slange** *en* (water) hose; **~stand** *en* water-level; **~sugende** *adj* ab'sorbent; **~tæt** *adj* watertight; *(om tøj)* waterproof; **~tårn** *et* water tower; **~varmer** *en* water heater; **~vogn** *en: være på ~vognen* be on the (water) wagon; **~værk** *et: et ~værk* a waterworks.
vane *en* habit; *have for* ~ *at gøre ngt* have a habit of doing sth; *af gammel* ~ from habit.
vanedannende *adj* habit-forming.
vanesag *en* question of habit.
vanfør *adj* dis'abled.
vanille *en* va'nilla; **~stang** *en* va'nilla pod.
vanke *v: der ~r et godt måltid* you will get a good meal.
vanlig *adj* usual, customary.
vanrøgt *en* ne'glect; **~e** *v* ne'glect.
vanskabt *adj* de'formed.
vanskelig *adj* difficult, hard; *jeg kan ~t forestille mig at...* I find· it hard to imagine that...; **~gøre** *v* complicate.
vanskelighed *en* difficulty; *komme i ~er* get· into trouble; *uden ~er* with'out any trouble (,difficulties).
vant *adj (sædvanlig)* usual; *være bedre* ~ be used to better things; ~ *til at gøre ngt* used to doing sth.
vante *en* mitten.
vantrives *v: de* ~ they don't thrive.
vantro *adj (undrende, tvivlende)* in'credulous.
vanvare *en: af* ~ inad'vertently.
vanvid *et* madness, in'sanity; *han driver mig til* ~ he is driving me mad; *det glade* ~ sheer madness.
vanvittig *adj* mad, in'sane, crazy; *have ~t travlt* be terribly busy; *det*

var ~ sjovt! it was a scream! *te sig som en ~* be'have like mad; *~t lækker* (S) way out.

vanære *en/v* dis'grace.

vare *en* product; *(enkelt)* article; *~r* goods, merchandise; *bringe ~r ud* de'liver goods; *tage ngt for gode ~r* take· sth at face value; *våde ~r* liquor; *tage ~ på ngt* take· care of sth.

vare *v* last; *(om tid)* take·; *turen ~r tre timer* the trip takes three hours; *krigen ~de i fem år* the war lasted for five years; *det ~r længe før det bliver sommer* it is a long time until summer; *~ ved* go· on, con'tinue.

vare... *sms:* **~deklaration** *en* in'formative label; *(vedr. indhold af fødevarer etc)* (de'scription of) contents; **~hus** *et* de'partment store; **~mærke** *et* trade-mark; **~prøve** *en* sample; **~tage** *v* take· care of, at'tend to; **~tægt** *en* care; **~tægtsfængsel** *et* re'mand (centre); **~tægtsfængsle** *v* re'mand (into custody); **~vogn** *en* van.

variant *en* variant *(til* on).

variation *en* vari'ation *(over* on).

variere *v* vary.

varieté *en* va'riety; *(om selve teatret)* music hall, va'riety theatre.

varig *adj* lasting, permanent; **~hed** *en* du'ration; *(løbetid, fx for kontrakt)* term; *af kortere ~hed* of short du'ration.

varm *adj* warm; *(stærkere)* hot; *de ~e lande* the tropics; *et ~t bad* a hot bath; *~t vand* hot water; *løbe (,køre) ~ (om motor etc)* run· hot; *få ~ mad* get· a hot meal; *have det ~t* feel· warm; *klæde sig ~t på* dress up warmly; *være ~ på en (,ngt)* fancy sby (,sth).

varme *en* heat; *(fig)* warmth; *lukke i (,op) for ~n* turn the heating on (,off); *to graders ~* two de'grees above zero // *v* heat, warm; *~ maden i ovnen* warm up the food in the oven; *~ op (sport)* warm up; *~ huset op* heat (,warm) up the house; *~ sig* get· warm; **~apparat** *et* radiator; *(elek)* e'lectric heater; **~blæser** *en* fan heater; **~bølge** *en* heatwave; **~dunk** *en* hot-water bottle; **~mester** *en (dvs. vicevært)* janitor; **~måler** *en* calo'rimeter; **~ovn** *en* stove, heater; **~pude** *en* e'lectric (heat) pad; **~tæppe** *et* e'lectric blanket.

varmluftsovn *en* circotherm oven.

varmtvandshane *en* hot-water tap.

varsel *et* warning, notice; *(spådom etc)* omen; *med kort ~* at short notice.

varsle *v* notify; *(spå etc)* augur.

varsom *adj* careful, cautious; **~hed** *en* caution.

varte *v: ~ en op* wait on sby; *~ op ved bordet* wait at table.

vartegn *et (for by etc)* symbol.

varulv *en* werewolf *(pl:* -wolves).

vase *en* vase.

vask *en (det at vaske)* washing; *(vasketøj)* laundry; *(køkkenvask)* sink; *(håndvask)* hand basin; *hælde ngt i ~en* pour sth down the sink; *gå i ~en (fig)* go· down the drain; *lægge tøj til ~* put· clothes in the wash.

vaskbar *adj* washable; *(om vægbeklædning etc)* spongeable.

vaske *v* wash; *~ hænder* wash one's hands; *~ tøj* do· the washing; *~ væggen af* wash (,sponge) down the walls; *~ op* do· the dishes; *kjolen kan ikke ~s* the dress won't wash; *~ sig* (have a) wash; **~anvisning** *en* washing in'structions *pl;* **~balje** *en* washbowl; **~bjørn** *en* ra'coon; **~klud** *en* facecloth; **~kumme** *en* (wash-)basin; **~kælder** *en sv.t.* laundry room; **~maskine** *en* washing-machine; **~pulver** *et* washing-powder; **~ri** *et* laundry; **~skind** *et* chamois ['ʃæmi]; **~suger** *en* plunger; **~svamp** *en* sponge; **~tøj** *et* laundry, washing; **~ægte** *adj* (colour)fast; *(fig)* genuine.

vat *et* cotton wool; *(pladevat)* wadding.

vaterpas *et* spirit level.

vatnisse *en* softy, sissy.

vatpind *en* cotton swab.

vattere *v* pad, quilt; *~t stof* quilted ma'terial; *~t tæppe* quilt; **vattering** *en* padding, quilting.

vattæppe *et* quilt.
ve *en* labour pain; *have ~er* be in labour; *dit ~ og vel* your welfare.
ved *præp (om sted)* at; *(henne ~)* by; *(i nærheden af)* near; *(om tid)* at; *(om middel, grund)* by; *(se også de enkelte ord som ~ forbindes med); vil du standse ~ rådhuset?* will you stop at the town hall? *de bor ~ vandet* they live by the sea; *~ midnat* at midnight; *den drives ~ elektricitet* it is run by elec'tricity; *røre ~ ngt* touch sth; *~ siden af ngt* next to sth, be'side sth; *han bor inde ~ siden af* he lives next door; *ikke ville være ~ det* not want to ad'mit it; *være ~ at gøre ngt* be doing sth; *mens du nu er ~ det...* while you are 'at it...; *han var lige ~ at drukne* he nearly drowned; *være ~ at blive søvnig* be getting sleepy; *jeg var ~ at eksplodere* I nearly blew up; *det er det dumme ~ det* that's what's so stupid about it.
vedbend *en* ivy.
vedblive *v* con'tinue, go· on; **~nde** *adv* still.
vederlag *et (som forlanges)* charge; *(som ydes)* compen'sation.
vederlagsfrit *adv* free of charge.
vedholdende *adj* per'sistent.
vedhæng *et* ap'pendage; *(smykke)* pendant.
vedkende *v: ~ sig* ac'knowledge; *ikke ville ~ sig* re'fuse to ac'knowledge.
vedkomme *v* con'cern; *det ~r ikke dig* it is none of your con'cern (,business).
vedkommende *en* the person con'cerned // *adj* con'cerned; *for mit ~* for my part; *jeg for mit ~ synes det er rart* I for one think it is nice.
vedligeholde *v* keep·, main'tain; *(holde i gang)* keep· up; *huset er pænt (,dårligt) vedligeholdt* the house is in good (,bad) re'pair; **~lse** *en* maintenance, re'pair.
vedlægge *v* en'close; *vedlagt fremsendes...* en'closed you will find...
vedrøre *v* con'cern; **~nde** *præp* con'cerning, as re'gards.
vedtage *v* a'gree to, de'cide; *(ved afstemning, parl)* carry; *de vedtog at gøre det* they a'greed (,de'cided) to do it; *forslaget blev ~t* the motion was carried; *~ en lov* pass an act; **~lse** *en* de'cision; carrying.
vedtægter *pl* rules, regu'lations.
vedvarende *adj* con'tinued, constant; *~ energi* re'newable energy // *adv* still.
vegetabilsk *adj* vegetable.
vegetar *en*, **vegetarisk** *adj* vege'tarian.
vegne *s: alle ~* everywhere; *vi kommer ingen ~* we are not getting anywhere; *på mine ~* on my be'half; *på embeds ~* of'ficially.
vej *en* road; *(vejlængde, afstand)* way, distance; *finde ~* find· one's way; *gå sin ~* go· away; *hele ~en* all the way; *der er lang ~ til Rom* it is a long way to Rome; *er der lang ~ til stranden?* is it far to the beach? *vise en ~* show sby the way; *gå nye ~e (fig)* tread· new paths; *gå sine egne ~e* go· one's own way; *de gik hver sin ~* they went their separate ways; *hen ad ~en* along the road; *(fig)* as you go along; *gå af ~en* get· out of the way; *ikke gå af ~en for ngt (fig)* stop at nothing; *rydde en (,ngt) af ~en* get· rid of sby (,sth); *komme i ~en for en* get· in sby's way; *være i ~en* stand· in the way; *hvad er der i ~en?* what is the matter? what is wrong? *der er ngt i ~en med bilen* there is sth wrong with the car; *være på ~ til et sted* be on one's way to some place; *skaffe ngt til ~e* pro'cure sth; *huset ligger ved ~en* the house is by the roadside.
vejarbejde *et* roadworks *pl; (på skilt også)* road up; **vejarbejder** *en* roadmender.
vejbane *en* carriageway; *(på flersporet vej)* lane.
vejbelægning *en* road surface.
vejbred *en (bot)* 'plantain.
veje *v* weigh; *hvor meget ~r du?* how much do you weigh? *~ kartofler af* weigh out po'tatoes; *kufferten ~r*

en del the suitcase is rather heavy; *~ for og imod* weigh the pros and cons; *det ~r tungt på ham* it is a heavy load on his shoulders.

vejgrøft *en* ditch.

vejkant *en* roadside; *(rabat)* shoulder.

vejkryds *et: et ~* a crossroads.

vejlede *v* guide; *(undervise)* in'struct; *~nde pris* recom'mended price; **~r** *en* guide; in'structor.

vejledning *en* guidance; in'struction.

vejmelding *en* road re'port.

vejning *en* weighing.

vejr *et* weather; *(ånde)* breath; *få ~et* breathe; *holde ~et* hold· one's breath; *tabe ~et* lose· one's breath; *trække ~et* breathe; *dårligt ~* bad weather; *godt ~* fine weather; *i ~et* up; *med bunden i ~et* upside down; *ryge i ~et (dvs. eksplodere)* blow· up; *stige til ~s* go· up; **~bidt** *adj* - weatherbeaten.

vejre *v* scent.

vejr... *sms:* **~forandring** *en* a change in the weather; **~hane** *en* weathercock; **~kort** *et* weather chart; **~melding** *en* weather re'port; **~trækning** *en* breathing; **~udsigt** *en* weather forecast.

vej... *sms:* **~skilt** *et* road sign; **~spærring** *en* road block; **~sving** *et* road bend; **~træ** *et* roadside tree; **~viser** *en (skilt)* road sign, signpost; *(bog)* di'rectory.

veksel *en (merk)* bill of ex'change; **~erer** *en* stockbroker; **~kurs** *en* rate of ex'change; **~strøm** *en* alternating current (AC); **~virkning** *en* inter'action.

veksle *v* change; *(udveksle)* ex'change; *(skiftes)* alternate; *~ fem pund til pence* change five pounds into pence; **vekslen** *en* change; alter'nation.

vel *et* welfare, well-being; *det almene ~* the common good; *det er til dit eget ~* it is for your own good.

vel *adj/adv* well; *(forhåbentlig)* I hope, hopefully; *(formentlig)* probably; *(lidt for, lovlig)* rather; *(bestemt)* surely; *han kommer ~ til tiden?* I hope he'll be on time; *vi bliver ~ nødt til at gøre det* I sup'pose we will have to do it; *han er lidt ~ storsnudet* he is a bit stuck-up; *~ er det sandt!* sure it is true! *du gør det ~ ikke?* you won't do it, will you? *du er ~ ikke syg?* you are not ill, are you? *~ at mærke* mind you; *han er ~ nok rar!* how nice he is! *du har vel ikke £5?* you don't happen to have £5, do you?

velbefindende *et* well-being.

velbegavet *adj* bright, in'telligent.

velbehag *et* pleasure, well-being.

velbeholden *adj (om person)* safe and sound; *(om ting)* in'tact.

velbekomme *interj (bruges ikke i forb. med måltider; i andre forb.:) tak for lån af blyanten! - velbekomme!* thanks for lending me your pencil! - you are welcome!

velbjærget *adj* well off.

velcrolukning *en* Velcro ® fastening.

velegnet *adj* suitable *(til* for); *(om person)* well qualified *(til* for).

velfortjent *adj* 'well-de'served.

velfærd *en* welfare.

velfærdssamfund *et* affluent so'ciety, welfare state.

velgørende *adj (behagelig)* re'freshing; *(godgørende)* charitable; *til ~ formål* for charity; **~hed** *en* charity.

velgører *en (om mand)* bene'factor; *(om kvinde)* bene'factress.

velgående *et: i bedste ~* safe and sound.

velhavende *adj* wealthy, well off; *(om samfund)* affluent.

velholdt *adj* well-kept; *(om hus også)* in good re'pair.

velkendt *adj* vell-known.

velkommen *adj* welcome; *byde en ~* welcome sby.

velkomst *en* welcome.

velkonserveret *adj (om person)* 'well-pre,served.

velkvalificeret *adj* well-qualified.

vellidt *adj* popular.

vellignende *adj* life-like.

vellykket *adj* suc'cessful; *være ~* be a suc'cess.

vellyst *en* sensu'ality; **~ig** *adj* sensual.

vellønnet *adj* well-paid.

velmenende *adj* well-meaning.
velment *adj* well-meant.
velopdragen *adj* well-bred; *(som opfører sig godt)* 'well-be,haved; **~hed** *en* good manners *pl.*
veloplagt *adj* in good form, fit *(til* for); **~hed** *en* fitness.
velour *en* ve'lour.
velset *adj* welcome.
velsigne *v* bless.
velsignelse *en* blessing; *en guds ~ af ngt* an a'bundance of sth.
velskabt *adj* well-made.
velsmagende *adj* savoury, de'licious.
velstand *en* wealth, affluence.
velstillet *adj* well off.
veltalende *adj* eloquent.
veltalenhed *en* eloquence.
veltilpas *adj* comfortable.
veludrustet *adj* 'well-e'quipped; *(seksuelt om mand)* well-hung.
velunderrettet *adj* 'well-in'formed.
velvalgt *adj* well-chosen.
velvilje *en* be'nevolence, goodwill.
velvillig *adj* be'nevolent, kind.
velvære *et* well-being.
vemod *en* sadness.
vemodig *adj* sad.
ven *en* friend; *blive ~ner med* make· friends with; *de er blevet gode ~ner igen* they have made (it) up; *få ~ner* make· friends; *være ~ner* be friends; *det er en af min mors ~ner* he (,she) is a friend of my mother's.
vende *v* turn; *(om vind)* shift; *~ hjem* re'turn home; *huset ~r mod syd* the house faces south; *~ om* turn back; *~ op og ned på ngt* turn sth upside down; *~ sig* turn; *~ sig om* turn around; *~ ryggen til en* turn one's back on sby; *~ tilbage* re'turn; *køkkenet ~r ud mod gården* the kitchen looks out on the courtyard.
vendekreds *en* tropic; *Krebsens (,Stenbukkens) ~* the Tropic of Cancer (,Capricorn).
vendepunkt *et* turning point.
vending *en (drejning)* turning; *(ændring)* turn; *(talemåde)* turn of speech; *i en snæver ~* at a pinch; *være hurtig i ~en* be quick; *være langsom i ~en* be slow.
vene *en* vein.
Venedig *s* Venice.
venetiansk *adj* Ve'netian.
veninde *en* friend; *(kæreste)* girl friend.
venlig *adj* kind; *vær så ~ at...* please...; *vil du være så ~ at gøre det?* will you please do it? *det er vel nok ~t af Dem!* how kind of you! -**venlig** -friendly.
venlighed *en* kindness; *tak for ~en!* thank you for your kindness!
venskab *et* friendship; *knytte ~ med en* make· friends with sby; **~e·lig** *adj* friendly; **~s·by** *en* twin town.
venstre *en: en lige ~* a straight left // *adj* left; *på ~ hånd* on the left hand; *i ~ side af vejen* on the left (hand side of the road); *til ~* left, to the left; *til ~ for* to the left of; *dreje til ~* turn left; *holde til ~* keep· left; **~drejning** *en (pol)* shift to the left; **~fløjen** *s* the left wing; **~håndet** *adj* left-handed; **~kørsel** *en* driving on the left; **~orienteret** *adj* left-wing; **~styring** *en (auto)* left-hand-drive.
vente *s: have ngt i ~* have sth coming; *være i ~* be ex'pected // *v* wait; *(forvente)* ex'pect; *~ at ngt sker* ex'pect sth to happen; *~ og se* wait and see; *lade en ~* keep· sby waiting; *vent lidt!* wait a minute! *du kan ~ dig!* you just wait! *~ med at gøre ngt* put· off doing sth; *~ på* wait for; *~ på at ngt sker* wait for sth to happen; *lade ~ på sig* be a long time in coming; *~ sig ngt* ex'pect sth; *hun ~r sig* she is ex'pecting; **~kjole** *en* ma'ternity dress; **~liste** *en* waiting list; **~tid** *en* wait; **~tøj** *et* ma'ternity wear; **~værelse** *et* waiting room.
ventil *en* valve.
ventilation *en* venti'lation; **~s·anlæg** *et* venti'lation system.
ventilator *en* 'ventilator; *(som drejer rundt)* fan.
ventilere *v* 'ventilate *(også fig).*
ventilgummi *et* valve tubing.
veranda *en* ve'randa.
verbum *et* verb.
verden *en* world; *hele ~* the whole

world, all the world; *ude i den store ~* in the big wide world; *den tredje ~* the Third World; *fra hele ~* from all over the world; *ikke for alt i ~* not for the world; *hvad i al ~!* what on earth! *så er det ude af ~!* that takes care of that! *~ går ikke under af den grund* it is not the end of the world; *han lever i sin egen ~* he lives in a world of his own; *sætte børn til ~* bring· children into the world.

Verdensbanken *s* the World Bank.

verdens... *sms:* **~berømt** *adj* world-famous; **~del** *en* continent; **~hav** *et* ocean; **~historie** *en* world history; **~hjørne** *et* di'rection; *fra alle ~hjørner* from all four corners of the world; **~kendt** *adj* world-known; **~kort** *et* world map; **~krig** *en* world war; **~mester** *en* world champion; **~mesterskab** *et* world championship; *(fodb)* World Cup; **~omspændende** *adj* global; **~rekord** *en* world 'record; **~rum** *et* space; **~udstilling** *en* world exhibition.

verdslig *adj* secular, wordly.

verificere *v* verify.

veritabel *adj* veritable.

vermut *en* vermouth.

vers *et* verse; *(strofe)* stanza; *på ~* in verse.

versemål *et* metre.

versere *v* circulate.

version *en* version.

vertikal *adj* 'vertical.

vest *en (tøj)* waistcoat.

vest *en (verdenshjørne)* west; *~ for* (to the) west of; *fra ~* from the west; *mod ~* west, westwards; *huset vender mod ~* the house faces west.

Vestblokken *s* the Western Bloc.

vestenvind *en* west wind.

Vesterhavet *s* the North Sea; **vesterhavs-** North-Sea *(fx fiskeri* fishing).

Vesteuropa *s* Western Europe; **vesteuropæisk** *adj* West Euro'pean.

Vestindien *s* the West Indies; **vestindisk** *adj* West-Indian, Carib'bean.

vestkyst *en* west coast.

vestlig *adj* western; west; **vestligst** *adj* westernmost.

vestmagterne *pl* the Western powers.

vestpå *adv* west; westwards; *(i vest)* in the west.

vesttysk *adj* West German; **Vesttyskland** *s* West Germany.

veteran *en* 'veteran; **~bil** *en* vintage car.

veto *et* veto *(pl:* -es); *nedlægge ~ mod ngt* veto sth; **~ret** *en: have ~ret* have a veto.

vi *pron* we; *~ to* we two, the two of us.

via *præp* via, by.

viadukt *en* viaduct.

vibe *en (zo)* lapwing, peewit.

vibration *en* vi'bration.

vibrere *v* vi'brate.

viceformand *en* vice-chairman *(pl:* -men), vice-president *(for* of).

vicepræsident *en* vice-president.

vicevært *en* janitor, caretaker.

vid *adj* wide; *(om tøj)* loose; *(om nederdel)* full; *stå på ~ gab* be wide open; *kendt i ~e kredse* widely known; *(se også vidt).*

vidde *en* width; *(åben strækning)* ex'panse; *en nederdel med ~* a full skirt.

vide *v* know·; *jeg ved (det) ikke* I don't know·; *jeg ved det godt* I know·; *man kan aldrig ~* you never know·; *~ besked med ngt* know· about sth; *ved du hvad?* do you know what? *der blev både danset og drukket og hvad ved jeg* there was dancing and drinking and... you name it; *det ved jeg nu ikke rigtig* I'm not so sure about that; *få ngt at ~* be told sth, learn sth; *hvor ved du det fra?* how do you know? *jeg gad ~ om...* I wonder whether (,if)...; *det vil jeg ikke ~ af* I won't have that.

viden *en* knowledge.

vidende *et: mod bedre ~* against one's better judgment; *uden mit ~* with'out my knowing.

videnskab *en (især natur~)* science; *de humanistiske ~er* the hu'manities; **~e·lig** *adj* scien'tific; **~s·mand** *en* scientist.

videobånd *et* video tape.

videomaskine *en* video, VCR.

videospil *et* video game.

videre *adj/adv (længere frem)* farther, further; *(sammen med verbum)* on *(fx gå ~* go· on); *(mere, yderligere)* further; *(mere vid)* wider; *give ngt ~* pass sth on; *lad os se at komme ~* let's get on; *sende ngt ~* send· sth on; *han er ikke ~ rar* he is not very nice; *der skete ikke ngt ~* nothing much happened; *indtil ~* until further notice; *(dvs. hidtil)* so far; *og så ~* and so on, etc; *uden ~* just like that; without further a'do.

videreforhandle *v* re'sell·.

videreføre *v* con'tinue.

videregående *adj* ad'vanced.

videst *adj/adv* widest; farthest; *i ordets ~e forstand* in every sense of the word.

vidne *et* witness; *blive indkaldt som ~* be summoned as a witness; *være ~ til ngt* witness sth // *v (i retten)* give· evidence; *~ om (dvs. tyde på)* indicate; *(dvs. aflægge vidnesbyrd)* testify to.

vidnesbyrd *et (tegn, bevis)* evidence; *(udtalelse)* testimony; *(attest)* cer'tificate; *(i skolen)* school re'port; *aflægge ~s·byrd om ngt* testify to sth.

vidneskranke *en* witness box.

vidt *adv* far, wide; *(fig)* widely; *det ville føre for ~ at…* it would be taking things to far to…; *gå for ~* go· too far; *for så ~* for that matter; *(egentlig)* really; *hvor ~ (dvs. om)* whether; *være lige ~* be back to square one; *så ~ jeg ved* as far as I know; *ikke så ~ jeg ved* not that I know of; *det kunne høres ~ og bredt* it was heard for miles a'round.

vidtgående *adj* ex'tensive.

vidtløftig *adj (dvs. langtrukken)* long-winded; *han er en ~løftig herre (dvs. har mange affærer)* he is a great one for the ladies; *(dvs. går meget ud og morer sig)* he likes his fun.

vidtrækkende *adj* far-reaching.

vidtstrakt *adj* ex'tensive.

vidunder *et* wonder; **~barn** *et* child prodigy.

vidunderlig *adj* wonderful.

vidvinkelobjektiv *et (foto)* wide-angle lens.

vie *v (ægtevie)* marry; *(indvie)* consecrate; *(hellige)* dedicate.

vielse *en* wedding; **~s·attest** *en* marriage licence; **~s·ring** *en* wedding ring.

vifte *en* fan // *v* wave; *(med ~)* fan; *~ med ngt* wave sth.

vig *en* creek.

vige *v* give· way, yield *(for* to); *ikke ~ tilbage for ngt* stop at nothing; **~plads** *en (på vej)* lay-by; **~pligt** *en: ~pligt for trafik for højre* right of way for traffic from the right.

vigte *v: ~ sig* show off; *~ sig med ngt* show sth off; *(tøj etc)* sport sth.

vigtig *adj (af betydning)* im'portant; *(storsnudet)* stuck-up, con'ceited; *det ~ste* the most im'portant thing; **~hed** *en* im'portance; con'ceit; *af største ~hed* of the utmost im'portance.

vigør *en: være i fuld ~* be a'live and kicking.

vikar *en* substitute; *(kontor~)* temp.

vikariat *et* temporary job.

vikariere *v* substitute *(for* for), re'place.

viking *en* Viking; **~e·skib** *et* Viking ship; **~e·tiden** *s* the Viking age.

vikle *v* wind·, twist; *~ garn (op)* wind· yarn; *~ ngt sammen* roll sth up; *~ sig ind i ngt* get· en'tangled in sth.

viktualiehandel *en* delica'tessen (shop).

vild *adj* wild; *(brutal, grusom)* savage; *~e (mennesker)* savages; *~e dyr* wild animals; *han blev helt ~ (dvs. vred)* he went off his head; *fare ~* lose· one's way; *være ~ med ngt* be crazy about sth; *vokse ~t (om plante)* grow· wild; *løbe som en ~* run· like mad; *~ forvirring* chaos.

vildelse *en* de'lirium; *tale i ~* be de'lirious.

vildlede *v* mis'lead·; **~nde** *adj* mis'leading.

vildmark *en* wilderness.

vildnis *et (tæt krat, fig)* tangle.

vildrede *s: være i ~* be at a loss; *(i uorden)* be in a tangle.

vildskab *en* wildness.
vildspor *et: være på ~* be on the wrong track.
vildsvin *et* wild boar.
vildt *et* game; *(dyrekød)* venison; **~handler** *en* poulterer; **~tyv** *en* poacher; **~voksende** *adj* wild.
vilje *en* will; *få sin ~* have one's own way; *gøre ngt med ~* do· sth on purpose; *jeg gjorde det ikke med ~* I didn't mean to do it; *ikke med min gode ~* not if I can help it; *ikke med min bedste ~* not for the life of me; *mod min ~* against my will; **~styrke** *en* will-power; **~stærk** *adj* strong-willed; **~svag** *adj* weak-willed.
vilkår *pl (forudsætninger)* con'ditions; *(omstændigheder)* circumstances; *på de ~* under those circumstances; *ikke på ~* not under any circumstances.
vilkårlig *adj (tilfældig)* hap'hazard; *(hvilken som helst)* any; *(valgt)* arbitrary; **~hed** *en* hap'hazardness; arbitrariness.
villa *en* house; *(stor)* villa; *(lille, især på landet)* cottage; **~kvarter** *et* resi'dential area.
ville *v (hjælpeverbum) vil, ville:* will, would; *(efter* I *og* we) shall, should; *(ønske, have til hensigt)* want, will; *(gerne ville)* be willing to; *han vil ikke* he won't; *hvad vil han?* what does he want? *han vil ud* he wants to get out; *hvad enten han vil eller ej* whether he wants to or not; *vil de komme?* will they come? *hvis du vil* I you want to; *som du vil* as you like; *vil du med?* are you coming too? *uden at ~ det* with'out wanting to; *hvis jeg var dig, ~ jeg glemme det* if I were you, I should forget it; *(se også gerne).*
villig *adj* willing; **~hed** *en* willingness.
vimpel *en* streamer.
vims *adj* nimble.
vimse *v* bustle *(rundt* about).
vin *en* wine; **~avler** *en* wine-grower; **~bjergsnegl** *en* edible snail; *(på menu)* e'scargot.
vind *en* wind; *~en blæser* the wind is blowing; *~en vender* the wind is shifting; *med ~en* with the wind; *mod ~en* against the wind; **~blæst** *adj* wind-swept; **~drejning** *en* shift of the wind.
vinde *v* win·; *(opnå også)* gain; *(vikle)* wind·; *~ sejr* gain the victory; *prøve at ~ tid* play for time; *~ i kortspil* win· at cards; *~ i tipning* win· the pools; *~ ind på en* gain on sby; *~ med 3-2* win· by three to two; *~ over en* beat· sby.
vindebro *en* drawbridge.
vindeltrappe *en* spiral staircase.
vinder *en* winner.
vinding *en (gevinst)* profit, gain; *(snoning)* winding; *(i skrue)* thread.
vind... *sms:* **~jakke** *en* windcheater; **~kraft** *en* wind energy; **~mølle** *en* windmill; **~møllepark** *en* wind farm, wind park; **~pose** *en* windsock; **~pust** *et* puff of wind; **~retning** *en* di'rection of the wind.
vindrue *en* grape; **~klase** *en* bunch of grapes.
vind... *sms:* **~spejl** *et* windscreen; **~stille** *s/adj* calm; **~styrke** *en* wind-force; *~styrke 6* force 6; **~stød** *et* gust of wind; **~tæt** *adj* windproof.
vindue *et* window; *kigge ind ad ~et* look in at the window; *kigge ud ad ~et* look out of the window; **~s·karm** *en* window-sill; **~s·plads** *en* window seat; **~s·pudser** *en* window cleaner; **~s·rude** *en* window pane; **~s·skraber** *en (af gummi)* squeegee; **~s·visker** *en* windscreen wiper.
vindyrkning *en* winegrowing.
vineddike *en* wine vinegar.
vinflaske *en* wine bottle.
vinge *en* wing; *gå på ~rne (om fly)* take· off; *baske med ~rne* flap one's wings; **~fang** *et* wing span.
vin... *sms:* **~glas** *et* wineglass; **~gummi** *et* fruit gum; **~gård** *en* vineyard ['vinjəd]; **~handel** *en* wine shop; **~handler** *en* wine merchant; **~høst** *en* vintage.
vink *et (tegn)* sign; *(med hånden)* wave; *(antydning, tip)* hint; *give en et ~* give· sby a hint; *han lystrer hendes mindste ~* he is at her beck and call.

vinke *v (som hilsen)* wave (one's hand); *(give tegn)* beckon; *~ ad en* beckon sby; *~ til en* wave to sby.

vinkel *en* angle; *en ret ~* a right angle; *se ngt fra en ny ~* see· sth from an'other angle; **~formet** *adj* angled; **~måler** *en* pro'tractor; **~ret** *adj: ~ret på* at right angles to; **~stue** *en* L-shaped room.

vin... *sms:* **~kort** *et* wine list; **~kælder** *en* wine cellar; **~mark** *en* vineyard ['vinjəd]; **~ranke** *en* vine; **~smagning** *en* wine-tasting; **~stok** *en* vine.

vinter *en* winter; *i ~ (dvs. sidste ~)* last winter; *(dvs. denne ~)* this winter; *om ~en* in (the) winter; *til ~* next winter; **~dag** *en* winter's day; **~dæk** *et* winter tyre; **~gæk** *en* snowdrop; **~have** *en* con'servatory; **~lege** *pl (vinter-OL)* Winter O'lympics; **~sport** *en* winter sports *pl;* **~sportssted** *et* ski re'sort; **~tøj** *et* winter clothing.

vinyl *et* vinyl.

viol *en* violet.

violet *adj (blå~)* violet; *(rød~)* purple.

violin *en* 'violin; *(spille ~)* play the violin; **~bygger** *en* violin maker.

violinist *en* violin player, vio'linist.

vippe *en (til svømmeudspring)* diving board; *(på legeplads)* seesaw; *det er lige på ~n* it is touch and go // *v* rock; *(på legeplads)* seesaw; *(tippe)* tip.

vips *interj: og ~ var de gift* and all of a sudden they were married.

vipstjært *en* wagtail.

virak *en (halløj)* fuss; *(hyldest)* homage.

viril *adj* virile; **virilitet** *en* vi'rility.

virke *v* work, act; *(forekomme)* look, seem; *bremsen ~r ikke* the brake does not work; *hun ~r rar* she seems nice; *~ som* act as; *(om person)* work as.

virkelig *adj* real; *i det ~e liv* in real life // *adv* really; *nej, ~?* oh, really? *han er ~ dygtig* he is really good; **~gøre** *v* realize.

virkelighed *en* re'ality; *i ~en* in re'ality, actually; *blive til ~* become· a re'ality; *(gå i opfyldelse)* come· true; **~s·fjern** *adj* out of touch with reality, airy-fairy; **~s·tro** *adj* rea'listic.

virkning *en* ef'fect; *have ~* have an ef'fect; *være uden ~* have no ef'fect; **~s·fuld** *adj* ef'fective; **~s·løs** *adj* inef'fective.

virksom *adj* active.

virksomhed *en (aktivitet)* ac'tivity; *(funktion)* action; *(foretagende)* business, firm; *(fabrik)* factory, works; **~s·ledelse** *en* management; **~s·leder** *en* manager.

virtuos *en* virtu'oso // *adj* brilliant.

virus *en* virus *(pl:* vira); *(edb)* bug; **~sygdom** *en* virus dis'ease.

virvar *et* chaos, con'fusion.

vis *adj* certain; *(sikker)* sure; *den ~se død* certain death; *en ~ hr. Massey* a certain Mr Massey; *i ~se tilfælde* in some cases; *til en ~ grad* to a certain de'gree; *være ~ på ngt* be sure of sth; *(se også vist).*

visdom *en* wisdom.

visdomstand *en* wisdom tooth *(pl:* teeth).

vise *en* song; *(folke~)* ballad // *v* show; *det vil tiden ~* time will show; *~ en vej* show sby the way; *~ af (ved sving)* signal; *~ ngt frem* show sth; *(pralende)* show sth off; *~ en ud* show sby out; *~ sig* ap'pear, turn up; *(vigte sig)* show off; *det ~r sig at...* it ap'pears that; *~ sig at være en skurk* turn out to be a crook; *det vil ~ sig* we shall see.

viser *en (på vægt etc)* needle; *(på ur)* hand; *den lille ~* the hour hand; *den store ~* the minute hand.

visesanger *en* singer, folksinger.

vished *en* certainty; *få ~ for at...* get· to know for sure that...; *skaffe sig ~* make· sure.

vision *en* 'vision.

visir *et (på hjelm)* visor.

visit *en* visit, call; *aflægge ~ hos en* pay· sby a visit.

visitere *v* search; *(krops~)* frisk.

visitkort *et* visiting card.

viske *v: ~ ngt ud (med viskelæder)*

e'rase sth, rub sth out; *(med klud)* wipe sth out; **~læder** *et* e'raser; **~stykke** *et* dishcloth.

vismand *en* wise man *(pl:* men); *økonomisk ~ (kan oversættes)* eco'nomic ad'viser to the Danish government.

visne *v* wither, die.

vissen *adj* withered, dead.

vist *adv (bestemt)* certainly; *(~ nok)* probably; *de kommer ~ ikke* they probably won't come; *jo ~!* oh, yes! certainly! *han hedder ~ Adam* he's called Adam, I think; *det er ganske ~ sent, men…* of course it's late, but…

vistnok *adv* I think; *han er ~ fraskilt* he is di'vorced, I think.

visuel *adj* visual; *~le hjælpemidler* visual aids.

visum *et* visa; *søge ~ til…* ap'ply for a visa to…

vital *adj* 'vital; *(om person)* vigorous.

vitamin *et* vitamin; *B-~* vitamin B; **~mangel** *en* vitamin de'ficiency; **~rig** *adj* rich in vitamins.

vitrine *en (møbel)* dis'play cabinet; *(til udstilling)* showcase.

vits *en* joke.

vittig *adj* witty.

vittighed *en* joke; **~s·tegning** *en* car'toon.

vod *et (til fiskeri)* dragnet; *trække ~ (i havnen)* drag (the harbour).

vogn *en (bil)* car; *(heste~)* wagon, cart; *(vare~)* van; *(last~)* lorry; *(taxa)* taxi; *(person~ i tog)* carriage; *(gods~)* goods wagon; *(bagage~)* trolley; *(indkøbs~)* shopping trolley; *(i supermarked)* supermarket trolley; **~bane** *en (på vej* lane; **~dæk** *et (på færge)* car deck; **~ladning** *en (om lastbil)* lorry load; **~mand** *en (med transportfirma)* haulage con'tractor; *(hyrevognsejer)* taxi owner; *(fragtmand)* carrier; **~park** *en* fleet of cars.

vogte *v* watch, guard; *~ sig* take· care; *~ sig for ngt* be'ware of sth; *~ sig for at* take· care not to.

vogter *en* keeper; *(af får)* shepherd; *(fig)* guardian.

vokal *en* vowel // *adj* vocal.

voks *et* wax; **~dug** *en* oilcloth.

vokse *v* grow·; *~ fra sit tøj* out'grow· one's clothes; *~ fra hinanden* grow· a'part; *gælden ~r med 20% om året* the debt grows by 20 per cent a year; *~ op* grow· up; *~ en over hovedet* out'grow· sby; *~ sammen (om sår)* heal; *~ sig stor* grow· big.

voksen *en* grown-up, adult; *de voksne* the grown-ups, the adults // *adj* grown-up, adult; *blive ~n* grow· up; *han er opgaven ~* he is equal to the task; **~undervisning** *en* adult edu'cation.

vokseværk *et* growing pains *pl.*

vokskabinet *et: et ~* a waxworks.

vold *en (jord~)* em'bankment; *(magt)* power; *(voldsomhed)* violence; *bruge ~* use violence; *være i ens ~* be in sby's power; *med ~* by force.

volde *v* cause.

voldelig *adj* violent.

voldgift *en* arbi'tration; **~s·mand** *en* 'arbitrator; **~s·ret** *en* court of arbi'tration.

voldgrav *en* moat.

volds… *sms:* **~handling** *en* act of violence; **~mand** *en* as'sailant; *(som slår folk ned på gaden etc)* thug; **~metoder** *pl* violent means.

voldsom *adj* violent; *(enorm)* im'mense; *(om regn, sne etc)* heavy; **~hed** *en* violence.

voldsramt *adj (om hustru el. barn)* battered.

voldsvideo *en* video nasty.

voldtage *v* rape.

voldtægt *en* rape; **~s·forbryder** *en* rapist.

voliere *en* aviary.

volt *en* volt.

volumen *et* volume.

voluminøs *adj* vo'luminous.

vom *en* paunch.

vor *se vores.*

vorden *s: være i sin ~* be in the making.

vordende *adj* future; *hans ~ hustru* his future bride; *en ~ mor* an ex'pectant mother.

vores *(vor, vort, vore(s)) pron* our;

(*stående alene*) ours; *det er* ~ *bil* it is our car; *bilen er* ~ the car is ours.
Vorherre God, the Lord.
vort *se vores.*
vorte *en* wart.
votere *v* vote; (*om nævninge*) con'sider the verdict.
vove *v* (*turde*) dare; (*risikere*) risk; ~ *på* dare to; *det kan du lige* ~ *på!* don't you dare! ~ *sig ind på ngt* venture into sth; ~ *sig for langt ud* venture too far; **~hals** *en* daredevil.
vovet *adj* daring.
vovse *en* doggie.
vrag *et* wreck.
vrage *v* re'ject; *vælge og* ~ pick and choose.
vraggods *et* wreckage.
vralte *v* waddle; **vralten** *en* waddle.
vrang *en* (*vrangside*) wrong side; *vende* ~*en ud* turn the wrong side out, turn inside out // *adj: strikke* ~ purl; *to ret og to* ~ knit two, purl two; **~forestilling** *en* de'lusion; **~maske** *en* purl; **~side** *en* wrong side; **~strikning** *en* purl knitting.
vranten *adj* surly.
vred *adj* angry; *blive* ~ *over ngt* get· angry at sth; *blive* ~ *på en* get· angry with sby.
vrede *en* anger; (*raseri*) rage; *gøre ngt i* ~ do· sth in anger.
vride *v* twist; (*tøj, hænder*) wring·; ~ *halsen om på en* wring· sby's neck; ~ *hjernen* rack one's brains; ~ *om på foden* twist one's ankle; ~ *sig* writhe; ~ *og vende sig* twist and turn; **~maskine** *en* wringer.
vrikke *v* wriggle; ~ *med ørerne* wriggle one's ears; ~ *om på foden* twist one's ankle.
vrimle *v* team, swarm (*med, af* with).
vrimmel *en* swarm.
vrinske *v* neigh; **vrinsken** *en* neigh(ing).
vrisse *v* snap (*ad* at).
vrist *en* instep.
vræl *et* yell, roar; **~e** *v* yell, roar.
vrænge *v* sneer (*ad* at).
vrøvl *et* nonsense; (*besvær*) trouble; *gøre* ~ *over ngt* com'plain about sth; *sådan ngt* ~*!* what nonsense! **~e** *v* talk nonsense.
vugge *en* cradle // *v* rock; **~døden** *s* cot death; **~sang** *en* lullaby; **~stue** *en* crèche, day nursery.
vulgær *adj* vulgar.
vulkan *en* vol'cano (*pl:* -es).
vulkanisere *v* (*om dæk*) retread.
vulkanudbrud *et* vol'canic e'ruption.
vurdere *v* estimate; (*fig*) e'valuate.
vurdering *en* estimate; evalu'ation; *efter min* ~ in my o'pinion; **~s·mand** *en* sur'veyor; **~s·pris** *en* estimated price.
VVS-mand *en* plumber.
væbne *v* arm; ~*de styrker* armed forces.
vædde *v* bet· (*om* on); *skal vi* ~*?* do you want to bet (on it)? *jeg tør* ~ *på at han...* I bet· (you) he...; ~ *£5 med en om at...* bet· sby £5 that...
væddeløb *et* race; **~s·bane** *en* racing track; (*til heste*) racecourse.
væddemål *et* bet; *indgå et* ~ make· a bet.
vædder *en* (*zo*) ram; *Vædderen* (*astr*) Aries.
væde *en* moisture // *v* moisten.
væg *en* wall; *hænge ngt op på* ~*gen* hang· sth on the wall.
væge *en* wick.
vægelsindet *adj* fickle, moody.
væggetøj *et* bedbugs *pl.*
væglampe *en* wall lamp.
vægmaleri *et* mural (painting).
vægre *v:* ~ *sig ved at gøre ngt* re'fuse to do sth.
vægring *en* re'fusal.
vægt *en* (*det ngt vejer; tyngde*) weight; (*apparat til at veje på*) scales; *Vægten* (*astr*) Libra; *i løs* ~ in bulk; *tabe i* ~ lose· weight; *tage på i* ~ put· on weight; *passe på* ~*en* watch one's figure; *lægge* ~ *på at gøre ngt* set· great store by doing sth; **~afgift** *en* (*auto*) road tax.
vægter *en* night watchman (*pl:* -men).
vægtfylde *en* spe'cific gravity.
væg til væg-tæppe *et* carpeting.
vægtløftning *en* weight-lifting.
vægtløs *adj* weightless.
vægtning *en* weighting.
vægtstang *en* lever.

vægttab *et* weight loss.
vægtæppe *et (gobelin)* tapestry; *(mindre pynte~)* wallhanging.
væk *adv* a'way; *(borte også)* gone; *blive ~ (dvs. forsvinde)* disap'pear; *(om person)* be lost; *(holde sig væk)* stay a'way; *langt ~* far a'way.
vække *v* wake· (up); *(kalde på for at vække)* call; *(frembringe)* a'rouse, ex'cite, cause; *væk mig kl. 7* please call me at 7; *~ forargelse* cause a scandal; *~ mistanke* a'rouse su'spicion; *~ til eftertanke* give· food for thought; *~ en til live (dvs. genoplive)* re'suscitate sby; *(dvs. sætte liv i)* a'rouse sby.
vækkelse *en* re'vival.
vækkeur *et* a'larm clock; *sætte ~et til at ringe kl. 6* set· the alarm for 6 o'clock.
vækning *en* calling; *(tlf)* wake-up service.
vækst *en* growth; *være høj af ~* be tall; *i ~* growing; **~hus** *et* greenhouse.
væld *et: et ~ af* lots of, (H) a multitude of.
væ1dig *adj (stor)* e'normous, im'mense; *det ser ~ godt ud* it looks awfully good.
vælge *v* choose·; *(~ ud, udsøge sig)* pick, se'lect; *(ved valg)* e'lect; *~ mellem flere vine* choose· from (,between) several wines; *~ en til præsident* e'lect sby president.
vælger *en* voter, e'lector; **~møde** *et* e'lection meeting.
vælling *en* gruel.
vælte *v (med objekt)* up'set·; *(selv ~, falde)* fall· (over); *(~ frem, fx om vand)* pour; *~ et glas* up'set· (,knock over) a glass; *~ regeringen* bring· down the government; *~ ens planer* up'set· sby's plans; *sneen ~de ned* there was a heavy snowfall; *~ ansvaret over på en* shift the responsi'bility to sby; *~ ngt på gulvet* push sth on to the floor; *~ med cyklen* have a fall with one's bicycle; *~ sig i ngt* be rolling in sth.
væmmelig *adj* nasty, dis'gusting.
væmmelse *en* dis'gust.
væmmes *v: væmmes ved ngt* be dis'gusted at sth.
vænne *v* ac'custom; *~ en af med ngt* make· sby to give up (,stop) sth; *~ en til (at gøre) ngt* ac'custom sby to (doing) sth; *~ sig af med at ryge* give· up smoking; *~ sig til at gøre ngt* get· used to doing sth.
værd *adj* worth; *det er det ikke ~* it is not worth it; *det er ~ at overveje* it is worth thinking about; *det er ikke ~ at vi gør det* we had better not do it; *tror du det er ~ at risikere det?* do you think we ought to risk it? *den er mange penge ~* it is worth a lot of money.
værdi *en* value; *af stor ~* of great value; *til en ~ af 500 kr.* to the value of 500 kr.; *~er (ejendom)* valuables; *(papirer)* se'curities; **~fuld** *adj* valuable.
værdig *adj* worthy; *(om persons fremtræden)* dignified; *være ~ til* be worthy of.
værdige *v: ikke ~ en et blik* not deign to look at sby.
værdigenstande *pl* valuables.
værdighed *en* dignity; *det var under hans ~* it was be'neath him.
værdigt *adv* with dignity.
værdiløs *adj* worthless.
værdipapirer *pl* se'curities.
værdsætte *v* ap'preciate.
være *v* be; *(som hjælpeverbum)* have; *hvem er det?* who is it? *det er mig* it is me; *~ læge* be a doctor; *han er i Skotland* he is in Scotland; *det kan ~ at de har glemt os* they may· have for'gotten us; *det kan ~ det samme* it does not matter, never mind; *de er lige kommet hjem* they have just come home; *~ til (dvs. eksistere)* ex'ist; *hvad er den æske til?* what is that box for? *den er til at lægge øreringe i* it is for putting earrings in; *der kan ~ en halv liter i glasset* the glass holds a pint; *kassen kan ikke ~ her* there is not room for the box.
værelse *et* room; *hun er på sit ~* she is in her room; *en femværelses lejlighed* a five-room flat.
værft *et* shipyard.

værge *en* guardian // *v:* ~ *for sig* de'fend oneself; **-løs** *adj* de'fenceless.
værk *et* work; *(el~, gas~ etc)* works; **-fører** *en* foreman *(pl:* -men).
værksted *et* workshop (også *fig);* **-s·teater** *et* workshop theatre.
værktøj *et* tool; *han har en masse* ~ he has lots of tools; **-s·kasse** *en* toolbox; **-s·maskine** *en* ma'chine tool.
værn *et (forsvar)* de'fence; *(beskyttelse)* pro'tection.
værne *v* de'fend; pro'tect *(mod* from, against); **-pligt** *en* com'pulsory military service; **-pligtig** *en* conscript.
værre *adj* worse; *han er en* ~ *en* he is a bad one; *du er en* ~ *idiot* you are a damned fool.
værsgo *interj (når man giver en ngt)* here you are; *(når man lader en vælge selv)* help your'self; *(når maden er færdig)* the meal (,dinner, lunch etc) is ready; *må jeg være med? - ja,* ~*!* may I join you? - yes, of course! ~ *at sidde ned!* do sit down!.
værst *adj* worst; *det* ~*e er at...* the worst thing is that...; *i* ~*e fald* at worst; *det er ikke så* ~ *(dvs. ret godt)* it is not bad at all; *det var ikke det* ~*e der kunne ske* it could have been worse.
vært *en (husejer, kroejer)* landlord; *(ved privat selskab)* host; **-inde** *en* landlady; hostess.
værtshus *et* pub, inn; **-turné** *en* pub crawling.
værtsland *et* host country.
væsen *et (skabning)* creature, being; *(beskaffenhed, natur)* nature; *(optræden)* manners *pl; (etat)* service, de'partment; *gøre stort* ~ *ud af ngt* make· a fuss about sth.
væsentlig *adj* es'sential; *(betragtelig)* con'siderable; *i det* ~*e* es'sentially // *adv* con'siderably; *(meget)* much.
væske *en* liquid.
vættelys *et* thunderstone.
væv *en* loom // *et (vævet stof)* tissue; *(net)* web; **-e** *v* weave·; *(vrøvle)* ramble; **-er** *en* weaver // *adj* agile; **-eri** *et* (textile) mill; **-ning** *en* weaving.
våben *et* weapon; *(om krigsvåben, pl)* arms; *(heraldisk)* (coat of) arms; *handle med* ~ trade in arms; *nedlægge våbnene* lay· down arms; **-fabrik** *en* arms factory; **-hus** *et (ved kirke)* porch; **-kapløb** *et* arms race; **-skjold** *et* coat of arms; **-stilstand** *en (foreløbig)* cease'fire; *(endelig)* armistice.
våd *adj* wet; *blive* ~ *i håret* get· one's hair wet; *det er* ~*t i vejret* it is a wet day; **-dragt** *en* wetsuit.
vådeskud *et* acci'dental shot.
vådområde *et* wetland.
vådserviet *en* moist tissue, (F) wet one.
våge *en (i is)* hole in the ice // *v (holde sig vågen)* wake, be a'wake; ~ *over en* watch over sby.
vågeblus *et* pilot light.
vågen *adj* a'wake; *(på vagt)* vigilant; *(kvik)* bright; *holde sig* ~ keep· a'wake; ~ *interesse* keen interest.
vågne *v* wake· (up).
vår *et (til dyne etc)* cover; *(forår,* H) spring.
vås *et* nonsense; **-e** *v* talk nonsense.

W

wagon *en (jernb)* carriage.
waliser *en* Welshman *(pl:* -men); ~*ne* the Welsh; **walisisk** *adj* Welsh.
Warszawa *s* 'Warsaw.
wc *et* toilet, lavatory, (F) loo; *gå på* ~ go· to the toilet (,bathroom); *skylle ud i wc'et (dvs. trække i snoren)* flush the toilet; *skylle ngt ud i wc'et* flush sth down the toilet; **-bræt** *et* toilet seat; **-kumme** *en* toilet bowl; **-papir** *et* toilet paper.
weekend *en* weekend; *vi var væk i* ~*en* we were away for the weekend; *vi skal til Paris i* ~*en* we are going to Paris over (,for) the weekend; *forlænget* ~ long weekend; **-kuffert** *en* overnight bag.
whisky *en (skotsk)* whisky; *(irsk)* whiskey; *(amerikansk)* bourbon; *en*

tør ~ a neat whisky; *en* ~ *med isterninger* a whisky on the rocks; **~sjus** *en* whisky and soda.
Wien *s* Vienna.
wiener *en* Vien'nese; **~brød** *et* Danish pastry; **~vals** *en* Vien'nese waltz.
wire *en* cable.

X

x *et* x; *hr. X* Mr. X; *gøre ngt x antal gange* do· sth x number of times.
x-akse *en* x-axis.
xylofon *en* 'xylophone.

Y

y-akse *en* y-axis.
yalelås *en* Yale lock.
yde *v (give)* yield; *(præstere)* do·; *(betale)* pay·; ~ *sit bedste* do· one's best; ~ *en bistand* help sby; **~dygtig** *adj* pro'ductive; *(om motor etc)* powerful; **~evne** *en* ca'pacity; *(om fx motor)* per'formance.
ydelse *en (udbytte etc)* yield; *(præstation)* per'formance; *(social ~)* benefit; *(tjeneste~)* service; *(betaling)* payment.
yderbane *en* outside lane.
yderlig *adj* near the edge; **~ere** *adj/adv* further.
yderliggående *adj* ex'tremist.
yderlighed *en: fra den ene* ~ *til den anden* from one ex'treme to the other; *gå til ~er* go· to extremes.
yderside *en* outside; *(om fx hus)* ex'terior.
yderst *adj* ex'treme; *(udvendig)* outer; *våd fra* ~ *til inderst* wet through; *det ~e højre (pol)* the ex'treme right; *ligge på sit ~e* be dying; *i ~e nødstilfælde* if the worst comes to the worst; *gøre sit ~e* do one's utmost // *adv* ex'tremely, most.
ydmyg *adj* humble; **~e** *v* hu'miliate.
ydmygelse *en* humili'ation.
ydmygende *adj* hu'miliating.
ydmyghed *en* hu'mility.
ydre *et* outside; *(udseende)* ap'pearance; *ligne en af* ~ be like sby to look at // *adj* outer, outside; ex'ternal; ~ *fjender* foreign (,ex'ternal) enemies; *det* ~ *rum* outer space.
yen *en* yen.
ymer *en sv.omtr.t.* junket.
ynde *en* charm // *v* like; **~fuld** *adj* graceful.
ynder *en* lover, ad'mirer *(af* of).
yndet *adj* popular.
yndig *adj* lovely.
yndling *en* favourite; **yndlings-** favourite, pet.
yndlingsbeskæftigelse *en* favourite occu'pation.
yngel *en* brood; *(om fisk)* fry.
yngle *v* breed·; *(om penge)* multiply; **~tid** *en* breeding season.
yngling *en* youth; *(sport)* junior.
yngre *adj* younger *(end* than); *(ret ung)* youngish.
yngst *adj* youngest.
ynk *en: det er den rene* ~ it is pa'thetic.
ynke *v* pity *(en* sby); **~lig** *adj* pitiful, pa'thetic; *gøre en ~lig figur* be a sorry sight.
yoga *en* yoga.
yoghurt *en* yoghurt.
yppe *v:* ~ *kiv* start an argument.
ypperlig *adj* su'perb, excellent.
ytre *v (vise)* show; *(udtale)* ex'press, speak·; *hun ~de et ønske* she ex'pressed a de'sire; *han ~de ikke ngt om det* he did not utter a word about it.
ytring *en (udtalelse)* re'mark, 'comment; *(demonstration)* manifes'tation; **~s·frihed** *en* freedom of ex'pression.
yver *et* udder.

Z

zar *en* tsar.
zebra *en* zebra; **~striber** *pl (fodgængerovergang)* zebra crossing.
zenit *et* zemith.
zink *en* zinc; **~salve** *en* zinc ointment.
zobel *en* sable.
zone *en* zone; *(takst~)* fare stage; **~terapi** *en* zone therapy, reflex'ology.
zoolog *en* zo'ologist.

zoologi *en* zo'ology; **zoologisk** *adj* zoo'logical; ~ *have* zoo.
zoome *v* zoom.
zoomlinse *en* zoom lens.

Æ

æble *et* apple; *stridens* ~ the apple of con'tention; *bide i det sure* ~ swallow the bitter pill; **~blomst** *en* apple blossom; **~kerne** *en* apple pip; **~mos** *en* apple sauce; **~most** *en* apple juice; **~skive** *en (kan oversættes:)* apple dumpling; **~skrog** *et* apple core; **~skræl** *en* apple peel; **~vin** *en (kan oversættes:)* strong cider.
æde *v* eat·; *(neds)* stuff oneself, gobble; ~ *ngt i sig igen* take· sth back; **~dolk** *en* glutton; **~gilde** *et* blow-out.
ædel *adj* noble; *ædle metaller* precious metals; *de ædlere dele* the private parts; **~gran** *en* silver fir.
ædelmodig *adj* mag'nanimous; **~hed** *en* magna'nimity.
ædelse *en* grub.
ædelsten *en* precious stone.
æderi *et* gluttony, guzzling.
ædru *adj* sober; *pinligt* ~ stone-cold sober.
ædruelig *adj* sober; **~hed** *en* soberness.
æg *et* egg; *behandle en som et råddent* ~ handle sby with kid gloves; *lægge et* ~ lay· an egg // *en (på kniv)* edge; *(på stof)* selvedge.
ægge... *sms:* **~blomme** *en* egg yolk; **~bæger** *et* egg cup; **~deler** *en* egg slicer; **~hvide** *en* egg white; **~hvidestof** *et* protein; **~kage** *en* omelet; **~leder** *en* fal'lopian tube; **~skal** *en* egg shell; **~stok** *en* ovary.
ægløsning *en* ovu'lation.
ægte *adj* real, genuine; *(om guld etc også)* pure; *en* ~ *brøk* a proper fraction.
ægtefælle *en* spouse.
ægtepar *et* married couple.
ægteskab *et* marriage; *hun har tre børn af første* ~ she has three children by her first husband; *født uden for* ~ ille'gitimate; **ægteskabelig** *adj* married.
ægteviet *adj* lawful.
ægæisk *adj: Det Ægæiske Hav* the Ae'gean (Sea).
ækel *adj* nasty; *en* ~ *karl* a nasty piece of work.
ækvator *en* the E'quator.
ækvivalent *en/adj* e'quivalent.
ælde *en* age; *dø af* ~ die of old age.
ældgammel *adj* ancient.
ældre *pl* elderly (people) // *adj* older; *(om søn, datter etc også)* elder; *(ret gammel)* rather old; *(om person)* elderly; *(tidligere)* earlier; *hun er 15 år* ~ *end han* she is 15 years older than he; *den* ~ *stenalder* the earlier Stone Age; **~diskriminering** *en* ageism; **~forsorg** *en* care of the elderly.
ældst *adj* oldest; *(om søn, datter også)* eldest.
ælling *en* duckling; *den grimme* ~ the Ugly Duckling.
ælte *et (pløre)* mud // *v (om dej)* knead.
æltning *en* kneading.
ændre *v* change, alter; ~ *mening* change one's mind; ~ *på* change; ~ *sig* change.
ændring *en* change.
ængste *v:* ~ *en* a'larm sby; ~*s* be a'larmed; **~lig** *adj* anxious *(for* about); *(af væsen)* timid.
ængstelse *en* an'xiety.
ænse *v: hun* ~*de ham ikke* she had no eye for him; *uden at* ~... re'gardless of...
æra *en* era.
ærbar *adj* de'mure; **~hed** *en* modesty.
ærbødig *adj* re'spectful, reverent; ~*st (i brev)* Yours faithfully; **~hed** *en* re'spect, 'deference.
ære *en* honour; *(anerkendelse)* credit; *det er al* ~ *værd at han...* it does him credit that he...; *tage* ~*n for ngt* take· the credit for sth; *hvad skylder man* ~*n?* to what do I owe this honour? *på* ~ *og samvittighed!* on my honour! *til* ~ *for* in honour of; ~ *den som* ~*s bør* honour where honour is due; *vi har den* ~ *at ind-*

byde Dem til... (H) we re'quest the honour of your company at... // *v* honour; *det ~de medlem (parl)* the Honourable member.
ærefrygt *en* awe; **~indgydende** *adj* 'awe-in,spiring.
ærefuld *adj* honourable.
ærekrænkende *adj* de'famatory.
æres... *sms:* **~bevisning** *en* honour; **~doktor** *en* honorary doctor; **~gæst** *en* guest of honour; **~hverv** *et* honorary office; **~medlem** *et* honorary member; **~ord** *et* word of honour; *på ~ord* cross my heart and hope to die; **~runde** *en* lap of honour; **~sag** *en* matter of honour; **~vagt** *en* guard of honour.
ærgerlig *adj* an'noying; *(som ærgrer sig)* an'noyed *(over* at; *på* with); *det var da ~t* how an'noying.
ærgerrig *adj* am'bitious; **~hed** *en* am'bition.
ærgre *v* an'noy; *~ sig* be an'noyed *(over* at); **~lse** *en* an'noyance, worry.
ærinde *et* errand; *være ude i andet ~* be after sth else.
ærke... *sms:* **~biskop** *en* archbishop; **~engel** *en* archangel; **~fjende** *en* arch-fiend.
ærlig *adj* honest, frank; *(oprigtig)* sin'cere, straightforward; *det er en ~ sag* it is no crime; *~t spil* fair play; **~hed** *en* honesty.
ærligt *adv* honestly; sin'cerely; *det har du ~t fortjent (dvs. det har du godt af)* it serves you right; *(dvs. det er en fair belønning)* you really de'served it; *~t talt* honestly; *helt ~t* to be quite frank.
ærme *et* sleeve; *uden ~r* sleeveless; *smøge ~rne op* roll up one's sleeves; *ryste ngt ud af ~t* pro'duce sth just like that; **~gab** *et* armhole; **~linning** *en* cuff.
ært *en* pea.
ærtebælg *en* pea pod.
ærværdig *adj* venerable; **~hed** *en* venera'bility.
æsel *et* donkey; **~øre** *et (i bog)* dog-ear.
æske *en* box; *en ~ tændstikker* a box of matches.
æstetisk *adj* aes'thetic.
æter *en* ether.
æterisk *adj* e'thereal.
ætse *v* cor'rode; *(med syre)* etch; **~nde** *adj* caustic.
ævl *et* rubbish; **~e** *v* talk rubbish; *~e løs* blether.
ævred *s: opgive ~* give· up.

Ø

ø *en* island; *de britiske ~er* the British Isles.
øbo(er) *en* islander.
øde *adj* de'serted, empty; *en ~ ø* a 'desert island // *v: ~ ngt væk* waste sth.
ødegård *en* 'derelict farmhouse.
ødelagt *adj* ruined, spoiled; *(gået i stykker)* broken; *(udslidt)* worn out.
ødelægge *v* ruin, spoil; *(med vilje)* de'stroy; *(slå i stykker)* break·, smash; **~lse** *en* de'struction; *(skade)* damage; *store ~lser* ex'tensive damage.
ødemark *en* wilderness.
ødsel *adj* ex'travagant; *(som gerne giver væk)* lavish; **~hed** *en* ex'travagance; lavishness.
ødsle *v* be ex'travagant; *~ ngt væk* squander (,waste) sth; *~ sine penge på en* lavish one's money on sby.
øg *et (gammel hest)* nag, jade.
øge *v* in'crease *(med* by); *(om tøj)* add to; **~navn** *et* nickname.
øges *v* in'crease.
øget *adj* added.
øgle *en* lizard.
øgruppe *en* group of islands.
øhav *et* archi'pelago.
øje *et* eye; *lukke øjnene* close one's eyes *(for* to); *jeg har ikke lukket et ~* I did not sleep a wink; *åbne øjnene* open one's eyes; *gøre store øjne* be all eyes; *så langt ~t rækker* as far as the eye can see; *øjnene var ved at falde ud af hovedet på ham* his eyes nearly popped out; *jeg har ikke øjne i nakken* I don't have eyes in the back of my head; *have ~ for ngt* have an eye for sth; *for øjnene af naboerne* in front of the neighbours;

i mine øjne in my view, as I see it; *se i øjnene at...* face the fact that...; *se en lige i øjnene* look sby in the eye; *holde ~ med ngt* keep· an eye on sth; *jeg har set ham med egne øjne* I have seen him with my own eyes; *med bind for øjnene* blindfolded; *holde øjnene åbne (dvs. holde udkig)* keep· one's eyes peeled; *få ~ på ngt* spot sth, see· sth; *have et godt ~ til en* have an eye on sby; *lave øjne til en* make· eyes at sby; *under fire øjne* in private.

øjeblik *et* moment; *(et kort nu)* instant; (F) second, minute; *et ~!* just a moment! just a second! *vent et ~* wait a minute; *for ~ket* at the moment; *i det ~* at that moment; *i samme ~ som...* the moment...; *i sidste ~* at the last moment; *om et ~* in a minute; *få et ~* in no time.

øjeblikkelig *adj* im'mediate, instant; *(nuværende)* present; *(som snart går over)* temporary // *adv* instantly, at once.

øjebliksbillede *et* snapshot.

øjemål *et: efter ~* by eye.

øjen... *sms:* **~bryn** *et* eyebrow; *løfte ~brynene* raise one's eyebrows; **~dråber** *pl* eye drops; **~glas** *et* eye bath; **~kontakt** *en* visual contact; **~læge** *en* eye specialist; **~låg** *et* eyelid; **~skygge** *en* eyeshadow.

øjensynlig *adj* ap'parent // *adv* ap'parently.

øjenvidne *et* eyewitness.

øjenvippe *en* eyelash.

øjeæble *et* eyeball.

øjne *v* see·.

økolog *en* e'cologist.

økologi *en* e'cology; **økologisk** *adj* eco'logical.

økonom *en* e'conomist.

økonoma *en* catering officer.

økonomi *en* e'conomy; *(som fag)* eco'nomics; *(økonomiske forhold)* fi'nances *pl;* **~ministerium** *et* Ministry of Eco'nomic Af'fairs.

økonomisere *v: ~ med ngt* e'conomize on sth.

økonomisk *adj* eco'nomic; *(sparsommelig)* eco'nomical.

økse *en* axe.

øl *en* beer; *(pilsner)* lager; *lyst ~* light beer; *~ fra fad* draught beer; *købe fem ~* buy· five beers; *det var lige til ~let* it was a scrape; **~dåse** *en* beer can; **~flaske** *en* beer bottle; **~gær** *en* brewer's yeast; **~kapsel** *en* beer-bottle cap; **~kasse** *en* beer crate.

øllebrød *en* soup made of bread and sweet beer.

ølmave *en* beer belly.

øloplukker *en* bottle opener.

øm *adj* sore; *(kærlig)* tender; *være ~ i benene* have sore legs; *være ~ over ngt* be very con'cerned about sth; *et ~t punkt* a sore spot *(også fig).*

ømentalitet *en* insu'larity.

ømfindtlig *adj* sensitive.

ømhed *en (smerte)* pain, ache; *(kærlighed)* love; *(varme følelser)* af'fection.

ømme *v: ~ sig* moan.

ømskindet *adj* sensitive.

ønske *et* wish, de'sire; *efter ~ (dvs. som man vil)* as de'sired; *(dvs. som det skal være)* satis'factory // *v* wish; *(ville have, ville)* want; *~ en godt nytår* wish sby a happy New Year; *~ en til lykke* con'gratulate sby *(med* on); *De ~r? (i butik)* can I help you? *som De ~r* as you please; *jeg ville ~ det var sommer* I wish it were summer; *~ sig ngt* wish for sth; *~ sig ngt til jul* want sth for Christmas; **~barn** *et (som er planlagt)* planned child; **~drøm** *en* pipedream; **~koncert** *en* musical re'quest programme.

ønskelig *adj* de'sirable.

ønskeseddel *en* list of gift wishes.

ønsket *adj* de'sired, wanted.

ønsketænkning *en* wishful thinking.

ønskværdig *adj* de'sirable.

ør *adj (svimmel)* dizzy; *(rundt på gulvet)* con'fused.

øre *et* ear; *(mønt)* øre; *have ~ for ngt* have an ear for sth; *holde en i ~rne* keep· a tight rein on sby; *spidse ~r* prick up one's ears; *have meget om ~rne* have a lot on one's plate; *døv på det ene ~* deaf in one ear; *være*

lutter ~ be all ears; *ikke en rød* ~ not a penny; *være forelsket til op over begge* ~*r* be head over heels in love; **-døvende** *adj* ear-splitting; **-flip** *en* earlobe; **-gang** *en* auditory ca'nal; **-læge** *en* ear specialist; **-mærke** *v* earmark.
ørenlyd *en: få* ~ make· oneself heard.
ørentvist *en* earwig.
ørepine *en* earache.
ørering *en* earring.
øresnegl *en (tv)* earpiece.
ørestik *en* stud earring.
Øresund *s* the Sound.
øretæve *en* box on the ear, slap (on the face); *give en en* ~ slap sby's face; *få en* ~ *(fig)* get· a smack in the eye; **-indbydende** *adj: han er* ~*indbydende* he makes my fingers itch.
ørevarmer *en* earmuff; *(på hue)* ear flap.
ørevoks *et* earwax.
ørige *et* archi'pelago.
ørken *en* 'desert; **-dannelse** *en* desertifi'cation.
ørn *en* eagle; *være en* ~ *til ngt* be a wizard at sth; **-e·næse** *en* aquiline nose; **-e·unge** *en* eaglet.
ørred *en* trout *(pl:* ~*)*.
øse *en (mar)* bale; (S, *om bil)* racy car // *v* scoop; *(mar)* bale; *det* ~*r ned* it is pouring down; ~ *suppe op* dish up soup.
øsken *en* eye.
øsregn *en* downpour; **-e** *v: det* ~*er* it is pouring down.
øst *en/adv* east; ~ *for* (to the) east of; *i* ~ in the east; *mod* ~ *(dvs. østpå)* eastwards; *(dvs. som vender mod* ~*)* facing east; **østasiatisk** *adj* East Asian.
Østblokken *s* the Eastern bloc.
Østdanmark *s* Eastern Denmark.
Østen *s* the East; *det Fjerne* ~ the Far East.
østenvind *en* east wind.
østerlandsk *adj* ori'ental.
østers *en* oyster; **-banke** *en* oyster bed.
Østersøen *s* the Baltic (Sea); **øster-sø-** Baltic.
Østeuropa *s* Eastern Europe; **øst-europæisk** *adj* Eastern Euro'pean.
østfra *adv* from the east.
østkyst *en* east coast.
østland *et* East Euro'pean country.
østlig *adj* east; *(om vind)* eastern.
østpå *adv* east, eastwards; *(i den østlige del af landet)* in the east.
Østrig *s* Austria; **østriger** *en,* **østrigsk** *adj* Austrian.
øve *v* practise; *(opøve)* train; *(gøre, volde)* do·; ~ *hærværk* vandalize; ~ *vold* use violence; ~ *sig på ngt* practise sth; **-hæfte** *et* exercise book.
øvelse *en* practice; *(enkelt øvelse, fx i gymnastik)* exercise; *have* ~ *i ngt* be practised in sth.
øverst *adj* top, topmost; *(fig)* highest // *adv* at the top; ~*e etage* top floor; ~ *i højre hjørne* in the top right-hand corner; *stå* ~ *på listen* top the list; *fra* ~ *til nederst* from top to bottom; **-befalende** *en* com'mander-in-chief.
øvet *adj* ex'perienced.
øvre *adj* upper.
øvrig *adj: det (, de)* ~*e* the rest; *for* ~*t (dvs. apropos)* by the way; *(dvs. ellers)* otherwise; *(dvs. imidlertid)* how'ever.
øvrigheden *s* the au'thorities *pl.*

Å

å *en* stream; *(stor, bred)* river; *(lille, smal)* brook.
åben *adj* open; *(om person også)* frank, open-minded; *være* ~ *over for ngt* be open to sth; *stå* ~ be open; *lade døren stå* ~ leave· the door open; *holde længe* ~*t* be open late; *holde* ~*t hus* keep· open house; ~ *ild* open fire; *på det åbne hav* in the open sea; *det åbne marked* the open market.
åbenbar *adj* evident; **-e** *v* re'veal; ~*e sig* ap'pear.
åbenbaring *en* reve'lation.
åbenbart *adv (helt klart)* evidently, obviously; *(tilsyneladende)* ap'parently.
åbenhjertig *adj* frank, candid.

åbenlys *adj* open, unconcealed; *(tydelig)* obvious.
åbne *v* open (up); *(låse op)* un'lock; ~ *sig* open (up); ~ *for en* open the door to sby; *det banker - gider du lige ~?* sby is knocking - will you answer the door? ~ *for vandet (,fjernsynet)* turn on the water (,television).
åbning *en* opening; *(hul)* hole; **~s·tider** *pl (i butik)* opening hours *(om kontor)* business hours.
ådsel *et* carcass; **~grib** *en* vulture.
åg *et* yoke (også *fig)*.
åger *en* usury; **~karl** *en* usurer; **~pris** *en* ex'orbitant price; *betale ~pris* pay· through your nose.
åh *interj* oh; ~ *ja* well, yes; ~ *jo!* please! ~ *hold op!* oh come now!
åkande *en* waterlily.
ål *en* eel.
åleglat *adj (fig)* slick.
ålejern *et* eelspear.
ånd *en* spirit, mind; *(spøgelse)* ghost; *en ond* ~ an evil spirit; *store ~er (om personer)* great minds; *opgive ~en* give· up the ghost; *se ngt i ~en* see· sth in one's mind's eye; *når ~en kommer over ham* when he is in the mood.
ånde *en: holde en i* ~ keep· sby occupied // *v* breathe; ~ *lettet op* breathe again.
åndedræt *et* respi'ration; *kunstigt* ~ arti'ficial respi'ration.
åndedrætsbesvær *et* difficulty in breathing.
åndelig *adj* spiritual, mental; ~ *føde* food for the mind; ~ *leder* spiritual leader.
åndeløs *adj* breathless.
åndenød *en* difficulty in breathing.
ånds... *sms:* **~arbejder** *en* brainworker; **~evner** *pl* mental faculties; **~forladt** *adj* dull; *(uopfindsom)* uni'maginative; **~fraværelse** *en* absent-mindedness; **~fraværende** *adj* absent-minded; **~frisk** *adj* mentally sound; **~nærværelse** *en* presence of mind; **~nærværende** *adj* quick-witted, resolute; **~svag** *adj (idiotisk)* stupid.
år *et* year; *være 20* ~ be twenty (years old); *blive 30 (~)* be thirty; *hvert* ~ every year; *hvert femte* ~ every five years; *i* ~ this year; *i de senere* ~ in recent years; *han er oppe i ~ene* he is getting on in years; *i en alder af 30 år* at the age of thirty; *et ~s tid* a year or so; *om et* ~ in a year; *om ~et* a year; *en gang om ~et* once a year; *£50 om ~et* £50 a year; *en dreng på otte* ~ an eight-year old boy; *næste* ~ next year; *sidste* ~ last year; *der er to ~s garanti* there's a two-year guaran'tee; **~bog** *en* yearbook.
åre *en (mar)* oar; *(blod~)* vein; *(puls~)* artery; *(i træ)* grain; **~forkalkning** *en* arterioscle'rosis; **~gaffel** *en* rowlock; **~knude** *en* varicose vein; **~tag** *et* stroke; **~told** *en* tholepin.
årevis: *i* ~ for years.
årgang *en (aldersklasse)* year; *(af tidsskrift etc)* volume; *(af vin)* vintage.
årgangsvin *en* vintage wine.
århundrede *et* century; *i ~r* for centuries; **~skifte** *et: ved ~skiftet* at the turn of the century.
-årig *(om alder)* ...-year old; *(om varighed)* ...-year; *en 10-årig dreng* a 10-year old boy; *en femårig aftale* a five-year a'greement.
årlig *adj* annual, yearly // *adv* annually, a year; *fire gange* ~ four times a year.
årring *en (i træ)* annual ring.
årrække *en: i en* ~ for (a number of) years.
årsag *en* cause *(til* of), reason *(til* for); *(anledning)* oc'casion *(til* for); *af den* ~ for that reason; *give* ~ *til* give· cause for; *~en til at...* the reason why...
års... *sms:* **~basis** *en: på ~basis* on an annual basis; **~beretning** *en* annual re'port; **~dag** *en* anni'versary *(for* of); **~indtægt** *en* annual income; **~kontigent** *et* annual sub'scription; **~møde** *et* annual meeting; **~prøve** *en* annual exami'nation; **~skifte** *et* turn of the year; **~tal** *et* year; **~tid** *en* season; *det er koldt efter ~tiden* it is cold for the time of the year.

årti *et* decade.
årtusinde *et* mil'lennium.
årvågen *adj* vigilant.
ås *en* ridge.
åsted *et:* ~*et* the scene of the crime.